# Shooter's Bible®



***ABOUT OUR COVER***

The 25-35 Winchester featured on our cover (top) is the Model 1894 Deluxe Rifle fitted with round takedown barrel, full magazine and engraved silver-plated receiver and frame; the stock is checkered, deluxe burled walnut with crescent buttplate. The Winchester 1894 Deluxe Rifle on the bottom is a 38-55 caliber featuring extremely rare casehardened frame, octagonal takedown barrel, full magazine, and checkered deluxe burled-walnut stock with shotgun buttplate.

***ASK YOUR BOOKSELLER OR SPORTING GOODS DEALER FOR THESE OTHER FINE PUBLICATIONS FROM STOEGER***

**ADVANCED BOWHUNTING** by Roger Maynard
**ADVANCED MUZZLELOADER'S GUIDE** by Toby Bridges
**AMERICA'S GREAT GUNMAKERS** by Wayne Von Zwoll
**ANGLER'S GUIDE TO JIGS AND JIGGING** by Ken Oberrecht
**ANTIQUE GUNS: THE COLLECTOR'S GUIDE,** 2nd Edition, by John Traister
**BLACK POWDER GUIDE,** 2nd Edition, by George C. Nonte Jr.
**BOB CHURCH'S GUIDE TO NEW FLY PATTERNS** by Bob Church
**BOOK OF THE 22: THE ALL-AMERICAN CALIBER** by Sam Fadala
**CLASSIC BIKES** by Peter Henshaw
**CLASSIC SALMON FLIES** by Mikael Frodin
**THE COMPLETE BOOK OF DEER HUNTING** by Byron W. Dalrymple
**THE COMPLETE FISH COOKBOOK** by Dan & Inez Morris
**COMPLETE GUIDE TO PHYSICAL FITNESS** by Kiell & Frelinghuysen
**DECEIVING TROUT** by John Parsons
**DRESS 'EM OUT** by Captain James A. Smith
**FIBERGLASS ROD MAKING** by Dale P. Clemens
**FIREARMS DISASSEMBLY WITH EXPLODED VIEWS** by John Karns & John Traister
**THE FLYTIER'S COMPANION** by Mike Dawes
**THE FLYTIER'S MANUAL** by Mike Dawes
**FLYTYERS MASTERCLASS** by Oliver Edwards
**GAME COOKBOOK,** New Revised Edition, by Geraldine Steindler
**GREAT SHOOTERS OF THE WORLD** by Sam Fadala
**GUNSMITHING AT HOME** by John E. Traister
**GUN TRADER'S GUIDE,** 18th Edition
**THE HANDBOOK OF FLYTYING** by Peter Gathercole
**HANDLOADER'S GUIDE** by Stanley W. Trzoniec
**HANDLOADER'S MANUAL OF CARTRIDGE CONVERSION** by John J. Donnelly
**THE HANDY SPORTSMAN** by Loring D. Wilson
**HOW TO BUY AND SELL USED GUNS** by John Traister
**HUNTING PREDATORS FOR HIDES & PROFIT** by Wilf E. Pyle
**LEGENDARY SPORTING RIFLES** by Sam Fadala
**MATCHING THE HATCH** by Ernest G. Schwiebert, Jr.
**MODERN BERETTA FIREARMS** by Gene Gangarosa, Jr.
**MODERN WATERFOWL GUNS & GUNNING** by Don Zutz
**P-38 AUTOMATIC PISTOL** by Gene Gangarosa, Jr.
**PETER DEANE'S GUIDE TO FLYTYING**
**PISTOL GUIDE** by George C. Nonte Jr.
**THE PRACTICAL BOOK OF KNIVES** by Ken Warner
**PRECISION HANDLOADING** by John Withers
**RELOADER'S GUIDE,** 3rd Edition, by R. A. Steindler
**REVOLVER GUIDE** by George C. Nonte Jr.
**RIFLE GUIDE** by Sam Fadala
**SHOOTER'S BIBLE 1940 REPRODUCTION**
**TAXIDERMY GUIDE,** 3rd Edition, by Russell Tinsley
**TO RISE A TROUT** by John Roberts
**THE ULTIMATE IN RIFLE ACCURACY** by Glenn Newick

NEW!

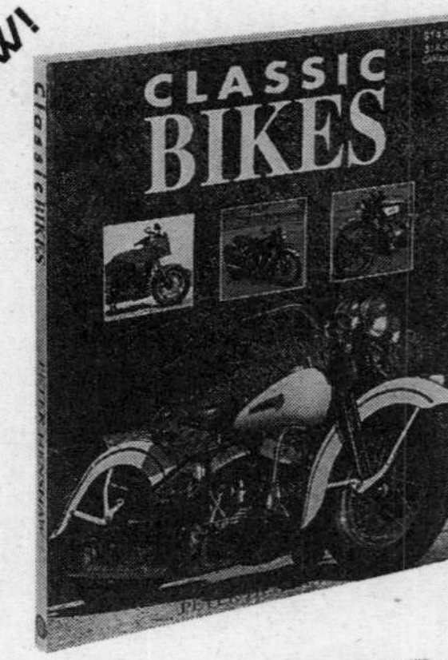


NEW!

NEW!

NEW!

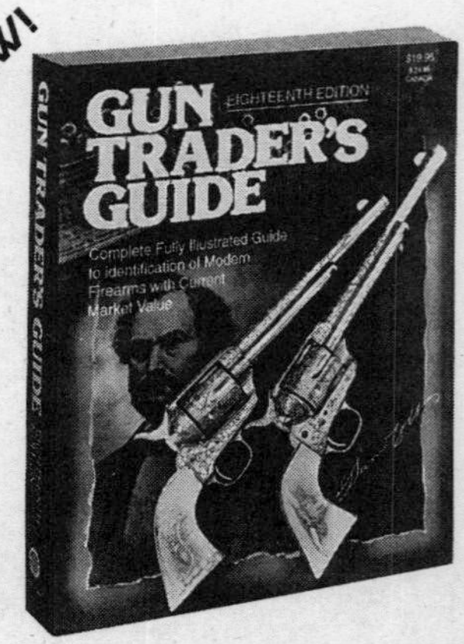

# Shooter's Bible®

**NO. 87**
**1996 EDITION**

**EDITOR:**
William S. Jarrett

**PRODUCTION & DESIGN:**
Charlene Cruson Step

**FIREARMS CONSULTANTS:**
Bill Meade
Vincent A. Pestilli
Paul Rochelle

**COVER PHOTOGRAPHER:**
Ray Wells

**PUBLISHER:**
David C. Perkins

**PRESIDENT**
Brian T. Herrick

**STOEGER PUBLISHING COMPANY**

Every effort has been made to record specifications and descriptions of guns, ammunition and accessories accurately, but the Publisher can take no responsibility for errors or omissions. The prices shown for guns, ammunition and accessories are manufacturers' suggested retail prices (unless otherwise noted) and are furnished for information only. These were in effect at press time and are subject to change without notice. Purchasers of this book have complete freedom of choice in pricing for resale.



Published by Stoeger Publishing Company
5 Mansard Court
Wayne, New Jersey 07470

Library of Congress Catalog Card No.: 63-6200
International Standard Book No.: 0-88317-181-3

Manufactured in the United States of America

In the United States:
Distributed to the book trade and to the sporting goods trade by
Stoeger Industries
5 Mansard Court
Wayne, New Jersey 07470

In Canada:
Distributed to the book trade and to the sporting goods trade by
Stoeger Canada Ltd.
1801 Wentworth Street, Unit 16
Whitby, Ontario, L1N 8R6, Canada

# Contents

# FOREWORD

As we approach the start of a new millennium, the most popular buzz word seems to be "change"—political as well as social. This 87th edition of SHOOTER'S BIBLE certainly reinforces the validity of that catchword, for these days "change" is apparent throughout the firearms industry.

Some things, though, remain the same. For example, we've repeated the popular "50 Years Ago in Shooter's Bible" feature for the ninth year in a row, including a review of that year's important events (1946, in this case). The articles that follow remain a blend of the old and new in shooting sports. Wayne van Zwoll offers some good advice on selecting new lightweight gear for big-game hunting, and Ralph Quinn weighs in with a piece on the importance of high-quality barrel making for top rifle accuracy. Toby Bridges describes some of the new products now available to muzzleloaders, and Don Lewis, another old friend of SHOOTER'S BIBLE, contributes a solid piece on how modern benchrest tools can fine-tune a varmint rifle better than ever.

As for the "old," we offer Steve Irwin's collection of those great wooden shotshell boxes and their contents—"nostalgic reminders of a time when game was more plentiful and bag limits were more generous." Author Jim Casada takes a reminiscent look at one of America's greatest outdoor writers, Robert Ruark, whose book, "The Old Man and the Boy," remains a classic of its kind. Finally, Wilf Pyle writes on the recently revised practice of hunting with a rifle-handgun combination, and which combos are lasting. Following these articles, you're invited to peruse through our Manufacturers Showcase, which contains a broad selection of products for shooters and gun enthusiasts of all types.

That leads us into the Specifications section, where we introduce several new manufacturers along with a few who've closed up shop during the past year. The former include Stone Mountain Arms, Cumberland Mountain Arms, UFA Teton (all blackpowder manufacturers), County Shotguns, Benton & Brown Rifles, and Precision Small Arms handguns. Gone from these pages are Parker- Hale, Churchill, Heym, Eagle Arms, KDF and Carl Gustaf.

The Sights and Scopes category, which includes more than 20 manufacturers and suppliers, adds Quarton to its list. And Thompson/Center, already well known for its handguns and rifles, joins our Reloading section. Those who are interested in ammunition and ballistics data will find 25 pages of resource tables and illustrations.

Finally, the Reference section, which is also updated each year, includes a lineup of new books of interest to shooting and gun enthusiasts, a Directory of Manufacturers and Suppliers, a list of discontinued models, and the all-important Caliberfinder and Gunfinder indexes. These will enable readers to find quickly and easily any of the guns that appear in SHOOTER'S BIBLE 1996 by caliber and model. All you have to do is "let your fingers do the walking."

As in the past, we hope you enjoy and benefit from this newest edition to our long line of annual publications. We welcome your suggestions and look forward to hearing from you

William S. Jarrett
*Editor*

## Articles

# 50 YEARS AGO IN SHOOTER'S BIBLE

With World War II at an end, the firearms and ammunitions industries turned their attention to the needs of average sportsmen, many of whom were former military personnel who had never before participated in the shooting sports. As the government lifted wartime price ceilings, supplies quickly became exhausted as demand increased.

A. F. Stoeger Jr. was now president of the Stoeger Arms Corporation and publisher of SHOOTER'S BIBLE. His father, A. F. Stoeger Sr., owner and founder of the company, had passed away in August 1945. The 1946 edition was therefore dedicated to him—the man who had "conceived the idea of the SHOOTER'S BIBLE and who, up to the end, remained its guiding spirit."

The demand for new firearms of all kinds that year ran far ahead of supplies, but the factories were humming, and new products were on the drawing boards. Because of the dearth of supplies, the new publisher noted, "Practically all the parts listed in the 'Gun Parts' section are immediately available . . . this should be a great boon to individuals and gunsmiths alike."

Some new products were available, of course. In the 1946 edition, for example, Winchester's Model 71 Big Game Rifle was listed for sale at $88.70, and Remington was selling its Model 81 Standard Grade for $109.40. Marlin touted its full line of rifles and shotguns as "the best Marlin guns in 76 years."

In addition to reprinting several pages as they appeared in the 1946 edition of SHOOTER'S BIBLE, we've continued our popular feature called "1946 In Review," which records the year's important news and sports events month by month. You'll find these nuggets of information in the boxes that appear at the top of the next 12 pages. We hope this section and the articles that follow will prove enjoyable as well as informative.

## 1946 IN REVIEW

***JANUARY:** In its third straight Rose Bowl appearance, Southern California is upset by Alabama, 34–14. Army is named National Collegiate Champion in football for 1945. The United Nations holds its first session in New York. Angela Lansbury and Judy Garland star in "The Harvey Girls."*

# COLT MATCH TARGET WOODSMAN

**Cal. .22 Long Rifle**

**6½" HEAVY BARREL**

**FIXED FRONT SIGHT . . .**
**RUGGED 2-WAY ADJUSTABLE REAR SIGHT**

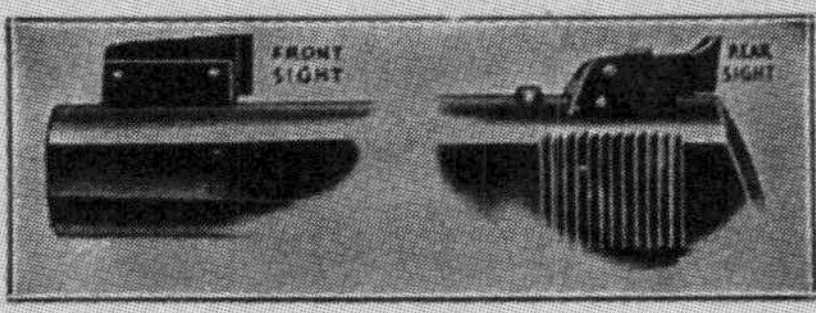


The new Woodsman has a perfect set of sights. The front sight is fixed Kelly type with full face and completely stippled.

The rear sight is NEW with adjustments for both elevation and windage. Both front and rear sights are exceptionally strong and rugged.

### SPECIFICATIONS

Ammunition: .22 Long Rifle Greased Cartridges, Regular or High Speed • Magazine Capacity: 10 cartridges • Action: Hand finished. Velvet smooth • Barrel: Of special weighted design. Slightly tapered, with flat sides • Length of Barrel: 6½ inches • Length over All: 11 inches • Distance Between Sights: 9¼ inches • Weight: 36 ounces • Sights: Front fixed sight. Rear sight adjustable, with adjustments for both elevation and windage • Trigger: Grooved. Of special design, with excess travel and backlash removed • Stocks: Specially designed to extend below bottom strap • Finish: Blued. Top of barrel, receiver and slide stippled. Rear of slide and receiver also stippled.

So perfectly has this Woodsman been designed, that it is hard to believe that seven full ounces have been added to its weight. The balance is absolutely perfect, with the weight in just the proper spot to boost timed and rapid fire scores. It's a streamlined job . . . thoroughly modern in every way.

The muzzle of the barrel is flat, with a slight tapering toward the rifling such as found on the most expensive rifles. To eliminate glare and light reflection the top of the barrel, receiver, and slide, as well as both sights have all been stippled to a fine dull finish. So has the rear of the slide and receiver.

The action of the Match Target Woodsman is super smooth, and has been hand-honed to a velvet finish that only Colt craftsmen could produce. The pull is smooth as glass . . . the let-off quick, sharp and without creep. Even the backlash has been removed. It's the smoothest thing out in .22 pistols.

No expense has been spared to make this the World's Finest Target Pistol . . . the arm that has been designed BY Expert Shooters FOR Expert Shooters.

# OFFICIAL POLICE REVOLVER

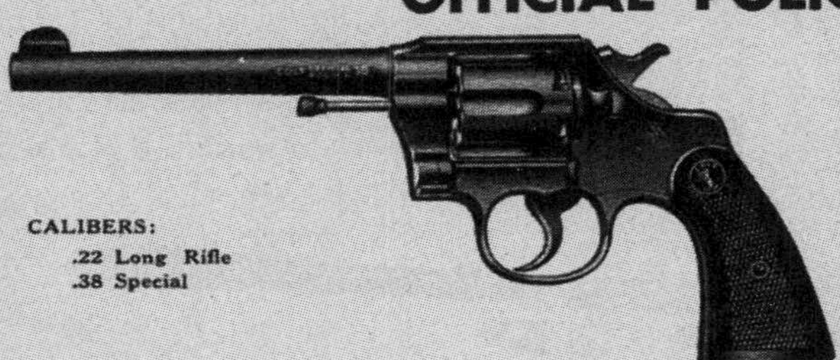

**CALIBERS:**
**.22 Long Rifle**
**.38 Special**

### SPECIFICATIONS: Caliber .38 Special

Ammunition:
.38 Short Colt; .38 Long Colt; .38 Colt Special; .38 S. & W. Special (full and mid-range loads); .38 Colt Special High Speed; .38 S. & W. Special High Speed and .38-44 S. & W. Special cartridges in .38 special model.

Lengths of Barrel: 2, 4, 5, 6 inches.

Length Over All: With 6 inch barrel, 11¼ inches.

Weight: With 6 inch barrel, 34 ounces.

Sights: Fixed type, stippled

Trigger and Hammer Spur: Checked. Stocks: Checked Walnut.

Finish: Blued or Nickel. Top of frame matted to prevent light reflection.

**Price .........................$36.75**

The COLT Official Police Revolver is without any question the world's outstanding police arm. This popular service model is famous for its ruggedness, and its ability to stand up under the severe abuse it receives at the sides of police officers the world over. Built on the .41 caliber frame it has ample strength to meet any requirements—and the .38 Special cartridges for which it is chambered offer sufficient power to meet any emergency. The Official Police is furnished with the Colt Positive Safety Lock—which makes accidental discharge impossible. Full size grip, perfect balance, special matted top. Also chambered for .22 Long Rifle cartridges to allow police officers, economical target practice with a small caliber model that is otherwise identical with their regular service arm.

### SPECIFICATIONS: Caliber .22

Ammunition: .22 Long Rifle cartridges. Regular or High Speed.

Length of Barrel: 6 inches only.

Length Over All: 11¼ inches.

Weight: 38 ounces.

Sights: Fixed type, stippled.

Cylinder: Embedded Head Type.

Stocks: Checked Walnut.

Finish: Blued only.

Top of frame matted to prevent light reflection.

Trigger and Hammer Spur: Checked.

**Price .........................$42.00**

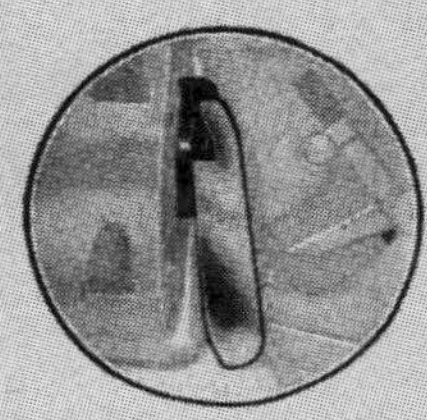

**Colt "Two Point" Hand**

*You have possibly often wondered what device was used in Colt Revolvers to hold the cylinder chamber and the barrel so rigidly and so perfectly in line. This result is obtained through the use of the **Colt "Two Point" Hand** found only in Colt Revolvers.*

*FEBRUARY: Bob Hope, Bing Crosby and Dorothy Lamour appear in their first "Road" movie, "Road to Utopia." IBM introduces its electronic calculator—called ENIAC—a new machine with no moving parts. Wartime price ceilings on arms and ammunition are lifted, causing prices to increase by 15 percent.*

# SAVAGE AUTOMATIC SHOTGUNS

## MODEL 720
**12 and 16 Gauge**

### STANDARD GRADE—5 Shot

The Standard Grade has the same general specifications as the Upland Sporter, except that it weighs 4 oz. more. It has a magazine capacity of four shells, with one shell in chamber giving five shots. A wood plug is furnished to reduce magazine capacity to two shells—with one shell in chamber, maximum of gun is three shots, complying with Federal Law regarding capacity of automatic shotguns when used on migratory birds.

Price .................................................. **$76.25**
Raised Solid Matted Rib, Extra .................... **13.45**

### UPLAND SPORTER—3 Shot

The Upland Sporter is a new three-shot automatic especially designed for field shooting. It is light to carry, fast in action and easy to point. The receiver is artistically decorated and this with the special checkering on stock and forearm combine to make an attractive arm for field use. It excels in ease of operation, shooting qualities and all-around dependability.

BARRELS—12 gauge, 26, 28 and 30-inch lengths; 16 gauge, 26, 28 and 30-inch lengths. Full, modified or cylinder bore. Plain round.

STOCK—Selected American walnut. Full pistol grip checkered on grip and forestock. Push-button type safety in rear of trigger guard. Magazine capacity two shells, with one in chamber, giving three shots. Receiver channeled and matted in line of sight. Friction ring adjustment for light and heavy loads. Receiver artistically decorated. Weight, 16 gauge, about 7½ pounds; 12 gauge, about 8 pounds.

Price .................................................. **$76.25**
Raised solid matted rib, extra .................... **13.45**

## MODEL 720-P
**12 and 16 Gauge**

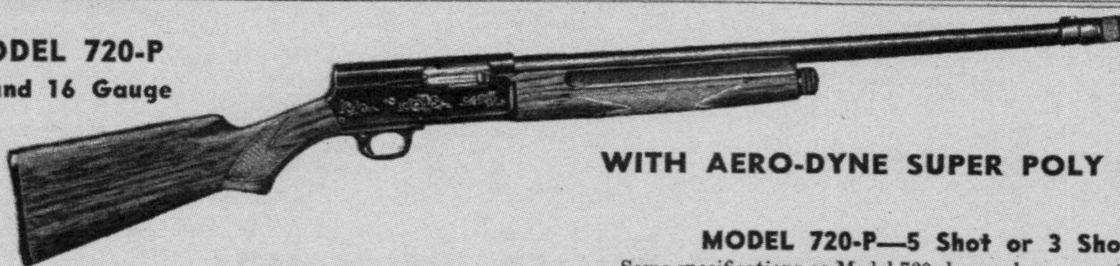

## WITH AERO-DYNE SUPER POLY CHOKE

### MODEL 740-P—Skeet Model. 3 Shot

Made in the same specifications as the Model 720-P, described above except that it has a fancy American Walnut stock, oil finish, full capped pistol grip elaborately checkered and a special beavertail fore-end, also elaborately checkered.

WEIGHT—About 8¼ pounds.

Price .................................................. **$95.55**

### MODEL 720-P—5 Shot or 3 Shot

Same specifications as Model 720 shown above except as follows:

Aero-Dyne Super Poly Choke built integral with barrel and equipped with Bev-L-Blok front sight.

Furnished only with 28" over-all barrel.

The Poly Choke is a device at the muzzle of barrel with finger adjustable sleeve so the shooter can instantly change to any choke desired. Nine distinct adjustments can be obtained from cylinder to full choke.

Price .................................................. **$90.00**

## MODEL 720-C
**12 and 16 Gauge**

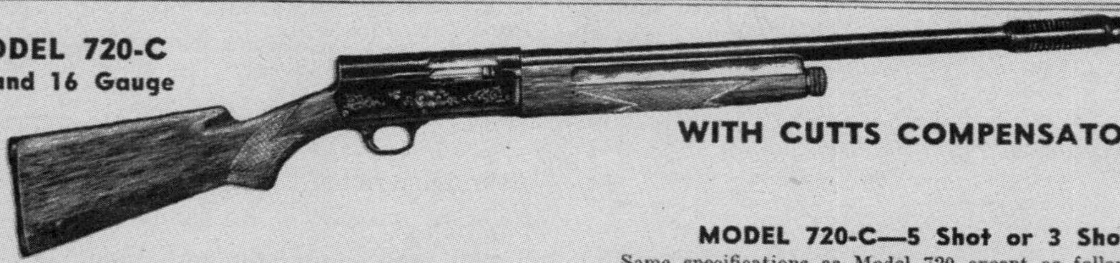

## WITH CUTTS COMPENSATOR

### MODEL 740-P—Skeet Model. 3 Shot

Special barrel with Cutts Compensator attached. 27" over-all length with Compensator and Spreader Tube. Compensator furnished with Spreader Tube and No. 705 Full Choke Tube. Stock 14" length. 2⅝" drop at heel. Selected American Walnut, oil finish. Full capped pistol grip, checkered. Special large beavertail fore-end of selected American Walnut, elaborately checkered. Magazine capacity two shells with one in chamber giving three shots.

WEIGHT—About 8¼ pounds.

Price .................................................. **$102.00**

### MODEL 720-C—5 Shot or 3 Shot

Same specifications as Model 720 except as follows: Special Barrel with Cutts Compensator attached, furnished with two choke tubes. Over-all barrel length 27" when fitted with compensator with spreader tube. Over-all barrel length 28" when fitted with compensator with No. 705 full-choke tube. Modified choke tube will be substituted if specified. Compensator regularly made of blued steel. Can be furnished made of aluminum alloy on special order.

The Cutts Compensator, when attached to the muzzle of shotguns, reduces recoil from 35% to 46% and provides a means of securing various chokes in one barrel by changing the choke tubes which screw on the end of the compensator.

**Price** .................................................. **$93.75**

MARCH: *Behind Bob Kurland, Oklahoma A&M defeats California, 52–35 for the NCAA Basketball Championship. Winston Churchill announces that an "Iron Curtain" now separates Communist Russia from the Free World. Smith & Wesson introduces its new line of "Masterpiece" revolvers.*

# WINCHESTER Lever Action and Self-Loading Rifles

TRADE MARK

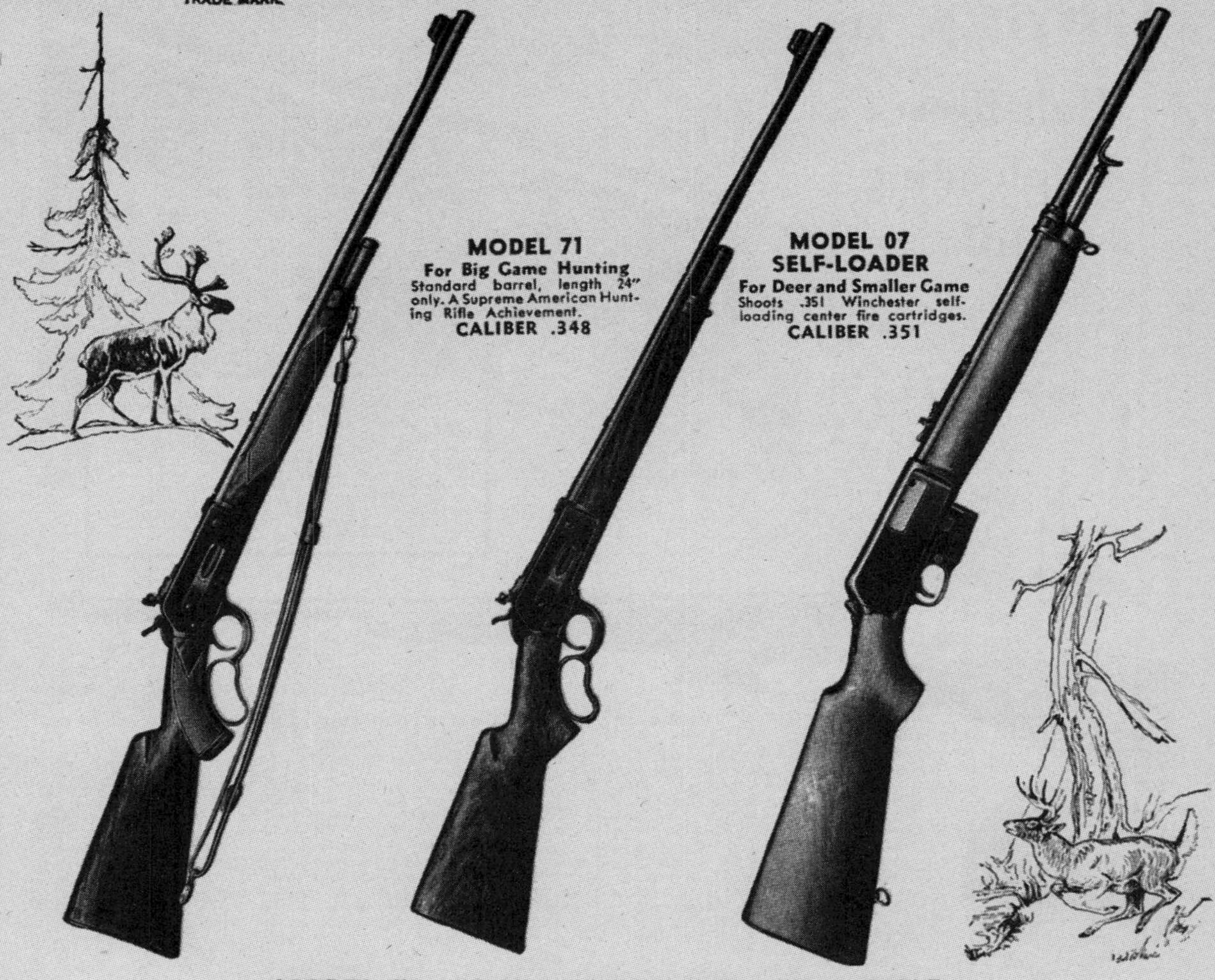
MODEL 71
For Big Game Hunting
Standard barrel, length 24" only. A Supreme American Hunting Rifle Achievement.
CALIBER .348
MODEL 07
SELF-LOADER
For Deer and Smaller Game
Shoots .351 Winchester self-loading center fire cartridges.
CALIBER .351

## MODEL 71—LEVER ACTION REPEATING RIFLE

**SOLID FRAME ONLY.**

This model offers new advantages for big game hunters. The gun is built for its own high efficiency cartridge—the Winchester Model 71 with the new 86 Golden-Jubilee action. The gun is single calibre and has a cartridge which combines greater ballistic efficiency, broader adaptability, higher velocity with medium to abundant bullet weight, with flat trajectory. Increased killing power is obtained with balanced increase of bullet speed, weight & diameter; reducing loss of triple gain.

Winchester Proof Steel barrel. Sporting type pistol grip walnut stock with semi-beavertail fore-end. Bead front-sight on ramp-sight base. Removable sight cover. Winchester rear peep sight No. 98A. Option of Winchester 22K sporting rear sight instead of 98A. N.R.A. leather gun sling, 1" wide. Weight about 8 lbs.

**PRICES:**

| | |
|---|---|
| Model 71 Rifle with Bead front sight and Winchester 22K sporting rear sight, as illustrated.............. | $88.70 |
| Model 71 Rifle with Bead front sight and Winchester 98A peep sight, as illustrated....................... | 88.70 |
| Model 71 Rifle without checkering, gun sling and swivels with Winchester 22K sporting rear sight............ | 77.40 |
| Model 71 Rifle without checkering, gun sling and swivels with Winchester 98A peep sight .................... | 77.40 |

**BIG GAME HUNTERS FAVORITES**

APRIL: *Herman Keiser captures the Masters golf tournament by one stroke over Ben Hogan. Seven new members are inducted into baseball's Hall of Fame, including "Iron Man" McGinnity, Eddie Plank and the three Chicago infielders who made famous the phrase "Tinkers-to-Evers-to-Chance."*

# Remington WOODSMASTER

## MODEL 81

### High-Power Autoloading Rifle

**No Noise Between Shots**

An important feature of the Model 81 autoloading rifle is that there is no mechanical noise between shots; because the action works so quickly that the sound of the action while reloading cannot be heard above the report of the shot. If the first shot misses, an animal is not always aware of the hunter's presence. Although startled, he may not move but will stand perfectly still trying to determine where the shot came from. With the Model 81, the shooter has a chance to get in another shot.

***For All North American Big Game***

***Made in 30, 35 Remington and 300 Savage Calibers***

*Half Pistol Grip*

*Streamlined Fore-end*

The Remington "Woodsmaster" Model 81 is a high power big game rifle that combines speed of action, power, accuracy, and perfect fire control. The autoloading action enables the big game hunter to pour out five shots as fast as he can pull the trigger. You just pull the trigger for each shot, never taking your eye or aim from the target. There is no other big game hunting rifle that offers this type of autoloading, locked-breech action in combination with such a powerful selection of cartridges. Made in 30, 35 Remington and 300 Savage calibers, the Model 81 is the ideal high power rifle to bring down running game. There is only one thing to think about—accurate aiming—in order to hit the game as it runs. Automatic loading does all the rest, leaving you all set for your next shot.

The barrel and action are locked together until the bullet has left the muzzle. Thus the locked-breech action assures positive safety and no loss of power. The full energy of the cartridge is delivered in the flight of the bullet and utmost accuracy is assured. Other safety features include two lugs on the bolt which lock in the barrel extension with great strength, and the conveniently located thumb safety.

The "Woodsmaster" Model 81 excels also in handling qualities and outside design. Note particularly the half pistol grip, streamlined fore-end and other features that contribute to perfect balance and easy handling. Stock and fore-end are especially designed to give fast handling qualities. The rifle is loaded simply by opening the action and pushing five cartridges down into the magazine. After the last shot is fired the action remains open, ready for quick reloading. The magazine is unloaded by pulling the operating handle back and forth until the rifle is empty. Single loading is quick and simple—just drop a cartridge on top of the magazine and release the action. The Model 81 takes down easily, by removing the fore-end and loosening the take-down screw. Length taken down is only 23 inches.

From butt to muzzle the Model 81 "Woodsmaster" upholds the Remington standards of excellence. Simplicity and reliability under all conditions make it an outstanding big game rifle. It will deliver five shots accurately in two seconds, and this means you can throw more than five tons of lead energy at a charging grizzly before he can get close to you. What game could stand up under such terrific power?

### SPECIFICATIONS

"Standard" Grade. Takedown, hammerless, solid breech. Double locking lugs. Made for 30, 35 Remington and 300 Savage calibers, all center fire and rimless. 22 inch barrel. American walnut stock and fore-end. Shotgun style steel butt plate, deeply checkered to prevent slipping. Half pistol grip. Streamlined fore-end. Step adjustable sporting rear sight. White metal bead front sight. Magazine holds 5 cartridges. Length, taken down, 23 inches. Weight about 8¾ pounds.

| | |
|---|---|
| **No. 81A** "Standard" Grade | $109.40 |
| **No. 81B** "Special" Grade | 123.35 |
| **No. 81D** "Peerless" Grade | 252.45 |
| **No. 81E** "Expert" Grade | 352.35 |
| **No. 81F** "Premier" Grade | 452.15 |
| **7/8" Leather Sling Strap,** Whelen type, with hooks and eyes, extra | 3.65 |

***MAY: The Indianapolis 500 auto race is run for the first time since 1941. George Robson wins, averaging 114.82 mph. Assault captures both the Kentucky Derby and the Preakness horse races. "Annie Get Your Gun," starring Ethel Merman, opens on Broadway. The first jet fighter plane is built in England.***

*JUNE: Assault wins the Belmont Stakes to become only the sixth horse to win racing's Triple Crown. Joe Louis knocks out Billy Conn for his 22d successful defense of the heavyweight boxing title. Lloyd Mangrum defeats Vic Ghezzi and Byron Nelson by one stroke after the three men tied in the first playoff round of the U.S. Open golf tournament.*

# FOX SHOTGUNS

## FOX MODEL B

The new Fox Model B has the features of light weight, stream-line design, perfect balance and superior shooting qualities.
**ACTION**—Two trigger, extractor type. Lightning-fast coil spring, hammer and sear design.
**BARRELS**—Alloy forged steel, proof tested. Chambered for 2¾" shells, except .410 bore which is chambered for 3" shells. 12 gauge 26", 28" and 30" barrels; 16 gauge 26" and 28" barrels; 20 gauge 26" and 28" barrels; .410 bore 26" barrels. Barrels bored right modified choke, left full choke, except .410 bore, which are both full choke. Other standard borings furnished to order at no additional charge.
**STOCK**—American walnut, stream-line design. Checkered pistol grip. Fluted comb. Length about 14"; drop at heel about 2¾". Hard rubber butt plate.
**FRAME**—Black gun-metal finish. Shock-proof bolting.
**WEIGHT**—12 gauge, 7¼ to 7½ lbs. 16 gauge, 6¼ to 6½ lbs. 20 gauge, 6 to 6¼ lbs. .410 bore, 5¾ to 6 lbs.
Price .......................................... **$34.50**

## STERLINGWORTH GRADE

Owing to the simplicity of mechanism, all superfluous metal in frame is eliminated, giving the gun a perfect balance and at the same time leaving plenty of metal in barrels, where strain is the greatest. The Fox system of boring is responsible for uniform pattern and maximum penetration attained in all Fox guns.

Special alloy forged steel Barrels, adapted to smokeless or black powders, American Walnut stock; full pistol grip; genuine hard rubber butt plate. Any other barrel borings if desired at no extra charge.

Without Automatic Shell Ejector .......................... **$66.50**
With Automatic Shell Ejector .......................... **84.75**

STERLINGWORTH DE LUXE, fitted with Jostam Anti-Flinch Recoil Pad and two Lyman ivory bead sights. Made in 28, 30 or 32 inch barrels. Any boring at no additional charge. Barrels regularly furnished bored right modified and left full choke.
Non-Ejector price .......................... **$71.25**
Sterlingworth Deluxe with Ejector .......................... **89.00**

| Weight 12 Gauge | Weight 16 Gauge | Weight 20 Gauge | Barrel Length | Boring of Barrels | | Length Stock | Drop Stock |
|---|---|---|---|---|---|---|---|
| | | | | Right | Left | | |
| 7¾ to 8¼ lbs. | 6½ to 7 lbs. | 6¼ to 6¾ lbs. | 32" | Full | Full | 14" | 2¾" |
| 7¼ to 7¾ lbs. | 6½ to 6¾ lbs. | 6¼ to 6½ lbs. | 30" | Mod. | Full | 14" | 2¾" |
| 7 to 7½ lbs. | 6¼ to 6½ lbs. | 6 to 6¼ lbs. | 28" | Mod. | Full | 14" | 2¾" |
| 6⅞ to 7¼ lbs. | 6 to 6¼ lbs. | 5¾ to 6 lbs. | 26" | Cyl. | Mod. | 14" | 2¾" |

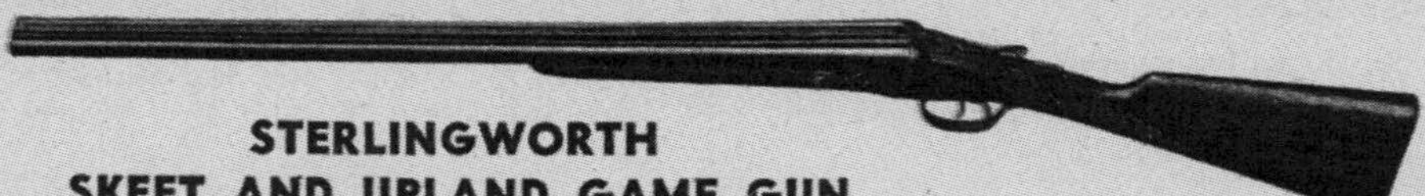

## STERLINGWORTH SKEET AND UPLAND GAME GUN

To meet the demand for a moderately priced skeet and upland game double gun we have produced the famous Fox-Sterlingworth gun in this new straight grip model with 26 or 28 inch barrels bored: right, skeet cylinder; left, quarter choke. This is a standard stock model possessing the features of skeet boring and stock design, heretofore available only in custom-built guns.
**BARRELS**—Special alloy forged steel; boring, right barrel, skeet cyl.; left barrel, mod. choke.
**STOCK**—American walnut, straight grip. Length 14 inches, drop at heel 2⅝ inches.
**FRAME**—Forged ordnance steel; case hardened finish; ornamented with fine line engraving.
**ACTION**—Two trigger, extractor type.
**WEIGHT**—12 gauge about 7 pounds. 16 gauge about 6 pounds. 20 gauge about 5¾ pounds.
Sterlingworth Skeet and Upland Game Gun.............. **$73.85**
With Automatic Ejectors.......................... **91.85**
Full Beaver-Tail Forend, extra .......................... **14.80**
Fox-Kautzky Selective Single Trigger, extra .......... **28.20**
Recoil Pad, extra .......................... **4.70**
Ivory Bead Sights, extra.......................... **1.45**

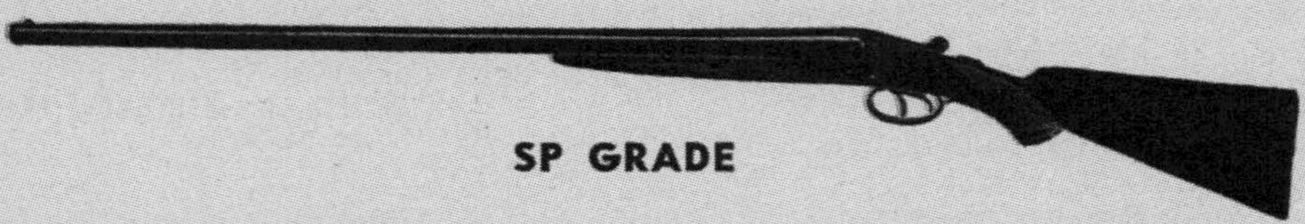

## SP GRADE



**NO FOX DOUBLES UNTIL 1947—OLD PRICES SHOWN ONLY FOR REFERENCE**

*JULY: Ted Williams blasts two home runs to lead the American League over the National League, 12–0 in the 13th annual All-Star game. Yvon Petra of France wins the men's Wimbledon tennis championship; Pauline Betz takes the women's cup. The U.S. Federal Reserve announces that half of all Americans earn less than $2,000 a year.*

# HIGH STANDARD AUTOMATIC PISTOLS

## GENERAL SPECIFICATIONS

The High Standard .22 calibre Automatic Pistol is of modern construction and design. It has all the features desired by the target shooter and sportsman. This pistol comes now in 6 different styles giving the shooter a selection never had before. This pistol can be taken down for cleaning very easily without using any tool whatsoever. All models will take low pressure as well as all standard makes of high speed ammunition.

Manufactured by gun mechanics who have had a lifetime of experience in producing firearms. Carefully inspected and tested. Guaranteed to be reliable and accurate.

## HAMMER MODELS "H"

There are some shooters who have always handled a revolver that have become used to an outside hammer and who would have changed to an automatic pistol except that all .22 caliber automatic pistols have formerly been of the hammerless type. With this in view a line of visible hammer pistols has been brought out. There is a little shorter hammer fall and a trigger pull that will show less variation with continued shooting. This is brought out by the fact that one of the most prominent shooters in the country states that in five thousand rounds his trigger pull has not changed more than 4 ounces, which is remarkable.

## HAMMERLESS

**MODEL B .22 L.R.**
**MODEL C .22 SHORT**

**(Model B with 4½" or 6¾" Bbl.)**
**Model C with 6¾" Bbl. only**

## HAMMER

**MODEL H-B .22 L.R.**

**Barrel 4½" or 6¾"**

## MODELS B, H-B, C, AND S-B

There is not a pistol on the market that can equal the High Standard Model "B" at the same price. The reputation of the manufacturers has been built up on the workmanship and quality of material that goes into this fine pistol plus accuracy excelled by none. An automatic that will handle both low pressure and high speed ammunition. Buy one, and see for yourself the pleasure and enjoyment you can get with this fine pistol using the inexpensive .22 caliber long rifle rimfire cartridges. Powerful enough for small game and sufficiently accurate for fine target work.

Model C is identical to model B, but for .22 short only.

### SPECIFICATIONS

Calibre .22 Long Rifle, barrel 6¾" or 4½", with fixed Patridge sights, magazine capacity 10 shot. Comes with black hard rubber grips, checkered. Comes with heavy barrel, small bore, deep rifling for extreme accuracy penetration and long wear. Weight: 31 oz.

| | |
|---|---|
| Model B with 6¾" barrel, cal. .22 L.R., price | $25.00 |
| Model B with 4½" barrel, cal. .22 L.R., price | 25.00 |
| Model C with 6¾" barrel, cal. .22 short | 25.00 |
| Model H-B with 6¾" barrel, cal. .22 L.R., price | 25.00 |
| Model H-B with 4½" barrel, cal. .22 L.R., price | 25.00 |

## MODELS A AND H-A

The High Standard Manufacturing Company were the first to bring out the new .22 caliber automatic long handle pistols. Realizing that the grip on the .22 automatic was too short for the average hand we spent a great deal of time and money in developing our new long handle models and at the same time added new features such as the automatic slide lock, adjustable rear sight and walnut grips. The Model "A" is practically the same as the Model "B" with the exception of the features mentioned above. It has the same barrel. The automatic slide lock holds the action open when the last cartridge has been fired from the magazine. The adjustable rear sight is positively locked in position and cannot shoot loose. This pistol is recommended to the shooters who want something a little better than the Model "B" and with additional features.

### SPECIFICATIONS

Barrel—Small bore deep rifling for extreme accuracy, penetration, and long wear.

Sights—Patridge front with wide blade and special adjustable rear.

Safety—Positive.

Grips—Walnut, finely checkered.

Finish—Blued.

Takedown—Slide removed without the use of any tools for inspection and cleaning of barrel from the breech end. No loose parts, pins or screws to fall out.

Weight of pistol—Model A 36 oz.

## HAMMERLESS

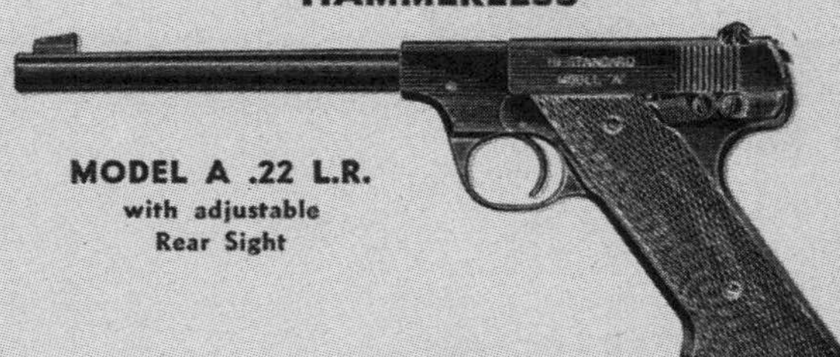

**MODEL A .22 L.R.**
**with adjustable**
**Rear Sight**

## HAMMER

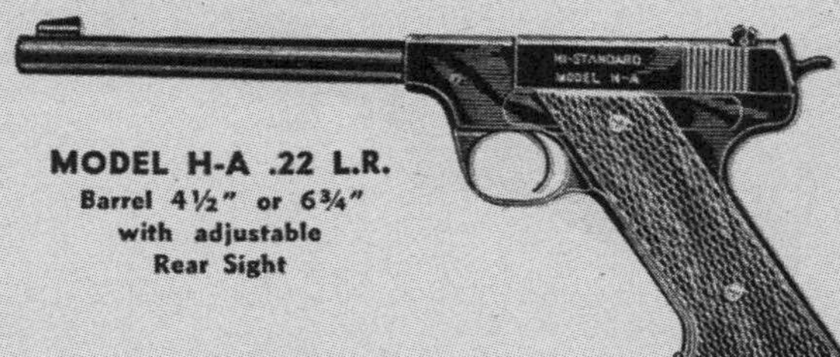

**MODEL H-A .22 L.R.**
**Barrel 4½" or 6¾"**
**with adjustable**
**Rear Sight**



**PISTOLS ON THIS PAGE NOT AVAILABLE UNTIL 1947**

***AUGUST: Ben Hogan easily defeats Ed "Porky" Oliver to capture the PGA golf tournament. China's communist leader, Mao Tse-Tung, declares all-out war against Chiang Kai-Shek. Humphrey Bogart and Lauren Bacall appear together for the first time in "The Big Sleep." Joe McCarthy defeats Robert LaFollette to become Wisconsin's junior senator.***

WINCHESTER
TRADE MARK

# MODEL 12
## SKEET GUN

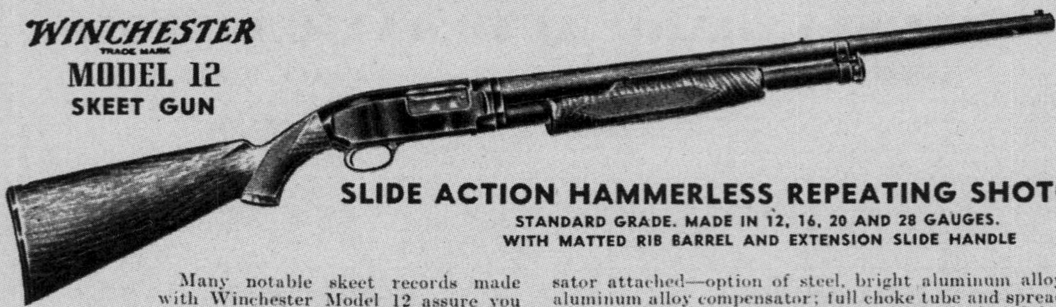

## SLIDE ACTION HAMMERLESS REPEATING SHOTGUN

**STANDARD GRADE. MADE IN 12, 16, 20 AND 28 GAUGES.**
**WITH MATTED RIB BARREL AND EXTENSION SLIDE HANDLE**

Many notable skeet records made with Winchester Model 12 assure you that if you like a repeater you will find this Standard Winchester Model 12 Skeet Gun exceptionally likeable both for skeet and for a lot of fast work in upland game shooting. Receiver sand blasted on top to prevent light refraction. Barrel, 26", with solid raised matted rib and the highly successful Winchester special Skeet Choke. Also furnished (A) in all gauges with plain barrel; (B) in 12 gauge only with 26¾" ventilated rib barrel; (C) in 12, 16 and 20 gauges with plain barrel with muzzle shoulder and Cutts Compensator attached—option of steel, bright aluminum alloy or blacked aluminum alloy compensator; full choke tube and spreader tube and special wrench included. Skeet stock with checkered full pistol grip and hard rubber cap. Checkered extension slide handle. Sights, Bradley ⅛" red bead front and metal middle; except on Compensator-equipped gun bead is metal.

Stock dimensions, 14" x 1½" x 2½" and 2" pitch. Regular 5-shot magazine. Removable magazine plug for limiting capacity to three shots. 28 gauge chambered for 2⅞" shells, all others for 2¾" shells. Approximate weights: 12 gauge 7¾ lbs., 16, 20 and 28 gauges 6¾ lbs. Take down.

**Order by symbol shown below**

| Symbol | Gauge | Barrel Length | Choke | Each | Symbol | Gauge | Barrel Length | Choke | Each |
|---|---|---|---|---|---|---|---|---|---|
| G1280S | 12 | 26" | Win. Skeet | $97.00 | G1236S | 12 | 26" | Win. Skeet | $84.75 |
| G1281S | 16 | 26" | Win. Skeet | | G1237S | 16 | 26" | Win. Skeet | |
| G1282S | 20 | 26" | Win. Skeet | | G1238S | 20 | 26" | Win. Skeet | |
| G1283S | 28 | 26" | Win. Skeet | | G1258SN | 28 | 26" | Win. Skeet | |

# MODEL 12
## SKEET GUN—TAKE-DOWN
**WITH VENTILATED RIB**
**12 Gauge Only**

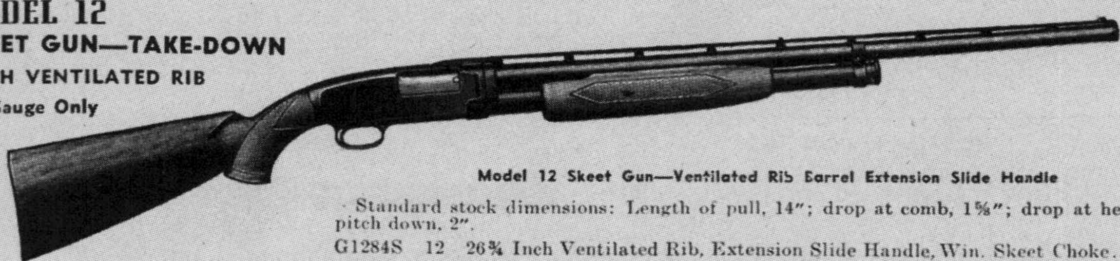

**Model 12 Skeet Gun—Ventilated Rib Barrel Extension Slide Handle**

Standard stock dimensions: Length of pull, 14"; drop at comb, 1⅝"; drop at heel, 2⅝"; pitch down, 2".

G1284S 12 26¾ Inch Ventilated Rib, Extension Slide Handle, Win. Skeet Choke. **$142.85**

# MODEL 12
## SKEET GUN—TAKE-DOWN
**WITH CUTTS COMPENSATOR**

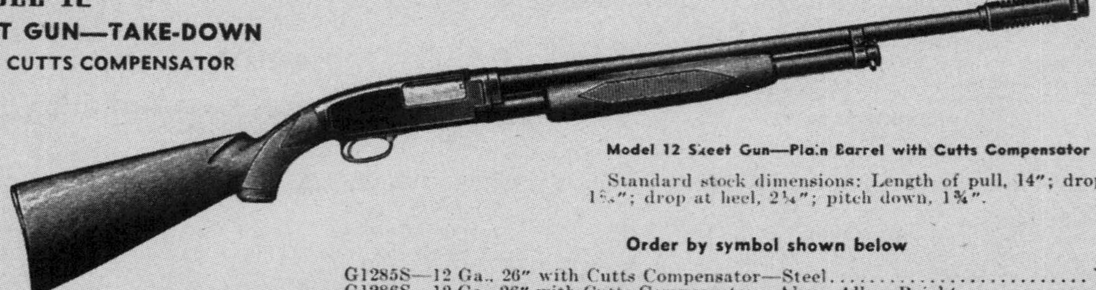

**Model 12 Skeet Gun—Plain Barrel with Cutts Compensator Attached**

Standard stock dimensions: Length of pull, 14"; drop at comb, 1⅝"; drop at heel, 2¼"; pitch down, 1¾".

**Order by symbol shown below**

| | | |
|---|---|---|
| G1285S—12 Ga., 26" with Cutts Compensator—Steel | .......... | $109.15 |
| G1286S—12 Ga., 26" with Cutts Compensator—Alum. Alloy, Bright | .......... | |
| G1287S—12 Ga., 26" with Cutts Compensator—Alum. Alloy, Blacked | .......... | |



**THE GUN FOR PUMP-HANDY SKEET SHOOTERS**

*SEPTEMBER: The first U.S. Women's Open golf tournament is won by Patty Berg over Betty Jameson. Jack Kramer beats Tom Brown to become the new U.S. lawn tennis champion, while Pauline Betz takes the women's title for the fourth time. The first Cannes Film Festival is held, with Billy Wilder's "The Lost Weekend" sharing top honors.*

# AMERICAN MUZZLE LOADING RIFLES

Revolutionary Flint Lock Rifle, used between 1760 to 1800, was made by J. Baer. The wood is polished butternut. Caliber of gun about .69. Type used by the pioneers for hunting and extensively used during the battles of the Revolution.

Typical Plains Rifle with under barrel supporting rib stock, made of birds eye maple. Gun made about 1845 by William Ogden, Owego, New York. (A. W. Spies was New York distributor for various gunsmiths.) Type favored by emigrants, pioneers and buffalo hunters.

Flint Lock Rifle commonly known as a "Squirrel Rifle," because of its small caliber. Unknown maker. Curly maple stock. Brass Patch Box. Silver inlays and escutcheons. Pennsylvania made. Between 1790 to 1810. Caliber about .36. Type used in early target matches and turkey shoots. An all around favorite.

Lehman of Lancaster is the maker. Simulated curly maple finish. This effect was obtained by wrapping impregnated cotton around the stock and then setting it afire. Percussion type, caliber about .45. Type used for trading with Indians. Worth its height in stacked pelts, hence its purposeful long length.

***OCTOBER:** The St. Louis Cardinals, after winning the first National League playoff series, win the 43d annual World Series, defeating the Boston Red Sox, 4 games to 3. Enos Slaughter scores the winning run in the last game by racing home from first base on a single by Harry Walker. Ice hockey star Gordie Howe scores his first goal in a record-setting career that lasts 34 years.*

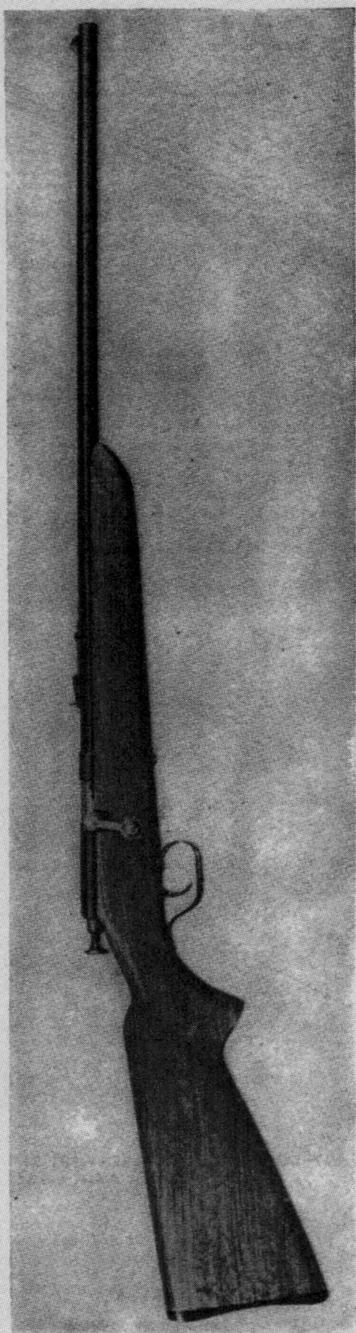

# The Best MARLIN GUNS in 76 Years

Marlin now offers the most sensational line of rifles and shotguns since the founding of the Company in 1870. From the new, custom-styled, low-priced .22's to the great new Model 90 Single Trigger Over & Under Shotgun (shown on page 61), advances and refinements feature the 1946 Marlin models. Long life, safety, accuracy and dependable performance, traditional with Marlin, are built into these new guns. Barrel bores are specially treated to discourage corrosion or rust. Every rifle is targeted and its action tested at the plant. All Marlin high power rifles and shotguns are proof-tested with extra heavy loads. Marlin offers the best guns and the best values in its 76-year history!

**NEW CUSTOM STYLE BUTTSTOCKS**

Marlin designers introduce this year the new custom style, one-piece buttstock, with fluted comb and semi-beaver tail forearm. Featured on all but one model of Marlin's popular-priced .22's, these man-size, custom-style buttstocks are outstanding for appearance and feel.

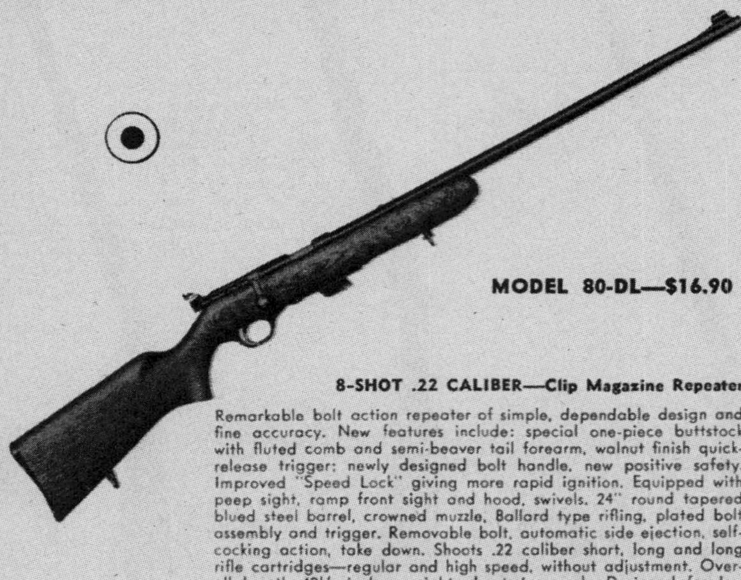

**MODEL 80-DL—$16.90**

**8-SHOT .22 CALIBER—Clip Magazine Repeater**

Remarkable bolt action repeater of simple, dependable design and fine accuracy. New features include: special one-piece buttstock with fluted comb and semi-beaver tail forearm, walnut finish quick-release trigger; newly designed bolt handle, new positive safety. Improved "Speed Lock" giving more rapid ignition. Equipped with peep sight, ramp front sight and hood, swivels. 24" round tapered blued steel barrel, crowned muzzle, Ballard type rifling, plated bolt assembly and trigger. Removable bolt, automatic side ejection, self-cocking action, take down. Shoots .22 caliber short, long and long rifle cartridges—regular and high speed, without adjustment. Overall length 42½ inches weight about 6 pounds. Designed for low mount telescopes.

**MODEL 80-C—$15.25**

Same general specifications as Model 80-DL but with Rocky Mountain type rear sight, bead front sight, no swivels.

← **MODEL 100—$8.65** **(Illustrated)**

**SINGLE SHOT BOLT ACTION .22 CAL. RIFLE**

24" round tapered blued steel barrel, crowned muzzle, Ballard type rifling. Shoots .22 cal. short, long and long rifle cartridges, regular and high speed. Walnut finish, full pistol grip stock; "non-slip" shaped, rubber butt plate. Removable bolt for quick cleaning. Rebounding striker for safety, automatic ejection. Flush take down screw, plated bolt assembly and trigger. Partridge type front sight. Overall length 40½ inches; weight about 4½ pounds.

©

**QUALITY AT LOW PRICE**

***NOVEMBER:** The National Horse Show returns to New York's Madison Square Garden for the first time since 1941. Over 400,000 coal miners, led by John L. Lewis, go on strike. Myrna Loy and Frederick March star in "The Best Years of Our Lives." The French government declares martial law against Vietnam and orders the first bombing raid over Hanoi.*

*DECEMBER: The Chicago Bears win the NFL championship, 24–14 over the New York Giants. Army's great running back, Glenn Davis, is awarded the Heisman Trophy. Chester Carlson files for a patent on his new electrostatic printing process, later marketed as the "Xerox" machine. W. C. Fields, the great film comedian, dies on Christmas day.*

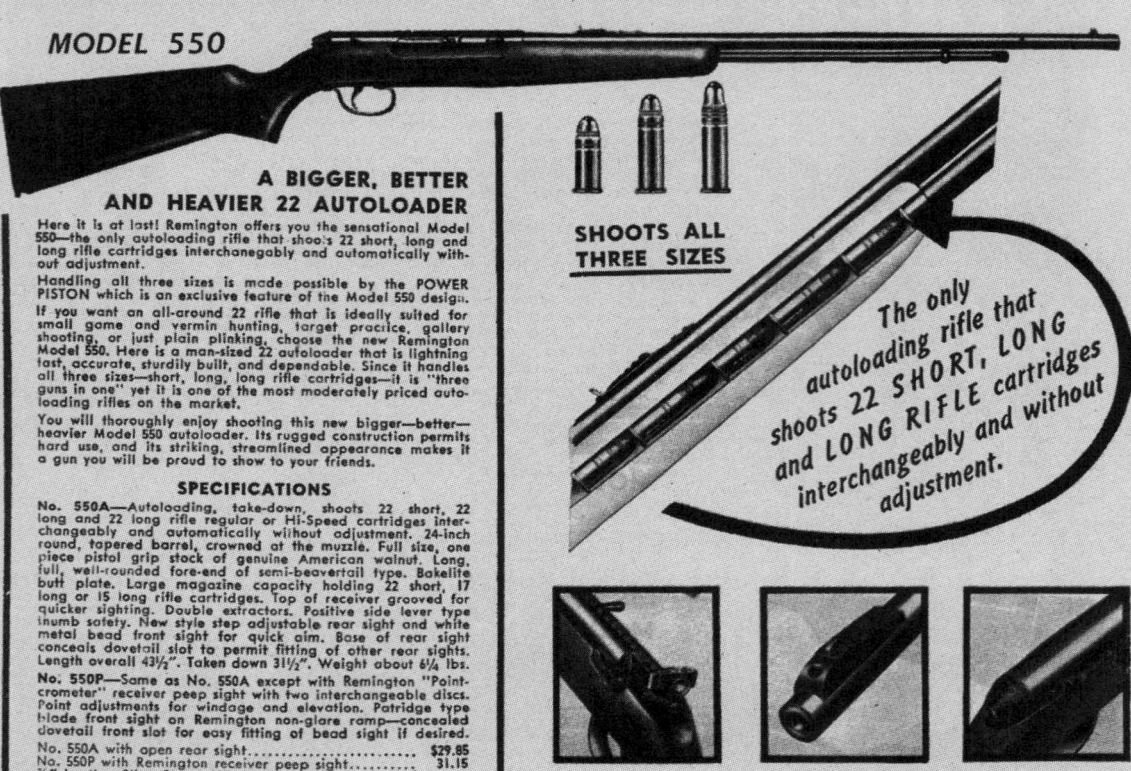

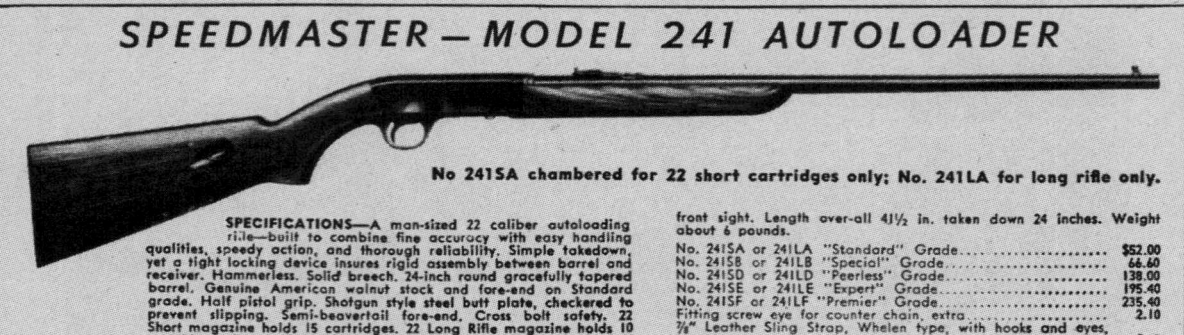

# LIGHTEN UP!

*by Wayne van Zwoll*

Anyone who has ever tried to move a piano knows you can't think about where you're going if you also have to think about what you're carrying. With a piano, you need only think about the next step. On a hunt, you must also consider your mission. For hunting demands that you pay attention to the woods around you, that you stay alert and move fluidly. When you're tired, you can't hunt well—and extra, unnecessary weight is one of the things that make you tired.

The first things you must get rid of are the following misconceptions: that weight only matters in the mountains, when you're climbing; and that an ounce is only an ounce. The fact is weight affects your hunt even when you're sitting in a tree stand or driving a swamp for whitetails. The weight of your bow or gun determines how it holds in your hand; the weight of your backpack can impair your ability to keep your footing while crossing a stream. Extra weight in your daypack can not only slow you down on an alpine ascent, it can gradually sap your energy in flatland coverts as well.

The simple truth is: weight can sneak up on you. A friend, frustrated by his own inability to keep up with a younger, more vigorous hiking partner, surreptitiously slipped small stones into his unsuspecting partner's pack at each rest stop. By the end of the day, this poor fellow was carrying an extra five pounds. The weight went unnoticed, however, because it comprised only a small percentage of total pack weight. The stones were added incrementally, without increasing bulk or altering balance.

Most of the time, though, such added weight translates into extra bulk and shifts in balance. These factors alone can make a hunter aware of heavier loads. Four ounces added to the sole of your hunting shoe can be immediately noticeable; but four pounds of books on a piano you're trying to carry may produce no perceptible weight increase. An ounce is an ounce only by definition. The difference between a well-balanced rifle and one that handles like a wooden plank may lie in the subtle distribution of ounces. Weight carried close to your back is more manageable than weight jammed into a rear pack pocket, far from the center of gravity.

In the early days, hunters and trappers had to put up with a lot of weight. Rifles were heavy then, because steel lacked the strength of modern metals. Bullets didn't travel as fast, either, so they had to be bigger to kill big game. Barrels were long, too, and there were no aluminum trigger guards, no hollow synthetic stocks. Heavy wool blankets were needed to fend off the cold;

*Hunters should use a strong, external-frame pack like this Kelty, with its single, top-opening main compartment and side pockets. This bag will carry 120 pounds of boned meat. With such a load, the wide, padded waist belt is invaluable.*

there were no down-filled bags of rip-stop nylon. Our early hunters used tin and cast-iron cooking utensils, canvas tents and wooden packframes. Not until backpacking became popular during the 1960s did lightweight outdoor gear become an industry in itself.

Oddly enough, hunters have been especially slow to pick up on these weight savings. And when hunters do decide to pare ounces, they're often the wrong ones. Recently, a hunter was observed practicing at a range with a custom-built bolt gun on which he'd mounted a big, expensive scope. Panels had been cut from the receiver wall, presumably to give the gun a skeleton effect and

*Climbing for big game is almost an athletic endeavor. Physical conditioning and the proper gear and clothing are more important than feverish attention to weight savings. Lightweight rifles are fun to carry but won't settle as quickly as heavier guns when it's time to shoot.*

to shave weight. The short, fluted barrel was slim enough to double as a marshmallow stick. Moreover, the synthetic stock lacked enough bulk to ensure a firm grip during recoil. Finally, the hunter's rifle appeared too small for the scope, which was mounted well above the receiver so that its large, objective bell could clear the barrel.

During a lull, I asked this fellow how much his rifle weighed. "Five and a half pounds," he boasted. That was not counting the 30mm scope, which doubtless weighed two pounds. I hefted the rifle and found it very light and top-heavy, making it nearly impossible to control from a standing position. The trigger broke cleanly

*This stainless barrel on a .338 rifle is fluted to reduce weight without compromising stiffness. The rifle shoots accurately and has fine balance. Light barrels are hard to steady when you're in a hurry to shoot and breathing hard.*

enough, but before that happened, the pressure caused by my tightening finger induced tremors in the rifle.

### BARREL WEIGHT AND LENGTH: WHAT TO LOOK FOR

Weight in a rifle can be useful. Properly distributed, it lends agility to a gun. A broomstick is light, but it doesn't have that near-tangible sense of purpose one feels when an English shotgun is thrown to the shoulder. Perfect balance can make a rifle seem lighter than it actually is when carried.

Weight also helps steady a rifle. Even when you're not winded, your pulse and muscle tremors can destabilize your hold. Competitive shooters install the heaviest barrels necessary to counteract this movement. While thick barrel steel is a liability on the trail, it helps settle the rifle when you pop over a steep ridge and spot a retreating buck. Some hunters prefer a rifle that's balanced with a slight tip toward the muzzle. A few ounces up front will steady a barrel almost as effectively as adding weight along its entire length.

If you double the stabilizing effect of a heavy barrel, compare the feel of a lightweight hunting rifle to that of a long-barreled muzzleloader or a heavy target gun. Try aiming and dry-firing them, then run in place for a few minutes before dry-firing them again. Long, fat barrels may be impractical for most big-game hunting, but there's little sense in choosing a barrel so light that it compromises your ability to hit the target. If you can't do that, you might as well leave the rifle back at camp.

Barrel weights are designated numerically, ranging from #1 (very slim) to #5 (target). Most commercial rifles come with #3 barrels, a few with #4s and #2s. I prefer #4 barrels because my standing position is wobbly and the extra ounces improve my shooting. A #4 barrel on a .338 built by Intermountain Arms (Boise, Idaho) is especially impressive. It weighs slightly less than an unfluted barrel but offers a muzzle-heavy tilt and a stiffness that enhances minute-of-angle accuracy. Most hunters prefer light barrels; but occasionally you'll find someone hunkered on the crest of a ridge with a 15-pound rifle chambered for a cartridge with an intercontinental range. He scans distant hills through powerful glasses, waiting for a deer or an elk to expose a rib he can quarter in his super-size, trajectory-compensating scope.

To me, that's not hunting. Still, it's getting a lot of attention from those who like long shooting and don't want to pare pounds from their rifles. One accomplished shooter showed up at an elk camp recently with a Mauser wearing a straight #5 barrel, a bipod and a 6.5-20x scope. When I asked how he planned to carry this gear into and out of steep canyons where the elk lived, he assured one and all that he'd bear the load cheerfully. To this man's credit, he did maintain his good humor, but the 14-pound rifle slowed him down considerably. Fortunately, we spotted a handsome bull on the second day out. The man got his shot at 200 yards, but the bullet was badly placed. As the elk climbed an exposed ridge, the hunter swung his unwieldy rifle and missed his follow-up shots. Only after the animal had stopped and bedded were we able to kill and recover it. This shooter learned a good lesson that day: that being equipped for shooting elk at long range is not the same as being prepared to hunt elk. The elk he shot could have been killed with one bullet from a 7-pound .308 with iron sights.

Barrel length is as important a factor as barrel diameter. Not only does it help determine weight and balance, it affects bullet speed as well. Most factory rifles come with 22- and 24-inch barrels. Either is appropriate for cartridges like the .30-06. Some velocity is lost with the shorter tube; but how much is hard to say (the rule stipulates 40 fps per inch). It all depends on case dimensions, powder type, initial bullet velocity and the original barrel length.

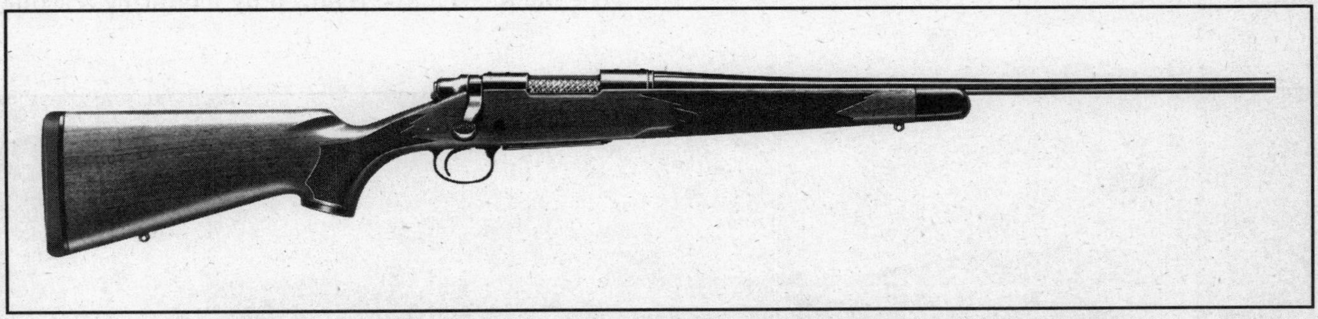

***Short-action rifles like this Remington Model 700 Mountain, chambered for 243 Win., 257 Roberts, 7mm-08 Rem. and 308 Win., work well in the timber, where quick shooting is often of great value.***

When cutting a barrel down from 22 to 21 inches, a small-bore, high-velocity cartridge like the .257 Weatherby Magnum can be expected to lose more than 40 fps. But a .35 Whelen barrel might not lose 40 fps when its chopped from 24 to 23 inches. I own two rifles with identical barrels chambered in .30-06 Improved. The 23-inch tube delivers, on average, 100 fps more velocity than the 22-inch; but why the spread is so large remains a mystery.

Long barrels make rifles too muzzle-heavy and are more likely to hang up in tree limbs. Most experienced hunters opt for reasonably long barrels: 24 inches for the .30-06 family of calibers and 25 inches for medium-bore magnums like the .338. The same applies to standard long-action rounds with slender, heavy bullets and slow powders (the .25-06 and improved versions of the .270 and .280).

For small-bore magnums, a 26-inch barrel is a popular choice. A 27-inch barrel on a .340 Weatherby or a .308 Norma is simply too long for hunting. Barrels that are 22 or 23 inches long work fine for short-action cases like the 7mm-08 and its parent, the .308 Winchester. They're also useful with big-bore rounds of greater capacity: the .35 Whelen and .350 Remington Magnum. These cartridges were designed for the timber, where quick shooting is often of greater value than a fast bullet. Besides, the medium-fast powders considered appropriate for wide-mouth cases don't require long bores to accelerate their payloads.

Other metal parts of a rifle can be trimmed or replaced with lighter materials to reduce weight. There's nothing wrong with an aluminum floor plate, or a magazine box with lots of holes in it, but don't expect any significant weight savings. The same applies to punching out chunks of the receiver wall, or hollowing the bolt handles. On the other hand, rubber buttpads are not only lighter, they're more functional than those made of steel. Some shooters use aluminum scope bases and lightweight rings like Weaver Tip-Offs to pare ounces. Other good choices are the slim steel Conetrols and beefier Leupold Dual Dovetails.

## SCOPES, STOCKS AND BINOCULARS

Significant weight reduction and improved rifle balance can be realized by mounting a scope

*A 4x scope like this Burris is all the scope a hunter needs for any North American big-game hunting. A scope in 4x weighs less than popular variables and can be mounted lower.*

of low, fixed magnification. The more popular variables with oversize objectives and 30mm tubes have claimed surprising market share of late—but they're not needed for big-game hunting. A 4x scope is scope enough and won't cost a lot of money; and it's more trouble-free by design than any variable. My one-inch alloy tubes are all mounted low for quick aiming and for keeping rifle weight between my hands where it belongs. A 4x scope weighs roughly 10 ounces, depending on make and model; but a 3.5-10x variable runs 20 to 50 percent heavier.

Installing a synthetic stock can reduce a rifle's weight, provided the right one is chosen. Some solid synthetic stocks are as heavy and sturdy as wood, while the more costly, foam-filed models weigh less. The biggest advantage of synthetic stocks is their stability in wet weather and during changes in temperature and humidity. So if you care more about performance than looks, synthetic stocks make sense. For those who prefer wood, consider glass-bedding the recoil lug (if not already done) and routing or drilling out some wood to tune the rifle's balance. With wood or synthetic stocks, you can also glass in lead shot to boost weight or shift the balance point.

Some hunters install thickly padded, loopless carrying straps on their rifles. These are bulky, though, and useless for shooting. Military slings are more functional but heavy, and their brass claws can mar your rifle stock. A sling available through Brownells (Montezuma, Iowa) is lightweight and quickly adjustable for shooting with a minimum of hardware. Like all functional slings, it's made of leather (nylon is too slippery).

How much should a big-game rifle weigh? That depends on the style of hunting, the rifle's chambering, and how much the hunter wants to carry. Iron-sighted rifles should weigh 7 to 8 pounds and scoped rifles 8 to 9 (loaded, with sling attached). That's more than a lot of hunters want to lug into the woods, but these criteria allow for a barrel of reasonable length and weight, plus a stock of sample proportions. If the stock fits, recoil shouldn't be a problem. Most factory rifles require little or nothing to attain these weight ranges. In sum, trimming rifle weight may not result in net benefits afield; but paying attention to weight distribution in your rifle most certainly will improve your chances.

***Binoculars should weigh less than 30 ounces, with an objective diameter of 35mm to 40mm and an exit pupil of 5mm. A short strap keeps the glasses high on the body to minimize swinging and neck strain.***

Binoculars are another item that can add substantial weight to your hunting kit. To shave ounces, some hunters choose mini-binoculars, with 24mm to 28mm objective lenses. Such small lenses can be a handicap, though, because in the popular 8x to 10x magnifications they provide exit pupils of only 2.4mm or 3.5mm (exit pupil is the arithmetic result of dividing binocular magnification by the objective lens diameter in millimeters; a bigger exit pupil allows more light to come through the lenses). For hunting, it's best to insist on an exit pupil of at least 4mm, preferably 5mm. That means a 7x35 or an 8x40 glass.

*A spotting scope needs a tripod. For extra duty, attach a shooting bag filled with styrofoam pellets. It makes a super rifle rest in sagebrush country.*

Zeiss and other high-quality 10x40 glasses certainly work well in open country, but they're hard to hold steady offhand and they don't have the field or exit pupil for quick, low-light glassing in thick timber. Swarovski makes fine 8x30 glasses that are small and lightweight, while offering an exit pupil that's sufficient for most hunting. Fifty-millimeter objectives admit more light, and in 7x glasses they give an exit pupil as big as your eyes can use, even in the dark. But they're too bulky and heavy for many shooters. Most binoculars should weigh under 30 ounces.

***Snow mandates layered clothes and stout, water-resistant boots. In steep country like this, you'll tire quickly in bulky, heavy clothes. The wind "on top" can be fierce, so comfortable clothing is a must.***

Glasses with 35mm and 40mm objectives generally fit below that cap, with 8x30s crowding 20 ounces. Incidentally, there's no significant weight difference between porro-prism and roof-prism binoculars of the same optical quality and specifications. Porro-prisms are bulkier, but they provide wider objective spacing that, theoretically, helps one judge distance.

Some hunters contend that a spotting scope is needed to hunt in open country. While it surely provides a better look at game, it won't replace your binoculars. Further, when mounted on a tripod (as it should) a spotting scope is a heavy, cumbersome thing. Actually, you can save ounces by the bushel when you leave a spotting scope at home. It can be a useful tool, though, when one is hunting pronghorn or when you're glassing great distances without moving much. But on a deer or elk hunt, a spotting scope isn't really necessary.

Another commodity best left behind is a sheath knife. Knives are made of steel, and steel is heavy—so choose the smallest knife that will suffice. A folding, lock-back Gerber with a single blade just under 4 inches long is ideal. So is a pocket-knife with 2½-inch blades. For deer hunting, leave that big knife at home and take the pocket models.

Extra ammunition can also be left behind with the Bowie knife and spotting scope. Hunters commonly carry a box of cartridges, sometimes two. But if you're serious about hunting, you'll have zeroed your rifle well before the trip and practiced with it. That way, you'll not take shots that shouldn't be attempted; i.e., you'll shoot only once or twice at each animal you kill. But because there's a small chance you might drop your rifle and knock the scope askew, you might take a handful of extras for an emergency zeroing session—say, eight cartridges in a soft leather belt pouch and three or four more in the rifle.

### *CLOTHES CAN MAKE THE HUNTER*

It's best to buy clothes with comfort in mind. Forget about weight. Clothes should protect you, keep you warm and dry and in good spirits so you can concentrate on your hunt, and that's that. Even heavy boots can be a bargain. They can protect your feet from moisture and sharp rocks, and support your ankles on rock slides.

If you're packing a camp in, instead of hunting from trailhead each day, you can save weight by using a down-filled sleeping bag instead of one that features synthetic filler. If you expect sleeping in wet conditions, though, buy a top-quality synthetic-filled bag. The semimummy-type makes efficient use of material without holding you immobile. In any event, for most hunting situations you'll want the warmest bag you can tie to a packframe.

While a daypack, beltpack or fannypack carries plenty of what's needed for a day's hunt—food, knife, flashlight, compass and first-aid items—a backpack is still needed to haul camp in and meat out. Again, weight isn't as important as comfort or function. Consider only external-frame packs with welded joints and a broad, padded waistbelt. Internal-frame packs or external frames of plastic are not stiff enough to carry big loads. Packframes are made in different sizes for people of different dimensions, so try on several before buying. A lower cargo ledge and top extension aren't necessary, but they do offer more places to tie things. A single, full-depth, top-loading packbag with roomy outside pouches on

***The biggest weight savings for most hunters can be achieved through pre-season exercise that burns fat. Walk up hills. Jog or bicycle three times a week. Reduce sugars and fats in your diet.***

the sides and top for maps, food and other items is ideal. The cavernous main compartment of a Kelty packbag can hold 120 pounds of meat and as much clothing as you'd want to carry in and out of the mountains. The fewer zippers and ties to get stuck, the better. Your warm, dry fingers may open those new fasteners easily at point of purchase; but the woods, weather, moisture and dirt can make simple jobs difficult indeed.

Be smart. Assemble everything you'll need well before a hunt. Throwing everything into your packbag at the last minute is sure to burden you with unnecessary gear—much less leave you without something of real value. It's good to have several changes of socks, but one wool shirt is enough for a week's hunt. Silk underwear weighs less than cotton, it performs the same function, and it stays odor-free longer.

### *THE IMPORTANCE OF CUTTING BODY WEIGHT*

Collectively, hunters tote more excess weight under their skin than in their packs or rifles. If you're overweight by 10 pounds, does it make any sense in fluting your barrel to remove 10 ounces? Flab on one's midsection serves no purpose; it only slows you down. Of all the things you can do to boost energy and stamina and improve mobility, nothing matches a physical fitness program—preferably one that starts months before the season opens. Restricting your diet or straining your muscles just before a hunt will only leave you sore and weak. Walking, jogging or bicycling for an hour on alternate days will build your heart and lung capacities and take off excess weight. And do some calisthenics each morning to tone your body.

You don't have to starve to lose weight, either. Cutting back on sugars and fats is enough, given moderate exercise. Avoid bacon, sausage and other greasy meats. Leave the margarine and mayonnaise off those sandwiches and avoid sugar in your cereal and coffee. Eschew anything that's deep-fried or chocolate; buy hard rolls instead of donuts; drink water, not soda or beer. Skip desserts and eat fruit instead.

Eating habits aren't easy to change, of course; but if you commit to a better diet, you'll eventually find yourself attracted to healthful foods. You won't want the sweet snacks and fatty entrees anymore. On the trail, don't count calories; but do maintain a nutritious diet. Carry raisins, cheese and bagels in zip-lock bags. These items can take a pounding in a pack without disintegrating and can be eaten a little at a time. For variety, add apples, nuts or granola bars. And always carry a plastic canteen of water so you can drink often enough without having to search for clean water sources. It's easy to dehydrate at high elevations in cold weather, because you seldom feel thirsty. Water may add a pound per pint to your load, but it is crucial to your hunt and health.

***You don't have to be a young athlete to hunt steep country effectively. Getting in shape and packing lightly helps keep hunters alert and successful.***

While hunting slowly is hunting well in

choice coverts, you'll find that the ability to vary your pace without pain is an asset. Groups of elk may be bunched miles apart. You might want to cross a canyon quickly to stalk a mule deer you spotted at a distance, or loop a big field to approach downwind in pursuit of a whitetail buck. Your most promising hunting spot at dawn may be a saddle a half-mile climb from camp; or you may want to stake out a meadow at twilight three miles below camp. Traveling light not only allows you to move faster, it extends your hunting range. It also improves your agility in the timber so you can move quietly. And it enables you to reach new territory quickly should a stalk turn sour and your prey escapes.

Smart hunters choose their equipment and clothing with care, making sure that it's heavy enough to serve its purpose, but no heavier or bulkier than necessary. They also work hard to condition their bodies, realizing that weight is an important part of the job. Hunters who bring home game consistently are equally efficient in carrying only what they need to the hunt. They also know that sometimes the right weight isn't necessarily the minimum weight.

***WAYNE VAN ZWOLL is a writer known for his expertise on big-game hunting and the technical aspects of shooting. He has written for most of the major sporting magazines, including Field & Stream, Sports Afield, and Rifle and Bugle. He has authored three books:*** **Mastering Mule Deer** ***(1988, North American Hunting Club),*** **America's Great Gunmakers,** ***(1992, Stoeger Publishing) and*** **Elk Rifles, Cartridges and Hunting Tactics** ***(1993). No stranger to the high country, van Zwoll has been a wildlife agent with the Washington State Dept. of Game and a field director for the Rocky Mountain Elk Foundation. He has also served as editor of Kansas Wildlife magazine and is currently working on his doctorate in wildlife management.***

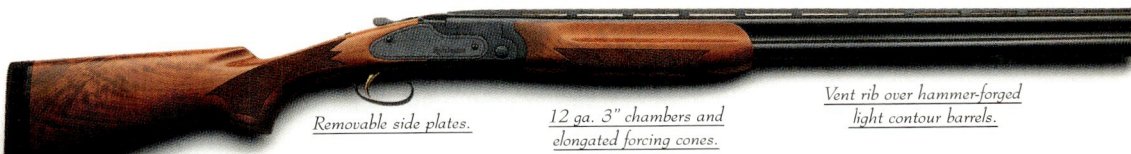

# New Crown Grade™ Model 500

**The affordable Mossberg 500 Shooting System™ now looks better than shotguns costing much more.**

Classically designed and cut-checkered, the new Crown Grade Buttstock and Forend transform Mossberg's most popular shotgun. There is even a Crown Grade Dual Comb® Stock for slug shooters. The Model 500 is already well known for its ability to shrug off the abuse of hard hunting. Now, we've added the good looks of a premium model, but we've done it without the premium price. In fact, one look tells you that the Crown Grade Model 500 is a better value than ever.

**New Quiet Carry® Action Bars and OFM Camo make Crown Grade guns better hunters, too!**

Every Crown Grade Model 500 comes with our new Quiet Carry slide. This spring-loaded, dual action bar system eliminates "slide rattle", even after the gun is broken-in. The new OFM Woodland camo pattern is remarkably effective; and because it's from Mossberg, it is remarkably priced. Our popular Bird & Deer, Dual Barrel Combos give hunters even more value.

**Plus, an important feature you'll probably never use: The Mossberg Ten Year Limited Warranty.**

After more than 30 years and 4 million guns in the field, the Mossberg 500 has proven itself in the harshest conditions. That extraordinary track record is why we can back every new Crown Grade Model 500 with a Ten Year Limited Warranty. Look at the features, the performance, the price and then look at the warranty. Nobody backs pump guns better than Mossberg.

1919–1994 MOSSBERG® 75 YEARS

MOSSBERG Ten Year LIMITED WARRANTY

**Mossberg Shooting Systems are always in season.**

O.F. Mossberg & Sons, Inc. • 7 Grasso Ave. • P.O. Box 497 • North Haven, CT 06473-9844



Safety and safe firearms handling is everyone's responsibility.

Carol Vaillancourt, Colt Customer Service Representative and 1994 Connecticut State Sporting Clays Ladies Champion, knows responsible firearms handling includes regular practice. Her small frame .380 Mustang, designed for personal protection, is no exception.

Small gun convenience, with big gun performance. That's why. The .380 Models offer Colt® quality performance in a compact, portable frame. Choose from 11 models, including 3 "Pocketlites", for just the right size, weight, feel and look. Despite its small size, you can

still count on Colt Craftsmanship for built-in quality, such as the three patented safety systems and locked breech. That's the quality that makes it a Colt.

Get your FREE Colt Firearms and Wearables Catalogs at your Colt Dealer today. Or call 1-800-962-COLT.

QUALITY MAKES IT A COLT.™

COLT

Warning: Never chamber a round until you are ready to shoot. Read and follow manual accompanying each firearm. Free manuals available on request. © 1995

FINLAND
sako
WORLD CLASS RIFLES
COMMITMENT TO EXCELLENCE—A SAKO TRADITION

# SHOOTING STEEL: SECRETS OF RIFLE ACCURACY

*by Ralph F. Quinn*

To dedicated hunters and seasoned benchrest competitors, a quality barrel is the heart and soul of an accurate rifle. When the chips are down you can only hold on the target and pull the trigger with all the skill and experience you possess. From there on, it's up to the built-in accuracy of your rifle. Granted that proper bedding of wood to metal and precision loads are also essential to good results, but what puts the bullet in motion so that it flies true to the mark is that rifled steel tube. Once the barrel imparts the proper spin/rotation and balance without impairing the ballistic shape of the bullet, you have a winner. Otherwise, accuracy will literally go down the tube.

The importance that rifling design and ballistic coefficient (the ability of a bullet to overcome resistance to air in flight) play in the accuracy game cannot be overestimated. Every modern shooter should be aware of some facts about modern rifling, which many think of as something that was developed in the 18th century. Actually, it came into use as far back as the 15th century. From the muzzleloading matchlock period to the introduction of breechloading cartridge guns, there ensued a constant period of experimentation with rifling and bullet designs, including Joseph Whitworth's fitted-bullet and hexagonal rifling, Captain Minie's conical bullet dubbed the "minnie ball," and John Jacobs's four-rib bullets and rifling.

But it wasn't until the late 1800s that the value of the rifled barrel was generally recognized. At that time, a British rifleman named William Metford developed a new method of rifling, one that accelerated the bullet's rate of rotation as it moved through the barrel. This gyroscopic effect on the bullet was, without question, a major step toward stable, repeatable accuracy.

At about the same time, American barrelmakers began showing off their own new rifling designs, among the most celebrated being Harry Pope's system. The shape of his rifling was basically shallow, flat-bottomed grooves cut with painstaking care. Because Pope's barrels proved so accurate, shooters flocked in droves to adopt his style, yet only a few competitors were able to gain access to the Holy Grail of barrelmaking. Actually, Pope's design wasn't all that significant: it was the time, care and attention to detail lavished on each job that made his design so accurate. Thus it is with any barrel, regardless of the rifling method used.

Shortly after the turn of the century, the U.S. and England had adopted the Enfield type of rifling, which stipulated that the radius of the groove bottom be identical to the radius of the bullet diameter. Because this rifling method was the easiest to manufacture, it gradually took hold. Then around the start of World War I, a genius named Charles Newton came up with a parabolic or "rachet" rifling design wherein only one side of each land was cut. This same style of rifling had been introduced in England earlier, but Newton was the first to recognize and implement what proved to be an excellent system.

Aficionados of the accuracy game, whether hunters or target competitors, constantly debate the subject of shooting steel and the inherent qualities of cut-rifling vs. buttoned or hammer-forged lands and grooves. Press a top-flight shooter on the subject and he will most likely admit there is basically no inherent superiority of one barrel or rifling type over another. Any tube that is properly stress-relieved, that is, made of quality rifle-grade steel (stainless or chrome-molybdenum, "chrome-moly" for short), and that has smooth, honed bores, can be counted on to produce good accuracy.

For most sportsmen, gaining access to the precision shooting fraternity is largely a matter of selecting a barrel manufacturer who is currently in favor among benchrest circles for mating barrel to action. Going that route, however, does not provide any real insight into the process of barrelmaking or, more importantly, what makes a barrel work; i.e., what type of steel rifling design and rate of twist are used. Since the angle or twist rate (expressed in inches per revolution) is dictated by the manufacturer, any discussion of the subject can only lead to confusion. In short, bullets that are short and stout require a slower rate of twist to stabilize than do bullets that are long and slender.

### *MAKING A QUALITY BARREL*

A quality barrel begins in the mill, where the steel is manufactured. With limited product demand and few foundries providing gun-grade alloys, most barrel shops simply aren't large enough to demand the grade of steel required to make a quality product. But for firearms manufacturers and big barrel companies who are in a position to buy a complete "melt" up to 30,000 pounds, the mills will formulate the steel to their specs, thereby controlling the quality of the end product. Clean steel translates into better stability during heat treatment and is equally important to machineability and finish during manufacture.

On the other hand, small operations must buy their steel on the open market, with the hope that the quality of steel they're buying will be suitable for barrelmaking. Quality control becomes an ongoing process of testing and retooling, lot to lot; but that same process slows down the manufacturing end and makes it tough for small outfits to compete. Many shooters today mistakenly equate production numbers with quality. Make no mistake, a poorly cut-rifled barrel is no better than the average buttoned one, and the best production buttoned barrel you can buy could be the equal of a quality cut-rifled tube.

Depending on caliber and PSI breech pressures, manufacturers select one of three steels for producing barrels: For .22 rimfire and other low-pressure rounds, carbon steel like #1137 is used. With high-pressure centerfire cartridges—.243s to 30-06s—the standard is #4140 chrome-moly. Target barrels are typically fashioned from a

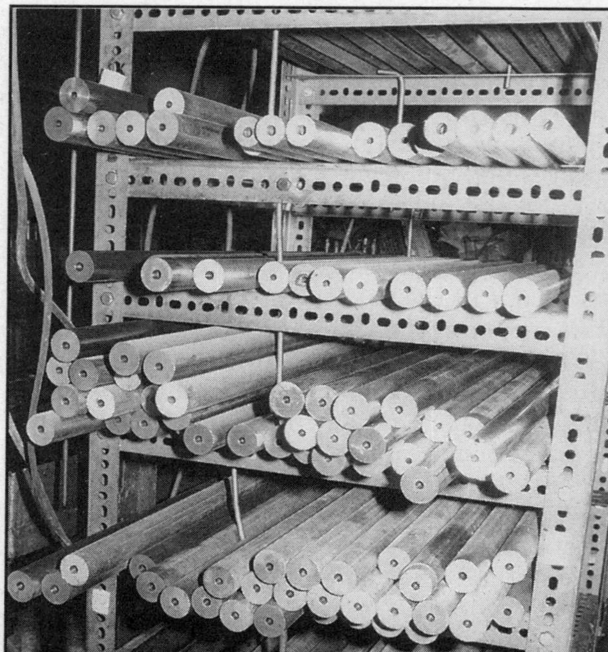

*Rifled blanks are ready for stress relief prior to contouring. This process prevents "trumpeting" and keeps bore diameter uniform, breech to bore.*

*A worker at McGowen Barrel Company pull-reams a barrel prior to honing. The purpose is to remove microscopic metal particles so as to prevent fouling and promote accuracy.*

proprietary stainless alloy called "416R." Many current production hunting rifles sport stainless barrels and receivers, such as Ruger's Model MK II All-Weather, Remington's popular Model 700 Synthetic, and Browning's Stainless Stalker.

Once the steel bars are received from the mill, they are heat-treated to normalize or anneal the metal before rifling. The normalizing process removes potential stress points that may cause warping or bending during production. Major production shops and companies that supply barrels to the gun-building trade—Wilson Arms, Shilen, Hart, for example—do their own heat-treating to keep the process running smoothly. Smaller shops typically buy steel bars already rolled, cut, heat-treated and stress-relieved.

After the steel bar is cut to length, the ends are faced and the breech center marked for drilling. The blank is then trued to run free of vibration. With the work rotating from 1,000 to

2,000 rpm, a stationary V-shaped tungsten carbide bit works its way through the bar at .001 inch per revolution. As the blank progresses, an oil coolant is forced up the drill shaft, carrying away the metal chips. When steel quality and bar rotation are uniform, the bit tends to center itself, resulting in a bore that is straight and true.

During the drilling operation, metal tracings are left along the entire bore. Before the rifling process can progress further, these microscopic particles must be removed by reaming; otherwise, the barrel will foul quickly and accuracy will be short-lived. Bore reamers are typically long, four-fluted affairs, designed to be pulled or pushed through the barrel. The reamer is attached to a shaft, which rotates at low rpms. Again, the barrel is held stationary as the work progresses.

Button-rifle manufacturers, such as Hart, Wilson, Douglas, Shilen and McGowen, prefer pull-reaming because it yields consistent dimen-

*The rotary honing setup, as shown here, smooths and brings bore diameter to uniform dimensions, an essential step if the barrel is to prove accurate.*

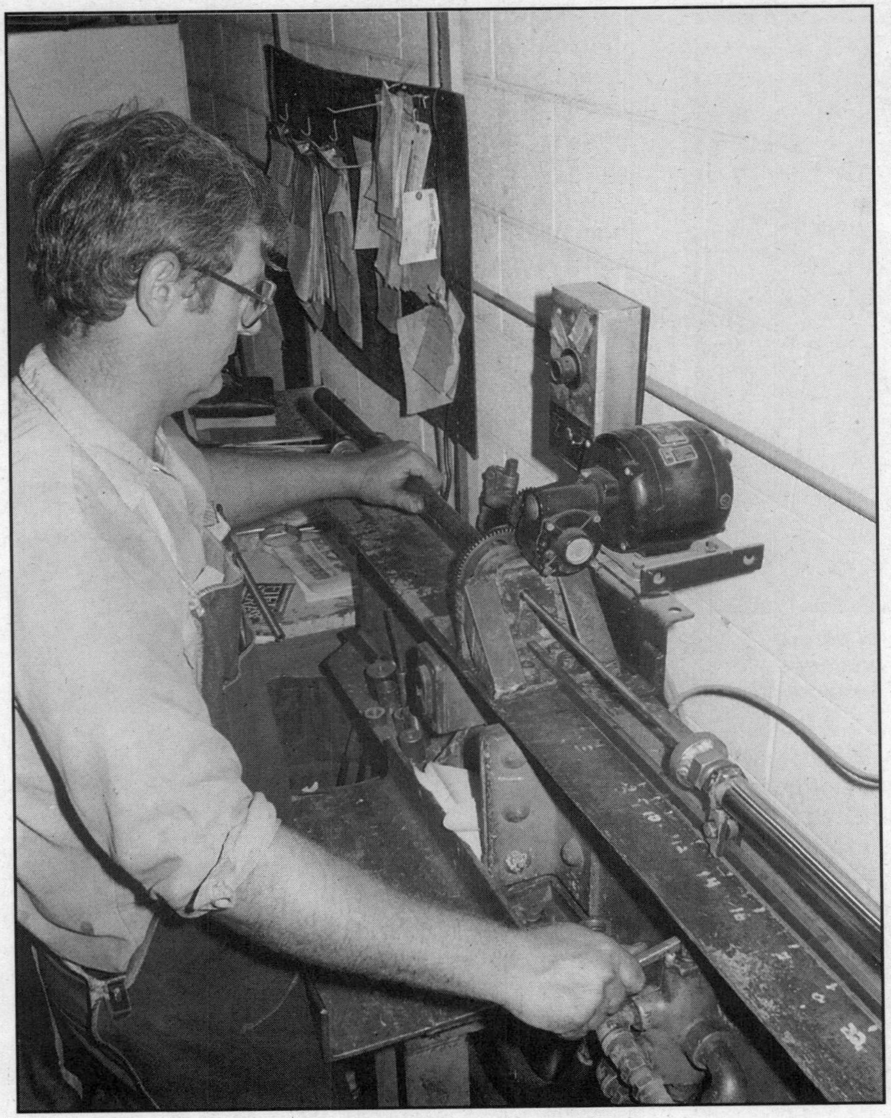

*This skilled worker is pull-buttoning a honed barrel. This process yields identical bores, barrel to barrel, throughout production runs.*

sions and simplifies the matching of button size to bore diameter. Push-reaming yields better surface finishes, but it's practical only for smaller calibers (.17, .22, 6mm). To ensure accuracy, a uniform bore diameter and smooth finish are essential. Some top-of-the line barrels made in the U.S. and Europe are honed or lead-lapped before rifling. Barrels made by Steyr-Mannlicher are both honed and electro-polished to a mirror-like finish prior to hammer (rotary) boring. As you might expect, accuracy is excellent.

### *HOW RIFLING IS CUT*

At this point, most manufacturers put their blanks through similar methods and machinery to prep the steel for rifling. After this, the process and handling vary according to the rifling method used. Keep in mind, too, that the quality of the tooling, machinery maintenance and attention to detail also make a difference in the finished product.

The oldest and perhaps most widely used form of rifling is called "cut." As its name in-

***A production lathe rough-turns a barrel before chambering. Proper stress relief can prevent widening of the muzzle as the metal is removed.***

dicates, the rifling is cut by a single-edged tool that works each groove in turn until the rifling has reached its full depth. During production, a rifling rod extends from a lathe, driving a spindle through the barrel muzzle to the breech. A ratchet feed pushes up the rifling knife (or hook-cutter) and the rod is pulled slowly through the steel. Each pass slices .0001 to .0003 of steel from the groove. Once the pass is complete, the knife depresses and returns to the breech.

As the work progresses, the chucked barrel is automatically indexed for degrees or grooves. A preset taper bar establishes the pitch and turn. It takes some 25–30 passes to cut each groove to the proper depth, so the process is very slow. Harry Pope and other famous barrelmakers of the later 19th century often took several days to rifle a barrel; today, the same process is completed in about one hour. Cut-rifling is quite labor-intensive, and therefore expensive; but then, how do you put a price on accuracy? For those who have the urge to own a cut barrel, plenty of quality makers are in business to serve you. The final results, though, always depend largely on the care and dedication of the maker.

***Button Rifling.*** During World War II, considerable pressure was put on government arsenals to create barrel production methods that yielded greater output than either cut or broaching (in which all grooves are cut at once) without increasing labor costs. It took sweat, perseverance and lots of ingenuity to get the job done, but two of the most common methods of rifling barrels in use today—button and hammer forging—owe their beginning to that wartime edict.

Just who invented the original button-rifling process is open to question. In the U.S., the process was developed by Remington Arms under the guidance of Mike Walker, a rifle engineer who was employed there, and whose name is on U.S. patents covering the process. After the war ended, however, several captured German weapons were found rifled

***In pull-button rifling, a tungsten carbide "button" is silver brazed to pull the rod. The steel that's displaced (as the grooves are formed) is forced into flutes machined on the button surface, creating lands.***

by this same "button" method. Whoever the inventor, this rifling process single-handedly revolutionized the postwar firearms industry, particularly the custom gunsmithing trade.

Here's how the process works. After a barrel blank has been drilled, it's reamed, honed or polished for smoothness and uniformity. A button made of tungsten carbide, with the rifling ground in reverse on its perimeter, is pushed or pulled through the barrel by hydraulic pressure. The steel that's displaced (as the grooves are formed) is then forced into indentations machined on the button. These become the lands.

Using quality steels, a trained worker can turn out hundreds of barrels in a single day with virtually identical bores, each one capable of accuracy that would have astounded the legendary barrelmakers of yesteryear. But perhaps the most important factor is reduced production costs, making quality shooting steel available to thousands of sportsmen worldwide.

The push method of button rifling is currently used by G. R. Douglas, Hart, Pac-Nor and Wilson Arms. In this method, a pilot lead aligns with a trailer on which the rifling design is ground. Schneider, McMillan, Shilen, McGowen Barrel Company, Savage Arms and Miroku Arms (Browning) all use the pull-button process, in which the button is silver-brazed to a pull rod.

In either process, proper stress relief is essential to assure that the bore will not "trumpet," or widen toward the muzzle after being rough-contoured. For this reason, some button manufacturers heat-treat the blank after rifling to reduce scaling and keep the bore diameter as uniform as possible from breech to bore. According to more than one expert, the muzzle of an accurate barrel should be smaller than the breech end. With modern air-gauging equipment capable of measuring in ten-thousandths of an inch, it's possible to mark the blank accordingly, then proceed.

*The button-rifling process for .30 caliber requires the following (left to right): honing rod; pull button rod; fluted bore reamer; V-shaped drill.*

Some target barrel manufacturers also stress-relieve their barrels after straightening. The purpose here is to reduce the tendency of the barrel to "walk" or regain "memory" when being fired. Douglas, however, prefers not to straighten barrels in the belief that it's better for the bullet to go through a barrel with a long curve than a lot of short ones.

***Rotary-forging.*** The last of the production

**TYPES OF RIFLING**
**(Cross-sectional View)**

**Metford Progressive Gain Twist** | **Pope-type Square Groove and Lands** | **Newton "Ratchet"** | **Enfield 4-Groove**

rifling techniques—rotary-forging—was developed in Germany in the 1930s. It was later exported to world markets when an Austrian firm designed cold-forging machinery for the firearms industry. As the name suggests, a hammer squeezes or forges the barrel steel around a carbide mandrel into which the lands and grooves are ground. As the blank is hammered, the mandrel is withdrawn. The entire process takes about three minutes, with the final product requiring minimum machining to achieve the proper finish dimensions.

Today, a wide number of U.S. manufacturers use roto-forging. These include U.S. Repeating Arms, Remington, Sturm, Ruger and Co., Weatherby and, in Europe, Steyr, Sako and Heckler & Koch. Due to the compacted molecular structure of hammer-forged steel, the bores tend to constrict when contoured. Some feel that this tapering, or "choke," at the muzzle, plus sloped lands for reducing bullet deformation, deliver superior accuracy, higher velocities and increased barrel life. From this writer's personal experience, out-of-the-box, off-the-shelf rifles from Steyr-Mannlicher, Sako, Remington and Weatherby all provide superior accuracy.

One advantage offered by button and hammer-forged barrels lies in a bore that's smoother than can be produced in cut-rifling. In top-of-the-line barrels, this is certainly true. The bores of target barrels made by Hart, McMillan, Douglas and Shilen are mirror-smooth, as are those of Sako, Steyr and Heckler & Koch. It's hard to believe, but one of the earliest and longest-lasting complaints about button barrels was that they were too smooth. The apparent absence of well-defined lands and grooves led to fic-

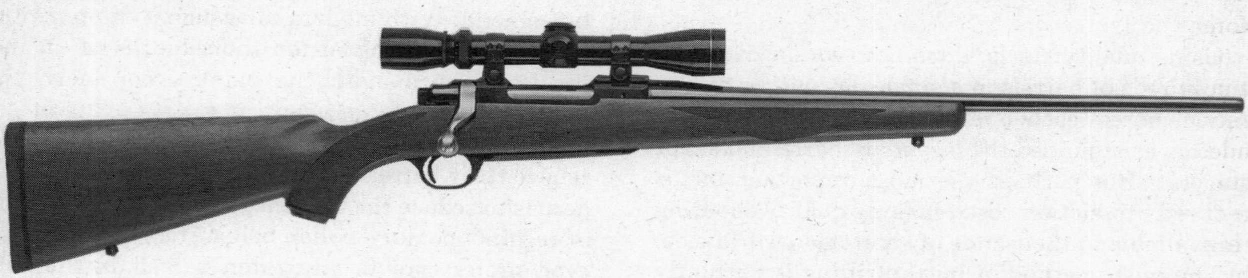

***The current production Ruger M-77 Mark II Bolt Action rifle uses a hammer-forged barrel. Taper-bore resulting from cold-swaging helps promote accuracy.***

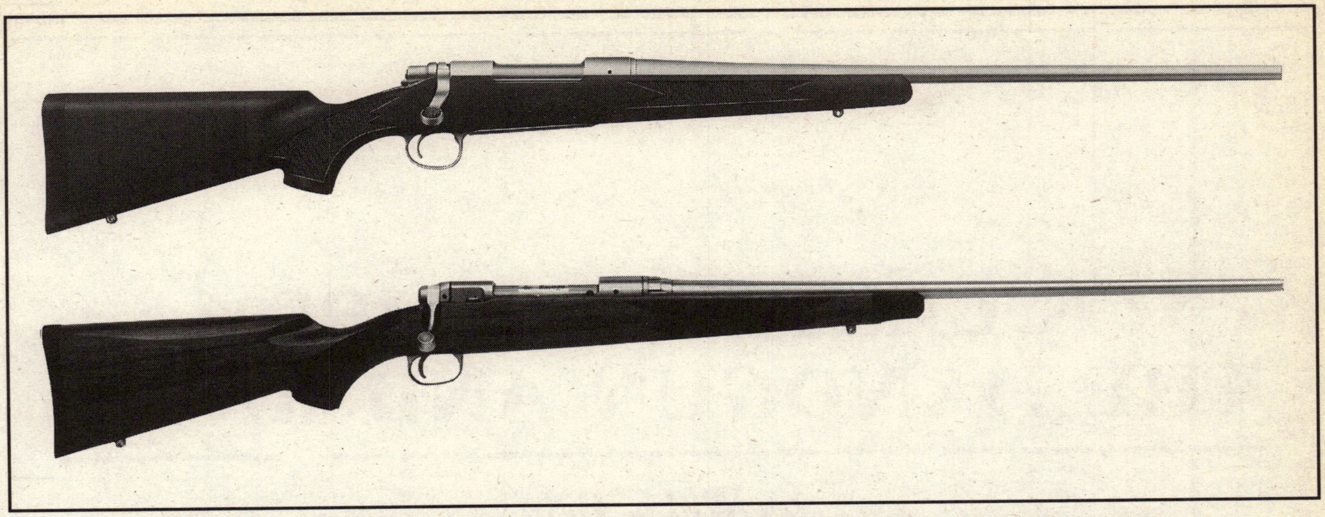

*While superior accuracy plus resistance to corrosion are two alleged advantages of stainless steel, stainless barrels undeniably have a superior finish and the smoothest bores regardless of the rifling method used. Remington's Model 700 BDL SS (top photo) and Savage's Model 116 US "Ultra Stainless" (bottom photo) both feature a stainless barrel and receiver.*

titious tales of shallow rifling incapable of stabilizing a heavy bullet. It took the benchrest fraternity to show the error of such thinking, when virtually every record in the National Bench Rest Association (NBRA) belonged to competitors who used button-rifled barrels.

With the strong marketing trend toward the sale of armored rifles (i.e., those with stainless barrels and receivers), the question arises whether the Remington 700 Synthetic, Browning's Stainless Stalker, Ruger's All Weather, et al, offer superior accuracy plus resistance to corrosion. The major advantage of stainless steels, like the 416R variety, is that barrels made from the alloy have a superior mirror finish and the smoothest bore regardless of the rifling method. They will, however, pit when subjected to chlorates or when ammonia-based cleaners are left in the bore too long. More stainless rifles have been damaged by sloppy cleaning methods than any other reason. Whether stainless barrels provide an extended accuracy life compared to those fashioned from #4140 steel (chambered for moderate calibers like the 7mm-08, .308 or .270) is debatable. However, in high-intensity chambering—like the .257 Weatherby, 7mm Remington Magnum and .338 Winchester—stainless barrels should prove beneficial.

If the purchase of a custom or factory rifle is a possibility in the near future, keep in mind that exacting manufacturing standards and quality steels are what make rifle barrels accurate, not rifling systems alone. When materials and workmanship are both of high quality, and when physical properties of bore finish are identical and dimensions uniform, muzzle to breech accuracy potential is assured. From that point on, it's up to the shooter to perform.

*RALPH F. QUINN for the past 20 years has been an award-winning, full-time freelance outdoor writer and video producer. His credits in major publications include Rifle, Rifle and Shotgun Sport Shooting, Petersen's Hunting, American Rifleman, Wing & Shot, Aquafield Hunting and Shooting, Sigarms Quarterly, and Handgunning, among others. As a dedicated centerfire competitor he regularly participates in both silhouette and benchrest events. Much of the information offered in this article derives from 34 years of rifle-building with his father, J.P. Quinn, a top gunsmith and machinist.*

# A LASTING COMBO: THE HANDGUN AND RIFLE

**by Wilf E. Pyle**

For most shooters, the image of a rugged outdoorsman carrying a trusted rifle along with a hip-slung handgun lies somewhere in the inaccessible romantic reaches of our minds. The real picture—often associated with old ammunition or firearms advertising—varies with the times. Early illustrations spanning several decades and recent reproductions of old calendars come to mind. One in particular features an early cowboy—revolver at his side—blazing away at marauding cattle thieves with his Winchester rifle. Another picture shows a lone mountain hunter shooting his Remington across a meadow at a distant ram, a Colt pistol held tight at his side. Still another features a northern trapper plying his trade within easy reach of his trusty Winchester and a cartridge belt sporting a pistol. Finally, there comes to mind the picture of an early northern explorer mushing over frozen barrens with a Model 92 Winchester in its scabbard and a handgun at his hip. All elicit the same romantic theme of man against nature armed with both rifle and handgun, suggesting that preparedness meant facility with two kinds of firearms. Even then, ammunition and firearms advertisers knew how to arouse the public's interest and capture its attention.

The combination of rifle and handgun as a personal support system originated with the American West, not in Continental or British hunting literature. Only here, in our most recent illustrations and written references to the Western era, do characters appear outfitted with both rifle and pistol. Even in the art and photography of fighting men created during the American Civil War, the rifle and handgun appeared together infrequently. In the military, handguns are usually associated with officers, while rifles remain the purview of enlisted men. Recent publications reveal such combinations only on Americans as they explore the jungles of Africa.

In pioneer times, though, the ability to interchange one kind of ammunition between two kinds of firearms was considered quite useful. You only had to buy and keep on hand a single kind of ammunition. The pistol was viewed as a backup to the rifle, so one type of ammunition was thought to be smart. It was commonly held that a single cartridge belt, box or ammo pouch could feed two firearms with different purposes in mind. This reduced confusion in the field and made transporting and managing cartridges much more efficient. The military never learned this lesson of expedience and prudence; only the Western pioneer saw the logic and reaped the benefits.

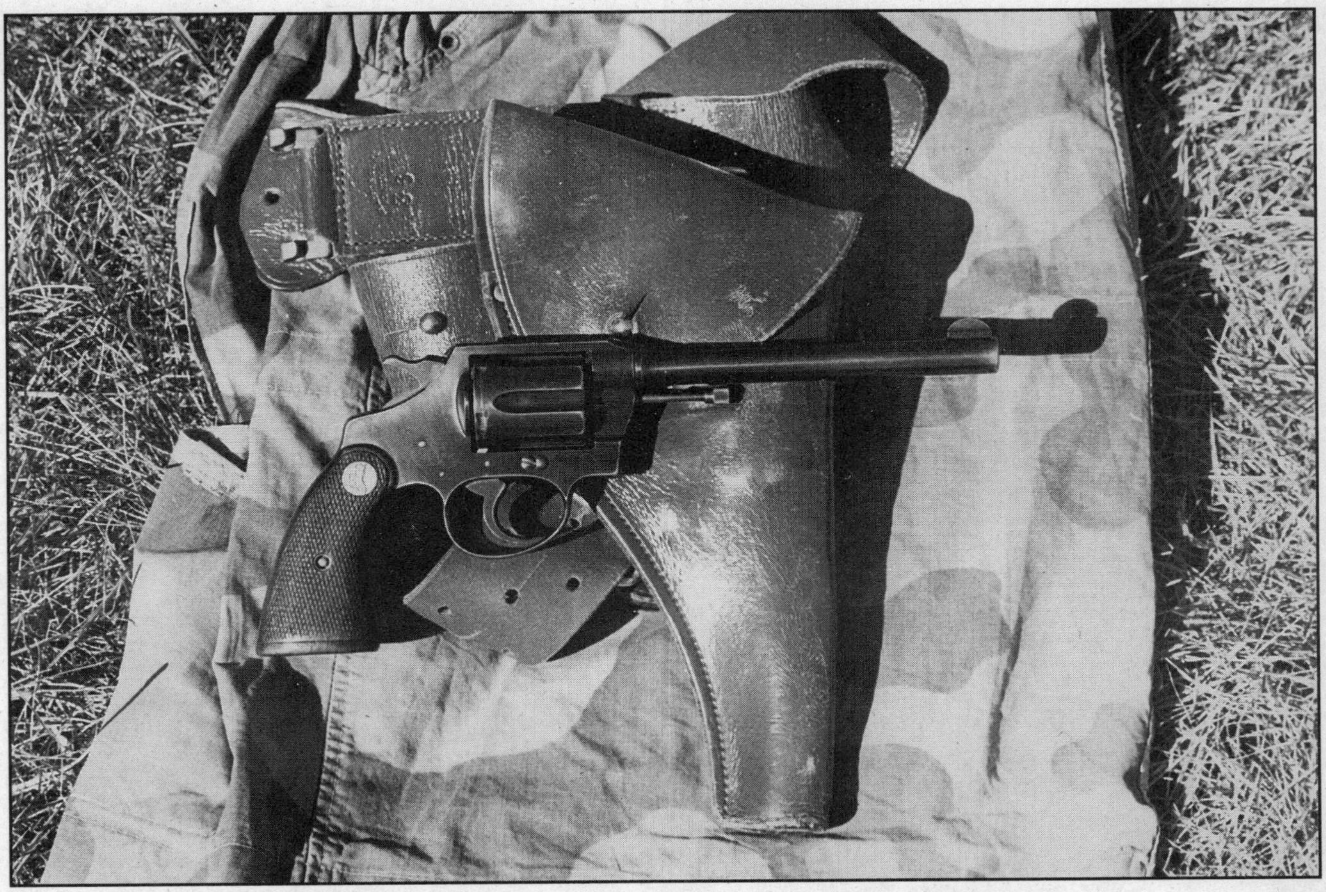

*This 32-20 Colt Police Positive Special revolver works well with Winchester's 30-06 Model 70 hunting rifle.*

One classic example was the 44-40 cartridge that fed both the Model 73 Winchester and the Colt Peacemaker. Early low pressure cartridges, like the 38-40 or 44-40, were excellent cartridges for such use. The most popular firearms designs at that time favored low-powered cartridges. Indeed, firearms companies offered different loadings of many early blackpowder pistol-rifle cartridges well suited to this dual role. For example, early hunters could choose the 44-40 in heavy or light load, with the latter clearly meant for revolver use and as a plinking load in rifles. The pistol was primarily used as a backup tool or a close-quarters, personal-defense weapon. Secondarily, its role was that of dispatching short-range predators or keeping down wounded game animals. Only when necessary was it used for defending the hearth or warning off would-be highwaymen.

In more modern times, these requirements have been less pronounced. Rifle cartridges are now significantly more powerful than standard revolver cartridges. Also, as conditions changed, fewer shooting and hunting opportunities arose where the handgun could substitute for a rifle. Early concerns about storage, transportation and the mixing of different cartridges also became less of a logistics problem. More importantly, the relationship between the rifle and the handgun changed. The handgun is no longer thought of as an understudy to the rifle. Today, several handgun cartridges offer power similar to many early rifle cartridges. Handgun design has changed, too, especially over the past 20 years. Witness the evolution of thicker, stiffer barrels, larger grips, improved sights and beefed-up accessories—all improving accuracy and extending the range potential of even the most modest handgun cartridge. As a result, handguns now stand on their own as tools for hunting or self-defense.

Today, just about any handgun cartridge can share pocket space with any rifle cartridge without concern for supply or interchangeability. Think of the handgun and rifle as a pair of tools, used together, that in combination extend our enjoyment in the field and support our hunting efforts. Much is written about selecting rifles, and even more about choosing handguns. But nothing is said about the rifle and pistol in combination with each other. Lost is the fact that things change in the hunting fields when one is equipped with both handgun and rifle.

Roles need to be clarified and ground rules set. First of all, the rifle remains the main powerhouse in the hunting fields of the world. The rule of thumb is to select rifle, action and caliber based on range, game and conditions. Handgun choice is based on similar criteria, but with its specialized use well defined. For our purposes, the handgun must serve for informal target prac-

*Because rifle cartridges are now significantly more powerful than standard revolver cartridges, fewer shooting and hunting opportunities are available where the handgun substitutes for a rifle.*

*A revolver offers an effective backup to the rifle. Plinking, short-range shooting and taking farm animals are top functions for any handgun used by a hunter.*

tice, dispatching wounded big game, and taking small game for sport or the pot. In a pinch, it might take a deer from a blind or provide a short-range shot, assuring a clean kill.

With an understanding of the history, and assuming there's consensus on the criteria for selecting any handgun and rifle, an amazing observation can be made concerning modern firearms design: there are few really good choices left. In one sense, modern handgun design has evolved so that the handgun can only play specialized roles; i.e., self-defense, target, hide-out, plinking and hunting. Rifles have also taken another role, one that tends toward assault rifle configurations rather than as hunting arms. Shooters are fortunate that many older handguns and rifles are still around to fit the combination role under discussion.

### TRUSTED RIFLE-HANDGUN COMBINATIONS

Personal preference is a big factor in selecting any combination of rifle and handgun. Going afield with what you've got is as American today as it was in pioneer times; and it's practical enough to cover most bases. Matching handgun to rifle (and vice-versa) is also an opportunity to express even greater personal preference. Let's illustrate by looking at some personal preferences in rifle and handgun combinations. Be forewarned, this is heady stuff for the traditionalists, but hunters and beginners will like some of the choices and the thinking that lies behind them.

What would you combine with a Winchester Model 70 hunting rifle in 30-06? There's no question: a 32-20, such as the Colt Police Positive Special. While revolvers like this one have only recently achieved limited collector status, they are, as a group, incredibly accurate in this caliber. They will also easily provide good one-shot kills on small game out to 60 or so yards, and they'll serve for a few close-range shots on deer and antelope taken from blinds. The Colt Police Positive Special, which was made between 1910 and 1950, meets all the criteria, it's lightweight, and it's easy to carry.

Selecting lightweight handguns for use in a support role is critical for those who hunt on foot or from horseback. My favorite Colt Police Positive Special weighs slightly over five ounces, even with six fully loaded cartridges in place. The point is, a lightweight handgun that shoots well for you in a mid-range caliber will match well with any standard deer-hunting cartridge.

The 32-20, extolled as an excellent small-game round, has regained some popularity recently. Originally loaded by both UMC and Winchester (and currently by Remington), the 32-20 featured several commercial loads for nearly every purpose. A high-velocity version carried the clear warning: *for rifles in good condition only.* A generation of early hunters were paranoid about using high-velocity loads in their Colts and Smith & Wessons. It was just as well. Their pistols were becoming rare antiques; indeed, warnings probably did much to save these guns from day-to-day use and preserved them for the future. Nothing needs to be said about selecting a Winchester Model 70 in 30-06 as a basic deer, bear and occasional antelope cartridge. The 32-20, on the other hand, is less familiar. Considered an old cartridge, it is still readily available, simply because so many old firearms are still in use. It's also surprisingly accurate in a handgun; moreover, it features low report and low recoil. The standard loading produced 1222 fps and moved a 115-grain flat-nosed bullet, which tumbled relentlessly upon contact with any small game and delivered a shock effect way out of proportion to velocity and bullet design. As a result, the 32-20 is still available, with the return of the Marlin attesting to its longevity. Any hunter going afield with his 30-06 backed up with a 32-20 is well prepared for most field situations.

***38 Specials and 357 Magnums.*** Many shooters would feel more comfortable choosing a 38 Special as a match for most any hunting rifle. Today, this round is much maligned, being passed over as a police and military cartridge. In favor of a more powerful 9mm and the newer line of 10mm's. Indeed, the 38 Special has probably experienced more commercial reloadings and offerings than any other since brass cartridges were first produced. The modern versions are the best ever, though, filling the handgun support role quite effectively. By the way, this cartridge has a characteristic that few shooters recognize, one that any hunter with outdoor experience under varying field conditions readily appreciates. Its size and design make it easy to find and grab a handful in one's pocket or pack.

The Colt Diamondback in 38 Special matches readily to any mid-level caliber hunting rifle. This lightweight, smaller-framed pistol, when teamed with a Model 70 Featherweight Winchester in 257 Roberts, for example, makes a smashing combination for varmints and small game. Both cartridges are considered mild, offering a combination that youngsters and women can enjoy shooting.

Whereas handguns are called upon to take deer-sized and larger game, the 357 Magnum is the least powerful cartridge one should consider. A better choice is the 41 or 44 Magnum, especially for hunters moving up to close-range bear or down to mid-sized elk. As a backup gun to a rifle, larger-framed magnum handguns can be a bit much to carry; but for hunts requiring little walking, they're the way to go. The Contender, offered in a variety of calibers, is also useful; unfortunately, it limits the hunter to one shot only.

The Colt Python and Smith & Wesson Model 27 are the standard references for wheel guns in 357 Magnum. Both are easily teamed with any deer rifle to meet the criteria for a hunting rifle-pistol combination. The longish 357 cartridge can never interchange accidentally with a rifle cartridge. It also offers the same advantage enjoyed

***Few semiautomatic hunting rifle designs are available, but those lucky enough to own or borrow a Model 100 Winchester Carbine can match it effectively with Browning's workhorse Model P-35.***

by the pioneers of allowing interchangeability when teamed with the Marlin 1894CS, also in 357 Magnum. Some things never change.

Those who look for the excitement of a quick repeat shot can easily determine the pistol side of the equation, but the rifle side is sometimes more difficult. Remington's excellent Model 7400 or the Voere Model 2185/2FSN are good hunting cartridges. Overall, fewer semiautomatic hunting rifle designs are available, but those who own or can borrow a Model 100 Winchester Carbine in 284 are fortunate indeed. Matched with Browning's workhorse Model P-35 in any of its current configurations, the Model 100 provides shooters with all they could hope for: quick repeat shots with adequate killing power in the rifle, and enough handgun power to take small game or dispatch wounded animals.

***The Lever Action Rifle.*** Any discussion of matching rifles with handguns should include lever-action rifles. Match a 30-30 in a Marlin or Winchester with a Ruger New Model Single Six in 32 Magnum and the bridge between old and new is crossed in one swoop. The flat-sided levers are still best for travel on horseback or pickup truck, and the plough- handled Ruger positions the butt in a way that assures quick access from any hip holster. While the 30-30 is a known quantity, the 32 Magnum is less familiar to most shooters. Conceived as a cartridge for handguns and available initially in late Harrington & Richardson models (before the firm was restructured), the 32 Magnum offers muzzle velocity and striking energy slightly above the 38 Special (but well below the 357 Magnum).

The big power-hitter among combinations is the Browning Model 81 lever-action rifle in 7mm Remington Magnum matched with an equally large handgun in 44 Magnum. By comparison, the world judges handgun performance in 44 Magnum by Smith & Wesson's Model 29, a big-bore pistol that can deliver target quality shooting. Many shooters can't handle full-load 44 Magnum pistols, however, without a lot of practice and experience. Dedicated 44 Magnum fans abound, though, because they know that any handgun in 44 Magnum makes an excellent match with any hunting rifle. A 44 is good on varmints as well as deer, they'll insist, claiming that the 44 Magnum is the only cartridge that truly backs up a hunting rifle. In any event, the 7mm Remington Magnum Model 81 Browning lever and Model 29 Smith & Wesson represent the most powerful rifle-handgun combination available for big-game hunting almost anywhere in the U.S.

For bear hunters, or those who perceive an advantage in using the same bullet in both handgun and rifle, there's another interesting matchup: Marlin's Model 444S and any 44 Magnum handgun, both of which use the same 240-grain softpoint bullet. For reloaders, this means only one kind of bullet need be on hand. The Marlin rifle has a reputation for taking short-range bear, while the 44 Magnum is adequate for black bear. The 444 offers about 590 fps more velocity than the 44 Magnum, but part of that difference is due to barrel length. Any hunter going after black bear over bait or from a stand is adequately

***Storing and transporting arms and ammunition is less of a problem today than in our great grandfather's time. The need to ensure one kind of ammunition that fits both rifle and handgun has become less important.***

*The Colt Python in 357 Magnum matches well with many hunting rifles, thus providing the outdoorsman a solid combination that can accommodate different hunting applications.*

armed with this powerful combination.

In gopher fields, the 222 Remington cartridge is a fine intermediate range performer when the crosswinds are down and the field mirages are up. Sako's heavy-barreled Varmint Rifle has the extra barrel weight and wider forearm a shooter needs to compete effectively with the wind in making shots count at long range. On short-range shots, Harrington & Richardson's newly revised Model 999 handgun (once called the Sportsman) works just fine when shooting at gophers. For those who elect to restrict their diet to 22 centerfires, several interesting combinations are available to suit the needs of plinkers and target shooters. The salad days of my own youth were spent shooting an Ithaca Model 15 semiautomatic rifle matched up with a single-shot Savage Model 101 handgun. The latter resembled a six-shooter, right down to the fake bullets in its fake aluminum cylinder—but was it fun!

As we've seen, there are plenty of good reasons for going afield with a rifle-handgun combination. Like the pioneers before us, we can cover more bases and enjoy more shooting opportunities with this combo. The practice of having a backup gun is as valid today as it was in the past. Flexibility and choice are the key elements for shooters who venture afield armed with handgun and rifle. Remember, too, that nostalgic trip we took—about having a handgun at the side and a rifle in the hand. The skilled hunter who ventures out alone into wild places armed with two kinds of firearms has good reason for those feelings of confidence and independence.

***WILF PYLE is an avid sportsman who has hunted nearly all game species with a wide variety of firearms. A well-known authority on sporting arms and reloading, he has a passion for sporting rifles and their designs. His books include*** **Small Game and Varmint Hunting** ***and*** **Hunting Predators for Hides and Profit** ***(Stoeger Publishing). He has also co-authored*** **The Hunter's Book of the Pronghorn Antelope** ***(New Century).***

# THE MAN WHO CHANGED MUZZLELOADING

***by Toby Bridges***

Muzzleloading, currently recognized as one of the fastest growing of all the shooting and hunting sports, is also one of the fastest changing. The frontloaders that are now enjoying the greatest popularity are a far cry from the reproduction models we knew only 20 years ago. While nostalgia continues to play a role, the main reason why today's shooters are turning to the slow-to-load blackpowder rifle is not only because it offers the challenge of mastering a firearms design that is centuries old—it's because these new blackpowder shooters are whitetail deer hunters who want to expand their hunting opportunities by taking advantage of the special muzzleloading seasons now sanctioned in all but a handful of states.

The 1990s breed of muzzleloading shooters could care less about the historic design of the muzzleloader. They simply demand a frontloading rifle that can deliver optimum muzzleloading performance on deer and other big game—and they're getting it. That's because some significant changes have evolved in muzzleloading design, so that now many muzzleloading hunting rifles can perform on a par with out-of-the-box centerfire hunting rifles.

And the one rifle that has done more than any other to change how the serious whitetail deer hunter looks at muzzleloading is the Knight MK-85. Designed by Missouri gunsmith William A. "Tony" Knight, the Knight MK-85 at first glance bears little resemblance to the long, heavy and awkward frontloading rifles of traditional side-hammer design. In fact, it displays all the classic lines of a bolt-action centerfire rifle, not to mention the handling characteristics and safeties of a modern firearm, one that can produce 1½-inch groups at 100 yards.

Considering Tony Knight's extensive gunsmithing background, the success of his MK-85 should come as no surprise. Before turning his attention to the design and construction of a new and better muzzleloading hunting rifle, Knight specialized in custom work based on Remington's Model 600 carbines. His reputation for building handsome and accurate short deer hunting rifles eventually carried over into the creation of several muzzleloading whitetail rifles that bear his name.

It all began during the late 1970s and early 1980s when several of Knight's friends took up muzzleloading in order to enjoy the new muzzleloading elk seasons sanctioned by the Rocky Mountain states. Loading and shooting the traditional reproduction muzzleloader was a new experience for these hunters. More often than not,

***At first glance, the earliest prototype of the Knight rifle bears little resemblance to the muzzleloader now carried by several hundred thousand blackpowder hunters. Still, this handmade original by William A. Knight established the basis for a new muzzleloading hunting rifle design.***

however, they returned from their hunts with horror stories about how the guns failed to fire in bad weather and how cumbersome they were to carry all day at high altitudes. There were also the limitations imposed by an ignition system that relied on only a half-cock notch as a safety. All these shortcomings caused Tony Knight to shift his attention to the design of a brand new muzzleloading rifle for the hunter.

Knight began by whittling on the stock and machining the metal parts for his first muzzleloader during the winter of 1983. The prototype was made from a piece of walnut tree cut down on the family farm, an inexpensive Numrich Arms barrel (with a slow one-turn-in-66 inches rifling twist), a handmade trigger and a set of

***The Knight MK-85 prototype was the first to incorporate a hammer that cocked from the rear. Other features included a removable breechplug, a secondary safety at the rear of the hammer, and a trigger taken from a sporting Mauser rifle.***

Remington sights. This and two subsequent prototypes featured a unique in-line percussion ignition system in which the nipple was positioned directly in the rear center of the breechplug. Fire from an exploding cap shot directly into the powder charge through an extremely short, straight flash channel. Ignition was spontaneous and more "sure-fire" than muzzleloaders of traditional side-hammer design could produce. In addition, Knight used a plunger-style hammer that rode inside the receiver, much like the bolt of a modern centerfire rifle. This design allowed the installation of a modern thumb-operated safety and scope bases on top of the hand-machined receiver.

Knight's rifles, which were also fitted with barrels that had been turned round and tapered, weighed in at slightly more than seven pounds, a major improvement over most traditional reproduction rifles on the market. Still another appealing feature was the fully removable breechplug for easier cleaning. In little more than a minute, this muzzleloader could be totally dismantled and cleaned from the breech end, just like a modern centerfire.

When Knight began to design his final prototype, he decided to add a second safety. This rifle—built with a trigger taken from a sporting Mauser—featured a safety that could be slipped into the "on" position before the plunger-style hammer was pulled back into the "cocked" position (earlier prototypes had featured a handle on the side of the hammer for cocking). This fourth prototype could be cocked simply by pulling back on the rear of the hammer. Knight's new design also had a second safety in the form of a hammer block, which was nothing more than a collar that could be moved forward or rearward on a threaded area located at the rear of the hammer. When turned into the forward position, this secondary safety prevented the hammer from falling far enough forward to strike a capped nipple.

By the end of 1984, Knight's redesigned muzzleloading rifle sported some very refined lines, a modern stock design complete with rubber recoil pad, and an adjustable rear sight. It was also lightweight, had an easy-handling barrel length, and a fast rifling twist that spun at the rate of one-turn-in-48 inches. Thus, in 1985, Knight finally introduced his rifle to muzzleloading hunters everywhere as the "Knight MK-85." Total production that first year amounted to only 25 rifles—and they weren't shipped until November.

***Knight muzzleloading rifles are well built, displaying the classic lines of quality centerfire hunting rifles.***

Since then, a number of refinements have been added to the original design, but Knight's basic concept has not changed. Small improvements have been made in nipple design and better configuration of the removable breechplug, but the principle of Knight's in-line percussion ignition system has remained the same. Newer models utilize large rifle primers for ignition instead of standard No. 11 percussion caps, but most changes from one model to the next have been purely cosmetic, not functional.

During the past decade, the company has continued its search for a better, more accurate rifle barrel. The 25 rifles produced in 1985, along with about half of the 200 rifles built the following year, were offered in .50 caliber only. These early reproduction guns, which gave relatively good accuracy, were built with Bauska barrels featuring a one-turn-in-48-inches rifling twist using both the patched round ball and the conical "maxi-style" lead bullets. Another noteworthy development around that time was the introduction of small plastic sabots that enabled blackpowder shooters to load and fire a wide range of jacketed and non-jacketed pistol bullets from their large-bored muzzleloading rifles. Muzzleload Magnum Products (Harrison, Arkansas) developed the system which immediately gave blackpowder hunters several hundred different .44- and .45-caliber handgun bullets to choose from for their .50- or .54-caliber muzzleloaders.

By 1986, Knight's company—Modern Muzzleloading, Inc.—began making barrels with a much faster rate of rifling twist. Saboted bullets, he reasoned correctly, would quickly gain popularity among blackpowder hunters, so he made the change to a one-turn-in-32 inches as the standard rate of twist for all Knight rifles. That same year the company also began offering the rifle in limited numbers in calibers .45 and .54. Later in the spring of 1987, the rate of rifling twist was changed once more to an even faster one-turn-in-28 inches. It was then that Knight's rifles really began to gain recognition as "The most accurate production muzzleloaders in the world." At last, here was a muzzleloader right out of the box that could outshoot many production centerfire hunting rifles at 100 yards.

Meanwhile, Knight's continuing search for a better barrel resulted in several changes. First, the company went to Lothar Walther in Germany for its barrels, then to McMillan and Competition Limited. By 1990, all Knight rifle barrels were being manufactured in New Hampshire by the Green Mountain Rifle Barrel Company. Up to then, they'd been built with button-rifled barrels; but since 1990 they've featured precision cut-rifled barrels, thus improving the frontloader's reputation for exceptional accuracy even more.

In early 1988 after moving into a larger plant in Lancaster, Missouri, production of Knight muzzleloading rifles topped the 1,000 mark; and by the spring of 1990, the operation moved again, this time to Centerville, Iowa, where the company continues to operate. In 1991, Tony Knight sold his company to Nebraska businessman L. Dale Watley, whose two sons, Loy and Bruce Watley, now run the operation. Knight, however, remains on board overseeing legislative issues, media promotions, and still newer product designs. While the company won't readily divulge the number of guns it has built since that first year, it's estimated that nearly 200,000 rifles built by Modern

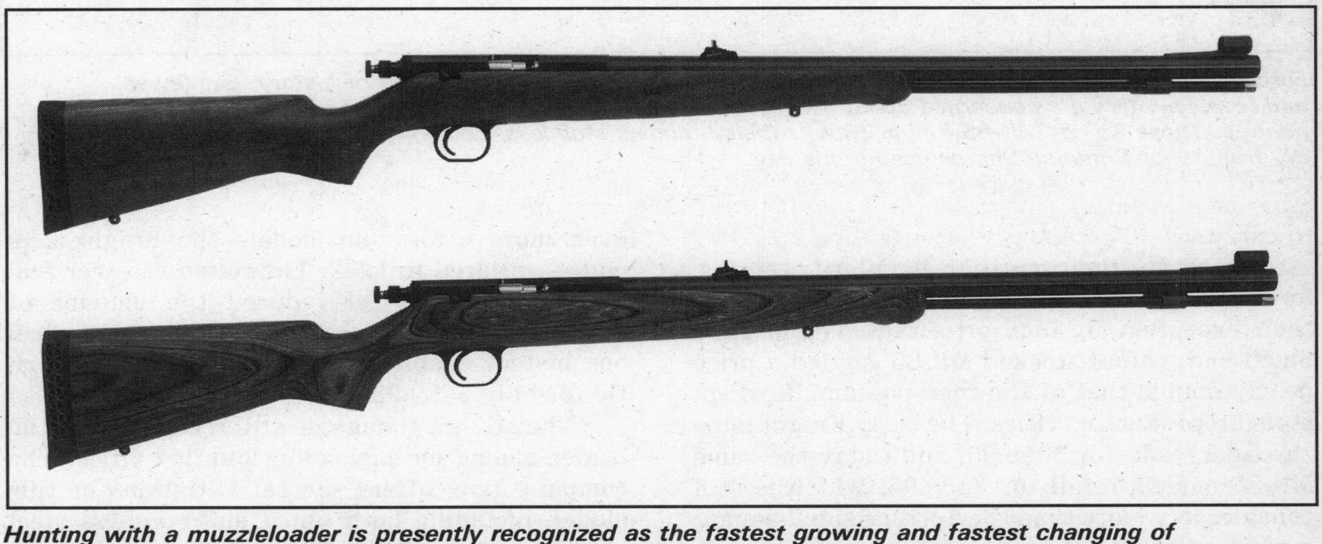

***Hunting with a muzzleloader is presently recognized as the fastest growing and fastest changing of today's shooting sports. A fascination with hunting whitetail deer is the main reason why these modern in-line percussion Knight MK-85's are becoming the guns of choice. Above is the Knight MK-85 Hunter (the current version of the original MK-85); below is the Knight MK-85 Stalker.***

Muzzleloading are in the hands of blackpowder hunters across the country.

Compared to most traditional side-hammer muzzleloading rifles that have been on the market for the past 20 years or more, the Knight rifle represents a vast improvement in the design of muzzleloading hunting rifles. The lightest model in the current line tips the scales at only 6 pounds, while the heaviest weighs in at about 7 pounds. Compared to the 9- and 10-pound half-stock frontloaders that were the choice of muzzleloading hunters before the modern in-line rifles appeared, the Knight rifles are indeed a delight to carry.

To reach their current popularity status, however, these frontloaders had to overcome their exceptionally high price tags. The original blued and walnut-stocked MK-85 carried a price nearly double that of the then-popular Hawken-styled reproduction rifles. The early Knight muzzleloaders sold for $349.95, and today the same MK-85 models retail for $559.95, which is still considerably more than the average side-hammer reproduction rifle.

Over the past couple of years, though, Modern Muzzleloading has introduced several lower-priced models. For example, in 1992 the company hit the market with its BK-92 Black Knight, a rifle that contained most of the features of the MK-85 but at a more affordable price. The new gun was still made with the cut-rifled Green Mountain barrel, and it had the same receiver and many of the same internal parts as the most costly MK-85. But by using a more economical method for producing the stock along with a less costly version of the Timney trigger found on the MK-85, Modern Muzzleloading was able to market its in-line percussion muzzleloading rifle for about one-third less than the walnut-stocked MK-85. An even more affordable model—the Knight Legend—appeared in 1993. The round receiver featured on this model reduced the amount of machining required and its more economical beech stock enabled the company to retail the rifle for only $289.95.

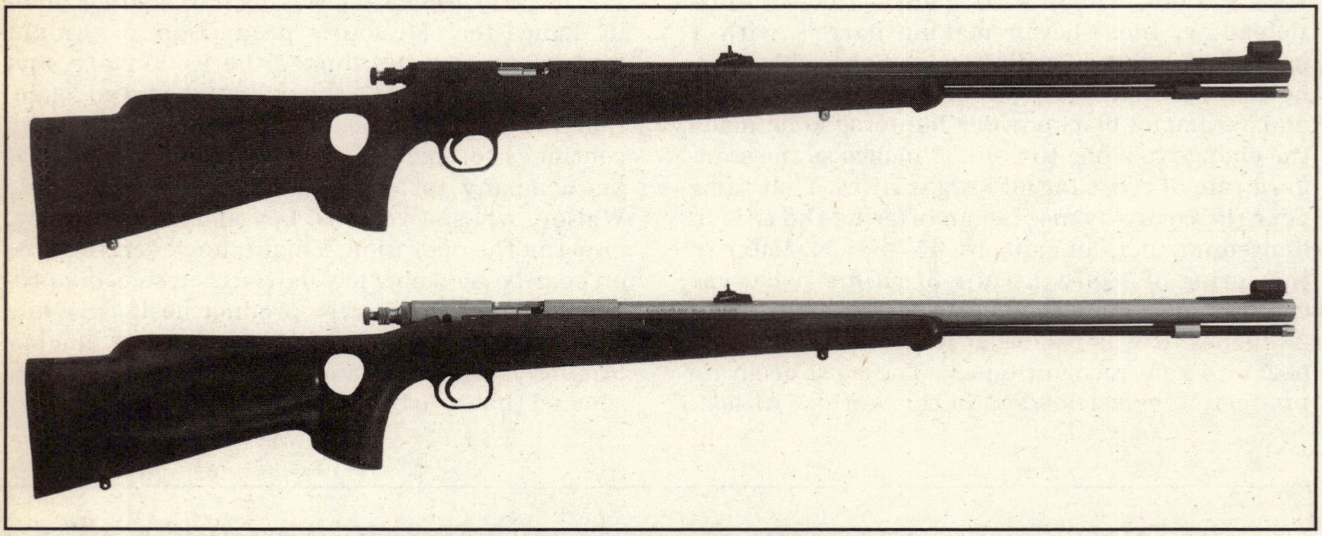

***For many blackpowder shooters, muzzleloading still offers a way to relive a bit of history. But fewer and fewer hunters are concerned about the historical correctness of the muzzleloaders they carry for hunting. These Knight MK-85 Knight Hawks (blued, above; stainless, below), for example, are a far cry from what Christian Sharps used in his day.***

The MK-85, though, is still recognized as the leader among muzzleloading hunting rifles. The company now offers several variations of this model, including both blued and stainless steel versions. Depending on which variation is selected, the rifle comes with a walnut, laminated or composite stock. One version is even available with a modernistic composite thumbhole stock that makes this frontloader look even less like a muzzleloader.

Two other recent entries from Modern Muzzleloading are the MK-95 Magnum Elite and the MK-86 Multiple Barrel System. The former boasts the hottest ignition system available on a muzzleloading hunting rifle. Instead of a No. 11 percussion cap, this innovative frontloader utilizes a large-rifle or magnum-large rifle primer for ignition. A simple hammer and bolt arrangement allows the shooter to chamber a small plastic capsule containing the rifle primer. Not only does this ignition system add considerably more fire into the powder charge, it allows the primer to be carried in a closed ignition system for protection from foul weather.

The new Multiple Barrel System features interchangeable barrels that allow blackpowder hunters to change from a .50- or .54-caliber frontloading rifle to a muzzleloading 12-gauge shotgun in a matter of minutes. In either rifle caliber, and with an optional shotgun barrel, the MK-86 enables the hunter to take the same gun after big game, wild turkey or small game simply by switching barrels.

There's even a well-designed in-line percussion muzzleloading pistol on the market. Called "The Hawkeye," it's built with all the features that have made Knight rifles famous, including a removable breechplug, double safeties and cut-rifled barrel. Available in .50-caliber only, this pistol was designed for blackpowder big-game hunters who are looking for an extra challenge. Using the hottest loads, this frontstuffer nearly duplicates the ballistics of a .44-magnum revolver.

Tony Knight didn't really invent the in-line ignition system—but he did perfect it. Through the years, a number of in-line ignition muzzleloading guns have been manufactured, including a few flintlock guns dating from the 1700s. And since around 1970, some in-line rifles have predated Knight's in-line ignition system, including the Eusopus Pacer, a frontloader that was way ahead of its time. As late as the early 1980s, Michigan Arms produced the Wolverine, still another innovative in-line ignition muzzleloader utilizing No. 209 shotgun primers for sure-fire ignition.

For one reason or another, these innovative in-line muzzleloading rifles have failed to appeal to modern-day blackpowder hunters. Generally speaking, they failed to produce the accuracy and performance demanded by the serious hunter, or their actions were poorly designed, making them difficult to operate reliably. The Knight rifles, on the other hand, gave muzzleloaders what they wanted: a serious deer rifle that just happened to load from the front. As a result, Knight rifles have spawned a whole new segment of the muzzleloading market. One of the first to follow the trend was the Apollo imported from Spain by Connecticut Valley Arms. White Shooting Systems (Roosevelt, Utah) and Gonic Arms (Gonic, New Hampshire) also offer modernistic in-line percussion hunting rifles. And Thompson/Center Arms, which did much to popularize muzzleloading hunting with its traditionally styled Hawken rifles during the 1970s, is marketing some modern in-line percussion hunting rifles of its own.

Whether the muzzleloading industry as a whole will switch over to the more modern in-line ignition rifles remains to be seen. The trend is headed in that direction as newer and better muzzleloading seasons offer big-game hunters more opportunities to hunt. For many, of course, there will always be an historical tie to the past; but for the present, the in-line percussion rifle remains the wave of the future.

***TOBY BRIDGES has been hunting with muzzleloading guns since the 1960s. His blackpowder hunts have rewarded him with dozens of big-game trophies, including black bear, wild boar, elk, mule deer, pronghorn antelope and even several buffalo. A veteran freelance writer and former editor of*** **Black Powder Gun Digest*****, Bridges is now associated full time with Modern Muzzle Loading Inc. (Centerville, Iowa) in the company's market development program.***

# FINE-TUNING VARMINT RIFLES—BENCHREST STYLE

***by Don Lewis***

When serious handloaders began testing reloads by firing 5-shot, 100-yard groups from a benchrest, it soon became apparent that there was more to accuracy than just weighing a powder charge to the nth degree. During that period when handloaders were using conventional methods and equipment and being as precise as possible, a nagging factor still persisted: groups weren't shrinking no matter how much care and precision went into each round.

By the mid-1960s, benchrest competitors were paying close attention to case preparation. Not much thought had been given to primer pocket conditioning, primer seating and outside neck-turning. Benchrest competitors learned that these steps were just as important as weighing the powder charge. Unfortunately, the tools required for these operations were not readily available. Reloading equipment manufacturers were producing high-quality loading presses, powder measures and die sets; but not much was offered to seat a primer the same in every case, gauge and size the flash hole, deburr the flash hole inside the case, and measure the bullet's relationship to the throat (known as seating depth).

The modern factory varmint rifle is as accurate as many benchrest rigs of the late 1940s. Back then, benchrest competitors were trying to stay below the one-inch mark on a consistent basis at 100 yards. In 1948, the Donaldson Trophy was won with a 10-shot, 200-yard group that measured under 1½ inches. That's about a ¾-inch group at 100 yards. In 1964, a world-record 5-shot, 100-yard group measured .143″. Several years ago, a friend fired a 5-shot, 100-yard group that measured .210 thousands of an inch (.250 is ¼-inch). While the tiny ragged hole looked like a winner, it scored 12th in a line of 15 shooters.

It's fair to say that benchrest competitors leave no stone unturned in their constant quest for the ultimate in accuracy. At 100 yards, individual group sizes have shrunk below one hundred thousandths of an inch. Even a 25-shot aggregate (five 5-shot groups) over several days of shooting will be well under ½ inch. This proves that one-hole accuracy is possible at 100 yards under controlled conditions from precision shooters using custom-made benchrest rifles topped with high-power scopes.

This type of accuracy is not a product of sheer luck; it comes from eliminating all the variables that tend to affect accuracy. Everything from the rifle to the cartridge used plays a major role. No matter how skilled a shooter is or how precisioned the rifle is, the case/primer/powder/bullet combination has to be free of even the smallest defect to produce a winning target.

The primer, which is the ignition system, is factory produced, but factory primers—especially benchrest primers—are highly dependable. Today's powders are manufactured under controlled conditions that make them uniform in burning. Benchrest bullets are literally handmade and are held to incredibly close tolerances, usually well below .0003 (three ten thousandths of an inch) in concentricity.

### *USING BENCHREST TOOLS FOR CASE PREPARATION*

Cartridge cases—factory-made ones—are mass produced, so it's literally impossible for them to have the same dimensions. Primer pockets are first punched, then primer flash holes are punched (or pierced) through the bottom of the primer pocket. The pockets won't be the same depth or diameter, and punching flash holes through the bottom of the pocket concaves the bottom slightly. This process also leaves burrs and irregularities on the bottom of the flash hole inside the case. Case necks may vary in thickness and high spots can appear on the outside of the neck. Trivial as these things may seem, they have to be corrected to assure benchrest accuracy.

*In modifying primer pockets, a Primer Pocket Turning Fixture (made by Custom Products) is used. The shell is held firmly in a shell holder, allowing the cutter to enter the pocket straight and square. It takes only seconds to "true" the primer pocket.*

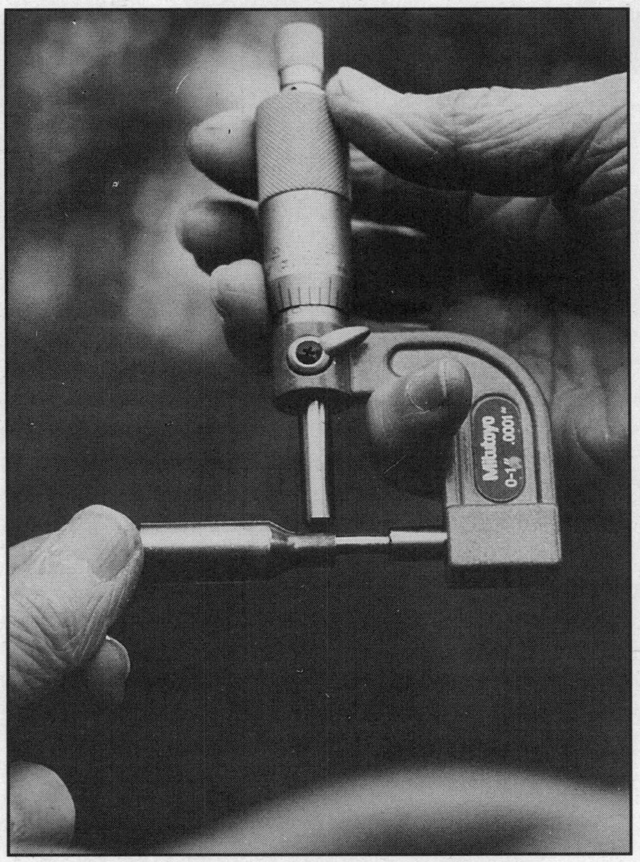


*By using benchrest tools for case preparation and certain benchrest loading procedures, the varmint hunter can improve the accuracy of his rifle. Here the K&M Ball Micrometer measures the thickness of a case's neck wall. Neck walls must be the same thickness around their entire circumference.*

The average heavy-barrel varmint rifle will never perform to the same degree of accuracy as does a benchrest rig. Still, by using some benchrest tools for case preparation and certain benchrest loading procedures, the varmint hunter can enhance his success ratio in the field. It's not the intent here to condemn conventional reloading tools. Over a 40-year period, this writer has loaded tens of thousands of high-performance reloads on a variety of factory presses, dies and other mass-produced factory equipment. It's just that benchrest tools are normally handmade by craftsmen who are dedicated shooters, and who

*This powder measure made by Neil Jones is guaranteed to achieve consistency of loads.*

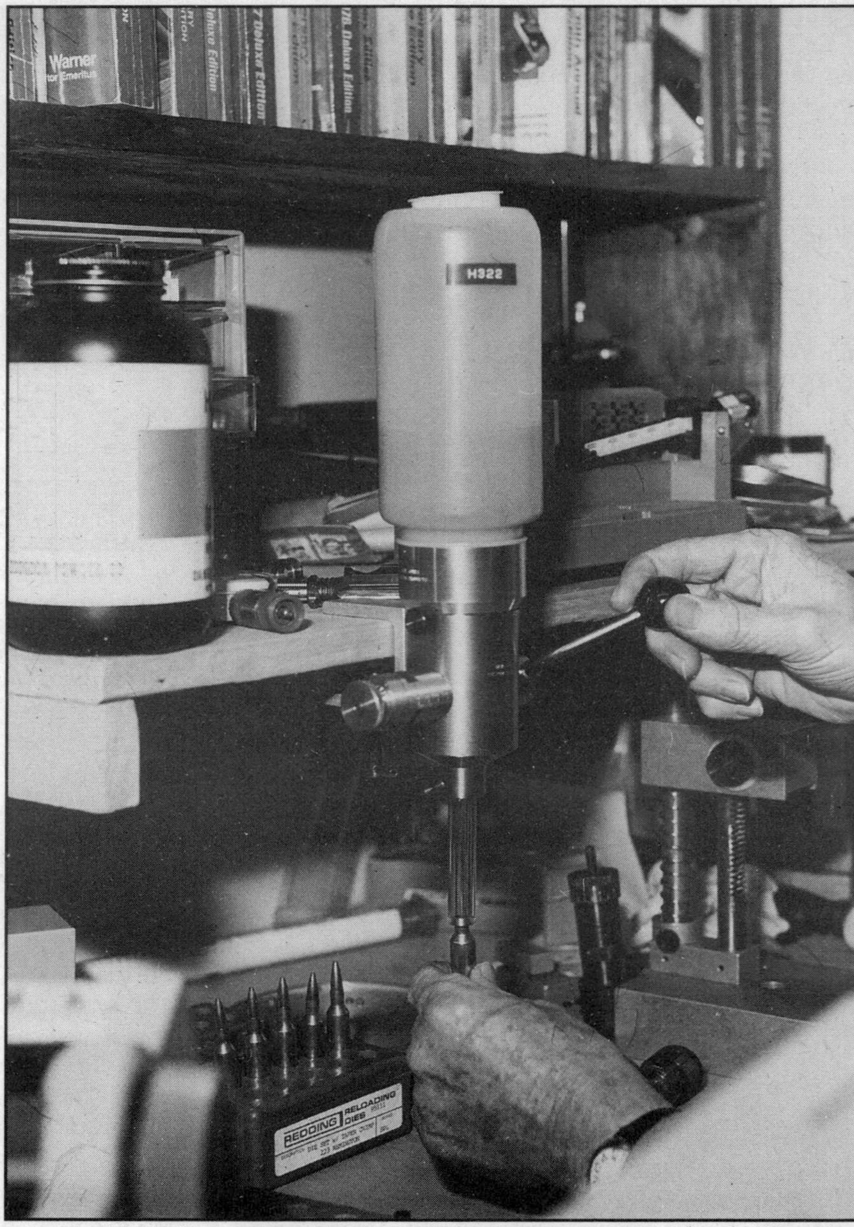


know what is required from a handload to obtain accuracy.

For instance, Neil Jones's handmade Micro Powder Measure costs several times more than conventional powder measures, but the company claims that its measure is made of tool steel and is 100% machined. It has no rough casting surfaces, thus assuring smooth powder flow through the measure. The cutting edges in the body of the measure have been designed to cut through the most difficult powders with ease. The measuring drum is guaranteed to repeat itself from one predetermined, recorded setting to another, and charges can be varied without the need to check on a powder scale. Most of all, the measure is consistent—and consistency is mandatory in reloading the accurate round.

Case preparation years ago consisted of

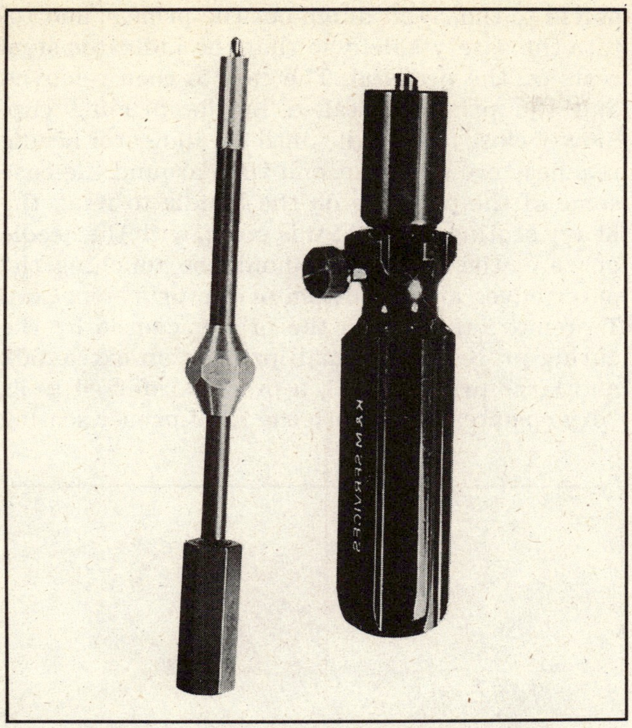

***The K&M Flash Hole Uniformer (left) has a reversible sliding dowel that fits both large and small case mouths. The K&M Primer Pocket modifying tool (right) features a square shoulder for the shellhead to butt against. This enables the cutter to hold square with the primer pocket and assures a flat cut on the bottom. It also prevents elongation of the pocket diameter.***

cleaning residue out of the primer pocket. A variety of homemade tools were used, such as filing the blade of a screwdriver to fit the primer pocket, whittling a Popsickle stick down to size, or gluing a bit of emery paper on the end of a round dowel pin. The object was to get the dirt off the bottom of the primer pocket. Even factory primer pocket cleaning tools worked on the same principle. The drawback with all of these tools was their lack of a shoulder to butt against the shellhead, thereby holding the tool square and in alignment with the primer pocket. With tools that had cutters on the side, the primer pocket became elongated, preventing the primer from being seated tight in the pocket. Many blowouts and gas leaks were caused by loose primers.

K&M's Primer Pocket Correction Tool has a shoulder and is hand-held; but it also has a tungsten carbide cutter and is factory set to an optimum depth of .131-inch for large primers and .122-inch for small primers. It's adjustable for other depths as well. The shellhead is held square against a precision-ground face or shoulder. Another Primer Pocket Turning Fixture made by Custom Products is bench-mounted and holds the case squarely in a modified Lee Shell Holder, allowing the cutter to enter the pocket straight and square. The crank shaft and bearing sleeves are hardened and ground to prevent shaft wobble. The tool utilizes 3/8-inch diameter carbide inserts in three sizes—Large Rifle, Small Rifle and Large Pistol. The cutters are factory set for optimum depth, but are adjustable. Both tools not only clean the burned residue from the bottom of the pocket, they also cut the outer edges of the primer pocket square so that the primer anvil legs may rest against them—an important function indeed.

After modifying the primer pocket, the next step is to remove the internal burrs around the bottom of the flash hole. The K&M Flash Hole Uniformer reams the flash hole to a uniform diameter while at the same time deburring and chamfering the bottom of the hole. The unique feature of this tool is its preset depth stop surrounding the tool steel cutter. Cases do not have to be trimmed to an exact length; and the operation is controlled in reference to the inside-bottom of the case, not the case mouth.

## *PRIMERS AND PRIMER SEATING*

In the early days of handloading, most handloaders did not understand the makeup of a primer, which is more complex than it looks. The

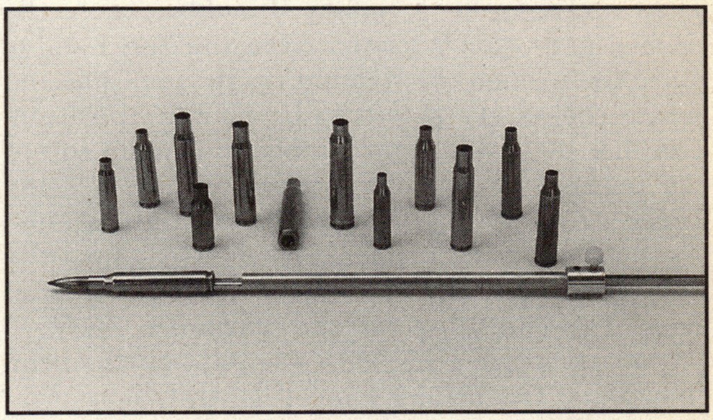

***A cartridge case is screwed onto the end of a Stony Point Chamber-All Gauge.***

primer consists of a metal cup, priming mix, foil cover and an anvil. For safety reasons, the priming mix is installed in a "wet" state, covered with a piece of foil, and the anvil is then pushed in against the wet mix. During the curing (drying/hardening) process, the mix shrinks, leaving a gap between the mix pellet and the top of the cap; in other words, the anvil is not set tight against the priming mix. The blow from the firing pin has to be strong enough to push the cap top down on the mix with enough strength left over to ignite the mix. This process can cause misfires and poor ignition.

The final step in the resizing operation was usually primer seating, the object being to seat the primer deep enough in the pocket to prevent the primer from protruding out of the shell pocket. This would cut down the chance for an accidental discharge should a protruding firing pin scrape across it. Not much emphasis was placed on primer seating beyond that point. Today, a great deal of emphasis is placed on seating primers, since not all primer pockets are the same depth; nor are all primers the same height, even from the same box. With a benchrest seating tool such as the K&M Deluxe Primer/Gauge, each primer can be seated to the exact thousandths of an inch. K&M's Primer/Gauge is a hand-type primer seating tool that incorporates a dial indicator, the stem of which rests on a primer-holding pedestal. Basically, it measures in one operation the depth of the primer pocket and the height of the primer to be used.

The K&M Primer/Gauge is fairly simply to operate. First, place a case whose primer pocket has been trued or modified and close the handle. Then rotate a plastic safety shield to expose the primer pedestal. Without releasing the handle, place the primer, anvil down, on the pedestal and rotate the safety shield to its original position. The dial indicator stem is now resting on top of the primer. The primer punch, or probe, being under strong spring pressure, is held tight against the bottom of the primer pocket. Next, turn the face of the dial indicator until the needle is on zero. This nullifies all the variables such as primer pocket depth, primer height and shell rim thickness. The primer pocket depth is now measured along with the height of the primer.

With the handle still closed, rotate the safety shield to the right, dump out the primer, and rotate the safety shield so that the indicator stem rests on the pedestal. The case is then removed and the primer installed in the priming cup. Slowly close the handle until the indicator needle reaches zero on its second time around. Release some of the pressure on the handle to relax the heavy seating force. At this point, with the needle on zero, the anvil legs should be touching the outer edges at the bottom of the primer pocket. To remove the gap in the primer caused by the curing process, seat small primers an extra .002 and large primers .003, a process referred to as "dry compression." With the K&M primer seating tool, each primer is mated to the primer pocket in which it will be used.

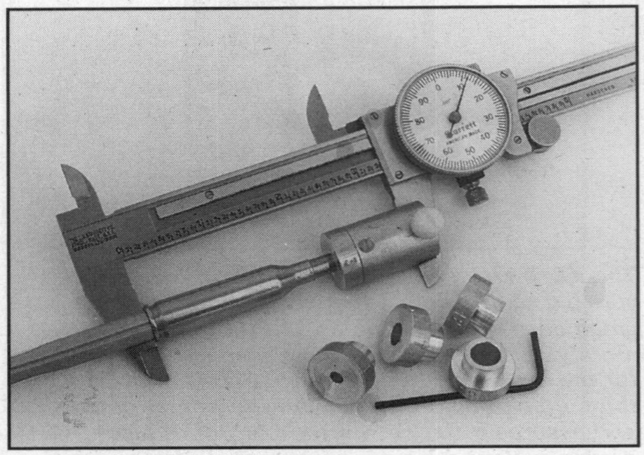

***A vernier caliper equipped with a dial indicator is used in connection with Stoney Point's Chamber-All Gauge to measure the distance between the shellhead to the bullet's ogive.***

Some handloaders ream the inside of the case neck, which can actually defeat the purpose. The reamer tends to follow an off-center hole. It's the outside of the neck that needs to be turned. The K&M Neck Turner is a precision tool with a cutting-knife adjusting screw whose compound thread is equal to 440 turns to the inch (compared to the usual 40 turns found on a micrometer). Tolerances can thus be held to an incredible .0001 of an inch.

The case holder uses Lee Shell Holders for different diameter shellheads. Place a case in the correct shell holder and turn the tool's handle

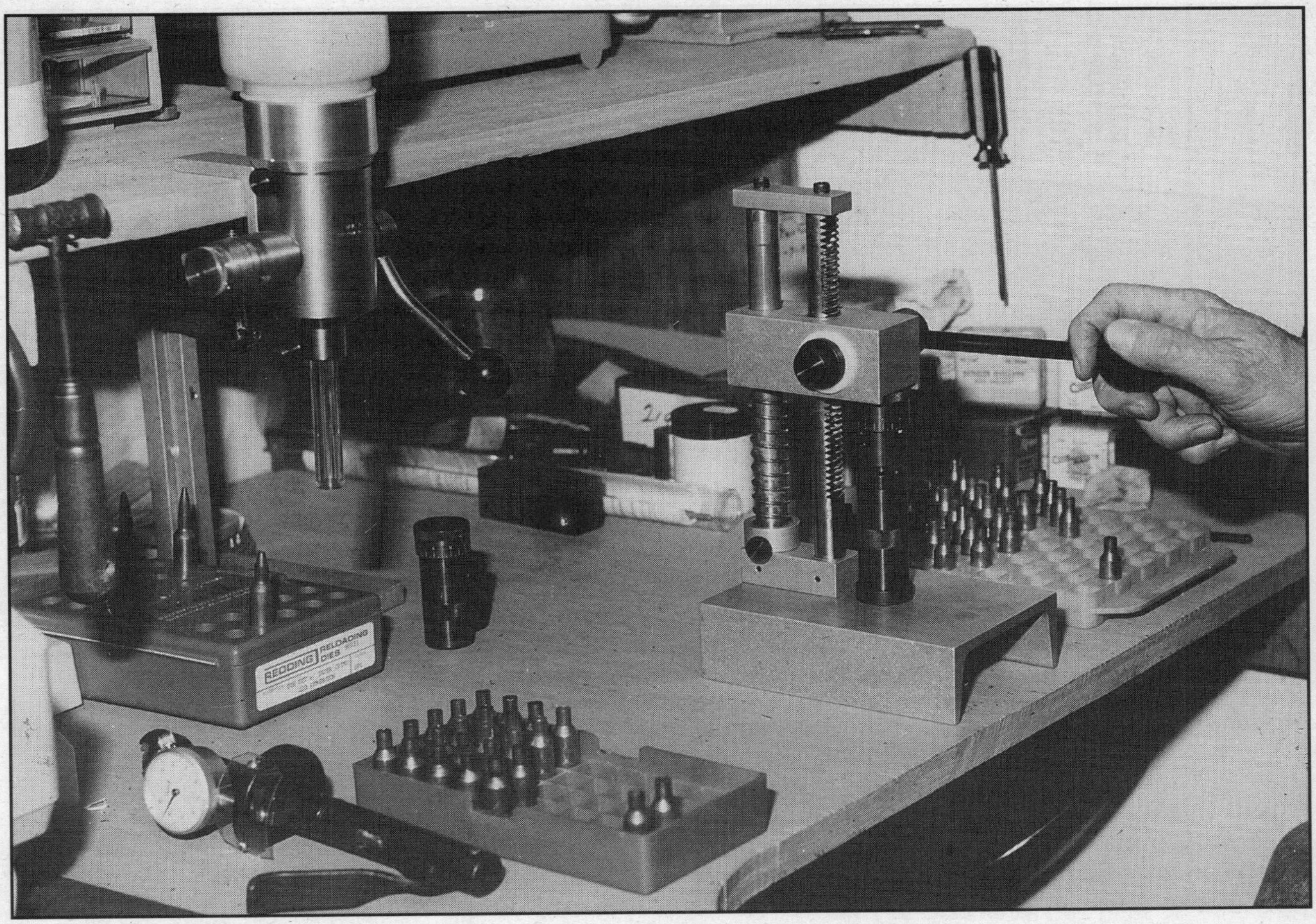

***Benchrest reloading tools do not require a strong bench. The author, whose setup is on 3/4" plywood, is seating bullets with Neil Jones's Arbor Press and Seating Die.***

clockwise until a plunger pushes hard against the shellhead. The case now is firmly locked in the tool. Loosen the cutter clamp screw and, with the correct pilot in the cutting tool, slip the mouth of a fired case (not resized) over the pilot. Then slowly turn the cutter adjustment until it just touches the brass at the front of the case neck. Remove the case and, using the hash marks on the body of the cutting tool, advance the cutter one mark, or .002. Tighten the cutter adjustment lock screw, slip the case over the pilot, and push the case mouth against the cutting tool. Holding the cutter assembly in the left hand, turn the tool's handle clockwise while at the same time pushing the case into the cutter. Cut only the flat neck area; cutting into the shoulder could weaken the case. Measure the wall thickness with a ball micrometer; if there are still high spots, move the cutting knife one-half hash mark. Continue until the desired amount of brass has been removed.

## *SEATING THE BULLET*

Bullet seating depth has always been a controversial subject, especially for competition shooters and varmint hunters. Big-game hunters must seat the bullet deep enough to work through a rifle's detachable or internal magazine. The argument is over whether the bullet's ogive (pronounced o-jive) should touch the rifling, or if there should be a "gap" between the ogive and the rifling.

Seating depth is very important. It influences accuracy and it causes significant changes in velocities and chamber pressures. It's a known fact:

***Bald Eagle's front windage rest has both elevation and windage adjustments, plus leveling screws. The rear bag has a flat between its ears for the rifle to ride in during recoil. The rifle shown is a Peightal Custom Thumbholder in Remington 6mmBR caliber, with Simmons 6x20X scope.***

a load that's considered safe with a gap can become dangerous by increasing the overall length to the point where the bullet's ogive actually touches the lands and groves (rifling). Once that's accomplished, a distinct ring (caused by the rifling) forms around the ogive. This doesn't guarantee accuracy, however, and the round may be unsafe in certain rifles.

The problem with seating a bullet correctly is the degree of difficulty in measuring where the bullet's ogive is in relationship to the rifling. Even measuring the overall length of a cartridge with a caliper (from bullet point to end of shellhead) doesn't guarantee how much gap there is between the bullet and the rifling. Measuring from the bullet's tip is not wise, because tips vary in length and can be damaged or distorted. The only accurate measurement is from the ogive to the shellhead. A bullet's ogive is the rounded, or pointed forward portion. It's that part of the bullet found forward of the flat bearing surface, regardless of shape. To be more technical, it's the radius of the curve of the bullet tip.

The problem in getting precise measurements has been solved with the introduction of Stoney Point Product's Chamber-All Gauge and Bullet Comparator. This tool, called an OAL (overall length) Gauge, is used in conjunction with a vernier caliper that incorporates a dial indicator (it can also determine firearm throat dimensions and throat erosion). In using the OAL Gauge, a factory modified case is screwed onto the end of the gauge. The neck of the modified case—with its primer pocket drilled out and threaded—is opened slightly, allowing the bullet to slide through without friction. The factory furnishes one case (of your choice) from among a total of 35 cases. Wildcat, custom chamber or "non-standard" cases can be factory modified for a precision fit.

To use the OAL Gauge, install a comparator with the correct bullet diameter insert to the traveling blade of a vernier caliper. After screwing the modified case onto the gauge, slip the bullet of choice into the case neck. Push the traveling rod (plunger) in the gauge against the base of the bullet until only the tip protrudes. Tighten the lock screw against the rod; then, with the bolt removed, push the cartridge into the chamber (it's wise to clean the chamber prior to measuring). Loosen the lock screw on the plunger and gently push against the plunger until the bullet is moved through the case neck, its ogive touching the rifling. Lightly tap the end of the plunger three times with the index finger, being careful not to drive the bullet into the rifling. Then, while maintaining a light pressure against the end of the plunger, tighten the plunger lock screw and remove both gauge and cartridge from the action. It's a good idea to run a cleaning rod through the barrel until it touches the end of the bullet. By pushing the rod and pulling on the gauge, the entire assembly can be removed in one sweep. Don't worry if the bullet falls out of the modified case—the plunger is locked into the proper distance.

With the assembly removed, the maximum overall-length cartridge that will fit the firearm (using the selected bullet) can be measured. The cartridge represents a loaded round with the bullet just touching the throat (lands and grooves). By using the comparator, an exact measurement can be taken from the bullet's ogive to the case shellhead. Both measurements on the dial indicator should be recorded for future references. However, every kind of bullet—even the same weight bullets—will have a different length according to where the ogives contact the rifling.

Is a gap necessary? According to one expert, "Seating a bullet without free travel (on or into the rifling) requires developing a load with a reduced powder charge and working up or down

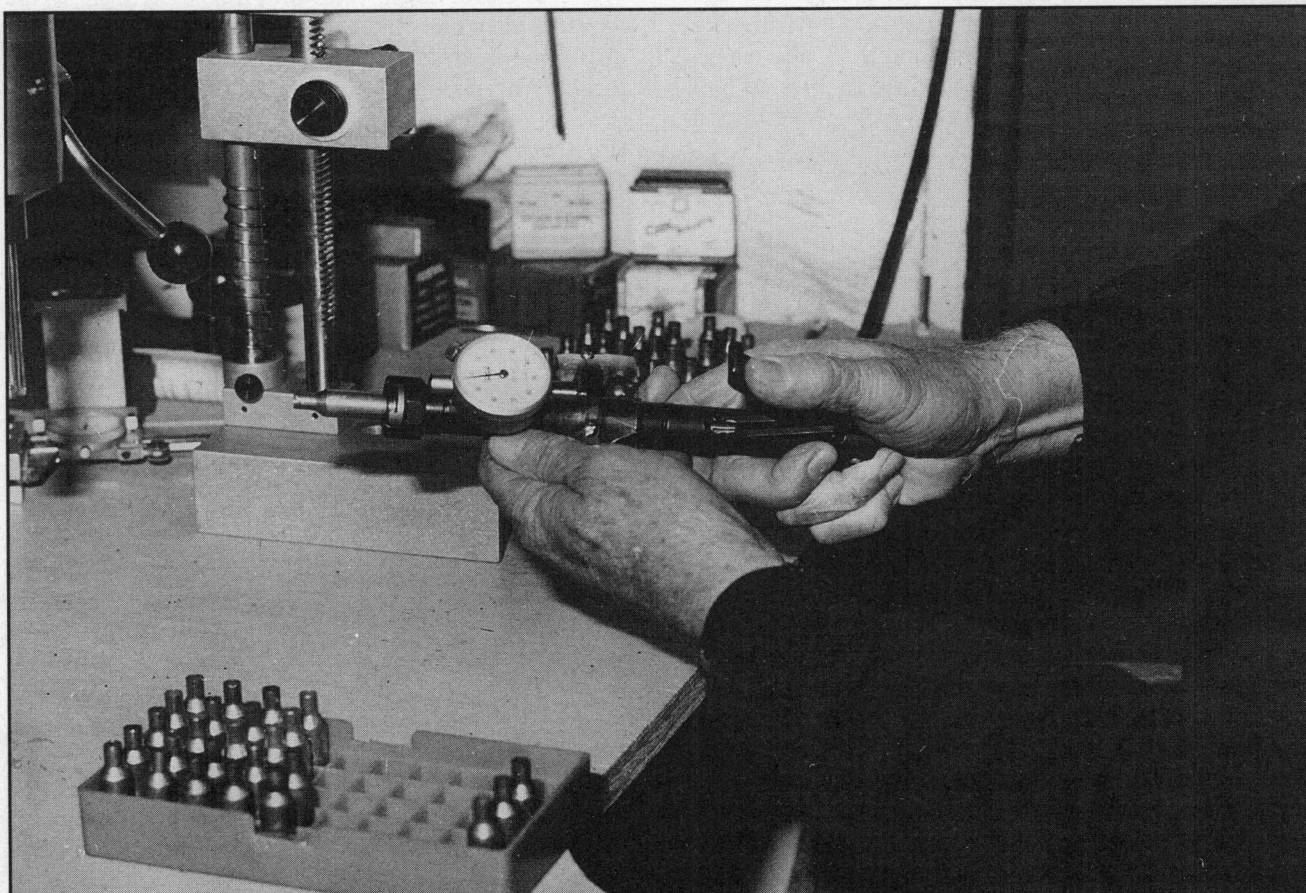

***With this K&M Deluxe Primer Seater, the dial indicator allows the handloader to hold seating tolerances to exact thousandths of an inch, with every primer seated the same.***

*Using the Neil Jones Target Measuring tool, the handloader can measure targets the way benchrest competitors do, thanks to the dial indicator and caliper shown at right.*

until a load is found that is both safe and accurate. . . it's doubtful that loads on or into the rifling will result in improvements in accuracy. Instead, they'll most likely result in loss of accuracy. A minimal free-travel is always required to produce an accurate load."

### GET A GOOD REST!

Even an accurate rifle with top- quality reloads can produce poor results if fired from a poor rest setup. Benchrest shooters discovered long ago that sand bags under the forearm and stock left a lot to be desired. To get top performance, an adjustable front rest coupled with a properly designed rear rest is required. The Bald Eagle Standard Windage Rest and a newly designed rear bag have all the requirements needed for precision shooting. Made of aircraft aluminum, the double-rise front rest weighs just under 8 pounds. Instead of being pulled up manually, the primary elevation adjustment is made with a rack and pinion. A mariner wheel can be turned for minor elevation adjustments. An adjusting knob effortlessly moves the top of the front rest left or right for minor windage adjustments. No shifting of the rear bag is necessary to align the rifle on the target. Once the rear bag is moved, a different angle of recoil over the ears is created, preventing the rifle from tracking the same from shot to shot. That's why it's important to have the capability of making minor windage adjustments on the front rest instead of shifting the rear bag.

The Bald Eagle rear bag also features a flat located between its ears, acting like a channel or guidance system for the rifle to ride in and allowing the rifle to move straight back during recoil. Flyers can occur when the rifle stock and the groove in the rear bag are not running parallel with each other. This new rear bag is larger and higher than most standard models. The extra bulk helps stabilize the bag, while the additional height allows the shooter to get down behind the rifle. Remember, "A good group starts with a good rest," and you can write that in stone.

***DON LEWIS is a retired corporate credit manager who currently tests and evaluates firearms and shooting gear. A regular contributor to* SHOOTER'S BIBLE, *Lewis writes gun-related articles for other publications, including Handloader's Digest, and Central Pennsylvania Afield. He has written the gun column for The Pennsylvania Game News for the past 30 years and is now outdoor writer for Leader Times. Lewis also contributed to Varmint Hunter magazine and Pennsylvania Woods & Waters. His most recent book,* The Shooter's Corner, *was published by the Pennsylvania Game Commission.***

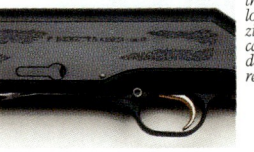

LUGER®

REG. U.S. PAT. OFF.

# STAINLESS STEEL

# AMERICAN EAGLE

**YESTERDAY'S TRADITION - TODAY'S TECHNOLOGY**

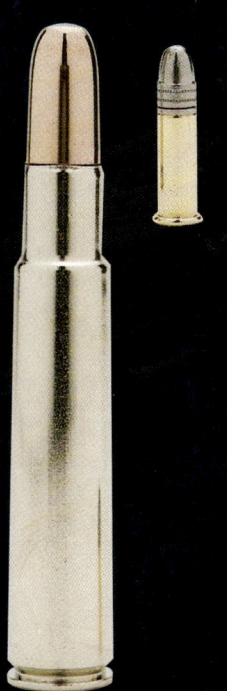

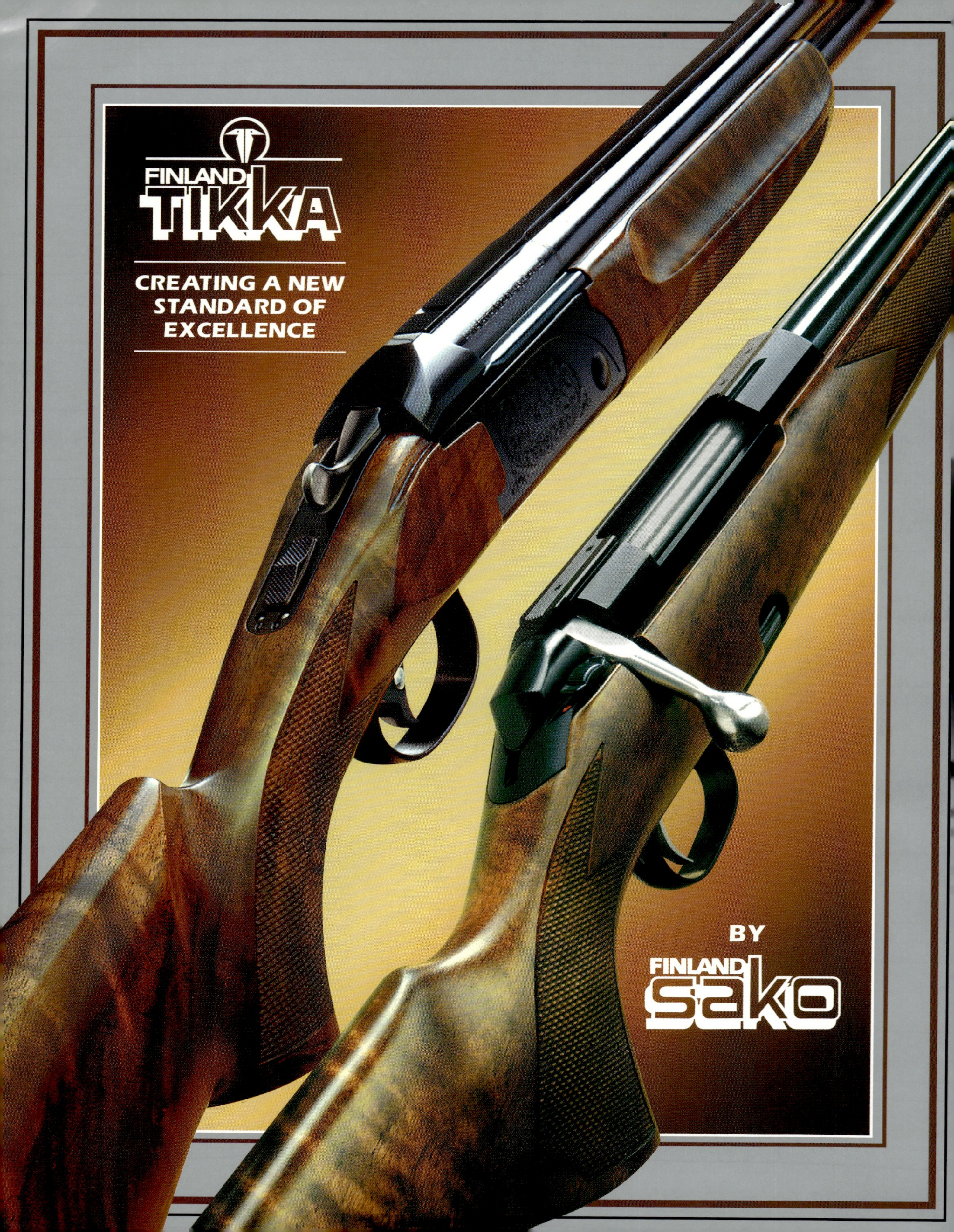
FINLAND TIKKA
CREATING A NEW STANDARD OF EXCELLENCE
BY
FINLAND sako

# ROBERT RUARK: THE "OLD MAN'S BOY"

***by Jim Casada***

"Anybody who reads this book is bound to realize that I had a real fine time as a boy." Thus did Robert Chester Ruark introduce his bestselling book, *The Old Man and the Boy* (1957). The best and brightest of those wonderful boyhood days of his were spent hunting and fishing with the "Old Man" of the book's title, Captain Edward Hall Adkins, who was Ruark's maternal grandfather. Their timeless partnership became one of hands reaching out across a generation, linking the very old and the very young. It became even more special when Ruark subsequently shared his experiences with millions of enthralled readers.

So touching and telling are the stories in *The Old Man and the Boy* and its sequel, *The Old Man's Boy Grows Older* (1961), they constitute a pretty sound case for considering Ruark among America's greatest outdoor writers. Certainly his books should be read and cherished by all those who savor the sights, sounds and smells of the great outdoors. Moreover, Ruark's finest work on Africa, *Horn of the Hunter* (1953), is arguably as good as anything ever written on sport in the "Dark Continent." Many people who are well-versed in this category of sporting literature feel it transcends even Ernest Hemingway's highly acclaimed *Green Hills of Africa.* Add to these works Ruark's posthumously published collection, *Use Enough Gun: On Hunting Big Game* (1966), plus literally hundreds of magazine pieces, there's no question he must rank as one of the giants among America's sporting writers.

Born on December 29, 1915, in Southport, North Carolina, Ruark was the son of a bookkeeper, Robert Chester Ruark Sr., and Charlotte Adkins, a school teacher. Thanks primarily to his reminiscences in the "Old Man and the Boy" stories, along with the obviously autobiographical overtones of his novel, *Poor No More* (1959), we know considerably more about the years of Ruark's adolescence than is normally the case. By his own account, Ruark's boyhood was indeed idyllic. Even when the family moved from rural Southport to the nearby port city of Wilmington, there was ample opportunity to join his grandfather afield. The "Old Man" was in every respect the sort of role model and mentor every sportsman should have. An endearing figure and a veritable storehouse of dry wit, homespun philosophy and practical wisdom, Captain Adkins patiently shared his lifetime of hard-won outdoor knowledge with the "Boy." The Old Man could be vinegary at times, though, as when the young Ruark neglected the basics of gun safety. But at heart he was a good and gentle figure of great humanity. While at first glance he may have

*Robert Ruark made this sketch of his maternal grandfather, Captain Edward Hall Adkins, whom he once described as "the orneriest son of a bitch I've ever known." Ruark spent the brightest days of his boyhood hunting and fishing with the "Old Man."*

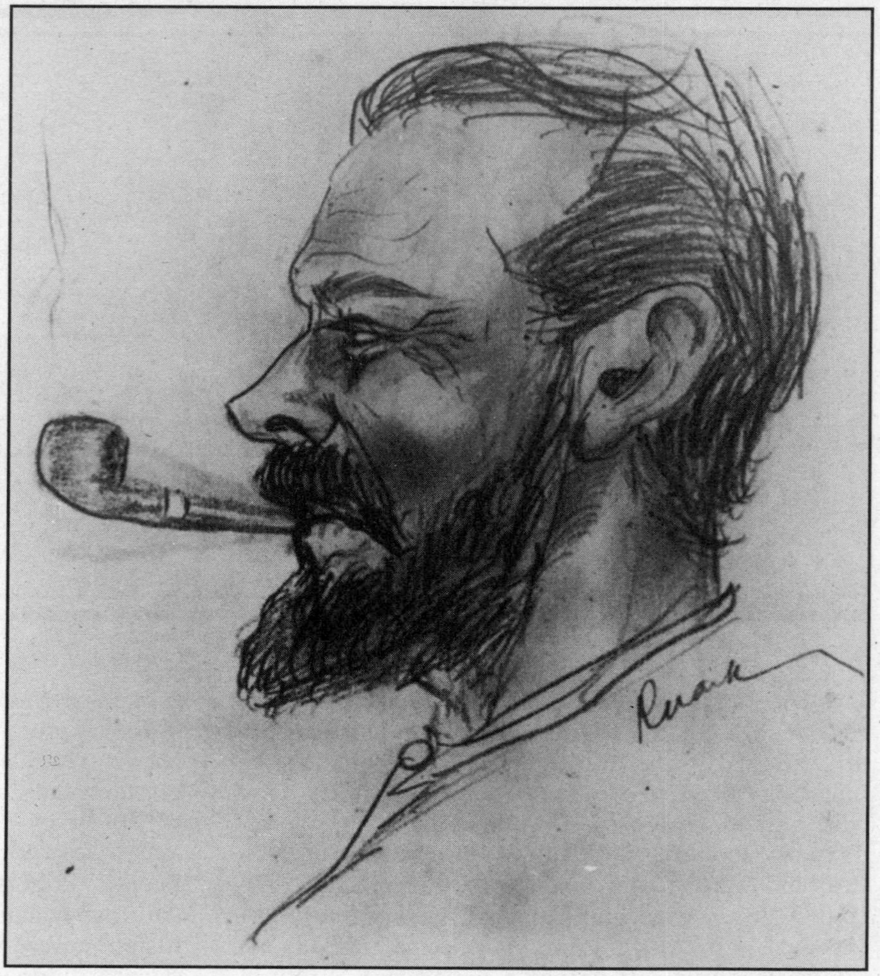


seemed a bit rough around the edges, underneath that salty, scruffy exterior lay a shrewd mind and a carefully nurtured intellect. As Ruark wrote: "He knows pretty well everything."

Drawing on the guile developed in a lifetime of hunting experiences, and putting to good use his abilities as a born teacher, the Old Man imbued Ruark with a genuine love for, and practical knowledge of, the outdoors. Together they hunted, side by side, almost everything that ran, climbed or flew in that coastal section of North Carolina. There were even ventures farther afield to Louisiana's Cajun country and Maryland's Eastern Shore. Mostly they hunted with shotguns, with quail and waterfowl looming large in their avian quests.

Although Ruark already knew a good deal about rifles through his familiarity with a .22, and while he learned early the basics of shotgunning, such as lead and swing on doves, no aspect of the sporting pleasures he enjoyed under the Old Man's tutelage was more rewarding and meaningful than wingshooting. Ruark's comments on bobwhites and bird dogs leave the astute reader little doubt that he knew—and knew well—the delights of upland game hunting. He was taught to deal with quail in a special way, because "Bobwhite is a gentleman, and you have to approach him as gentleman to gentleman." The Old Man considered quail to be almost members of the family, and he expected his student to respect them accordingly:

You treat it [a covey of quail] right, and it stays there with you for all the years you live. It works in and around your garden, and it eats the bugs and it whistles every evening and cheers you up. It keeps your dogs happy, because they've got something to play with, and when you shoot it, you shoot just so many and then you don't shoot it anymore that year, because you got to leave some seed birds to breed a new covey for next year. There ain't nothing as nice as taking the gun down off the hook and going out to look for a covey of quail you got a good chance to find. . . The bobwhite doesn't weigh but about five ounces, but every ounce of him is pure class. He's smart as a whip, and every time you go up against him you're proving something about yourself.

*In 1938, Ruark had become a reporter at the Daily News in Washington, D.C. When World War II hit, he joined the U.S. Navy, continuing to write. Some of his pieces written in the European theater attracted a great deal of attention, enabling him to join the Scripps-Howard Alliance shortly after the war's end.*

*As a member of the Scripps-Howard Alliance, Ruark produced upwards of 4,000 newspaper columns, totaling an estimated 2.8 million words. He once boasted that he could turn out a daily column in 15 minutes or less, and he delighted onlookers by proving it. On one occasion, while on assignment in Rome, he wrote 16 pieces in one sitting.*

The Old Man used "Gentleman Bob" to teach his pupil all sorts of lessons. There was a first-class chewing out when the Boy was caught easing the safety off on his gun before a covey got up. And on another never-to-be-forgotten occasion, the Old Man palmed a couple of shells into the youngster's gun and told him to "fry" fire it. The Old Man was desperately anxious for the youngster to prove himself a true sportsman in every sense, one worthy of matching wits with quail. The first time the Boy got a chance to shoot at a rising bevy of bobwhites, "I walked in past the dog," he wrote years later, "and the birds came up like rockets on the Fourth, and I did what most people do at first. I shot at all of them all at the same time. I fired both barrels and nothing dropped."

Ruark's first experience on cock pheasants was similarly memorable:

*A talented artist in his own right, Ruark works on the illustrations for one of his own books.*

There was an outraged squawk inside the brambles, a rapid beating of wings, and something—it might have been a bird or possibly the Graf Zeppelin—erupted in my general direction. It seemed to be less than a hundred yards long, and I could swear it was not actually breathing fire. Otherwise I never saw such a production in my life. I shot at this thing twice, and it went away with very little damage, although one tail feather got dislodged, very possibly due to the imminence of the molting season.

When it came to the myriad mysteries of bird dogs, the Old Man imparted this sage advice:

There ain't nothing anybody can tell a good dog that the dog don't know better than the man. I reckon it's the dog's business to know his business. . . If a man is really intelligent, there's practically nothing a good dog can't teach him. But a dumb man can't learn anything from a smart dog, while a dumb dog can occasionally learn something from a smart man.

Ruark's grandfather had some well-defined thoughts on what it took to bring out the best in a bird dog. Those who lost their temper with an impetuous and rambunctious hound were well advised to keep one of the Old Man's maxims constantly in mind: "A man who's got to break a dog don't deserve the dog." Anyone who's ever enjoyed the privilege of working afield with the "dog of a lifetime" can readily identify with another of the Old Man's sayings on the subject: "The loss of a dog is felt more keenly because a portion of the human dies with the beast."

Along with this ample exposure to pointers and partridges, there remained plenty of hunting for waterfowl, while doves, deer and turkeys all came in for their share of attention. Yet Ruark, who'd been taught so wisely and well, had his eyes set on sporting horizons well beyond the game immediately at hand. From an early age he had dreamed of an African safari, a desire spurred on by reading classic works on the subject by such legendary figures as Fred Selous and "Karamojo" Bell. He dreamed of gunning sand grouse with gleaming Purdey shotguns and of taking Africa's "Big Five" with English-made double rifles.

### RUARK FACES A HARSHER WORLD

Ruark's years with the Old Man were sadly all too few. Captain Adkins died when the Boy was only 15. As Ruark gratefully acknowledges in two poignant tales that conclude the first volume and open the second of his *Old Man and the Boy* series, his grandfather's death did not come on the opening day of bird season: "All He Left Me Was the World." He knew, possibly as a boy and certainly as a man, that he'd been singularly blessed throughout his childhood.

It suddenly occurred to me that I was educated before I saw a college. I made up my mind right then that someday I would learn to be a writer and write some of the stuff the Old Man had taught me. There was only one thing I had to do first, and that was to get educated and make enough money to buy back the old yellow-painted square house (which had been lost to creditors, thanks to the Old Man's illness and the onset of the Great Depression) with its mockingbird in the magnolia and its pecan trees in the backyard.

Born with a tenacious capacity for hard work, Ruark entered the University of North Carolina before he reached his 16th birthday. Gone were those halcyon days spent with the Old Man and "All the honorary uncles, black and white" who had loomed so large in his early years. A harsher world now faced Ruark, and in time he learned the truth taught by a fellow Tar Heel writer, Thomas Wolfe: "You can't go home again." In a vicarious sense, though, Ruark did go back home repeatedly, sharing with his readers the lore and wisdom the Old Man had given him. In so doing, he helped recapture for all his readers some precious moments from their own childhoods.

At college, according to a fellow student, Ruark was ". . . the most guileless boy I ever knew. He was skinny as a boat pole in those days. The biggest thing about him was his grin." He began writing for various college publications, such as Yackety Yack, Carolina Magazine and the Buccaneer. Later, he managed to scrape together sufficient funds to join Phi Kappa Sigma fraternity. He completed his degree in journalism in 1935, graduating near the top of his class. Then, while still in his teens, he launched his career as a writer, first as a reporter for the Hamlet News-Messenger. Somehow, he found time to court and wed a young interior decorator named Virginia Webb. By then, in the summer of 1938, Ruark had become a reporter at the Daily News in Washington, D.C., working under the guidance of its Managing Editor, Ernie Pyle, who later gained worldwide fame as a reporter during World War II.

In the ensuing years, Ruark's ascendancy in the newspaper world can only be described as meteoric. Some of his pieces written in the European theater during World War II attracted a great deal of attention, enabling him to join the Scripps-Howard Alliance shortly after war's end. There he produced upwards of 4,000 newspaper columns, totaling an estimated 2.8 million words. Ruark once boasted that he could turn out a daily column in 15 minutes or less, and he delighted onlookers by proving it. On one occasion, while on assignment in Rome, he wrote 16 pieces in one sitting. In addition to his prodigious output of newspaper articles, Ruark turned out innumerable magazine articles and 13 books. By the early 1950s, he'd become something of a celebrity. He moved to New York, became a regular at Toot Shor's restaurant, drank free champagne at the Stork Club, lived in an expensive penthouse, and dressed his wife in mink. He knew everybody, from Bernie Baruch to Frank Costello, and yet he grew desperately unhappy. He realized he was writing for dollars, not posterity, and it hurt.

### THE DREAMS COME TRUE

Finally Ruark summoned up enough courage to break away from his newspaper career and pursue instead his boyhood dream of going on African safari. Hemingway had always been his hero; indeed, the two men were so similar in physical appearance that they could easily have passed for brothers. Their lifestyles and writing styles were similar as well. Time magazine even went so far as to suggest unflatteringly that "If

***Ruark rejoices about a successful pheasant hunt with an unidentified partner.***

***As a young hunter, Ruark dreamed of an African safari. When that dream finally came to fruition, he relished in every waking hour. Here is "Bwana Ruark" after a triumphant moment subduing the mighty Cape buffalo.***

Ernest Hemingway had not existed. . . it would be difficult to see how Robert Ruark could ever have been invented."

In any event, there's no denying Hemingway's influence when it came time for Ruark's first African adventure. After hiring the noted white hunter, Harry Selby, he set out to follow the literary and sporting footsteps that had produced such masterpieces as *The Snows of Kilimanjaro* and *The Green Hills of Africa.*

Africa revitalized Ruark in a most remarkable way. For the rest of his life, the title of one of his stories, "I've Got to Go Back," ran through his mind as a constant refrain, luring him back to East Africa again and again. At this point in his writing career, Ruark turned to the genre in which he proved truly masterful—sporting literature—producing what was far and away the best of his early books, *Horn of the Hunter,* in which Ruark lived out his boyhood dream in de-

*Ruark's electrifying experiences in Africa of course led to his recapturing them on paper.* Horn of the Hunter *(1953) is considered his finest work on Africa and as good as anything ever written about it, including Hemingway's books. Here Ruark photographs a giant snake caught while on safari.*

lightful fashion. Indeed, it was a book of such power that it captured the hearts of hunters everywhere. Not surprisingly, first editions of that classic have become prized collector's items fetching premium prices.

While on safari, Ruark's keen journalistic eye observed Africa's seething racial conflicts, which bubbled beneath the surface and eventually resulted in Kenya's bloody Mau Mau rebellion. Drawing heavily on his observations, Ruark wrote a controversial and highly successful novel, *Something of Value* (1955), which later was made into a blockbuster movie that drew heavy criticism for its garishness and gore. One reviewer even suggested "It was a trip through an abattoir. The stench overwhelms the mind. Worse, it remains." Another critic characterized the book as "literally horrible," and there was even talk of banning it in Britain. Ruark frankly acknowledged these allegations in his Foreword: "There is much blood in this book. There is much killing. But the life of Africa was washed early by blood, and its ground was, and still is, fertilized by the blood of its people and its animals." Most readers agreed with John Barkham of The New York Times Book Review, who wrote that it was a "huge and frightening novel" of great power and almost irresistible appeal. The fact that book royalties, movie rights, translations and excerpts made Ruark more than a million dollars tells the real tale of its impact.

During the same period, while *Horn of the Hunter* and another highly successful book, *Something of Value,* were being written, Ruark launched his "Old Man and the Boy" series. For a decade, beginning in 1952, each issue of Field & Stream carried these tales, which helped lead the magazine to unprecedented heights of popularity. He also wrote numerous outdoor pieces for True, Collier's, Playboy, The Saturday Evening Post, and other periodicals. It was the "Old Man" sagas, though, that guaranteed Ruark's place in posterity, and rightly so. The stories were spicy, sprinkled liberally with the Old Man's pithy language and Ruark's own vivid recall of other earthy aphorisms and the salty characters who uttered them. Throughout the series, the Old Man dispensed wit and wisdom mixed with ample doses of practical philosophy on the outdoors and life in general. Ruark once said, "I don't evaluate myself as a heavy thinker," but through the medium of the Old Man he dispensed a wealth of deep thought that went to the heart of what the sporting experience is all about.

### *DEATH OF A MAN AND A LEGEND*

Ruark, the man, unfortunately ignored much of the Old Man's sage advice. On the surface, the late 1950s and early 1960s were good times for Ruark, who was seemingly at the height of his powers as a writer. The collected stories that form the two *Old Man* volumes were published along with two major novels, *Poor No More* (1959) and *Uhuru: A Novel of Africa* (1962). In the midst of these literary triumphs, several developments arose that spelled future disaster for Ruark. One was the death of his idol and good friend, Ernest Hemingway. In his memory, Ruark wrote two ar-

***Ruark is photographed in Spain with his showy Rolls Royce after his blockbuster novels made him rich.***

### *BOOKS BY AND ABOUT RUARK*

Ruark's books are listed below chronologically by year of publication. Those marked with an asterisk (*) deal primarily with sport (*Something of Value,* while not so designated, also falls into this category to some degree, centering as it does in large measure around safari-related matters in East Africa).

*Grenadine Etching: Her Life and Loves* (Doubleday, 1947)
*I Didn't Know It Was Loaded* (Doubleday, 1948)
*One For the Road* (Doubleday, 1949)
*Grenadine's Spawn* (Doubleday, 1952)
**Horn of the Hunter* (Doubleday, 1953)
*Something of Value* (Doubleday, 1955)
**The Old Man and the Boy* (Holt, 1957)
*Poor No More* (Holt, 1959)
**The Old Man's Boy Grows Older* (Holt, 1961)
*Uhuru: A Novel of Africa* (McGraw, 1962)
*The Honey Badger* (McGraw, 1965)
**Use Enough Gun: On Hunting Big Game* (New American Library, 1966)
*Women* (New American Library, 1967)
**Robert Ruark's Africa* edited by Michael McIntosh (Countrysport Press, 1991)

The last three books, which were published posthumously, are collections from Ruark's magazine articles. The deluxe, limited edition (500 copies) of *Robert Ruark's Africa* contains one story that does not appear in the regular edition. To date, only one book has been written about Ruark. Called *Someone of Value,* it was written by Hugh Foster and published in 1992 in a signed, limited edition of 1000 copies. Unfortunately, this biography pays scant attention to Ruark as a sportsman or sporting writer. His personal papers now reside in the Southern Historical Collection at the University of North Carolina at Chapel Hill.

***Ruark as he appeared in the late 1950s. On the surface, the late 1950s and early 1960s were good times for the author, who was seemingly at the height of his powers as a writer. But his soul was troubled and his liver became ravaged by years of overindulgence.***

ticles—both of which unfortunately are largely forgotten—on the death of the man whom he called "the master." Along with the profound impact of Hemingway's suicide, Ruark was further troubled by the breakup of his marriage of two decades. "Ginny," as he referred to his former wife, had always been a stabilizing factor in his life. Once she was gone, Ruark's problems multiplied exponentially.

Tired of New York, which he once described as "a can of worms," he had used his new-found wealth to buy a castle in Spain. More African safaris, a shikar in India, and even a sporting trip to Australia filled his months. Although he had completely abandoned newspaper work, Ruark had continued to write at a frenetic pace. Still, there were ample hints of what was coming to anyone who looked closely. As early as 1957, he revealed in writing that his soul was troubled: "Time just seems to fly away for a boy. That, I s'pose, is why one day you wake up suddenly and you ain't a boy any longer."

Recognition of his own mortality and the disappearance of youth's sweet innocence had hit Ruark hard. He abandoned his long-time association with Field & Stream and his name disappeared from the magazine's masthead in the early 1960s. He'd become a heavy drinker, a problem he had battled throughout most of his adult life, despite his grandfather's earlier warnings on the subject.

Finally, in June of 1965, Ruark was flown from Spain to London and there, on July 1, his liver, ravaged by years of abuse, failed. Still several months short of his 50th birthday, Ruark died. As a friend commented: "Thank God he did not live to be impotent, old and sick like Hemingway." Instead, he had to an appreciable degree achieved his stated goal in life: "I started out to be a man. . . glad, sad, occasionally triumphant." In the sense that he enabled sporting posterity to know and cherish those grand days he experienced with the Old Man, Ruark was unquestionably triumphant. He left every lover of nature, every hunter, a bountiful legacy.

***JIM CASADA is co-editor of Turkey & Turkey Hunting magazine and serves on the staffs of several other publications, including North American Fisherman, Southern Outdoors, and Sporting Classics. He is also the editor of several books, including the long-forgotten writings of Fred Selous (*****see SHOOTER'S BIBLE 1995). *****Casada is the author of* **Modern Fly Fishing** *and currently serves as secretary-treasurer of the Outdoor Writers Association of America and as Chairman of the Board of the Southeastern Outdoor Press Association. Recently he began editing a series of books, called* **The Lost Classics,** *which will reprint the works of great sporting writers never before published in book form. The first volume, from which Casada has drawn this article, features Robert Ruark.***

# THE ARTISTRY OF SHOTSHELL BOXES

**by R. Stephen Irwin, M.D.**

There's no doubt about it: life isn't what it used to be half a century or more ago. Trains ran on time, windshield wipers were operated by hand, and tires were inflated by a hand pump. Ice blocks were carried home on the car bumper and cardboard fans were supplied in the church pews during the summer months. The general store had its cracker and pickle barrels, its pot-bellied stove, and frequently it doubled as the post office. Quinine and castor oil were considered wonder drugs and vaccinations were still suspect. People had stimulating hobbies, like collecting string, tinfoil and cigar bands. Lunch was called dinner and dinner was called supper. And for those who carried a favorite shotgun in the back of their Ford truck, a box of shells cost only a dollar.

In the tiny Indiana farming town where I grew up, I'd stop in at Hanna's Hardware on Saturday mornings before walking out to my hunting area. As often as not, some of the local comedians would be sitting on a bench back by the nail bins. "You'd better take along some 8s, Steve," one of them would comment. "There's likely a covey of quail in the fencerow behind Lester Wharton's place. And don't just be thinkin' rabbits. You can reload after you walk the corn field and get to the gate."

Without waiting for my reply, Wink Hanna, the store owner, would slide a box of Remington Shur Shot #6s and another full of Western Xpert #8s down the counter. The front of the Remington box featured an illustration of a bristling setter at point.

Not long ago, I bought some shells at a local emporium for $14.95 a box. The boxes were plainly marked: "gauge 12-inches 2¾–1¼ oz. steel shot-shot 4." There were no flushing pheasants, no shattering clay targets or ducks with their wings set to grace these drab, contemporary-type shell boxes. Warnings printed on the top flap admonished me to point the muzzle in a safe direction, to check for barrel obstruction, to wear eye and ear protection, to keep out of reach of children and, last, to exercise care when eating game because shot could cause tooth damage.

I'm willing to admit that those modern shells I bought may have represented a far superior product than the ones I purchased in my youth at Hanna's Hardware—but they sure weren't as colorful and attractive. Indeed, those old shotshell boxes rekindle the flavor of those days gone by and some have even become eminently collectible. After all, they've evolved for over a century, with nearly an infinite variety of manufacturers, distributors, gauges and loads in-

volved. It's extremely unlikely that any collector will ever have samples of them all. The game, bird dog and hunting scenes on the boxes have actually become miniature art forms capable of exhibiting considerable artistic appeal.

### *IN THE BEGINNING . . .*

The history of shell boxes is as fascinating as it is elusive. Advertisements in early sporting magazines are a good source of information, and a study of these ads reveals a number of brands for which no boxes are known to exist. For the avid collector, this represents a rare challenge.

When the breechloading shotgun was first introduced in the 1860s, there was no factory loaded ammunition—only empty cases—first brass and then paper. Loading tools were quite primitive and early breechloading shooters were further discouraged by the fact that considerable variation in casings existed among the manufacturers. Some were known as a "loose fit," while others were so large for the gauge that it was often difficult to chamber them.

Although metal casings might endure many firings before they split, ruptured or became overused, they still required new primers after each firing, and these always seemed to be in short supply. Some models had a screw-off (removable) head for primer replacement, the threads of which soon became so corroded the case was worthless. Hence, reloading cases for the new-fangled breechloader was infinitely more complicated than, and entirely different from, pouring powder and shot down a muzzleloader.

REMINGTON
HEAVY
DUCK LOAD
REMINGTON
Remington
NITRO CLUB
GAME LOADS
REMINGTON UMC
12 GA.
Remington
8 CH.
QUAIL LOAD
Also for DOVES and WOODCOCK
NITRO CLUB Wetproof

25
WINCHESTER
NUBLACK
LOADED BLACK POWDER SHELLS

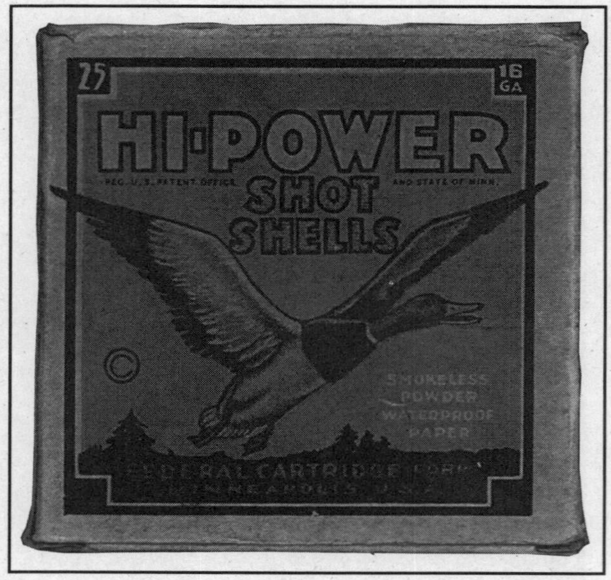
25
16 GA
HI-POWER
REG. U.S. PATENT OFFICE
AND STATE OF MINN.
SHOT SHELLS
SMOKELESS POWDER WATERPROOF PAPER

WINCHESTER
TRADE MARK
RANGER
LOADED SHOT SHELLS
SMOKELESS
STAYNLESS

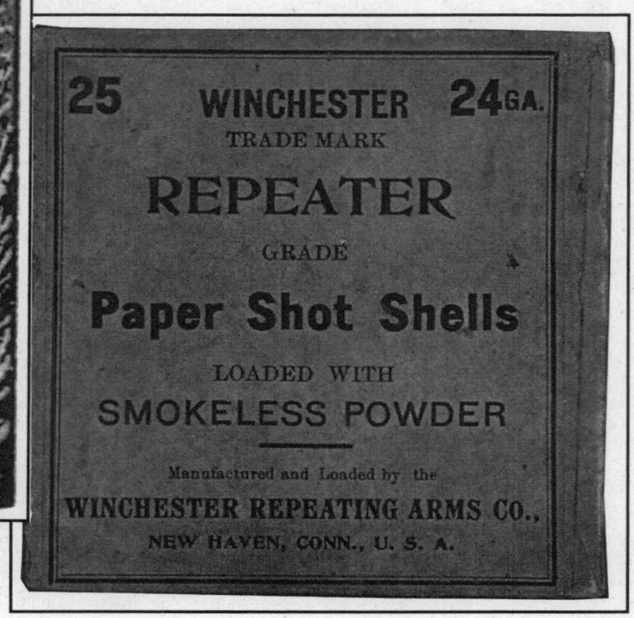
25
WINCHESTER
24GA.
TRADE MARK
REPEATER
GRADE
Paper Shot Shells
LOADED WITH
SMOKELESS POWDER
Manufactured and Loaded by the
WINCHESTER REPEATING ARMS CO.,
NEW HAVEN, CONN., U. S. A.

12 CLIMAX GA.
US
AMMUNITION
UNITED STATES CARTRIDGE CO.
SHOT SHELLS
LOWELL, MASS.
U.S.A.

WINCHESTER-Western
DUCK & PHEASANT LOAD

FEDERAL
25 TRADE MARK 12 GA
Monark
REG. U. S. PAT. OFF.
F.C.C.
FEDERAL CARTRIDGE CORPORATION

Western
Shotgun Shells
SMOKELESS POWDER — NON-CORROSIVE PRIMERS
MADE IN U. S. A.

The first paper shell cases were imported from England by Lancaster and Needham. But C.D. Leet of Springfield, Massachusetts, was the first to make the paper shell in America, followed closely by the Delaware Cartridge Co. and U.M.C. (Union Metallic Cartridge Co.). Those first paper shells were flimsy affairs that were easily ruined by wetness and lacked the hard-hitting qualities of brass-cased loads. In the long run, brass cases proved less expensive than paper simply because they lasted longer. Then in 1884, Winchester began selling 12-gauge paper shells for $11 per thousand, whereas the same gauge brass shell cost $10 per hundred. During the 1880s, the popularity of brass versus paper casings was about equal, and both were rapidly being improved. Paper casings started getting the edge after a waterproof case was developed simply by shellacking it. Both the paper and brass casings were supplied to retailers in square boxes with ten rows of ten shells, making a total of 100 cases. Often these boxes indicated a price-per-shell, suggesting this was the way most hunters purchased their shell cases.

A demand for pre-loaded shells soon spawned two industries: the case maker and the shotshell loader. The latter was usually a gunsmith or the owner of a sporting goods store. Whether large or small, these firms each developed their own label and distinctive box for packaging their products. Then, in 1883, Frank Chamberlin, founder of the Chamberlin Cartridge and Target Co. (Cleveland, Ohio), invented the first truly automatic loading machine, which turned out to be the genesis of the factory loaded shotshell.

### *THE 25-SHELL BOX ARRIVES*

The 100-shell box reigned supreme for many years, even seeing limited use as late as the 1950s. Eventually, the popularity of factory-loaded shotshells sounded the death knell for the 100-shell box. That many loaded shotshells were simply too heavy for the original lightweight cardboard boxes. Thus did the familiar 25-shell capacity box become the industry standard.

Most of the early shotshell companies that used the 100-shell boxes never entered the loaded shotshell market. However, the large ammunition companies used the 100-capacity boxes for empty cases and, temporarily, for loaded shells as well. Multicolor printing was not readily available during the era of 100-shell boxes, so they are usually not very colorful. Still, they are appealing because of their graceful script and choice of wording.

In the late 1880s, Union Metallic Cartridge Company, United States Cartridge Co. and Winchester Repeating Arms Company all produced extra-fancy and remarkably colorful 100-shell boxes, known as "Christmas boxes." Presumably designed for the Christmas trade, these boxes remain the most outstanding examples of shotshell packaging in existence, commanding in turn a hefty price among collectors.

The original 25-shell box consisted of two pieces—a lid and a bottom. The box was sealed by a wraparound paper containing the graphics and printing. In the 1930s, a transition occurred when a one-piece, folded-style box bearing the printed design and label took over. Although the occasional one-piece box continues to show artistic merit, it is the earlier two-piece boxes that

mark the real heyday of pleasing designs on shotshell boxes, the kind that cause serious collectors to dig deep into their wallets to buy them.

With their delightful sporting scenes, the shotshell boxes, as represented on these pages, provide nostalgic reminders of a time when game was more plentiful, bag limits were more generous, hunting was a bigger part of our lives, and there was still a fencerow behind Lester Wharton's place.

***DR. STEPHEN IRWIN** combines his love of big-game hunting and sport fishing with his artistic eye and talent for writing. From his home in Montana, he writes on the history of hunting and fishing as well as such specialized topics as antique fishing lures, duck decoys, Kentucky flintlocks and sporting art. His articles have appeared in most of the major outdoor publications. He has also authored the book,* **The Providers: Hunting and Fishing Methods of the Indians and Eskimos.** *This is Dr. Irwin's seventh in a series of articles for* **SHOOTER'S BIBLE.**

# MANUFACTURERS' SHOWCASE

## GATLING GUN BUILDER'S PACKAGE

Complete plans for the 22-caliber Long Rifle Gatling are now available thru RG-G, Inc. Fully dimensioned and toleranced to-scale blueprints are included with a 40-page instruction booklet that lists materials and explains each part and how it is made. Includes drawings and instructions for making rifled barrels, wooden spoked wheels, and all internal parts. No castings are required. The finished piece has 10 rifled barrels and is 3′ (long) x 2′ (tall). Plans for the gun and carriage are **$58.48** (priority postage within the U.S. included; overseas air add $14.00). Materials kits are also available. Send checks or money orders only. Include a self-addressed card and mail to:

**RG-G, Inc.**
P.O. Box 1261, Conifer, CO 80433-1261
Tel. or Fax: 303-697-4154

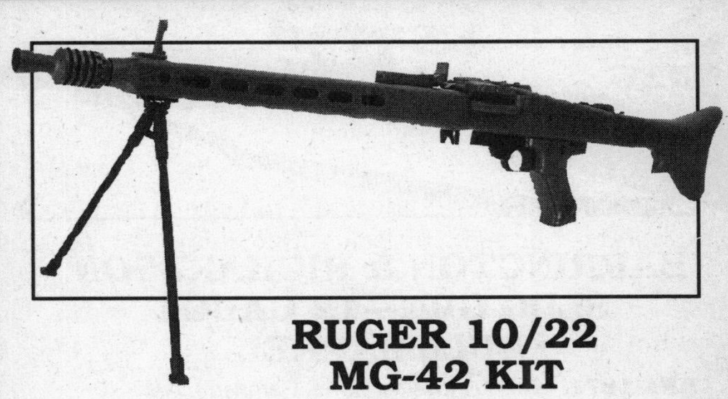

## RUGER 10/22 MG-42 KIT

Transform your Ruger 10/22 into a 2/3 replica WWII MG-42 with Glaser's new stock kit. Requires only simple tools, 15 minutes and no permanent alterations to your rifle. The assembled MG-42 has adjustable sights and weighs no more than the stock rifle. Glaser's Featherweight Bipod adds the final authentic touch to your new MG-42. This bipod is the strongest, lightest one made and comes with a LIFETIME warranty, plus all the hardware needed to mount it on Colt AR series rifles or any sporter rifle with a sling swivel mount. Hidden and quick detachable mounting accessories are also available. For brochure, contact:

**Glaser Safety Slug, Inc.**
P.O. Box 8223, Foster City, CA 94404
Tel: 1-800-221-3489

## GLASER SAFETY SLUG AMMO

GLASER SAFETY SLUG's state-of-the-art, professional-grade personal defense ammunition is now offered in two bullet styles: BLUE uses a #12 compressed shot core for maximum ricochet protection, and SILVER uses a #6 compressed shot core for maximum penetration. The manufacturing process results in outstanding accuracy, with documented groups of less than an inch at 100 yards! That's why GLASER has been the top choice of professional and private law enforcement agencies worldwide for over 15 years. Currently available in every caliber from 25 ACP through 30-06, including 40 S&W, 10mm, 223 and 7.62 × 39. For a free brochure contact:

**GLASER SAFETY SLUG, INC.,**
P.O. Box 8223, Foster City, CA 94404

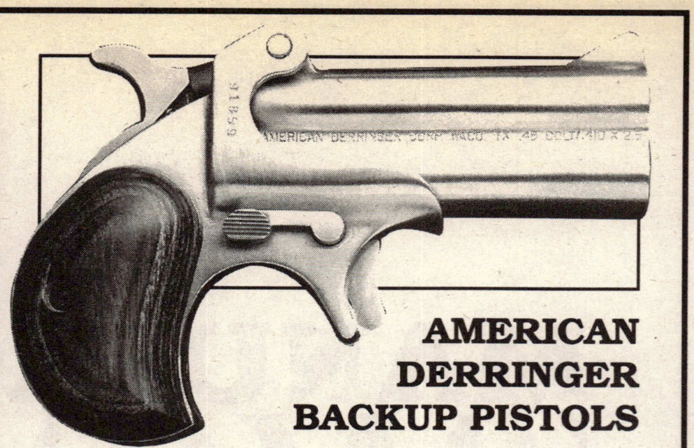

## AMERICAN DERRINGER BACKUP PISTOLS

Designed to be the ultimate in short-range backup pistols, this gun has no equal. Over 10 years were spent in developing and refining this pistol to make it the finest derringer ever manufactured. The smallest and most powerful pocket pistol ever made, it is built from the finest high-tensile strength stainless steel—strong enough to handle the 44-Magnum cartridge if you are man enough to shoot it! Over 60 different rifle and pistol calibers are available. Classic styling and smooth lines give these derringers a classic look.

**AMERICAN DERRINGER CORPORATION**
127 N. Lacy Drive, Waco, Texas 76705
Tel: 817-799-9111 Fax: 817-799-7935

# MANUFACTURERS' SHOWCASE

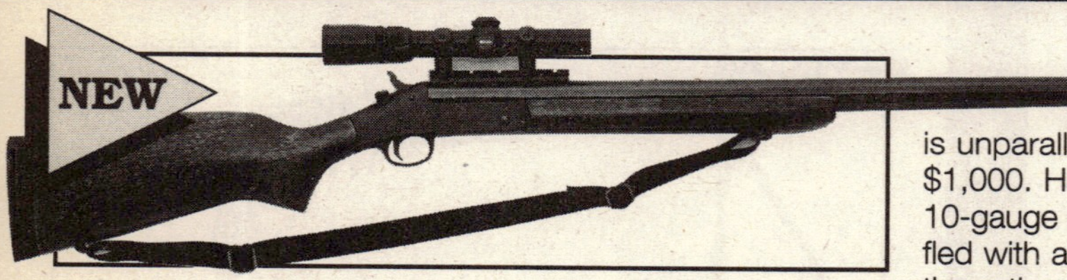


## HARRINGTON & RICHARDSON SLUG GUN—12 GAUGE BULL BARREL

**H&R 1871, INC.** 60 Industrial Rowe, Gardner, MA 01440
Tel: 508-632-9393

H&R's new Model SB2-980 ULTRA Slug Hunter is the first rifled slug gun to use a heavy target-style barrel. The result is unparalleled accuracy found only in custom slug guns costing over $1,000. H&R's ULTRA slug gun is built on a 10-gauge action, using a 10-gauge barrel blank that is under-bored to 12 gauge and then fully rifled with a 1:35″ twist. This allows for an extra-heavy barrel profile, with the action providing the extra weight and strength to moderate recoil.

The 980 ULTRA also features: factory-mounted Weaver-style scope base, Monte Carlo stock of dark walnut-stained American hardwood, vent recoil pad, sling swivels and a black nylon sling. Receiver is matte-black finished; barrel is low-luster blued. Suggested retail price: **$224.95**

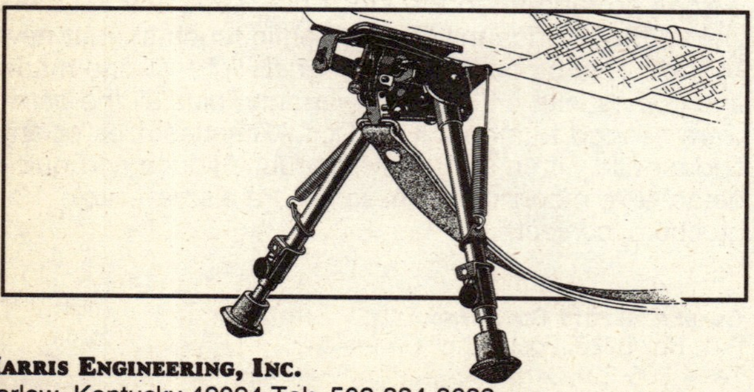

**HARRIS ENGINEERING, INC.**
Barlow, Kentucky 42024 Tel: 502-334-3633

## HARRIS ENGINEERING INC. BIPODS

HARRIS bipods clamp securely to most stud-equipped bolt-action rifles and are quick-detachable. With adapters, they can fit other guns as well. HARRIS bipods are the result of time-proven design and quality, and are made with heat-treated steel and hard alloys. Folding legs on the bipods have completely adjustable spring-return extensions (except Model LM). The sling swivel attaches to the clamp. Series S Bipods rotate 45 degrees for instant leveling on uneven ground. The hinged base has tension adjustment and buffer springs to eliminate tremor or looseness in the crotch area of the bipod. Otherwise, all Series S models are similar to the non-rotating Series 1A2.

# MANUFACTURERS' SHOWCASE

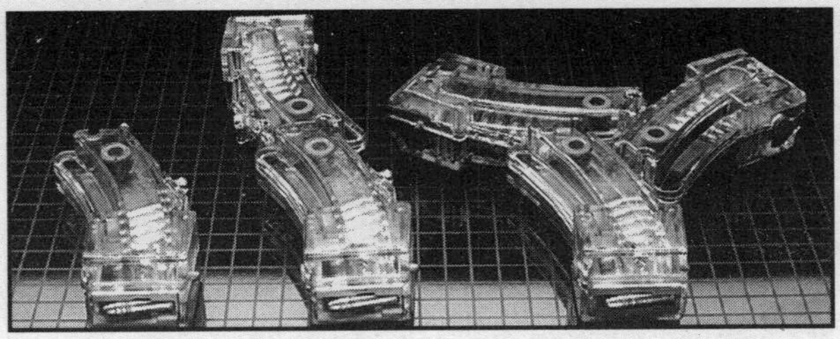

## BUTLER CREEK'S HOT LIPS HIGH-CAPACITY BANANA MAGAZINE

BUTLER CREEK now offers its Hot Lips magazine in a new 10-round capacity. Hot Lips provides 10-shot capacity for Ruger 10/22, 77/22 and AMT rifles. Jungle clip available for 20 rounds or Star Clip for 30 rounds. The separately molded feed-lip design ensures superior dependability and a longer life, while the constant force spring design has never made loading your ammunition easier! This magazine is also available with our precision-designed stainless steel feed lips (Steel Lips). Lifetime Warranty! FREE CATALOG . . . just for mentioning you saw our ad in SHOOTER'S BIBLE.

**BUTLER CREEK CORPORATION**
290 Arden Drive, Belgrade, MT 59714
Tel: 406-388-1356 Fax: 406-388-7204

## BUTLER CREEK'S NEW "SPORTER" FULL-LENGTH SEMIAUTO STOCKS

NEW for 1995 is the Marlin Sporter Stock for Marlin Models 60 and 70 .22 rimfires. These new featherweight stocks feature a Monte Carlo-style comb, schnabel forearm, double palm swells, raised diamond checkering and are suited for both right- and left-handed shooters. Available in both standard or deluxe texturized finishes with our crescent-shaped rifle recoil pad and swivel studs. Lifetime Warranty! FREE CATALOG. . . just for mentioning you saw our ad in SHOOTER'S BIBLE.

**BUTLER CREEK CORPORATION**
290 Arden Drive , Belgrade, MT 59714
Tel: 406-388-1356 Fax: 406-388-7204

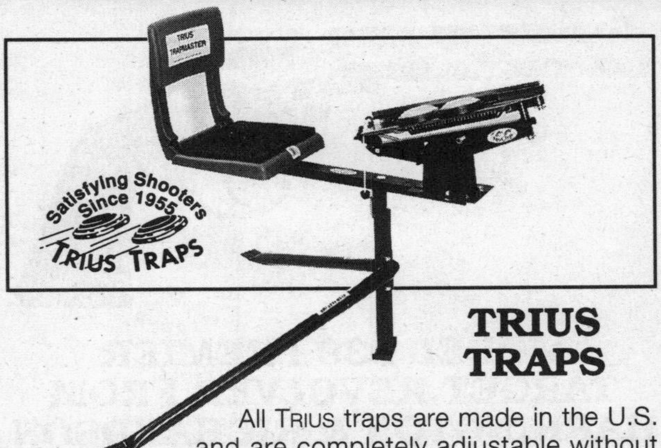


## TRIUS TRAPS

All TRIUS traps are made in the U.S. and are completely adjustable without tools. TRIUS has set the standard for the industry for 40 years. From "behind-the-barn" shooters to upstart Sporting/Hunters' clay ranges, our easy cocking, lay-on loading makes TRIUS traps simple to operate. Singles, doubles plus piggy-back doubles offer unparalleled variety. **Birdshooter**: quality at a budget price—now with high angles retainer. **Model 92**: a bestseller with high-angle clip and can thrower. **TrapMaster** (shown): sit-down comfort plus pivoting action. TRIUS also offers five Sporting/Hunters' clay models made to throw all targets, including "rabbits."

**TRIUS PRODUCTS, INC.**
P.O. Box 25, Cleves, Ohio 45002
Tel: 513-941-5682 Fax: 513-941-7970

## DON'T RELOAD WITHOUT IT

The most important piece of reloading equipment you'll ever buy isn't a press or a chronograph. It's a book: the *Accurate Smokeless Powder Loading Guide, Number One.* Features 345 pages of pressure-tested reloading data, articles and technical information to help you get the most out of your favorite gun.

Order your copy today by sending a check or money order for **$18.95** (plus $2 for shipping and handling) to:

**ACCURATE ARMS RELOADING MANUAL**
Box 167, Dept. SB, McEwen, TN 37101
Tel: 1-800-416-3006 (toll-free customer service line)

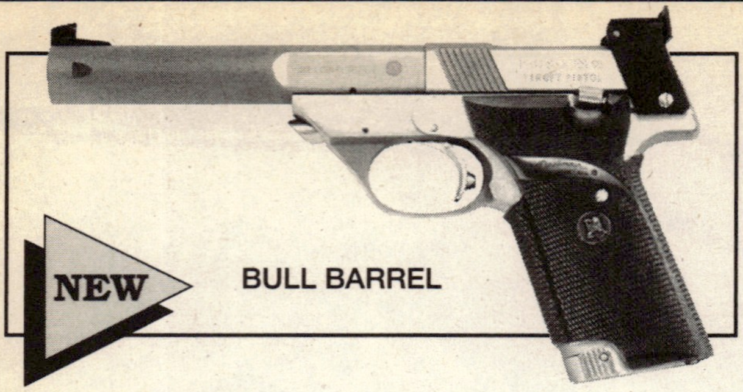


## PRO SERIES 95

Precision target pistols designed for the knowledgeable, advanced target shooter. Destined to be among the world's most popular competitive pistols, the PRO SERIES 95 features: military grip • interchangeable barrels • fully adjustable target sights • trigger pull adjustment • trigger travel adjustment • automatic slide lock and Pachmayr rubber grips. The bull barrel model sports the military bracket rear sight . . . acclaimed by many competitive shooters as the most reliable sighting system developed. Contact:

**Stoeger Industries**
5 Mansard Court, Wayne, NJ 07470
Tel: 201-872-9500 Fax: 201-872-2230

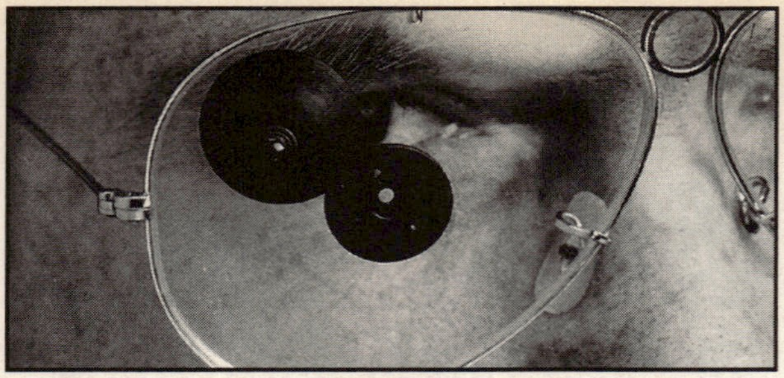

## CLEAR SIGHTS FOR PISTOL SHOOTERS

If you can read the Shooter's Bible, watch television or drive a car, you can focus on your target and pistol sights simultaneously — even if you wear bifocals or trifocals — by using the Merit Optical Attachment.

The Optical Attachment has a variable diameter aperture that will increase your eyes' depth of field and provide a clear sight picture. It mounts on your eyeglasses with a suction cup, so it requires no gunsmithing and adds no weight to your pistol. When not in use, it pivots out of your line of vision. Call or write for a free brochure of all Merit sighting aids.

**Merit Corporation**
P.O. Box 9044, Schenectady, NY 12309
Tel: 518-346-1420

# MANUFACTURERS' SHOWCASE

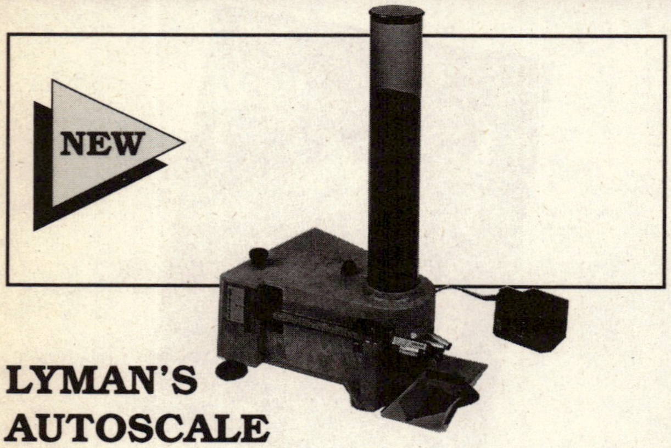


## LYMAN'S AUTOSCALE

Lyman's new Autoscale is a reloader's dream come true. This remarkable product represents a major breakthrough in handloading technique. Simply set the Autoscale to the desired grain weight, push the start button and it dispenses the exact powder charge into the powder pan . . . over and over again. It is faster and more accurate than any "benchrest" micrometer-type powder measure. The heart of the Autoscale is a solid-state electronic light-emitting diode and sensor, which controls the powder feeding tubes. This patented system assures fast, accurate loads for years. For more information, please contact:

**Ed Schmitt, Lyman Products Corp.**
Route 147, Middlefield, CT 06455
Tel: 1-800-22-LYMAN (toll free)

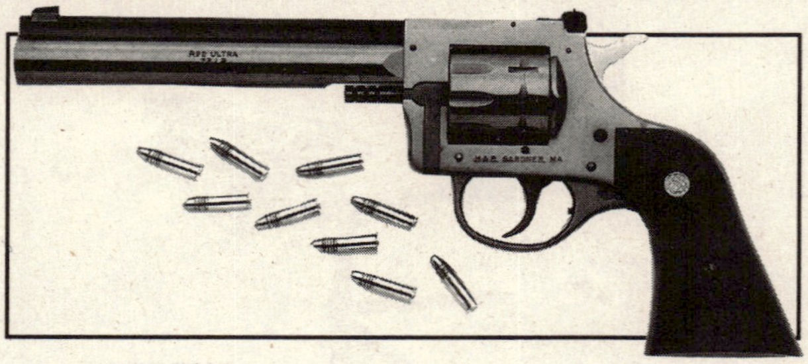

## MODEL 939 PREMIER TARGET REVOLVER FROM HARRINGTON & RICHARDSON

Harrington & Richardson's double-action 939 Premier Target revolver features a 9-shot, swing-out cylinder, 6″ heavy target-grade barrel with barrel rib and fully adjustable sights. Chambered for 22 Short, Long and Long Rifle cartridges, the 939 has a deeply recessed barrel crown that protects the critical rifling at the point where it is most vulnerable to damage. The two-piece walnut-stained hardwood grips are western-styled and accent the high-polish, traditional deep blue metal. The transfer bar safety system virtually eliminates unplanned discharges. Contact:

**H&R 1871, Inc.**
60 Industrial Rowe, Gardner, MA 01440
Tel: 508-632-9393

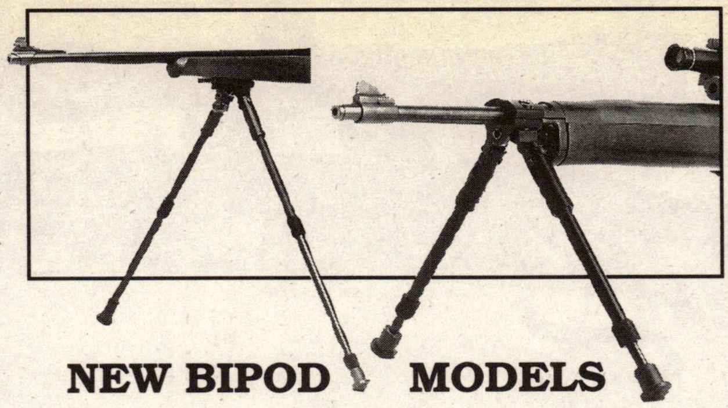

## NEW BIPOD MODELS

B-SQUARE bipods are now available in several models. The Rigid Bipod is available with Swivel Stud "Sporter" or Barrel Clamp "Service" attachment. The "Tilt" Bipod provides the same rigid support "canting" from side to side for fine-tuning your aim. "Tilt" bipods are also available with both swivel stud and barrel clamp attachment. The "Roto-Tilt" Bipod offers everything you could want in a bipod: rigid support, side-to-side "canting," swivels in a 30-degree angle, enabling the shooter to follow perfectly aimed shots. Available with swivel stud attachment only. All bipods available in blue or stainless and feature an Unlimited Leg Extension System with 7-inch leg extenders (sold separately). For more info, call or write:

**B-SQUARE CO.**
P.O. Box 11281, Fort Worth, TX 76110
Tel: 1-800-433-2909 (toll-free) or 817-923-0964

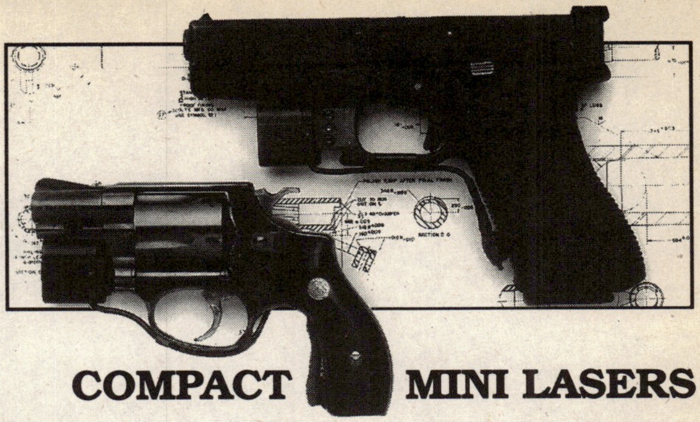

## COMPACT MINI LASERS

B-SQUARE introduces the little laser that is big on performance. At only 1.1″ x 1.1″ x .6″, the Compact Mini Laser delivers 5mW of power (Class IIIa), while operating on common A76 size batteries (lithium or alkaline). Visibility is 1.0″ at 25 yards. Features an omnidirectional screw-type aiming method with windage and elevation adjustments and is the only laser with an "Air-Lock" feature. Moisture-proof and shock-resistant, the B-SQUARE Compact Mini Laser carries a lifetime warranty. Service is available simply by calling B-SQUARE. Mounting systems are available for trigger guard, under barrel, and long guns. The vertical T-Slot design makes them quick-detachable and ensures no change in zero. Contact:

**B-SQUARE CO.**
P.O. Box 11281, Fort Worth, TX 76110
Tel: 1-800-433-2909 (toll-free) or 817-923-0964

# MANUFACTURERS' SHOWCASE

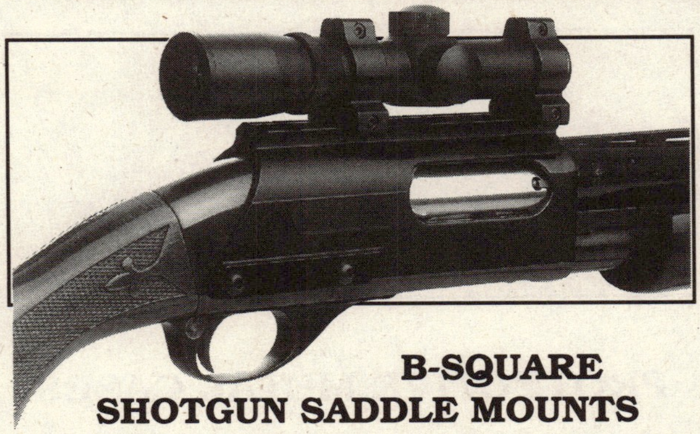

## B-SQUARE SHOTGUN SADDLE MOUNTS

B-SQUARE Shotgun Saddle Mounts are now available for most popular 12-gauge guns. These newly designed mounts straddle the receiver and fit the top of the gun tightly. All mounts have a standard dovetail base and "see-thru" design allowing continued use of the gun's sight. Standard dovetail rings can be used. B-SQUARE shotgun mounts do not require gunsmithing, have a blued finish, and attach to the gun's side with included hardware. Mounts available for: Remington 870/1100; Mossberg 500, 5500 and 835; Winchester 1400/1300/1200; Ithaca 37/87; and Browning A-5 shotguns. The mounts retail for **$49.95** at your local dealer, or call B-SQUARE toll-free for a FREE catalog.

**B-SQUARE CO.**
P.O. Box 11281, Fort Worth, TX 76110
Tel: 1-800-433-2909 (toll-free) or 817-923-0964

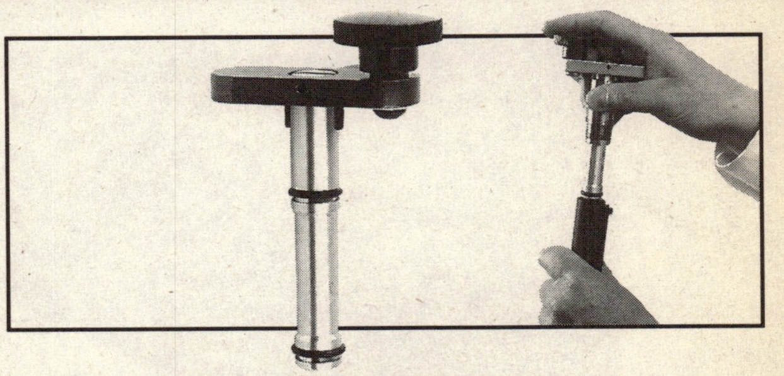

## CHOKE TUBE SPEED WRENCH

The Texas Twister© Choke Tube Speed Wrench from B-SQUARE is currently available for most 12-gauge shotguns. The wrench inserts into the choke tube so it can be cranked out of the bore. A bore guide prevents crooked starts and damaged threads. The T-handle is designed to break stubborn tubes loose so they can be cranked out quickly and easily. Texas Twister© wrenches are available for Briley, Beretta, Browning, Mossberg, Weatherby, Remington, Ruger, SKB and Winchester 12-gauge shotguns. Retail price is **$29.95** at your local dealer, or call B-SQUARE toll-free. A catalog featuring the complete line of B-SQUARE products is available on request.

**B-SQUARE CO.**
P.O. Box 11281, Fort Worth, TX 76110
Tel: 1-800-433-2909 (toll-free) or 817-923-0964

**WIDEVIEW**

## NEW BLACKPOWDER MOUNT

The new WIDEVIEW Black Powder Mount pictured above fits the Thompson/Center Renegade and Hawken rifles with no drilling or tapping. The barrel still comes off for easy cleaning, and the original iron sight is used. With WIDEVIEW's Ultra Precision See-Thru mounts included, you may use a scope or iron sights. No hammer modification is needed.

**WIDEVIEW SCOPE MOUNT CORP.**
13535 South Highway 16, Rapid City, SD 57701
Tel: 605-341-3220 Fax: 605-341-9142

# MANUFACTURERS' SHOWCASE

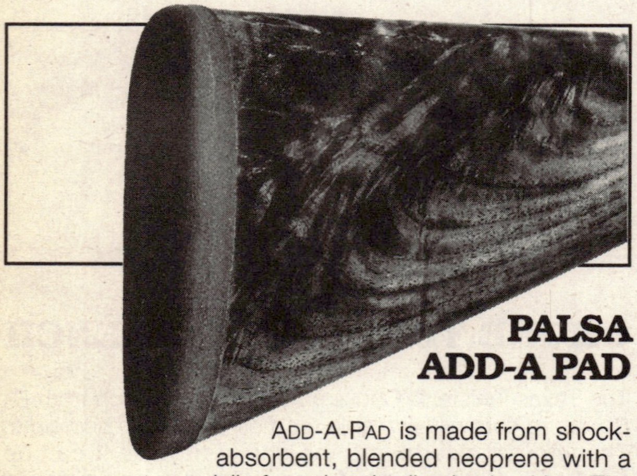

## PALSA ADD-A PAD

ADD-A-PAD is made from shock-absorbent, blended neoprene with a specially formulated adhesive backing. The ADD-A-PAD can be quickly installed simply by pressing a pad on the end of the butt, trimming it with a knife, then sanding it to the exact shape of the stock. The package includes two 1/4-inch and one 1/2-inch pads, thus allowing the use of any pad or combination of pads. The result is an economical "do-it-yourself" pad that looks professionally installed. ADD-A-PAD costs **$10.95** with complete instructions. Call or write for more information.

**PALSA OUTDOOR PRODUCTS**
P.O. Box 81336, Lincoln, Nebraska 68501-1336
Tel: 402-488-5288 Fax: 402-488-2321

## PROTECTIVE METAL CASES

A complete line of Protective Metal Transport/Shipping Cases are available through ICC (IMPACT CASE COMPANY) and KK AIR INTERNATIONAL. Both lines are products of KNOUFF & KNOUFF, INC. In addition to the "flat case" design, three-piece and "Trunk"-style cases are part of the standard lines. KK AIR also manufactures customized cases to each owner's sizing and specifications. These case products are designed for STRENGTH, with third-party handling in mind, and are "proven." For detailed specification sheets, contact:

**KNOUFF & KNOUFF, INC.**
P.O. Box 9912, Spokane, WA 99209
Tel: 1-800-262-3322 (toll-free)

## ADJUSTABLE HUNTING APERTURE

No need for a ghost ring or a pocketful of apertures. The MERIT Hunting Disc opening varies from .022 to .155 diameter with a turn of the knurled face, providing a clear front sight and target under the changing light conditions of hunting. The aperture, similar to the iris shutter of a camera, is designed specifically to withstand the recoil of heavy caliber rifles.

Complete satisfaction is guaranteed. Write or call for a FREE brochure describing all MERIT sighting aids.

**MERIT CORPORATION**
P.O. Box 9044, Schenectady, NY 12309
Tel: 518-346-1420

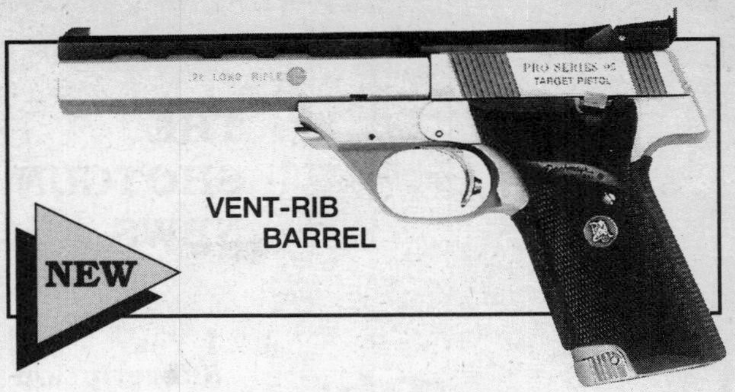


## PRO SERIES 95

Destined to be among the world's most popular competitive pistols, the PRO SERIES 95 are precision target pistols designed for the knowledgeable, advanced target shooter. Features include: military grip • interchangeable barrels • fully adjustable target sights • trigger pull adjustment • trigger travel adjustment • automatic slide lock and Pachmayr rubber grips. The vent-rib model features a full-length vent rib, which produces the most positive sighting plane for the advanced competitor. Contact:

**STOEGER INDUSTRIES**
5 Mansard Court, Wayne, NJ 07470
Tel: 201-872-9500 Fax: 201-872-2230

# MANUFACTURERS' SHOWCASE

## NEW CALIBERS FOR AMT'S COMPACT DAO PISTOL

AMT's acclaimed compact .45 ACP Double Action Only auto pistol is now offered in three new popular calibers. While the original Backup remains the smallest semiautomatic ever produced in .45 ACP caliber, the additional caliber options now include 9mm, .38 Super and .40 S&W. The 9mm and .38 Super models both weigh 25 ounces, each with a magazine capacity of six. The .40 S&W model weighs in at 24 ounces, with a magazine capacity of five. This latest pistol features AMT's smooth Double Action Only engineering of the compact .380 Backup and comes in stainless steel with checkered black fiberglass grips.

**AMT (ARCADIA MACHINE & TOOL, INC.)**
6226 Santos Diaz St., Irwindale, CA 91702
Tel: 818-334-6629

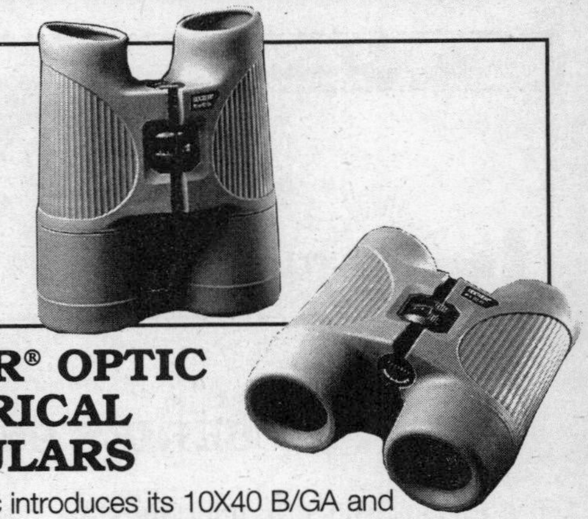

## DOCTER® OPTIC ASPHERICAL BINOCULARS

DOCTER® OPTIC introduces its 10X40 B/GA and 8X32 B/GA Aspherical, the first generation of binoculars to offer sharper, more brilliant and true-to-life imaging because of the lenses' aspherical form, which provides six-image correction parameters. A multi-level, phase-correction coating of all glass-to-air surfaces optimizes color fidelity and light transmission. The roof-prism construction allows for a compact, ergonomic design that fits the hand comfortably. Its resilient rubber armoring makes it shock-absorbent and slip-proof. The rugged diecast aluminum body is completely sealed, making it impervious to dust and all climatic conditions. 30-YEAR warranty!

**DOCTER® OPTIC TECHNOLOGIES, INC.**
4685 Boulder Highway, Suite A, Las Vegas, NV 89121
Tel: 1-800-290-3634 Fax: 702-898-3737

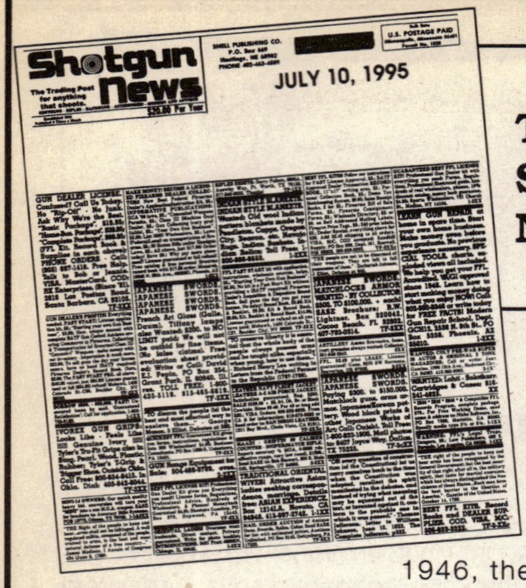


## THE SHOTGUN NEWS

**1-Year Subscription (36 issues) FOR ONLY $22.00**

Established in 1946, the Shotgun News offers some of the finest gun buys in the United States. Published three times each month, with over 150,000 readers, this national publication has helped thousands of gun enthusiasts locate, buy, trade and sell antique, modern, military and sporting firearms and accessories. As the cover says, Shotgun News is "The Trading Post for Anything That Shoots." Call TOLL FREE and receive your one-year subscription (use your Master or Visa card).

**The Shotgun News**
P.O Box 669, Hastings, NE 68902
Tel: 1-800-345-6923 (toll free) or 402-463-4589

## DOUG TURNBULL GUN RESTORATION

Doug Turnbull Restoration continues to offer bone charcoal colorcase work plus nitre bluing. Turnbull will match the original case colors produced by Winchester, Colt, Marlin, Parker, LC Smith, Ansley Fox and other noted manufacturers, without reassembly problems. Also available is charcoal blue, known as Carbona or machine blue, a pre-war finish used by most makers.

Turnbull also now offers new Winchester 94, 94-22, Ruger SA, Browning Citori and others, all casecolored with their own traditional process. Production work with single run control. Partial or complete restoration. Prepolished parts also finished. Contact:

**Doug Turnbull Restoration**
6426 Co. Rd. 30, P.O. Box 471, Bloomfield, NY 14469
Tel: 717-657-6338

# MANUFACTURERS' SHOWCASE

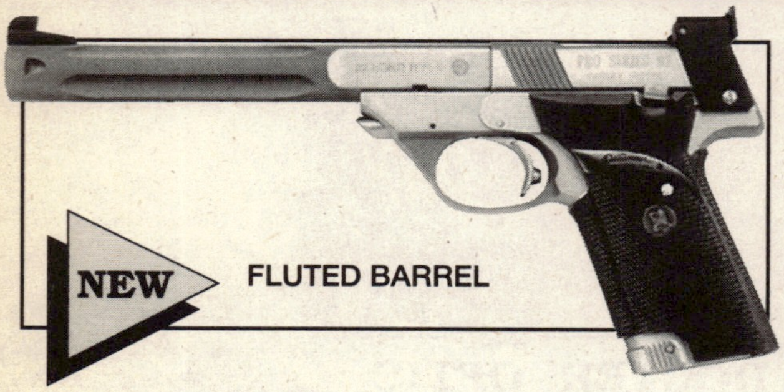


## PRO SERIES 95

The PRO SERIES 95 handguns are precision target pistols designed for the knowledgeable, advanced target shooter. Destined to be among the world's most popular competitive pistols, this new series features: military grip • interchangeable barrels • fully adjustable target sights • trigger pull adjustment • trigger travel adjustment • automatic slide lock and Pachmayr rubber grips. The fluted barrel model features the military bracket rear sight . . . acclaimed by many competitive shooters as the most reliable sighting system developed. Contact:

**Stoeger Industries**
5 Mansard Court, Wayne, NJ 07470
Tel: 201-872-9500 Fax: 201-872-2230

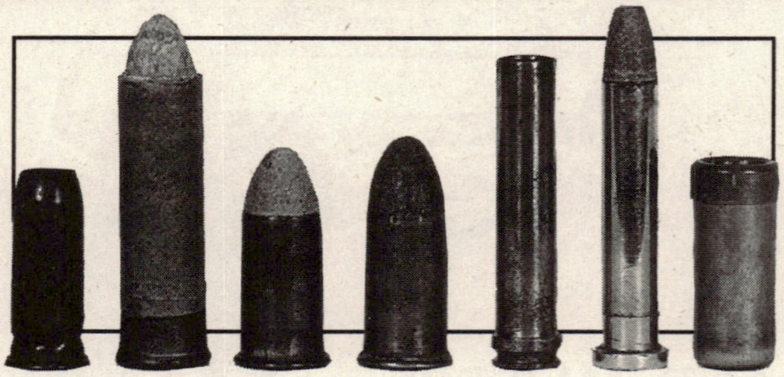

## CARTRIDGES FOR COLLECTORS

Tillinghast's "Cartridges for Collectors List" contains over 1,000 cartridges for sale: patent ignition, rimfire, pistol, rifle and shotgun. It also lists American and foreign books and catalogs available. Send **$2.00** for a single cartridge list.

Also offered is the *Antique Ammunition Price Guide #1*—8½ x 11, 64 pages, well illustrated. Regular price: **$6.00**; special price: **$3.50** prepaid.
The cartridge list is FREE with the purchase of the price guide. Write to:

**Gaye D. Tillinghast**
Box 405, Hancock, NH 03449

# FREE! RELOADING CATALOG FROM MIDWAY

Free three-month subscription to our reloading catalog. If you reload for rifle or pistol, you need our free 64-page catalog containing thousands of products from more than 100 manufacturers. We offer one of the world's largest selections of reloading and shooting products. FREE. Call or write:

**MIDWAY**
5875-D Van Horn Tavern Rd., Columbia, MO 65203
Tel: 1-800-243-3220 (toll-free)

# QUARTON OUTSHINES ALL OTHERS

QUARTON'S BEAMSHOT is a top-of-the-line laser sight that easily attaches to a rifle, shotgun, pistol or revolver. Constructed of aircraft aluminum, this sturdy unit is powered with an easily obtainable 3-volt lithium battery, giving the operator a 20-hour constant "on" usage. The unit weighs only 3.8 ounces, is activated by a simple pressure switch, and has a range of 300 to 800 yards. In addition to the laser sight, the BEAMSHOT kit includes a lithium battery, a 5-inch pressure switch, a mount for the gun of your choice, and a one-year warranty. All at an incredibly competitive price! Call, fax or write:

**QUARTON USA, LTD. CO.**
7042 Alamo Downs Pkwy., Suite 250, San Antonio, TX 78238
Tel: 210-520-8430 Fax: 210-520-8433

# MANUFACTURERS' SHOWCASE

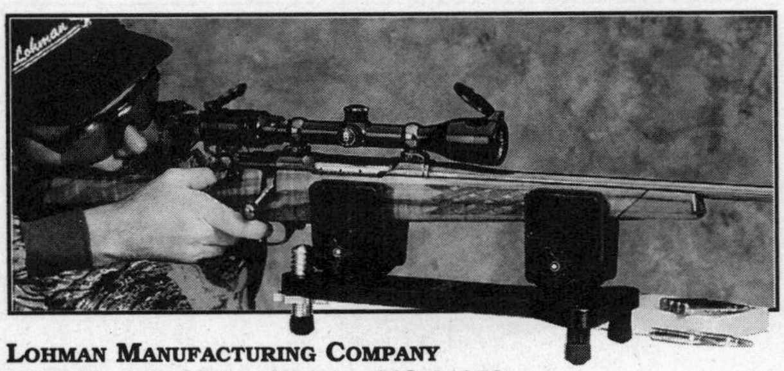

**LOHMAN MANUFACTURING COMPANY**
4500 Doniphan Drive, Neosho, MO 64850
Tel: 417-451-4438 Fax: 417-451-2576

## LOHMAN'S POPULAR SIGHT-VISE SSV-2

Ideal for all caliber guns, the Sight-Vise SSV-2 from LOHMAN is a precision instrument that makes accurate rifle sighting and shotgun patterning easy. Adjustable dual clamps hold the gun stock firmly, regardless of size or shape, while the unit's soft, padded jaws prevent stock-marring. An adjustable rear post is provided for precise aiming.

The U.S.-made Sight-Vise SSV-2 is extremely sturdy. Its wide, stable base helps reduce recoil and increase the shooter's confidence and accuracy. Extra lead shot can be added to the base for extra support and stability. The Sight-Vise can also be used to secure the gun for cleaning, scope mounting and repair work.

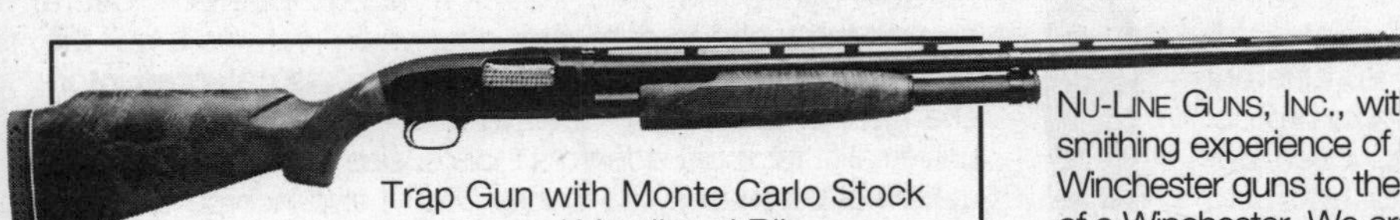

Trap Gun with Monte Carlo Stock and Ventilated Rib

## NU-LINE REPAIR AND GUNSMITHING

**NU-LINE INC.**
1053 Caulks Hill Rd., Harvester, MO 63303
Tel: 314-441-4500 or 314-447-4500

NU-LINE GUNS, INC., with old-world craftsmanship and a combined gunsmithing experience of more than 150 years, can repair or refurbish most Winchester guns to the high standard and quality workmanship expected of a Winchester. We are here to serve YOU. If you purchased the gun, or it was handed down from your father or grandfather, you'll want to put it in our trusted hands. Along with the complete gun, send a letter stating your request. We will make an in-depth inspection and submit a written estimate. Our estimate fee will be waived if the estimate is approved.

NU-LINE also carries a huge inventory of Winchester gun parts—current and obsolete—along with a large selection of screw-in choke tubes.

## KOWA HIGH RESOLUTION SPOTTING SCOPES

The KOWA TSN Series with 77mm lens offers a wider-than-usual field of view and increased light-gathering capabilities of no less than 60% over conventional 60mm spotting scopes. The TSN series is also capable of high-quality photo applications. There are eight different interchangeable eye pieces (bayonet mount), dust- and moisture-protection glass and a built-in sunshade. Available in straight, 45° off-set, multi-coated or multi-coated fluorite objective lens.

**KOWA OPTIMED, INC.**
20001 S. Vermont Ave., Torrance, CA 90502
Tel: 310-327-1913 Fax: 310-327-4177



# MANUFACTURERS' SHOWCASE

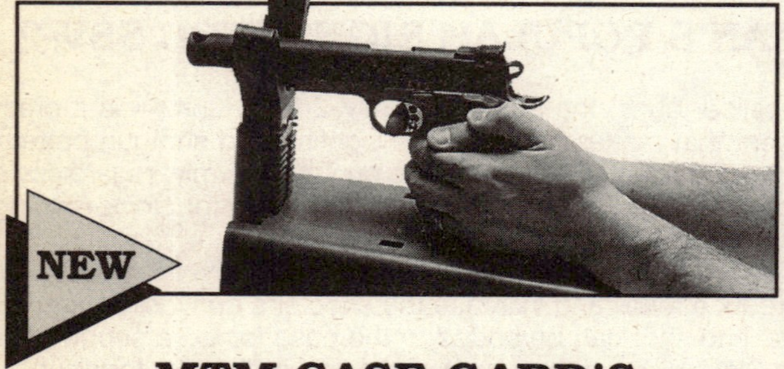


## MTM CASE-GARD'S NEW PISTOL REST

MTM CASE-GARD introduces its new PR-30 fully adjustable pistol rest. The adjustable all-plastic pistol rest is so versatile it will accommodate everything from a derringer to a 14" Contender. The base locks into the fork at 20 different positions. Rubber padding is molded to the fork to protect your handgun. When not in use, the fork has been designed to clip onto the bottom of the base for compact storage. This new product and many other items for the shooting sports can be seen in our 1995 catalog. For further information contact:

**MTM CASE-GARD CORP.**
P.O. Box 14117, Dayton, OH 45413
Tel: 513-890-7461

## DESANTIS GUNNY SACK II STYLE R-71

DESANTIS HOLSTER & LEATHER GOODS, INC., announces the release of its new "Gunny Sack II". Manufactured completely of durable nylon, the Gunny Sack II has a zippered closure around the weapon compartment, which features a pull tab on both sides to allow for easy opening. Its patented interchangeable holster system is available in two sizes to ensure a universal fit for most sidearms (holster size should be specified at time of purchase). The Gunny Sack II also incorporates two smaller zippered compartments for credentials, cuffs, spare magazine or personal items. Available in black, royal blue and three new colors: navy blue, forest green and burgundy. Black leather and natural suede offered at extra cost. Contact:

**DESANTIS HOLSTER & LEATHER GOODS, INC.**
P.O. Box 2039, New Hyde Park, NY 11040-0701
Tel: 516-354-8000 Fax: 516-354-7501

## DESANTIS UPGRADES A CLASSIC

For over two decades, DESANTIS has provided law-enforcement professionals with a reliable shoulder to lean on. Now, the classic DESANTIS Slant Shoulder Rig has been updated and redesigned to meet the needs of the '90s. Crafted from top-grain cowhide, this exceptionally comfortable rig features a four-point swiveling harness and a screw-tensioning device. New options include provisions for dual belt tie-down straps and an open muzzle design for use with a variety of arms. Made for revolvers and autoloaders, our models fit guns chambered for .380 ACP up to .44 Magnum. To obtain a catalog detailing the entire line, contact:

**DESANTIS HOLSTER & LEATHER GOODS, INC.**
P.O. Box 2039, New Hyde Park, NY 11040-0701
Tel: 516-354-8000 Fax: 516-354-7501

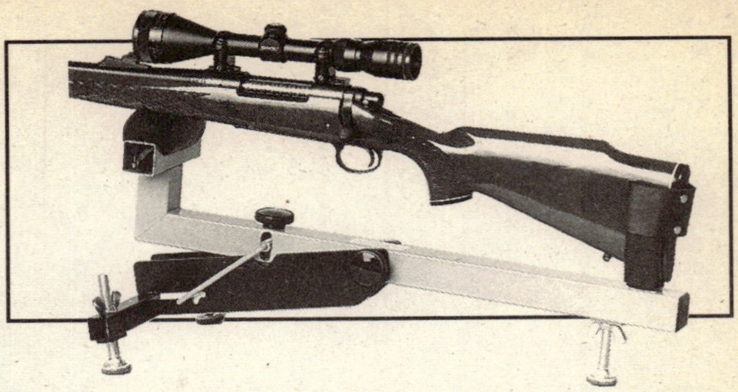

## BENCH MASTER RIFLE REST

The Bench Master Rifle Rest is a rugged, compact and highly adjustable rifle-shooting accessory—one that offers precision line-up and recoil reduction when sighting in a rifle, testing ammunition or shooting varmints. It features three course positions totaling 5½", with 1½" fine adjustment in each course position, plus leveling and shoulder height adjustments for maximum control and comfort. Because of its unique design, the Bench Master can easily double as a rifle vise for scope mounting, bore sighting and cleaning. It comes with a LIFETIME Warranty and a list price of only **$119.95**. For a free brochure, call or write:

**DESERT MOUNTAIN MFG.**
P.O. Box 2767, Columbia Falls, MT 59912-2767

# MANUFACTURERS' SHOWCASE

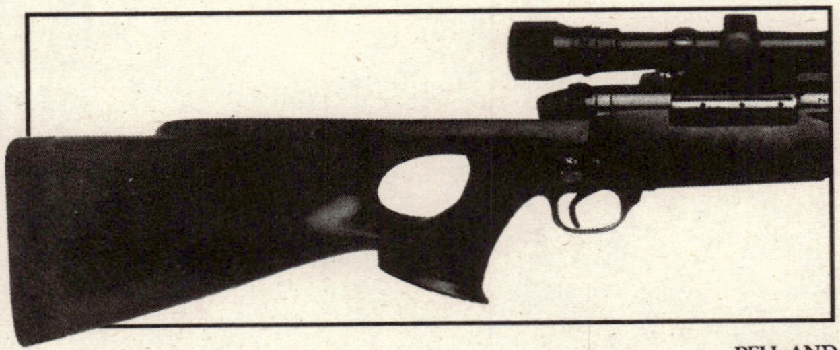

## BELL & CARLSON COMPOSITE GUN STOCKS

BELL AND CARLSON

All DURALITE, CARBELITE™ and PREMIER gun stocks are composed of hand-placed layers of Kevlar, graphite and fiberglass. The stocks are bound with structural urethane and chopped fiberglass throughout the entire cavity. This creates a dramatic reduction in felt recoil to the shoulder and allows for a secure solid feel when firing. BELL & CARLSON composite stocks are engineered to stand up to hard use, temperature extremes and moisture. All stocks are factory-fit to standard barrel contours as listed in our current model section. To find out more about our complete product line, write or call for a free catalog.

**BELL & CARLSON**
Dept. SB96, 509 N. 5th, Atwood, Kansas 67730
Tel: 913-626-3204

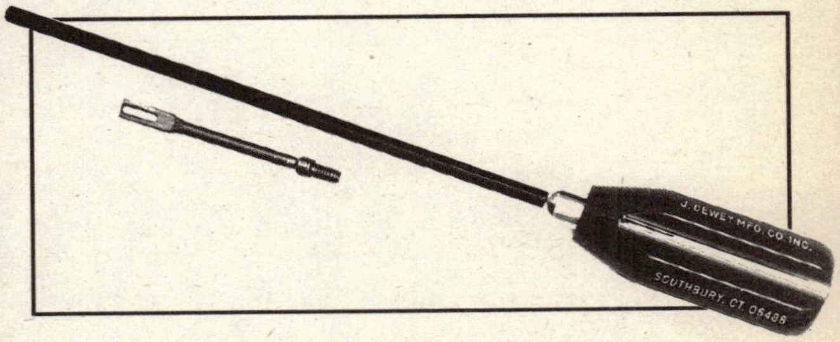


## NYLON-COATED GUN CLEANING RODS

J. DEWEY cleaning rods have been used by the U.S. Olympic shooting team and the benchrest community for over 20 years. These one-piece, spring-tempered, steel-based rods will not gall delicate rifling or damage the muzzle area of front-cleaned firearms. Each nylon-coated rod comes with a non-breakable plastic handle supported by ball-bearings for ease of cleaning. The brass cleaning jags are designed to pierce the center of the cleaning patch or wrap around the knurled end to keep the patch centered in the bore. Available from 17-caliber to shotgun bore size in several lengths. For more information, contact:

**J. DEWEY MANUFACTURING CO., INC.**
P.O. Box 2014, Southbury, CT 06488
Tel: 203-264-3064 Fax: 203-598-3119

# NEW P229 .357 SIG

## .357 SIG Ballistics
## 125gr JHP and 125gr FMJ

**Velocity (fps)**

| Muzzle | 25 | 50 | 75 | 100 YDS |
|---|---|---|---|---|
| 1350 | 1265 | 1190 | 1130 | 1080 |

**Energy (ft/lbs)**

| Muzzle | 25 | 50 | 75 | 100 YDS |
|---|---|---|---|---|
| 510 | 445 | 395 | 355 | 325 |

**Mid-Range Trajectory (inches)**

| 25 | 50 | 75 | 100 YDS |
|---|---|---|---|
| 0.2 | 0.7 | 1.6 | 3.1 |

**SIGARMS**

*ENGINEERED RELIABILITY*

SIGARMS, INC
Industrial Drive
Corporate Park
Exeter, NH 03833

FINLAND
SAKO
FINNFIRE .22 L.R.
THE TERM "PREMIUM .22 RIMFIRE RIFLE" HAS BEEN REDEFINED WITH THE INTRODUCTION OF THE SAKO FINNFIRE .22 L.R. BOLT ACTION RIFLE

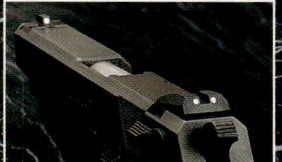

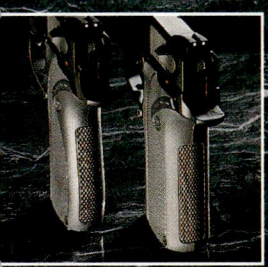

STOEGER IGA
SHOTGUNS
RUGGED. RELIABLE. PERFORMANCE AT AN AFFORDABLE PRICE!

# Handguns



For addresses and phone numbers of manufacturers and distributors included in this section, turn to *DIRECTORY OF MANUFACTURERS AND SUPPLIERS* at the back of the book.

# AMERICAN ARMS

**ESCORT .380 ACP**
**$312.00**

**SPECIFICATIONS**
**Caliber:** .380 ACP
**Capacity:** 7-shot magazine
**Barrel length:** $3\frac{3}{8}$"
**Overall length:** $6\frac{1}{8}$"
**Weight:** 19 oz. **Width:** $\frac{13}{16}$"
**Sights:** Fixed; low profile
**Features:** Stainless-steel frame, slide & trigger; nickel-steel barrel; soft polymer grips; loaded chamber indicator

**MODEL CX-22 DA**
**SEMIAUTO $213.00**

**SPECIFICATIONS**
**Caliber:** 22 LR
**Capacity:** 8-shot clip
**Barrel length:** $3\frac{1}{3}$" **Overall length:** $6\frac{1}{3}$"
**Weight:** 22 oz. (empty)
**Sights:** Fixed; blade front, "V"-notch rear
**Grip:** Black polymer
Also available:
**MODEL PX-22** (7-shot magazine): **$206.00**

**MODEL P-98 CLASSIC**
**SEMIAUTO $229.00**

**SPECIFICATIONS**
**Caliber:** 22 LR
**Capacity:** 8-shot clip
**Barrel length:** 5" **Overall length:** $8\frac{1}{8}$"
**Weight:** 26 oz. (empty)
**Sights:** Fixed blade front; adjustable square-notch rear
**Grip:** Black polymer

**MODEL PK-22 DA**
**SEMIAUTO $213.00**

**SPECIFICATIONS**
**Caliber:** 22 LR
**Capacity:** 8-shot clip
**Barrel length:** $3\frac{1}{3}$"
**Overall length:** $6\frac{1}{3}$"
**Weight:** 22 oz. (empty)
**Sights:** Fixed; blade front, "V"-notch rear
**Grip:** Black polymer

**REGULATOR SA**
**REVOLVER $328.00**
**TWO-CYLINDER SET $374.00**

**SPECIFICATIONS**
**Calibers:** 45 Long Colt, 44-40, 357 Mag.
**Barrel lengths:** $4\frac{3}{4}$", $5\frac{1}{2}$" and $7\frac{1}{2}$"
**Overall length:** $8\frac{1}{16}$"
**Weight:** 2 lb. 3 oz. ($4\frac{3}{4}$" barrel)
**Sights:** Fixed **Safety:** Half cock
**Features:** Brass trigger guard and backstrap; two-cylinder combos avail. (45 L.C./45 ACP and 44-40/44 Special)
Also available:
**BUCKHORN SA.** Same as Regulator but with stronger frame for 44 Rem. Mag. .................... **$359.00**
**REGULATOR DELUXE** w/blued steel backstrap and trigger guard ......................... **$374.00**

# AMERICAN DERRINGER PISTOLS

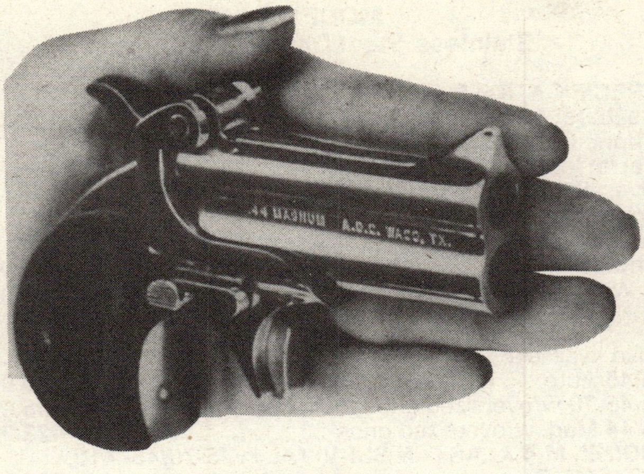


### MODEL 1

**SPECIFICATIONS**
**Calibers:** See below
**Action:** Single action w/automatic barrel selection
**Capacity:** 2 shots
**Barrel length:** 3″ **Overall length:** 4.82″
**Weight:** 15 oz. (in 45 Auto)

| **Calibers:** | **Prices** |
|---|---|
| 22 Long Rifle w/rosewood grips | **$245.00** |
| 32 Magnum/32 S&W Long | **255.00** |
| 32-20 | **245.00** |
| 357 Magnum w/rosewood grips | **257.00** |
| 357 Maximum w/rosewood grips | **265.00** |
| 38 Special w/rosewood grips | **245.00** |
| 38 Super w/rosewood grips | **253.00** |
| 38 Special +P+ (Police) | **253.00** |
| 38 Special Shot Shells | **253.00** |
| 380 Auto, 9mm Luger | **245.00** |
| 10mm Auto, 40 S&W, 45 Auto, 30 M-1 Carbine | **257.00** |
| 45-70 (single shot) | **312.00** |
| 45 Colt, 2½″ Snake (45-cal. rifled barrel), 44-40 Win., 44 Special | **320.00** |
| 45 Win. Mag., 44 Magnum, 41 Magnum | **385.00** |
| 30-30 Win., 357 Mag., 45/.410, 223 Rem. Comm. Ammo dual calibers | **375.00** |

Also available:
**MODEL 7 Ultra Lightweight (7½ oz.) Single Action (not shown)**

| | |
|---|---|
| 22 LR, 22 Mag. Rimfire, 32 Mag./32 S&W Long, 38 Special, 380 Auto | **$240.00** |
| 44 Special | **500.00** |

**MODEL 10 (10 oz.)**
**(not shown)**

| | |
|---|---|
| 38 Special (SS Barrel) | **$240.00** |
| 45 Auto (SS Barrel) | **257.00** |
| 45 Colt (SS Barrel) | **320.00** |

**MODEL 11 Lightweight (11 oz.) Double Derringer**

| | |
|---|---|
| 22 LR, 22 Mag. Rim., 32 Mag./SW, 38 Special, 380 Auto | **$225.00** |

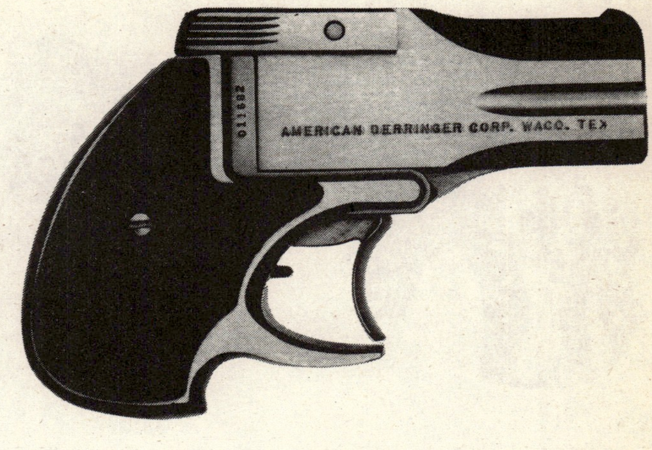


### 38 DOUBLE ACTION DERRINGER (14.5 oz.)

| | |
|---|---|
| 38 Special | **$300.00** |
| 9mm Luger | **325.00** |
| 357 Magnum, 40 S&W | **350.00** |

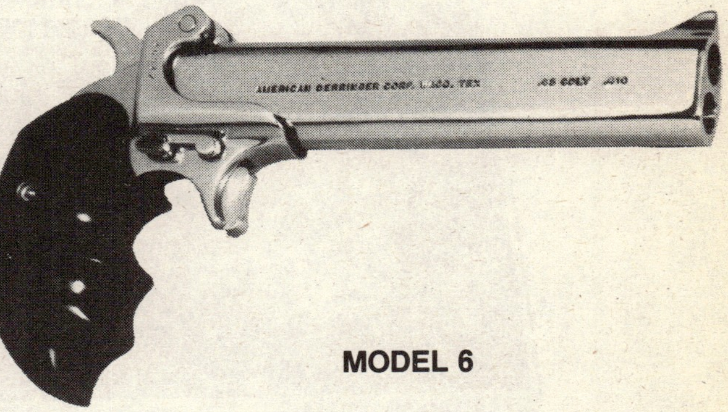

MODEL 6

### MODEL 6
### Stainless Steel Double Derringer

**SPECIFICATIONS**
**Calibers:** 22 Win. Mag., 357 Mag., .410, 45 Auto, 45 Colt
**Capacity:** 2 shots
**Barrel length:** 6″
**Overall length:** 8.2″
**Weight:** 21 oz.

| **Price:** | |
|---|---|
| 22 Win. Mag. | **$300.00** |
| 357 Mag. | **312.50** |
| 45 Auto | **345.00** |
| 45/.410, 45 Colt | **362.50** |

MODEL 4

## MODEL 4
### Stainless Steel Double Derringer

**SPECIFICATIONS**
**Calibers:** 45 Colt and 3″ .410
**Capacity:** 2 shots
**Barrel length:** 4.1″
**Overall length:** 6″
**Weight:** 16.5 oz.
**Finish:** Satin or high-polish stainless steel
**Price:** . . . . . . . . . . . . . . . . . . . . . . . . . . . . . . . . . . . . **$352.00**
With oversized grips . . . . . . . . . . . . . . . . . . . . **382.00**

Also available:
In 45 Auto, 45 Colt, 357 Mag., 357 Maximum . . . . **$369.00**
In 45-70 w/oversized grips, both barrels . . . . . . . . . **495.00**
In 44 Mag. w/oversized grips . . . . . . . . . . . . . . . . . **422.00**
**MODEL M-4 ALASKAN SURVIVAL** in 45-70/45-.410, 45-70/45 Colt . . . . . . . . . . . . . . . . . . . . . . . . . . . . . . . . **387.50**

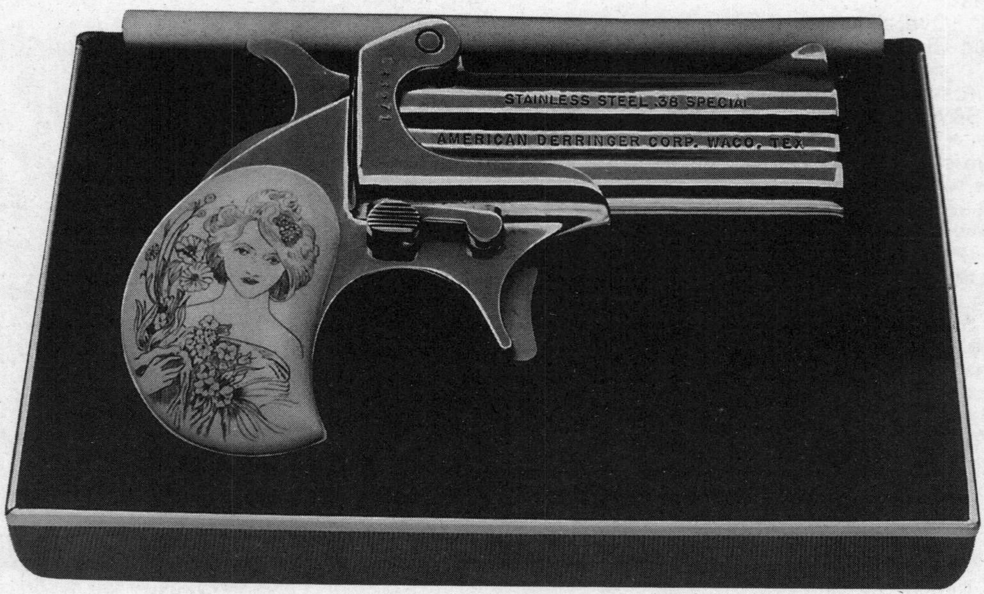


LADY DERRINGER
Stainless Steel Double

Also available:
**LADY DERRINGER** (Stainless Steel Double)
38 Special . . . . . . . . . . . . . . . . . . . . . . . . . . . . . . . . . **$235.00**
32 Mag. . . . . . . . . . . . . . . . . . . . . . . . . . . . . . . . . . . **255.00**
357 Mag. . . . . . . . . . . . . . . . . . . . . . . . . . . . . . . . . . **275.00**
45 Colt . . . . . . . . . . . . . . . . . . . . . . . . . . . . . . . . . . **320.00**

### 125th ANNIVERSARY DOUBLE DERRINGER COMMEMORATIVE (1866–1991) (not shown)

38 Special (Brass) . . . . . . . . . . . . . . . . . . . . . . . . . **$255.00**
44-40 or 45 Colt (Brass) . . . . . . . . . . . . . . . . . . . . **320.00**

# AMT PISTOLS

## BACKUP
**$449.99 (All Calibers)**

**SPECIFICATIONS**
**Calibers:** 380 ACP (9mm Short), 38 Super, 40 S&W, 45 ACP
**Capacity:** 5-shot (40 S&W, 45 ACP); 6-shot (other calibers)
**Barrel length:** 3″
**Overall length:** 5¾″
**Weight:** 23 oz.
**Width:** 1″
**Features:** Locking-barrel action, checkered fiberglass grips, grooved slide sight

**BACKUP (.380 or 9mm Short)**

## 380 BACKUP II
**$309.99 (Single Action)**
**$329.95 (Double Action)**

**SPECIFICATIONS**
**Caliber:** 380 ACP
**Capacity:** 5 shots
**Barrel length:** 2½″
**Overall length:** 5″
**Weight:** 18 oz.
**Width:** 11/16″
**Sights:** Open
**Grips:** Carbon fiber

**.380 BACKUP II**

## 1911 GOVERNMENT 45 ACP LONGSLIDE (not shown)
**$595.99**

**SPECIFICATIONS**
**Caliber:** 45 ACP
**Capacity:** 7 shots
**Barrel length:** 7″
**Overall length:** 10½″
**Weight:** 46 oz.
**Sights:** 3-dot, adjustable
**Features:** Wide adjustable trigger; Neoprene wraparound grips
Also available:
**Conversion Kit** . . . . . . . . . . . . . . . . . . . . . . . . . . . . **$299.99**

## 1911 GOVERNMENT MODEL
**$489.99**

**SPECIFICATIONS**
**Caliber:** 45 ACP
**Capacity:** 7 shots
**Barrel length:** 5″
**Overall length:** 8½″
**Weight:** 38 oz.
**Width:** 1¼″
**Sights:** Fixed
**Features:** Long grip safety; rubber wraparound Neoprene grips; beveled magazine well; wide adjustable trigger
Also available:
**1911 HARDBALLER.** Same specifications as Standard Model, but with adjustable sights and matte rib
**Price:** . . . . . . . . . . . . . . . . . . . . . . . . . . . . . . . . **$549.99**
**Conversion Kit** . . . . . . . . . . . . . . . . . . . . . . . . . . **279.00**

**1911 GOVERNMENT**

# AMT PISTOLS

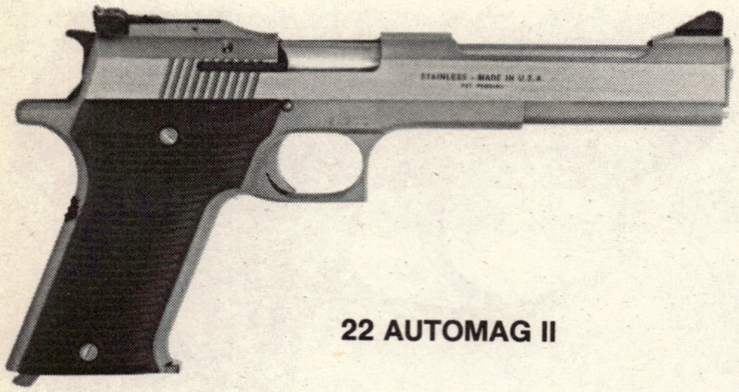

22 AUTOMAG II

## 22 AUTOMAG II RIMFIRE MAGNUM
## $405.95

The only production semiautomatic handgun in this caliber, the Automag II is ideal for the small-game hunter or shooting enthusiast who wants more power and accuracy in a light, trim handgun. The pistol features a bold open-slide design and employs a unique gas-channeling system for smooth, trouble-free action.

**SPECIFICATIONS**
**Caliber:** 22 Rimfire Magnum
**Barrel lengths:** 3 3/8″, 4 1/2″ or 6″
**Magazine capacity:** 9 shots (4 1/2″ & 6″), 7 shots (3 3/8″)
**Weight:** 32 oz. (6″), 30 oz. (4 1/2″), 24 oz. (3 3/8″)
**Sights:** Adjustable (white outline rear; red ramp)
**Features:** Squared trigger guard; grooved carbon fiber grips

## AUTOMAG III
## $469.79

**SPECIFICATIONS**
**Caliber:** 30 M1 Carbine
**Capacity:** 8 shots
**Barrel length:** 6 3/8″
**Overall length:** 10 1/2″
**Weight:** 43 oz.
**Sights:** Adjustable
**Grips:** Carbon fiber
**Finish:** Stainless steel

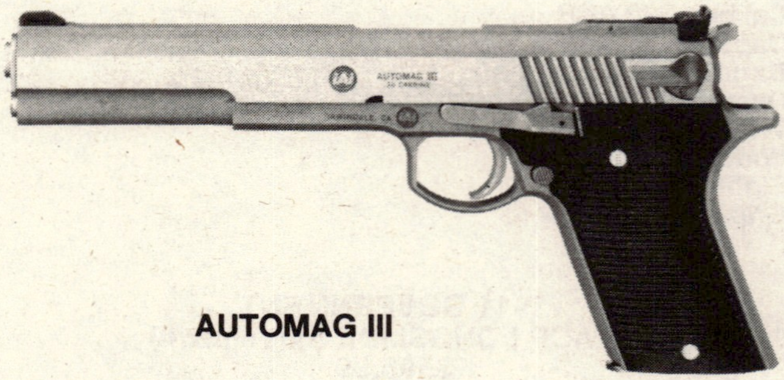

AUTOMAG III

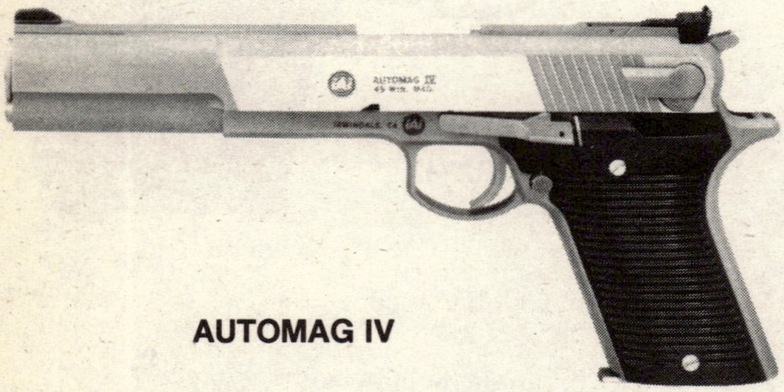

AUTOMAG IV

## AUTOMAG IV
## $699.99

**SPECIFICATIONS**
**Caliber:** 45 Win. Mag.
**Capacity:** 7 shots
**Barrel lengths:** 6 1/2″
**Overall length:** 10 1/2″
**Weight:** 46 oz.
**Sights:** Adjustable
**Grips:** Carbon fiber
**Finish:** Stainless steel

## AUTOMAG V
## $899.99

**SPECIFICATIONS**
**Caliber:** 50
**Capacity:** 5 shot
**Barrel length:** 6 1/2″
**Overall length:** 10 1/2″
**Weight:** 46 oz.
**Sights:** Adjustable

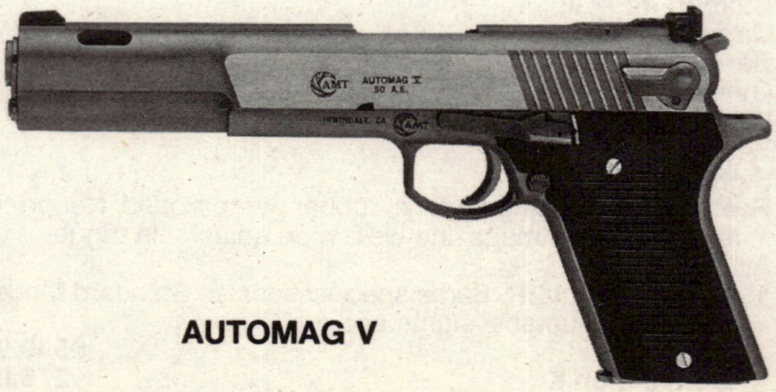

AUTOMAG V

# ANSCHUTZ PISTOLS

EXEMPLAR BOLT-ACTION PISTOL

**EXEMPLAR**
**$558.00**

**SPECIFICATIONS**
**Caliber:** 22 Long Rifle
**Capacity:** 5-shot clip
**Barrel length:** 10″
**Overall length:** 19″
**Weight:** 3 1/3 lbs.
**Action:** Match 64
**Trigger pull:** 9.85 oz., two-stage adjustable
**Safety:** Slide
**Sights:** Hooded ramp post front; open notched rear; adjustable for windage and elevation
**Stock:** European walnut

Also available:
**EXEMPLAR LEFT** featuring right-hand operating bolt.
**Price:** . . . . . . . . . . . . . . . . . . . . . . . . . . . . . . . . . . **$558.00**

**EXEMPLAR XIV**
**$562.00**

**SPECIFICATIONS**
**Caliber:** 22 Long Rifle
**Capacity:** 5-shot clip
**Barrel length:** 14″
**Overall length:** 23″
**Weight:** 4.15 lbs.
**Action:** Match 64
**Trigger pull:** 9.85 oz., two-stage
**Safety:** Slide

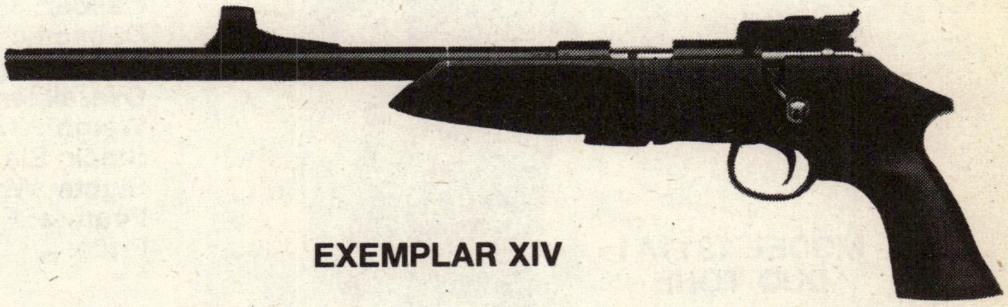

EXEMPLAR XIV

**EXEMPLAR HORNET**
**$995.00**

A centerfire version with Match 54 action.

**SPECIFICATIONS**
**Caliber:** 22 Hornet
**Capacity:** 5-shot clip
**Trigger pull:** 19.6 oz.
**Barrel:** 10″
**Overall length:** 20″
**Weight:** 4.35 lbs.
**Features:** Tapped and grooved for scope mounting; wing safety

EXEMPLAR HORNET

# AUTO-ORDNANCE PISTOLS

## MODEL 1911A1 THOMPSON

**SPECIFICATIONS**
**Calibers:** 45 ACP, 9mm, 10mm and 38 Super
**Capacity:** 9 rounds (9mm, 10mm & 38 Super); 7 rounds (45 ACP)
**Barrel length:** 5″
**Overall length:** 8½″
**Weight:** 39 oz.
**Sights:** Blade front; rear adjustable for windage
**Stock:** Checkered plastic with medallion
**Prices:**

| | |
|---|---|
| In 9mm and 38 Super | **$415.00** |
| In 10mm | **420.95** |
| In 45 ACP | **388.95** |
| Satin nickel or Duo-Tone finish (45 cal. only) | **405.00** |
| **PIT BULL MODEL** (45 ACP w/3½″ barrel) | **420.95** |
| **WW II PARKERIZED PISTOL** (45 cal. only) | **379.25** |
| **DELUXE MODEL** (45 cal. only) | **405.00** |

**MODEL 1911A1 THOMPSON (9mm)**

**MODEL 1911A1 DUO-TONE**

## MODEL 1911 "THE GENERAL" (not shown)

**SPECIFICATIONS**
**Caliber:** 45 ACP
**Capacity:** 7 rounds
**Barrel length:** 4½″
**Overall length:** 7¾″
**Weight:** 37 oz.
**Stock:** Black textured, rubber wraparound with medallion
**Sights:** White 3-dot system
**Feature:** Full-length recoil guide system
**Price:** . . . . . . . . . . **$427.95**

## MODEL 1911A1 COMPETITION

**SPECIFICATIONS**
**Calibers:** 45 ACP and 38 Super
**Weight:** 42 oz.
**Barrel length:** 5″
**Overall length:** 10″
**Stock:** Rubber wraparound
**Sights:** White 3-dot system
**Features:** Full-length recoil spring guide system, Videcki adjustable speed trigger; extended combat ejector; Hi-ride beavertail grip safety
**Price:** . . . . . . . . . . **$615.00**

**MODEL 1911A1 COMPETITION**

# BERETTA PISTOLS

## COMPACT FRAME PISTOLS

**MODEL 8000/8040
COUGAR**

### COUGAR SERIES
### MODEL 8000 (9mm)
### MODEL 8040 (40 cal.)

Beretta's 8000/8040 Cougar Series semiautomatics use a proven locked-breech system with a rotating barrel. This design makes the pistol compact and easy to conceal and operate with today's high-powered 9mm and 40-caliber ammunition. When the pistol is fired, the initial thrust of recoil energy is partially absorbed as it pushes slide and barrel back, with the barrel rotating by cam action against a tooth on the rigid central block. When the barrel has turned about 30 degrees, the locking lugs on the barrel clear the locking recesses, which free the slide to continue rearward. The recoil spring absorbs the remaining recoil energy as the slide extracts and ejects the spent shell casing, rotates the hammer, and then reverses direction to chamber the next round. By channeling part of the recoil energy into barrel rotation and by partially absorbing the barrel and slide recoil shock through the central block before it is transferred to the frame, the Cougar shows an unusually low felt recoil.

**SPECIFICATIONS**
**Calibers:** 9mm and 40 semiauto
**Capacity:** 10
**Action:** Double/Single or Double Action only
**Barrel length:** 3.6″
**Overall length:** 7″
**Weight:** 33.5 oz.
**Overall height:** 5.5″
**Sight radius:** 5.2″
**Sights:** Front and rear sights dovetailed to slide
**Finish:** Bruniton/Plastic
**Features:** Firing-pin block; chrome-lined barrel; short recoil, rotating barrel; anodized aluminum alloy frame

**Prices:**
Double action only . . . . . . . . . . . . . . . . . . . . . . . . **$611.00**
Double or Single action . . . . . . . . . . . . . . . . . . . . . **636.00**

# BERETTA PISTOLS

## SMALL FRAME PISTOLS

### MODEL 21 BOBCAT DA SEMIAUTOMATIC
**$235.00 ($247.00 Nickel)**

A safe, dependable, accurate small-bore pistol in 22 LR or 25 Auto. Easy to load with its unique barrel tip-up system.

**SPECIFICATIONS**
**Caliber:** 22 LR or 25 Auto. **Magazine capacity:** 7 rounds (22 LR); 8 rounds (25 Auto). **Overall length:** 4.9″. **Barrel length:** 2.4″. **Weight:** 11.5 oz. (25 ACP); 11.8 oz. (22 LR) **Sights:** Blade front; V-notch rear. **Safety:** Thumb operated. **Grips:** Plastic or Walnut. **Frame:** Forged aluminum.
Also available:
**Model 21 Engraved** . . . . . . . . . . . . . . . . . . . . . . . . . **$294.00**
W/Plastic grips, matte black finish . . . . . . . . . . . . . . **194.00**

MODEL 21 BOBCAT

MODEL 950 BS JETFIRE

### MODEL 950 BS JETFIRE SINGLE-ACTION SEMIAUTOMATIC

**SPECIFICATIONS**
**Caliber:** 25 ACP. **Barrel length:** 2.4″. **Overall length:** 4.7″. **Overall height:** 3.4″. **Safety:** External, thumb-operated **Magazine capacity:** 8 rounds. **Sights:** Blade front; V-notch rear. **Weight:** 9.9 oz. **Frame:** Forged aluminum.
**Prices:**
**Model 950 BS** . . . . . . . . . . . . . . . . . . . . . . . . . . . . . **$187.00**
**Model 950 BS** Nickel . . . . . . . . . . . . . . . . . . . . . . . **221.00**
**Model 950 EL** Engraved . . . . . . . . . . . . . . . . . . . . **267.00**
**Model 950 BS** Plastic grips, matte black finish . . . **159.00**

## MEDIUM FRAME PISTOLS

### MODEL 84 CHEETAH

This pistol is pocket size with a large magazine capacity. The first shot (with hammer down, chamber loaded) can be fired by a double-action pull on the trigger without cocking the hammer manually.

The pistol also features a favorable grip angle for natural pointing, positive thumb safety (designed for both right- and left-handed operation), quick takedown (by means of special takedown button) and a conveniently located magazine release. Black plastic grips. Wood grips extra.

**SPECIFICATIONS**
**Caliber:** 380 Auto (9mm Short). **Weight:** 23.3 oz. (approx.). **Barrel length:** 3.8″. (approx.) **Overall length:** 6.8″. (approx.) **Sights:** Fixed front and rear. **Magazine capacity:** 10 rounds. **Height overall:** 4 1/4″ (approx.).
**Prices:**
**Model 84** w/Bruniton/Plastic . . . . . . . . . . . . . . . . . **$529.00**
**Model 84** w/Bruniton/Wood . . . . . . . . . . . . . . . . . . **557.00**
**Model 84** w/Nickel/Wood . . . . . . . . . . . . . . . . . . . . **600.00**

MODEL 84 CHEETAH

# BERETTA PISTOLS

## MEDIUM FRAME PISTOLS

### MODEL 85 CHEETAH

This double-action semiautomatic pistol features walnut or plastic grips, matte black finish on steel slide, barrel and anodized forged aluminum, ambidextrous safety and a single line 8-round magazine.

**SPECIFICATIONS**
**Caliber:** 380 Auto (9mm Short). **Barrel length:** 3.82″. **Weight:** 21.9 oz. (empty). **Overall length:** 6.8″. **Overall height:** 4.8″. **Capacity:** 8 rounds. **Sights:** Blade integral with slide (front); square-notched bar, dovetailed to slide (rear).
**Prices:**
**Model 85** w/Bruniton/Plastic .................. **$486.00**
**Model 85** w/Bruniton/Wood .................. **514.00**
**Model 85** w/Nickel/Wood .................. **551.00**

Also available:
**Model 87** in 22 LR. **Capacity:** 7. Straight blow-back, open slide design. **Width:** 1.3″. **Overall height:** 4.7″. **Weight:** 20.1 oz. **Finish:** Blued with wood. .................. **$493.00**

MODEL 85 CHEETAH

MODEL 86 CHEETAH

### MODEL 86 CHEETAH

**SPECIFICATIONS**
**Caliber:** 380 Auto. **Barrel length:** 4.4″. **Overall length:** 7.3″. **Capacity:** 8 rounds. **Weight:** 23.3 oz. **Sight radius:** 4.9″. **Overall height:** 4.8″. **Overall width:** 1.4″. **Grip:** Walnut. **Features:** Same as other Medium Frame, straight blow-back models, plus safety and convenience of a tip-up barrel (rounds can be loaded directly into chamber without operating the slide).
**Price:** (w/Bruniton finish) .................. **$514.00**

### MODEL 89 GOLD STANDARD

This sophisticated single-action, target pistol features an eight-round magazine, adjustable target sights, and target-style contoured walnut grips with thumbrest.

**SPECIFICATIONS**
**Caliber:** 22 LR. **Capacity:** 8 rounds. **Barrel length:** 6″. **Overall length:** 9½″. **Height:** 5.3″. **Weight:** 41 oz. ....... **$736.00**

MODEL 89 GOLD STANDARD

# BERETTA PISTOLS

## LARGE FRAME PISTOLS

MODEL 92F (9mm)

MODEL 92D

MODEL 96

### MODELS 92FS (9mm) & 96 (40 Cal.)

**SPECIFICATIONS**
**Calibers:** 9mm and 40 cal.
**Capacity:** 10
**Action:** Double/Single
**Barrel length:** 4.9″
**Overall length:** 8.5″
**Weight:** 34.4 oz.
**Overall height:** 5.4″
**Overall width:** 1.5″
**Sights:** Integral front; windage adjustable rear; 3-dot or tritium night sights
**Grips:** Wood, plastic or rubber
**Finish:** Bruniton (also available in blued, stainless or gold)
**Features:** Chrome-lined bore; visible firing-pin block; open slide design; safety drop catch (half-cock); combat trigger guard; external hammer; reversible magazine release

Also available:
**MODELS 92D** (9mm) and **96D** (40 cal.). Same specifications but in DA only and with Bruniton finish and plastic grips only. Also features chamber loaded indicator on extractor; bobbed external hammer; "slick" slide (no external levers)
**MODEL CENTURION** (9mm and 40 cal.). Same as above but with more compact upper slide and barrel assembly. **Barrel length:** 4.3″. **Overall length:** 7.8″. **Weight:** 33.2 oz.

| **Models** | **Prices** |
|---|---|
| **Model 92FS Plastic** | **$ 626.00** |
| (Wood grips **$20.00** additional) | |
| **Model 92F Stainless** w/3-dot sights | **757.00** |
| **Model 92FS Plastic Centurion** | |
| 9mm/40 cal. w/3-dot sights | **626.00** |
| w/tritium sights | **680.00** |
| **Model 92D** (DA only, bobbed hammer) | |
| w/3-dot sights | **586.00** |
| w/tritium sight | **676.00** |
| Deluxe gold-plated engraved | **5429.00** |
| **Model 92F-EL** Stainless | **1243.00** |
| **Model 96** w/3-dot sights | **643.00** |
| w/tritium sights | **733.00** |
| **Model 96D** (DA only) | **607.00** |
| w/tritium sights | **697.00** |
| **Model 96 Centurion** | **643.00** |
| w/tritium sights | **733.00** |

### BRIGADIER

The new Brigadier is a variant of the Beretta 92/96 Series of 9mm and 40-caliber pistols. It features removable front sights and a reconfigured high slide wall profile that reduces felt recoil and improves sight alignment between shots.

**SPECIFICATIONS**
**Calibers:** 9mm and 40 cal.
**Capacity:** 10 rounds
**Barrel length:** 4.9″
**Weight:** 35.3 oz.
**Sights:** 3-dot sight system
**Finish:** Matte black Bruniton
**Price:** To be announced

MODEL 92/96 BRIGADIER

# BERNARDELLI PISTOLS

## MODEL PO18 TARGET PISTOL
**$560.00 (Black Plastic)**
**$620.00 (Chrome)**

**SPECIFICATIONS**
**Caliber:** 9mm
**Capacity:** 16 rounds
**Barrel length:** 4.8″ **Overall length:** 8.25″
**Weight:** 34.2 oz.
**Sights:** Low micrometric sights adjustable for windage and elevation. **Sight radius:** 5.4″
**Features:** Thumb safety decocks hammer; magazine press button release reversible for right- and left-hand shooters; hardened steel barrel; can be carried cocked and locked; squared and serrated trigger guard and grip; frame and barrel forged in steel and milled with CNC machines; manual thumb, half cock, magazine and auto-locking firing-pin block safeties; low-profile 3-dot interchangeable combat sights

## MODEL PO18 COMPACT TARGET PISTOL
**$665.00 (Black Plastic)**
**$610.00 (Chrome)**

**SPECIFICATIONS**
**Calibers:** 380 and 9mm
**Capacity:** 14 rounds
**Barrel length:** 4″
**Overall length:** 7.44″
**Weight:** 31.7 oz.
**Sight radius:** 5.4″
**Grips:** Walnut or plastic
**Features:** Same as Model PO18

## MODEL PO10 TARGET PISTOL
**$825.00**

**SPECIFICATIONS**
**Caliber:** 22 LR
**Capacity:** 5 or 10 rounds
**Barrel length:** 5.9″
**Weight:** 40 oz.
**Sights:** Interchangeable front sight; rear sight adjustable for windage and elevation
**Sight radius:** 7 1/2″
**Features:** All steel construction; external hammer with safety notch; external slide catch for hold-open device; inertia safe firing pin; oil-finished walnut grips for right- and left-hand shooters; matte black or chrome finish; pivoted trigger with adjustable weight and take-ups

# BERSA AUTOMATIC PISTOLS

**THUNDER 9 DOUBLE ACTION**
**$491.95 (Duo-Tone) $524.95 (Satin Nickel)**
**$474.95 (Matte)**

**SPECIFICATIONS**
**Caliber:** 9mm **Capacity:** 10 rounds
**Action:** Double
**Barrel length:** 4″ **Overall length:** 7 3/8″
**Weight:** 30 oz. **Height:** 5 1/2″
**Sights:** Blade front (integral w/slide); fully adjustable rear
**Safety:** Manual, firing pin and decocking lever
**Grips:** Black polymer
**Finish:** Matte blue, satin nickel or duo-tone
**Features:** Reversible extended magazine release; adjustable trigger release; "Link-Free" design system (ensures positive lockup); instant disassembly; ambidextrous slide release

**THUNDER 9 DOUBLE ACTION**

**THUNDER 22**

**THUNDER 380**

**SERIES 95**

**THUNDER 22**
**$308.95 (Blue) $341.95 (Satin Nickel)**

**SPECIFICATIONS**
**Caliber:** 22 LR **Capacity:** 10 rounds
**Action:** Double
**Barrel length:** 3 1/2″ **Overall length:** 6 5/8″
**Weight:** 24 1/2 oz.
**Sights:** Notched-bar dovetailed rear; blade integral with slide front
**Safety:** Manual firing pin
**Grips:** Black polymer

**THUNDER 380**
**$308.95 (Blue) $341.95 (Satin Nickel)**
**$324.95 (Duo-Tone)**

**SPECIFICATIONS**
**Caliber:** 380 ACP **Capacity:** 7 rounds
**Barrel length:** 3 1/2″ **Overall length:** 6 5/8″
**Weight:** 25.75 oz.
**Sights:** Notched-bar dovetailed rear; blade integral with slide front
**Safety:** Manual firing pin
**Grips:** Rubber
**Finish:** Blue, satin nickel, duo-tone
Also available:
**THUNDER 380 PLUS** (26 oz.; 10 shots) **Prices: $367.95** (Matte); **$408.00** (Satin Nickel); **$384.95** (Duo-Tone)

**SERIES 95**
**$274.95 (Matte) $291.95 (Nickel)**

**SPECIFICATIONS**
**Caliber:** 380 ACP **Capacity:** 7 rounds
**Action:** Double
**Barrel length:** 3 1/2″ **Overall length:** 6 5/8″
**Weight:** 23 oz.
**Sights:** Notched-bar dovetailed rear; blade integral with slide front
**Safety:** Manual firing pin
**Grips:** Black polymer
**Finish:** Matte blue, satin nickel

# BROWNING AUTOMATIC PISTOLS

9mm HI-POWER SINGLE ACTION

## HI-POWER SINGLE ACTION

Both the 9mm and 40 S&W models come with either a fixed-blade front sight and a windage-adjustable rear sight or a non-glare rear sight, screw adjustable for both windage and elevation. The front sight is an 1/8-inch-wide blade mounted on a ramp. The rear surface of the blade is serrated to prevent glare. All models have an ambidextrous safety. See table below for specifications and prices.

### HI-POWER SPECIFICATIONS

| Model | Sights | Grips | Barrel Length | Overall Length | Overall Width | Overall Height | Weight[2] | Mag. Cap.[1] | Prices |
|---|---|---|---|---|---|---|---|---|---|
| **Mark III** | Fixed | Molded | 4 3/4″ | 7 3/4″ | 1 3/8″ | 5″ | 32 oz. | 10 | **$524.95** |
| **Standard** | Fixed | Walnut | 4 3/4″ | 7 3/4″ | 1 3/8″ | 5″ | 32 oz. | 10 | **556.95** |
| **Standard** | Adj. | Walnut | 4 3/4″ | 7 3/4″ | 1 3/8″ | 5″ | 32 oz. | 10 | **605.95** |
| **HP-Practical** | Fixed | Pachmayr | 4 3/4″ | 7 3/4″ | 1 3/8″ | 5″ | 36 oz. | 10 | **599.95** |
| **HP-Practical** | Adj. | Pachmayr | 4 3/4″ | 7 3/4″ | 1 3/8″ | 5″ | 36 oz. | 10 | **649.95** |
| **Silver Chrome** | Adj. | Pachmayr | 4 3/4″ | 7 3/4″ | 1 3/8″ | 5″ | 36 oz. | 10 | **619.95** |
| **Capitan (9mm only)** | Adj. | Walnut | 4 3/4″ | 7 3/4″ | 1 3/8″ | 5″ | 32 oz. | 10 | **659.95** |

*[1] 9mm magazine capacity listed. Magazine capacity of 40 S&W is 10.*
*[2] 9mm weight listed. Overall weight of the 40 S&W Hi-Power is 3 oz. heavier than the 9mm.*

## MODEL BDM 9mm DOUBLE ACTION

Browning's Model BDM (for Browning Double Mode) pistol provides shooters with convenience and safety by combining the best advantages of double-action pistols with those of the revolver. In just seconds, the shooter can set the BDM to conventional double-action "pistol" mode or to the all-new double-action "revolver" mode.

**SPECIFICATIONS**
**Caliber:** 9mm Luger
**Capacity:** 10 rounds
**Barrel length:** 4.73″
**Overall length:** 7.85″
**Weight:** 31 oz. (empty)
**Sight radius:** 6.26″
**Sights:** Low-profile front (removable); rear screw adjustable for windage; includes 3-dot sight system
**Finish:** Matte blue
**Features:** Dual-purpose ambidextrous decocking lever/safety designed with a short stroke for easy operation (also functions as slide release); contoured grip is checkered on all four sides
**Price:** . . . . . . . . . . . . . . . . . . . . . . . . . . . . . . **$594.95**

MODEL BDM 9mm DOUBLE ACTION

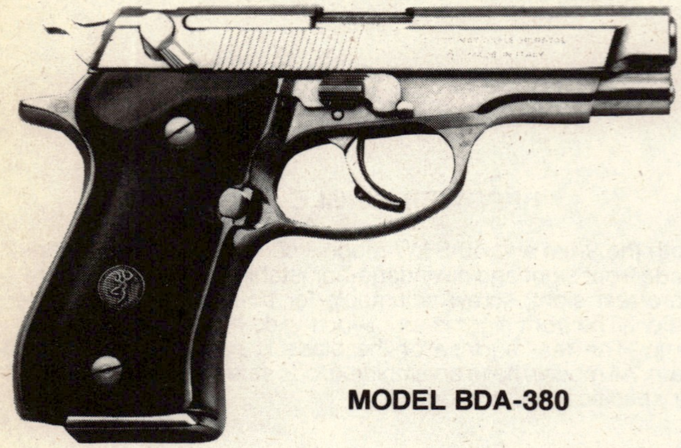

MODEL BDA-380

BUCK MARK 5.5 TARGET

MICRO BUCK MARK

## MODEL BDA-380

A high-powered, double-action semiautomatic pistol with fixed sights in 380 caliber.

**SPECIFICATIONS**
**Capacity:** 10 shots
**Barrel length:** 3 13/16″
**Overall length:** 6 3/4″
**Weight:** 23 oz.
**Sights:** Fixed
**Grips:** Walnut
**Prices:**
Nickel Finish .................. **$577.95**
Blued Finish .................. **536.95**

### BUCK MARK SEMIAUTOMATIC PISTOL SPECIFICATIONS (22 LR)

| Model | Finish | Sights | Barrel Length | Overall Length | Overall Width | Overall Height | Sight Radius | Weight Unloaded | Mag. Cap. |
|---|---|---|---|---|---|---|---|---|---|
| Standard | Matte Blue | Pro Target | 5 1/2" | 9 1/2" | 1 5/16" | 5 3/8" | 8" | 36 oz. | 10 |
| Nickel | Nickel Plated | Pro Target | 5 1/2" | 9 1/2" | 1 5/16" | 5 3/8" | 8" | 36 oz. | 10 |
| Plus | Matte Blue | Pro Target | 5 1/2" | 9 1/2" | 1 5/16" | 5 3/8" | 8" | 36 oz. | 10 |
| Micro Standard | Matte Blue | Pro Target | 4" | 8" | 1 5/16" | 5 3/8" | 6 1/4" | 32 oz. | 10 |
| Micro Nickel | Nickel Plated | Pro Target | 4" | 8" | 1 5/16" | 5 3/8" | 6 1/4" | 32 oz. | 10 |
| Micro Plus | Matte Blue | Pro Target | 4" | 8" | 1 5/16" | 5 3/8" | 6 1/4" | 32 oz. | 10 |

### BUCK MARK 5.5 FIELD AND TARGET (22 LR)

| Model | Finish | Sights | Barrel Length | Overall Length | Overall Width | Overall Height | Sight Radius | Weight Unloaded | Mag. Cap. |
|---|---|---|---|---|---|---|---|---|---|
| 5.5 Field | Matte Blue | Pro Target | 5 1/2" | 9 5/8" | 1 5/8" | 6 5/16" | 8 1/4 | 35 1/2 oz. | 10 |
| 5.5 Gold Target | Gold/Blue | Pro Target | 5 1/2" | 9 5/8" | 1 5/8" | 6 5/16" | 8 1/4 | 35 1/2 oz. | 10 |
| 5.5 Target Blued | Matte Blue | Pro Target | 5 1/2" | 9 5/8" | 1 5/8" | 6 5/16" | 8 1/4 | 35 1/2 oz. | 10 |
| 5.5 Nickel Target | Nickel/Blue | Pro Target | 5 1/2" | 9 5/8" | 1 5/8" | 6 5/16" | 8 1/4 | 35 1/2 oz. | 10 |

# CHARTER ARMS REVOLVERS



## BULLDOG PUG 44 SPECIAL

**SPECIFICATIONS**
**Caliber:** 44 Special. **Capacity:** 5 shots. **Type of action:** Single and double. **Barrel length:** 2½″ shrouded. **Overall length:** 7″. **Height:** 5″. **Weight:** 19.5 oz. (21 oz. w/neoprene grips). **Grips:** Neoprene or American walnut hand-checkered bulldog grips. **Sights:** Patridge-type, 9/64″ wide front; square-notched rear. **Finish:** High-luster Service Blue or stainless steel. **Hammer:** Spur or pocket.

**Prices:**
Blued finish Pug .............................. **$267.50**
Nickel (Electroless) Pug .............................. **289.50**
Also available:
**357 Mag.** (18 oz.), 2.2″ shrouded barrel .............. **$273.50**

BULLDOG PUG
44 SPECIAL

## OFF-DUTY

**SPECIFICATIONS**
**Calibers:** 22 LR, 22 Mag. and 38 Special. **Capacity:** 5 shots. **Type of action:** Single and double. **Barrel length:** 2″ shrouded. **Overall length:** 6¼″. **Height:** 4¼″. **Weight:** 16 oz. (38 Special); 19 oz. (22 LR & 22 Mag.). **Grips:** Walnut or combat. **Sights:** Patridge-type ramp front (with "red dot" feature); square-notch rear on stainless.

**Prices:**
Blued finish .............................. **$199.00**
Nickel (Electroless) 22 LR & 22 Mag. .............. **239.75**
In 38 Special .............................. **247.20**

OFF-DUTY 38 SPECIAL

## LADY ON-DUTY (not shown)
## $219.25

**SPECIFICATIONS**
**Calibers:** 32 S&W and 38 Special. **Capacity:** 6 shots (32 S&W), 5 shots (38 Special). **Barrel length:** 2″. **Overall length:** 6¼″. **Weight:** 16 oz. **Grips:** Rosewood.

## POLICE UNDERCOVER

**SPECIFICATIONS**
**Caliber:** 32 H&R Magnum and 38 Special. **Capacity:** 6 shots. **Type of action:** Single and double. **Barrel length:** 2″. **Height:** 4½″. **Weight:** 17½ oz. (2″ barrel) and 19 oz. (4″ barrel.) **Grips:** Checkered walnut panel. **Sights:** Patridge-type ramp front; square-notch rear. **Finish:** Blue.

**Prices:**
Blued .............................. **$237.75**
Nickel (Electroless) .............................. **252.00**

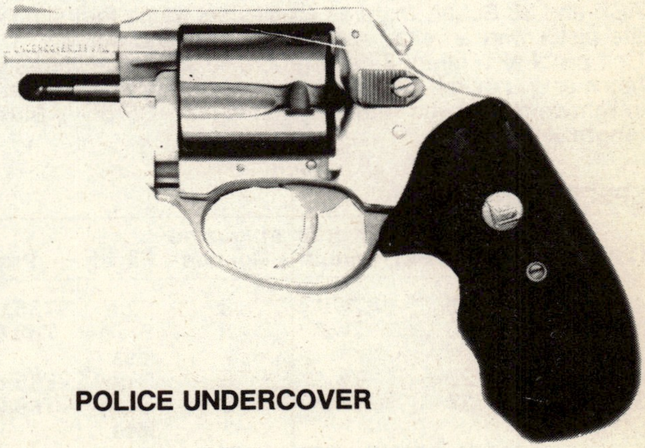

POLICE UNDERCOVER

# COLT AUTOMATIC PISTOLS

## DOUBLE EAGLE MK SERIES 90

**SPECIFICATIONS**
**Caliber:** 45 ACP
**Capacity:** 8 rounds
**Barrel lengths:** 5″ (Std.); 4¼″ (D.E. Combat Commander); 3½″ (D.E. Officer's ACP)
**Overall length:** 8½″ (Std.); 7¾″ (D.E. Combat Commander); 7¼″ (D.E. Officer's ACP)
**Weight:** 35 to 39 oz. (approx.)
**Sights:** WDS with sight radius 5¼″ (Officer's ACP) to 6½″ (Std.)
**Prices:**
**DOUBLE EAGLE** .......... **$727.00**
**D.E. COMBAT COMMANDER** .......... **727.00**
**D.E. OFFICER'S ACP** .......... **727.00**

**DOUBLE EAGLE**

**MODEL M1991A1**

## MODEL M1991A1 PISTOL

**SPECIFICATIONS**
**Caliber:** 45 ACP
**Capacity:** 7 rounds
**Barrel length:** 5″
**Overall length:** 8½″
**Sight radius:** 6½″
**Grips:** Black composition
**Finish:** Parkerized
**Features:** Custom-molded carry case
**Price: $538.00**

Also available:
**COMPACT M1991A1** with 3½″ barrel .......... **$538.00**
**COMMANDER M1991A1** with 4¼″ barrel and 7-round capacity .......... **538.00**

## COMBAT COMMANDER MKIV SERIES 80

The semiautomatic Combat Commander, available in 45 ACP and 38 Super, features an all-steel frame that supplies the pistol with an extra measure of heft and stability. This Colt pistol also offers 3-dot high-profile sights, lanyard-style hammer and thumb and beavertail grip safety. Also available in lightweight version with alloy frame (45 ACP only). **Barrel length:** 4¼″.

**SPECIFICATIONS**

| Caliber | Weight (ounces) | Overall Length | Magazine Rounds | Finish | Price |
|---|---|---|---|---|---|
| 45 ACP | 36 | 7¾″ | 8 | Blue | $735.00 |
| 45 ACP | 36 | 7¾″ | 8 | Stainless | 789.00 |
| 45 ACP LW | 27½ | 7¾″ | 8 | Blue | 735.00 |
| 38 Super | 37 | 7¾″ | 9 | Stainless | 789.00 |

**COMBAT COMMANDER**
**4¼″ barrel only**

# COLT AUTOMATIC PISTOLS

## MKIV SERIES 80

### GOLD CUP NATIONAL MATCH

**SPECIFICATIONS**
**Caliber:** 45 ACP
**Capacity:** 7 and 8 rounds
**Barrel length:** 5″ **Overall length:** 8½″
**Weight:** 39 oz.
**Sights:** Colt Elliason sights; adjustable rear for windage and elevation
**Hammer:** Serrated rounded hammer
**Stock:** Rubber combat
**Finish:** Colt blue, stainless or "Ultimate" bright stainless steel
**Prices:** $ **937.00** Blue
**1003.00** Stainless steel
**1073.00** Bright stainless
Also available:
**COMBAT ELITE** in 45 ACP or 38 Super; features Accro Adjustable sights, beavertail grip safety. **Price: $895.00**

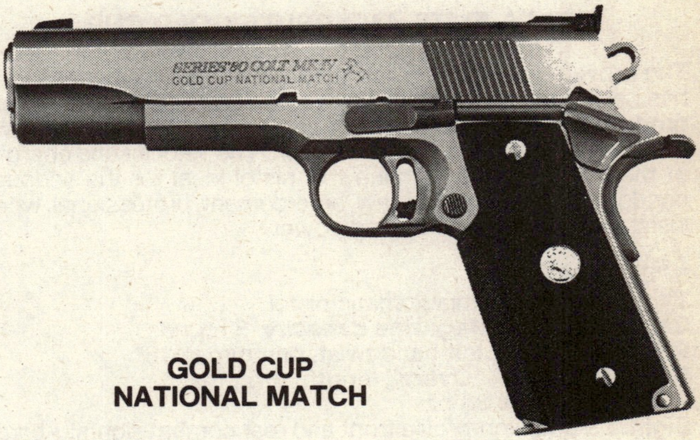


GOLD CUP
NATIONAL MATCH

GOVERNMENT MODEL

### GOVERNMENT MODEL MKIV SERIES 80 SEMIAUTOMATIC

These full-size automatic pistols with 5-inch barrels are available in 45 ACP and 38 Super. The Government Model's special features include high-profile 3-dot sights, grip and thumb safeties, and rubber combat stocks.

**SPECIFICATIONS**
**Calibers:** 38 Super and 45 ACP
**Capacity:** 9 rounds (38 Super); 8 rounds (45 ACP)
**Barrel length:** 5″ **Overall length:** 8½″
**Weight:** 38 oz. (45 ACP), 39 oz. (38 Super)
**Prices: $735.00** 45 ACP blue
**789.00** 45 ACP stainless
**863.00** 45 ACP bright stainless
**735.00** 38 Super blue
**789.00** 38 Super stainless
**863.00** 38 Super bright stainless

### GOVERNMENT MODEL 380 MKIV SERIES 80 SEMIAUTOMATIC

This scaled-down version of the 1911A1 Colt Government Model does not include a grip safety. It incorporates the use of a firing-pin safety to provide for a safe method to carry a round in the chamber in a "cocked-and-locked" mode. Available in matte stainless-steel finish with black composition stocks.

**SPECIFICATIONS**
**Caliber:** 380 ACP
**Magazine capacity:** 7 rounds
**Barrel length:** 3.25″ **Overall length:** 6″
**Height:** 4.4″
**Weight** : 21.75 oz. (empty)
**Sights:** Fixed ramp blade front; fixed square-notched rear
**Grip:** Composition stocks
**Prices: $462.00** Blue
**493.00** Stainless steel
Also available:
**POCKETLITE MODEL** (14¾ oz.), blue finish only. **$462.00**

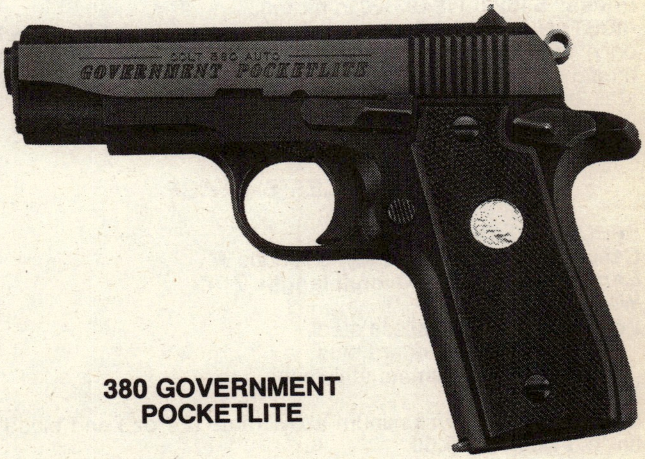


380 GOVERNMENT
POCKETLITE

# COLT AUTOMATIC PISTOLS

## MKIV SERIES 80

### DELTA ELITE AND DELTA GOLD CUP

The proven design and reliability of Colt's Government Model has been combined with the powerful 10mm auto cartridge to produce a highly effective shooting system for hunting, law enforcement and personal protection. The velocity and energy of the 10mm cartridge make this pistol ideal for the serious handgun hunter and the law enforcement professional who insist on downrange stopping power.

**SPECIFICATIONS**
**Type:** 0 Frame, semiautomatic pistol
**Caliber:** 10mm **Magazine capacity:** 8 rounds
**Rifling:** 6 groove, left-hand twist, one turn in 16″
**Barrel length:** 5″ **Overall length:** 8½″
**Weight (empty):** 38 oz.
**Sights:** 3-dot, high-profile front and rear combat sights; Accro rear sight adjustable for windage and elevation (on Delta Gold Cup only)
**Sight radius:** 6½″ (3-dot sight system), 6¾″ (adjustable sights)
**Grips:** Rubber combat stocks with Delta medallion
**Safety:** Trigger safety lock (thumb safety) is located on left-hand side of receiver; grip safety is located on backstrap; internal firing-pin safety
**Price: $807.00 ($860.00 Stainless)**

### COLT MUSTANG .380

This backup automatic has four times the knockdown power of most 25 ACP automatics. It is a smaller version of the 380 Government Model.

**SPECIFICATIONS**
**Caliber:** 380 ACP **Capacity:** 6 rounds
**Barrel length:** 2¾″ **Overall length:** 5½″
**Height:** 3.9″ **Weight:** 18.5 oz.
**Prices: $462.00** Standard, blue
**493.00** Stainless steel
Also available:
**MUSTANG POCKETLITE 380** with aluminum alloy receiver; ½″ shorter than standard Govt. 380; weighs only 12.5 oz. **Prices: $462.00 ($493.00** in nickel).
**MUSTANG PLUS II** features full grip length (Govt. 380 model only) with shorter compact barrel and slide (Mustang .380 model only); **weight:** 20 oz. **Prices: $443.00** blue; **$473.00** stainless steel.

### COLT OFFICER'S 45 ACP

**SPECIFICATIONS**
**Caliber:** 45 ACP **Capacity:** 6 rounds
**Barrel length:** 3½″ **Overall length:** 7¼″
**Weight:** 34 oz.
**Prices: $789.00** Stainless steel
**735.00** Standard blue
**863.00** Ultimate stainless
Also available:
**OFFICER'S LW** w/aluminum alloy frame (24 oz.) and blued finish. **Price: $735.00**

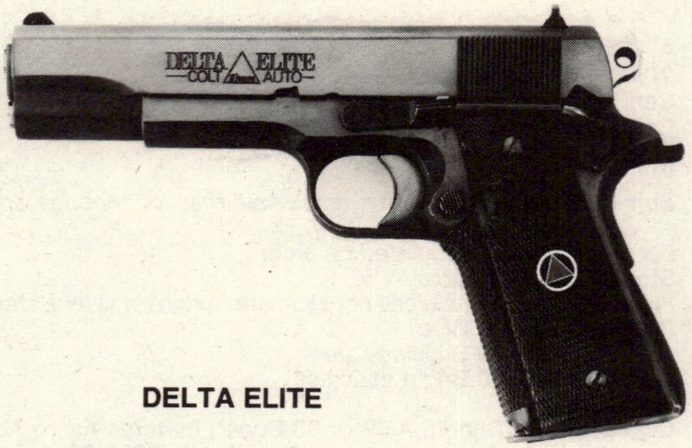


**DELTA ELITE**

Also available:
**DELTA GOLD CUP.** Same specifications as Delta Elite, except 39 oz. weight and 6¾″ sight radius. Stainless. **$1027.00**

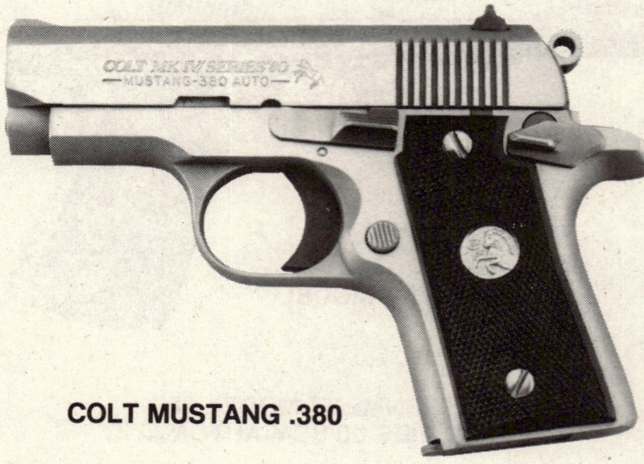


**COLT MUSTANG .380**

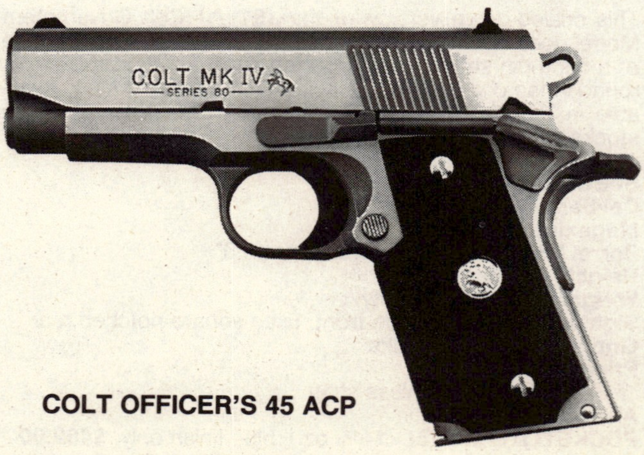


**COLT OFFICER'S 45 ACP**

# COLT PISTOLS/REVOLVERS

## CADET SEMIAUTOMATIC DA

**SPECIFICATIONS**
**Caliber:** 22 LR **Capacity:** 10 rounds
**Barrel length:** $4\frac{1}{2}$″ **Overall length:** $8\frac{5}{8}$″
**Weight:** $33\frac{1}{2}$ oz.
**Sight radius:** 5.75″
**Grips:** Rubber polymer
**Finish:** Stainless steel
**Price: $248.00**
Also available:
**COLT .22 TARGET** w/6″ barrel. **Weight:** $40\frac{1}{2}$ oz. **Sight radius:** $9\frac{1}{4}$″. **Sights:** Removable front, adjustable rear. **Price:** To be determined.

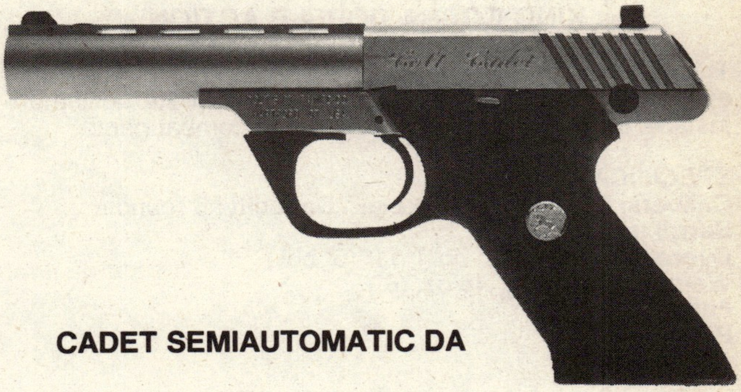

CADET SEMIAUTOMATIC DA

## DETECTIVE SPECIAL

Introduced in 1927, the Colt Detective Special has earned a legendary reputation in the law enforcement field and for personal protection. Constructed of forged, high-strength alloy steel, the updated Detective Special is based on the Colt "D" frame.

**SPECIFICATIONS**
**Caliber:** 38 Special **Capacity:** 6 rounds
**Barrel length:** 2″ **Overall length:** 7″
**Weight:** 21 oz.
**Sights:** Ramp front
**Grips:** Black composition
**Finish:** Blue
**Price: $400.00**
Also available:
**POLICE POSITIVE. Barrel length:** 4″. **Overall length:** 9″. **Weight:** 25 oz. **Price: $400.00**

DETECTIVE SPECIAL

SINGLE ACTION ARMY
(Nickel Finish)

## SINGLE ACTION ARMY REVOLVER

Colt's maintains the tradition of quality and innovation that Samuel Colt began more than a century and a half ago. Single Action Army revolvers continue to be highly prized collectible arms and are offered in full nickel finish or in Royal Blue with color casehardened frame, without engraving, unless otherwise specified by the purchaser. Grips are American walnut.
**Price:** . . . . . . . . . . . . . . . . . . . . . . . . . . . . . . . . . . **$1213.00**

**SINGLE ACTION ARMY SPECIFICATIONS**

| Caliber | Bbl. Length (inches) | Finish | Approx. Weight (ozs.) | O/A Length (inches) | Grips | Medal-lions |
|---|---|---|---|---|---|---|
| 45LC | $4\frac{3}{4}$ | CC/B | 40 | $10\frac{1}{4}$ | BCE | Gold |
| 45LC | $4\frac{3}{4}$ | N | 40 | $10\frac{1}{4}$ | BCE | Nickel |
| 45LC | $5\frac{1}{2}$ | CC/B | 42 | 11 | BCE | Gold |
| 45LC | $5\frac{1}{2}$ | N | 42 | 11 | BCE | Nickel |
| 45LC | $7\frac{1}{2}$ | CC/B | 43 | 13 | BCE | Gold |
| 45LC | $7\frac{1}{2}$ | N | 43 | 13 | BCE | Nickel |
| 44-40 | $4\frac{3}{4}$ | CC/B | 40 | $10\frac{1}{4}$ | BCE | Gold |
| 44-40 | $4\frac{3}{4}$ | N | 40 | $10\frac{1}{4}$ | BCE | Nickel |
| 44-40 | $5\frac{1}{2}$ | CC/B | 42 | 11 | BCE | Gold |
| 44-40 | $5\frac{1}{2}$ | N | 42 | 11 | BCE | Nickel |
| 44-40 | $7\frac{1}{2}$ | CC/B | 43 | 13 | BCE | Gold |
| 44-40 | $7\frac{1}{2}$ | N | 43 | 13 | BCE | Nickel |
| 38-40 | $4\frac{3}{4}$ | CC/B | 40 | $10\frac{1}{4}$ | BCE | Gold |
| 38-40 | $4\frac{3}{4}$ | N | 40 | $10\frac{1}{4}$ | BCE | Nickel |
| 38-40 | $5\frac{1}{2}$ | CC/B | 42 | 11 | BCE | Gold |
| 38-40 | $5\frac{1}{2}$ | N | 42 | 11 | BCE | Nickel |

N—Nickel CC/B—Colorcase frame/Royal Blue cylinder & barrel
BCE—Black Composite Eagle

## KING COBRA DOUBLE ACTION

This "snake" revolver features a solid barrel rib, full-length ejector rod housing, red ramp front sight, white outline adjustable rear sight and "gripper" rubber combat grips.

**SPECIFICATIONS**
**Calibers:** 357 Mag./38 Special **Capacity:** 6 rounds
**Barrel length:** 4″ or 6″
**Overall length:** 9″ (4″ bbl.); 11″ (6″ bbl.)
**Weight:** 42 oz. (4″); 46 oz. (6″)
**Finish:** Stainless
**Price: $455.00**

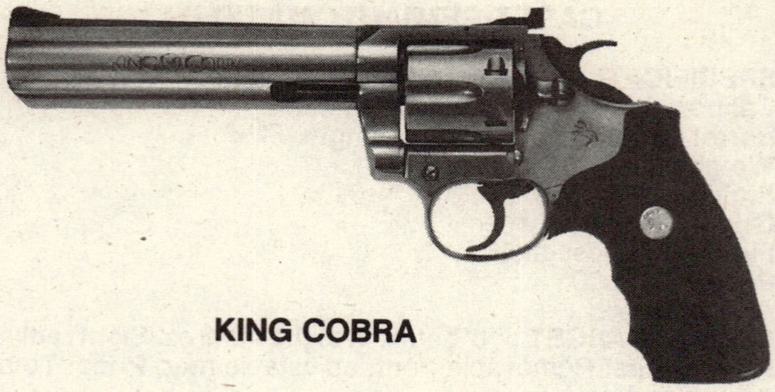

**KING COBRA**

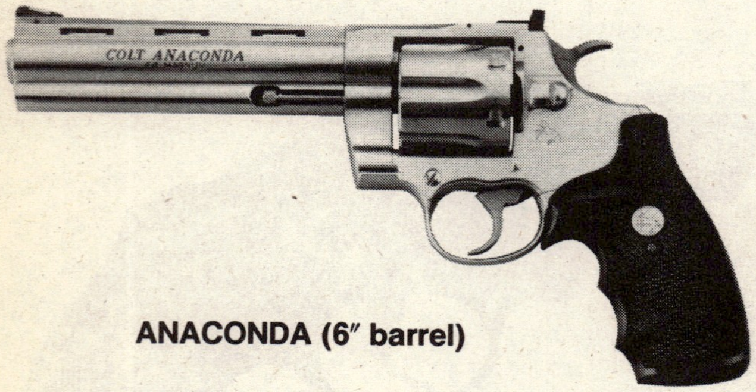


**ANACONDA (6″ barrel)**

## ANACONDA DOUBLE ACTION

**SPECIFICATIONS**
**Calibers:** 44 Magnum/44 Special and 45 Colt (6″ and 8″ barrel only)
**Capacity:** 6 rounds
**Barrel length:** 4″, 6″ or 8″
**Overall length:** $9\frac{5}{8}$″, $11\frac{5}{8}$″, $13\frac{5}{8}$″
**Weight:** 47 oz. (4″), 53 oz. (6″), 59 oz. (8″)
**Sights:** Red insert front; adjustable white outline rear
**Sight radius:** $5\frac{3}{4}$″ (4″), $7\frac{3}{4}$″ (6″), $9\frac{3}{4}$″ (8″)
**Grips:** Black neoprene combat-style with finger grooves
**Finish:** Matte stainless steel
**Price: $612.00**

**MODEL 38SF-VI**

## COLT MODEL 38 SF-VI

**SPECIFICATIONS**
**Caliber:** 38 Special **Capacity:** 6 rounds
**Barrel length:** 2″ **Overall length:** 7″
**Weight:** 21 oz.
**Sight radius:** 4″
**Grips:** Black composition
**Finish:** Stainless steel
**Price:** To be determined

## PYTHON PREMIUM DOUBLE ACTION

The Colt Python revolver, suitable for hunting, target shooting and police use, is chambered for the powerful 357 Magnum cartridge. Python features include ventilated rib, fast cocking, wide-spur hammer, trigger and rubber grips, adjustable rear and ramp-type front sights, grooved.

**SPECIFICATIONS**
**Calibers:** 357 Mag./38 Special
**Barrel length:** 4″, 6″ or 8″
**Overall length:** $9\frac{1}{2}$″, $11\frac{1}{2}$″, $13\frac{1}{2}$″
**Weight:** 38 oz. (4″); $43\frac{1}{2}$ oz. (6″); 48 oz. (8″)
**Stocks:** Rubber combat (4″) or rubber target (6″, 8″)
**Finish:** Colt high-polish royal blue, stainless steel and "Ultimate" bright stainless steel

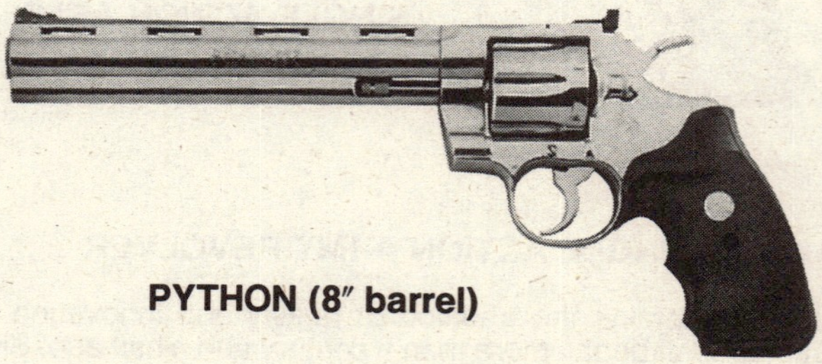

**PYTHON (8″ barrel)**

**Prices: $815.00** Royal Blue
**904.00** Stainless steel
**935.00** "Ultimate" Bright Stainless Steel

# COONAN ARMS

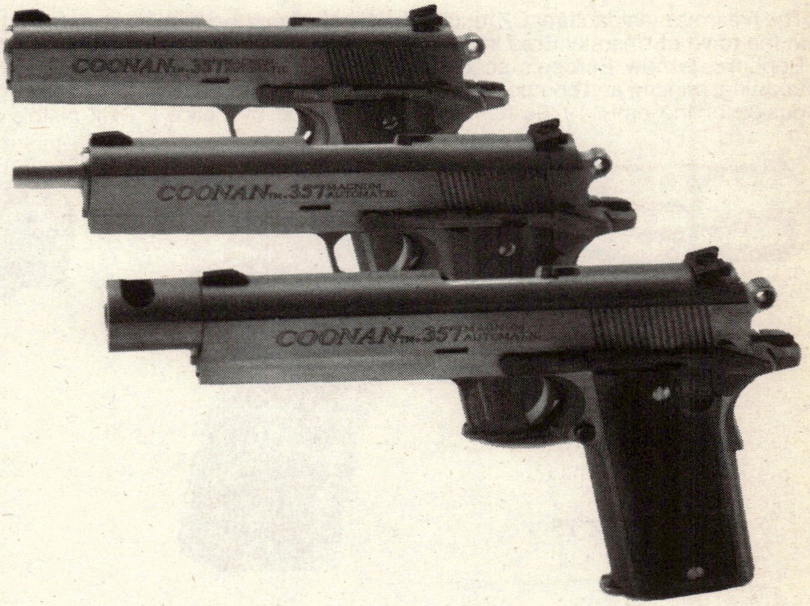

**357 MAGNUM PISTOL**
**5″ Barrel (top)**
**6″ Barrel (middle)**
**Compensated Barrel (bottom)**

## 357 MAGNUM PISTOL

**SPECIFICATIONS**
**Caliber:** 357 Magnum
**Magazine capacity:** 7 rounds + 1
**Barrel length:** 5″ (6″ or Compensated barrel optional)
**Overall length:** 8.3″
**Weight:** 48 oz. (loaded)
**Height:** 5.6″
**Width:** 1.3″
**Sights:** Ramp front; fixed rear, adjustable for windage only
**Grips:** Smooth black walnut (checkered grips optional)
**Finish:** Stainless steel and alloy steel
**Features:** Linkless barrel; recoil-operated; extended slide catch and thumb lock
**Prices:** With 5″ barrel . . . . . . . . . . . . . . . . . . . . . . **$720.00**
With 6″ barrel . . . . . . . . . . . . . . . . . . . . . . . . . . . **755.00**
With Compensated barrel . . . . . . . . . . . . . . . . . . . **999.00**

## "CADET" COMPACT MODEL

**SPECIFICATIONS**
**Caliber:** 357 Magnum
**Magazine capacity:** 6 rounds + 1
**Barrel length:** 3.9″
**Overall length:** 7.8″
**Weight:** 39 oz.
**Height:** 5.3″
**Width:** 1.3″
**Sights:** Ramp front; fixed rear, adjustable for windage only
**Grips:** Smooth black walnut
**Features:** Linkless bull barrel; full-length guide rod; recoil-operated (Browning falling-block design); extended slide catch and thumb lock for one-hand operation
**Price:** . . . . . . . . . . . . . . . . . . . . . . . . . . . . . . . . . **$841.00**

**"CADET" COMPACT**

# CZ PISTOLS

The firearms manufacturer CZ, established in 1936 and located in the town of Uhersky Brod in the eastern part of the Czech Republic, is now Europe's second largest manufacturer of sporting, hunting and competitive firearms. The classic CZ 75 design of the early 1970s has been widely used by police departments in more countries around the world than any other firearm. It has been unavailable in the U.S. for many years because of government prohibitions against importing arms from Communist countries. With the lifting of the Iron Curtain, CZ pistols can now be sold in this country once again.

**CZ 75**

**CZ 75 COMPACT**

**MODEL CZ 75**
**$499.00 ($549.00 in Nickel)**

**SPECIFICATIONS**
**Caliber:** 9mm Luger
**Capacity:** 10 shots
**Barrel length:** 4.7″ **Overall length:** 8.1″
**Weight:** 34.3 oz.
**Grips:** Black polymer
**Finish:** Black polymer or nickel

Also available:
**MODEL CZ 75 COMPACT. Weight:** 32 oz. **Barrel:** 3.9″. **Capacity:** 10 shots. **Grips:** Checkered walnut.
**Price:** . . . . . . . . . . . . . . . . . . . . . . . . . . . . . . . . . . **$519.00**
**MODEL CZ 85.** Same as above, except for ambidextrous slide release and safety levers. **Price:** . . . . . . . . **$529.00**
**MODEL CZ 85 COMBAT.** Same as above, but features adjustable rear sight, extended magazine release button, no magazine break. **Price:** . . . . . . . . . . . . . . . . . . . . **$619.00**

**CZ 85 STANDARD**

**MODEL CZ 83**
**$389.00**

**SPECIFICATIONS**
**Caliber:** 380 (9mm Browning)
**Capacity:** 10 shots
**Barrel length:** 3.8″
**Weight:** 26.2 oz.
**Finish:** High-polish blue

**CZ 83**

# DAEWOO PISTOLS

## MODEL DP51
**$400.00**

**SPECIFICATIONS**
**Caliber:** 9mm Parabellum
**Capacity:** 10 rounds
**Barrel length:** 4.1 **Overall length:** 7 1/2″
**Weight:** 28 oz.
**Muzzle velocity:** 1150 fps
**Sights:** Blade front (1/8″); square notch rear, drift adjustable with 3 self-luminous dots
**Safety:** Ambidextrous manual safety, automatic firing-pin block
**Feature:** Patented Fastfire action with light 5–6 lb. trigger pull for first-shot accuracy

Also available:
**MODEL DP51C COMPACT.** 3.6″ barrel (7″ overall). **Weight:** 26 oz. **Height:** 4 1/2″. **Price: $445.00**
**MODEL DP51S.** Same specifications as above, except weight is 27 oz., height is 4.8″.

MODEL DP51C COMPACT

## MODEL DH40
**$450.00**

**SPECIFICATIONS**
**Caliber:** 40 S&W
**Capacity:** 10 rounds
**Barrel length:** 4.1″ **Overall length:** 7 1/2″
**Weight:** 32 oz. **Height:** 4.8″
**Width:** 1.38″
**Firing mode:** Double, single or FastFire, Tri-Action

MODEL DH40

## MODEL DH380 (not shown)
**$410.00**

**SPECIFICATIONS**
**Caliber:** 380 ACP
**Capacity:** 8 rounds
**Barrel length:** 3.8″ **Overall length:** 6.7″
**Weight:** 24 oz. **Height:** 4.1″
**Width:** 1.2″

## MODEL DP52 PISTOL
**$380.00**

**SPECIFICATIONS**
**Caliber:** 22 LR
**Capacity:** 10 rounds
**Barrel length:** 3.8″ **Overall length:** 6.7″
**Weight:** 23 oz.
**Width:** 1.18″
**Sights:** 1/8″ front blade; drift adjustable rear (3 white-dot system)

MODEL DP52

# DAVIS PISTOLS

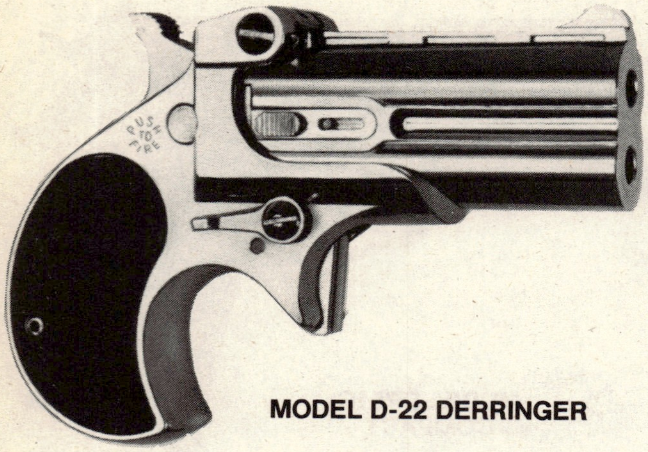

MODEL D-22 DERRINGER

## D-SERIES DERRINGERS
## $75.00

**SPECIFICATIONS**
**Calibers:** 22 LR, 22 Mag., 25 Auto, 32 Auto
**Capacity:** 2 shot
**Barrel length:** 2.4″
**Overall length:** 4″
**Height:** 2.8″
**Weight:** 9.5 oz.
**Grips:** Laminated wood
**Finish:** Black teflon or chrome

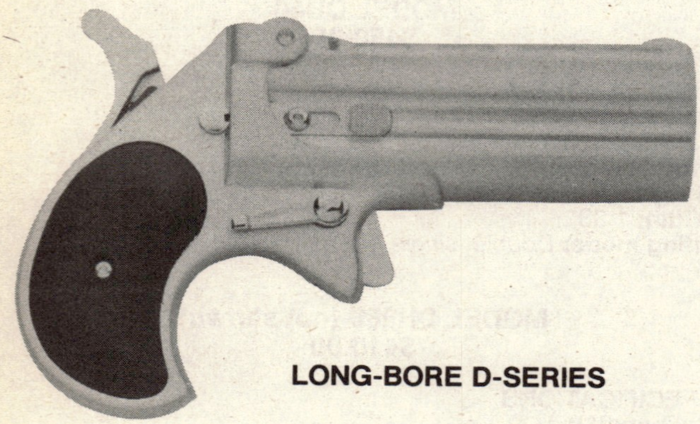

LONG-BORE D-SERIES

## LONG-BORE D-SERIES
## $104.00

**SPECIFICATIONS**
**Calibers:** 22 Mag., 9mm
**Capacity:** 2 rounds
**Barrel length:** 3.5″
**Overall length:** 5.4″
**Overall height:** 3.31″
**Weight:** 16 oz.

Also available:
**BIG-BORE 38 SPECIAL D-SERIES. Calibers:** 32 H&R Magnum, 38 Special. **Barrel length:** 2.75″. **Overall length:** 4.65″. **Weight:** 14 oz. **Price: $98.00**

## MODEL P-32
## $87.50

**SPECIFICATIONS**
**Caliber:** 32 Auto
**Magazine capacity:** 6 rounds
**Barrel length:** 2.8″ **Overall length:** 5.4″
**Height:** 4″ **Weight** (empty): 22 oz.
**Grips:** Laminated wood
**Finish:** Black teflon or chrome

## MODEL P-380 (not shown)
## $98.00

**SPECIFICATIONS**
**Caliber:** 380 Auto
**Magazine capacity:** 5 rounds
**Barrel length:** 2.8″
**Overall length:** 5.4″
**Height:** 4″
**Weight:** 22 oz. (empty)

MODEL P-32

## LASERAIM ARMS

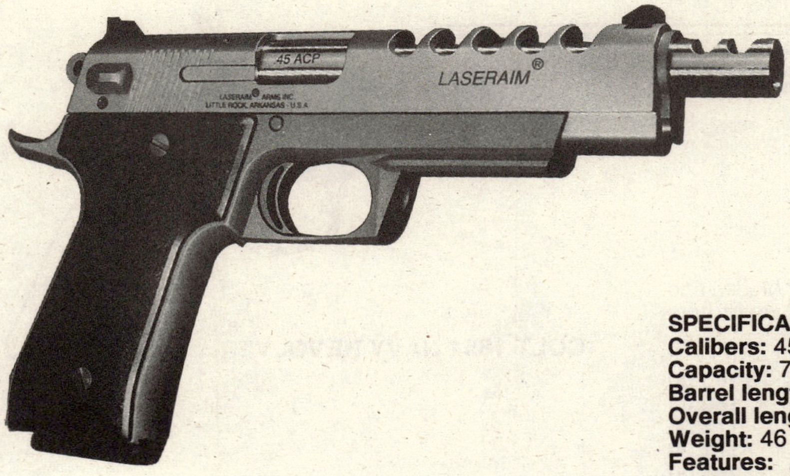


### LASERAIM SERIES I PISTOLS

The Series I pistol features a dual port compensated barrel and vented slide to reduce recoil and improve control. Other features include stainless-steel construction, ramped barrel, accurized barrel bushing and fixed sights (Laseraim's "HOT-DOT" sight or Auto Illusion electronic red dot sight available as options).

**SPECIFICATIONS**
**Calibers:** 45 ACP, 10mm
**Capacity:** 7+1 (45 ACP) and 8+1 (10mm)
**Barrel lengths:** 3⅞" and 5½"
**Overall length:** 8¾" (3⅞") and 10½"
**Weight:** 46 oz. (3⅞") and 52 oz.
**Features:** Adjustable Millet sights, ambidextrous safety, beavertail tang, non-glare slide serration, beveled magazine well, extended slide release
**Price:** . . . . . . . . $629.00
w/Adjustable Sights) . . . . . . . . 659.00

Also available:
**DREAM TEAM** w/Laseraim Laser, fixed sights, HOTDOT . . . . . . . . **$794.95**

### LASERAIM SERIES III PISTOLS

The Series III pistol features a ported barrel and slide to reduce recoil and improve control. Includes stainless-steel construction, ramped barrel, accurized barrel bushing and comes with adjustable and laser sights (optional).

**SPECIFICATIONS**
**Calibers:** 45 ACP and 10mm
**Capacity:** 8+1 (10mm) and 7+1 (45 ACP)
**Barrel length:** 5" **Overall length:** 7⅝"
**Weight:** 43 oz.
**Overall height:** 5⅝"
**Features:** Same as Series I
**Price:** . . . . . . . . **$599.00**
w/Adjustable Sights . . . . . . . . **629.00**

Also available:
**SERIES II** w/3⅜" or 5" barrel, fixed sights . . . . . . . **$499.00**
w/Adjustable sights, add . . . . . . . . **30.00**

# EMF/DAKOTA

## SINGLE ACTION REVOLVERS

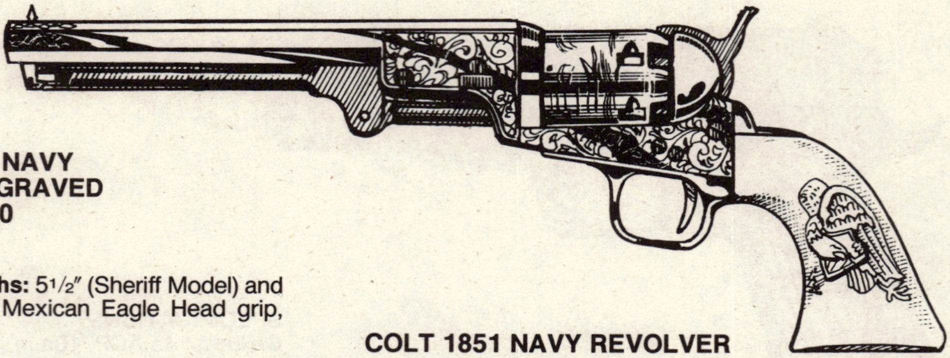

COLT 1851 NAVY REVOLVER

**COLT 1851 NAVY FACTORY ENGRAVED $339.00**

**SPECIFICATIONS**
**Calibers:** 36 and 44. **Barrel lengths:** 5 1/2" (Sheriff Model) and 7 1/2". **Features:** Polyivory grips, Mexican Eagle Head grip, brass or steel.
Also available:

| | |
|---|---|
| **1851 Navy Brass Frame** | **$140.00** |
| Engraved | **160.00** |
| With nickel trim | **172.00** |
| With steel frame | **172.00** |
| Engraved | **285.00** |

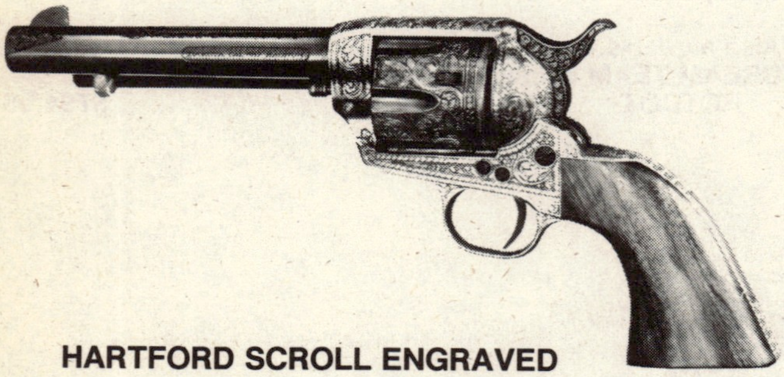

HARTFORD SCROLL ENGRAVED

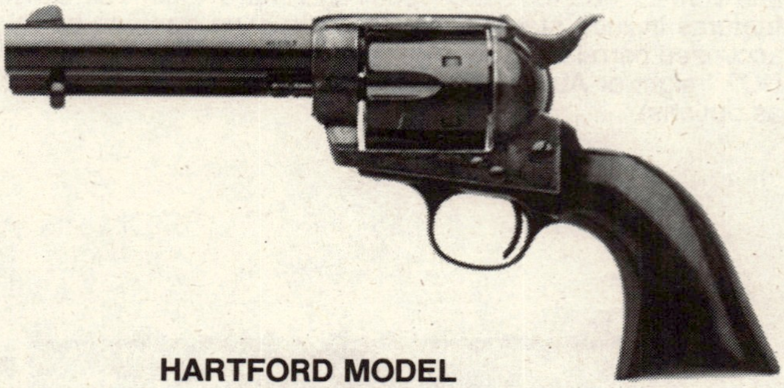

HARTFORD MODEL

**HARTFORD SCROLL ENGRAVED SINGLE ACTION REVOLVER $840.00 ($1000.00 in Nickel)**

**SPECIFICATIONS**
**Calibers:** 22, 45 Long Colt, 357 Magnum, 44-40. **Barrel lengths:** 4 5/8", 5 1/2" and 7 1/2". **Features:** Classic original-type scroll engraving.

**HARTFORD MODELS $600.00 ($680.00 in Nickel)**

EMF's Hartford Single Action revolvers are available in the following calibers: 32-20, 38-40, 44-40, 44 Special and 45 Long Colt. **Barrel lengths:** 4 3/4", 5 1/2" and 7 1/2". All models feature steel back straps, trigger guards and forged frame. Identical to the original Colts.

**HARTFORD MODELS "CAVALRY COLT" AND "ARTILLERY" $655.00**

The Model 1873 Government Model Cavalry revolver is an exact reproduction of the original Colt made for the U.S. Cavalry in caliber 45 Long Colt with barrel length of 7 1/2". The Artillery Model has 5 1/2" barrel.
Also available:
**Sheriff's Model** (3 1/2" barrel) .................... **$655.00**

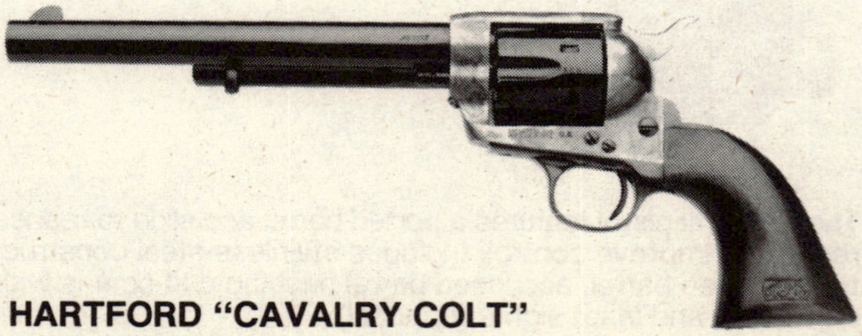

HARTFORD "CAVALRY COLT"

# EMF/DAKOTA

**MODEL 1873 $460.00**
**($560.00 w/Extra Cylinder)**

**SPECIFICATIONS**
**Calibers:** 44-40, 357 Mag., 45 Long Colt. **Barrel lengths:** 4³/₄″, 5¹/₂″, 7¹/₂″. **Finish:** Engraved models, blue or nickel. **Special feature:** Each gun is fitted with second caliber.

**DAKOTA TARGET**
**$500.00**

**SPECIFICATIONS**
**Calibers:** 45 Long Colt, 357 Magnum, 22 LR. **Barrel lengths:** 5¹/₂″ and 7¹/₂″. **Finish:** Polished blue. **Special features:** Casehardened frame, one-piece walnut grips, brass back strap, ramp front blade target sight and adjustable rear sight.

**1873 DAKOTA SINGLE ACTION**
**REVOLVER $460.00 ($585.00 in Nickel)**

**SPECIFICATIONS**
**Calibers:** 357 Mag., 44-40, 45 Long Colt. **Barrel lengths:** 4³/₄″, 5¹/₂″ and 7¹/₂″. **Finish:** Blued, casehardened frame. **Grips:** One-piece walnut. **Features:** Set screw for cylinder pin release; parts are interchangeable with early Colts.

**PINKERTON DETECTIVE SA**
**$680.00**

**SPECIFICATIONS**
**Caliber:** 45 Long Colt. **Barrel length:** 4″. **Grip:** Bird's-head.

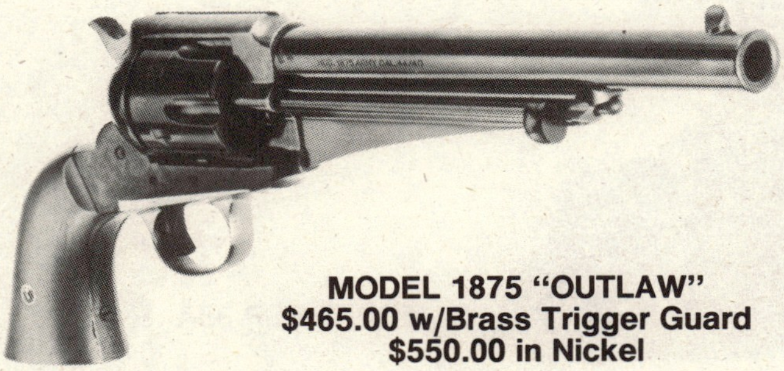

**MODEL 1875 "OUTLAW"**
**$465.00 w/Brass Trigger Guard**
**$550.00 in Nickel**

**SPECIFICATIONS**
**Calibers:** 44-40, 45 Long Colt, 357. **Barrel length:** 5¹/₂″ and 7¹/₂″. **Finish:** Blue or nickel. **Special features:** Casehardened frame, walnut grips; an exact replica of the Remington No. 3 revolver produced from 1875 to 1889.

| | |
|---|---|
| Factory Engraved Model (7¹/₂″ bbl.) | **$600.00** |
| In nickel | **710.00** |
| With steel trigger guard | **475.00** |

**MODEL 1890 REMINGTON POLICE**
**$470.00 w/Brass Trigger Guard**
**$560.00 in Nickel**

**SPECIFICATIONS**
**Calibers:** 44-40, 45 Long Colt and 357 Magnum. **Barrel length:** 5³/₄″. **Finish:** Blue or nickel. **Features:** Original design (1891–1894) with lanyard ring in buttstock; casehardened frame; walnut grips.

| | |
|---|---|
| Engraved Model | **$620.00** |
| In nickel | **725.00** |
| With steel trigger guard | **480.00** |

# ERMA TARGET ARMS

## MODEL 777 SPORTING REVOLVER

**SPECIFICATIONS**
**Caliber:** 357 Magnum
**Capacity:** 6 cartridges
**Barrel length:** 4″ and 5½″
**Overall length:** 9.7″ and 11.3″
**Weight:** 43.7 oz. w/5½″ barrel
**Sight radius:** 6.4″ and 8″
**Grip:** Checkered walnut
**Price:** $1019.00

Also available:
**MODEL 773 MATCH** (32 S&W Wadcutter). Features 6″ barrel, 6-shot capacity, adjustable match grip, micrometer rear sight (adjustable for windage and elevation), interchangeable front and rear sight blades, adjustable trigger and polished blued finish. **Weight:** 47.3 oz. **Price:** . . . **$1068.00**

**MODEL 777 STANDARD**

**MODEL ESP 85A JUNIOR 22 LR**
**$1295.00**

**MODEL ESP 85A**

## MODEL ESP 85A AUTOLOADING COMPETITION PISTOLS

**SPECIFICATIONS**
**Caliber:** 22 LR or 32 S&W Wadcutter
**Action:** Semiautomatic
**Capacity:** 5 cartridges (8 in 22 LR optional)
**Barrel length:** 6″
**Overall length:** 10″
**Weight:** 37 oz.
**Sight radius:** 7.8″
**Sights:** Micrometer rear sight; fully adjustable interchangeable front and rear sight blade (.13/.16″)
**Grip:** Checkered walnut grip with thumbrest
**Prices:**
**ESP 85A MATCH** 32 S&W . . . . . . . . . . **$1790.00**
Target adjustable grip, **add** . . . . . . . . . . **180.50**
Left hand, **add** . . . . . . . . . . **203.25**
**ESP 85A MATCH** 22 LR . . . . . . . . . . **1695.00**
**ESP 85A CHROME MATCH** 22 LR . . . . . . . . . . **1890.00**
In 32 S&W . . . . . . . . . . **2095.00**
**Conversion Units** 22 LR . . . . . . . . . . **882.00**
In 32 S&W . . . . . . . . . . **1068.00**
**Chrome Slide** (22 LR) . . . . . . . . . . **1068.00**
In 32 S&W . . . . . . . . . . **1253.00**

# EUROPEAN AMERICAN ARMORY

**ASTRA MODEL A-70**
**$360.00 (Blue)**
**$385.00 (Nickel or Stainless Steel)**

**SPECIFICATIONS**
**Calibers:** 9mm and 40 S&W
**Capacity:** 8 rounds (9mm), 7 rounds (40 S&W)
**Barrel length:** 3½″
**Overall length:** 6½″
**Weight:** 23.3 oz.
**Finish:** Blue, nickel or stainless steel

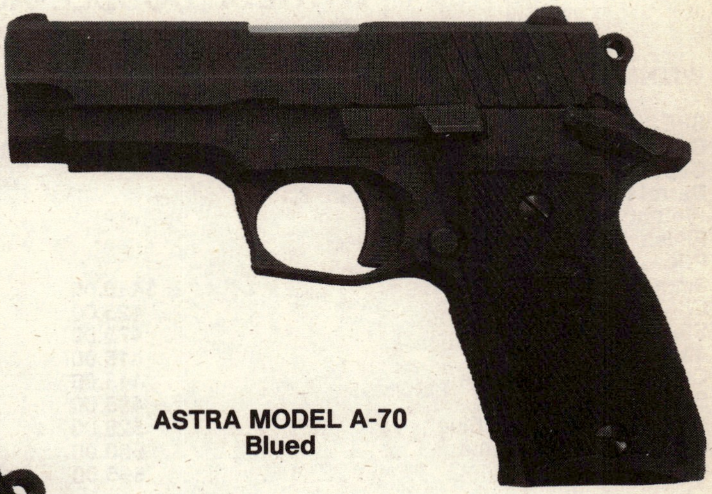

**ASTRA MODEL A-70**
**Blued**

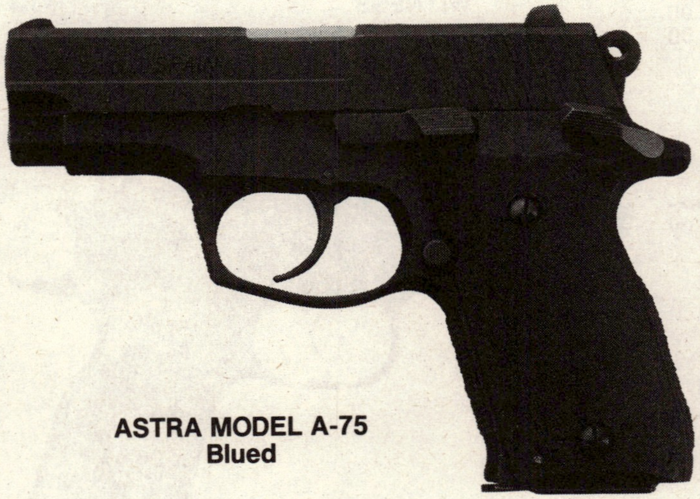

**ASTRA MODEL A-75**
**Blued**

**ASTRA MODEL A-75**
**$415.00 (Blue)**
**$445.00 (Nickel or Stainless Steel)**

**SPECIFICATIONS**
**Calibers:** 9mm, 40 S&W and 45 ACP
**Capacity:** 8 rounds (7 in 45 ACP & 40 S&W)
**Barrel length:** 3½″
**Overall length:** 6½″
**Weight:** 31 oz. (23½ oz. in Featherweight model)
**Finish:** Blue, nickel or stainless steel
Also available:
**Featherweight 9mm** . . . . . . . . . . . . . . . . . . . . **$445.00**

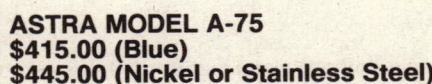

**ASTRA MODEL A-100**
**$445.00 (Blue)**
**$475.00 (Nickel or Stainless Steel)**
**$475.00 (Featherweight 9mm)**

**SPECIFICATIONS**
**Calibers:** 9mm, 40 S&W and 45 ACP
**Capacity:** 10 rounds
**Barrel length:** 3.75″
**Overall length:** 7″
**Weight:** 34 oz.
**Finish:** Blue, nickel or stainless steel

**ASTRA MODEL A-100**
**Blued**

# EUROPEAN AMERICAN ARMORY

## WITNESS DOUBLE-ACTION PISTOLS

### WITNESS

**SPECIFICATIONS**
**Calibers:** 9mm, 38 Super, 40 S&W and 45 ACP
**Capacity:** 10 rounds
**Barrel length:** 4½″ **Overall length:** 8.1″
**Weight:** 33 oz.
**Finish:** Blue, chrome, stainless steel
**Prices:**

| | |
|---|---|
| **9mm** Blue | **$410.00** |
| Chrome or blue/chrome | **425.00** |
| Stainless steel | **475.00** |
| **40 S&W** Blue | **415.00** |
| Chrome or blue/chrome | **445.00** |
| Stainless steel | **495.00** |
| **45 ACP or 38 Super** Blue | **525.00** |
| Chrome or blue/chrome | **550.00** |
| Stainless steel | **595.00** |

**WITNESS**

### WITNESS FAB

This all-steel semiautomatic pistol features a special ambidextrous hammer drop safety/decocker system now required by many law enforcement agencies.

**SPECIFICATIONS**
**Calibers:** 9mm, 40 S&W, 45 ACP (full size only)
**Capacity:** 10 rounds
**Barrel length:** 4½″ (3⅝″ Compact)
**Overall length:** 8.1″ (4½″ Compact)
**Weight:** 33 oz. (30 oz. Compact)
**Finish:** Blue, hard chrome or Duo-Tone
**Optional:** Tritium night sights; extended magazine release; rubber grips
**Prices:**

| | |
|---|---|
| **9mm** Blue (full and Compact) | **$395.00** |
| **40 S&W** Blue (full and Compact) | **425.00** |
| **45 ACP Blue** | **475.00** |

**WITNESS FAB**

**WITNESS GOLD TEAM**

### WITNESS GOLD TEAM

**SPECIFICATIONS**
**Calibers:** 9mm, 40 S&W, 38 Super, 9×21mm, 45 ACP
**Capacity:** 10 rounds
**Barrel length:** 5¼″ **Overall length:** 10½″
**Weight:** 38 oz.
**Finish:** Hard chrome
**Features:** Triple chamber comp, S/A trigger, extended safety competition hammer, checkered front strap and backstrap, low-profile competition grips, square trigger guard
**Price:** . . . . . . **$2195.00**

DEMAND
"THE DIFFERENCE"®
THE
D
DIFFERENCE
Lifetime
Replacement Coverage!
Ask your dealer for details
"The Difference"® is not a manufacturer's warranty.

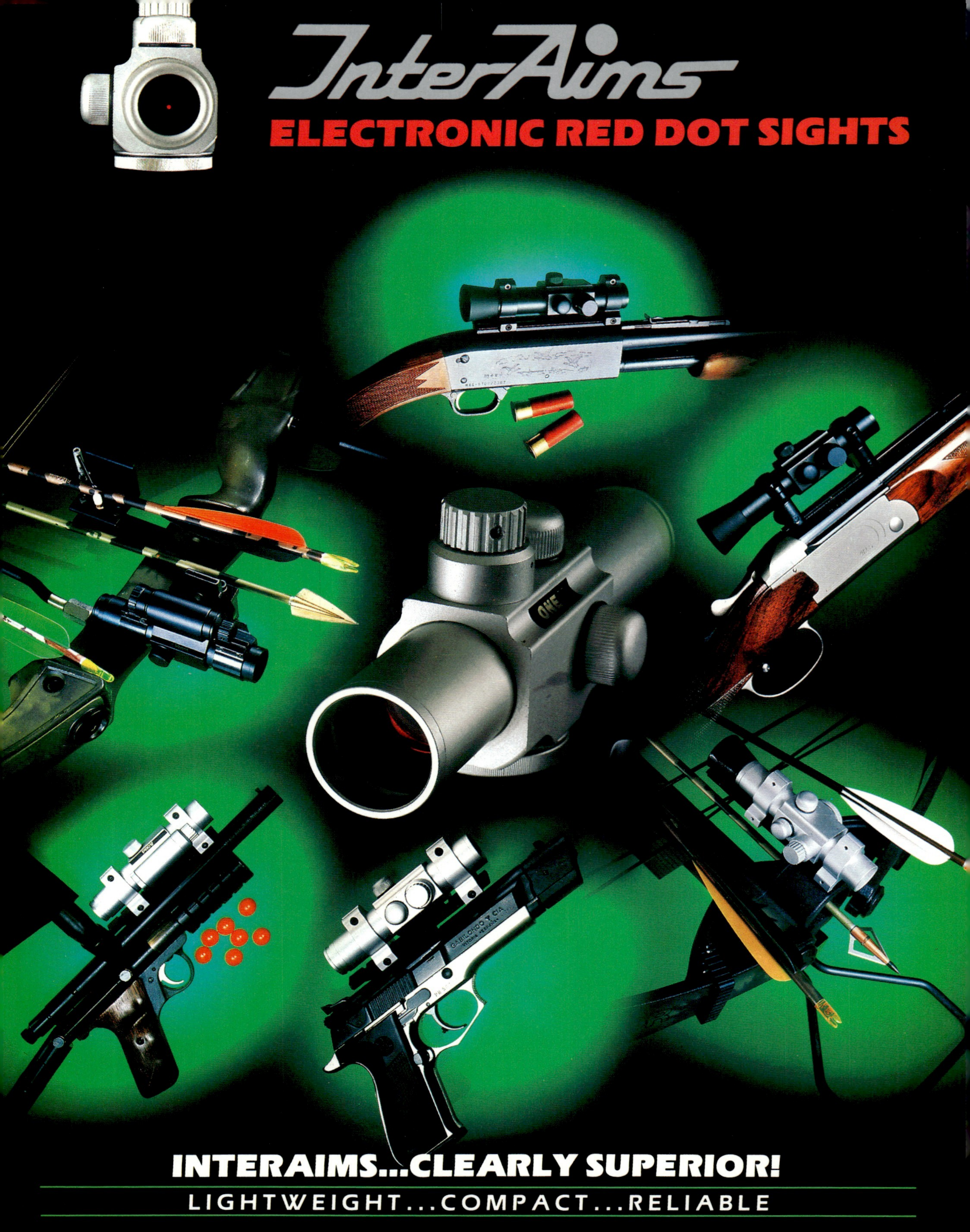
InterAims
ELECTRONIC RED DOT SIGHTS
INTERAIMS...CLEARLY SUPERIOR!
LIGHTWEIGHT...COMPACT...RELIABLE

# EUROPEAN AMERICAN ARMORY

## EUROPEAN SINGLE ACTION COMPACTS

**SPECIFICATIONS**
**Calibers:** 380 ACP and 32 ACP
**Capacity:** 7 rounds
**Barrel length:** $3\frac{7}{8}$″ **Overall length:** $6\frac{1}{2}$″
**Weight:** 26 oz.
**Finish:** Blue or chrome
**Prices:**
**32 ACP & 380 ACP** Blue .......... **$160.00**
Chrome finish .......... **175.00**
**EUROPEAN LADY 380 ACP** Blue/gold .......... **225.00**

EUROPEAN SA COMPACT

## WITNESS SUBCOMPACT (not shown)

**SPECIFICATIONS**
**Calibers:** 9mm, 38 Super, 40 S&W, 45 ACP. **Capacity:** 10 rounds. **Barrel length:** 3.66″. **Overall length:** 7.24″. **Weight:** 30 oz. **Finish:** Blue or chrome.

**Prices:**
**9mm** Blue .......... **$410.00**
Chrome .......... **425.00**
**40 S&W** Blue .......... **415.00**
Chrome .......... **445.00**
**45 ACP** Blue .......... **525.00**

## WINDICATOR DOUBLE ACTION (STANDARD GRADE)

**SPECIFICATIONS**
**Calibers:** 22 LR, 22 LR/22 WMR, 38 Special, 357 Mag.
**Capacity:** 6 rounds (38 Special only); 8 rounds (22 LR and 22 LR/22 WMR)
**Barrel length:** 2″, 4″ or 6″
**Finish:** Blue only
**Features:** Swing-out cylinder; black rubber grips; hammer block safety
**Prices:**
22 LR w/4″ barrel .......... **$200.00**
22 LR w/6″ barrel .......... **210.00**
22 LR/22 WMR w/4″ barrel .......... **257.00**
22 LR/22 WMR w/6″ barrel .......... **268.00**
38 Special w/2″ barrel .......... **179.00**
38 Special w/4″ barrel .......... **207.00**
357 Mag. w/2″ barrel .......... **195.00**
357 Mag. w/4″ barrel .......... **225.00**

WINDICATOR REVOLVER

BIG BORE BOUNTY HUNTER SINGLE ACTION

## BIG BORE BOUNTY HUNTER SA

**SPECIFICATIONS**
**Calibers:** 357 Mag., 45 Long Colt and 44 Mag.
**Capacity:** 6 rounds
**Barrel length:** $4\frac{1}{2}$″, $5\frac{1}{2}$″ or $7\frac{1}{2}$″
**Sights:** Fixed
**Finish:** Blue, color casehardened, chrome
**Features:** Transfer bar safety, 3-position hammer; hammer-forged barrel; walnut grips
**Prices:**
Blued .......... **$300.00**
Color casehardened receiver .......... **310.00**
Chrome .......... **345.00**

# EUROPEAN AMERICAN ARMORY

**BENELLI MODEL MP90S TARGET PISTOL**
**$1295.00 (22LR) $1495.00 (32 WC)**

This match-grade silhouette pistol features a chromium/molybdenum steel subframe and bolt, fully adjustable grip (with no internal moving parts), modular firing system and a barrel axis that maintains alignment with the shooter's forearm and shoulder. Trigger is adjustable for take-up and breaking point, longitudinally or axially, without altering other trigger adjustments. Extra-large ejection port dissipates gas/reduces recoil.

**SPECIFICATIONS**
**Calibers:** 22 LR or 32 Wadcutter
**Capacity:** 5 rounds (detachable magazine)
**Barrel length:** 4.33″ **Overall length:** 11.7″
**Weight:** 41.3 oz.
**Finish:** Blued barrel and frame
**Grip:** Adjustable, contoured wooden target grip
Also available:
**BENELLI MODEL MP95E.** Same specifications as above, but w/o target trigger and grip. **Price: $550.00** (22 LR blue or chrome); **$617.00** (32 WC blue or chrome).

# FEATHER HANDGUNS

**GUARDIAN ANGEL PISTOL**
**$119.95**

The Guardian Angel is a compact, lightweight handgun built to last with virtually all stainless-steel parts. It features an interchangeable dropping block that slips easily in and out of the top of the frame with the push of a button. The double-action firing mechanism automatically chooses the next barrel for instant response on the second shot. Safety features include a full trigger guard, a loading-block safety that automatically disengages for firing only when the block is firmly in place; and a passive internal firing-pin-block safety that is always "on" and disengages only when the trigger is pulled almost fully forward. The gun cannot fire because of an accidental fall or blow.

**SPECIFICATIONS**
**Calibers:** 22 LR and 22 WMR
**Capacity:** 2 rounds (removable block)
**Barrel length:** 2″ **Overall length:** 5″
**Weight:** 12 oz.

**GUARDIAN ANGEL PISTOL**

# FREEDOM ARMS

MODEL 252 REVOLVER
SILHOUETTE CLASS 10″ BARREL

**SPECIFICATIONS**
**Caliber:** 22 LR (optional 22 Magnum cylinder)
**Barrel lengths:** 5 1/8″, 7 1/2″ (Varmint Class) and 10″ (Silhouette Class)
**Sights:** Silhouette competition sights (Silhouette Class); adjustable rear express sight; removable front express blade
**Grips:** Black micarta (Silhouette Class); black and green laminated hardwood (Varmint Class)
**Finish:** Stainless steel
**Features:** Dual firing pin; lightened hammer; pre-set trigger stop; accepts all sights and/or scope mounts
**Prices:**
**Silhouette Class** (10″ barrel) . . . . . . . . . . . . . . . . **$1432.00**
**Varmint Class** (5 1/8″ & 7 1/2″ barrels . . . . . . . . . . . . **1384.00**
**22 Mag. Cylinder** . . . . . . . . . . . . . . . . . . . . . . . . **311.50**

## SILHOUETTE/COMPETITION MODELS (not shown)

**SPECIFICATIONS**
**Calibers:** 357 Magnum and 44 Rem. Mag.
**Barrel lengths:** 9″ (357 Mag.) and 10″ (44 Rem. Mag.)
**Sights:** Silhouette competition **Grips:** Pachmayr
**Trigger:** Pre-set stop; trigger over travel screw
**Finish:** Field Grade
**Price:** . . . . . . . . . . . . . . . . . . . . . . . . . . . . . . **$1304.35**

MODEL 353 REVOLVER
FIELD GRADE 7 1/2″ BARREL

**SPECIFICATIONS**
**Caliber:** 357 Magnum
**Action:** Single action **Capacity:** 5 shots
**Barrel lengths:** 4 3/4″, 6″, 7 1/2″, 9″
**Sights:** Removable front blade; adjustable rear
**Grips:** Pachmayr Presentation grips (Premier Grade has impregnated hardwood grips
**Finish:** Nonglare Field Grade (standard model); Premier Grade brushed finish (all stainless steel)
**Prices:**
**Field Grade** . . . . . . . . . . . . . . . . . . . . . . . . . . **$1216.00**
**Premier Grade** . . . . . . . . . . . . . . . . . . . . . . . . . **1564.00**

454 CASULL FIELD GRADE

MODEL 555 PREMIER GRADE (50 AE)

## 454 CASULL & MODEL 555 PREMIER & FIELD GRADES

**SPECIFICATIONS**
**Calibers:** 454 Casull, 44 Rem. Mag.
**Action:** Single action **Capacity:** 5 rounds
**Barrel lengths:** 4 3/4″, 6″, 7 1/2″, 10″
**Overall length:** 14″ (w/7 1/2″ barrel)
**Weight:** 3 lbs. 2 oz. (w/7 1/2″ barrel)
**Safety:** Patented sliding bar
**Sights:** Notched rear; blade front (optional adjustable rear and replaceable front blade)
**Grips:** Impregnated hardwood or rubber Pachmayr
**Finish:** Brushed stainless
**Features:** Patented interchangeable forcing cone bushing (optional); ISGW silhouette, Millett competition and express sights are optional; SSK T'SOB 3-ring scope mount optional; optional cylinder in 454 Casull, 45 ACP, 45 Win. Mag. (**$311.50**)
**Prices:**
**MODEL FA-454AS Premier Grade**
W/adjustable sights . . . . . . . . . . . . . . . . . . . . . **$1612.00**
W/fixed sights . . . . . . . . . . . . . . . . . . . . . . . . . **1507.00**
44 Remington w/adjustable sights . . . . . . . . . . . . **1564.00**
**MODEL FA-454FGAS Field Grade**
With stainless-steel matte finish, adj. sight, Pachmayr presentation grips . . . . . . . . . . **1263.00**
W/fixed sights . . . . . . . . . . . . . . . . . . . . . . . . . **1171.00**
44 Remington w/adjustable sights . . . . . . . . . . . . **1216.00**
With fixed sights . . . . . . . . . . . . . . . . . . . . . . . **1462.00**
**MODEL 555 Premier** 50 Action Express . . . . . . . **1612.00**
**MODEL 555 Field** . . . . . . . . . . . . . . . . . . . . . . **1263.00**

# GLOCK PISTOLS

**MODEL 17**
**$608.95**

**MODEL 17L COMPETITION**
**$806.75**

**SPECIFICATIONS**
**Caliber:** 9mm Parabellum
**Magazine capacity:** 17 rounds (19 rounds optional)*
**Barrel length:** $4^1/_2$″ (hexagonal profile with right-hand twist
**Overall length:** 7.32″
**Weight:** 22 oz. (without magazine)
**Sights:** Fixed or adjustable rear sights
Also available:
**MODEL 19 COMPACT** 15 rounds. **Barrel length:** 4″. **Overall length:** 6.85″. **Weight:** 21 oz. **Price:** . . . . . . . . . . . **$608.95**
**MODEL 21** in 45 ACP (13 round capacity). **Price:** . . . **670.50**

**SPECIFICATIONS**
**Caliber:** 9mm Parabellum
**Magazine capacity:** 17 rounds*
**Barrel length:** 6.02″ **Overall length:** 8.85″
**Weight:** 23.35 oz. (without magazine)
**Sights:** Fixed or adjustable rear sights
Also available:
**MODEL 22** (Sport and Service models) in 40 S&W. **Overall length:** 7.32″. **Capacity:** 15 rounds. **Price:** . . . . . **$608.95**
**MODEL 23** (Compact Sport and Service models) in 40 S&W. **Barrel length:** 4″. **Overall length:** 6.85″. **Capacity:** 13 rounds. **Price:** . . . . . . . . . . . . . . . . . . . . . . . . . . **$608.95**

**MODEL 20**
**$670.50**

**MODEL 24 COMPETITON**
**$806.00 ($850.00 w/Compensated Barrel)**

**SPECIFICATIONS**
**Caliber:** 10mm
**Magazine capacity:** 15 rounds*
**Action:** Double action
**Barrel length:** 4.6″ **Overall length:** 7.59″
**Height:** 5.47″ (w/sights)
**Weight:** 27.68 oz. (empty)
**Sights:** Fixed or adjustable
**Features:** 3 safeties, "safe-action" system, polymer frame

**SPECIFICATIONS**
**Caliber:** 40 S&W
**Capacity:** 15 rounds*
**Barrel length:** 6.02″ **Overall length:** 8.85″
**Weight:** 26.5 oz. (empty)
**Safety:** Manual trigger safety; passive firing block and drop safety
**Finish:** Matte (Tenifer process); nonglare

* For law enforcement and military use only.

# GRENDEL PISTOLS

**MODEL P-12**
**$175.00 ($195.00 in Nickel)**

**SPECIFICATIONS**
**Caliber:** 380 ACP
**Capacity:** 12 rounds
**Barrel length:** 3″
**Overall length:** 5.3″
**Weight:** 13 oz. (empty)
**Sight radius:** 4½″
**Features:** Low inertia safety hammer system; glass reinforced Zytel magazine; solid steel slide w/firing pin and extractor; polymer DuPont ST-800 grip

MODEL P-12

# HÄMMERLI U.S.A. PISTOLS

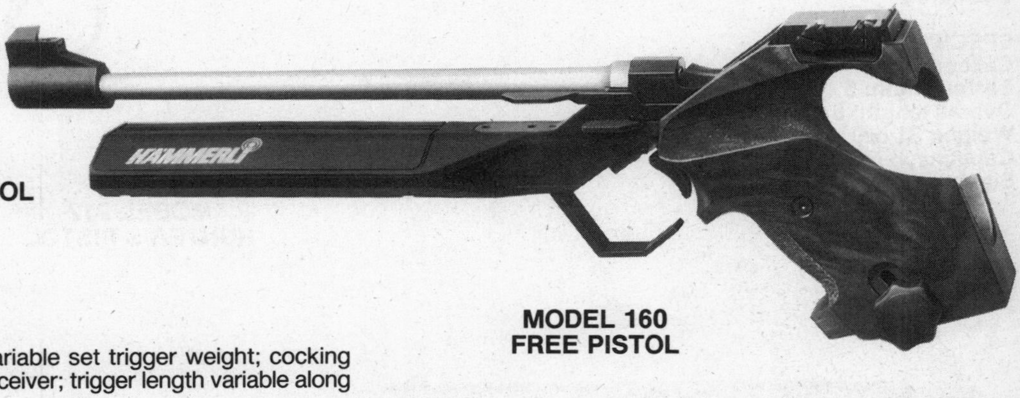


MODEL 160 FREE PISTOL

**MODEL 160 FREE PISTOL**
**$2034.00**

**SPECIFICATIONS**
**Caliber:** 22 LR
**Overall length:** 17.2″
**Weight:** 45.6 oz.
**Trigger action:** Infinitely variable set trigger weight; cocking lever located on left of receiver; trigger length variable along weapon axis
**Sights:** Sight radius 14.8″; micrometer rear sight adj. for windage and elevation
**Locking action:** Martini-type locking action w/side-mounted locking lever
**Barrel:** Free floating, cold swaged precision barrel w/low axis relative to the hand
**Ignition:** Horizontal firing pin (hammerless) in line w/barrel axis; firing-pin travel 0.15″
**Grips:** Selected walnut w/adj. hand rest for direct arm to barrel extension

**MODEL 162 ELECTRONIC PISTOL**
**$2189.00**

**SPECIFICATIONS:**
Same as **Model 160** except trigger action is electronic.
**Features:** Short lock time (1.7 milliseconds between trigger actuation and firing-pin impact), light trigger pull and extended battery life.

MODEL 162 ELECTRONIC

**MODEL 208S**
**STANDARD PISTOL**
**$1768.00**

**SPECIFICATIONS:**
**Caliber:** 22 LR
**Barrel length:** 6″
**Overall length:** 10.2″
**Weight:** 37.3 oz. (w/accessories)
**Capacity:** 9 rounds
**Sight radius:** 8.3″
**Sights:** Micrometer rear sight w/notch width; standard front blade

**MODEL 208S**
**STANDARD PISTOL**

**MODEL 212 HUNTER'S PISTOL**
**$1395.00**

**SPECIFICATIONS**
**Caliber:** 22 LR
**Barrel length:** 5″
**Overall length:** 8.6″
**Weight:** 31 oz.
**Capacity:** 8 rounds
**Sights:** Blade front; notched rear

**MODEL 212**
**HUNTER'S PISTOL**

**MODEL 280 TARGET PISTOL**

**MODEL 280 TARGET PISTOL**
**$1558.00 ($1747.00 in 32 S&W)**

**SPECIFICATIONS**
**Calibers:** 22 LR and 32 S&W
**Capacity:** 6 rounds (22 LR); 5 rounds (32 S&W)
**Barrel length:** 4.58″
**Weight:** (excluding counterweights) 34.92 oz. (22 LR); 38.8 oz. (32 S&W)
**Sight radius:** 8.66″
Also available:
**MODEL 280 TARGET PISTOL COMBO**

| | |
|---|---|
| With carrying case | **$2606.00** |
| Conversion Unit (22 LR) | **748.00** |
| In 32 S&W | **928.00** |

# HARRINGTON & RICHARDSON

## MODEL 939 PREMIER TARGET REVOLVER $184.95

The Model 939 Premier is a double-action revolver with nine-shot swing-out cylinder and features a heavy target-grade barrel with barrel rib.

**SPECIFICATIONS**
**Calibers:** 22 Short, Long, Long Rifle
**Action:** Double
**Capacity:** 9 rounds
**Sights:** Fully adjustable
**Features:** Two-piece walnut-stained hardwood western-styled grip frame profile, transfer bar system; made of high-quality ferrous metals

**MODEL 939 PREMIER TARGET REVOLVER**

**MODEL 949 CLASSIC WESTERN**

## MODEL 949 CLASSIC WESTERN REVOLVER $184.95

With true Western styling, the double-action Model 949 features a color casehardened frame and backstrap, loading gate, shrouded ejector rod and transfer bar safety system.

**SPECIFICATIONS**
**Calibers:** 22 Short, Long and Long Rifle
**Capacity:** 9 rounds
**Barrel length:** 5½″ or 7½″ (case colored)
**Sights:** Windage adjustable rear sight
**Grips:** Two-piece walnut-stained hardwood

## SPORTSMAN 999 REVOLVER $279.95

**SPECIFICATIONS**
**Calibers:** 22 Short, Long, Long Rifle
**Action:** Single and double
**Capacity:** 9 rounds
**Barrel lengths:** 4″ and 6″ (both fluted)
**Weight:** 30 oz. (w/4″ barrel); 34 oz. (w/6″ barrel)
**Sights:** Windage adjustable rear; elevation adjustable front
**Grips:** Walnut-finished hardwood
**Finish:** Blue
**Features:** Top-break loading with auto shell ejection

**SPORTSMAN 999 REVOLVER**

# HECKLER & KOCH PISTOLS

**MODEL HK USP**

**MODEL P7K3**

**SPECIFICATIONS**
**Calibers:** 9mm, 45 ACP and 40 S&W
**Capacity:** 10 + 1
**Operating system:** Short recoil, modified Browning action
**Barrel length:** 4.25″ **Overall length:** 7.64″
**Weight:** 1.74 lbs. (40 S&W); 1.66 lbs. (9mm)
**Height:** 5.35″ **Sights:** Adjustable 3-dot
**Grips/stock:** Polymer receiver and integral grips
**Prices:**

| | |
|---|---|
| 9mm & 40 S&W | **$636.00** |
| W/control lever on right | **656.00** |
| 45 ACP | **696.00** |
| W/control lever on right | **716.00** |
| Universal Tactical Pistol Light (**UTL**) | **225.00** |

**SPECIFICATIONS**
**Calibers:** 22 LR, 380 **Capacity:** 8 rounds
**Barrel length:** 3.8″ **Overall length:** 6.3″
**Weight:** 1.65 lbs. (empty)
**Sight radius:** 5.5″ **Sights:** Adjustable rear
**Price: $1100.00**
Also available:
**22 LR Conversion Kit $544.00**; Tritium Sights (orange, yellow or green rear with green front) **$88.00**

**MODEL P7M8**
**SELF-LOADING PISTOL**

**SPECIFICATIONS**
**Caliber:** 9mm×19 (Luger) **Capacity:** 8 rounds
**Barrel length:** 4.13″ **Overall length:** 6.73″
**Weight:** 1.75 lbs. (empty)
**Sight radius:** 5.83″ **Sights:** Adjustable rear
**Finish:** Blue or nickel **Price: $1141.00**
Also available:
**MODEL P7M13** with same barrel length, but slightly longer overall (6.9″), heavier (1.87 lbs.) and 13-round capacity. Blue or nickel finish. **$1330.00**

**MODEL P7M10**

**SPECIFICATIONS**
**Caliber:** 40 S&W **Capacity:** 10 rounds
**Operating system:** Recoil operated; retarded inertia bolt
**Barrel length:** 4.13″ **Overall length:** 6.9″
**Weight:** 2.69 lbs. (empty)
**Sights:** Adjustable rear
**Finish:** Blue or nickel
**Price: $1315.00**

# HERITAGE MANUFACTURING

**ROUGH RIDER SINGLE ACTION (4¾″, 6½″, 9″ barrels)**

**ROUGH RIDER SINGLE ACTION w/Bird's-Head Grip (3¾″ & 4¾″ barrels only)**

**SENTRY DOUBLE ACTION**

## SENTRY DOUBLE ACTION
## $124.95 – $134.95

**SPECIFICATIONS**
**Calibers:** 22 LR, 22 Mag., 38, 9mm
**Capacity:** 6 rounds (22 Mag., 38) and 8 rounds (22 LR, 22 Mag.)
**Barrel length:** 2″ or 4″
**Weight:** 21 oz.
**Sights:** Ramped front, fixed rear
**Grips:** Black polymer **Finish:** Blue or nickel
**Features:** Internal hammer block; additional safety plug in cylinder

## MODEL H25B/H25G SEMIAUTOMATIC

**SPECIFICATIONS**
**Caliber:** 25 ACP **Capacity:** 6 rounds
**Barrel length:** 2¼″ **Weight:** 15 oz.
**Grips:** Smooth hardwood (H25B); checkered walnut (H25G)
**Sights:** Fixed
**Features:** Exposed hammer w/half-cock position; gold trigger, safety and hammer (H25G)
**Prices:**
**Model H25B** . . . . . . . . . . . . . . . . . . . . **$74.95**
**Model H25G** . . . . . . . . . . . . . . . . . . . . **84.95**

## ROUGH RIDER SINGLE ACTION

**SPECIFICATIONS**
**Caliber:** 22 LR or 22 LR/22 WMR
**Capacity:** 6 rounds
**Barrel lengths:** 3¾″, 4¾″, 6½″, 9″
**Weight:** 31 to 38 oz.
**Sights:** Blade front, fixed rear
**Grips:** Goncalo Alves
**Finish:** Blue or nickel
**Features:** Rotating hammer block safety; brass accent screws
**Prices:**
**22 LR** (3¾″, 4¾″, 6½″ barrel) Blued . . . . . . . . . . **$105.00**
With 9″ barrel . . . . . . . . . . . . . . . . . . . . **119.95**
Nickel (all bbl. lengths) . . . . . . . . . . . . . . . . **149.00**
**22 LR/22 WRM Combo** (4¾″, 6½″ barrel) . . . . . . . **119.95**
With 9″ barrel only . . . . . . . . . . . . . . . . . . **134.95**
With nickel, **add** . . . . . . . . . . . . . . . . . . **25.00**

**HERITAGE MODEL H25B**

# HI-STANDARD

## HIGH STANDARD PISTOLS

### SUPERMATIC CITATION
**$425.00 (5½″ Barrel)**
**$445.00 (7¾″ Barrel)**

SUPERMATIC CITATION

**SPECIFICATIONS**
**Caliber:** 22 LR
**Capacity:** 10 rounds
**Barrel lengths:** 5½″ and 7¾″
**Overall length:** 9½″ and 11¾″
**Weight:** 44 oz. (46 oz. w/7¾″ bbl.)
**Finish:** Blued or Parkerized

Also available:
**CITATION MS** Recoil-operated semiautomatic. **Barrel length:** 10″. **Overall length:** 14″. **Weight:** 49 oz. **Features:** Gold-plated trigger; slide lock lever; push-button takedown system; adjustable trigger; drilled and tapped for Weaver-style scope base. **Price:** . . . . . . . . . . . . . . . . . . . . . . . . **$516.00**

### SUPERMATIC TROPHY
**$516.00 (5½″ Barrel)**
**$536.00 (7¼″ Barrel)**

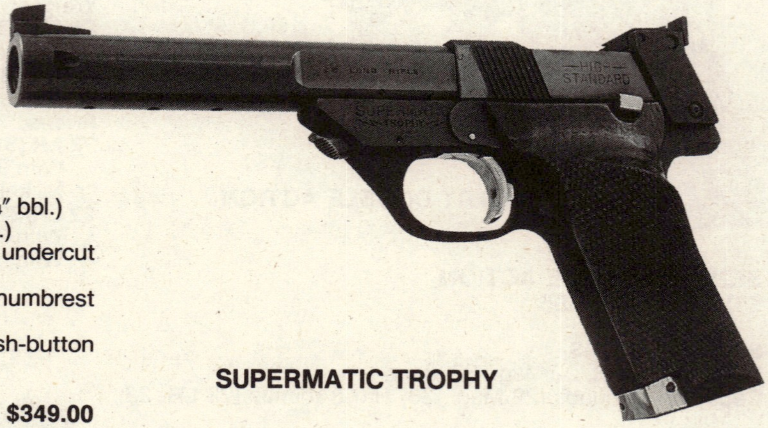

SUPERMATIC TROPHY

**SPECIFICATIONS**
**Caliber:** 22 LR
**Capacity:** 10 rounds
**Action:** Recoil-operated semiautomatic
**Barrel length:** 5½″ bull or 7¼″ fluted
**Overall length:** 9½″ (w/5½″ bbl.) and 11¼″ (w/7¼″ bbl.)
**Weight:** 44 oz. (w/5½″ bbl.) and 46 oz. (w/7¼″ bbl.)
**Sights:** Click-adjustable rear for windage/elevation; undercut ramp front
**Grips:** Checkered American walnut with right-hand thumbrest (left-hand optional)
**Features:** Gold-plated trigger; slide lock lever; push-button takedown system; magazine release
Also available:
**.22 Short Conversion Kit** . . . . . . . . . . . . . . . . . . . . **$349.00**

### SUPERMATIC TOURNAMENT
**$395.00**

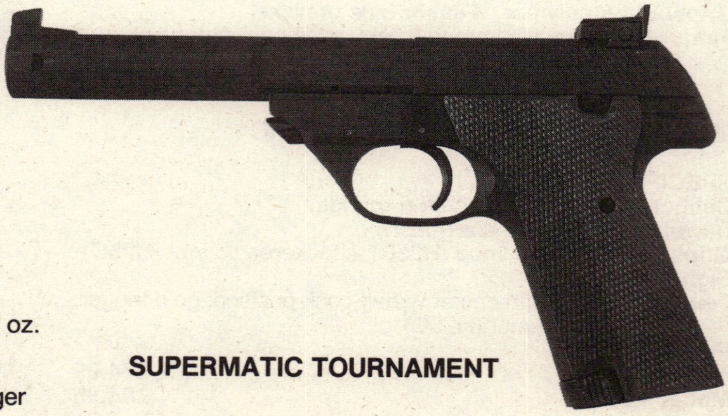

SUPERMATIC TOURNAMENT

**SPECIFICATIONS**
**Caliber:** 22 LR
**Capacity:** 10 rounds
**Barrel lengths:** 4½″, 5½″ and 6¾″
**Overall length:** 8½″, 9½″ and 10¾″
**Weight:** 43 oz. (w/4½″ bbl.); 44 oz. (w/5½″ bbl.); and 45 oz. (w/6¾″ bbl.)
**Finish:** Parkerized frame
**Features:** Fully adjustable rear sight; non-adjustable trigger

# HI-STANDARD

## HIGH STANDARD PISTOLS

VICTOR

### VICTOR 22 LR
### $532.00

**SPECIFICATIONS**
**Caliber:** 22 LR
**Capacity:** 10 rounds
**Barrel lengths:** 4 1/2″ and 5 1/2″
**Overall length:** 8 1/2″ and 9 1/2″
**Weight:** 45 oz. (w/4 1/2″ bbl.); 46 oz. (w/5 1/2″ bbl.)
**Finish:** Blued or Parkerized frame
**Features:** Optional steel rib; click-adjustable sights for windage and elevation; optional barrel weights
Also avaliable:
**22 Short Conversion Kit** 5 1/2″ barrel w/vent rib, slide, two magazines . . . . . . . . . . . . . . . . . . . . . . . . . . . . . **$397.00**

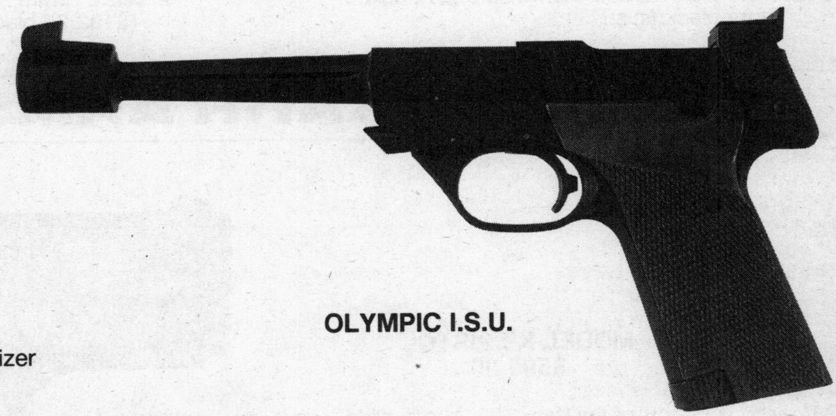

OLYMPIC I.S.U.

### OLYMPIC I.S.U.
### $625.00

**SPECIFICATIONS**
**Caliber:** 22 LR
**Capacity:** 5 rounds
**Action:** Recoil-operated semiautomatic
**Barrel length:** 6 3/4″ tapered w/integral stabilizer
**Overall length:** 10 3/4″
**Weight:** 45 oz.
**Sights:** Click-adjustable rear for windage/elevation; undercut ramp front
**Grips:** Checkered American walnut with thumbrest
**Features:** Blued trigger; slide lock lever; adjustable trigger (weight of pull and travel); detachable barrel weights and brackets; Sure-Grip stippling on grip front and backstrap

Also available:
**OLYMPIC MILITARY** in 22 Short with 5 1/2″ bull barrel and lightweight high-strength aluminum alloy slide, plus precision carbon steel frame. **Price:** . . . . . . . . . . . . . . . . . . **$504.00**

### SPORT KING (not shown)
### $325.00

**SPECIFICATIONS**
**Caliber:** 22 LR
**Capacity:** 10 rounds
**Barrel lengths:** 4 1/2″ and 6 3/4″
**Overall length:** 8 1/2″ and 10 3/4″
**Weight:** 44 oz. (w/4 1/2″ bbl.); 46 oz. (w/6 3/4″ bbl.)
**Sights:** Fixed rear (slide mounted); blade front
**Grips:** Checkered American walnut (ambidextrous)
**Finish:** Parkerized
**Features:** Blued trigger; slide lock lever; magazine release; push-button barrel takedown system

# HI-POINT FIREARMS

MODEL 9mm
$139.95

380 POLYMER

**SPECIFICATIONS**
**Caliber:** 9mm Parabellum
**Capacity:** 9 shots
**Barrel length:** 4 1/2″
**Overall length:** 7.72″
**Weight:** 42 oz.
**Sights:** 3-dot type
**Features:** Quick on-off thumb safety; nonglare military black finish

Also available:
**MODEL 45** in 45 ACP. Same specifications as the 9mm, except w/7-shot capacity and two-tone Polymer finish. **Price: $148.95**
**MODEL 40** in 40 S&W. Same specifications as the 45 ACP w/8-shot capacity. **Price: $148.95**
**MODEL 380 POLYMER** w/3 1/2″ barrel and 8-shot capacity. **Price: $148.95**
**MODEL 9mm COMPACT** w/3 1/2″ barrel. **Price: $124.95 ($132.95** black polymer)

# KAHR ARMS

**MODEL K9 PISTOL**
**$595.00**

All key components of the Kahr K9—frame, slide, barrel, etc.—are made from 4140 steel, allowing the pistol to chamber reliably and fire virtually any commercial 9mm ammo, including +P rounds. The frame and sighting surfaces are matte blued, and the sides of the slide carry a polished blue finish. The grips are crafted from exotic wood.

The unique trigger system holds the striker in a partially cocked state; then, a pull of the trigger completes the cocking cycle and releases the striker. Recoil on firing partially cocks the striker for the next trigger pull. This design allows a lighter-than-normal "DA" pull that is consistent from shot to shot. A trigger-activated firing-pin block prevents accidental discharge. Like a double-action revolver, no other safeties are needed.

MODEL K9 PISTOL

**SPECIFICATIONS**
**Caliber:** 9mm and 9mm+P
**Capacity:** 7 rounds
**Barrel length:** 3 1/2″
**Overall length:** 6″
**Weight:** 25 oz. (empty)
**Sights:** Drift-adjustable, low-profile white bar-dot combat sights
**Grips:** Textured polymer
**Finish:** Nonglare blued; polished slide; matte frame and sighting surface

# KBI PISTOLS

### MODEL PSP-25
**$249.00 ($299.00 Hard Chrome)**

**SPECIFICATIONS**
**Caliber:** 25 ACP
**Capacity:** 6 rounds
**Barrel length:** 2 1/8″
**Overall length:** 4 1/8″
**Weight:** 9.5 oz. (empty)
**Height:** 2 7/8″
**Finish:** Blue or chrome
**Features:** Dual safety system; all-steel construction

**MODEL PSP-25**

### FEG MODEL PJK-9HP
**$349.00 ($429.00 Chrome)**

**SPECIFICATIONS**
**Caliber:** 9mm Luger Parabellum
**Magazine capacity:** 13 rounds
**Action:** Single
**Barrel length:** 4 3/4″
**Overall length:** 8″
**Weight:** 21 oz.
**Grips:** Hand-checkered walnut
**Safety:** Thumb safety
**Sights:** 3-dot system
**Finish:** Blue or chrome
**Features:** Two 13-round magazines, cleaning rod

**FEG MODEL PJK-9HP**

### FEG MODEL SMC-380/SMC-918
**$279.00**

**SPECIFICATIONS**
**Calibers:** 380 ACP, 9mm Makarov (9×18)
**Capacity:** 6 rounds
**Action:** Double
**Barrel length:** 3 1/2″
**Overall length:** 6 1/8″
**Weight:** 18 1/2 oz.
**Safety:** Thumb safety
**Grips:** Black composite
**Features:** High-luster blued steel slide; blue anodized aluminum alloy frame

**FEG MODEL SMC-380**

# KBI HANDGUNS

**FEG GKK-45 AUTO PISTOL**
**$399.00**

**SPECIFICATIONS**
**Calibers:** 45 ACP and 40 S&W
**Capacity:** 8 rounds (9 rounds in 40 S&W)
**Barrel length:** 4 1/8″
**Overall length:** 7 3/4″
**Weight:** 36 oz.
**Sights:** 3-dot, blade front; rear adjustable for windage
**Stock:** Hand-checkered walnut
**Features:** Double action; polished blue or hard chrome finish; combat trigger guard; two magazines and cleaning rod standard

**FEG GKK-45**

**FEG SMC-22 AUTO PISTOL**
**$279.00**

**SPECIFICATIONS**
**Calibers:** 22 LR and 380 ACP
**Capacity:** 6 rounds (380 ACP) or 8 rounds (22 LR)
**Barrel length:** 3 1/2″
**Overall length:** 6 1/8″
**Weight:** 18 1/2 oz.
**Stock:** Checkered composition w/thumbrest
**Sights:** Blade front; rear adjustable for windage
**Features:** Alloy frame; steel slide; double action; blue finish; two magazines and cleaning rod standard

**FEG SMC-22**

**BAIKAL IJ-70 AUTO PISTOL**
**$199.00 (9×18, 8 shots)**
**$239.00 (9×18, 10 shots)**
**$249.00 (380, 10 shots)**

**SPECIFICATIONS**
**Calibers:** 9×18 Makarov, 380 ACP
**Capacity:** 8 or 10 rounds
**Barrel length:** 4″
**Overall length:** 6 1/4″
**Weight:** 25 oz. (26 oz. w/10 rounds)
**Stock:** Checkered composition
**Sights:** Blade front; rear adjustable for windage and elevation
**Features:** Double action; all steel; frame-mounted safety with decocker; two magazines, cleaning rod, universal tool and leather holster standard

**BAIKAL IJ-70**
**(9×18)**

# KIMBER PISTOLS

MODEL .45 PISTOL

## MODEL CLASSIC .45

This Chip McCormick-inspired pistol is made in the U.S.A. by the famous riflemaker, Kimber. The new firearm comes in four versions—Custom, Custom Stainless, Custom Royal and Gold Match—according to differences in sights, grips and capacity.

**SPECIFICATIONS**
**Caliber:** 45 ACP
**Capacity:** 8 (10 also in Gold Match)
**Barrel length:** 5″
**Overall length:** 8.5″
**Sights:** McCormick low-profile combat type (Bo-Mar sights only in Gold Match model)
**Finish:** Polished blue (Custom Royal & Gold Match); matte black oxide (Custom); matte stainless steel (Custom Stainless)
**Features:** Lowered and flared ejection port; slide machined from solid steel; premium match-grade hammer-forged barrel and bushing; front serration; ultra-lightweight composite premium match trigger; relief cut under trigger guard; extended combat-style thumb safety; flat main spring housing; beveled magazine well; hard synthetic grips

| Models | Prices |
|---|---|
| **CUSTOM** | **$575.00** |
| **CUSTOM STAINLESS** | **650.00** |
| **ROYAL** | **715.00** |
| **GOLD MATCH** | **925.00** |

# L.A.R. GRIZZLY

## MARK I GRIZZLY

**45 Win Mag $920.00 357 Magnum $933.00**

This semiautomatic pistol is a direct descendant of the tried and trusted 1911-type .45 automatic, but with the added advantage of increased caliber capacity.

**SPECIFICATIONS**
**Calibers:** 45 Win. Mag., 45 ACP, 357 Mag., 10mm
**Barrel lengths:** 5.4″ and $6\frac{1}{2}$″
**Overall length:** $10\frac{1}{2}$″
**Weight (empty):** 48 oz.
**Height:** $5\frac{3}{4}$″
**Sights:** Fixed, ramped blade (front); fully adjustable for elevation and windage (rear)
**Magazine capacity:** 7 rounds
**Grips:** Checkered rubber, nonslip, combat-type
**Safeties:** Grip depressor, manual thumb, slide-out-of-battery disconnect
**Materials:** Mil spec 4140 steel slide and receiver with noncorrosive, heat-treated, special alloy steels for other parts

Also available:

| | |
|---|---|
| **Grizzly 44 Magnum Mark 4** w/adj. sights | **$933.00** |
| **Grizzly Win Mag Conversion Units** | |
| In 45 Win. Mag., 45 ACP, 10mm | **214.00** |
| In 357 Magnum | **228.00** |
| **Win Mag Compensator** | **110.00** |
| In 50 caliber | **120.00** |

**MARK 4 GRIZZLY 44 MAG.**

**GRIZZLY WIN MAG $6\frac{1}{2}$″ BARREL**

**GRIZZLY WIN MAG 8″ BARREL**

**GRIZZLY 50 MARK 5**

Also available:
**GRIZZLY WIN MAG** (8″ and 10″ barrels)

| | |
|---|---|
| **Model G-WM8** (8″ barrel in 45 Win. Mag., 45 ACP or 357/45 Grizzly Win. Mag. | **$1313.00** |
| **Model G357M8** (8″ barrel in 357 Magnum) | **1337.50** |
| **Model G-WM10** (10″ barrel in 45 Win. Mag., 45 ACP or 357/45 Grizzly Win. Mag. | **1375.00** |
| **Model G357M10** (10″ barrel in 357 Magnum) | **1400.00** |

## GRIZZLY 50 MARK 5
**$1060.00**

**SPECIFICATIONS**
**Caliber:** 50 AE
**Capacity:** 6 rounds
**Barrel lengths:** 5.4″ and 6.5″
**Overall length:** $10\frac{5}{8}$″
**Sights:** Fixed front; fully adjustable rear

# LLAMA AUTOMATIC PISTOLS

SMALL-FRAME 380 AUTOMATIC
(Deep Blue Finish)
$258.95

MAX-I
COMPACT IX-D 45
$349.95

**SPECIFICATIONS**
**Calibers:** 9mm and 45 Auto
**Capacity:** 9 shots (9mm); 7 shots (45 Auto)
**Barrel length:** $4^1/_4$" ($5^1/_4$" Government Model)
**Overall length:** $7^7/_8$" ($8^1/_2$" Government Model)
**Weight:** 34 oz. (36 oz. Government Model)
**Sights:** 3-dot combat
**Finish:** Non-glare combat matte
**Price:** .......... **$349.95**
10-shot Model .......... **399.95**
7-shot 45 Govt. Model .......... **366.95**

## LLAMA AUTOMATIC PISTOL SPECIFICATIONS

| **Type:** | **Small-Frame** | **IX-D Compact-Frame** | **IX-C Government Model** |
|---|---|---|---|
| **Calibers:** | 380 Auto | 45 Auto | 45 Auto |
| **Frame:** | Precision machined from high-strength steel | Precision machined from high-strength steel | Precision machined from high-strength steel |
| **Trigger:** | Serrated | Serrated | Serrated |
| **Hammer:** | External; wide spur, serrated | External; military style | External; military style |
| **Operation:** | Straight blow-back | Locked breech | Locked breech |
| **Loaded Chamber Indicator:** | Yes | Yes | Yes |
| **Safeties:** | Extended manual & grip safeties | Extended manual & grip safeties | Extended manual & grip safeties |
| **Grips:** | Matte black polymer | Anatomically designed rubber grips | Anatomically designed rubber grips |
| **Sights:** | Partridge-type front; sq.-notch rear | 3-dot combat sights | 3-dot combat sights |
| **Sight Radius:** | $4^1/_4$" | $6^1/_4$" | $6^1/_4$" |
| **Magazine Capacity:** | 7 shots | 10 shots | 10 shots |
| **Weight:** | 23 oz. | 39 oz. | 41 oz. |
| **Barrel Length:** | $3^{11}/_{16}$" | $4^1/_4$" | $5^1/_8$" |
| **Overall Length:** | $6^1/_2$" | $7^7/_8$" | $8^1/_2$" |
| **Height:** | $4^3/_8$" | $5^7/_{16}$" | $5^5/_{16}$" |
| **Finish:** | Standard: High-polished, deep blue. Deluxe: Satin chrome | Non-glare combat matte | Non-glare combat matte |

# AMERICAN EAGLE LUGER®

AMERICAN EAGLE LUGER®

## 9mm AMERICAN EAGLE LUGER® STAINLESS STEEL

It is doubtful that there ever was a pistol created that evokes the nostalgia or mystique of the Luger® pistol. Since its beginnings at the turn of the 20th century, the name Luger® conjures memories of the past. Stoeger Industries is indeed proud to have owned the name Luger® since the late 1920s and is equally proud of the stainless-steel version that graces this page.

The "American Eagle" name was introduced around 1900 to capture the American marketplace. It served its purpose well, the name having become legendary along with the Luger® name. The "American Eagle" inscribed on a Luger® also distinguishes a firearm of exceptional quality over some inexpensive models that have been manufactured in the past.

Constructed entirely of stainless steel, the gun is available in 9mm Parabellum only, with either a 4″ or 6″ barrel, each with deeply checkered American walnut grips.

The name Luger®, combined with Stoeger's reputation of selling only quality merchandise since 1918, assures the owner of complete satisfaction.

**SPECIFICATIONS**
**Caliber:** 9mm Parabellum
**Capacity:** 7 + 1
**Barrel length:** 4″ (P-08 Model); 6″ (Navy Model)
**Overall length:** 8¼″ (w/4″ bbl.), 10¼″ (w/6″ bbl.)
**Weight:** 30 oz. w/4″ barrel, 32 oz. w/6″ barrel
**Grips:** Deeply checkered American walnut
**Features:** All stainless-steel construction
**Price:** . . . . . . . . . . . . . . . . . . . . . . . . . . . . . . **$695.00**

# MAGNUM RESEARCH

## DESERT EAGLE PISTOLS

| SPECIFICATIONS | 357 MAGNUM | 41/44 MAGNUM |
|---|---|---|
| Length, with 6-inch barrel | 10.6 inches | 10.6 inches |
| Height | 5.6 inches | 5.7 inches |
| Width | 1.25 inches | 1.25 inches |
| Trigger reach | 2.75 inches | 2.75 inches |
| Sight radius (wh 6-inch barrel) | 8.5 inches | 8.5 inches |
| Additional available barrels | 14 inch | 14 inch & 10 inch |
| Weight | See below | See below |
| Bore rifling — Six rib | Polygonal: 1 turn in 14 inches | Polygonal: 1 turn in 18 inches |
| Method of operation | Gas operated | Gas operated |
| Method of locking | Rotating bolt | Rotating bolt |
| Magazine capacity | 9 rounds (plus one in chamber) | 8 rounds (plus one in chamber) |

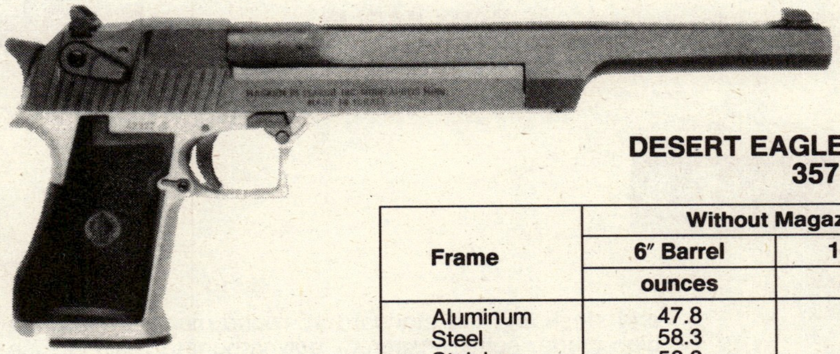

**DESERT EAGLE (10″ Barrel)**

## DESERT EAGLE — WEIGHT TABLES
### 357 Magnum

| Frame | Without Magazine | | With Empty Magazine | |
|---|---|---|---|---|
| | 6″ Barrel | 14″ Barrel | 6″ Barrel | 14″ Barrel |
| | ounces | ounces | ounces | ounces |
| Aluminum | 47.8 | 55.0 | 51.9 | 59.1 |
| Steel | 58.3 | 65.5 | 62.4 | 96.6 |
| Stainless | 58.3 | 65.5 | 62.4 | 69.6 |

### 41/44 Magnum

| Frame | Without Magazine | | With Empty Magazine | |
|---|---|---|---|---|
| | 6″ Barrel | 14″ Barrel | 6″ Barrel | 14″ Barrel |
| | ounces | ounces | ounces | ounces |
| Aluminum | 52.3 | 61.0 | 56.4 | 65.1 |
| Steel | 62.8 | 71.5 | 66.9 | 75.6 |
| Stainless | 62.8 | 71.5 | 66.9 | 75.6 |

## DESERT EAGLE PISTOLS

**357 MAGNUM**
**$789.00 Standard Parkerized Finish (6″ Barrel)**
**839.00 Stainless Steel (6″)**
**939.00 Standard (10″ barrel)**
**989.00 Stainless (10″ barrel)**
**949.00 Standard (14″ barrel)**
**999.00 Stainless (14″ barrel)**

**41 MAGNUM (6″ Barrel)**
**$899.00 Standard Black**
**949.00 Stainless Steel Frame**

**44 MAGNUM (6″, 10″, 14″ Barrels)**
**$ 899.00 Standard Parkerized Finish**
**949.00 Stainless Steel (6″ Barrel)**
**1099.00 Standard (10″ Barrel)**
**1159.00 Stainless (10″ Barrel)**
**1119.00 Standard (14″ Barrel)**
**1169.00 Stainless (14″ Barrel)**

**DESERT EAGLE 50 MAGNUM**
**$1249.00**

**Barrel length:** 10½″; **Capacity:** 7 rounds; **weight:** 72.4 oz.; **height:** 5.9″; **sight radius:** 8.3″

# MAGNUM RESEARCH

## BABY EAGLE PISTOL
**$569.00**

**SPECIFICATIONS**
**Calibers:** 9mm, 40 S&W, 41 AE
**Capacity:** 10 rounds
**Barrel length:** 4.72″ **Overall length:** 8.14″
**Weight:** 35.27 oz. (empty)
**Sights:** Combat
**Features:** Double action; extra-long slide rail; combat-style trigger guard; decocking safety; polygonal rifling; ambidextrous thumb safety; all-steel construction
Also available:
**Conversion Kit** (9mm to 41 AE) . . . . . . . . . . . . . . . **$239.00**

## BABY EAGLE 9mm PISTOL VARIATIONS
**$569.00 (10-round capacity)**

1. With Frame-mounted safety, black finish
2. With Frame-mounted Safety & Short Barrel (3.62″)
3. With Frame-mounted Safety, Short Barrel & Short Grip

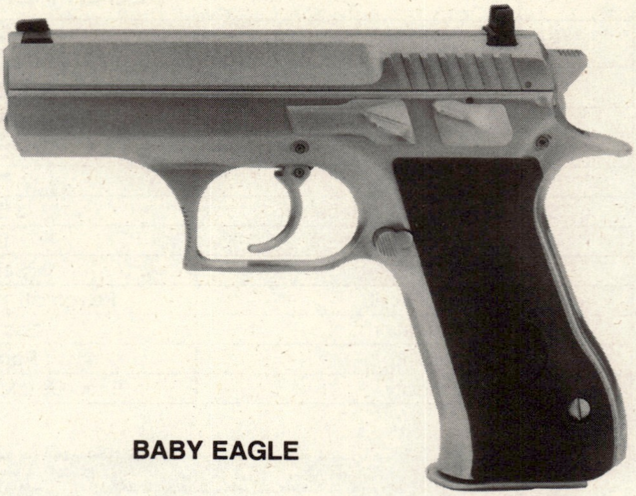

**BABY EAGLE**

**MOUNTAIN EAGLE**

## MOUNTAIN EAGLE
**$239.00**

This affordable, lightweight triangular-barreled pistol with minimum recoil is ideal for plinkers, target shooters and varmint hunters. The barrel is made of hybrid injection-molded polymer and steel, and the standard 15-round magazine is made of high-grade, semitransparent polycarbonate resin. It uses a constant force spring to load all 15 rounds easily. The receiver is made of machined T-6 alloy.

**SPECIFICATIONS**
**Caliber:** 22 LR
**Barrel length:** 6″ **Overall length:** 10.6″
**Weight:** 21 oz. (unloaded)
**Sights:** Standard orange in front, black in rear (adjustable for windage and elevation
**Grip:** One-piece injection-molded, checkered conventional contour side panels, horizontally textured front and back panels
Also available:
**TARGET EDITION** with 8″ barrel, 2-stroke target trigger, jeweled bolt, adj. sights, range case . . . . . . . . . . . . **$279.00**

## LONE EAGLE SINGLE SHOT BARRELED ACTION
**$254.00**

This specialty pistol is designed for hunters, silhouette enthusiasts, long-range target shooters and other marksmen. The pistol can fire 14 different calibers of ammunition. Available with interchangeable 14-inch barreled actions. **Calibers:** 22 Hornet, 22-250, 223 Rem., 243 Rem., 30-06, 30-30, 308 Win., 35 Rem., 357 Maximum, 358 Win., 44 Mag., 444 Marlin, 7mm-08, 7mm Bench Rest.

**LONE EAGLE**

Also available:
**LONE EAGLE** with barreled action in calibers 7mm-08, 308 or 30-06. Features integral muzzle brake, silver matte Ecoloy II satin finish, satin scope mount and travel case . . **$399.00**

# McMILLAN

WOLVERINE

## WOLVERINE PISTOL
**$1700.00**

This competition-ready pistol is built and designed around the 1911 Colt auto pistol frame. Two models—the **Combat** and **Competition Match**—are available with metal finish options (electroless nickel, NP³, black Teflon and deep blue), plus wood or Pachmayr grips. Other features include: a compensator integral to the barrel; round burr-style hammer; oversized button-style catch for quick clip release; high grip system to reduce muzzle rise and felt recoil; knurled backstrap and low-profile adjustable sights; skeletonized aluminum trigger with hand-tuned medium weight pull.

**SPECIFICATIONS**
**Calibers:** 45 ACP, 45 Italian, 38 Super, 38 Wadcutter, 9mm, 10mm
**Action:** Single
**Barrel length:** 6″ (5″ in Officer's Model)

# MITCHELL ARMS

GOLD SERIES

## 1911 GOLD SERIES
**$535.00 (8-Shot)**
**$685.00 (10-Shot)**

Mitchell Arms offers two models of its new competition 45-caliber pistols: a standard 8-round model and a "wide body" 10-round model. Innovations include a bull barrel/slide lockup; full-length guide rod recoil assembly, extended ambisafety, adjustable trigger, replaceable front sights and beveled magazine wells. Plus the same grip angle as the original 1911 pistols, which matches Mitchell's 22-caliber competition target pistols.

The Gold Series standard model accepts virtually every 8-round single-stack 1911-type 45 ACP magazine (pistols acquired by law-enforcement agencies and U.S. Military also accept double-stack 13-round magazines). Options include stainless steel or high blue finish, fixed or fully adjustable rear sights, replaceable combat-type front sights, American walnut or blue rubberized competition grips.

Additional specifications, which are similar to the former Signature Series (*see* SHOOTER'S BIBLE 1995), can be obtained directly from Mitchell Arms (*see* Directory of Manufacturers and Suppliers).

# MITCHELL ARMS

## TARGET PISTOLS

### VICTOR II

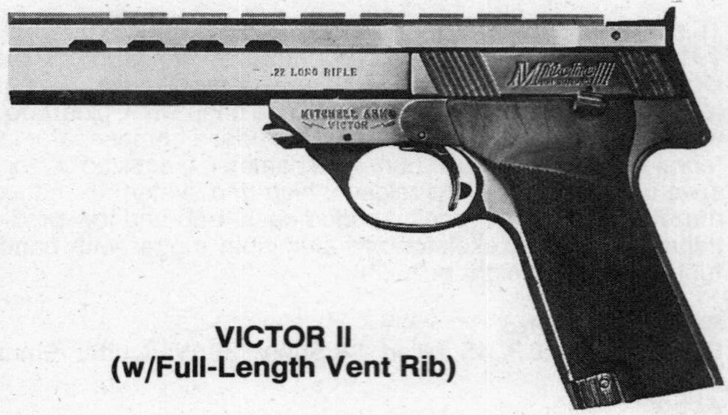


**VICTOR II (w/Full-Length Vent Rib)**

**SPECIFICATIONS**
**Caliber:** 22 LR
**Barrel lengths:** 4 1/2″ (full-length vent rib only) and 5 1/2″
**Sights:** Rib-mounted
**Grips:** Military-style with thumbrest; full checkered American walnut
**Frame:** Stippled grip, front and rear
**Trigger:** Adjustable for both travel and weight; gold-plated
**Features:** Push-button barrel takedown; gold-filled marking; safety, magazine and slide lock; left- or right-hand styles
**Prices:**
W/full-length dovetail rib (5 1/2″ bbl.) . . . . . . . . . . . . . **$650.00**
W/full-length vent rib (both barrels) . . . . . . . . . . . . . **595.00**
W/full-length vent rib/Weaver-style base . . . . . . . . . **675.00**
Detachable barrel weights (2 or 3 oz.) **add** . . . . . . . **20.00**

### TROPHY II

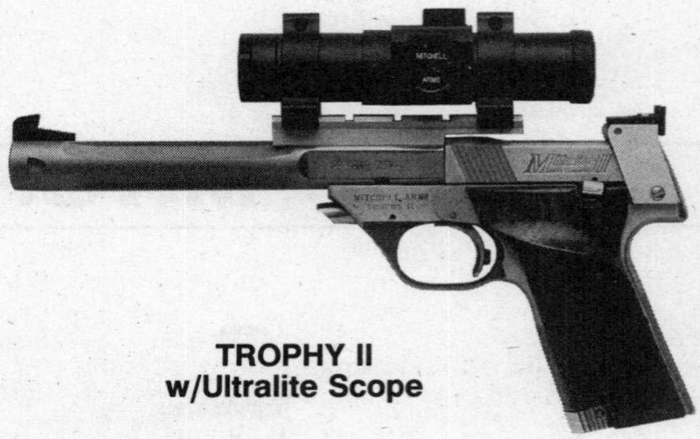

**TROPHY II w/Ultralite Scope**

**SPECIFICATIONS**
**Caliber:** 22 LR
**Barrel length:** Interchangeable 5 1/2″ (Bull) or 7 1/4″ (Fluted)
**Sights:** Bridge rear; frame mounted on rails
**Grips:** Military-style
**Trigger:** Adjustable for travel and weight; gold-plated
**Features:** Full checkered American walnut thumbrest grips; push-button barrel takedown; all roll marks gold filled; stippled grip frame (front and rear); gold-plated trigger, safety, magazine release and slide lock
**Price:** Royal blue or stainless . . . . . . . . . . . . . . . . **$498.00**
Red-dot scope ultralite w/rings; click adj., 4 oz. . . . **199.95**

Also available:
**CITATION II.** Same specifications as Trophy II, except finish is satin stainless or satin blue with nickel-plated trigger, safety, mag. release and slide lock. **Price:** . . . . . **$489.00**

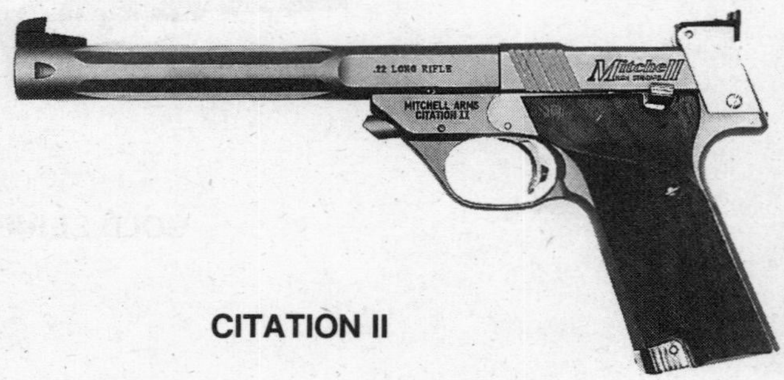


**CITATION II**

### SHARPSHOOTER II

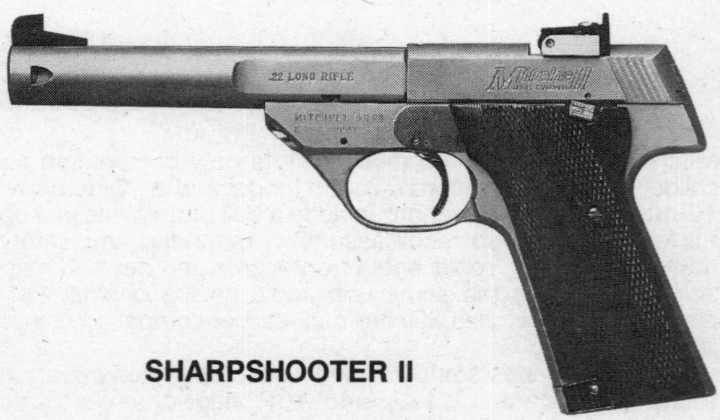


**SHARPSHOOTER II**

**SPECIFICATIONS**
**Caliber:** 22 Rimfire
**Barrel length:** 5 1/2″ bull barrel
**Sights:** Slide-mounted adjustable rear
**Features:** Push-button takedown; special barrel weights (optional); smooth grip frame; satin finish
**Price:** . . . . . . . . . . . . . . . . . . . . . . . . . . . . . . . . . . **$395.00**

# MITCHELL ARMS PISTOLS

## SPORT KING II
**$325.00**

This 22-caliber pistol is designed for plinkers, woodsmen and beginner target shooters. The Sport King II comes with either a 6.75″ or 4.5″ tapered crowned barrel, each with the original High Standard quick-change barrel system, which allows nearly instantaneous barrel changes. Other features include a wide trigger; black tactile rubber grips; drift adjustable rear sight; ramp front sight; and a military grip angle. Options include a wide variety of wooden target grips, scopes and barrel weights.

Additional specifications may be obtained directly from Mitchell Arms (*see* Directory of Manufacturers and Suppliers).

**SPORT KING II**
**6¾″ Barrel**

## OLYMPIC I.S.U.
**$599.00**

**SPECIFICATIONS**
**Caliber:** 22 Short, Long
**Barrel length:** 6¾″ w/integral stabilizer
**Sights:** Bridge rear sight; frame-mounted on rails
**Trigger:** Adjustable for travel and weight
**Grips:** Full checkered with thumbrest
**Finish:** Royal blue or stainless steel
**Features:** Push-button barrel takedown; stippled grip frame (front and rear); military-style grip; adjustable barrel weights

**OLYMPIC I.S.U.**

**ALPHA 45 AUTO**

## ALPHA SERIES
**$685.00 (10-Shot) $689.00 (Double Action Only)**
**$725.00 (Stainless Steel)**

The Alpha Series, which draws its inspiration from John Browning's Model 1911, contains its trigger action in a removable sideplate module, much like that of a revolver. With three different interchangeable trigger modules available, this pistol can be converted easily to double-action-only, single-action-only or Duplex Action, S/A and D/A. Alpha accepts its own 10-round, double-column 45 ACP magazine and any single-column, 8-round 45 ACP 1911-style magazine.

Alpha's Race gun features include: extended ambidextrous safety • extended slide lock • serrated combat hammer • beveled magazine well • replaceable dovetail-style front sights (fully adjustable rear sights optional) • heavy bull barrel • frame-mounted fire control switch (decocker/safety) • and full wraparound design grip mounted without screws, angled to match the Colt 1911.

Additional specifications may be obtained directly from Mitchell Arms (*see* Directory of Manufacturers and Suppliers).

# MITCHELL ARMS REVOLVERS

GUARDIAN II
4″ Barrel

GUARDIAN II
6″ Barrel

**GUARDIAN DOUBLE ACTION**
**$275.00 ($305.00 w/Target Grip)**

Mitchell Arms' 38-caliber Guardian revolver shares many of the same design and performance features of the 357 Titan series, including a target hammer, shrouded ejector rod, and smooth trigger action set to 12 lbs. in double action and 3 lbs. in single action. **Barrel lengths:** 4″ or 6″. Flat-bottomed wood grips and adjustable target sights; or the 4″ (only) combat model with fixed sights, combat-style rubber grips and low-profile ejector rod housing.

Additional specifications may be obtained directly from Mitchell Arms (*see* Directory of Manufacturers and Suppliers).

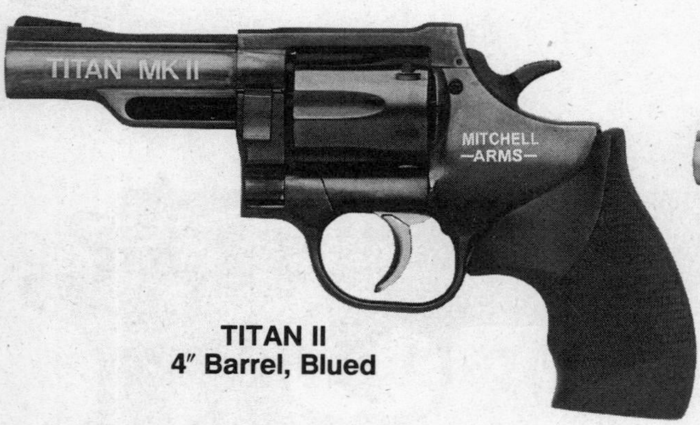


TITAN II
4″ Barrel, Blued

TITAN II
6″ Barrel, Stainless

**TITAN DOUBLE-ACTION SERIES**
**$339.00 (Blue)**
**$429.00 (Stainless)**

Mitchell's Titan Series is chambered for the 357 Magnum cartridge and incorporates such features as a target hammer, shrouded ejector rod, and trigger action set to 12 lbs. in double action and 3 lbs. in single action. Available in stainless steel or blued steel construction, fitted with combat-style or target grips, and fixed (Titan II) or adjustable rear sights with a ramp front sight (Titan III). **Barrel lengths:** 4″ and 6″.

Additional specifications may be obtained directly from Mitchell Arms (*see* Directory of Manufacturers and Suppliers).

# MOA MAXIMUM PISTOL

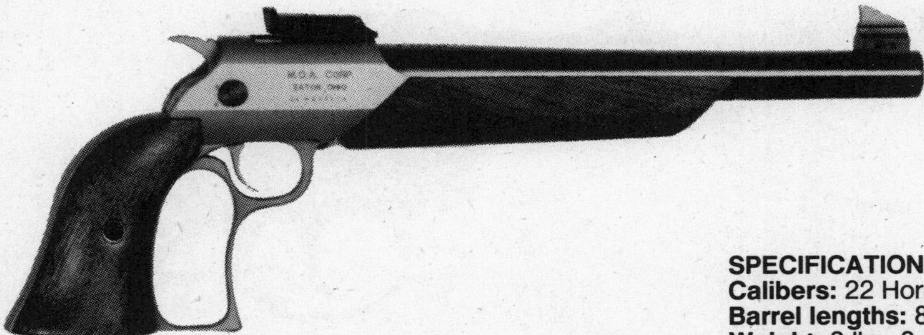

MAXIMUM

**SPECIFICATIONS**
**Calibers:** 22 Hornet to 358 Win.
**Barrel lengths:** 8½″, 10½″ and 14″
**Weight:** 3 lbs. 8 oz. (8¾″ bbl.); 3 lbs. 13 oz. (10½″ bbl.); 4lbs. 3 oz. (14″ bbl.)
**Prices:**

| | |
|---|---|
| Stainless receiver, blued barrel | **$653.00** |
| Stainless receiver and barrel | **711.00** |
| Extra barrels (blue) | **180.00** |
| Stainless | **244.00** |
| Muzzle brake | **125.00** |

This single-shot pistol with its unique falling-block action performs like a finely tuned rifle. The single-piece receiver of stainless steel is mated to a Douglas barrel for optimum accuracy and strength.

# NAVY ARMS REPLICAS

1873 SINGLE ACTION

### 1873 COLT-STYLE SINGLE-ACTION REVOLVERS

The classic 1873 Single Action is the most famous of all the "six shooters." From its adoption by the U.S. Army in 1873 to the present, it still retains its place as America's most popular revolver. **Calibers:** 44-40 or 45 Long Colt. **Barrel lengths:** 3″, 4¾″, 5½″ or 7½″. **Overall length:** 10¾″ (5½″ barrel). **Weight:** 2¼ lbs. **Sights:** Blade front; notch rear. **Grips:** Walnut.
**Price:** .................................... **$390.00**

### 1873 U.S. CAVALRY MODEL (not shown)

An exact replica of the original U.S. Government issue Colt Single-Action Army, complete with Arsenal stampings and inspector's cartouche. **Caliber:** 45 Long Colt. **Barrel length:** 7½″. **Overall length:** 13¼″. **Weight:** 2 lbs. 7 oz. **Sights:** Blade front; notch rear. **Grips:** Walnut.
**Price:** .................................... **$480.00**

### 1895 U.S. ARTILLERY MODEL (not shown)

Same specifications as the U.S. Cavalry Model, but with a 5½″ barrel as issued to Artillery units. **Caliber:** 45 Long Colt.
**Price:** .................................... **$480.00**

1875 SCHOFIELD REVOLVER

### 1875 SCHOFIELD REVOLVER

A favorite side arm of Jesse James and General George Armstrong, the 1875 Schofield revolver was one of the legendary handguns of the Old West. **Caliber:** .44-40, 45 LC. **Barrel lengths:** 5″ (Wells Fargo Model) or 7″ (U.S. Cavalry Model). **Overall length:** 10¾″ or 12¾″. **Weight:** 2 lbs. 7 oz. **Sights:** Blade front; notch rear. **Features:** Top-break, automatic ejector single action.
**Price:** .................................... **$795.00**

# NEW ENGLAND FIREARMS

**STANDARD REVOLVER**
**$129.95 ($139.95 in Nickel)**

**SPECIFICATIONS**
**Calibers:** 22 S, L or LR
**Capacity:** 9 shots
**Barrel lengths:** 2½″ and 4″
**Overall length:** 7″ (2½″ barrel) and 8½″ (4″ barrel)
**Weight:** 25 oz. (2½″ bbl.) and 28 (4″ bbl.)
**Sights:** Blade front; fixed rear
**Grips:** American hardwood, walnut finish
**Finish:** Blue or nickel

Also available:
In 5-shot 32 H&R Mag., 32 S&W, 32 S&W Long. **Weight:** 23 oz. (2½″ barrel); 26 oz. (8½″ barrel).
**Blued finish** . . . . . . . . . . . . . . . . . . . . . . . . . . . . . **$129.95**
**Nickel finish** (2½″ bbl. only) . . . . . . . . . . . . . . . . . . . . **139.95**

**STANDARD MODEL (22 LR, 2½″ Barrel)**

**ULTRA MAG.**

**ULTRA MODEL (6″ Barrel)**

**ULTRA AND ULTRA MAG. REVOLVERS**
**$165.95**

**SPECIFICATIONS**
**Calibers:** 22 Short, Long, Long Rifle (Ultra); 22 Win. Mag. (Ultra Mag.)
**Capacity:** 9 shots (22 LR); 6 shots (22 Win. Mag.)
**Barrel lengths:** 4″ and 6″
**Overall length:** 10⅝″
**Weight:** 36 oz. (6″ barrel)
**Sights:** Blade on rib front; fully adjustable rear
**Grips:** American hardwood, walnut finish

Also available:
**LADY ULTRA** in 5-shot 32 H&R Magnum. **Barrel length:** 3″. **Overall length:** 7¼″. **Weight:** 31 oz. **Price:** . . . . . . **$165.95**

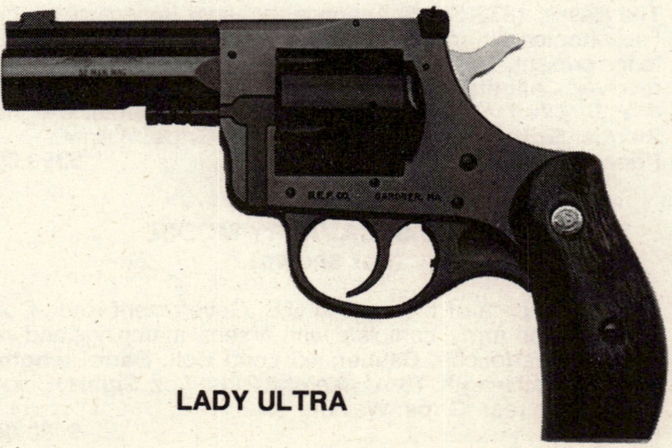

**LADY ULTRA**

# NORTH AMERICAN ARMS

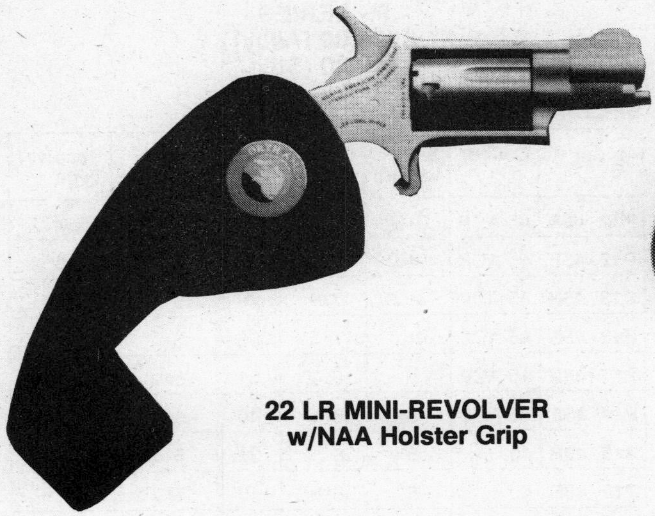

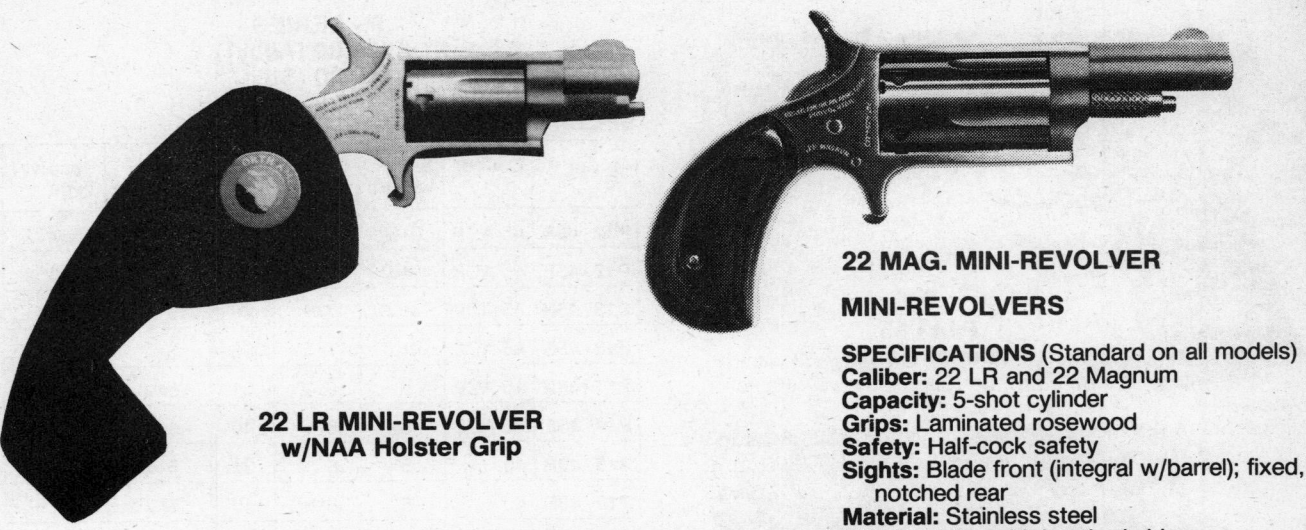

22 LR MINI-REVOLVER
w/NAA Holster Grip

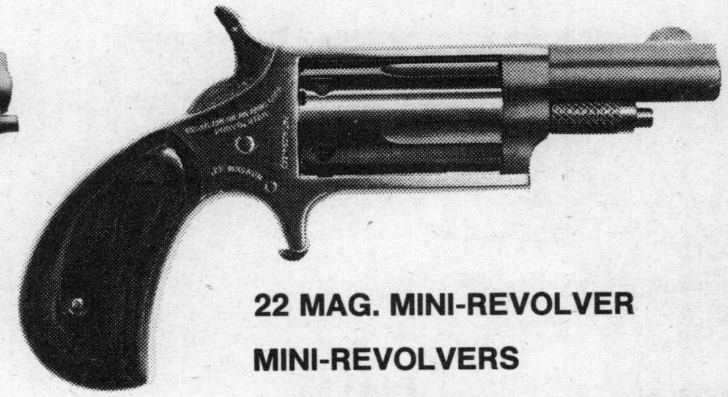

22 MAG. MINI-REVOLVER

## MINI-REVOLVERS

**SPECIFICATIONS** (Standard on all models)
**Caliber:** 22 LR and 22 Magnum
**Capacity:** 5-shot cylinder
**Grips:** Laminated rosewood
**Safety:** Half-cock safety
**Sights:** Blade front (integral w/barrel); fixed, notched rear
**Material:** Stainless steel
**Finish:** Matte with brushed sides

### SPECIFICATIONS: MINI-REVOLVERS & MINI-MASTER SERIES

| Model | Weight | Barrel Length | Overall Length | Overall Height | Overall Width | Prices |
|---|---|---|---|---|---|---|
| NAA-MMT-M | 10.7 oz. | 4″ | 7 3/4″ | 3 7/8″ | 7/8″ | $279.00 |
| NAA-MMT-L | 10.7 oz. | 4″ | 7 3/4″ | 3 7/8″ | 7/8″ | 279.00 |
| *NAA-BW-M | 8.8 oz. | 2″ | 5 7/8″ | 3 7/8″ | 7/8″ | 235.00 |
| *NAA-BW-L | 8.8 oz. | 2″ | 5 7/8″ | 3 7/8″ | 7/8″ | 235.00 |
| NAA-22LR** | 4.5 oz. | 1 1/8″ | 4 1/4″ | 2 3/8″ | 13/16″ | 157.00 |
| NAA-22LLR** | 4.6 oz. | 1 5/8″ | 4 3/4″ | 2 3/8 | 13/16″ | 157.00 |
| *NAA-22MS | 5.9 oz. | 1 1/8″ | 5″ | 2 7/8″ | 7/8″ | 178.00 |
| *NAA-22M | 6.2 oz. | 1 5/8″ | 5 3/8″ | 2 7/8″ | 7/8″ | 178.00 |

* Available with Conversion Cylinder chambered for 22 Long Rifle ** Available with holster grip (**$188.00**)

## MINI-MASTER SERIES

**SPECIFICATIONS** (Standard on all models)
**Calibers:** 22 LR (NAA-MMT-L, NAA-BW-L) and 22 Magnum (NAA-MMT-M, NAA-BW-M)
**Barrel:** Heavy vent
**Rifling:** 8 land and grooves, 1:12 R.H. button broach twist
**Grips:** Oversized black rubber
**Cylinder:** Bull
**Sights:** Front integral with barrel; rear Millett adjustable white outlined (elevation only) or low-profile fixed

**MINI-MASTER NAA-BW
BLACK WIDOW
$249.00**

**MINI-MASTER NAA-MMT-M
(22 Mag. 4″ Barrel)
$279.00**

# PARA-ORDNANCE

**P14 • 45**
**With 5″ Barrel**

**MODEL P12 • 45 COMPACT**
**With 3½″ Barrel**

**P • SERIES**
**$700.00 (Alloy)**
**$745.00 (Steel)**

**SPECIFICATIONS**

| Model # | Caliber | Barrel Length | Overall Length | Wt. (Oz.) | Height (w/mag.) | Receiver Type |
|---|---|---|---|---|---|---|
| **P12·45R** | 45 ACP | 3½″ | 7⅛″ | 26 | 5″ | Alloy |
| **P12·45E** | 45 ACP | 3½″ | 7⅛″ | 34 | 5″ | Steel |
| **P13·45R** | 45 ACP | 4¼″ | 7¾″ | 28 | 5¼″ | Alloy |
| **P13·45E** | 45 ACP | 4¼″ | 7¾″ | 36 | 5¼″ | Steel |
| **P14·45R** | 45 ACP | 5″ | 8½″ | 31 | 5¾″ | Alloy |
| **P14·45E** | 45 ACP | 5″ | 8½″ | 40 | 5¾″ | Steel |
| **P16·40R** | 40 | 5″ | 8½″ | 31 | 5¾″ | Alloy |
| **P16·40E** | 40 | 5″ | 8½″ | 40 | 5¾″ | Steel |

All models have matte black finish. For recreational purposes, magazine capacities are restricted to 10 rounds.

# PRECISION SMALL ARMS

**Model PSP-25**
**$249.00**

**SPECIFICATIONS**
**Type:** Single action, self-loading, blow-back, semiautomatic; all-steel construction; manufactured in the U.S.
**Caliber:** 25 ACP **Capacity:** 6 + 1 round in chamber
**Ignition system:** Striker fired
**Barrel length:** 2.13″
**Rifling:** 6 lands and grooves; right-hand twist
**Overall length:** 4.11″ **Height:** 2.88″
**Weight (unloaded):** 9.5 oz.
**Radius:** 3.54″
**Safety Systems:** Manual frame-mounted safety; magazine safety; cocking indicator
**Sights:** Blade front, 0.03″ width (0.9mm); fixed V-notched rear
**Trigger:** Smooth faced, single stage, draw bar; 0.20″ width; 5.25 lbs. pull weight
**Grips:** Composition; black polymer
**Finish:** Highly polished black oxide
**Options:** Polished stainless-steel frame, slide and barrel; industrial hard chrome, chromium nitrate and gold finish; various grips; engraved limited editions; integrated laser with soft grip

**PSP-25**

# ROSSI REVOLVERS

MODEL 68 "S"
Nickel

MODEL M88 "S"
2″ Barrel

**MODEL 68 "S" SERIES**
**$234.00 (3″ Barrel)**
**$246.00 (2″ Barrel)**
**$238.00 Nickel (3″ Barrel)**

**SPECIFICATIONS**
**Caliber:** 38 Special
**Capacity:** 5 rounds
**Barrel lengths:** 2″ and 3″
**Overall length:** 6 1/2″ (2″ barrel); 7 1/2″ (3″ barrel)
**Weight:** 21 oz. (2″ barrel); 23 oz. (3″ barrel)
**Finish:** Blue or nickel

**MODEL M88 "S" SERIES**
**$265.00 (3″ Barrel)**
**$281.00 (2″ Barrel)**

**SPECIFICATIONS**
**Caliber:** 38 Special
**Capacity:** 5 rounds, swing-out cylinder
**Barrel lengths:** 2″ and 3″
**Overall length:** 6 1/2″ (2″ barrel); 7 1/2″ (3″ barrel)
**Weight:** 21 oz. (2″); 23 oz. (3″)
**Sights:** Ramp front, square-notched rear adjustable for windage
**Grips:** Wood or rubber (2″ barrel only)
**Finish:** Stainless steel

MODEL 515
22 MAG.

MODEL 518
22 LR

**MODELS 515 and 518**
**$281.00 (22 LR)**
**$296.00 (22 Mag.)**

**SPECIFICATIONS**
**Calibers:** 22 LR (**Model 518**) and 22 Mag. (**Model 515**)
**Capacity:** 6 rounds
**Barrel length:** 4″ **Overall length:** 9″
**Weight:** 30 oz.

# ROSSI REVOLVERS

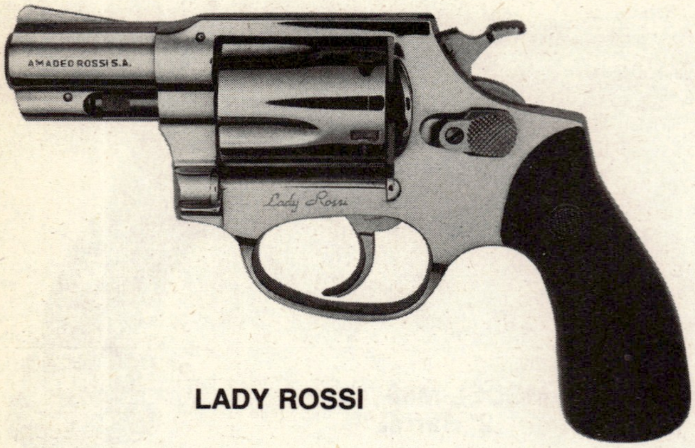


LADY ROSSI

MODEL 720
COVERT SPECIAL

**LADY ROSSI**
**$312.00**

**SPECIFICATIONS**
**Caliber:** 38 Special **Capacity:** 5 rounds
**Barrel lengths:** 2″ and 3″
**Overall length:** 6½″ (2″ bbl.); 7½″ (3″ bbl.)
**Weight:** 21 oz. (2″ bbl.); 23 oz. (3″ bbl.)
**Grips:** Rosewood
**Finish:** Stainless steel
**Features:** Fixed sights, velvet bag

**MODEL 720 (not shown)**
**$320.00**

**SPECIFICATIONS**
**Caliber:** 44 S&W Special **Capacity:** 5 shots
**Barrel length:** 3″ **Overall length:** 8″
**Weight:** 27½ oz.
**Sights:** Adjustable rear; red insert front
**Finish:** Stainless steel
**Features:** Rubber combat grips; full ejector rod shroud

Also available:
**MODEL 720 COVERT SPECIAL.** Double action only, hammerless, notched sight channel in frame. **Price: $320.00**

MODEL 851

MODEL 971
Blue

**MODEL 851**
**$281.00**

**SPECIFICATIONS**
**Caliber:** 38 Special **Capacity:** 6 rounds
**Barrel length:** 4″ **Overall length:** 7½″
**Weight:** 30 oz.
**Frame:** Medium
**Finish:** Stainless

**MODEL 971**
**$281.00 Blue (4″ Barrel)**
**$320.00 Stainless**

**SPECIFICATIONS**
**Caliber:** 357 Magnum or 38 Special
**Capacity:** 6 rounds
**Barrel lengths:** 2½″, 4″ and 6″
**Overall length:** 8 5/16″ w/2½″ bbl.; 9 3/16″ w/4″ bbl.; 11 3/16″ w/6″ bbl.
**Weight:** 22 oz. (2½″ bbl.); 35.4 oz. (4″ bbl.); 40.5 oz. (6″ bbl.)
**Finish:** Blued (4″ barrel only) or stainless steel

Also available:
**MODEL 971 COMPACT GUN.** 357 Mag. only w/3″ barrel. **Capacity:** 6 shots. **Weight:** 32 oz. **Finish:** Stainless only.
**Price:** .................................... **$320.00**

# RUGER REVOLVERS

BLUED REDHAWK REVOLVER

## BLUED STEEL REDHAWK REVOLVER

The popular Ruger Redhawk® double-action revolver is available in an alloy steel model with blued finish in 44 Magnum caliber. Constructed of hardened chrome-moly and other alloy steels, this Redhawk is satin polished to a high lustre and finished in a rich blue.

| Catalog Number | Caliber | Barrel Length | Overall Length | Approx. Weight (Ounces) | Price |
|---|---|---|---|---|---|
| **RUGER BLUED REDHAWK REVOLVER** | | | | | |
| RH-445 | 44 Mag. | 5½″ | 11″ | 49 | **$475.00** |
| RH-44 | 44 Mag. | 7½″ | 13″ | 54 | **475.00** |
| RH-44R* | 44 Mag. | 7½″ | 13″ | 54 | **512.00** |

* Scope model, with Integral Scope Mounts, 1″ Ruger Scope rings.

STAINLESS REDHAWK REVOLVER

## STAINLESS REDHAWK DOUBLE-ACTION REVOLVER

There is no other revolver like the Ruger Redhawk. Knowledgeable sportsmen reaching for perfection in a big bore revolver will find that the Redhawk demonstrates its superiority at the target, whether silhouette shooting or hunting. The scope sight model incorporates the patented Ruger integral Scope Mounting System with 1″ stainless steel Ruger scope rings.

| Catalog Number | Caliber | Barrel Length | Overall Length | Approx. Weight (Ounces) | Price |
|---|---|---|---|---|---|
| **RUGER STAINLESS REDHAWK REVOLVER** | | | | | |
| KRH-445 | 44 Mag. | 5½″ | 11″ | 49 | **$532.00** |
| KRH-44 | 44 Mag. | 7½″ | 13″ | 54 | **532.00** |
| KRH-44R* | 44 Mag. | 7½″ | 13″ | 54 | **574.00** |

* Scope model, with Integral Scope Mounts, 1″ Stainless Steel Ruger Scope rings.

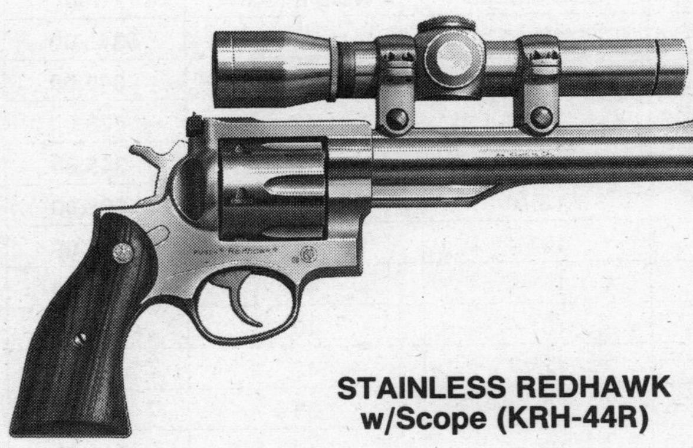

STAINLESS REDHAWK w/Scope (KRH-44R)

## SUPER REDHAWK STAINLESS DOUBLE-ACTION REVOLVER

The **Super Redhawk** double-action revolver in stainless steel features a heavy extended frame with 7½″ and 9½″ barrels. Cushioned grip panels contain Goncalo Alves wood grip panel inserts to provide comfortable, nonslip hold. Comes with integral scope mounts and 1″ stainless steel Ruger scope rings.

**SPECIFICATIONS**
**Caliber:** 44 Magnum
**Barrel length:** 7½″ and 9½″
**Overall length:** 13″ w/7½″ bbl.; 15″ w/9½″ bbl.
**Weight (empty):** 53 oz. (7½″ bbl.); 58 oz. (9½″ bbl.)
**Sight radius:** 9½″ (7½″ bbl.); 11¼″ (9½″ bbl.)
**Finish:** Stainless steel; satin polished

**KSRH-7** (7½″ barrel) . . . . . . . . . . . . . . . . **$574.00**
**KSRH-9** (9½″ barrel) . . . . . . . . . . . . . . . . **574.00**

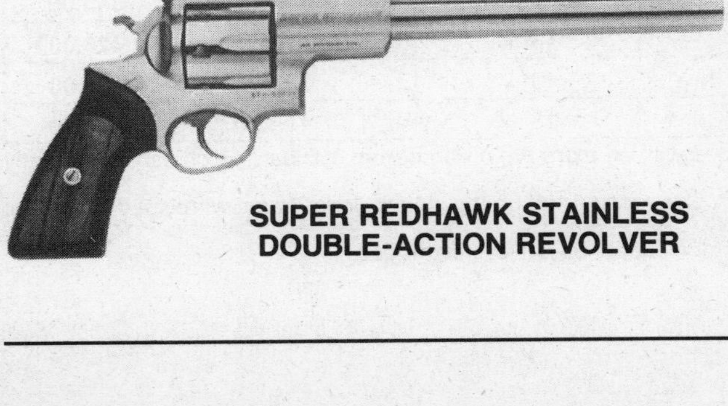

SUPER REDHAWK STAINLESS DOUBLE-ACTION REVOLVER

# RUGER SINGLE-ACTION REVOLVERS

**VAQUERO SINGLE ACTION**
**$419.00**

**SPECIFICATIONS:**
**VAQUERO SINGLE-ACTION REVOLVER**

| Catalog Number | Caliber | Barrel Length | Overall Length | Weight (Ounces) | Finish* |
|---|---|---|---|---|---|
| BNV40 | 44-40 | 4 5/8″ | 10 1/4″ | 39 | CB |
| KBNV40 | 44-40 | 4 5/8″ | 10 1/4″ | 39 | SSG |
| BNV405 | 44-40 | 5 1/2″ | 11 1/2″ | 40 | CB |
| KBNV405 | 44-40 | 5 1/2″ | 11 1/2″ | 40 | SSG |
| BNV407 | 44-40 | 7 1/2″ | 13 1/8″ | 41 | CB |
| KBNV407 | 44-40 | 7 1/2″ | 13 1/8″ | 41 | SSG |
| BNV475 | 44 Mag. | 5 1/2″ | 11 1/2″ | 40 | CB |
| KBNV475 | 44 Mag. | 5 1/2″ | 11 1/2″ | 40 | SSG |
| BNV477 | 44 Mag. | 7 1/2″ | 13 1/8″ | 41 | CB |
| KBNV477 | 44 Mag. | 7 1/2″ | 13 1/8″ | 41 | SSG |
| BNV44 | 45 LC | 4 5/8″ | 10 1/4″ | 39 | CB |
| KBNV44 | 45 LC | 4 5/8″ | 10 1/4″ | 39 | SSG |
| BNV455 | 45 LC | 5 1/2″ | 11 1/2″ | 40 | CB |
| KBNV455 | 45 LC | 5 1/2″ | 11 1/2″ | 40 | SSG |
| BNV45 | 45 LC | 7 1/2″ | 13 1/8″ | 41 | CB |
| KBNV45 | 45 LC | 7 1/2″ | 13 1/8″ | 41 | SSG |

* Finish: high-gloss stainless steel (SSG); color-cased finish on steel cyl. frame w/blued steel grip, barrel, cylinder (CB). LC = Long Colt.

**SPECIFICATIONS: NEW MODEL BLACKHAWK AND BLACKHAWK CONVERTIBLE***

| Cat. Number | Caliber | Finish** | Bbl. Length | O.A. Length | Weight (Oz.) | Price |
|---|---|---|---|---|---|---|
| BN31 | .30 Carbine | B | 7 1/2″ | 13 1/8″ | 44 | **$345.00** |
| BN34 | .357 Mag. + + | B | 4 5/8″ | 10 3/8″ | 40 | **345.00** |
| KBN34 | .357 Mag. + + | SS | 4 5/8″ | 10 3/8″ | 40 | **428.00** |
| BN36 | .357 Mag. + + | B | 6 1/2″ | 12 1/4″ | 42 | **345.00** |
| KBN36 | .357 Mag. + + | SS | 6 1/2″ | 12 1/2″ | 42 | **428.00** |
| BN34X* | .357 Mag. + + | B | 4 5/8″ | 10 3/8″ | 40 | **365.00** |
| BN36X* | .357 Mag. + + | B | 6 1/2″ | 12 1/4″ | 42 | **365.00** |
| GKBN34 | .357 Mag. + + | HGSS | 4 5/8″ | 10 3/8″ | 40 | **428.00** |
| GKBN36 | .357 Mag. + + | HGSS | 6 1/2″ | 12 1/4″ | 42 | **428.00** |
| BN41 | .41 Mag. | B | 4 5/8″ | 10 1/4″ | 38 | **345.00** |
| BN42 | .41 Mag. | B | 6 1/2″ | 12 1/8″ | 40 | **345.00** |
| BN44 | .45 Long Colt | B | 4 5/8″ | 10 1/4″ | 39 | **345.00** |
| KBN44 | .45 Long Colt | SS | 4 5/8″ | 10 1/4″ | 39 | **428.00** |
| BN455 | .45 Long Colt | B | 5 1/2″ | 11 1/8″ | 39 | **345.00** |
| BN45 | .45 Long Colt | B | 7 1/2″ | 13 1/8″ | 41 | **345.00** |
| KBN45 | .45 Long Colt | SS | 7 1/2″ | 13 1/8″ | 41 | **428.00** |
| GKBN44 | .45 Long Colt | HGSS | 4 5/8″ | 10 1/4″ | 39 | **428.00** |
| GKBN45 | .45 Long Colt | HGSS | 7 1/2″ | 13 1/8″ | 41 | **428.00** |

* Convertible: Designated by an X in the Catalog Number, this model comes with an extra 9mm Parabellum cylinder, which can be instantly interchanged without the use of tools. Price includes the extra cylinder.
** Finish: blued (B); stainless steel (SS); high-gloss stainless steel (HGSS); color-cased finish on the steel cylinder frame with blued steel grip, barrel, and cylinder (CB).
+ + Revolvers chambered for the .357 Magnum cartridge also accept factory-loaded .38 Special cartridges.

# RUGER REVOLVERS

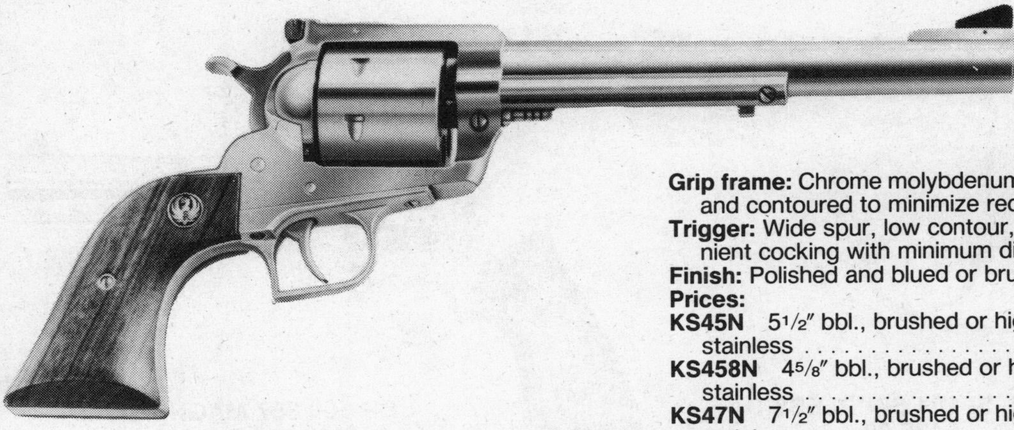

## NEW MODEL SUPER BLACKHAWK SINGLE-ACTION REVOLVER

**SPECIFICATIONS**
**Caliber:** 44 Magnum; interchangeable with 44 Special
**Barrel lengths:** 5½", 7½", 10½"
**Overall length:** 13⅜" (7½" barrel)
**Weight:** 48 oz. (7½" bbl.) and 51 oz. (10½" bbl.)
**Frame:** Chrome molybdenum steel or stainless steel
**Springs:** Music wire springs throughout
**Sights:** Patridge style, ramp front matted blade ⅛" wide; rear sight click-adjustable for windage and elevation
**Grip frame:** Chrome molybdenum or stainless steel, enlarged and contoured to minimize recoil effect
**Trigger:** Wide spur, low contour, sharply serrated for convenient cocking with minimum disturbance of grip
**Finish:** Polished and blued or brushed satin stainless steel
**Prices:**
**KS45N** 5½" bbl., brushed or high-gloss stainless . . . . . **$435.00**
**KS458N** 4⅝" bbl., brushed or high-gloss stainless . . . . . **435.00**
**KS47N** 7½" bbl., brushed or high-gloss stainless . . . . . **435.00**
**GKS47N** 7½" bbl., steel grip frame, high-gloss stainless . . . . . **435.00**
**GKS459** 5½" bbl., steel grip frame, high-gloss stainless . . . . . **435.00**
**GKS458N** 4⅝" bbl., steel grip frame, high-gloss stainless . . . . . **435.00**
**KS411N** 10½" bull bbl., stainless steel . . . . . **435.00**
**KSH7NH** 7½" bbl., scope rings, stainless . . . . . **498.00**
**S45N** 5½" bbl., blued . . . . . **398.00**
**S458N** 4⅝" bbl., blued . . . . . **398.00**
**S47N** 7½" bbl., blued . . . . . **398.00**
**S411N** 10½" bull bbl., blued . . . . . **398.00**

**FIXED SIGHT NEW MODEL SINGLE-SIX (W/Extra Cylinder)**

## NEW MODEL SUPER SINGLE-SIX REVOLVER

**SPECIFICATIONS**
**Caliber:** 22 LR (fitted with WMR cylinder)
**Barrel lengths:** 4⅝", 5½", 6½", 9½"; stainless steel model in 5½" and 6½" lengths only
**Weight** (approx.): 33 oz. (with 5½" barrel); 38 oz. (with 9½" barrel)
**Sights:** Patridge-type ramp front sight; rear sight click adjustable for elevation and windage; protected by integral frame ribs. Fixed sight model available with 5½" or 6½" barrel (same prices as adj. sight models).
**Finish:** Blue, stainless steel or high-gloss stainless
**Prices:**
In blue . . . . . **$298.00**
In brushed or high-gloss stainless steel (convertible 5½" and 6½" barrels only) . . . . . **378.00**

Also available:
**BEARCAT SINGLE ACTION** with 4" barrel, walnut grips
Blue . . . . . **$298.00**
Stainless . . . . . **325.00**

**NEW MODEL SINGLE-SIX SSM™**

## NEW MODEL SINGLE-SIX SSM™ REVOLVER

**SPECIFICATIONS**
**Caliber:** 32 Magnum; also handles 32 S&W and 32 S&W Long
**Barrel lengths:** 4⅝", 5½", 6½", 9½"
**Weight** (approx.): 34 oz. (with 6½" barrel)
**Price:** . . . . . **$298.00**

# RUGER REVOLVERS

**MODEL SP101 SPURLESS DA**
**$428.00**

**GP-100 357 MAGNUM**
**6″ Heavy Barrel**

### SPECIFICATIONS SP101 REVOLVERS

| Catalog Number | Caliber | Cap.* | Sights | Barrel Length | Approx. Wt. (Oz.) |
|---|---|---|---|---|---|
| KSP-221 | 22 LR | 6 | A | 2¼″ | 32 |
| GKSP-221 | 22 LR | 6 | A | 2¼″ | 32 |
| KSP-240 | 22 LR | 6 | A | 4″ | 33 |
| KSP-241 | 22 LR | 6 | A | 4″ | 34 |
| GKSP-241 | 22 LR | 6 | A | 4″ | 34 |
| KSP-3231 | 32 Mag. | 6 | A | 3¹⁄₁₆″ | 30 |
| GKSP-3231 | 32 Mag. | 6 | A | 3¹⁄₁₆″ | 30 |
| KSP-3241 | 32 Mag. | 6 | A | 4″ | 33 |
| GKSP-3241 | 32 Mag. | 6 | A | 4″ | 33 |
| KSP-921 | 9mm×19 | 5 | F | 2¼″ | 25 |
| GKSP-921 | 9mm×19 | 5 | F | 2¼″ | 25 |
| KSP-931 | 9mm×19 | 5 | F | 3¹⁄₁₆″ | 27 |
| GKSP-931 | 9mm×19 | 5 | F | 3¹⁄₁₆″ | 27 |
| KSP-821 | 38+P | 5 | F | 2¼″ | 25 |
| GKSP-821 | 38+P | 5 | F | 2¼″ | 25 |
| KSP-821L | 38+P | 5 | F | 2¼″ | 26 |
| GKSP-821L | 38+P | 5 | F | 2¼″ | 26 |
| KSP-831 | 38+P | 5 | F | 3¹⁄₁₆″ | 27 |
| GKSP-831 | 38+P | 5 | F | 3¹⁄₁₆″ | 27 |
| KSP-321X** | 357 Mag. | 5 | F | 2¼″ | 25 |
| GKSP-321X** | 357 Mag. | 5 | F | 2¼″ | 25 |
| KSP-321XL** | 357 Mag. | 5 | F | 2¼″ | 25 |
| GKSP-321XL** | 357 Mag. | 5 | F | 2¼″ | 25 |
| KSP-331X** | 357 Mag. | 5 | F | 3¹⁄₁₆″ | 27 |
| GKSP-331X** | 357 Mag. | 5 | F | 3¹⁄₁₆″ | 27 |

* Indicates cylinder capacity
** Revolvers chambered for .357 Magnum also accept 38 Special cartridges.
Model KSP-240 has short shroud; all others have full. Spurless hammer models are designated by "L" in catalog no. "G" before a catalog no. indicates high-gloss finish models.

## GP-100 DA 357 MAGNUM

The GP-100 is designed for the unlimited use of 357 Magnum ammunition in all factory loadings; it combines strength and reliability with accuracy and shooting comfort. (Revolvers chambered for the 357 Magnum cartridge also accept the 38 Special cartridge.)

### SPECIFICATIONS

| Catalog Number | Finish | Sights† | Shroud†† | Barrel Length | Wt. (Oz.) | Price |
|---|---|---|---|---|---|---|
| GP-141 | B | A | F | 4″ | 41 | **$425.00** |
| GP-160 | B | A | S | 6″ | 43 | **425.00** |
| GP-161 | B | A | F | 6″ | 46 | **425.00** |
| GPF-331 | B | F | F | 3″ | 36 | **408.00** |
| GPF-340 | B | F | S | 4″ | 37 | **408.00** |
| GPF-341 | B | F | F | 4″ | 38 | **408.00** |
| KGP-141 | SS | A | F | 4″ | 41 | **459.00** |
| GKGP-141 | SSG | A | F | 4″ | 41 | **459.00** |
| KGP-160 | SS | A | S | 6″ | 43 | **459.00** |
| KGP-161 | SS | A | F | 6″ | 46 | **459.00** |
| GKGP-161 | SSG | A | F | 6″ | 46 | **459.00** |
| KGPF-330 | SS | F | S | 3″ | 35 | **442.00** |
| KGPF-331 | SS | F | F | 3″ | 36 | **442.00** |
| GKGPF-33 | SSG | F | F | 3″ | 36 | **442.00** |
| KGPF-340 | SS | F | S | 4″ | 37 | **442.00** |
| KGPF-341 | SS | F | F | 4″ | 38 | **442.00** |
| GKGPF-34 | SSG | F | F | 4″ | 38 | **442.00** |
| KGPF-840* | SS | F | S | 4″ | 37 | **442.00** |
| KGPF-841* | SS | F | F | 4″ | 38 | **442.00** |

* 38 Special only. B = blued; SS = stainless; SSG = high-gloss stainless. † A = adjustable; F = fixed. †† F = full; S = short.

# RUGER REVOLVERS

BISLEY SINGLE-ACTION
TARGET GUN

## BISLEY SINGLE-ACTION TARGET GUN

The Bisley single-action was originally used at the British National Rifle Association matches held in Bisley, England, in the 1890s. Today's Ruger Bisleys are offered in two frame sizes, chambered from 22 LR to 45 Long Colt. These revolvers are the target-model versions of the Ruger single-action line.

**Special features:** Unfluted cylinder rollmarked with classic foliate engraving pattern (or fluted cylinder without engraving); hammer is low with smoothly curved, deeply checkered wide spur positioned for easy cocking.

**Prices:**
22 LR or 32 Magnum .......................... **$345.00**
357 Mag., 41 Mag., 44 Mag., 45 Long Colt ...... **415.00**

## BISLEY SPECIFICATIONS

| Catalog Number | Caliber | Barrel Length | Overall Length | Sights | Approx. Wt. (Oz.) |
|---|---|---|---|---|---|
| RB22AW | 22 LR | 6 1/2″ | 11 1/2″ | Adj. | 41 |
| RB32W | 32 Mag. | 6 1/2″ | 11 1/2″ | Fixed* | 41 |
| RB32AW | 32 Mag. | 6 1/2″ | 11 1/2″ | Adj. | 41 |
| RB35W | 357 Mag. | 7 1/2″ | 13″ | Adj. | 48 |
| RB41W | 41 Mag. | 7 1/2″ | 13″ | Adj. | 48 |
| RB44W | 44 Mag. | 7 1/2″ | 13″ | Adj. | 48 |
| RB45W | 45 Long Colt | 7 1/2″ | 13″ | Adj. | 48 |

* Dovetail rear sight adjustable for windage only.

## THE NEW BEARCAT
**$298.00 (Blued)**
**$325.00 (Stainless)**

THE NEW BEARCAT

Originally manufactured between 1958 and 1973, the new .22-rimfire single-action Bearcat features an all-steel precision investment-cast frame, patented transfer bar mechanism, and two cylinders—one in 22 LR and the other engineered specifically for 22 WMR. The New Bearcat also has walnut grips with the Ruger medallion.

**SPECIFICATIONS**
**Calibers:** 22 LR and 22 WMR (extra cylinder)
**Barrel length:** 4″
**Grips:** Walnut
**Finish:** Blued chrome-moly steel or high-gloss stainless steel

# RUGER P-SERIES PISTOLS

MODEL KP94 9mm
($5^3/_4$" Barrel)

MODEL KP89DC

## P-SERIES PISTOLS

**GENERAL SPECIFICATIONS** (see also table below for additional specifications and prices)
**Barrel length:** $4^1/_2$"
**Overall length:** $7^7/_8$"
**Weight:** 36 oz. (empty magazine)
**Height:** $5^1/_2$" **Width:** $1^1/_2$"
**Sight radius:** 5"
**Sights:** 3-dot system
**Features:** Oversized trigger guard with curved trigger-guard bow; slide stop activated automatically on last shot (w/ magazine in pistol); all stainless steel models made with "Terhune Anticorro" steel for maximum corrosion resistance

### SPECIFICATIONS: P-SERIES PISTOLS

| Cat. Number | Model | Finish | Caliber | Mag. Cap. | Price |
|---|---|---|---|---|---|
| P89 | Manual Safety | Blued | 9mm | 10 | **$410.00** |
| KP89 | Manual Safety | Stainless | 9mm | 10 | **452.00** |
| P89DC | Decock-Only | Blued | 9mm | 10 | **410.00** |
| KP89DC | Decock-Only | Stainless | 9mm | 10 | **452.00** |
| KP89DAO | Double-Action-Only | Stainless | 9mm | 10 | **452.00** |
| KP90 | Manual Safety | Stainless | 45 ACP | 7 | **488.65** |
| KP90DC | Decock-Only | Stainless | 45 ACP | 7 | **488.65** |
| KP93DC | Decock-Only | Stainless | 9mm | 10 | **520.00** |
| KP93DAO | Double-Action-Only | Stainless | 9mm | 10 | **520.00** |
| KP94 | Manual Safety | Stainless | 9mm | 10 | **520.00** |
| KP94DC | Decock-Only | Stainless | 9mm | 10 | **520.00** |
| KP94DAO | Double-Action-Only | Stainless | 9mm | 10 | **520.00** |
| KP944 | Manual Safety | Stainless | 40 Auto | 11 | **520.00** |
| KP944DC | Decock-Only | Stainless | 40 Auto | 11 | **520.00** |
| KP944DAO | Double-Action-Only | Stainless | 40 Auto | 11 | **520.00** |

# RUGER 22 AUTOMATIC PISTOLS

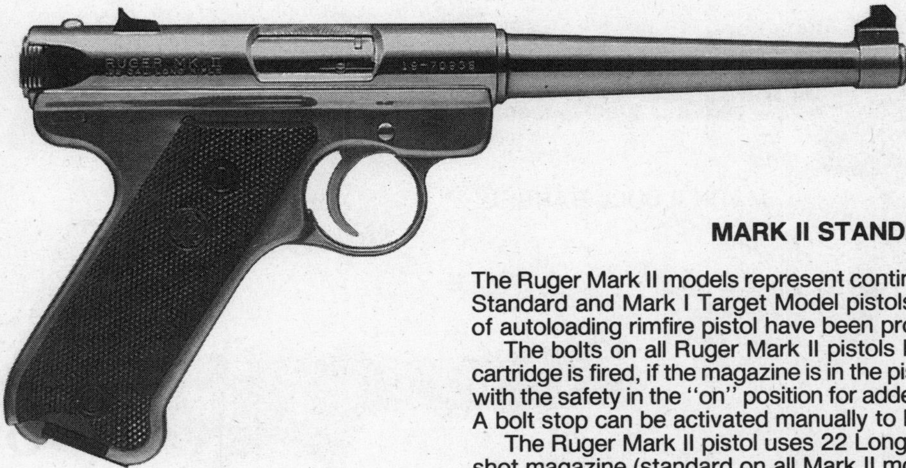

**MARK II STANDARD MODEL STAINLESS**

## MARK II STANDARD MODEL

The Ruger Mark II models represent continuing refinements of the original Ruger Standard and Mark I Target Model pistols. More than two million of this series of autoloading rimfire pistol have been produced since 1949.

The bolts on all Ruger Mark II pistols lock open automatically when the last cartridge is fired, if the magazine is in the pistol. The bolt can be operated manually with the safety in the "on" position for added security while loading and unloading. A bolt stop can be activated manually to lock the bolt open.

The Ruger Mark II pistol uses 22 Long Rifle ammunition in a detachable, 10-shot magazine (standard on all Mark II models except Model 22/45, whose 10-shot magazine is not interchangeable with other Mark II magazines). Designed for easy insertion and removal, the Mark II magazine is equipped with a magazine follower button for convenience in reloading.

For additional specifications, please see the chart on the next page.

**MARK II GOVERNMENT MODEL**

**MARK II TARGET MODEL**

# RUGER 22 AUTOMATIC PISTOLS

MARK II BULL BARREL

MARK II 22/45
w/Zytel Frame

22/45 TARGET
MODEL P-512
(w/11-degree angle)

**SPECIFICATIONS: RUGER 22 MARK II PISTOLS**

| Catalog Number | Model* | Finish** | Barrel Length | Overall Length | Approx. Wt. (Oz.) | Price |
|---|---|---|---|---|---|---|
| MK-4 | Std. | B | 4 3/4″ | 8 5/16″ | 35 | **$252.00** |
| KMK-4 | Std. | SS | 4 3/4″ | 8 5/16″ | 35 | **330.25** |
| KP-4 | Std. | SS | 4 3/4″ | 8 13/16″ | 28 | **280.00** |
| MK-6 | Std. | B | 6″ | 10 5/16″ | 37 | **252.00** |
| KMK-6 | Std. | SS | 6″ | 10 5/16″ | 37 | **330.25** |
| MK-678 | Target | B | 6 7/8″ | 11 1/8″ | 42 | **310.50** |
| KMK-678 | Target | SS | 6 7/8″ | 11 1/8″ | 42 | **389.00** |
| P-512 | Bull | B | 5 1/2″ | 9 3/4″ | 42 | **237.50** |
| MK-512 | Bull | B | 5 1/2″ | 9 3/4″ | 42 | **310.50** |
| KMK-512 | Bull | SS | 5 1/2″ | 9 3/4″ | 42 | **389.00** |
| KP-512 | Bull | SS | 5 1/2″ | 9 3/4″ | 35 | **330.00** |
| MK-10 | Bull | B | 10″ | 14 5/16″ | 51 | **294.50** |
| KMK-10 | Bull | SS | 10″ | 14 5/16″ | 51 | **373.00** |
| MK-678G | Bull | B | 6 7/8″ | 11 1/8″ | 46 | **356.50** |
| KMK-678G | Bull | SS | 6 7/8″ | 11 1/8″ | 46 | **427.25** |
| KMK-678GC | Bull | SS | 6 7/8″ | 11 1/8″ | 45 | **441.00** |

* Model: Std. = standard  ** Finish: B = blued; SS = stainless steel

# SIG-SAUER PISTOLS

MODEL P220 "AMERICAN"

## MODEL P220 "AMERICAN"

**SPECIFICATIONS**
**Calibers:** 38 Super, 45 ACP
**Capacity:** 9 rounds; 7 rounds in 45 ACP
**Barrel length:** 4.4″
**Overall length:** 7.79″
**Weight (empty):** 26½ oz.; 25.7 oz. in 45 ACP
**Finish:** Blue or K-Kote
**Prices:**

| | |
|---|---|
| Blued | **$805.00** |
| W/"Siglite" night sights | **905.00** |
| W/K-Kote finish | **850.00** |
| W/K-Kote and "Siglite" night sights | **950.00** |

## MODEL P225

**SPECIFICATIONS**
**Caliber:** 9mm Parabellum
**Capacity:** 8 rounds
**Barrel length:** 3.9″
**Overall length:** 7.1″
**Trigger:** DA/SA or DA only
**Weight (empty):** 26.1 oz.
**Finish:** Blue or K-Kote
**Prices:**

| | |
|---|---|
| Blued finish | **$780.00** |
| Blued w/"Siglite" night sights | **880.00** |
| W/K-Kote | **850.00** |
| W/K-Kote and "Siglite" night sights | **950.00** |

MODEL P225

MODEL P226

## MODEL P226

**SPECIFICATIONS**
**Caliber:** 9mm Parabellum
**Capacity:** 10 rounds
**Barrel length:** 4.4″
**Overall length:** 7¾″
**Weight (empty):** 26.5 oz.
**Triggers:** DA/SA or DA only
**Finish:** Blue or K-Kote
**Prices:**

| | |
|---|---|
| Blued finish | **$825.00** |
| Blued w/"Siglite" night sights | **925.00** |
| W/K-Kote | **875.00** |
| K-Kote w/"Siglite" night sights | **975.00** |

# SIG-SAUER PISTOLS

MODEL P228

## MODEL P228

**SPECIFICATIONS**
**Caliber:** 9mm
**Capacity:** 10 rounds
**Barrel length:** 3.9″
**Overall length:** 7.1″
**Weight (empty):** 26.1 oz.
**Trigger: DA/SA or DA only**
**Finish:** Blue or K-Kote
**Prices:**

| | |
|---|---|
| Blued finish | **$825.00** |
| Blued w/"Siglite" night sights | **925.00** |
| W/K-Kote | **875.00** |
| W/K-Kote and "Siglite" night sights | **975.00** |

## MODEL P229

**SPECIFICATIONS**
**Calibers:** 9mm, 357 and 40 S&W
**Capacity:** 10 rounds
**Barrel length:** 3.9″
**Overall length:** 7.1″
**Weight (empty):** 27.54 oz.
**Trigger:** DA/SA or DA only
**Finish:** Stainless steel, black frame in aluminum alloy
**Features:** Stainless steel slide; DA/SA or DA only; automatic firing-pin lock
**Prices:**

| | |
|---|---|
| **Model P229** | **$875.00** |
| W/"Siglite night sight | **975.00** |

MODEL P229

MODEL P230

## MODEL P230

**SPECIFICATIONS**
**Caliber:** 9mm Short (380 ACP)
**Capacity:** 7 rounds
**Barrel length:** 3.6″
**Overall length:** 6.6″
**Weight (empty):** 16.2 oz.; 20.8 oz. in stainless steel
**Finish:** Blued or stainless steel
**Prices:**

| | |
|---|---|
| Blued finish | **$510.00** |
| Stainless steel | **595.00** |

# SMITH & WESSON PISTOLS

## COMPACT SERIES

### MODEL 3900 COMPACT SERIES

**SPECIFICATIONS**
**Caliber:** 9mm Parabellum DA Autoloading Luger
**Capacity:** 8 rounds
**Barrel length:** 3½″
**Overall length:** 6⅞″
**Weight (empty):** 25 oz.
**Sights:** Post w/white dot front; fixed rear adj. for windage only w/2 white dots. Adjustable sight models include micrometer click, adj. for windage and elevation w/2 white dots. Deduct **$25** for fixed sights.
**Finish:** Blue (Model 3914); satin stainless (Model 3913)
**Prices:**
**MODEL 3913** . . . . . . . . . . . . . . . . . . . . . . . . . . . . **$622.00**
**MODEL 3914** . . . . . . . . . . . . . . . . . . . . . . . . . . . . **562.00**
**MODEL 3913 LADYSMITH** (stainless) . . . . . . . . . . **640.00**
**MODEL 3953** (Double action only, stainless) . . . . . . **622.00**

**MODEL 3913 DA**
**Stainless**

### MODEL 4000 COMPACT SERIES (not shown)

**SPECIFICATIONS**
**Caliber:** 40 S&W
**Capacity:** 8 rounds
**Barrel length:** 3½″
**Overall length:** 7″
**Weight:** 27 oz.
**Sights:** White dot front; fixed w/2-dot rear
**Price:** . . . . . . . . . . . . . . . . . . . . . . . . . . . . . . . . . **$722.00**

**MODEL 4516 COMPACT**

### MODEL 4500 COMPACT SERIES

**SPECIFICATIONS**
**Caliber:** 45 ACP
**Capacity:** 7 rounds
**Barrel length:** 3¾″
**Overall length:** 7¼″
**Weight:** 34 oz.
**Sights:** White dot front; fixed w/2-dot rear
**Price:** . . . . . . . . . . . . . . . . . . . . . . . . . . . . . . . . . **$774.00**

### MODEL 6900 COMPACT SERIES

**SPECIFICATIONS**
**Caliber:** 9mm Parabellum DA Autoloading Luger
**Capacity:** 12 rounds
**Barrel length:** 3½″
**Overall length:** 6⅞″
**Weight (empty):** 26½ oz.
**Sights:** Post w/white dot front; fixed rear, adj. for windage only w/2 white dots
**Grips:** Delrin one-piece wraparound, arched backstrap, textured surface
**Finish:** Blue (Model 6904); clear anodized/satin stainless (Model 6906)
**Prices:**
**MODEL 6904** . . . . . . . . . . . . . . . . . . . . . . . . . . . . **$614.00**
**MODEL 6906** . . . . . . . . . . . . . . . . . . . . . . . . . . . . **677.00**
**MODEL 6906** Fixed Novak night sight . . . . . . . . . . **788.00**
**MODEL 6946** DA only, fixed sights . . . . . . . . . . . . **677.00**

**MODEL 6906 DA**
**Stainless**

# SMITH & WESSON PISTOLS

## FULL-SIZE DOUBLE-ACTION PISTOLS

Smith & Wesson's double-action semiautomatic Third Generation line includes the following features: fixed barrel bushing for greater accuracy • smoother trigger pull plus a slimmer, contoured grip and lateral relief cut where trigger guard meets frame • three-dot sights • wraparound grips • beveled magazine well for easier reloading • ambidextrous safety lever secured by spring-loaded plunger • low-glare bead-blasted finish.

**MODEL 4006**
**With Fixed Sight**

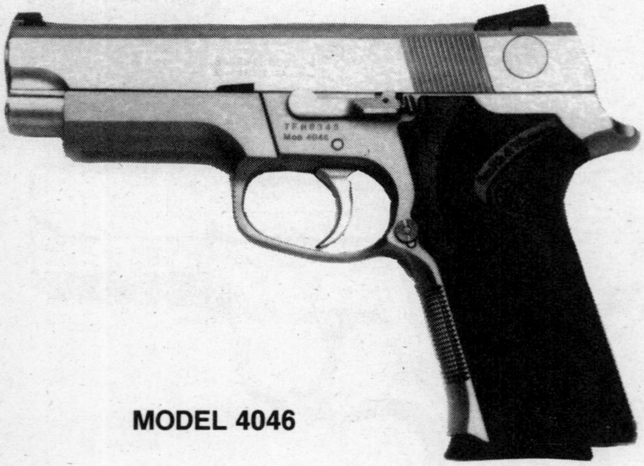

**MODEL 4046**

### MODEL 4000 SERIES

**SPECIFICATIONS**
**Caliber:** 40 S&W
**Capacity:** 11 rounds
**Barrel length:** 4″
**Overall length:** 7 7/8″
**Weight:** 38 1/2 oz. (with fixed sights)
**Sights:** Post w/white dot front; fixed or adjustable w/white 2-dot rear
**Grips:** Straight backstrap, Xenoy wraparound
**Finish:** Stainless steel
**Prices:**
**MODEL 4006** w/fixed sights . . . . . . . . . . **$745.00**
Same as above w/adj. sights . . . . . . . . . . **775.00**
w/fixed night sight . . . . . . . . . . **855.00**
**MODEL 4043** Double action only . . . . . . . . . . **727.00**
**MODEL 4046** w/fixed sights, DA only . . . . . . . . . . **745.00**
Double action only, fixed Tritium night sight . . . . **855.00**

### MODEL 4500 SERIES

**SPECIFICATIONS**
**Caliber:** 45 ACP Autoloading DA
**Capacity:** 8 rounds (Model 4506); 7 rounds (Model 4516)
**Barrel lengths:** 5″ (Model 4506); 3 3/4″ (Model 4516)
**Overall length:** 8 5/8″ (Model 4506); 7 1/8″ (Model 4516)
**Weight (empty):** 38 1/2 oz. (Model 4506); 34 1/2 oz. (Model 4516)
**Sights:** Post w/white-dot front; fixed rear, adj. for windage only. Adj. sight incl. micrometer click, adj. for windage and elevation w/2 white dots. Add **$29.00** for adj. sights.
**Grips:** Delrin one-piece wraparound, arched backstrap, textured surface
**Finish:** Satin stainless
**Prices:**
**MODEL 4506** w/adj. sights, 5″ bbl. . . . . . . . . . . **$806.00**
With fixed sights . . . . . . . . . . **774.00**
**MODEL 4566** w/4 1/4″ bbl., fixed sights . . . . . . . . . . **774.00**
**MODEL 4586** DA only, 4 1/4″ bbl., fixed sights . . . . . **774.00**

**MODEL 4506-1**
**Adjustable Sight**

# SMITH & WESSON PISTOLS

## FULL-SIZE DOUBLE-ACTION PISTOLS

### MODEL 5900 SERIES

**SPECIFICATIONS**
**Caliber:** 9mm Parabellum DA Autoloading Luger
**Capacity:** 15 rounds
**Barrel length:** 4″
**Overall length:** 7½″
**Weight (empty):** 28½ oz. (Models 5903, 5904, 5946); 37½ oz. (Model 5906); 38 oz. (Model 5906 w/adj. sight)
**Sights:** Front, post w/white dot; fixed rear, adj. for windage only w/2 white dots. Adjustable sight models include micrometer click, adj. for windage and elevation w/2 white dots.
**Finish:** Blue (Model 5904); satin stainless (Models 5903 and 5906)
**Prices:**
**MODEL 5903** Satin stainless .................... **$690.00**
**MODEL 5904** Blue .................... **642.00**
**MODEL 5906** Satin stainless .................... **742.00**
With fixed sights .................... **707.00**
With Tritium night sight .................... **817.00**
**MODEL 5946** Double action only .................... **707.00**

**MODEL 5906 DA Stainless**

**MODEL 411**

### MODEL 411

**SPECIFICATIONS**
**Caliber:** 40 S&W
**Capacity:** 11 rounds + 1
**Barrel length:** 4″
**Overall length:** 7½″
**Weight:** 29.4 oz.
**Sights:** Post w/white dot front; fixed rear
**Grips:** One-piece Xenoy straight backstrap
**Features:** Right-hand slide-mounted manual safety; decocking lever; aluminum alloy frame; blue carbon steel slide; non-reflective finish
**Price:** .................... **$525.00**

### MODEL 910

**SPECIFICATIONS**
**Caliber:** 9mm
**Capacity:** 10 rounds
**Barrel length:** 4″
**Overall length:** 7⅜″
**Weight:** 28 oz.
**Sights:** Post front; fixed rear
**Grips:** Straight backstrap
**Safety:** External, single side
**Finish:** Matte blue
**Features:** Carbon steel slide; alloy frame
**Price:** .................... **$467.00**
Also available:
**MODEL 909** (9 rounds) w/curved backstrap. **Price: $443.00**

**MODEL 910**

# SMITH & WESSON TARGET PISTOLS

### MODEL NO. 41 RIMFIRE
**$753.00 (Blue Only)**

**SPECIFICATIONS**
**Caliber:** 22 LR **Magazine capacity:** 12 rounds
**Barrel lengths:** 5½″ and 7″ **Weight:** 44 oz. (5½″ barrel)
**Sights:** Front, ⅛″ Patridge undercut; rear, S&W micrometer click sight adjustable for windage and elevation
**Grips:** Checkered walnut with modified thumbrest, equally adaptable to right- or left-handed shooters
**Finish:** S&W Bright blue
**Trigger:** .365″ width; S&W grooving, adj. trigger stop

MODEL NO. 41

### MODEL 422 RIMFIRE 22 SA
**$235.00 (Fixed Sight)**
**$290.00 (Adjustable Sight)**

**SPECIFICATIONS**
**Caliber:** 22 LR **Capacity:** 12 rounds (magazine furnished)
**Barrel lengths:** 4½″ and 6″
**Overall length:** 7½″ (4½″ barrel) and 9″ (6″ barrel)
**Weight:** 22 oz. (4½″ barrel) and 23 oz. (6″ barrel)
**Grips:** Plastic (field version) and checkered walnut w/S&W monogram (target version)
**Front sight:** Serrated ramp w/.125″ blade (field version); Patridge w/.125″ blade (target version)
**Rear sight:** Fixed sight w/.125″ blade (field version): adjustable sight w/.125″ blade (target version)
**Hammer:** .250″ internal **Trigger:** .312″ serrated
Also available:
**MODEL 622.** Same specifications as Model 422 in stainless steel. **Price: $284.00.** (Add **$53.00** for adj. sights).

MODEL 422

MODEL 2213
"SPORTSMAN"

### MODEL 2213/2214 RIMFIRE "SPORTSMAN"
**$269.00 (Blue) $314.00 (Stainless)**

**SPECIFICATIONS**
**Caliber:** 22 LR. **Capacity:** 8 rounds. **Barrel length:** 3″. **Overall length:** 6⅛″. **Weight:** 18 oz. **Finish:** Stainless steel slide w/ alloy frame (**Model 2214** has blued carbon steel slide w/alloy frame)

### MODEL 2206
**$327.00 (Fixed Sights)**
**$385.00 (Adj. Sights)**

**SPECIFICATIONS**
**Caliber:** 22 LR. **Capacity:** 12 rounds. **Barrel length:** 6″. **Overall length:** 9″. **Weight:** 39 oz. **Finish:** Stainless steel.
Also available:
**Model 2206 TARGET** w/adj. target sight, drilled and tapped. **Price: $433.00**

MODEL 2206 TARGET

# SMITH & WESSON PISTOLS

## SIGMA SERIES

Smith & Wesson's Sigma Series is the product of several years' effort to produce a series of pistols that has resulted in 12 patent applications. These pistols are a combination of traditional craftsmanship and the latest technological advances that allow the guns to be assembled without the usual "fitting" process required for other handguns, a method that results in complete interchangeability of parts.

The polymer frame design for the Sigma Series provides unprecedented comfort and pointability. The low barrel centerline combined with the ergonomic design means low muzzle flip and fast reaction for the next shot.

**SIGMA SERIES MODEL SW40F**

**SPECIFICATIONS**
**Calibers:** 40 S&W and 9mm
**Capacity:** 10 rounds; 15- and 17-round magazines available for law-enforcement personnel only
**Barrel length:** 4½"
**Overall length:** 7.4"
**Weight (empty):** 26 oz.
**Height:** 5.6"
**Width:** 1.3"
**Sight radius:** 6.4"
**Sights:** 3-dot system (Tritium night sights available)
**Features:** Custom carrying case standard; internal striker firing system; corrosion-resistant slide; field-stripping to four components only; front and backstrap checkering; carbon steel magazine w/Teflon-filled electroless-nickel coating; integral thumbrest
**Price:**
**9mm** . . . . . . . . . . . . . . . . . . . . **$593.00**
**40 S&W** . . . . . . . . . . . . . . . . . . . . **697.00**

# SMITH & WESSON REVOLVERS

## SMALL FRAME

**MODEL 60LS LADYSMITH**
**38 S&W Special**

### LADYSMITH HANDGUNS
### MODEL 36-LS $408.00 (Blue)
### MODEL 60-LS $461.00 (Stainless)

**SPECIFICATIONS**
**Caliber:** 38 S&W Special
**Capacity:** 5 shots
**Barrel length:** 2″
**Overall length:** $6\frac{5}{16}$″
**Weight:** 20 oz.
**Sights:** Serrated ramp front; fixed notch rear
**Grips:** Contoured laminated rosewood
**Finish:** Glossy deep blue or stainless
**Features:** Both models come with soft-side LadySmith carry case

### MODEL 36
### 38 CHIEFS SPECIAL
### $377.00

**MODEL 37**
**CHIEFS SPECIAL AIRWEIGHT**
**38 S&W Special**

**SPECIFICATIONS**
**Caliber:** 38 S&W Special
**Capacity:** 5 shots
**Barrel length:** 2″ or 3″
**Overall length:** $6\frac{1}{2}$″ with 2″ barrel
**Weight:** $19\frac{1}{2}$ oz. (2″ barrel); $21\frac{1}{2}$ oz. (3″ barrel)
**Sights:** Serrated ramp front; fixed, square-notch rear
**Grips:** Checkered walnut Service
**Finish:** S&W blue carbon steel or nickel
**Features:** .312″ smooth combat-style trigger; .240″ service hammer
**MODEL 37 CHIEFS SPECIAL AIRWEIGHT:** Same as Model 36, except finish is blue or nickel aluminum alloy; **weight:** $13\frac{1}{2}$ oz.; 2″ barrel only

| | |
|---|---|
| Blue | **$412.00** |
| With nickel finish | **428.00** |

### MODEL 60
### 38 CHIEFS SPECIAL, STAINLESS
### $431.00 (2″ Barrel) $458.00 (3″ Barrel)

**MODEL 60**
**38 CHIEFS SPECIAL**

**SPECIFICATIONS**
**Caliber:** 38 S&W Special
**Capacity:** 5 shots
**Barrel lengths:** 2″ and 3″
**Overall length:** $6\frac{5}{16}$″ (2″ barrel); $7\frac{1}{2}$″ (3″ barrel)
**Weight:** $19\frac{1}{2}$ oz. (2″ barrel); $21\frac{1}{2}$ oz. (3″ barrel); $24\frac{1}{2}$ oz. (3″ full lug barrel)
**Sights:** Micrometer click rear, adj. for windage and elevation; pinned black front (3″ full lug model only); standard sights as on Model 36
**Grips:** Checkered walnut Service with S&W monograms; Santoprene combat-style on 3″ full lug model
**Finish:** Stainless steel
**Features:** .312″ smooth combat-style trigger (.347″ serrated trigger on 3″ full lug model); .240″ service hammer (.375″ semitarget hammer on 3″ full lug model)

# SMITH & WESSON REVOLVERS

## SMALL FRAME

### 38 CENTENNIAL "AIRWEIGHT" MODEL 442
**$427.00 (Blue) $442.00 (Nickel)**

**SPECIFICATIONS**
**Caliber:** 38 S&W Special
**Capacity:** 5 rounds
**Barrel length:** 2″
**Overall length:** 6 7/16″
**Weight:** 15.8 oz.
**Sights:** Serrated ramp front; fixed, square-notch rear
**Finish:** Matte blue or satin nickel

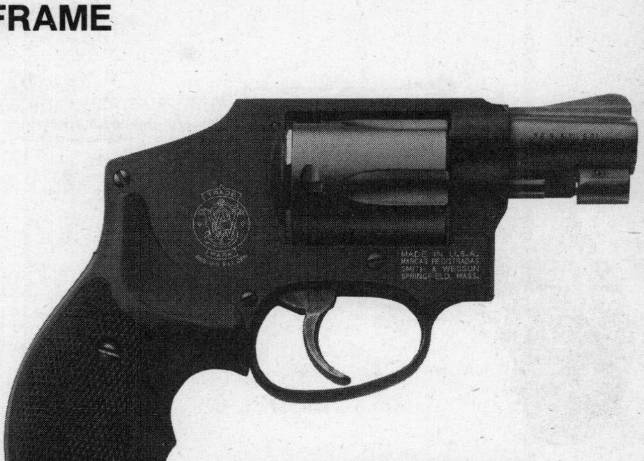

MODEL 442 38 SPECIAL

### 38 BODYGUARD "AIRWEIGHT" MODEL 38 (not shown)
**$444.00 Blue $460.00 Nickel**

**SPECIFICATIONS**
**Caliber:** 38 S&W Special
**Capacity:** 5 shots
**Barrel length:** 2″
**Overall length:** 6 3/8″
**Weight:** 14 oz.
**Sights:** Front, fixed 1/10″ serrated ramp; square-notch rear
**Grips:** Checkered walnut Service with S&W monograms
**Finish:** S&W blue or nickel aluminum alloy

### 38 BODYGUARD MODEL 49
**$409.00 (not shown)**

**SPECIFICATIONS**
**Caliber:** 38 S&W Special
**Capacity:** 5 shots
**Barrel length:** 2″
**Overall length:** 6 1/4″
**Weight (empty):** 20 oz.
**Sights:** Serrated ramp front; fixed, square-notch rear
**Finish:** S&W blue

### MODEL 649 BODYGUARD
**$469.00**

**SPECIFICATIONS**
**Caliber:** 38 S&W Special
**Capacity:** 5 shots
**Barrel length:** 2″
**Overall length:** 6 1/4″
**Weight:** 20 oz.
**Sights:** Serrated ramp front; fixed, square-notch rear
**Grips:** Round butt; checkered walnut Service
**Finish:** Stainless steel

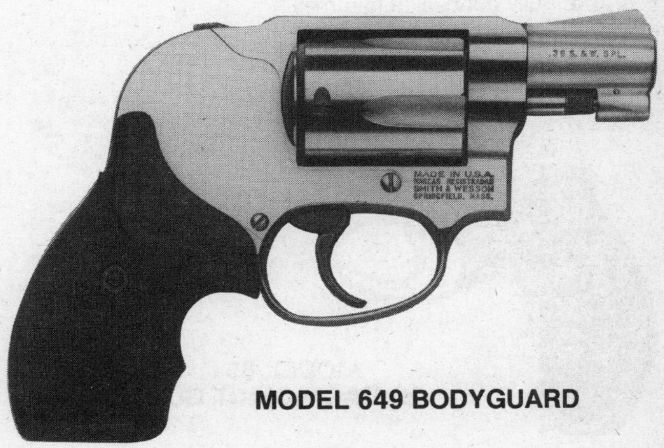

MODEL 649 BODYGUARD

# SMITH & WESSON REVOLVERS

## SMALL FRAME

MODEL 63

### MODEL 63 22/32 KIT GUN
**$458.00 (2″ Barrel)**
**$462.00 (4″ Barrel)**

**SPECIFICATIONS**
**Caliber:** 22 Long Rifle **Capacity:** 6 shots
**Barrel lengths:** 2″ and 4″
**Weight:** 22 oz. (2″ barrel); 24 1/2 oz. (4″ barrel)
**Sights:** 1/8″ red ramp front sight; rear sight is black stainless steel S&W micrometer click, square-notch, adjustable for windage and elevation
**Grips:** Square butt
**Finish:** Satin stainless

MODEL 640

### MODEL 640
**$469.00**

**SPECIFICATIONS**
**Caliber:** 357 Magnum **Capacity:** 5 rounds
**Barrel length:** 2 1/8″ **Overall length:** 6 3/4″
**Weight:** 25 oz.
**Sights:** Pinned black ramp front; fixed, square-notch rear
**Features:** Fully concealed hammer; smooth hardwood service stock

### MODEL 940 CENTENNIAL (not shown)
**$474.00**

**SPECIFICATIONS**
**Caliber:** 9mm Parabellum **Capacity:** 5 rounds
**Barrel length:** 2″ **Overall length:** 6 7/16″
**Weight:** 23 oz.
**Sights:** Serrated ramp front; fixed, square-notch rear
**Grips:** Santoprene combat grips
**Feature:** Fully concealed hammer

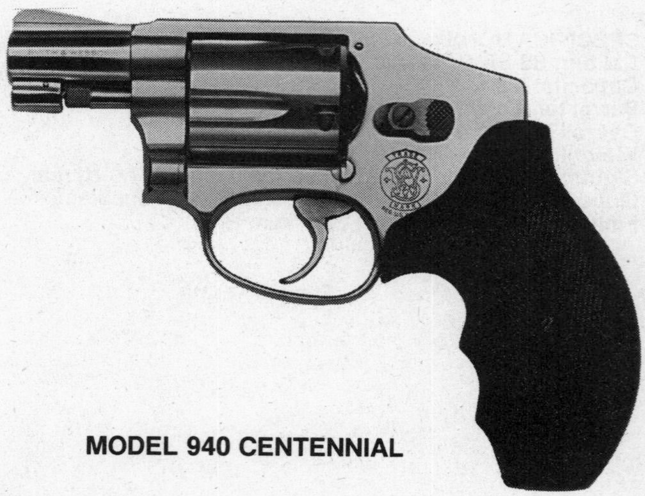

MODEL 940 CENTENNIAL

MODEL 651
22 MAGNUM KIT GUN

### 22 MAGNUM KIT GUN MODEL 651
**$460.00**

**SPECIFICATIONS**
**Caliber:** 22 Magnum **Capacity:** 6 shots
**Barrel length:** 4″ **Overall length:** 8 11/16″
**Weight:** 24 1/2 oz.
**Sights:** Red ramp front; micrometer click rear, adjustable for windage and elevation
**Grips:** Checkered premium hardwood Service
**Finish:** Stainless steel
**Features:** .375″ hammer; .312″ smooth combat trigger

# SMITH & WESSON REVOLVERS

## MEDIUM FRAME

MODEL 10 HEAVY BARREL

### 38 MILITARY & POLICE
### MODEL 10
**$383.00 (2″ Bbl.) $390.00 (4″ Bbl.)**

**SPECIFICATIONS**
**Caliber:** 38 S&W Special **Capacity:** 6 shots
**Barrel lengths:** 2″, 4″ (also 4″ heavy barrel)
**Weight:** 33½ oz. with 4″ barrel
**Sights:** Front, fixed ⅛″ serrated ramp; square-notch rear
**Grips:** Checkered walnut Service with S&W monograms, round or square butt
**Finish:** S&W blue

### 38 MILITARY & POLICE STAINLESS
### MODEL 64
**$415.00 (2″ Bbl.) $423.00 (3″ & 4″ Bbl.)**

**SPECIFICATIONS**
**Calibers:** 38 S&W Special, 38 S&W Special Mid Range
**Capacity:** 6 shots
**Barrel lengthS:** 4″ heavy barrel, square butt; 3″ heavy barrel, round butt; 2″ regular barrel, round butt
**Overall length:** 9¼″ w/4″ bbl.; 7⅞″ w/3″ bbl.; 6⅞″ w/2″ bbl.
**Weight:** 28 oz. w/2″ barrel; 30½ oz. w/3″ bbl.; 33½ oz. w/4″ bbl.
**Sights:** Fixed, ⅛″ serrated ramp front; square-notch rear
**Grips:** Checkered walnut Service with S&W monograms
**Finish:** Satin stainless

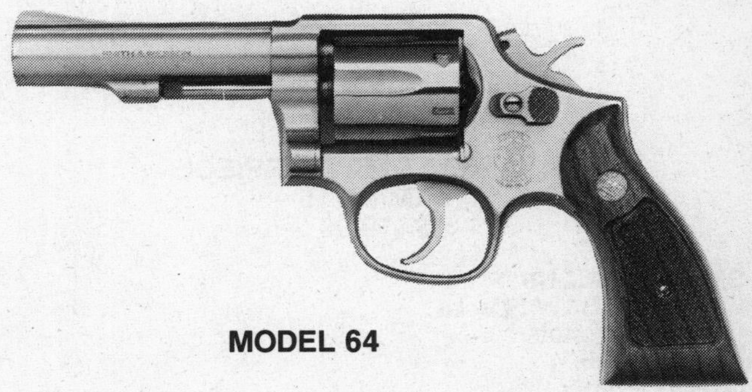

MODEL 64

### 357 MILITARY & POLICE
### MODEL 13 (HEAVY BARREL)
**$394.00**

**SPECIFICATIONS**
**Calibers:** 357 Magnum and 38 S&W Special
**Capacity:** 6 shots
**Barrel lengths:** 3″ and 4″ **Overall length:** 9¼″ (w/4″ bbl.)
**Weight:** 34 oz. (w/4″ bbl.)
**Sights:** Front, ⅛″ serrated ramp; square-notch rear
**Grips:** Checkered walnut service with S&W monograms, square butt (3″ barrel has round butt)
**Finish:** S&W blue

MODEL 13

MODEL 65

### 357 MILITARY & POLICE
### MODEL 65 (HEAVY BARREL)
**$427.00**

**SPECIFICATIONS**
Same specifications as Model 13, except **Model 65** is stainless steel. Available with matte finish.
Also available:
**MODEL 65 LADYSMITH.** Same specifications as **Model 65** but with 3″ barrel only. Also features rosewood laminate stock, glass beaded. **Price:** . . . . . . . . . . . . . . . . . . . . . . . . **$461.00**

# SMITH & WESSON REVOLVERS

## MEDIUM FRAME

MODEL 14

### K-38 MASTERPIECE MODEL 14 $465.00

**SPECIFICATIONS**
**Caliber:** 38 S&W Special
**Barrel length:** 6″ full lug barrel
**Overall length:** 11 1/8″
**Weight:** 47 oz.
**Sights:** Micrometer click rear, adjustable for windage and elevation; pinned black Patridge-style front
**Grips:** Combat-style premium hardwood
**Finish:** Blue carbon steel
**Features:** .500 target hammer; .312″ smooth combat trigger

### 38 COMBAT MASTERPIECE MODEL 15 $419.00

**SPECIFICATIONS**
**Caliber:** 38 S&W Special
**Capacity:** 6 shots
**Barrel length:** 4″
**Overall length:** 9 5/16″
**Weight (loaded):** 32 oz.
**Sights:** Serrated ramp front; S&W micrometer click sight adjustable for windage and elevation
**Grips:** Checkered walnut Service with S&W monograms
**Finish:** S&W blue
**Features:** .375″ semitarget hammer; .312″ smooth combat-style trigger
Also available:
**MODEL 67.** Same specifications as above but w/red ramp front sight and adj. rear sight; stainless steel. **Price: $467.00**

MODEL 15

MODEL 617

### K-22 MASTERPIECE MODEL 617 $460.00 (4″ barrel) $490.00 (6″ barrel) $501.00 (8 3/4″ barrel)

**SPECIFICATIONS**
**Caliber:** 22 Long Rifle
**Capacity:** 6 shots
**Barrel length:** 4″, 6″ or 8 3/8″
**Overall length:** 9 1/8″ (4″ barrel); 11 1/8″ (6″ barrel); 13 1/2″ (8 3/8″ barrel)
**Weight (loaded):** 42 oz. with 4″ barrel; 48 oz. with 6″ barrel; 54 oz. with 8 3/8″ barrel
**Sights:** Front, 1/8″ plain Patridge; rear, S&W micrometer click sight adjustable for windage and elevation
**Grips:** Checkered walnut Service with S&W monograms
**Finish:** S&W blue

# SMITH & WESSON REVOLVERS

## MEDIUM FRAME

MODEL 19

### 357 COMBAT MAGNUM
### MODEL 19
**$416.00 (2½" Bbl.) $426.00 (4" Bbl.)**
**$430.00 (6" Barrel)**

**SPECIFICATIONS**
**Caliber:** 357 S&W Magnum (actual bullet dia. 38 S&W Spec.)
**Capacity:** 6 shots
**Barrel lengths:** 2½", 4" and 6"
**Overall length:** 9½" w/4" bbl.; 7½" w/2½" bbl.; 11⅜" w/6" bbl.
**Weight:** 30½ oz. (2½" bbl.); 36 oz. (4" bbl.); 39 oz. (6" bbl.)
**Sights:** Front, ⅛" Baughman Quick Draw on 2½" or 4" bbl., ⅛" Patridge on 6" bbl.; rear, S&W Micrometer Click, adjustable for windage and elevation
**Grips:** Checkered Goncalo Alves Target with S&W monograms
**Finish:** S&W bright blue
**Features:** 2½"-barrel model has round butt and synthetic grip

### 357 COMBAT MAGNUM
### MODEL 66
**$466.00 (2½" Bbl.) $471.00 (4" & 6" Bbl.)**

**SPECIFICATIONS**
**Caliber:** 357 Magnum (actual bullet dia. 38 S&W Spec.)
**Capacity:** 6 shots
**Ammunition:** 357 S&W Magnum, 38 S&W Special Hi-Speed, 38 S&W Special, 38 S&W Special Mid Range
**Barrel lengths:** 4" or 6" with square butt; 2½" with round butt
**Overall length:** 7½" w/2½" bbl.; 9½" w/4" bbl.; 11⅜" w/6" bbl.
**Weight:** 30½ oz. w/2½" bbl.; 36 oz. w/4" bbl.; 39 oz. w/6" bbl.
**Sights:** Front, ⅛"; rear, S&W Red Ramp on ramp base, S&W Micrometer Click, adjustable for windage and elevation; white outline rear
**Grips:** Checkered Goncalo Alves target with square butt and S&W monograms
**Trigger:** S&W grooving with an adjustable trigger stop
**Finish:** Satin stainless

MODEL 66

### DISTINGUISHED COMBAT MAGNUM
### MODEL 586 (not shown)
**$457.00 (4" Bbl.) $461.00 (6" Bbl.)**

**SPECIFICATIONS**
**Caliber:** 357 Magnum
**Capacity:** 6 shots
**Barrel lengths:** 4" and 6"
**Overall length:** 9 9/16" w/4" bbl.; 11 5/16" w/6" bbl.
**Weight:** 41 oz. w/4" bbl.; 46 oz. w/6" bbl.
**Sights:** Front, S&W Red Ramp; rear, S&W Micrometer Click, adjustable for windage and elevation; white outline notch. Option with 6" barrel only—plain Patridge front with black outline notch; for white outline rear sight, add **$4.00**
**Grips:** Checkered Goncalo Alves with speedloader cutaway
**Finish:** S&W Blue

# SMITH & WESSON REVOLVERS

## MEDIUM FRAME

MODEL 686

MODEL 686 POWERPORT

### MODEL 686
### $481.00 – $530.00

Same specifications as **Model 586** (see preceding page), except also available with 2 1/2″ barrel (35 3/4 oz.) and 8 3/8″ barrel (53 oz.). All models have stainless steel finish, combat or target stock and/or trigger; adjustable sights optional.

### MODEL 686 POWERPORT

Same general specifications as the **Model 686,** except this revolver features 6″ ported barrel, Hogue synthetic grips and black-pinned Patridge front sight.

## LARGE FRAME

### 44 MAGNUM MODEL 29
### $554.00 (6″ Bbl.) $566.00 (8 3/8″ Bbl.)

**SPECIFICATIONS**
**Caliber:** 44 Magnum **Capacity:** 6 shots
**Barrel lengths:** 6″ and 8 3/8″
**Overall length:** 11 7/8″ with 6″ bbl.; 13 7/8″ with 8 3/8″ bbl.
**Weight:** 47 oz. w/6″ bbl.; 51 1/2 oz. w/8 3/8″ bbl.
**Sights:** Front, Red Ramp on ramp base; rear, S&W Micrometer Click, adjustable for windage and elevation; white outline notch
**Grips:** Checkered, highly grained hardwood, target type
**Hammer:** Checkered target type
**Trigger:** Grooved target type
**Finish:** Blued carbon steel

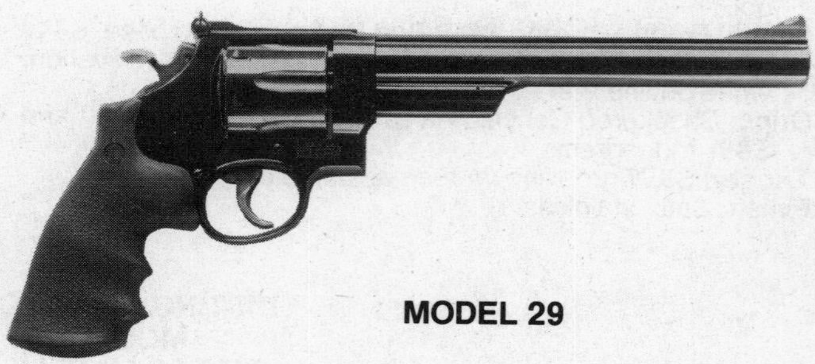

MODEL 29

### MODEL 625 (not shown)
### $597.00

**SPECIFICATIONS**
**Caliber:** 45 ACP **Capacity:** 6 shots
**Barrel length:** 5″ full lug barrel **Overall length:** 10 3/8″
**Weight (empty):** 45 oz.
**Sights:** Front, Patridge on ramp base; S&W Micrometer Click rear, adjustable for windage and elevation
**Grips:** Pachmayr SK/GR gripper, round butt
**Finish:** Stainless steel

# SMITH & WESSON REVOLVERS

## LARGE FRAME

MODEL 629

### MODEL 629
**$587.00 (4″ Bbl.) $592.00 (6″ Bbl.)**
**$606.00 (8 3/8″ Barrel)**

**SPECIFICATIONS**
**Calibers:** 44 Magnum, 44 S&W Special
**Capacity:** 6 shots
**Barrel lengths:** 4″, 6″, 8 3/8″
**Overall length:** 9 5/8″, 11 3/8″, 13 7/8″
**Weight (empty):** 44 oz. (4″ bbl.); 47 oz. (6″ bbl.); 51 1/2 oz. (8 3/8″ bbl.)
**Sights:** S&W Red Ramp front; plain blade rear w/S&W Micrometer Click, adjustable for windage and elevation; scope mount
**Grips:** Checkered hardwood target or synthetic
**Finish:** Stainless steel

### MODEL 629 CLASSIC
**$629.00 (5″ & 6 1/2″ Bbl.)**
**$650.00 (8 3/8″ Bbl.)**

**SPECIFICATIONS**
**Calibers:** 44 Magnum, 44 S&W Special
**Capacity:** 6 rounds
**Barrel lengths:** 5″, 6 1/2″, 8 3/8″
**Overall length:** 10 1/2″, 12″, 13 7/8″
**Weight:** 51 oz. (5″ bbl.); 52 oz. (6 1/2″ bbl.); 54 oz. (8 3/8″ bbl.)

Also available:
**MODEL 629 CLASSIC DX.** Same features as the **Model 629 Classic** above, plus two sets of grips and five interchangeable front sights and proof target.
With 6 1/2″ barrel ........................... **$811.00**
With 8 3/8″ barrel ........................... **838.00**

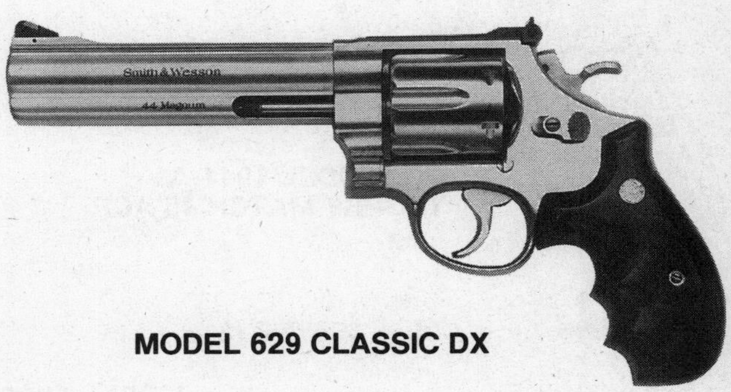


MODEL 629 CLASSIC DX

MODEL 657

### MODEL 657 STAINLESS
**$528.00**

**SPECIFICATIONS**
**Caliber:** 41 Magnum
**Capacity:** 6 shots
**Barrel length:** 6″
**Overall length:** 11 3/8″
**Weight (empty):** 48 oz.
**Sights:** Front, serrated ramp on ramp base; rear, blue S&W Micrometer Click, adjustable for windage and elevation
**Finish:** Satin stainless steel

# SPRINGFIELD PISTOLS

MODEL 1911-A1
STANDARD

MODEL 1911-A1
MIL-SPEC COMPACT 45 ACP

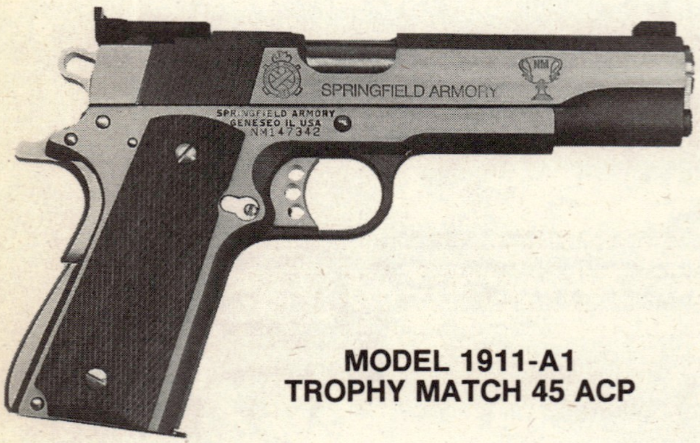


MODEL 1911-A1
TROPHY MATCH 45 ACP

MODEL 1911-A1
CHAMPION

## MODEL 1911-A1 STANDARD

An exact duplicate of the M1911-A1 pistol that served the U.S. Armed Forces for more than 70 years, this model has been precision manufactured from forged parts, including a forged frame, then hand-assembled.

**SPECIFICATIONS**
**Calibers:** 9mm Parabellum, 38 Super and 45 ACP
**Capacity:** 9 + 1 in chamber (9mm/38 Super); 8 + 1 in chamber (45 ACP)
**Barrel length:** 5″ **Overall length:** 8.59″
**Weight:** 35.62 oz.
**Trigger pull:** 5 to 6.5 lbs.
**Sight radius:** 6.281″
**Rifling:** 1 turn in 16; right-hand, 4-groove (9mm); left-hand, 6-groove (45 ACP)

| **MODEL 1911-A1** | **Prices** |
|---|---|
| 45 ACP/9mm, Blued | **$515.00** |
| 45 ACP, Parkerized finish | **459.00** |
| 45 ACP, Stainless finish | **555.00** |
| 9mm, Blued | **545.00** |
| 9mm, Stainless finish | **570.00** |
| **1911-A1 TROPHY MATCH 45 ACP** | |
| Blued | **919.00** |
| Stainless Steel | **951.00** |
| **1911-A1 DEFENDER** w/fixed combat sights, skeletonized hammer, walnut grips, beveled magazine well, extended thumb safety, 45 ACP, Bi-Tone | **958.00** |
| **1911-A1 CHAMPION** with shortened (1″) slide and barrel, 45 ACP, stainless finish | **565.00** |
| With Blued finish | **525.00** |
| MD-1 .380, Parkerized | **424.00** |
| MD-1 .380, Blued | **449.00** |
| Mil-Spec 45 ACP Parkerized | **459.00** |
| **1911-A1 38 SUPER** | |
| Mil-Spec Blued finish | **515.00** |
| Standard, blued | **545.00** |

# SPRINGFIELD PISTOLS

1911-A1 ULTRA COMPACT
BI-TONE

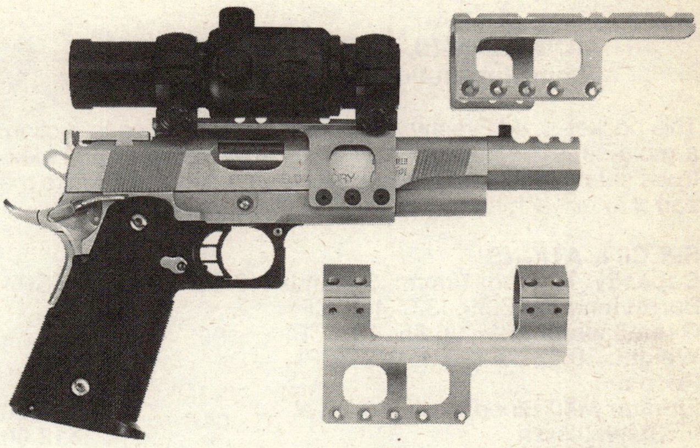

HIGH-CAPACITY FULL-HOUSE RACEGUN
$3322.00

## MODEL 1911-A1 COMPACT, HIGH-CAPACITY AND FACTORY COMP MODELS

| Models | Prices |
|---|---|
| **1911-A1 COMPACT 45 ACP** | |
| Blued finish | **$ 525.00** |
| Stainless finish | **565.00** |
| Lightweight 45 ACP w/matte finish | **525.00** |
| Mil-Spec 45 ACP Parkerized | **459.00** |
| V-10 Compact 45 ACP (ported), Bi-Tone | **637.00** |
| **ULTRA COMPACT** | |
| 45 Bi-Tone | **549.00** |
| MD-1 Lightweight .380, matte finish | **449.00** |
| **HIGH-CAPACITY COMPACT 45 ACP** | |
| Blued finish | **609.00** |
| Stainless finish | **648.00** |
| **1911-A1 FACTORY COMP** Blued | |
| In 38 Super | **949.00** |
| In 45 ACP | **915.00** |
| **PDP SERIES HIGH CAPACITY FACTORY COMP** | |
| In 45 ACP | **1049.00** |
| In 38 caliber | **1074.00** |

## SPECIFICATIONS

**Calibers:** 45 ACP, 9×25 Dillon, 38 Super (custom calibers available on request)
**Capacity:** 15+1 rounds (45 ACP); 17+1 rounds (9×25 Dillon); 17+1 (38 Super)
**Barrel:** Custom match-grade barrel, match-grade chamber and leade
**Sights:** Bo-Mar rear, dovetail front; Springfield scope mount (optional extra); C-More "heads-up display" optical sight (optional extra)
**Safeties:** Extended ambidextrous thumb safety, recessed hammer beavertail grip safety
**Compensator:** Progressive triple port expansion chamber design, tapered cone system
**Trigger pull:** $3^1/_2$ lbs.
**Checkering:** 20 or 30 lines per inch (custom on request) on frontstrap, trigger guard, mainspring housing

Other custom Raceguns available include:

| | |
|---|---|
| **Trophy Master Distinguished** (45 ACP) | **$2717.00** |
| **Trophy Master Distinguished "Limited"** (45 ACP) | **2606.00** |
| **Trophy Master Expert** (45 ACP, 9mm, 38 Super) | **1915.00** |
| **Trophy Master "Limited Class"** | **1804.00** |
| **N.R.A. PPC** | **1632.00** |
| **Springfield Custom "Carry Gun"** (45 ACP) | **1388.00** |
| **Basic Competition Pistol** (45 ACP) | **1439.00** |
| **Competition** | **1598.00** |
| **National Match Hardball Pistol** (45 ACP) | **1485.00** |
| **Bull's-Eye Wadcutter Pistol** (45 ACP) | **1665.00** |

1911-A1 V10 COMPACT

1911-A1 HIGH-CAPACITY
STANDARD

# STAR AUTOMATIC PISTOLS

## MODELS M40, M43 & M45 FIRESTAR
## 9mm Parabellum, 40 S&W or 45 ACP

This pocket-sized Firestar pistol features all-steel construction, a triple-dot sight system (fully adjustable rear) and ambidextrous safety. The Acculine barrel design reseats and locks the barrel after each shot. Checkered rubber grips.

**SPECIFICATIONS**
**Capacity:** 7 rounds (9mm); 6 rounds (40 S&W and 45 ACP)
**Barrel lengths:** 3.39″ (3.6″ 45 ACP)
**Overall length:** 6½″ (6.85″ 45 ACP)
**Weight:** 30.35 oz. (35 oz. 45 ACP)
**Prices:**

| | |
|---|---|
| **Firestar M40** Blued finish, 40 S&W | **$486.00** |
| Starvel finish | **513.00** |
| **Firestar M43** Blued finish, 9mm | **469.00** |
| Starvel finish, 9mm | **496.00** |
| **Firestar M45** Blued finish, 45 ACP | **516.00** |
| Starvel finish, 45 ACP | **543.00** |

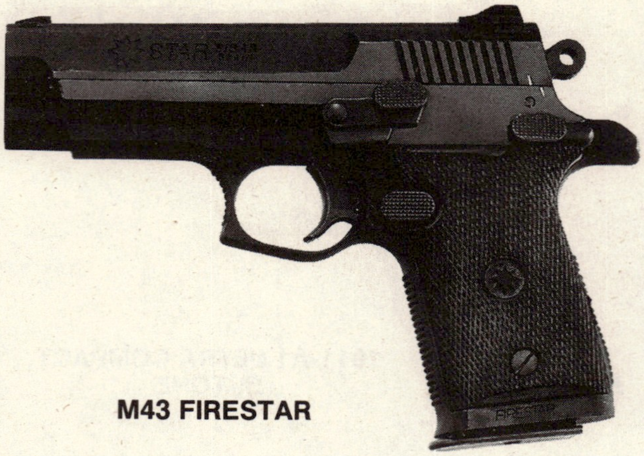

M43 FIRESTAR

## FIRESTAR PLUS

The new Firestar Plus featues enlarged magazine capacity, lightweight alloy frame, fast button-release magazine, large grip and ambidextrous safety. It also has a triple-dot sight system, tight-lock Acculine barrel for positive barrel/slide alignment and an all-steel slide that glides on internal rails machined inside the frame.

**SPECIFICATIONS**
**Calibers:** 9mm Parabellum, 40 S&W, 45 ACP
**Capacity:** 10 rounds
**Barrel length:** 3.39″
**Overall length:** 6.5″
**Weight:** 30.35″
**Finish:** Blued or Starvel
**Prices:**

| | |
|---|---|
| 9mm blued | **$507.00** |
| Starvel finish | **533.00** |
| 40 S&W blued | **527.00** |
| Starvel finish | **554.00** |
| 45 ACP blued | **554.00** |
| Starvel finish | **580.00** |

FIRESTAR PLUS

## ULTRASTAR

The Ultrastar features a slim profile, light weight and first-shot, double-action speed. The use of polymers makes this pistol exceptionally strong and durable. Other features include a triple-dot sight system, ambidextrous two-position manual safety (safe and safe decock), all-steel internal mechanism and barrel, slide-mounted on rails inside frame.

**SPECIFICATIONS**
**Caliber:** 9mm Parabellum **Capacity:** 9 rounds
**Barrel length:** 3.57″ **Overall length:** 7″
**Weight:** 26 oz.
**Price: $547.00**

ULTRASTAR

# STOEGER PISTOLS

## PRO SERIES 95

The PRO SERIES 95 are precision target pistols designed for the knowledgeable, advanced target shooter. Destined to be among the world's most popular competitive pistols, the PRO SERIES 95 features 10-round capacity in 22 Long Rifle caliber, plus:

- interchangeable barrels
- fully adjustable target sights
- trigger pull adjustment
- trigger travel adjustment
- automatic slide lock
- Pachmayr military-style rubber grips
- stainless-steel finish

The vent-rib model features a full-length vent rib that produces the most positive sighting plane for the advanced competitor.

The bull-barrel and fluted-barrel models feature the military bracket rear sight, acclaimed by many competitive shooters as the most reliable sighting system developed.

**Optional:**
Walnut target grips with thumbrest . . . . . . . . . . . . . . . **$40.00**
Stainless-steel magazine (10 rounds): . . . . . . . . . . . . . **$32.00**

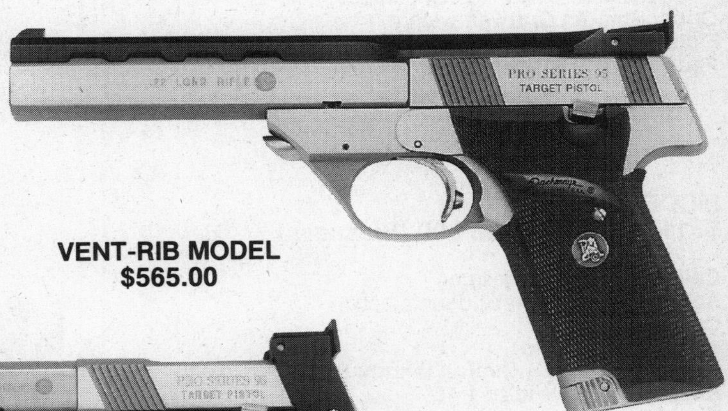


**VENT-RIB MODEL**
**$565.00**

**BULL-BARREL MODEL**
**$460.00**

**FLUTED-BARREL MODEL**
**$490.00**

### SPECIFICATIONS PRO SERIES 95

| MODEL | BBL. LGTH. | O/A LGTH. | REAR SIGHT | SIGHT RADIUS | WT./OZ. |
|---|---|---|---|---|---|
| **Vent Rib** | 5½″ | 9¾″ | ON RIB | 8¾″ | 47 |
| **Bull Barrel** | 5½″ | 9¾″ | ON BRACKET | 8¾″ | 45 |
| **Fluted Barrel** | 7¼″ | 11¾″ | ON BRACKET | 10″ | 45 |

# TAURUS PISTOLS

### MODEL PT-58
**$462.00 (Blue) $526.00 (Stainless)**

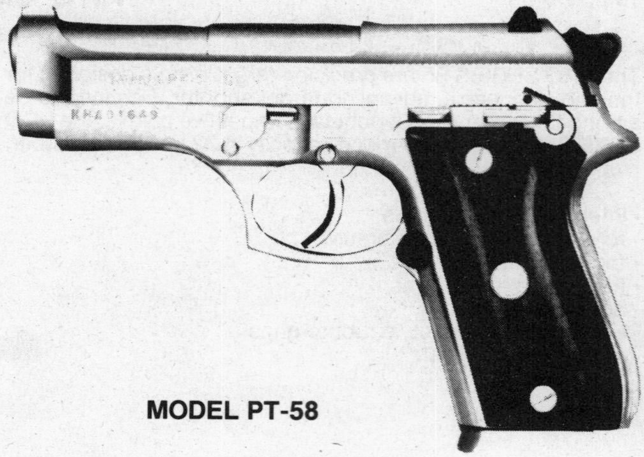

MODEL PT-58

**SPECIFICATIONS**
**Caliber:** 380 ACP
**Action:** Semiautomatic double action
**Capacity:** 10 + 1
**Barrel length:** 4″
**Overall length:** 7.2″
**Weight:** 30 oz.
**Hammer:** Exposed
**Sights:** Front, drift adjustable; rear, notched bar dovetailed to slide, 3-dot combat
**Grips:** Smooth Brazilian walnut
**Finish:** Blue, satin nickel or stainless steel
**Features:** Tri-position safety system

### MODEL PT-92 AF
**$511.00 (Blue) $582.00 (Stainless)**

MODEL PT-92 AF

**Caliber:** 9mm Parabellum
**Action:** Semiautomatic double action
**Capacity:** 10 + 1
**Hammer:** Exposed
**Barrel length:** 5″ **Overall length:** 8 1/2″
**Height:** 5.39″ **Width:** 1.45″
**Weight:** 34 oz. (empty)
**Rifling:** R.H., 6 grooves
**Sights:** Front, fixed; rear, drift adjustable, 3-dot combat
**Safeties:** (a) Ambidextrous manual safety locking trigger mechanism and slide in locked position; (b) half-cock position; (c) inertia-operated firing pin; (d) chamber-loaded indicator
**Slide:** Hold open upon firing last cartridge
**Grips:** Smooth Brazilian walnut
**Finish:** Blue, satin nickel or stainless steel

Also available:
**MODEL PT-99.** Same specifications as Model PT 92, but has micrometer click-adjustable rear sight. **$554.00** Blue; **$606.00** Stainless
**MODEL PT-99AFD Deluxe Shooter's Pak** w/extra magazine & custom case. **$542.00** Blue; **$610.00** Stainless

### MODEL PT-92 AFC
**$511.00 (Blue) $582.00 (Stainless)**

MODEL PT-92 AFC

**SPECIFICATIONS**
**Caliber:** 9mm Parabellum **Capacity:** 10 + 1
**Barrel length:** 4.25″ **Overall length:** 7.5″
**Weight:** 31 oz.
**Sights:** Fixed front; drift-adjustable rear, 3-dot combat
**Grips:** Brazilian hardwood
**Slide:** Last shot held open
**Safety:** Manual, ambidextrous hammer drop; inertia firing pin; chamber load indicator
**Finish:** Blue, satin nickel or stainless steel

# TAURUS PISTOLS

## MODEL PT 22
**$193.00 (Blue)**
**$201.00 (Nickel)**

**SPECIFICATIONS**
**Caliber:** 22 LR
**Action:** Semiautomatic
**Capacity:** 9 shots
**Barrel length:** 2³/₄″
**Overall length:** 5¹/₄″
**Weight:** 12.3 oz.
**Sights:** Fixed
**Grips:** Brazilian hardwood
**Finish:** Blue

Also available:
**MODEL PT 25.** Same price and specifications as Model PT 22, except magazine holds 9 rounds in 25 ACP.

## MODEL PT 101
**$564.00 (Blue)**
**$644.00 (Stainless)**

**SPECIFICATIONS**
**Caliber:** 40 S&W
**Capacity:**10 + 1
**Barrel length:** 5″ **Overall length:** 8¹/₂″
**Weight:** 34 oz. (empty)
**Sights:** Micrometer click-adjustable rear sight
**Grips:** Brazilian hardwood
**Finish:** Blue, satin nickel or stainless steel

Also available:
**MODEL PT 100.** Same specifications as Model PT 101, but has fixed sights. **Prices: $522.00** Blue; **$592.00** Stainless
**MODEL PT-100/101D Deluxe Shooter's Pak** w/extra magazine & custom case. **Prices: $551.00** Blue; **$622.00** Stainless

## MODEL PT-908
**$511.00 (Blue)**
**$582.00 (Stainless)**

**SPECIFICATIONS**
**Caliber:** 9mm Parabellum
**Action:** Double action
**Capacity:** 8 shot
**Barrel length:** 3.8″ **Overall length:** 7.05″
**Weight:** 30 oz.
**Sights:** Drift adjustable front and rear, 3-dot combat
**Grips:** Rubber
**Finish:** Blue, satin nickel or stainless steel

## MODEL PT-945
**$570.00 (Blue)**
**$646.00 (Stainless)**

**SPECIFICATIONS**
**Caliber:** 45 ACP **Capacity:** 8 shots
**Barrel length:** 4.25″ **Overall length:** 7.48″
**Weight:** 29.5 oz.
**Action:** Semiautomatic double
**Sights:** Drift-adjustable front and rear; 3-dot combat
**Grips:** Santoprene II
**Safety features:** Manual safety; ambidextrous; chamber load indicator; intercept notch; firing-pin block; floating firing pin
**Finish:** Blue or stainless

# TAURUS REVOLVERS

### MODEL 44

**SPECIFICATIONS**
**Caliber:** 44 Mag. **Capacity:** 6 rounds
**Barrel length:** 4″ (heavy, solid); 6½″ and 8⅜″ (vent. rib)
**Weight:** 44¾ oz. (4″); 52½ oz. (6½″); 57¼ oz. (8⅜″)
**Sights:** Serrated ramp front; rear micrometer click, adjustable for windage and elevation
**Grips:** Brazilian hardwood
**Finish:** Blue or stainless steel
**Features:** Compensated barrel; transfer bar safety
**Prices:**

| | |
|---|---|
| 4″ barrel blue | **$439.00** |
| stainless steel | **499.00** |
| 6½″ and 8⅜″ blue | **457.00** |
| stainless steel | **520.00** |

### MODEL 65 (2½″ Barrel)
**$299.00 (Blue)**
**$369.00 (Stainless)**

**SPECIFICATIONS**
**Caliber:** 357 Magnum
**Capacity:** 6 shot
**Action:** Double
**Barrel lengths:** 2½″, 4″
**Weight:** 34 oz. (4″)
**Sights:** Rear square notched; serrated front ramp
**Grips:** Brazilian hardwood
**Finish:** Royal blue or stainless

### MODEL 66
**$329.00 (Blue)**
**$405.00 (Stainless)**

**SPECIFICATIONS**
**Caliber:** 357 Magnum
**Action:** Double
**Capacity:** 6 shot
**Barrel lengths:** 2½″, 4″, 6″
**Weight:** 35 oz. (4″ barrel)
**Sights:** Serrated ramp front; rear, micrometer click adjustable for windage and elevation
**Grips:** Brazilian hardwood
**Finish:** Royal blue or stainless steel
**Prices:**
With Recoil Compensator

| | |
|---|---|
| 4″ and 6″ Blue | **$323.00** |
| 4″ and 6″ Stainless | **403.00** |

### MODEL 83
**$274.00 (Blue)**
**$319.00 (Stainless)**

**SPECIFICATIONS**
**Caliber:** 38 Special
**Action:** Double
**Capacity:** 6 shot
**Barrel length:** 4″
**Weight:** 34 oz.
**Sights:** Patridge-type front; rear, micrometer click adjustable for windage and elevation
**Grips:** Brazilian hardwood
**Finish:** Blue

# TAURUS REVOLVERS

MODEL 80

**MODEL 80**
**$260.00 (Blue)**
**$308.00 (Stainless)**

**SPECIFICATIONS**
**Caliber:** 38 Special
**Capacity:** 6 shot
**Action:** Double
**Barrel lengths:** 3″, 4″
**Weight:** 30 oz. (4″ barrel)
**Sights:** Notched rear; serrated ramp front
**Grips:** Brazilian hardwood
**Finish:** Blue or stainless

MODEL 82

**MODEL 82**
**$260.00 (Blue)**
**$308.00 (Stainless)**

**SPECIFICATIONS**
**Caliber:** 38 Special
**Capacity:** 6 shot
**Action:** Double
**Barrel lengths:** 3″, 4″
**Weight:** 34 oz. (4″ barrel)
**Sights:** Notched rear; serrated ramp front
**Grips:** Brazilian hardwood
**Finish:** Blue or stainless

MODEL 941

**MODEL 94**
**$303.00 (Blue)**
**$350.00 (Stainless)**

**SPECIFICATIONS**
**Caliber:** 22 LR
**Number of shots:** 9
**Action:** Double
**Barrel lengths:** 3″ and 4″
**Weight:** 25 oz. (w/4″ barrel)
**Sights:** Serrated ramp front; rear micrometer click adjustable for windage and elevation
**Grips:** Brazilian hardwood
**Finish:** Blue or stainless steel

Also available:
**MODEL 941** in 22 Magnum, 8-shot capacity; ejector shroud.
In blue . . . . . . . . . . . . . . . . . . . . . . . . . . . . . . . . . . **$326.00**
In stainless steel . . . . . . . . . . . . . . . . . . . . . . . . . . . **378.00**

# TAURUS REVOLVERS

**MODEL 85**
**$284.00 (Blue)**
**$343.00 (Stainless Steel)**

**SPECIFICATIONS**
**Caliber:** 38 Special
**Capacity:** 5 shot
**Action:** Double
**Barrel length:** 2″ and 3″ **Weight:** 21 oz. (2″ barrel)
**Sights:** Notched rear sight, fixed sight
**Grips:** Brazilian hardwood
**Finish:** Blue or stainless steel
Also available:
**MODEL 85CH.** Same specifications as Model 85, except has concealed hammer and 2″ barrel only.
**Prices: $284.00** (Blue); **$343.00** (Stainless Steel)

**MODEL 96**
**$370.00**

**SPECIFICATIONS**
**Caliber:** 22 LR
**Capacity:** 6 shot
**Action:** Double
**Barrel length:** 6″
**Weight:** 34 oz.
**Sights:** Patridge-type front; rear, micrometer click adjustable for windage and elevation
**Grips:** Brazilian hardwood
**Finish:** Blue only

**MODEL 431**
**$295.00 (Blue)**
**$362.00 (Stainless)**

**SPECIFICATIONS**
**Caliber:** 44 Special
**Capacity:** 5 shot
**Action:** Double
**Barrel lengths:** 2″, 3″ or 4″ w/ejector shroud; heavy, solid rib barrel
**Weight:** 35 oz. (4″ barrel)
**Sights:** Notched rear; serrated ramp front
**Safety:** Transfer bar
**Grips:** Brazilian hardwood
**Finish:** Blue or stainless steel

**MODEL 441**
**$307.00 (Blue)**
**$386.00 (Stainless)**

**SPECIFICATIONS**
**Caliber:** 44 Special
**Capacity:** 5 shot
**Action:** Double
**Barrel lengths:** 3″, 4″ or 6″ w/ejector shroud; heavy, solid rib barrel
**Weight:** 40¼ oz. (6″ barrel)
**Sights:** Serrated ramp front; rear, micrometer click adjustable for windage and elevation
**Safety:** Transfer bar
**Grips:** Brazilian hardwood
**Finish:** Blue or stainless steel

# TAURUS REVOLVERS

MODEL 605

MODEL 607

**MODEL 605**
**$305.00 (Blue)**
**$369.00 (Stainless)**

**SPECIFICATIONS**
**Caliber:** 357 Magnum/38 Special
**Capacity:** 5 shot
**Barrel length:** 2.25″
**Weight:** 24.5 oz.
**Sights:** Notched rear; serrated ramp front
**Grips:** Santoprene I
**Safety:** Transfer bar
**Finish:** Blue or stainless

**MODEL 607**
**$439.00 (Blue 4″)**
**$457.00 (Blue 6½″)**
**$499.00 (Stainless 4″)**
**$520.00 (Stainless 6½″)**

**SPECIFICATIONS**
**Caliber:** 357 Magnum/38 Special
**Capacity:** 7 shot
**Barrel lengths:** 4″ (heavy solid rib) and 6½″ (vent rib)
**Weight:** 44 oz. (w/4″ barrel)
**Sights:** Notched rear; serrated ramp front
**Safety:** Transfer bar
**Grips:** Santoprene I
**Finish:** Blue or stainless
**Feature:** Compensated barrel

MODEL 669

**MODEL 669**
**$338.00 (4″ and 6″ Blue)**
**$414.00 (4″ and 6″ Stainless)**

**SPECIFICATIONS**
**Caliber:** 357 Magnum
**Capacity:** 6 shot
**Action:** Double
**Barrel lengths:** 4″ and 6″
**Weight:** 37 oz. (4″ barrel)
**Sights:** Serrated ramp front; rear, micrometer click adjustable for windage and elevation
**Grips:** Brazilian hardwood
**Finish:** Royal blue or stainless
**Features:** Recoil compensator (optional) **$19.00** additional

MODEL 689 STAINLESS

**MODEL 689**
**$352.00 (Blue)**
**$428.00 (Stainless)**

The Model 689 has the same specifications as the Model 669, except vent rib is featured.

# TEXAS ARMS

## DEFENDER DERRINGER

This single-action derringer is the first to feature a rebounding hammer and retracting firing pins. This system, along with the positive crossbolt safety, makes this derringer safer than any others. Its spring-loaded cammed locking lever provides a tighter barrel/frame fit, assuring faster and easier loading and unloading. An interchangeable barrel system allows different caliber barrels to be used on the same gun frame.

**SPECIFICATIONS**
**Calibers:** 9mm Luger, 357 Magnum, 38 Special, 44 Magnum, 45 Auto, 45 LC/.410 shotshell
**Barrel length:** 3″ (octagonal)
**Overall length:** 5″
**Weight:** 21 oz.
**Height:** 3.75″
**Width:** 1.25″ across grips
**Finish:** Bead-blasted, gun-metal grey
**Features:** Removable trigger guard; automatic shell extractor; improved grip angle distributes recoil
**Price:** . . . . . . . . . . . . . . . . . . . . . . . . . **$299.00**

DEFENDER DERRINGER

# THOMPSON/CENTER

CONTENDER HUNTER

## CONTENDER HUNTER

Chambered in the most popular commercially loaded cartridges available to handgunners.

**SPECIFICATIONS**
**Calibers:** 7-30 Waters, 223 Rem., 30-30 Win., 35 Rem., 45-70 Government, 375 Win. and. 44 Rem. Mag.
**Barrel length:** 14″
**Overall length:** 16″
**Weight:** 4 lbs. (approx.)
**Features:** T/C Muzzle Tamer (to reduce recoil); a mounted T/C Recoil Proof 2.5X scope w/lighted reticle, QD sling swivels and nylon sling, plus suede leather carrying case
**Price:** . . . . . . . . . . . . . . . . . . . . . . . . . . . . . . . . . . . . **$765.00**

# THOMPSON/CENTER

BULL BARREL

## CONTENDER BULL BARREL MODELS

These pistols with 10-inch barrel feature fully adjustable Patridge-style iron sights. All stainless-steel models (including the Super "14" and Super "16" below) are equipped with Rynite finger-groove grip with rubber recoil cushion and matching Rynite forend, plus Cougar etching on the steel frame.

**Standard and Custom calibers available:** 22 LR, 22 Hornet, 22 Win. Mag., 223 Rem., 300 Whisper, 30-30 Win., 32-20 Win., 7mm T.C.U., 357 Mag., 357 Rem. Max., 44 Mag. and 45 Colt/.410

**Bull Barrel** (less internal choke) . . . . . . . . . . **$450.00–460.00**
**Bull Barrel** Stainless . . . . . . . . . . . . . . . . . . **480.00–490.00**
Standard calibers w/internal choke 45 Colt/.410 . . . **455.00**
**Vent Rib Model** . . . . . . . . . . . . . . . . . . . . . . . **470.00**
With **Match Grade Barrel** (22 LR only) . . . . . . . . . **460.00**

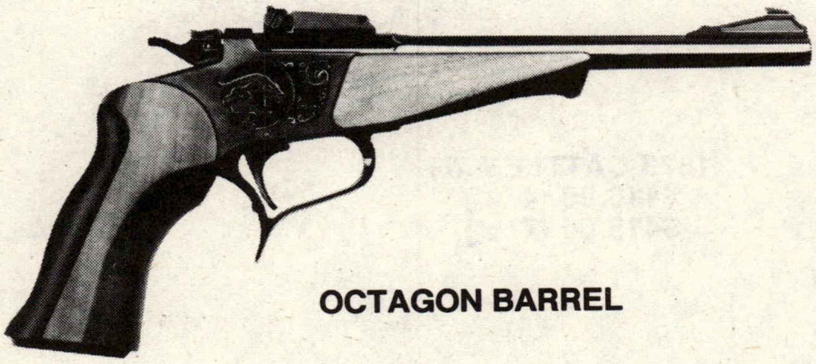

OCTAGON BARREL

## CONTENDER OCTAGON BARREL MODELS

This standard barrel is interchangeable with any model listed here. Available in 10-inch length, it is supplied with iron sights. Octagon barrel is available in 22 LR. No external choke.
**Price:** . . . . . . . . . . . . . . . . . . . . . . . . . . . . . **$450.00**

CONTENDER SUPER "14"
STAINLESS STEEL

## CONTENDER SUPER "14" MODELS

Chambered in 10 calibers (22 LR, 22 LR Match Grade Chamber, 22 Hornet, 223 Rem., 7-30 Waters, 300 Whisper, 30-30 Win., 35 Rem., 375 Win. and 44 Mag.), this gun is equipped with a 14-inch bull barrel, fully adjustable target rear sight and Patridge-style ramped front sight with $13\frac{1}{2}$-inch sight radius.

**Overall length:** $18\frac{1}{4}$". **Weight:** $3\frac{1}{2}$ lbs.
**Prices:**
Blued . . . . . . . . . . . . . . . . . . . . . . . . . . . . . **$460.00–490.00**
Stainless . . . . . . . . . . . . . . . . . . . . . . . . . . . **490.00–500.00**
**14" Vent Rib Model** in 45 Colt/.410, blue . . . . . . . . **490.00**
Stainless . . . . . . . . . . . . . . . . . . . . . . . . . . . **520.00**

## CONTENDER SUPER "16" VENTILATED RIB/INTERNAL CHOKE MODELS (not shown)

Featuring a raised ventilated ($\frac{7}{16}$-inch wide) rib, this Contender model is available in 45 Colt/.410 caliber. A patented detachable choke ($1\frac{7}{8}$ inches long) screws into the muzzle internally.
**Barrel length:** $16\frac{1}{4}$" inches.

**Prices:**
Blued . . . . . . . . . . . . . . . . . . . . . . . . . . . . . **$495.00**
Stainless . . . . . . . . . . . . . . . . . . . . . . . . . . . **525.00**
**10" Vent Rib Model** w/internal choke, blue . . . . . . . **470.00**
Stainless . . . . . . . . . . . . . . . . . . . . . . . . . . . **500.00**

# A. UBERTI REPLICAS

### 1871 ROLLING BLOCK TARGET PISTOL

**SPECIFICATIONS**
**Calibers:** 22 LR, 22 Magnum, 22 Hornet, 357 Mag., 45 L.C.
**Capacity:** Single shot
**Barrel length:** 9½″ (half-octagon/half-round or full round Navy Style)
**Overall length:** 14″ **Weight:** 2.75 lbs.
**Sights:** Fully adjustable rear; ramp front or open sight on Navy Style barrel
**Grip and forend:** Walnut
**Trigger guard:** Brass
**Frame:** Color casehardened steel

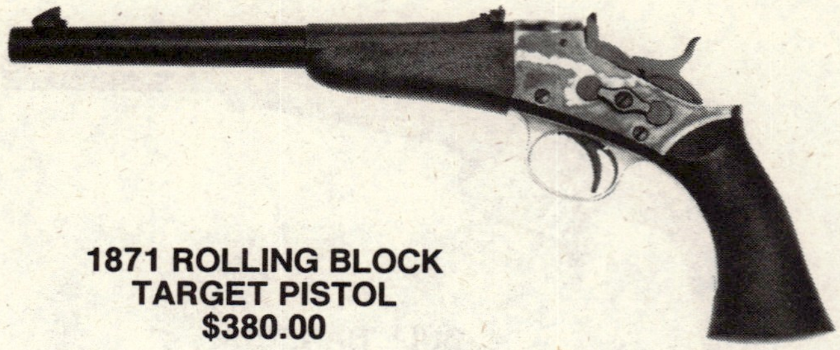

**1871 ROLLING BLOCK TARGET PISTOL**
**$380.00**

### 1873 CATTLEMAN S.A.

**SPECIFICATIONS**
**Calibers:** 38-40, 357 Magnum, 44 S&W Special, 44-40, 45 L.C., 45 ACP
**Capacity:** 6 shots
**Barrel lengths:** 3″, 4¾″, 5½″, 7½″ round, tapered; 18″ (Buntline)
**Overall length:** 10¾″ w/5½″ barrel
**Weight:** 2.42 lbs.
**Grip:** One-piece walnut
**Frame:** Color casehardened steel; also available in charcoal blue or nickel
Also available:
45 L.C./45 ACP Convertible . . . . . . . . . . . . . . . . **$425.00**

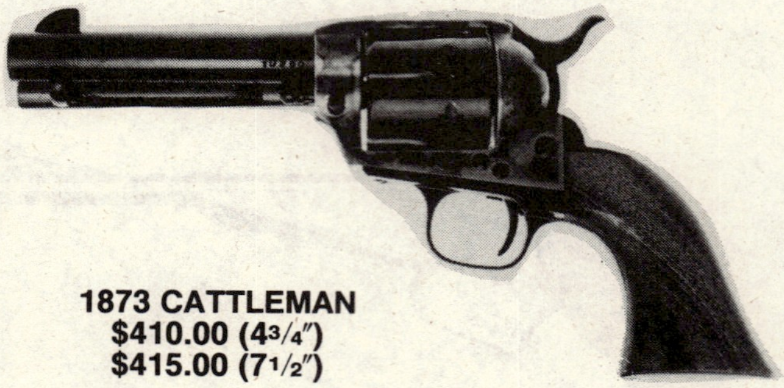

**1873 CATTLEMAN**
**$410.00 (4¾″)**
**$415.00 (7½″)**

**1875 "OUTLAW"/1890 POLICE**
**$405.00**

### 1875 "OUTLAW"/1890 POLICE

**SPECIFICATIONS**
**Calibers:** 357 Magnum, 44-40, 45 ACP, 45 Long Colt
**Capacity:** 6 shots
**Barrel lengths:** 5½″, 7½″ round, tapered
**Overall length:** 13¾″ **Weight:** 2.75 lbs.
**Grips:** Two-piece walnut
**Frame:** Color casehardened steel
Also available:
In nickel plate . . . . . . . . . . . . . . . . . . . . . . . . . **$450.00**
45 L.C./45 ACP Convertible . . . . . . . . . . . . . . . **450.00**

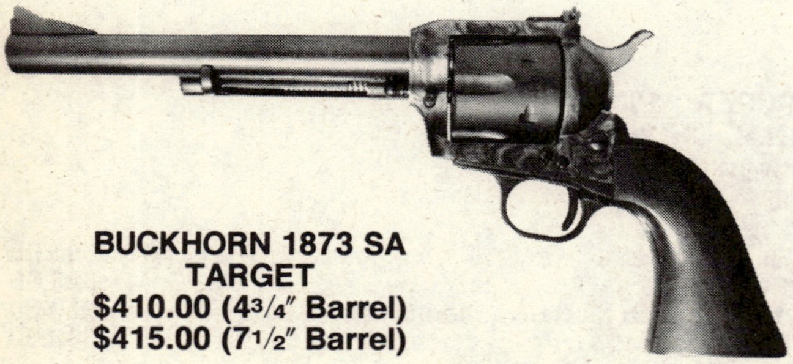

**BUCKHORN 1873 SA TARGET**
**$410.00 (4¾″ Barrel)**
**$415.00 (7½″ Barrel)**

### BUCKHORN 1873 SINGLE ACTION TARGET

**SPECIFICATIONS**
**Caliber:** 44 Magnum **Capacity:** 6 shots
**Barrel length:** 4¾″, 6″ or 7½″ round, tapered
**Overall length:** 11¾″ **Weight:** 2.5 lbs.
**Sights:** Open or target
**Finish:** Black
Also available:
In nickel plate . . . . . . . . . . . . . . . . . . . . . . . . . . **$455.00**
44-40 Mag. Convertible . . . . . . . . . . . . . . . . . . **460.00**
**BUCKHORN BUNTLINE** . . . . . . . . . . . . . . . . . **448.00**
Convertible . . . . . . . . . . . . . . . . . . . . . . . . . . . . **499.00**

# UNIQUE PISTOLS

## MODEL DES 69U
**$1295.00**

**SPECIFICATIONS**
**Caliber:** 22 LR
**Capacity:** 5- or 6-shot magazine
**Barrel length:** 5.9″
**Overall length:** 11.2″
**Weight:** 40.2 oz. (empty)
**Height:** 5.5″
**Width:** 1.97″
**Sights:** Micrometric rear; lateral and vertical correction by clicks
**Safety:** Manual
**Features:** Orthopedic French walnut grip with adjustable hand rest; external hammer

Also available:
**Model DES 32U** in 32 S&W Long Wadcutter. Designed for centerfire U.I.T. and military rapid fire. Other specifications same as Model DES 69U. **Price:** .......... **$1295.00**

## MODEL I.S. INTERNATIONAL SILHOUETTE
**$1095.00**

**SPECIFICATIONS**
**Calibers:** 22 LR, 22 Magnum, 7mm TCU, 357 Magnum, 44 Magnum
**Barrel length:** 10″
**Overall length:** 14.5″
**Weight:** 38 oz.
**Height:** 6.5″
**Width:** 1.5″
**Sights:** Micrometric rear; lateral and vertical correction by clicks; interchangeable front sight; dovetailed grooves for scope
**Features:** French walnut grip; interchangeable shroud/barrel assembly; external hammer; firing adjustments

Also available:
**International Sport** w/light alloy frame in 22 LR and 22 Mag.
**Price:** .................................... **$795.00**

## MODEL DES 2000U
**$1450.00**

**SPECIFICATIONS**
**Caliber:** 22 Short
**Barrel length:** 5.9″
**Overall length:** 11.4″
**Weight:** 43.4 oz. (empty)
**Height:** 5.3″
**Width:** 1.97″
**Sights:** Micrometric rear; lateral and vertical correction by clicks
**Features:** French walnut grips with adjustable hand rest; left-hand grips available; external hammer; dry firing device; slide stop catch; antirecoil device

# WALTHER PISTOLS

The Walther double-action system combines the principles of the double-action revolver with the advantages of the modern pistol without the disadvantages inherent in either design.

Models PPK and PPK/S differ only in the overall length of the barrel and slide. Both models offer the same features, including compact form, light weight, easy handling, and absolute safety. Both models can be carried with a loaded chamber and closed hammer, but ready to fire either single- or double-action. Both models are provided with a live round indicator pin to signal a loaded chamber. An automatic internal safety blocks the hammer to prevent accidental striking of the firing pin, except with a deliberate pull of the trigger. Sights are provided with white markings for high visibility in poor light. Rich Walther blue/black finish is standard, and each pistol is complete with an extra magazine with finger-rest extension.

MODEL PPK & PPK/S

### MODEL PPK & PPK/S

**SPECIFICATIONS**
**Caliber:** 380 ACP
**Capacity:** 6 rounds (PPK), 7 rounds (PPK/S)
**Barrel lengths:** 3.8″ (PPK); 5″ (PPK/S)
**Overall length:** 6.7″ (PPK); 8 1/2″ (PPK/S)
**Height:** 4.28″
**Weight:** 23 oz. (PPK); 28 oz. (PPK/S)
**Finish:** Walther blue or stainless steel
**Price:** . . . . . . . . . . . . . . . . . . . . . . . . . . . . . . . . . . . **$651.00**

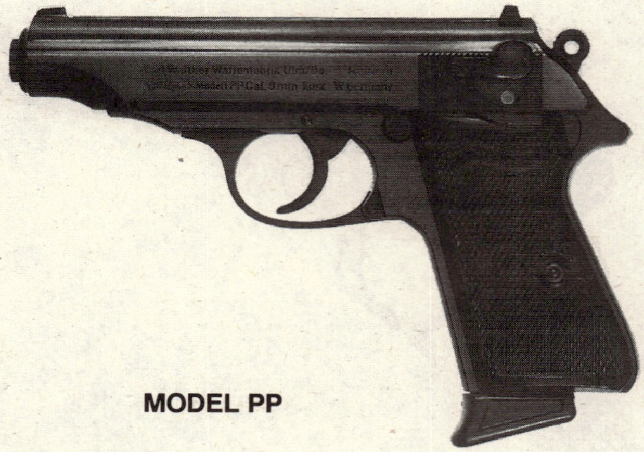

MODEL PP

### MODEL PP DOUBLE ACTION

**SPECIFICATIONS**
**Calibers:** 32 ACP and 380 ACP
**Capacity:** 7 rounds
**Barrel length:** 3.8″ (32 ACP)
**Overall length:** 6.7″ (32 ACP)
**Weight:** 23 oz. (32 ACP)
**Finish:** Walther blue
**Price:** . . . . . . . . . . . . . . . . . . . . . . . . . . . . . . . . . . . **$1206.00**

### MODEL TPH DOUBLE ACTION

Walther's Model TPH is considered by government agents and professional lawmen to be one of the top undercover/backup guns available. A scaled-down version of Walther's PP-PPK series.

**SPECIFICATIONS**
**Calibers:** 22 LR and 25 ACP
**Capacity:** 6 rounds
**Barrel length:** 2.3″
**Overall length:** 5.3″
**Weight:** 14 oz.
**Finish:** Walther blue or stainless steel
**Price:** (All models) . . . . . . . . . . . . . . . . . . . . . . . . . . . . **$486.00**

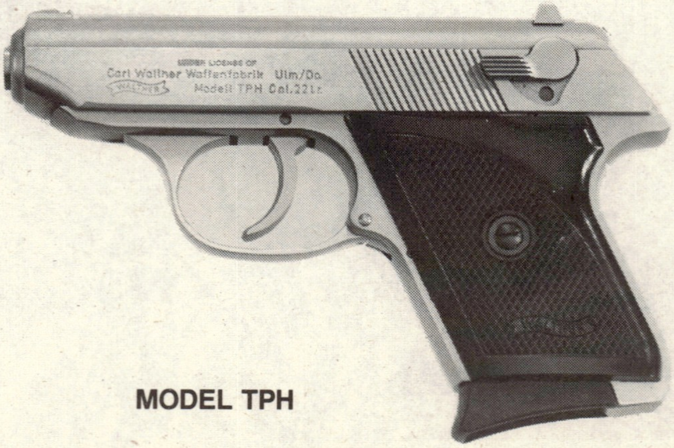

MODEL TPH

# WALTHER PISTOLS

## MODEL P-38 DOUBLE ACTION

The Walther P-38 is a double-action, locked-breech, semiautomatic pistol with an external hammer. Its compact form, light weight and easy handling are combined with the superb performance of the 9mm Luger Parabellum cartridge. The P-38 is equipped with both a manual and automatic safety, which allows it to be carried safely while the chamber is loaded.

**SPECIFICATIONS**
**Caliber:** 9mm Parabellum
**Capacity:** 8 rounds
**Barrel length:** 5″
**Overall length:** 8 1/2″
**Weight:** 28 oz.
**Finish:** Blue
**Price:** . . . . . . . . . . . . . . . . . . . . . . . . . . . . . . . . . . . . . . **$824.00**

**MODEL P-38**

## MODEL P-5 DA

**SPECIFICATIONS**
**Caliber:** 9mm Parabellum
**Capacity:** 8 rounds
**Barrel lengths:** 3.1″ (Compact) and 3.5″
**Overall length:** 6.6″ (Compact) and 7″
**Weight:** 26.5 oz. (3.1″ barrel); 28 oz. (3.5″ barrel)
**Finish:** Blue
**Features:** Four automatic built-in safety functions; lightweight alloy frame; supplied with two magazines
**Price:** . . . . . . . . . . . . . . . . . . . . . . . . . . . . . . . . . . . . . **$1096.00**

**MODEL P-5 DA**

# DAN WESSON REVOLVERS

## 357 MAGNUM REVOLVERS

Introduced in 1935, the 357 Magnum is still the top-selling handgun caliber. It makes an excellent hunting sidearm, and many law enforcement agencies have adopted it as a duty caliber. Take your pick of Dan Wesson 357s; then, add to its versatility with an additional barrel assembly option to alter it to your other needs.

**SPECIFICATIONS**
**Action:** Six-shot double and single action. **Ammunition:** 357 Magnum, 38 Special Hi-speed, 38 Special Mid-range. **Typical dimension:** 4″ barrel revolver, 9¼″×5¾″. **Trigger:** Smooth, wide tang (3/8″) with overtravel adjustment. **Hammer:** Wide spur (3/8″) with short double-action travel. **Sights: Models 14 and 714,** 1/8″ fixed serrated front; fixed rear integral with frame. **Models 15 and 715,** 1/8″ serrated interchangeable front blade; red insert standard, yellow and white available; rear notch (.125, .080, or white outline) adjustable for windage and elevation; graduated click. 10″ barrel assemblies have special front sights and instructions. **Rifling:** Six lands and grooves, right-hand twist, 1 turn in 18.75 inches (2½″ thru 8″ lengths); six lands & grooves, right-hand twist, 1 turn in 14 inches (10″ bbl.). **Note:** All 2½″ guns shipped with undercover grips. 4″ guns are shipped with service grips and the balance have oversized target grips.

**Price:**
**Pistol Pac Models** 357 Magnum ....... **$629.00** (Blue) to **$922.00** (Stainless)

### 357 MAGNUMS

| Model | Type | Barrel Lengths/ Weight in Ounces | | | | | Finish |
|---|---|---|---|---|---|---|---|
| | | 2½″ | 4″ | 6″ | 8″ | 10″ | |
| 14-2 | Service | 30 | 34 | 38 | NA | NA | BB |
| 15-2 | Target | 32 | 36 | 40 | 44 | 50 | BB |
| 15-2V | Target | 32 | 35 | 39 | 43 | 49 | BB |
| 15-2VH | Target | 32 | 37 | 42 | 47 | 55 | BB |
| 714 | Service | 30 | 34 | 38 | NA | NA | SSS |
| 715 | Target | 32 | 36 | 40 | 45 | 50 | SSS |
| 715-V | Target | 32 | 35 | 40 | 43 | 49 | SSS |
| 715-VH | Target | 32 | 37 | 42 | 49 | 55 | SSS |

* BB=Brite Blue. SSS=Satin Stainless Steel.

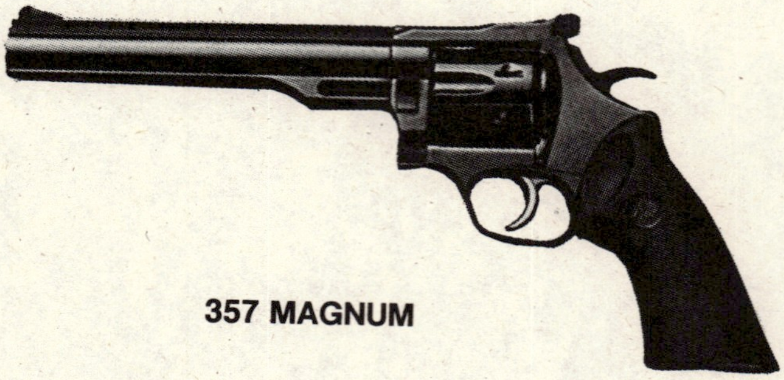

357 MAGNUM

## 38 SPECIAL REVOLVERS

For decades a favorite of security and law enforcement agencies, the 38 special still maintains it's reputation as a fine caliber for sportsmen and target shooters. Dan Wesson offers a choice of barrel lengths in either service or target configuration.

**SPECIFICATIONS**
**Action:** Six-shot double and single action. **Ammunition:** 38 Special Hi-speed, 38 Special Mid-range. **Typical dimension:** 4″ barrel revolver, 9¼″ × 5¾″. **Trigger:** Smooth, wide tang (3/8″) with overtravel adjustment. **Hammer:** Wide spur (3/8″) with short double travel. **Sights:** Models 8 and 708, 1/8″ fixed serrated front; fixed rear integral with frame. Models 9 and 709, 1/8″ serrated interchangeable front blade; red insert standard, yellow and white available; rear, standard notch (.125, .080, or white outline) adjustable for windage and elevation; graduated click. **Rifling:** Six lands and grooves, right-hand twist, 1 turn in 18.75 inches. **Note:** All 2½″ guns shipped with undercover grips. 4″ guns are shipped with service grips and the balance have oversized target grips.

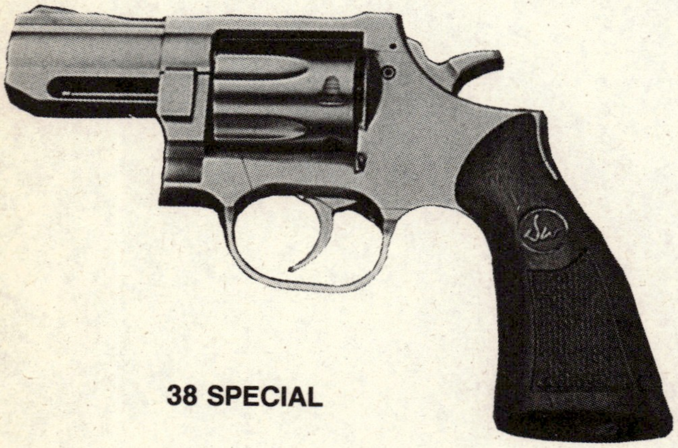

38 SPECIAL

**Price:**
**Pistol Pac Models** 38 Special .......... **$629.00** (Blue) to **$922.00** (Stainless)

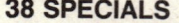

### 38 SPECIALS

| Model | Type | Barrel Lengths/ Weight in Ounces | | | | Finish |
|---|---|---|---|---|---|---|
| | | 2½″ | 4″ | 6″ | 8″ | |
| 8-2 | Service | 30 | 34 | 38 | NA | BB |
| 9-2 | Target | 32 | 36 | 40 | 44 | BB |
| 9-2V | Target | 32 | 35 | 39 | 43 | BB |
| 9-2VH | Target | 32 | 37 | 42 | 47 | BB |
| 708 | Service | 30 | 34 | 38 | NA | SSS |
| 709 | Target | 32 | 36 | 40 | 44 | SSS |
| 709-V | Target | 32 | 35 | 39 | 43 | SSS |
| 709-VH | Target | 32 | 37 | 42 | 47 | SSS |

* BB=Brite Blue. SSS=Satin Stainless Steel.

# DAN WESSON REVOLVERS

## 22 SILHOUETTE REVOLVER

**SPECIFICATIONS**
This six-shot, single-action-only revolver is available with 10″ vented or vent heavy barrel assembly; incorporates a new cylinder manufacturing process that enhances the inherent accuracy of the Wesson revolver. Shipped with a combat-style grip, .080 narrow notch rear sight blade, a Patridge-style front sight blade to match. **Caliber:** 22 rimfire. **Type:** Target. **Weight:** 55 to 62 oz. **Finish:** Bright blue or stainless steel.
**Price:** ............................ **$474.00 to $532.00**

22 SILHOUETTE REVOLVER

## FIXED BARREL REVOLVERS
**$289.00–$319.00 (Service Model)**
**$322.00–$370.00 (Target Model)**

These revolvers retain the advantages of a barrel in tension (minimal barrel whip) without the interchangeable features of earlier Wesson models.

**SPECIFICATIONS**
**Calibers:** 357 Magnum and 38 Special. **Capacity:** 6 shots. **Barrel lengths:** 3″, 4″, 5″ and 6″ (Target); 2½″ and 4″ (Service). **Overall length:** 8¾″ w/3″ barrel; 11¾″ w/6″ barrel. **Height:** 5¾″. **Weight:** 37 oz. to 45 oz. **Sight radius:** 5⅛″ (3″); 8⅛″ (6″). **Sights:** Adjustable rear target (Target model); fixed service sight (Service model). **Finish:** Brushed stainless steel or High Brite Blue (Target); brushed stainless steel or satin blue (Service).

Also available in 44 Mag./44 Special. **Barrel lengths:** 4″, 5″, 6″ and 8″. **Price: $447.00** (Blue); **$508.00** (Stainless).

357 MAG. FIXED BARREL REVOLVER

## .45 PIN GUN
**$654.00–$762.00**

**SPECIFICATIONS**
**Caliber:** 45 Auto. **Barrel length:** 5″ (5.28″ compensated shroud). **Overall length:** 12½″. **Weight:** 54 oz. **Sight radius:** 8.375″. **Finish:** Brushed stainless steel or High Brite Blue steel.

.45 PIN GUN

# DAN WESSON REVOLVERS

357 SUPER MAG

**SPECIFICATIONS**
**Action:** Six-shot double and single action. **Ammunition:** 357 Maximum. **Overall length:** 14.375″ with 8″ barrel. **Height:** 6.5″. **Trigger:** Clean let-off, wide tang with overtravel adjustment. **Hammer:** Wide spur with short double-action travel. **Sights:** 1/8″ serrated interchangeable front blade; red insert standard, yellow and white available; rear, new interchangeable blade (.125 or optional .080); screwdriver adjustable for windage and elevation. **Rifling:** Six lands and grooves, right-hand twist, 1 in 18 3/4 inches.

**SPECIFICATIONS**

| Model | Caliber | Type | Barrel Lengths/ Weight in Ounces | | | Finish | Prices* |
|---|---|---|---|---|---|---|---|
| | | | 6″ | 8″ | 10″ | | |
| 740-V | 357 Max | Target | 59.5 | 64 | 65 | Stainless | $502.00–$704.00 |
| 740-VH | 357 Max | Target | 62 | 72 | 76 | Stainless | |
| 740-V8S | 357 Max | Target | | 62 | | Stainless | |

*** Model 40** (Blue): **$488.00–613.00**

32/32-20 MAGNUM SIX SHOT

This target and small-game gun offers a high muzzle velocity and a flat trajectory for better accuracy. **Action:** Six-shot double and single. **Calibers:** 32 H&R Magnum, 32 S&W Long, 32 Colt new police cartridges interchangeable. **Barrel length:** 4″. **Overall length:** 9 1/4″ (w/4″ barrel). **Trigger:** Smooth, wide tang (3/8″) w/overtravel adjustment. **Hammer:** Wide spur (3/8″) w/short double-action travel. **Sights:** Front—1/8″ serrated, interchangeable blade, red insert standard (yellow and white available); rear—interchangeable blade for wide or narrow notch sight picture (wide notch standard, narrow notch available), adj. for windage and elevation, graduated click. **Rifling:** Six lands and grooves, right-hand twist 1:18 3/4″. **Finish:** Blue or stainless steel.

**SPECIFICATIONS**

| Model | Caliber | Type | Barrel Lengths/ Weight in Ounces | | | | Finish | Pistol Pac Prices* |
|---|---|---|---|---|---|---|---|---|
| | | | 2 1/2″ | 4″ | 6″ | 8″ | | |
| 32 | .32 Magnum | Target | 35 | 39 | 43 | 48 | BB | $653.00–$870.00 |
| 32V | .32 Magnum | Target | 35 | 39 | 43 | 48 | BB | |
| 32VH | .32 Magnum | Target | 35 | 40 | 46 | 53 | BB | |
| 732 | .32 Magnum | Target | 35 | 39 | 43 | 48 | SSS | $712.00–$922.00 |
| 732V | .32 Magnum | Target | 35 | 39 | 43 | 48 | SSS | |
| 732VH | .32 Magnum | Target | 35 | 40 | 46 | 53 | SSS | |

# DAN WESSON REVOLVERS

## 41, 44 MAGNUM AND 45 COLT REVOLVERS

The Dan Wesson 41, 44 Magnum and 45 Colt revolvers are available with a patented "Power Control" to reduce muzzle flip. Each has a one-piece frame and patented gain bolt for maximum strength.

**SPECIFICATIONS**
**Action:** Six-shot double- and single-action. **Typical dimension:** 6″ barrel revolver, 12″×6.″ **Trigger:** Smooth, wide tang (3/8″) with overtravel adjustment. **Hammer:** Wide checkered spur with short double-action travel. **Sights:** Front, 1/8″ serrated interchangeable blade; red insert standard, yellow and white available; rear, standard notch (.125, .080, or white outline) adjustable for windage and elevation; click graduated. **Rifling:** Eight lands and grooves, right-hand twist, 1 turn in 18.75 inches.
**Prices:**
**Pistol Pac Models** (All calibers)
Blue . . . . . . . . . . . . . . . . . . . . . . . . . . . . . . . . . . . . . **$678.00–731.00**
Stainless Steel . . . . . . . . . . . . . . . . . . . . . . . . **785.00–839.00**

| Model | Caliber | Type | Barrel Lengths/ Weight in Ounces | | | | Finish |
|---|---|---|---|---|---|---|---|
| | | | 4″ | 6″ | 8″ | 10″* | |
| 41-V | 41 Magnum | Target | 48 | 53 | 58 | 64 | BB |
| 41-VH | 41 Magnum | Target | 49 | 56 | 64 | 69 | BB |
| 44-V | 44 Magnum | Target | 48 | 53 | 58 | 64 | BB |
| 44-VH | 44 Magnum | Target | 49 | 56 | 64 | 69 | BB |
| 741-V | 41 Magnum | Target | 48 | 53 | 58 | 64 | SSS |
| 741-VH | 41 Magnum | Target | 49 | 56 | 64 | 69 | SSS |
| 744-V | 44 Magnum | Target | 48 | 53 | 58 | 64 | SSS |
| 744-VH | 44 Magnum | Target | 49 | 56 | 64 | 69 | SSS |
| 745-V | 45 Colt | Target | 48 | 53 | 58 | 64 | SSS |
| 745-VH | 45 Colt | Target | 49 | 56 | 64 | 69 | SSS |

* BB=Brite Blue. SSS=Satin Stainless Steel.

41/44 MAGNUM AND 45 COLT REVOLVERS

## 445 SUPERMAG REVOLVERS

With muzzle velocities in the 1650 fps range, and chamber pressures and recoil comparable to the 44 Magnum, the 445 Supermag has already won considerable renown in silhouette competition. As a hunting cartridge, it is more than adequate for any species of game on the American continent. **Action:** Six-shot double and single. **Type:** Target. **Caliber:** 445 Supermag. **Overall length:** 14.375″ w/8″ barrel. **Trigger:** Clean let-off, widg tane with overtravel adjustment. **Hammer:** Wide spur with short double-action travel. **Sights:** 1/8″ serrated, interchangeable front blade, red insert standard (yellow and white available); rear—interchangeable blade for wide or narrow notch sight picture, wide notch standard (narrow notch available), adj. for windage and elevation. **Rifling:** Six lands and grooves, right-hand twist 1:18 3/4″.

| Model | Barrel Lengths/ Weight in Ounces | | | Finish | Prices |
|---|---|---|---|---|---|
| | 6″ | 8″ | 10″ | | |
| 445-V | 59.5 | 62 | 65 | BB | $551.00–$619.00 |
| 445-VH | 62 | 72 | 76 | BB | |
| 445-VHS | — | 64 | — | BB | |
| 445-VS | — | 60 | 64 | BB | |
| 7445-V | 59.5 | 62 | 65 | SS | $596.00–$687.00 |
| 7445-VH | 62 | 72 | 76 | SS | |
| 7445-VHS | — | 64 | — | SS | |
| 7445-VS | — | 60 | 64 | SS | |

* BB=Brite Blue. SS=Stainless Steel.

445 SUPERMAG

# DAN WESSON REVOLVERS

## 22 RIMFIRE

Built on the same frames as the Dan Wesson 357 Magnum, these 22 rimfires offer the heft and balance of fine target revolvers. Affordable fun for the beginner or the expert.

**SPECIFICATIONS**
**Action:** Six-shot double and single action. **Ammunition:** Models 22 & 722, 22 Long Rifle. **Typical dimension:** 4″ barrel revolver, 9¼″×5¾″. **Trigger:** Smooth, wide tang (3/8″) with overtravel adjustment. **Hammer:** Wide spur (3/8″) with short double-action travel. **Sights:** Front, 1/8″ serrated, interchangeable blade; red insert standard, yellow and white available; rear, standard wide notch (.125, .080, or white outline) adjustable for windage and elevation; graduated click. **Rifling:** Models 22 and 722, six lands and grooves, right-hand twist, 1 turn in 12 inches. **Note:** All 2½″ guns are shipped with undercover grips. 4″ guns are shipped with service grips and the balance have oversized target grips.

| Model | Caliber | Type | Barrel Lengths/ Weight in Ounces | | | | Finish |
|---|---|---|---|---|---|---|---|
| | | | 2¼″ | 4″ | 6″ | 8″ | |
| 22 | 22 LR | Target | 36 | 40 | 44 | 49 | BB |
| 22-V | 22 LR | Target | 36 | 40 | 44 | 49 | BB |
| 22-VH | 22 LR | Target | 36 | 41 | 47 | 54 | BB |
| 722 | 22 LR | Target | 36 | 40 | 44 | 49 | SSS |
| 722-V | 22 LR | Target | 36 | 40 | 44 | 49 | SSS |
| 722-VH | 22 LR | Target | 36 | 41 | 47 | 54 | SSS |

* BB=Brite Blue. SSS=Satin Stainless Steel.

**Prices:**
**Pistol Pac Model 22** . . . . . . . . . . . . . . . . . **$653.00** (Blue)—
**$923.00** (Stainless)

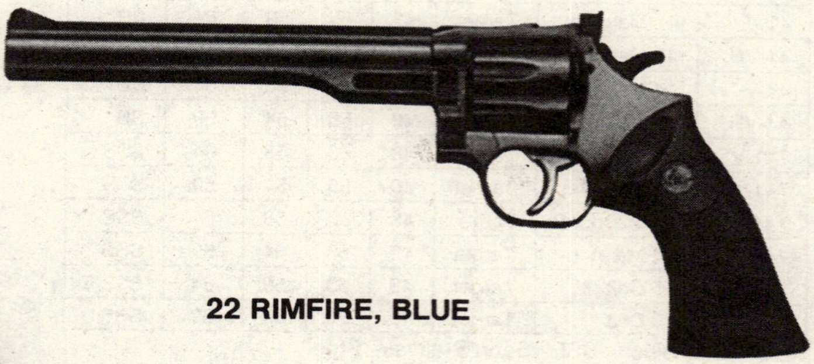

22 RIMFIRE, BLUE

22 RIMFIRE, STAINLESS

## MODEL 738+P "L'IL DAN"
## $340.00

This new 5-shot double-action revolver uses a .38+P cartridge and features fixed sights plus Pauferro wood or rubber grips. Overall length is 6½ inches and weight is 24.6 ounces.

**SPECIFICATIONS**
**Caliber:** 38 + P. **Capacity:** 5 shots. **Barrel length:** 6½″. **Weight:** 24.6 oz. **Sights:** Fixed. **Finish:** Stainless steel or blue. **Grip:** Pauferro wood or rubber.

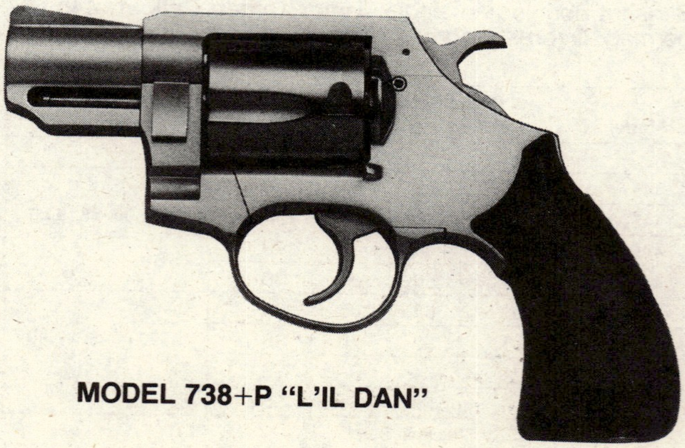

MODEL 738+P "L'IL DAN"

# DAN WESSON REVOLVERS

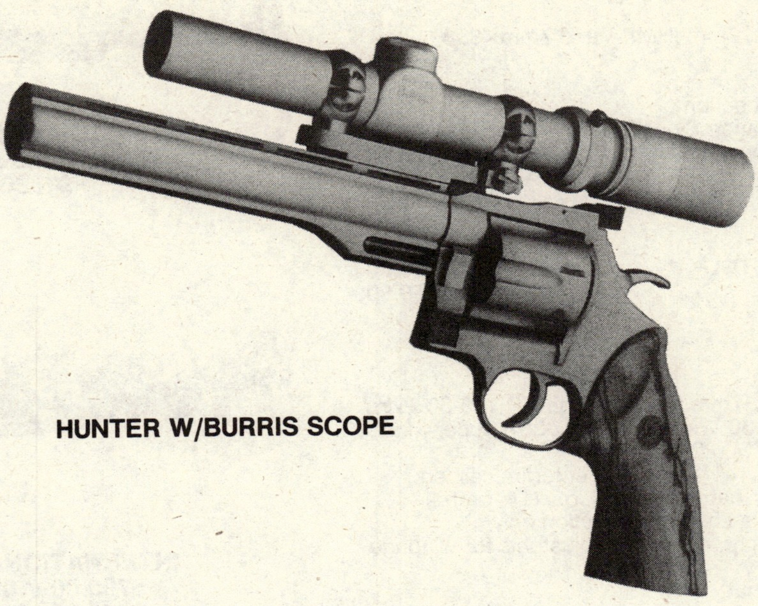

HUNTER W/BURRIS SCOPE

## HUNTER SERIES

**Open Hunter:** Features a dovetailed Iron Sight Gunworks rear sight for quick target acquisition. The Alan Taylor throated 7½ inch barrel provides improved accuracy.
**Compensated Open Hunter:** For those who prefer open sights and less muzzle flip for quick follow-up shots. A shorter barrel (6″ with 7″ shroud) retains sight radius while allowing compensator system.
**Scoped Hunter:** No open sights and a 7½-inch barrel. Features a Burris base and rings mounted on shroud. Drilled, tapped and factory mounted.
**Compensated Scoped Hunter:** Same specifications as above, but with 6-inch barrel (7-inch shroud).

**GENERAL SPECIFICATIONS**
**Calibers:** 44 Magnum (Buck Series); 445 Super Mag. (Grizzly Series); 357 Super Mag. (Varmint Series); 41 Mag. (Boar Series)
**Barrel lengths:** See above
**Shrouds:** Vent heavy on Open and Scoped Hunter; full round (Lightweight) on Compensated models (approx. 1″ longer than inner barrel); non-fluted cylinder
**Overall length:** Approx. 14″
**Weight:** 4 lbs. (approx.)
**Action:** Double and single (creep-free)
**Grips:** Hogue rubber, finger-grooved
**Finish:** Bright blue steel or satin stainless steel
**Prices:**

| | |
|---|---|
| **Open Hunter** | **$805.00** |
| w/Stainless Steel | **849.00** |
| **Open Hunter Compensated** | **837.00** |
| w/Stainless Steel | **880.00** |
| **Scoped Hunter** | **838.00** |
| w/Stainless Steel | **881.00** |
| **Scoped Hunter Compensated** | **870.00** |
| w/Stainless Steel | **914.00** |

## SUPER RAM SILHOUETTE REVOLVER (not shown)
**$807.00 ($850.00 in .41 Supermag and .357 Max.)**

Wesson's new Super Ram features a modified Iron Sight Gun Works rear sight and a front sight that is hooded to prevent glare. The revolver also offers as standard equipment an Allen Taylor throated barrel. This combination—a faster rate of twist and Allen Taylor throating—helps stabilize the bullet for greater accuracy. A factory trigger is also standard, bringing the single action to 2½ pounds (approx.). The Super Ram has a fixed barrel configuration with the barrel-to-cylinder gap set at the factory. Each unit is factory-certified to meet the four-pound weight requirement. **Calibers:** 357 Max., 44 Magnum and 41 Supermag.

For additional specifications, contact Dan Wesson (see Directory of Manufacturers and Suppliers).

# WICHITA ARMS PISTOLS

**SPECIFICATIONS**
**Calibers:** 308 Win. F.L., 7mm IHMSA and 7mm×308
**Barrel length:** $14\frac{15}{16}$″
**Weight:** $4\frac{1}{2}$ lbs.
**Action:** Single-shot bolt action
**Sights:** Wichita Multi-Range Sight System
**Grips:** Right-hand center walnut grip or right-hand rear walnut grip
**Features:** Glass bedded; bolt ground to precision fit; adjustable Wichita trigger
Also available:
**WICHITA CLASSIC PISTOL** .................. **$3450.00**
**Engraved Model** ........................... **4850.00**

**SILHOUETTE PISTOL**
**(Right-Hand Rear Grip)**
**$1350.00**

**SPECIFICATIONS**
**Calibers:** 7-30 Waters, 7mm Super Mag., 7R (30-30 Win. necked to 7mm), 30-30 Win., 357 Mag., 357 Super Mag., 32 H&H Mag., 22 RFM, 22 LR
**Barrel lengths:** 10″ and 14″ ($10\frac{1}{2}$″ for centerfire calibers)
**Weight:** 3 lbs. 2 oz. (10″ barrel); 4 lbs. 7 oz. (14″ barrel)
**Action:** Top-break, single-shot, single action only
**Sights:** Patridge front sight; rear sight adjustable for windage and elevation
**Grips and Forend:** Walnut
**Safety:** Crossbolt

**INTERNATIONAL PISTOL**
**$700.00 (10″ Barrel)**
**$775.00 (14″ Barrel)**

# WILDEY PISTOLS

## WILDEY PISTOLS

These gas-operated pistols are designed to meet the needs of hunters who want to use handguns for big game. The Wildey pistol includes such features as: • Ventilated rib • Reduced recoil • Double-action trigger mechanism • Patented hammer and trigger blocks and rebounding fire pin • Sights adjustable for windage and elevation • Stainless construction • Fixed barred for increased accuracy • Increased action strength (with 3-lug and exposed face rotary bolt) • Selective single or autoloading capability • Ability to handle high-pressure loads

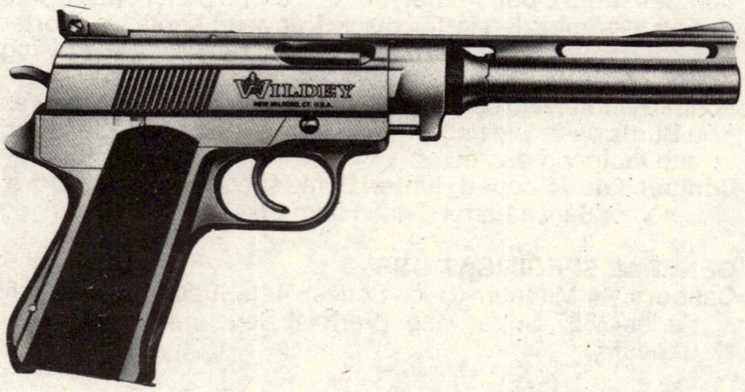

**SPECIFICATIONS**
**Calibers:** 45 Win. Mag., 475 Wildey Mag.
**Capacity:** 7 shots
**Barrel lengths:** 5″, 6″, 7″, 8″, 10″, 12″
**Overall length:** 11″ with 7″ barrel
**Weight:** 64 oz. with 5″ barrel
**Height:** 6″

**SURVIVOR MODEL** in 45 Win. Mag. **Prices**
5″, 6″ or 7″ models ........................ **$1295.00**
Same model w/8″ or 10″ barrels ............. **1295.00**
With square trigger guard, **add** ............ **35.00**
With new vent rib, **add** ..................... **30.00**
**SURVIVOR MODEL** in 475 Wildey Mag.
8″ or 10″ barrels ............................ **1316.00**
With square trigger guard, **add** ............ **35.00**
With new vent rib, **add** ..................... **30.00**

**HUNTER MODEL** in 45 Win. Mag.
8″, 10″ or 12″ barrels ....................... **$1400.00**
With square trigger guard, **add** ............ **35.00**
**HUNTER MODEL** in 475 Wildey Mag.
8″ or 10″ barrels ............................ **1400.00**
With 12″ barrel .............................. **1449.00**
W/square trigger guard (8″, 10″, 12″ barrels)
**add** ......................................... **35.00**

Also available:
Interchangeable barrel extension assemblies **$523.00** (5″ barrel) to **$648.95** (12″ barrel).

# Rifles

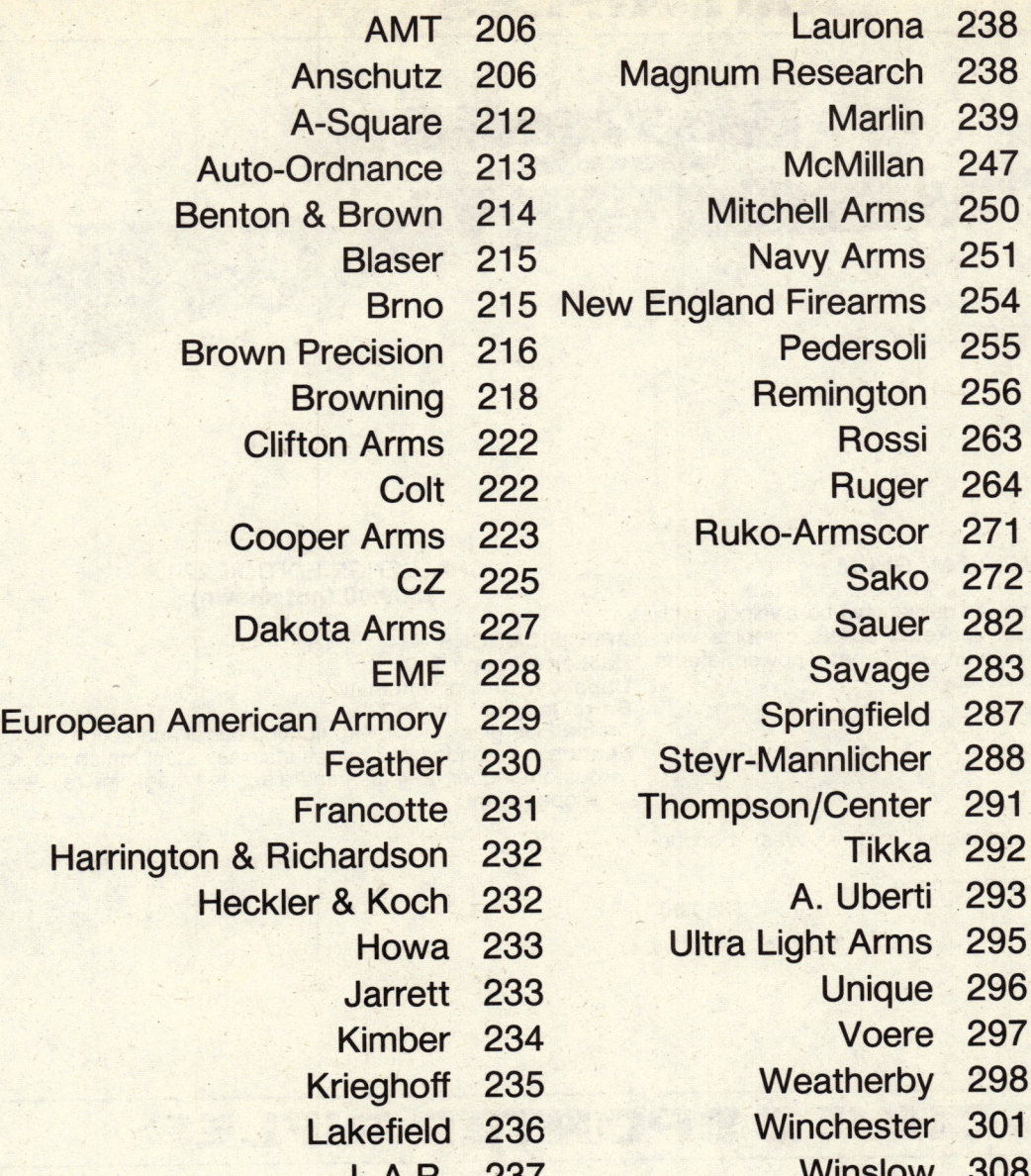

For addresses and phone numbers of manufacturers and distributors included in this section, turn to *DIRECTORY OF MANUFACTURERS AND SUPPLIERS* at the back of the book.

# AMT RIFLES

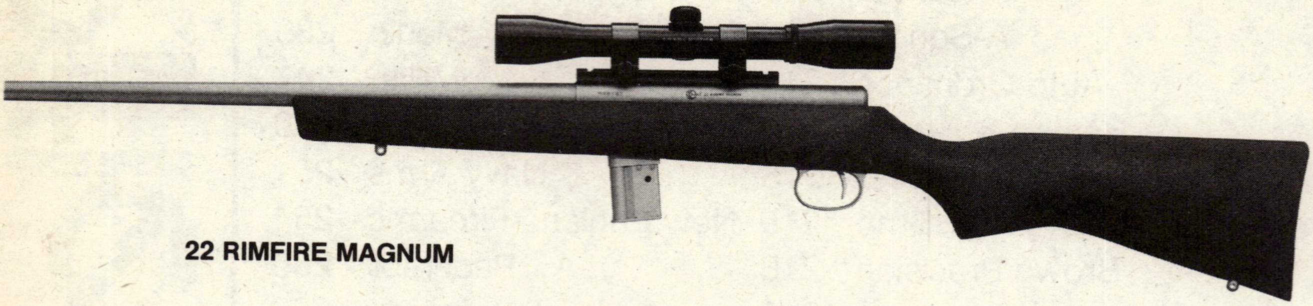

22 RIMFIRE MAGNUM

### 22 RIMFIRE MAGNUM

AMT's new rimfire magnum rifle delivers big-bore velocity with minimum cost ammunition. Jacketed bullets combine with magnum velocity to yield high impact. Greater power flattens trajectory and improves accuracy.

**SPECIFICATIONS**
**Caliber:** 22 Rimfire Magnum
**Capacity:** 10 rounds
**Barrel length:** 20″
**Weight:** 6 lbs.
**Sights:** No sights; drilled and tapped for 87-A Weaver scope mount base
**Features:** Stainless steel construction
**Price:** . . . . . . . . . . . . . . . . . . . . . . . . . . . . . . . . . . . . . . . **$369.00**

### CHALLENGE EDITION 22 LR
### $899.00 (not shown)

**SPECIFICATIONS**
**Caliber:** 22 Long Rifle
**Capacity:** 10-shot automatic
**Barrel lengths:** 18″ or 22″
**Stock:** Fiberglass stock with floating barrel and action
**Features:** Threaded bull barrel; stainless steel match grade; custom trigger (2–4 lbs.) and extended magazine release; scope mount

# ANSCHUTZ SPORTER RIFLES

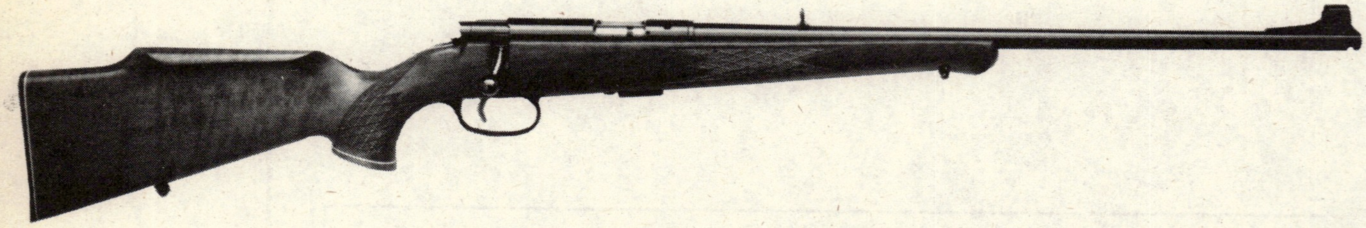

**MODEL 1700D CUSTOM $1364.00 (22 LR)**
**$1534.00 (22 Hornet & 222 Rem.)**
**$1230.00 (22 LR Featherweight)**
**$1460.00 (22 LR Featherweight Deluxe)**

# ANSCHUTZ SPORTER RIFLES



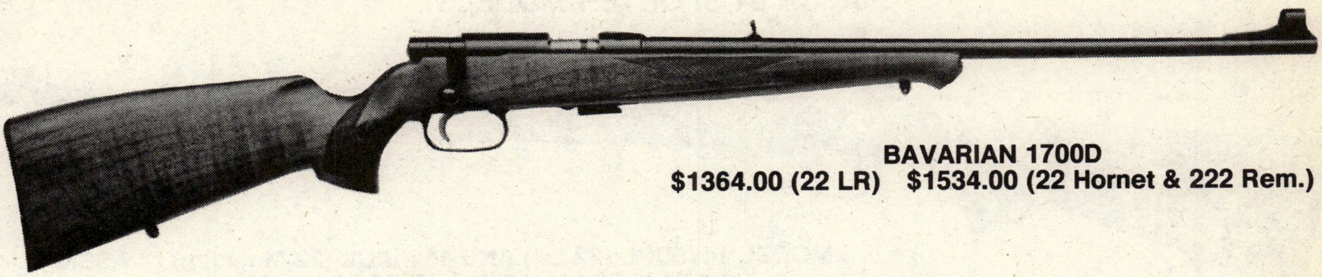

**BAVARIAN 1700D**
**$1364.00 (22 LR) $1534.00 (22 Hornet & 222 Rem.)**

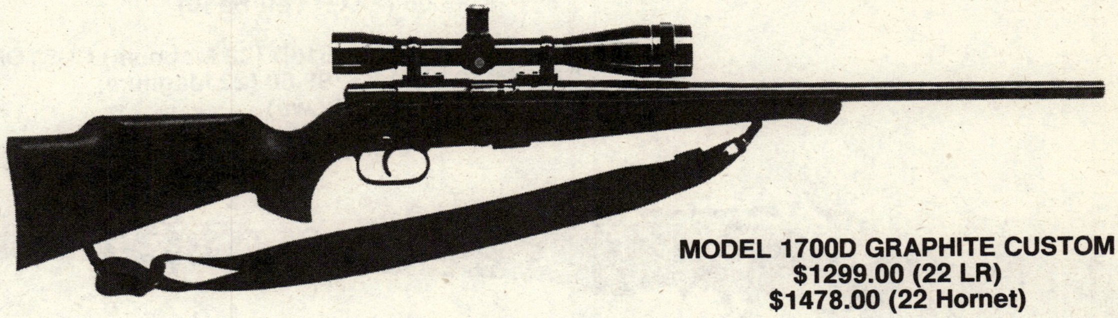

**MODEL 1700D GRAPHITE CUSTOM**
**$1299.00 (22 LR)**
**$1478.00 (22 Hornet)**

**MANNLICHER 1733D**
**$1657.00**

## SPECIFICATIONS

| *Specifications:* | | 1700D Bavarian | 1700D Custom | 1733D Mannlicher | 1700D Graphite Custom | | 1700D FWT | 1700D FWT Deluxe |
|---|---|---|---|---|---|---|---|---|
| | | .22 LR, .22 Hornet, | .222 Rem. | .22 Hornet | .22 Hornet | .22 LR | .22 LR | .22 LR |
| Length: | Overall | 43" | 43" | 39" | 41" | 41" | 41" | 41" |
| | Barrel | 24" | 24" | 19w" | 22" | 22" | 22" | 22" |
| | Pull | 14" | 14" | 14" | 14" | 14" | 14" | 14" |
| Drop at: | Comb | 1¼" | 1¼" | 1¼" | 1¼" | 1¼" | 1¼" | 1¼" |
| | Monte Carlo | 1" | | 1¼" | 1" | 1" | 1" | 1" |
| | Heel | 1½" | 1½" | 2⅜" | 1½" | 1½" | 1½" | 1½" |
| Average weight: | | 7½ lbs. | 7½ lbs. | 6¼ lbs. | 7½ lbs. | 7½ lbs. | 6¼ lbs. | 6¼ lbs. |
| Trigger: | Single stage 5096 (.222 Rem. 5095) | • | • | • | • | • | • | • |
| | Adjustable* for creep and overtravel | • | • | • | • | • | • | • |

# ANSCHUTZ SPORTER RIFLES

## MATCH 64 SPORTER MODELS

**MODEL 1416DCL (22 LR) AND 1516DCL (22 Magnum) CLASSIC**
**$748.00 (1416DCL) $763.00 (1516DCL)**
**$785.00 (22 LR Left Hand)**

**MODEL 1416D (22 LR) AND 1516D (22 Magnum) CUSTOM**
**$785.00 (22 LR) $799.00 (22 Magnum)**
**(not shown)**

**1418D MANNLICHER**
**$1159.00 (22 LR)**

**MODEL 1518D MANNLICHER**
**$1170.00 (22 Magnum)**

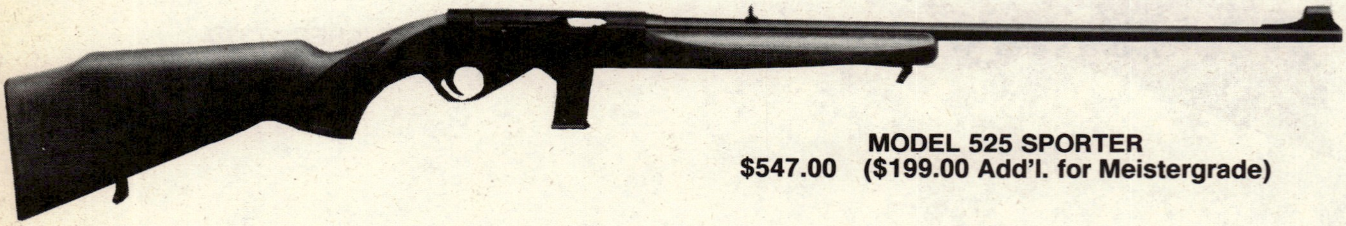

**MODEL 525 SPORTER**
**$547.00 ($199.00 Add'l. for Meistergrade)**

### SPECIFICATIONS

| MODEL | Classic 1416D** 1516D | Custom 1416D 1516D | Mannlicher* 1418D 1518D | Model 525 Sporter |
|---|---|---|---|---|
| Length—Overall | 41″ | 41″ | 38″ | 43″ |
| Barrel | 22 1/2″ | 22 1/2″ | 19 3/4″ | 24″ |
| Pull | 14″ | 14″ | 14″ | 14″ |
| Drop at—Comb | 1 1/4″ | 1 1/4″ | 1 1/4″ | 1 1/8″ |
| Monte Carlo | 1 1/2″ | 1 1/2″ | 1 1/2″ | 1 3/4″ |
| Heel | 1 1/2″ | 2 1/2″ | 2 1/2″ | 2 5/8″ |
| Average Weight | 5 1/2 lbs. | 6 lbs. | 5 1/2 lbs. | 6 1/2 lbs. |
| Rate of Twist Right Hand—one turn in 16.5″ for .22 LR; 1–16″ for .22 Mag | | | | |
| Takedown Bolt Action With Removable Firing Pin | • | • | • | |
| 3/4″ Swivel | | | • | • |
| Swivel Studs | • | • | | |

# ANSCHUTZ MATCH RIFLES

**MODEL BR-50 BENCH REST RIFLE**
**$3312.00**

**SPECIFICATIONS**
**Caliber:** 22 LR.
**Barrel length:** 19¾″ without muzzle weight; 23″ with muzzle weight.
**Overall length:** 37¾″ – 42½″
**Weight:** 11 lbs.
**Trigger:** No. 5015 two-stage adjustable target trigger (3.9 oz. weight).
**Stock:** European hardwood with adjustable spacers.

**BIATHLON RIFLES SPECIFICATIONS**

| | SuperMatch Model 2013 | Model 1827BT Biathlon Rifle | Model 54.18MS Fortner Silhouette Rifle |
|---|---|---|---|
| Barrel length - O/D: | 19.7/27.2" - 15/16" | 21.5" - 3/4" | 21" - 3/4" |
| Overall length: | 43" - 45.5" | 41" | 41.3" |
| Overall length to hook/buttplate: | 49.6" - 51.2" | 41" | 41.3" |
| Stock: | International Adj. palm rest Adj. hand rest | Biathlon European walnut | Fibergrain® Meets all sanctioned competition rules |
| Cheekpiece: | Adjustable | Adjustable | Fixed |
| Recommended sights: | 7020/20 | 6827 (included) | Scope |
| Weight (approx.) : | 15.5 lbs. (w/o sights) | 8.8 lbs. (w/sights) | 8.0 lbs. |
| Trigger: | #5018 | #5020 | #5020 |
| Stage: | Two | Two | Two |
| Factory set weight: | 3.9 oz. | 1 lb., 3.5 oz. | 1 lb., 3.5 oz. |
| Adjustable weight*: | 2.1 - 8.6 oz. | 3.5 oz. - 2 lbs. | 3.5 oz. - 2 lbs. |

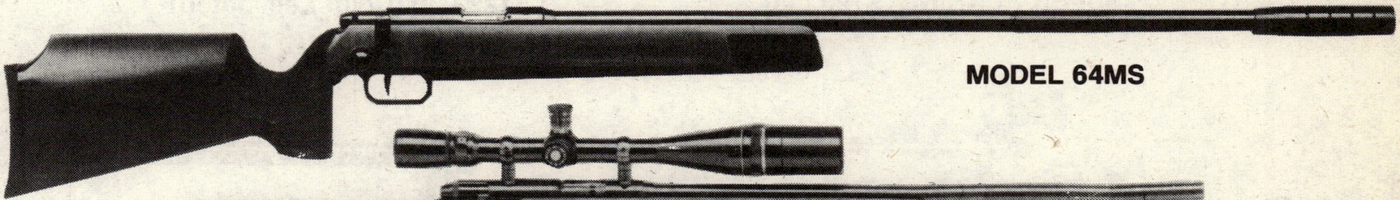

**MODEL 64MS**

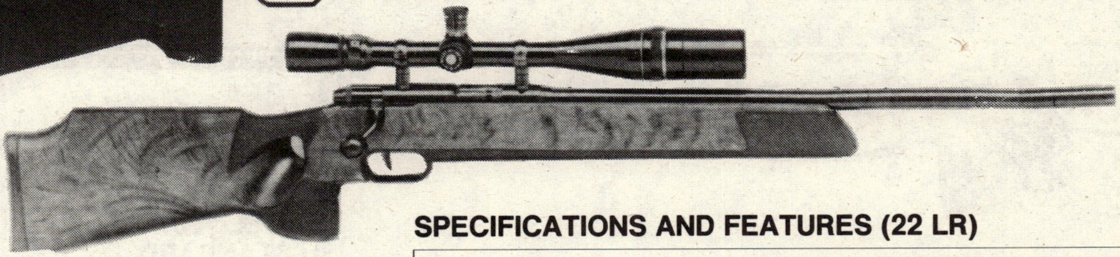

**MODEL 54.18MS-REP DELUXE**

**SPECIFICATIONS AND FEATURES (22 LR)**

| | 54.18MS | 54.18MS REP Deluxe | 64MS |
|---|---|---|---|
| Action: | SuperMatch 54 | SuperMatch 54 rep.* | Match 64 |
| Overall length: | 41.3" | 41 -49" | 39.3" |
| Barrel length: | 22.5" | 22 - 30" (19.3" rifled) | 21.5" |
| Length of pull: | 13.7" | 13.7" | 13.5" |
| Drop at comb: | 1.5" | 1.5" | 1.5" |
| Average weight: | 9 lbs., 4 oz. | 7 lbs., 12 oz. | 8 lbs., 2 oz. |
| Trigger: | #5018 | #5018 | #5091 |
| Stage: | Two | Two | Two |
| Factory adjustment weight: | 3.9 oz. | 3.9 oz. | 10 oz. |
| Adjustable weight**: | 2.1 - 8.6 oz. | 2.1 - 8.6 oz. | 9.2 - 10.6 oz. |
| Safety: | Slide | Slide | Slide |
| True left-hand model available: | ● | | ● |

*Single shot clip adaptor available. **By qualified gunsmith only.

**METALLIC SILHOUETTE RIFLES**

**Prices:**

| | |
|---|---|
| **64MS** | **$ 987.00** |
| Left Hand | **1037.00** |
| **54.18MS** | **1579.00** |
| Left Hand | **1675.00** |
| **54.18MS-REP** | **2066.00** |
| **54.18MS-REP DELUXE** | **2450.00** |
| **54.18MS FORTNER** | **3855.00** |
| Left Hand | **4168.00** |

# ANSCHUTZ INT'L. TARGET RIFLES

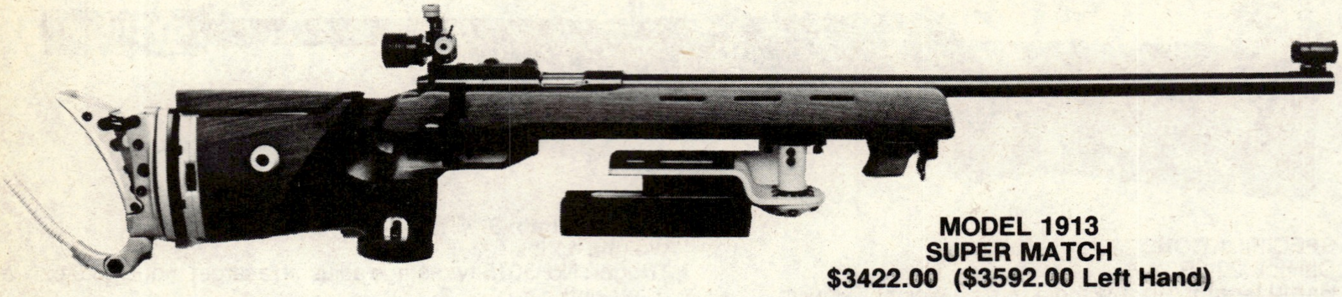

**MODEL 1913**
**SUPER MATCH**
**$3422.00 ($3592.00 Left Hand)**

**MODEL 1910 SUPER MATCH II**
**(not shown)**
**$2967.00 ($3116.00 Left Hand)**

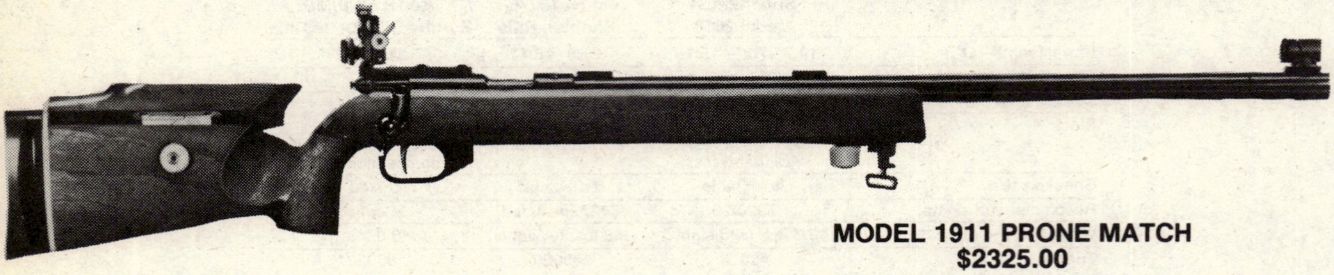

**MODEL 1911 PRONE MATCH**
**$2325.00**

**MODEL 1808DRT (not shown)**
**SUPER RUNNING $1963.00**

**MODEL 1903D (not shown)**
**$1163.00 ($1221.00 Left Hand)**
**$1293.00 (Color Laminated)**

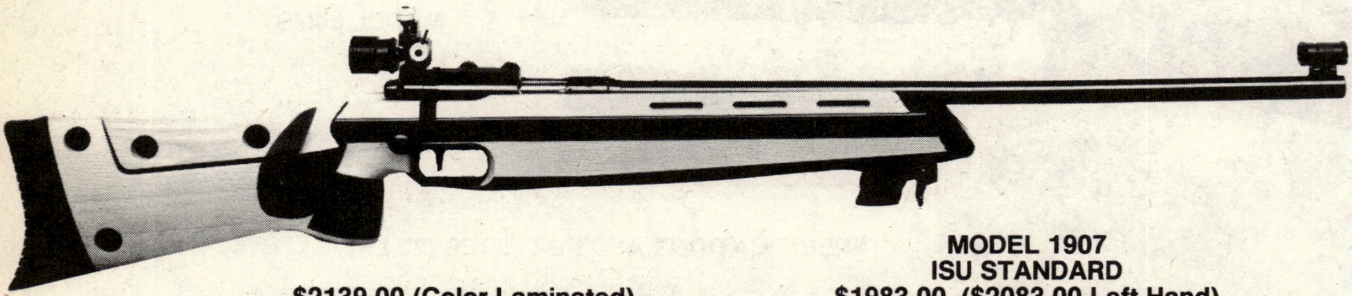

**MODEL 1907**
**ISU STANDARD**
**$1983.00 ($2083.00 Left Hand)**
**$2060.00 (Walnut) $2164.00 (Walnut L.H.)**

**$2139.00 (Color Laminated)**
**$2246.00 (Color Laminated L.H.)**

## INTERNATIONAL MATCH RIFLES: SPECIFICATIONS AND FEATURES

| | Model 1913 | Model 1907 | SuperMatch Model 2007 | Model 1808D-RT | Models 1911, 1910 | Model 1903 | Model BR-50 | Model 2002 | Achiever ST Junior Match |
|---|---|---|---|---|---|---|---|---|---|
| Barrel length: | 27.2" | 26" | 19.7/27.2" | 19.3/32.5" | 27.2" | 25.5" | 19.7/22.9" | 16.5/25.2" | 22" |
| Barrel O/D: | 15/16" | 7/8" | 15/16" | 7/8" | 15/16" | 11/16" | 15/16" | n/a | 3/4" |
| Overall length: | 43.7" - 46" | 44.5" | 45.7" | 50" | 45.7" | 43.3" | 41.3" | 42.5 | 38.7" |
| Stock: | International | Standard ISU | Standard ISU | Thumbhole | Prone, Int'l. | Standard ISU | Bench rest | Standard ISU | Standard ISU |
| Cheekpiece: | Adjustable | Adjustable | Adjustable | Adjustable | Adjustable | Adjustable | Adjustable | Adjustable | Fixed |
| Recommended sights: | #7020/20 | #7020/20 | #7020/20 | Scope | #7020/20 | #6823 | Scope | #6834 (incl.) | Sight Set #2 |
| Weight (approx.) : | 15.5 lbs. | 10.8 lbs. | 11.9 lbs. | 9.3 lbs. | 11.9, 13.7 lbs. | 9.9 lbs. | 11.5 lbs. | 10.8 lbs. | 6.5 lbs. |
| Trigger: | #5018 | #5018 | #5018 | #5020D | #5018 | #5098 | #5018 | #5021 | #5066 |
| Stage: | Two | Two | Two | One | Two | Two | Two | Two | Two |
| Factory set weight: | 3.5 oz. | 3.5 oz. | 3.5 oz. | 1.2 lbs. | 3.5 oz. | 10 oz. | 3.5 oz. | 3.5 oz. | 2.6 lbs. |
| Adjustable weight*: | 2.1 - 8.6 oz. | 2.1 - 8.6 oz.. | 2.1 - 8.6 oz.. | 3.5 oz..- 2.2 lbs. | 2.1 - 8.6 oz. | 9.2 - 10.6 oz. | 2.1 - 8.6 oz. | 2.1 - 8.6 oz. | |

# ANSCHUTZ TARGET RIFLES

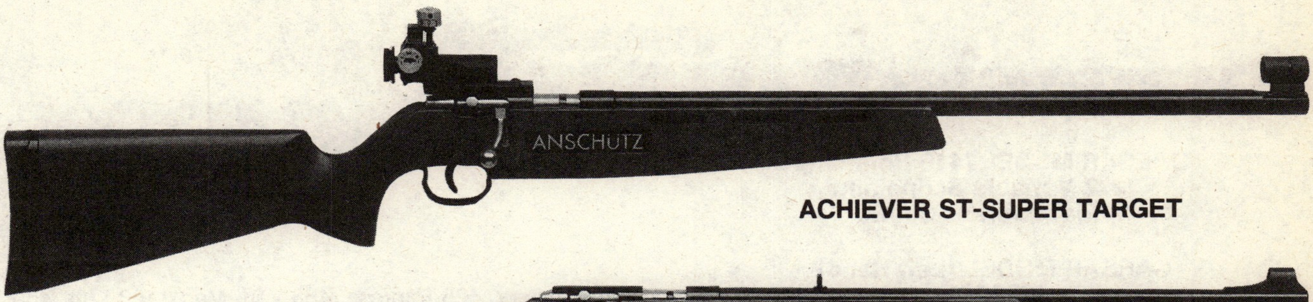


**ACHIEVER ST-SUPER TARGET**

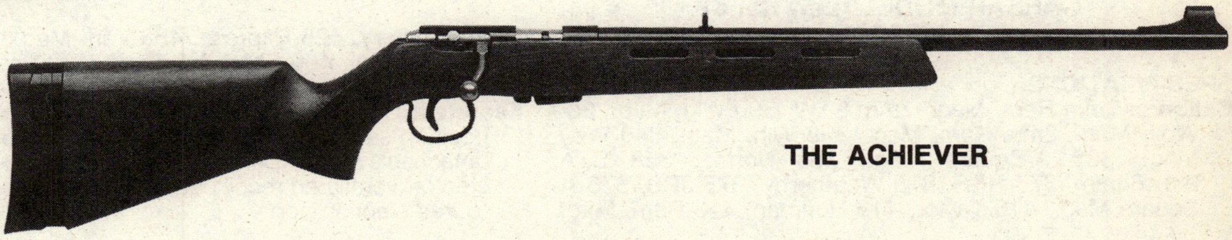

**THE ACHIEVER**

## THE ACHIEVER
## $399.00

This rifle has been designed especially for young shooters and is equally at home on range or field. It meets all NRA recommendations as an ideal training rifle.

**SPECIFICATIONS**
**Caliber:** 22 LR **Capacity:** 5- or 10-shot clips available
**Action:** Mark 2000-type repeating
**Barrel length:** $19\frac{1}{2}$" **Overall length:** $35\frac{1}{2}$"–$36\frac{2}{3}$"
**Weight:** 5 lbs.
**Trigger:** #5066-two stage (2.6 lbs.)
**Safety:** Slide
**Sights:** Hooded ramp front; Lyman folding-leaf rear, adjustable for elevation
**Stock pull:** $11\frac{7}{8}$"–13"
**Stock:** European hardwood
Also available:
**ACHIEVER ST-SUPER TARGET.**
**Barrel length:** 22". **Overall length:** $38\frac{3}{4}$".
**Weight:** $6\frac{1}{2}$ lbs.
**Price: $485.00**

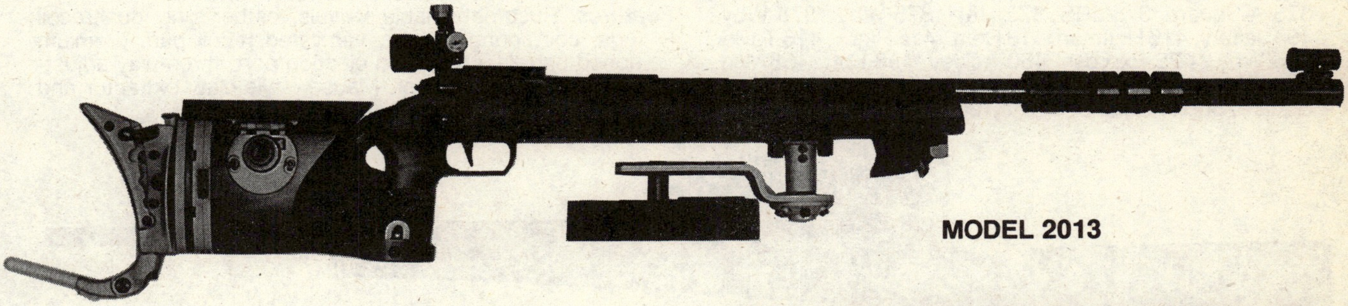

**MODEL 2013**

## MODEL 2013 SUPER MATCH 54
## $4067.00 ($4270.00 Left Hand)

**SPECIFICATIONS**
**Caliber:** 22 LR
**Barrel length:** $19\frac{3}{4}$" **Overall length:** 43" to $45\frac{1}{2}$"
**Weight:** 12.5 lbs. (without sights)
**Trigger:** #5018, two-stage, 3.9 oz. (factory set wt.)
**Sights:** #6802 Set
**Stock:** International with adjustable palm rest and hand rest
**Feature:** Adjustable cheekpiece

## MODEL 2007 SUPER MATCH 54 ISU STANDARD
## $2881.00 ($3025.00 Left Hand)
## $2961.00 (Walnut, Standard, Short or Extra Short) (not shown)

**SPECIFICATIONS**
**Caliber:** 22 LR
**Barrel length:** $19\frac{3}{4}$" **Overall length:** $43\frac{1}{2}$" to $44\frac{1}{2}$"
**Weight:** 10.8 lbs. (without sights)
**Trigger:** #5018, two-stage, 3.9 oz. (factory set wt.)
**Sights:** #6802 Set
**Stock:** Standard ISU
**Feature:** Adjustable cheekpiece

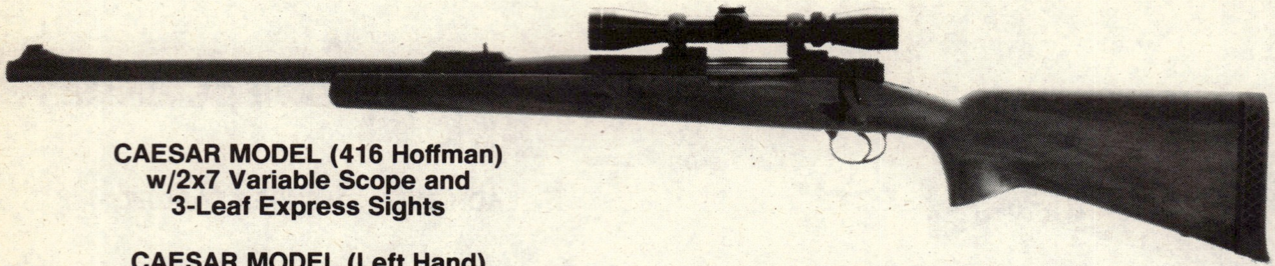

**CAESAR MODEL (416 Hoffman) w/2x7 Variable Scope and 3-Leaf Express Sights**

**CAESAR MODEL (Left Hand) $2995.00**

**SPECIFICATIONS**

**Calibers:** 7mm Rem. Mag., 7mm STW, 300 Win. Mag., 300 Wby. Mag., 8mm Rem. Mag., 338 Win. Mag., 340 Wby. Mag., 338 A-Square Mag., 358 Norma, 358 STA, 9.3×64mm, 375 H&H, 375 Weatherby, 375 JRS, 375 A-Square Mag., 416 Taylor, 416 Hoffman, 416 Rem. Mag., 404 Jeffery, 425 Express, 458 Win. Mag., 458 Lott, 450 Ackley Mag., 460 Short A-Square, 470 Capstick and 495 A-Square Mag.

**Features:** Selected Claro walnut stock with oil finish; three-position safety; three-way adjustable target trigger; flush detachable swivels; leather sling; dual recoil lugs; coil spring ejector; ventilated recoil pad; premium honed barrels; contoured ejection port

**HANNIBAL MODEL (416 Rigby) w/2xLER Scope and 3-Leaf Express Sights**

**HANNIBAL MODEL $2995.00**

**SPECIFICATIONS**

**Calibers:** 300 Petersen, 8mm Rem. Mag., 338 Win., 340 Wby., 338 A-Square Mag., 358 Norma Mag., 358 STA, 9.3×64, 375 A-Square, 375 JRS, 375 H&H, 375 Wby., 378 Wby., 404 Jeffery, 416 Hoffman, 416 Rem., 416 Rigby, 416 Taylor, 416 Wby., 425 Express, 450 Ackley, 458 Lott, 458 Win., 460 Short A-Square, 460 Wby., 470 Capstick, 495 A-Square, 500 A-Square, 577 Tyrannosaur

**Barrel lengths:** 20″ to 26″

**Length of pull:** 12″ to 15¼″

**Finish:** Deluxe walnut stock; oil finish; matte blue

**Features:** Flush detachable swivels, leather sling, dual recoil lugs, coil spring ejector, ventilated recoil pad, premium honed barrels, contoured ejection port, three-way adjustable target-style trigger, Mauser-style claw extractor and controlled feed, positive safety

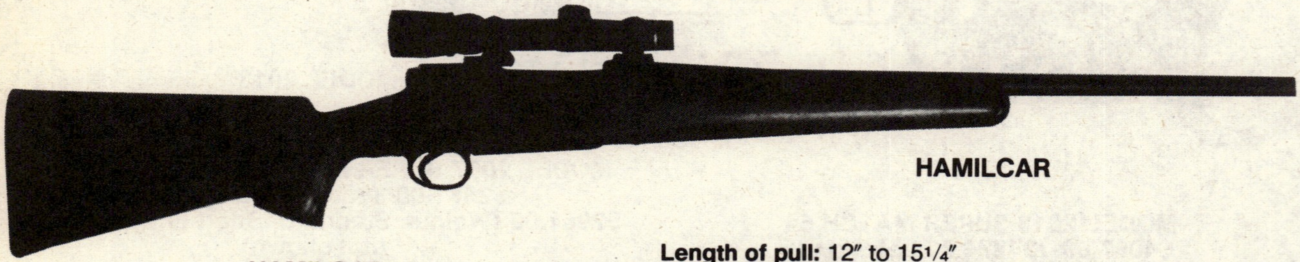

**HAMILCAR**

**HAMILCAR $2995.00**

**SPECIFICATIONS**

**Calibers:** 25-06, 257 Wby., 6.5×55 Swedish, 264 Win., 270 Win., 270 Wby., 7×57 Mauser, 280 Rem., 7mm Rem., 7mm Wby., 7mm STW, 30-06, 300 Win., 300 Wby., 338-06, 9.3×62

**Barrel lengths:** 20″ to 26″

**Length of pull:** 12″ to 15¼″

**Finish:** Deluxe walnut stock; oil finish; matte blue

**Features:** Flush detachable swivels; leather sling, coil spring ejector, vent. recoil pad; honed barrels; contoured ejection port; target-style adjustable trigger; Mauser-style claw extractor; controlled feed; positive safety

Also available:

**GHENGHIS KHAN MODEL** in 22-250, 243 Win., 6mm Rem. 25-06. Features benchrest-quality heavy taper barrel and coil-chek stock. **Price: $2495.00**

# AUTO-ORDNANCE

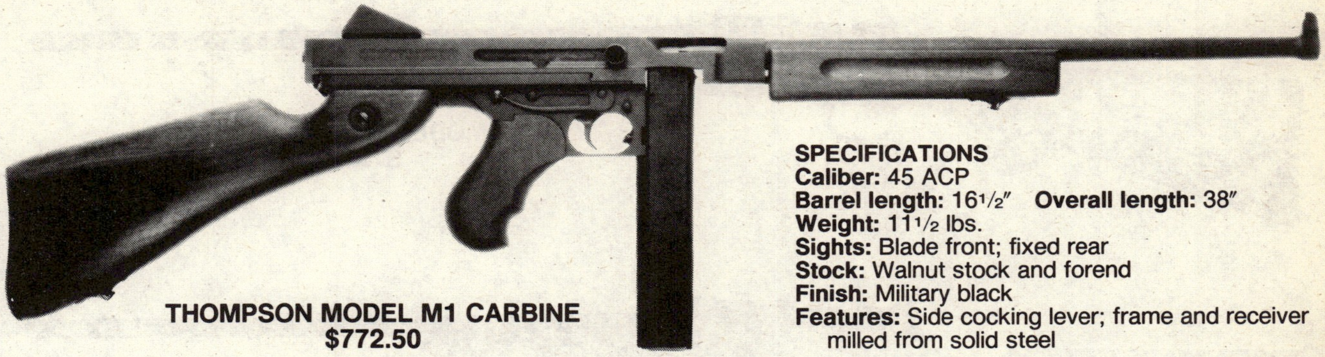

**THOMPSON MODEL M1 CARBINE**
**$772.50**

**SPECIFICATIONS**
**Caliber:** 45 ACP
**Barrel length:** 16 1/2″ **Overall length:** 38″
**Weight:** 11 1/2 lbs.
**Sights:** Blade front; fixed rear
**Stock:** Walnut stock and forend
**Finish:** Military black
**Features:** Side cocking lever; frame and receiver milled from solid steel

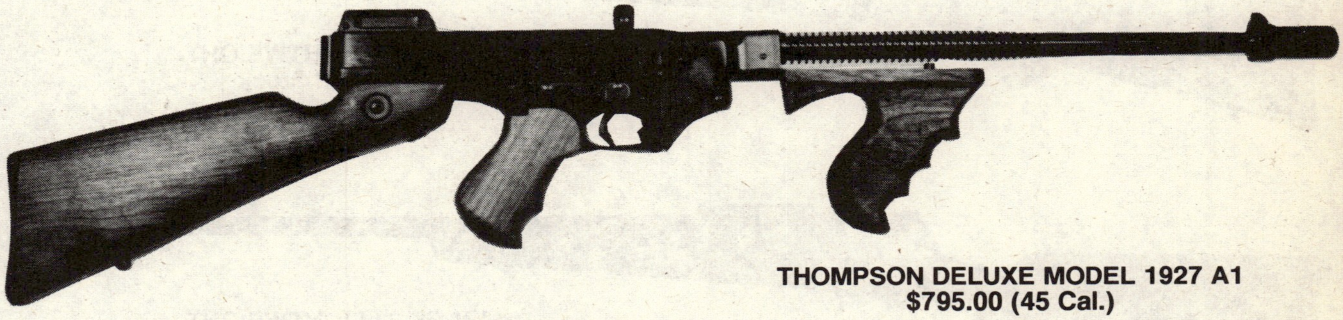

**THOMPSON DELUXE MODEL 1927 A1**
**$795.00 (45 Cal.)**

**SPECIFICATIONS**
**Caliber:** 45 ACP
**Barrel length:** 16″ **Overall length:** 42″
**Weight:** 11 1/2 lbs.
**Sights:** Blade front; open rear adjustable
**Stock:** Walnut stock; vertical forend

Also available:
**THOMPSON 1927A1C LIGHTWEIGHT** (45 cal.). Same as the 1927A1 model, but 20% lighter. **Price:**. . . . . . . . **$767.00**

**VIOLIN CARRYING CASE (for gun, drum & extra magazines) $105.00**

RIFLES

# BENTON & BROWN FIREARMS

MODEL 93 BOLT ACTION
STANDARD

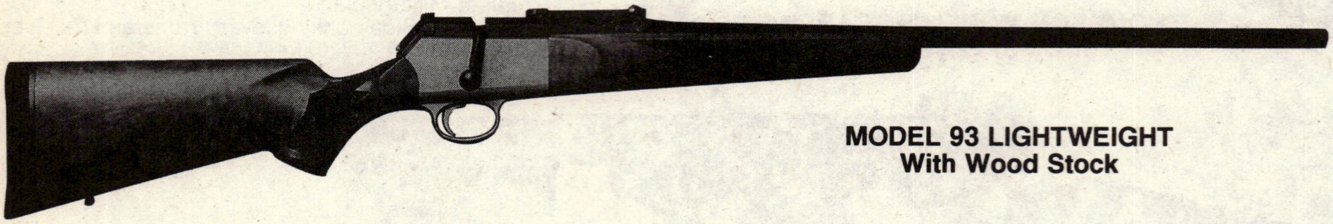

MODEL 93 LIGHTWEIGHT
With Wood Stock

MODEL 93 LIGHTWEIGHT
With Fiberglass Stock

## MODEL 93 BOLT ACTION

**SPECIFICATIONS**
**Calibers:**
*Standard*—243 Win., 6mm Rem., 25-06, 270 Win., 280 Rem., 30-06, 308
*Magnum*—257 Wby. Mag., 264 Win., 7mm Rem., 300 Win., 300 Wby., 338 Win., 340 Wby., 375 H&H
**Barrel length:** 22″ (24″ Magnum)
**Overall length:** 41″ (43″ Magnum)
**Weight:** 8½ lbs. (Standard); 7 lbs. (Lightweight)
**Action:** Short bolt action with 3 massive locking lugs; cartridge case head completely enclosed in bolt head; 60-degree bolt-handle uplift; crisp trigger
**Stock:** Two-piece fancy walnut or fiberglass; forend has oil finish; 20 lines-per-inch borderless hand-cut checkering; solid black recoil pad **Length of pull:** 13¾″
**Safety:** Locks firing pin and bolt handle
**Scope mounts:** Factory-fitted low profile one-piece steel scope mount for 1″ diameter scope
**Features:** Interchangeable barrels with scope mounts; custom-fitted case; interchangeable standard and magnum-caliber bolt assemblies; two-piece takedown design does not require re-zeroing when rifle is reassembled; left-handed models available

**Prices:**
**MODEL 93** Standard & Magnum calibers, wood stock . . . . . **$2075.00**
With Fiberglass Stock . . . . . **1875.00**
Interchangeable Barrels w/Scope Mount . . . . . **450.00**
Complete bolt assembly . . . . . **400.00**

# BLASER RIFLES

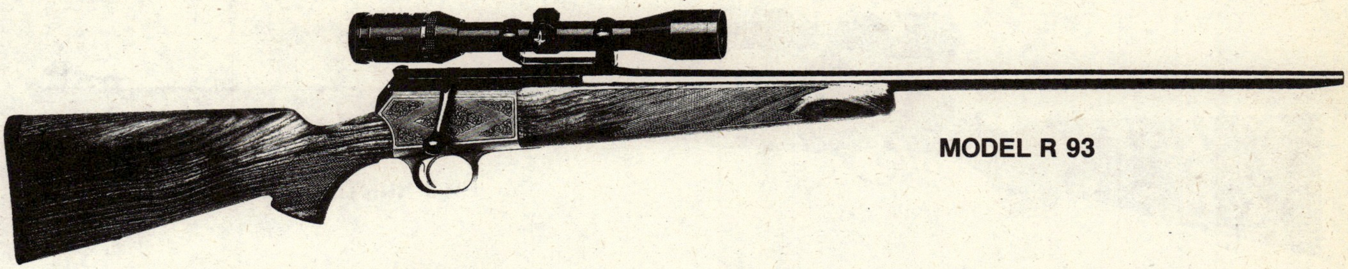

MODEL R 93

## MODEL R 93 BOLT ACTION

**SPECIFICATIONS**
**Calibers:** (interchangeable)
**Standard:** 22-250, 243 Win., 270 Win., 30-06, 308 Win.
**Magnum:** 257 Weatherby Mag., 264 Win. Mag., 7mm Rem. Mag., 300 Win. Mag., 300 Wby. Mag., 338 Win. Mag., 375 H&H, 416 Rem. Mag.
**Varmint:** 222 Rem., 223
**Barrel lengths:** 22″ (Standard) and 24″ (Magnum)
**Overall length:** 40″ (Standard) and 42″ (Magnum)
**Weight:** (w/scope mounts) 7 lbs. (Standard) and $7\frac{1}{4}$ lbs. (Magnum)
**Safety:** Cocking slide
**Stock:** Two-piece Turkish walnut stock and forend; solid black recoil pad, hand-cut checkering (18 lines/inch, borderless)
**Length of pull:** $13\frac{3}{4}$″
**Prices:**

| | |
|---|---|
| **Standard Model** | **$2800.00** |
| Interchangeable barrels | **550.00** |
| **Deluxe Model** | **3100.00** |
| **Super Deluxe Model** | **3500.00** |



# BRNO RIFLES

MODEL ZKM 611

## MODEL ZKM 611
**$569.00**

This premium semiautomatic rifle in 22 WMR caliber features a hammer-forged barrel, 6-round magazine, checkered walnut stock and forend, single thumb-screw takedown, and a grooved receiver for scope mounting. The rear sight is mid-mounted and the front sight is hooded. The action has a lightweight precision spring and large bolt to improve accuracy while practically eliminating felt recoil. Accessories include additional 6-round and 10-round magazines and custom-built ring mounts.

**SPECIFICATIONS**
**Caliber:** 22 WMR
**Capacity:** 6 or 10 rounds
**Barrel length:** 20″
**Overall length:** 37″
**Weight:** 6 lbs. 2 oz.
**Features:** High cheekpiece stock; sling swivels; quick-detach magazine

# BROWN PRECISION RIFLES

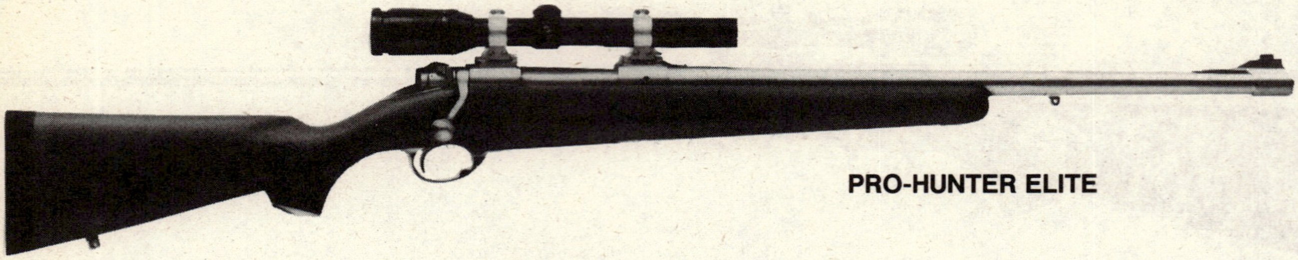

PRO-HUNTER ELITE

## PRO-HUNTER ELITE

Designed for the serious game hunter or guide, this version of Brown Precision's Pro-Hunter rifle is custom built, utilizing standard features and equipment. The rifle begins as a Winchester Model 70 Super Grade action with controlled feed claw extractor. The action is finely tuned for smooth operation, and a Speedlock firing-pin spring is installed. The trigger is tuned to crisp let-off at each customer's specified weight. A Shilen Match Grade stainless-steel barrel is custom crowned at the desired barrel length and hand-fitted to the action. A barrel band front QD sling swivel is attached permanently to the barrel.

The Pro-Hunter Elite features the customer's choice of express rear sight or custom Dave Talley removable peep sight and banded front ramp sight with European dovetail and replaceable brass bead. An optional flip-up white night sight is also available, as is a set of Dave Talley detachable T.N.T. scope mount rings and bases installed with Brown's Magnum Duty 8×40 screws.

All metal parts are finished in either matte electroless nickel or black Teflon. The barreled action is glass bedded to a custom Brown Precision fiberglass stock. Brown's Alaskan configuration stock features a Dave Talley trapdoor grip cap designed to carry the rear peep sight and/or replacement front sight beads. A premium 1″ recoil-reducing buttpad is installed, and the stock painted according to customer choice. Weight ranges from 7 to 15 lbs., depending on barrel length, coutour and options.

Optional equipment includes custom steel drop box magazine, KDF or Answer System muzzle brake, Mag-Na-Port, Zeiss, Swarovski or Leupold scope and Americase aluminum hard case. **Price** ........................ **$3370.00**

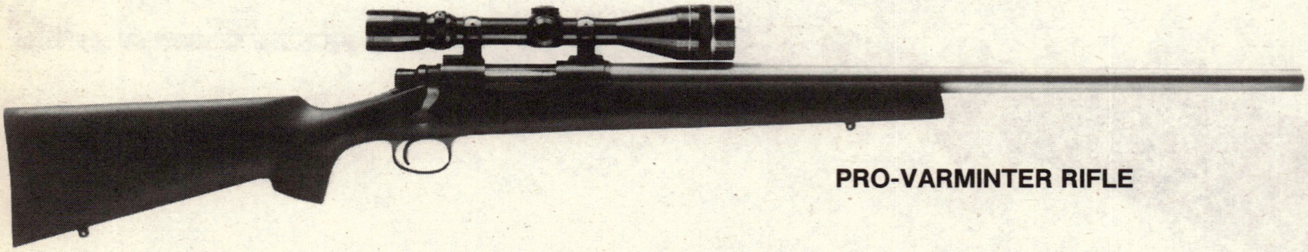

PRO-VARMINTER RIFLE

## PRO-VARMINTER RIFLE

The standard Pro-Varminter is built on the Remington 700 or Remington 40X action (right or left hand) and features a hand-fitted Shilen Match Grade Heavy Benchrest stainless-steel barrel in bright or bead-blasted finish. The barreled action is custom-bedded in Brown Precision's Varmint Special Hunter Bench or 40X Benchrest-style custom fiberglass, Kevlar or graphite stock.

Other standard features include custom barrel length and contour, trigger tuned for crisp pull to customer's specified weight, custom length of pull, and choice of recoil pad. Additional options include metal finishes, muzzle brakes, Leupold target or varmint scopes and others.

**Prices:**

Right-hand Model 700 Action ................ **$1790.00**
For Left-hand Model, **add** ................ **100.00**
40X Action ................ **2290.00**

BROWN PRECISION RIFLES

## HIGH COUNTRY YOUTH RIFLE

This custom rifle has all the same features as the standard High Country rifle, but scaled-down to fit the younger or smaller shooter. Based on the Remington Model 7 barreled action, it is available in calibers .223, .243, 7mm-08, 6mm and .308. The rifle features a fiberglass, Kevlar or graphite stock shortened to fit. As the shooter grows, the stock can be lengthened, a new recoil pad installed and the stock refinished. Custom features and options include choice of actions, custom barrels, chamberings, muzzle brakes, metal finishes, scopes and accessories.

All Youth Rifles include a deluxe package of shooting, reloading and hunting accessories and information to increase a young shooter's interest. **Price:** starts at ...... **$1290.00**

## TACTICAL ELITE RIFLE

Brown Precision's Tactical Elite is built on a Remington 700 action and features a bead-blasted Shilen Select Match Grade Heavy Benchrest Stainless Steel barrel custom-chambered for .223 Remington, .308 Winchester, .300 Winchester Magnum (or any standard or wildcat caliber). A nonreflective custom black Teflon metal finish on all metal surfaces ensures smooth bolt operation and 100 percent weatherproofing. The barreled action is bedded in a target-style stock with high rollover comb/cheekpiece, vertical pistol grip and palmswell. The stock is an advanced, custom fiberglass/Kevlar/graphite composite for maximum durability and rigidity. QD sling swivel studs and swivels are included on the stock. Standard stock paint color is flat black (camouflage patterns are also available).

Other standard features include: three-way adjustable buttplate/recoil pad assembly with length of pull, vertical and cant angle adjustments, custom barrel length and contour, and trigger tuned for a crisp pull to customer's specifications. Options include muzzle brakes, Leupold or Kahles police scopes, and others, and are priced accordingly.

**Price:** ...................................... **$2595.00**

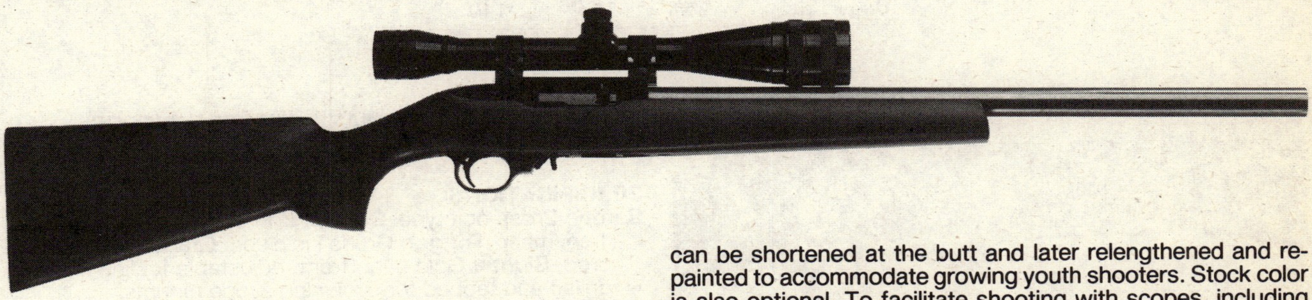

## CUSTOM TEAM CHALLENGER

This custom rifle was designed for use in the Chevy Trucks Sportsman's Team Challenge shooting event. It's also used in metallic silhouette competition as well as in the field for small game and varmints. Custom built on the Ruger 10/22 semiautomatic rimfire action, which features an extended magazine release, a simplified bolt release and finely tuned trigger, this rifle is fitted with either a Brown Precision fiberglass or Kevlar stock with custom length of pull up to 15″. The stock can be shortened at the butt and later relengthened and repainted to accommodate growing youth shooters. Stock color is also optional. To facilitate shooting with scopes, including large objective target or varmint scopes, the lightweight stock is of classic styling with a high comb. The absence of a cheekpiece accommodates either right- or left-handed shooters, while the stock's flat-bottom, 1¾″-wide forearm ensures maximum comfort in both offhand and rest shooting. Barrels are custom-length Shilen Match Grade .920″ diameter straight or lightweight tapered.

**Prices:**

With blued action/barrel ..................... **$ 937.00**
With blued action/stainless barrel .............. **997.00**
With stainless action/stainless barrel ........... **1044.00**

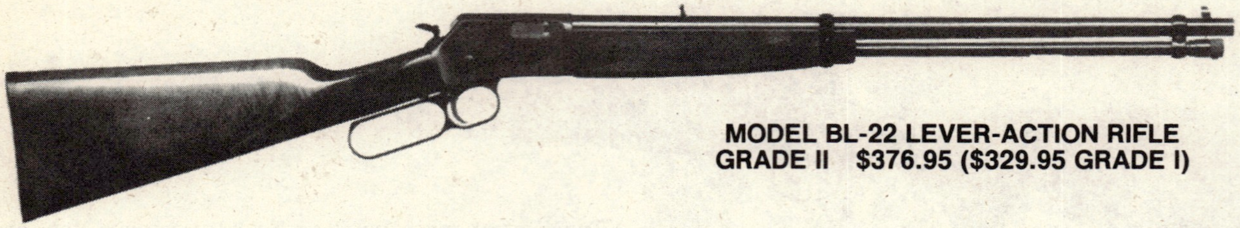

**MODEL BL-22 LEVER-ACTION RIFLE GRADE II $376.95 ($329.95 GRADE I)**

### RIMFIRE RIFLE SPECIFICATIONS

| Model | Caliber | Barrel Length | Sight Radius | Overall Length | Average Weight |
|---|---|---|---|---|---|
| A-Bolt 22 Mag Gr. I | 22 WMR | 22" | — | 40 1/4" | 5 lbs. 9 oz. |
| A-Bolt 22 Mag Gr. I w/sights | 22 WMR | 22" | 17 5/8" | 40 1/4" | 5 lbs. 9 oz. |
| A-Bolt 22 Gold Medallion[1] | 22 Long Rifle | 22" | — | 40 1/4" | 5 lbs. 9 oz. |
| A-Bolt 22 Grade I | 22 Long Rifle | 22" | — | 40 1/4" | 5 lbs. 9 oz. |
| A-Bolt 22 Gr. I w/sights | 22 Long Rifle | 22" | 17 5/8" | 40 1/4" | 5 lbs. 9 oz. |
| Semi-Auto 22 Grade I & Grade VI | 22 Long Rifle | 19 1/4" | 16 1/4" | 37" | 4 lbs. 4 oz. |
| BL-22 Grade I & Grade II | 22 Long Rifle, Long, Short | 20" | 15 3/8" | 36 3/4" | 5 lbs. |

[1] *No sight models only.*

### STOCK DIMENSIONS

| | Semi-Auto | BL-22 | A-Bolt 22 |
|---|---|---|---|
| Length of Pull | 13 3/4" | 13 1/2" | 13 3/4" |
| Drop at Comb | 1 3/16" | 5/8" | 3/4" |
| Drop at Heel | 2 5/8" | 2 1/4" | 1 1/2" |

**GRADE VI ENGRAVED (24-Karat Gold Plated)**

**22 SEMIAUTOMATIC RIMFIRE RIFLES GRADES I AND VI**

**SPECIFICATIONS**
**Safety:** Cross-bolt type. **Capacity:** 11 cartridges in magazine, 1 chamber. **Trigger:** Grade I is blued; Grade VI is gold colored. **Sights:** Gold bead front, adjustable folding leaf ear; drilled and tapped for Browning scope mounts.
**Stock & Forearm:** Grade I, select walnut with checkering (18 lines/inch); Grade VI, high-grade walnut with checkering (22 lines/inch). See table above for additional specifications.
**Prices:**
**Grade I** . . . . . . . . . . . . . . . . . . . . . . . . . **$379.95**
**Grade VI (blued or greyed receiver** . . . . . . . . . . **780.00**

# BROWNING RIFLES

MODEL 1885 LOW WALL RIFLE

## SPECIFICATIONS MODEL 1885 LOW WALL OR HIGH WALL $895.00

| Calibers | Barrel Length | Sight Radius | Overall Length | Approximate Weight | Rate of Twist (R. Hand) |
|---|---|---|---|---|---|
| **High Wall** | | | | | |
| 22-250 Rem. | 28" | — | 43 1/2" | 8 lbs. 13 oz. | 1 in 14" |
| 270 Win. | 28" | — | 43 1/2" | 8 lbs. 12 oz. | 1 in 10" |
| 30-06 Sprg. | 28" | — | 43 1/2" | 8 lbs. 12 oz. | 1 in 10" |
| 7mm Rem. Mag. | 28" | — | 43 1/2" | 8 lbs. 11 oz. | 1 in 9½" |
| 45-70 Govt. | 28" | 21 1/2" | 431/2" | 8 lbs. 14 oz. | 1 in 20" |
| **Low Wall** | | | | | |
| 22 Hornet | 24" | — | 39 1/2" | 6 lbs. 4 oz. | 1 in 16" |
| 223 Rem. | 24" | — | 39 1/2" | 6 lbs. 4 oz. | 1 in 12" |
| 243 Win. | 24" | — | 39 1/2" | 6 lbs. 4 oz. | 1 in 10" |

MODEL A-BOLT 22 BOLT ACTION

**Action:** Short throw bolt. Bolt cycles a round with 60° of bolt rotation. Firing pin acts as secondary extractor and ejector, snapping out fired rounds at prescribed speed. **Magazine:** Five and 15-shot magazine standard. Magazine/clip ejects with a push on magazine latch button. **Trigger:** Gold colored, screw adjustable. Preset at approx. 4 lbs. **Stock:** Laminated walnut, classic style with pistol grip. **Sights:** Available with or without sights. Ramp front and adjustable folding-leaf rear on open sight model. **Scopes:** Grooved receiver for 22 mount. Drilled and tapped for full-size scope mounts. See preceding page for additional specifications.

**Prices:**
**Grade I** (22 Magnum, open sights) . . . . . . . . . . . . **$479.95**
**Grade I** (22 Magnum without sights) . . . . . . . . . . **469.95**
**Grade I** (22 LR, no sights) . . . . . . . . . . . . . . . . . . . **404.95**
**Grade I** (22 LR, open sights) . . . . . . . . . . . . . . . . . **417.95**
**Gold Medallion Model** (22 LR, no sights) . . . . . . . . **539.95**

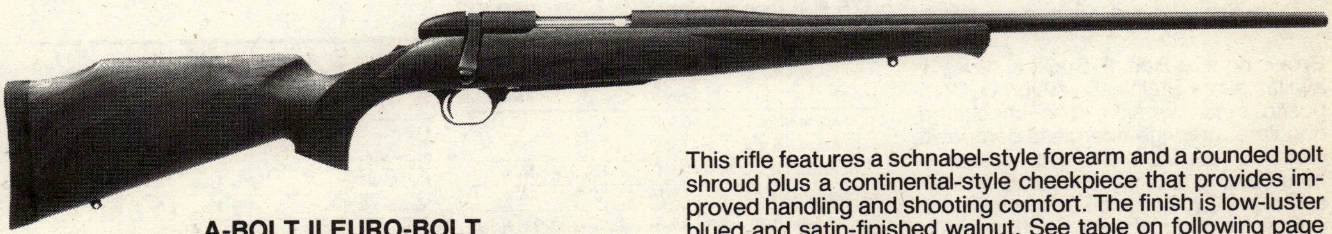

**A-BOLT II EURO-BOLT**
**$784.95 (No Sights) $877.95 (w/BOSS)**

This rifle features a schnabel-style forearm and a rounded bolt shroud plus a continental-style cheekpiece that provides improved handling and shooting comfort. The finish is low-luster blued and satin-finished walnut. See table on following page for additional specifications and A-Bolt II models.

# BROWNING RIFLES

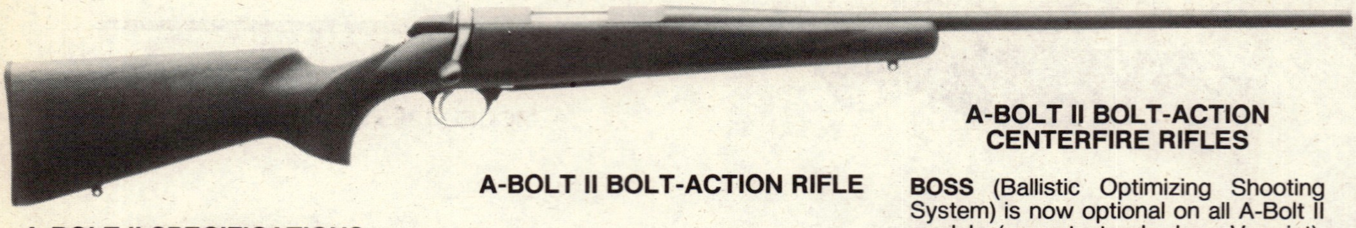

A-BOLT II BOLT-ACTION RIFLE

## A-BOLT II SPECIFICATIONS

| Caliber | Rate of Twist (R. Hand) | Magazine Capacity | Hunter | Gold Medal. | Medal. | Micro-Medal. | Euro-Bolt | Stainless Stalker | Comp. Stalker | Varmint |
|---|---|---|---|---|---|---|---|---|---|---|
| LONG ACTION MAGNUM CALIBERS | | | | | | | | | | |
| 375 H&H | 1 in 12" | 3 | | | ● | | | ● | | |
| 338 Win. Mag. | 1 in 10" | 3 | ● | | ● | | | ● | ● | |
| 300 Win. Mag. | 1 in 10" | 3 | ● | ● | ● | ● | | ● | ● | |
| 7mm Rem. Mag. | 1 in 9 1/2" | 3 | ● | ● | ● | ● | ● | ● | ● | |
| LONG ACTION STANDARD CALIBERS | | | | | | | | | | |
| 25-06 Rem. | 1 in 10" | 4 | ● | | ● | ● | | ● | ● | |
| 270 Win. | 1 in 10" | 4 | ● | ● | ● | ● | ● | ● | ● | |
| 280 Rem. | 1 in 10" | 4 | ● | | ● | ● | | ● | ● | |
| 30-06 Sprg. | 1 in 10" | 4 | ● | ● | ● | ● | ● | ● | ● | |
| SHORT ACTION CALIBERS | | | | | | | | | | |
| 243 Win. | 1 in 10" | 4 | ● | | ● | ● | ● | ● | ● | |
| 308 Win. | 1 in 12" | 4 | ● | | ● | ● | ● | ● | ● | ● |
| 284 Win. | 1 in 10" | 4 | | | | ● | | | | |
| 7mm-08 Rem. | 1 in 9 1/2" | 4 | ● | | ● | ● | | ● | ● | |
| 257 Roberts | 1 in 9 1/2" | 4 | | | | ● | | | | |
| 22-250 Rem. | 1 in 14" | 4 | ● | | ● | ● | ● | ● | ● | ● |
| 223 Rem. | 1 in 12" | 4 | ● | | ● | ● | | ● | ● | ● |
| 22 Hornet | 1 in 16" | 4 | | | | ● | | | | |

*Standard caliber capacity is four rounds in magzine, one in chamber. Magnum calibers and Micro-Medallion 284: Three in magazine, one in chamber. Boss equipped A-Bolt II's not available with open sights except 375 H&H Stainless Stalker and Medallion.*
** Magazine capacity of 223 Rem. is up to five rounds on Micro-Medallion and up to six rounds on other models.*

## A-BOLT II BOLT-ACTION CENTERFIRE RIFLES

**BOSS** (Ballistic Optimizing Shooting System) is now optional on all A-Bolt II models (except standard on Varmint). BOSS adjusts barrel vibrations to allow a bullet to leave the rifle muzzle at the most advantageous point in the barrel oscillation, thereby fine-tuning accuracy with any brand of ammunition regardless of caliber.

**Scopes:** Closed. Clean tapered barrel. Receiver is drilled and tapped for a scope mount; or select **Hunter** model has open sights.

**Prices:**
**Gold Medallion** no sights, BOSS ... **$997.95**
**Gold Medallion** no sights ... **904.95**
**Medallion** no sights, BOSS ... **765.95**
**Medallion** no sights ... **672.95**
**Medallion** L.H., no sights, BOSS ... **792.95**
**Medallion** L.H., no sights ... **699.95**
**Medallion 375 H&H** no sights, BOSS ... **872.95**
**Medallion 375 H&H** open sights ... **779.95**
**Medallion 375 H&H** L.H., no sights, BOSS ... **899.95**
**Medallion 375 H&H** L.H., open sights ... **806.95**
**Micro Medallion** no sights ... **672.95**
**Euro-Bolt** no sights, BOSS ... **877.95**
**Euro-Bolt** no sights ... **784.95**

A-BOLT II STAINLESS STALKER

## A-BOLT II STALKER SERIES

Browning's A-Bolt II Stalker series is available in a Stainless version or Composite stock version. The checkered, nonglare, graphite-fiberglass composite stock resists the nicks and scrapes of hard hunting and is resistant to weather and humidity. Its recoil-absorbing properties also make shooting a more pleasant experience.

**STALKER SERIES** — **Prices**
**Stainless Stalker**
No sights, BOSS ... **$842.95**
No sights ... **749.95**
L.H., no sights, BOSS ... **865.95**
L.H., no sights ... **772.95**
375 H&H, BOSS ... **945.95**
375 H&H, open sights ... **852.95**
375 H&H, L.H., BOSS ... **$972.95**
375 H&H, L.H., open sights ... **879.95**
**Varmint,** hvy. bbl., BOSS, gloss or satin/matte finish ... **894.95**
**Composite Stalker,** no sights, BOSS ... **687.95**
**Composite Stalker,** no sights ... **594.95**

| Length | Overall Length | Barrel | Sight Radius* |
|---|---|---|---|
| Long Action Mag. Cal. | 46 3/4" | 26" | 18" |
| Long Action Std. Cal. | 42 3/4" | 22" | 18" |
| Short Action Cal. | 41 3/4" | 22" | 16" |
| Micro-Medallion | 39 9/16" | 20"** | — |

**Open sights available on A-Bolt Hunter and all models in 375 H&H.*
***22 Hornet Micro-Medallion has a 22" barrel.*
*BOSS equipped rifles have the same dimensions.*

| Model | Long Action Magnum Calibers | Long Action Standard Calibers | Short Action Calibers |
|---|---|---|---|
| Composite/Stainless Stalkers | 7 lbs. 3 oz. | 6 lbs. 11 oz. | 6 lbs. 4 oz. |
| Micro-Medallion | | | 6 lbs. 1 oz. |
| Gold Medallion | 7 lbs. 11 oz. | 7 lbs. 3 oz. | |
| Medallion & Hunter | 7 lbs. 3 oz. | 6 lbs. 11 oz. | 6 lbs. 7 oz. |
| Varmint | | | 9 lbs. |
| Euro-Bolt II | 7 lbs. 6 oz. | 6 lbs. 14 oz. | |

# BROWNING RIFLES

**MODEL 81 BLR HIGH POWER**
**$549.95 (Short Action)**
**$579.95 (Long Action)**

## MODEL 81 BLR SPECIFICATIONS

| Calibers | Barrel Length | Magazine Capacity[1] | Sight Radius | Overall Length | Approximate Weight | Rate of Twist (R. Hand) |
|---|---|---|---|---|---|---|
| **LONG ACTION CALIBERS** | | | | | | |
| 270 Win. | 22" | 4 | 17 3/4" | 43 1/8" | 8 lbs. 8 oz. | 1 in 10" |
| 30-06 Sprg. | 22" | 4 | 17 3/4" | 43 1/8" | 8 lbs. 8 oz. | 1 in 10" |
| 7mm Rem. Magnum | 24" | 4 | 19 3/4" | 44 1/2" | 8 lbs. 13 oz. | 1 in 9 1/2" |
| **SHORT ACTION CALIBERS** | | | | | | |
| 223 Rem. | 20" | 4 | 17 3/4" | 39 3/4" | 6 lbs. 15 oz. | 1 in 12" |
| 22-250 Rem. | 20" | 4 | 17 3/4" | 39 3/4" | 6 lbs. 15 oz. | 1 in 14" |
| 243 Win. | 20" | 4 | 17 3/4" | 39 3/4" | 7 lbs. 2 oz. | 1 in 10" |
| 284 Win. | 20" | 3 | 17 3/4" | 39 3/4" | 7 lbs. | 1 in 10" |
| 7mm-08 Rem. | 20" | 4 | 17 3/4" | 39 3/4" | 7 lbs. | 1 in 9 1/2" |
| 308 Win. | 20" | 4 | 17 3/4" | 39 3/4" | 7 lbs. | 1 in 12" |

*[1] Number of cartridges the magazine holds when locked in the rifle with the bolt closed. The maximum magazine capacity can vary when outside of the rifle.*

**BAR MARK II SAFARI**

## BAR MARK II SAFARI SEMIAUTOMATIC RIFLES

The BAR has been upgraded to include an engraved receiver, a redesigned bolt release, new gas and buffeting systems, and a removable trigger assembly. Additional features include: crossbolt safety with enlarged head; hinged floorplate, 4-shot capacity in Standard models (1 in chamber); gold trigger; select walnut stock and forearm with cut-checkering and swivel studs; 13 3/4″ length of pull; 2″ drop at heel; 1 5/8″ drop at comb; and a recoil pad (magnum calibers only).

## SPECIFICATIONS BAR MARK II SAFARI

| Model | Calibers | Magazine Capacity | Barrel Length | Sight Radius* | Overall Length | Average Weight | Rate of Twist (Right Hand) |
|---|---|---|---|---|---|---|---|
| Magnum | 338 Win. Mag. | 3 | 24" | 19 1/2" | 45" | 8 lbs. 6 oz. | 1 in 12" |
| Magnum | 300 Win Mag. | 3 | 24" | 19 1/2" | 45" | 8 lbs. 6 oz. | 1 in 9 1/2" |
| Magnum | 7mm Rem Mag. | 3 | 24" | 19 1/2" | 45" | 8 lbs. 6 oz. | 1 in 9 1/2" |
| Standard | 30-06 Sprg. | 4 | 22" | 17 1/2" | 43" | 7 lbs. 6 oz. | 1 in 9 1/2" |
| Standard | 270 Win. | 4 | 22" | 17 1/2" | 43" | 7 lbs. 9 oz. | 1 in 9 1/2" |
| Standard | 308 Win. | 4 | 22" | 17 1/2" | 43" | 7 lbs. 9 oz. | 1 in 12" |
| Standard | 243 Win. | 4 | 22" | 17 1/2" | 43" | 7 lbs. 10 oz. | 1 in 9 1/2" |

**Non-BOSS models are available with or without open sights. All models drilled and tapped for scope mounts. BOSS-equipped BAR's not available with open sights.*
*BAR Mark II specifications are the same with or without the BOSS, except the 338 Win. Mag. which is 5 1/2 ozs. heavier and has a 26 " barrel.*

**Prices:**
**Standard Calibers,** no sights, BOSS . . . . . . . . . . . . . . . . **$722.95**
Open sights, no BOSS . . . . . . **694.95**
No sights, no BOSS . . . . . . . . **679.95**
**Magnum Calibers** no sights, BOSS . . . . . . . . . . . . . . . . **822.95**
Open sights . . . . . . . . . . . . . . **744.95**
No sights, no BOSS . . . . . . . . **729.95**

# CLIFTON ARMS

**SCOUT RIFLE**
**$2750.00**

Several years ago, in response to Colonel Jeff Cooper's concept of an all-purpose rifle, which he calls the "Scout Rifle," Clifton Arms developed the integral, retractable bipod and its accompanying state-of-the-art composite stock. Further development resulted in an integral butt magazine well for storage of cartridges inside the buttstock. These and other components make up the Clifton Scout Rifle.

**SPECIFICATIONS**
**Calibers:** 243, 7mm-08, 30-06, 308, 350 Rem. Mag.
**Barrel length:** 19″ to 19$^1/_2$″ (longer or shorter lengths available; made with Shilen stainless premium match-grade steel)
**Weight:** 7 to 8 lbs.
**Sights:** Forward-mounted Burris 2$^3/_4$X Scout Scope attached to integral scope base pedestals machined in the barrel; Warne rings; reserve iron sight is square post dovetailed into a ramp integral to the barrel, plus a large aperture "ghost ring" mounted on the receiver bridge.
**Features:** Standard action is Ruger 77 MKII stainless; metal finish options include Poly-T, NP3 and chrome sulphide; left-handed rifles available.

# COLT RIFLES

**LIGHTWEIGHTS**
**$987.00**

The Colt Match Target Lightweight semiautomatic rifle fires from a closed bolt, is easy to load and unload, and has a buttstock and pistol grip made of tough nylon. A round, ribbed handguard is fiberglass-reinforced to ensure better grip control. **Calibers:** 223 Rem., 7.62×39mm and 9mm. **Barrel length:** 16″. **Overall length:** 34$^1/_2$″ (35$^1/_2$″ in 7.62×39mm). **Weight:** 7.1 lbs. **Capacity:** 5 rounds.

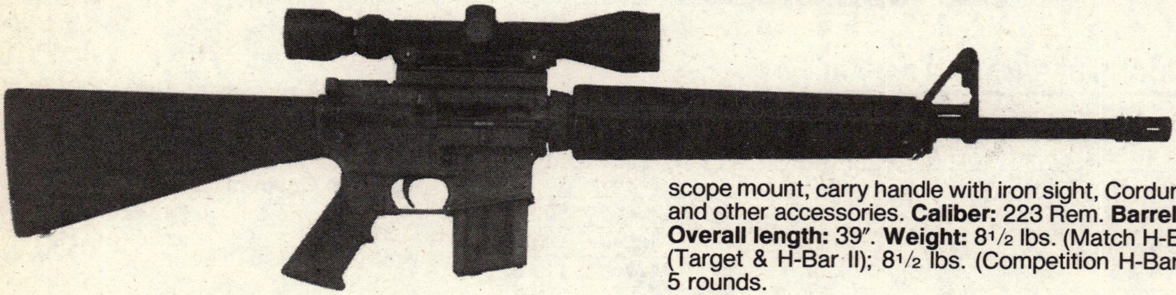

**MATCH TARGET RIFLES**

The Colt Target and H-Bar rifles are range-selected for top accuracy. They have a 3-9x rubber armored variable-power scope mount, carry handle with iron sight, Cordura nylon case and other accessories. **Caliber:** 223 Rem. **Barrel length:** 20″. **Overall length:** 39″. **Weight:** 8$^1/_2$ lbs. (Match H-Bar); 7$^1/_2$ lbs. (Target & H-Bar II); 8$^1/_2$ lbs. (Competition H-Bar). **Capacity:** 5 rounds.

**Prices:**

| | |
|---|---|
| **MATCH H-BAR** | **$1067.00** |
| **TARGET** | **1019.00** |
| **COMPETITION H-BAR** | **1073.00** |
| **COMPETITION H-BAR II** | **1044.00** |

# COOPER ARMS RIFLES

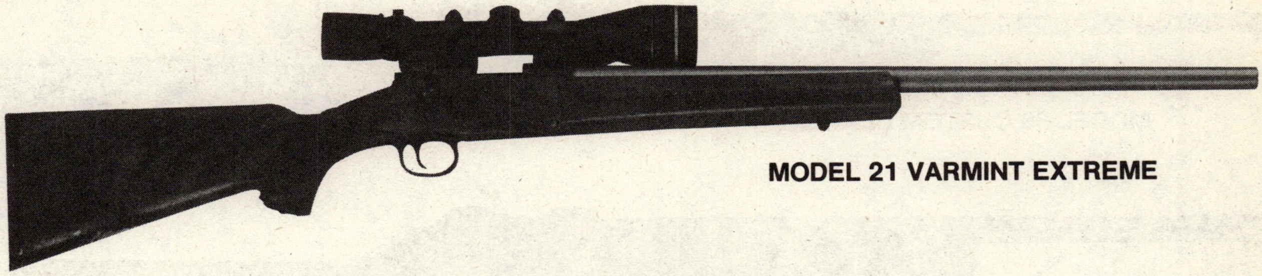

MODEL 21 VARMINT EXTREME

**MODEL 21 VARMINT EXTREME**

**SPECIFICATIONS**
**Calibers:** 17 Rem., 17 Mach IV, 221 Fireball, 222 Rem., 222 Rem. Mag., 22 PPC, 223
**Barrel length:** 24″
**Stock:** AAA Claro walnut; flared oval forearm
Other specifications same as Model 36 RF.
**Price** .................................... **$1495.00**

Also available:
**MODEL 21 BENCHREST.** Same as above, but in 223 and 22 PPC only; competition step crown and match chamber, chrome-moly barrel.
**Price** .................................... **$1695.00**

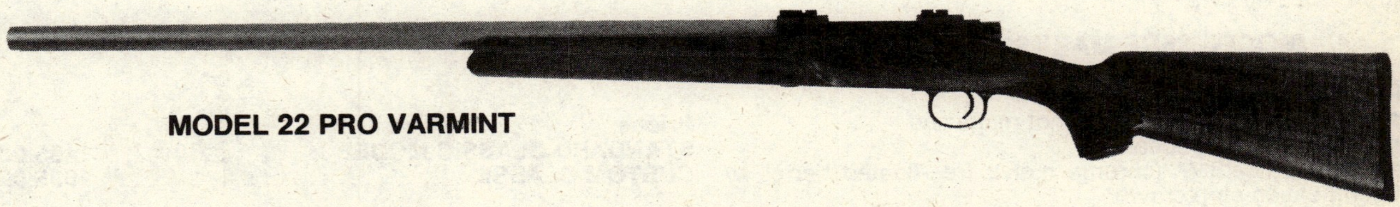

MODEL 22 PRO VARMINT

**MODEL 22 PRO VARMINT EXTREME**

**SPECIFICATIONS**
**Calibers:** 22-250, 220 Swift, 243, 25-06, 308, 6mm PPC
**Capacity:** Single shot
**Barrel length:** 24″
**Action:** 3 front locking lug; glass-bedded
**Trigger:** Single-stage Match, fully adjustable; Jewell 2-stage (optional)
**Stock:** McMillan black-textured synthetic, beaded, w/Monte Carlo cheekpiece; 4-panel checkering print; Pachmayr recoil pad
**Prices:**
**MODEL 22 PRO VARMINT EXTREME** ......... **$1595.00**
**BENCH REST II TRIGGER** ................. **1695.00**
**BLACK JACK (SYNTHETIC SPORTER)** ...... **1395.00**

RIFLES

# COOPER ARMS RIFLES

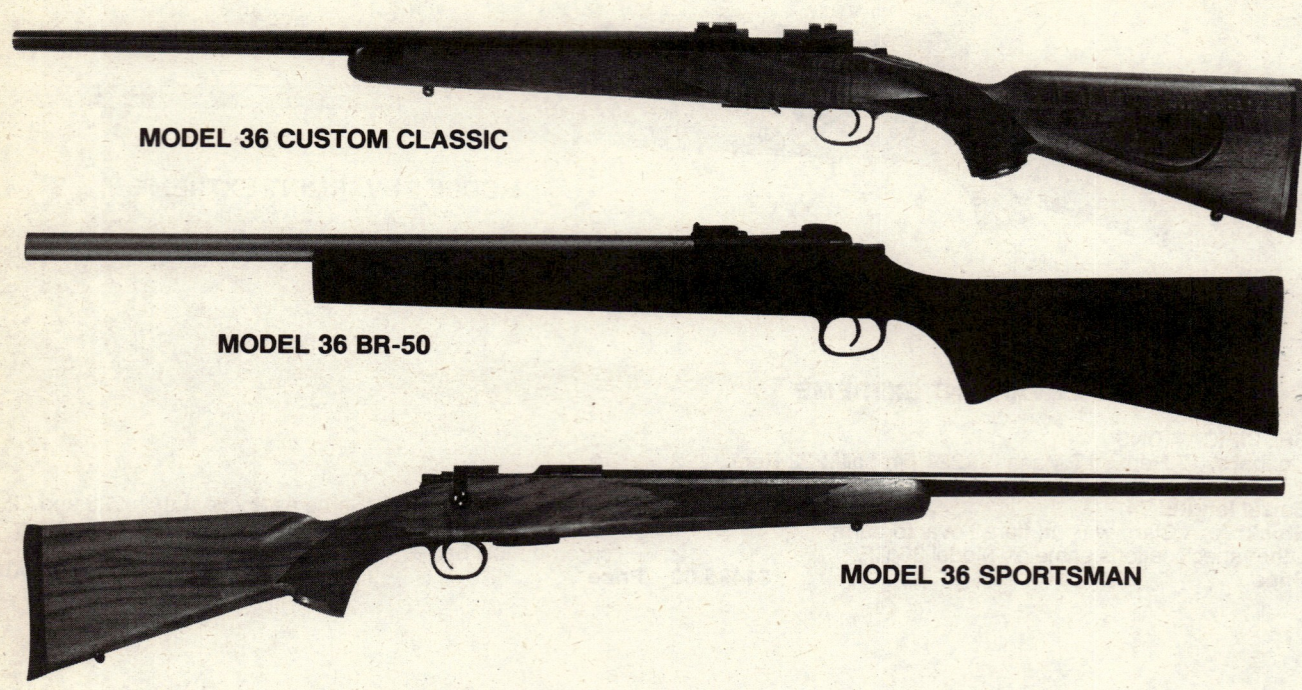

MODEL 36 CUSTOM CLASSIC

MODEL 36 BR-50

MODEL 36 SPORTSMAN

MODEL 36RF MARKSMAN SERIES

**SPECIFICATIONS**
**Caliber:** 22 LR **Capacity:** 5-shot magazine
**Action:** bolt-action repeater
**Barrel length:** $23\frac{3}{4}$″ (chrome moly); free-floated barrel w/ competition step crown
**Stock:** AA Claro walnut (AAA Claro walnut in Custom and Custom Classic models; Custom Classic has ebony forend tip)
**Features:** Glass-beaded adjustable trigger; bases and rings optional; 3 mid-locking lugs

**Prices:**
**STANDARD CLASSIC MODEL** ............... **$1495.00**
**CUSTOM CLASSIC** ........................ **1695.00**

Also available:
**MODEL 36 RF/CF FEATHERWEIGHT:** Same specifications as Model 36 RF, but weighs $6\frac{1}{2}$ lbs. ........ **$1595.00**
**MODEL 36 RF BR-50:** Same specifications as Model 36 RF, but w/22″ stainless steel bbl. 6.8 lbs. ........ **1595.00**

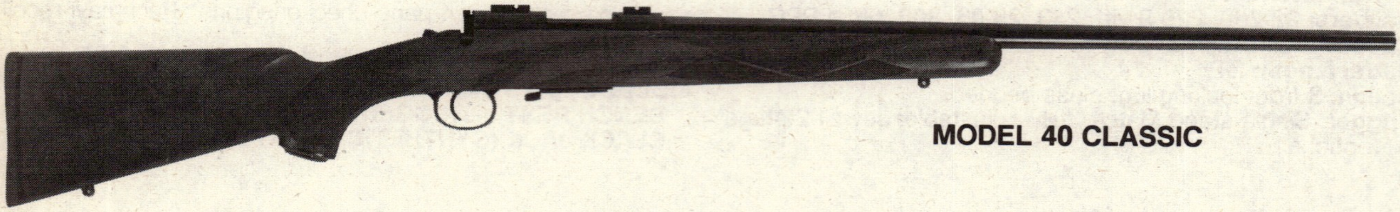

MODEL 40 CLASSIC

MODEL 40 CLASSIC

**SPECIFICATIONS**
**Calibers:** 17 CCM, 17 Ackley Hornet, 22 Hornet, 22K Hornet, 22 CCM
**Capacity:** 4-shot clip (Hornets); 5-shot clip (CCM)
**Action:** 3 mid-locking lug, bolt-action repeater; glass-bedded
**Barrel length:** 23.75″
**Trigger:** Single-stage match, fully adjustable (Jewell two-stage optional)
**Rate of twist:** 1-in-14″ (22 cal.); 1-in-10″ (17 cal.)
**Features:** Chrome-moly Match-Grade barrel, free floated; competition step crown
**Stock:** Oil-finished AAA Claro walnut w/steel grip cap, Pachmayr recoil pad and 22-LPI borderless wraparound ribbon checkering

**Prices:**
**CLASSIC** ................................ **$1495.00**
**CUSTOM CLASSIC** ........................ **1695.00**
**CLASSIC VARMINTER** ..................... **1695.00**

# CZ RIFLES

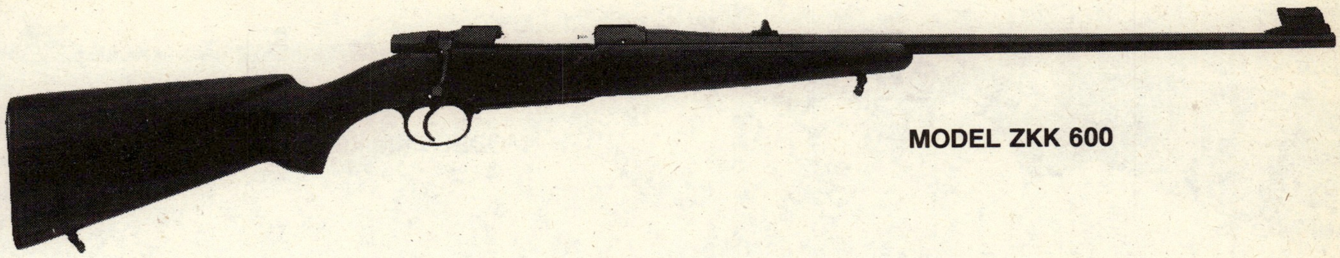

MODEL ZKK 600

## MODEL ZKK 600

**SPECIFICATIONS**
**Calibers:** 30-06, 270 Win.
**Capacity:** 5 rounds
**Action:** Medium
**Barrel length:** 23.62″ **Overall length:** 43.7″
**Weight:** 7.25 lbs.
**Price:** . . . . . . . . . . . . . . . . . . . . . . **$589.00**

Also available:
**MODEL ZKK 601.** Same specifications as Model ZKK 600 except **Calibers:** 243 Win., 308 Win.

RIFLES

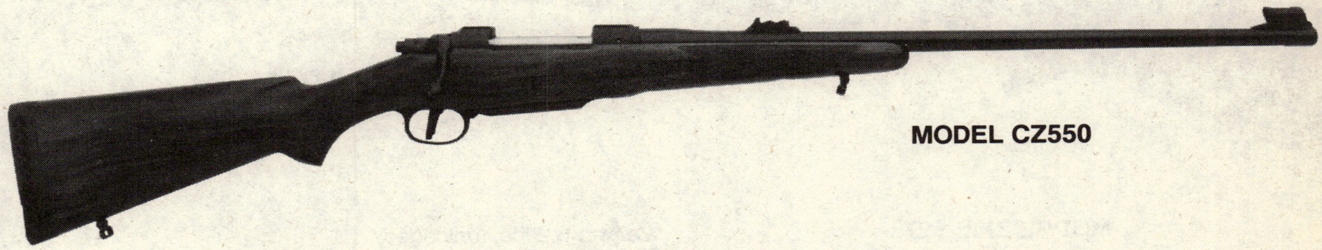

MODEL CZ550

## MODEL CZ550

**SPECIFICATIONS**
**Calibers:** 243 Win., 270 Win., 308 Win., 7×57, 7mm Rem., 300 Win. Mag.
**Capacity:** 4 rounds
**Barrel length:** 23.62″
**Weight:** 7.26 lbs.
**Sights:** None
**Stock:** High comb
**Features:** Single-set trigger; 3-position safety
**Price:** . . . . . . . . . . . . . . . . . . . . . . **$649.00**

## MODEL ZKK 602
**(not shown)**

**SPECIFICATIONS**
**Calibers:** 375 H&H and 458 Win.
**Capacity:** 4 rounds
**Barrel length:** 25″
**Overall length:** 45.28″
**Weight:** 9.25 lbs.
**Sight radius:** 19.5″
**Stock:** Walnut
**Sights:** Open (grooved to accommodate scope mount)
**Features:** Single-stage trigger
**Price:** . . . . . . . . . . . . . . . . . . . . . . **$799.00**

# CZ RIFLES

MODEL ZKM 452 2E DELUXE

### MODEL ZKM 452

**SPECIFICATIONS**
**Calibers:** 22 LR, 22 Win. Mag.
**Capacity:** 5 or 10 rounds (22 LR); 6 or 10 rounds (22 Win. Mag.)
**Barrel length:** 24.82″ **Overall length:** 42.64″
**Weight:** 6.56 lbs. (unloaded)
**Sights:** Mechanical sights; machined receiver for custom ring mounts
**Stock:** Beechwood (Standard); walnut (Deluxe)
**Finish:** Lacquer
**Prices:**
**Standard Model** .......... **$299.00**
**Deluxe Model** .......... **399.00**

MODEL ZKM 527

### MODEL ZKM 527

**SPECIFICATIONS**
**Calibers:** 22 Hornet, 222 Rem., 223 Rem.
**Capacity:** 5 rounds
**Barrel length:** 23.6″ (standard or heavy).
**Overall length:** 42.4″
**Weight:** 6.2 lbs. (unloaded)
**Sights:** Open (grooved to accept scope)
**Stock:** Luxury sport stock w/cheekpiece
**Features:** Mauser-type bolt and non-rotating claw extractor; hammer-forged barrel; integral dovetail scope bases with recoil stop; detachable 5-round magazine; silent safety
**Price:** .......... **$629.00**

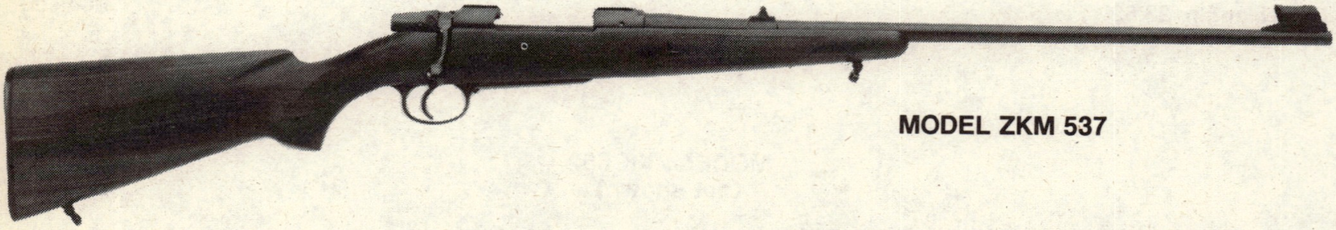

MODEL ZKM 537

### MODEL ZKM 537

**SPECIFICATIONS**
**Calibers:** 270 Win., 30-06 (fixed magazine); 243 Win., 308 Win. (detachable magazine)
**Capacity:** 4 rounds (243 Win., 308 Win.); 5 rounds (270 Win., 30-06)
**Barrel length:** 23.6″ (20.5″ w/full stock)
**Overall length:** 44.7″ (41.6″ w/full stock)
**Weight (unloaded):** 7.26 lbs. (6.85 lbs. w/full stock)
**Safety:** Thumb safety (locks trigger and bolt)
**Sights:** Mechanical sights; machined receiver for custom ring mounts
**Stock:** Checkered walnut or synthetic
**Features:** Streamlined bolt shroud w/cocking indicator; integral dovetail scope bases w/recoil stop; controlled-feed claw extractor; forged, one-piece bolt
**Price:** .......... **$649.00**
With full stock .......... **709.00**

# DAKOTA ARMS

DAKOTA 76 AFRICAN GRADE

## DAKOTA 76 RIFLES

**SPECIFICATIONS**
**Calibers:**
**Safari Grade:** 338 Win. Mag., 300 Win. Mag., 375 H&H Mag., 458 Win. Mag.
**Classic Grade:** 22-250, 257 Roberts, 270 Win., 280 Rem., 30-06, 7mm Rem. Mag., 338 Win. Mag., 300 Win. Mag., 375 H&H Mag., 458 Win. Mag.
**African Grade:** 404 Jeffery, 416 Dakota, 416 Rigby, 450 Dakota
**Varmint Grade:** 22 Hornet, 22 PPC, 22-250, 220 Swift, 222 Rem. Mag., 223, 6mm PPC
**Barrel lengths:** 21″ or 23″ (Clas.); 23″ only (Saf.); 24″ (Varm. and Afr.)
**Weight:** 7 1/2 lbs. (Classic); 9 1/2 lbs. (African); 8 1/2 lbs. (Safari)
**Safety:** Three-position striker-blocking safety allows bolt operation with safety on
**Sights:** Ramp front sight; standing-leaf rear
**Stock:** Medium-fancy walnut stock fitted with 1″ black recoil pad (Classic); fancy walnut stock with ebony forend tip and recoil pad (Safari)

**Prices:**
| | |
|---|---|
| **Varmint Grade** | $2300.00 |
| **Classic Grade** | 2500.00 |
| **Safari Grade** | 3300.00 |
| **African Grade** | 3750.00 |
| **Barreled actions:** | |
| Classic Grade | 1750.00 |
| Varmint Grade | 1750.00 |
| Safari Grade | 2000.00 |
| African Grade | 2500.00 |
| **Actions:** | |
| Classic Grade | 1500.00 |
| Varmint Grade | 1500.00 |
| Safari Grade | 1600.00 |

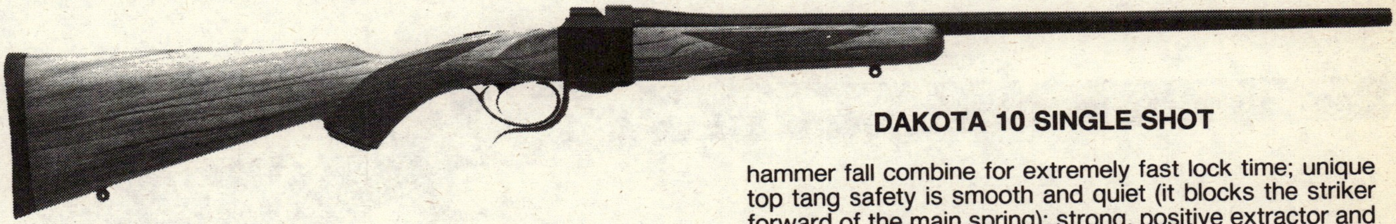

## DAKOTA 10 SINGLE SHOT

**SPECIFICATIONS**
**Calibers:** Most rimmed/rimless commercially loaded types
**Barrel length:** 23″ **Overall length:** 39 1/2″ **Weight:** 5 1/2 lbs.
**Features:** Receiver and rear of breech block are solid steel without cuts or holes for maximum lug area (approx. 8 times more bearing area than most bolt rifles); crisp, clean trigger pull (trigger plate is removable, allowing action to adapt to single set triggers); straight-line coil-spring action and short hammer fall combine for extremely fast lock time; unique top tang safety is smooth and quiet (it blocks the striker forward of the main spring); strong, positive extractor and manual ejector adapted to rimmed or rimless cases.

| | |
|---|---|
| **Price:** | $2500.00 |
| **Barreled actions** | 1850.00 |
| **Actions only** | 1500.00 |

Also available:
| | |
|---|---|
| **DAKOTA 10 MAGNUM SINGLE SHOT** | $2750.00 |
| Barreled actions | 1850.00 |
| Actions only | 1660.00 |

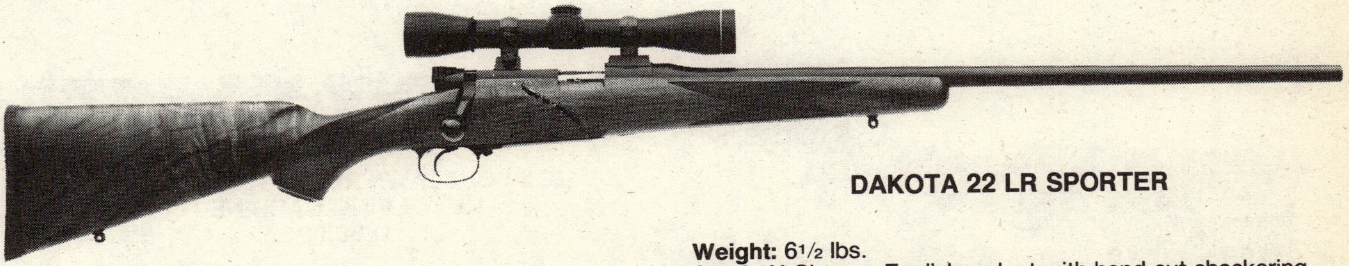

## DAKOTA 22 LR SPORTER

**SPECIFICATIONS**
**Calibers:** 22 LR **Capacity:** 5-round clip
**Barrel length:** 22″ (chrome-moly, 1 turn in 16″)
**Weight:** 6 1/2 lbs.
**Stock:** X Claro or English walnut with hand-cut checkering
**Features:** Plain bolt handle; swivels and single screw studs; 1/2-inch black pad; 13 5/8″ length of pull

| | |
|---|---|
| **Price:** | $1500.00 |
| **Barreled actions** | 1200.00 |

# EMF REPLICA RIFLES

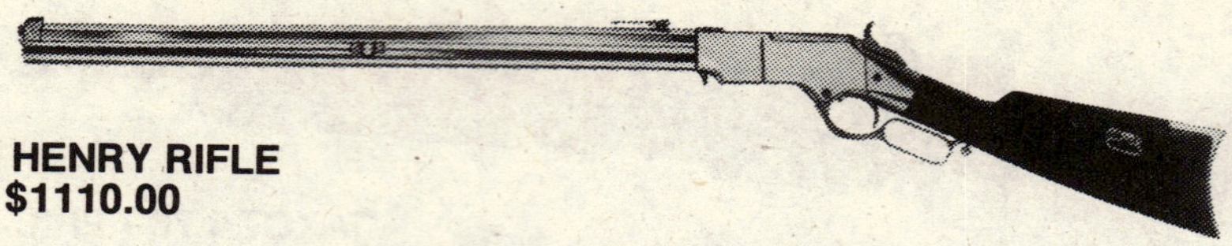

### 1860 HENRY RIFLE
**$1110.00**

This lever-action rifle was patented by B. Tyler Henry and produced by the New Haven Arms Company, where Oliver Winchester was then president (he later gave his name to future models and the company itself). Production was developed between 1860 and 1865, with serial numbers 1 to 12000 (plus 2000 additional units in 1866, when the Winchester gun first appeared).

**SPECIFICATIONS**
**Calibers:** 44-40 and 45 LC
**Barrel length:** 24¼″; upper half-octagonal w/magazine tube in one-piece steel
**Overall length:** 43¾″ **Weight:** 9¼ lbs.
**Stock:** Varnished American walnut wood
**Features:** Polished brass frame; brass buttplate

### MODEL 1866 YELLOW BOY RIFLE & CARBINE
**$848.00 (Rifle) $825.00 (Carbine)**

These exact reproductions of guns used over 100 years ago are available in 45 Long Colt, 38 Special and 44-40. Both carbine and rifle are offered with blued finish, walnut stock and brass frame.

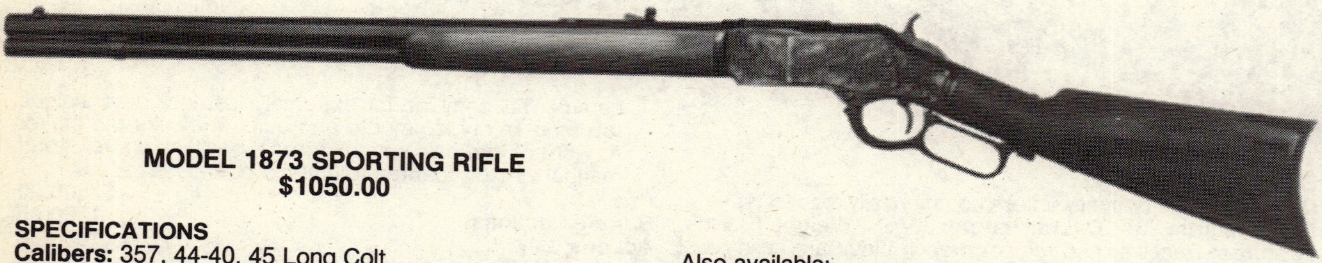

### MODEL 1873 SPORTING RIFLE
**$1050.00**

**SPECIFICATIONS**
**Calibers:** 357, 44-40, 45 Long Colt
**Barrel length:** 24¼″ octagonal **Overall length:** 43¼″
**Weight:** 8.16 lbs.
**Features:** Magazine tube in blued steel; frame is casehardened steel; stock and forend are walnut wood

Also available:
**MODEL 1873 CARBINE.** Same features as the 1873 Sporting Rifle, except in 45 Long Colt only with 19″ barrel, overall length 38¼″ and weight 7.38 lbs. **Price: $1020.00; $1050.00** Casehardened

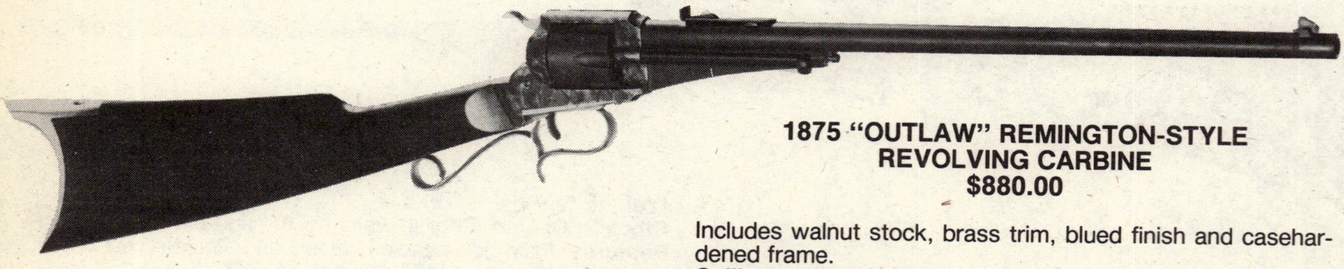

### 1875 "OUTLAW" REMINGTON-STYLE REVOLVING CARBINE
**$880.00**

Includes walnut stock, brass trim, blued finish and casehardened frame.
**Calibers:** 45 Long Colt
**Barrel length:** 20″ **Overall length:** 38″
**Weight:** 5 lbs.

# EUROPEAN AMERICAN ARMORY

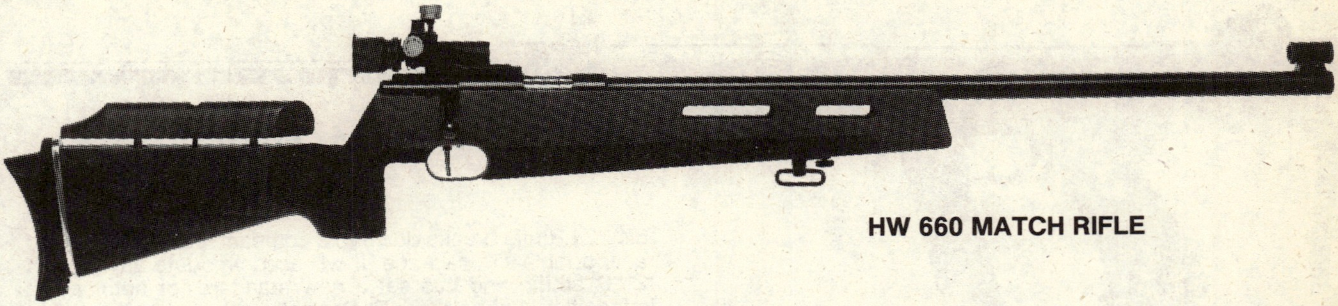

HW 660 MATCH RIFLE

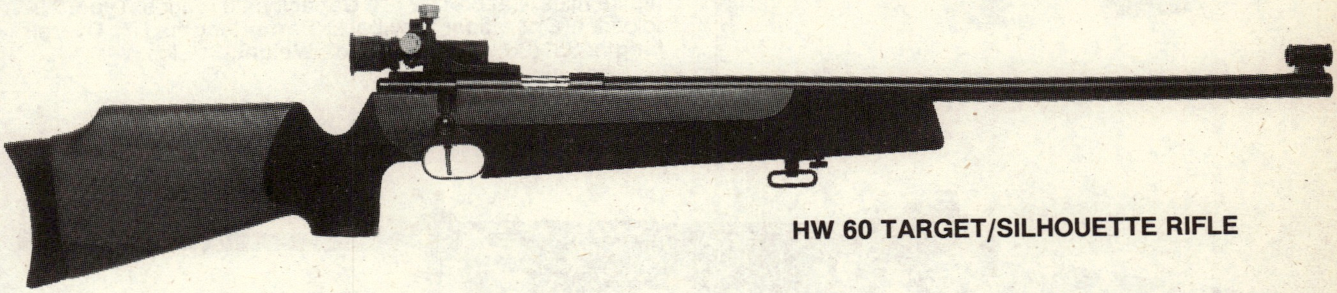

HW 60 TARGET/SILHOUETTE RIFLE



## HW 660 MATCH RIFLE (SINGLE SHOT) $795.00

**SPECIFICATIONS**
**Caliber:** 22 LR
**Barrel length:** 26.8″
**Overall length:** 45.7″
**Weight:** 10.8 lbs.
**Sights:** Match-type aperture rear; hooded ramp front
**Finish:** Blue
**Stock:** Stippled walnut

**Features:** Adjustable match trigger; push-button safety; stippled walnut stock with adjustable buttplate and comb; left-handed stock available

Also available:
**HW 60 TARGET RIFLE.** Same specifications as Model HW 660, except with target stock. **Price:** ......... **$695.00**
**HW 60 LEFT-HAND** ........................ **850.00**

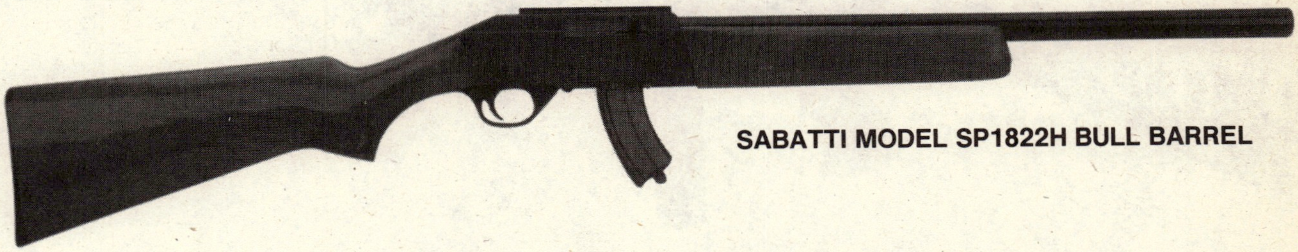

SABATTI MODEL SP1822H BULL BARREL

**SPECIFICATIONS**
**Caliber:** 22 LR
**Capacity:** 10 rounds (detachable magazine)
**Barrel length:** 18½″
**Overall length:** 37½″
**Weight:** 7.15 lbs.
**Sights:** No sights
**Price: BULL BARREL** ........................ **$204.95**

# FEATHER RIFLES

**MODEL AT-22**
**$249.95**

This 22 LR rifle breaks down to a compact, easy-to-stow and transportable 17″ package. It will accommodate any kind of 22 LR ammo and has set a new standard for autoloading rimfire rifles. **Caliber:** 22 LR. **Capacity:** 20 rounds. **Type:** Autoloader. **Operation:** Blowback. **Barrel length:** 17″. **Overall length:** 35″ (26″ w/stock folded). **Weight:** 3½ lbs.

**MODEL F2 AT-22**

Also available:
**MODEL F2 AT-22.** Same as Model AT-22 but with fixed buttstock made of high-impact polymer for a more traditional look.
**Price:** .......................................... **$279.95**

**MODEL F9 AT-9**
**$525.00**

Same specifications as the Model AT-9, but with fixed buttstock made of high-impact polymer for a more traditional look.

**MODEL AT-9 (not shown)**
**$499.00**

Feather's AT-9 offers 3″ groups or less at 50 yards using standard, fully adjustable sights. Ideal for competitive use in rapid-fire events like pin shooting, weekend plinking or personal security. **Caliber:** 9mm. **Capacity:** 25 rounds. **Type:** Autoloader. **Operation:** Blowback. **Barrel length:** 17″. **Overall length:** 35″ (26½″ w/stock folded). **Weight:** 5 lbs.

# FRANCOTTE RIFLES

August Francotte rifles are available in all calibers for which barrels and chambers are made. All guns are custom made to the customer's specifications; there are no standard models. Most bolt-action rifles use commercial Mauser actions; however, the magnum action is produced by Francotte exclusively for its own production. Side-by-side and mountain rifles use either boxlock or sidelock action. Francotte system sidelocks are back-action type. Options include gold and silver inlay, special engraving and exhibition and museum grade wood. Francotte rifles are distributed in the U.S. by Armes de Chasse (see Directory of Manufacturers and Distributors for details).

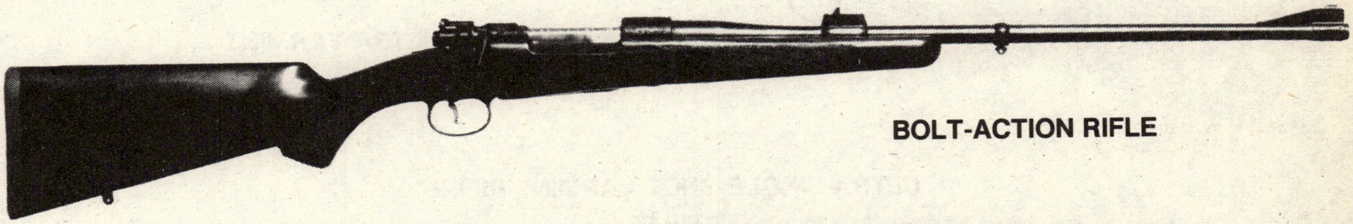

BOLT-ACTION RIFLE

**SPECIFICATIONS**
**Calibers:** 17 Bee, 7×64, 30-06, 270, 222R, 243W, 308W, 375 H&H, 416 Rigby, 460 Weatherby, 505 Gibbs
**Barrel length:** To customer's specifications
**Weight:** 8 to 12 lbs., or to customer's specifications
**Stock:** A wide selection of wood in all possible styles according to customer preferences
**Engraving:** Per customer specifications
**Sights:** All types of sights and scopes

| **BOLT-ACTION RIFLES** | **Prices** |
|---|---|
| Standard Bolt Action (30-06, 270, 7×64, etc.) | **$5,572.00** |
| Short Bolt Action (222R, 243W, etc.) | **6,930.00** |
| African Action (416 Rigby, 460 Wby., etc.) | **9,960.00** |
| Magnum Action (300 WM, 338 WM, 375 H&H, 458 WM | **6,180.00** |

| **BOXLOCK SIDE-BY-SIDE DOUBLE RIFLES** | **Prices** |
|---|---|
| Std. boxlock double rifle (9.3×74R, 8×57JRS, 7×65R, etc.) | **$11,513.00** |
| Std. boxlock double (Magnum calibers) | **15,293.00** |
| Optional sideplates, **add** | **1,700.00** |

| **SIDELOCK S/S DOUBLE RIFLES** | |
|---|---|
| Std. sidelock double rifle (9.3×74R, 8×57JRS, 7×65R, etc.) | **$30,000.00** |
| Std. sidelock double (Magnum calibers) | **27,761.00** |
| Special safari sidelock | **Price on request** |

| **MOUNTAIN RIFLES** | |
|---|---|
| Standard boxlock | **$9,186.00** |
| Std. boxlock (Mag. & rimless calibers) | **Price on request** |
| Optional sideplates, **add** | **1,158.00** |
| Standard sidelock | **20,538.00** |

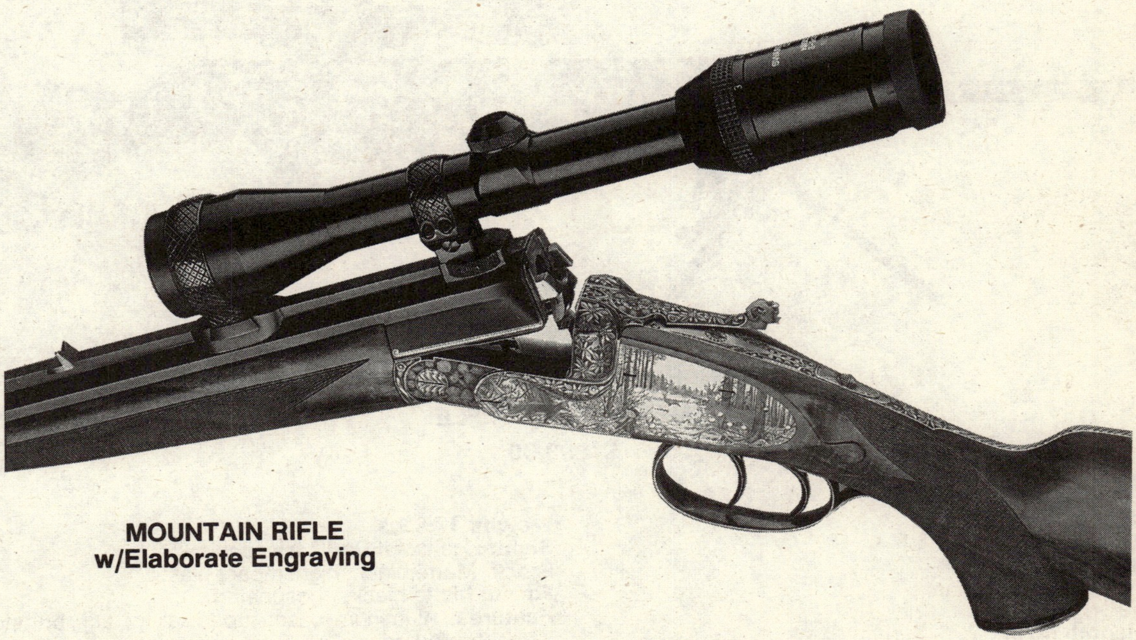

MOUNTAIN RIFLE
w/Elaborate Engraving

RIFLES

# HARRINGTON & RICHARDSON

ULTRA VARMINT

**ULTRA SINGLE-SHOT VARMINT RIFLE**

**$249.95**

**SPECIFICATIONS**
**Caliber:** 223 Rem.
**Action:** Break-open; side lever release; positive ejection
**Barrel length:** 22″ heavy varmint profile
**Weight:** 7 to 8 lbs.
**Sights:** None (scope mount included)
**Length of pull:** 14$^{1}/_{4}$″
**Drop at comb:** 1$^{1}/_{4}$″
**Drop at heel:** 1$^{1}/_{8}$″

**Forend:** Semi-beavertail
**Stock:** Monte Carlo; hand-checkered curly maple
**Features:** Sling swivels on stock and forend; patented transfer bar safety; automatic ejection; hammer extension; rebated muzzle; Uncle Mike recoil pad

Also available: **ULTRA HUNTER** w/Cinnamon Laminate Stock.
**Caliber:** 25-06 (26″ barrel); 308 Win. (22″ barrel)

# HECKLER & KOCH RIFLES

**MODEL HK PSG-1 HIGH PRECISION MARKSMAN'S RIFLE**

**$1093.00**

**SPECIFICATIONS**
**Caliber:** 308 (7.62mm)
**Capacity:** 5 rounds
**Barrel length:** 25.6″
**Rifling:** 4 groove, polygonal
**Twist:** 12″, right hand
**Overall length:** 47.5″

**Weight:** 17.8 lbs.
**Sights:** Hensoldt 6×42 telescopic
**Stock:** Matte black, high-impact plastic
**Finish:** Matte black, phosphated
**Features:** Aluminum case; tripod; sling; adj. buttstock and contoured grip

## HOWA LIGHTNING RIFLES

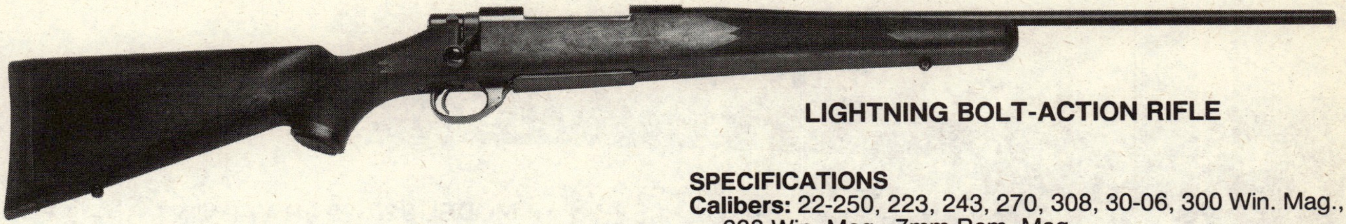

LIGHTNING BOLT-ACTION RIFLE

The rugged mono-bloc receivers on all Howa rifles are machined from a single billet of high carbon steel. The machined steel bolt boasts dual-opposed locking lugs and triple relief gas ports. Actions are fitted with a button-release hinged floorplate for fast reloading. Premium steel sporter-weight barrels are hammer-forged. A silent sliding thumb safety locks the trigger for safe loading or clearing the chamber. The stock is ultra-tough polymer.

**SPECIFICATIONS**
**Calibers:** 22-250, 223, 243, 270, 308, 30-06, 300 Win. Mag., 338 Win. Mag., 7mm Rem. Mag.
**Capacity:** 5 rounds (3 in Magnum)
**Barrel length:** 22″ (24″ in Magnum)
**Overall length:** 42″
**Weight:** 7½ lbs. (7.75 lbs. in Magnum)
**Price:**
**Standard Model** .......... $469.00
In Magnum calibers .......... 486.00
**Barreled Actions** .......... 347.00
In Magnum calibers .......... 364.00

## JARRETT CUSTOM RIFLES

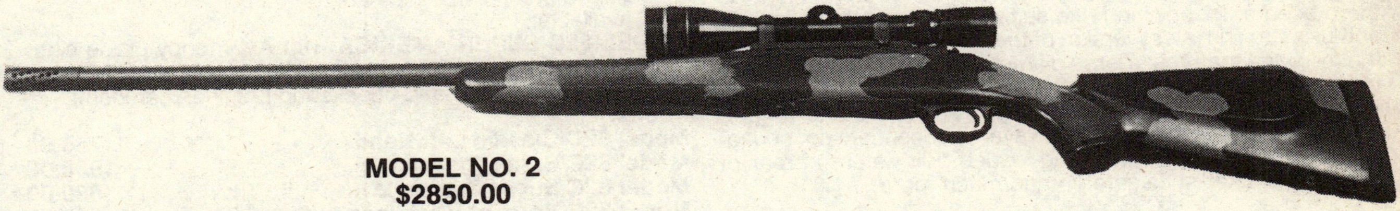

**MODEL NO. 2**
**$2850.00**

This lightweight rifle—called the "Walkabout"—is based on Remington's Model 7 receiver. It is available in any short-action caliber and is pillar-bedded into a McMillan Model 7-style stock.

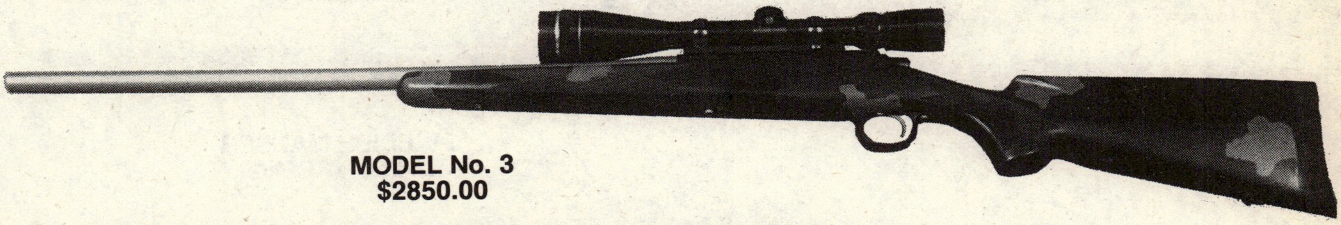

**MODEL No. 3**
**$2850.00**

Jarrett's Standard Hunting Rifle uses McMillan's fiberglass stock and is made primarily for hunters of big game and varmints.

**MODEL NO. 4 (not shown)**
**$6000.00**

This model—the "Professional Hunter"—is based on a Winchester controlled round-feed Model 70. It features a quarter rib and iron sights and comes with two Leupold scopes with quick-detachable scope rings. A handload is developed for solids and soft points (40 rounds each). It is then pillar-bedded into a McMillan fiberglass stock. Available in any Magnum caliber.

**COWDEN RIFLE (not shown)**
**$1575.00**

Cowden Gunworks (a division of Jarrett Rifles) beds each action into a camo McMillan stock using poured pillars, then installs a recoil pad with a 13½″ length of pull. Stock options include the Mountain Rifle, Remington Classic and the Marksman. A Jarrett stainless-steel barrel in #3 or #6 taper is fitted and chambered for any standard caliber. Crowned at 24″, it is then bead-blasted for a stain finish. Action lapping and trigger adjustment are standard.

# KIMBER RIFLES

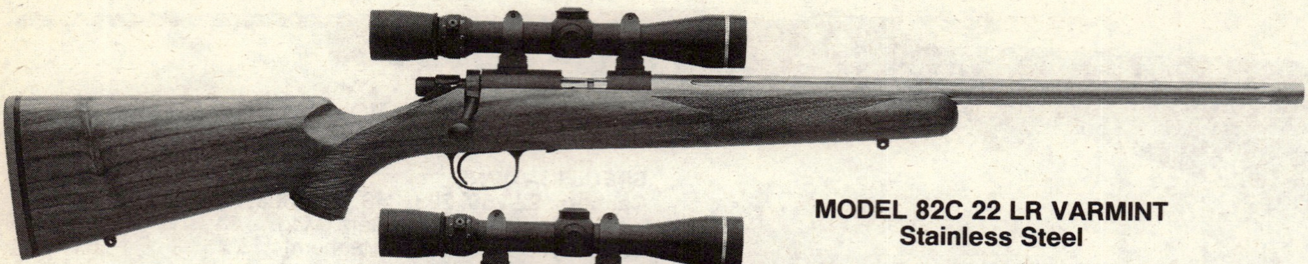

MODEL 82C 22 LR VARMINT
Stainless Steel

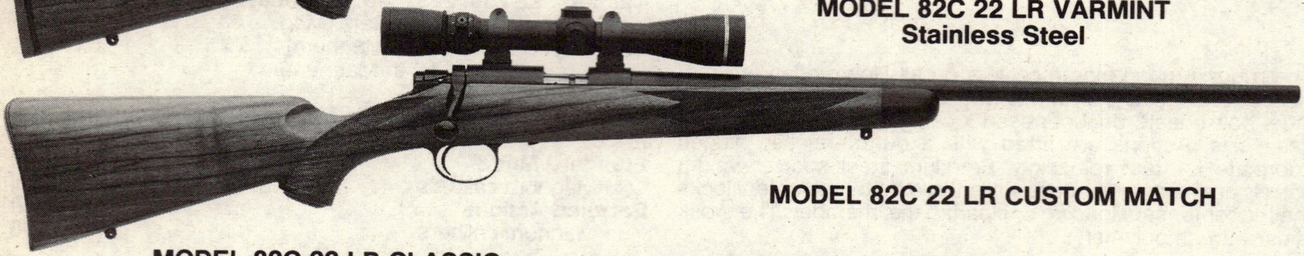

MODEL 82C 22 LR CUSTOM MATCH

## MODEL 82C 22 LR CLASSIC
## $696.00

The Kimber 22 Long Rifle Model 82, first introduced in 1980, became a leader in the resurgence of interest in premium-grade rimfire rifles. Not since the demise of the original American-made Winchester 52 Sporter 30 years earlier had there been a .22 sporting rifle suitable for serious rimfire rifle enthusiasts. The latest version of the Kimber Model 82 includes the following features: a large diameter receiver, fully machined from solid steel and threaded at the front • a rear locking bolt with twin horizontally opposed lugs • a single-stage trigger, adjustable for pressure and overtravel • independent coil spring-operated bolt stop • coil spring-loaded bolt detent in rear of receiver • rocker-style safety • and much more.

**SPECIFICATIONS**
**Caliber:** 22 LR **Capacity:** 4-shot clip (10-shot optional)
**Barrel length:** 21″ (1 turn in 16″)
**Overall length:** 40½″ **Weight:** 6½ lbs.
**Stock:** Standard grade claro walnut
**Length of pull:** 13½″
**Features:** Red rubber buttpad w/Kimber insignia; plain buttstock (no cheekpiece); hand checkering (20 lines per inch); polished steel pistol-grip cap

Also available:
**MODEL 82C SUPER AMERICA** with AAA fancy-grade claro walnut; genuine ebony forend tip; beaded cheekpiece; black rubber buttstock; hand-checkering (20 lines per inch).

**Prices:**

| | |
|---|---|
| **Model 82C Classic Left Hand** | **$ 785.00** |
| **Model 82C Super Classic** | **1090.00** |
| **Model 82C Super Classic L.H.** | **1090.00** |
| **Model 82C Varmint (Stainless w/fluted bbl.)** | **885.00** |
| **Model 82C Super America** | **1175.00** |
| **Model 82C Custom Match** | **1850.00** |

SWEDISH MAUSER
22-250 VARMINT

## SWEDISH MAUSER 98

**SPECIFICATIONS**
**Calibers:** Sporters—243 Win., 6.5×55mm, 308 Win.; Heavy Barrel Models—22-250 and 308 Win. (SS Varmint), 308 Win. (Hvy. Barrel)
**Capacity:** 5 shots
**Action:** Mauser, front-locking bolt action, cock on closing
**Barrel length:** 22″ (Sporters); 25″ (Heavy barrel models)
**Overall length:** 41.5″ (Sporters); 44.5″ (Heavy barrel models)
**Weight:** 7.25 lbs. (Sporters); 8.25 lbs. (SS Varmint) and 9.25 lbs. (Hvy. Barrel)
**Trigger:** Two-stage military trigger
**Stock:** Ramline™ Syn-Tech™ synthetic plastic "krinkle" finish; lifetime guarantee; length of pull 13.5″
**Finish:** Satin silver or matte blue (Sporters); stainless barrel w/matte blue action (SS Varmint); matte blue (Hvy. Barrel)

**Prices:**

| | |
|---|---|
| **SPORTERS** | |
| 243 or 308 Sporter (matte blue) | **$400.00** |
| Same as above in satin silver | **450.00** |
| 6.5×55mm matte blue | **325.00** |
| Same as above in satin silver | **355.00** |
| **HEAVY BARREL MODELS** | |
| 22-250 SS Varmint | **495.00** |
| 308 SS Varmint | **510.00** |
| 308 Heavy Barrel | **450.00** |

# KRIEGHOFF DOUBLE RIFLES



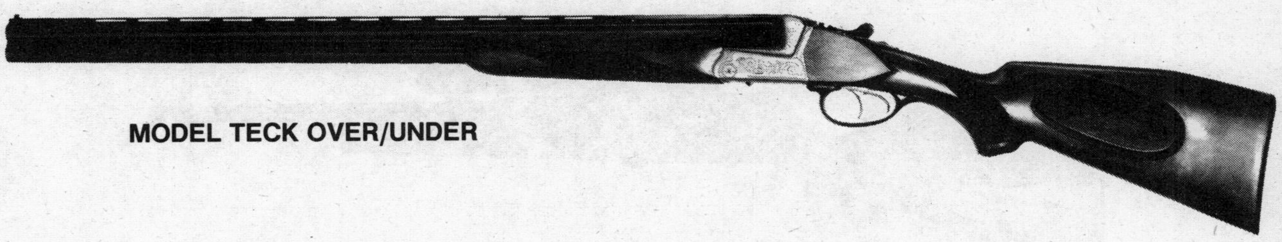

## MODEL TECK OVER/UNDER

**SPECIFICATIONS**
**Calibers:** 308, 30-06, 300 Win. Mag., 9.3×74R, 8×57JRS, 7×65R, 458 Win. Mag.
**Barrel length:** 25″
**Weight:** 7½ lbs.
**Action:** Boxlock; double greener-type crossbolt and double-barrel lug locking, steel receiver
**Triggers:** Double triggers; single trigger optional
**Safety:** Located on top tang
**Sights:** Open sight with right-angle front sight
**Stock:** German-styled with pistol grip and cheekpiece; oil-finished (14⅜″ long)
**Finish:** Nickel-plated steel receiver with satin grey finish
**Prices:**
**MODEL TECK** (Boxlock) 458 Win. Mag. . . . . . . . **$11,450.00**
**TECK-HANDSPANNER** (16 ga. receiver only; 7×65R, 30-06, 308 Win.) . . . . . . . . . . . . . . . . . **10,970.00**
Also available:
**TRUMPF SBS** (Side-by-side boxlock) . . . . . . . . . **16,150.00**

## ULM OVER/UNDER (not shown)

**SPECIFICATIONS**
**Calibers:** 308 Win., 30-06, 300 Win. Mag., 375 H&H, 458 Win. Mag.
**Barrel length:** 25″
**Weight:** 7.8 lbs.
**Triggers:** Double triggers (front trigger=bottom; rear trigger=upper
**Safety:** Located on top tang
**Sights:** Open sight w/right-angle front sight
**Stock:** German-styled with pistol grip and cheekpiece; oil-finished (14⅜″ long); semi-beavertail forend
**Prices:**
**ULM** (Sidelock) . . . . . . . . . . . . . . . . . . . . . . . . **$13,500.00**
**ULM PRIMUS** (Deluxe Sidelock) . . . . . . . . . . . . . **20,950.00**

## CLASSIC SIDE-BY-SIDE DOUBLE RIFLE $6895.00 (not shown)

Krieghoff's new Classic Side-by-Side offers many features, including: Short opening angle for fast loading . . . compact action with reinforced sidewalls . . . sliding, self-adjusting wedge for secure bolt . . . large underlugs . . . automatic hammer safety . . . horizontal firing-pin placement . . . Purdey-style extension between barrels.

**SPECIFICATIONS**
**Calibers:** 308 Win., 30-06, 30R Blaser, 8×57JRS/RS, 9.3×74R, 375 H&H, 458 Win. Mag., 416 Rigby, 470 N.E., 500 N.E.
**Barrel length:** 23½″
**Trigger:** Double triggers with front set trigger standard
**Weight:** 7½ to 11 lbs. (depending on caliber and wood density)
**Options:** 21½″ barrel; Combi-Cocking Device; double-set triggers; automatic set trigger release; engraved sideplates
Also available: **CLASSIC BIG BOAR** in 375 H&H, 416 Rigby, 458 WH, 470 NE and 500 NE. Standard features include Combi-Cocking device (for automatic re-cocking), hinged front trigger, nonremovable muzzle wedge. **Price: $8995.00**

# LAKEFIELD SPORTING RIFLES

## SPECIFICATIONS

**MODEL 90B BIATHLON**
**$558.95 ($614.95 Left Hand)**

**MODEL 92S SILHOUETTE**
**$379.95 ($417.95 Left Hand)**

| **Model:** | **90B** | **92S** |
|---|---|---|
| **Caliber:** | .22 Long Rifle Only | .22 Long Rifle |
| **Capacity:** | 5-shot metal magazine | 5-shot metal magazine |
| **Action:** | Self-cocking bolt action, thumb-operated rotary safety | Self-cocking bolt action, thumb-operated rotary safety |
| **Stock:** | One-piece target-type stock with natural finish hardwood; comes with clip holder, carrying & shooting rails, butt hook and hand stop | One-piece high comb, target-type with walnut finish hardwood |
| **Barrel Length:** | 21″ w/snow cover | 21″ |
| **Sights:** | Receiver peep sights with 1/4 min. click micrometer adjustments; target front sight with inserts | None (receiver drilled and tapped for scope base) |
| **Overall Length:** | 39 5/8″ | 39 5/8″ |
| **Approx. Weight:** | 8 1/4 lbs. | 8 lbs. |

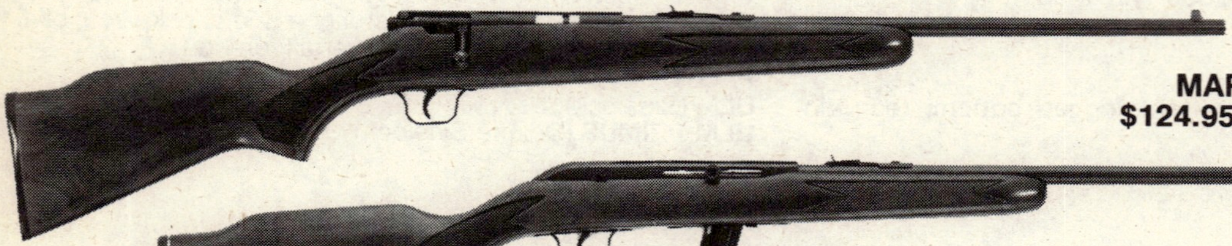

**MARK I SINGLE SHOT**
**$124.95 ($137.95 Left Hand)**

**MODEL 64B SEMIAUTO**
**$138.95**

Also available:
**MARK I "SMOOTH BORE"** (20 3/4″ barrel) . . . . . . . . **$124.95**
Left Hand . . . . . . . . . . . . . . . . . . . . . . . . . **137.95**
**MARK I YOUTH** (19″ barrel) . . . . . . . . . . . . . . . **124.95**
Left Hand . . . . . . . . . . . . . . . . . . . . . . . . . **137.95**
**MARK II & MARK II YOUTH** (19″ barrel) . . . . . . . . . **133.95**
**MARK II LEFT HAND** (20 1/2″ barrel) . . . . . . . . . . **146.95**

## SPECIFICATIONS

| **Model:** | **MARK I** | **MARK II** | **64B** |
|---|---|---|---|
| **Caliber:** | .22 Short, Long or Long Rifle | .22 Long Rifle only | .22 Long Rifle only |
| **Capacity:** | Single shot | 10-shot clip magazine | 10-shot clip magazine |
| **Action:** | Self-cocking bolt action, Thumb-operated rotary safety | Self-cocking bolt action Thumb-operated rotary safety | Semiautomatic side ejection, bolt hold-open device, thumb-operated rotary safety |
| **Stock:** | One Piece, Walnut Finish Hardwood, Monte Carlo Type with Full Pistol Grip. Checkering on Pistol Grip and Forend. | | |
| **Barrel Length:** | 20 3/4″ | 20 3/4″ | 20 1/4″ |
| **Sights:** | Open bead front sight, adjustable rear sight, receiver grooved for scope mounting. | | |
| **Overall Length:** | 39 1/2″ | 39 1/2″ | 40″ |
| **Approx. Weight:** | 5 1/2 lbs. | 5 1/2 lbs. | 5 1/2 lbs. |

# LAKEFIELD SPORTING RIFLES

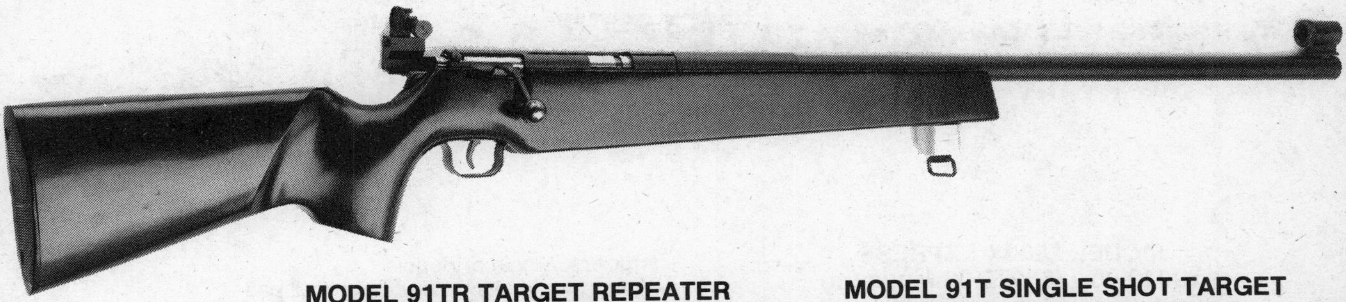

**MODEL 91TR TARGET REPEATER**
**$474.95 ($521.95 Left Hand)**

**MODEL 91T SINGLE SHOT TARGET**
**$445.95 ($489.95 Left Hand)**

| Model | 91TR | 91T |
|---|---|---|
| Caliber: | .22 Long Rifle | .22 Short, Long or Long Rifle |
| Capacity | 5-shot clip magazine | Single shot |
| Action: | Self-cocking bolt action, thumb-operated rotary safety | Self-cocking bolt action, thumb-operated rotary safety |
| Stock: | One-piece, target-type with walnut finish hardwood (also available in natural finish); comes with shooting rail and hand stop | One-piece, target-type walnut finish hardwood (also available in natural finish); comes with shootng rail and hand stop |
| Sights: | Receiver peep sights with 1/4 min. click micrometer adjustments, target front sight with inserts | Receiver peep sights with 1/4 min. click micrometer adjustments, target front sight with inserts |
| Overall Length: | 43 5/8″ | 43 5/8″ |
| Approx. Weight: | 8 lbs. | 8 lbs. |



# L.A.R. GRIZZLY RIFLE

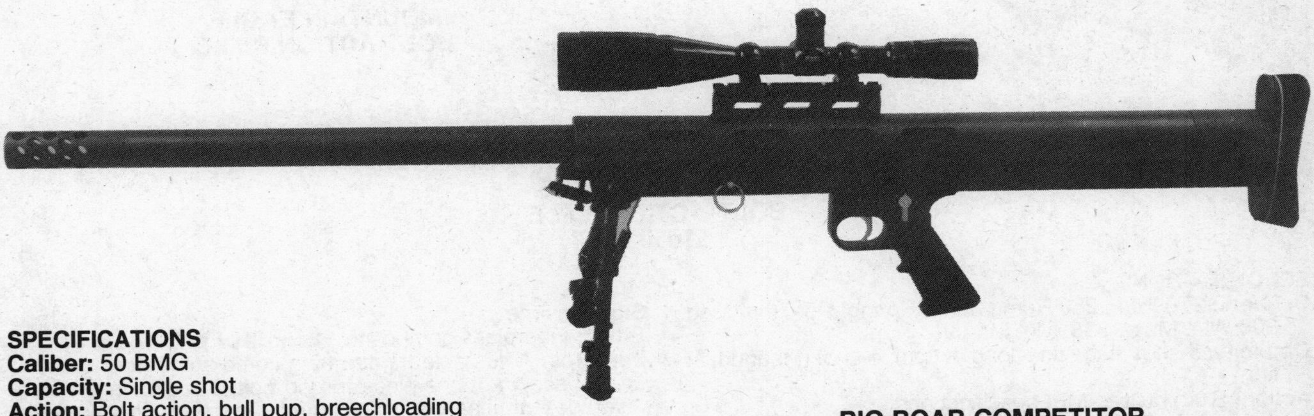

**SPECIFICATIONS**
**Caliber:** 50 BMG
**Capacity:** Single shot
**Action:** Bolt action, bull pup, breechloading
**Barrel length:** 36″
**Overall length:** 45 1/2″
**Weight:** 28.4 lbs.
**Safety:** Thumb safety
**Features:** All-steel construction; receiver made of 4140 alloy steel, heat-treated to 42 R/C; bolt made of 4340 alloy steel; low recoil (like 12 ga. shotgun)

**BIG BOAR COMPETITOR**
**$2400.00**

# LAURONA RIFLES

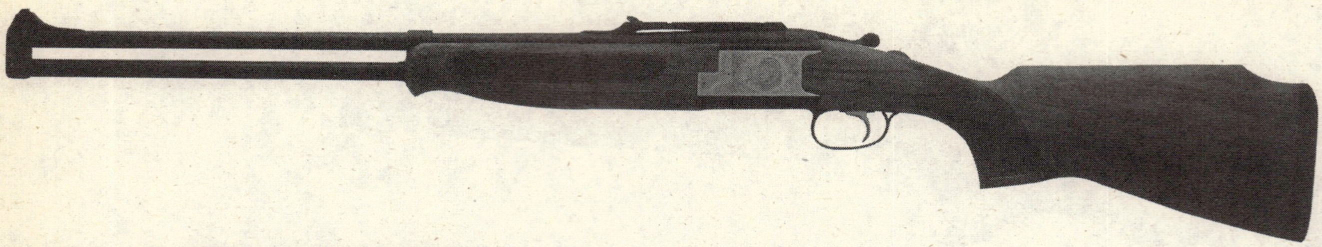

**MODEL 2000X EXPRESS**
**$2919.00 ($3279.00 Magnum)**

**SPECIFICATIONS**
**Calibers:** 9.3×74R, 30-06 Spfd., 8×57 JRS, 8×75 RS, 375 H&H Mag.
**Barrel length:** 23.8″ (25″ in 375 H&H Mag.)
**Weight:** 8½ lbs. (8.15 lbs. in 9.3×74R)
**Triggers:** Single or double
**Stock:** Monte Carlo w/rubber recoil pad
**Drop at comb:** 14″ **Drop at heel:** 20.25″
**Features:** Tulip forend; automatic ejectors (or extractors); high alloy full-length hinge pin; anti-rust matte black chrome; hand-checkered select-grade walnut with nonglare finish; engravings on receivers; convergency adjustment; drilled and tapped for Leupold mounts

# MAGNUM RESEARCH

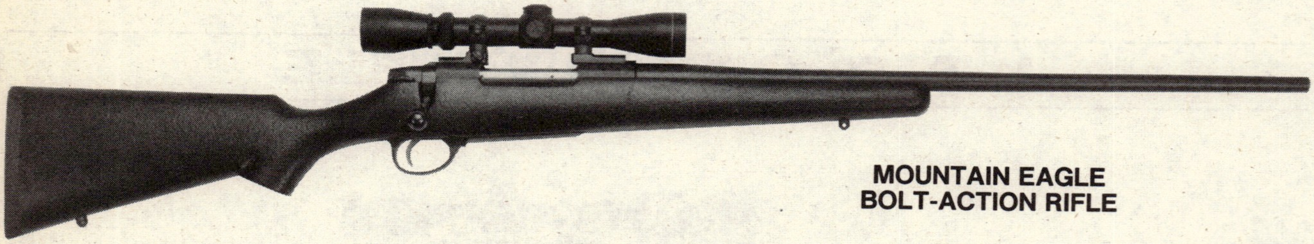

**MOUNTAIN EAGLE BOLT-ACTION RIFLE**

**MOUNTAIN EAGLE**
**BOLT-ACTION RIFLE**
**$1650.00**

**SPECIFICATIONS**
**Calibers:** 270 Win., 280 Rem., 30-06 Springfield, 7mm Mag., 300 Win. Mag., 338 Win. Mag.
**Capacity:** 5-shot magazine (long action); 4-shot (Magnum action)
**Action:** Sako-built to MRI specifications
**Barrel length:** 24″ with .004″ headspace tolerance
**Overall length:** 44″
**Weight:** 7 lbs. 13 oz.
**Sights:** None
**Stock:** Fiberglass composite **Length of pull:** 13⅝″
**Features:** Adjustable trigger; high comb stock (for mounting and scoping); one-piece forged bolt; free-floating, match-grade, cut-rifles, benchrest barrel; recoil pad and sling swivel studs; Platform Bedding System front lug; pillar-bedded rear guard screw; lengthened receiver ring; solid steel hinged floorplate

# MARLIN 22 RIFLES

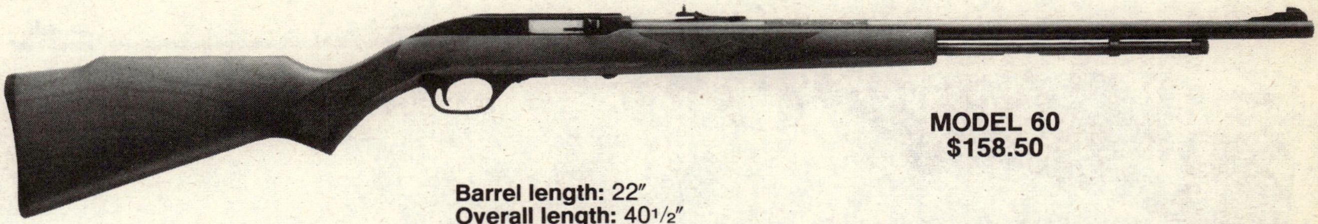

**MODEL 60**
**$158.50**

**SPECIFICATIONS**
**Caliber:** 22 Long Rifle
**Capacity:** 14-shot tubular magazine with patented closure system
**Barrel length:** 22″
**Overall length:** 40½″
**Weight:** 5½ lbs.
**Sights:** Ramp front sight; adjustable open rear, receiver grooved for scope mount
**Action:** Self-loading; side ejection; manual and automatic "last-shot" hold-open devices; receiver top has serrated, nonglare finish; crossbolt safety
**Stock:** One-piece Maine birch Monte Carlo stock, press-checkered, with full pistol grip; Mar-Shield® finish

**MODEL 60SS**
**$237.00**

**SPECIFICATIONS**
**Caliber:** 22 Long Rifle
**Capacity:** 14 rounds
**Barrel length:** 22″
**Overall length:** 40½″
**Weight:** 5½ lbs.
**Sights:** Adjustable folding semibuckhorn rear; ramp front sight with high-visibility post and removable Wide Scan™ hood
**Stock:** Laminated two-tone Maine birch with nickel-plated swivel studs and rubber rifle buttpad
**Features:** Micro-Groove® rifling; side ejection; manual bolt hold-open; automatic last-shot bolt hold-open; crossbolt safety

**MODEL 70HC**
**$167.25**

**SPECIFICATIONS**
**Caliber:** 22 Long Rifle
**Capacity:** Two 7-shot clip magazines
**Barrel length:** 18″
**Overall length:** 36¾″
**Weight:** 5½ lbs.
**Action:** Self-loading; side ejection; manual bolt hold-open; receiver top has serrated, nonglare finish; crossbolt safety
**Sights:** Adjustable open rear, ramp front; receiver grooved for scope mount
**Stock:** Press-checkered Monte Carlo walnut-finished Maine birch w/full pistol grip and Mar-Shield® finish

# MARLIN 22 RIFLES

**MODEL 70PSS "PAPOOSE"**
**$224.75**

**SPECIFICATIONS**
**Caliber:** 22 Long Rifle
**Capacity:** 7-shot clip
**Barrel length:** 16¼″
**Overall length:** 35¼″
**Weight:** 3¼ lbs.
**Action:** Self-loading; side ejection; manual bolt hold-open; crossbolt safety; stainless-steel breech bolt and barrel
**Sights:** Screw adjustable open rear; ramp front; receiver grooved for scope mount
**Stock:** Black fiberglass-filled synthetic with abbrev. forend, nickel-plated swivel studs and molded-in checkering

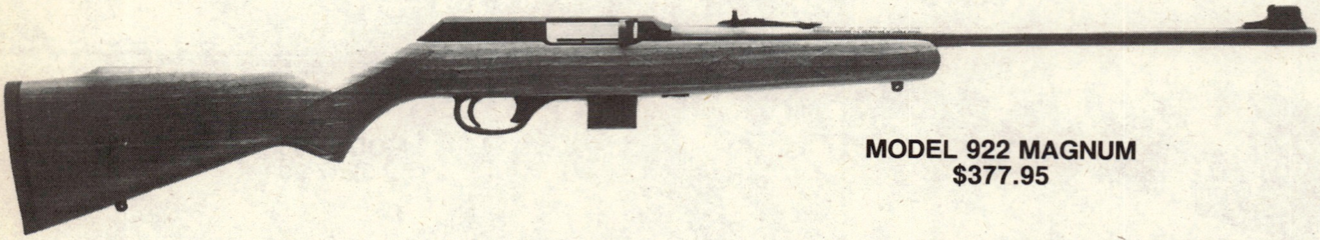

**MODEL 922 MAGNUM**
**$377.95**

**SPECIFICATIONS**
**Caliber:** 22 Win. Mag. Rimfire
**Capacity:** 7-shot clip magazine
**Barrel length:** 20½″
**Overall length:** 39¾″
**Weight:** 6½ lbs.
**Sights:** Adjustable semibuckhorn rear; ramp front sight with brass bead and removable Wide-Scan hood™
**Stock:** Monte Carlo checkered American black walnut with rubber rifle buttpad and swivel studs
**Features:** Side ejection; manual bolt hold-open; automatic last-shot bolt hold-open; magazine safety; Garand-type safety; Micro-Groove® rifling

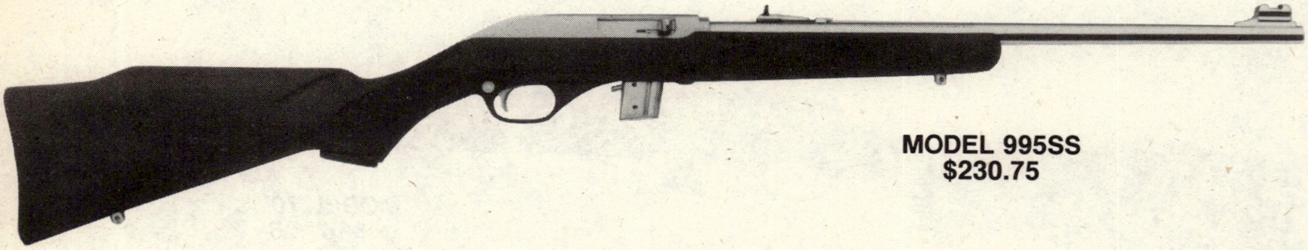

**MODEL 995SS**
**$230.75**

**SPECIFICATIONS**
**Caliber:** 22 Long Rifle
**Action:** Self-loading
**Capacity:** 7-shot nickel-plated clip magazine
**Barrel:** 18″ stainless steel with Micro-Groove® rifling (16 grooves)
**Overall length:** 36¾″
**Weight:** 5 lbs.
**Stock:** Black fiberglass-filled synthetic with nickel-plated swivel studs and molded-in checkering
**Sights:** Screw-adjustable open rear; ramp front with high-visibility orange post; cutaway Wide-Scan™ hood
**Features:** Receiver grooved for tip-off scope mount; stainless-steel breech-bolt and barrel; crossbolt safety

# MARLIN BOLT-ACTION RIFLES

**MARLIN 15YN "LITTLE BUCKAROO™" Single Shot 22 Beginner's Rifle**
**$162.80**

**SPECIFICATIONS**
**Caliber:** 22 Short, Long or Long Rifle
**Capacity:** Single shot
**Action:** Bolt action; easy-load feed throat; thumb safety; red cocking indicator
**Barrel length:** 16¼″ (16 grooves)
**Overall length:** 33¼″
**Weight:** 4¼ lbs.
**Sights:** Adjustable open rear; ramp front sight
**Stock:** One-piece walnut-finished press-checkered Maine birch Monte Carlo w/full pistol grip; tough Mar-Shield® finish

**MODEL 25MN**
**$192.50**

**SPECIFICATIONS**
**Caliber:** 22 WMR (not interchangeable w/other 22 cartridges)
**Capacity:** 7-shot clip magazine
**Barrel length:** 22″ with Micro-Groove® rifling
**Overall length:** 41″
**Weight:** 6 lbs.
**Sights:** Adjustable open rear, ramp front sight; receiver grooved for scope mount
**Stock:** One-piece walnut-finished press-checkered Maine birch Monte Carlo w/full pistol grip; Mar-Shield® finish

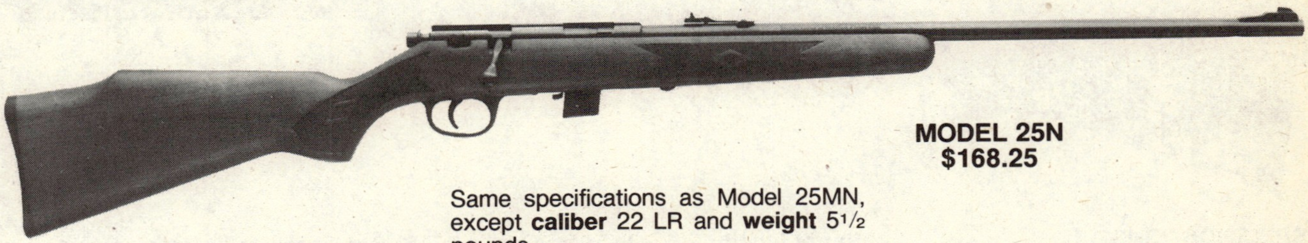

**MODEL 25N**
**$168.25**

Same specifications as Model 25MN, except **caliber** 22 LR and **weight** 5½ pounds.

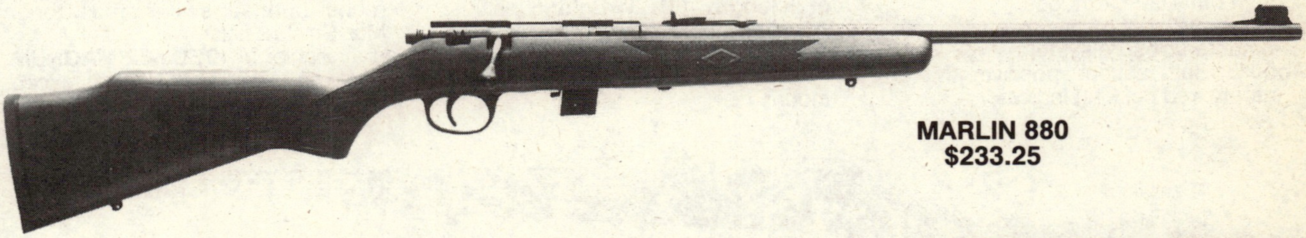

**MARLIN 880**
**$233.25**

**SPECIFICATIONS**
**Caliber:** 22 Long Rifle
**Capacity:** 7-shot clip magazine
**Action:** Bolt action; positive thumb safety; red cocking indicator
**Barrel:** 22″ with Micro-Groove® rifling (16 grooves)
**Sights:** Adj. folding semibuckhorn rear; ramp front w/Wide-Scan™ hood; receiver grooved for scope mount
**Overall length:** 41″ **Weight:** 5½ lbs.
**Stock:** Checkered Monte Carlo American black walnut with full pistol grip; Mar-Shield® finish; rubber buttpad; swivel studs

Also available: **MODEL 880SS.** Same as Model 880, in stainless steel (weight 6 lbs.). **$249.25**
**MODEL 881.** Same as Model 880, except w/tubular mag. holding 17 22 LR cartridges. **Weight:** 6 lbs. **$242.95**

# MARLIN BOLT-ACTION RIFLES

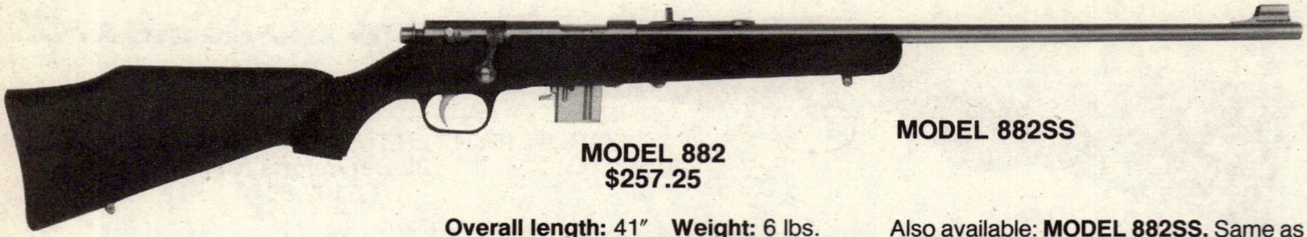

MODEL 882SS

**MODEL 882**
**$257.25**

**SPECIFICATIONS**
**Caliber:** 22 Win. Mag.
**Action:** Bolt action; thumb safety; red cocking indicator
**Capacity:** 7-shot clip
**Barrel length:** 22″
**Overall length:** 41″ **Weight:** 6 lbs.
**Sights:** Adj. semibuckhorn folding rear; ramp front w/brass bead and Wide-Scan™ front sight hood
**Stock:** Monte Carlo American black walnut with swivel studs; full pistol grip; classic cut-checkering; rubber rifle buttpad

Also available: **MODEL 882SS.** Same as Model 882, except stainless-steel barrel, receiver front breechbolt striker knob and trigger stud; orange front sight post; black fiberglass-filled synthetic stock w/nickel-plated swivel studs and molded-in checkering. **$274.50**

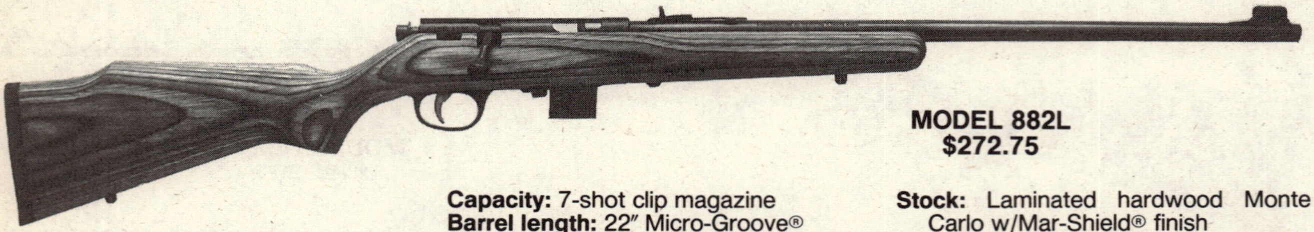

**MODEL 882L**
**$272.75**

**SPECIFICATIONS**
**Caliber:** 22 WMR (not interchangeable with other 22 cartridges)
**Capacity:** 7-shot clip magazine
**Barrel length:** 22″ Micro-Groove®
**Overall length:** 41″ **Weight:** 6 1/4 lbs.
**Sights:** Ramp front w/brass bead and removable Wide-Scan™ hood; adj. folding semibuckhorn rear
**Stock:** Laminated hardwood Monte Carlo w/Mar-Shield® finish
**Features:** Swivel studs; rubber rifle butt pad; receiver grooved for scope mount; positive thumb safety; red cocking indicator

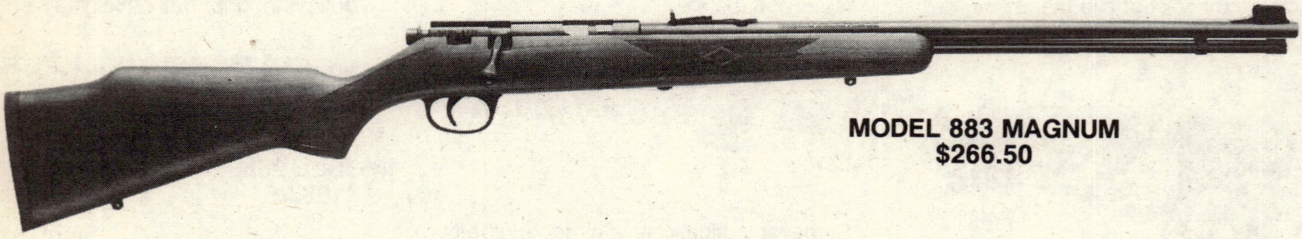

**MODEL 883 MAGNUM**
**$266.50**

**SPECIFICATIONS**
**Caliber:** 22 WMR (not interchangeable with other 22 cartridges)
**Capacity:** 12-shot tubular magazine with patented closure system
**Action:** Bolt action; positive thumb safety; red cocking indicator
**Barrel length:** 22″ with Micro-Groove® rifling (20 grooves)
**Overall length:** 41″ **Weight:** 6 lbs.
**Sights:** Adjustable folding semibuckhorn rear; ramp front with Wide-Scan™ hood; receiver grooved for scope mount
**Stock:** Checkered Monte Carlo American black walnut with full pistol grip; rubber buttpad; swivel studs; tough Mar-Shield® finish
Also available: **MODEL 882 MAGNUM.** Same as Model 883 Magnum, except with 7-shot clip magazine. **$257.25**

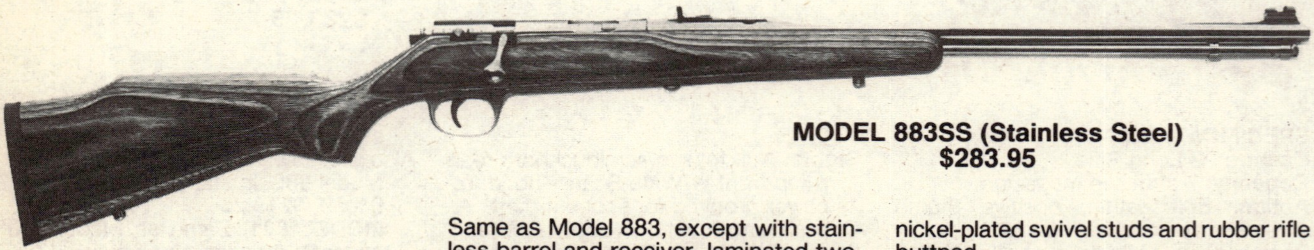

**MODEL 883SS (Stainless Steel)**
**$283.95**

Same as Model 883, except with stainless barrel and receiver, laminated two-tone brown Maine birch stock with nickel-plated swivel studs and rubber rifle buttpad.

# MARLIN RIFLES



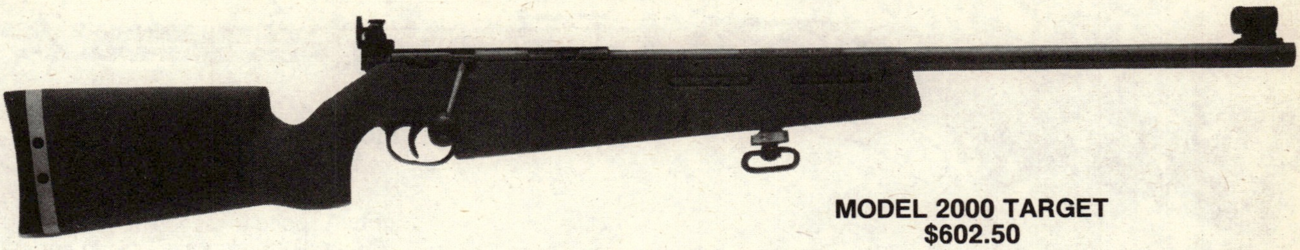

**MODEL 2000 TARGET**
**$602.50**

**SPECIFICATIONS**
**Caliber:** 22 Long Rifle
**Capacity:** Single-shot; 5-shot Summer Biathlon adapter kit available
**Action:** Bolt action, 2-stage target trigger, red cocking indicator
**Barrel length:** Heavy 22″ Micro-Groove w/match chamber, recessed muzzle
**Overall length:** 41″ **Weight:** 8 lbs.
**Sights:** Hooded Lyman front sight with 10 aperture inserts; fully adjustable Lyman target rear peep sight
**Stock:** High-comb "Carbelite" (fiberglass/Kevlar) w/stipple-finished forearm and pistol grip. Blue baked epoxy enamel finish. Buttplate adjustable for length of pull, height and angle. Aluminum forearm rail with forearm stop and quick-detachable swivel

**MODEL 9 CAMP CARBINE**
**$404.25**

**SPECIFICATIONS**
**Caliber:** 9mm
**Capacity:** 4-shot clip (12-shot avail.)
**Action:** Self-loading. Manual bolt hold-open. Garand-type safety, magazine safety, loaded chamber indicator. Solid-top, machined steel receiver is sandblasted to prevent glare, and is drilled/tapped for scope mounting.
**Barrel length:** 16½″ with Micro-Groove® rifling
**Overall length:** 35½″ **Weight:** 6¾ lbs.
**Sights:** Adjustable folding rear, ramp front sight with high-visibility, orange front sight post; Wide-Scan™ hood.
**Stock:** Walnut finished hardwood with pistol grip; tough Mar-Shield™ finish; rubber rifle buttpad; swivel studs

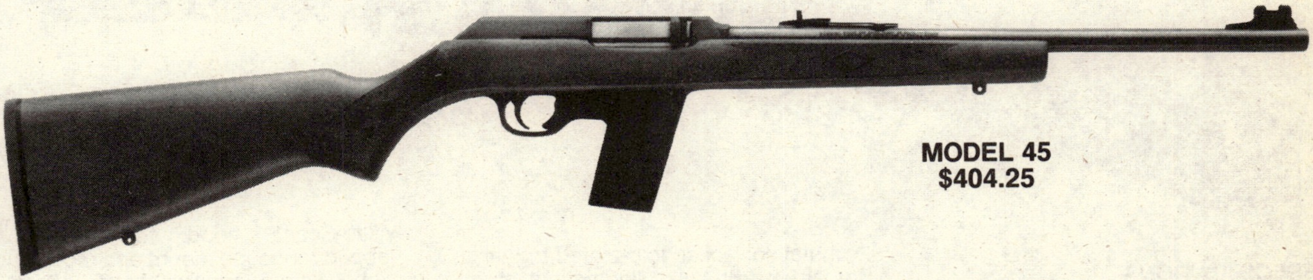

**MODEL 45**
**$404.25**

**SPECIFICATIONS**
**Caliber:** 45 Auto
**Capacity:** 7-shot clip
**Barrel length:** 16½″
**Overall length:** 35½″
**Weight** 6.75 lbs.
**Sights:** Adjustable folding rear; ramp front sight with high-visibility, orange front sight post; Wide-Scan™ hood
**Stock:** Press-checkered walnut-finished Maine birch with pistol grip; rubber rifle buttpad; swivel studs

# MARLIN LEVER-ACTION CARBINES

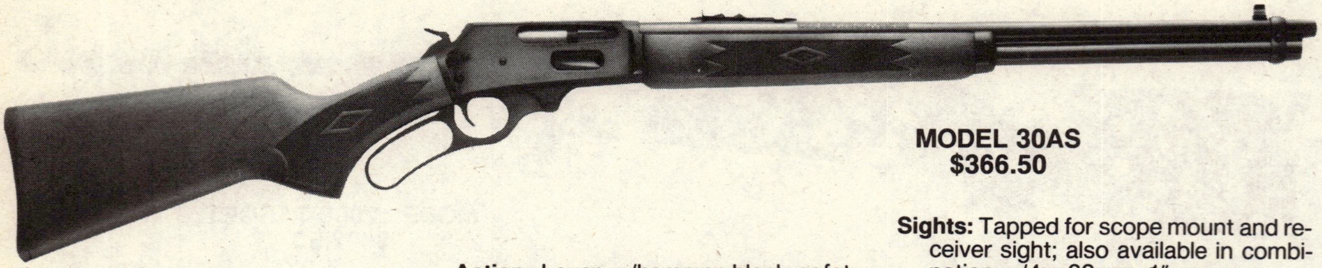

**MODEL 30AS**
**$366.50**

**SPECIFICATIONS**
**Caliber :** 30-30
**Capacity:** 6-shot tubular magazine
**Action:** Lever w/hammer block safety; solid top receiver w/side ejection
**Barrel length:** 20″ w/Micro-Groove®
**Overall length:** 38¹/₄″ **Weight:** 7 lbs.
**Sights:** Tapped for scope mount and receiver sight; also available in combination w/4x, 32mm, 1″ scope
**Stock:** Walnut-finished Maine birch stock w/pistol grip; pressed checkering; Mar-Shield® finish

**MARLIN GOLDEN 39AS**
**$431.95**

The Marlin lever-action 22 is the oldest (since 1891) shoulder gun still being manufactured.

**Solid Receiver Top.** You can easily mount a scope on your Marlin 39 by screwing on the machined scope adapter base provided. The screw-on base is a neater, more versatile method of mounting a scope on a 22 sporting rifle. The solid top receiver and scope adapter base provide a maximum in eye relief adjustment. If you prefer iron sights, you'll find the 39 receiver clean, flat and sandblasted to prevent glare. Exclusive brass magazine tube

**Micro-Groove® Barrel.** Marlin's famous rifling system of multi-grooving has consistently produced fine accuracy because the system grips the bullet more securely, minimizes distortion, and provides a better gas seal.

And the Model 39 maximizes accuracy with the heaviest barrels available on any lever-action 22.

**SPECIFICATIONS**
**Caliber:** 22 Short, Long and Long Rifle
**Capacity:** Tubular magazine holds 26 Short, 21 Long and 19 LR cartridges
**Action:** Lever; solid top receiver; side ejection; one-step takedown; deeply blued metal surfaces; receiver top sandblasted to prevent glare; hammer block safety; rebounding hammer
**Barrel:** 24″ with Micro-Groove® rifling (16 grooves)
**Overall length:** 40″ **Weight:** 6¹/₂ lbs.
**Sights:** Adjustable folding semibuckhorn rear, ramp front sight with new Wide-Scan™ hood; solid top receiver tapped for scope mount or receiver sight; scope adapter base; offset hammer spur for scope use—works right or left
**Stock:** Two-piece cut-checkered American black walnut w/fluted comb; full pistol grip and forend; blued-steel forend cap; swivel studs; grip cap; white butt and pistol-grip spacers; Mar-Shield® finish; rubber buttpad

**MODEL 39TDS TAKEDOWN**
**$443.25 (Incl. Carrying Case)**

**SPECIFICATIONS**
**Caliber:** 22 Short, Long or Long Rifle
**Capacity:** Tubular mag. holds 16 Short, 12 Long or 11 LR cartridges
**Action:** Lever action; solid top receiver; side ejection; rebounding hammer; one-step take-down; deep blued metal surfaces; gold-plated trigger
**Barrel length:** 16¹/₂″ lightweight barrel (16 grooves)
**Overall length:** 32⁵/₈″
**Weight:** 5¹/₄ lbs.
**Safety** Hammer block safety
**Sights:** Adjustable semibuckhorn folding rear, ramp front with brass bead and Wide-Scan™ hood; top receiver tapped for scope mount and receiver sight; scope adapter base; offset hammer spur (right or left hand) for scope use
**Stock:** Two-piece cut-checkered straight-grip American black walnut w/scaled-down forearm and blued steel forend cap; Mar-Shield® finish

# MARLIN LEVER-ACTION CARBINES

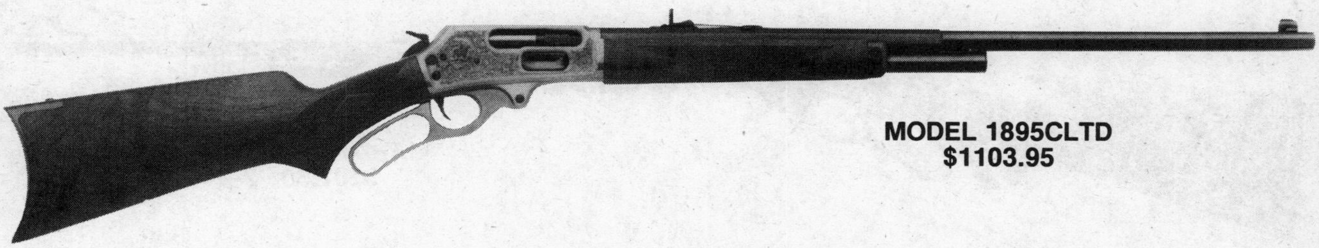

**MODEL 1895CLTD**
**$1103.95**

**SPECIFICATIONS**
**Caliber:** 45-70 Government
**Capacity:** 4-shot tubular magazine
**Action:** Lever; solid top receiver w/side ejection; receiver and lever engraved and finished in "French Gray"
**Barrel length:** 24″ half-round/half-octagon w/Micro-Groove® rifling (12 groove)
**Overall length:** 43″ **Weight:** 7½ lbs.
**Sights:** Marble semibuckhorn rear and blade front
**Stock:** Semi-fancy American black walnut w/cut-checkering; steel forend cap and inletted steel wraparound buttplate

**MARLIN 1894S**
**$454.80**

**SPECIFICATIONS**
**Calibers:** 44 Rem. Mag./44 Special, 45 Colt
**Capacity:** 10-shot tubular magazine
**Action:** Lever action w/square finger lever; hammer block safety
**Barrel length:** 20″ w/ Micro-Groove®
**Sights:** Ramp front sight w/brass bead; adjustable semibuckhorn folding rear and Wide-Scan™ hood; solid-top receiver tapped for scope mount or receiver sight
**Overall length:** 37½″
**Weight:** 6 lbs.
**Stock:** Checkered American black walnut stock w/Mar-Shield™ finish; blued steel forend cap; swivel studs

**MARLIN 1894CS 357 MAGNUM**
**$454.80**

**SPECIFICATIONS**
**Calibers:** 357 Magnum, 38 Special
**Capacity:** 9-shot tubular magazine
**Action:** Lever action w/square finger lever; hammer block safety; side ejection; solid top receiver; deeply blued metal surfaces; receiver top sandblasted to prevent glare
**Barrel length:** 18½″ with Micro-Groove® rifling (12 grooves)
**Sights:** Adjustable semibuckhorn folding rear, bead front; solid top receiver tapped for scope mount or receiver sight; offset hammer spur for scope use—adjustable for right or left hand
**Overall length:** 36″
**Weight:** 6 lbs.
**Stock:** Cut-checkered straight-grip two-piece American black walnut w/white buttplate spacer; Mar-Shield® finish; swivel studs

# MARLIN LEVER-ACTION CARBINES

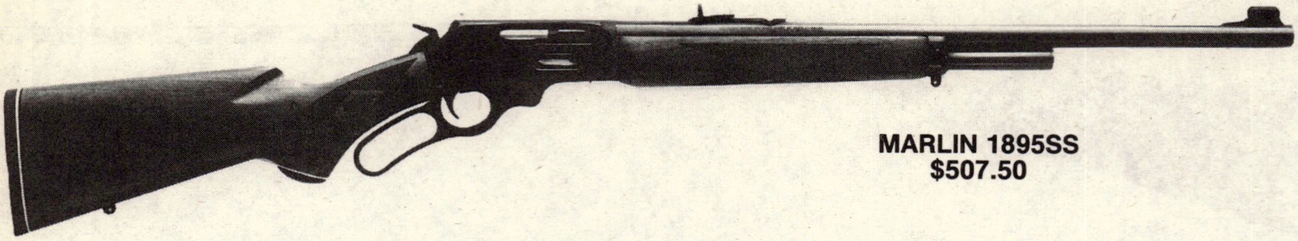

**MARLIN 1895SS**
**$507.50**

**SPECIFICATIONS**
**Caliber:** 45-70 Government
**Capacity:** 4-shot tubular magazine
**Action:** Lever action; hammer block safety; receiver top sandblasted to prevent glare
**Barrel:** 22″ Micro-Groove® barrel
**Sights:** Ramp front sight w/brass bead; adjustable semibuckhorn folding rear and Wide-Scan™ hood; receiver tapped for scope mount or receiver sight
**Overall length:** 40 1/2″
**Weight:** 7 1/2 lbs.
**Stock:** Checkered American black walnut pistol-grip stock w/rubber rifle buttpad and Mar-Shield® finish; white pistol grip, butt spacers; swivel studs

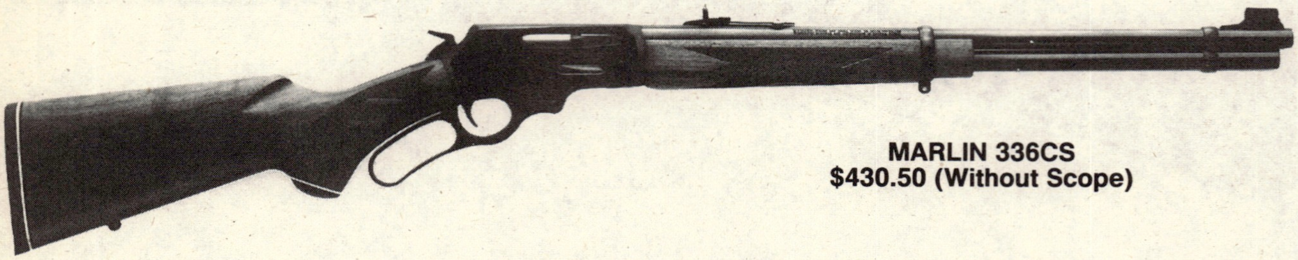

**MARLIN 336CS**
**$430.50 (Without Scope)**

**SPECIFICATIONS**
**Calibers:** 30-30 Win., and 35 Rem.
**Capacity:** 6-shot tubular magazine
**Action:** Lever action w/hammer block safety; deeply blued metal surfaces; receiver top sandblasted to prevent glare
**Barrel:** 20″ Micro-Groove® barrel
**Sights:** Adjustable folding semibuckhorn rear; ramp front sight w/brass bead and Wide-Scan™ hood; tapped for receiver sight and scope mount; offset hammer spur for scope use (works right or left)
**Overall length:** 38 1/2″
**Weight:** 7 lbs.
**Stock:** Checkered American black walnut pistol-grip stock w/fluted comb and Mar-Shield® finish; rubber rifle buttpad; swivel studs

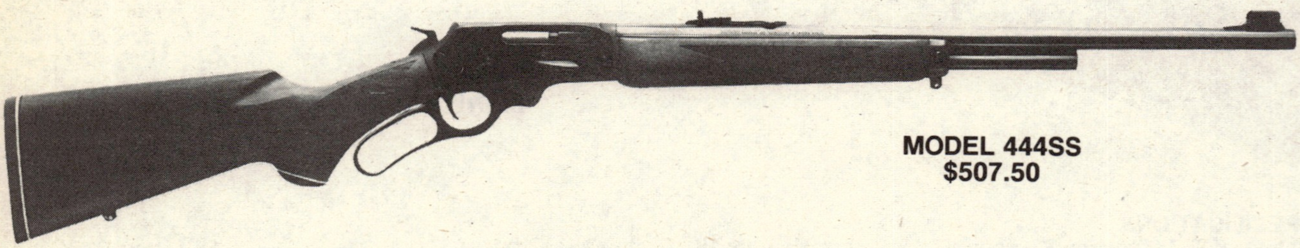

**MODEL 444SS**
**$507.50**

**SPECIFICATIONS**
**Caliber:** 444 Marlin
**Capacity:** 5-shot tubular magazine
**Barrel:** 22″ Micro-Groove®
**Overall length:** 40 1/2″
**Weight:** 7 1/2 lbs.
**Stock:** Checkered American black walnut pistol grip stock with rubber rifle buttpad; swivel studs
**Sights:** Ramp front sight with brass bead and Wide-Scan® hood; adjustable semibuckhorn folding rear; receiver tapped for scope mount or receiver sight

# McMILLAN SIGNATURE RIFLES

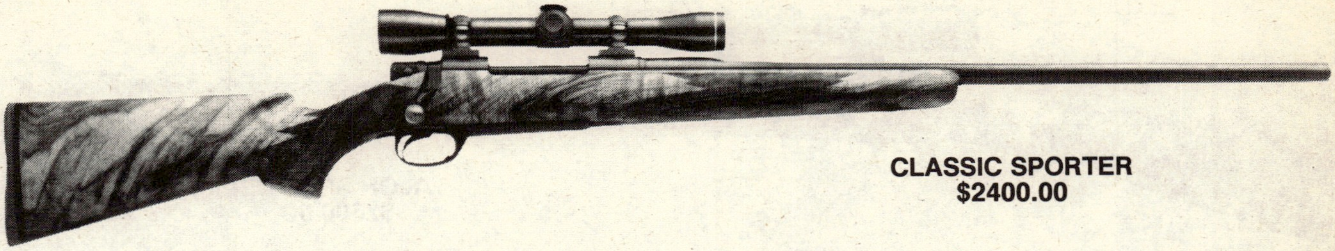

**CLASSIC SPORTER**
**$2400.00**

**SPECIFICATIONS**
**Calibers:**
**Model SA:** 22-250, 243, 6mm Rem., 6mm BR, 7mm BR, 7mm-08, 284, 308, 350 Rem. Mag.
**Model LA:** 25-06, 270, 280 Rem., 30-06
**Model MA:** 7mm STW, 7mm Rem. Mag., 300 Win. Mag., 300 Weatherby, 300 H&H, 338 Win. Mag., 340 Weatherby, 375 H&H, 416 Rem.

**Capacity:** 4 rounds; 3 rounds in magnum calibers
**Weight:** 7 lbs; 7 lbs. 9 oz. in long action
**Barrel lengths:** 22″, 24″, 26″
**Options:** Fibergrain; wooden stock, optics, 30mm rings, muzzle brakes, steel floor plates, iron sights

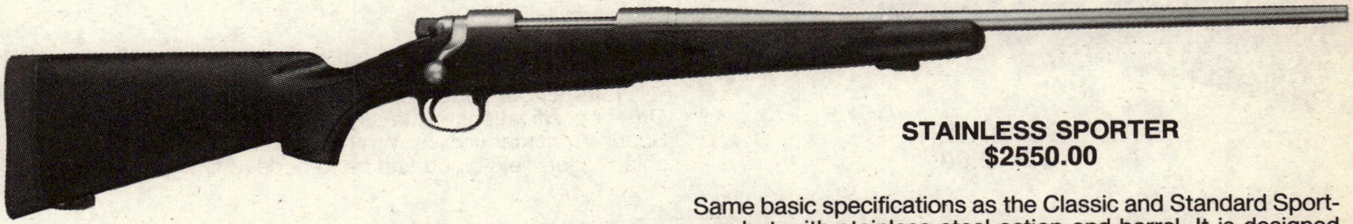

**STAINLESS SPORTER**
**$2550.00**

Same basic specifications as the Classic and Standard Sporters, but with stainless steel action and barrel. It is designed to withstand the most adverse weather conditions. Accuracy is guaranteed (3 shot in ½″ at 100 yards). Choice of wood, laminate or McMillan fiberglass stock.

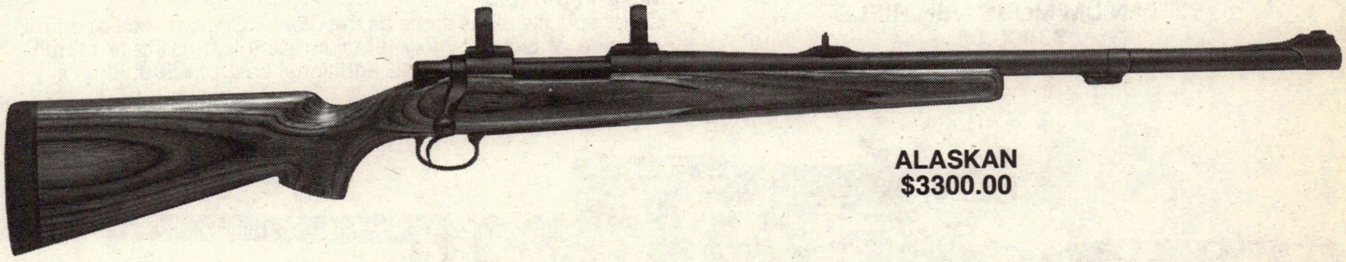

**ALASKAN**
**$3300.00**

**SPECIFICATIONS**
**Calibers:**
**Model LA:** 270, 280, 30-06
**Model MA:** 7mm Rem. Mag., 300 Win. Mag., 300 H&H, 300 Weatherby, 358 Win., 340 Weatherby, 375 H&H, 416 Rem.

Other specifications same as the Classic Sporter, except McMillan action is fitted to a match-grade barrel, complete with single-leaf rear sight, barrel band front sight, 1″ detachable rings and mounts, steel floorplate, electroless nickel finish. Monte Carlo stock features cheekpiece, palm swell and special recoil pad.
Also available: Stainless Steel Receiver, **add** ..... **$150.00**

# McMILLAN SIGNATURE RIFLES

**TALON SPORTER**
**$2600.00**

The all-new action of this model is designed and engineered specifically for the hunting of dangerous (African-type) game animals. Patterned after the renowned pre-64 Model 70, the Talon features a cone breech, controlled feed, claw extractor, positive ejection and three-position safety. Action is available in chromolybdenum and stainless steel. Drilled and tapped for scope mounting in long, short or magnum, left or right hand.

Same basic specifications as McMillan's Signature series, but offered in the following **calibers:**
**Standard Action:** 22-250, 243, 6mm Rem., 6mm BR, 7mm BR, 7mm-08, 284, 308, 350 Rem. Mag.
**Long Action:** 25-06, 270, 280 Rem., 30-06
**Magnum Action:** 7mm STW, 7mm Rem. Mag., 300 Win. Mag., 300 Weatherby, 300 H&H, 338 Win. Mag., 340 Weatherby, 375 H&H, 416 Rem.

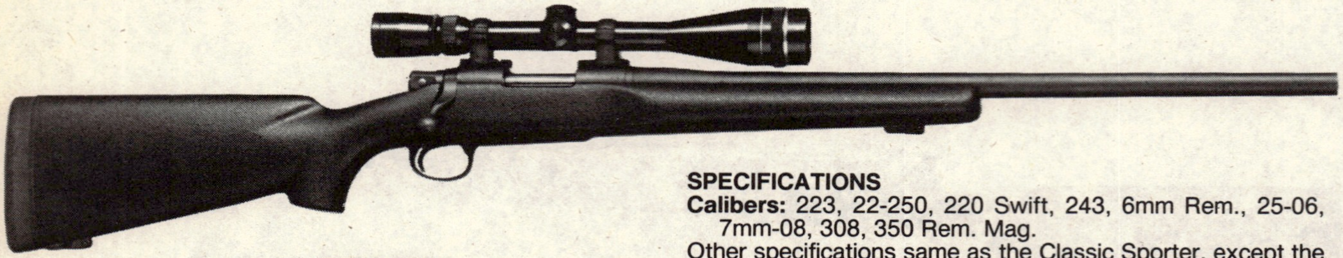

**VARMINTER**
**$2400.00**

**SPECIFICATIONS**
**Calibers:** 223, 22-250, 220 Swift, 243, 6mm Rem., 25-06, 7mm-08, 308, 350 Rem. Mag.
Other specifications same as the Classic Sporter, except the Super Varminter comes with heavy contoured barrel, adjustable trigger, field bipod and hand-bedded fiberglass stock.

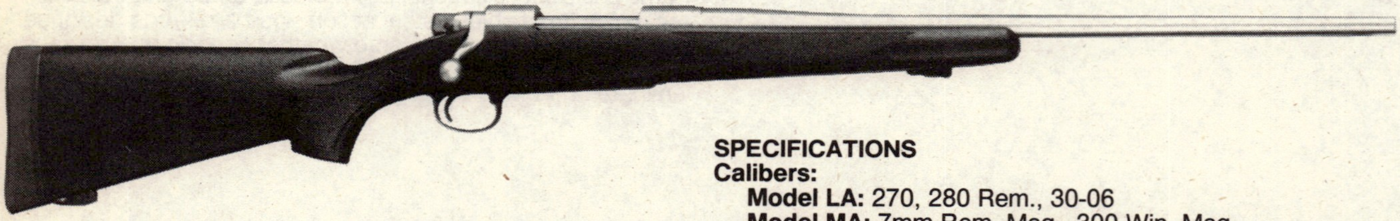

**TITANIUM MOUNTAIN RIFLE**
**$3000.00**
**$3600.00 w/Titanium Barrel**

**SPECIFICATIONS**
**Calibers:**
**Model LA:** 270, 280 Rem., 30-06
**Model MA:** 7mm Rem. Mag., 300 Win. Mag.
**Weight:** 5 1/2 lbs.
Other specifications same as the Classic Sporter, except barrel is made of chrome-moly (titanium alloy light contour match-grade barrel is available at additional cost of **$500.00**).

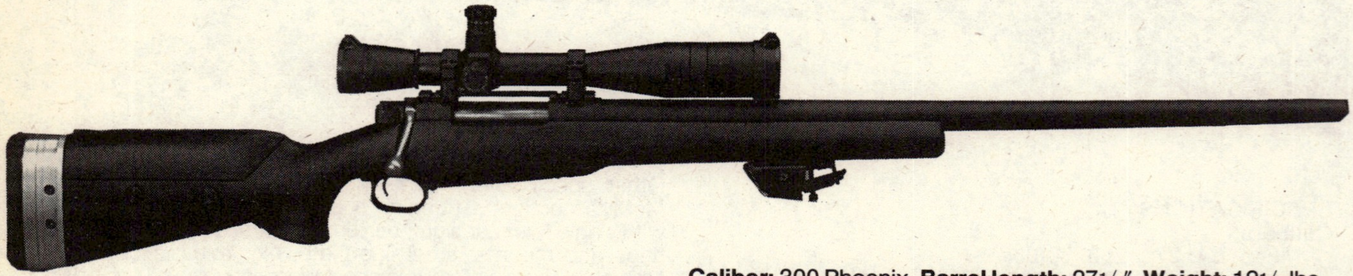

**.300 PHOENIX**
**$2995.00**

**Caliber:** 300 Phoenix. **Barrel length:** 27 1/2". **Weight:** 12 1/2 lbs. **Stock:** Fiberglass with adjustable cheekpiece. **Feature:** Available in left-hand action.

# McMILLAN SIGNATURE RIFLES

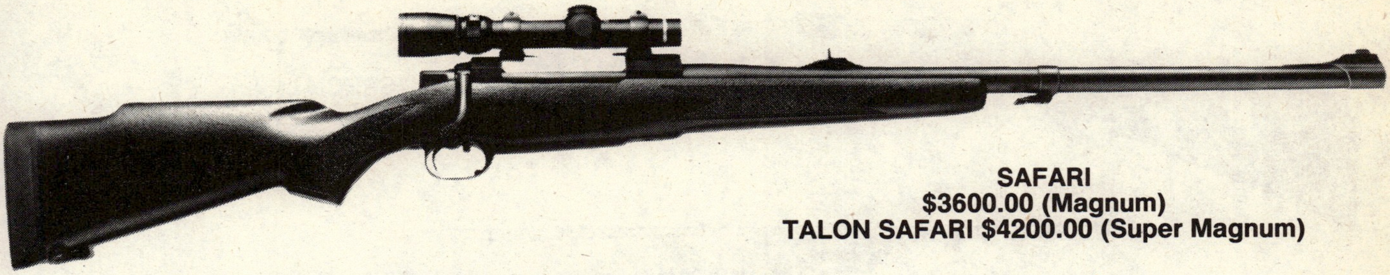

**SAFARI**
**$3600.00 (Magnum)**
**TALON SAFARI $4200.00 (Super Magnum)**

**SPECIFICATIONS**
**Calibers:**
**Magnum:** 300 Win. Mag., 300 Weatherby, 300 H&H, 338 Win. Mag., 340 Weatherby, 375 H&H, 404 Jeffrey, 416 Rem., 458 Win.
**Super Magnum:** 300 Phoenix, 338 Lapua, 378 Wby., 416 Rigby, 416 Wby., 460 Wby.

Other specifications same as the Classic Sporter, except for match-grade barrel, positive extraction McMillan Safari action, quick detachable 1″ scope mounts, positive locking steel floorplate, multi-leaf express sights, barrel band ramp front sight, barrel band swivels, and McMillan's Safari stock.



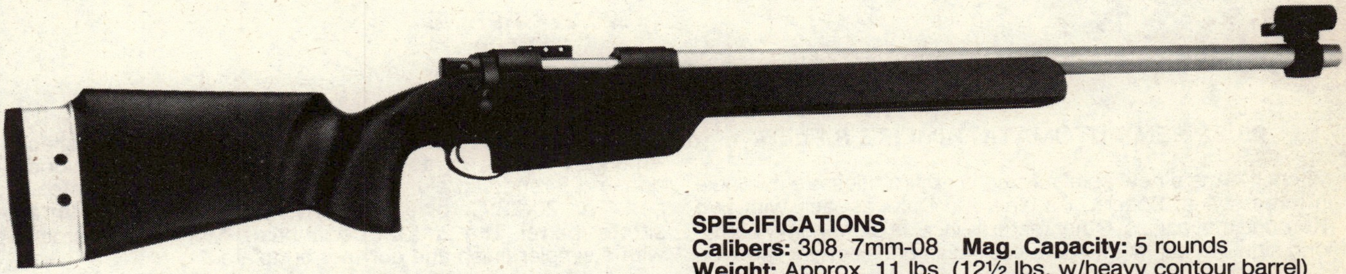

**NATIONAL MATCH RIFLE**
**$2600.00**

**SPECIFICATIONS**
**Calibers:** 308, 7mm-08 **Mag. Capacity:** 5 rounds
**Weight:** Approx. 11 lbs. (12½ lbs. w/heavy contour barrel)
Available for right-hand shooters only. Features modified ISU fiberglass stock with adjustable butt plate, stainless steel match barrel with barrel band and Tompkins front sight; McMillan repeating bolt action with clip shot and Canjar trigger. Barrel twist is 1:12″.

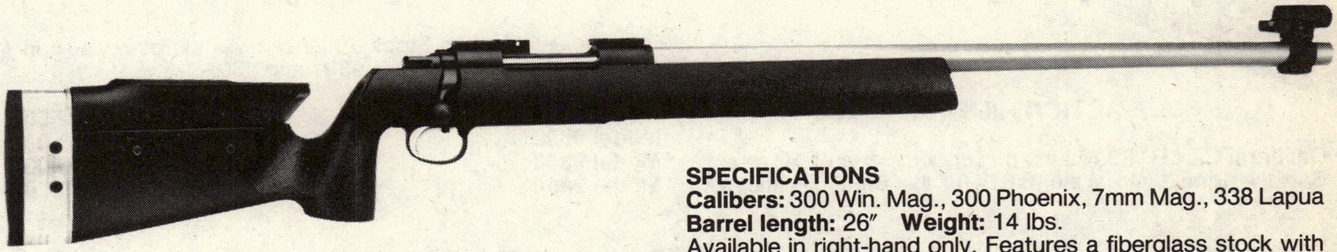

**LONG RANGE RIFLE**
**$2600.00**

**SPECIFICATIONS**
**Calibers:** 300 Win. Mag., 300 Phoenix, 7mm Mag., 338 Lapua
**Barrel length:** 26″ **Weight:** 14 lbs.
Available in right-hand only. Features a fiberglass stock with adjustable butt plate and cheekpiece. Stainless steel match barrel comes with barrel band and Tompkins front sight. McMillan solid bottom single-shot action and Canjar trigger. Barrel twist is 1:12″.

**McMILLAN BENCHREST RIFLE**
**$2800.00 (not shown)**

**SPECIFICATIONS**
**Calibers:** 6mm PPC, 243, 6mm BR, 6mm Rem., 308
Built to individual specifications to be competitive in hunter, light varmint and heavy varmint classes. Features solid bottom or repeating bolt action, Canjar trigger, fiberglass stock with recoil pad, stainless steel match-grade barrel and reloading dies. Right- or left-hand models.

# MITCHELL ARMS

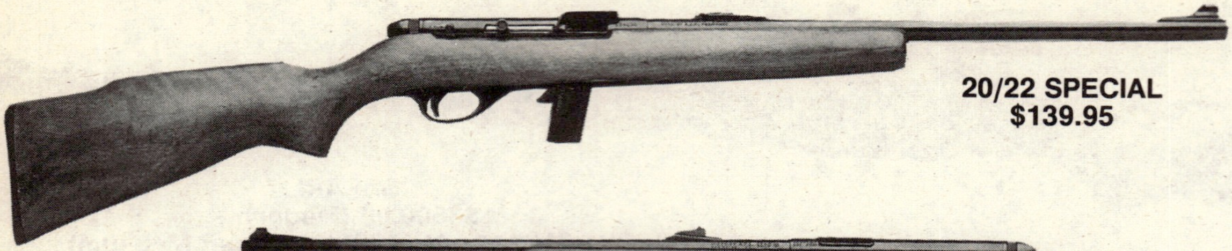

20/22 SPECIAL
$139.95

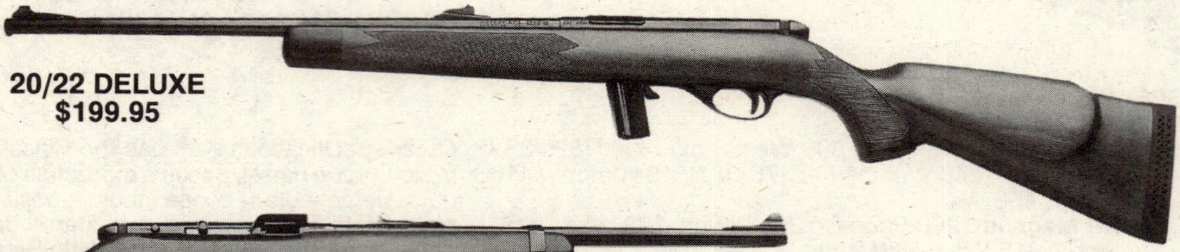

20/22 DELUXE
$199.95

20/22 CARBINE
$179.00

## 20/22 SEMIAUTOMATIC RIMFIRE RIFLES

Mitchell Arms's new semiautomatic rimfire rifles are available in three styles: Special, Carbine and Deluxe, each with two 10-round magazines. Other features include extra-heavy barrel, long sight radius, high-blue barrel finish and receiver grooved for scope mount. The Deluxe model sports a highly finished American walnut Monte Carlo stock, contrasting rosewood grip and forend cap plus fine-line checkering and thick recoil pad. The 20/22 Carbine is essentially the same rifle with a shorter barrel. The 20/22 Special has a Monte Carlo stock with a simpler finish and polymer buttplate.

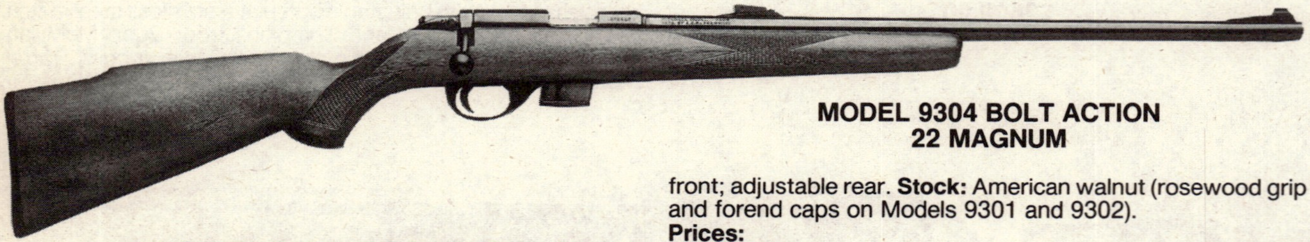

MODEL 9304 BOLT ACTION
22 MAGNUM

## BOLT-ACTION RIMFIRE RIFLES

**Calibers:** 22 LR, 22 Magnum. **Capacity:** 5 and 10 rounds. **Barrel length:** 22½". **Weight:** 6.5–6.7 lbs. **Sights:** Ramp bead front; adjustable rear. **Stock:** American walnut (rosewood grip and forend caps on Models 9301 and 9302).

**Prices:**

| | |
|---|---|
| **Model 9301** | **$312.50** |
| **Model 9302** | **325.00** |
| **Model 9303** | **275.00** |
| **Model 9304** | **289.00** |

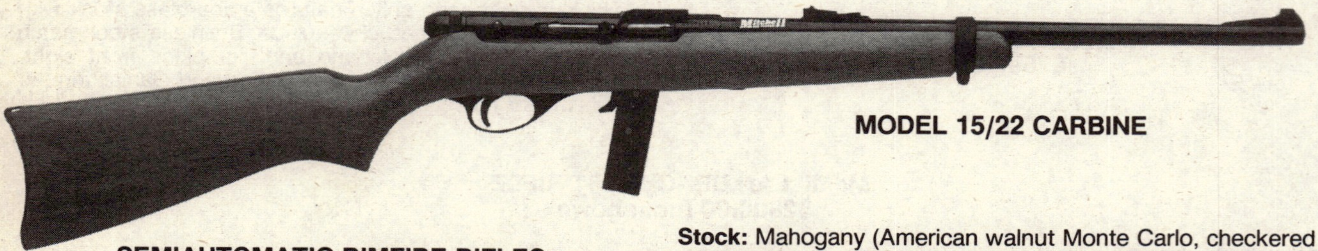

MODEL 15/22 CARBINE

## SEMIAUTOMATIC RIMFIRE RIFLES

**Caliber:** 22 LR. **Capacity:** 15 and 30 rounds. **Barrel length:** 20½". **Weight:** 6.4 lbs. **Sights:** Ramp front; adjustable rear. **Stock:** Mahogany (American walnut Monte Carlo, checkered rosewood grip and forend cap on Model 15/22D).

| | |
|---|---|
| **Prices:** | **$159.95** |
| **Model 15/22D** | **199.95** |
| **Model 15/22 SP** w/plastic buttplate | **139.95** |

# NAVY ARMS REPLICA RIFLES



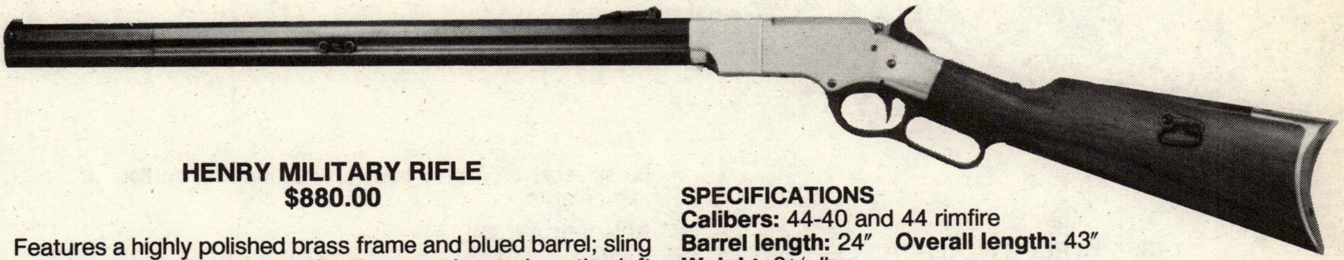

**HENRY MILITARY RIFLE**
**$880.00**

Features a highly polished brass frame and blued barrel; sling swivels to the original specifications are located on the left side.

**SPECIFICATIONS**
**Calibers:** 44-40 and 44 rimfire
**Barrel length:** 24″ **Overall length:** 43″
**Weight:** 9¼ lbs.
**Stock:** Walnut

Same specifications as the Henry Rifle, except with iron frame. Available with blued or casehardened receiver.

**IRON FRAME HENRY**
**$895.00**

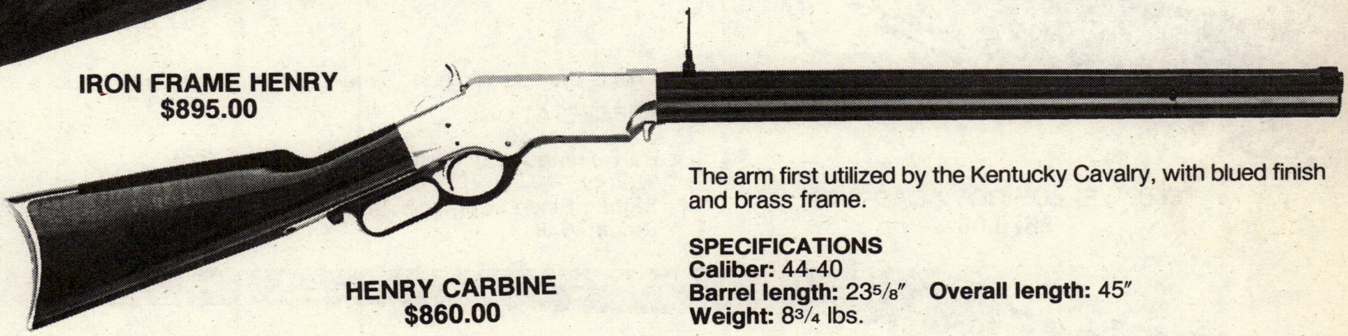

**HENRY CARBINE**
**$860.00**

The arm first utilized by the Kentucky Cavalry, with blued finish and brass frame.

**SPECIFICATIONS**
**Caliber:** 44-40
**Barrel length:** 23⅝″ **Overall length:** 45″
**Weight:** 8¾ lbs.

This short, lightweight lever-action arm is ideal for the hunter.

**SPECIFICATIONS**
**Caliber:** 44-40
**Barrel length:** 16½″ **Overall length:** 34½″
**Weight:** 7¼ lbs.

**HENRY TRAPPER MODEL**
**$860.00**

**1874 SHARPS SNIPER RIFLE**
**$1055.00**

A replica of the 1874 three-band sharpshooter's rifle.

**Caliber:** .45–70
**Barrel length:** 30″ **Overall length:** 46¾″
**Weight:** 8 lbs. 8 oz. **Stock:** Walnut
**Features:** Double-set triggers; casehardened receiver; patchbox and furniture
Also available:
**Single Trigger Infantry Model** . . . . . . . . . . . . . . . . . **$990.00**

# NAVY ARMS REPLICA RIFLES

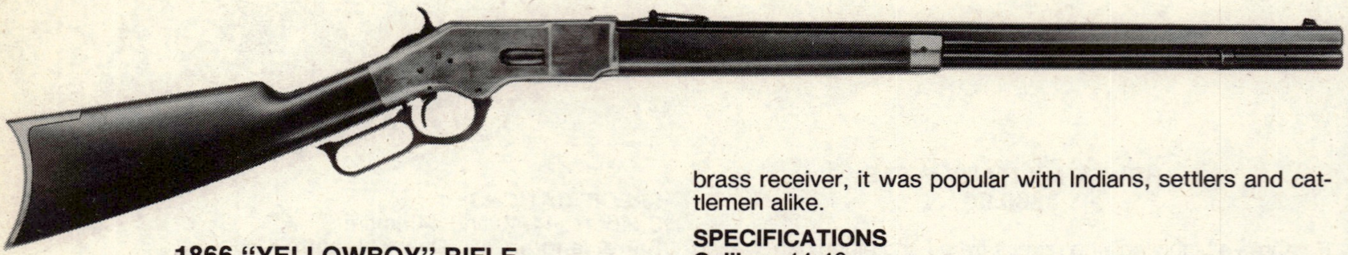

**1866 "YELLOWBOY" RIFLE**
**$675.00**

The 1866 model was Oliver Winchester's improved version of the Henry rifle. Called the "Yellowboy" because of its polished brass receiver, it was popular with Indians, settlers and cattlemen alike.

**SPECIFICATIONS**
**Caliber:** 44-40
**Barrel length:** 24″ full octagon **Overall length:** 42½″
**Weight:** 8½ lbs.
**Sights:** Blade front; open ladder rear
**Stock:** Walnut

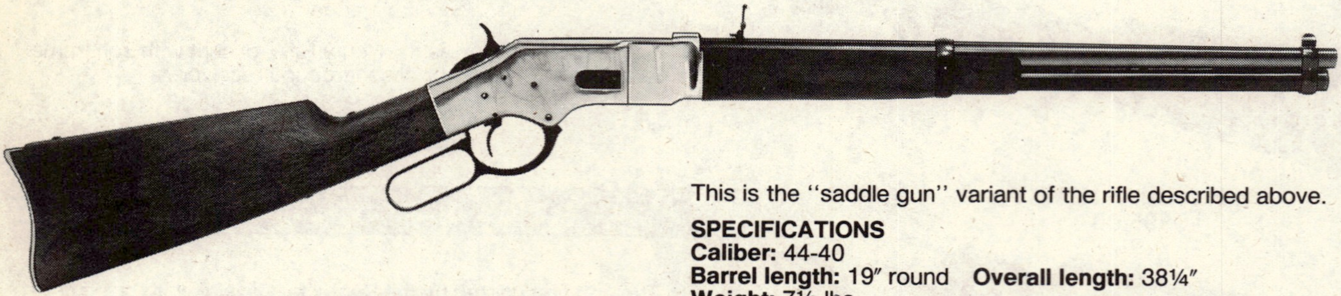

**1866 "YELLOWBOY" CARBINE**
**$670.00**

This is the "saddle gun" variant of the rifle described above.

**SPECIFICATIONS**
**Caliber:** 44-40
**Barrel length:** 19″ round **Overall length:** 38¼″
**Weight:** 7¼ lbs.
**Sights:** Blade front; open ladder rear
**Stock:** Walnut

**1873 WINCHESTER SPORTING RIFLE**
**$900.00**

This replica of the state-of-the-art Winchester 1873 Sporting Rifle features a checkered pistol grip, buttstock, casehardened receiver and blued octagonal barrel.

**SPECIFICATIONS**
**Caliber:** 44-40 or 45 LC
**Barrel length:** 24″ or 30″
**Overall length:** 48¾″ (w/30″ barrel)
**Weight:** 8 lbs. 14 oz.
**Sights:** Blade front; buckhorn rear

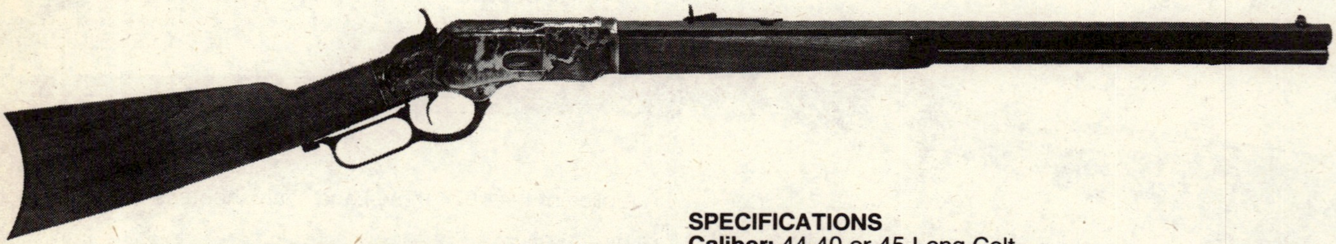

**1873 WINCHESTER-STYLE RIFLE**
**$790.00**

Known as "The Gun That Won the West," the 1873 was the most popular lever-action rifle of its time. This fine replica features a casehardened receiver.

**SPECIFICATIONS**
**Caliber:** 44-40 or 45 Long Colt
**Barrel length:** 24″ **Overall length:** 43″
**Weight:** 8¼ lbs.
**Sights:** Blade front; open ladder rear
**Stock:** Walnut
Also available: **1873 WINCHESTER-STYLE CARBINE**
(19″ barrel) . . . . . . . . . . . . . . . . . . . . . . . . . . . . . **$820.00**

# NAVY ARMS REPLICA RIFLES

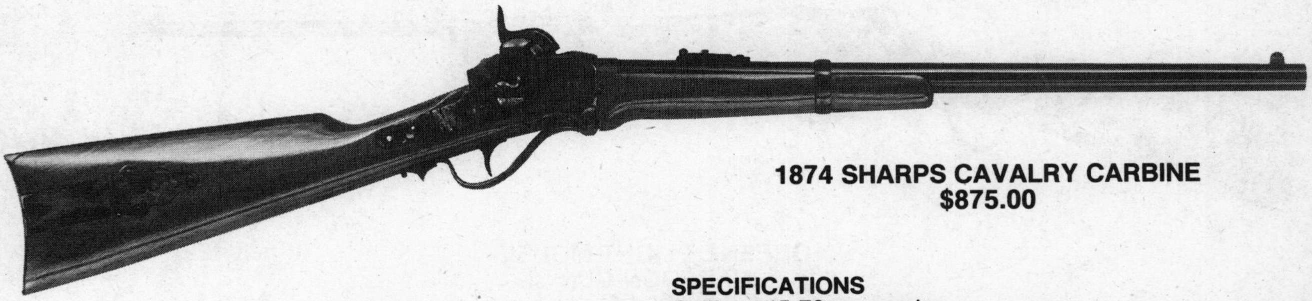

**1874 SHARPS CAVALRY CARBINE**
**$875.00**

This cavalry carbine version of the Sharps rifle features a side bar and saddle ring.

**SPECIFICATIONS**
**Caliber:** 45-70 percussion
**Barrel length:** 22″ **Overall length:** 39″
**Weight:** 7¾ lbs.
**Sights:** Blade front; military ladder rear
**Stock:** Walnut



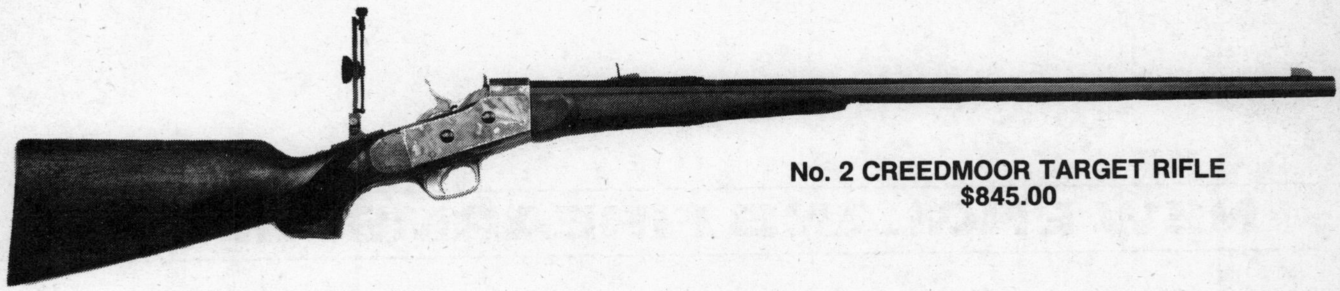

**No. 2 CREEDMOOR TARGET RIFLE**
**$845.00**

This reproduction of the Remington No. 2 Creedmoor Rifle features a color casehardened receiver and steel trigger guard, tapered octagon barrel, and walnut forend and buttstock with checkered pistol grip.

**SPECIFICATIONS**
**Caliber:** 45-70
**Barrel length:** 30″, tapered **Overall length:** 46″
**Weight:** 9 lbs.
**Sights:** Globe front, adjustable Creedmoor rear
**Stock:** Checkered walnut stock and forend

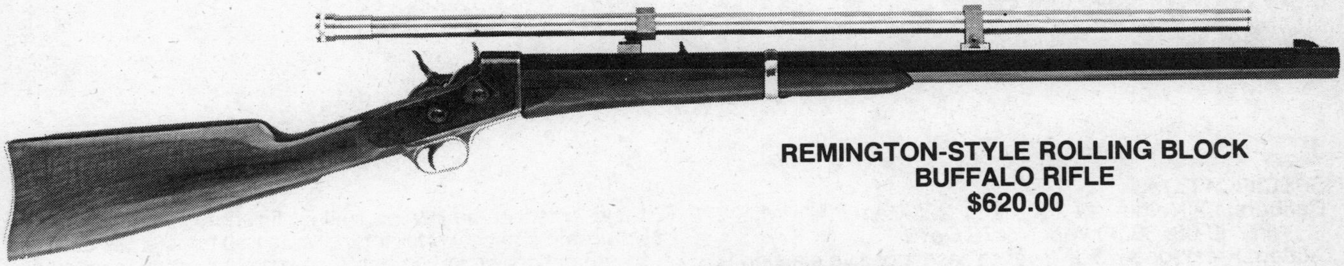

**REMINGTON-STYLE ROLLING BLOCK**
**BUFFALO RIFLE**
**$620.00**

This replica of the rifle used by buffalo hunters and plainsmen of the 1800s features a casehardened receiver, solid brass trigger guard and walnut stock and forend. The tang is drilled and tapped to accept the optional Creedmoor sight.

**SPECIFICATIONS**
**Caliber:** 45-70
**Barrel length:** 26″ or 30″; full octagon or half-round
**Sights:** Blade front, open notch rear
**Stock:** Walnut stock and forend
**Feature:** Shown with optional 32½″ Model 1860 brass telescopic sight **$210.00**; Compact Model (18″) is **$200.00**

# NAVY ARMS RIFLES

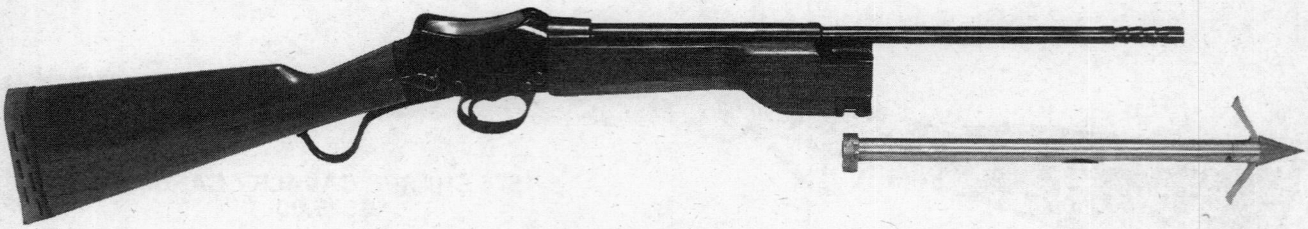

GREENER LIGHT MODEL
HARPOON GUN
**$995.00**

Designed for large game fish, the Greener Harpoon gun utilizes the time-proven Martini action. The complete outfit consists of gun, harpoons, harpoon lines, line release frames, blank cartridges and cleaning kit—all housed in a carrying case.

**SPECIFICATIONS**
**Caliber:** 38 Special (blank)
**Barrel length:** 20″ **Overall length:** 36″
**Weight:** 6 lbs. 5 oz. **Stock:** Walnut

# NEW ENGLAND FIREARMS RIFLES

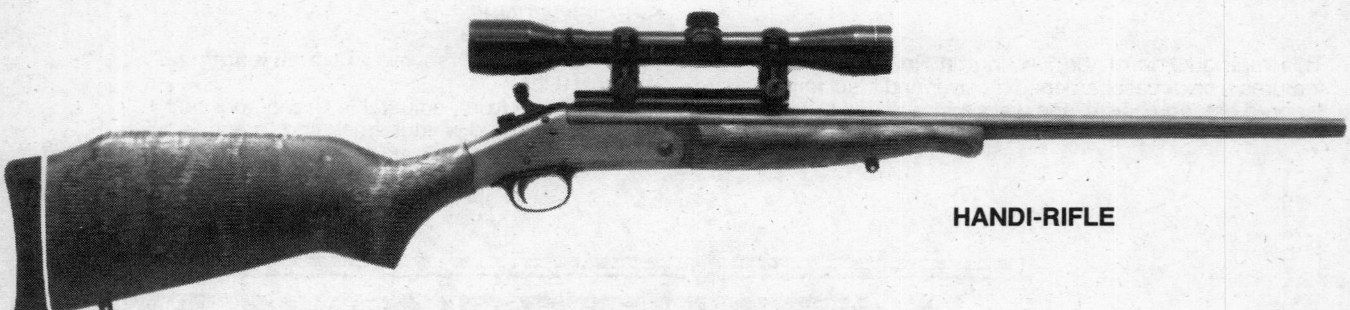

HANDI-RIFLE

**SPECIFICATIONS**
**Calibers:** 22 Hornet, 22-250 Rem., 223 Rem., 243 Win., 270 Win., 30-06, 30-30 Win., 45-70 Govt.
**Action:** Break-open; side lever release; positive ejection
**Barrel length:** 22″
**Weight:** 7 lbs.
**Sights:** Ramp front; fully adjustable rear; tapped for scope mounts (22 Hornet, 30-30 Win. and 45-70 Govt. only)
**Length of pull:** 14 1/4″
**Drop at comb:** 1 1/2″ (1 1/4″ in Monte Carlo)
**Drop at heel:** 2 1/8″ (1 1/8″ in Monte Carlo)
**Stock:** American hardwood, walnut finish; full pistol grip
**Features:** Semi-beavertail forend; patented transfer bar safety; automatic ejection; rebated muzzle; hammer extension; sling swivel studs on stock and forend

**Prices:**
In 223 Rem., blue . . . . . . . . . . **$199.95**
In 223 Rem., Bull, blued . . . . . . . . . . **204.95**
In 22-250 Rem., 22 Hornet, 243 Win., 270 Win. 30-06, 30-30 Win., 45-70 Govt. . . . . . . . . . . **204.95**

# PEDERSOLI REPLICA RIFLES



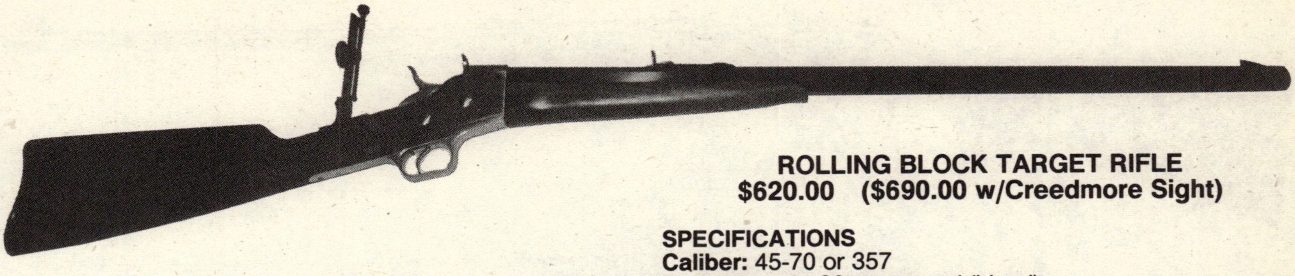

**ROLLING BLOCK TARGET RIFLE**
**$620.00 ($690.00 w/Creedmore Sight)**

**SPECIFICATIONS**
**Caliber:** 45-70 or 357
**Barrel length:** 30″ octagonal (blued)
**Weight:** 9 1/2 lbs. (45-70); 10 lbs. (357)
**Sights:** Adjustable rear sight; tunnel modified front (all models designed for fitting of Creedmore sight)

Also available:
**Cavalry, Infantry, Long Range Creedmoor** . . . . . . **$550.00**

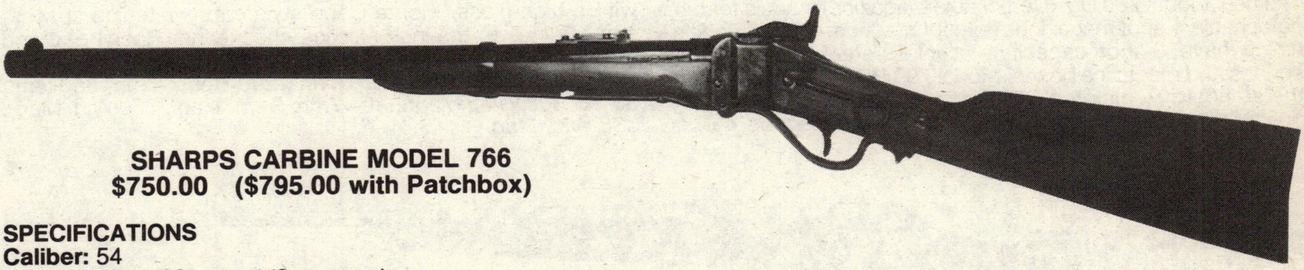

**SHARPS CARBINE MODEL 766**
**$750.00 ($795.00 with Patchbox)**

**SPECIFICATIONS**
**Caliber:** 54
**Barrel length:** 22″ round (6 grooves)
**Overall length:** 39″
**Weight:** 7 1/2 lbs.
**Sights:** Fully adjustable rear; fixed front

Also available:
**Sharps 1859 Military Rifle** (set trigger, 30″ barrel, 8.4 lbs.).
**Price:** . . . . . . . . . . . . . . . . . . . . . . . . . . . . . . . . . . **$895.00**

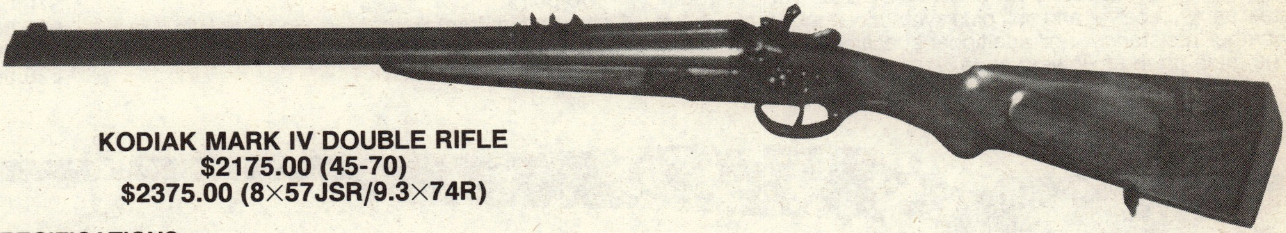

**KODIAK MARK IV DOUBLE RIFLE**
**$2175.00 (45-70)**
**$2375.00 (8×57JSR/9.3×74R)**

**SPECIFICATIONS**
**Calibers:** 45-70, 9.3×74R, 8×57JSR
**Barrel length:** 22″ (24″ 45-70)
**Overall length:** 39″ (40 1/2″ 45-70)
**Weight:** 8.24 lbs. (9.7 lbs. 45/70)

Also available:
**Kodiak Mark IV** w/interchangeable 20-ga. barrel . **$4100.00**
In 8×57JSR or 9.3×74R . . . . . . . . . . . . . . . . . . **4325.00**

# REMINGTON BOLT-ACTION RIFLES

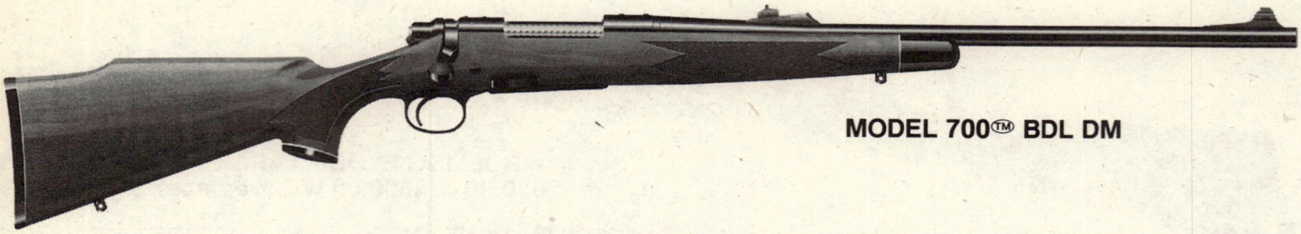

**MODEL 700™ BDL DM**

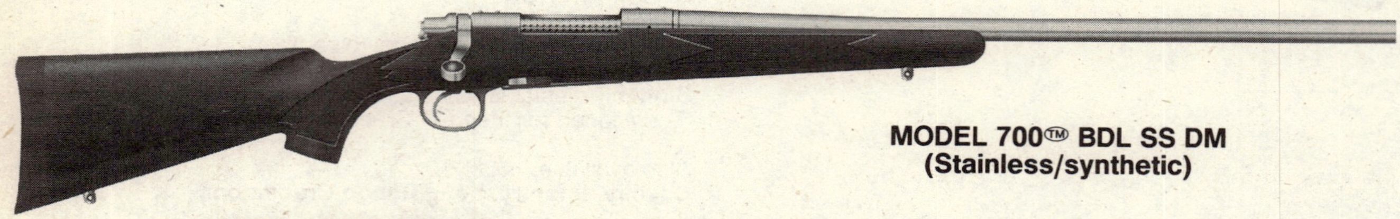

**MODEL 700™ BDL SS DM (Stainless/synthetic)**

## MODEL 700™ BDL DM
## $603.00 ($629.00 Magnum)

The new Model 700 DM (Detachable Magazine) models feature detachable 4-shot magazines (except magnum-caliber models, which have 3-shot capacity), stainless-steel latches, latch springs and magazine boxes. Model 700 BDL DM rifles feature the standard Remington BDL barrel contour with 22″ barrels on standard caliber models and 24″ barrels on magnum caliber rifles. All barrels feature a hooded front sight and adjustable rear sight. Polished blued-metal finish is used throughout, along with a high-gloss, Monte Carlo-style cap, white line spacers and 20 lines-to-the-inch skipline checkering. Recoil pad and swivel studs are included. **Calibers:** Standard—6mm Rem., 25-06 Rem., 243 Win., 270 Win., 280 Rem., 7mm-08 Rem., 30-06, 308 Win.; Magnum—7mm Rem. Mag., 300 Win. Mag., 338 Win. Mag.

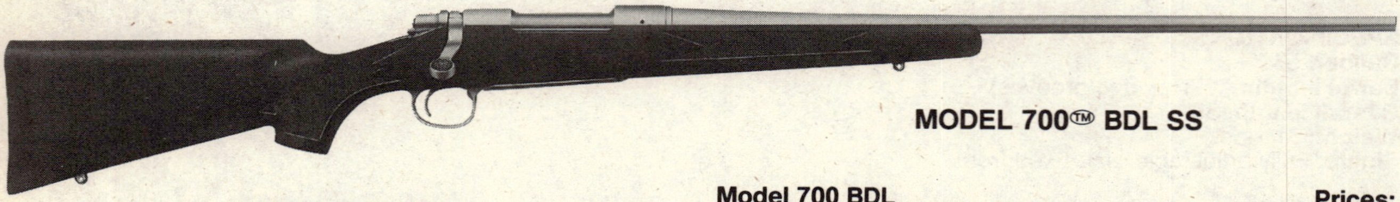

**MODEL 700™ BDL SS**

## MODEL 700™ BDL

This Model 700 features the Monte Carlo American walnut stock finished to a high gloss with fine-cut skipline checkering. Also includes a hinged floorplate, sling swivels studs, hooded ramp front sight and adjustable rear sight. Also available in stainless synthetic version (Model 700 BDL SS) with stainless-steel barrel, receiver and bolt plus synthetic stock for maximum weather resistance. For additional specifications, see Model 700 table on the following page.

| **Model 700 BDL** | **Prices:** |
|---|---|
| In 17 Rem., 7mm Rem. Mag., 300 Win. Mag., 338 Win. Mag. | **$576.00** |
| In 222 Rem., 22-250 Rem., 223 Rem., 243 Win., 25-06 Rem., 270 Win., 280 Rem., 30-06, 308 Win. | **549.00** |
| Left Hand in 22-250 Rem., 243 Win., 270 Win., 30-06 | **576.00** |
| Left Hand in 7mm Rem. Mag. and 338 Win. Mag. | **603.00** |
| **Model BDL SS (Stainless Synthetic)** | **603.00** |
| In Magnum calibers | **629.00** |

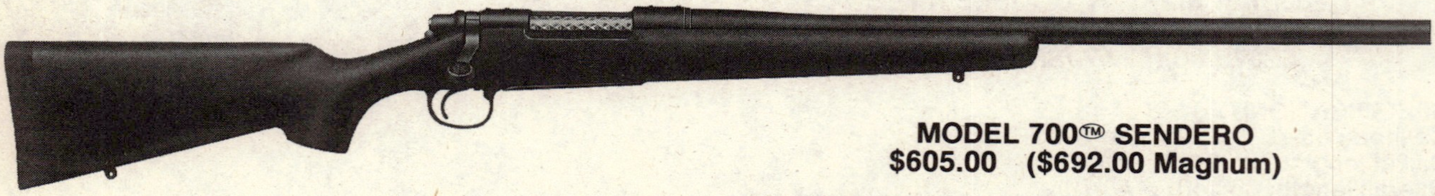

**MODEL 700™ "SENDERO SPECIAL"**

## MODEL 700™ SENDERO
## $605.00 ($692.00 Magnum)

Remington's Sendero rifle combines the accuracy features of the Model 700 Varmint Special with long action and magnum calibers for long-range hunting. The 26″ barrel has a heavy varmint profile and features a spherical concave crown. For additional specifications, see table on the following page.

# REMINGTON BOLT-ACTION RIFLES

**MODEL 700 BDL VARMINT LAMINATED STOCK**

## MODEL 700™ VS VARMINT SYNTHETIC BOLT-ACTION CENTERFIRE RIFLE

With heavy barrel, synthetic stock and aluminum bedding block ........................ **$665.00**
With stainless fluted barrel and synthetic stock in 220 Swift, 22-250 Rem. 223 Rem., 308 Win. . . **798.00**

Also available:
**MODEL 700 BDL VARMINT LAMINATED STOCK (VLS)** in 222 Rem., 22-250 Rem., 223 Rem., 243 Win. and 308 Win. ........................................ **$585.00**



## SPECIFICATIONS MODEL 700

| | | | Overall Length/Avg. Wt. (lbs.) | | | | | | | | | Twist |
|---|---|---|---|---|---|---|---|---|---|---|---|---|
| | | | | | | | | | | Varmint Synthetic[1] | | R-H, 1 |
| Calibers | Magazine Capacity | Barrel Length | Mtn Rifle (DM) | Sendero™ [1] (26" Barrel) | BDL Stainless Synthetic (DM) | BDL Stainless Synthetic | ADL & BDL | BDL (DM) | VLS (Varmint Laminated Stock)[1] | (26" Heavy BBL) | (26" Stainless Fluted BBL) | turn in |
| 17 Remington | 5 | 24" | — | — | — | — | 43 ⅝"/7 ¼ | — | — | — | — | 9" |
| 220 Swift | 4 | 26" | — | — | — | — | — | — | — | 45 ¾"/9 | 45 ¾"/8 ½ | 14" |
| 222 Remington | 5 | 24" | — | — | — | — | 43 ⅝"/7 ¼ | — | 45 ½"/9 ⅜ | — | — | 14" |
| 22-250 Remington | 4 | 24" | — | — | — | — | 43 ⅝"/7 ¼ | — | 45 ½"/9 ⅜ | 45 ¾"/9 | 45 ¾"/8 ½ | 14" |
| | 4 | 24" | — | — | — | — | 43 ⅝"/7 ¼ | — | — | — | — | 14" |
| 223 Remington | 5 | 24" | — | — | — | — | 43 ⅝"/7 ¼ | — | 45 ½"/9 ⅜ | 45 ¾"/9 | 45 ¾"/8 ½ | 12" |
| 6mm Remington | 4 | 22" | — | — | — | — | — | 41 ¾"/7 ¼ | — | — | — | 9 ⅛" |
| | 4 | 24" | — | — | 43 ½"/7 | — | — | — | — | — | — | 9 ⅛" |
| 243 Win. | 4 | 22" | 41 ¾"/6 ⅜ | — | — | — | 41 ⅝"/7 ¼ | 41 ¾"/7 ¼ | — | — | — | 9 ⅛" |
| | 4 | 22" | — | — | — | — | 41 ⅝"/7 ¼ | 41 ¾"/7 ¼ | — | — | — | 9 ⅛" |
| | 4 | 24" | — | — | 43 ½"/7 | — | — | — | 45 ½"/9 ⅜ | — | — | 9 ⅛" |
| 25-06 Remington | 4 | 24" | — | 45 ¾"/9 | 44 ½"/7 ⅜ | — | 44 ½"/7 ¼ | 44½"/7 ⅜ | — | — | — | 10" |
| | 4 | 22" | 42 ½"/6 ⅜ | — | — | — | — | — | — | — | — | 10" |
| 270 Win. | 4 | 22" | 42 ½"/6 ⅜ | — | — | — | 42 ½"/7 ¼ | 42 ½"/7 ⅜ | — | — | — | 10" |
| | 4 | 22" | — | — | — | — | 42 ½"/7 ¼ | 42 ½"/7 ⅜ | — | — | — | 10" |
| | 4 | 24" | — | 45 ¾"/9 | 44 ½"/7 ⅜ | 44 ½"/7 ¼ | — | — | — | — | — | 10" |
| 280 Remington | 4 | 22" | 42 ½"/6 ⅜ | — | — | — | 42 ½"/7 ¼ | 42 ½"/7 ⅜ | — | — | — | 9 ¼" |
| | 4 | 24" | — | — | 44 ½"/7 ⅜ | 44 ½"/7 ¼ | — | — | — | — | — | 9 ¼" |
| 7mm-08 Remington | 4 | 22" | 41 ¾"/6 ⅜ | — | — | — | — | 41 ¾"/7 ¼ | — | — | — | 9 ¼" |
| | 4 | 22" | — | — | — | — | — | 41 ¾"/7 42 ½"/7 ⅜ | — | — | — | 9 ¼" |
| | 4 | 24" | — | — | 43 ½"/7 | — | — | — | — | — | — | 9 ¼" |
| 7mm Rem. Mag. | 3 | 24" | — | 45 ¾"/9 | 44 ½"/7 ½ | 44 ½"/7 ½ | 44 ½"/7 ½ | 44 ½"/7 ¾ | — | — | — | 9 ¼" |
| | 3 | 24" | — | — | — | — | 44 ½"/7 ½ | 44 ½"/7 ¾ | — | — | — | 9 ¼" |
| 30-06 | 4 | 22" | 42 ½"/6 ⅜ | — | — | — | 42 ½"/7 ¼ | 42 ½"/7 ⅜ | — | — | — | 10" |
| | 4 | 22" | — | — | — | — | 42 ½"/7 ¼ | 42 ½"/7 ¼ | — | — | — | 10" |
| | 4 | 24" | — | — | 44 ½"/7 ⅜ | 44 ½"/7 ¼ | — | — | — | — | — | 10" |
| 308 Win. | 4 | 22" | — | — | — | — | 41 ⅝"/7 ¼ | 41 ¾"/7 ¼ | — | — | — | 10" |
| | 4 | 24" | — | — | 43½"/7 | — | — | — | 45 ½"/9 ⅜ | 45 ¾"/9 | 45 ¾"/8 ½ | 12" |
| | 4 | 22" | — | — | — | — | 41 ⅝"/7 ¼ | — | — | — | — | 10" |
| 300 Win. Mag. | 3 | 24" | — | 45 ¾"/9 | 44½"/7 ½ | 44 ½"/7 ½ | 44 ½"/7 ½ | 44½"/7 ¾ | — | — | — | 10" |
| | 3 | 24" | — | — | — | — | — | 44½"/7 ¾ | — | — | — | 10" |
| 300 Wby. Mag. | 3 | 24" | — | — | 44½"/7 ½ | — | — | — | — | — | — | 12" |
| 338 Win. Mag. | 3 | 24" | — | — | 44½"/7 ½ | — | — | — | — | — | — | 10" |
| | 3 | 24" | — | — | — | — | — | 44½"/7 ¾ | — | — | — | 10" |
| Stock Dimensions: Length of Pull | | | 13 ⅜" | 13 ⅜" | 13 ⅜" | 13⅜" | 13 ⅜" | 13 ⅜" | 13 ½" | 13 ⅜" | 13 ⅜" | |
| Drop at Comb (from centerline of bore) | | | ⅜" | ⅝" | ½" | ½" | ½" | ½" | 15/16" | ⅝" | ⅝" | |
| Drop at Heel (from centerline of bore) | | | ⅜" | ⅝" | ⅜" | ⅜" | 1 ⅜" | 1 ⅜" | 13/16" | ⅝" | ⅝" | |

[1]Sendero™, Varmint Laminated Synthetic, Varmint Synthetic Stainless Fluted and Varmint Synthetic equipped with a 26" barrel only. LH = Left Hand. All Model 700™ and Model Seven™ rifles come with sling swivel studs. The BDL, ADL, and Seven™ (except Seven™ chambered for 17 Remington) are furnished with sights. The BDL Stainless Synthetic, Mountain Rifle, Classic, and Varmint guns have clean barrels. All Remington centerfire rifles are drilled and tapped for scope mounts.

# REMINGTON BOLT-ACTION RIFLES

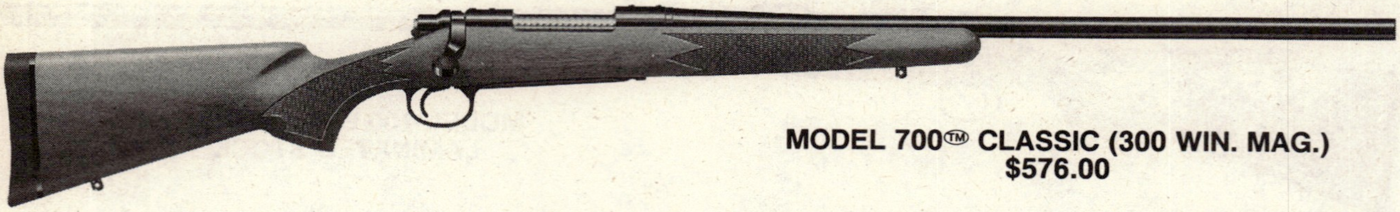

## MODEL 700™ CLASSIC (300 WIN. MAG.)
## $576.00

Since Remington's series of Model 700 Classics began in 1981, the company has offered this model in a special chambering each year. The 300 Win. Mag. was introduced in 1963 for the Model 70 bolt-action rifle following the development of the 338 Win. Mag., 30-338 Wildcat and 308 Norma Mag. The 300 Win. Mag. has a slightly longer body and a shorter neck than its predecessors and is recommended for all North American big-game hunting. The Model 700 Classic features an American walnut, straight-comb stock without a cheekpiece for rapid mounting, better sight alignment and reduced felt recoil. A hinged magazine floorplate, sling swivel studs and satin wood finish with cut-checkering are standard, along with 24″ barrel and 1:10″ twist. Receivers drilled/tapped for scope mounts.

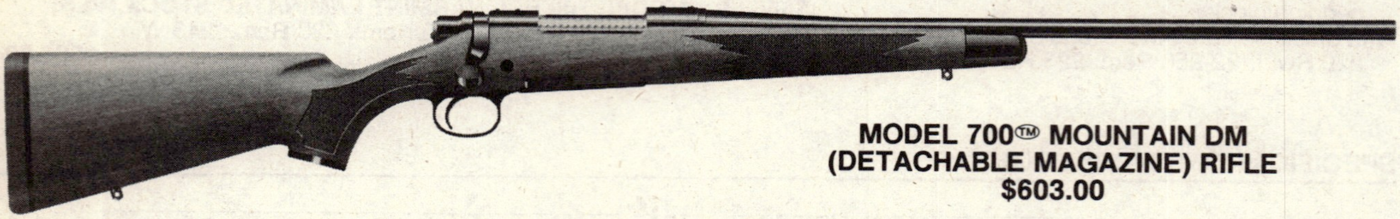

## MODEL 700™ MOUNTAIN DM (DETACHABLE MAGAZINE) RIFLE
## $603.00

The new Remington Model 700 MTN DM rifle features the traditional mountain rifle-styled stock with a pistol grip pitched lower to position the wrist for a better grip. The cheekpiece is designed to align the eye for quick, accurate sighting. The American walnut stock has a hand-rubbed oil finish and comes with a brown recoil pad and deep-cut checkering. The Model 700 MTN DM also features a lean contoured 22″ barrel that helps reduce total weight to 6.75 pounds. (no sights). All metalwork features a glass bead-blasted, blued-metal finish. **Calibers:** 243 Win., 25-06 Rem., 270 Win., 7mm-08 Rem., 280 Rem and 30-06 Springfield.

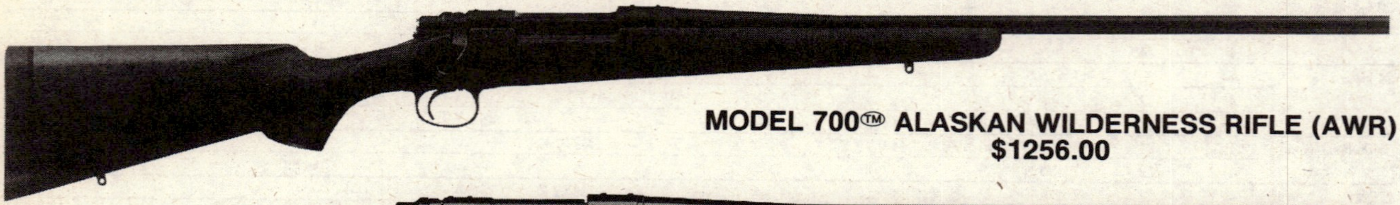

## MODEL 700™ ALASKAN WILDERNESS RIFLE (AWR)
## $1256.00

## MODEL 700™ AFRICAN PLAINS RIFLE (APR)
## $1466.00

Both these custom-built rifles have the same stock dimensions, rate of twist and custom magnum barrel contour. The AWR model features a Kevlar-reinforced composite stock, while the APR has a laminated classic wood stock. Specifications are listed in the table below.

### SPECIFICATIONS MODEL 700™ APR AND AWR

| | | | | | |
|---|---|---|---|---|---|
| **Model 700™APR (African Plains Rifle)** | | | | | |
| 7mm Remington Mag. | 3 | 26" | 46 ½" | 7 ¾ | 9 ¼" |
| 300 Win. Mag. | 3 | 26" | 46 ½" | 7 ¾ | 10" |
| 300 Wby. Mag. | 3 | 26" | 46 ½" | 7 ¾ | 12" |
| 338 Win. Mag. | 3 | 26" | 46 ½" | 7 ¾ | 10" |
| 375 H&H. Mag. | 3 | 26" | 46 ½" | 7 ¾ | 12" |
| **Model 700™AWR (Alaskan Wilderness Rifle)** | | | | | |
| 7mm Remington Mag. | 3 | 24" | 44 ½" | 6 ¾ | 9 ¼" |
| 300 Win. Mag. | 3 | 24" | 44 ½" | 6 ¾ | 10" |
| 300 Wby. Mag. | 3 | 24" | 44 ½" | 6 ¾ | 12" |
| 338 Win. Mag. | 3 | 24" | 44 ½" | 6 ¾ | 10" |
| 375 H&H Mag. | 3 | 24" | 44 ½" | 6 ¾ | 12" |

# REMINGTON BOLT-ACTION RIFLES



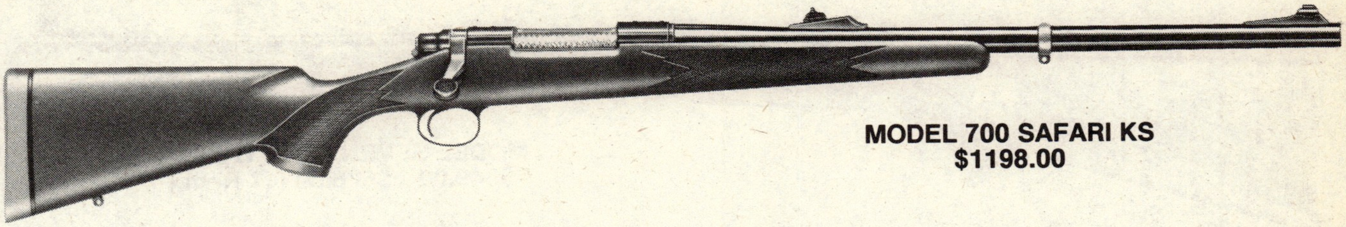

**MODEL 700 SAFARI KS**
**$1198.00**

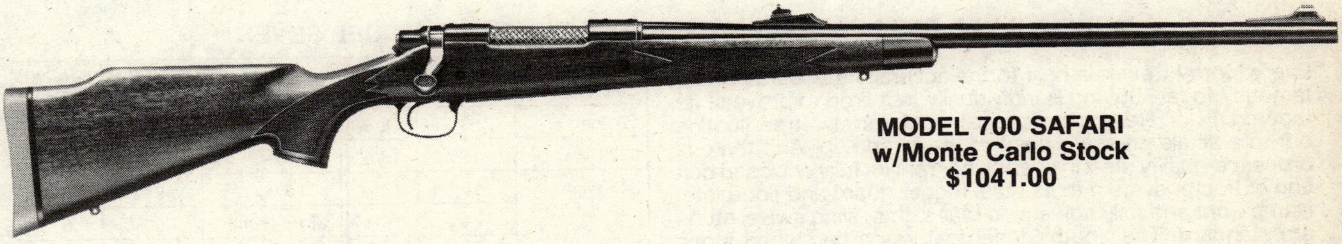

**MODEL 700 SAFARI**
**w/Monte Carlo Stock**
**$1041.00**

**Model 700™ Safari Grade** bolt-action rifles provide big-game hunters with a choice of either wood or synthetic stocks. Model 700 Safari Monte Carlo (with Monte Carlo comb and cheekpiece) and Model 700 Safari Classic (with straight-line classic comb and no cheekpiece) are the satin-finished wood-stock models. Both are decorated with hand-cut checkering 18 lines to the inch and fitted with two reinforcing crossbolts covered with rosewood plugs. The Monte Carlo model also has rosewood pistol-grip and forend caps. All models are fitted with sling swivel studs and 24″ barrels. Synthetic stock has simulated wood-grain finish, reinforced with Kevlar® (KS). **Calibers:** 8mm Rem. Mag., 375 H&H Magnum, 416 Rem. Mag. and 458 Win. Mag. **Capacity:** 3 rounds. **Average weight:** 9 lbs. **Overall length:** 44½″. **Rate of twist:** 10″ (8mm Rem. Mag.); 12″ (375 H&H Mag.); 14″ (416 Rem. Mag., 458 Win. Mag.).

**MODEL 40-XR KS SPORTER**
**Target Rimfire Position Rifle w/Kevlar Stock**
**$1316.00**

**Action:** Bolt action, single shot
**Caliber:** 22 Long Rifle rimfire **Capacity:** Single loading
**Barrel:** 24″ medium weight target barrel countersunk at muzzle. Drilled and tapped for target scope blocks. Fitted with front sight base
**Bolt:** Artillery style with lockup at rear; 6 locking lugs, double extractors
**Overall length:** 43½″ **Average weight:** 10½ lbs.
**Sights:** Optional at extra cost; Williams Receiver No. FPTK and Redfield Globe front match sight
**Safety:** Positive serrated thumb safety
**Receiver:** Drilled and tapped for receiver sight
**Trigger:** Adjustable from 2 to 4 lbs.
**Stock:** Position style with Monte Carlo, cheekpiece and thumb groove; five-way adj. buttplate and full-length guide rail

Also available:
**MODEL 40-XR BR** with 22″ stainless-steel barrel (heavy contour), 22 LR match chamber and bore dimensioms. Receiver and barrel drilled and tapped for scope mounts (mounted on green, Du Pont Kevlar reinforced fiberglass benchrest stock. Fully adjustable trigger (2 oz. trigger optional).
**Price:**.......................................... **$1400.00**
(Additional target rifles are available through Remington's Custom Shop.)

# REMINGTON BOLT-ACTION RIFLES

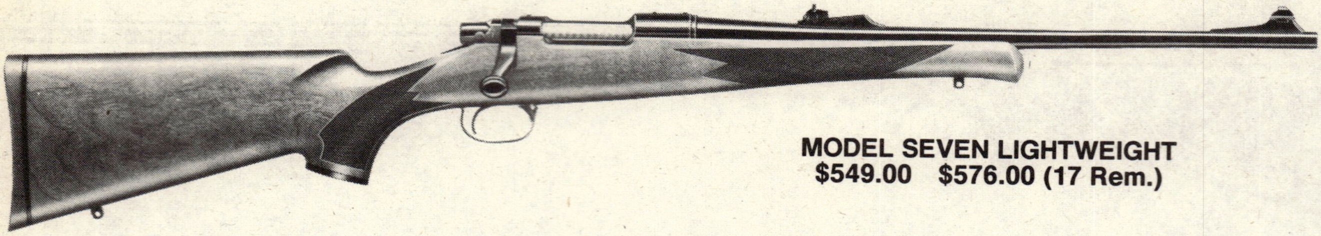

**MODEL SEVEN LIGHTWEIGHT**
**$549.00 $576.00 (17 Rem.)**

## MODEL SEVEN RIFLES

Every **Model Seven** is built to the accuracy standards of the famous Model 700 and is individually test fired to prove it. Its tapered 18½″ Remington special steel barrel is free floating out to a single pressure point at the forend tip. And there is ordnance-quality steel in everything from its fully enclosed bolt and extractor system to its steel trigger guard and floorplate. Ramp front and fully adjustable rear sights, sling swivel studs are standard. The Youth Model features a hardwood stock that is 1 inch shorter for easy control. Chambered in 243 Win. and 7mm-08 for less recoil. See table at right for additional specifications.

## SPECIFICATIONS MODEL SEVEN™

| Calibers | Clip Mag. Capacity | Barrel Length | Overall Length | Twist R-H 1 Turn In | Avg. Wt. (lbs.) |
|---|---|---|---|---|---|
| 17 Rem. | 5 | 18½″ | 37¾″ | 9″ | 6¼ |
| 223 Rem. | 5 | 18½″ | 37¾″ | 12″ | 6¼ |
| 243 Win. | 4 | 18½″ | 37¾″ | 9⅛″ | 6¼ |
| | 4 | 18½″ | 36¾″ (Youth) | 9⅛″ | 6 |
| | 4 | 20″ | 39¼″ | 9⅛″ | 6¼ |
| 6mm Rem. | 4 | 18½″ | 37¾″ | 9⅛″ | 6¼ |
| 7mm-08 Rem. | 4 | 18½″ | 37¾″ | 9¼″ | 6¼ |
| | 4 | 18½″ | 36¾″ (Youth) | 9¼″ | 6 |
| | 4 | 20″ | 39¼″ | 9¼″ | 6¼ |
| 308 Win. | 4 | 18½″ | 37¾″ | 10″ | 6¼ |
| | 4 | 20″ | 39¼″ | 10″ | 6¼ |

Stock Dimensions: 13 3/16″ length of pull, 9/16″ drop at comb, 5/16″ drop at heel. Youth gun has 12½″ length of pull. 17. Rem. provided without sights.
*Note:* New Model Seven Mannlicher and Model Seven KS versions are available from the Remington Custom Shop through your local dealer.

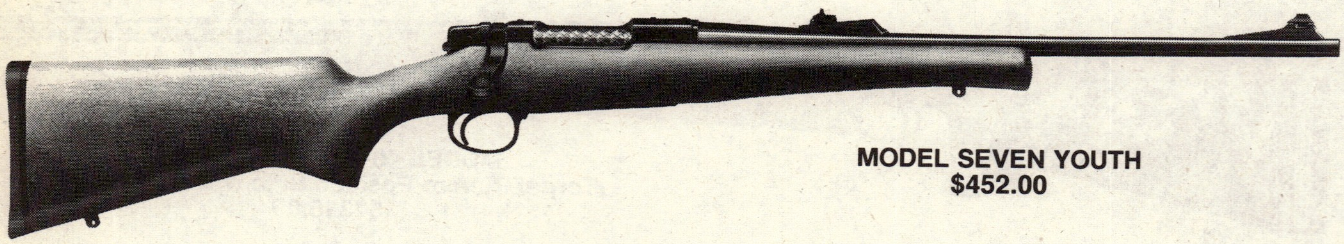

**MODEL SEVEN YOUTH**
**$452.00**

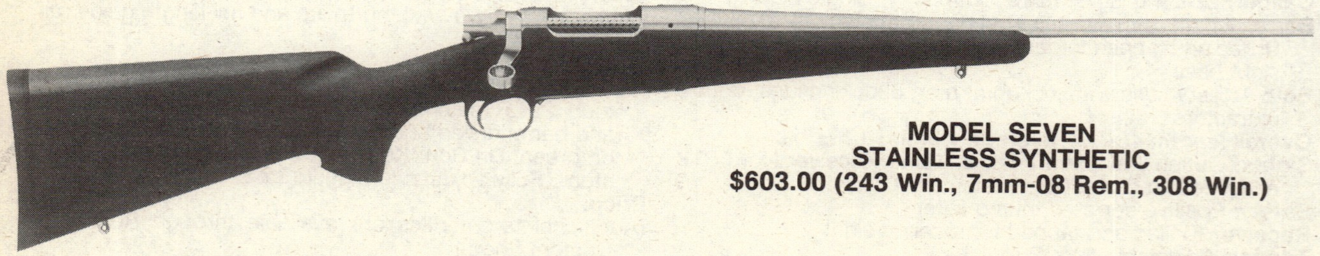

**MODEL SEVEN**
**STAINLESS SYNTHETIC**
**$603.00 (243 Win., 7mm-08 Rem., 308 Win.)**

# REMINGTON REPEATING RIFLES

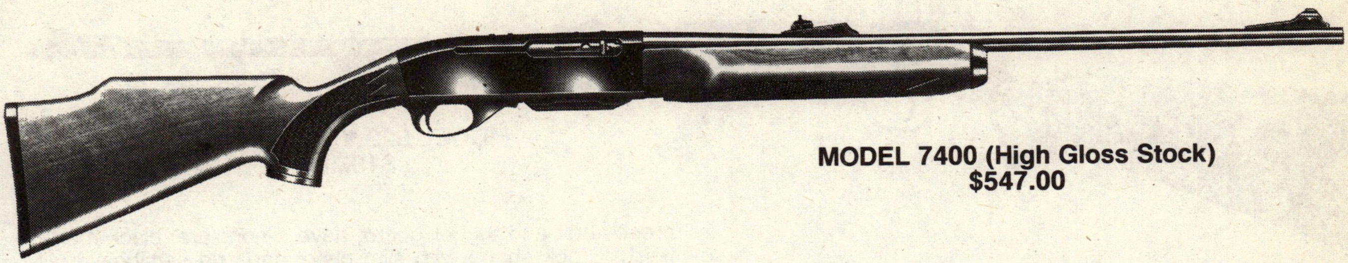

**MODEL 7400 (High Gloss Stock)**
**$547.00**

**Calibers:** 243 Win., 270 Win., 280 Rem., 30-06, 308 Win., 35 Whelen and 30-06 Carbine (see below)
**Capacity:** 5 centerfire cartridges (4 in the magazine, 1 in the chamber); extra 4-shot magazine available
**Action:** Gas-operated; receiver drilled and tapped for scope mounts
**Barrel lengths:** 22″ (18½″ in 30-06 Carbine)
**Weight:** 7½ lbs. (7¼ lbs. in 30-06 Carbine and 35 Whelen)
**Overall length:** 42″ (39⅛″ in 30-06 Carbine)
**Sights:** Standard blade ramp front; sliding ramp rear
**Stock:** Satin or high-gloss (270 Win. and 30-06 only) walnut stock and forend; curved pistol grip; also available with Special Purpose nonreflective finish (270 Win. and 30-06 only)
**Length of pull:** 13⅜″
**Drop at heel:** 2¼″ **Drop at comb:** 1 13/16″



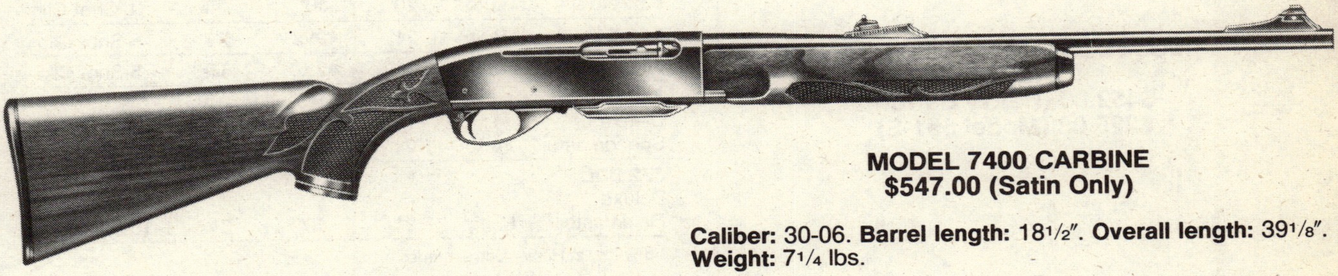

**MODEL 7400 CARBINE**
**$547.00 (Satin Only)**

**Caliber:** 30-06. **Barrel length:** 18½″. **Overall length:** 39⅛″.
**Weight:** 7¼ lbs.

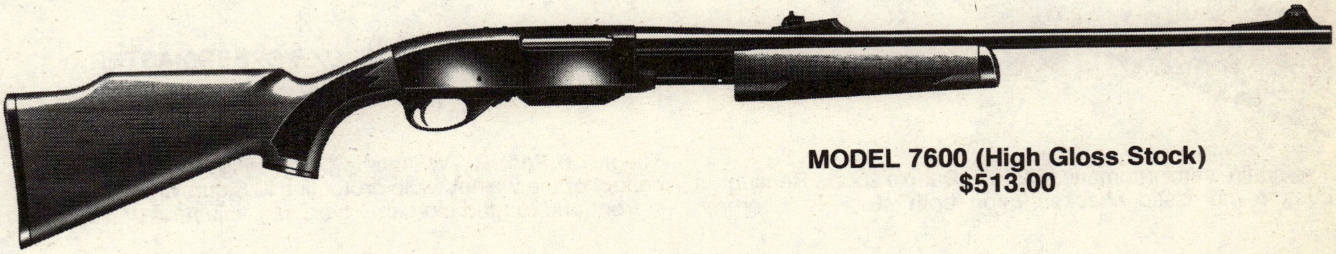

**MODEL 7600 (High Gloss Stock)**
**$513.00**

**Calibers:** 243 Win., 270 Win., 280 Rem., 30-06, 308 Win., 35 Whelen, and 30-06 Carbine
**Capacity:** 5-shot capacity in all six calibers (4 in the removable magazine, 1 in the chamber)
**Action:** Pump action
**Barrel length:** 22″ (18½″ in 30-06 Carbine)
**Overall length:** 42″ (39⅛″ in 30-06 Carbine)
**Weight:** 7½ lbs. (7¼ lbs. in 30-06 Carbine and 35 Whelen)
**Sights:** Standard blade ramp front sight; sliding ramp rear, both removable
**Stock:** Satin or high-gloss walnut; also available with Special Purpose nonreflective finish
**Length of pull:** 13⅜″
**Drop at heel:** 15/16″ **Drop at comb:** 9/16″

Also available:
**MODEL 7600 CARBINE** with 18½″ barrel; chambered for 30-06 cartridge. **Price** . . . . . . . . . . . . . . . . . . . . . . **$513.00**

# REMINGTON RIMFIRE RIFLES

**MODEL 522 VIPER (22 LR)**
**$165.00**

Remington's autoloading rimfire rifle utilizes a strong lightweight stock of PET resin that is impervious to changing temperatures and humidity. The receiver is made of a Du Pont high-tech synthetic. All exposed metalwork, including barrel, breech bolt and trigger guard, have a nonglare, black matte finish. Stock shape with slim pistol grip and semibeavertail forend is proportioned to fit the size and stature of younger or smaller shooters. Other features include: factory-installed centerfire-type iron sights, detachable clip magazine, safety features, primary and secondary sears in trigger mechanism and a protective ejection port shield.

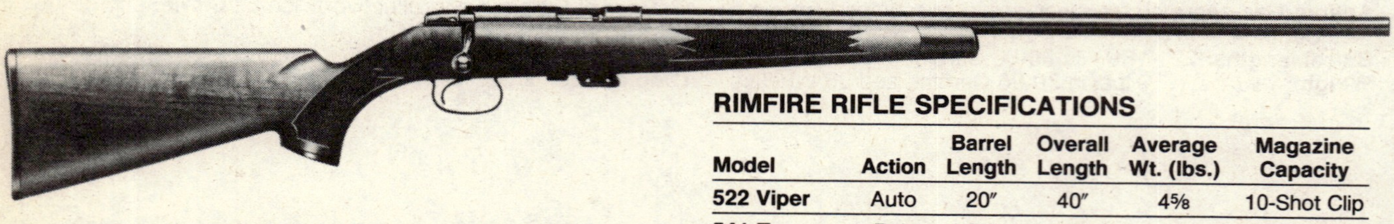

**MODEL 541-T BOLT ACTION**
**$425.00**
**$452.00 (Heavy Barrel)**
**$225.00 (Model 581-S)**

**RIMFIRE RIFLE SPECIFICATIONS**

| Model | Action | Barrel Length | Overall Length | Average Wt. (lbs.) | Magazine Capacity |
|---|---|---|---|---|---|
| **522 Viper** | Auto | 20″ | 40″ | 4⅝ | 10-Shot Clip |
| **541-T** | Bolt | 24″ | 42½″ | 5⅞* | 5-Shot Clip |
| **581-S** | Bolt | 24″ | 42½″ | 5⅞ | 5-Shot Clip |
| **552 BDL** Deluxe Speedmaster | Auto | 21″ | 40″ | 5¾ | 15 Long Rifle |
| **572 BDL** Deluxe Fieldmaster | Pump | 21″ | 40″ | 5½ | 15 Long Rifle |

* 6½ lbs. in Heavy Barrel model

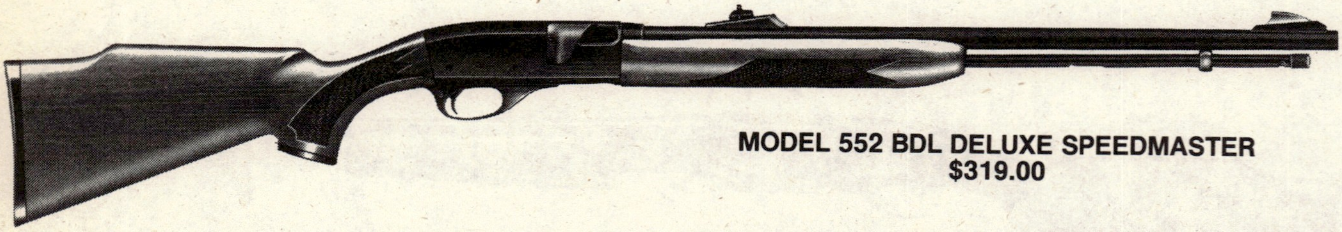

**MODEL 552 BDL DELUXE SPEEDMASTER**
**$319.00**

The rimfire semiautomatic 552 BDL Deluxe sports Remington custom-impressed checkering on both stock and forend. Tough Du Pont RK-W lifetime finish brings out the lustrous beauty of the walnut while protecting it. Sights are ramp-style in front and rugged big-game type fully adjustable in rear.

**MODEL 572 BDL DELUXE FIELDMASTER**
**$332.00**

Features of this rifle with big-game feel and appearance are: Du Pont's tough RK-W finish; centerfire-rifle-type rear sight fully adjustable for both vertical and horizontal sight alignment; big-game style ramp front sight; Remington impressed checkering on both stock and forend.

# ROSSI RIFLES

## PUMP-ACTION GALLERY GUNS

**MODEL M62 SAC CARBINE**
**$226.00 ($243.00 Nickel)**

**SPECIFICATIONS**
**Caliber:** 22 LR **Capacity:** 12 rounds
**Barrel length:** $16\frac{1}{2}$″ **Overall length:** $32\frac{3}{4}$″
**Weight:** $4\frac{1}{4}$″
**Finish:** Blue or nickel

**MODEL M62 SA**
**$226.00 ($243.00 Nickel)**
**$251.00 (w/Octagonal Bbl.)**

**SPECIFICATIONS**
**Caliber:** 22 LR **Capacity:** 13 rounds
**Barrel length:** 23″ **Overall length:** $39\frac{1}{4}$″
**Weight:** $5\frac{1}{2}$″ lbs.
**Finish:** Blue or nickel
Also available:
**Model 59** 22 Magnum (10 rds., blue only) . . . . . . . . **$276.00**

## LEVER-ACTION OLD WEST CARBINES

**MODEL M92 SRC**

**MODEL M92 SRS**
**$347.00 (not shown)**

**SPECIFICATIONS**
**Caliber:** 38 Special or 357 Magnum
**Capacity:** 8 rounds
**Barrel length:** 16″
**Overall length:** 33″
**Weight:** $5\frac{3}{4}$ lbs.
**Finish:** Blue

**MODEL M92 SRC**
**$347.00**

**SPECIFICATIONS**
**Caliber:** 38 Special or 357 Magnum **Capacity:** 10 rounds
**Barrel length:** 20″ **Overall length:** 37″
**Weight:** 6 lbs.
**Finish:** Blue
Also available:
**Model M92** (44-40 and 45 L.C.) . . . . . . . . . . . . . . . **$364.00**

# RUGER CARBINES

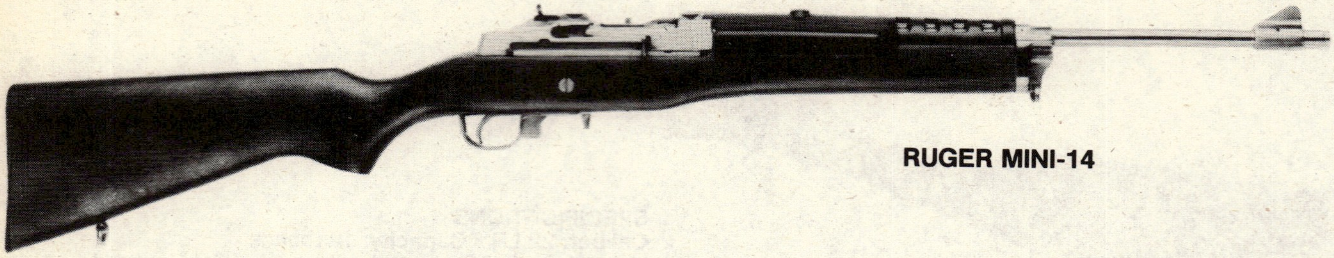

RUGER MINI-14

**Mechanism:** Gas-operated, semiautomatic. **Materials:** Heat-treated chrome molybdenum and other alloy steels as well as music wire coil springs are used throughout the mechanism to ensure reliability under field-operating conditions. **Safety:** The safety blocks both the hammer and sear. The slide can be cycled when the safety is on. The safety is mounted in the front of the trigger guard so that it may be set to Fire position without removing finger from trigger guard. **Firing pin:** The firing pin is retracted mechanically during the first part of the unlocking of the bolt. The rifle can only be fired when the bolt is safely locked. **Stock:** One-piece American hardwood reinforced with steel liner at stressed areas. Sling swivels standard. Handguard and forearm separated by air space from barrel to promote cooling under rapid-fire conditions. **Field stripping:** The Carbine can be field-stripped to its eight (8) basic subassemblies in a matter of seconds and without use of special tools.

**MINI-14 SPECIFICATIONS**
**Caliber:** 223 (5.56mm). **Barrel length:** 18½″. **Overall length:** 37¼″. **Weight:** 6 lbs. 8 oz. **Magazine:** 5-round, detachable box magazine. **Sights:** Rear adj. for windage/elevation.
**Prices:**
**Mini-14/5** Blued . . . . . . . . . . **$516.00**
**K-Mini-14/5** Stainless Steel . . . . . . . . . . **569.00**
(Scopes rings not included)

MINI-14 RANCH RIFLE

**SPECIFICATIONS**
**Caliber:** 223 (5.56mm). **Barrel length:** 18½″. **Overall length:** 37¼″. **Weight:** 6 lbs. 8 oz. **Magazine:** 5-round detachable box magazine. **Sights:** Fold-down rear sight; 1″ scope rings
**Prices:**
**Mini-14/5R** Blued . . . . . . . . . . **$556.00**
**K-Mini-14/5R** Stainless Steel . . . . . . . . . . **609.00**

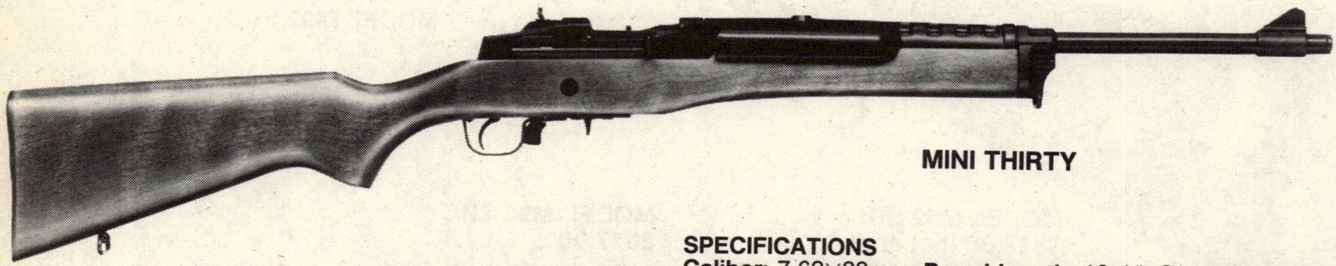

MINI THIRTY

This modified version of the Ruger Ranch rifle is chambered for the 7.62 × 39mm Soviet service cartridge. Designed for use with telescopic sights, it features low, compact scope-mounting for greater accuracy and carrying ease, and a buffer in the receiver. Sling swivels are standard.

**SPECIFICATIONS**
**Caliber:** 7.62×39mm. **Barrel length:** 18½″. **Overall length:** 37⅛″. **Weight:** 6 lbs. 14 oz. (empty). **Magazine capacity:** 5 shots. **Rifling:** 6 grooves, R.H. twist, 1:10″. **Finish:** Blued or stainless. **Stock:** One-piece American hardwood w/steel liners in stressed areas. **Sights:** Blade front; peep rear.
**Prices:**
In Blue . . . . . . . . . . **$556.00**
In Stainless steel . . . . . . . . . . **609.00**

# RUGER CARBINES

STANDARD 10/22 CARBINE

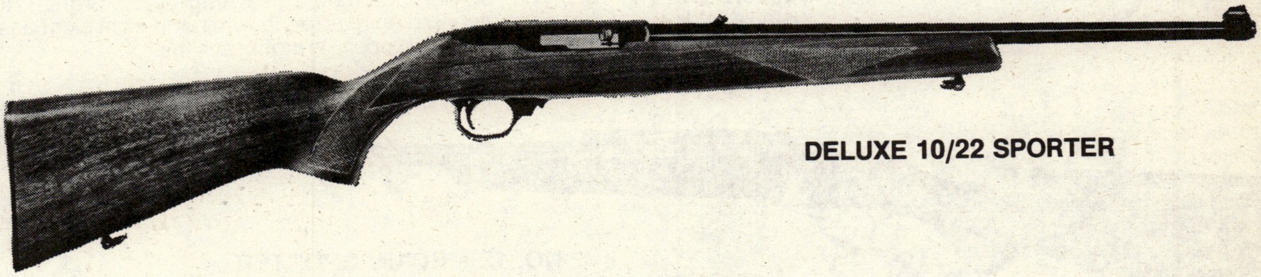

DELUXE 10/22 SPORTER

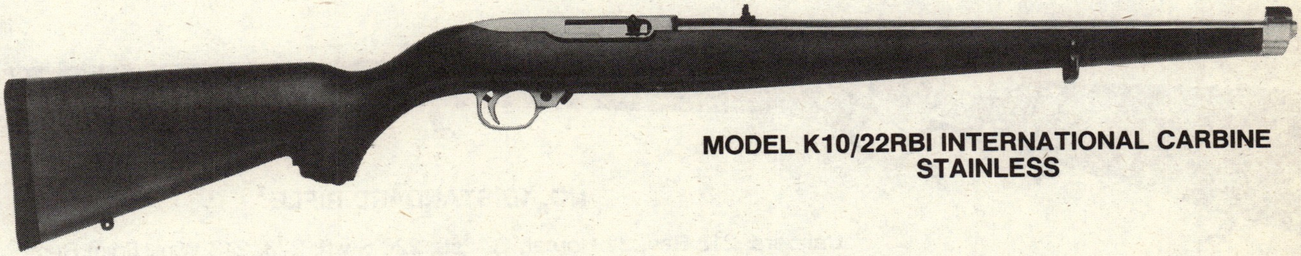

MODEL K10/22RBI INTERNATIONAL CARBINE STAINLESS

## MODEL 10/22 CARBINE 22 LONG RIFLE

Construction of the 10/22 Carbine is rugged and follows the Ruger design practice of building a firearm from integrated sub-assemblies. For example, the trigger housing assembly contains the entire ignition system, which employs a high-speed, swinging hammer to ensure the shortest possible lock time. The barrel is assembled to the receiver by a unique dual-screw dovetail system that provides unusual rigidity and strength—and accounts, in part, for the exceptional accuracy of the 10/22.

**SPECIFICATIONS**
**Mechanism:** Blow-back, semiautomatic. **Caliber:** 22 LR, high-speed or standard-velocity loads. **Magazine:** 10-shot capacity, exclusive Ruger rotary design; fits flush into stock. **Barrel:** 18½", assembled to the receiver by dual-screw dovetail mounting for added strength and rigidity. **Overall length:** 37¼". **Weight:** 5 lbs. **Sights:** 1/16" brass bead front; single folding-leaf rear, adjustable for elevation; receiver drilled and tapped for scope blocks or tip-off mount adapter (included). **Trigger:** Curved finger surface, 3/8" wide. **Safety:** Sliding cross-button type; safety locks both sear and hammer and cannot be put in safe position unless gun is cocked. **Stocks:** 10/22 RB is birch; 10/22 SP Deluxe Sporter is American walnut. **Finish:** Polished all over and blued or anodized or brushed satin bright metal.

**Model 10/22 RB Standard** (Birch carbine stock) . . **$207.00**
**Model 10/22 DSP Deluxe** (Hand-checkered American walnut) . . . . . . . . . . . . . . . . . . . . . . . . . . **274.00**
**Model K10/22 RB Stainless** . . . . . . . . . . . . . . . . . . . . **248.00**
**Model K10/22 RBI International Carbine** w/full-length hardwood stock, stainless-steel bbl. . . . . . **282.00**
**MODEL 10/22 RBI International Carbine** w/blued barrel . . . . . . . . . . . . . . . . . . . . . . . . . . **202.00**

# RUGER SINGLE-SHOT RIFLES

The following illustrations show the variations currently offered in the Ruger No. 1 Single-Shot Rifle Series. Ruger No. 1 rifles have a Farquharson-type falling-block action and select American walnut stocks. Pistol grip and forearm are hand-checkered to a borderless design. Price for any listed model is **$665.00** (except the No. 1 RSI International Model: **$688.00**). Barreled Actions (blued only): **$450.00**

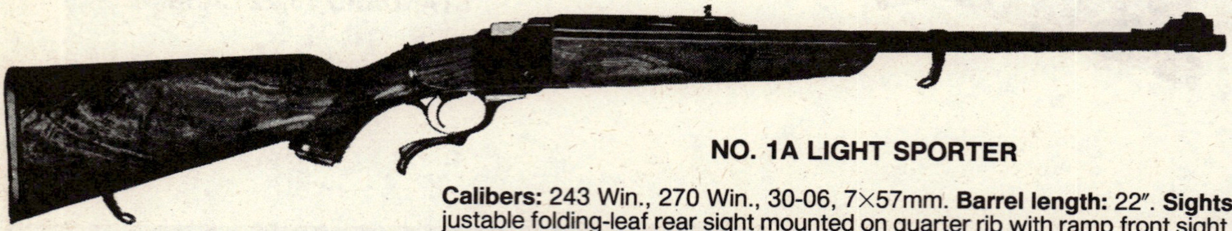

**NO. 1A LIGHT SPORTER**

**Calibers:** 243 Win., 270 Win., 30-06, 7×57mm. **Barrel length:** 22″. **Sights:** Adjustable folding-leaf rear sight mounted on quarter rib with ramp front sight base and dovetail-type gold bead front sight; open. **Weight:** 7 1/4 lbs.

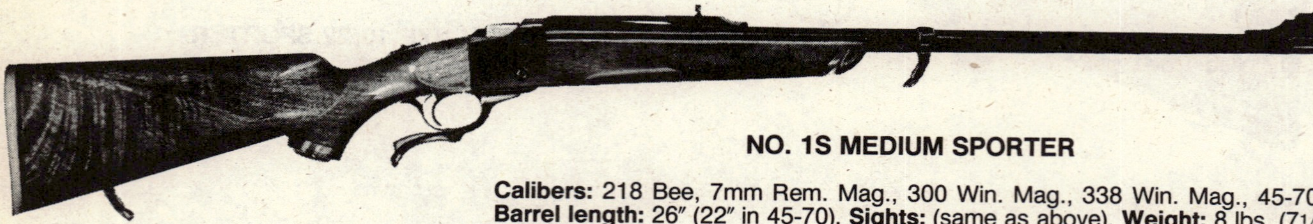

**NO. 1S MEDIUM SPORTER**

**Calibers:** 218 Bee, 7mm Rem. Mag., 300 Win. Mag., 338 Win. Mag., 45-70. **Barrel length:** 26″ (22″ in 45-70). **Sights:** (same as above). **Weight:** 8 lbs. (7 1/4 lbs. in 45-70).

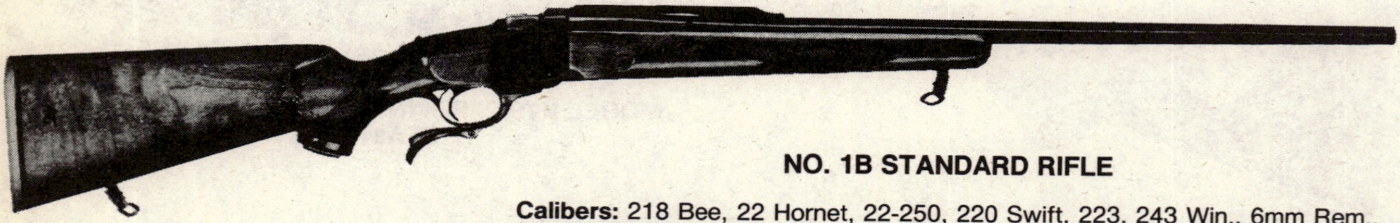

**NO. 1B STANDARD RIFLE**

**Calibers:** 218 Bee, 22 Hornet, 22-250, 220 Swift, 223, 243 Win., 6mm Rem., 25-06, 257 Roberts, 270 Win., 270 Wby. Mag., 7mm Rem. Mag., 280, 30-06, 300 Win. Mag., 300 Wby. Mag., 338 Win. Mag. **Barrel:** 26″. **Sights:** Ruger 1″ steel tip-off scope rings. **Weight:** 8 lbs.

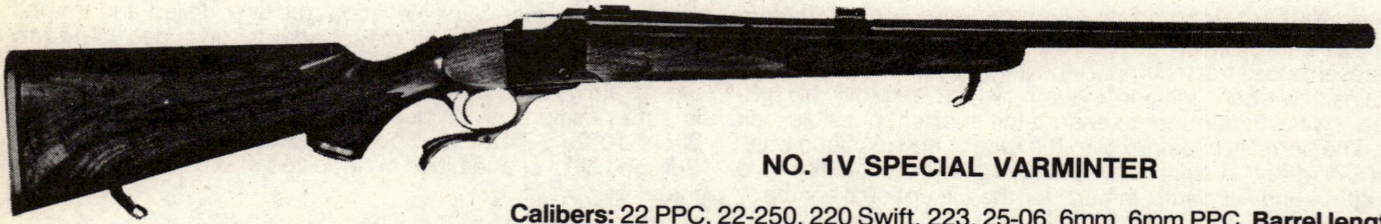

**NO. 1V SPECIAL VARMINTER**

**Calibers:** 22 PPC, 22-250, 220 Swift, 223, 25-06, 6mm, 6mm PPC. **Barrel length:** 24″ (26″ in 220 Swift). **Sights:** Ruger target scope blocks, heavy barrel and 1″ tip-off scope rings. **Weight:** 9 lbs.

Also available:
**NO. 1H TROPICAL RIFLE** (24″ heavy barrel) in 375 H&H Mag., 404 Jeffery, 458 Win. Mag., 416 Rigby and 416 Rem. Mag.
**NO 1. RSI INTERNATIONAL** (20″ lightweight barrel) in 243 Win., 270 Win., 30-06 and 7×57mm

# RUGER BOLT-ACTION RIFLES



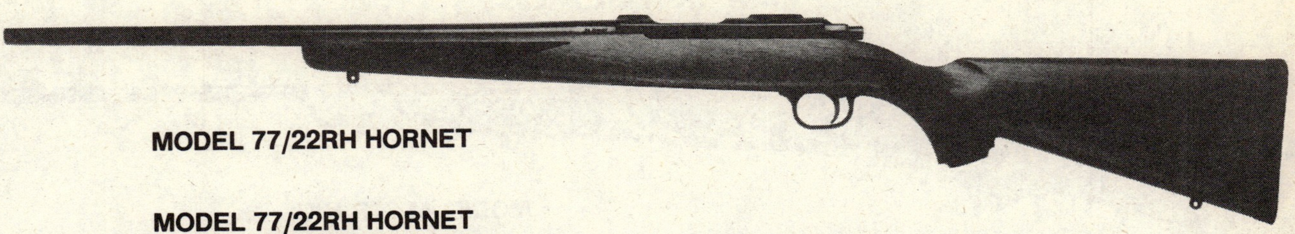

MODEL 77/22RH HORNET

## MODEL 77/22RH HORNET
**$452.00 ($469.00 w/Sights)**

The Model 77/22RH is Ruger's first truly compact centerfire bolt-action rifle. It features a 77/22 action crafted from heat-treated alloy steel. Exterior surfaces are blued to match the hammer-forged barrel. The action features a right-hand turning bolt with a 90-degree bolt throw, cocking on opening. Fast lock time (2.7 milliseconds) adds to accuracy. A three-position swing-back safety locks the bolt; in its center position firing is blocked, but bolt operation and safe loading and unloading are permitted. When fully forward, the rifle is ready to fire. The American walnut stock has recoil pad, grip cap and sling swivels installed. One-inch diameter scope rings fit integral bases.

**SPECIFICATIONS**
**Caliber:** 22 Hornet
**Capacity:** 6 rounds (detachable rotary magazine)
**Barrel length:** 20″ **Overall length:** 40″
**Weight:** 6 lbs. (unloaded)
**Sights:** Single folding-leaf rear; gold bead front
**Length of pull:** 13¾″
**Drop at heel:** 2⅜″ **Drop at comb:** 2″
**Finish:** Polished and blued, matte, nonglare receiver top
Also available: **MODEL K77/22VH.** Varmint model w/stainless-steel heavy barrel, laminated American hardwood stock.
**Price:** (w/o sights) . . . . . . . . . . . . . . . . . . . . . . . . **$525.00**

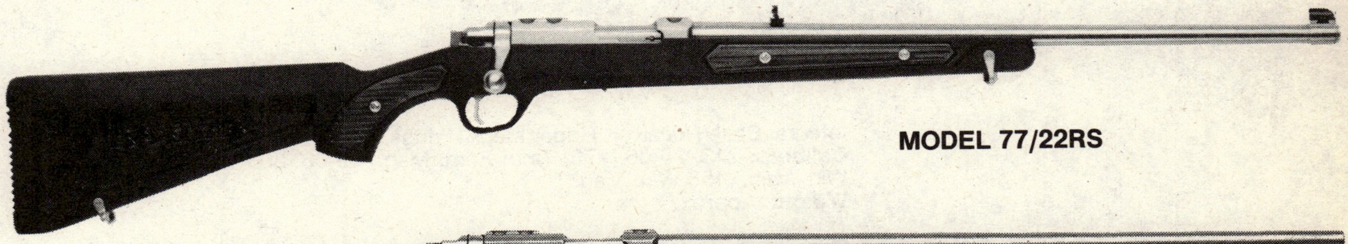

MODEL 77/22RS

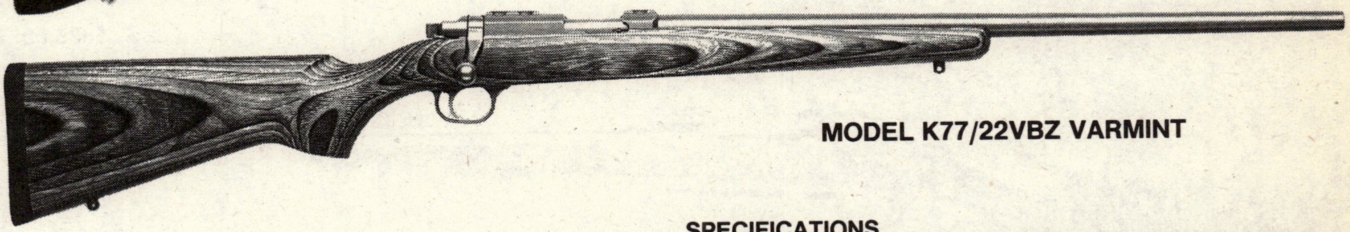

MODEL K77/22VBZ VARMINT

## MODEL 77/22 RIMFIRE RIFLE

The Ruger 22-caliber rimfire 77/22 bolt-action rifle has been built especially to function with the patented Ruger 10-Shot Rotary Magazine concept. The magazine throat, retaining lips, and ramps that guide the cartridge into the chamber are solid alloy steel that resists bending or deforming.

The 77/22 weighs just under six pounds. Its heavy-duty receiver incorporates the integral scope bases of the patented Ruger Scope Mounting System, with 1-inch Ruger scope rings. With the 3-position safety in its "lock" position, a dead bolt is cammed forward, locking the bolt handle down. In this position the action is locked closed and the handle cannot be raised.

All metal surfaces are finished in nonglare deep blue or satin stainless. Stock is select straight-grain American walnut, hand checkered and finished with durable polyurethane.

An All-Weather, all-stainless steel **MODEL K77/22RS** features a stock made of glass-fiber reinforced Zytel. **Weight:** Approx. 6 lbs.

**SPECIFICATIONS**
**Calibers:** 22 LR and 22 Magnum. **Barrel length:** 20″. **Overall length:** 39¼″. **Weight:** 6 lbs. (w/o scope, magazine empty).
**Feed:** Detachable 10-Shot Ruger Rotary Magazine.
**Prices:**
**77/22R** Blue, w/o sights, 1″ Ruger rings . . . . . . . . . **$431.00**
**77/22RM** Blue, walnut stock, plain barrel, no sights, 1″ Ruger rings, 22 Mag. . . . . . . . . . . . **431.00**
**77/22RS** Blue, sights included, 1″ Ruger rings . . . . **458.00**
**77/22RSM** Blue, American walnut, iron sights . . . . **458.00**
**K77/22-RP** Synthetic stock, stainless steel, plain barrel with 1″ Ruger rings . . . . . . . . . . . . . . . **431.00**
**K77/22-RMP** Synthetic stock, stainless steel, plain barrel, 1″ Ruger rings . . . . . . . . . . . . . . . . . . **431.00**
**K77/22-RSP** Synthetic stock, stainless steel, gold bead front sight, folding-leaf rear, Ruger 1″ rings . . . . . . . . . . . . . . . . . . . . . . . . . . . . . . . **458.00**
**K77/22RSMP** Synthetic stock, metal sights, stainless . . . . . . . . . . . . . . . . . . . . . . . . . . . . **458.00**
**K77/22VBZ Varmint** Laminated stock, scope rings, heavy barrel, stainless . . . . . . . . . . . . . . . **499.00**

# RUGER BOLT-ACTION RIFLES

## MARK II SERIES

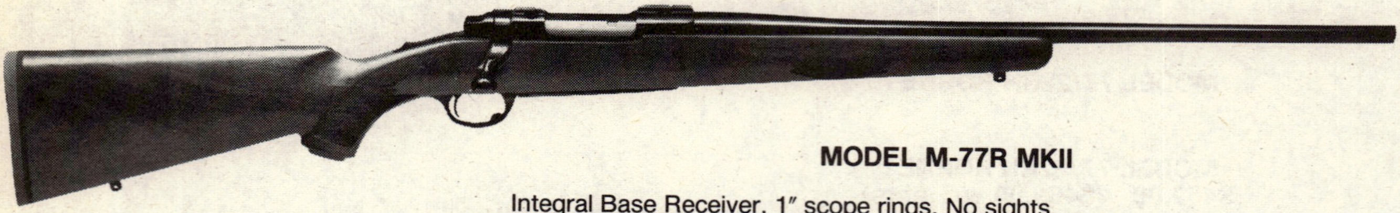

### MODEL M-77R MKII

Integral Base Receiver, 1″ scope rings. No sights.
**Calibers:** (Long action) 6mm Rem., 6.5×55mm, 7×57mm, 257 Roberts, 270, 280 Rem., 30-06 (all with 22″ barrels); 7mm Rem. Mag., 300 Win. Mag., 338 Win. Mag. (all with 24″ barrels); and (Short Stroke action) 223, 243, 308 (22″ barrels).
**Weight:** Approx. 7 lbs.

**Price:** .......... **$574.00**
Also available: **M-77LR MKII** (Left Hand).
**Calibers:** 270, 30-06, 7mm Rem. Mag., 300 Win. Mag. .......... **574.00**

### MODEL M-77RS MKII

Integral Base Receiver, Ruger steel 1″ rings, open sights.
**Calibers:** 243, 25-06, 270, 7mm Rem. Mag., 30-06, 300 Win. Mag., 308, 338 Win. Mag., 458 Win. Mag.
**Weight:** Approx. 7 lbs.

**Price:** .......... **$635.00**

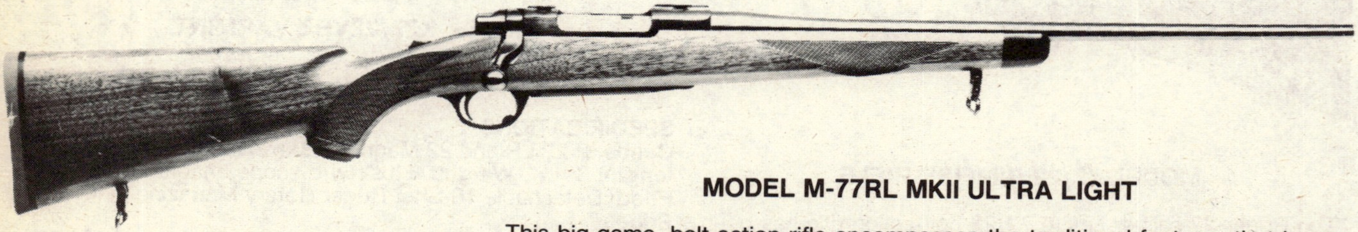

### MODEL M-77RL MKII ULTRA LIGHT

This big-game, bolt-action rifle encompasses the traditional features that have made the Ruger M-77 one of the most popular centerfire rifles in the world. It includes a sliding top tang safety, a one-piece bolt with Mauser-type extractor and diagonal front mounting system. American walnut stock is hand-checkered in a sharp diamond pattern. A rubber recoil pad, pistol-grip cap and studs for mounting quick detachable sling swivels are standard. Available in both long- and short-action versions, with Integral Base Receiver and 1″ Ruger scope rings.
**Calibers:** 223, 243, 257, 270, 30-06, 308.
**Barrel length:** 20″. **Weight:** Approx. 6 lbs.

**Price:** .......... **$610.00**

## MARK II SERIES

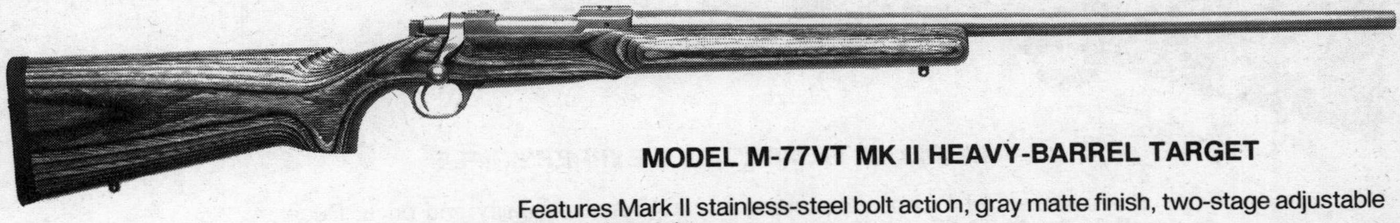

### MODEL M-77VT MK II HEAVY-BARREL TARGET

Features Mark II stainless-steel bolt action, gray matte finish, two-stage adjustable trigger. No sights.
**Calibers:** 22 PPC, 22-250, 220 Swift, 6mm PPC, 223, 243, 25-06 and 308.
**Barrel length:** 26″, hammer-forged, free-floating stainless steel. **Weight:** 9 3/4 lbs.
**Stock:** Laminated American hardwood with flat forend.

**Price: KM-77VT MK II** . . . . . . . . . . . . . . . . . . . . . . . . . . . . . **$684.00**

### M-77 II MARK II ALL-WEATHER

**KM-77RP MK II ALL-WEATHER** Receiver w/integral dovetails to accommodate Ruger 1″ rings, no sights, stainless steel, synthetic stock.
**Calibers:** 223, 22-250, 243, 270, 280, 30-06, 7mm Rem. Mag., 300 Win. Mag., 308, 338 Win. Mag. . . . . . . . . . . . . . . . . . . . **$574.00**
**KM-77RSP MK II ALL-WEATHER** Receiver w/integral dovetails to accommodate Ruger 1″ rings, metal sights, stainless steel, synthetic stock.
**Calibers:** 243, 270, 7mm Rem. Mag., 30-06, 300 Win. Mag., 338 Win. Mag. . . . . . . . . . . . . . . . . . . . . . . . . . **635.00**

### RUGER 77RSM MK II MAGNUM RIFLE

This "Bond Street" quality African safari hunting rifle features a sighting rib machined from a single bar of steel; Circassian walnut stock with black forend tip; steel floorplate and latch; a new Ruger Magnum trigger guard with floorplate latch designed flush with the contours of the trigger guard (to eliminate accidental dumping of cartridges); a three-position safety mechanism (*see* illustrations); Express rear sight; and front sight ramp with gold bead sight.
**Calibers:** 375 H&H, 416 Rigby. **Capacity:** 4 rounds (375 H&H) and 3 rounds (416 Rigby). **Barrel length:** 22″. **Overall length:** 42 1/8″. **Barrel thread diameter:** 1 1/8″. **Weight:** 9 1/4 lbs. (375 H&H); 10 1/4 lbs. (416 Rigby).

**Price:** . . . . . . . . . . . . . . . . . . . . . . . . . . . . . . . . . . **$1550.00**

# RUGER BOLT-ACTION RIFLES

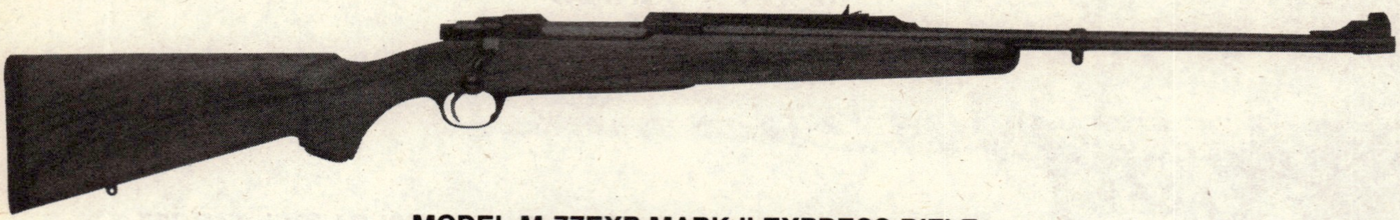

## MODEL M-77EXP MARK II EXPRESS RIFLE

For shooters who prefer a sporting rifle of premium quality and price, Ruger offers the M-77 Mark II Express rifle. Its stock is precision machined from a single blank of French walnut. Forend and pistol grip are hand-checkered in a diamond pattern with 18 lines per inch. Hardened alloy steel grip cap, trigger guard and floorplate plus a black buttpad of live rubber, black forend cap and steel studs for quick detachable sling swivels are standard.

Action is standard short or long length in blued chrome-moly steel with stainless-steel bolt. A fixed blade-type ejector working through a slot under the left locking lug replaces the plunger-type ejector used in the earlier M-77 models. A three-position wing safety allows the shooter to unload the rifle with safety on. The trigger guard houses the patented floorplate latch, which holds the floorplate closed securely to prevent accidental dumping of cartridges into the magazine.

An integral, solid sight rib extends from the front of the receiver ring. Machined from a solid chrome-moly steel barrel blank, the rib has cross serrations on the upper surface to reduce light reflections. Each rifle is equipped with open metal sights. A blade front sight of blued steel is mounted on a steel ramp with curved rear surface serrated to reduce glare. Rear sights (adjustable for windage and non-folding) are mounted on the sighting rib. The forward rear sight is folding and adjustable for windage. A set of Ruger 1″ scope rings with integral bases is standard.

**Calibers:** 270, 30-06, 7mm Rem. Mag., 300 Win. Mag., 338 Win. Mag. **Barrel length:** 22″. **Capacity:** 4 rounds (3 rounds in Magnum). **Overall length:** 42 1/8″. **Weight:** 7 1/2 lbs. (avg., loaded). **Length of pull:** 13 1/2″.

**Price:** .................................................. **$1550.00**

## MODEL M-77RSI INTERNATIONAL MANNLICHER

Mannlicher-type stock, Integral Base Receiver, open sights, Ruger 1″ steel rings. **Calibers:** 243, 270, 30-06, 308. **Barrel length:** 18″. **Weight:** Approx. 6 lbs.

**Price** .................................................. **$642.00**

# RUKO-ARMSCOR RIFLES

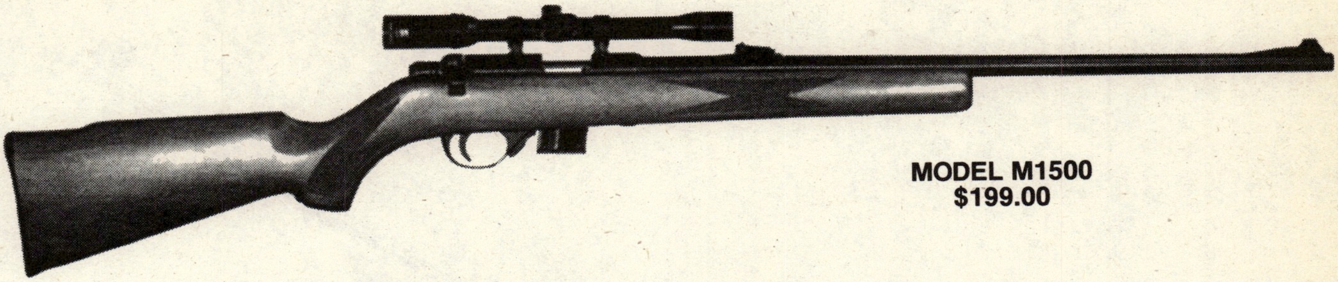

**MODEL M1500**
**$199.00**

**SPECIFICATIONS**
**Type:** Bolt action deluxe
**Caliber:** 22 Win. Mag.
**Capacity:** 5 rounds
**Barrel length:** 21 1/2″
**Overall length:** 41 1/4″
**Weight:** 6.8 lbs.
**Trigger pull:** 14″
**Stock:** Mahogany
**Finish:** Blued



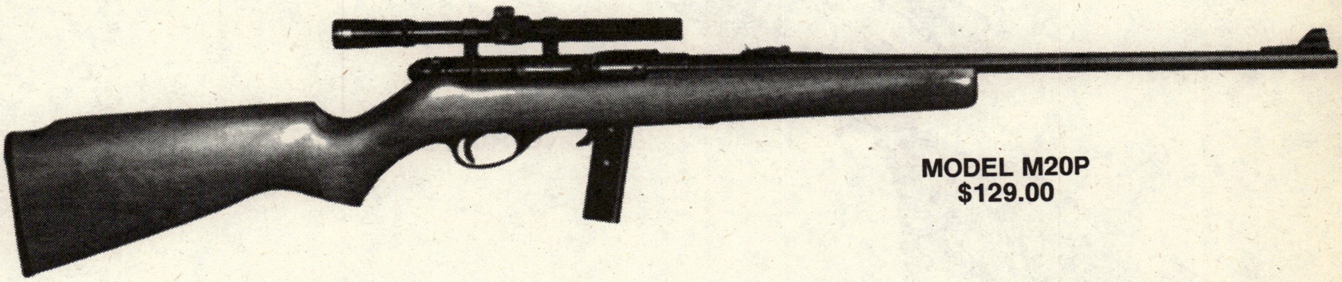

**MODEL M20P**
**$129.00**

**SPECIFICATIONS**
**Type:** Semiautomatic
**Caliber:** 22 LR
**Capacity:** 15 or 30 rounds
**Barrel length:** 21″
**Overall length:** 39 3/4″
**Weight:** 6 1/2 lbs.
**Trigger pull:** 13″
**Stock:** Mahogany
**Finish:** Blued

Also available:
**MODEL M2000** with deluxe stock . . . . . . . . . . . . . . . **$139.00**
**MODEL M20C** (16 1/2″ barrel; 5 1/4″ lbs.) . . . . . . . . . . **159.00**

# SAKO RIFLES

FINNFIRE
22 LONG RIFLE

## FINNFIRE 22 LR BOLT-ACTION RIFLE
## $715.00

SAKO of Finland, acclaimed as the premier manufacturer of bolt-action centerfire rifles,presents its .22 Long Rifle Finnfire. Designed by engineers who use only state-of-the-art technology to achieve both form and function and produced by craftsmen to exacting specifications, this premium grade bolt-action rifle exceeds the requirements of even the most demanding firearm enthusiast.

The basic concept in the design of the Finnfire was to make it as similar to its "big brothers" as possible—just scaled down. For example, the single-stage adjustable trigger is a carbon copy of the trigger found on any other big-bore hunting model. The 22-inch barrel is cold-hammered to ensure superior accuracy. **Overall length:** 39 1/2". **Weight:** 5 1/4 lbs. **Rate of twist:** 16 1/2".

Other outstanding features include:
- European walnut stock
- Luxurious matte lacquer finish
- 50° bolt lift
- Free-floating barrel
- Integral 11mm dovetail for scope mounting
- Two-position safety that locks the bolt
- Cocking indicator
- Five-shot detachable magazine
- Ten-shot magazine available

*COMMITMENT TO EXCELLENCE — A SAKO TRADITION*

# SAKO RIFLES

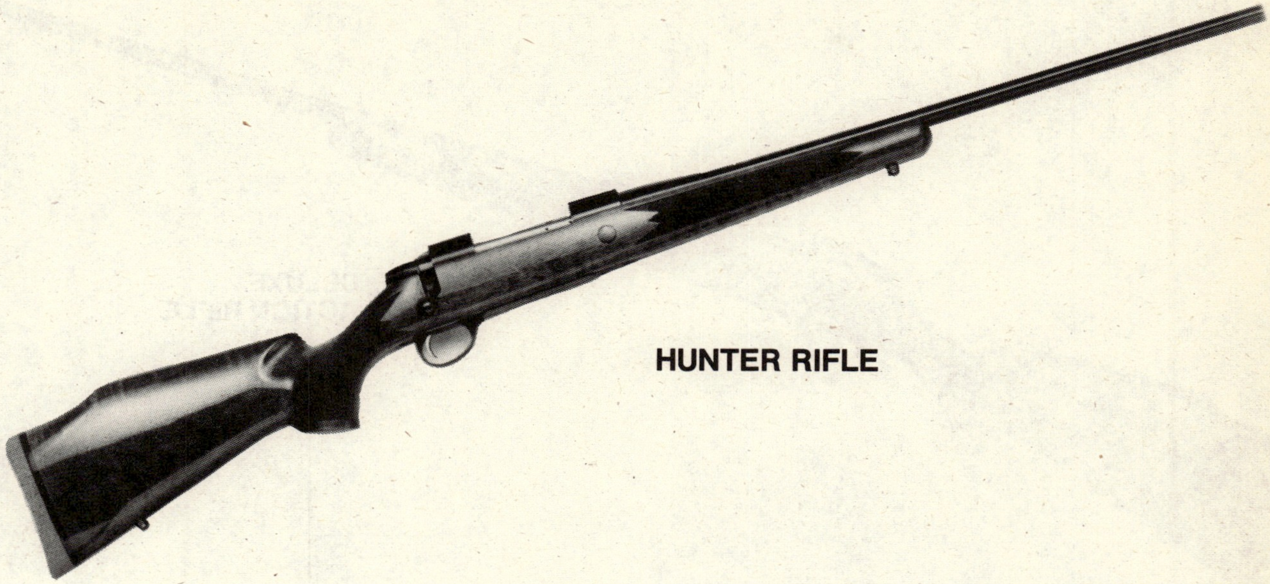

HUNTER RIFLE

RIFLES

### HUNTER LIGHTWEIGHT

Here's one case of less being more. SAKO has taken its famed bolt-action, centerfire rifle, redesigned the stock and trimmed the barrel contour. In fact, in any of the short action (S 491-1) calibers—17 Rem., 222 or 223 Rem.—the Hunter weighs in at less than 7 pounds, making it one of the lightest wood stock production rifles in the world.

The same cosmetic upgrading and weight reduction have been applied to the entire Hunter line in all calibers and action lengths, standard and magnum. All the precision, quality and accuracy for which this Finnish rifle has been so justly famous are still here. Now it just weighs less.

The SAKO trigger is a rifleman's delight—smooth, crisp and fully adjustable. If these were the only SAKO features, it would still be the best rifle available. But the real test that sets SAKO apart from all others is its truly outstanding accuracy.

While many factors can affect a rifle's accuracy, 90 percent of any rifle's accuracy potential lies in its barrel. And the creation of superbly accurate barrels is where SAKO excels.

The care that SAKO takes in the cold-hammering processing of each barrel is unparalleled in the industry. For example, after each barrel blank is drilled, it is diamond-lapped and then optically checked for microscopic flaws. This extra care affords the SAKO owner lasting accuracy and a finish that will stay "new" season after season.

You can't buy an unfired SAKO. Every gun is test fired using special overloaded proof cartridges. This test ensures the SAKO owner total safety and uncompromising accuracy. Every barrel must group within SAKO specifications or it's scrapped. Not recycled. Not adjusted. Scrapped. Either a SAKO barrel delivers SAKO accuracy, or it never leaves the factory.

And hand-in-hand with SAKO accuracy is SAKO beauty. Pistol-grip stocks are of genuine European walnut, flawlessly finished and checkered by hand. Also available with a matte lacquer finish.

**Prices:**

**Short Action (S 491-1)**

In 17 Rem., 222 Rem., 223 Rem. ............ **$1030.00**

**Medium Action (M 591)**

In 22-250 Rem., 7mm-08, 243 Win. & 308 Win. ............ **1030.00**

**Long Action (L 691)**

In 25-06 Rem., 270 Win., 280 Rem., 30-06 ..... **1060.00**

In 7mm Rem. Mag., 300 Win. Mag., 338 Win. Mag. ............ **1080.00**

In 300 Wby. Mag., 375 H&H Mag., 416 Rem. Mag. ............ **1075.00**

**LEFT-HANDED MODELS** (Matte Lacquer Finish)

**Medium Action (M 591)**

In 22-250 Rem., 7mm-08, 243 Win. & 308 Win. ............ **$1110.00**

**Long Action (L 691)**

In 25-06 Rem., 270 Win., 280 Rem., 30-06 ..... **1145.00**

In 7mm Rem. Mag., 300 Win. Mag., 338 Win. Mag. ............ **1160.00**

In 300 Wby. Mag., 375 H&H Mag., 416 Rem. Mag. ............ **1175.00**

# SAKO RIFLES

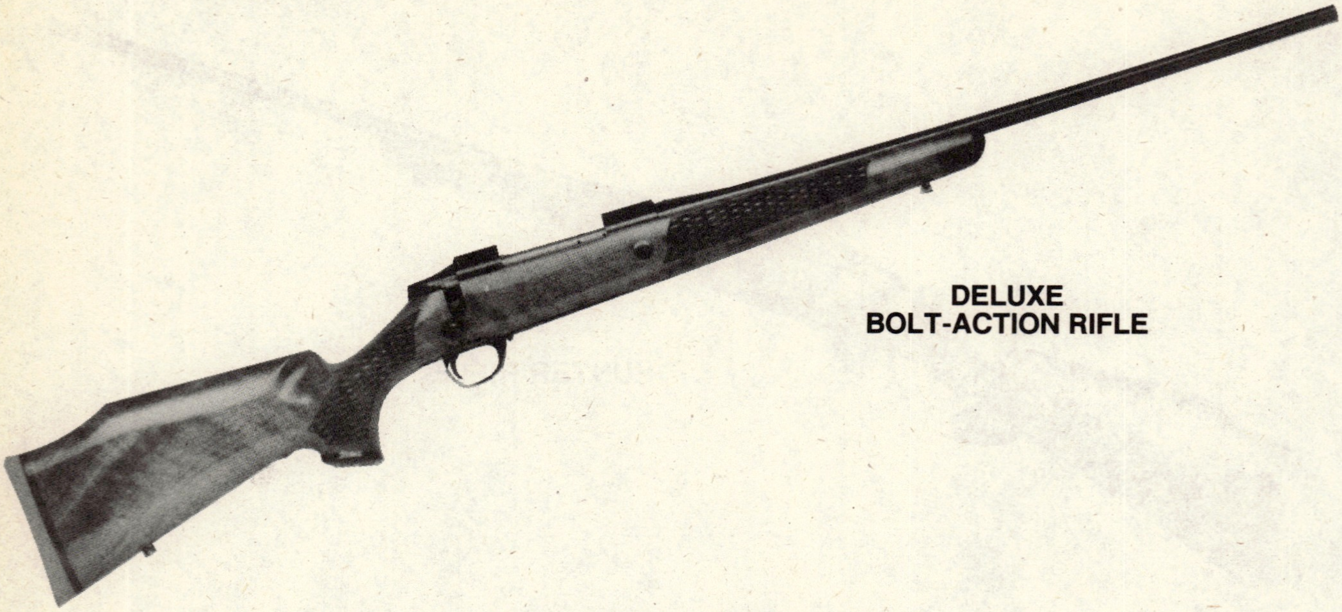

DELUXE
BOLT-ACTION RIFLE

## DELUXE BOLT-ACTION

All the fine-touch features you expect of the deluxe grade SAKO are here—beautifully grained French walnut, superbly done high-gloss finish, hand-cut checkering, deep rich bluing and rosewood forend tip and grip cap. And of course the accuracy, reliability and superior field performance for which SAKO is so justly famous are still here too. It's all here—it just weighs less than it used to. Think of it as more for less.

In addition, the scope mounting system on these SAKOs is among the strongest in the world. Instead of using separate bases, a tapered dovetail is milled into the receiver, to which the scope rings are mounted. A beautiful system that's been proven by over 20 years of use. SAKO Original Scope Mounts and SAKO scope rings are available in short/medium, and high in one-inch and 30mm.

**Prices:**

**Short Action (S 491)**

In 17 Rem., 222 Rem. & 223 Rem. .......... **$1445.00**

**Medium Action (M 591)**

In 22-250 Rem., 243 Win., 7mm-08 and 308 Win. .......... **1445.00**

**Long Action (L 691)**

In 25-06 Rem., 270 Win., 280 Rem., 30-06 .......... **1480.00**

In 7mm Rem. Mag., 300 Win. Mag. & 338 Win. Mag. .......... **1495.00**

In 300 Wby. Mag., 375 H&H Mag., 416 Rem. Mag. .......... **1515.00**

## SUPER DELUXE

SAKO offers the Super Deluxe for the most discriminating gun buyer. This one-of-a-kind beauty is available on special order.

**SUPER DELUXE .......... $3030.00**

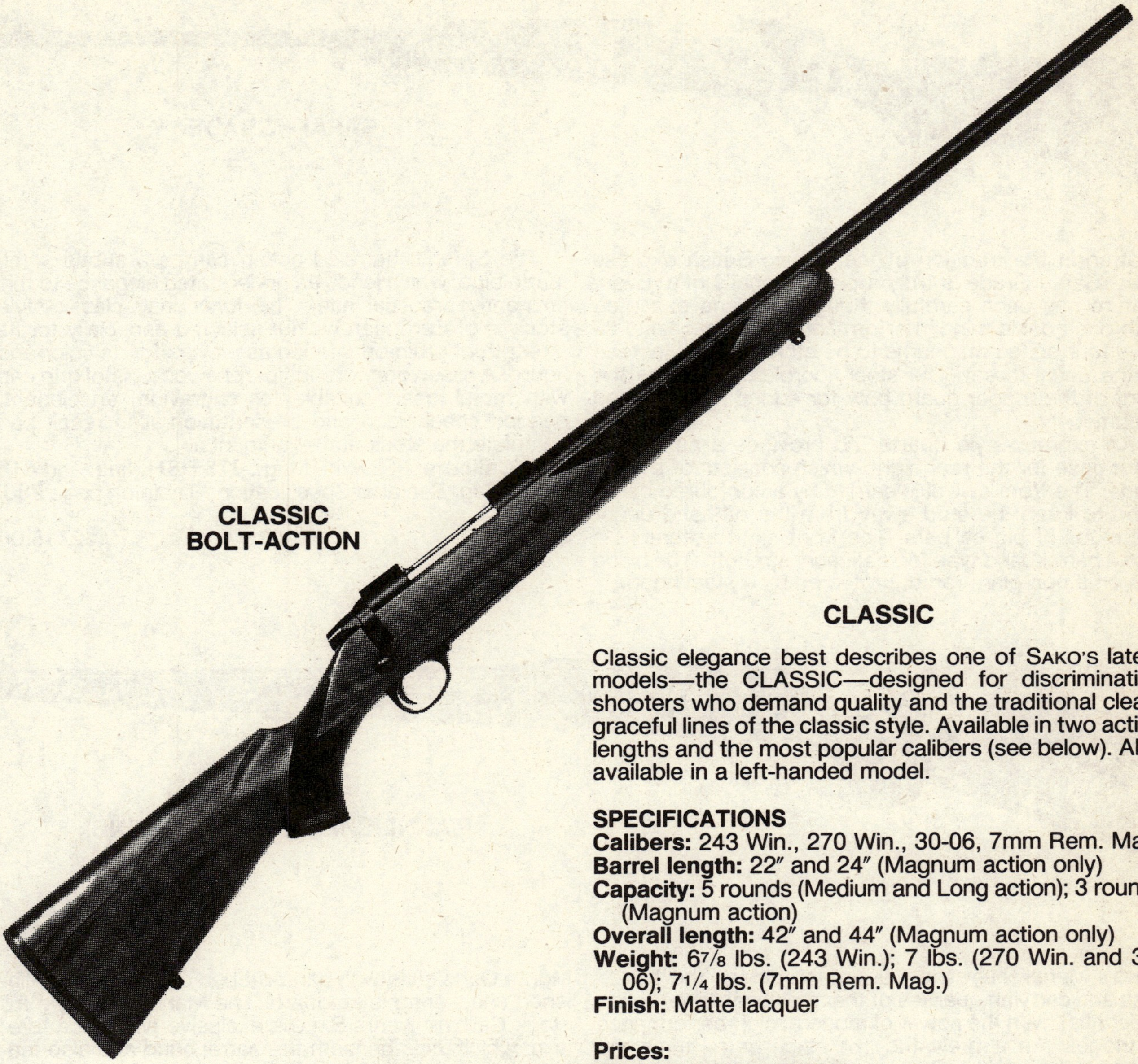

CLASSIC
BOLT-ACTION



## CLASSIC

Classic elegance best describes one of SAKO'S latest models—the CLASSIC—designed for discriminating shooters who demand quality and the traditional clean, graceful lines of the classic style. Available in two action lengths and the most popular calibers (see below). Also available in a left-handed model.

**SPECIFICATIONS**
**Calibers:** 243 Win., 270 Win., 30-06, 7mm Rem. Mag.
**Barrel length:** 22″ and 24″ (Magnum action only)
**Capacity:** 5 rounds (Medium and Long action); 3 rounds (Magnum action)
**Overall length:** 42″ and 44″ (Magnum action only)
**Weight:** 6 7/8 lbs. (243 Win.); 7 lbs. (270 Win. and 30-06); 7 1/4 lbs. (7mm Rem. Mag.)
**Finish:** Matte lacquer

**Prices:**
**Medium Action (M 591)**
In 243 Win. . . . . . . . . . . . . . . . . . . . . . . . . . . . . . **$1030.00**
**Long Action (L 691)**
In 270 Win., 30-06 . . . . . . . . . . . . . . . . . . . . . . . **1060.00**
In 7mm Rem. Mag. . . . . . . . . . . . . . . . . . . . . . . . . **1080.00**

# SAKO RIFLES/CARBINES

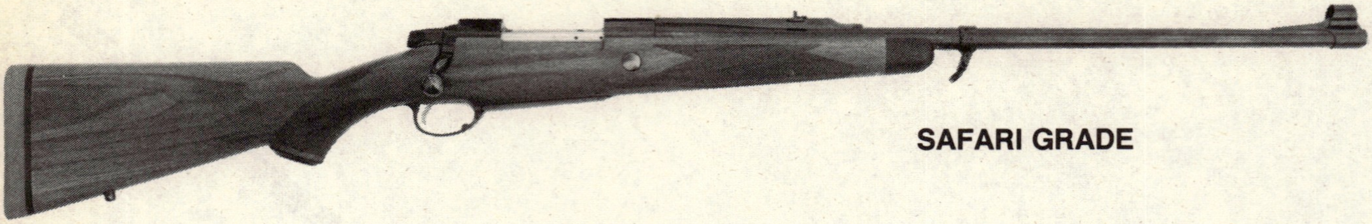

SAFARI GRADE

Crafted in the tradition of the classic British express rifles, Safari Grade is truly a professional's rifle. Every feature has been carefully thought out and executed with one goal in mind: performance. The magazine allows four belted magnums to be stored inside (instead of the usual three). The steel floorplate straddles the front of the trigger guard bow for added strength and security.

An express-style quarter rib provides a rigid, non-glare base for the rear sight, which consists of a fixed blade. The front swivel is carried by a contoured barrel band to keep the stud away from the off-hand under the recoil of big calibers. The front sight assembly is also a barrel-band type for maximum strength. The blade sits on a non-glare ramp, protected by a steel hood.

The Safari's barreled action carries a subtle semi-matte blue, which lends an understated elegance to this eminently practical rifle. The functional, classic-style stock is of European walnut selected especially for its strength of grain orientation as well as for its color and figure. A rosewood forend tip, rosewood pistol grip cap with metal insert suitable for engraving, an elegant, beaded cheekpiece and presentation-style recoil pad complete the stock embellishments.

In **Calibers:** 338 Win. Mag., 375 H&H Mag. and 416 Rem. Mag. See also Specifications Table on page 280.

**Price:** . . . . . . . . . . . . . . . . . . . . . . . . . . . . **$2715.00**

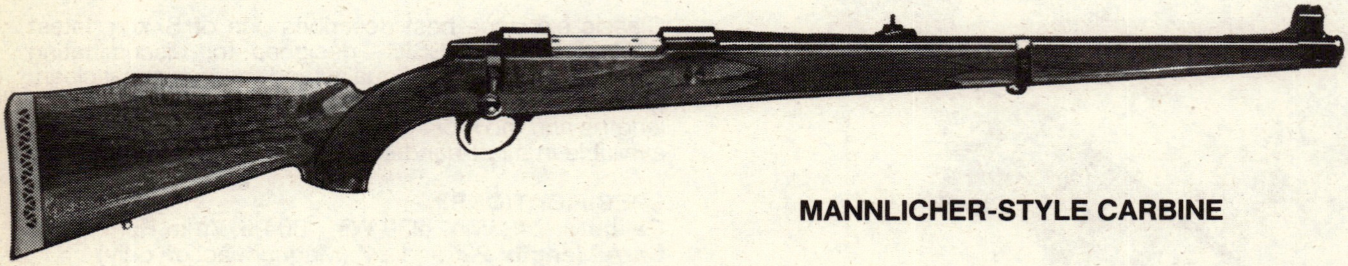

MANNLICHER-STYLE CARBINE

SAKO's Mannlicher-style Carbine combines the handiness and carrying qualities of the traditional, lever-action "deer rifle" with the power of modern, high-performance cartridges. An abbreviated 18½-inch barrel trims the overall length of the Carbine to just over 40 inches in the Long Action (L 691) calibers, and 38 inches in the Medium Action (M 591) calibers. Weight is a highly portable 7 pounds and 6½ pounds, respectively (except in the 338 and 375 H&H calibers, which measure 7½ pounds).

As is appropriate for a rifle of this type, the Carbine is furnished with an excellent set of open sights; the rear is fully adjustable for windage, while the front is a non-glare, serrated ramp with protective hood.

The Mannlicher Carbine is available in the traditional wood stock of European walnut done in a contemporary Monte Carlo style with hand-rubbed oil finish. Hand-finished checkering is standard. The Mannlicher-style full stock Carbine wears SAKO's exclusive two-piece forearm, which joins beneath the barrel band and also features an oil finish. This independent forward section of the forearm eliminates the bedding problems normally associated with the full forestock. A blued steel muzzle cap puts the finishing touches on this European-styled Carbine.

**Prices:**

**Medium Action (M 591)**

In 243 Win. and 308 Win. . . . . . . . . . . . . . . . . . . . . **$1245.00**

**Long Action (L 691)**

In 270 Win. and 30-06 . . . . . . . . . . . . . . . . . . . . . **1285.00**

In 338 Win. Mag. . . . . . . . . . . . . . . . . . . . . . . . . **1300.00**

In 375 H&H Mag. . . . . . . . . . . . . . . . . . . . . . . . . **1320.00**

# SAKO RIFLES

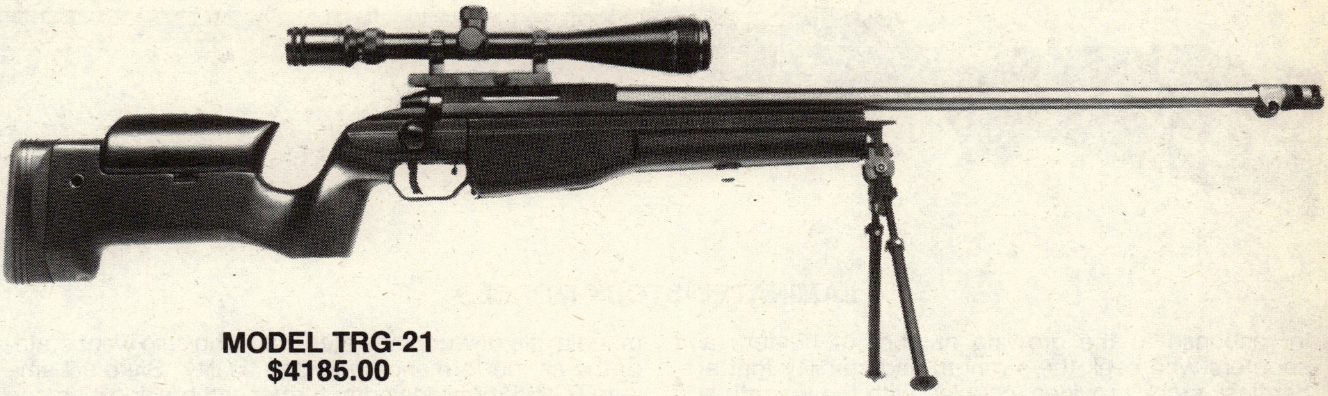

**MODEL TRG-21**
**$4185.00**

SAKO, known for manufacturing the finest and most accurate production sporting rifles available today, presents the ultimate in sharpshooting systems: the **TRG-21 Target Rifle.** Designed for use when nothing less than total precision is demanded, this new SAKO rifle features a cold-hammer forged receiver, "resistance-free" bolt, stainless-steel barrel and a fully adjustable polyurethane stock. Chambered in .308 Win. A wide selection of optional accessories is also available. Designed, crafted and manufactured in Finland. For additional specifications, see the table on page 280.

- Cold-hammer forged receiver
- "Resistance-free" bolt
- Cold-hammer forged, stainless steel barrel
- Three massive locking lugs
- 60° bolt lift
- Free-floating barrel
- Detachable 10-round magazine
- Fully adjustable cheekpiece
- Infinitely adjustable buttplate
- Adjustable two-stage trigger pull
- Trigger adjustable for both length and pull
- Trigger also adjustable for horizontal or vertical pitch
- Safety lever inside the trigger guard
- Reinforced polyurethane stock

**Optional features:**
- Muzzle brake
- Quick-detachable one-piece scope mount base
- Available with 1" or 30mm rings
- Collapsible and removable bipod rest
- Quick-detachable sling swivels
- Wide military-type nylon sling

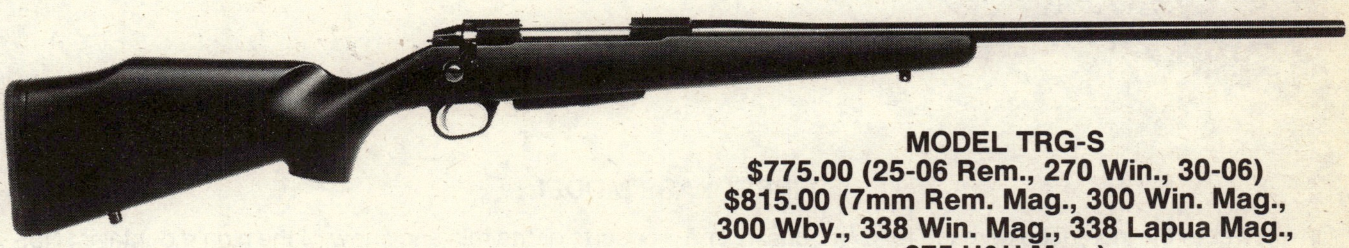

**MODEL TRG-S**
**$775.00 (25-06 Rem., 270 Win., 30-06)**
**$815.00 (7mm Rem. Mag., 300 Win. Mag., 300 Wby., 338 Win. Mag., 338 Lapua Mag., 375 H&H Mag.)**

The TRG-S has been crafted and designed around SAKO's highly sophisticated and extremely accurate TRG-21 Target Rifle (above). The "resistance-free" bolt and precise balance of the TRG-S, plus its three massive locking lugs and short 60-degree bolt lift, are among the features that attract the shooter's attention. Also of critical importance is the cold-hammer forged receiver—unparalleled for strength and durability. The detachable 5-round magazine fits securely into the polyurethane stock. The stock, in turn, is molded around a synthetic skeleton that provides additional support and maximum rigidity. For additional specifications, see page 280.

# SAKO RIFLES

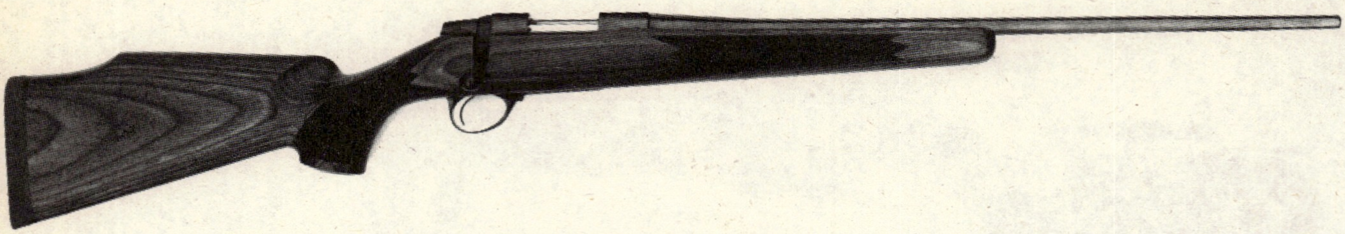

## LAMINATED STOCK MODELS

In response to the growing number of hunters and shooters who seek the strength and stability that a fiberglass stock provides, coupled with the warmth and feel of real wood, SAKO features its Laminated Stock models.

Machined from blanks comprised of 36 individual layers of 1/16-inch hardwood veneers that are resin-bonded under extreme pressure, these stocks are virtually inert. Each layer of hardwood has been vacuum-impregnated with a permanent brown dye. The bisecting of various layers of veneers in the shaping of the stock results in a contour-line appearance similar to a piece of slab-sawed walnut. Because all SAKO Laminated Stocks are of real wood, each one is unique, with its own shading, color and grain.

These stocks satisfy those whose sensibilities demand a rifle of wood and steel, but who also want state-of-the-art performance and practicality. SAKO's Laminated Stock provides both, further establishing it among the most progressive manufacturers of sporting rifles—and the *only* one to offer hunters and shooters their choice of walnut, fiberglass or laminated stocks in a wide range of calibers.

**Prices:**
**Medium Action (M 591)**
In 22-250, 243 Win., 308 Win. and 7mm-08 . . . . **$1200.00**
**Long Action (L 691)**
In 25-06 Rem., 270 Win., 280 Rem. & 30-06 . . . **1255.00**
In 7mm Rem. Mag., 300 Win. Mag. and 338 Win. Mag. . . . . . . . . **1275.00**
In 375 H&H Mag., 416 Rem. Mag. . . . . . . . . . . **1295.00**

## FIBERCLASS MODEL

In answer to the increased demand for SAKO quality and accuracy in a true "all-weather" rifle, this fiberglass-stock version of the renowned SAKO barreled action has been created. Long since proven on the bench rest circuit to be the most stable material for cradling a rifle, fiberglass is extremely strong, light in weight, and unaffected by changes in weather. Because fiberglass is inert, it does not absorb or expel moisture; hence, it cannot swell, shrink or warp. It is impervious to the high humidity of equatorial jungles, the searing heat of arid deserts or the rain and snow of the high mountains. Not only is this rifle lighter than its wood counterpart, it also appeals to the performance-oriented hunter who seeks results over appearance.

**Prices:**
**Long Action (L 691)**
In 25-06 Rem., 270 Win., 280 Rem., 30-06 . . . . . **$1360.00**
In 7mm Rem. Mag., 300 Win. Mag. and 338 Win. Mag. . . . . . . . . **1375.00**
In 375 H&H Mag., 416 Rem. Mag. . . . . . . . . . . **1395.00**

# SAKO RIFLES

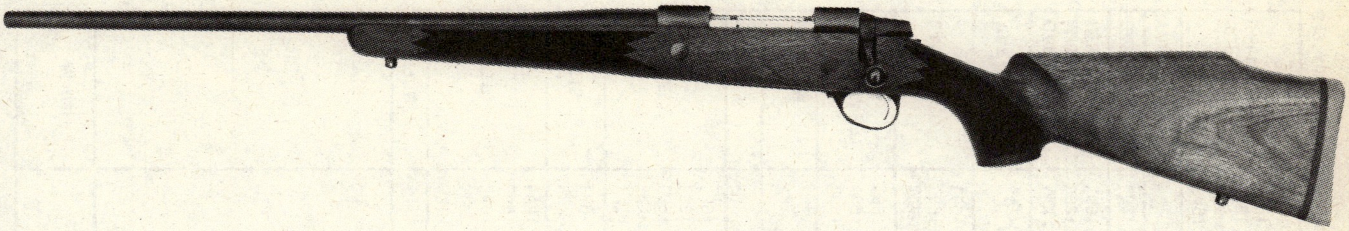

## LEFT-HANDED MODELS

SAKO's Left-Handed models are based on mirror images of the right-handed models SAKO owners have enjoyed for years; the handle, extractor and ejection port all are located on the port side. Naturally, the stock is also reversed, with the cheekpiece on the opposite side and the palm swell on the port side of the grip.

Otherwise, these guns are identical to the right-handed models. That means hammer-forged barrels, one-piece bolts with integral locking lugs and handles, integral scope mount rails, adjustable triggers and Mauser-type inertia ejectors.

SAKO's Left-Handed rifles are available in all Long Action models, while the Hunter grade is available in both Medium and Long Action. The Hunter Grade carries a durable matte lacquer finish with generous-size panels of hand-cut checkering, a presentation-style recoil pad and sling swivel studs installed.

**Prices:**
**Hunter Lightweight (Medium Action)**
In 22-250 Rem. 243 Win., 308 Win., 7mm-08 . . . **$1110.00**
**Hunter Lightweight (Long Action)**
In 25-06, 270 Win., 280 Rem. & 30-06 . . . . . . . . **1145.00**
In 7mm Rem. Mag., 300 Win. Mag. and 338 Win. Mag. . . . . . . . . . . . . . . . . . . . . . . . . **1160.00**
In 300 Wby. Mag., 375 H&H Mag. and 416 Rem. Mag. . . . . . . . . . . . . . . . . . . . . . . . . **1175.00**

## VARMINT

The SAKO Varmint is specifically designed with a prone-type stock for shooting from the ground or bench. The forend is extra wide to provide added steadiness when rested on sandbags or makeshift field rests.

**Calibers:**
Short Action—17 Rem., 222 Rem., 223 Rem.
Medium Action—22-250, 243 Win., 7mm-08, 308 Win.

**Price:** . . . . . . . . . . . . . . . . . . . . . . . . . . . . . . **$1215.00**

# SAKO RIFLES

| Model | Action | Left-handed | Dimensions: Total length (inches) | Dimensions: Barrel length (inches) | Dimensions: Weight (lbs) | Stock Finish: Lacquered | Stock Finish: Matte Lacquered | Stock Finish: Oiled | Stock Finish: Reinforced polyurethane | Sights: Without sights | Sights: Open sights | Sights: Scope mount rails | Mag.: Magazine capacity | Buttplate: Rubber recoil pad |
|---|---|---|---|---|---|---|---|---|---|---|---|---|---|---|
| FINNFIRE | | | 39½ | 22 | 5¼ | | ■ | | | ■ | ■ | ■ | 5*** | |
| HUNTER | S491 | | 41½ | 21¼ | 6¼ | | ■ | | | ■ | | ■ | 6 | ■ |
| | M591 | ■ | 42½ | 21¾ | 6½ | | ■ | | | ■ | | ■ | 5 | ■ |
| | L691 | ■ | 44 | 22 | 7¾ | | ■ | | | ■ | | ■ | 5 | ■ |
| | L691 | ■ | 46 | 24 | 7¾ | | ■ | | | ■ | ■ | ■ | 4 | ■ |
| | L691 | ■ | 46 | 24 | 8¼ | | ■ | | | ■ | ■ | ■ | 4 | ■ |
| CLASSIC | M591 | | 42½ | 21¾ | 6 | | ■ | | | ■ | | ■ | 5 | ■ |
| | L691 | ■ | 44 | 24 | 7½ | | ■ | | | ■ | | ■ | 4 | ■ |
| DELUXE | S491 | | 41½ | 21¼ | 6¼ | ■ | | | | ■ | | ■ | 6 | ■ |
| | M591 | | 42½ | 21¾ | 6½ | ■ | | | | ■ | | ■ | 5 | ■ |
| | L691 | ■ | 44 | 22 | 7¾ | ■ | | | | ■ | | ■ | 5 | ■ |
| | L691 | ■ | 46 | 24 | 7¾ | ■ | | | | ■ | | ■ | 4 | ■ |
| | L691 | ■ | 46 | 24 | 8¼ | ■ | | | | ■ | | ■ | 4 | ■ |
| TRG-S | * | | 45½ | 22 | 7¾ | | | | ■ | | | ■ | 5 | ■ |
| TRG-S MAGNUM | * | | 47½ | 24 | 7¾ | | | | ■ | | | ■ | ** | ■ |
| FIBERCLASS | L691 | | 44 | 22 | 7¼ | | | | | ■ | | ■ | 5 | ■ |
| | L691 | | 46 | 24 | 7¼ | | | | | ■ | | ■ | 4 | ■ |
| | L691 | | 46 | 24 | 8 | | | | | ■ | | ■ | 4 | ■ |
| LAMINATED | M591 | | 42½ | 21¾ | 6½ | | ■ | | | ■ | | ■ | 5 | ■ |
| | L691 | | 44 | 22 | 7¾ | | ■ | | | ■ | | ■ | 5 | ■ |
| | L691 | | 46 | 24 | 7¾ | | ■ | | | ■ | | ■ | 4 | ■ |
| VARMINT | S491 | | 43½ | 23 | 8½ | | | ■ | | ■ | | ■ | 6 | ■ |
| | M591 | | 43½ | 23 | 8½ | | | ■ | | ■ | | ■ | 5 | ■ |
| CARBINE MANNLICHER STYLE | M591 | | 39½ | 18½ | 6 | | | ■ | | | ■ | ■ | 5 | ■ |
| | L691 | | 40½ | 18½ | 7¼ | | | ■ | | | ■ | ■ | 5 | ■ |
| | L691 | | 40½ | 18½ | 7¾ | | | ■ | | | ■ | ■ | 3 | ■ |
| SAFARI | L691 | | 44 | 23½ | 8¼ | | | ■ | | | ■ | ■ | 4 | ■ |
| TRG-21 | * | | 46½ | 25¾ | 10½ | | | | ■ | | | ■ | 10 | ■ |
| SUPER DELUXE | S491 | | 41½ | 21¼ | 6¼ | ■ | | | | ■ | | ■ | 6 | ■ |
| | M591 | | 42½ | 21¾ | 6½ | ■ | | | | ■ | | ■ | 5 | ■ |
| | L691 | | 44 | 22 | 7¾ | ■ | | | | ■ | | ■ | 5 | ■ |
| | L691 | | 46 | 24 | 7¾ | ■ | | | | ■ | | ■ | 4 | ■ |
| | L691 | | 46 | 24 | 8¼ | ■ | | | | ■ | | ■ | 4 | ■ |

Caliber/Rate of Twist

| Model | Action | 17 Rem/10″ | 22 LR/16.5″ (Finnfire) | 222 Rem/14″ | 223 Rem/12″ | 22-250 Rem/14″ | 243 Win/10″ | 308 Win/12″ | 7mm-08/9½″ | 25-06 Rem/10″ | 270 Win/10″ | 280 Rem/10″ | 30-06/10″ | 7mm/Rem Mag/9½″ | 300 Win Mag/10″ | 300 Wby Mag/10″ | 338 Win Mag/10″ | 338 Lapua/12″ | 375 H&H Mag/12″ | 416 Rem Mag/14″ |
|---|---|---|---|---|---|---|---|---|---|---|---|---|---|---|---|---|---|---|---|---|
| FINNFIRE | | | ■ | | | | | | | | | | | | | | | | | |
| HUNTER | S491 | ■ | | ■ | ■ | | | | | | | | | | | | | | | |
| | M591 | | | | | ■ | ■ | ■ | ■ | | | | | | | | | | | |
| | L691 | | | | | | | | | ■ | ■ | ■ | ■ | | | | | | | |
| | L691 | | | | | | | | | | | | | ■ | ■ | ■ | ■ | | ■ | |
| | L691 | | | | | | | | | | | | | | | | | | | ■ |
| CLASSIC | M591 | | | | | | ■ | | | | | | | | | | | | | |
| | L691 | | | | | | | | | | ■ | | ■ | ■ | | | | | | |
| DELUXE | S491 | ■ | | ■ | ■ | | | | | | | | | | | | | | | |
| | M591 | | | | | ■ | ■ | ■ | ■ | | | | | | | | | | | |
| | L691 | | | | | | | | | ■ | ■ | ■ | ■ | | | | | | | |
| | L691 | | | | | | | | | | | | | ■ | ■ | ■ | ■ | | ■ | |
| | L691 | | | | | | | | | | | | | | | | | | | ■ |
| TRG-S | * | | | | | | | | | ■ | ■ | | ■ | | | | | | | |
| TRG-S MAGNUM | * | | | | | | | | | | | | | ■ | ■ | ■ | ■ | ■ | ■ | |
| FIBERCLASS | L691 | | | | | | | | | ■ | ■ | ■ | ■ | | | | | | | |
| | L691 | | | | | | | | | | | | | ■ | ■ | | ■ | | ■ | |
| | L691 | | | | | | | | | | | | | | | | | | | ■ |
| LAMINATED | M591 | | | | | ■ | ■ | ■ | ■ | | | | | | | | | | | |
| | L691 | | | | | | | | | ■ | ■ | ■ | ■ | | | | | | | |
| | L691 | | | | | | | | | | | | | ■ | ■ | | ■ | | ■ | |
| VARMINT | S491 | ■ | | ■ | ■ | | | | | | | | | | | | | | | |
| | M591 | | | | | ■ | ■ | ■ | ■ | | | | | | | | | | | |
| CARBINE MANNLICHER STYLE | M591 | | | | | | ■ | ■ | | | | | | | | | | | | |
| | L691 | | | | | | | | | | ■ | | ■ | | | | | | | |
| | L691 | | | | | | | | | | | | | | | | ■ | | ■ | |
| SAFARI | L691 | | | | | | | | | | | | | | | | ■ | | ■ | ■ |
| TRG-21 | * | | | | | | | ■ | | | | | | | | | | | | |
| SUPER DELUXE | S491 | ■ | | ■ | ■ | | | | | | | | | | | | | | | |
| | M591 | | | | | ■ | ■ | ■ | ■ | | | | | | | | | | | |
| | L691 | | | | | | | | | ■ | ■ | ■ | ■ | | | | | | | |
| | L691 | | | | | | | | | | | | | ■ | ■ | ■ | ■ | | ■ | |
| | L691 | | | | | | | | | | | | | | | | | | | ■ |

S491 formerly AI; M591 formerly AII; L691 formerly AV *Cold-Hammer Forged Receiver **5 except for the .375 H&H which is 4 ***10 round optional

# SAKO ACTIONS

Only by building a rifle around a SAKO action do shooters enjoy the choice of three different lengths, each scaled to a specific family of cartridges. The S 491-1 (Short) action is miniaturized in every respect to match the 222 family, which includes everything from 17 Remington to 223 Remington. The M 591 (Medium) action is scaled down to the medium-length cartridges of standard bolt face—22-250, 243, 308, 7mm-08 or similar length cartridges. The L 691 (Long) action is offered in either standard or Magnum bolt face and accommodates cartridges of up to 3.65 inches in overall length, including rounds like the 300 Weatherby and 375 H&H Magnum. **For left-handers, the Medium and Long actions are offered in either standard or Magnum bolt face.** All actions are furnished in-the-white only.



**S 491 SHORT ACTION** (formerly AI-1)
**$535.00**

**CALIBERS:**
**17 Rem., 222 Rem.**
**222 Rem. Mag.**
**223 Rem.**

**S 491-PPC SHORT ACTION**
**HUNTER: $535.00**
**$615.00 SINGLE SHOT**

**CALIBERS:**
**22 PPC**
**6 PPC**

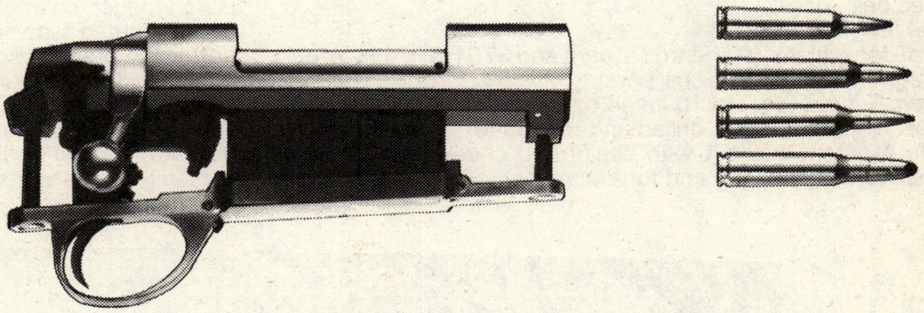

**M 591 MEDIUM ACTION** (formerly AII-1)
**$535.00**

**CALIBERS:**
**22-250 Rem. (M 591-3)**
**243 Win.**
**308 Win.**
**7mm-08**

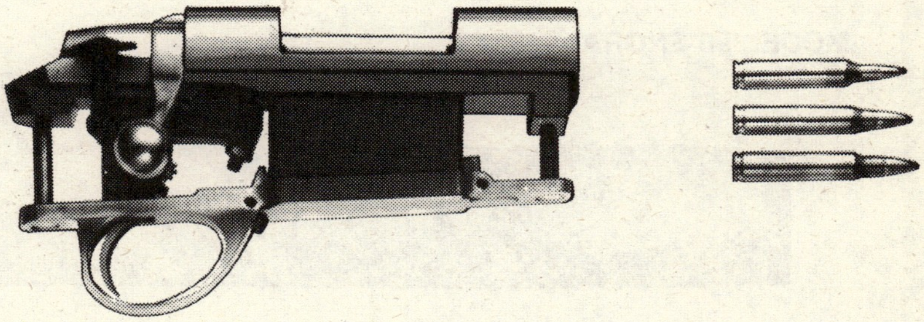

**L 691 LONG ACTION** (formerly AV-4)
**$535.00**

**CALIBERS:**
**25-06 Rem. (L 691-1)**
**270 Win. (L 691-1)**
**280 Rem. (L 691-1)**
**30-06 (L 691-1)**
**7mm Rem. Mag. (L 691-4)**
**300 Win. Mag. (L 691-4)**
**300 Wby. Mag. (L 691-4)**
**338 Win. Mag. (L 691-4)**
**375 H&H Mag. (L 691-4)**
**416 Rem. Mag. (L 691-4)**

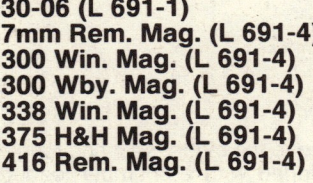

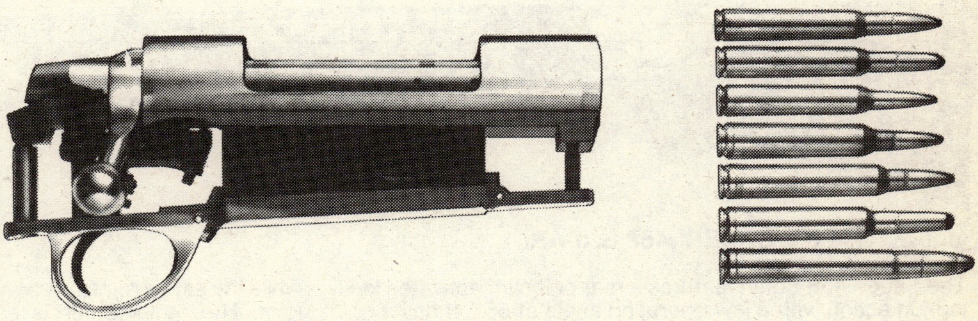

Also available:
**LEFT-HANDED ACTIONS**
**Medium and Long: $565.00**

# SAUER RIFLES

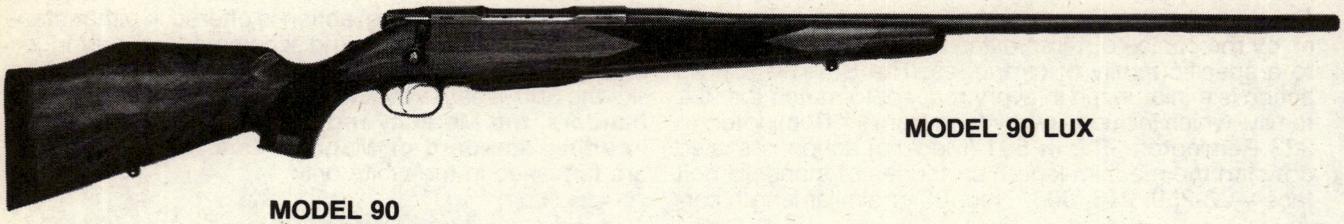

MODEL 90 LUX

MODEL 90
**$1190.00**

**SPECIFICATIONS**
**Calibers:** 25-06, 270, 30-06, 7mm Rem. Mag., 300 Win. Mag., 300 Wby. Mag., 338 Win., 375 H&H and 458 Win. Mag. (see below)
**Barrel length:** 24″ or 26″
**Overall length:** 44″ (standard calibers and 375 H&H, 458 Win. Mag.; 46 1/8″ (for other calibers)
**Weight:** 7 lbs. 12 oz. to 10 lbs. 6 oz. (458 Win. Mag.)
**Sights:** None furnished; drilled and tapped for scope mount
**Stock:** Monte Carlo cut with sculptured cheekpiece, hand-checkered pistol grip and forend, rosewood pistol grip cap and forend tip, black rubber recoil pad, and fully inletted sling swivel studs.
**Features:** Rear bolt cam-activated locking lug action; jeweled bolt with an operating angle of 65°; fully adjustable gold-plated trigger; chamber loaded signal pin; cocking indicator; tang-mounted slide safety with button release; bolt release button (to operate bolt while slide safety is engaged); detachable 3 or 4-round box magazine; sling side scope mounts; leather sling (extra)
**Engravings:** Four distinctive hand-cut patterns on gray nitride receiver, trigger housing plate, magazine plate and bolt handle (extra). **Prices on request.**

MODEL 90 ENGRAVING #2

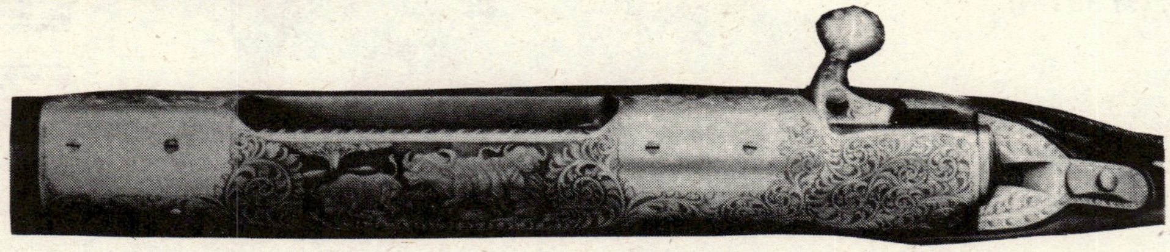

MODEL 90 ENGRAVING #4

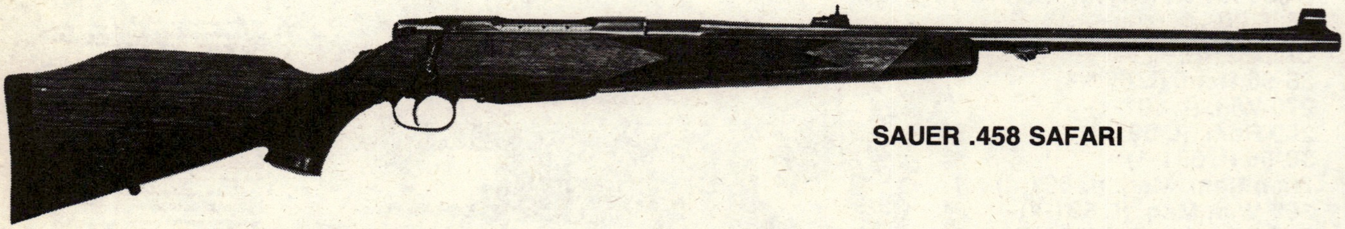

SAUER .458 SAFARI

SAUER .458 SAFARI

The Sauer .458 Safari features a rear bolt cam-activated locking-lug action with a low operating angle of 65°. It has a gold plated trigger, jeweled bolt, oil finished bubinga stock and deep luster bluing. Safety features include a press bottom slide safety that engages the trigger sear, toggle joint and bolt. The bolt release feature allows the sportsman to unload the rifle while the safety remains engaged to the trigger sear and toggle joint. The Sauer Safari is equipped with a chamber loaded signal pin for positive identification. Specifications include: **Barrel Length:** 24″ (heavy barrel contour). **Overall length:** 44″. **Weight:** 10 lb. 6 oz. **Sights:** Williams open sights (sling swivels included). **Price:** . . . . . . . . . . . . . . . . . . . . . . . . . . . . **$1650.00**

# SAVAGE RIFLES

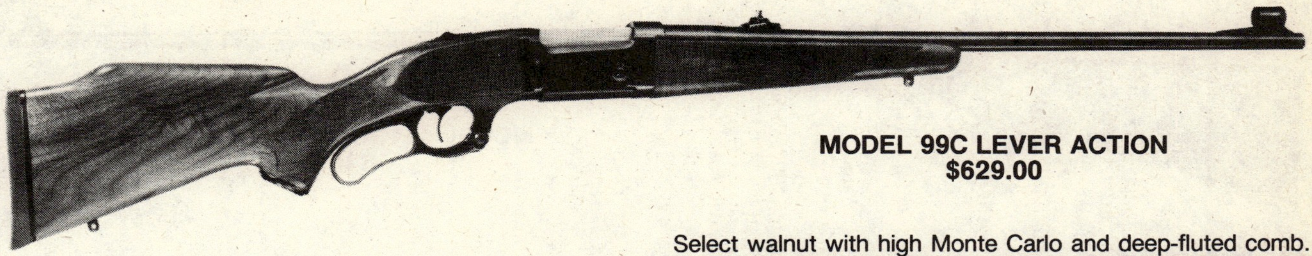

## MODEL 99C LEVER ACTION
**$629.00**

Clip magazine allows for the chambering of pointed, high-velocity big-bore cartridges. **Calibers:** 243 Win., 308 Win. **Action:** Hammerless, lever action, top tang safety. **Magazine:** Detachable clip; holds 4 rounds plus 1 in the chamber. **Stock:** Select walnut with high Monte Carlo and deep-fluted comb. Cut-checkered stock and forend with swivel studs. Recoil pad and pistol grip cap. **Sights:** Detachable hooded ramp front sight, bead front sight on removable ramp adjustable rear sight. Tapped for top mount scopes. **Barrel length:** 22″. **Overall length:** 42 3/4″. **Weight:** 7 3/4 lbs.

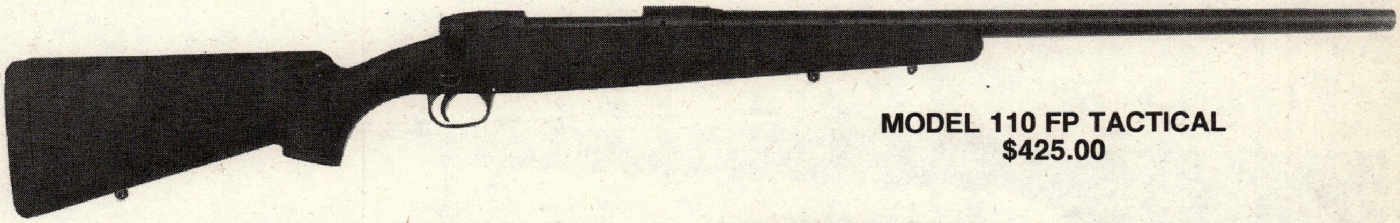

## MODEL 110 FP TACTICAL
**$425.00**

**SPECIFICATIONS**
**Calibers:** 223 Rem., 25-06 Rem., 308 Win., 7mm Rem. Mag., 300 Win. Mag.
**Capacity:** 5 rounds (1 in chamber)
**Barrel length:** 24″ (w/recessed target-style muzzle)
**Overall length:** 45 1/2″
**Weight:** 8 1/2 lbs.
**Sights:** None; drilled and tapped for scope mount
**Features:** Black matte nonreflective finish on metal parts; bolt coated with titanium nitride; stock made of black graphite/fiberglass filled composite with positive checkering

## MODEL 110CY (not shown)
**$362.00**

**SPECIFICATIONS**
**Calibers:** 223 Rem., 243 Win., 270 Win., 300 Savage, 308 Win.
**Capacity:** 5 rounds (1 in chamber); top-loading internal magazine
**Barrel length:** 22″ blued
**Overall length:** 42 1/2″
**Weight:** 6 1/2 lbs.
**Sights:** Adjustable: drilled and tapped for scope mounts
**Stock:** High comb, walnut-stained hardwood w/cut checkering and short pull

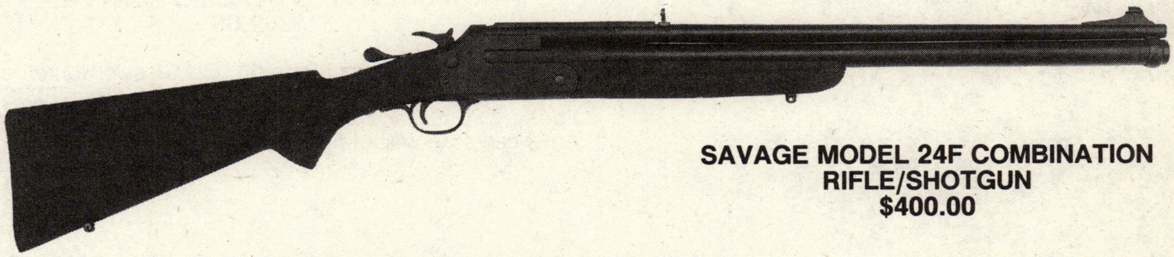

## SAVAGE MODEL 24F COMBINATION RIFLE/SHOTGUN
**$400.00**

### SPECIFICATIONS MODEL 24F COMBINATION RIFLE/SHOTGUN

| O/U Comb. Model | Gauge/ Caliber | Choke | Chamber | Barrel Length | O.A. Length | Twist R.H. | Stock |
|---|---|---|---|---|---|---|---|
| 24F-20<br>24F-12 | 12 or 20/22 LR | Modified Barrel | 3″ | 24″ | 40 1/2″ | 1 in 14″ | Black Graphite Fiberglass Polymer |
| | 12 or 20/22 Hornet | | | | | 1 in 14″ | |
| | 12 or 20/223 | | | | | 1 in 14″ | |
| | 12 or 20/30-30 | | | | | 1 in 12″ | |

**MODEL 111GC CLASSIC HUNTER**
**$407.00**

**SPECIFICATIONS**
**Calibers:** 270 Win., 30-06 Springfield, 7mm Rem. Mag., 300 Win. Mag.
**Capacity:** 5 rounds (4 rounds in Magnum calibers)
**Overall length:** 43½″ (45½″ Magnum calibers)
**Weight:** 6⅜ lbs.
**Sights:** Adjustable
**Stock:** American-style walnut-finished hardwood; cut checkering
**Features:** Detachable staggered box-type magazine; left-hand model available

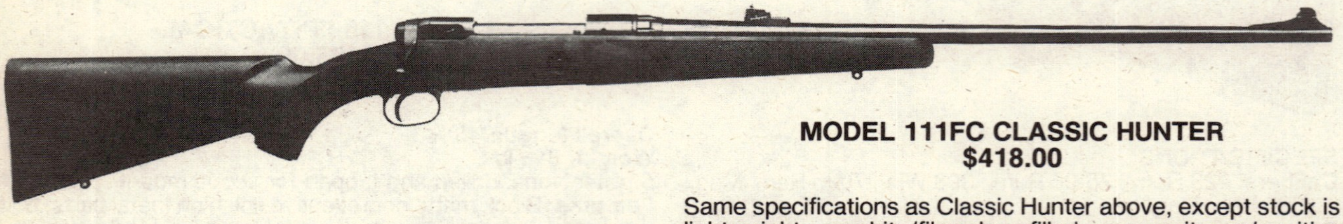

**MODEL 111FC CLASSIC HUNTER**
**$418.00**

Same specifications as Classic Hunter above, except stock is lightweight graphite/fiberglass-filled composite w/positive checkering. **Calibers:** 270 Win., 30-06 Spfld., 7mm Rem. Mag. and 300 Win. Mag.

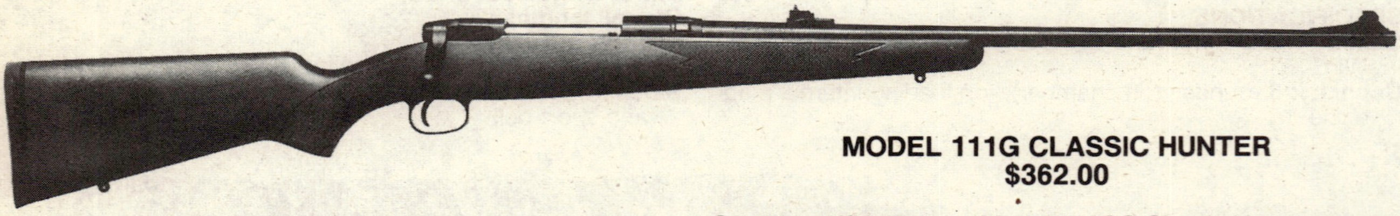

**MODEL 111G CLASSIC HUNTER**
**$362.00**

Same specifications as Model 111GC Classic Hunter, except available also in **calibers** 22-250 Rem., 223 Rem., 243 Win., 25-06, 250 Savage, 300 Savage, 308, 7mm-08. Stock is American-style walnut-finished hardwood with cut checkering.

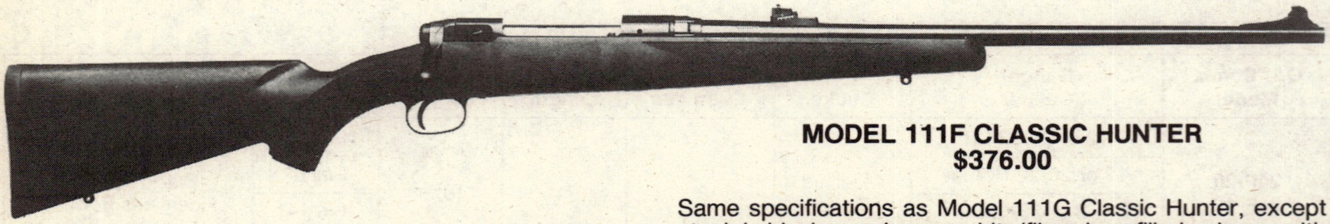

**MODEL 111F CLASSIC HUNTER**
**$376.00**

Same specifications as Model 111G Classic Hunter, except stock is black nonglare graphite/fiberglass-filled polymer with positive checkering. Left-hand model available.

# SAVAGE CENTERFIRE RIFLES



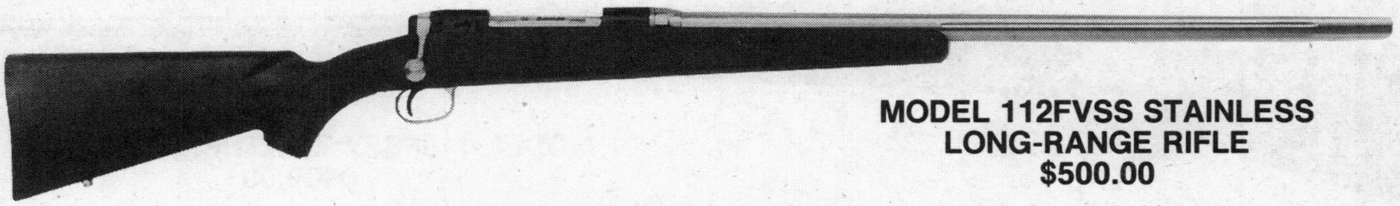

**MODEL 112FVSS STAINLESS LONG-RANGE RIFLE**
**$500.00**

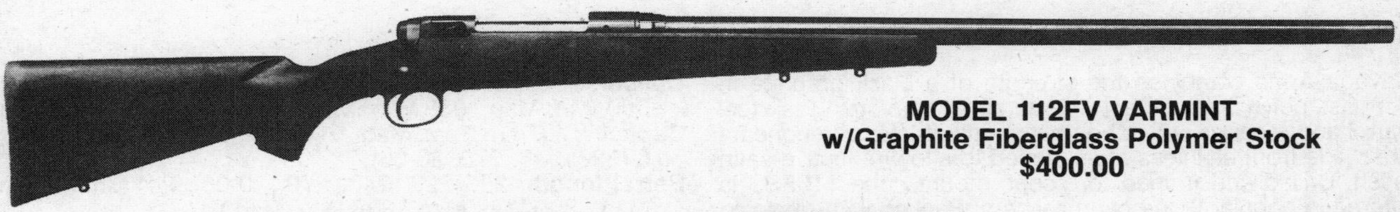

**MODEL 112FV VARMINT**
**w/Graphite Fiberglass Polymer Stock**
**$400.00**

**SPECIFICATIONS**
**Calibers:** 22-250 Rem., 223 Rem., 25-06 Rem., 7mm Rem. Mag., 300 Win. Mag. (Single-shot model available in 220 Swift)
**Capacity:** 5+1
**Barrel length:** 26" fluted, stainless steel
**Overall length:** 47½"
**Weight:** 8⅞ lbs.
**Sights:** Graphite/fiberglass-filled composite w/positve checkering

**MODEL 112BVSS VARMINT**
**$525.00 (not shown)**

**SPECIFICATIONS**
**Calibers:** 22-250 Rem., 223 Rem. (Single-shot model also available in 220 Swift)
**Capacity:** 5+1
**Barrel length:** 26" fluted heavy barrel, stainless steel
**Overall length:** 47½"
**Weight:** 8⅞ lbs.
**Sights:** None; drilled and tapped
**Stock:** Laminated hardwood w/high comb; ambidextrous grip

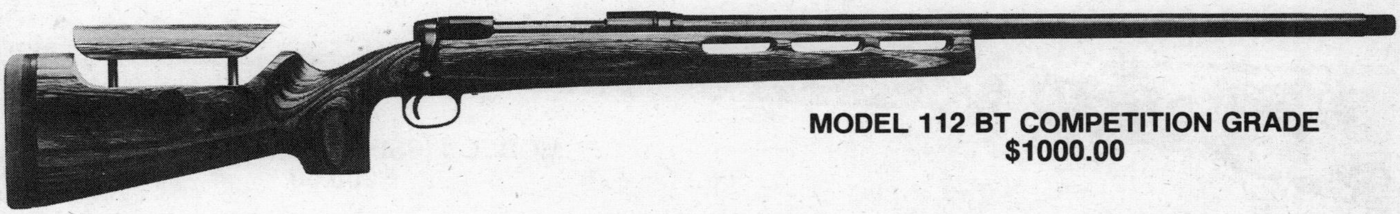

**MODEL 112 BT COMPETITION GRADE**
**$1000.00**

**SPECIFICATIONS**
**Calibers:** 223 Rem. and 308 Win. Mag. (single-shot available in 300 Win. Mag.)
**Capacity:** 5+1
**Barrel length:** 26"; blackened stainless steel w/recessed target-style muzzle
**Overall length:** 47½" **Weight:** 10⅞ lbs.
**Stock:** Laminated brown w/straight comb

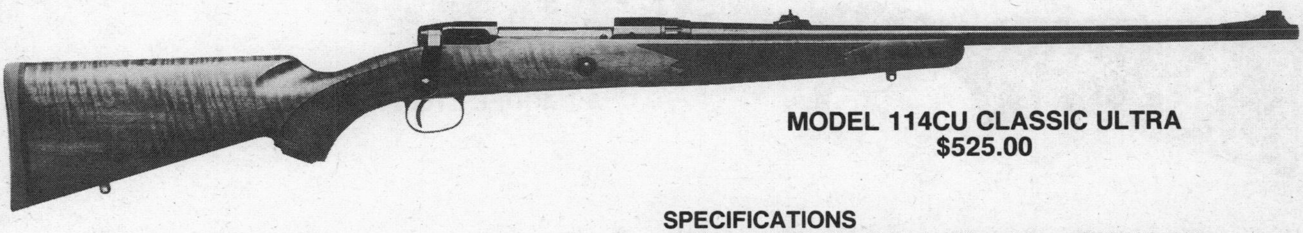

**MODEL 114CU CLASSIC ULTRA**
**$525.00**

Savage's Model 114CU is a high-grade sporting firearm designed with a straight classic American black walnut stock. Cut checkering, fitted grip cap and recoil pad are complemented by a high-gloss luster metal polish finish. The staggered box-type magazine is removed with a push of a button, making loading and reloading quick and easy.

**SPECIFICATIONS**
**Calibers:** 270, 30-06, 7mm Rem Mag., 300 Win. Mag.
**Capacity:** 4 rounds (Magnum); 5 rounds (270 and 30-06)
**Barrel length:** 22" (270 and 30-06) and 24" (Magnum)
**Overall length:** 43½" (270 and 30-06) and 45½" (Magnum)
**Weight:** 7½ lbs. (270 and 30-06) and 7¾ lbs. (Magnum)
**Sights:** Deluxe adjustable; receivers drilled and tapped for scope mounts **Length of pull:** 13½"

# SAVAGE CENTERFIRE RIFLES

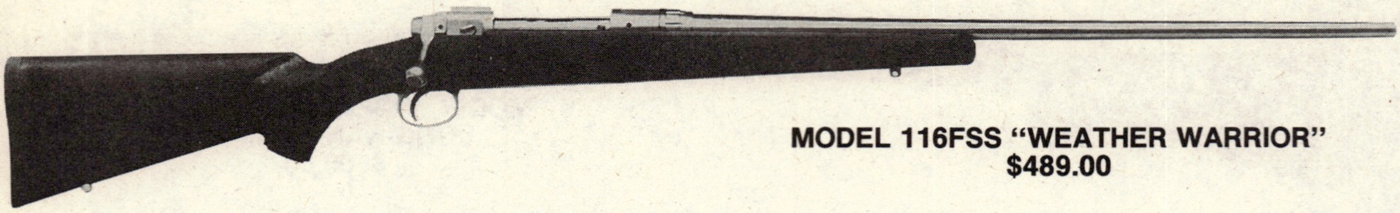

## MODEL 116FSS "WEATHER WARRIOR"
**$489.00**

Savage Arms combines the strength of a black graphite fiberglass polymer stock and the durability of a stainless-steel barrel and receiver in this bolt-action rifle. Major components are made from stainless steel, honed to a low reflective satin finish. Drilled and tapped for scope mounts, the 116FSS is offered in popular long-action calibers. Packed with gunlock, ear puffs and target. Left-hand model available.

**SPECIFICATIONS**
**Calibers:** 223, 243, 270, 30-06, 308 Win., 7mm Rem Mag., 300 Win. Mag., 338 Win. Mag.
**Capacity:** 4 (7mm Rem. Mag., 300 Win. Mag., 338 Win. Mag.); 5 (223, 243, 270, 30-06)
**Barrel length:** 22″ (223, 243, 270, 30-06); 24″ (7mm Rem. Mag., 300 Win. Mag., 338 Win. Mag.)
**Overall length:** 43½″–45½″ **Weight:** 6½ lbs.

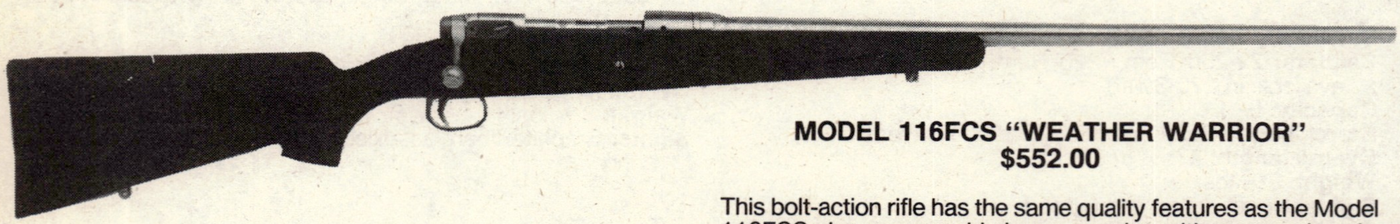

## MODEL 116FCS "WEATHER WARRIOR"
**$552.00**

This bolt-action rifle has the same quality features as the Model 116FSS plus a removable box magazine with recessed push-button release for ease in loading and unloading. Left-hand model available.

## MODEL 116SE SAFARI EXPRESS
**$900.00**

**SPECIFICATIONS**
**Calibers:** 300 Win. Mag., 338, 425 Express, 458
**Capacity:** 4 rounds (1 in chamber)
**Barrel length:** 24″ stainless steel w/AMB
**Overall length:** 45½″ **Weight:** 8½ lbs.
**Sights:** 3-leaf express
**Stock:** Classic-style select-grade walnut w/cut checkering; ebony tip; stainless-steel crossbolts; internally vented recoil pad

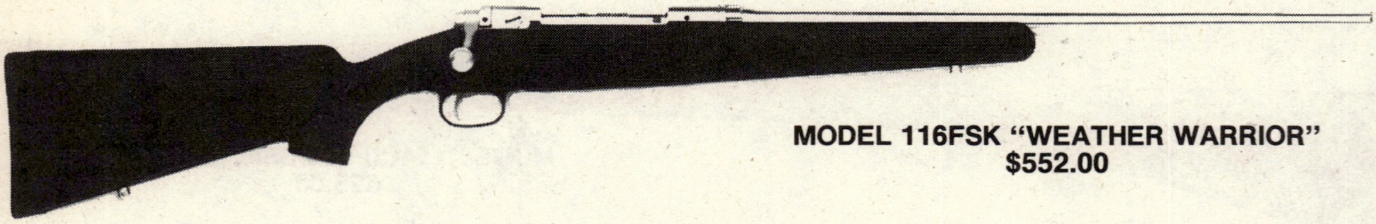

## MODEL 116FSK "WEATHER WARRIOR"
**$552.00**

Features a compact barrel with "shock suppressor" that reduces average linear recoil by more than 30% without loss of Magnum stopping power. Left-hand model available.

**SPECIFICATIONS**
**Calibers:** 270 Win., 30-06 Sprg., 7mm Rem. Mag., 300 Win. Mag., 338 Win. Mag.
**Capacity:** 5 rounds (4 in Magnum)
**Barrel length:** 22″ **Overall length:** 43½″
**Weight:** 6½ lbs.

Also available:
**MODEL 116FSAK.** Same specifications as above except includes adj. muzzle brake. **Price:** . . . . . . . . . . . . . **$581.00**

# SPRINGFIELD RIFLES

## M1A STANDARD

**SPECIFICATIONS**
**Caliber:** 308 Win./7.62mm NATO (243 or 7mm-08 optional)
**Capacity:** 5-, 10- or 20-round box magazine
**Barrel length:** 22″ **Rifling:** 6 groove, RH twist, 1 turn in 11″
**Overall length:** 44⅓″ **Weight:** 9 lbs.
**Sights:** Military square post front; military aperture rear, adjustable for windage and elevation
**Sight radius:** 26¾″
**Finish:** Walnut
**Price:** . . . . . . . . . . . . . . . . . . . . . . . . . . . . . . . . . **$1329.00**

Also available:
**BASIC M1A RIFLE** w/painted black fiberglass stock, caliber 308 only. **Price:** . . . . . . . . . . . . . . . . . . . . . . . . . . . **$1199.00**

## M1A NATIONAL MATCH

**Features:** Comes with National Match barrel, flash suppressor, gas cylinder, special glass-bedded walnut stock and match-tuned trigger assembly.
**Price:** . . . . . . . . . . . . . . . . . . . . . . . . . . . . . . . . . **$1670.00**

Also available:
**M1A SUPER MATCH.** Features heavy match barrel and permanently attached figure-8-style operating rod guide, plus special heavy walnut match stock, longer pistol grip and contoured area behind rear sight for better grip.
**Price:** . . . . . . . . . . . . . . . . . . . . . . . . . . . . . . . . . **$1980.00**

**SPECIFICATIONS**
**Caliber:** 243 Win., 308 Win., 7mm-08 Win.
**Barrel length:** 22″
**Overall length:** 44.375″
**Trigger pull:** 4½ lbs.
**Weight:** 10 lbs. (11 lbs. in Super Match)

## M1A-A1 BUSH RIFLE

**SPECIFICATIONS**
**Caliber:** 308 Win./7.62mm, 243 or 7mm-08 Win.
**Barrel length:** 18″ (w/o flash suppressor)
**Overall length:** 40.5″
**Weight:** 8.75 lbs. **Sight radius:** 26¾″
**Prices:**
With walnut stock . . . . . . . . . . . . . . . . . . . . . . . . . **$1359.00**
With black fiberglass . . . . . . . . . . . . . . . . . . . . . . . **1349.00**

# STEYR-MANNLICHER RIFLES

## SPORTER SERIES

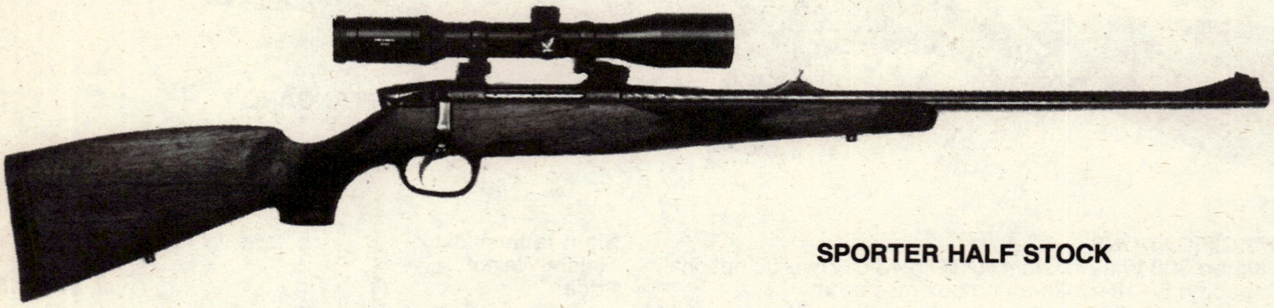

SPORTER HALF STOCK

SPORTER FULL STOCK

### SPORTER SERIES

All Sporter models feature hand-checkered wood stocks, a five-round detachable rotary magazine, and a choice of single or double-set triggers. M actions are available in left-hand models. S (Magnum) action are available in half stock only.

**SPECIFICATIONS**
**Calibers:** See table on the following page
**Barrel length:** 20″ (Full Stock); 23.6″ (Half Stock)
**Overall length:** 39″ (Full)
**Weight:**
Model SL—6.16 lbs. (Full) and 6.27 lbs. (Half Stock)
Model L—6.27 lbs. (Full) and 6.38 lbs. (Half)
Model M—6.82 lbs. (Full) and 7 lbs. (Half).
**Features:** SL and L Models have rifle-type rubber butt pad

**Prices:**
**Models SL, L, M** Full Stock . . . . . . . . . . . . . . . . . . $2179.00
**Models SL, L, M** Half Stock . . . . . . . . . . . . . . . . . . 2023.00
**Model MIII Left Hand** Full Stock . . . . . . . . . . . . . . 2335.00
**Model MIII Left Hand** Half Stock . . . . . . . . . . . . . . 2179.00
**Model MIII Professional** (w/black synthetic half stock, 23.6″ barrel and no sights) . . . . . . . . . . . 995.00
Same as above w/stippled checkered European wood stock (270 Win. and 30-06 calibers) . . . 1125.00
**Varmint Rifle** Half stock, 26″ heavy barrel . . . . . . 2179.00
**Jagd Match** Laminated half stock, 23.6″ barrel in 222 Rem., 243 Win., 308 Win. . . . . . . . . . . . . . . . 2275.00
**Magnum,** Half stock, 26″ barrel in 7mm Rem. Mag., 300 Win. Mag., 375 H&H . . . . . . . . . . . . . . . . . 2179.00

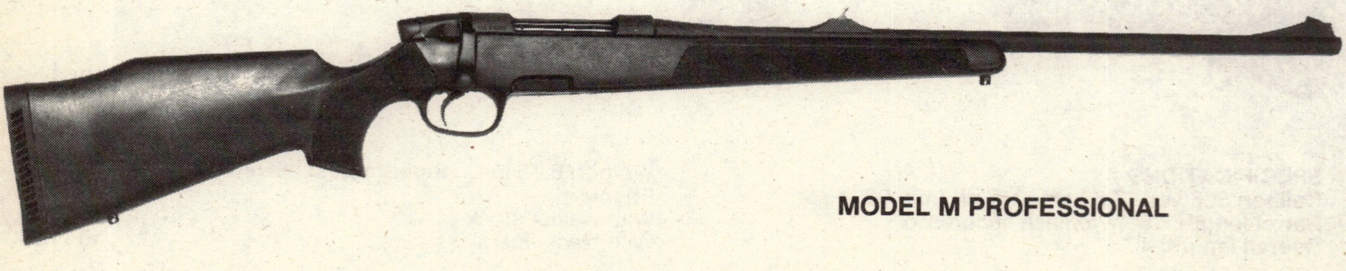

MODEL M PROFESSIONAL

# STEYR-MANNLICHER RIFLES

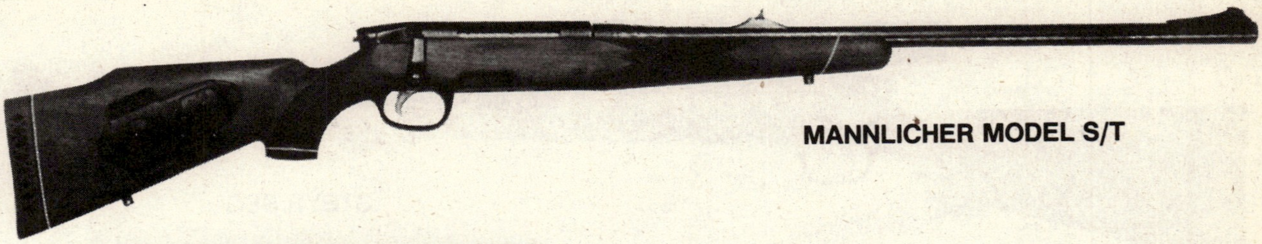

**MANNLICHER MODEL S/T**

**MANNLICHER MODEL S-S/T MAGNUM**

The Mannlicher S/T is a heavy-barreled version of the Sporter S Model designed specifically for big game hunting. It features a hand-checkered walnut stock, five-round rotary magazine, optional butt stock magazine, and double-set or single trigger. **Calibers:** See table below. **Barrel length:** 26″. **Weight:** 8.36 lbs. (Model S); 9 lbs. (Model S/T).

**Prices:**
**Model S** .................................... $2179.00
**Model S/T** (w/optional butt magazine) .......... 2335.00

RIFLES

## SPORTER & LUXUS SERIES CALIBERS SPECIFICATIONS

| MODELS: | 222 Rem. | 222 Rem. Mag. | 223 Rem. | 243 Win. | 25-06 | 308 Win. | 6.5 × 55 | 6.5 × 57 | 270 Win. | 7 × 64 | 30-06 Spr. | 9.3 × 62 | 6.5 × 68 | 7mm Rem. Mag. | .300 Win. Mag. | 8 × 685S | 9.3 × 64 | .375 H & H Mag. | 458 Win. Mag. |
|---|---|---|---|---|---|---|---|---|---|---|---|---|---|---|---|---|---|---|---|
| **Sporter (SL)** | • | • | • | | | | | | | | | | | | | | | | |
| **(L)** | | | | • | | • | | | | | | | | | | | | | |
| **(M)** | | | | | | | • | • | • | • | • | • | | | | | | | |
| **S** | | | | | | | | | | | | | • | • | • | • | • | • | |
| **S/T** | | | | | | | | | | | | | | | | | | • | • |
| **Mill Professional** | | | | | • | | | | • | • | • | | | | | | | | |
| **Luxus (L)** | | | | • | | • | | | | | | | | | | | | | |
| **(M)** | | | | | | | • | • | • | • | • | • | | | | | | | |
| **(S)** | | | | | | | | | | | | | • | • | • | • | | | |
| **Varmint (not shown)** | • | | | | | | | | | | | | | | | | | | |
| **Jagd Match** | • | | | • | | • | | | | | | | | | | | | | |

* Also available in 9.3 × 64

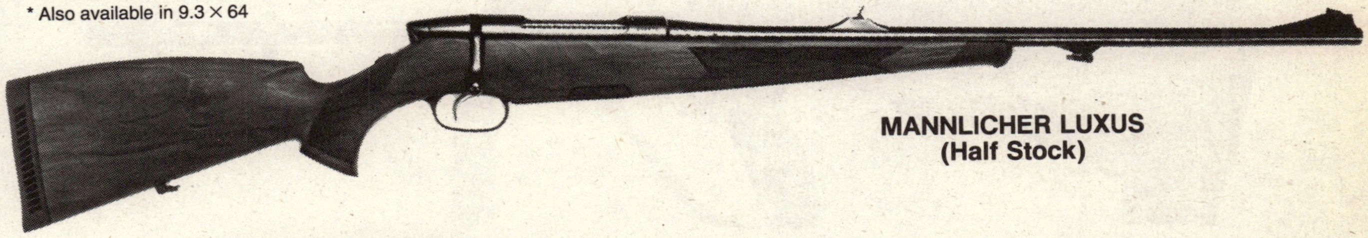

**MANNLICHER LUXUS (Half Stock)**

**MANNLICHER LUXUS**

The Mannlicher Luxus is the premier rifle in the Steyr lineup. It features a hand-checkered walnut stock, smooth action, combination shotgun set trigger, steel in-line three-round magazine (detachable), rear tang slide safety, and European-designed receiver. **Calibers:** See table above. **Barrel length:** 20″ (Full Stock); 23.6″ (Half Stock).

**Prices:**
**Luxus Models**
Half Stock .................................... $2648.00
Full Stock .................................... 2804.00
**Luxus S (Magnum) Models** (26″ barrel, Half Stock only) .................................... 2804.00

# STEYR-MANNLICHER RIFLES

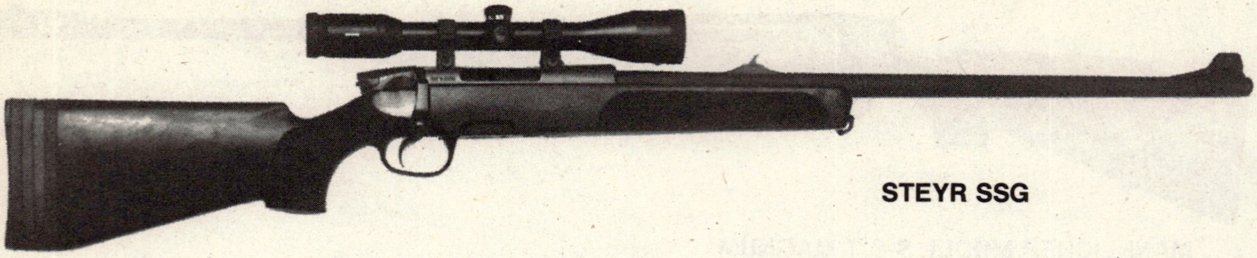

STEYR SSG

The Steyr SSG features a black synthetic Cycolac stock (walnut optional), heavy Parkerized barrel, five-round standard (and optional 10-round) staggered magazine, heavy-duty milled receiver. **Calibers:** 243 Win. and 308 Win. **Barrel length:** 26″. **Overall length:** 44.5″. **Weight:** 8.5 lbs. **Sights:** Iron sights; hooded ramp front with blade adjustable for elevation; rear standard V-notch adjustable for windage. **Features:** Sliding safety; 1″ swivels.

**Prices:**
**Model SSG-PI** Cycolac half-stock (26″ bbl. in 308 Win.) .......... **$1995.00**
**Model SSG-PII** (20″ or 26″ heavy bbl. in 308 Win.) .......... **1995.00**
**Model SSG P-IV Urban** in 308 Win. w/16¾″ heavy barrel .......... **2660.00**
**Model SSG Marksman Scope Mount** .......... **244.00**

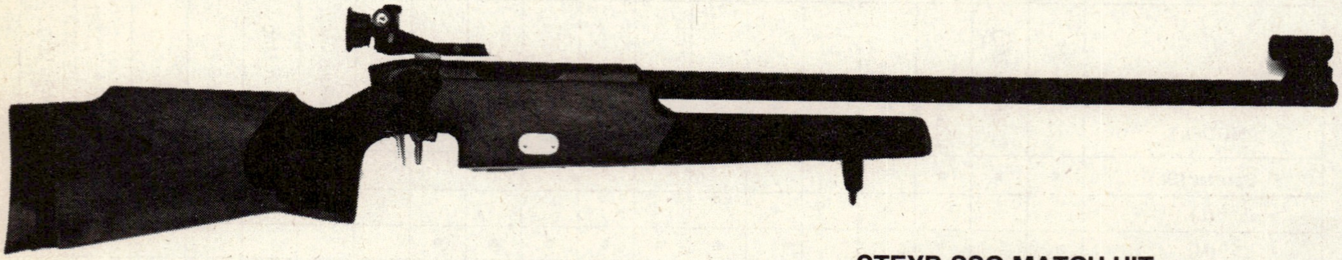

STEYR SSG MATCH UIT

Designed especially for target competition, the Steyr Match UIT features a walnut competition stock, stipple-textured pistol grip, adjustable straight and wide trigger, adjustable first-stage trigger pull, enlarged bolt handle for rapid fire, cold hammer-forged barrel, and non-glare band for sighting.
**Caliber:** 308 Win. **Overall length:** 44″. **Weight:** 10 lbs.

**Prices:**
**Steyr Match SPG-UIT** .......... **$3995.00**
10-shot magazine .......... **143.00**
**Model SPG-CISM** .......... **4295.00**
**Model SPG-T** .......... **3695.00**

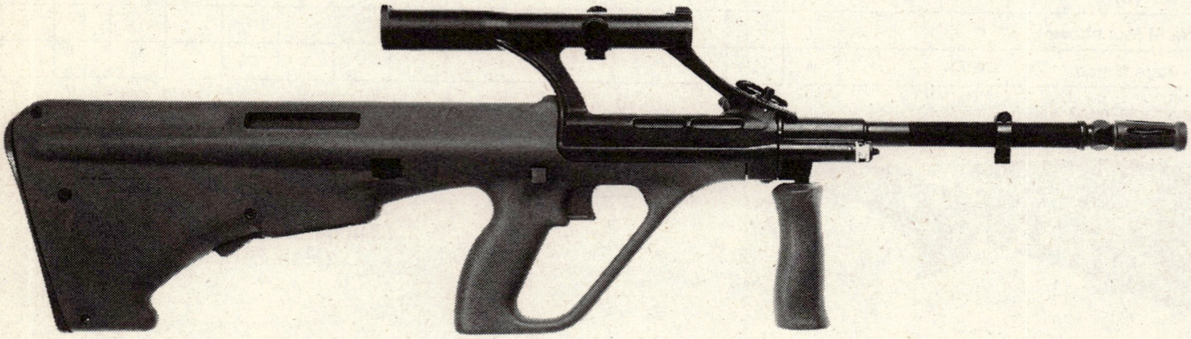

AUG S.A. SEMIAUTOMATIC RIFLE

**SPECIFICATIONS**
**Caliber:** 223 **Capacity:** 30-round magazine
**Barrel length:** 16″
**Price:** .......... **$1685.00**
Also available: **AUG** Special Receiver w/Stanag Scope Mount .......... **695.00**

# THOMPSON/CENTER RIFLES

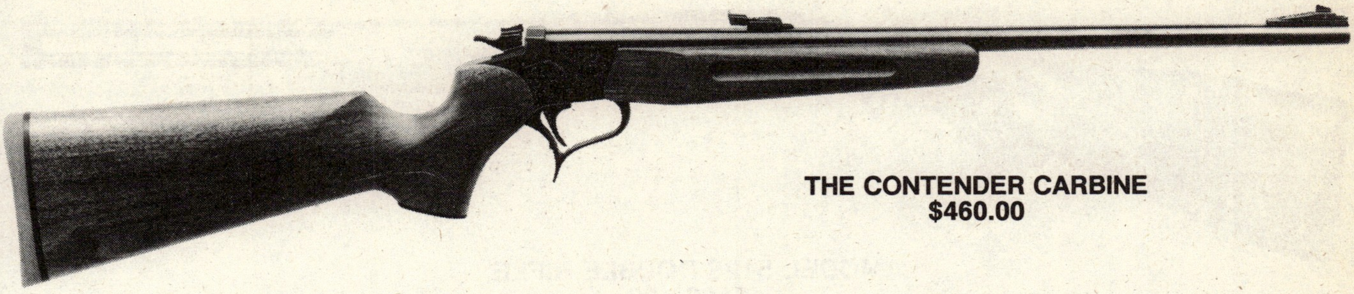

**THE CONTENDER CARBINE**
**$460.00**

Available in 8 **calibers:** 17 Rem., 22 LR, 22 LR Match, 22 Hornet, 223 Rem., 7×30 Waters, 30-30 Win. and 375 Win. **Barrels** are 21 inches long and are interchangeable, with adjustable iron sights and tapped and drilled for scope mounts. **Weight:** Only 5 lbs. 3 oz.

Also available:

**Contender Vent Rib Carbine**
With standard walnut stock . . . . . . . . . . . . . . . . . . **$500.00**
With 21″ 17 Rem. barrel . . . . . . . . . . . . . . . . . . . . . **530.00**

**Contender Youth Model Carbine** (22 LR and 223 Rem.)
W/16¼″ bbl., walnut Youth stock . . . . . . . . . . . **$465.00**
**Contender Carbine**
w/Match Grade 22 LR barrel . . . . . . . . . . . . . . . . . **510.00**

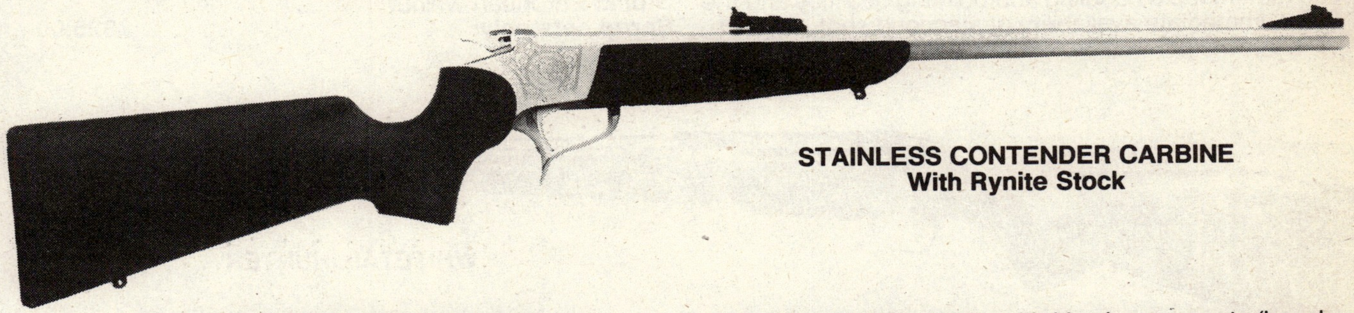

**STAINLESS CONTENDER CARBINE**
**With Rynite Stock**

## CONTENDER CARBINE STAINLESS

Available in 22 LR, 22 Hornet, 223 Rem., 7-30 Waters, 30-30 Win., 375 Win., and .410 bore. Same specifications as standard model, with walnut or Rynite stock. All stainless-steel components interchange readily with blued components (barrels and frames can be mixed or matched).

**Prices:**
**Stainless Carbine Standard** . . . . . . . . . . . . . . . . . . . **$495.00**
**Stainless Carbine w/vent rib** (.410 ga.) . . . . . . . . . **520.00**

**CONTENDER CARBINE KIT**
**Walnut Stock**

## CONTENDER CONVERSION KIT

Available in 22LR, 22 Hornet, 223 Rem., 30-30 Win. and .410 smoothbore. Each kit contains a buttstock, blued 21″ barrel, forend and sights.

**Prices:**
With walnut stock . . . . . . . . . . . . . . . . . . . . **$300.00–$330.00**
Rynite stock, stainless-steel barrel . . . . . . **320.00– 345.00**

# TIKKA RIFLES

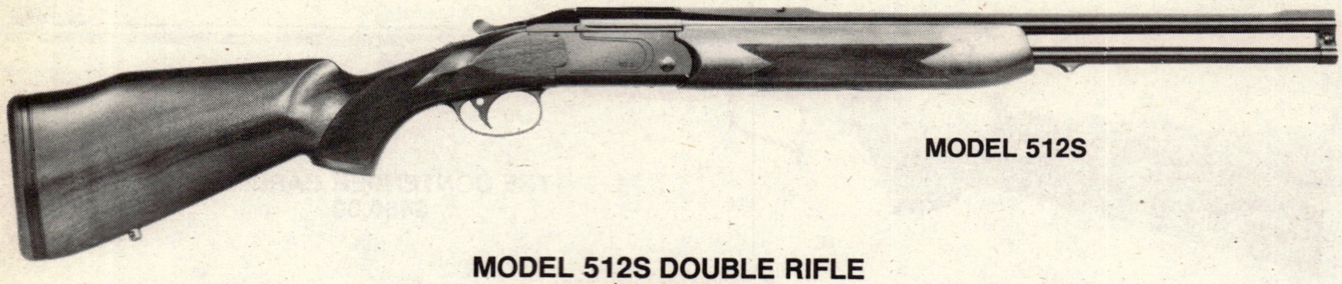

MODEL 512S

## MODEL 512S DOUBLE RIFLE
## $1525.00

The renowned Valmet 512S line of fine firearms is now being produced under the TIKKA brand name and is being manufactured to the same specifications as the former Valmet. As a result of a joint venture entered into by SAKO Ltd., the production facilities for these firearms are now located in Italy. The manufacture of the 512S series is controlled under the rigid quality standards of SAKO Ltd., with complete interchangeability of parts between firearms produced in Italy and Finland. TIKKA'S double rifle offers features and qualities no other action can match: rapid handling and pointing qualities and the silent, immediate availability of a second shot. As such, this model overcomes the two major drawbacks usually associated with this type of firearm: price and accuracy. Automatic ejectors on 9.3×74R only.

**SPECIFICATIONS**
**Calibers:** 308 Win., 30-06, 9.3×74R
**Barrel length:** 24″
**Overall length:** 40″
**Weight:** 8 1/2 lbs.
**Stock:** European walnut
**Barrel sets only:** . . . . . . . . . . . . . . . . . . . . . . . . . . **$825.00**

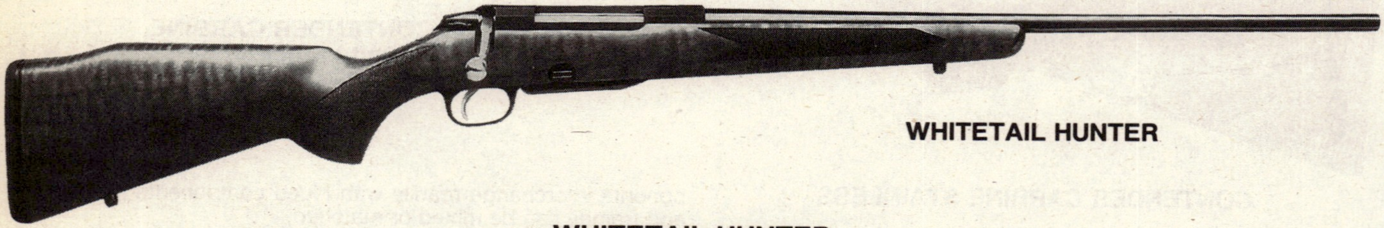

WHITETAIL HUNTER

## WHITETAIL HUNTER
## $535.00 ($560.00 Magnum)

**SPECIFICATIONS**
**Calibers:** 22-250, 223, 243, 308 (Medium); 25-06, 270, 30-06 (Long); 7mm Mag., 300 Win. Mag., 338 Win. Mag.
**Capacity:** 3 rounds (5 rounds optional); detachable magazine
**Barrel length:** 22 1/2″ (24 1/2″ Magnum)
**Overall length:** 42″ (Medium); 42 1/2″ (Long); 44 1/2″ (Magnum)
**Weight:** 7 lbs. (Medium); 7 1/4 lbs. (Long); 7 1/2 lbs. (Magnum)
**Sights:** No sights; integral scope mount rails; drilled and tapped
**Safety:** Locks trigger and bolt handle
**Features:** Oversized trigger guard; short bolt throw; customized spacer system; walnut stock w/matte lacquer finish; cold hammer-forged barrel

# A. UBERTI REPLICAS

ALL UBERTI FIREARMS AVAILABLE IN SUPER GRADE, PRESTIGE AND ENGRAVED FINISHES



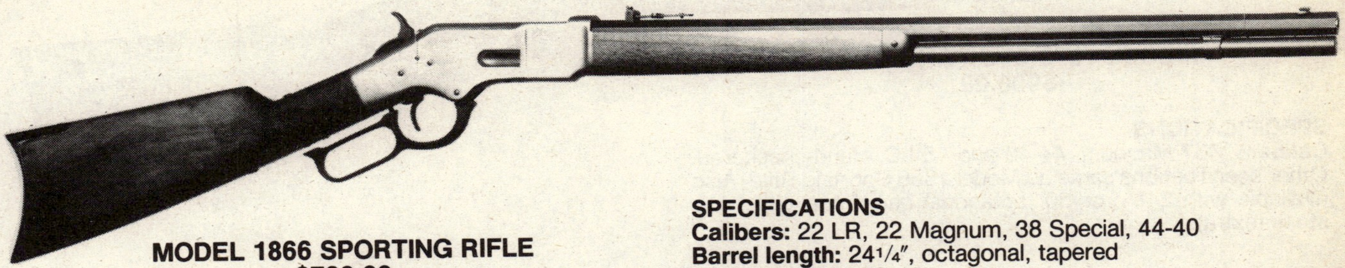

**MODEL 1866 SPORTING RIFLE**
**$780.00**

**SPECIFICATIONS**
**Calibers:** 22 LR, 22 Magnum, 38 Special, 44-40
**Barrel length:** 24 1/4″, octagonal, tapered
**Overall length:** 43 1/4″
**Weight:** 8.16 lbs.
**Frame:** Elevator and buttplate in brass
**Stock:** Walnut
**Sights:** Vertically adjustable rear; horizontally adjustable front

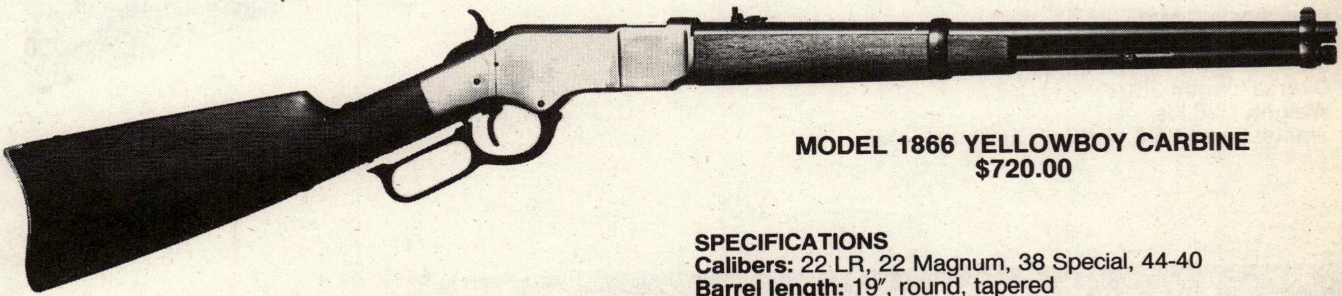

**MODEL 1866 YELLOWBOY CARBINE**
**$720.00**

The first gun to carry the Winchester name, this model was born as the 44-caliber rimfire cartridge Henry and is now chambered for 22 LR and 44-40.

**SPECIFICATIONS**
**Calibers:** 22 LR, 22 Magnum, 38 Special, 44-40
**Barrel length:** 19″, round, tapered
**Overall length:** 38 1/4″
**Weight:** 7.380 lbs.
**Frame:** Brass
**Stock and forend:** Walnut
**Sights:** Vertically adjustable rear; horizontally adjustable front

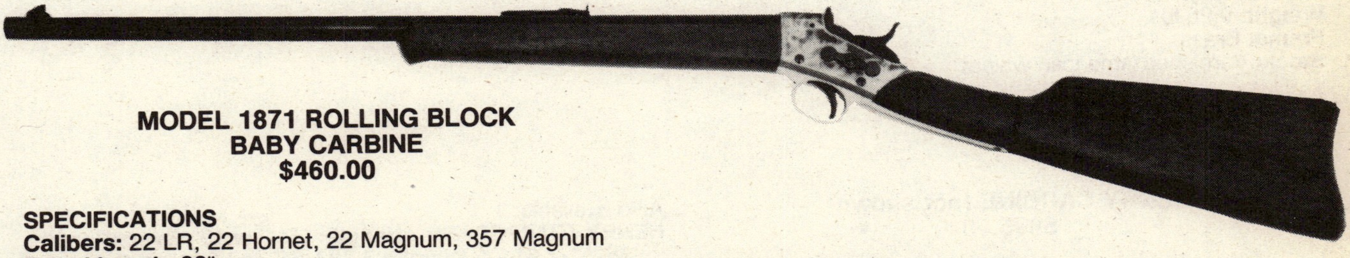

**MODEL 1871 ROLLING BLOCK**
**BABY CARBINE**
**$460.00**

**SPECIFICATIONS**
**Calibers:** 22 LR, 22 Hornet, 22 Magnum, 357 Magnum
**Barrel length:** 22″
**Overall length:** 35 1/2″
**Weight:** 4.85 lbs.
**Stock & forend:** Walnut
**Trigger guard:** Brass
**Sights:** Fully adjustable rear; ramp front
**Frame:** Color-casehardened steel

# A. UBERTI REPLICAS

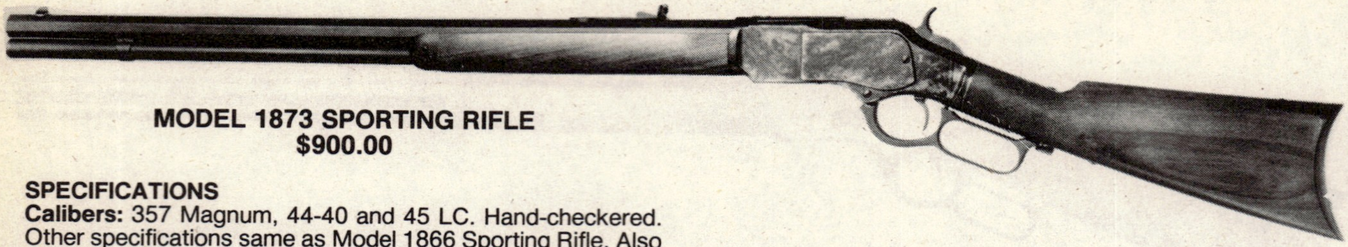

**MODEL 1873 SPORTING RIFLE**
**$900.00**

**SPECIFICATIONS**
**Calibers:** 357 Magnum, 44-40 and 45 LC. Hand-checkered. Other specifications same as Model 1866 Sporting Rifle. Also available with 24 1/4″ or 30″ octagonal barrel and pistol-grip stock (extra).

**1873 CARBINE**
**$890.00**

**SPECIFICATIONS**
**Calibers:** 357 Mag., 44-40, 45 LC
**Barrel length:** 19″ round, tapered
**Overall length:** 38 1/4″
**Weight:** 7.38 lbs.
**Sights:** Fixed front; vertically adjustable rear

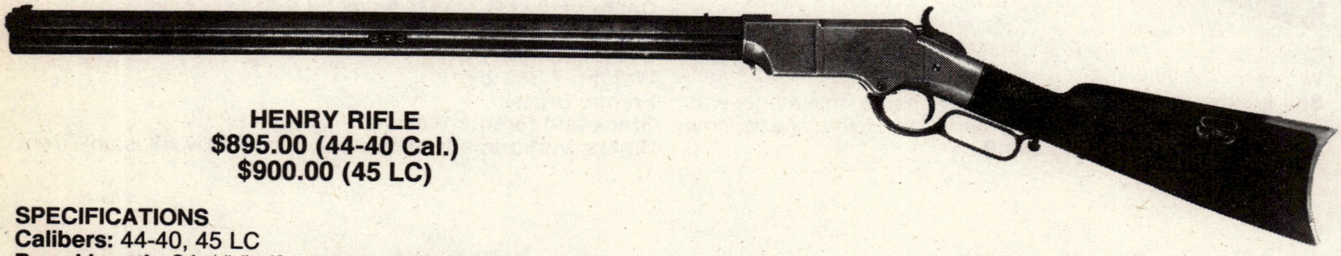

**HENRY RIFLE**
**$895.00 (44-40 Cal.)**
**$900.00 (45 LC)**

**SPECIFICATIONS**
**Calibers:** 44-40, 45 LC
**Barrel length:** 24 1/4″ (half-octagon, with tubular magazine)
**Overall length:** 43 3/4″
**Weight:** 9.26 lbs.
**Frame:** Brass
**Stock:** Varnished American walnut

**HENRY CARBINE (not shown)**
**$895.00**

**SPECIFICATIONS**
**Caliber:** 44-40 **Capacity:** 12 shots
**Barrel length:** 22 1/4″ **Weight:** 9.04 lbs.

Also available:
**HENRY TRAPPER. Barrel length:** 16 1/4″ or 18″. **Overall length:** 35 3/4″ or 37 3/4″. **Weight:** 7.383 lbs. or 7.934 lbs. **Capacity:** 8 or 9 shots. **Price: $900.00**
**HENRY RIFLE w/Steel Frame** (24 1/4″ barrel; 44/40 cal.). **Price: $950.00**

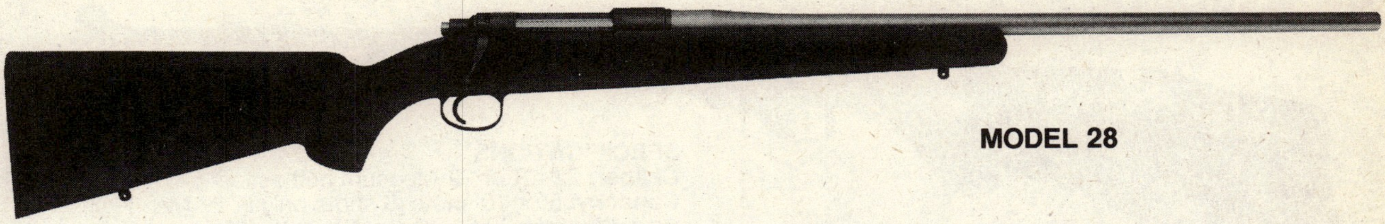

MODEL 28

MODEL 20
MOUNTAIN RIFLE

**MODEL 20 SERIES**
**$2400.00 ($2500.00 Left Hand)**

**SPECIFICATIONS**
**Calibers (Short Action):** 6mm Rem., 17 Rem., 22 Hornet, 222 Rem., 222 Rem. Mag., 22-250 Rem., 223 Rem., 243 Win., 250-3000 Savage, 257 Roberts, 257 Ackley, 7×57 Mauser, 7×57 Ackley, 7mm-08 Rem., 284 Win., 300 Savage, 308 Win., 358 Win.
**Barrel length:** 22″
**Weight:** 4.75 lbs.
**Safety:** Two-position safety allows bolt to open or lock with sear blocked
**Stock:** Kevlar/Graphite composite; choice of 7 or more colors

Also available:
**MODEL 24 SERIES** (Long Action) in 270 Win., 30-06, 25-06, 7mm Express **Weight:** $5\frac{1}{4}$ lbs.
**Barrel length:** 22″ .......................... **$2600.00**
Same as above in Left-Hand Model ......... **2700.00**
**MODEL 28 SERIES** (Magnum Action) in 264 Win., 7mm Rem., 300 Win., 338 **Weight:** $5\frac{3}{4}$ lbs.
**Barrel length:** 24″ .......................... **2900.00**
Same as above in Left-Hand Model ......... **3000.00**
**MODEL 40 SERIES** (Magnum Action) in 300 Wby. and 416 Rigby. **Weight:** $7\frac{1}{2}$ lbs.
**Barrel length:** 26″ .......................... **2900.00**
Same as above in Left-Hand Model ......... **3000.00**

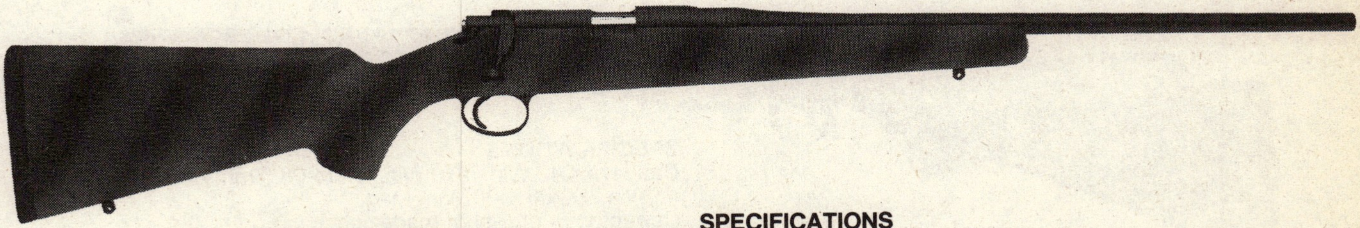

**MODEL 20 RF**
**(Single Shot or Repeater)**
**$800.00**

**SPECIFICATIONS**
**Caliber:** 22 LR
**Barrel length:** 22″ (Douglas Premium #1 Contour)
**Weight:** $5\frac{1}{2}$ lbs.
**Sights:** None (drilled and tapped for scope)
**Stock:** Composite

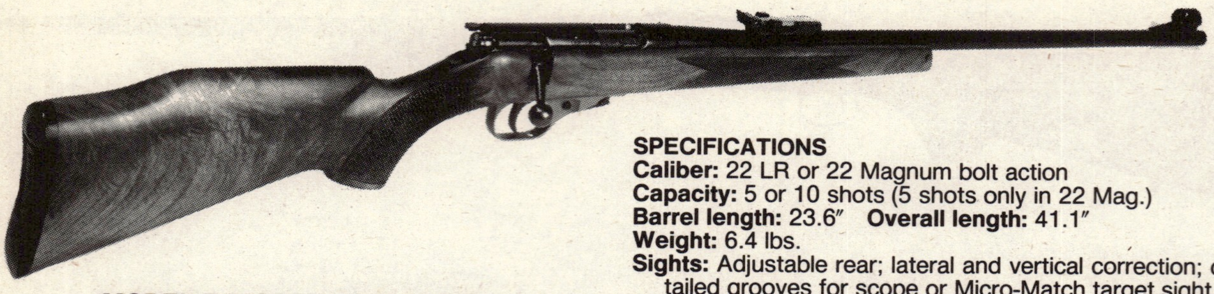

**SPECIFICATIONS**
**Caliber:** 22 LR or 22 Magnum bolt action
**Capacity:** 5 or 10 shots (5 shots only in 22 Mag.)
**Barrel length:** 23.6″ **Overall length:** 41.1″
**Weight:** 6.4 lbs.
**Sights:** Adjustable rear; lateral and vertical correction; dovetailed grooves for scope or Micro-Match target sight
**Features:** French walnut Monte Carlo stock; firing adjustment safety (working in firing pin)

**MODEL T DIOPTRA SPORTER**
**$650.00**

**SPECIFICATIONS**
**Caliber:** 22 LR
**Barrel length:** 25.6″ **Overall length:** 44.1″
**Weight:** 10.4 lbs.
**Sights:** Micro-Match target sight
**Stock:** French walnut
**Features:** Adjustable buttplate and cheek rest; fully adjustable firing; left-hand stock and action available

**MODEL T UIT STANDARD RIFLE**
**$1250.00**

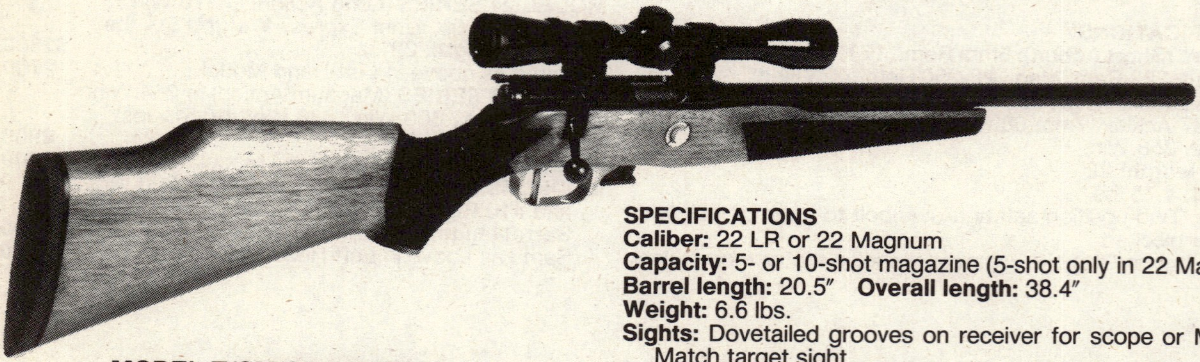

**SPECIFICATIONS**
**Caliber:** 22 LR or 22 Magnum
**Capacity:** 5- or 10-shot magazine (5-shot only in 22 Mag.)
**Barrel length:** 20.5″ **Overall length:** 38.4″
**Weight:** 6.6 lbs.
**Sights:** Dovetailed grooves on receiver for scope or Micro-Match target sight
**Stock:** French walnut Monte Carlo stock (left-hand stock available)

**MODEL T/SM SILHOUETTE**
**$750.00**

**SPECIFICATIONS**
**Calibers:** 243 Win., 270 Win., 7mm-08, 7mm Rem. Mag., 308 Win., 30-06, 300 Win. Mag.
**Capacity:** 3- or 5-shot magazine
**Barrel length:** 24″ bolt action (interchangeable barrel)
**Overall length:** 44.8″ **Weight:** 8.4 lbs.
**Sights:** Dovetailed grooves on receiver for scope
**Stock:** French walnut Monte Carlo stock (left-hand stock available)

**MODEL TGC CENTERFIRE**
**$1090.00**

# VOERE RIFLES

BENCHREST RIFLE

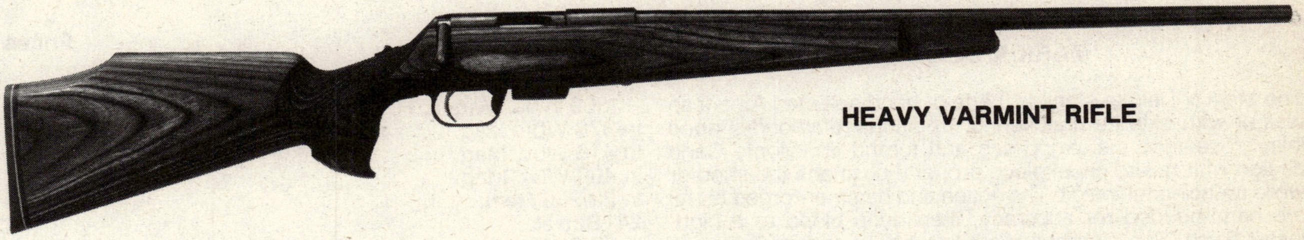

HEAVY VARMINT RIFLE

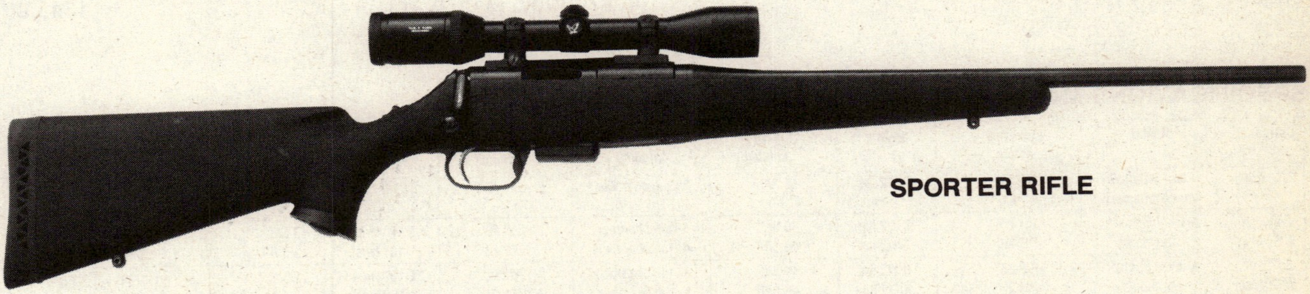

SPORTER RIFLE

**MODEL VEC 91 LIGHTNING BOLT**
**$1995.00 $1495.00 w/Synthetic Stock**
**$1695.00 Heavy Barrel Varmint w/Laminated Stock**
**$1995.00 Benchrest Model**

This first factory-made high-power caseless ammunition sporting and hunting rifle features two small batteries capable of delivering 5,000 shots. The rifle will not fire unless the bolt is fully closed with the sliding safety in forward fire position. The trigger let-off is adjustable for 5 ounces to 7 pounds by an adjustment screw in the trigger guard. A free-floating barrel ensures a high level of accuracy. The rifle features a bolt action with twin forward locking lugs, a double protector from gas leaks, a two-stage fully adjustable electrical trigger, and electronic ignition.

**SPECIFICATIONS**
**Caliber:** 223 UCC caseless ammo **Capacity:** 5-shot
**Barrel length:** 20″ (22″ Heavy Varmint)
**Overall length:** 39″
**Weight:** 6 lbs.
**Safety:** Top tang sliding safety
**Sights:** Fixed post ramp front; open rear adjustable for windage and elevation
**Stock:** Select walnut, hand-cut checkered pistol-grip stock with schnabel forend (modified Bavarian buttstock); hand-rubbed oil finish; vented recoil pad; detachable sling swivels

# WEATHERBY MARK V RIFLES

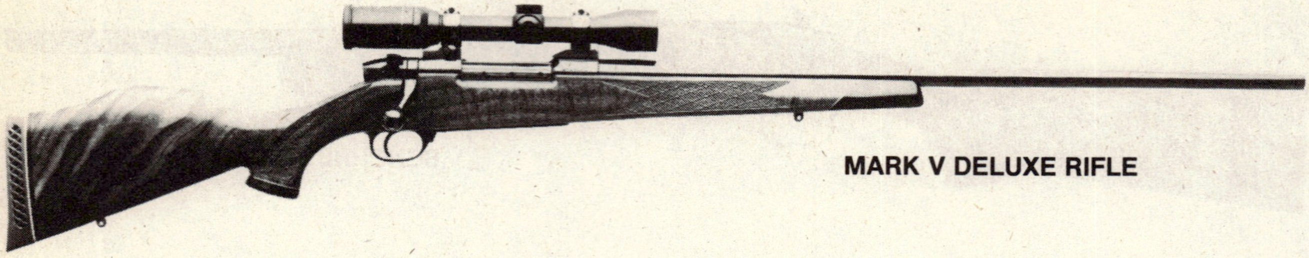

MARK V DELUXE RIFLE

## MARK V DELUXE

The Mark V Deluxe stock is made of hand-selected American walnut with skipline checkering, traditional diamond-shaped inlay, rosewood pistol-grip cap and forend tip. Monte Carlo design with raised cheekpiece properly positions the shooter while reducing felt recoil. The action and hammer-forged barrel are hand-bedded for accuracy, then deep blued to a high-luster finish. See also specifications below and on following page.

| Calibers | Prices |
|---|---|
| **26″ Barrel:** | |
| In 240 Wby. Mag., 257 Wby. Mag., 7mm Wby. Mag., 300 Wby. Mag. (L.H. also), 340 Wby. Mag. | **$1343.00** |
| In 378 Wby. Mag. | **1415.00** |
| In 416 Wby. Mag. | **1459.00** |
| In 460 Wby. Mag. | **1799.00** |
| In 22-250 Rem. | **1297.00** |
| **24″ Barrel:** | |
| In 30-06 Spfld. | **1343.00** |
| In 270 Wby. Mag. (L.H.) | **1343.00** |

### SPECIFICATIONS MARK V RIFLES

| Caliber | Model | Barrelled Action | Weight * | Overall Length | Magazine Capacity | Barrel Length/ Contour | Rifling | Length of Pull | Drop at Comb | Monte Carlo | Drop at Heel |
|---|---|---|---|---|---|---|---|---|---|---|---|
| 22 - .250 | Mark V Deluxe Varmintmaster† | RH 26" | 6 1/2 lbs. | 45 3/8" | 3+1 in chamber | 26" #2 | 1 - 14" twist | 13 1/2" | 3/4" | 3/8" | 1 1/4" |
| .240 WBY Mag. | Mark V Deluxe† | RH 26" | 8 1/2 lbs. | 46 5/8" | 4+1 in chamber | 26" #2 | 1-10" twist | 13 5/8" | 7/8" | 3/8" | 1 3/8" |
| | Lazermark† | RH 26" | 8 1/2 lbs. | 46 5/8" | 4+1 in chamber | 26" #2 | 1-10" twist | 13 5/8" | 7/8" | 3/8" | 1 3/8" |
| .257 WBY Mag. | Mark V Sporter | RH 26" | 8 1/2 lbs. | 46 5/8" | 3+1 in chamber | 26" #2 | 1-10" twist | 13 5/8" | 1" | 1/2" | 1 5/8" |
| | Eurosport | RH 26" | 8 1/2 lbs. | 46 5/8" | 3+1 in chamber | 26" #2 | 1-10" twist | 13 5/8" | 1" | 1/2" | 1 5/8" |
| | Mark V Deluxe | RH 26" | 8 1/2 lbs. | 46 5/8" | 3+1 in chamber | 26" #2 | 1-10" twist | 13 5/8" | 7/8" | 3/8" | 1 3/8" |
| | Euromark | RH 26" | 8 1/2 lbs. | 46 5/8" | 3+1 in chamber | 26" #2 | 1-10" twist | 13 5/8" | 7/8" | 3/8" | 1 3/8" |
| | Lazermark | RH 26" | 8 1/2 lbs. | 46 5/8" | 3+1 in chamber | 26" #2 | 1-10" twist | 13 5/8" | 7/8" | 3/8" | 1 3/8" |
| | Synthetic | RH 26" | 8 lbs. | 46 5/8" | 3+1 in chamber | 26" #2 | 1-10" twist | 13 5/8" | 7/8" | 1/2" | 1 1/8" |
| | Stainless | RH 26" | 8 lbs. | 46 5/8" | 3+1 in chamber | 26" #2 | 1-10" twist | 13 5/8" | 7/8" | 1/2" | 1 1/8" |
| .270 WIN. | Mark V Sporter† | RH 22" | 7 1/2 lbs. | 42 5/8" | 4+1 in chamber | 22" #1 | 1-10" twist | 13 5/8" | 1" | 5/8" | 1 5/8" |
| | Weathermark† | RH 22" | 7 1/2 lbs. | 42 5/8" | 4+1 in chamber | 22" #1 | 1-10" twist | 13 1/2" | 7/8" | - | 1 1/8" |
| | Alaskan† | RH 22" | 7 1/2 lbs. | 42 5/8" | 4+1 in chamber | 22" #1 | 1-10" twist | 13 1/2" | 7/8" | - | 1 1/8" |
| .270 WBY Mag. | Mark V Sporter | RH 26" | 8 1/2 lbs. | 46 5/8" | 3+1 in chamber | 26" #2 | 1-10" twist | 13 5/8" | 1" | 1/2" | 1 5/8" |
| | Eurosport | RH 26" | 8 1/2 lbs. | 46 5/8" | 3+1 in chamber | 26" #2 | 1-10" twist | 13 5/8" | 1" | 1/2" | 1 5/8" |
| | Mark V Deluxe | RH 26" | 8 1/2 lbs. | 46 5/8" | 3+1 in chamber | 26" #2 | 1-10" twist | 13 5/8" | 7/8" | 3/8" | 1 3/8" |
| | Mark V Deluxe† | LH 24" | 8 1/2 lbs. | 44 5/8" | 3+1 in chamber | 24" #1 | 1-10" twist | 13 5/8" | 7/8" | 3/8" | 1 3/8" |
| | Euromark | RH 26" | 8 1/2 lbs. | 46 5/8" | 3+1 in chamber | 26" #2 | 1-10" twist | 13 5/8" | 7/8" | 3/8" | 1 3/8" |
| | Lazermark | RH 26" | 8 1/2 lbs. | 46 5/8" | 3+1 in chamber | 26" #2 | 1-10" twist | 13 5/8" | 7/8" | 3/8" | 1 3/8" |
| | Synthetic | RH 26" | 8 lbs. | 46 5/8" | 3+1 in chamber | 26" #2 | 1-10" twist | 13 5/8" | 7/8" | 1/2" | 1 1/8" |
| | Stainless | RH 26" | 8 lbs. | 46 5/8" | 3+1 in chamber | 26" #2 | 1-10" twist | 13 5/8" | 7/8" | 1/2" | 1 1/8" |
| 7mm Rem. Mag. | Mark V Sporter | RH 24" | 8 lbs. | 44 5/8" | 3+1 in chamber | 24" #2 | 1-9 1/4" twist | 13 5/8" | 1" | 1/2" | 1 5/8" |
| | Eurosport | RH 24" | 8 lbs. | 44 5/8" | 3+1 in chamber | 24" #2 | 1-9 1/4" twist | 13 5/8" | 1" | 1/2" | 1 5/8" |
| | Synthetic | RH 24" | 8 lbs. | 44 5/8" | 3+1 in chamber | 24" #2 | 1-9 1/4" twist | 13 5/8" | 7/8" | 1/2" | 1 1/8" |
| | Stainless | RH 24" | 8 lbs. | 44 5/8" | 3+1 in chamber | 24" #2 | 1-9 1/4" twist | 13 5/8" | 7/8" | 1/2" | 1 1/8" |
| 7mm WBY Mag. | Mark V Sporter | RH 26" | 8 1/2 lbs. | 46 5/8" | 3+1 in chamber | 26" #2 | 1-10" twist | 13 5/8" | 1" | 1/2" | 1 5/8" |
| | Eurosport | RH 26" | 8 1/2 lbs. | 46 5/8" | 3+1 in chamber | 26" #2 | 1-10" twist | 13 5/8" | 1" | 1/2" | 1 5/8" |
| | Mark V Deluxe | RH 26" | 8 1/2 lbs. | 46 5/8" | 3+1 in chamber | 26" #2 | 1-10" twist | 13 5/8" | 7/8" | 3/8" | 1 3/8" |
| | Euromark | RH 26" | 8 1/2 lbs. | 46 5/8" | 3+1 in chamber | 26" #2 | 1-10" twist | 13 5/8" | 7/8" | 3/8" | 1 3/8" |
| | Lazermark | RH 26" | 8 1/2 lbs. | 46 5/8" | 3+1 in chamber | 26" #2 | 1-10" twist | 13 5/8" | 7/8" | 3/8" | 1 3/8" |
| | Synthetic | RH 26" | 8 lbs. | 46 5/8" | 3+1 in chamber | 26" #2 | 1-10" twist | 13 5/8" | 7/8" | 1/2" | 1 1/8" |
| | Stainless | RH 26" | 8 lbs. | 46 5/8" | 3+1 in chamber | 26" #2 | 1-10" twist | 13 5/8" | 7/8" | 1/2" | 1 1/8" |
| .30-06 Springfield | Mark V Sporter† | RH 22" | 7 1/2 lbs. | 42 5/8" | 4+1 in chamber | 22" #1 | 1-10" twist | 13 5/8" | 1" | 5/8" | 1 5/8" |
| | Mark V Deluxe† | RH 24" | 8 lbs. | 44 5/8" | 4+1 in chamber | 24" #1 | 1-10" twist | 13 5/8" | 5/8" | 1/4" | 1 1/8" |
| | Lazermark† | RH 24" | 8 lbs. | 44 5/8" | 4+1 in chamber | 24" #1 | 1-10" twist | 13 5/8" | 5/8" | 1/4" | 1 1/8" |
| | Weathermark† | RH 22" | 7 1/2 lbs. | 42 5/8" | 4+1 in chamber | 22" #1 | 1-10" twist | 13 1/2" | 7/8" | - | 1 1/8" |
| | Alaskan† | RH 22" | 7 1/2 lbs. | 42 5/8" | 4+1 in chamber | 22" #1 | 1-10" twist | 13 1/2" | 7/8" | - | 1 1/8" |

# WEATHERBY MARK V RIFLES

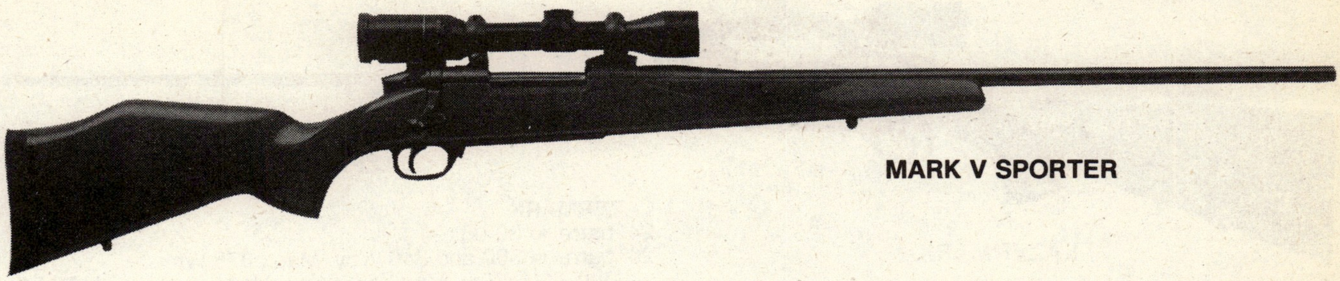

MARK V SPORTER



## MARK V SPORTER

**Calibers** **Prices**

**26″ Barrel:**

In 257 Wby. Mag., 270 Wby. Mag., 7mm Wby. Mag., 300 Wby. Mag., 340 Wby. Mag. . . . . . . . . . . . . **$878.00**

**24″ Barrel:**

In 7mm Rem. Mag., 300 Win. Mag., 338 Win. Mag. **825.00**

In 375 H&H . . . . . . . . . . . . . . . . . . . . . . . . . . . . . . **937.00**

Also available: **EUROSPORT.** Same specifications and prices but with hand-rubbed satin oil finish.

## SPECIFICATIONS MARK V RIFLES (CONT.)

| Caliber | Model | Barrelled Action | Weight * | Overall Length | Magazine Capacity | Barrel Length/ Contour | Rifling | Length of Pull | Drop at Comb | Monte Carlo | Drop at Heel |
|---|---|---|---|---|---|---|---|---|---|---|---|
| .300 Win Mag. | Mark V Sporter | RH 24" | 8 lbs. | 44 5/8" | 3+1 in chamber | 24" #2 | 1-10" twist | 13 5/8" | 1" | 1/2" | 1 5/8" |
| | Eurosport | RH 24" | 8 lbs. | 44 5/8" | 3+1 in chamber | 24" #2 | 1-10" twist | 13 5/8" | 1" | 1/2" | 1 5/8" |
| | Synthetic | RH 24" | 8 lbs. | 44 5/8" | 3+1 in chamber | 24" #2 | 1-10" twist | 13 5/8" | 7/8" | 1/2" | 1 1/8" |
| | Stainless | RH 24" | 8 lbs. | 44 5/8" | 3+1 in chamber | 24" #2 | 1-10" twist | 13 5/8" | 7/8" | 1/2" | 1 1/8" |
| .300 WBY Mag. | Mark V Sporter | RH 26" | 8 1/2 lbs. | 46 5/8" | 3+1 in chamber | 26" #2 | 1-10" twist | 13 5/8" | 1" | 1/2" | 1 5/8" |
| | Eurosport | RH 26" | 8 1/2 lbs. | 46 5/8" | 3+1 in chamber | 26" #2 | 1-10" twist | 13 5/8" | 1" | 1/2" | 1 5/8" |
| | Mark V Deluxe | RH 26" | 8 1/2 lbs. | 46 5/8" | 3+1 in chamber | 26" #2 | 1-10" twist | 13 5/8" | 7/8" | 3/8" | 1 3/8" |
| | Mark V Deluxe† | LH 26" | 8 1/2 lbs. | 46 5/8" | 3+1 in chamber | 26" #2 | 1-10" twist | 13 5/8" | 7/8" | 3/8" | 1 3/8" |
| | Euromark | RH 26" | 8 1/2 lbs. | 46 5/8" | 3+1 in chamber | 26" #2 | 1-10" twist | 13 5/8" | 7/8" | 3/8" | 1 3/8" |
| | Lazermark | RH 26" | 8 1/2 lbs. | 46 5/8" | 3+1 in chamber | 26" #2 | 1-10" twist | 13 5/8" | 7/8" | 3/8" | 1 3/8" |
| | Lazermark† | LH 26" | 8 1/2 lbs. | 46 5/8" | 3+1 in chamber | 26" #2 | 1-10" twist | 13 5/8" | 7/8" | 3/8" | 1 3/8" |
| | Synthetic | RH 26" | 8 lbs. | 46 5/8" | 3+1 in chamber | 26" #2 | 1-10" twist | 13 5/8" | 7/8" | 1/2" | 1 1/8" |
| | Stainless | RH 26" | 8 lbs. | 46 5/8" | 3+1 in chamber | 26" #2 | 1-10" twist | 13 5/8" | 7/8" | 1/2" | 1 1/8" |
| .338 Win Mag. | Mark V Sporter | RH 24" | 8 lbs. | 44 5/8" | 3+1 in chamber | 24" #2 | 1-10" twist | 13 5/8" | 1" | 1/2" | 1 5/8" |
| | Eurosport | RH 24" | 8 lbs. | 44 5/8" | 3+1 in chamber | 24" #2 | 1-10" twist | 13 5/8" | 1" | 1/2" | 1 5/8" |
| | Synthetic | RH 24" | 8 lbs. | 44 5/8" | 3+1 in chamber | 24" #2 | 1-10" twist | 13 5/8" | 7/8" | 1/2" | 1 1/8" |
| | Stainless | RH 24" | 8 lbs. | 44 5/8" | 3+1 in chamber | 24" #2 | 1-10" twist | 13 5/8" | 7/8" | 1/2" | 1 1/8" |
| .340 WBY Mag. | Mark V Sporter | RH 26" | 8 1/2 lbs. | 46 5/8" | 3+1 in chamber | 26" #2 | 1-10" twist | 13 5/8" | 1" | 1/2" | 1 5/8" |
| | Eurosport | RH 26" | 8 1/2 lbs. | 46 5/8" | 3+1 in chamber | 26" #2 | 1-10" twist | 13 5/8" | 1" | 1/2" | 1 5/8" |
| | Mark V Deluxe | RH 26" | 8 1/2 lbs. | 46 5/8" | 3+1 in chamber | 26" #2 | 1-10" twist | 13 5/8" | 7/8" | 3/8" | 1 3/8" |
| | Euromark | RH 26" | 8 1/2 lbs. | 46 5/8" | 3+1 in chamber | 26" #2 | 1-10" twist | 13 5/8" | 7/8" | 3/8" | 1 3/8" |
| | Lazermark | RH 26" | 8 1/2 lbs. | 46 5/8" | 3+1 in chamber | 26" #2 | 1-10" twist | 13 5/8" | 7/8" | 3/8" | 1 3/8" |
| | Synthetic | RH 26" | 8 lbs. | 46 5/8" | 3+1 in chamber | 26" #2 | 1-10" twist | 13 5/8" | 7/8" | 1/2" | 1 1/8" |
| | Stainless | RH 26" | 8 lbs. | 46 5/8" | 3+1 in chamber | 26" #2 | 1-10" twist | 13 5/8" | 7/8" | 1/2" | 1 1/8" |
| .375 H&H Mag. | Mark V Sporter | RH 24" | 8 1/2 lbs. | 44 5/8" | 3+1 in chamber | 24" #3 | 1-12" twist | 13 5/8" | 1" | 1/2" | 1 5/8" |
| | Eurosport | RH 24" | 8 1/2 lbs. | 44 5/8" | 3+1 in chamber | 24" #3 | 1-12" twist | 13 5/8" | 1" | 1/2" | 1 5/8" |
| | Synthetic | RH 24" | 8 lbs. | 44 5/8" | 3+1 in chamber | 24" #3 | 1-12" twist | 13 5/8" | 7/8" | 1/2" | 1 1/8" |
| | Stainless | RH 24" | 8 lbs. | 44 5/8" | 3+1 in chamber | 24" #3 | 1-12" twist | 13 5/8" | 7/8" | 1/2" | 1 1/8" |
| .378 WBY Mag. | Mark V Deluxe | RH 26" | 9 1/2 lbs. | 46 5/8" | 2+1 in chamber | 26" #3 | 1-12" twist | 13 7/8" | 7/8" | 3/8" | 1 3/8" |
| | Lazermark | RH 26" | 9 1/2 lbs. | 46 5/8" | 2+1 in chamber | 26" #3 | 1-12" twist | 13 7/8" | 7/8" | 3/8" | 1 3/8" |
| **.416 WBY Mag. | Mark V Deluxe | RH 26" | 9 1/2 lbs. | 46 3/4" | 2+1 in chamber | 26" #3 | 1-14" twist | 13 7/8" | 7/8" | 3/8" | 1 3/8" |
| | Euromark | RH 26" | 9 1/2 lbs. | 46 3/4" | 2+1 in chamber | 26" #3 | 1-14" twist | 13 7/8" | 7/8" | 3/8" | 1 3/8" |
| | Lazermark | RH 26" | 9 1/2 lbs. | 46 3/4" | 2+1 in chamber | 26" #3 | 1-14" twist | 13 7/8" | 7/8" | 3/8" | 1 3/8" |
| **.460 WBY Mag. | Mark V Deluxe | RH 26" | 10 1/2 lbs. | 46 3/4" | 2+1 in chamber | 26" #4 | 1-16" twist | 14" | 7/8" | 3/8" | 1 3/8" |
| | Lazermark | RH 26" | 10 1/2 lbs. | 46 3/4" | 2+1 in chamber | 26" #4 | 1-16" twist | 14" | 7/8" | 3/8" | 1 3/8" |

Safari Grade Custom and Crown Custom rifles are also available. Consult your Weatherby dealer or the Weatherby Custom Shop for specifications.

*Weight approximate. Varies due to stock density and bore diameter. ** Available with Weatherby Accubrake only.

# WEATHERBY MARK V RIFLES

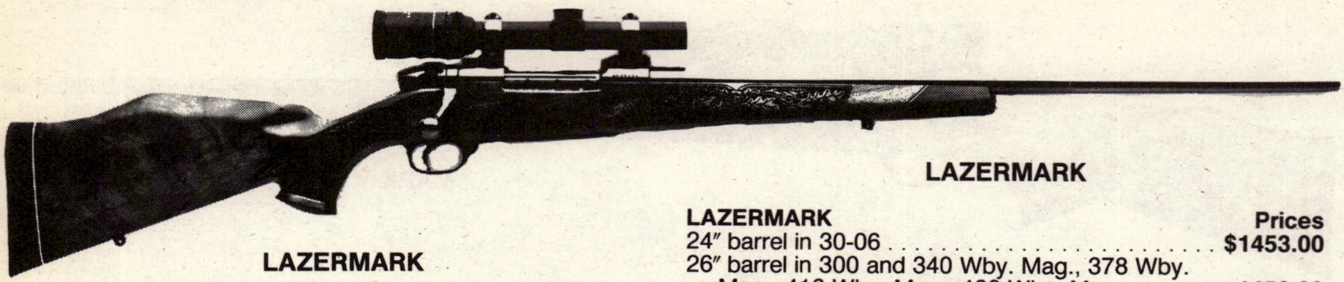

LAZERMARK

## LAZERMARK

| LAZERMARK | Prices |
|---|---|
| 24″ barrel in 30-06 | $1453.00 |
| 26″ barrel in 300 and 340 Wby. Mag., 378 Wby. Mag., 416 Wby. Mag., 460 Wby. Mag. | 1453.00 |

MARK V STAINLESS

## MARK V STAINLESS

Features 400 Series stainless steel. The action is hand-bedded to a lightweight, injection-molded synthetic stock. A custom floorplate on stainless-steel trigger guard with engraved flying "W" monogram is standard.

| MARK V STAINLESS | Prices |
|---|---|
| In 257 Wby. Mag., 270 Wby. Mag., 7mm Wby. Mag., 300 Wby. Mag., 340 Wby. Mag. | $ 960.00 |
| In 7mm Rem. Mag., 300 Win. Mag., 338 Win. Mag. | 925.00 |
| In 375 H&H | 1094.00 |

MARK V SYNTHETIC

## MARK V SYNTHETIC

Features an injection-molded synthetic stock with dual-tapered checkered forearm. Comes with custom floorplate release/trigger guard assembly and engraved flying "W" monogram.

| MARK V SYNTHETIC | Prices |
|---|---|
| In 257 Wby. Mag., 270 Wby. Mag., 7mm Wby. Mag., 300 Wby. Mag., 340 Wby. Mag. | $727.00 |
| In 7mm Rem. Mag., 300 Win. Mag., 338 Win. Mag. | 695.00 |
| In 375 H&H | 827.00 |

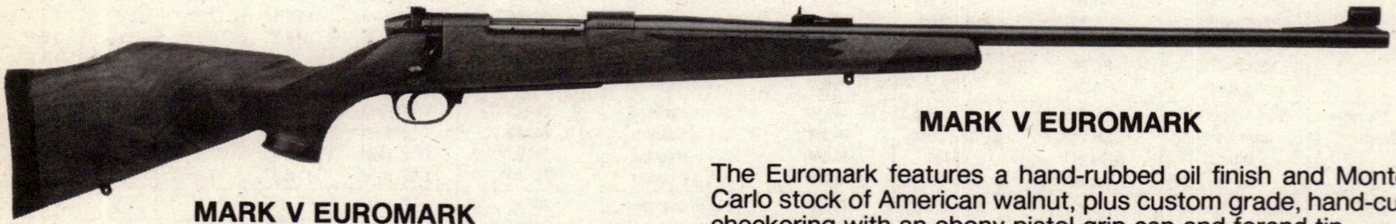

MARK V EUROMARK

## MARK V EUROMARK

The Euromark features a hand-rubbed oil finish and Monte Carlo stock of American walnut, plus custom grade, hand-cut checkering with an ebony pistol-grip cap and forend tip.

| EUROMARK | Prices |
|---|---|
| In 257 Wby. Mag., 270 Wby. Mag., 7 Wby. Mag. | $1245.00 |
| In 300 Wby. Mag., 340 Wby. Mag. | 1318.00 |
| In 416 Wby. Mag. | 1866.00 |

FOR COMPLETE SPECIFICATIONS ON THE ABOVE RIFLES, PLEASE SEE THE TABLES ON THE PREVIOUS PAGES.

# WINCHESTER BOLT-ACTION RIFLES



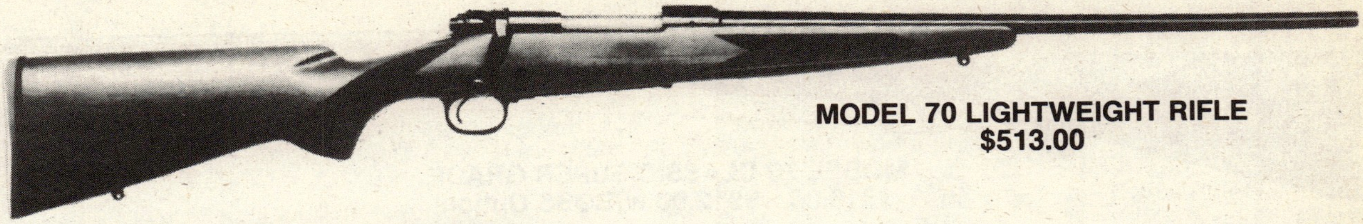

**MODEL 70 LIGHTWEIGHT RIFLE**
**$513.00**

## SPECIFICATIONS MODEL 70 LIGHTWEIGHT

| Model | Caliber | Magazine Capacity (A) | Barrel Length | Overall Length | Nominal Length Of Pull | Nominal Drop At Comb | Nominal Drop At Heel | Nominal Weight (Lbs.) | Rate of Twist 1 Turn In |
|---|---|---|---|---|---|---|---|---|---|
| **70 WALNUT** | 223 Rem. | 6 | 22″ | 42 | 13 1/2″ | 9/16″ | 7/8″ | 6 3/4 | 12″ |
| | 243 Win. | 5 | 22 | 42 | 13 1/2 | 9/16 | 7/8 | 6 7/8 | 10 |
| Checkered, | 270 Win. | 5 | 22 | 42 1/2 | 13 1/2 | 9/16 | 7/8 | 7 | 10 |
| No Sights | 30-06 Spgfld. | 5 | 22 | 42 1/2 | 13 1/2 | 9/16 | 7/8 | 7 | 10 |
| | 308 Win. | 5 | 22 | 42 | 13 1/2 | 9/16 | 7/8 | 6 3/4 | 12 |

(A) For additional capacity, add one round in chamber when ready to fire. Drops are measured from center line of bore. Rate of twist is right-hand. No sights.

## SPECIFICATIONS MODEL 70 FEATHERWEIGHT CLASSIC $602.00

| Model | Caliber | Magazine Capacity* | Barrel Length | Overall Length | Nominal Length Of Pull | Nominal Drop At Comb | Nominal Drop At Heel | Nominal Weight (Lbs.) | Rate of Twist 1 Turn In |
|---|---|---|---|---|---|---|---|---|---|
| **70 WALNUT FEATHERWEIGHT CLASSIC** | 22-250 Rem. | 5 | 22 | 42 | 13 1/2 | 9/16 | 7/8 | 7 | 14″ |
| | 243 Win. | 5 | 22 | 42 | 13 1/2 | 9/16 | 7/8 | 7 | 10 |
| | 308 Win. | 5 | 22 | 42 | 13 1/2 | 9/16 | 7/8 | 7 | 12 |
| | 7mm-08 Rem. | 5 | 22 | 42 | 13 1/2 | 9/16 | 7/8 | 7 | 10 |
| | 270 Win. | 5 | 22 | 42 | 13 1/2″ | 9/16 | 7/8 | 7 1/4 | 10 |
| *Standard Grade Walnut* | 280 Rem. | 5 | 22 | 42 | 13 1/2″ | 9/16 | 7/8 | 7 1/4 | 10 |
| *Controlled Round Feeding* | 30-06 Spfld. | 5 | 22 | 42 | 13 1/2″ | 9/16 | 7/8 | 7 1/4 | 10 |

* For additional capacity, add one round in chamber when ready to fire. Drops are measured from center line of bore. Rate of twist is right-hand.

**MODEL 70 CLASSIC SM**
**(Synthetic Composite Stock, Matte)**
**$602.00**
**$699.00 w/BOSS System**
**$653.00 (375 H&H MAGNUM)**

## SPECIFICATIONS MODEL 70 CLASSIC SM (SYNTHETIC STOCK; CONTROLLED ROUND FEED)

| Caliber | Magazine Capacity | Barrel Length | Overall Length | Nominal Length Of Pull | Nominal Drop At Comb | Nominal Drop At Heel | Nominal Weight (Lbs.) | Rate of Twist 1 Turn In | Bases Rings or Sights |
|---|---|---|---|---|---|---|---|---|---|
| 270 Win. | 5 | 24 | 44 3/4″ | 13 3/4″ | 9/16″ | 7/8″ | 7 3/8 | 10″ | |
| 30-06 Spfld. | 5 | 24 | 44 3/4 | 13 3/4 | 9/16 | 7/8 | 7 3/8 | 10 | |
| 7mm Rem. Mag. | 3 | 26 | 44 3/4 | 13 3/4 | 9/16 | 7/8 | 7 5/8 | 9 1/2 | |
| 300 Win. Mag. | 3 | 26 | 44 3/4 | 13 3/4 | 9/16 | 7/8 | 7 5/8 | 10 | |
| 338 Win. Mag. | 3 | 26 | 44 3/4 | 13 3/4 | 9/16 | 7/8 | 7 5/8 | 10 | |
| 375 H&H Mag.* | 3 | 24 | 44 3/4″ | 13 3/4 | 9/16 | 7/8 | 8 | 12 | Sights |

* Not available in BOSS models

# WINCHESTER BOLT-ACTION RIFLES

**MODEL 70 CLASSIC SUPER GRADE**
**$816.00 $912.00 w/BOSS Option**

The Winchester Model 70 Classic Super Grade features a bolt with true claw-controlled feeding of belted magnums. The stainless-steel claw extractor on the bolt grasps the round from the magazine and delivers it to the chamber and later extracts the spent cartridge. A gas block doubles as bolt stop, and the bolt guard rail assures smooth action. Winchester's 3-position safety and field-strippable firing pin are standard equipment. Other features include a satin-finish select walnut stock with sculptured cheekpiece; all-steel bottom metal; and chrome molybdenum barrel with cold hammer-forged rifling for optimum accuracy. Now available with BOSS System (**$912.00; $750.00** in Stainless). Specifications are listed in the tables below.

## SPECIFICATIONS WINCHESTER MODEL 70 CLASSIC SUPER GRADE RIFLE

| Caliber | Magazine Capacity* | Barrel Length | Overall Length | Nominal Length of Pull | Nominal Drop at | | MC | Nominal Weight (Lbs.) | Rate of Twist 1 Turn in | Bases & Rings or Sights |
|---|---|---|---|---|---|---|---|---|---|---|
| | | | | | Comb | Heel | | | | |
| 270 Win. | 5 | 24" | 44 3/4" | 13 3/4" | 9/16" | 13/16" | — | 7 3/4 | 10" | B + R |
| 30-06 Spfld. | 5 | 24 | 44 3/4 | 13 3/4 | 9/16 | 13/16 | — | 7 3/4 | 10 | B + R |
| 7mm Rem. Mag. | 3 | 26 | 46 3/4 | 13 3/4 | 9/16 | 13/16 | — | 8 | 9 1/2 | B + R |
| 300 Win. Mag. | 3 | 26 | 46 3/4 | 13 3/4 | 9/16 | 13/16 | — | 8 | 10 | B + R |
| 338 Win. Mag. | 3 | 26 | 46 3/4 | 13 3/4 | 9/16 | 13/16 | — | 8 | 10 | B + R |

* For add'l' capacity, add one round in chamber when ready to fire. Drops are measured from center line of bore. R.H. rate of twist.

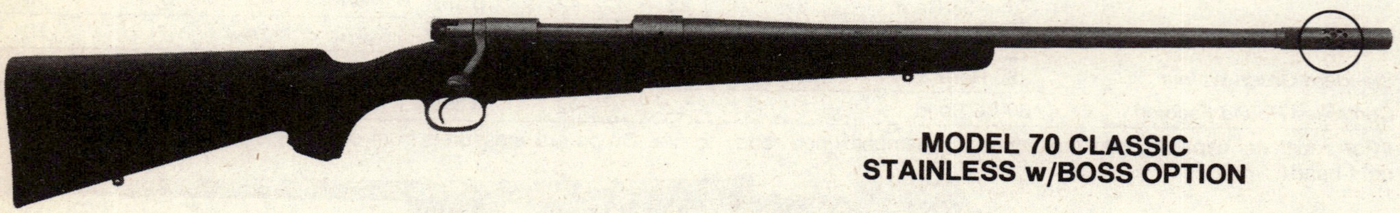

**MODEL 70 CLASSIC STAINLESS w/BOSS OPTION**

## MODEL 70 CLASSIC STAINLESS (SYNTHETIC COMPOSITE STOCK) $653.00 ($703.00 in 375 H&H Mag.)

| Caliber | Magazine Capacity | Barrel Length | Overall Length | Nominal Length Of Pull | Nominal Drop At | | Nominal Weight (Lbs.) | Rate of Twist 1 Turn In | Bases & Rings or Sights |
|---|---|---|---|---|---|---|---|---|---|
| | | | | | Comb | Heel | | | |
| 22-250 Rem. | 5" | 22" | 42 1/4" | 13 3/4" | 9/16" | 13/16" | 6 3/4 | 14" | — |
| 243 Win. | 5 | 22 | 42 1/4 | 13 3/4 | 9/16 | 13/16 | 6 3/4 | 10 | — |
| 308 Win. | 5 | 22 | 42 1/4 | 13 3/4 | 9/16 | 13/16 | 6 3/4 | 12 | — |
| 270 Win. | 5 | 24 | 44 3/4 | 13 3/4 | 9/16 | 13/16 | 7 1/4 | 10 | — |
| 30-06 Spfld. | 5 | 24 | 44 3/4 | 13 3/4 | 9/16 | 13/16 | 7 1/4 | 10 | — |
| 7mm Rem. Mag. | 3 | 26 | 46 3/4 | 13 3/4 | 9/16 | 13/16 | 7 1/2 | 9 1/2 | — |
| 300 Win. Mag. | 3 | 26 | 46 3/4 | 13 3/4 | 9/16 | 13/16 | 7 1/2 | 10 | — |
| 300 Wby. Mag. | 3 | 26 | 46 3/4 | 13 3/4 | 9/16 | 13/16 | 7 1/2 | 10 | — |
| 338 Win. Mag. | 3 | 26 | 46 3/4 | 13 3/4 | 9/16 | 13/16 | 7 1/2 | 10 | — |
| 375 H&H Mag.* | 3 | 24 | 44 3/4 | 13 3/4 | 9/16 | 13/16 | 7 1/4 | 12 | Sights |

* Not available with BOSS System

# WINCHESTER BOLT-ACTION RIFLES

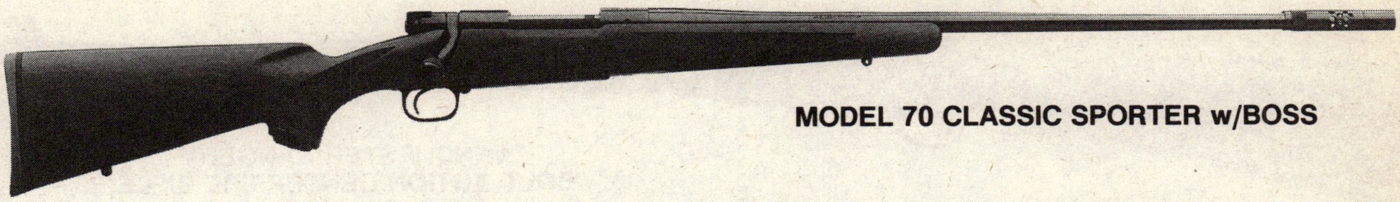

MODEL 70 CLASSIC SPORTER w/BOSS

**MODEL 70 CLASSIC SPORTER**
**$595.00 ($632.00 w/Sights)**
**$692.00 w/BOSS**

## SPECIFICATIONS MODEL 70 CLASSIC SPORTER

| Caliber | Magazine Capacity A | Barrel Length | Overall Length | Nominal Length Of Pull | Nominal Drop At Comb | Nominal Drop At Heel | Nominal Weight (Lbs.) | Rate of Twist 1 Turn In | Sights |
|---|---|---|---|---|---|---|---|---|---|
| **70 SPORTER** | | | | | | | | | |
| 25-06 Rem. | 5 | 24″ | 44 3/4″ | 13 3/4″ | 9/16″ | 13/16″ | 7 3/4 | 10″ | |
| 264-Win. Mag. | 3 | 26 | 46 3/4 | 13 3/4 | 9/16 | 13/16 | 8 | 9 | |
| 270 Win. | 5 | 24 | 44 3/4 | 13 3/4 | 9/16 | 13/16 | 7 3/4 | 10 | Sights |
| 270 Win. | 5 | 24 | 44 3/4 | 13 3/4 | 9/16 | 13/16 | 7 3/4 | 10 | |
| 270 Wby. Mag. | 3 | 26 | 46 3/4 | 13 3/4 | 9/16 | 13/16 | 8 | 10 | |
| 30-06 Spgfld. | 5 | 24 | 44 3/4 | 13 3/4 | 9/16 | 13/16 | 7 3/4 | 10 | Sights |
| 30-06 Spfld. | 5 | 24 | 44 3/4 | 13 3/4 | 9/16 | 13/16 | 7 3/4 | 10 | |
| 7mm Rem. Mag. | 3 | 26 | 46 3/4 | 13 3/4 | 9/16 | 13/16 | 8 | 9 1/2 | Sights |
| 7mm Rem. Mag. | 3 | 26 | 46 3/4 | 13 3/4 | 9/16 | 13/16 | 8 | 9 1/2 | |
| 300 Win. Mag. | 3 | 26 | 46 3/4 | 13 3/4 | 9/16 | 13/16 | 8 | 10 | Sights |
| 300 Win. Mag. | 3 | 26 | 46 3/4 | 13 3/4 | 9/16 | 13/16 | 8 | 10 | |
| 300 Wby. Mag. | 3 | 26 | 46 3/4 | 13 3/4 | 9/16 | 13/16 | 8 | 10 | |
| 338 Win. Mag. | 3 | 26 | 46 3/4 | 13 3/4 | 9/16 | 13/16 | 8 | 10 | Sights |

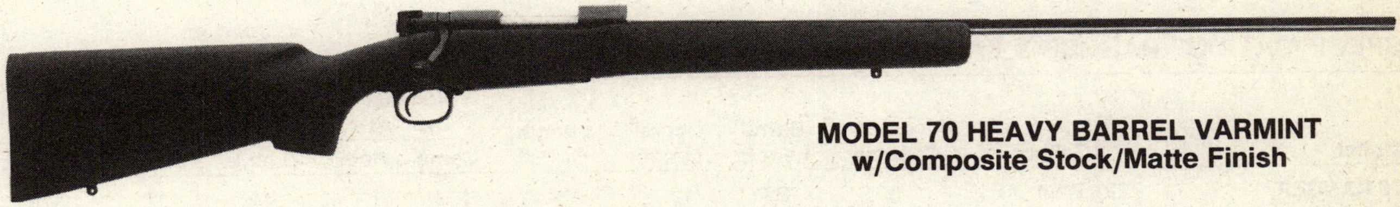

MODEL 70 HEAVY BARREL VARMINT
w/Composite Stock/Matte Finish

## MODEL 70 HEAVY BARREL VARMINT RIFLE SPECIFICATIONS Price: $742.00

| Caliber | Magazine Capacity (A) | Barrel Length | Overall Length | Nominal Length Of Pull | Nominal Drop At Comb | Nominal Drop At Heel | Nominal Weight (Lbs.) | Rate of Twist 1 Turn In | Sights |
|---|---|---|---|---|---|---|---|---|---|
| 220 Swift | 5 | 26″ | 46″ | 13 1/2″ | 3/4″ | 1/2″ | 10 3/4 | 14″ | — |
| 22-250 Rem. | 5 | 26 | 46 | 13 1/2 | 3/4 | 1/2 | 10 3/4 | 14 | — |
| 223 Rem. | 6 | 26 | 46 | 13 1/2 | 3/4 | 1/2 | 10 3/4 | 9 | — |
| 243 Win. | 5 | 26 | 46 | 13 1/2 | 3/4 | 1/2 | 10 3/4 | 10 | — |
| 308 Win. | 5 | 26 | 46 | 13 1/2 | 3/4 | 1/2 | 10 3/4 | 12 | — |

(A) For add'l. capacity, add one round in chamber when ready to fire. Drops are measured from center line of bore. R.H. rate of twist.

# WINCHESTER BOLT-ACTION RIFLES

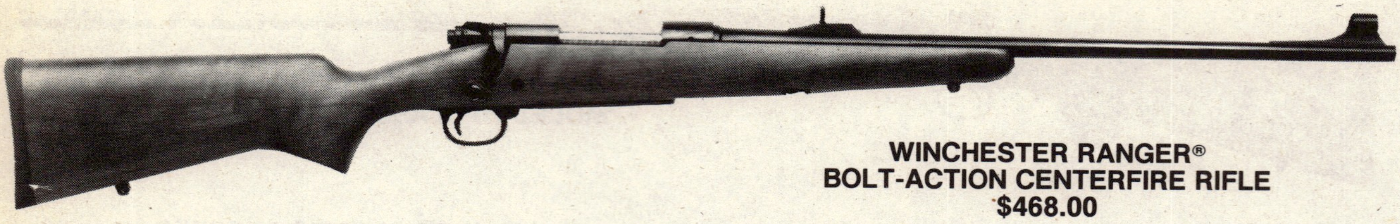

**WINCHESTER RANGER®**
**BOLT-ACTION CENTERFIRE RIFLE**
**$468.00**

The Ranger Bolt Action Rifle comes with an American hardwood stock, a wear-resistant satin walnut finish, ramp bead-post front sight, steel barrel, hinged steel magazine floorplate, three-position safety and engine-turned, anti-bind bolt. The receiver is drilled and tapped for scope mounting; accuracy is enhanced by thermoplastic bedding of the receiver. Barrel and receiver are brushed and blued.

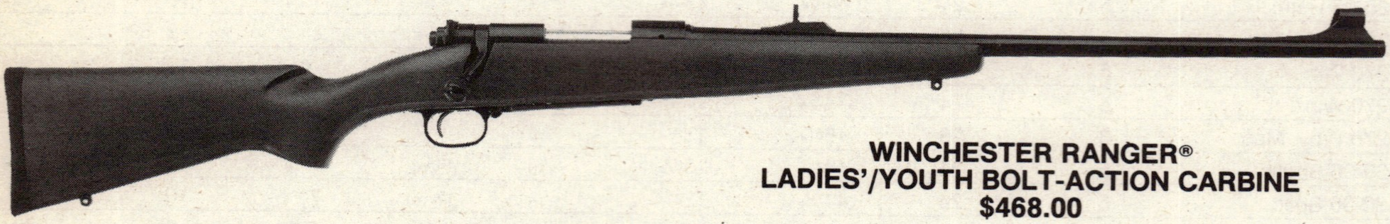

**WINCHESTER RANGER®**
**LADIES'/YOUTH BOLT-ACTION CARBINE**
**$468.00**

This carbine offers dependable bolt-action performance combined with a scaled-down design to fit the younger, smaller shooter. It features anti-bind bolt design, jeweled bolt, three-position safety, contoured recoil pad, ramped bead front sight, semibuckhorn folding-leaf rear sight, hinged steel magazine floorplate, and sling swivels. Receiver is drilled and tapped for scope mounting. Stock is of American hardwood with protective satin walnut finish. Pistol grip, length of pull, overall length and comb are all tailored to youth dimensions (see table).

### SPECIFICATIONS RANGER & LADIES' YOUTH RIFLES

| Model | Caliber | Magazine Capacity | Barrel Length | Overall Length | Nominal Length Of Pull | Nominal Drop At Comb | Nominal Drop At Heel | Nominal Weight (Lbs.) | Rate of Twist 1 Turn in | Bases & Rings Sights |
|---|---|---|---|---|---|---|---|---|---|---|
| **70 RANGER** | 223 Rem. | 6 | 22″ | 42″ | 13 1/2″ | 9/16″ | 7/8″ | 6 3/4 | 12″ | Sights |
| | 243 Win. | 5 | 22 | 42 | 13 1/2 | 9/16 | 7/8 | 6 3/4 | 10 | Sights |
| | 270 Win. | 5 | 22 | 42 1/2 | 13 1/2 | 9/16 | 7/8 | 7 | 10 | Sights |
| | 30-06 Spfld. | 5 | 22 | 41 1/2 | 13 1/2 | 9/16 | 7/8 | 7 | 10 | Sights |
| **70 RANGER LADIES/ YOUTH** | 243 Win. | 5 | 22 | 41 | 12 1/2 | 3/4 | 1 | 6 1/2 | 10 | Sights |
| | 308 Win. | 5 | 22 | 41 | 12 1/2 | 3/4 | 1 | 6 1/2 | 12 | Sights |

For add'l. capacity, add one round in chamber when ready to fire. Drops are measured from center line of bore. R.H. rate of twist.

# WINCHESTER RIFLES

## LEVER-ACTION CARBINES/RIFLES

**MODEL 94 STANDARD WALNUT RIFLE**

The top choice for lever-action styling and craftsmanship. Metal surfaces are highly polished and blued. American walnut stock and forearm have a protective stain finish with precise-cut wraparound checkering. It has a 20-inch barrel with hooded blade front sight and semibuckhorn rear sight.

**Prices:**
30-30 Win., checkered .......................... **$381.00**
w/o checkering .......................... **352.00**

**MODEL 94 WALNUT TRAPPER CARBINE**

With 16-inch short-barrel lever action and straight forward styling. Compact and fast handling in dense cover, it has a 5-shot magazine capacity (9 in 45 Colt or 44 Rem. Mag./44 S&W Special). **Calibers:** 30-30 Win., 357 Mag., 45 Colt, and 44 Rem. Mag./44 S&W Special.

**Prices:**
30-30 Winchester .......................... **$352.00**
357 Mag., 45 Colt, 44 Rem. Mag./44 S&W Spec. .......................... **372.00**

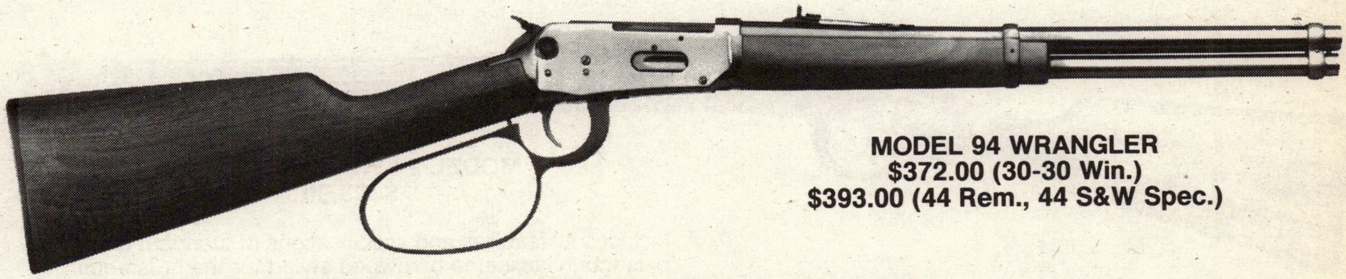

**MODEL 94 WRANGLER**
**$372.00 (30-30 Win.)**
**$393.00 (44 Rem., 44 S&W Spec.)**

### MODEL 94 SPECIFICATIONS (with 100th Anniversary Receiver Inscription)

| Model | Caliber | Magazine Capacity (A) | Barrel Length | Overall Length | Nominal Length Of Pull | Nominal Drop At Comb | Nominal Drop At Heel | Nominal Weight (Lbs.) | Rate of Twist 1 Turn in | Rings Sights |
|---|---|---|---|---|---|---|---|---|---|---|
| **94 CHECKERED WALNUT** | 30-30 Win. | 6 | 20″ | 37¾″ | 13½″ | 1⅛″ | 1⅞″ | 6½ | 12″ | Rifle |
| **94 STANDARD** | 30-30 Win. | 6 | 20 | 37¾ | 13½ | 1⅛ | 1⅞ | 6½ | 12 | Rifle |
| **94 TRAPPER CARBINE** | 30-30 Win. | 5 | 16 | 33¾ | 13½ | 1⅛ | 1⅞ | 6⅛ | 12 | Rifle |
| | 357 Mag. | 9 | 16 | 33¾ | 13½ | 1 1/16 | 1⅞ | 6⅛ | 16 | Rifle |
| | 44 Rem. Mag .44 S&W Spec. | 99 | 16 | 33¾ | 13½ | 1⅛ | 1⅞ | 6 | 38 | Rifle |
| | 45 Colt | 9 | 16 | 33¾ | 13½ | 1⅞ | 1⅞ | 6 | 38 | Rifle |
| **94 WRANGLER** | 30-30 Win. | 5 | 16 | 33¾ | 13½ | 1⅛ | 1⅞ | 6⅛ | 12 | Rifle |
| | 44 Rem. Mag .44 S&W Spec. | 99 | 16 | 33¾ | 13½ | 1⅛ | 1⅞ | 6 | 12 | Rifle |

(A) For additional capacity, add one round in chamber when ready to fire. Drops are measured from center line of bore. Rate of twist is right-hand.

# WINCHESTER RIFLES

## LEVER ACTION

### MODEL 94 RANGER
**$311.00 ($366.00 with Scope)**

**Model 94 Ranger** is an economical version of the Model 94. Lever action is smooth and reliable. In 30-30 Winchester, the rapid-firing six-shot magazine capacity provides two more shots than most other centerfire hunting rifles.

### MODEL 94 BIG-BORE WALNUT
**$393.00**

Winchester's powerful 307 and 356 hunting calibers combined with maximum lever-action power and angled ejection provide hunters with improved performance and economy.

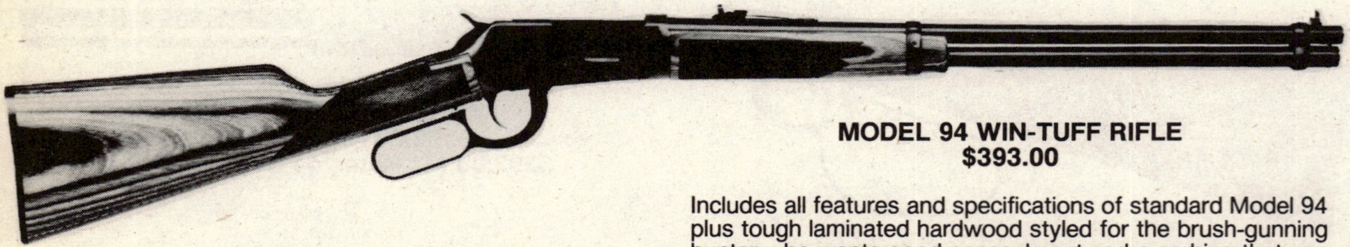

### MODEL 94 WIN-TUFF RIFLE
**$393.00**

Includes all features and specifications of standard Model 94 plus tough laminated hardwood styled for the brush-gunning hunter who wants good concealment and a carbine that can stand up to all kinds of weather.

### MODEL 94 SPECIFICATIONS

| Model | Caliber | Magazine Capacity (A) | Barrel Length | Overall Length | Nominal Length Of Pull | Nominal Drop At Comb | Nominal Drop At Heel | Nominal Weight (Lbs.) | Rate of Twist 1 Turn in | Sights |
|---|---|---|---|---|---|---|---|---|---|---|
| **94 WIN-TUFF** | 30-30 Win. | 6 | 20″ | 37¾″ | 13½″ | 1⅛″ | 1⅞″ | 6½ | 12″ | Rifle |
| **94 BIG BORE WALNUT** | 307 Win. | 6 | 20 | 37¼ | 13½ | 1⅛ | 1⅞ | 6½ | 12 | Rifle |
| | 356 Win. | 6 | 20 | 37¾ | 13½ | 1⅛ | 1⅞ | 6½ | 12 | Rifle |
| **RANGER** | 30-30 Win. | 6 | 20 | 37¾ | 13½ | 1⅛ | 1⅞ | 6½ | 12 | Rifle |
| Scope 4X32 and see-through mounts | 30-30 Win. | 6 | 20 | 37¾ | 13½ | 1⅛ | 1⅞ | 6½ | 12 | R/S |

(A) For additional capacity, add one round in chamber when ready to fire. Drops are measured from center line of bore. R/S-Rifle sights and Bushnell® Sportview™ scope with mounts. Rate of twist is right-hand.

## MODEL 9422 LEVER-ACTION RIMFIRE RIFLES

These Model 9422 rimfire rifles combine classic 94 styling and handling in ultra-modern lever action 22s of superb craftsmanship. Handling and shooting characteristics are superior because of their carbine-like size.

Positive lever action and bolt design ensure feeding and chambering from any shooting position. The bolt face is T-slotted to guide the cartridge with complete control from magazine to chamber. A color-coded magazine follower shows when the brass magazine tube is empty. Receivers are grooved for scope mounting. Other functional features include exposed hammer with half-cock safety, hooded bead front sight, semi-buckhorn rear sight and side ejection of spent cartridges.

Stock and forearm are American walnut with checkering, high-luster finish, and straight-grip design. Internal parts are carefully finished for smoothness of action.

**MODEL 9422 WALNUT**

Considered one of the world's finest production sporting arms, this lever-action rimfire (shown above) holds 21 Short, 17 Long or 15 Long Rifle cartridges.

**Model 9422 Walnut Magnum** gives exceptional accuracy at longer ranges than conventional 22 rifles. It is designed specifically for the 22 Winchester Magnum Rimfire cartridge and holds 11 cartridges.

**Model 9422 Win-Cam Magnum** features laminated nonglare, green-shaded stock and forearm. American hardwood stock is bonded to withstand all weather and climates. **Model 9422 Win-Tuff** is also availale to ensure resistance to changes in weather conditions, or exposure to water and hard knocks.

### SPECIFICATIONS MODEL 9422

| Model | Caliber | Magazine Capacity | Barrel Length | Overall Length | Nominal Length Of Pull | Nominal Drop At Comb | Nominal Drop At Heel | Nominal Weight (Lbs.) | Rate of Twist 1 Turn in | Sights | Prices |
|---|---|---|---|---|---|---|---|---|---|---|---|
| **9422 WALNUT** | 22 S, L, LR<br>22 WMR | 21 S,17 L, 15 LR11 | 20½ | 37⅛ | 13½ | 1⅛ | 1⅞ | 6¼ | 16 | Rifle | **$395.00**<br>**412.00** |
| **9422 WIN-TUFF** | 22 S, L, LR<br>22 WMR | 21 S, 17 L, 15 LR11 | 20½ | 37⅛ | 13½ | 1⅛ | 1⅞ | 6¼ | 16 | Rifle | **395.00**<br>**412.00** |
| **9422 WIN-CAM** | 22 WMR | 11 | 20½″ | 37⅛″ | 13½″ | 1⅛″ | 1⅞″ | 6¼ | 16″ | Rifle | **412.00** |

WMR = Winchester Magnum Rimfire. S=Short, L=Long, LR=Long Rifle. Drops are measured from center line of bore.

# WINSLOW RIFLES

**SPECIFICATIONS**
**Stock:** Choice of two stock models. **The Plainsmaster** offers pinpoint accuracy in open country with full curl pistol grip and flat forearm. **The Bushmaster** offers lighter weight for bush country; slender pistol with palm swell; beavertail forend for light hand comfort. Both styles are of hand-rubbed black walnut. Length of pull—13½ inches; plainsmaster ⅜ inch castoff; Bushmaster 3/16 inch castoff; all rifles are drilled and tapped to incorporate the use of telescopic sights; rifles with receiver or open sights are available on special order; all rifles are equipped with quick detachable sling swivel studs and whiteline recoil pad. All Winslow stocks incorporate a slight castoff to deflect recoil, minimizing flinch and muzzle jump. **Magazine:** Staggered box type, four shot. (Blind in the stock has no floorplate). **Action:** Mauser Mark X Action. **Overall length:** 43″ (Standard Model); 45″ (Magnum); all Winslow rifles have company name and serial number and grade engraved on the action and caliber engraved on barrel. **Barrel:** Douglas barrel premium grade, chrome moly-type steel; all barrels, 20 caliber through 35 caliber, have six lands and grooves; barrels larger than 35 caliber have eight lands and grooves. All barrels are finished to (.2 to .4) micro inches inside the lands and grooves. **Total weight** (without scope): 7 to 7½ lbs. with 24″ barrel in standard calibers 243, 308, 270, etc; 8 to 9 lbs. with 26″ barrel in Magnum calibers 264 Win., 300 Wby., 458 Win., etc. Winslow rifles are made in the following calibers:
**Standard cartridges:** 22-250, 243 Win., 244 Rem., 257 Roberts, 308 Win., 30-06, 280 Rem., 270 Win., 25-06, 284 Win., 358 Win., and 7mm (7×57).
**Magnum cartridges:** 300 Weatherby, 300 Win., 338 Win., 358 Norma, 375 H.H., 458 Win., 257 Weatherby, 264 Win., 270 Weatherby, 7mm Weatherby, 7mm Rem., 300 H.H., 308 Norma.
Left-handed models available in most calibers.

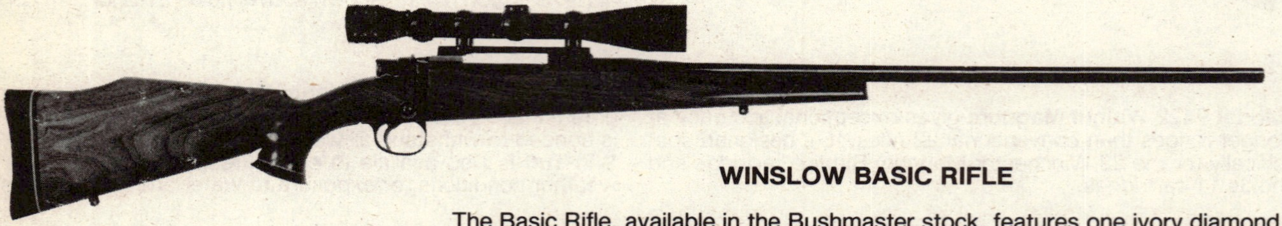

**WINSLOW BASIC RIFLE**

The Basic Rifle, available in the Bushmaster stock, features one ivory diamond inlay in a rose-wood grip cap and ivory trademark in bottom of forearm. Grade 'A' walnut jeweled bolt and follower.

**Price:** . . . . . . . . . . . . **from $1750.00**
With **Plainsmaster stock, add** . . . . . . . . . . . . **100.00**
**Left-hand model** . . . . . . . . . . . . **from 1850.00**

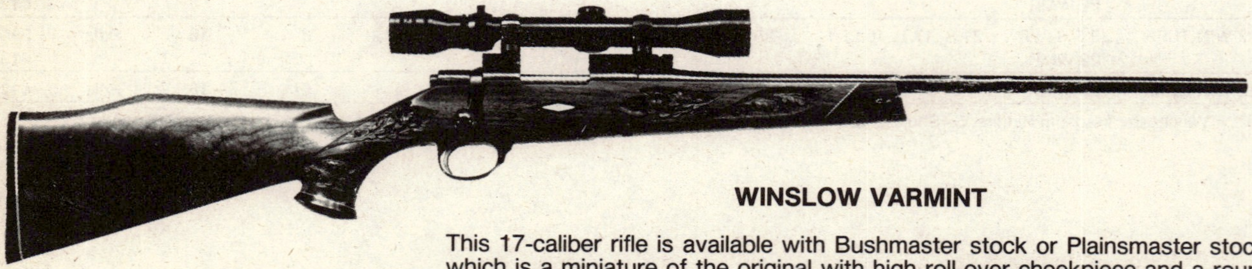

**WINSLOW VARMINT**

This 17-caliber rifle is available with Bushmaster stock or Plainsmaster stock, which is a miniature of the original with high roll-over cheekpiece and a round leading edge on the forearm, modified spoon billed pistol grip. Available in 17/222, 17/222 Mag. 17/233, 222 Rem. and 223. Regent grade shown.

**Prices:**
With **Bushmaster stock** . . . . . . . . . . . . **from $1750.00**
With **Plainsmaster stock, add** . . . . . . . . . . . . **100.00**
**Left-hand Model** . . . . . . . . . . . . **from 1850.00**

# Shotguns



For addresses and phone numbers of manufacturers and distributors included in this section, turn to *DIRECTORY OF MANUFACTURERS AND SUPPLIERS* at the back of the book.

# AMERICAN ARMS SHOTGUNS

SILVER I OVER AND UNDER
(W/Fixed Chokes & Extractors)

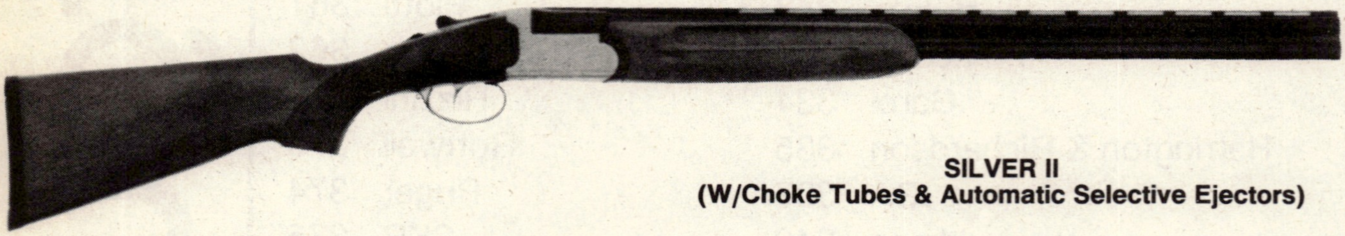

SILVER II
(W/Choke Tubes & Automatic Selective Ejectors)

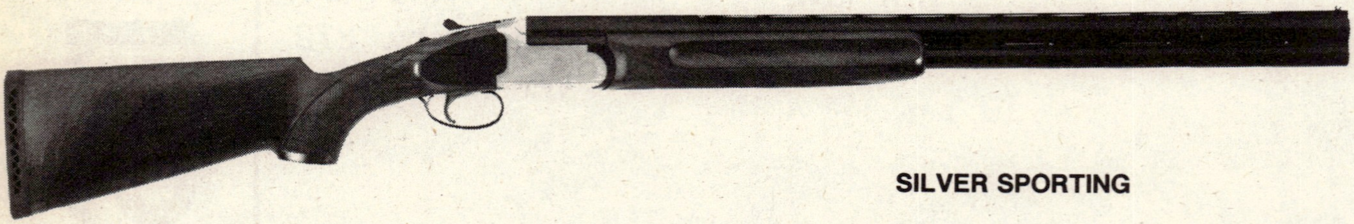

SILVER SPORTING

**SPECIFICATIONS**

| Model | Gauge | Bbl. Length | Chamber | Chokes | Avg. Weight | Prices |
|---|---|---|---|---|---|---|
| **Silver I** | 12<br>20 | 26″–28″<br>26″–28″ | 3″<br>3″ | IC/M-M/F<br>IC/M-M/F | 6 lbs. 15 oz.<br>6 lbs. 12 oz. | **$593.00** |
| | 28<br>.410 | 26″<br>26″ | 2¾″<br>3″ | IC/M<br>IC/M | 5 lbs. 14 oz.<br>6 lbs. 6 oz. | **658.00** |
| **Silver II** | 12<br>16<br>20 | 26″–28″<br>26″<br>26″ | 3″<br>2¾″<br>3″ | CT-3<br>IC/M<br>CT-3 | 6 lbs. 15 oz.<br>6 lbs. 13 oz.<br>6 lbs. 12 oz. | **748.00** |
| | 28<br>.410 | 26″<br>26″ | 2¾″<br>3″ | IC/M<br>IC/M | 5 lbs. 14 oz.<br>6 lbs. 6 oz. | **765.00** |
| **Silver Lite (not shown)** | 12<br>20<br>28 | 26″<br>26″<br>26″ | 3″<br>3″<br>2¾″ | CT-3<br>CT-3<br>IC/M | 6 lbs. 4 oz.<br>5 lbs. 12 oz.<br>6 lbs. | **984.00** |
| **Sporting** | 12 | 28″–30″ | 2¾″ | CTS | 7 lbs. 6 oz. | **937.00** |

CT-3 Choke Tubes IC/M/F  Cast Off = 3/8″  CTS = SK/SK/IC/M
Silver I and II: Pull = 14 1/8″; Drop at Comb = 1 3/8″; Drop at Heel = 2 3/8″
Silver Sporting: Pull = 14 3/8″; Drop at Comb = 1 1/2″; Drop at Heel = 2 3/8″

# AMERICAN ARMS SHOTGUNS

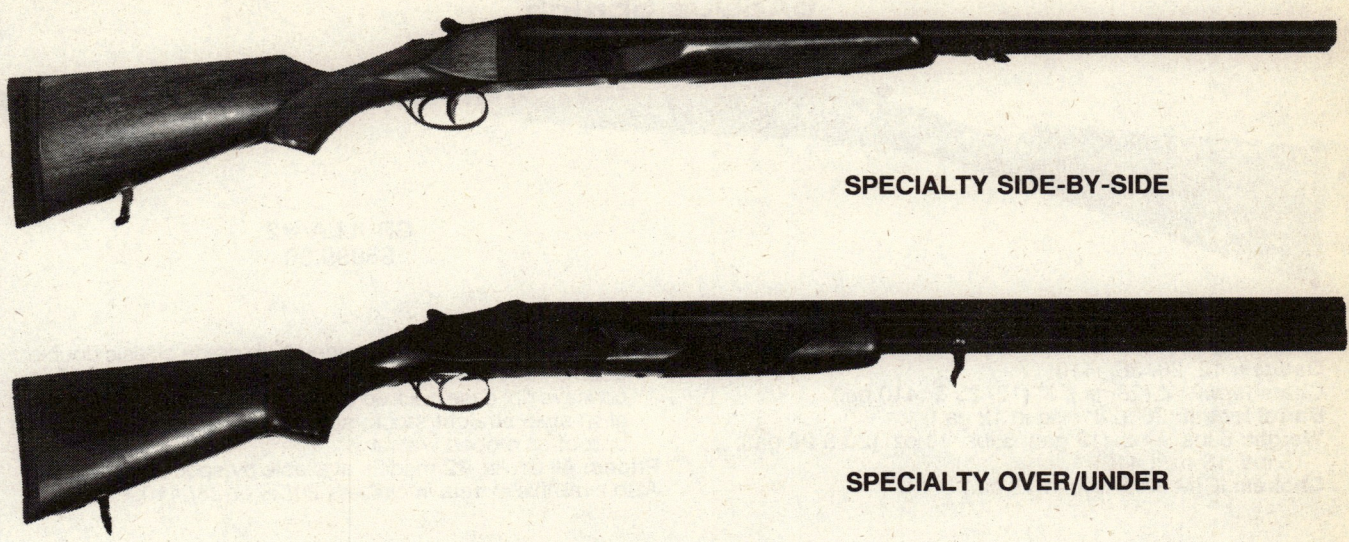

SPECIALTY SIDE-BY-SIDE

SPECIALTY OVER/UNDER

**SPECIFICATIONS**

| Model | Gauge | Bbl. Length | Chamber | Chokes | Avg. Wgt. | Prices |
|---|---|---|---|---|---|---|
| WT/OU | 10 | 26″ | 3½″ | CT-2 | 9 lbs. 10 oz. | $1029.00 |
| WS/OU | 12 | 28″ | 3½″ | CT-3 | 7 lbs. 2 oz. | 765.00 |
| TS/OU | 12 | 24″ | 3½″ | CT-3 | 6 lbs. 14 oz. | 765.00 |
| TS/SS | 12 | 26″ | 3½″ | CT-3 | 7 lbs. 6 oz. | 765.00 |
| CT-3 = Choke tubes IC/M/F. CT-2 = Choke tubes F/F. Drop at Comb = 1⅛″. Drop at Heel = 2⅜″. | | | | | | |

## BASQUE SERIES

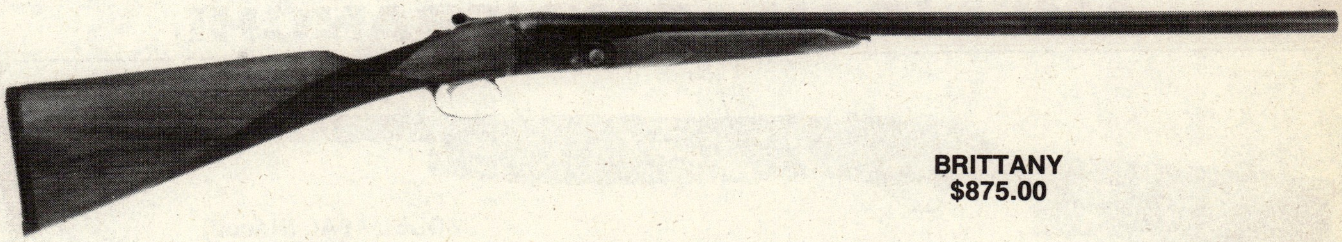

**BRITTANY**
**$875.00**

**SPECIFICATIONS**
**Gauges:** 12, 20
**Chamber:** 3″ **Chokes:** CT-3
**Barrel length:** 26″
**Weight:** 6 lbs. 7 ozs. (20 ga.); 6 lbs. 15 oz. (12 ga.)

**Features:** Engraved case-colored frame; single selective trigger with top tang selector; automatic selective ejectors; manual safety; hard chrome-lined barrels; walnut English-style straight stock and semi-beavertail forearm w/cut checkering and oil-rubbed finish; ventilated rubber recoil pad; and choke tubes with key

SHOTGUNS

# AMERICAN ARMS SHOTGUNS

## BASQUE SERIES

**GRULLA #2**
**$3099.00**

**SPECIFICATIONS**
**Gauges:** 12, 20, 28, .410
**Chambers:** 2 3/4″ (28 ga.); 3″ (12, 20 & .410 ga.)
**Barrel length:** 26″ (28″ also in 12 ga.)
**Weight:** 6 lbs. 4 oz. (12 ga.); 5 lbs. 11 oz. (20 & 28 ga.); 5 lbs. 13 oz. (.410)
**Chokes:** IC/M (M/F also in 12 ga.)

**Features:** Hand-fitted and finished high-grade classic double; double triggers; automatic selective ejectors; fixed chokes; concave rib; case-colored sidelock action w/engraving; English-style straight stock; splinter forearm and checkered butt of oil rubbed walnut
**Prices:** All Grulla #2 models available by special order only. Also available in sets in calibers 20/28 or 28/.410.

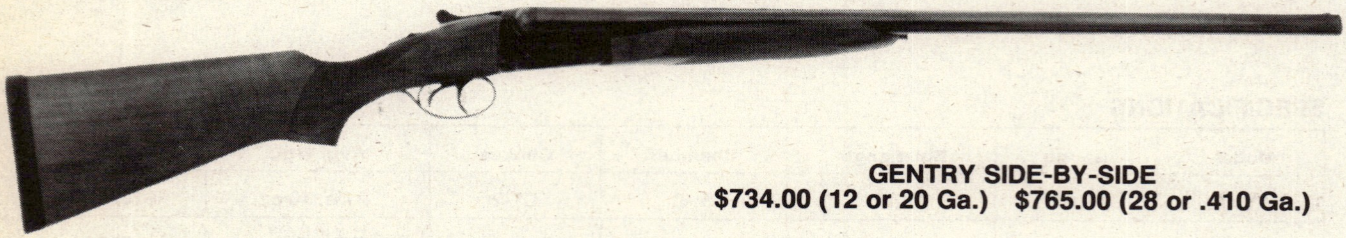

**GENTRY SIDE-BY-SIDE**
**$734.00 (12 or 20 Ga.) $765.00 (28 or .410 Ga.)**

Features boxlocks with engraved English-style scrollwork on side plates; one-piece, steel-forged receiver; chrome barrels; manual thumb safety; independent floating firing pin.

**SPECIFICATIONS**
**Gauges:** 12, 20, 28, .410
**Chambers:** 3″ (except 28 gauge, 2 3/4″)

**Barrel lengths:** 26″, choked IC/M (all gauges); 28″, choked M/F (12 and 20 gauges)
**Weight:** 6 lbs. 15 oz. (12 ga.); 6 lbs. 7 oz. (20 and .410 ga.); 6 lbs. 5 oz. (28 ga.)
**Drop at comb:** 1 3/8″ **Drop at heel:** 2 3/8″
**Other features:** Fitted recoil pad; flat matted rib; walnut pistol-grip stock and beavertail forend with hand-checkering; gold front sight bead

# AMERICAN ARMS/FRANCHI

**MODEL 48AL (Recoil)**
**$635.00**

**SPECIFICATIONS**
**Gauge:** 12/20 **Chamber:** 2 3/4″
**Action:** Single Action

**Barrel lengths:** 24″, 26″, 28″ **Choke:** Full
**Weight:** 5 1/2 to 6 1/2 lbs.
**Length of pull:** 14 1/4″
**Drop at comb:** 1 1/2″ **Drop at heel:** 2 3/8″

# AYA SHOTGUNS

## SIDELOCK SHOTGUNS

AYA sidelock shotguns are fitted with London Holland & Holland system sidelocks, double triggers with articulated front trigger, automatic safety and ejectors, cocking indicators, bushed firing pins, replaceable hinge pins and chopper lump barrels. Stocks are of figured walnut with hand-cut checkering and oil finish, complete with a metal oval on the buttstock for engraving of initials.

Exhibition grade wood is available as are many special options, including a true left-hand version and self-opener.

**Barrel lengths:** 26″, 27″, 28″ and 29″. **Weight:** 5 to 7 pounds, depending on gauge.

| Model | Prices |
|---|---|
| **MODEL 1:** Sidelock in 12 and 20 gauge with special engraving and exhibition quality wood | **$6181.00** |
| **MODEL 2:** Sidelock in 12, 16, 20, 28 gauge and .410 bore | **3219.00** |
| **MODEL 53:** Sidelock in 12, 16 and 20 gauge with 3 locking lugs and side clips | **4636.00** |
| **MODEL 56:** Sidelock in 12 gauge only with 3 locking lugs and side clips | **7209.00** |
| **MODEL XXV/SL:** Sidelock in 12 and 20 gauge only with Churchill-type rib | **3824.00** |

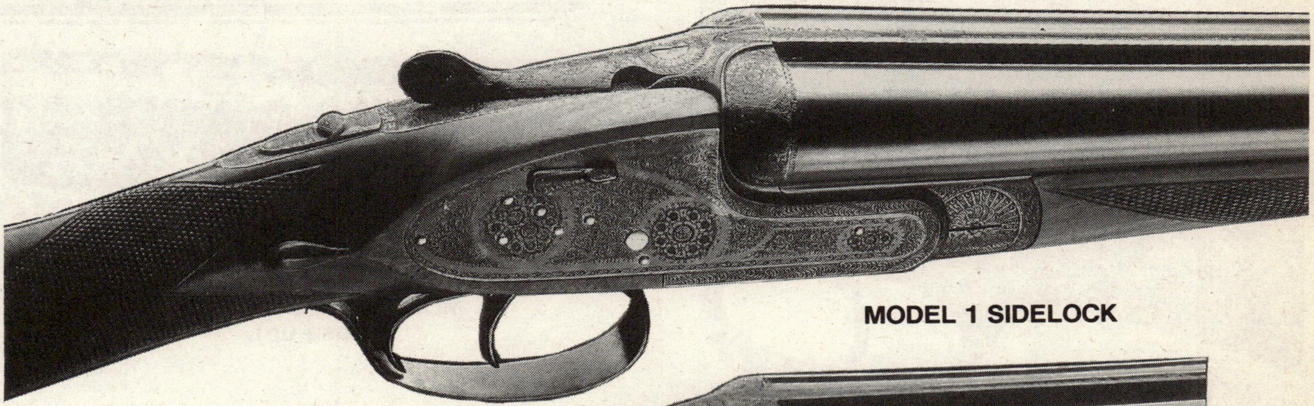

**MODEL 1 SIDELOCK**

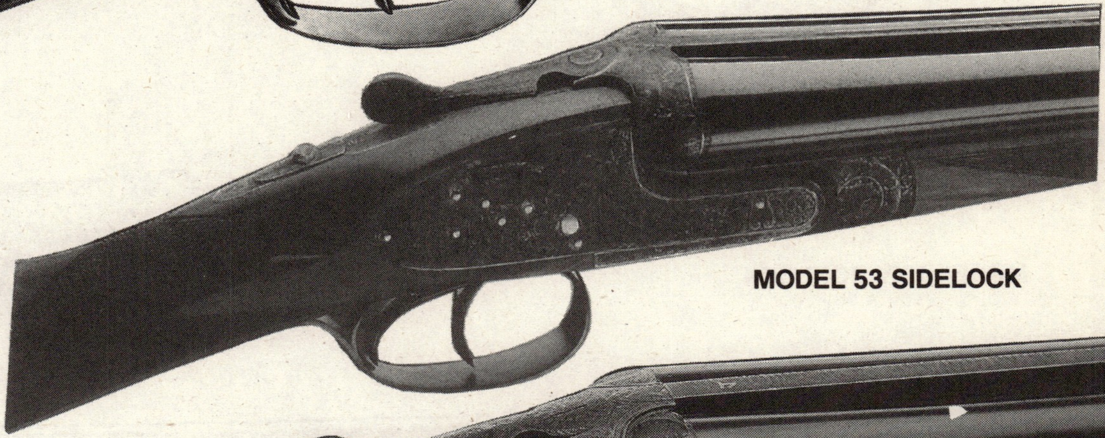

**MODEL 53 SIDELOCK**

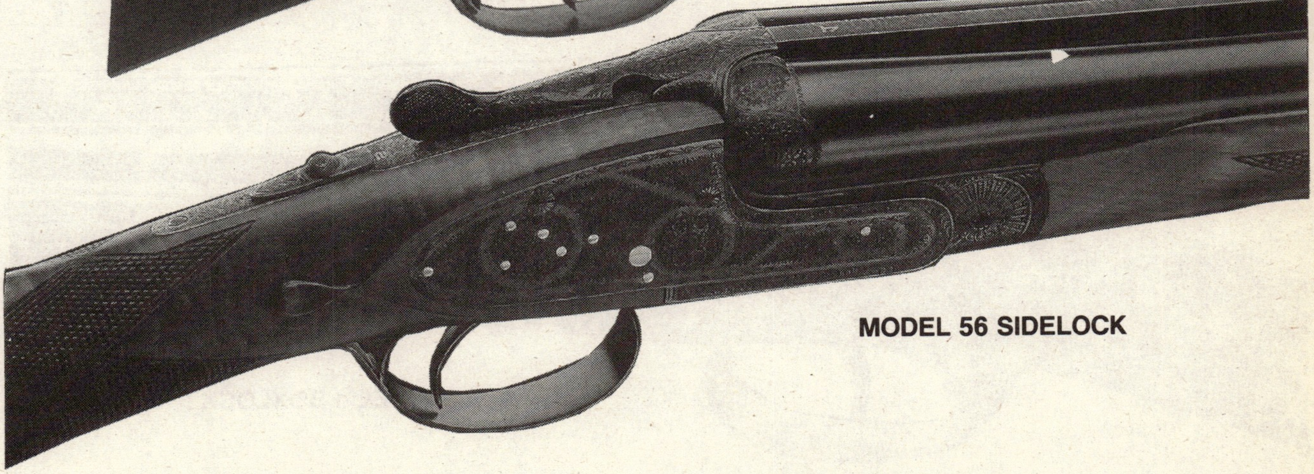

**MODEL 56 SIDELOCK**

# AYA SHOTGUNS

## BOXLOCK SHOTGUNS

AYA boxlocks use the Anson & Deeley system with double locking lugs, incorporating detachable cross pin and separate plate to allow easy access to the firing mechanism. Barrels are chopper lump, firing pins are bushed, plus automatic safety and ejectors and metal oval for engraving of initials.

**Barrel lengths:** 26″, 27″ and 28″. **Weight:** 5 to 7 pounds, depending on gauge.

| Model | Price |
|---|---|
| **MODEL XXV BOXLOCK:** 12 and 20 gauge only | $ 2,867.00 |
| **MODEL 4 BOXLOCK:** 12, 16, 20, 28, .410 ga. | 1,684.00 |
| **MODEL 4 DELUXE BOXLOCK:** Same gauges as above | 2,966.00 |
| **MODEL 37 SUPER A** | 13,842.00 |
| **MODEL AUGUSTA** | 24,899.00 |

**MODEL XXV BOXLOCK (Close-up)**

**MODEL XXV BOXLOCK**

**MODEL 4 BOXLOCK**

# BENELLI SHOTGUNS

## MODEL M1 SUPER 90 SERIES

*See table on the following page for all Benelli specifications.*



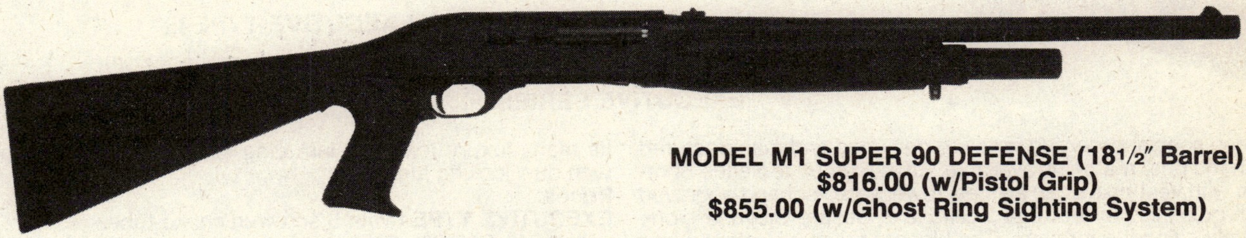

**MODEL M1 SUPER 90 DEFENSE (18½″ Barrel)**
**$816.00 (w/Pistol Grip)**
**$855.00 (w/Ghost Ring Sighting System)**

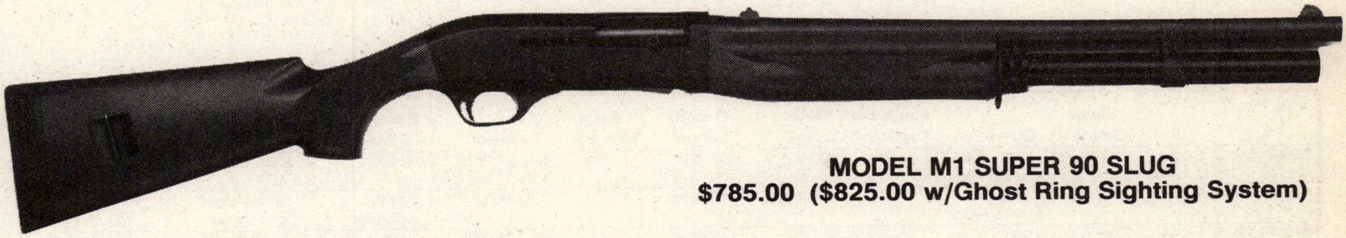

**MODEL M1 SUPER 90 SLUG**
**$785.00 ($825.00 w/Ghost Ring Sighting System)**

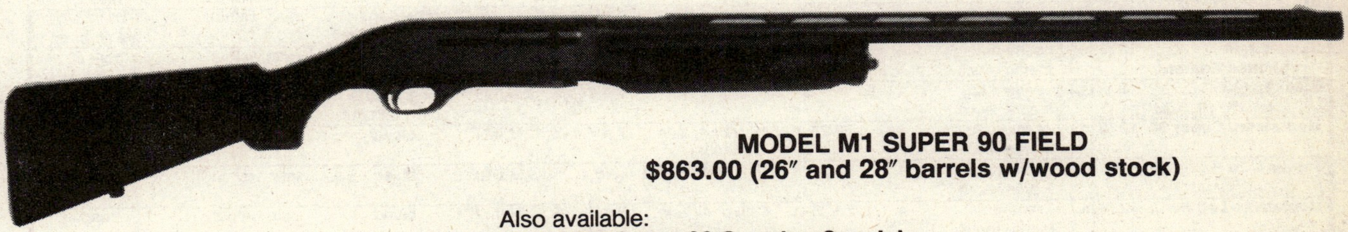

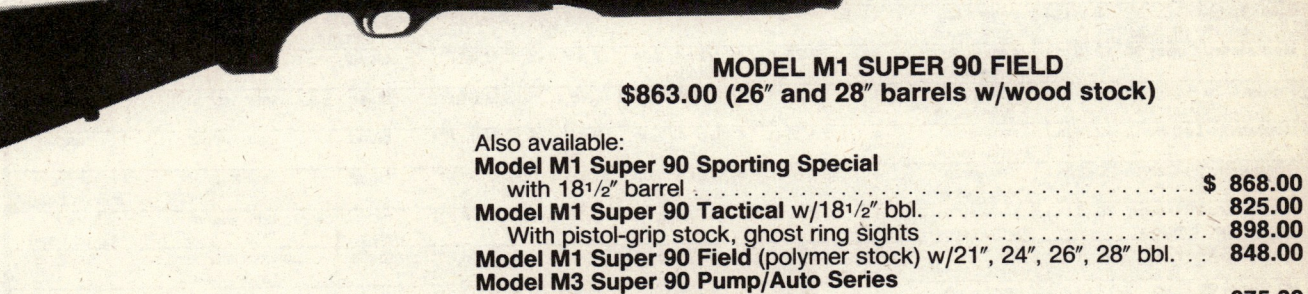

**MODEL M1 SUPER 90 FIELD**
**$863.00 (26″ and 28″ barrels w/wood stock)**

Also available:
**Model M1 Super 90 Sporting Special**
with 18½″ barrel . . . . . . . . . . **$ 868.00**
**Model M1 Super 90 Tactical** w/18½″ bbl. . . . . . . . . . **825.00**
With pistol-grip stock, ghost ring sights . . . . . . . . . . **898.00**
**Model M1 Super 90 Field** (polymer stock) w/21″, 24″, 26″, 28″ bbl. . . **848.00**
**Model M3 Super 90 Pump/Auto Series**
Standard stock, 19¾″ barrel . . . . . . . . . . **975.00**
w/Ghost Ring Sight and standard stock . . . . . . . . . . **1042.00**

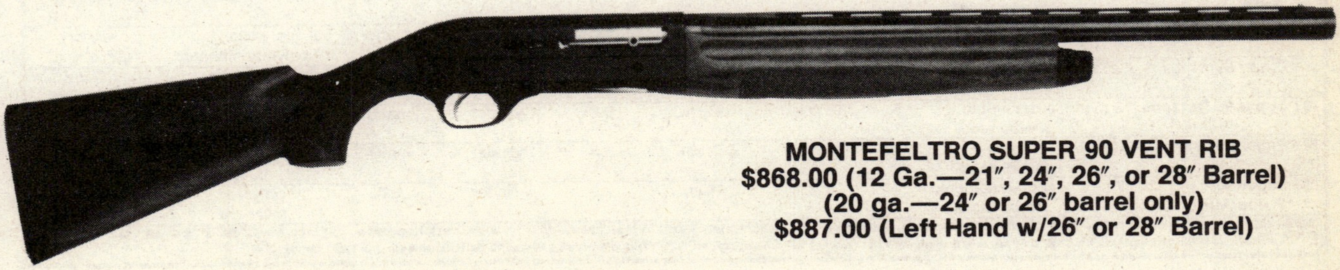

**MONTEFELTRO SUPER 90 VENT RIB**
**$868.00 (12 Ga.—21″, 24″, 26″, or 28″ Barrel)**
**(20 ga.—24″ or 26″ barrel only)**
**$887.00 (Left Hand w/26″ or 28″ Barrel)**

# BENELLI SHOTGUNS

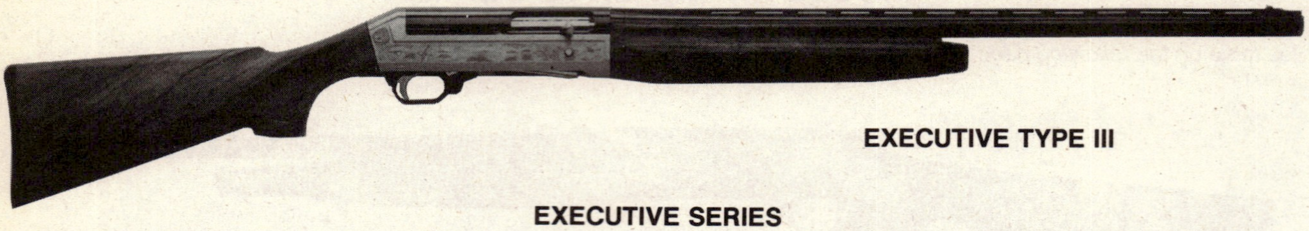

EXECUTIVE TYPE III

## EXECUTIVE SERIES

These special-order firearms are designed and manufactured with the best materials available. Each Executive Series Shotgun with vent rib has an all-steel tower receiver hand-engraved with gold inlay by Bottega Incisione di Cesare Giovanelli, one of Italy's finest engravers. The highest grade of walnut wood stocks is selected, and each can be custom-fitted with Benelli's drop adjustment kit. The Executive Series is engineered with all the features found on the Black Eagle Series Shotguns plus its many luxury features, including Montefeltro rotating bolt with dual locking lugs.

**Prices:**

**EXECUTIVE TYPE I** with 5 screw-in choke tubes and 21″, 24″, 26″, 28″ vent-rib barrels . . . . . . . . **$4375.00**

**EXECUTIVE TYPE II** . . . . . . . . . . . . . . . . . . . . . . . . **5000.00**

**EXECUTIVE TYPE III** . . . . . . . . . . . . . . . . . . . . . . . **5800.00**

### BENELLI SHOTGUN SPECIFICATIONS

| | Gauge (Chamber) | Operation | Magazine Capacity* | Barrel Length | Overall Length | Weight (in lbs.) | Choke | Receiver Finish | Stock | Sights |
|---|---|---|---|---|---|---|---|---|---|---|
| **Super Black Eagle** | 12 (3 1/2 in.) | semi-auto inertia recoil | 3 | 28 in. | 49 5/8 in. | 7.3 | S,IC,M,IM,F** | matte | satin walnut or polymer | front & mid rib bead |
| **Super Black Eagle** | 12 (3 1/2 in.) | semi-auto inertia recoil | 3 | 26 in. | 47 5/8 in. | 7.1 | S,IC,M,IM,F** | matte or blued | satin walnut or polymer | front & mid rib bead |
| **Super Black Eagle** | 12 (3 1/2 in.) | semi-auto inertia recoil | 3 | 24 in. | 45 5/8 in. | 7.0 | S,IC,M,IM,F** | matte | polymer | front & mid rib bead |
| **Super Black Eagle Custom Slug** | 12 (3 in.) | semi-auto inertia recoil | 3 | 24 in. | 45 1/2 in. | 7.6 | rifled barrel | matte | satin walnut or polymer | scope mount base |
| **Black Eagle Competition Gun** | 12 (3 in.) | semi-auto inertia recoil | 4 | 28/26 in. | 49 5/8 or 47 5/8 in. | 7.3/7 | S,IC,M,IM,F** | blued with etched receiver | satin walnut | front & mid rib bead |
| **Black Eagle Limited Edition** | 12 (3 in.) | semi-auto inertia recoil | 4 | 26 in. | 47 5/8 in | 7.3/7 | S,IC,M,IM,F** | blued with etched receiver | satin walnut | front & mid rib bead |
| **Black Eagle Executive I, II, III** | 12 (3 in.) | semi-auto inertia recoil | 4 | 26 in. | 47 5/8 in | 7.3/7 | S,IC,M,IM,F** | engraved & gold inlaid rec. | satin high grade walnut | front & mid rib bead |
| **Montefeltro Super 90** | 12 (3 in.) | semi-auto inertia recoil | 4 | 28/26 in. | 49 1/2 or 47 1/2 in. | 7.4/7 | S,IC,M,IM,F** | blued | satin walnut | bead |
| **Montefeltro Super 90** | 12 (3 in.) | semi-auto inertia recoil | 4 | 24/21 in. | 45 1/2 or 42 1/2 in. | 6.9/6.7 | S,IC,M,IM,F** | blued | satin walnut | bead |
| **Montefeltro Left Hand** | 12 (3 in.) | semi-auto inertia recoil | 4 | 28/26 in. | 49 1/2 or 47 1/2 in. | 7.4/7 | S,IC,M,IM,F** | blued | satin walnut | bead |
| **Montefeltro 20 Gauge** | 20 (3 in.) | semi-auto inertia recoil | 4 | 26/24 in. | 47 1/2 or 45 1/2 in. | 5.75/5.5 | S,IC,M,IM,F** | blued | satin walnut | front & mid rib bead |
| **Montefeltro 20 Gauge Limited Edition** | 20 (3 in.) | semi-auto inertia recoil | 4 | 26 in. | 47 1/2 in. | 5.75 | S,IC,M,IM,F** | nickel with gold | satin walnut | front & mid rib bead |
| **M1 Super 90 Field** | 12 (3 in.) | semi-auto inertia recoil | 3 | 28 in. | 49 1/2 in. | 7.4 | S,IC,M,IM,F** | matte | polymer standard or satin walnut | bead |
| **M1 Super 90 Field** | 12 (3 in.) | semi-auto inertia recoil | 3 | 26 in. | 47 1/2 in. | 7.3 | S,IC,M,IM,F** | matte | polymer standard or satin walnut | bead |
| **M1 Super 90 Field** | 12 (3 in.) | semi-auto inertia recoil | 3 | 24 in. | 45 1/2 in. | 7.2 | S,IC,M,IM,F** | matte | polymer standard | bead |
| **M1 Super 90 Field** | 12 (3 in.) | semi-auto inertia recoil | 3 | 21 in. | 42 1/2 in. | 7 | S,IC,M,IM,F** | matte | polymer standard | bead |
| **M1 Super 90 Sporting Special** | 12 (3 in.) | semi-auto inertia recoil | 3 | 18 1/2 in. | 39 3/4 in. | 6.5 | IC,M,F** | matte | polymer standard | ghost ring |
| **M1 Super 90 Tactical** | 12 (3 in.) | semi-auto inertia recoil | 5 | 18 1/2 in. | 39 3/4 in. | 6.5 | IC,M,F** | matte | polymer pistol grip*** or polymer standard | rifle or ghost ring |
| **M1 Super 90 Slug** | 12 (3 in.) | semi-auto inertia recoil | 5 | 18 1/2 in. | 39 3/4 in. | 6.5 | Cylinder | matte | polymer standard | rifle or ghost ring |
| **M1 Super 90 Defense** | 12 (3 in.) | semi-auto inertia recoil | 5 | 18 1/2 in. | 39 3/4 in. | 6.8 | Cylinder | matte | polymer pistol grip*** | rifle or ghost ring |
| **M1 Super 90 Entry** | 12 (3 in.) | semi-auto inertia recoil | 5 | 14 in. | 35 1/2 in. | 6.3 | Cylinder | matte | polymer pistol grip*** or polymer standard | rifle or ghost ring |
| **M3 Super 90 Pump/Auto** | 12 (3 in.) | semi-auto/pump inertia recoil | 7 | 19 3/4 in. | 41 in. | 7.9 | Cylinder | matte | polymer standard | rifle or ghost ring |

*Magazine capacity given for 2 3/4 inch shells, size variations among some brands may result in less capacity. **Skeet, Improved Cylinder, Modified, Improved Modified, Full
***CAUTION: Increasing magazine capacity to more than five rounds on M1 shotguns with pistol grip stocks violates provisions of the 1994 Crime Bill.

# BENELLI SHOTGUNS

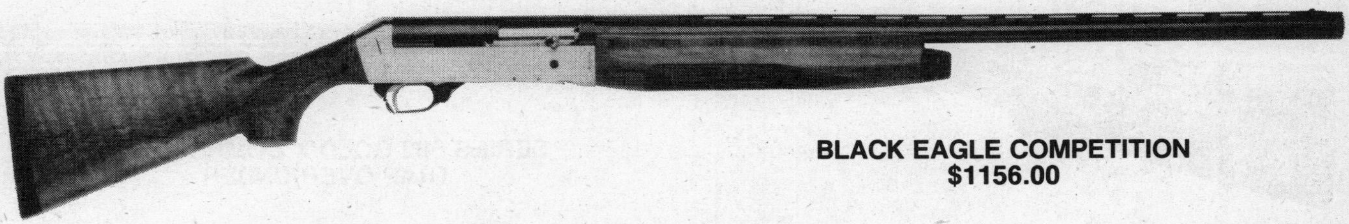

**BLACK EAGLE COMPETITION**
**$1156.00**

Benelli's Black Eagle Competition shotgun combines the best technical features of the Montefeltro Super 90 and the classic design of the old SL 80 Series. It comes standard with a specially designed two-piece receiver of steel and aluminum, adding to its reliability and resistance to wear. A premium high-gloss walnut stock and gold-plated trigger are included, along with a Montefeltro rotating bolt. The Black Eagle Competition has no complex cylinders and pistons to maintain. Features include etched receiver, competition stock and mid-rib bead.

Also available:
**Black Eagle Limited Edition.** One of 1,000 with 26″ vent-rib barrel and satin walnut stock. **Price:** . . . . . . . . . . **$2,000.00**

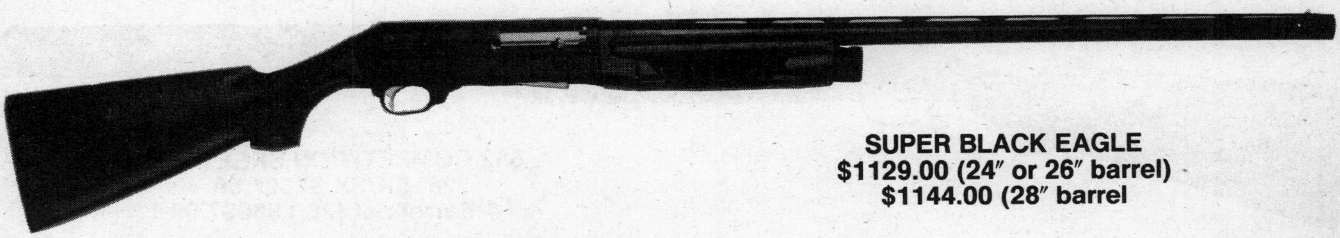

**SUPER BLACK EAGLE**
**$1129.00 (24″ or 26″ barrel)**
**$1144.00 (28″ barrel**

Benelli's Super Black Eagle shotgun offers the advantage of owning one 12-gauge auto that fires every type of 12 gauge currently available. It has the same balance, sighting plane and fast-swinging characteristics whether practicing on the sporting clays course with light target loads or touching off a 3 1/2″ Magnum steel load at a high-flying goose.

The Super Black Eagle also features a specially strengthened steel upper receiver mated to the barrel to endure the toughest shotgunning. The alloy lower receiver keeps the overall weight low, making this model as well balanced and point-able as possible. Distinctive high-gloss or satin walnut stocks and a choice of dull finish or blued metal add up to a universal gun for all shotgun hunting and sports.

**Stock:** Satin walnut (28″) with drop adjustment kit; high-gloss walnut (26″) with drop adjustment kit; or synthetic stock
**Finish:** Matte black finish on receiver, barrel and bolt (28″); blued finish on receiver and barrel (26″) with bolt mirror polished
**Features:** Montefeltro rotating bolt with dual locking lugs
For additional specifications, see table on previous page.

Also available:
**Custom Slug Gun** with 24″ E.R. Shaw rifled barrel for sabot-type slugs and polymer stock. **Price:** . . . . . . . . . . **$1171.00**

# BERETTA SHOTGUNS

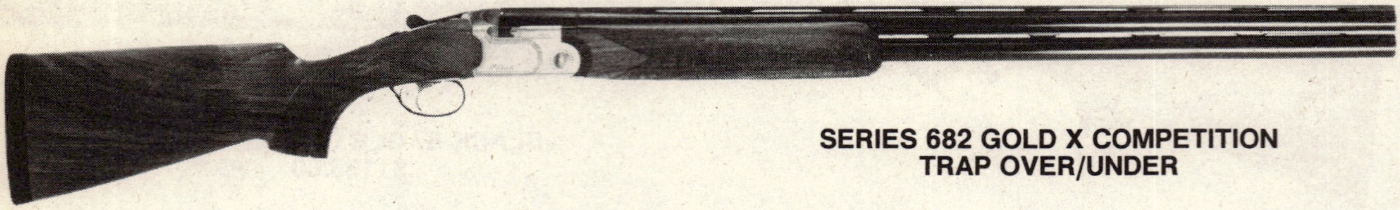

**SERIES 682 GOLD X COMPETITION TRAP OVER/UNDER**

Available in Competition Mono, Over/Under or Mono Trap Over/Under Combo Set, the 12-gauge 682X trap guns boast hand-checkered walnut stock and forend with International or Monte Carlo left- or right-hand stock.

**Features:** Adjustable gold-plated, single selective sliding trigger for precise length of pull fit; fluorescent competition front sight; step-up top rib; nonreflective black matte finish; low-profile improved boxlock action; manual safety with barrel selector; 2¾″ chambers; auto ejector; competition recoil pad buttplate; stock with silver oval for initials; silver inscription inlaid on trigger guard; handsome fitted case. **Weight:** Approx. 8 lbs.

| **Barrel length/Choke** | **Prices** |
|---|---|
| 30″ Imp. Mod./Full (Black) | **$2573.00** |
| 30″ or 32″ Mobilchoke® (Black) | **2650.00** |
| Top Single 32″ or 34″ Mobilchoke® | **2734.00** |
| "Live Bird" (Flat rib, Silver) | **2846.00** |
| Combo.: 30″ or 32″ Mobilchoke® (Top) | **3506.00** |
| 30″ IM/F (Top) | **3444.00** |
| 32″ Mobilchoke® (Mono) | **3506.00** |
| 30″ or 32″ Mobilchoke® ported | **3606.00** |

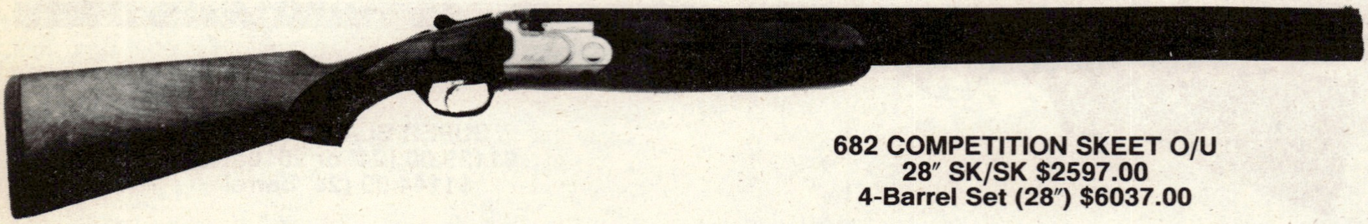

**682 COMPETITION SKEET O/U**
**28″ SK/SK $2597.00**
**4-Barrel Set (28″) $6037.00**

This skeet gun sports hand-checkered premium walnut stock, forged and hardened receiver, manual safety with trigger selector, auto ejector, stock with silver oval for initials, silver inlaid on trigger guard. Price includes fitted case.
**Gauges:** 12; 4-barrel sets in 12, 20, 28 and .410
**Action:** Low-profile hard chrome-plated boxlock
**Trigger:** Single adjustable sliding trigger
**Barrels:** 26″ or 28″ blued barrels with 2¾″ chambers
**Stock dimensions:** Length of pull 14¾″; drop at comb 1⅜″; drop at heel 2¼″
**Sights:** Fluorescent front and metal middle bead
**Weight:** Approx. 7½ lbs.

**MODEL 682 SUPER TRAP**

Beretta's 12-gauge over/under shotgun features a revolutionary adjustable stock. Comb is adjustable with interchangeable comb height adjustments. Length of pull is also adjustable with interchangeable butt pad spacers. Also features ported barrels and tapered step rib, satin-finished receiver and adjustable trigger.

**Barrel lengths:** 30″, 32″, 34″; chamber 2¾″
**Chokes:** Choice of Mobilchoke®, IM/F, Full

| **Models** | **Prices** |
|---|---|
| **Model 682 Super Trap O/U** (Mobilchoke®) | **$2976.00** |
| Same as above with IM/F choke | **2907.00** |
| **Model 682 Top Single Super Trap** | |
| 32″ barrel and Mobilchoke | **3156.00** |
| Same as above with Full choke | **3083.00** |
| **Model 682 Top Combo Super Trap** | **3907.00** |
| Same as above w/o Mobilchoke® | **3983.00** |

# BERETTA SHOTGUNS

## 12- AND 20-GAUGE SPORTING CLAYS

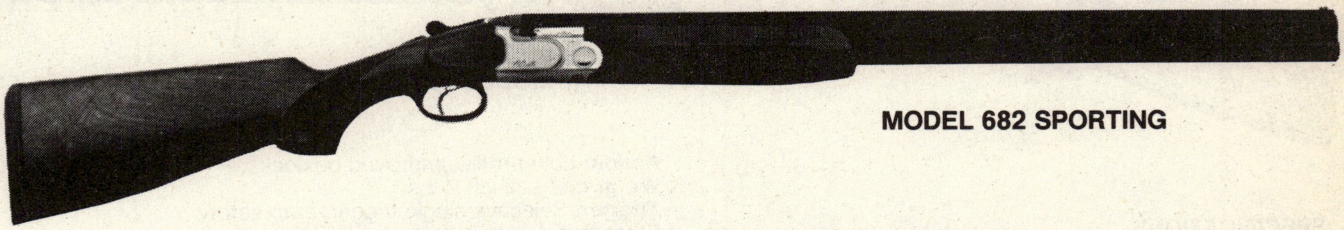

MODEL 682 SPORTING

### MODELS 682/686/687 SPORTING CLAYS

This competition-style shotgun for sporting clays features 28″ or 30″ barrels with four flush-mounted screw-in choke tubes (Full, Modified, Improved Cylinder and Skeet), plus hand-checkered stock and forend of fine walnut, 2¾″ or 3″ chambers and adjustable trigger. **Model 682 Continental Course Sporting** has tapered rib and schnabel forend. **Model 682 Super Sporting** has ported barrels, adjustable comb height inserts and length of pull. **Model 686 Onyx Sporting** has black matte receiver and **686 Silver Perdiz Sporting** has coin silver receiver with scroll engraving. **Model 687EL** has sideplates with scroll engraving.

| Models | Prices |
|---|---|
| **682 Sporting** | **$2915.00** |
| **682 Continental Course Sporting** | **2796.00** |
| **682 Super Sporting** | **3017.00** |
| **686 Onyx Sporting** | **1427.00** |
| **686 Silver Perdiz Sporting** | **1471.00** |
| **686 Silver Perdiz Sporting Combo** | **2687.00** |
| **687 Silver Perdiz Sporting** | **2354.00** |
| **687 Silver Pigeon Sporting Combo** | **3516.00** |
| **687EL** | **3320.00** |
| **687EELL Diamond Pigeon Sporting** | **4850.00** |

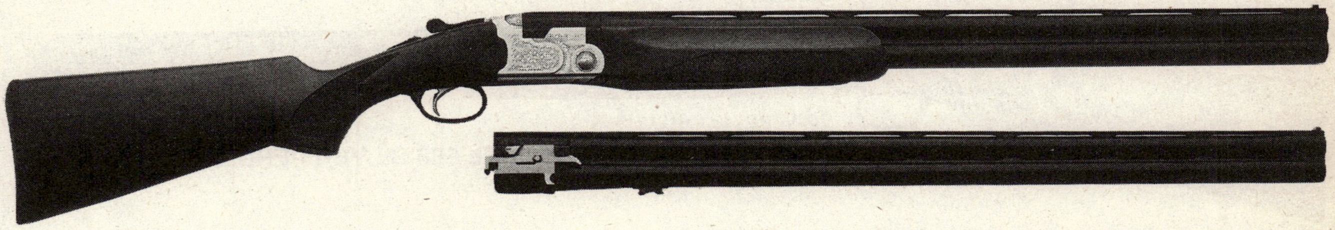

MODEL 686 SILVER PERDIZ SPORTING COMBO

### MODELS 686/687 SILVER PERDIZ/PIGEON SPORTING COMBO

This 12-gauge Beretta over/under features interchangeable 28″ and 30″ barrels for versatility in competition at different courses with short and long passing shots. **Chamber:** 3″. Mobilchoke® screw-in tube system. Prices listed above.



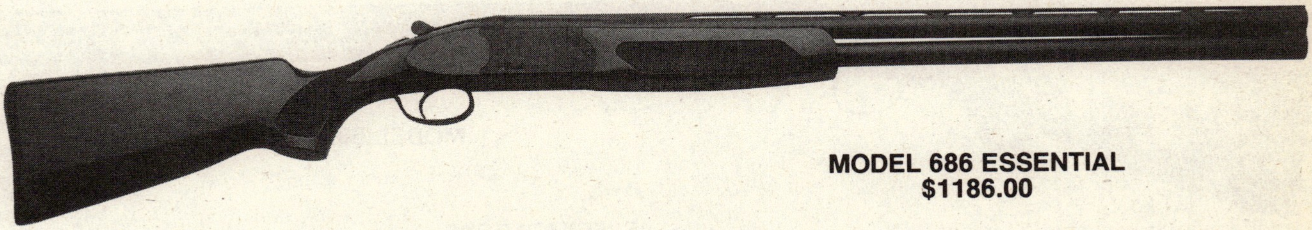

MODEL 686 ESSENTIAL
$1186.00

**SPECIFICATIONS**
**Gauge:** 12 (3″ chamber)
**Choke:** MC3 Mobilchoke® (F, M, IC)
**Barrel length:** 26″ or 28″ **Overall length:** 45.7″
**Weight:** 6.7 lbs.
**Stock:** American walnut
**Drop at comb:** 1.4″ **Drop at heel:** 2.2″
**Length of pull:** 14½″
**Features:** Matte black receiver

# BERETTA SHOTGUNS

**MODEL 686 SILVER PERDIZ FIELD**

**SPECIFICATIONS**
**Gauges:** 12, 20
**Barrels/chokes:** 26″ and 28″ with Mobilchoke® screw-in choke tubes

**Action:** Low-profile, improved boxlock
**Weight:** Less than 7 lbs.
**Trigger:** Selective single trigger, auto safety
**Extractors:** Auto ejectors
**Stock:** Choice walnut, hand-checkered and hand-finished with a tough gloss finish
**Price:** . . . . . . . . . . . . **$1427.00**

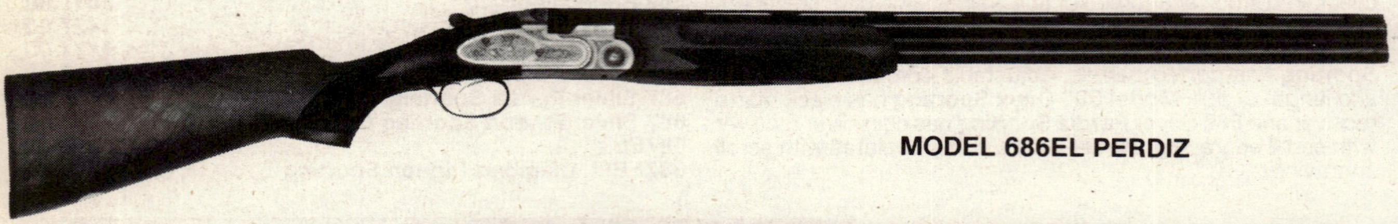

**MODEL 686EL PERDIZ**

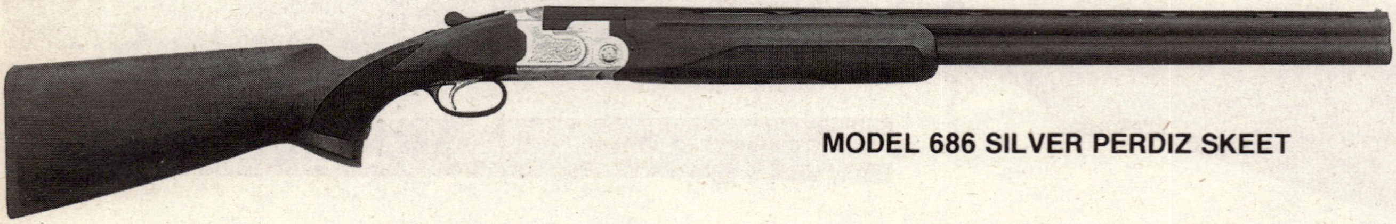

**MODEL 686 SILVER PERDIZ SKEET**

This 12- or 20-gauge over/under field gun features scroll engraving on sideplates, European walnut stock and forend, hard-chromed bores, Mobilchoke® system of interchangeable choke tubes, and gun case. **Price:** . . . . . . . . . . **$2266.00**

Also available:
**Model 686L Silver Perdiz** (28 ga.) with highly polished silver receiver, traditional blued finish 26″ barrels, and rubber recoil pad, plus Mobilchoke® **Price:** . . . . . . . . **$1399.00**

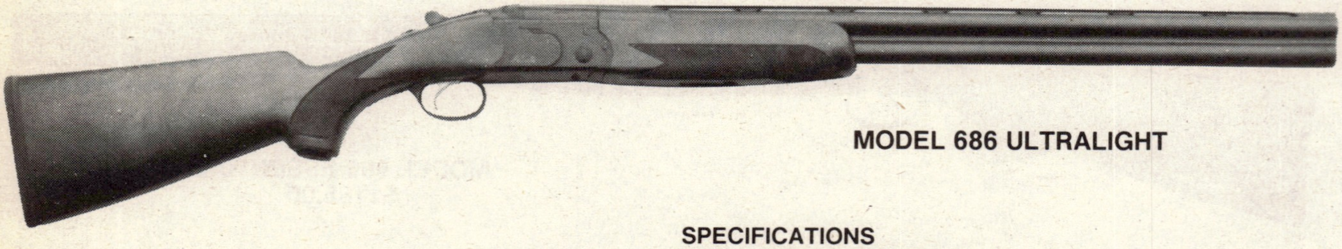

**MODEL 686 ULTRALIGHT**

This new 12-gauge over/under field gun features the payload of a 12-gauge gun in a 20-gauge weight (approx. 5 lbs. 13 oz.). Chambered for 2¾″, the Ultralight has a matte black finish on its receiver with a gold inlay of the P. Beretta signature.

**SPECIFICATIONS**
**Action:** Low-profile boxlock
**Barrel length:** 26″ or 28″
**Trigger:** Single, selective gold trigger
**Safety:** Automatic
**Stock:** Walnut, hand-checkered
**Price:** . . . . . . . . . . . . **$1574.00**

# BERETTA SHOTGUNS

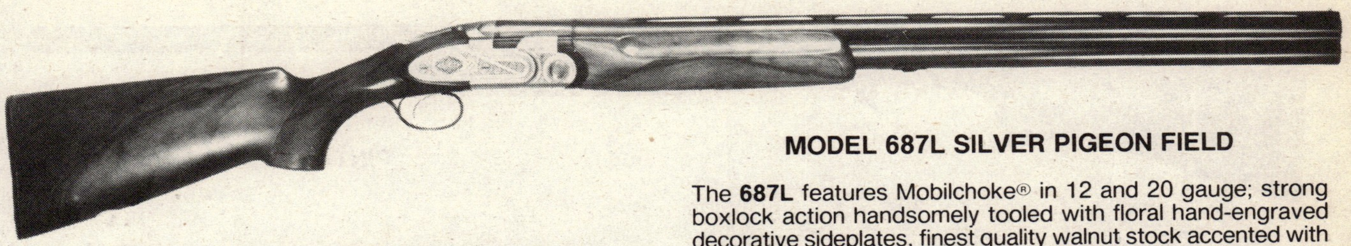

### MODEL 687L SILVER PIGEON FIELD

The **687L** features Mobilchoke® in 12 and 20 gauge; strong boxlock action handsomely tooled with floral hand-engraved decorative sideplates, finest quality walnut stock accented with silver monogram plate, selective auto ejectors and fitted case.
**Price:** . . . . . . . . . . . . . . . . . . . . . . . . . . . . . . . . . . . . . . . **$1927.00**

### MODEL 687EL GOLD PIGEON FIELD (not shown)

Features game-scene engraving on receiver with gold highlights. Available in 12, 20 gauge (28 ga. and .410 in small frame).

**SPECIFICATIONS**
**Barrels/chokes:** 26″ and 28″ with Mobilchoke®
**Action:** Low-profile improved boxlock
**Weight:** 6.8 lbs. (12 ga.)
**Trigger:** Single selective with manual safety
**Extractors:** Auto ejectors
**Prices:**
**Model 687EL** (12, 20, 28 ga.; 26″ or 28″ bbl.) . . . . **$3276.00**
**Model 687EL Small Frame** (.410) . . . . . . . . . . . . . **3423.00**

### MODEL 687EELL DIAMOND PIGEON $4764.00 (not shown)
### Model 687EELL Combo (20 and 28 ga.) $5287.00

In 12, 20 or 28 ga., this model features the Mobilchoke® choke system, a special premium walnut stock and exquisitely engraved sideplate with game-scene motifs.

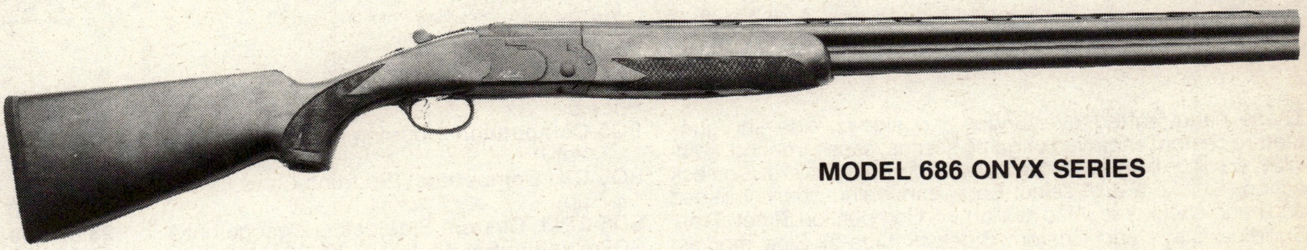

### MODEL 686 ONYX SERIES

**SPECIFICATIONS**
**Gauges:** 12, 20 **Chamber:** 3″
**Barrel lengths:** 26″ and 28″
**Chokes:** Mobilchoke® screw-in system
**Weight:** 6 lbs. 12 oz. (12 ga.); 6.2 lbs. (20 ga.)

**Stock:** American walnut with recoil pad (English stock available)
**Features:** Automatic ejectors; matte black finish on barrels and receiver to reduce glare
**Price:** . . . . . . . . . . . . . . . . . . . . . . . . . . . . . . . . . . . . . . . **$1399.00**

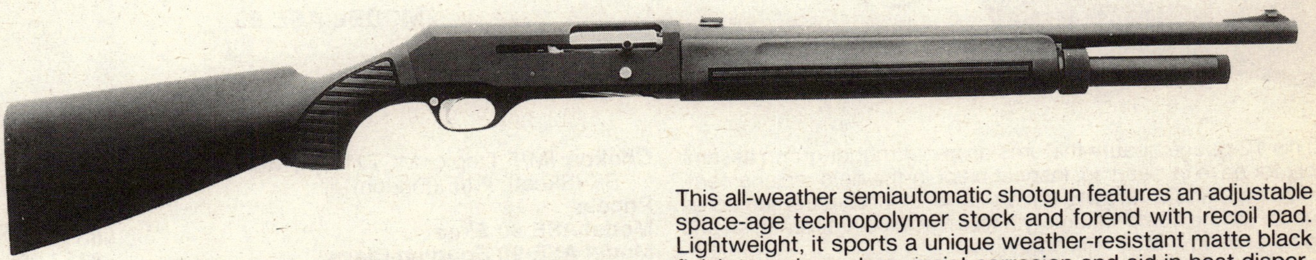

### MODEL 1201 FP RIOT
### $683.00

This all-weather semiautomatic shotgun features an adjustable space-age technopolymer stock and forend with recoil pad. Lightweight, it sports a unique weather-resistant matte black finish to reduce glare, resist corrosion and aid in heat dispersion; short recoil action for light and heavy loads. **Gauge:** 12. **Chamber:** 3″ (2 3/4″ or 3″ shells). **Capacity:** 7 rounds w/2 3/4″; 6 rounds w/3″. **Barrel length:** 20″. **Choke:** Cylinder (fixed). **Weight:** 6.3 lbs.

# BERETTA SHOTGUNS

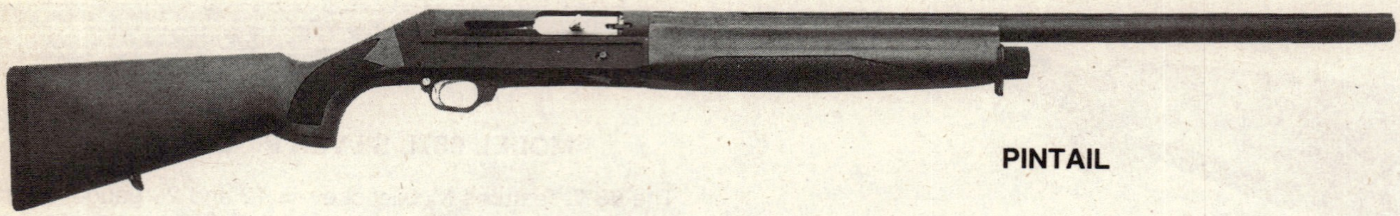

PINTAIL

This new 12-gauge semiautomatic shotgun with short-recoil operation is available with 24″ or 26″ barrels and Mobilchoke®. A slug version is also available with rifled sights and choke tube. Finish is nonreflective matte on all exposed wood and metal surfaces. Checkered walnut stock and forend; sling swivels.

**SPECIFICATIONS**
**Barrel lengths:** 24″, 26″; 24″ Slug
**Weight:** 7.3 lbs.
**Stock:** Walnut
**Sights:** Bead front on vent rib
**Price:** . . . . . . . . . . **$700.00**

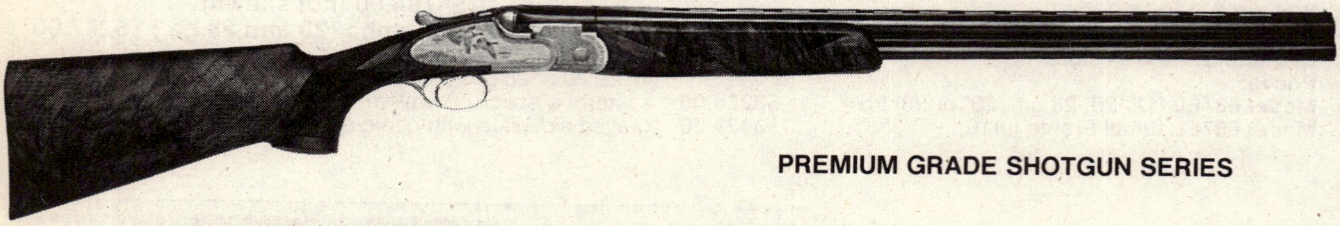

PREMIUM GRADE SHOTGUN SERIES

These hand-crafted over/under and side-by-side shotguns feature custom engraved or game scenes, casehardened, gold-inlay, scroll or floral patterns, all available on receivers. Sidelock action. Stocks are of select European walnut, hand-finished and hand-checkered. Also available in Competition Skeet, Trap, Sporting Clays and Custom Sidelock Side-by-Side models. Barrels are constructed of Boehler high-nickel antinit steel.
**Gauges:** 12, 20, 28, .410 **Chamber:** 2½″ or 3″

**Prices:**
**SO5 Competition** (Sporting Clays, Skeet, Trap) . . . . . . . . . . **$13,000.00**
**SO6 O/U Competition** (Sporting Clays, Skeet, Trap) . . . . . . . . . . **17,500.00**
**SO6 EELL Custom Sidelock** (12 gauge only) . . . **28,000.00**
**SO9 Custom Sidelock** (12, 20, 28, .410 ga.) . . . **31,000.00**
**452 EELL Custom Sidelock Side/Side** (12 ga.) . . . . . . . . . . **31,000.00**

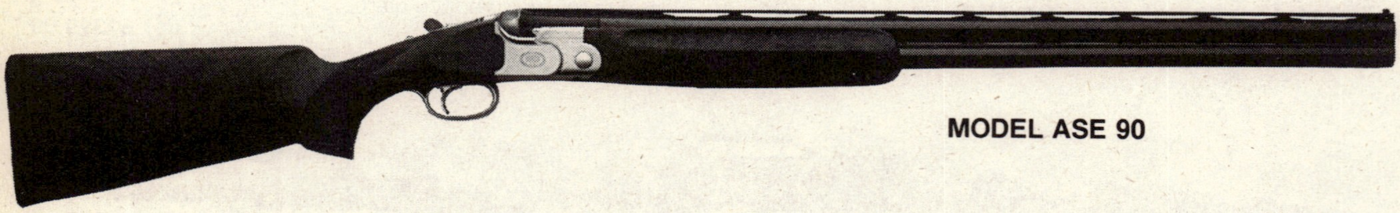

MODEL ASE 90

This 12-gauge beauty features drop-out trigger group assembly for ease in cleaning, inspection or in-the-field replacement. Also has wide ventilating top and side rib, hard-chromed bores and a strong competition-style receiver in coin-silver finish and gold etching with P. Beretta initials.

**SPECIFICATIONS**
**Barrel lengths:** 28″ (Pigeon, Skeet, Sporting Clays); 30″ (Trap and Sporting Clays); 30″ and 32″ Combo (Top Combo Trap); 30″ and 34″ Combo (Top Combo Trap)
**Chokes:** IM/F Trap or MCT (Trap); MC4 (Sporting Clays); SK/SK (Skeet); IM/F (Pigeon)
**Prices:**
**Model ASE 90 Skeet** . . . . . . . . . . **$8314.00**
**Model ASE 90 Sporting Clays** . . . . . . . . . . **8387.00**
**Model ASE 90 Trap** . . . . . . . . . . **8387.00**
**Model ASE 90 Trap Combo** . . . . . . . . . . **9763.00**

# BERETTA SHOTGUNS

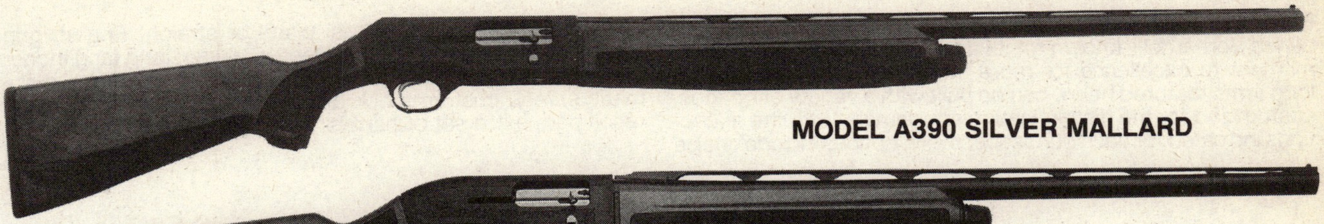

MODEL A390 SILVER MALLARD

MODEL A390 SPORTING

MODEL A390 TRAP

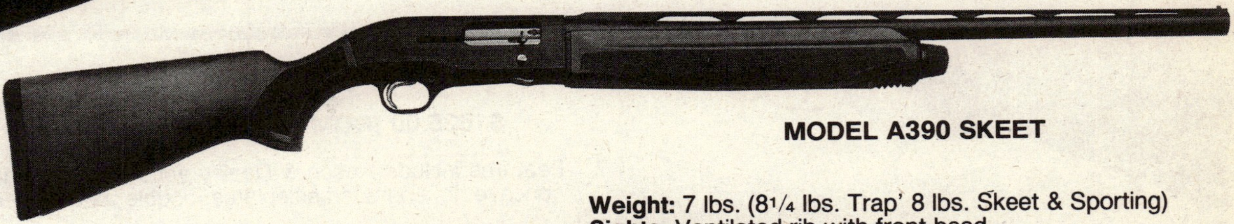

MODEL A390 SKEET

These gas-operated semiautomatics have an innovative gas system that handles a variety of loads. A self-regulating valve automatically adjusts gas pressure to handle anything from 2½″ target loads to heavy 3″ magnums. Matte finish models for turkey/waterfowl, slug and Deluxe models with gold-engraved receiver and deluxe wood are available. Also offered are **Model A390 Super Trap** and **A390 Super Skeet** with ported barrels and adjustable comb height and length of pull. New 390 Trap, Skeet and Sporting models have lower contour, walnut stock.

**SPECIFICATIONS**
**Gauge:** 12 **Action:** Locked breech, gas-operated
**Barrel lengths:** 24″, 26″, 28″, 30″; 22″ slug
**Weight:** 7 lbs. (8¼ lbs. Trap' 8 lbs. Skeet & Sporting)
**Sights:** Ventilated rib with front bead
**Safety:** Crossbolt (reversible)
**Prices:**

| | |
|---|---|
| **A390 Silver Mallard Field** | $ 779.00 |
| **A390 Waterfowl/Turkey** Matte Finish (Silver Mallard) | 779.00 |
| **A390 Gold Mallard** | 935.00 |
| **A390 Trap** | 821.00 |
| **A390 Trap (Ported)** | 907.00 |
| **A390 Super Trap** | 1256.00 |
| **A390 Skeet** (3″ chamber) | 779.00 |
| **A390 Skeet (Ported)** | 879.00 |
| **A390 Super Skeet** | 1203.00 |
| **A390 Sporting** | 807.00 |
| **A390 Sporting (Ported)** | 910.00 |

SHOTGUNS

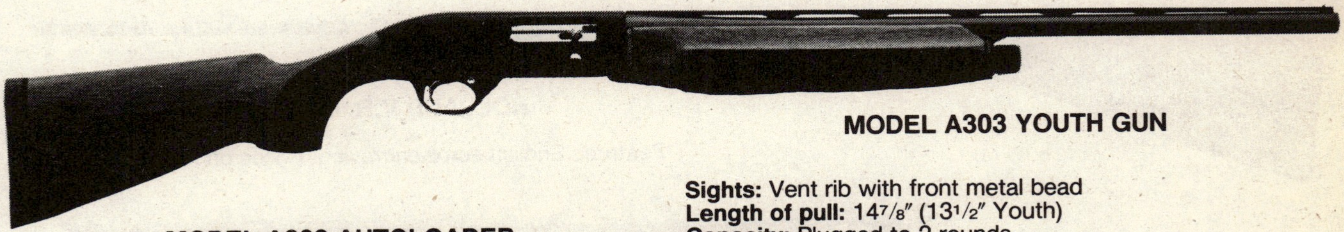

MODEL A303 YOUTH GUN

MODEL A303 AUTOLOADER

**SPECIFICATIONS**
**Gauges:** 12 and 20
**Barrel lengths:** 24″, 26″, 28″, 30″, 32″
**Weight:** 7 lbs. (12 gauge) and 6 lbs. (20 gauge)
**Safety:** Crossbolt
**Action:** Locked breech, gas-operated
**Sights:** Vent rib with front metal bead
**Length of pull:** 14⅞″ (13½″ Youth)
**Capacity:** Plugged to 2 rounds
**Prices:**

| | |
|---|---|
| **Upland** | $735.00 |
| **Field (English)** | 735.00 |
| **Youth** | 735.00 |
| **Skeet** | 735.00 |
| **Trap** | 735.00 |
| With Mobilchoke® F, IM, M | 775.00 |

# BERNARDELLI SHOTGUNS

Bernardelli shotguns are the creation of the Italian firm of Vincenzo Bernardelli, known for its fine quality firearms and commitment to excellence for more than a century. Most of the long arms featured below can be built with a variety of options, customized for the discriminating sportsman. With the exceptions indicated for each gun respectively, options include choice of barrel lengths and chokes; pistol or straight English grip stock; single selective or non-selective trigger; long tang trigger guard; checkered butt; beavertail forend; hand-cut rib; automatic safety; custom stock dimensions; standard or English recoil pad; extra set of barrels; choice of luggage gun case.

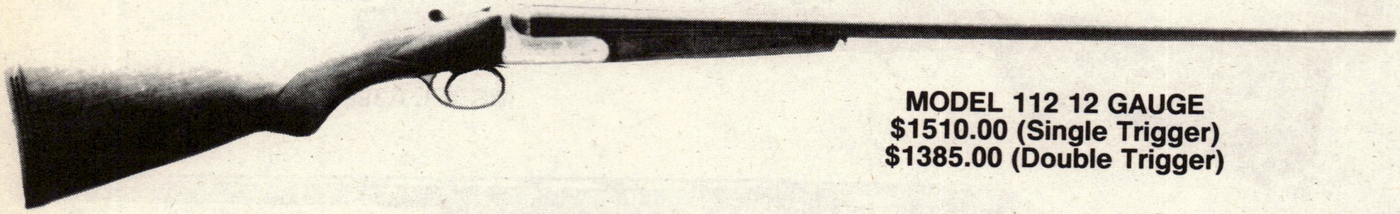

**MODEL 112 12 GAUGE**
**$1510.00 (Single Trigger)**
**$1385.00 (Double Trigger)**

Features extractors or automatic ejectors, English or half pistol-grip stock and splinter forend. **Barrel length:** 26¾″ (3″ chamber). **Choke:** Improved Cylinder and Improved Modified. **Safety:** Manual. **Weight:** 6½ lbs.
**Price:** (with ejector and multi-choke) . . . . . . . . . . **$1650.00**

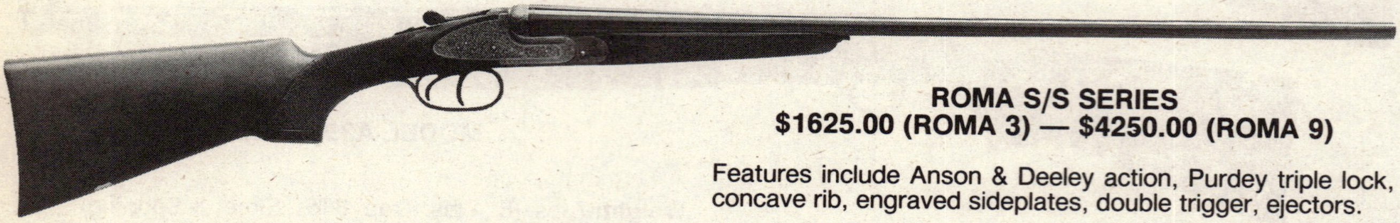

**ROMA S/S SERIES**
**$1625.00 (ROMA 3) — $4250.00 (ROMA 9)**

Features include Anson & Deeley action, Purdey triple lock, concave rib, engraved sideplates, double trigger, ejectors.

## HOLLAND & HOLLAND TYPE SIDELOCK SIDE-BY-SIDE

These 12-gauge Holland & Holland-style sidelock side-by-sides feature sidelocks with double safety levers, reinforced breech, three round Purdey locks, automatic ejectors, right trigger folding, striker retaining plates, best-quality walnut stock and finely chiselled high-grade engravings. The eight shotguns in this series differ only in the amount and intricacy of engravings.

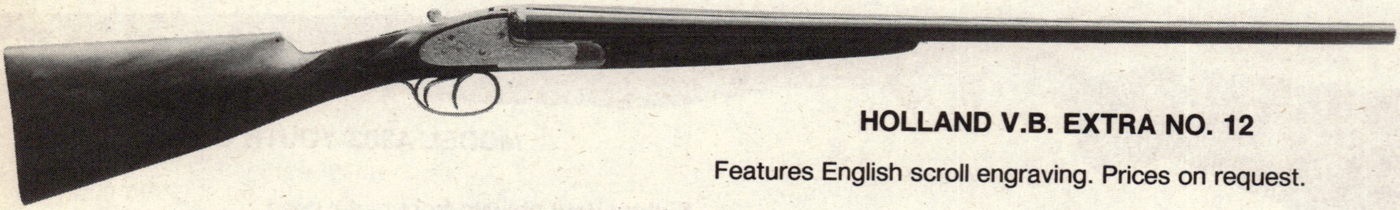

**HOLLAND V.B. EXTRA NO. 12**

Features English scroll engraving. Prices on request.

**HEMINGWAY S/S LIGHTWEIGHT**
**$1915.00 — $2200.00 (Deluxe)**

# BROWNING AUTOMATIC SHOTGUNS

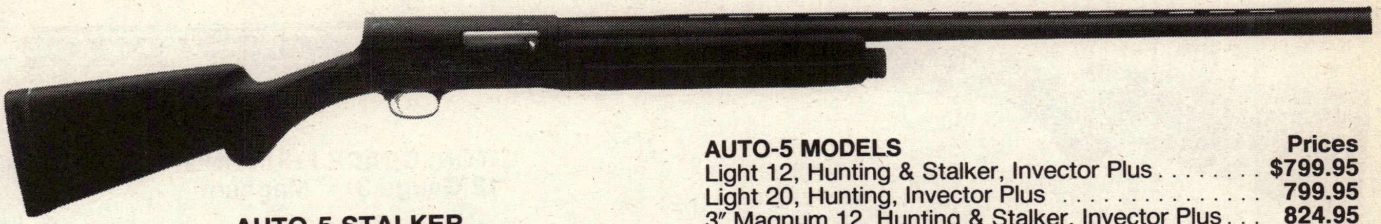

AUTO-5 STALKER

**AUTO-5 MODELS** — **Prices**

Light 12, Hunting & Stalker, Invector Plus . . . . . . . . **$799.95**
Light 20, Hunting, Invector Plus . . . . . . . . . . . . **799.95**
3″ Magnum 12, Hunting & Stalker, Invector Plus . . . **824.95**
3″ Magnum 12, Hunting, Invector Plus . . . . . . . . . . **824.95**
Light 12, Buck Special . . . . . . . . . . . . . . . . . . . . . . **789.95**
3″ Magnum 12 ga. Buck Special . . . . . . . . . . . . . . **814.95**
Extra Barrels . . . . . . . . . . . . . . . . . . . . . . . . **$282.95–292.95**

## SPECIFICATIONS AUTO-5 SHOTGUNS

| Model | Chamber | Barrel Length | Overall Length | Average Weight | Chokes Available |
|---|---|---|---|---|---|
| **12 GAUGE** | | | | | |
| Light | 2¾″ | 30″ | 49½″ | 8 lbs. 7 oz. | Invector-Plus |
| Light | 2¾″ | 28″ | 47½″ | 8 lbs. 4 oz. | Invector-Plus |
| Light | 2¾″ | 26″ | 45½″ | 8 lbs. 1 oz. | Invector-Plus |
| Lt. Buck Special | 2¾″ | 24″ | 43½″ | 8 lbs. | Slug/buckshot |
| Light | 2¾″ | 22″ | 41½″ | 7 lbs. 13 oz. | Invector-Plus |
| Magnum | 3″ | 32″ | 51¼″ | 9 lbs. 2 oz. | Invector-Plus |
| Magnum | 3″ | 30″ | 49¼″ | 8 lbs. 13 oz. | Invector-Plus |
| Magnum | 3″ | 28″ | 47¼″ | 8 lbs. 11 oz. | Invector-Plus |
| Magnum | 3″ | 26″ | 45¼″ | 8 lbs. 9 oz. | Invector-Plus |
| Mag. Buck Special | 3″ | 24″ | 43¼″ | 8 lbs. 8 oz. | Slug/buckshot |
| Light Stalker | 2¾″ | 28″ | 47½″ | 8 lbs. 4 oz. | Invector-Plus |
| Light Stalker | 2¾″ | 26″ | 45½″ | 8 lbs. 1 oz. | Invector-Plus |
| Magnum Stalker | 3″ | 30″ | 49¼″ | 8 lbs. 13 oz. | Invector-Plus |
| Magnum Stalker | 3″ | 28″ | 47¼″ | 8 lbs. 11 oz. | Invector-Plus |
| **20 GAUGE** | | | | | |
| Light | 2¾″ | 28″ | 47⅛″ | 6 lbs. 10 oz. | Invector |
| Light | 2¾″ | 26″ | 45¼″ | 6 lbs. 8 oz. | Invector |
| Magnum | 3″ | 28″ | 47¼″ | 7 lbs. 3 oz. | Invector |
| Magnum | 3″ | 26″ | 45¼″ | 7 lbs. 1 oz. | Invector |

## GOLD HUNTER & STALKER SEMIAUTOMATIC SHOTGUNS

### SPECIFICATIONS GOLD 12 AND 20 $699.95

| Gauge | Model | Barrel Length | Overall Length | Average Weight | Chokes Available |
|---|---|---|---|---|---|
| 12 | Hunting | 30" | 50½" | 7 lbs. 9 oz. | Invector-Plus |
| 12 | Hunting | 28" | 48½" | 7 lbs. 6 oz. | Invector-Plus |
| 12 | Hunting | 26" | 46½" | 7 lbs. 3 oz. | Invector-Plus |
| 20 | Hunting | 28" | 48¼" | 6 lbs. 14 oz. | Invector |
| 20 | Hunting | 26" | 46¼" | 6 lbs. 12 oz. | Invector |

Total capacity for 3″ loads is 3 shells in magazine, 1 in chamber; with 2½″ loads, 4 in magazine, 1 in chamber. Gold 12 ga. models have vent recoil pad; 20 ga. models have solid pad.

### SPECIFICATIONS GOLD 10 $959.95

| Chamber | Barrel Length | Overall Length | Average Weight | Chokes |
|---|---|---|---|---|
| 3½" | 30" | 52" | 10 lbs. 13 oz. | Standard Invector |
| 3½" | 28" | 50" | 10 lbs. 10 oz. | Standard Invector |
| 3½" | 26" | 48" | 10 lbs. 7 oz. | Standard Invector |

Extra barrels are available for **$249.95** (10 ga.) and **$259.95** (12 and 20 ga.).



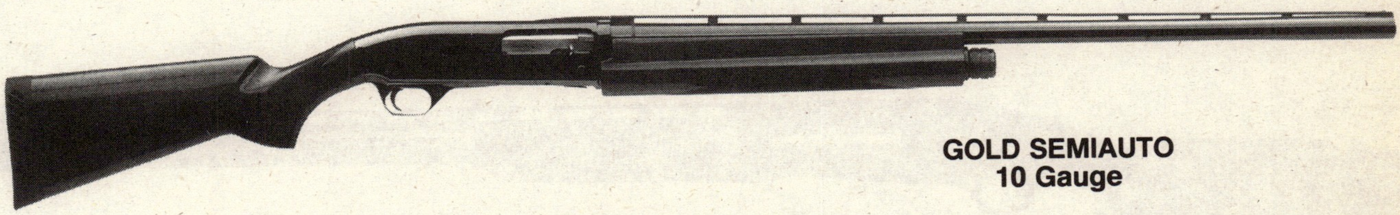

GOLD SEMIAUTO
10 Gauge

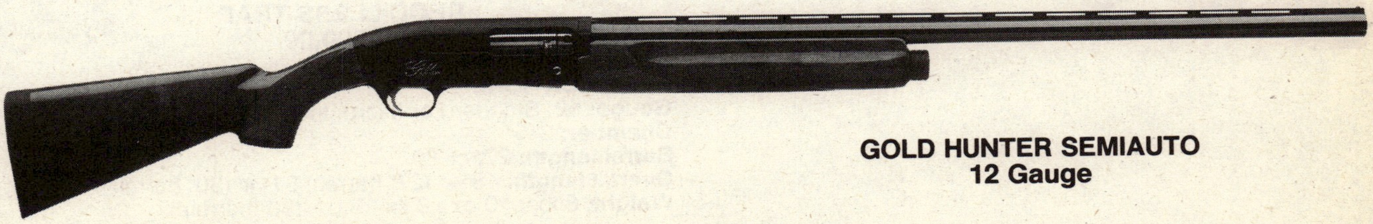

GOLD HUNTER SEMIAUTO
12 Gauge

# BROWNING CITORI SHOTGUNS

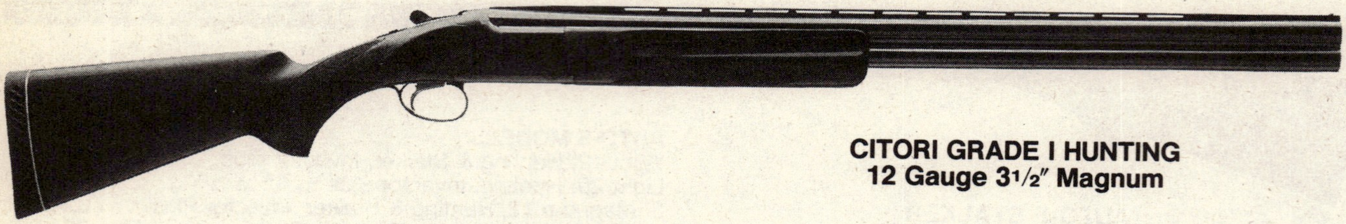

CITORI GRADE I HUNTING
12 Gauge 3 1/2" Magnum

## SPECIFICATIONS CITORI FIELD MODELS

| Gauge | Model | Chamber* | Barrel Length | Overall Length | Average Weight | Chokes Available[1] | Grades Available |
|---|---|---|---|---|---|---|---|
| 12 | Hunting | 3 1/2" Mag. | 30" | 47" | 8 lbs. 10 oz. | Invector-Plus | I |
| 12 | Hunting | 3 1/2" Mag. | 28" | 45" | 8 lbs. 9 oz. | Invector-Plus | I |
| 12 | Hunting | 3" | 30" | 47" | 8 lbs. 4 oz. | Invector-Plus | I |
| 12 | Hunting | 3" | 28" | 45" | 8 lbs. 1 oz. | Invector-Plus | I, III, VI |
| 12 | Hunting | 3" | 26" | 43" | 7 lbs. 15 oz. | Invector-Plus | I, III, VI |
| 12 | Lightning | 3" | 28" | 45" | 8 lbs. 1 oz. | Invector-Plus | I, GL, III, VI |
| 12 | Lightning | 3" | 26" | 43" | 7 lbs. 15 oz. | Invector-Plus | I, GL III, VI |
| 12 | Superlight | 2 3/4" | 28" | 45" | 6 lbs. 12 oz. | Invector-Plus | I, III, VI |
| 12 | Superlight | 2 3/4" | 26" | 43" | 6 lbs. 10 oz. | Invector-Plus | I, III, VI |
| 12 | Upland Special | 2 3/4" | 24" | 41" | 6 lbs. 11 oz. | Invector-Plus | I |
| 20 | Hunting | 3" | 28" | 45" | 6 lbs. 12 oz. | Invector-Plus | I, III, |
| 20 | Hunting | 3" | 26" | 43" | 6 lbs. 10 oz. | Invector-Plus | I, III, VI |
| 20 | Lightning | 3" | 28" | 45" | 6 lbs. 14 oz. | Invector-Plus | I, GL, III, VI |
| 20 | Lightning | 3" | 26" | 43" | 6 lbs. 9 oz. | Invector-Plus | I, GL, III, VI |
| 20 | Lightning | 3" | 24" | 41" | 6 lbs. 6 oz. | Invector-Plus | I |
| 20 | Micro Lightning | 2 3/4" | 24" | 41" | 6 lbs. 3 oz. | Invector-Plus | I, III, VI |
| 20 | Superlight | 2 3/4" | 26" | 43" | 6 lbs. | Invector-Plus | I, III, VI |
| 20 | Upland Special | 2 3/4" | 24" | 41" | 6 lbs. | Invector-Plus | I |
| 28 | Lightning | 2 3/4" | 28" | 45" | 6 lbs. 11 oz. | Invector | I |
| 28 | Lightning | 2 3/4" | 26" | 43" | 6 lbs. 10 oz. | Invector | I, GL, III, VI |
| 28 | Superlight | 2 3/4" | 26" | 43" | 6 lbs. 10 oz. | Invector | I, III, VI |
| .410 | Lightning | 3" | 28" | 45" | 7 lbs. | Invector | I |
| .410 | Lightning | 3" | 26" | 43" | 6 lbs. 14 oz. | Invector | I, GL, III, VI |
| .410 | Superlight | 3" | 28" | 45" | 6 lbs. 14 oz. | Invector | I |
| .410 | Superlight | 3" | 26" | 43" | 6 lbs. 13 oz. | Invector | I, III, VI |

[1]*Full & Modified Choke installed; Improved Cylinder and wrench included. GL=Gran Lightning grade.*

| Citori Field Models | Prices |
|---|---|
| **12 Ga. 3 1/2" Mag. Invector-Plus** | **$1350.00** |
| **12 & 20 Ga. Invector-Plus** | |
| Grade I Hunting | **1270.00** |
| Grade I Lightning | **1310.00** |
| Grade Superlight & Upland Spec. | **1320.00** |
| Grade I 20 Ga. Micro-Lightning | **1360.00** |
| Gran Lightning | **1780.00** |
| Grade III Hunting | **1875.00** |
| Grade III Lightning & Superlight | **1910.00** |
| Grade VI Hunting | **2715.00** |
| Grade VI Lightning & Superlight | **2780.00** |
| **28 Ga. & .410 Bore** | |
| Grade I Lightning | **1350.00** |
| Grade I Superlight | **1370.00** |
| Gran Lightning | **1875.00** |
| Grade III Lightning & Superlight | **2135.00** |
| Grade VI Lightning & Superlight | **2995.00** |

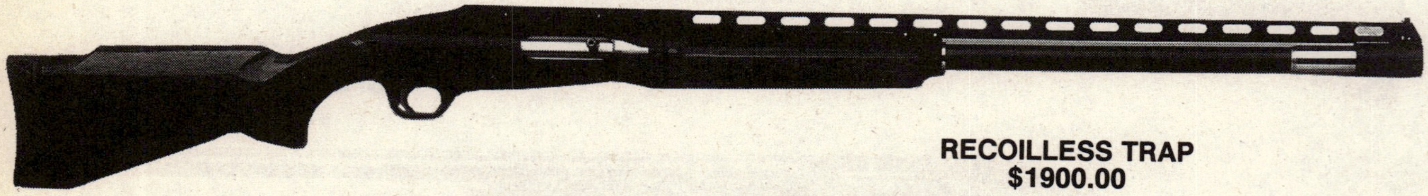

**RECOILLESS TRAP**
**$1900.00**

**SPECIFICATIONS**
**Gauge:** 12, Standard or Micro; Invector-Plus choke
**Chamber:** 2 3/4"
**Barrel length:** 27" or 30"
**Overall length:** 48 5/8" (27" barrel); 51 5/8" (30" barrel)
**Weight:** 8 lbs. 10 oz.; 8 lbs. 8 oz. (30" barrel)

# BROWNING CITORI SHOTGUNS

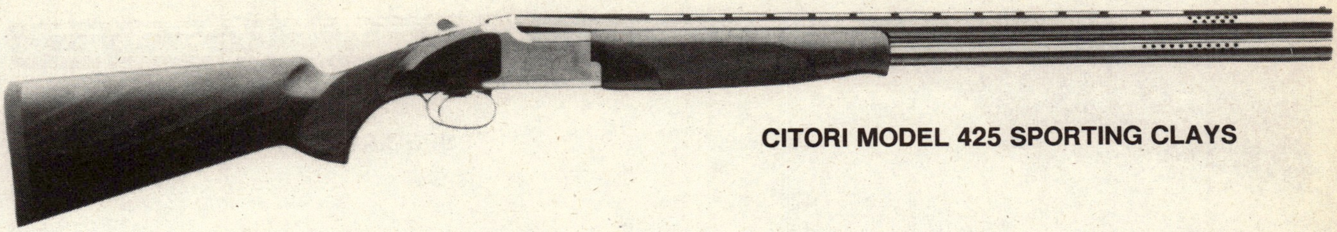

CITORI MODEL 425 SPORTING CLAYS

## SPECIFICATIONS SPECIAL SPORTING CLAYS, TRAP & SKEET AND LIGHTNING SPORTING

| Gauge | Model | Chamber | Barrel Length | Overall Length | Average Weight | Chokes | Grades Available |
|---|---|---|---|---|---|---|---|
| SPECIAL* | | | | | | | |
| 12 | Sporting Clays | 2 3/4" | 32" | 49" | 8 lbs. 5 oz. | Invector-Plus | I, Golden Clays |
| 12 | Sporting Clays | 2 3/4" | 30" | 47" | 8 lbs. 3 oz. | Invector-Plus | I, Golden Clays |
| 12 | Sporting Clays | 2 3/4" | 28" | 45" | 8 lbs. 1 oz. | Invector-Plus | I, Golden Clays |
| 12 | Trap (Conv.) | 2 3/4" | 32" | 49" | 8 lbs. 11 oz. | Invector-Plus | I, III, Golden Clays |
| 12 | Trap (Monte Carlo) | 2 3/4" | 32" | 49" | 8 lbs. 10 oz. | Invector-Plus | I, III, Golden Clays |
| 12 | Trap (Conv.) | 2 3/4" | 30" | 47" | 8 lbs. 7 oz. | Invector-Plus | I, III, Golden Clays |
| 12 | Trap (Monte Carlo) | 2 3/4" | 30" | 47" | 8 lbs. 6 oz. | Invector-Plus | I, III, Golden Clays |
| 12 | Skeet | 2 3/4" | 28" | 45" | 8 lbs. | Invector-Plus | I, III, Golden Clays |
| 12 | Skeet | 2 3/4" | 26" | 43" | 7 lbs. 15 oz. | Invector-Plus | I, III, Golden Clays |
| 20 | Skeet | 2 3/4" | 28" | 45" | 7 lbs. 4 oz. | Invector-Plus | I, III, Golden Clays |
| 20 | Skeet | 2 3/4" | 26" | 43" | 7 lbs. 1 oz. | Invector-Plus | I, III, Golden Clays |
| 28 | Skeet | 2 3/4" | 28" | 45" | 6 lbs. 15 oz. | Invector | I, III, Golden Clays |
| 28 | Skeet | 2 3/4" | 26" | 43" | 6 lbs. 10 oz. | Invector | I, III, Golden Clays |
| .410 | Skeet | 3" | 28" | 45" | 7 lbs. 6 oz. | Invector | I, III, Golden Clays |
| .410 | Skeet | 3" | 26" | 43" | 7 lbs. 3 oz. | Invector | I, III, Golden Clays |
| LIGHTNING SPORTING | | | | | | | |
| 12 | Sporting Clays | 3" | 30" | 47" | 8 lbs. 8 oz. | Invector-Pus | I, Golden Clays |
| 12 | Sporting Clays | 3" | 28" | 45" | 8 lbs. 6 oz. | Invector-Plus | I, Golden Clays |

*Invector=Invector Choke System — Sporting Clays models: Modified, Improved Cylinder and Skeet tube supplied. Trap models: Full, Improved Modified, Modified tube supplied. Skeet models: Skeet and Skeet tubes only supplied. Sets: 12 gauge Invector-Plus, Ported. *All target models are also available with optional adjustable comb.*

## CITORI SPORTING CLAYS, INVECTOR-PLUS Prices

**Model 425, 12 Gauge**

| | |
|---|---|
| Grade I, ported barrels | **$1690.00** |
| Grade I, adj. comb | **1890.00** |
| Golden Clays, ported barrels | **3150.00** |
| Golden Clays, adj. comb | **3350.00** |
| WSSF, Women's Model | **N/A** |

**Model 425, 20 Gauge**

| | |
|---|---|
| Grade I, ported barrels | **1690.00** |
| Grade I, adj. comb | **1890.00** |

**Model 425, 20 Gauge (cont.)**

| | |
|---|---|
| Golden Clays, ported barrels | **$3150.00** |
| Golden Clays, adj. comb | **3350.00** |

**Ultra Sporter**

| | |
|---|---|
| With ported barrels | **1640.00** |
| With adj. comb | **1840.00** |
| Golden Clays, ported barrels | **3050.00** |
| Golden Clays, adj. comb | **3250.00** |

SHOTGUNS

# BROWNING CITORI SHOTGUNS

SPECIAL SPORTING

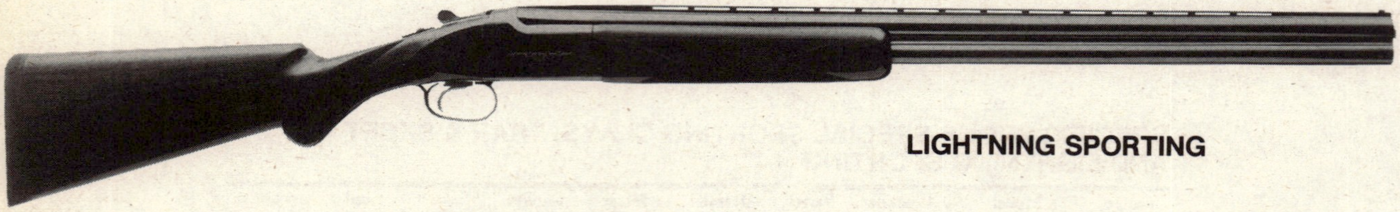

LIGHTNING SPORTING

## CITORI SPECIAL SPORTING AND LIGHTNING SPORTING

| **Special Sporting** | **Prices** |
|---|---|
| Grade I, ported barrels | $1490.00 |
| Grade I, ported bbls., adj. comb | 1690.00 |
| Golden Clays, ported barrels | 3050.00 |
| Golden Clays, adj. comb | 3250.00 |
| **Lightning Sporting** | |
| Grade I, high rib, ported bbl., 3″ | 1490.00 |
| **Lightning Sporting (cont.)** | |
| Grade I, high rib, adj. comb | $1690.00 |
| Grade I, low rib, ported bbls., 3″ | 1425.00 |
| Grade I, low rib, adj. comb | 1625.00 |
| Golden Clays, low rib, ported bbls., 3″ | 2945.00 |
| Golden Clays, low rib, adj. comb | 3145.00 |
| Golden Clays, high rib, ported bbls., 3″ | 3050.00 |
| Golden Clays, high rib, adj. comb | 3250.00 |

(See previous page for specifications)

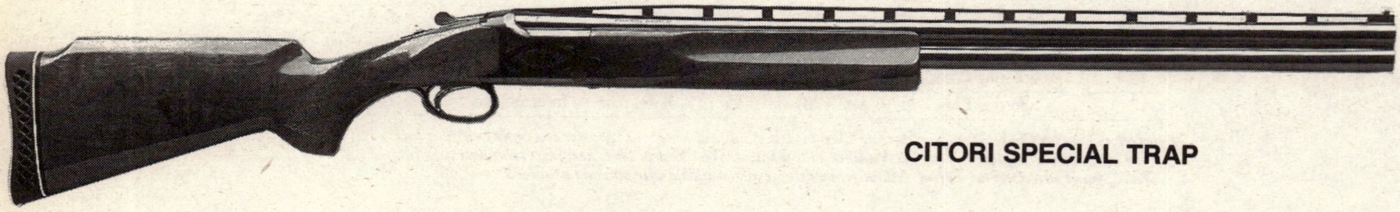

CITORI SPECIAL TRAP

## SPECIAL TRAP MODELS

| **12 Gauge, Invector-Plus, Ported Barrels** | **Prices** |
|---|---|
| Grade I, Monte Carlo stock | $1150.00 |
| Grade I, adj. comb | 1710.00 |
| Grade III, Monte Carlo stock | 2057.00 |
| Grade III, adj. comb | 2275.00 |
| Golden Clays, Monte Carlo stock | 3085.00 |
| Golden Clays, adj. comb | 3285.00 |

## SPECIAL SKEET MODELS

| **12 and 20 Gauge, Invector Plus, Ported Barrels** | **Prices** |
|---|---|
| Grade I, high post rib | $1510.00 |
| Grade I, high post rib, adj. comb | 1710.00 |
| Grade III, high post rib | 2075.00 |
| Grade III, high post rib, adj. comb | 2275.00 |
| Golden Clays, high post rib | 3085.00 |
| Golden Clays, high post rib, adj. comb | 3285.00 |
| **28 Ga. and .410 Bore Std. Invector** | |
| Grade I, high post rib | 1475.00 |
| Grade III, high post rib | 2080.00 |
| Golden Clays, high post rib | 3015.00 |

# BROWNING SHOTGUNS

BT-100 TRAP

## SPECIFICATIONS BT-100 AND BT-99 MAX

| Gauge | Model | Chamber | Barrel Length | Overall Length | Average Weight | Chokes | Grades Available |
|---|---|---|---|---|---|---|---|
| 12 | BT-100 | 2 3/4" | 34" | 50 1/2" | 8 lbs. 10 oz. | Invector Plus[1] | I, Stainless |
| 12 | BT-100 | 2 3/4" | 32" | 48 1/2" | 8 lbs. 9 oz. | Invector Plus[1] | I, Stainless |
| 12 | BT-100 Monte Carlo | 2 3/4" | 34" | 50 1/2" | 8 lbs. 10 oz. | Invector Plus | I, Stainless |
| 12 | BT-100 Monte Carlo | 2 3/4" | 32" | 48 1/2" | 8 lbs. 9 oz. | Invector Plus | I, Stainless |
| 12 | BT-100 Thumbhole | 2 3/4" | 34" | 50 3/4" | 8 lbs. 8 oz. | Invector Plus | I, Stainless |
| 12 | BT-100 Thumbhole | 2 3/4" | 32" | 48 3/4" | 8 lbs. 6 oz. | Invector Plus | I, Stainless |
| 12 | BT-99 MAX | 2 3/4" | 34" | 50 1/2" | 8 lbs. 10 oz. | Invector Plus | I, Stainless |
| 12 | BT-99 MAX | 2 3/4" | 32" | 48 1/2" | 8 lbs. 8 oz. | Invector Plus | I, Stainless |
| 12 | BT-99 MAX M-Carlo | 2 3/4" | 34" | 50 1/2" | 8 lbs. 9 oz. | Invector Plus | I, Stainless |
| 12 | BT-99 MAX M-Carlo | 2 3/4" | 32" | 48 1/2" | 8 lbs. 6 oz. | Invector Plus | I, Stainless |

*F=Full, M=Modified, IM=Improved Modified, S=Skeet, Invector=Invector Choke System — Invector-Plus Trap models: Full, Improved Modified, Modified, and wrench included.*
*[1] Also available with conventional full choke barrel.*

### STOCK DIMENSIONS BT-100

| | Adjustable Conventional | Thumbhole | Monte Carlo |
|---|---|---|---|
| Length of Pull | 14 3/8" | 14 3/8" | 14 3/8" |
| Drop at Comb | Adj.* | 1 3/4" | 1 9/16" |
| Drop at Monte Carlo | — | 1 1/4" | 1 7/16" |
| Drop at Heel | Adj.* | 2 1/8" | 2" |

**Adjustable Drop at Comb and Heel.*

### STOCK DIMENSIONS BT-99 MAX

| | Conventional | Monte Carlo |
|---|---|---|
| Length of Pull | 14 3/8" | 14 3/8" |
| Drop at Comb | 1 5/8" | 1 9/16" |
| Drop at Monte Carlo | — | 1 7/16" |
| Drop at Heel | 1 1/2" | 2" |

**BT-100 SINGLE BARREL TRAP Prices**

**Grade I, Invector-Plus**
Monte Carlo stock . . . . . . . . **$1900.00**
Adjustable comb . . . . . . . . **2100.00**
Full choke barrel . . . . . . . . **1855.00**
Full choke barrel, adj. comb . . . . . . . . **2055.00**

**Stainless, Invector-Plus**
Monte Carlo stock . . . . . . . . **2300.00**
Adjustable comb . . . . . . . . **2500.00**
Full choke barrel . . . . . . . . **2255.00**
Full choke barrel, adj. comb . . . . . . . . **2455.00**

**Trigger Assembly Replacement** . . . . . . . . **500.00**

**MODEL BT-99 MAX**
Grade I, ported bbls. . . . . . . **1495.95**
Stainless, ported bbls. . . . . . **1895.95**

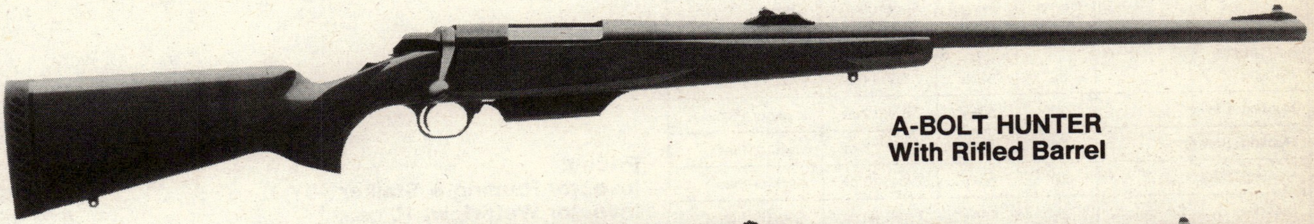

A-BOLT HUNTER
With Rifled Barrel

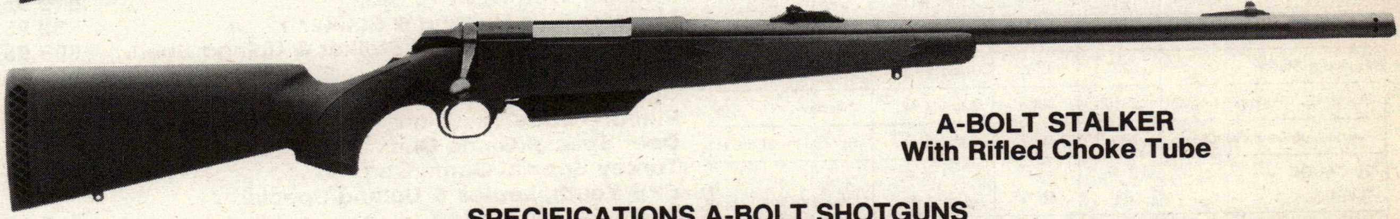

A-BOLT STALKER
With Rifled Choke Tube

## SPECIFICATIONS A-BOLT SHOTGUNS

| Model | Chamber | Magazine Capacity | Barrel Length | Overall Length | Average Weight | Choke/Barrel Available |
|---|---|---|---|---|---|---|
| Hunter/Choke Tube | 3" | 2[1] | 23" | 44 3/4" | 7 lbs. 2 oz. | Standard Invector* |
| Hunter/Rifled Barrel | 3" | 2[1] | 22" | 43 3/4" | 7 lbs. | Fully rifled barrel |
| Stalker/Choke Tube | 3" | 2[1] | 23" | 44 3/4" | 7 lbs. 2 oz. | Standard Invector* |
| Stalker/Rifled Barrel | 3" | 2[1] | 22" | 43 3/4" | 7 lbs. | Fully rifled barrel |

**Standard Invector interchangeable choke tube system: One rifled choke tube and one X-Full Turkey choke tube included.*
*[1] Total capacity is 2 shells in magazine, one in chamber.*

**A-BOLT SHOTGUNS Prices**

**Hunter**
With choke tube . . . . . . . . . **$789.95**
With rifled barrel . . . . . . . . . **839.95**

**Stalker**
With choke tube . . . . . . . . . **709.95**
With rifled barrel . . . . . . . . . **759.95**

# BROWNING SHOTGUNS

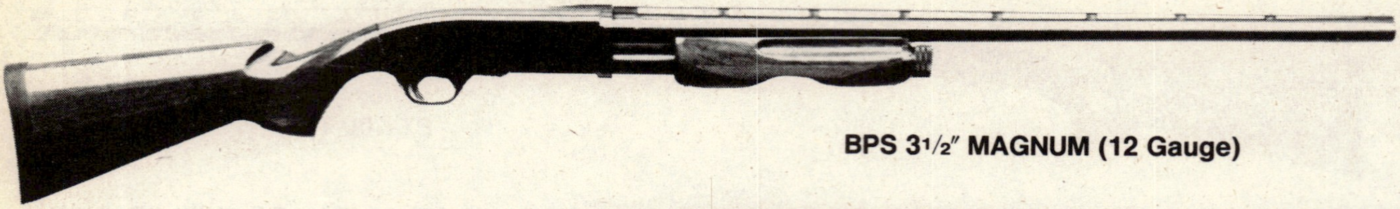

BPS 3½″ MAGNUM (12 Gauge)

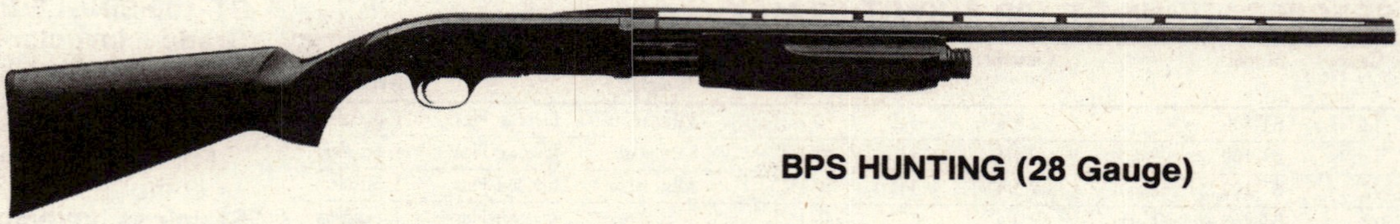

BPS HUNTING (28 Gauge)

## SPECIFICATIONS BPS MAGNUMS

| Gauge | Model | Chamber Length | Barrel Length | Overall Weight | Average Available | Chokes |
|---|---|---|---|---|---|---|
| 10 Magnum | Hunting & Stalker | 3½″ | 30″ | 51¾″ | 9 lbs. 8 oz. | Invector |
| 10 Magnum | Hunting & Stalker | 3½″ | 28″ | 49¾″ | 9 lbs. 6 oz. | Invector |
| 10 Magnum | Hunting & Stalker | 3½″ | 26″ | 47¾″ | 9 lbs. 4 oz. | Invector |
| 10 Magnum | Hunting & Stalker | 3½″ | 24″ | 45¾″ | 9 lbs. 4 oz. | Invector |
| 10 Magnum | Hunting Buck Special | 3½″ | 24″ | 45¾″ | 9 lbs. 2 oz. | Slug/Buckshot |
| 12, 3½″ Mag | Hunting & Stalker | 3½″ | 30″ | 51¾″ | 8 lbs. 12 oz. | Invector-Plus |
| 12, 3½″ Mag | Hunting & Stalker | 3½″ | 28″ | 49¾″ | 8 lbs. 9 oz. | Invector-Plus |
| 12, 3½″ Mag | Hunting & Stalker | 3½″ | 26″ | 47¾″ | 8 lbs. 6 oz. | Invector-Plus |
| 12, 3½″ Mag | Hunting & Stalker | 3½″ | 24″ | 45¾″ | 8 lbs. 3 oz. | Invector-Plus |
| 12, 3½″ Mag | Hunting Buck Special | 3½″ | 24″ | 45¾″ | 8 lbs. 7 oz. | Slug/Buckshot |

## SPECIFICATIONS BPS 12 & 20 GAUGE PUMP (3″)

| Model | Barrel Length | Overall Length | Average Weight | Chokes Available |
|---|---|---|---|---|
| **12 GAUGE** Hunting | 32″ | 52½″ | 7 lbs. 14 oz. | Invector-Plus |
| Hunting, Stalker | 30″ | 50¾″ | 7 lbs. 12 oz. | Invector-Plus |
| Hunting, Stalker | 28″ | 48¾″ | 7 lbs. 11 oz. | Invector-Plus |
| Hunting, Stalker | 26″ | 46¾″ | 7 lbs. 10 oz. | Invector-Plus |
| Standard Buck Special | 24″ | 44¾″ | 7 lbs. 10 oz. | Slug/Buckshot |
| Upland Special | 22″ | 42½″ | 7 lbs. 8 oz. | Invector-Plus |
| Hunting, Stalker | 22″ | 42½″ | 7 lbs. 7 oz. | Invector-Plus |
| Game Gun Turkey Special | 20½″ | 40⅞″ | 7 lbs. 7 oz. | Invector |
| Game Gun Deer Special | 20½″ | 40⅞″ | 7 lbs. 7 oz. | Special Inv./Rifled |
| **20 GAUGE** Hunting | 28″ | 48¾″ | 7 lbs. 1 oz. | Invector-Plus |
| Hunting | 26″ | 46¾″ | 7 lbs. | Invector-Plus |
| Youth/Ladies | 22″ | 41¾″ | 6 lbs. 11 oz. | Invector-Plus |
| Upland Special | 22″ | 42½″ | 6 lbs. 12 oz. | Invector-Plus |
| **28 GAUGE** Hunting* | 28″ | 48¾″ | 7 lbs. 1 oz. | Invector |
| Hunting* | 26″ | 46¾″ | 7 lbs. | Invector |

* 2¾″ chamber

**Prices:**

**Invector Hunting & Stalker** 10 ga. . . . . . . . . . . . . . **$639.95**
**Invector Waterfowl** 10 ga. . . . . . . . . . . . . . . . . . . **819.95**
**Invector-Plus Hunting & Stalker** 12 ga. . . . . . . . . **639.95**
**Invector-Plus Hunting, Stalker & Upland Spec.** . . **509.95**
**Buck Special** 12 ga. only . . . . . . . . . . . . . . . . . . **494.95**
**Buck Special** 10 ga. & 3½″ 12 ga. . . . . . . . . . . . . **644.95**
**Pigeon Grade** 12 ga. only . . . . . . . . . . . . . . . . . . **679.95**
**Deer Special Game Gun** . . . . . . . . . . . . . . . . . . . . **574.95**
**Turkey Special Game Gun** . . . . . . . . . . . . . . . . . . **544.95**
**BPS Youth, Ladies & Upland Special**
20 ga. only . . . . . . . . . . . . . . . . . . . . . . . . . . . . . . **398.95**
**Hunting, Youth, Ladies, Upland Spec.** 20 ga. . . . **509.95**
**Hunting** (Standard Invector), 20 ga. . . . . . . . . . . . **509.95**

# CONNECTICUT VALLEY CLASSICS

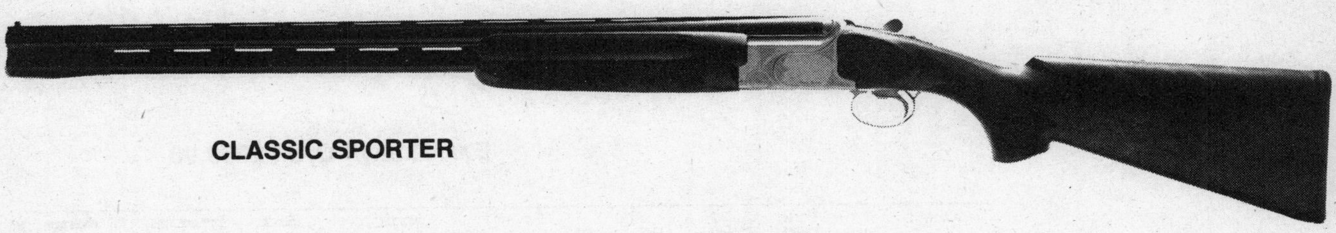

CLASSIC SPORTER

## CVC CLASSIC 101 SPORTER

The designers of the new CVC "Classic Sporter" and "Classic Waterfowler" trace their lineage back to the well-known "Classic Doubles" and Winchester over/under shotguns. They have used the proven strength and durability of the M-101 design and integrated these qualities with advanced engineering and manufacturing techniques. In addition to the basic specifications listed below, the CVC Classic models feature the following: Frame, monoblock and key integral parts are machined from solid steel bar stock. . . Tang spacer is an integral part of the frame to ensure rigid alignment for solid lockup of buttstock to frame. . . Chrome molybdenum steel barrels; chrome-lined bores and chambers (suitable for steel shot use). . . Barrels have elongated forcing cones for reduced recoil; interchangeable screw-in chokes included. . . Low-luster satin-finished stock and forend are of full, fancy-grade American black walnut and hand-checkered with fine-line engraving.

**Prices:**
**Classic Sporter Stainless . . . . . . . . . . . . . . . . . . $2995.00**

### CONNECTICUT VALLEY CLASSICS SPECIFICATIONS

| Model | Symbol | Gauge | Barrel Length | Overall Length | Length of Pull | Drop at Comb | Drop at Heel | Nominal Weight (lbs.) |
|---|---|---|---|---|---|---|---|---|
| Classic Sporter-Stainless | CV-SS28<br>CV-SS30<br>CV-SS32 | 12<br>12<br>12 | 28″<br>30″<br>32″ | 44 7/8″<br>46 7/8″<br>48 7/8″ | 14 1/2″<br>14 1/2″<br>14 1/2″ | 1 1/2″<br>1 1/2″<br>1 1/2″ | 2 1/8″<br>2 1/8″<br>2 1/8″ | 7 3/4<br>7 3/4<br>7 3/4 |

**Chambers:** All Connecticut Valley Classics have 3″ chambers. **Interchangeable Chokes:** All Connecticut Valley Classics have the internal CV Choke System, and each gun includes the following four chokes: Full, Modified, Improved Cylinder and Skeet. CV Choke Systems are fully compatible with previously manufactured Classic Doubles In-Choke and Winchoke interchangeable choke tubes.
**Interchangeable Choke System Options:** Two options are available at additional cost to the standard CV Choke System: CV Plus Choke System, a 2 3/8″ choke tube system for an extra 7/8″ choke length using the standard CV choke tube barrel threading; and the Briley Competition Choke System, a factory-installed 2 3/4″ flush-mounted system.

SHOTGUNS

# COUNTY SHOTGUNS

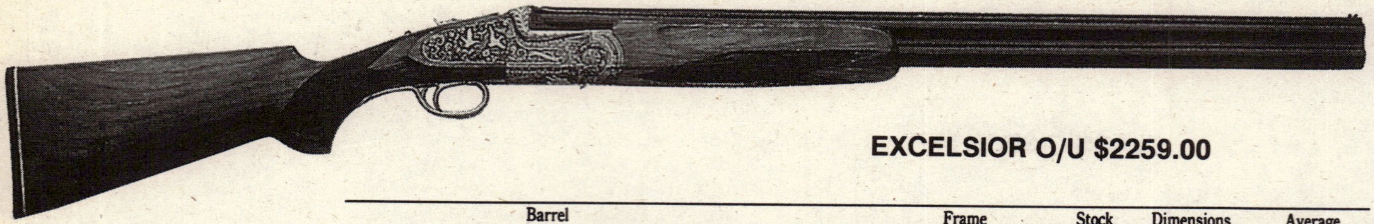

**EXCELSIOR O/U $2259.00**

| Gauge | Barrel Lenght | Chamber | Chokes | Rib | Ejector | Trigger | Frame Finish | Stock | Stock Lenght of pull | Dimensions Drop Comb | Dimensions At Heel | Average Weight lb | Average Weight oz |
|---|---|---|---|---|---|---|---|---|---|---|---|---|---|
| 12 | 28"-26" | 3" | MULTI. | 1/4" | ASE | ST | OS | FPG | 14⅛" | 1⅜" | 2⅜" | 7 | 3 |
| 20 | 26" | 3" | MULTI. | 1/4" | ASE | ST | OS | FPG | 14⅛" | 1⅜" | 2⅜" | 6 | 15 |

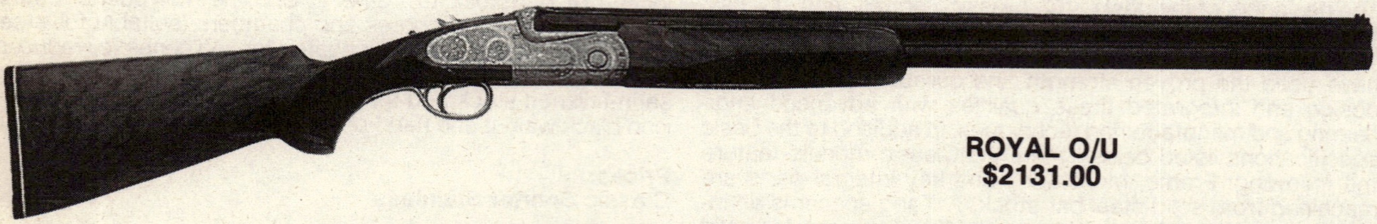

**ROYAL O/U**
**$2131.00**

| Gauge | Barrel Lenght | Chamber | Chokes | Rib | Ejector | Trigger | Frame Finish | Stock | Stock Lenght of pull | Dimensions Drop Comb | Dimensions At Heel | Average Weight lb | Average Weight oz |
|---|---|---|---|---|---|---|---|---|---|---|---|---|---|
| 12 | 28"-26" | 3" | MULTI. | 1/4" | ASE | ST | OS | FPG | 14⅛" | 1⅜" | 2⅜" | 7 | 3 |
| 20 | 26" | 3" | MULTI. | 1/4" | ASE | ST | OS | FPG | 14⅛" | 1⅜" | 2⅜" | 6 | 15 |

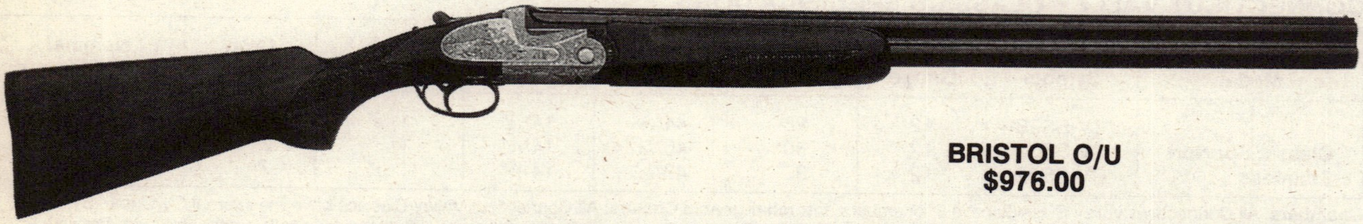

**BRISTOL O/U**
**$976.00**

| Gauge | Barrel Lenght | Chamber | Chokes | Rib | Ejector | Trigger | Frame Finish | Stock | Stock Lenght of pull | Dimensions Drop Comb | Dimensions At Heel | Average Weight lb | Average Weight oz |
|---|---|---|---|---|---|---|---|---|---|---|---|---|---|
| 12 | 28"-26" | 3" | M/F-IC/M MULTI. | 1/4" | ASE | SST | OS | FPG | 14⅛" | 1⅜" | 2⅜" | 7 | 1 |
| 20 | 26" | 3" | M/F-IC/M MULTI. | 1/4" | ASE | SST | OS | FPG | 14⅛" | 1⅜" | 2⅜" | 6 | 12 |

**MODEL FS-300 O/U**
**$1108.00**
**w/Monte Carlo Stock and Vent Middle Rib**

| Gauge | Barrel Lenght | Chamber | Chokes | Rib | Ejector | Trigger | Frame Finish | Stock | Stock Lenght of pull | Dimensions Drop Comb | Dimensions At Heel | Average Weight lb | Average Weight oz |
|---|---|---|---|---|---|---|---|---|---|---|---|---|---|
| 12 | 30" | 2¾" | IM/F | 3/8" | ASE | ST | OS | FPG | 14 5/16" | 1⅜" | 1½" | 8 | 2 |

# A.H. FOX SHOTGUNS

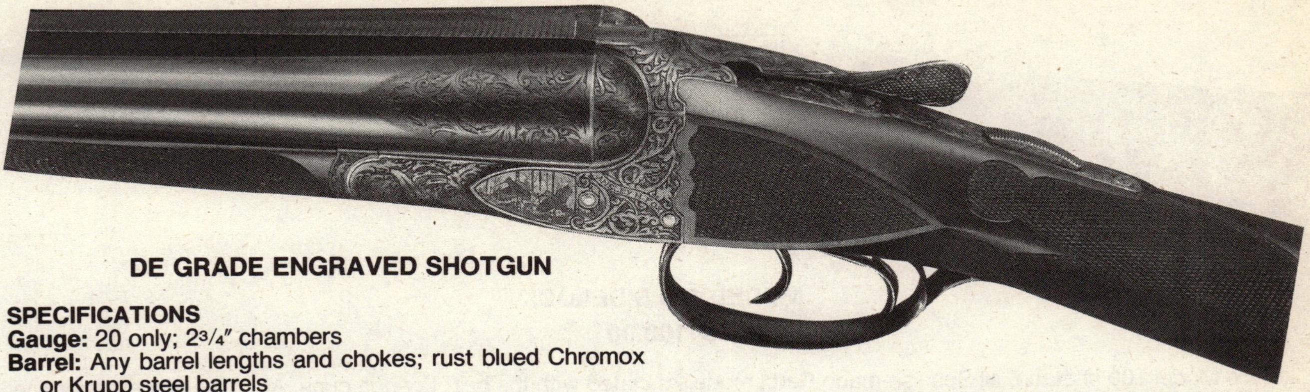

DE GRADE ENGRAVED SHOTGUN

**SPECIFICATIONS**
**Gauge:** 20 only; 2³/₄" chambers
**Barrel:** Any barrel lengths and chokes; rust blued Chromox or Krupp steel barrels
**Weight:** 5¹/₂ to 7 lbs.
**Stock:** Custom stock dimensions including cast; hand-checkered Turkish Circassian walnut stock and forend with hand-rubbed oil finish; straight grip, full pistol grip (with cap), or semi-pistol grip; splinter, schnabel or beavertail forend; traditional pad, hard rubber plate, checkered, or skeleton butt
**Features:** Boxlock action with automatic ejectors; scalloped, rebated and color casehardened receiver; double or Fox single selective trigger; hand-finished and hand-engraved. This is the same gun that was manufactured between 1905 and 1930 by the A.H. Fox Gun Company of Philadelphia, PA, now manufactured in the U.S. by the Connecticut Shotgun Mfg. Co. (New Britain, CT).
**Prices:**

| | |
|---|---|
| CE Grade* | $ 7,200.00 |
| XE Grade | 8,500.00 |
| DE Grade | 12,500.00 |
| FE Grade | 17,500.00 |
| Exhibition Grade | 25,000.00 |

* Grades differ in engraving and inlay, grade of wood and amount of hand finishing needed.

# FRANCOTTE SHOTGUNS

CLOSE-UP OF BOXLOCK S6

"CUSTOM" BOXLOCKS/SIDELOCKS

There are no standard Francotte models, since every shotgun is custom made in Belgium to the purchaser's individual specifications. Features and options include Anson & Deeley boxlocks or Auguste Francotte system sidelocks. All guns have custom-fitted stocks. Available are exhibition-grade stocks as well as extensive engraving and gold inlays. U.S. agent for Auguste Francotte of Belgium is Armes de Chasse (see Directory of Manufacturers and Distributors).

**SPECIFICATIONS**
**Gauges:** 12, 16, 20, 28, .410; also 24 and 32
**Chambers:** 2¹/₂", 2³/₄" and 3"
**Barrel length:** To customer's specifications
**Forend:** To customer's specifications
**Stock:** Deluxe to exhibition grade; pistol, English or half-pistol grip
**Prices:**

| | |
|---|---|
| **Basic Boxlock** | $ 9,710 |
| **Basic Boxlock** (28 & .410 ga.) | 10,710 |
| **Optional sideplates, add** | 1,158 |
| **Basic Sidelock** | 22,427 |
| **Basic Sidelock** (28 & .410 ga.) | 24,665 |

# GARBI SIDELOCK SHOTGUNS

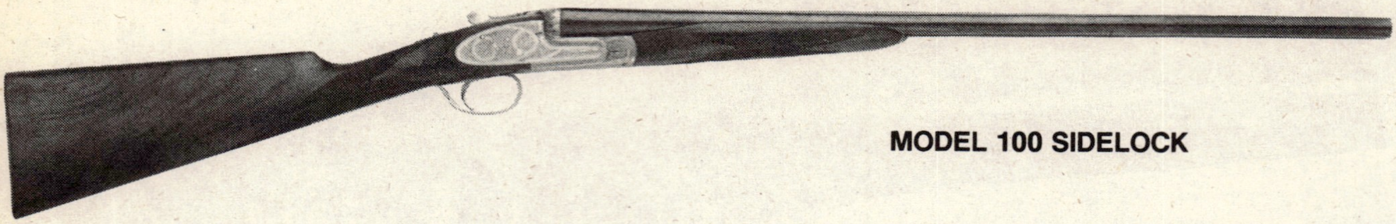

MODEL 100 SIDELOCK

## MODEL 100 SIDELOCK
## $4100.00

Like this Model 100 shotgun, all Spanish-made Garbi models featured here are Holland & Holland pattern sidelock ejector guns with chopper lump (demibloc) barrels. They are built to English gun standards with regard to design, weight, balance and proportions, and all have the characteristic "feel" associated with the best London guns. All of the models offer fine 24-line hand-checkering, with outstanding quality wood-to-metal and metal-to-metal fit. The Model 100 is available in 12, 16, 20 and 28 gauge and sports Purdey-style fine scroll and rosette engraving, partly done by machine.

## MODELS 101, 103A and 103B (not shown)

Available in 12, 16, 20, and 28 gauge, the sidelocks are handcrafted with hand-engraved receiver and select walnut straight grip stock.

**SPECIFICATIONS**

**Barrels:** 25″ to 30″ in 12 ga.; 25″ to 28″ in 16, 20 and 28 ga.; high-luster blued finish; smooth concave rib (optional Churchill or level, file-cut rib)

**Action:** Holland & Holland pattern sidelock; automatic ejectors; double triggers with front trigger hinged; casehardened

**Stock/forend:** Straight grip stock with checkered butt (optional pistol grip); hand-rubbed oil finish; classic (splinter) forend (optional beavertail)

**Weight:**
12 ga. Game, 6 lbs. 10 oz.–6 lbs. 14 oz.
12 ga. Pigeon or Wildfowl, about 7 lbs. 8 oz.
16 ga., 6 lbs. 6 oz.–6 lbs. 12 oz.
20 ga., 5 lbs. 15 oz.–6 lbs. 8 oz.
28 ga., 5 lbs. 10 oz.—5 lbs. 15 oz.

**Prices:**

| | |
|---|---|
| **Model 101** | **$5250.00** |
| **Model 103A** | **6550.00** |
| **Model 103B** | **9200.00** |

MODEL 200

## MODEL 200
## $8500.00

The **Model 200 double** is available in 12, 16, 20 or 28 gauge; features Holland-pattern stock ejector design, heavy-duty locks, heavy proof, Continental-style floral and scroll engraving, walnut stock.

## SINGLE-BARREL SHOTGUNS

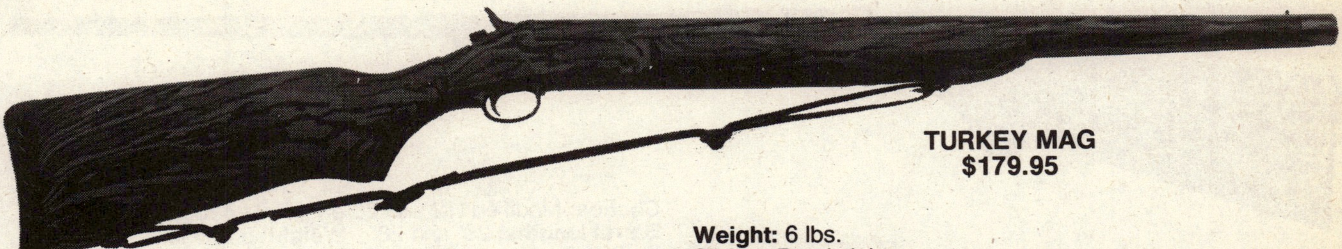

**TURKEY MAG**
**$179.95**

**SPECIFICATIONS**
**Gauge:** 12 (3½″ chamber); Turkey Full screw-in choke
**Barrel length:** 24″ **Overall length:** 40″
**Weight:** 6 lbs.
**Sights:** Bead sights
**Stock & forearm:** American hardwood with recoil pad; swivel and studs
**Finish:** Mossy Oak camo coverage and sling

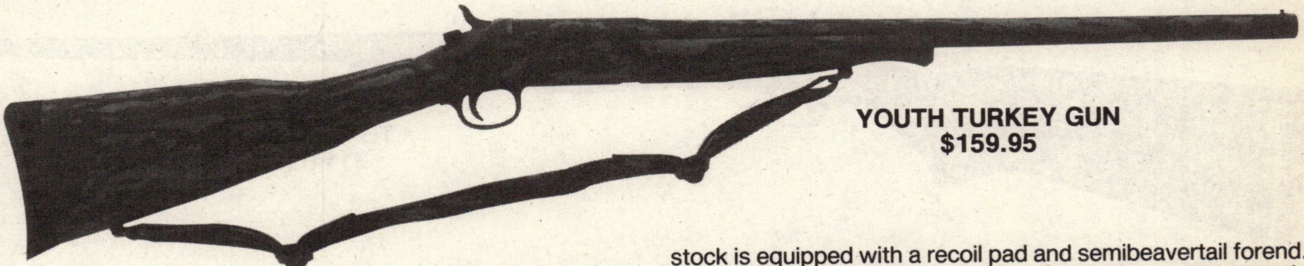

**YOUTH TURKEY GUN**
**$159.95**

This 20-gauge (3″ chamber) single shot has a 22″ full choke barrel with Realtree™ camo finish and sling. Its Thin Wrist stock is equipped with a recoil pad and semibeavertail forend. Other features include a transfer bar safety and automatic ejection. The weight is only 6 lbs., making it ideal for young shooters to hunt all types of game.

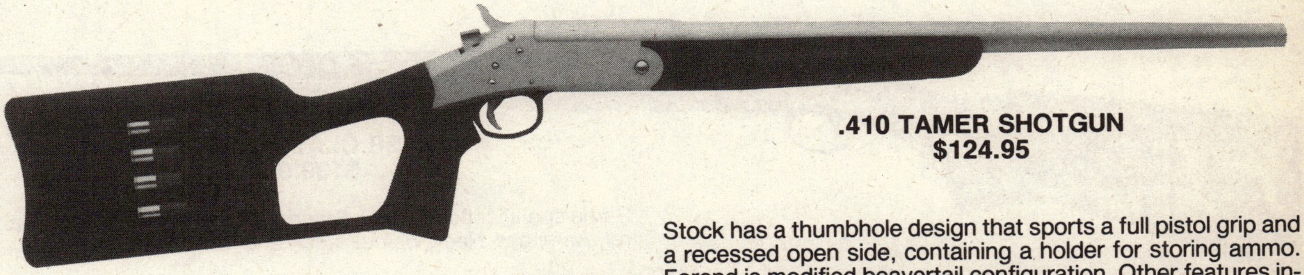

**.410 TAMER SHOTGUN**
**$124.95**

This barreled .410 snake gun features single-shot action, transfer bar safety and high-impact synthetic stock and forend. Stock has a thumbhole design that sports a full pistol grip and a recessed open side, containing a holder for storing ammo. Forend is modified beavertail configuration. Other features include a matte, electroless nickel finish. **Weight:** 5–6 lbs. **Barrel length:** 20″ (3″ chamber). **Choke:** Full.

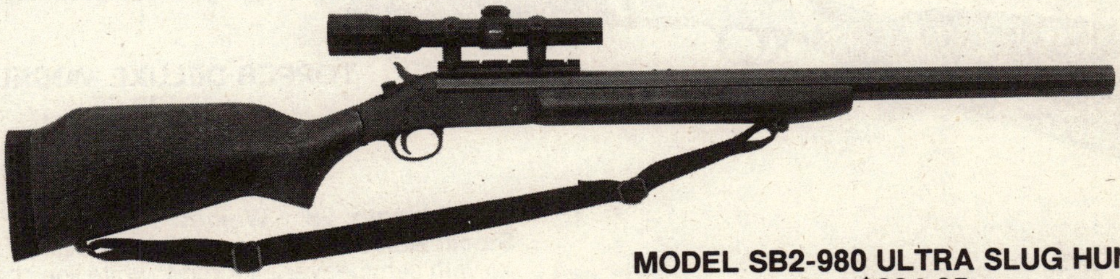

**MODEL SB2-980 ULTRA SLUG HUNTER**
**$224.95**

Features 12-gauge 24″ barrel, 3″ chamber, fully rifled slug barrel (HEAVY). Monte Carlo stock, scope rail, swivels and sling.

SHOTGUNS

# HARRINGTON & RICHARDSON

## SINGLE-BARREL SHOTGUNS

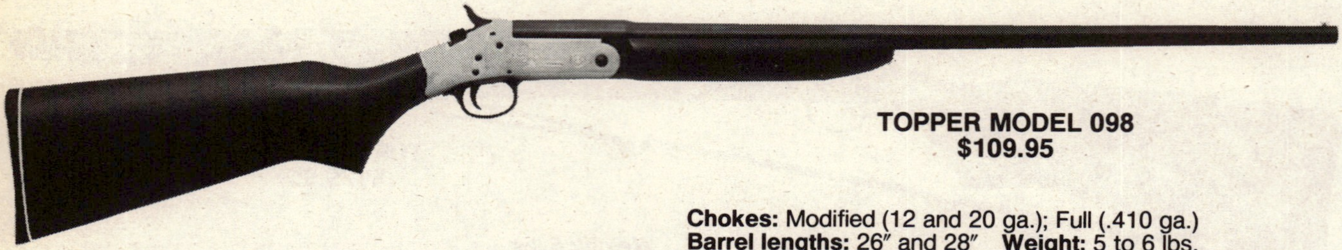

### TOPPER MODEL 098
**$109.95**

**SPECIFICATIONS**
**Gauges:** 12, 20 and .410 (3″ chamber); 16 and 28 ga. (2¾″ chamber)
**Chokes:** Modified (12 and 20 ga.); Full (.410 ga.)
**Barrel lengths:** 26″ and 28″ **Weight:** 5 to 6 lbs.
**Action:** Break-open; side lever release; automatic ejection
**Stock:** Full pistol grip; American hardwood; black finish with white buttplate spacer
**Length of pull:** 14½″

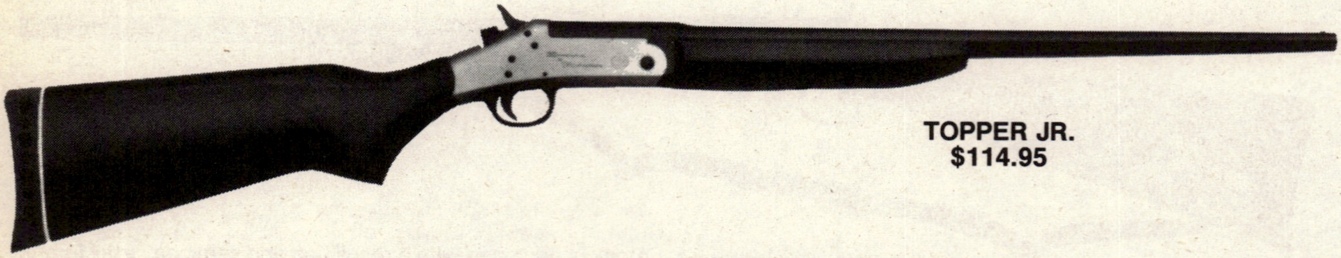

### TOPPER JR.
**$114.95**

**SPECIFICATIONS**
**Gauges:** 20 and .410 (3″ chamber)
**Chokes:** Modified (20 ga.); Full (.410 ga.)
**Barrel length:** 22″ **Weight:** 5 to 6 lbs.
**Stock:** Full pistol grip; American hardwood; black finish; white line spacer; recoil pad
**Finish:** Satin nickel frame; blued barrel

### TOPPER CLASSIC YOUTH
**$139.95**

Same specifications as the Standard Topper, but with 22″ barrel, American black walnut stock and 12½″ pull.

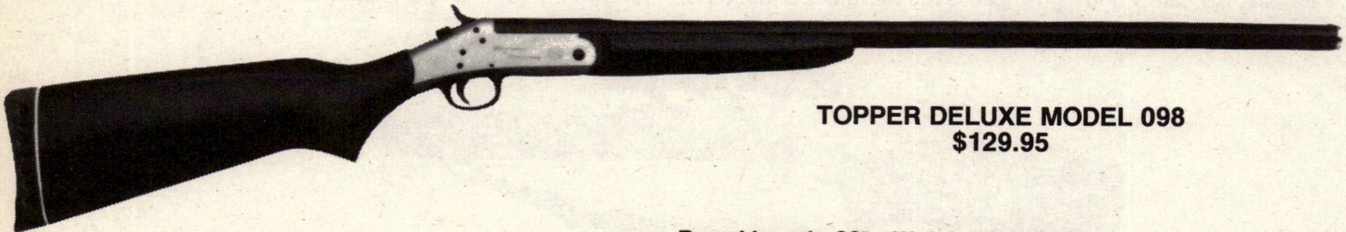

### TOPPER DELUXE MODEL 098
**$129.95**

**SPECIFICATIONS**
**Gauge:** 12 (3½″ chamber)
**Chokes:** Screw-in Modified (Full, Extra-Full Turkey and Steel Shot also available)
**Action:** Break-open; side lever release; positive ejection
**Barrel length:** 28″ **Weight:** 5 to 6 lbs.
**Stock:** American hardwood, black finish, full pistol-grip stock with semibeavertail forend; white line spacer; ventilated recoil pad
**Finish:** Satin nickel frame; blued barrel
Also available: **TOPPER DELUXE RIFLED SLUG GUN.** 12 ga., 28″ compensated choke, 3″, w/recoil pad and swivel studs

# IGA SHOTGUNS

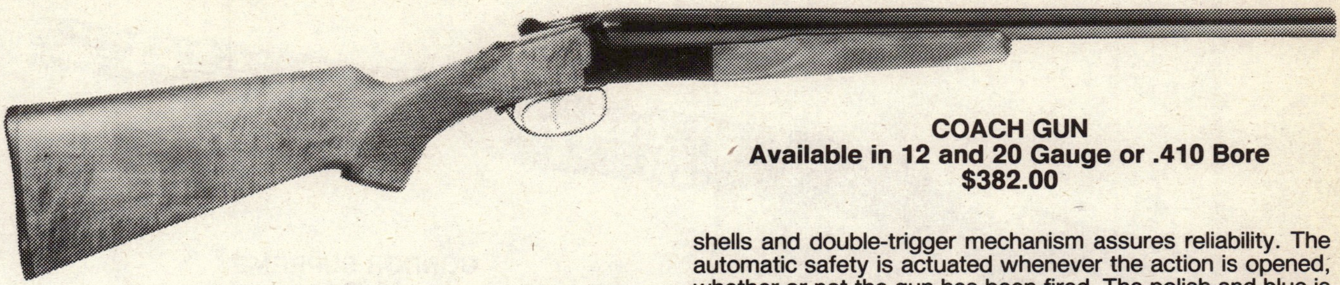

COACH GUN
**Available in 12 and 20 Gauge or .410 Bore**
**$382.00**

The **IGA CLASSIC SIDE-BY-SIDE COACH GUN** sports a 20-inch barrel. Lightning fast, it is the perfect shotgun for hunting upland game in dense brush or close quarters. This endurance-tested workhorse of a gun is designed from the ground up to give you years of trouble-free service. Two massive underlugs provide a super-safe, vise-tight locking system for lasting strength and durability. The mechanical extraction of spent shells and double-trigger mechanism assures reliability. The automatic safety is actuated whenever the action is opened, whether or not the gun has been fired. The polish and blue is deep and rich, and the solid sighting rib is matte-finished for glare-free sighting. Chrome-moly steel barrels with micro-polished bores give dense, consistent patterns. The classic stock and forend are of durable hardwood . . . oil finished, hand-rubbed and hand-checkered.

Improved Cylinder/Modified choking and its short barrel make the IGA coach gun the ideal choice for hunting in close quarters, security and police work. Three-inch chambers.

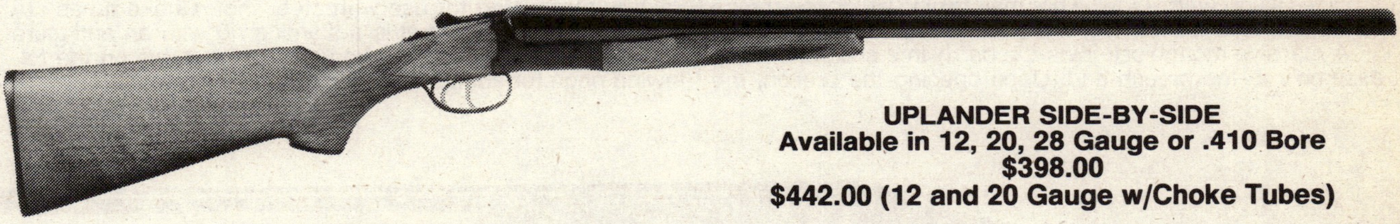

**UPLANDER SIDE-BY-SIDE**
**Available in 12, 20, 28 Gauge or .410 Bore**
**$398.00**
**$442.00 (12 and 20 Gauge w/Choke Tubes)**

The **IGA SIDE-BY-SIDE** is a rugged shotgun, endurance-tested and designed to give years of trouble-free service. A vise-tight, super-safe locking system is provided by two massive underlugs for lasting strength and durability. Two design features that make the IGA a standout for reliability are its positive mechanical extraction of spent shells and its traditional double-trigger mechanism. The safety is automatic in that every time the action is opened, whether or not the gun has been fired, the safety is actuated. The polish and bluing are deep and rich. The solid sighting rib carries a machined-in matte finish for glare-free sighting. Barrels are of chrome-moly steel with micro-polished bores to give dense, consistent patterns. The stock and forend are available with either traditional stock or the legendary English-style stock. Both are of durable Brazilian hardwood, oil-finished, hand-rubbed and hand-checkered.



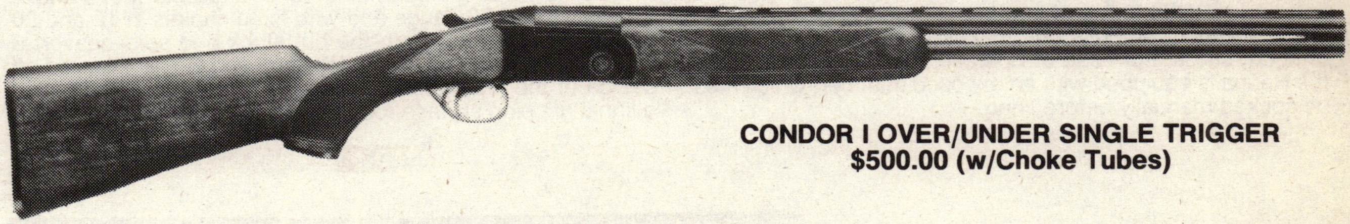

**CONDOR I OVER/UNDER SINGLE TRIGGER**
**$500.00 (w/Choke Tubes)**

The **IGA OVER/UNDER SINGLE TRIGGER** is a workhorse of a shotgun, designed for maximum dependability in heavy field use. The super-safe lock-up system makes use of a sliding underlug, the best system for over/under shotguns. A massive monobloc joins the barrel in a solid one-piece assembly at the breech end. Reliability is assured, thanks to the mechanical extraction system. Upon opening the breech, the spent shells are partially lifted from the chamber, allowing easy removal by hand. IGA barrels are of chrome-moly steel with micro-polished bores to give tight, consistent patterns. They are specifically formulated for use with steel shot where Federal migratory bird regulations require. Atop the barrel is a sighting rib with an anti-glare surface. The buttstock and forend are of durable hardwood, hand-checkered and finished with an oil-based formula that takes dents and scratches in stride.

The IGA **Condor I** over/under shotgun is available in 12 and 20 gauge with 26- and 28-inch barrels with choke tubes and 3-inch chambers; 12 and 20 gauge with 26- and 28-inch barrels choked IC/M and Mod./Full, 3-inch chambers.

Also available:
**Condor II O/U** in 12 gauge, double trigger, 26″ barrel IC/M or 28″ barrel M/F. **Price:** . . . . . . . . . . . . . . . . . . . . . . . . **$375.00**

# IGA SHOTGUNS

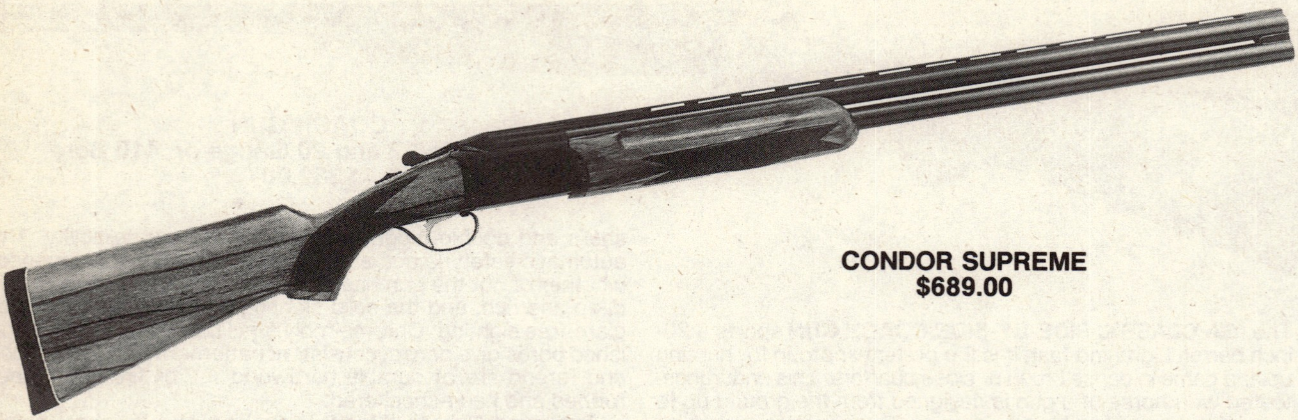

**CONDOR SUPREME**
**$689.00**

The IGA Condor Supreme truly complements its name. The stock is selected from upgraded Brazilian walnut, and the hand-finished checkering is sharp and crisp. A matte-laquered finish provides a soft warm glow, while maintaining a high resistance to dents and scratches.

A massive monoblock joins the barrel in a solid one-piece assembly at the breech end. Upon opening the breech, the automatic ejectors cause the spent shells to be thrown clear of the gun. The barrels are of moly-chrome steel with micro-polished bores to give tight, consistent patterns; they are specifically formulated for use with steel shot. Choke tubes are provided. Atop the barrel is a sighting rib with an anti-glare surface with both mid- and front bead. See table on the following page for additional specifications.

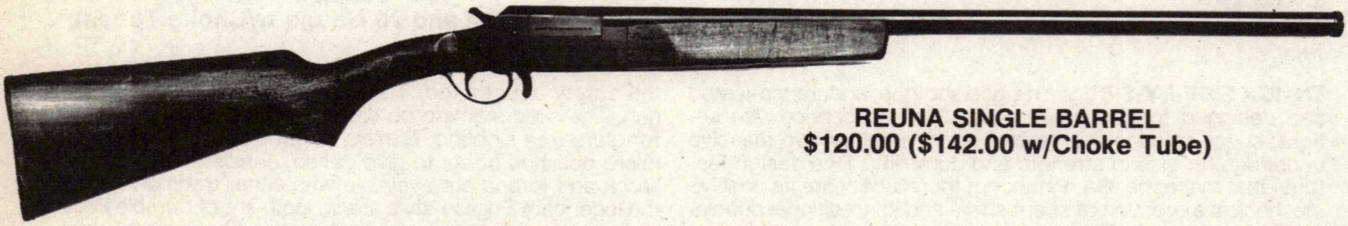

**REUNA SINGLE BARREL**
**$120.00 ($142.00 w/Choke Tube)**

IGA's entry-level single-barrel shotgun features a feeling of heft and quality not found in other shotguns similarly priced. Single mechanical extraction makes for convenient removal of spent shells. For ease of operation and maximum safety, the Reuna is equipped with an exposed hammer, which must be cocked manually before firing.

The Reuna single-barrel shotgun is available with a choke tube in 12 and 20 gauge and with fixed chokes in 12 and 20 gauge or .410 bore. Both the buttstock and semi-beavertail forearm are of durable Brazilian hardwood. The squared-off design of the firearm enhances stability and provides an additional gripping surface for greater comfort.

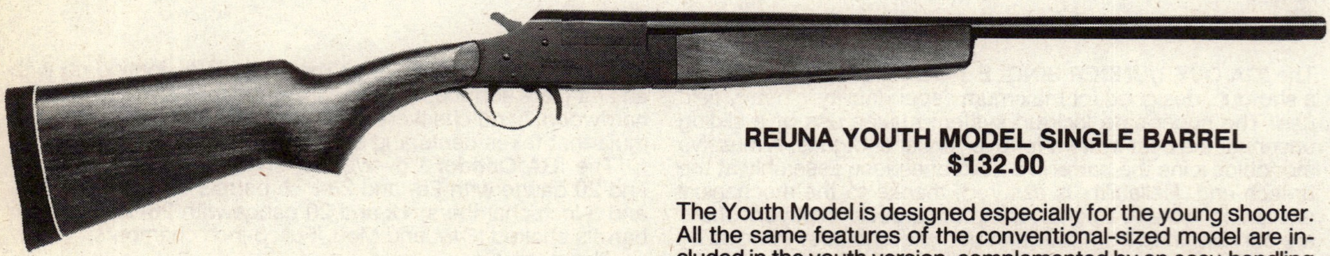

**REUNA YOUTH MODEL SINGLE BARREL**
**$132.00**

The Youth Model is designed especially for the young shooter. All the same features of the conventional-sized model are included in the youth version, complemented by an easy-handling shorter barrel (22″), shortened stock and ventilated recoil pad. In 20 gauge and .410 (Full choke).

# IGA SHOTGUNS

## IGA SHOTGUN SPECIFICATIONS

| | Gauge | | | | Barrel Length | | | | | Chokes | Other Specifications | | | | | Dimensions | | | |
|---|---|---|---|---|---|---|---|---|---|---|---|---|---|---|---|---|---|---|---|
| | 12 | 20 | 28 | 410 | 20″ | 22″ | 24″ | 26″ | 28″ | Fixed | Choke tubes | Chamber | Weight (lbs.) | Extractors | Triggers | Length of pull | Drop at comb | Drop at heel | Overall length |
| **Coach Gun** Side by Side | ■ | ■ | | ■ | ■ | | | | | IC/M | | 3″ | 6 3/4 | ■ | D.T. | 14 1/2″ | 1 1/2″ | 2 1/2″ | 36 1/2″ |
| **Uplander** Side by Side | ■ | ■ | | | | | | ■ | | IC/M | IC/M | 3″ | 7 1/2 | ■ | D.T. | 14 1/2″ | 1 1/2″ | 2 1/2″ | 42″ |
| **Uplander** Side by Side | ■ | ■ | | | | | | | ■ | M/F | M/F | 3″ | 7 1/2 | ■ | D.T. | 14 1/2″ | 1 1/2″ | 2 1/2″ | 44″ |
| **Uplander** Side by Side | | | ■ | | | | | ■ | | IC/M | | 2 3/4″ | 6 3/4 | ■ | D.T. | 14 1/2″ | 1 1/2″ | 2 1/2″ | 42″ |
| **Uplander** Side by Side | | | | ■ | | | | ■ | | F/F | | 3″ | 6 3/4 | ■ | D.T. | 14 1/2″ | 1 1/2″ | 2 1/2″ | 42″ |
| **English Stock** Side by Side | | ■ | | | | | ■ | ■ | | | IC/M | 3″ | 6 1/2 | ■ | D.T. | 14 1/2″ | 1 3/8″ | 2 3/8″ | 40″/42″ |
| **Condor Supreme** | ■ | ■ ■ | | | | | | ■ | ■ | | F, M IC | 3″ | 8 | ■ | S.T. | 14 1/2″ | 1 1/2″ | 2 1/2″ | 43 1/2″/ 45 1/2″ |
| **Condor I** Over/Under | ■ | ■ | | | | | | ■ | | IC/M | IC/M | 3″ | 8 | ■ | S.T. | 14 1/2″ | 1 1/2″ | 2 1/2″ | 43 1/2″ |
| **Condor I** Over/Under | ■ | ■ | | | | | | | ■ | M/F | M/F | 3″ | 8 | ■ | S.T. | 14 1/2″ | 1 1/2″ | 2 1/2″ | 45 1/2″ |
| **Condor II** Over/Under | ■ | | | | | | | ■ | | IC/M | | 3″ | 8 | ■ | D.T. | 14 1/2″ | 1 1/2″ | 2 1/2″ | 43 1/2″ |
| **Condor II** Over/Under | ■ | | | | | | | | ■ | M/F | | 3″ | 8 | ■ | D.T. | 14 1/2″ | 1 1/2″ | 2 1/2″ | 45 1/2″ |
| **Reuna** Single Barrel | ■ | | | | | | | | ■ | F | F | 3″ | 6 1/4 | ■ | | 14 1/2″ | 1 1/2″ | 2 1/2″ | 44 1/2″ |
| **Reuna** Single Barrel | ■ | | | | | | | ■ | | M | | 3″ | 6 1/4 | ■ | | 14 1/2″ | 1 1/2″ | 2 1/2″ | 42 1/2″ |
| **Reuna** Single Barrel | | ■ | | | | | | ■ | | F | F | 3″ | 6 1/4 | ■ | | 14 1/2″ | 1 1/2″ | 2 1/2″ | 42 1/2″ |
| **Reuna** Single Barrel | | | | ■ | | | | ■ | | F | | 3″ | 6 | ■ | | 14 1/2″ | 1 1/2″ | 2 1/2″ | 42 1/2″ |
| **Reuna-Youth Model** Single Barrel | | ■ | | ■ | | ■ | | | | F | | 3″ | 5 | ■ | | 13 | 1 1/2″ | 2 1/2″ | 37 |

* Condor Supreme equipped with automatic ejectors

SHOTGUNS

# ITHACA SHOTGUNS

For Specifications, see following page.

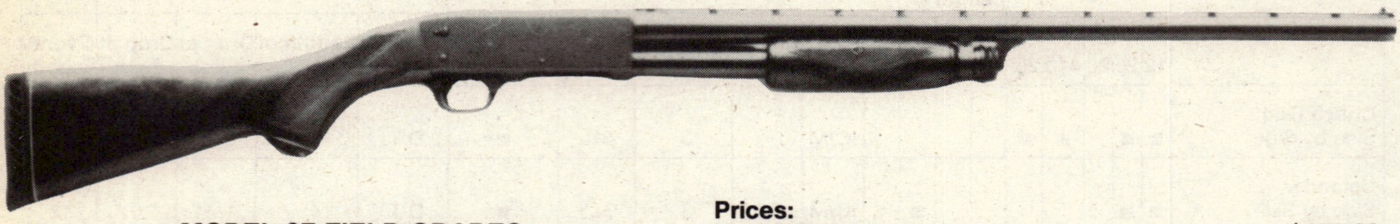

### MODEL 87 FIELD GRADES

Made in much the same manner as 50 years ago, Ithaca's Model 37 pump (now designated as Model 87) features Roto-forged barrels hammered from 11" round billets of steel, then triple-reamed, lapped and polished. The receivers are milled from a solid block of ordnance grade steel, and all internal parts—hammer, extractors, slides and carriers—are milled and individually fitted to each gun.

**Prices:**

| | |
|---|---|
| **Model 87 Basic** | **$477.00** |
| **Model 87 Supreme** | **808.50** |
| **Model 87 Deluxe Vent** | **533.25** |
| **Model 87 Camo Field** | **542.00** |
| **Model 87 English** | **545.50** |
| **Model 87 Turkey Field w/Tube** | **508.25** |
| **Model 87 Turkey Field w/Fixed Choke** | **465.75** |
| **Model 87 Turkey Field Camo w/Tube** | **550.75** |
| **Model 87 Turkey Field Camo w/Fixed Choke** | **508.25** |

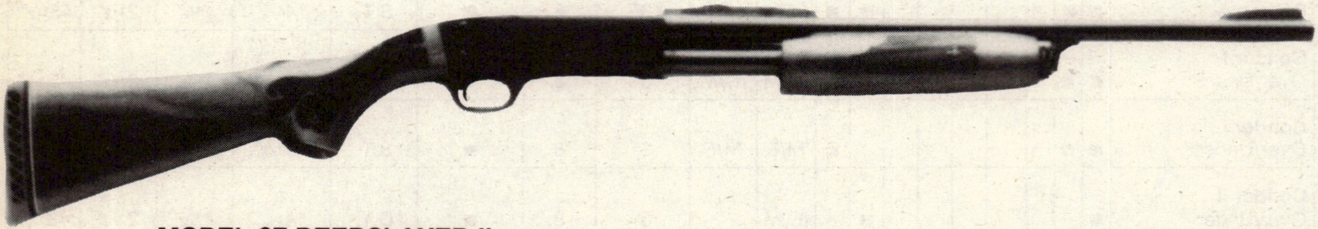

### MODEL 87 DEERSLAYER II

The first shotgun developed to handle rifled slugs successfully, the Deerslayer's design results in an "undersized" cylinder bore—from the forcing cone all the way to the muzzle. This enables the slug to travel smoothly down the barrel with no gas leakage or slug rattle. The new Deerslayer II features the world's first production rifled barrel for shotguns; moreover, the Deerslayer's barrel is permanently screwed into the receiver for solid frame construction, which insures better accuracy to about 85 yards.

**Prices:**

| | |
|---|---|
| **Deerslayer Smoothbore Basic** | **$424.50** |
| **Deerslayer Smoothbore Deluxe** | **464.75** |
| **Deerslayer DSR Deluxe** | **498.25** |
| **Deerslayer II Basic** | **464.75** |
| **Deerslayer II Brenneke** | **566.50** |

**MODEL 87 FIELD TURKEY GUN**
**(Camo-seal Finish)**

# ITHACA SHOTGUNS

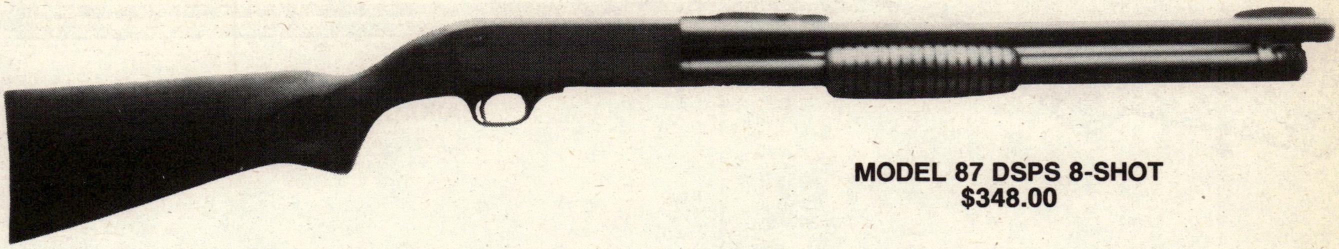

**MODEL 87 DSPS 8-SHOT**
**$348.00**

## SPECIFICATIONS ITHACA MODEL 87 SHOTGUNS

| Type | Gauge | Bbl In. | Chokes | Chamb. | Cap. | Wt. |
|---|---|---|---|---|---|---|
| Supreme | 12 | 30 | CT | 3″ | 5 | 7 |
| | 12 | 28 | CT | 3″ | 5 | 7 |
| | 12 | 26 | CT | 3″ | 5 | 7 |
| | 20 | 26 | CT | 3″ | 5 | 6.8 |
| Deluxe Vent | 12 | 30 | CT | 3″ | 5 | 7 |
| | 12 | 28 | CT | 3″ | 5 | 7 |
| | 12 | 26 | CT | 3″ | 5 | 7 |
| | 20 | 26 | CT | 3″ | 5 | 6.8 |
| English | 20 | 26 | CT | 3″ | 5 | 6.8 |
| | 20 | 24 | CT | 3″ | 5 | 6.8 |
| Camo Field | 12 | 28 | CT | 3″ | 5 | 7 |
| | 12 | 24 | CT | 3″ | 5 | 7 |
| | 12 | 28 | CT | 3″ | 5 | 7 |
| | 12 | 24 | CT | 3″ | 5 | 7 |
| Turkey Camo w/Tube | 12 | 24 | Full CT | 3″ | 5 | 7 |
| | 12 | 22 | Full CT | 3″ | 5 | 7 |
| Turkey Camo Fixed Choke | 12 | 24 | Full | 3″ | 5 | 7 |
| | 12 | 22 | Full | 3″ | 5 | 7 |
| Turkey Field w/Tube | 12 | 24 | Full CT | 3″ | 5 | 7 |
| | 12 | 22 | Full CT | 3″ | 5 | 7 |
| Turkey Field Fixed Choke | 12 | 24 | Full | 3″ | 5 | 7 |
| | 12 | 22 | Full | 3″ | 5 | 7 |
| Deerslayer SB Deluxe | 12 | 25 | DS | 3″ | 5 | 7 |
| | 20 | 20 | DS | 3″ | 5 | 7 |
| | 20 | 25 | DS | 3″ | 5 | 6.8 |
| | 20 | 20 | DS | 3″ | 5 | 6.8 |
| Deerslayer SB Basic | 12 | 25 | DS | 3″ | 5 | 7 |
| | 12 | 20 | DS | 3″ | 5 | 7 |
| | 20 | 25 | DS | 3″ | 5 | 6.8 |
| | 20 | 20 | DS | 3″ | 5 | 6 |
| Deerslayer DSR Deluxe | 12 | 25 | DSR | 3″ | 5 | 7 |
| | 12 | 20 | DSR | 3″ | 5 | 7 |
| | 20 | 25 | DSR | 3″ | 5 | 6.8 |
| | 20 | 20 | DSR | 3″ | 5 | 6.8 |

| Type | Gauge | Bbl In. | Chokes | Chamb. | Cap. | Wt. |
|---|---|---|---|---|---|---|
| Deerslayer II | 12 | 25 | DSR1 | 3″ | 5 | 7 |
| | 12 | 20 | DSR1 | 3″ | 5 | 7 |
| | 20 | 25 | DSR1 | 3″ | 5 | 6.8 |
| | 20 | 20 | DSR1 | 3″ | 5 | 6.8 |
| Deerslayer II Brenneke | 12 | 25 | DSR2 | 3″ | 5 | 7 |
| Extra Barrel Vent Rib | 12 | 30 | CTt | 3″ | N/A | 2.1 |
| | 12 | 28 | CT | 3″ | N/A | 2.1 |
| | 12 | 26 | CT | 3″ | N/A | 2.1 |
| | 12 | 24 | CT | 3″ | N/A | 2.1 |
| | 20 | 28 | CT | 3″ | N/A | 2 |
| | 20 | 26 | CT | 3″ | N/A | 2 |
| | 20 | 24 | CT | 3″ | N/A | 2 |
| Extra Barrel Deer SB | 12 | 25 | DS | 3″ | N/A | 2.1 |
| | 12 | 20 | DS | 3″ | N/A | 2.1 |
| | 20 | 25 | DS | 3″ | N/A | 2 |
| | 20 | 20 | DS | 3″ | N/A | 2 |
| Extra Barrel Deer DSR | 12 | 25 | DSR | 3″ | N/A | 2.1 |
| | 12 | 20 | DSR | 3″ | N/A | 2.1 |
| | 20 | 25 | DSR | 3″ | N/A | 2 |
| | 20 | 20 | DSR | 3″ | N/A | 2 |
| Hand Grip | 12 | 19 | CYL | 3″ | 5 | 6.5 |
| | 20 | 19 | CYL | 3″ | 5 | 6 |
| | 12 | 20 | CYL | 3″ | 8 | 5.5 |
| DSPS | 12 | 20 | DS | 3″ | 5 | 7 |
| | 12 | 19 | DS | 3″ | 5 | 7 |
| | 12 | 19 | DS | 3″ | 8 | 7 |
| | 12 | 20 | DSR1 | 3″ | 5 | 7 |
| | 12 | 25 | DSR1 | 3″ | 5 | 7 |
| M&P | 12 | 20 | CYL | 3″ | 5 | 7 |
| | 20 | 20 | CYL | 3″ | 5 | 6.5 |
| | 12 | 20 | CYL | 3″ | 8 | 7 |

CT = Full Mod IC Tubes; DS = Smooth Bore Deer; DSR = Rifled Bore Deer; DSR1 = Fixed Rifled Bore Deer 1/34; DSR2 = Fixed Rifled Bore Deer 1/25

# KBI SHOTGUNS

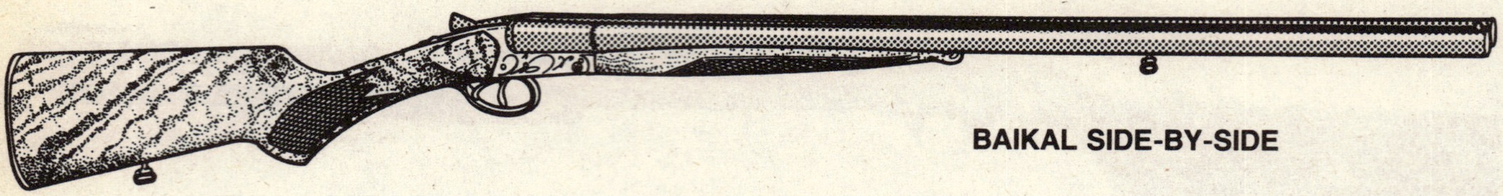

BAIKAL SIDE-BY-SIDE

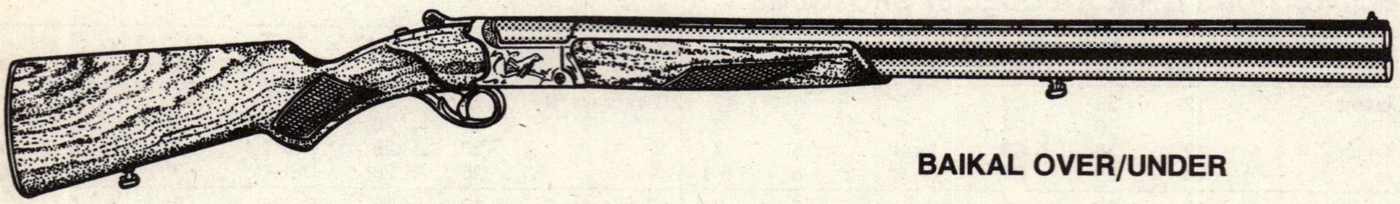

BAIKAL OVER/UNDER

### BAIKAL SHOTGUNS

Baikal shotguns are manufactured by Russian arms producers. The **Single Barrel** model has a chrome-lined barrel bore and chamber, non-auto safety and extractor with external disengaging lever. Available in 12 or 20 gauge. Additional specifications are listed in the table below.
12 or 20 gauge .............................. **$74.00**

The **Side by Side** model has chrome-lined barrels and chambers, and comes with double triggers and extractors.
28 gauge .............................. **$349.00**
20 gauge .............................. **369.00**

The **Over/Under** model features either double trigger and extractors or single-selective trigger and auto ejectors.
12 gauge, double triggers .............................. **$429.00**
12 gauge, single trigger, Auto Ejector .............................. **469.00**

### BAIKAL SHOTGUN SPECIFICATIONS

| Model | Article Number | Gauge | Barrel Length in. | Chamber in. | Chokes | Weight lb. |
|---|---|---|---|---|---|---|
| Single | GD1000 | 12 | 28 | 2¾″ | F | 6 |
| Single | GD1019 | 12 | 28 | 2¾″ | M | 6 |
| Single | GD1027 | 12 | 26 | 2¾″ | IC | 6 |
| Single | GD1035 | 20 | 28 | 3″ | F | 5½ |
| Single | GD1043 | 20 | 28 | 3″ | M | 5½ |
| Single | GD1051 | 20 | 26 | 3″ | IC | 5½ |
| Single | GD1078 | 410 | 26 | 3″ | F | 5½ |
| Side/Side—DT | GE1006 | 12 | 28 | 2¾″ | M/F | 6¾ |
| Side/Side—DT | GE1014 | 12 | 26 | 2¾″ | IC/F | 6¾ |
| Side/Side-DT | GE1022 | 12 | 20 | 2¾″ | Cyl./Cyl. | 6 |
| O/U—DT | GP1006 | 12 | 28 | 2¾″ | M/F | 7 |
| O/U—DT | GP1014 | 12 | 26 | 2¾″ | IC/F | 7 |
| O/U—SST | GP1065 | 12 | 28 | 2¾″ | M/F | 7 |
| O/U—SST | GP1073 | 12 | 26 | 2¾″ | IC/F | 7 |

# KRIEGHOFF SHOTGUNS

(See following page for additional Specifications and Prices)

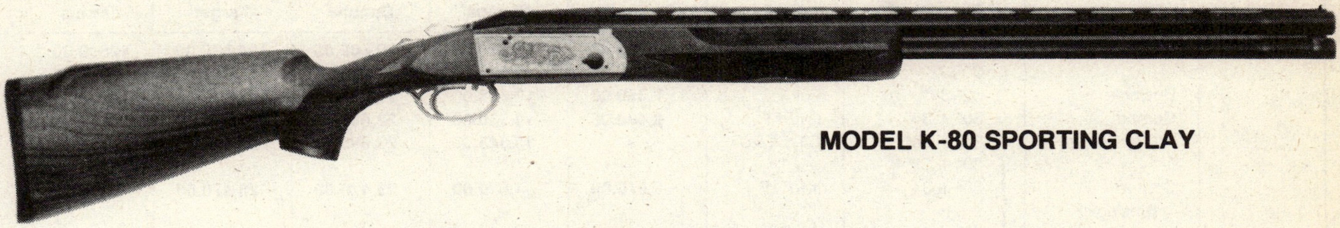

MODEL K-80 SPORTING CLAY

## MODEL K-80 TRAP, SKEET, SPORTING CLAY AND LIVE BIRD

**Barrels:** Made of Boehler steel; free-floating bottom barrel with adjustable point of impact; standard Trap and Live Pigeon ribs are tapered step; standard Skeet, Sporting Clay and International ribs are tapered or parallel flat.
**Receivers:** Hard satin-nickel finish; casehardened; blue finish available as special order
**Triggers:** Wide profile, single selective, position adjustable. Removable trigger option available (add'l **$1275.00**)
**Weight:** 8½ lbs. (Trap); 8 lbs. (Skeet)
**Ejectors:** Selective automatic
**Sights:** White pearl front bead and metal center bead
**Stocks:** Hand-checkered and epoxy-finished Select European walnut stock and forearm; quick-detachable palm swell stocks available in five different styles and dimensions
**Safety:** Push button safety located on top tang.
Also available:
**SKEET SPECIAL** (28″ and 30″ barrel; tapered flat or 8mm rib; 2 choke tubes). **Price: $7300.00** (Standard)

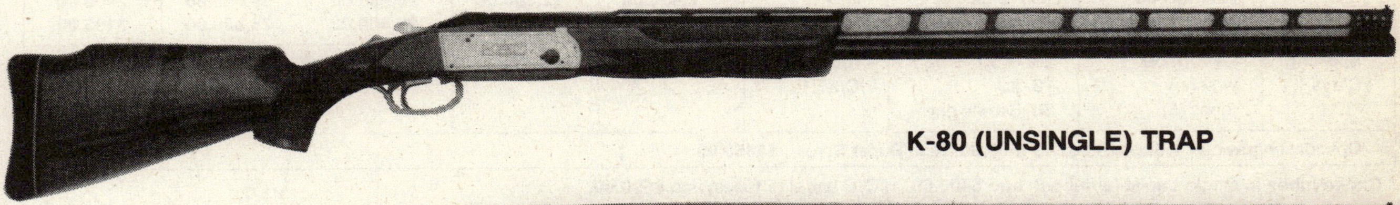

K-80 (UNSINGLE) TRAP

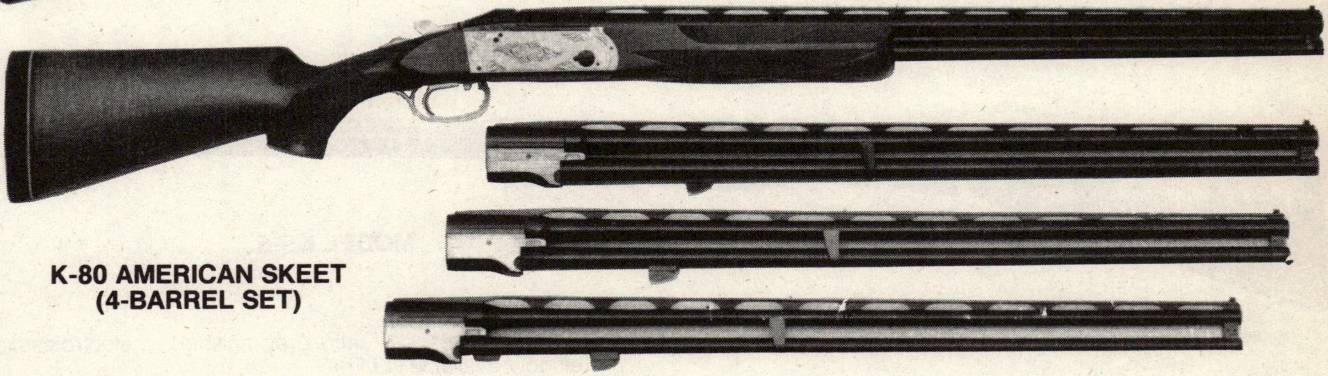

K-80 AMERICAN SKEET (4-BARREL SET)

## MODEL ULM-P
## O/U SIDELOCK LIVE PIGEON (not shown)
**$18,900.00 (Standard Grade) $26,000.00 (Bavaria Grade)**

**SPECIFICATIONS**
**Gauge:** 12
**Chamber:** 2¾″
**Barrel:** 28″ or 30″ long; tapered, ventilated rib
**Choke:** Top, Full; bottom, Imp. Mod.
**Trigger action:** Single trigger, non-selective bottom-top; hand-detachable sidelocks with coil springs; optional release trigger
**Stock:** Selected fancy English walnut, oil finish; length, 14⅜″; drop at comb, 1⅜″; optional custom-made stock
**Forearm:** Semi-beavertail
**Engraving:** Light scrollwork; optional engravings available
**Weight:** Approx. 8 lbs.
Also available in Skeet and Trap models

# KRIEGHOFF SHOTGUNS

## SPECIFICATIONS AND PRICES MODEL K-80 (see also preceding page)

| Model | Description | Bbl. Length | Choke | Standard | Bavaria | Danube | Gold Target | Extra Barrels |
|---|---|---|---|---|---|---|---|---|
| **Trap** | Over & Under | 30″/32″ | IM/F | $ 7,100.00 | $11,950.00 | $20,600.00 | $25,600.00 | $2800.00 |
| | | 30″/32″ | CT/CT | 7,725.00 | 12,575.00 | 21,225.00 | 26,225.00 | 3425.00 |
| | Unsingle | 32″/34″ | Full | 7,650.00 | 12,500.00 | 21,150.00 | 26,150.00 | 3350.00 |
| | Combo | 30″ + 34″ | IM/F&F | 9,480.00 | 14,330.00 | 22,980.00 | 27,980.00 | |
| | (Top Single) | 32″ + 34″ | CT/CT&CT | | 15,345.00 | 23,995.00 | 28,995.00 | |
| | Combo (Unsingle) | 30″ + 32″ / 30″ + 34″ | IM/F+F | 9,970.00 | 14,820.00 | 23,470.00 | 28,470.00 | 2850.00 |
| | | 32″ + 34″ | CT/CT&CT | 10,995.00 | 15,845.00 | 24,495.00 | 29,495.00 | 3250.00 |
| Optional Features:* | | | | | | | | |
| Screw-in chokes (O/U, Top or Unsingle) | | | **$400.00** | | | | | |
| Single factory release | | | **395.00** | | | | | |
| Double factory release | | | **695.00** | | | | | |
| **Skeet** | 4-Barrel Set | 28″/12 ga. | Tula | $15,950.00 | $20,800.00 | $29,450.00 | $34,450.00 | $2850.00 |
| | | 28″/20 ga. | Skeet | | | | | 2850.00 |
| | | 28″/28 ga. | Skeet | | | | | 2850.00 |
| | | 28″/.410 ga. | Skeet | | | | | 2850.00 |
| | 2-Barrel Set | 28″/12 ga. | Tula | 11,305.00 | 16,155.00 | 24,805.00 | 29,805.00 | 3990.00 |
| | Lightweight | 28″ + 30″/12 ga. | Skeet | 6,650.00 | 11,500.00 | N/A | N/A | 3990.00 |
| | Standardweight | 28″/12 ga. | Tula | 6,890.00 | 11,740.00 | 20,390.00 | 25,390.00 | 2850.00 |
| | | 28″ + 30″/12 ga. | Skeet | 6,650.00 | 11,500.00 | 20,150.00 | 25,150.00 | 2570.00 |
| | International | 28″/12 ga. | Tula | 7,450.00 | 12,300.00 | 20,950.00 | 25,950.00 | 2900.00 |
| | Skeet Special | | | 7,300.00 | 12,150.00 | 20,800.00 | 25,800.00 | 3195.00 |
| **Sporting Clays** | Over/Under w/screw-in tubes (5) | 28″ + 30″ + 32″/ 12 ga. | Tubes IC/ICTF | $7,850.00 | $12,700.00 | $21,350.00 | $26,350.00 | $3195.00 |
| | | 30″ Semi-Light | | | | | | 2800.00 |
| Optional engravings: Super Scroll **$1695.00**; Gold Super Scroll **$3850.00** | | | | | | | | |

*** Choke tubes in single barrel (w/tubes): add $400.00.** In O/U barrel (5 tubes) add **$590.00.**

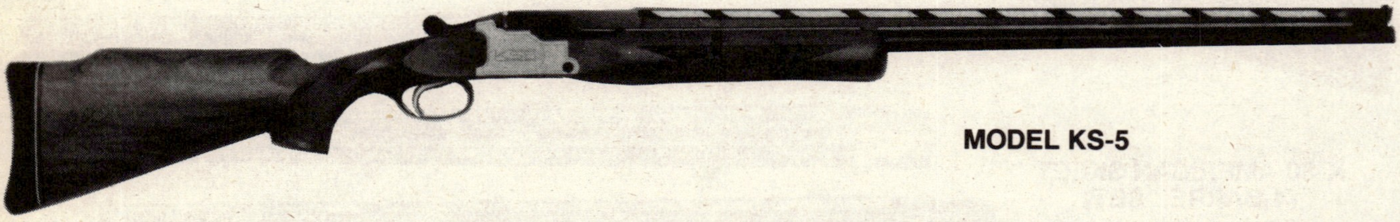

**MODEL KS-5**

The KS-5 is a single barrel trap gun with a ventilated, tapered and adjustable step rib, casehardened receiver in satin grey matte or blue, finished in electroless nickel. It features an adjustable point of impact by means of different optional fronthangers. Screw-in chokes and adjustable stock are optional. Trigger is adjustable externally for poundage.

**SPECIFICATIONS**
**Gauge:**12
**Chamber:** 2¾″
**Barrel length:** 32″ or 34″
**Choke:** Full; optional screw-in chokes
**Rib:** Tapered step; ventilated
**Trigger:** Weight of pull adjustable; optional release
**Receiver:** Casehardened; satin grey finished in electroless nickel; now available in blue
**Grade:** Standard; engraved models on special order
**Weight:** Approximately 8.6-8.8 lbs.
**Case:** Aluminum
**Prices:**
With full choke and case .................... **$3575.00**
With screw-in choke and case ............... **4350.00**
Screw-in choke barrels ....................... **2350.00**
Regular barrels .............................. **1950.00**
Special barrels (F) .......................... **2600.00**

Also available:
**KS-5 SPECIAL.** Same as **KS-5** except barrel has fully adjustable rib and stock. **Price: $4580.00** (add **$3000.00** for special screw-in choke barrel)

# MAGTECH SHOTGUNS

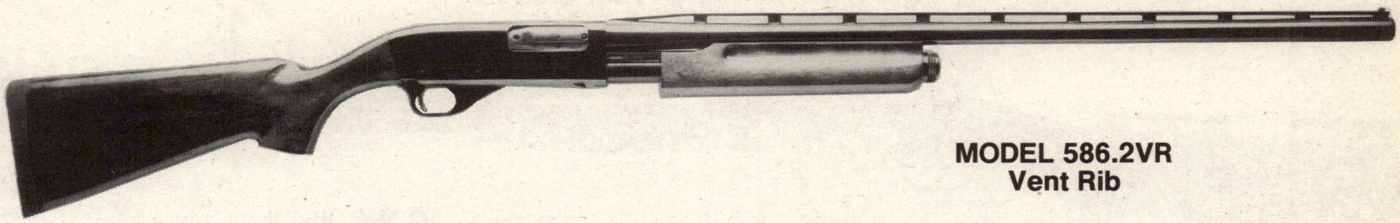

MODEL 586.2VR
Vent Rib

## MODEL 586.2VR SERIES

The new Magtech 586.2VR Series 12-gauge pump shotguns handle 2³/₄" and 3" magnum shells interchangeably and give the shooter custom features, including: • ordnance-grade, deep-blued steel receiver • double-action slide bars • hand-finished Brazilian Embuia wood stock and forearm • hammer-forged chrome-moly barrel • high-profile steel rib • brass mid-bead and ivory-colored front sight • chrome-plated bolt • screw-in Magchokes in IC, Mod. and Full • crossbolt safety • special magazine release for unloading without cycling round through the chamber

**SPECIFICATIONS**
**Gauge:** 12 (2³/₄" or 3" shells)
**Capacity:** 5 rounds (8 in Model 586.2P)
**Chokes:** Magchokes in IC, Mod. & Full (IC only in Model 586.2P)
**Barrel:** 26" and 28", vent rib (19" plain in Model 586.2P)
**Overall length:** 46¹/₄" and 48¹/₄" (39¹/₄" in Model 586.2P)
**Sights** Two beads (one bead in Model 586.2P)
**Prices:**
**MODEL 586.2VR26 and 586.2VR28** ........... **$255.00**
**MODEL 586.2P** ........................... **235.00**

# MARLIN SHOTGUNS

## MARLIN MODEL 55 GOOSE GUN
## $298.75

High-flying ducks and geese are the Goose Gun's specialty. The Marlin Goose Gun has an extra-long 36-inch full-choked barrel and Magnum capability, making it the perfect choice for tough shots at wary waterfowl. It also features a quick-loading 2-shot clip magazine, a convenient leather carrying strap and a quality ventilated recoil pad.

**SPECIFICATIONS**
**Gauge:** 12; 2³/₄" Magnum, 3" Magnum or 2³/₄" regular shells
**Choke:** Full **Capacity:** 2-shot clip magazine
**Action:** Bolt action; positive thumb safety; red cocking indicator
**Barrel length:** 36" **Overall length:** 56³/₄"
**Sights:** Bead front sight and U-groove rear sight
**Weight:** About 8 lbs.
**Stock:** Walnut-finish hardwood with pistol grip and ventilated recoil pad; swivel studs; tough Mar-Shield® finish

SHOTGUNS

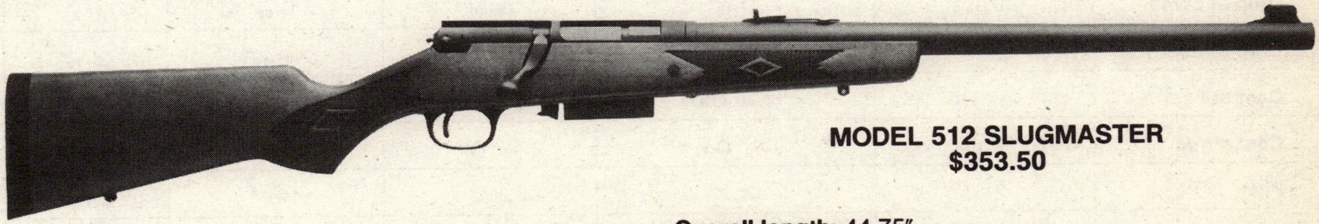

## MODEL 512 SLUGMASTER
## $353.50

**SPECIFICATIONS**
**Gauge:** 12 (up to 3" shells)
**Capacity:** 2-shot box magazine (+1 in chamber)
**Action:** Bolt action; thumb safety; red cocking indicator
**Barrel length:** 21" rifled (1:28" right-hand twist)
**Overall length:** 44.75"
**Weight:** 8 lbs. (w/o scope and mount)
**Sights:** Adjustable folding semi-buckhorn rear; ramp front with brass bead and removable Wide-Scan® hood; receiver drilled and tapped for scope mount
**Stock:** Walnut finished, press-checkered Maine birch w/pistol grip and Mar-Shield® finish, swivel studs, vent. recoil pad

# MAROCCHI SHOTGUNS

## CONQUISTA SHOTGUNS

**CONQUISTA**
**(12 Gauge, 2 3/4" Chambers)**

**CONQUISTA**
**SPORTING CLAYS GRADE III**

The Conquista 12-gauge over/under shotguns feature 2 3/4" chambers in 28", 30" or 32" barrels with 10mm concave, ventilated upper rib and classic middle rib; competition white front sight, automatic extractors/ejectors, Instajust selective trigger with 3.5–4.0 lbs. trigger pull (weight) and checkered (20 lines/inch) select American walnut stock. Additional specifications appear in the chart below.

### SPECIFICATIONS CONQUISTA SHOTGUNS

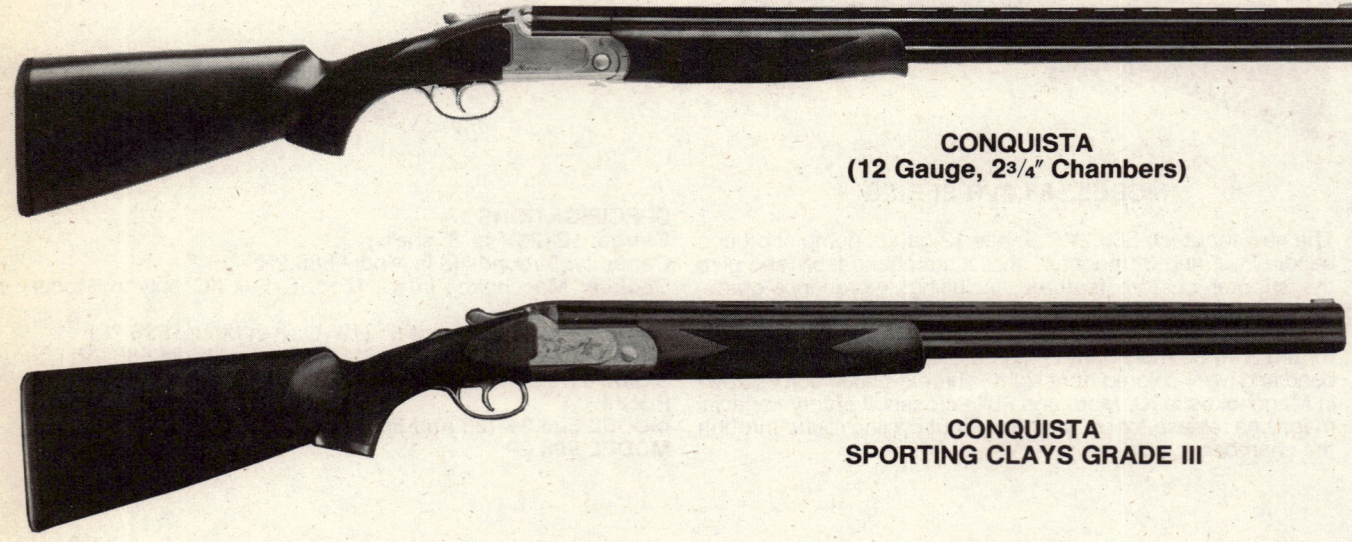

| MODEL | Sporting Clays | Sporting Clays (Left) | Lady Sport | Trap | Skeet |
|---|---|---|---|---|---|
| Barrel length | 28", 30", 32" | 28", 30", 32" | 28" | 30", 32" | 28" |
| Chokes | Contrechokes | Contrechokes | Contrechokes | Imp. Mod./Full | Skeet |
| Overall length | 45"–49" | 45"–49" | 44 3/8" | 47"–49" | 45" |
| Weight approx. | 7 7/8 lbs. | 7 7/8 lbs. | 7 1/2 lbs. | 8 1/4 lbs. | 7 3/4 lbs. |
| Drop at comb | 1 7/16" | 1 7/16" | 1 11/32" | 1 9/32" | 1 1/2" |
| Drop at heel | 2 3/16" | 2 3/16" | 2 9/32" | 1 11/16" | 2 3/16" |
| Cast at heel | 3/16" Off | 3/16" On | 3/16" Off | 3/16" Off | 3/16" Off |
| Cast at toe | 3/8" Off | 3/8" On | 3/8" Off | 5/16" Off | 5/16" Off |
| Pitch | 2 3/4" | 2 3/4" | 2 3/4" | 1 5/32" | 2 5/16" |
| Prices: Grade I | $1895.00 | $1945.00 | $1945.00 | $1895.00 | $1895.00 |
| Grade II | 2285.00 | 2335.00 | 2335.00 | 2285.00 | 2285.00 |
| Grade III | 3250.00 | 3300.00 | 3300.00 | 3250.00 | 3250.00 |

# MAVERICK OF MOSSBERG

## PUMP-ACTION SHOTGUNS

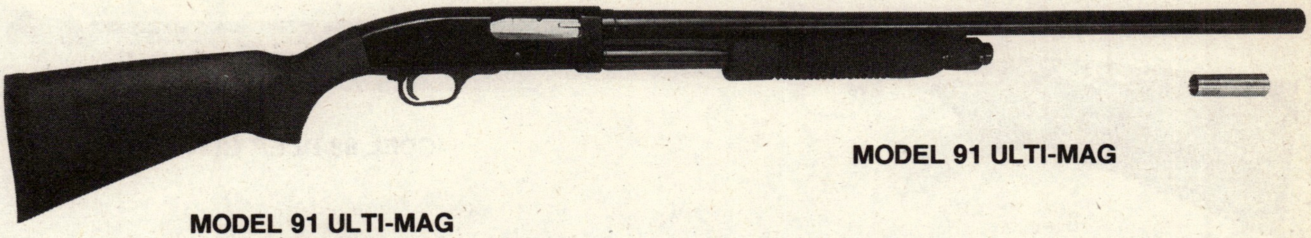

MODEL 91 ULTI-MAG

**MODEL 91 ULTI-MAG**
**$271.00**

**SPECIFICATIONS**
**Gauge:** 12 w/3½″ chamber; also fires 2¾″ and 3″ shells
**Capacity:** 6 shots (2¾″ shells)
**Barrel length:** 28″ vent rib **Overall length:** 48½″
**Weight:** 7.7 lbs.
**Choke:** Threaded for Accu-Mag tubes
**Features:** Crossbolt safety; rubber recoil pad; synthetic stock and forearm; dual slide bars; accessories interchangeable with Mossberg M835; cablelock included

MODEL 88 VENT RIB

**MODEL 88 VENT RIB**
**$241.00 w/Full or Mod. Barrel**
**$248.00 w/Threaded Barrel and Mod. Tube**

**SPECIFICATIONS**
**Gauge:** 12; 3″ chamber
**Capacity:** 6 shots (2¾″ shells)
**Barrel length:** 30″ Full Fixed, all others 28″
**Overall length:** 48″ w/28″ barrel
**Weight:** 7.2 lbs. w/28″ barrel
**Chokes:** Fixed or threaded for Accu-Choke
**Features:** Crossbolt safety; rubber recoil pad; synthetic stock and forearm; dual slide bars; accessories interchangeable with Mossberg M500; cablelock included

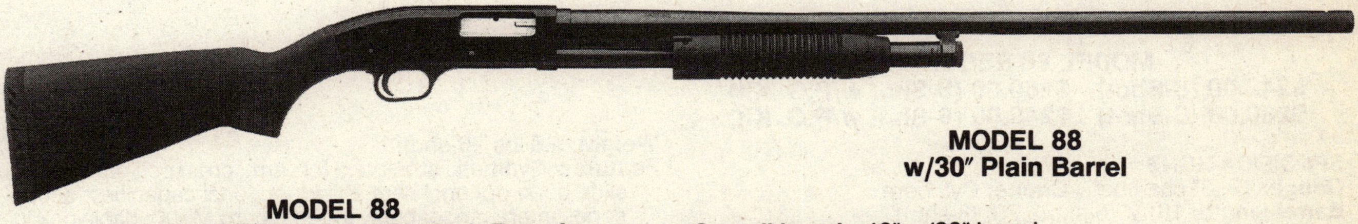

MODEL 88
w/30″ Plain Barrel

**MODEL 88**
**$230.00 w/30″ Full or 28″ Mod. Barrel**

**SPECIFICATIONS**
**Gauge:** 12; 3″ chamber
**Capacity:** 6 shots (2¾″ shells)
**Barrel length:** 30″ Full or 28″ Mod.
**Overall length:** 48″ w/28″ barrel
**Weight:** 7.1 lbs. w/28″ barrel
**Chokes:** Fixed, Full or Mod.
**Features:** Crossbolt safety; rubber recoil pad; synthetic stock and forearm; dual slide bars; accessories interchangeable with Mossberg M500; cablelock included

# MAVERICK OF MOSSBERG

## PUMP-ACTION SHOTGUNS

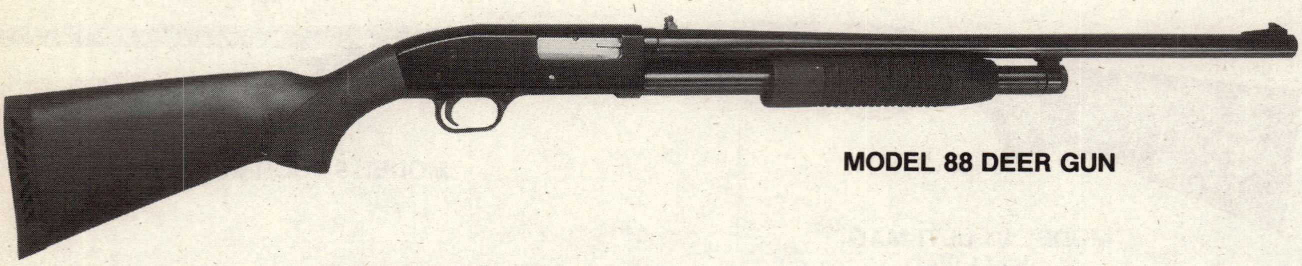

MODEL 88 DEER GUN

**MODEL 88 DEER GUN**
**$247.00**

**SPECIFICATIONS**
**Gauge:** 12; 3″ chamber
**Capacity:** 6 shots (2³/₄″ shells)
**Choke:** Cylinder bore
**Barrel length:** 24″ **Overall length:** 44″

**Weight:** 7 lbs.
**Sights:** Adjustable rear leaf and rifle-style front
**Features:** Crossbolt safety; rubber recoil pad; synthetic stock and forearm; dual slide bars; accessories interchangeable with Mossberg M500; cablelock included

MODEL 88 SECURITY (6-Shot)

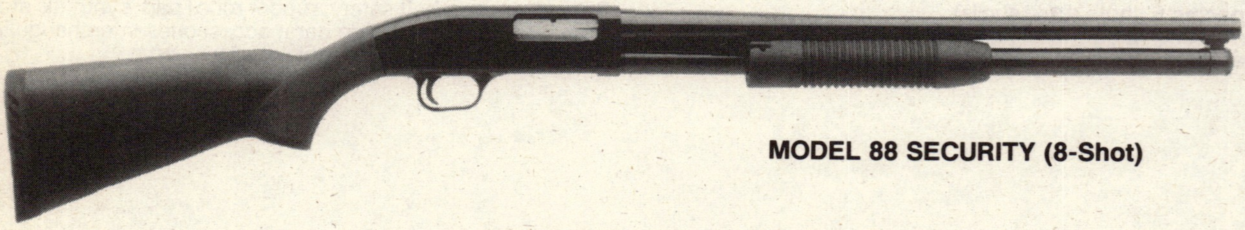

MODEL 88 SECURITY (8-Shot)

**MODEL 88 SECURITY**
**$246.00 (8-Shot) $260.00 (8-Shot w/P.G. Kit)**
**$230.00 (6-Shot) $246.00 (6-Shot w/P.G. Kit)**

**SPECIFICATIONS**
**Gauge:** 12; 3″ chamber **Choke:** Cyl. bore
**Barrel length:** 18¹/₂″ (6-shot); 20″ (8-shot)
**Overall length:** 28″ w/18¹/₂″ barrel

**Weight:** 5.6 lbs. (6-shot)
**Features:** Synthetic stock and forearm; crossbolt safety; dual slide bars; optional heat shield; optional capacities; accessories interchangeable with Mossberg M500; cablelock included

# MERKEL OVER/UNDER SHOTGUNS

Merkel over-and-unders are the first hunting guns with barrels arranged one above the other, and they have since proved to be able competitors of the side-by-side gun. Merkel superiority lies in the following details:

- Available in 12, 16 and 20 gauge (28 ga. in Model 201E with 26¾″ barrel)
- Lightweight from 6.4 to 7.28 lbs.
- The high, narrow forend protects the shooter's hand from the barrel in hot or cold climates
- The forend is narrow and therefore lies snugly in the hand to permit easy and positive swinging
- The slim barrel line provides an unobstructed field of view and thus permits rapid aiming and shooting.
- The over-and-under barrel arrangement reduces recoil error; the recoil merely pushes the muzzle up vertically.

All Merkel shotguns are manufactured by Jagd und Sportwaffen GmbH, Suhl, Thuringia, Germany; imported, distributed and retailed in the U.S. by GSI Inc. (see Directory of Manufacturers and Distributors).

**MODEL 200E BOXLOCK**

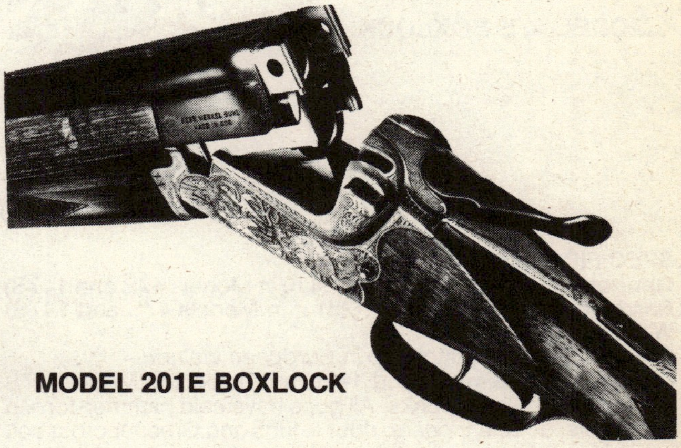

**MODEL 201E BOXLOCK**



### MERKEL OVER/UNDER SHOTGUN SPECIFICATIONS

**Gauges:** 12, 16, 20, 28
**Barrel lengths:** 26¾″ and 28″ (30″ also in Models 200SC, 201E and 203E)
**Weight:** 6.4 to 7.28 lbs.
**Stock:** English or pistol grip in European walnut
**Features:** Models 200E and 201E are boxlocks; Models 202E, 203E and 303E are sidelocks. All models include three-piece forearm, automatic ejectors, Kersten double crossbolt lock, Blitz action and single selective triggers.

**Prices:**
**MODEL 200E Boxlock** (w/scroll engraved casehardened receiver) . . . . . . . . . . . . . . . . . . . . $ 3,395.00
**MODEL 200ET Trap** (Full/Full) 12 ga. w/30″ barrel . . . . . . . . . . . . . . . . . . . . . . . . . 4,895.00
**MODEL 200SC Sporting Clays** 12 ga. (30″ only) . . . . . . . . . . . . . . . . . . . . . . . . . . . . . 6,995.00
Same as above w/Briley choke tubes . . . . . . . 7,495.00
**MODEL 201E Boxlock** (w/hunting scenes) . . . . . 4,895.00
**MODEL 201E** in 28 ga. (26¾″) . . . . . . . . . . . . . . 5,495.00
**MODEL 202E Sidelock** (w/hunting scenes) . . . . 8,895.00
**MODEL 203E Sidelock** (w/English-style engraving) . . . . . . . . . . . . . . . . . . . . . . . . . . . . 10,695.00

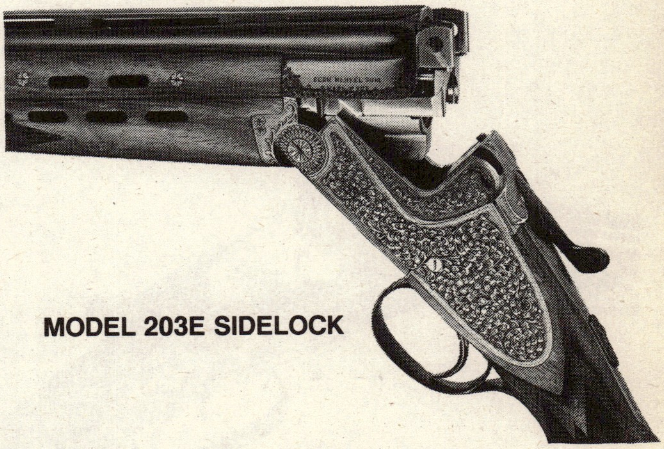

**MODEL 203E SIDELOCK**

**MODEL 303E Sidelock** (w/quick-detachable side-lock plates w/integral retracting hook . . . . . . . 19,995.00
**Also available: MERKEL O/U SHOTGUN/RIFLE COMBINATIONS** (Models 210E, 211E, 213E, 313E); 12, 16 & 20 ga. (2¾″ chamber) w/22 Hornet (12 ga. only) and 5.6×50R (16 & 20 ga.) . . . . . . . . . . . . . . . . . . . . 6,195.00–$20,695.00

# MERKEL SIDE-BY-SIDE SHOTGUNS

MODEL 47E BOXLOCK

MODEL 147E BOXLOCK

## SIDE-BY-SIDE SHOTGUNS

**SPECIFICATIONS**
**Gauges:** 12 and 20 (28 ga. and .410 in Models 47S and 147S)
**Barrel lengths:** 26″ and 28″ (25 1/2″ in Models 47S and 147S)
**Weight:** 6 to 7 lbs.
**Stock:** English or pistol grip in European walnut
**Features:** Models 47E and 147E are boxlocks; Models 47S and 147S are sidelocks. All guns have cold hammer-forged barrels, double triggers, double lugs and Greener crossbolt locking systems and automatic ejectors.

**Prices:**

| | |
|---|---|
| **MODEL 8** | **$1395.00** |
| **MODEL 47E** (Holland & Holland ejectors) | **1795.00** |
| **MODEL 122** (H&H ejectors, engraved hunting scenes) | **3795.00** |
| **MODEL 147** (H&H ejectors) | **1895.00** |
| **MODEL 147E** (engraved hunting scenes) | |
| 12, 16 & 20 ga. | **2295.00** |
| 28 ga. | **3195.00** |
| **MODEL 47S Sidelock** (H&H ejectors) | **4495.00** |
| **MODEL 147S Sidelock** | |
| 12, 16 & 20 ga. | **5595.00** |
| 28 ga. | **5795.00** |
| **MODEL 247S** (English-style engraving) | **6895.00** |
| **MODEL 347S** (H&H ejectors) | **7895.00** |
| **MODEL 447S** | **8995.00** |

MODEL 47S SIDE-BY-SIDE

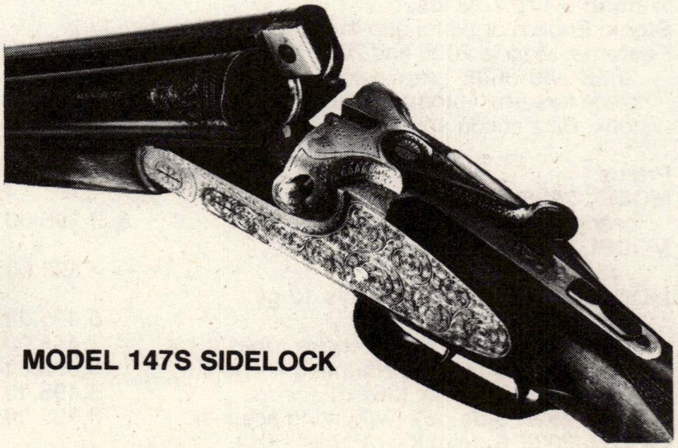

MODEL 147S SIDELOCK

# MOSSBERG PUMP SHOTGUNS

## MODEL 500 SPORTING

All Mossberg Model 500 pump-action shotguns feature Milspec tough, lightweight alloy receivers with "top thumb safety." Standard models include 6-shot capacity with 2¾" shells, cut-checkered stocks, Quiet Carry forearms, gold trigger, engraved receiver, blued or Marinecote metal finish and the largest selection of accessory barrels. All models include a Cablelock and 10-year limited warranty. Model 500 Combos feature walnut-finish stocks and blued metal.

### SPECIFICATIONS & PRICES MODEL 500 CROWN GRADE

| Ga. | Stock # | Bbl. Length | Bbl. Type | Sights | Chokes | Stock | Length O/A | Wt. | Q.D. Studs | Notes | Prices |
|---|---|---|---|---|---|---|---|---|---|---|---|
| 12 | 54120 | 28" | Vent Rib | 2 Beads | Accu-Choke | Walnut Finish | 48" | 7.2 | | I.C., Mod. & Full Tubes | **$299.00** |
| 12 | 58126 | 24" | Plain | Iron | Accu-Choke | Walnut Finish | 44" | 7.0 | Y | Mod. & X-Full Tubes | **285.00** |
| 12 | 58117 | 28" | Vent Rib | 2 Beads | Accu-Choke | Walnut Finish | 48" | 7.2 | | Mod. Tube Only | **281.00** |
| 12 | 58116 | 26" | Vent Rib | 2 Beads | Accu-Choke | Walnut Finish | 46" | 7.1 | | I.C. & Mod. Tubes | **281.00** |
| 20 | 58132 | 22" | Vent Rib | 2 Beads | Accu-Choke | Walnut Finish | 42" | 6.9 | | Mod. Tube Only, Bantam Stock | **281.00** |
| 20 | 54136 | 26" | Vent Rib | 2 Beads | Accu-Choke | Walnut Finish | 46" | 7.0 | | I.C., Mod. & Full Tubes | **299.00** |
| 20 | 58137 | 26" | Vent Rib | 2 Beads | Accu-Choke | Walnut Finish | 46" | 7.0 | | Mod. Tube Only | **281.00** |
| .410 | 50149 | 24" | Plain | 2 Beads | Full | Synthetic | 43" | 6.8 | | Fixed Choke, Bantam Stock | **285.00** |
| .410 | 58104 | 24" | Vent Rib | 2 Beads | Full | Walnut Finish | 44" | 6.8 | | Fixed Choke | **287.00** |
| 12 | 54032 | 24" | Trophy Slugster™ | None | Rifled Bore | Walnut Finish | 44" | 7.3 | Y | Dual-Comb™ Stock | **354.00** |
| 12 | 54044 | 24" | Slug | Iron | Rifled Bore | Walnut Finish | 44" | 7.0 | Y | | **326.00** |
| 12 | 58045 | 24" | Slug | Iron | Cyl. Bore | Walnut Finish | 44" | 7.0 | Y | | **288.00** |
| 12 | 50308 | 24" | Slug | Iron | Rifled Bore | Synthetic | 44" | 7.0 | Y | | **415.00** |
| 12 | 50309 | 24" | Trophy Slugster™ | None | Rifled Bore | Synthetic | 44" | 7.0 | Y | | **415.00** |
| 20 | 54033 | 24" | Trophy Slugster™ | None | Rifled Bore | Walnut Finish | 44" | 6.9 | Y | Dual-Comb™ Stock | **354.00** |
| 20 | 54051 | 24" | Slug | Iron | Rifled Bore | Walnut Finish | 44" | 6.9 | Y | | **326.00** |
| 20 | 58050 | 24" | Slug | Iron | Cyl. Bore | Walnut Finish | 44" | 6.9 | Y | | **288.00** |

### SPECIFICATIONS MODEL 500 COMBOS

| | | | | | | | | | | | |
|---|---|---|---|---|---|---|---|---|---|---|---|
| 12 | 54043 | 28"<br>24" | Vent Rib<br>Trophy Slugster™ | 2 Beads<br>None | Accu-Choke<br>Rifled Bore | Walnut Finish | 48" | 7.2 | Y | I.C., Mod. & Full Tubes<br>Dual-Comb™ Stock | **$406.00** |
| 12 | 54164 | 28"<br>24" | Vent Rib<br>Slug | 2 Beads<br>Iron | Accu-Choke<br>Rifled Bore | Walnut Finish | 48" | 7.2 | Y | I.C., Mod. & Full Tubes | **384.00** |
| 12 | 58483 | 28"<br>18.5" | Plain<br>Plain | Bead<br>Bead | Modified<br>Cyl. Bore | Walnut Finish | 48" | 7.2 | | Fixed Choke, Pistol Grip Kit | **312.00** |
| 20 | 54182 | 26"<br>24" | Vent Rib<br>Slug | 2 Beads<br>Iron | Accu-Choke<br>Rifled Bore | Walnut Finish | 46" | 7.0 | Y | I.C., Mod. & Full Tubes | **384.00** |
| 12 | 58158 | 28"<br>24" | Vent Rib<br>Slug | 2 Beads<br>Iron | Accu-Choke<br>Cyl. Bore | Walnut Finish | 48" | 7.2 | | Mod. Tube Only | **344.00** |
| 12 | 58169 | 28"<br>18.5" | Vent Rib<br>Plain | 2 Beads<br>Bead | Accu-Choke<br>Cyl. Bore | Walnut Finish | 48" | 7.2 | | Mod. Tube Only, Pistol Grip Kit | **334.00** |
| 20 | 58186 | 26"<br>18.5" | Vent Rib<br>Plain | 2 Beads<br>Bead | Accu-Choke<br>Cyl. Bore | Walnut Finish | 46" | 7.3 | | Mod. Tube Only, Pistol Grip Kit | **334.00** |
| .410 | 58456 | 24"<br>18.5" | Vent Rib<br>Plain | 2 Beads<br>Bead | Full<br>Cyl. Bore | Walnut Finish | 44" | 6.8 | | Fixed Choke, Pistol Grip Kit | **340.00** |
| 12 | 54153 | 24"<br>24" | Slug<br>Muzzleloader | Iron<br>Iron | Rifled Bore<br>Rifled Bore | Walnut Finish | 44" | 7.0 | | .50 Cal., 1/26" Right Hand Twist | **457.00** |

# MOSSBERG PUMP SHOTGUNS

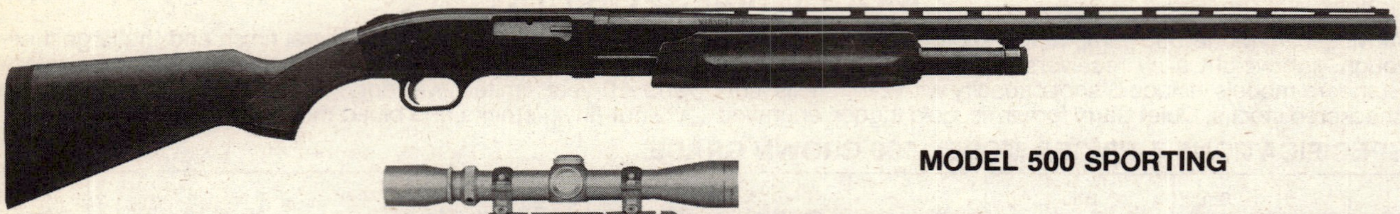

MODEL 500 SPORTING

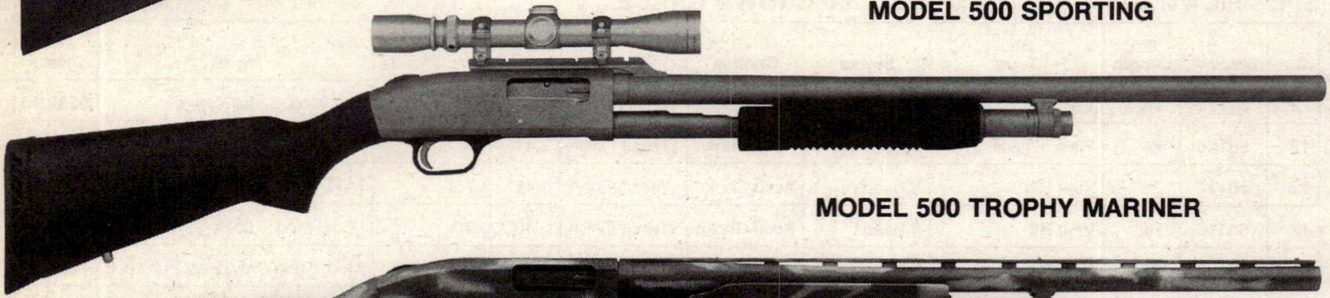

MODEL 500 TROPHY MARINER

MODEL 500 OFM WOODLAND CAMO

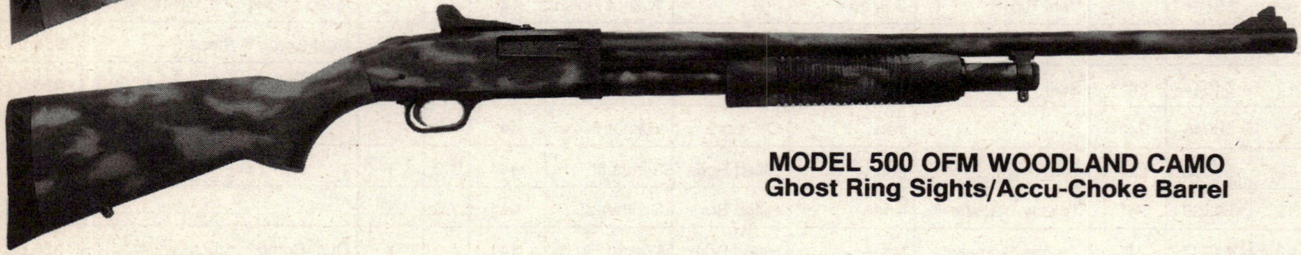

MODEL 500 OFM WOODLAND CAMO
Ghost Ring Sights/Accu-Choke Barrel

## SPECIFICATIONS MODEL 500 WOODLAND CAMO (6-shot)

| | | | | | | | | | | | |
|---|---|---|---|---|---|---|---|---|---|---|---|
| 12 | 50197 | 28″ | Vent Rib | 2 Beads | Accu-Choke | Synthetic | 48″ | 7.2 | Y | Mod. Tube only | $296.00 |
| 12 | 50193 | 28″ | Vent Rib | 2 Beads | Accu-Choke | Synthetic | 48″ | 7.2 | Y | I.C., Mod. & Full Tubes | 325.00 |
| 12 | 50195 | 24″ | Vent Rib | 2 Beads | Accu-Choke | Synthetic | 44″ | 7.1 | Y | I.C., Mod., Full & X-Full Tubes | 324.00 |
| 12 | 50196 | 24″ | Ghost Ring™ Sight | Ghost Ring™ | Accu-Choke | Synthetic | 44″ | 7.1 | Y | I.C., Mod. Full & X-Full Tubes | 384.00 |
| 20 | 50194 | 22″ | Vent Rib | 2 Beads | Accu-Choke | Synthetic | 42″ | 6.8 | Y | I.C., Mod. Full Tubes | 316.00 |
| 12 | 50213 | 28″<br>24″ | Vent Rib<br>Slug | 2 Beads<br>Iron | Accu-Choke<br>Rifled Bore | Synthetic | 48″ | 7.2 | Y | I.C., Mod. & Full Tubes | 415.00 |
| 12 | 50214 | 26″<br>24″ | Vent Rib<br>Slug | 2 Beads<br>Iron | Accu-Choke<br>Rifled Bore | Synthetic | 46″ | 6.9 | Y | I.C., Mod. & Full Tubes | 407.00 |

## MODEL 500 AMERICAN FIELD (Pressed Checkered, Blued Barrel)

| | | | | | | | | | | | |
|---|---|---|---|---|---|---|---|---|---|---|---|
| 12 | 50117 | 28″ | Vent Rib | 2 Beads | Accu-Choke | Walnut Finish | 48″ | 7.2 | | Mod. Tube Only | $278.00 |
| 20 | 50137 | 26″ | Vent Rib | 2 Beads | Accu-Choke | Walnut Finish | 46″ | 7.1 | | Mod. Tube Only | 278.00 |
| .410 | 50104 | 24″ | Vent Rib | 2 Beads | Full | Walnut Finish | 44″ | 7.0 | | Fixed Choke | 284.00 |
| 12 | 50044 | 24″ | Slug | Iron | Rifled Bore | Walnut Finish | 44″ | 7.0 | Y | | 324.00 |
| 12 | 50045 | 24″ | Slug | Iron | Cyl. Bore | Walnut Finish | 44″ | 7.0 | Y | | 285.00 |
| 20 | 50050 | 24″ | Slug | Iron | Cyl. Bore | Walnut Finish | 44″ | 7.0 | Y | | 285.00 |

## MODEL 500/590 SPECIAL PURPOSE

Since 1979, Mossberg's Special Purpose Models 500 and 590 have been the only pump shotguns that meet or exceed U.S. Government MILSPEC 3443D and 3443E requirements. These shotguns feature lightweight alloy receivers with ambidextrous "top thumb safety" button, walnut-finished wood or durable synthetic with Quiet Carry™ forearms, rubber recoil pads, dual extractors, two slide bars and twin cartridge stops. All models include a Cablelock™ and a 10-year limited warranty.

| Gauge | Barrel Length | Sight | Stock # | Finish | Stock | Capacity | Overall Length | Weight | Notes | Price |
|---|---|---|---|---|---|---|---|---|---|---|
| **MODEL 500/590 MARINER™** | | | | | | | | | | |
| 12 | 18.5″ | Bead | 50273 | Marinecote™ | Synthetic | 6 | 38.5″ | 6.8 | Includes Pistol Grip | $403.00 |
| 12 | 20″ | Bead | 50299 | Marinecote™ | Synthetic | 9 | 40″ | 7.0 | Includes Pistol Grip | 415.00 |
| 12 | 18.5″ | Ghost Ring™ | 50276 | Marinecote™ | Synthetic | 6 | 38.5″ | 6.8 | | 459.00 |
| 12 | 20″ | Ghost Ring™ | 50296 | Marinecote™ | Synthetic | 9 | 40″ | 7.0 | | 471.00 |
| **MODEL 500 SPECIAL PURPOSE** | | | | | | | | | | |
| 12 | 18.5″ | Bead | 50404 | Blue | Walnut Finish | 6 | 38.5″ | 6.8 | Includes Pistol Grip | $281.00 |
| 12 | 18.5″ | Bead | 50411 | Blue | Synthetic | 6 | 38.5″ | 6.8 | Includes Pistol Grip | 281.00 |
| 12 | 18.5″ | Bead | 50412* | Blue | Synthetic | 6 | 38.5″ | 6.8 | Mod. Tube only | 281.00 |
| 12 | 18.5″ | Bead | 50521 | Parkerized | Synthetic | 6 | 38.5″ | 6.8 | Includes Pistol Grip | 315.00 |
| 12 | 18.5″ | Bead | 50440 | Blue | Pistol Grip | 6 | 28″ | 5.6 | Includes Heat Shield | 272.00 |
| 20 | 18.5″ | Bead | 50451 | Blue | Walnut Finish | 6 | 38.5″ | 6.8 | Includes Pistol Grip | 281.00 |
| 20 | 18.5″ | Bead | 50452 | Blue | Synthetic | 6 | 38.5″ | 6.8 | Includes Pistol Grip | 279.00 |
| 20 | 18.5″ | Bead | 50450 | Blue | Pistol Grip | 6 | 28″ | 5.6 | | 272.00 |
| 20 | 18.5″ | Bead | 50330 | Blue | Pistol Grip | 6 | 28″ | 5.6 | Includes Camper Case | 306.00 |
| .410 | 18.5″ | Bead | 50455 | Blue | Pistol Grip | 6 | 28″ | 5.3 | | 279.00 |
| .410 | 18.5″ | Bead | 50335 | Blue | Pistol Grip | 6 | 28″ | 5.3 | Includes Camper Case | 312.00 |
| 12 | 20″ | Iron | 50570 | Blue | Walnut Finish | 8 | 40″ | 7.0 | Includes Pistol Grip | 304.00 |
| 12 | 20″ | Bead | 50564 | Blue | Walnut Finish | 8 | 40″ | 7.0 | Includes Pistol Grip | 281.00 |
| 12 | 20″ | Bead | 50576* | Blue | Synthetic | 8 | 38.5″ | 6.9 | Includes Mod. tube | 281.00 |
| 12 | 20″ | Bead | 50579 | Blue | Synthetic | 8 | 40″ | 7.0 | Includes Pistol Grip | 281.00 |
| 12 | 20″ | Bead | 50580 | Blue | Pistol Grip | 8 | 40″ | 7.0 | Includes Heat Shield | 272.00 |
| 20 | 20″ | Bead | 50581 | Blue | Synthetic | 8 | 38.5″ | 6.9 | Includes Pistol Grip | 279.00 |
| 20 | 20″ | Bead | 50582 | Blue | Pistol Grip | 8 | 28.5″ | 5.6 | | 272.00 |
| **MODEL 590 SPECIAL PURPOSE** | | | | | | | | | | |
| 12 | 20″ | Bead | 50645 | Blue | Synthetic | 9 | 40″ | 7.2 | w/Acc. Lug & Heat Shield | $329.00 |
| 12 | 20″ | Bead | 50650 | Blue | Speed Feed | 9 | 40″ | 7.2 | w/Acc. Lug & Heat Shield | 362.00 |
| 12 | 20″ | Bead | 50660 | Parkerized | Synthetic | 9 | 40″ | 7.2 | w/Acc. Lug & Heat Shield | 379.00 |
| 12 | 20″ | Bead | 50665 | Parkerized | Speed Feed | 9 | 40″ | 7.2 | w/Acc. Lug & Heat Shield | 412.00 |
| **MODEL 500/590 GHOST RING™** | | | | | | | | | | |
| 12 | 18.5″ | Ghost Ring™ | 50402 | Blue | Synthetic | 6 | 38.5″ | 6.8 | | $331.00 |
| 12 | 18.5″ | Ghost Ring™ | 50517 | Parkerized | Synthetic | 6 | 38.5″ | 6.8 | | 384.00 |
| 12 | 20″ | Ghost Ring™ | 50652 | Blue | Synthetic | 9 | 40″ | 7.2 | w/Acc. Lug | 379.00 |
| 12 | 20″ | Ghost Ring™ | 50662* | Parkerized | Synthetic | 9 | 40″ | 7.2 | w/Acc. Lug & Mod. Tube | 454.00 |
| 12 | 20″ | Ghost Ring™ | 50663 | Parkerized | Synthetic | 9 | 40″ | 7.2 | w/Acc. Lug | 432.00 |
| 12 | 20″ | Ghost Ring™ | 50668 | Parkerized | Speed Feed | 9 | 40″ | 7.2 | w/Acc. Lug | 465.00 |
| **HS 410 HOME SECURITY** | | | | | | | | | | |
| .410 | 18.5″ | Bead | 50359 | Blue | Synthetic | 6 | 39.5″ | 6.6 | Includes Vertical Foregrip | $295.00 |

* New models for 1995/6 include Accu-Choke; all others have Cyl. Bore.

SHOTGUNS

# MOSSBERG PUMP SHOTGUNS

## MODEL 835 ULTI-MAG

Mossberg's Model 835 Ulti-Mag pump action shotgun has a 3½" 12 gauge chamber but can also handle standard 2¾" and 3" shells. Field barrels are backbored for optimum patterns and felt recoil reduction. Cut checkered walnut and walnut-finished stocks and Quiet Carry™ forearms are standard, as are gold triggers and engraved receivers. Camo models are drilled and tapped for scope and feature detachable swivels and sling. All models include a Cablelock™ and 10-year limited warranty.

**MODEL 835 ULTI-MAG**

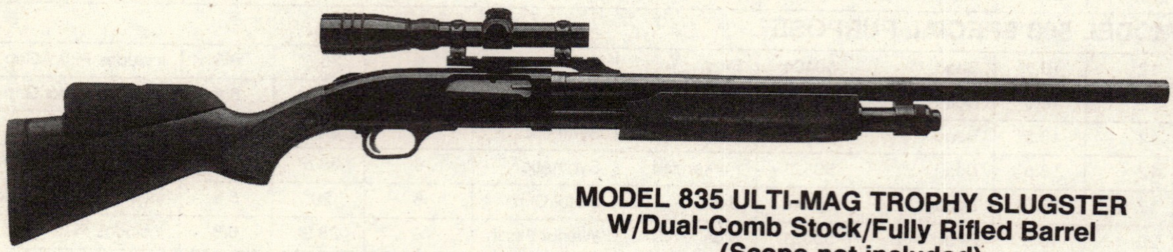

**MODEL 835 ULTI-MAG TROPHY SLUGSTER**
**W/Dual-Comb Stock/Fully Rifled Barrel**
**(Scope not included)**

**MODEL 835 ULTI-MAG**
**Mossy Oak™ Camo Finish**

### SPECIFICATIONS AND PRICES MODEL 835 ULTI-MAG (12 Gauge, 6 Shot)

| Ga. | Stock No. | Barrel Length | Type | Sights | Choke | Finish | Stock | O.A. Length | Wt. | Studs | Notes | Price |
|---|---|---|---|---|---|---|---|---|---|---|---|---|
| **Ulti-Mag™ 835 Crown Grade** | | | | | | | | | | | | |
| 12 | 64110 | 28" | Vent Rib | 2 Beads | Accu-Mag | Blue | Walnut | 48.5" | 7.7 | | 4 Tubes* & Dual-Comb™ Stock | $412.00 |
| 12 | 64132 | 24" | Trophy Slugster™ | None | Rifled Bore | Blue | Walnut | 44.5" | 7.3 | Y | Dual-Comb™ Stock | 434.00 |
| 12 | 64120 | 28" | Vent Rib | 2 Beads | Accu-Mag | Blue | Walnut | 48.5" | 7.7 | | 4 Tubes* | 404.00 |
| 12 | 68120 | 28" | Vent Rib | 2 Beads | Accu-Mag | Blue | Walnut Finish | 48.5" | 7.7 | | Mod. Tube Only | 310.00 |
| 12 | 68125 | 24" | Vent Rib | 2 Beads | Accu-Mag | Blue | Walnut Finish | 44.5" | 7.3 | | Mod. & X-Full Tubes | 310.00 |
| 12 | 64144 | 28"<br>24" | Vent Rib<br>Trophy Slugster™ | 2 Beads<br>None | Accu-Mag<br>Rifled Bore | Blue | Walnut | 48.5" | 7.7 | | 4 Tubes*<br>Dual-Comb™ Stock | 487.00 |
| 12 | 64145 | 28"<br>24" | Vent Rib<br>Slug | 2 Beads<br>Iron | Accu-Mag<br>Rifled Bore | Blue | Walnut | 48.5" | 7.7 | | 4 Tubes*<br>Dual-Comb™ Stock | 476.00 |
| 12 | 68160 | 28"<br>24" | Vent Rib<br>Slug | 2 Beads<br>Iron | Accu-Mag<br>Cyl. Bore | Blue | Walnut Finish | 48.5" | 7.7 | | Mod. Tube Only | 363.00 |
| **Ulti-Mag™ 835 Camo** | | | | | | | | | | | | |
| 12 | 60034 | 24" | Vent Rib | 2 Beads | Accu-Mag | Realtree® | Synthetic | 44.5" | 7.3 | Y | 4 Tube Turkey Pack** | 482.00 |
| 12 | 60434 | 24" | Vent Rib | 2 Beads | Accu-Mag | Mossy Oak® | Synthetic | 44.5" | 7.3 | Y | 4 Tube Turkey Pack** | 482.00 |
| 12 | 60035 | 28" | Vent Rib | 2 Beads | Accu-Mag | Realtree® | Synthetic | 48.5" | 7.7 | | 4 Tubes* | 482.00 |
| 12 | 60016 | 28" | Vent Rib | 2 Beads | Accu-Mag | OFM Woodland | Synthetic | 48.5" | | | 4 Tubes* | 441.00 |
| 12 | 68130 | 24" | Vent Rib | 2 Beads | Accu-Mag | OFM Woodland | Synthetic | 44.5" | 7.3 | Y | Mod. & X-Full Tubes | 332.00 |
| 12 | 60147 | 24"<br>24" | Vent Rib<br>Slug | 2 Beads<br>Iron | Accu-Mag<br>Rifled Bore | Realtree® | Synthetic | 44.5" | 7.3 | Y | 4 Tube Turkey Pack**<br>Includes Hard Case | 590.00 |
| 12 | 60148 | 28"<br>24" | Vent Rib<br>Slug | 2 Beads<br>Iron | Accu-Mag<br>Rifled Bore | OFM Woodland | Wood/Synthetic | 48.5" | 7.7 | Y | 4 Tubes*<br>Dual-Comb™ Stock | 515.00 |
| **Ulti-Mag™ 835 American Field (Pressed Checkering)** | | | | | | | | | | | | |
| 12 | 61120 | 28" | Vent Rib | 2 Beads | Accu-Mag | Blue | Walnut Finish | 48.5" | 7.7 | | Mod. Tube Only | 307.00 |

# MOSSBERG SHOTGUNS

## MODEL 9200 AUTOLOADERS

All Mossberg Model 9200 award-winning autoloader shotguns handle light 2³/₄″ or heavy 3″ magnum loads. Features include cut-checkered walnut stock and forearm, gold trigger, engraved receiver, top thumb safety, light weight and easy shooting. All models include a Cablelock™ and a 10-year Limited Warranty.

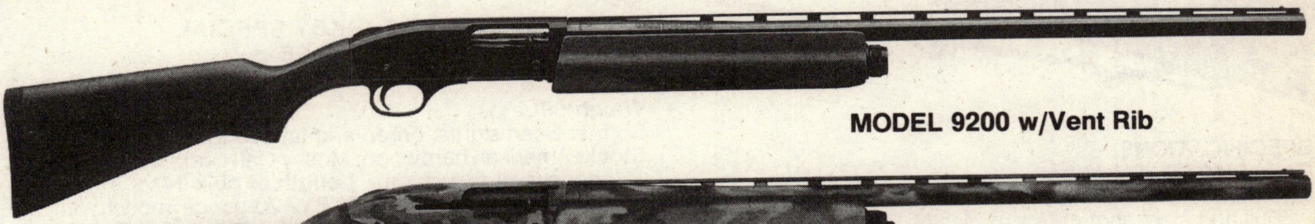

MODEL 9200 w/Vent Rib

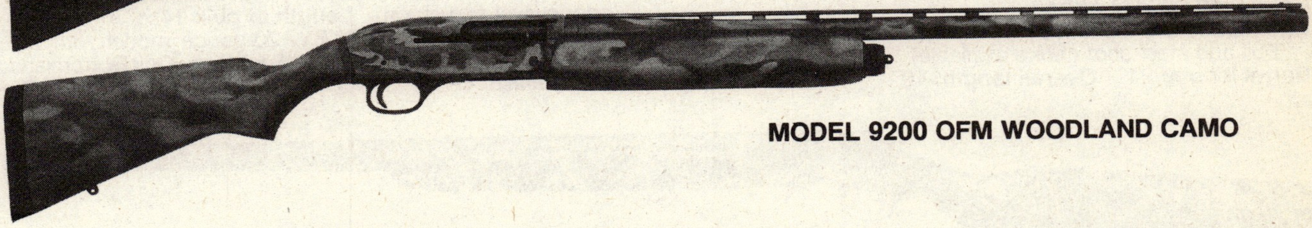

MODEL 9200 OFM WOODLAND CAMO

### SPECIFICATIONS AND PRICES MODEL 9200 (12 Gauge, 5 Shot)

| Ga. | Stock # | Bbl. Length | Bbl. Type | Sights | Choke | Finish | Stock | Length O.A. | Wt. | Q.D. Studs | Notes | Prices |
|---|---|---|---|---|---|---|---|---|---|---|---|---|
| **Model 9200 Crown Grade** | | | | | | | | | | | | |
| 12 | 49420 | 28" | Vent Rib | 2 Beads | Accu-Choke | Blue | Walnut | 48" | 7.7 | | I.C., Mod. & Full Tubes | $478.00 |
| 12 | 49425 | 24" | Vent Rib | 2 Beads | Accu-Choke | Blue | Walnut | 44" | 7.3 | | I.C., Mod. & Full Tubes | 478.00 |
| 12 | 49432 | 24" | Trophy Slugster™ | None | Rifled Bore | Blue | Walnut | 44" | 7.3 | Y | Dual-Comb™ Stock | 500.00 |
| 12 | 49444 | 24" | Slug | Iron | Rifled Bore | Blue | Walnut | 44" | 7.3 | | | 478.00 |
| 12 | 49403 | 26" | Vent Rib | 2 Beads | Accu-Choke | Blue | Walnut | 46" | 7.5 | | USST, I.C., Mod., Full & Skeet | 478.00 |
| 12 | 49406 | 18.5" | Plain | Bead | Mod. | Matte Blue | Synthetic | 39.5" | 7.0 | Y | Fixed Choke | 463.00 |
| **Model 9200 Camo** | | | | | | | | | | | | |
| 12 | 49434 | 24" | Vent Rib | 2 Beads | Accu-Choke | Mossy Oak® | Synthetic | 44" | 7.3 | Y | I.C., Mod., Full & X-Full Tubes | 562.00 |
| 12 | 49034 | 24" | Vent Rib | 2 Beads | Accu-Choke | Realtree®/Matte Blue | Synthetic | 44" | 7.3 | Y | I.C., Mod., Full & X-Full Tubes | 562.00 |
| 12 | 49491 | 28" | Vent Rib | 2 Beads | Accu-Choke | OFM Woodland | Synthetic | 48" | 7.7 | Y | I.C., Mod. & Full Tubes | 463.00 |
| 12 | 49466 | 28" | Vent Rib | 2 Beads | Acu-Choke | OFM Woodland | Synthetic | 48" | 7.7 | Y | I.C., Mod. & Full Tubes | 565.00 |
| | | 24" | Slug | Iron | Rifled Bore | OFM Woodland | | | | | | |
| 12 | 49443 | 28" | Vent Rib | 2 Beads | Acu-Choke | Blued | Walnut | 48" | 7.7 | | I.C., Mod. & Full Tubes | 591.00 |
| | | 24" | Trophy Slugger™ | None | Rifled Bore | | | | | | Dual-Comb™ Stock | |
| 12 | 49464 | 28" | Vent Rib | 2 Beads | Acu-Choke | Blued | Walnut | 48" | 7.7 | | I.C., Mod., & Full Tubes | 572.00 |
| | | 24" | Slug | Iron | Rifled Bore | | | | | | | |

SHOTGUNS

**MOSSBERG LINE LAUNCHER**
**$999.00** (**$735.00** Launcher Kit)

The Line Launcher is the first shotgun devoted to rescue and personal safety. It provides an early self-contained rescue opportunity for boaters, police and fire departments, salvage operations or whenever an extra-long throw of line is the safest alternative. This shotgun uses a 12-gauge blank cartridge to propel a convertible projectile with a line attached. With a floating head attached, the projectile will travel 250 to 275 feet. Removing the floating head increases the projectile range to approx. 700 feet. The braided 360-lb. test floating line is highly visible and is supplied inside on an 800′ coiled spool.

# NEW ENGLAND FIREARMS

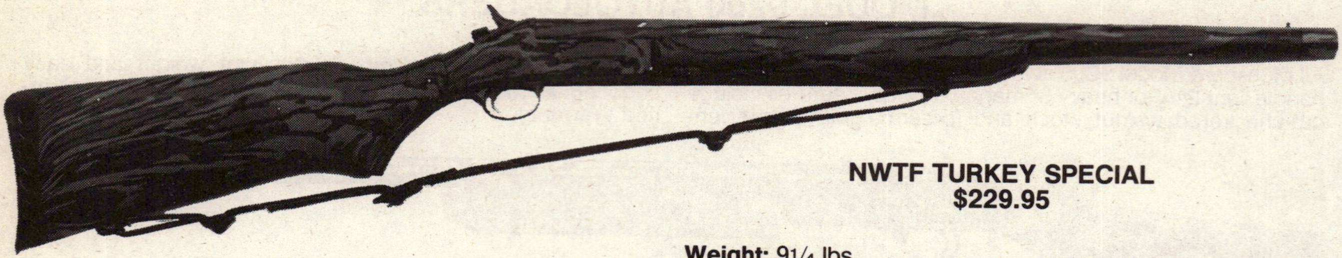

**NWTF TURKEY SPECIAL**
**$229.95**

**SPECIFICATIONS**
**Gauge:** 10 (3 1/2″ chamber)
**Chokes:** Screw-in chokes (Turkey Full Choke provided; Extra Full and steel shot choke available)
**Barrel length:** 24″ **Overall length:** 40″
**Weight:** 9 1/4 lbs.
**Sights:** Bead sights; drilled and tapped for scope mounting
**Stock:** American hardwood; Mossy Oak camo finish; full pistol grip; swivel and studs. **Length of pull:** 14 1/2″
Also available: **YOUTH TURKEY.** 20-gauge model with 22″ barrel and 3″ chamber, Mod. choke, Mossy Oak Bottomland Camo finish . . . . . . . . . . . . . . . . . . . . . . . . . . . . . . **$149.95**

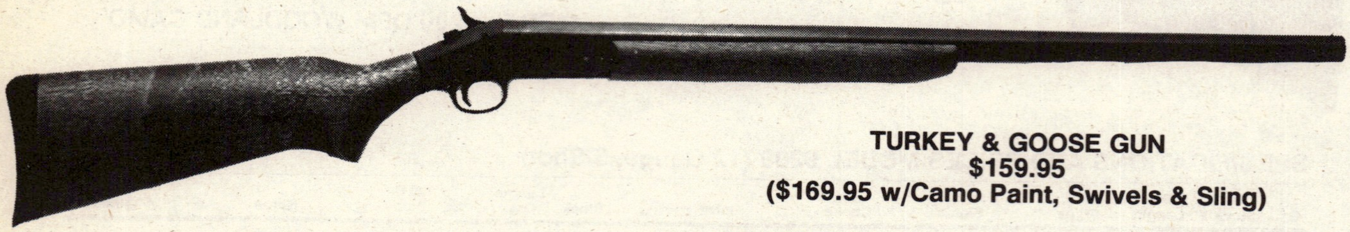

**TURKEY & GOOSE GUN**
**$159.95**
**($169.95 w/Camo Paint, Swivels & Sling)**

**SPECIFICATIONS**
**Gauge:** 10 (3 1/2″ chamber) **Choke:** Full
**Barrel length:** 28″ **Overall length:** 44″
**Weight:** 9 1/2 lbs.
**Sights:** Bead sights
**Stock:** American hardwood; walnut or camo finish; full pistol grip; ventilated recoil pad. **Length of pull:** 14 1/2″

**TRACKER II RIFLED SLUG GUN**
**$129.95**

**SPECIFICATIONS**
**Gauges:** 12 and 20 (3″ chamber) **Choke:** Rifled Bore
**Barrel length:** 24″ **Overall length:** 40″
**Weight:** 6 lbs.
**Sights:** Adjustable rifle sights
**Length of pull:** 14 1/2″
**Stock:** American hardwood; walnut or camo finish; full pistol grip; recoil pad; sling swivel studs
Also available:
**TRACKER SLUG GUN** w/Cylinder Bore: . . . . . . . . . . **$124.95**

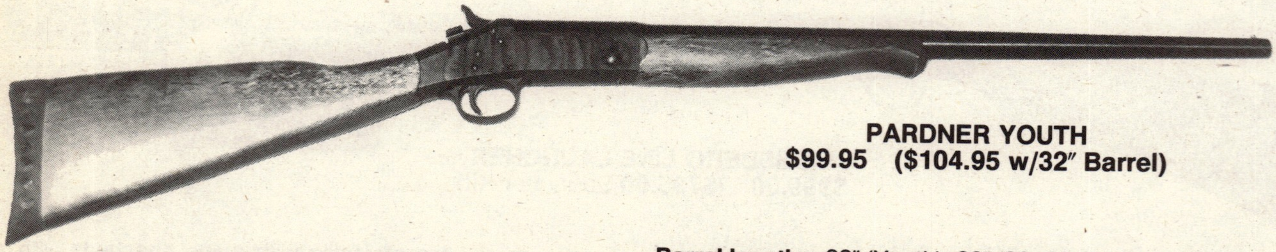

**PARDNER YOUTH**
**$99.95 ($104.95 w/32″ Barrel)**

**PARDNER SINGLE-BARREL SHOTGUNS**

**SPECIFICATIONS**
**Gauges:** 12, 16, 20, 28 and .410
**Barrel lengths:** 22″ (Youth); 26″ (20, 28, .410); 28″ (12 and 16 ga.), 32″ (12 ga.)
**Chokes:** Full (all gauges, except 28); Modified (12, 20 and 28 ga.)
**Chamber:** 2 3/4″ (16 and 28 ga.); 3″ (all others)

# PARKER REPRODUCTIONS

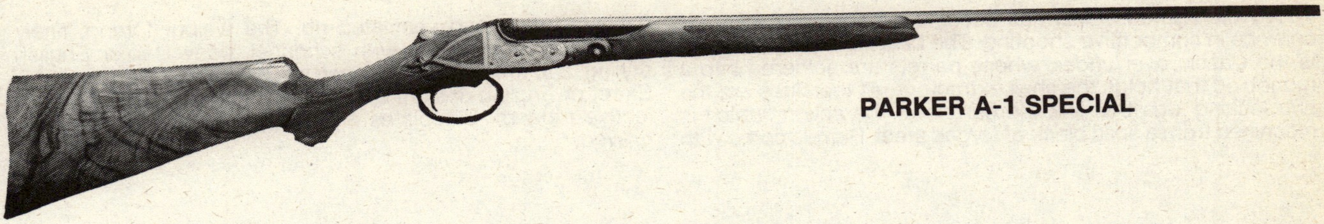

PARKER A-1 SPECIAL

Recognized by the shooting fraternity as the finest American shotgun ever produced, the Parker A-1 Special is again available. Exquisite engraving and rare presentation-grade French walnut distinguish the A-1 Special from any other shotguns in the world. Currently offered in 12 and 20 gauge, each gun is custom-fitted in its own oak and leather trunk case. Two models are offered: Hand Engraved and Custom Engraved. Also available in D Grade.

**Standard features:** Automatic safety, selective ejectors, skeleton steel butt plate, splinter forend, engraved snap caps, fitted leather trunk case, canvas and leather case cover, chrome barrel interiors, hand-checkering. The A-1 Special also features a 24k gold initial plate or pistol cap, 32 lines-per-inch checkering, selected wood and fine hand-engraving. Choose from single or double trigger, English or pistol grip stock (all models). Options include beavertail forend, additional barrels.

In addition to the A-1 Special, the D-Grade is available in 12, 20, 16/20 and 28 gauge. A 16-gauge, 28″ barrel can be ordered with a 20-gauge one or two-barrel set. The two-barrel sets come in a custom leather cased with a fitted over cover.

**Prices: D-GRADE**
One Barrel—12, 20, 28 gauge . . . . . . . . . . . . . . . **$3370.00**
Two-barrel set . . . . . . . . . . . . . . . . . . . . . . . . . . **4200.00**
16/20 Combo . . . . . . . . . . . . . . . . . . . . . . . . . . . **4870.00**
20/20/16 Combo . . . . . . . . . . . . . . . . . . . . . . . . **5630.00**

**SPECIFICATIONS**

| Gauge | Barrel Length | Chokes | Chambers | Drop At Comb | Drop At Heel | Length of Pull | Nominal Weight (lbs.) | Overall Length |
|---|---|---|---|---|---|---|---|---|
| 12 | 26″ | Skeet I & II or IC/M | 2 3/4″ | 1 3/8″ | 2 3/16″ | 14 1/8″ | 6 3/4 | 42 5/8″ |
| 12 | 28″ | IC/M or M/F | 2 3/4 & 3″ | 1 3/8″ | 2 3/16″ | 14 1/8″ | 6 3/4 | 44 5/8″ |
| 20 | 26″ | Skeet I & II or IC/M | 2 3/4″ | 1 3/8″ | 2 3/16″ | 14 3/8″ | 6 1/2 | 42 3/8″ |
| 20 | 28″ | M/F | 3″ | 1 3/8″ | 2 3/16″ | 14 3/8″ | 6 1/2 | 44 5/8″ |
| 16 on 20 frame | 28″ | Skeet I & II, IC/M or M/F | 2 3/4″ | 1 3/8″ | 2 3/16″ | 14 3/8″ | 6 1/4 | 44 5/8″ |
| 28 | 26″ | Skeet I & II or IC/M | 2 3/4″ | 1 3/8″ | 2 3/16″ | 14 3/8″ | 5 1/3 | 42 5/8″ |
| 28 | 28″ | M/F | 2 3/4 & 3″ | 1 3/8″ | 2 3/16″ | 14 3/8″ | 5 1/3 | 44 5/8″ |

* *Note:* The 16-gauge barrels are lighter than the 20-gauge barrels.

# PERAZZI SHOTGUNS

Today the name *Perazzi* has become synonymous with excellence in competitive shooting. The heart of the Perazzi line is the classic over/under, whose barrels are soldered into a monobloc that holds the shell extractors. At the sides are the two locking lugs that link the barrels to the action, which is machined from a solid block of forged steel. Barrels come with flat, step or raised ventilated rib. The walnut forend, finely checkered, is available with schnabel, beavertail or English styling, and the walnut stock can be of standard, Monte Carlo, Skeet or English design. Double or single nonselective or selective triggers. Sideplates and receiver are masterfully engraved.

## OVER/UNDER GAME MODELS

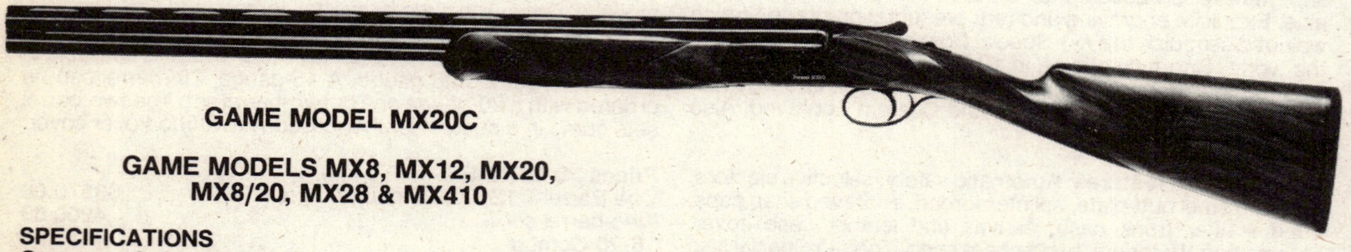

GAME MODEL MX20C

### GAME MODELS MX8, MX12, MX20, MX8/20, MX28 & MX410

**SPECIFICATIONS**
**Gauges:** 12, 20, 28 & .410
**Chambers:** 2¾″; also available in 3″
**Barrel lengths:** 26″ and 27½″
**Weight:** 6 lbs. 6 oz. to 7 lbs. 4 oz.
**Trigger group:** Nondetachable with coil springs and selective trigger
**Stock:** Interchangeable and custom; schnabel forend
**Prices:**

| | |
|---|---|
| **Standard Grade** | **$ 7,850.00–$15,700.00** |
| **SC3 Grade** | **13,300.00– 21,150.00** |
| **SCO Grade** | **22,700.00– 30,550.00** |
| **SCO Gold Grades** | **25,550.00– 33,400.00** |

## AMERICAN TRAP COMBO MODELS

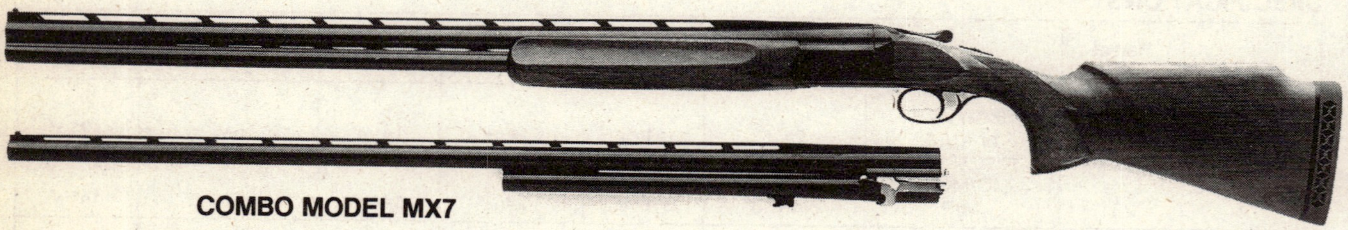

COMBO MODEL MX7

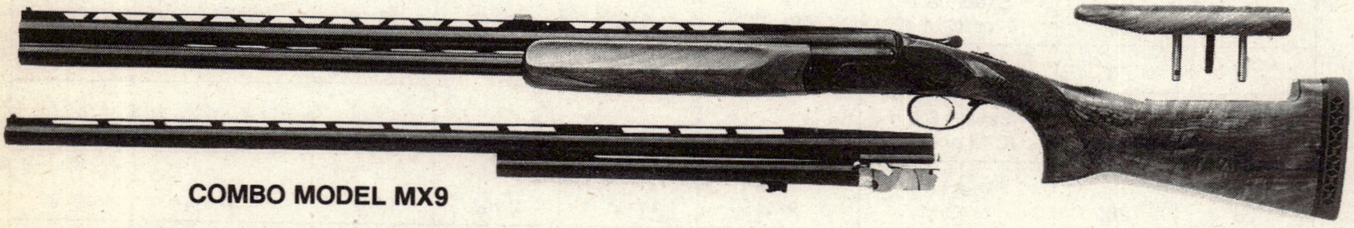

COMBO MODEL MX9

### AMERICAN TRAP COMBO MODELS MX6, MX7, MX9, MX10, MX8 SPECIAL, DB81 SPECIAL & GRANDAMERICA 1

**SPECIFICATIONS**
**Gauge:** 12 **Chamber:** 2¾″
**Barrel lengths:** 29½″ and 31½″ (O/U); 32″ and 34″ (single barrel) **Chokes:** Mod./Full (O/U); Full (single barrel)
**Weight (avg.):** 8 lbs. 6 oz.
**Trigger group:** Detachable and interchangeable with flat "V" springs
**Stock:** Interchangeable and custom; beavertail forend
**Prices:**

| | |
|---|---|
| **Standard Grade** | **$ 7,250.00–$13,700.00** |
| **SC3 Grade** | **17,250.00– 19,800.00** |
| **SCO Grade** | **27,550.00– 29,700.00** |
| **Gold Grade** | **30,550.00– 32,650.00** |

# PERAZZI SHOTGUNS

## AMERICAN TRAP SINGLE-BARREL MODELS

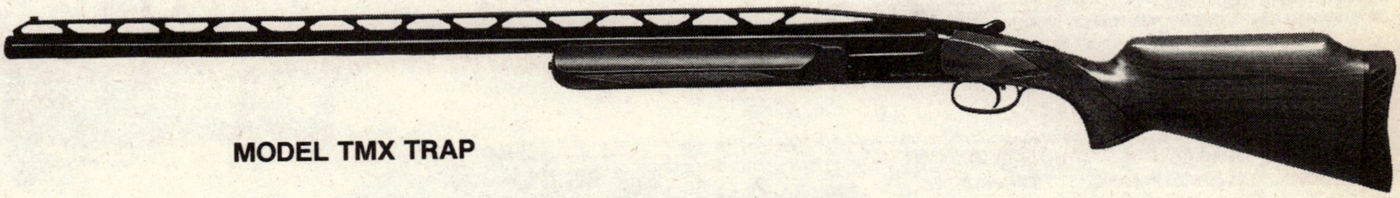

MODEL TMX TRAP

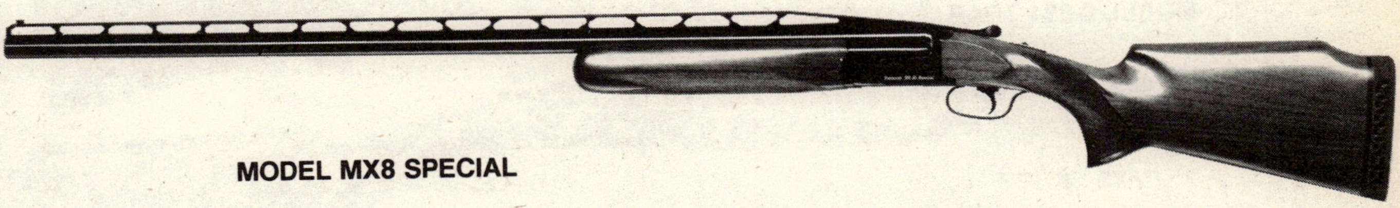

MODEL MX8 SPECIAL

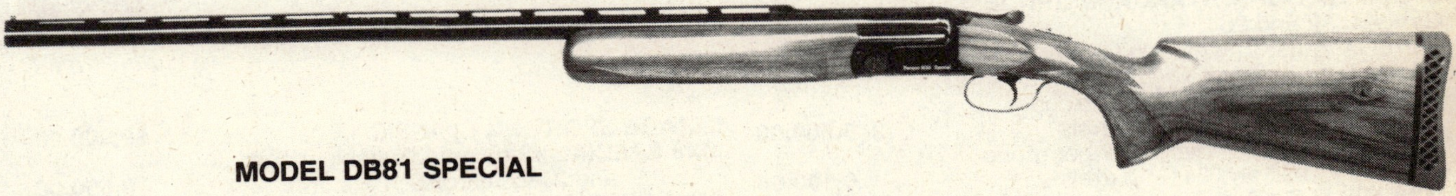

MODEL DB81 SPECIAL

SHOTGUNS

### AMERICAN TRAP SINGLE BARREL MODELS

### MX6, MX7, TM1 SPECIAL, TMX SPECIAL

**SPECIFICATIONS**
**Gauge:** 12
**Chamber:** 2³/₄″
**Barrel lengths:** 32″ and 34″
**Weight:** 8 lbs. 6 oz.
**Choke:** Full
**Trigger group:** Detachable and interchangeable with coil springs
**Stock:** Interchangeable and custom made
**Forend:** Beavertail
**Prices:**

| | |
|---|---|
| **Standard Grade** | $ 6,150.00–$ 7,030.00 |
| **SCO Grade** | 18,000.00– 18,200.00 |
| **Gold Grade** | 20,050.00– 20,250.00 |

# PERAZZI SHOTGUNS

## COMPETITION OVER/UNDER SHOTGUNS
### OLYMPIC, DOUBLE TRAP, SKEET, PIGEON & ELECTROCIBLES

MODEL MX10

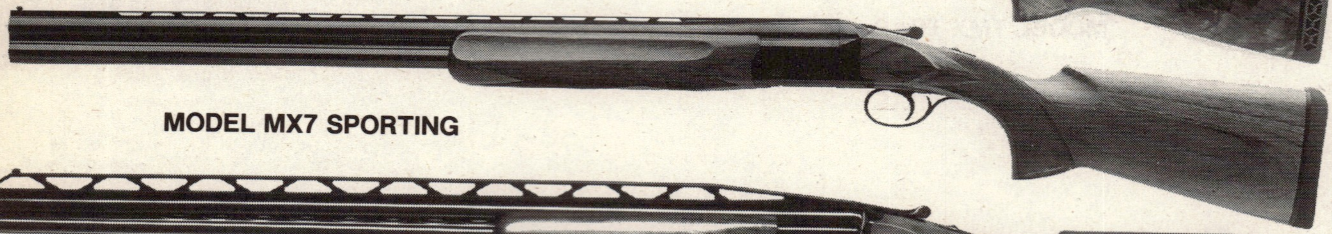

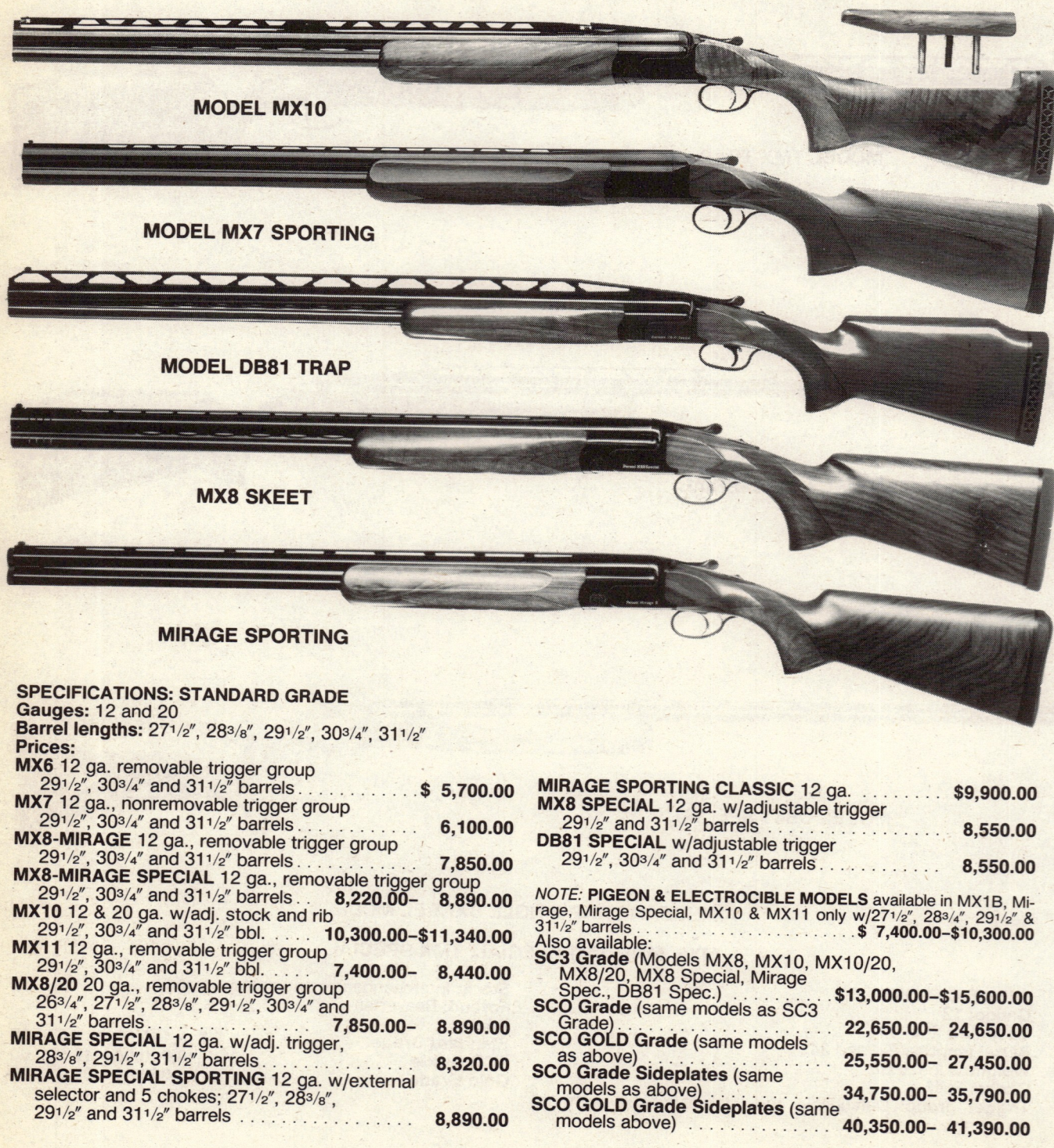

MODEL MX7 SPORTING

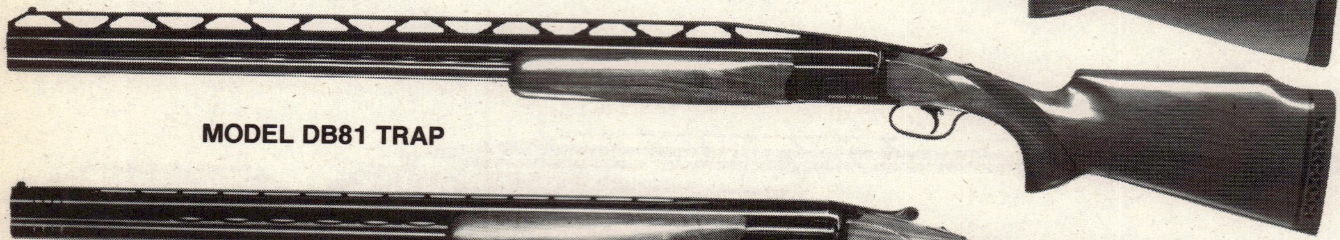

MODEL DB81 TRAP

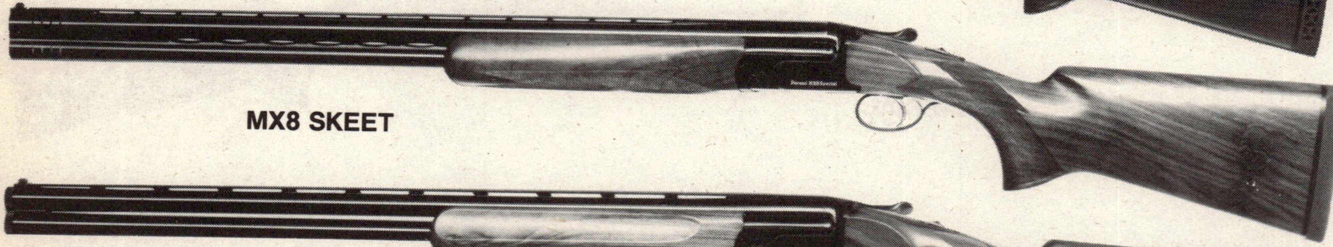

MX8 SKEET

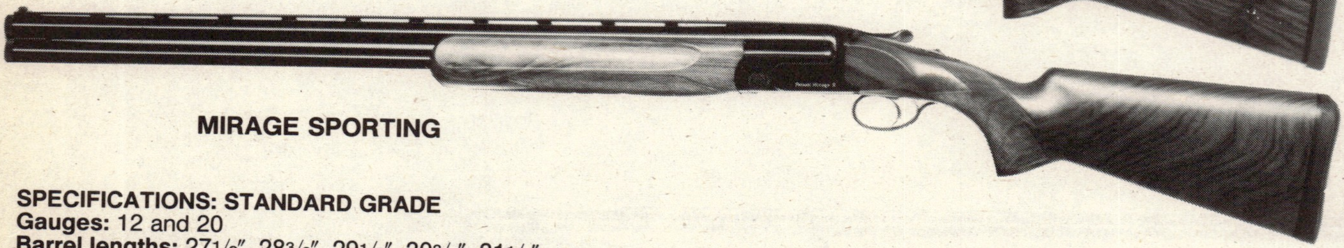

MIRAGE SPORTING

**SPECIFICATIONS: STANDARD GRADE**
**Gauges:** 12 and 20
**Barrel lengths:** 27½″, 28⅜″, 29½″, 30¾″, 31½″
**Prices:**

**MX6** 12 ga. removable trigger group 29½″, 30¾″ and 31½″ barrels ............ $ 5,700.00
**MX7** 12 ga., nonremovable trigger group 29½″, 30¾″ and 31½″ barrels ............ 6,100.00
**MX8-MIRAGE** 12 ga., removable trigger group 29½″, 30¾″ and 31½″ barrels ............ 7,850.00
**MX8-MIRAGE SPECIAL** 12 ga., removable trigger group 29½″, 30¾″ and 31½″ barrels .. 8,220.00– 8,890.00
**MX10** 12 & 20 ga. w/adj. stock and rib 29½″, 30¾″ and 31½″ bbl. ..... 10,300.00–$11,340.00
**MX11** 12 ga., removable trigger group 29½″, 30¾″ and 31½″ bbl. ..... 7,400.00– 8,440.00
**MX8/20** 20 ga., removable trigger group 26¾″, 27½″, 28⅜″, 29½″, 30¾″ and 31½″ barrels ............ 7,850.00– 8,890.00
**MIRAGE SPECIAL** 12 ga. w/adj. trigger, 28⅜″, 29½″, 31½″ barrels ............ 8,320.00
**MIRAGE SPECIAL SPORTING** 12 ga. w/external selector and 5 chokes; 27½″, 28⅜″, 29½″ and 31½″ barrels ............ 8,890.00

**MIRAGE SPORTING CLASSIC** 12 ga. ........ $9,900.00
**MX8 SPECIAL** 12 ga. w/adjustable trigger 29½″ and 31½″ barrels ............ 8,550.00
**DB81 SPECIAL** w/adjustable trigger 29½″, 30¾″ and 31½″ barrels ............ 8,550.00

*NOTE:* **PIGEON & ELECTROCIBLE MODELS** available in MX1B, Mirage, Mirage Special, MX10 & MX11 only w/27½″, 28¾″, 29½″ & 31½″ barrels ............ $ 7,400.00–$10,300.00

Also available:
**SC3 Grade** (Models MX8, MX10, MX10/20, MX8/20, MX8 Special, Mirage Spec., DB81 Spec.) ........ $13,000.00–$15,600.00
**SCO Grade** (same models as SC3 Grade) ............ 22,650.00– 24,650.00
**SCO GOLD Grade** (same models as above) ............ 25,550.00– 27,450.00
**SCO Grade Sideplates** (same models as above) ............ 34,750.00– 35,790.00
**SCO GOLD Grade Sideplates** (same models above) ............ 40,350.00– 41,390.00

# PIOTTI SHOTGUNS

One of Italy's top gunmakers, Piotti limits its production to a small number of hand-crafted, best-quality double-barreled shotguns whose shaping, checkering, stock, action and barrel work meets or exceeds the standards achieved in London before WWII. All of the sidelock models exhibit the same overall design, materials and standards of workmanship; they differ only in the quality of the wood, shaping and sculpturing of the action, type of engraving and gold inlay work and other details. The Model Piuma differs from the other shotguns only in its Anson & Deeley boxlock design. Piotti's new over/under model appears below.

**SPECIFICATIONS**
**Gauges:** 10, 12, 16, 20, 28, .410
**Chokes:** As ordered
**Barrels:** 12 ga., 25″ to 32″; other gauges, 25″ to 30″; chopper lump (demi-bloc) barrels with soft-luster blued finish; level, file-cut rib or optional concave
**Action:** Boxlock, Anson & Deeley; Sidelock, Holland & Holland pattern; both have automatic ejectors, double triggers with yielding front trigger (non-selective single trigger optional), coin finish or optional color casehardening
**Stock:** Hand-rubbed oil finish on straight grip stock with checkered butt (pistol grip optional)
**Forend:** Classic (splinter); optional beavertail
**Weight:** 5 lbs. 4 oz. (.410 ga.) to 8 lbs. 4 oz. (12 ga.)

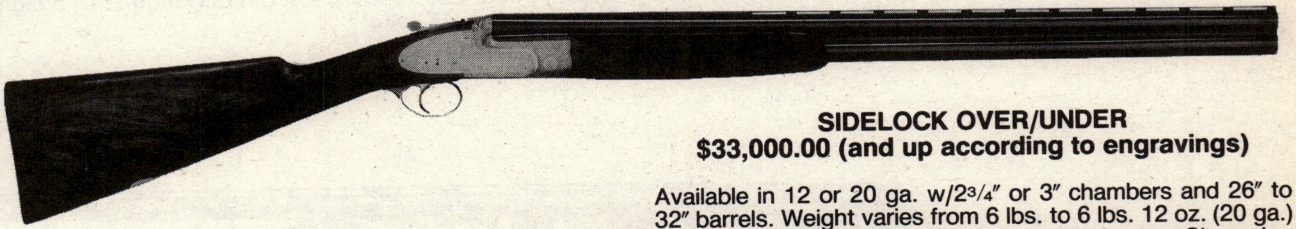

**SIDELOCK OVER/UNDER**
**$33,000.00 (and up according to engravings)**

Available in 12 or 20 ga. w/$2\frac{3}{4}$″ or 3″ chambers and 26″ to 32″ barrels. Weight varies from 6 lbs. to 6 lbs. 12 oz. (20 ga.) and 7–8 lbs. (12 ga.). Single or double triggers. Circassion (Turkish) wood

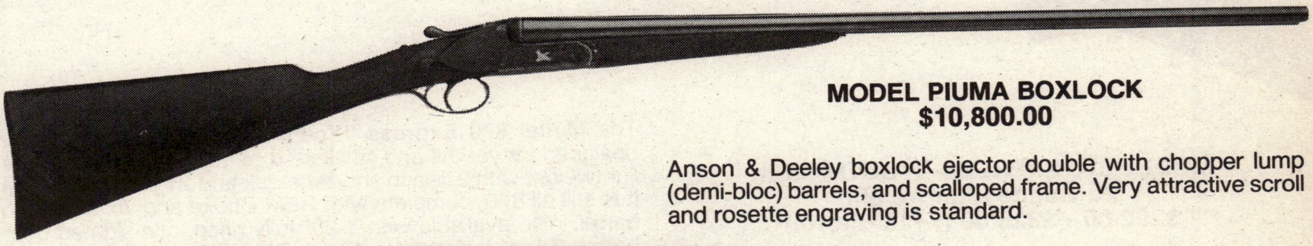

**MODEL PIUMA BOXLOCK**
**$10,800.00**

Anson & Deeley boxlock ejector double with chopper lump (demi-bloc) barrels, and scalloped frame. Very attractive scroll and rosette engraving is standard.

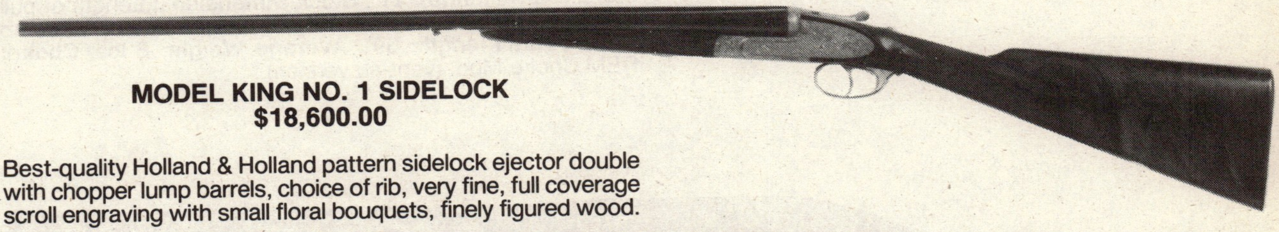

**MODEL KING NO. 1 SIDELOCK**
**$18,600.00**

Best-quality Holland & Holland pattern sidelock ejector double with chopper lump barrels, choice of rib, very fine, full coverage scroll engraving with small floral bouquets, finely figured wood.

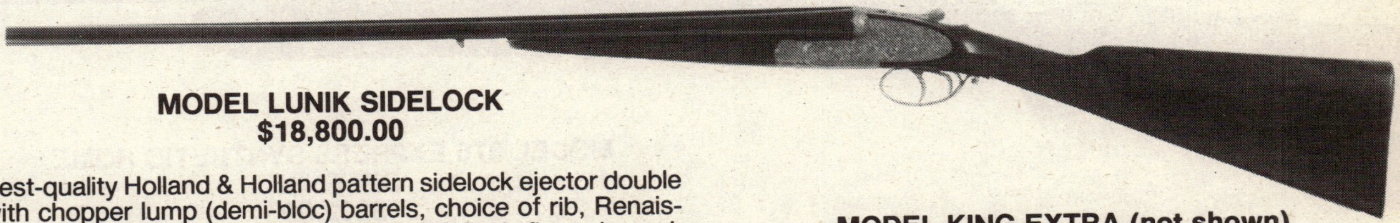

**MODEL LUNIK SIDELOCK**
**$18,800.00**

Best-quality Holland & Holland pattern sidelock ejector double with chopper lump (demi-bloc) barrels, choice of rib, Renaissance-style, large scroll engraving in relief, finely figured wood.

**MODEL KING EXTRA (not shown)**
**$26,500.00 (With Gold)**

Best-quality Holland & Holland pattern sidelock ejector double with chopper lump barrels, choice of rib and bulino game-scene engraving or game-scene engraving with gold inlays; engraved and signed by a master engraver.

# REMINGTON SHOTGUNS

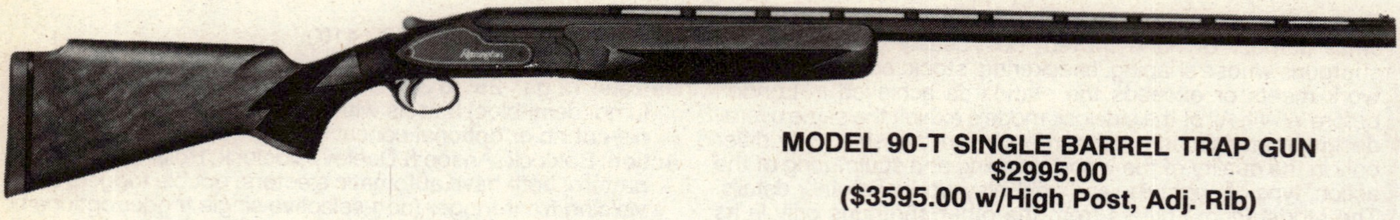

**MODEL 90-T SINGLE BARREL TRAP GUN**
**$2995.00**
**($3595.00 w/High Post, Adj. Rib)**

Remington's **Model 90-T Single Barrel Trap** features a top-lever release and internal, full-width, horizontal bolt lockup. Barrel is overbored, with elongated forcing cone, and is available in 34″ length. A medium-high, tapered, ventilated rib includes a white, Bradley-type front bead and stainless steel center bead. Choice of stocks includes Monte Carlo style with 1³/₈″, 1¹/₂″ or 1¹/₄″ drop at comb, or a conventional straight stock with 1¹/₂″ drop. Standard length of pull is 14³/₈″. Stocks and modified beavertail forends are made from semifancy American walnut. Wood finish is low-luster satin with positive, deep-cut checkering 20 lines to the inch. All stocks come with black, vented-rubber recoil pads. **Overall length:** 51″. **Weight:** Approx. 8³/₄ lbs. **Choke:** Full.

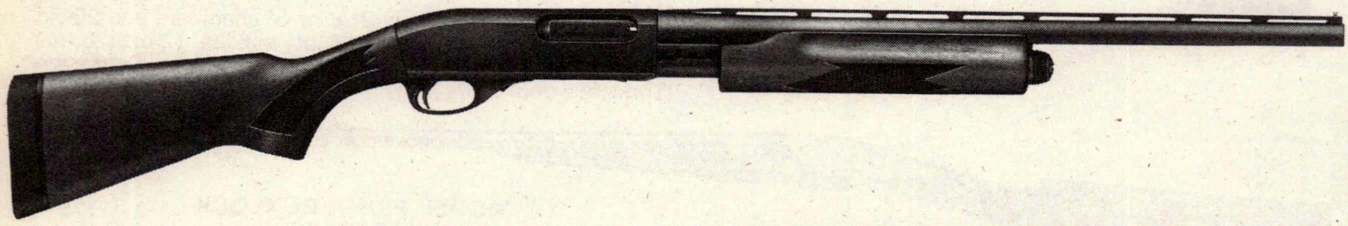

**MODEL 870 EXPRESS "YOUTH" GUN**
**20-Gauge Lightweight**
**$292.00 $325.00 (w/19″ Barrel)**

The **Model 870 Express "Youth" Gun** has been specially designed for youths and smaller-sized adults. It's a 20-gauge lightweight with a 1-inch shorter stock and 21-inch barrel. Yet it is still all 870, complete with REM Choke and ventilated rib barrel. Also available with a 20″ fully rifled, rifle-sighted deer barrel. **Barrel length:** 21″. **Stock Dimensions:** Length of pull 12¹/₂″ (including recoil pad); drop at heel; 2¹/₂″ drop at comb 1⁵/₈″. **Overall length:** 39″. **Average Weight:** 6 lbs. **Choke:** REM Choke-Mod. (vent-rib version).

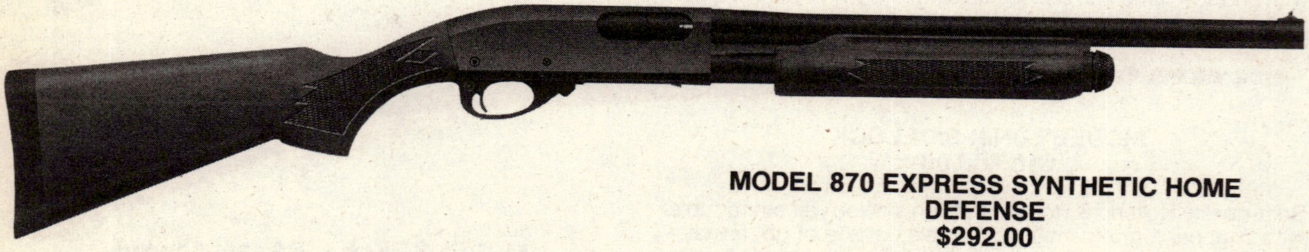

**MODEL 870 EXPRESS SYNTHETIC HOME DEFENSE**
**$292.00**

This new shotgun is designed specifically for home defense use. The 12-gauge pump-action shotgun features an 18″ barrel with Cylinder choke and front bead sight. Barrel and action have the traditional Express-style metal finish. The synthetic stock and forend have a textured black, nonreflective finish and feature positive checkering. **Capacity:** 4 rounds.

# REMINGTON PUMP SHOTGUNS

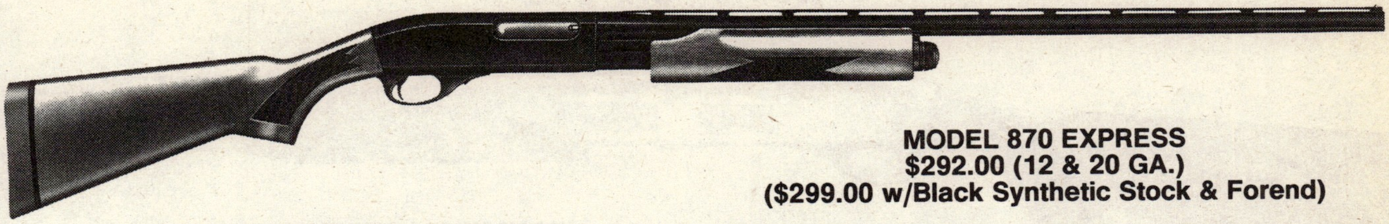

**MODEL 870 EXPRESS**
**$292.00 (12 & 20 GA.)**
**($299.00 w/Black Synthetic Stock & Forend)**

**MODEL 870 EXPRESS (20 GA.)**

**Model 870 Express** features the same action as the Wingmaster and is available with 3″ chamber and 26″ or 28″ vent-rib barrel. It has a hardwood stock with low-luster finish and solid buttpad. Choke is Modified REM Choke tube and wrench. **Overall length:** 48 1/2″ (28″ barrel). **Weight:** 7 1/4 lbs (26″ barrel).

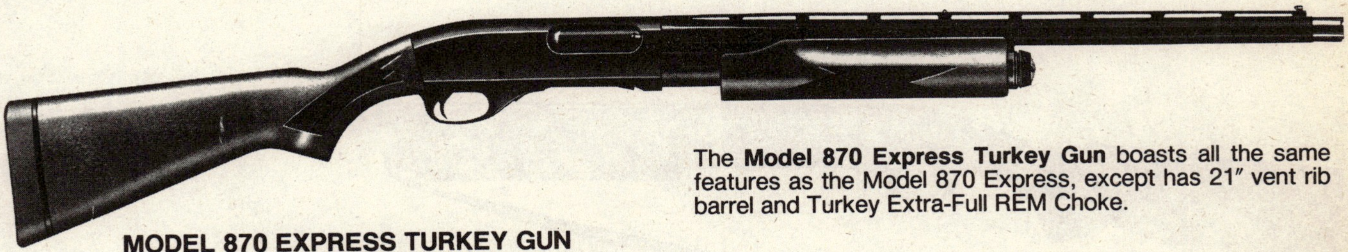

The **Model 870 Express Turkey Gun** boasts all the same features as the Model 870 Express, except has 21″ vent rib barrel and Turkey Extra-Full REM Choke.

**MODEL 870 EXPRESS TURKEY GUN**
**$305.00**

**MODEL 870 EXPRESS DEER GUN**
**$287.00 With Rifle Sights**
**($325.00 Fully Rifled)**

This 12-gauge, pump-action deer gun is for hunters who prefer open sights. Features a 20″ barrel, quick-reading iron sights, fixed Imp. Cyl. choke and Monte Carlo stock. Also available with fully rifled barrel.

**MODEL 870 EXPRESS COMBO (not shown)**
**$395.00**

The **Model 870 Express** in 12 and 20 gauge offers all the features of the standard Model 870, including twin-action bars, quick-changing 28″ barrels, REM Choke and vent rib plus low-luster, checkered hardwood stock and no-shine finish on barrel and receiver. The Model 870 Combo is packaged with an extra 20″ deer barrel, fitted with rifle sights and fixed, Improved Cylinder choke (additional REM chokes can be added for special applications). The 3-inch chamber handles all 2 3/4″ and 3″ shells without adjustment. **Weight:** 7 1/2 lbs.

SHOTGUNS

# REMINGTON PUMP SHOTGUNS

## SPECIAL PURPOSE

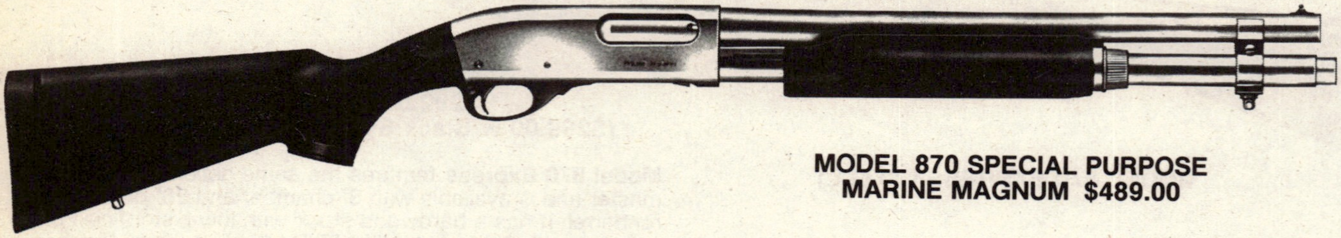

**MODEL 870 SPECIAL PURPOSE MARINE MAGNUM $489.00**

Remington's **Model 870 Special Purpose Marine Magnum** is a versatile, multipurpose security gun featuring a rugged synthetic stock and extensive, electroless nickel plating on all metal parts. This new shotgun utilizes a standard 12-gauge Model 870 receiver with a 7-round magazine extension tube and an 18″ cylinder barrel (38½″ overall) with bead front sight. The receiver, magazine extension and barrel are protected (inside and out) with heavy-duty, corrosion-resistant nickel plating. The synthetic stock and forend reduce the effects of moisture. The gun is supplied with a black rubber recoil pad, sling swivel studs, and positive checkering on both pistol grip and forend. **Weight:** 7½ lbs.

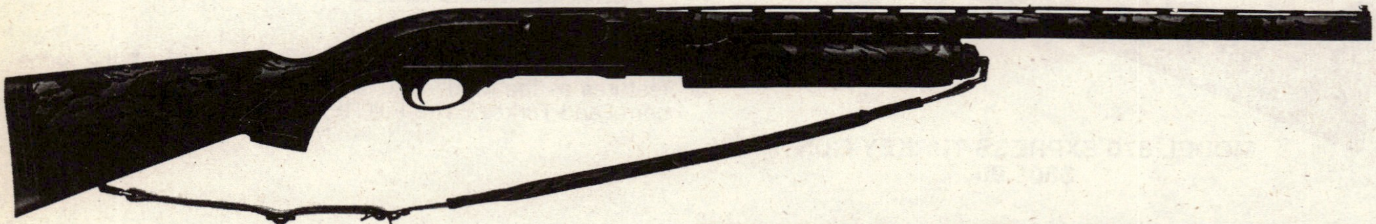

**MODEL 870 SPS-CAMO $465.00**

This Mossy Oak Bottomland™ Camo version of Model 11-87 and Model 870 Special Purpose Synthetic shotguns features a durable camo finish and synthetic stocks that are immune to the effects of ice, snow and mud. Available with a 26″ vent-rib barrel with twin bead sights and Imp. Cyl., Modified, and Full REM Choke tubes.

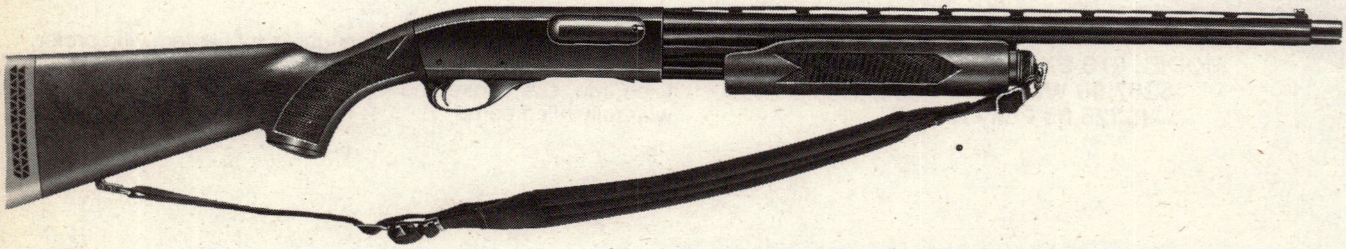

**MODEL 870 SPST ALL BLACK TURKEY GUN $399.00**

Same as the Model 870 SPS above, except with a 21″ vent-rib turkey barrel and Extra-Full REM Choke tube.
Also available:

| | |
|---|---|
| Mossy Oak Greenleaf Camo finish | **$479.00** |
| 20″ fully rifled cantilever deer barrel | |
| (All Black) | **467.00** |
| With Rem Choke | **425.00** |
| 20″ fully rifled deer barrel, rifle sights | **407.00** |

# REMINGTON PUMP SHOTGUNS

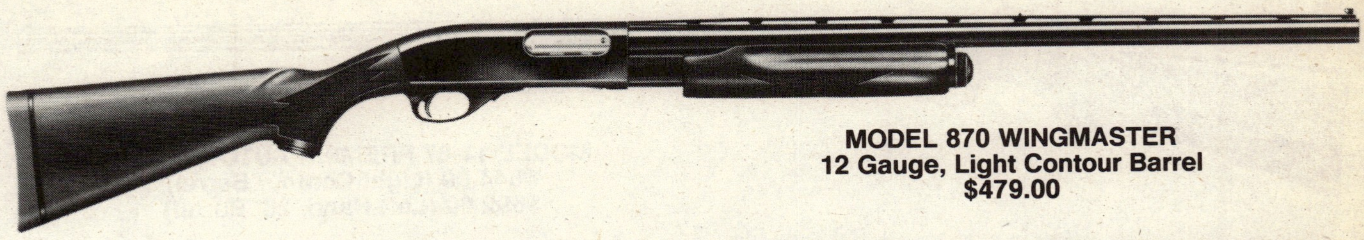

**MODEL 870 WINGMASTER**
**12 Gauge, Light Contour Barrel**
**$479.00**

This restyled **870 "Wingmaster"** pump has cut-checkering on its satin-finished American walnut stock and forend for confident handling, even in wet weather. Also available in Hi-Gloss finish. An ivory bead "Bradley"-type front sight is included. Rifle is available with 26", 28" and 30" barrel with REM Choke and handles 3" and 2¾" shells interchangeably. **Overall length:** 46½ (26" barrel), 48½" (28" barrel), 50½ (30" barrel). **Weight:** 7¼ lbs. (w/26" barrel).
Also available:
**MODEL 870 WINGMASTER.** 20 Ga. Lightweight (6½ lbs.), American walnut stock and forend. **Price:** ....... **$473.00**

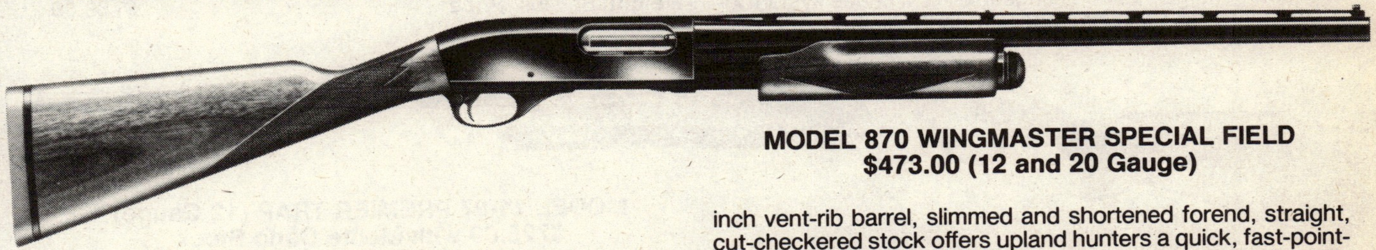

**MODEL 870 WINGMASTER SPECIAL FIELD**
**$473.00 (12 and 20 Gauge)**

The **Model 870 Wingmaster "Special Field"** shotgun combines the traditional, straight-stock styling of years past with features never before available on a Remington pump. Its 23-inch vent-rib barrel, slimmed and shortened forend, straight, cut-checkered stock offers upland hunters a quick, fast-pointing shotgun. The "Special Field" is chambered for 3-inch shells and will also handle all 2¾-inch shells interchangeably. Barrels will not interchange with standard 870 barrels. **Overall length:** 41½". **Weight:** 7 lbs. (12 ga.); 6¼ lbs. (20 ga.).

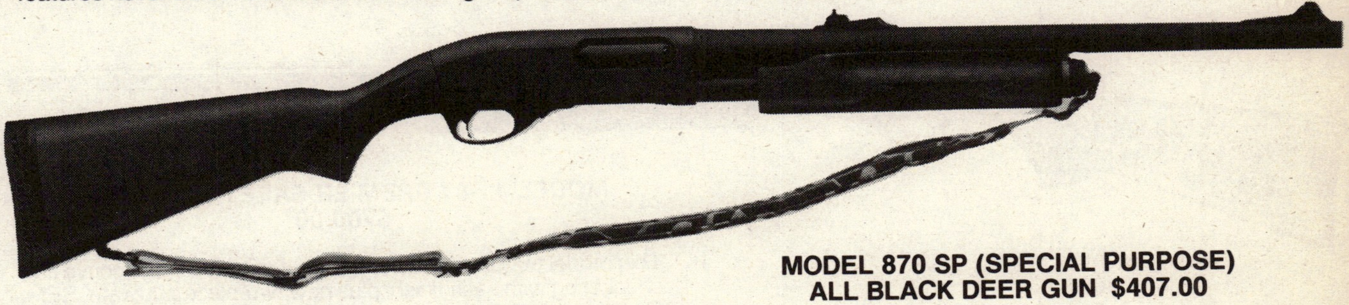

**MODEL 870 SP (SPECIAL PURPOSE)**
**ALL BLACK DEER GUN $407.00**

**Gauge:** 12. **Choke:** Fully rifled with rifle sights, recoil pad. **Barrel length:** 20". **Overall length:** 40½." **Average weight:** 7 lbs.

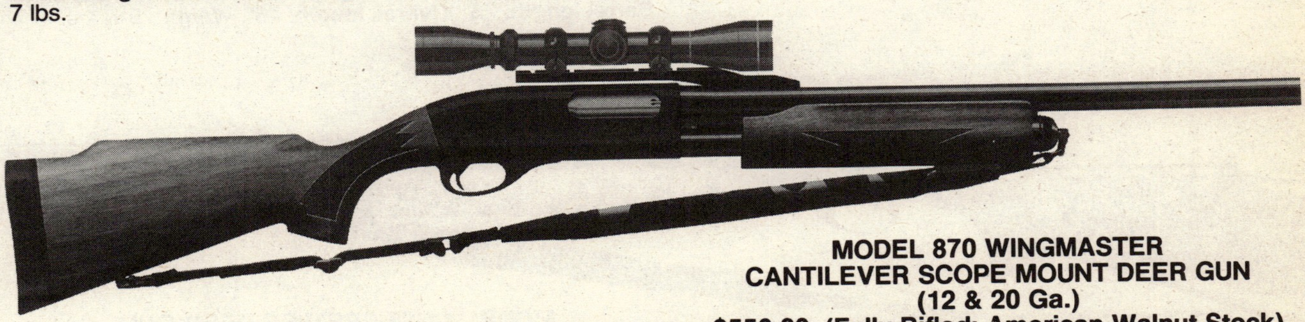

**MODEL 870 WINGMASTER**
**CANTILEVER SCOPE MOUNT DEER GUN**
**(12 & 20 Ga.)**
**$556.00 (Fully Rifled; American Walnut Stock)**

Also available: 28 ga. and .410 **Model 870 Wingmaster** models w/25" barrels (45½" overall), Full or Modified. **Weight:** 6 lbs. (6½ lbs. in .410). **Price:** ...................... **$504.00**

# REMINGTON AUTO SHOTGUNS

**MODEL 11-87 PREMIER AUTOLOADER**
**\$644.00 (Light Contour Barrel)**
**\$692.00 (Left Hand, 28″ Barrel)**

Remington's redesigned 12-gauge **Model 11-87 Premier Autoloader** features new, light-contour barrels that reduce both barrel weight and overall weight (more than 8 ounces). The shotgun has a standard 3-inch chamber and handles all 12-gauge shells interchangeably—from 2¾″ field loads to 3″ Magnums. The gun's interchangeable REM choke system includes Improved Cylinder, Modified and Full chokes. Select American walnut stocks with fine-line, cut-checkering in satin or high-gloss finish are standard. Right-hand models are available in 26″, 28″ and 30″ barrels (left-hand models are 28″ only). A two-barrel gun case is supplied.
Also available: 21″ fully rifled cantilever deer barrel (41″ overall).
**Weight:** 8½ lbs. **Price:** . . . . . . . . . . . . . . . . . . . . . . **\$706.00**

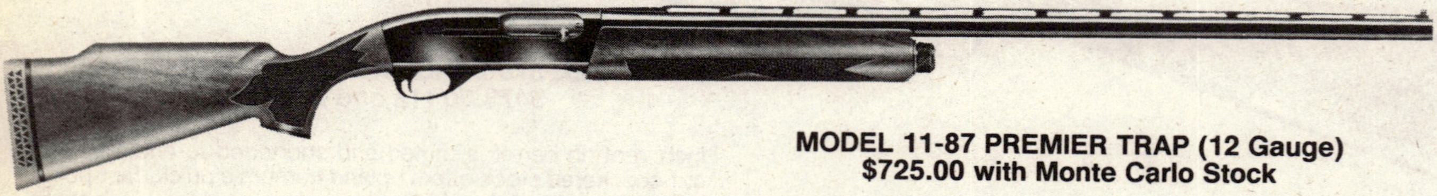

**MODEL 11-87 PREMIER TRAP (12 Gauge)**
**\$725.00 with Monte Carlo Stock**

A 30″ trap barrel (50½″ overall) offers trap shooters a REM Choke system with three interchangeable choke constrictions: trap full, trap extra full, and trap super full. **Weight:** 8¾ lbs.

**MODEL 11-87 PREMIER SKEET (12 Gauge)**
**\$700.00**

This model features American walnut wood and distinctive cut checkering with satin finish, plus new two-piece buttplate. REM Choke system includes option of two skeet chokes—skeet and improved skeet. Trap and skeet guns are designed for 12-gauge target loads and are set to handle 2¾″ shells only. **Barrel length:** 26″. **Overall length:** 46″. **Weight:** 8⅛ lbs.

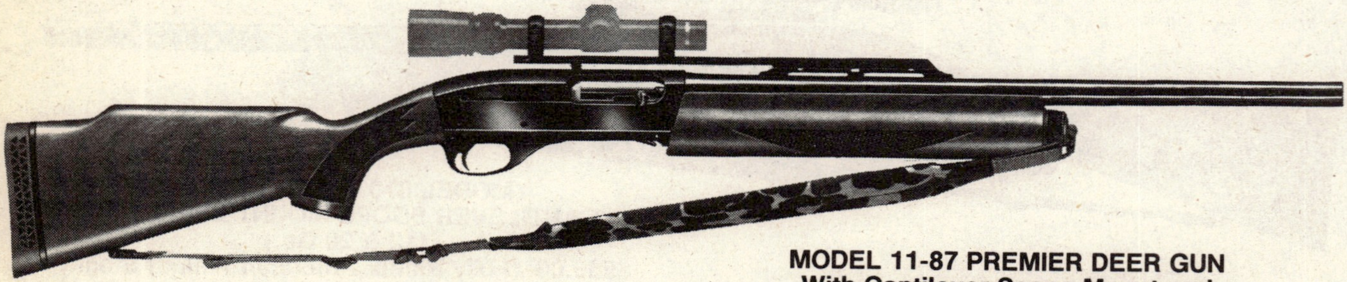

**MODEL 11-87 PREMIER DEER GUN**
**With Cantilever Scope Mount and**
**Fully Rifled 21″ Barrel**
**\$706.00 (Satin Finish)**

# REMINGTON AUTO SHOTGUNS

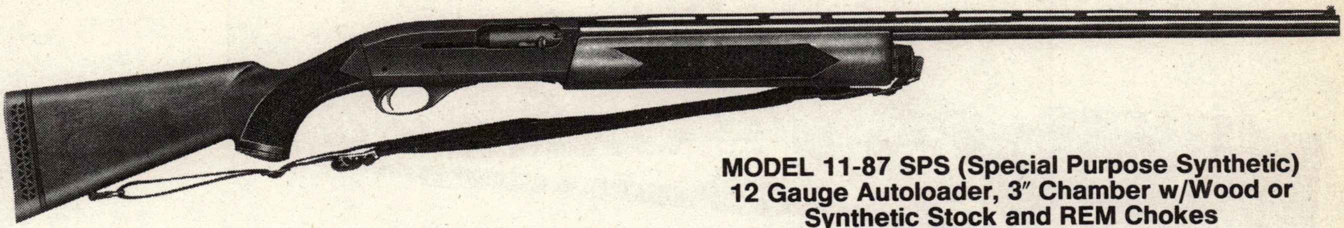

**MODEL 11-87 SPS (Special Purpose Synthetic)**
**12 Gauge Autoloader, 3″ Chamber w/Wood or Synthetic Stock and REM Chokes**
**26″ or 28″ Vent Rib Barrels**
**$625.00**

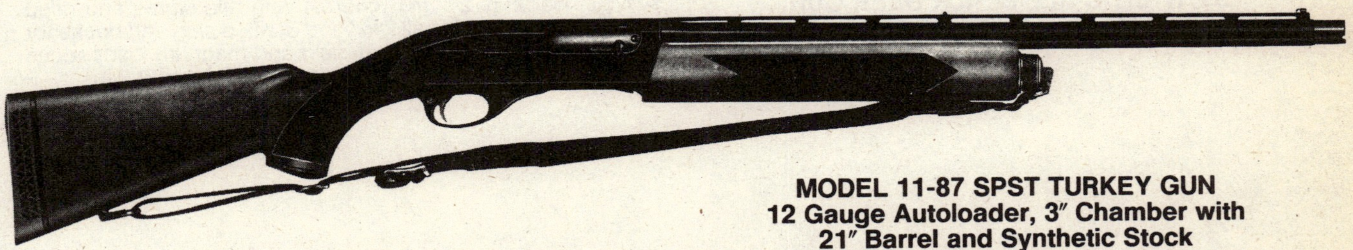

**MODEL 11-87 SPST TURKEY GUN**
**12 Gauge Autoloader, 3″ Chamber with 21″ Barrel and Synthetic Stock**
**Extra-Full REM Choke Turkey Tube**
**$639.00**
**$718.00 w/Mossy Oak Greenleaf Camo Finish**

**MODEL 11-87 SPS-CAMO**
**12 Gauge Autoloader, 3″ Chamber (26″ or 28″ barrel) with REM Chokes and Synthetic Stock In Mossy Oak Bottomland™ Camo**
**$705.00**

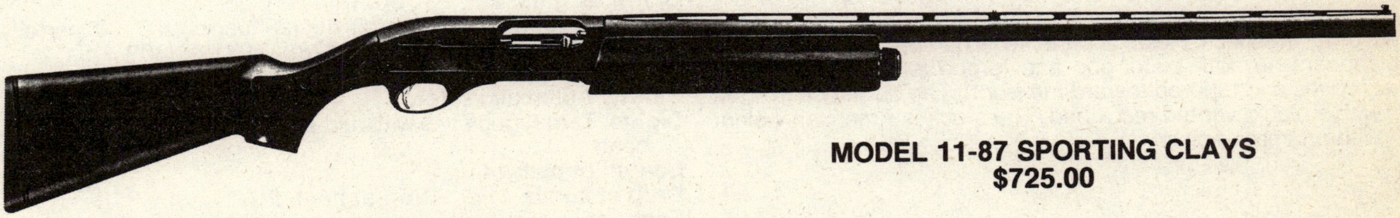

**MODEL 11-87 SPORTING CLAYS**
**$725.00**

Remington's new **Model 11-87 Premier Sporting Clays** features a target-grade, American walnut competition stock with a length of pull that is 3/16″ longer and 1/4″ higher at the heel. The tops of the receiver, barrel and rib have a nonreflective matte finish. The rib is medium high with a stainless mid-bead and ivory front bead. The barrel (26″ or 28″) has a lengthened forcing cone to generate greater pattern uniformity; and there are 5 REM choke tubes—Skeet, Improved Skeet, Improved Cylinder, Modified and Full. All sporting clays choke tubes have a knurled end extending .45″ beyond the muzzle for fast field changes. Both the toe and heel of the buttpad are rounded. **Weight:** 7 1/2 lbs. (26″); 7 5/8 lbs. (28″)

SHOTGUNS

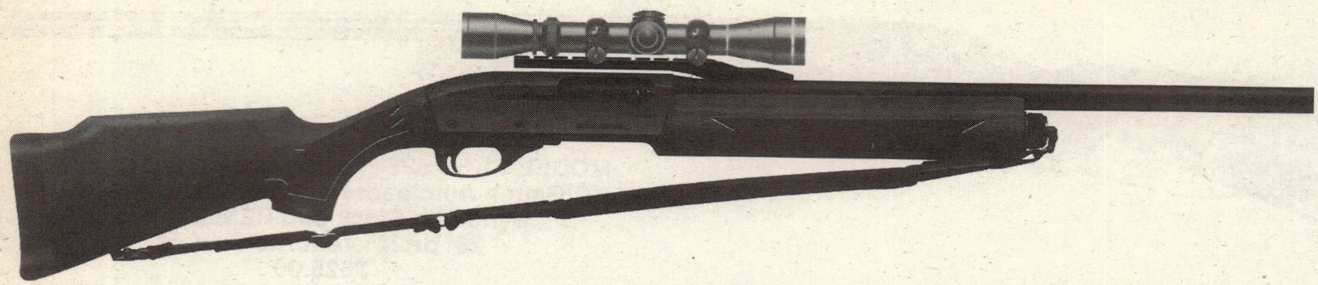

**MODEL 11-87 SPS SPECIAL PURPOSE SYNTHETIC ALL-BLACK DEER GUN**
**$625.00 (3″ Magnum) $647.00 (Fully Rifled)**

Features the same finish as other SP models plus a padded, camo-style carrying sling of Cordura nylon with Q.D. sling swivels. Barrel is 21″ (41″ overall) with rifle sights and rifled and IC choke (handles all 2 3/4″ and 3″ rifled slug and buckshot loads as well as high-velocity field and magnum loads; does not function with light 2 3/4″ field loads). **Weight:** 8 1/2 lbs.

**PEERLESS OVER/UNDER**
**with Vent Rib and Engraved Sideplates**

**PEERLESS OVER/UNDER SHOTGUN**
**$1225.00**

Practical, lightweight, well-balanced and affordable are the attributes of this Remington shotgun. Features include an all-steel receiver, boxlock action and removable sideplates (engraved with a pointer on one side and a setter on the other). The bottom of the receiver has the Remington logo, plus the words "Peerless, Field" and the serial number. Cut-checkering appears on both pistol grip and forend (shaped with finger grooves and tapered toward the front). The buttstock is fitted with a black, vented recoil pad. The stock is American walnut with an Imron finish.

**SPECIFICATIONS**
**Gauge:** 12 (3″ chamber)
**Chokes:** REM Choke System (1 Full, 1 Mod., 1 Imp. Cyl.)
**Barrel lengths:** 26″, 28″, 30″ with vent rib
**Overall length:** 43″ (26″ barrel); 45″ (28″ barrel); 47″ (30″ barrel)
**Weight:** 7 1/4 lbs. (26″); 7 3/8 lbs. (28″); 7 1/2 lbs. (30″)
**Trigger:** Single, selective, gold-plated
**Safety:** Automatic safety
**Sights:** Target gun style with mid-bead and Bradley-type front bead
**Length of pull:** 14 3/16″
**Drop at comb:** 1 1/2″ **Drop at heel:** 2 1/4″
**Features:** Solid, horseshoe-shaped locking bar with two rectangular lug extensions on either side of the barrel's mid-bore; fast lock time (3.28 milliseconds)

# REMINGTON AUTO SHOTGUNS

## MODEL 1100 AUTOLOADING SHOTGUNS

The Remington **Model 1100** is a 5-shot gas-operated autoloading shotgun with a gas-metering system designed to reduce recoil effect. This design enables the shooter to use all 2$\frac{3}{4}$-inch standard velocity "Express" and 2$\frac{3}{4}$-inch Magnum loads without any gun adjustments. Barrels, within gauge and versions, are interchangeable. The 1100 is made in gauges of 12, Lightweight 20, 28 and .410. All 12- and 20-gauge versions include REM Choke; interchangeable choke tubes in 26″ and 28″ (12 gauge only) barrels. The solid-steel receiver features decorative scroll work. Stocks come with fine-line checkering in a fleur-de-lis design combined with American walnut and a scratch-resistant finish. Features include white-diamond inlay in pistol-grip cap, white-line spacers, full beavertail forend, fluted-comb cuts, chrome-plated bolt and metal bead front sight. Made in the U.S.A.

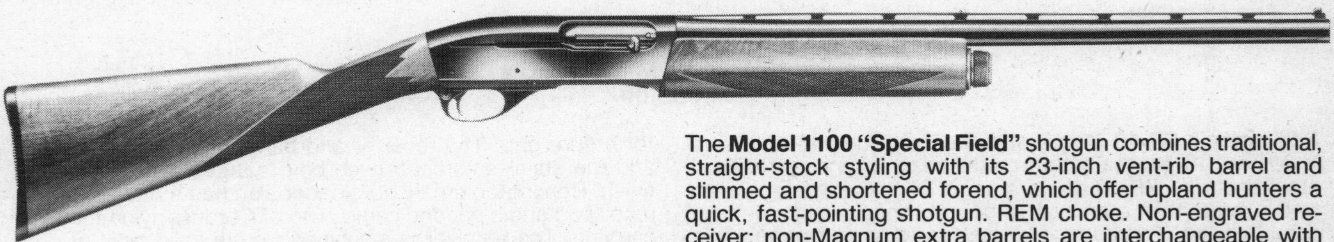

**MODEL 1100 SPECIAL FIELD (12 & 20 GA.)**
**$605.00**

The **Model 1100 "Special Field"** shotgun combines traditional, straight-stock styling with its 23-inch vent-rib barrel and slimmed and shortened forend, which offer upland hunters a quick, fast-pointing shotgun. REM choke. Non-engraved receiver; non-Magnum extra barrels are interchangeable with standard Model 1100 barrels. **Overall length:** 41″. **Stock dimensions:** Length of pull 14$\frac{1}{8}$″; drop at comb 1$\frac{1}{2}$″; drop at heel 2$\frac{1}{2}$″. **Weight:** 7$\frac{1}{4}$ lbs. (12 ga.); 6$\frac{1}{2}$ lbs. (20 ga.).

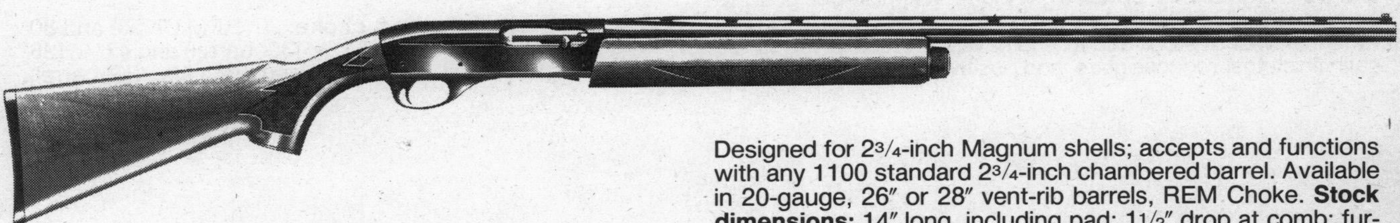

**MODEL 1100 LT-20**
**$605.00**

Designed for 2$\frac{3}{4}$-inch Magnum shells; accepts and functions with any 1100 standard 2$\frac{3}{4}$-inch chambered barrel. Available in 20-gauge, 26″ or 28″ vent-rib barrels, REM Choke. **Stock dimensions:** 14″ long, including pad; 1$\frac{1}{2}$″ drop at comb; furnished w/recoil pad. Satin or Hi-Gloss finish. **Weight:** About 7 lbs.

Also available: 3″ Magnum (28″ and satin finish only).

**MODEL 1100 DEER GUN**
**Lightweight 20 Gauge**
**$565.00**

Features 21-inch barrels with Improved Cylinder choke (choked for both rifled slugs and buck shot). Includes rifle sights, adjustable for windage and elevation, and recoil pad. **Weight:** 6$\frac{1}{2}$ lbs. **Overall length:** 41″.

Also available with fully rifled cantilever 21″ deer barrel. **Price: $682.00**

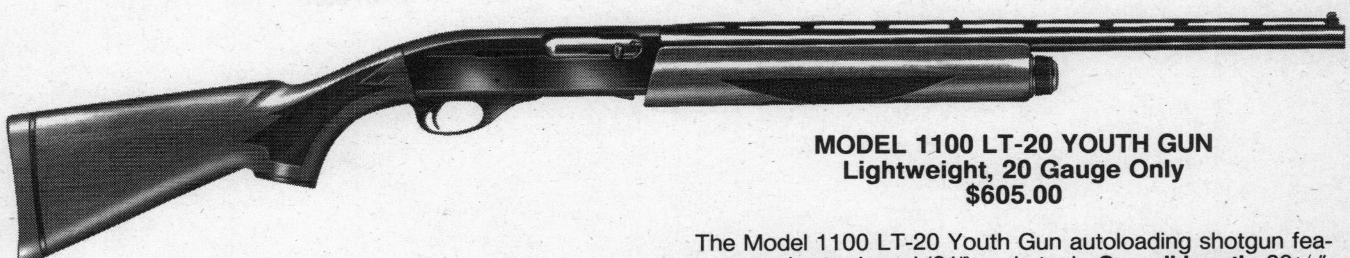

**MODEL 1100 LT-20 YOUTH GUN**
**Lightweight, 20 Gauge Only**
**$605.00**

The Model 1100 LT-20 Youth Gun autoloading shotgun features a shorter barrel (21″) and stock. **Overall length:** 39$\frac{1}{2}$″. **Weight:** 6$\frac{1}{2}$ lbs.

# REMINGTON AUTO SHOTGUNS

SP-10 MAGNUM SHOTGUN

**SP-10 MAGNUM SHOTGUN**
**$993.00**

Remington's **SP-10 Magnum** is the only gas-operated semiautomatic 10-gauge shotgun made today. Engineered to shoot steel shot, the SP-10 delivers up to 34 percent more pellets to the target than standard 12-gauge shotgun and steel shot combinations. This autoloader features a noncorrosive, stainless-steel gas system, in which the cylinder moves—not the piston. This reduces felt recoil energy by spreading the recoil over a longer time. The SP-10 has a 3/8″ vent rib with middle and front sights for a better sight plane. It is also designed to appear virtually invisible to the sharp eyes of waterfowl. The American walnut stock and forend have a protective, low-gloss satin finish that reduces glare, and positive deep-cut checkering for a sure grip. The receiver and barrel have a matte finish, and the stainless-steel breech bolt features a non-reflective finish. Remington's new autoloader also has a brown-vented recoil pad and a padded camo sling of Cordura nylon for easy carrying. The receiver is machined from a solid billet of ordnance steel for total integral strength. The SP-10 vented gas system reduces powder residue buildup and makes cleaning easier.

**Gauge:** 10. **Barrel lengths & choke:** 26″ REM Choke and 30″ REM Choke. **Overall length:** 51 1/2″ (30″ barrel) and 47 1/2″ (26″ barrel). **Weight:** 11 lbs. (30″ barrel) and 10 3/4 lbs. (26″ barrel).

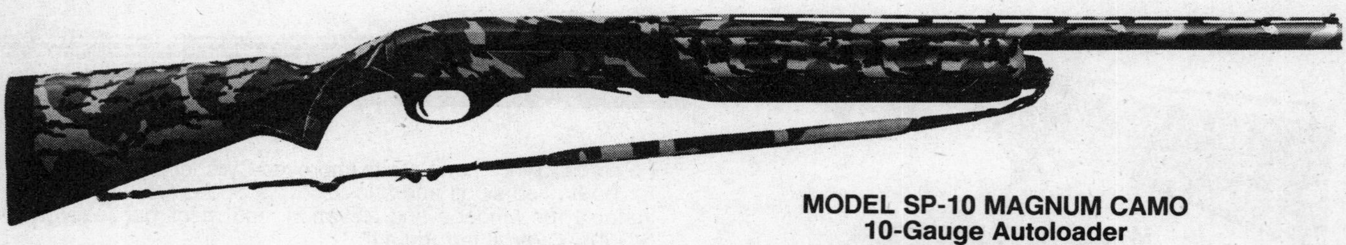

**MODEL SP-10 MAGNUM CAMO**
**10-Gauge Autoloader**
**with 23″ Vent-Rib Barrel**
**and Mossy Oak Bottomland Camo Pattern**
**$1078.00**

# RIZZINI SHOTGUNS

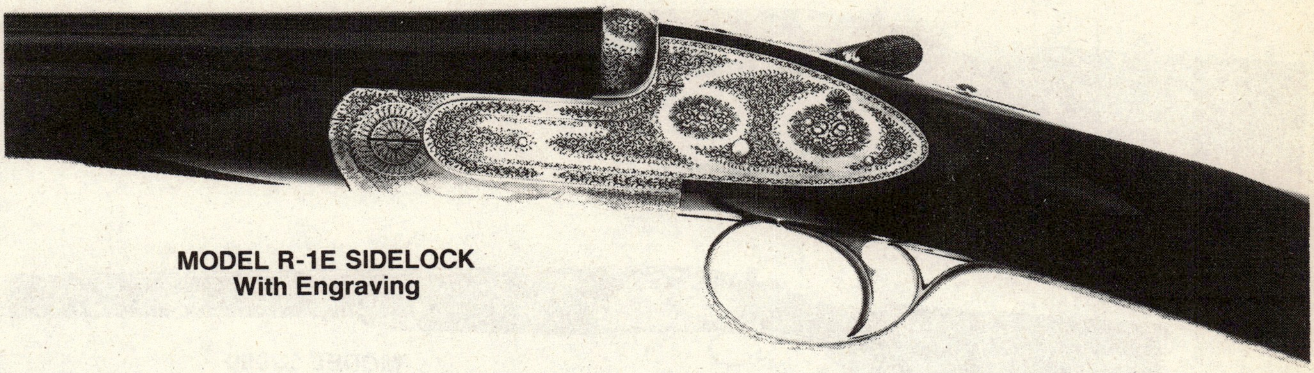

**MODEL R-1E SIDELOCK**
**With Engraving**

## MODEL R-1 and R-2 SHOTGUNS

Rizzini offers the **R-1,** a sidelock ejector, and **R-2,** an Anson & Deeley boxlock with a removable inspection plate on the bottom of the action. The basic price of these Rizzini shotguns includes the choice of single or double triggers and a fitted leather trunk case (but not the cost of engraving). A wide variety of ornamental and game scene engravings are available.

Multi-gauge two-barrel sets (supplied with a single forearm) are available in .410/28 ga., 28/20 ga. or 20/16 ga. The actions and locks are carefully shaped and polished. The stock finish is hand-rubbed oil applied after the stock is filled and sealed. Options include stock ovals, hand-detachable locks, rib type, barrel length, weight of gun, and more.

**SPECIFICATIONS**
**Gauges:** 12, 16, 20, 28, .410
**Barrel lengths:** 25″ to 28″ (28 ga. and .410); 25″ to 30″ (12, 16 and 20 ga.)
**Top ribs:** Straight matted concave ribs are standard; swamped smooth concave and level file cut ribs are optional
**Action:** Anson & Deeley boxlock with inspection plate (Model R-2 only); Holland & Holland-type sidelock (Model R-1 only)
**Weight:** 4 lbs. 14 oz. to 6 lbs. (28 and .410); 5 1/2 lbs. to 6 lbs. 12 oz. (20 ga.); 5 lbs. 12 oz. to 7 lbs. (16 ga.); 6 lbs. 4 oz. to 8 lbs. 4 oz. (12 ga.)
**Stock & Forearm:** High-luster hand-rubbed oil finish; straight-grip stock with checkered butt; classic forearm; pistol-grip stock and beavertail forearm optional
**Trigger:** Non-selective trigger (double trigger with front trigger hinged optional)
**Prices:**
**MODEL R-1** in 12, 16 or 20 ga.
(w/o engraving) . . . . . . . . . . **$38,800.00**
In 28 ga. or .410 (w/o engraving) . . . . . . . . . **43,800.00**
**MODEL R-2** in 12, 16 or 20 ga.
(w/o engraving) . . . . . . . . . . **23,000.00**
Engravings available:
Fine English scroll or ornamental with swans . . **8,500.00**
Fracassi-style ornamental . . . . . . . . . **18,800.00**

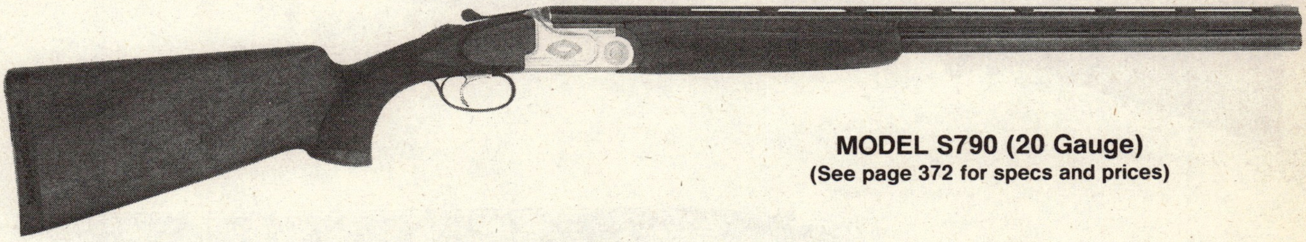

**MODEL S790 (20 Gauge)**
**(See page 372 for specs and prices)**

## MODEL 780 O/U SERIES

**MODEL S780N.** Double trigger, standard extractors. **Gauges:** 12 and 16. **Barrel length:** 27.3″. **Weight:** 6.4 lbs. **Features:** Schnabel forend. **Stock:** Standard walnut. **Price: $1650.00**
**MODEL S780 EM.** Single selective trigger, standard ejectors. **Gauges:** 12, 16, 20, 28, 36. **Barrel lengths:** 26″ and 27.3″. **Weight:** 6.25 lbs. (20, 28 and 36 ga.); 6.8 lbs. (12 and 16 ga.). **Price:** . . . . . . . . . . **$1300.00**
**MODEL 780 EML.** Same specifications as above, but in 12 and 16 ga. only. **Weight:** 6.8 lbs. **Price:** . . . . . . **$1450.00**
**MODEL S780 EMEL.** Same specifications as above, but with hand finishing and hand engraving. **Price:** . . . . **$7100.00**

## MODEL S782 SERIES

**MODEL S782.** Single selective trigger, ejectors, sideplates. **Gauges:** 12 and 16. **Barrel lengths:** 26″ and 27.3″. **Weight:** 6.9 lbs. **Price:** . . . . . . . . . . **$1550.00**
**MOODEL S782 EML.** Same specifications as above, but with select walnut stock. **Price:** . . . . . . . . . **$1900.00**
**MODEL S782 EM SLUG.** Same features as above except **Gauges:** 12 and 20. **Barrel lengths:** 24″ and 25.75″. **Weight:** 6.6 lbs. **Price:** . . . . . . . . . . **$3000.00**

# RIZZINI SHOTGUNS

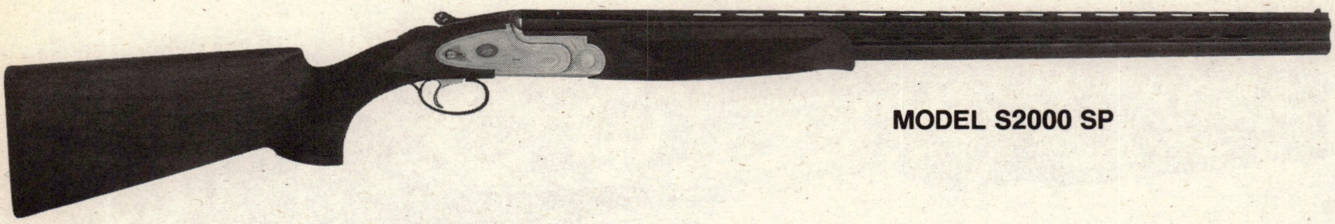

MODEL S2000 SP

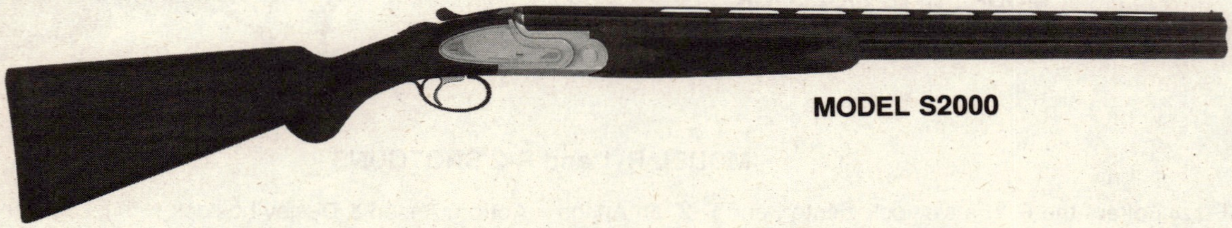

MODEL S2000

## TRAP, SKEET & SPORTING MODELS

**MODEL S780 SKEET. Gauge:** 12. **Barrel lengths:** 26.1″ and 27.3″. **Weight:** 7 lbs. Same features as Model S780 Series. **Price:** . . . . . . . . . . . . . . . . . . . . . . . . . . . . . . . . **$1450.00**

**MODEL S780 TRAP.** Stock is standard walnut. **Barrel length:** 29.25″. **Weight:** 7.8 lbs. **Price:** . . . . . . . . . . . . . . **$1450.00**

**MODEL S780 SPORTING.** Same features and specifications as Model S780N except **Gauge:** 12. **Weight:** 7.25 lbs. Features sporting-style forend. **Price:** . . . . . . . . . . **$1450.00**

**MODEL S790 SKEET SL.** Same specifications as above with select walnut stock. **Weight:** 7½ lbs. **Price:** . . **$2050.00**

**MODEL S790 TRAP SL.** Same features as above but with select walnut stock **Weight:** 7.9 lbs. **Price:** . . . **$2050.00**

**MODEL S790 SL.** Same as above, but with select walnut stock. **Weight:** 7.4 lbs. **Price:** . . . . . . . . . . . . . . . . . . . . . **$2050.00**

**MODEL S790 EL.** Same as above but with hand finishing and hand engraving. **Weight:** 8.15 lbs. Select walnut stock. **Price:** . . . . . . . . . . . . . . . . . . . . . . . . . . . . . . . . . . . . . **$5650.00**

**MODEL S2000 TRAP.** Same specifications as above, but with select walnut stock, sideplates, single trigger and automatic ejector. **Gauges:** 12 and 20. **Price:** . . . . . . . . . **$2100.00**

**MODEL S2000 SP.** Same specifications as above, but with select walnut stock, sideplates, single trigger, automatic ejector and double vent ribs. **Gauges:** 12 and 20.

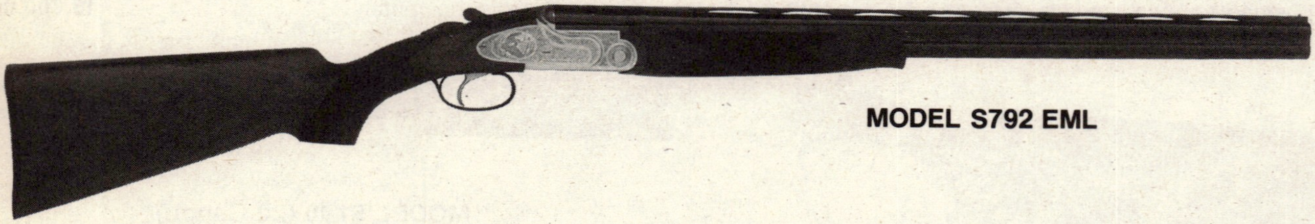

MODEL S792 EML

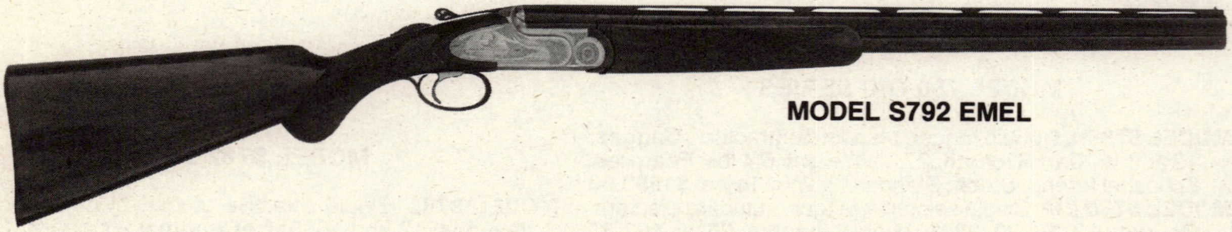

MODEL S792 EMEL

Also available:

**MODEL S792 EML.** Single selective trigger, ejectors, sideplates. **Gauges:** 20, 28, 36. Schnabel forend. **Weight:** 6 lbs. **Price:** . . . . . . . . . . . . . . . . . . . . . . . . . . . . . . . **$1800.00**

**MODEL S792 EMEL.** Same as above, except in 20 gauge only. **Weight:** 6.1 lbs. Hand finishing and hand engraving. **Price:** . . . . . . . . . . . . . . . . . . . . . . . . . . . . . . . . . . . . . . **$7600.00**

**MODEL S792 TRAP SL.** Same as other trap models, but in 20 gauge only. **Price:** . . . . . . . . . . . . . . . . . . . . . **$1900.00**

# ROTTWEIL SHOTGUNS

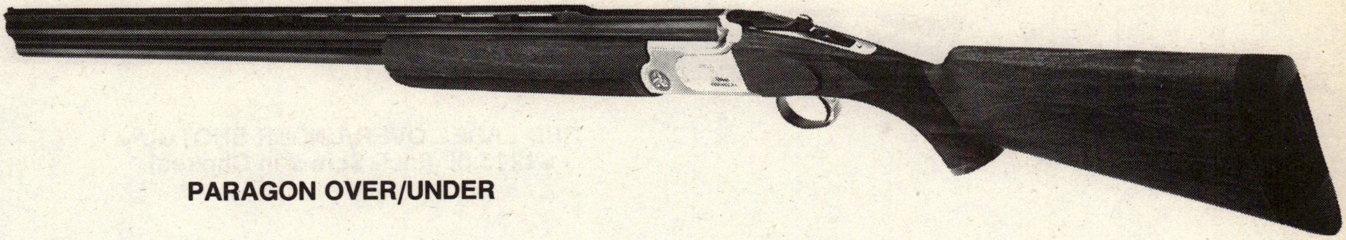

PARAGON OVER/UNDER

## ROTTWEIL PARAGON

This concept in shotgun systems, trap, skeet and sporting clays includes the following features: Detachable and interchangeable trigger action with superimposed hammers • Safety action on trigger and sears • Spring-loaded self-adjusting wedges • Ejector can be turned on and off at will • Top lever convertible for right- and left-handed shooters • Interchangeable firing pins (without disassembly) • Length and weight of barrels selected depending on application (see below) • Module system: Fully interchangeable receiver, barrels, stocks trigger action and forends • Select walnut stocks

**Barrel lengths:**

| | | | |
|---|---|---|---|
| Field & Skeet | 27½″ | Sporting | 28½″ |
| American Skeet | 28″ | Trap | 29″ & 30″ |
| Parcours | 28⅜″ | American Trap Single | 32″ & 34″ |

**Price:** . . . . . . . . . . **\$5,200.00** to **\$7,200.00**

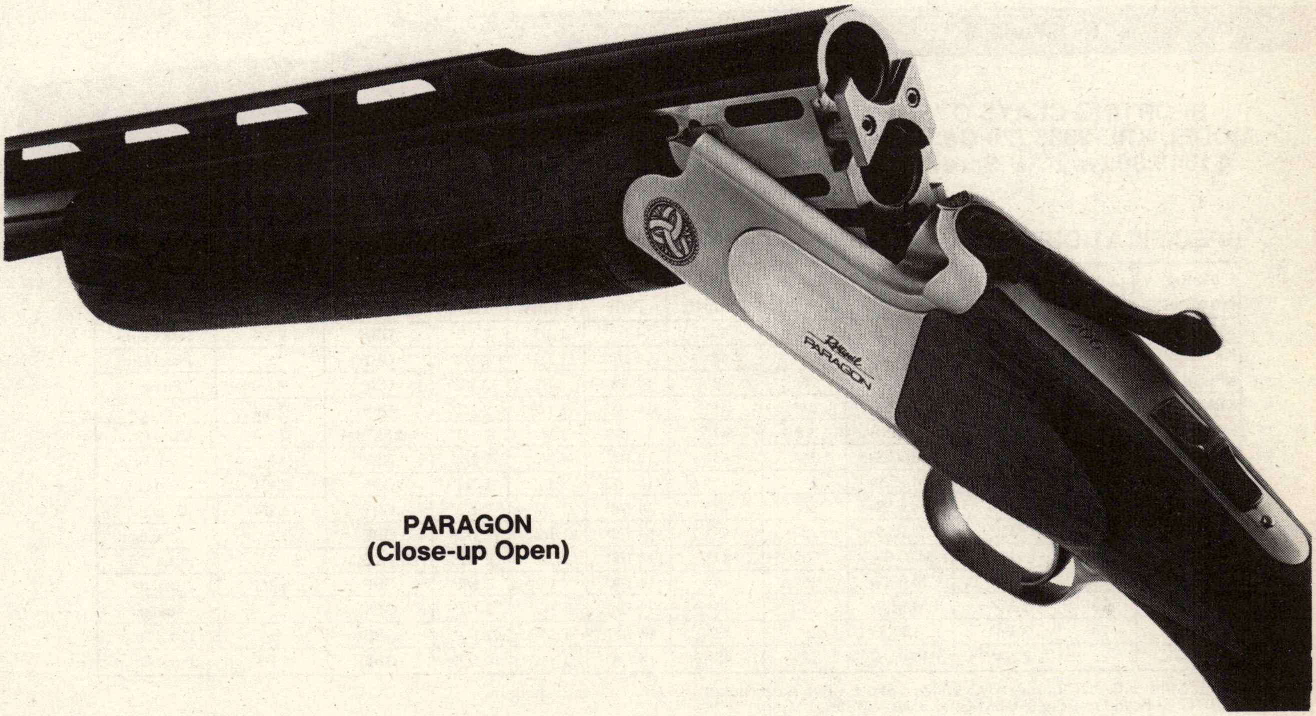


PARAGON
(Close-up Open)

SHOTGUNS

# RUGER SHOTGUNS

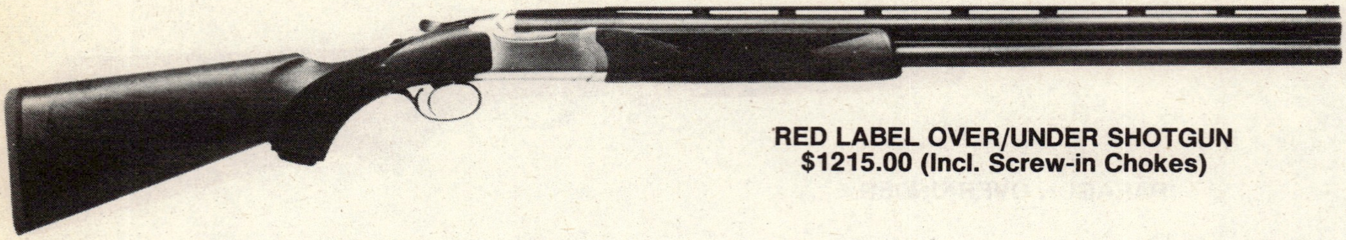

**RED LABEL OVER/UNDER SHOTGUN**
**$1215.00 (Incl. Screw-in Chokes)**

These shotguns are made of hardened chrome molybdenum, other alloy steels and music wire coil springs. Features include boxlock action with single-selective mechanical trigger, selective automatic ejectors, automatic top safety, free-floating vent rib with serrated top surface to reduce glare, standard brass bead front sight, and stainless steel receiver. Stock and semi-beavertail forearm are shaped from American walnut with hand-cut checkering (20 lines per inch). Pistol-grip cap and rubber recoil pad are standard, and all wood surfaces are beautifully finished. Available in 12 or 20 gauge with 3″ chambers.

**Screw-in choke inserts.** Designed especially for the popular 12-gauge "Red Label" over/under shotgun. Easily installed with a key wrench packaged with each shotgun. Choke fits flush with the muzzle. Every shotgun is equipped with a Full, Modified, Improved Cylinder and two Skeet screw-in chokes. The muzzle edge of the chokes has been slotted for quick identification in or out of the barrels. Full choke has 3 slots; Modified, 2 slots; Improved Cylinder, 1 slot (Skeet has no slots).

For additional specifications, please see table below.

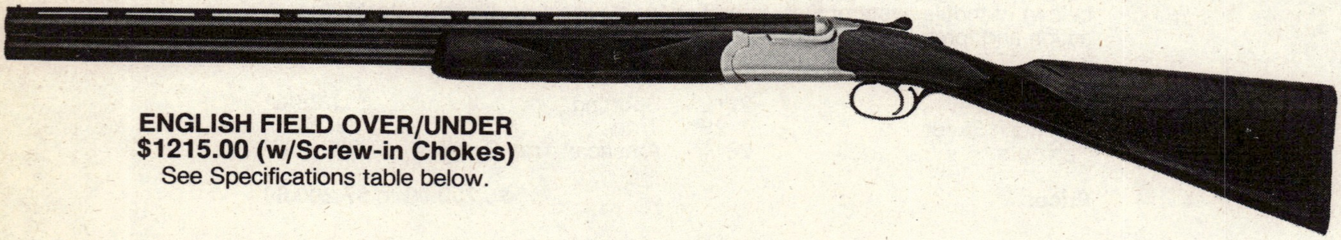

**ENGLISH FIELD OVER/UNDER**
**$1215.00 (w/Screw-in Chokes)**
See Specifications table below.

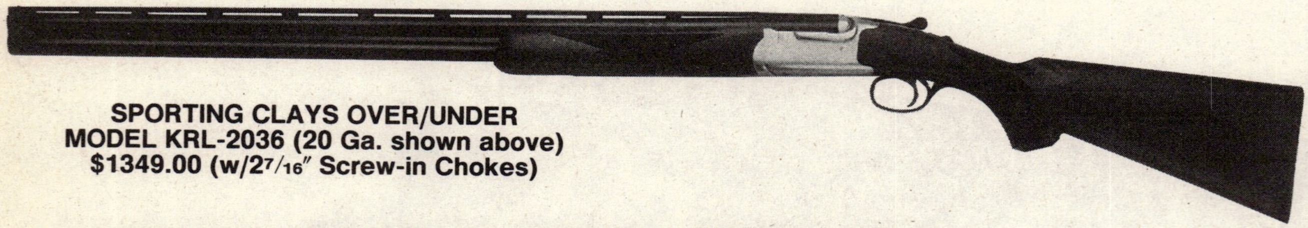

**SPORTING CLAYS OVER/UNDER**
**MODEL KRL-2036 (20 Ga. shown above)**
**$1349.00 (w/2 7/16″ Screw-in Chokes)**

## SPECIFICATIONS RED LABEL AND SPORTING CLAYS OVER/UNDERS

| Catalog Number | Gauge | Chamber | Choke* | Barrel Length | Overall Length | Length Pull | Drop Comb | Drop Heel | Sights** | Approx. Wt. (lbs.) | Type Stock |
|---|---|---|---|---|---|---|---|---|---|---|---|
| KRL-1226 | 12 | 3" | F,M,IC,S+ | 26" | 43" | 14 1/8" | 1 1/2" | 2 1/2" | GBF | 7 3/4 | Pistol Grip |
| KRL-1227 | 12 | 3" | F,M,IC,S+ | 28" | 45" | 14 1/8" | 1 1/2" | 2 1/2" | GBF | 8 | Pistol Grip |
| KRLS-1226 | 12 | 3" | F,M,IC,S+ | 26" | 43" | 14 1/8" | 1 1/2" | 2 1/2" | GBF | 7 1/2 | Straight |
| KRLS-1227 | 12 | 3" | F,M,IC,S+ | 28" | 45" | 14 1/8" | 1 1/2" | 2 1/2" | GBF | 7 3/4 | Straight |
| KRL-1236 | 12 | 3" | M,IC,S+ | 30" | 47" | 14 1/8" | 1 1/2" | 2 1/2" | GBF/GBM | 7 3/4 | Pistol Grip |
| KRL-2029 | 20 | 3" | F,M,IC,S+ | 26" | 43" | 14 1/8" | 1 1/2" | 2 1/2" | GBF | 7 | Pistol Grip |
| KRL-2030 | 20 | 3" | F,M,IC,S+ | 28" | 45" | 14 1/8" | 1 1/2" | 2 1/2" | GBF | 7 1/4 | Pistol Grip |
| KRLS-2029 | 20 | 3" | F,M,IC,S+ | 26" | 43" | 14 1/8" | 1 1/2" | 2 1/2" | GBF | 6 3/4 | Straight |
| KRLS-2030 | 20 | 3" | F,M,IC,S+ | 28" | 45" | 14 1/8" | 1 1/2" | 2 1/2" | GBF | 7 | Straight |
| KRL-2036 | 20 | 3" | M,IC,S+ | 30" | 47" | 14 1/8" | 1 1/2" | 2 1/2" | GBF/GBM | 7 | Pistol Grip |
| KRLS-2826 | 28 | 2 3/4" | F,M,IC,S+ | 26" | 43" | 14 1/8" | 1 1/2" | 2 1/2" | GBF | 5 7/8 | Straight |
| KRLS-2827 | 28 | 2 3/4" | F,M,IC,S+ | 28" | 45" | 14 1/8" | 1 1/2" | 2 1/2" | GBF | 6 | Straight |
| KRL-2826 | 28 | 2 3/4" | F,M,IC,S+ | 26" | 43" | 14 1/8" | 1 1/2" | 2 1/2" | GBF | 6 | Pistol Grip |
| KRL-2827 | 28 | 2 3/4" | F,M,IC,S+ | 28" | 45" | 14 1/8" | 1 1/2" | 2 1/2" | GBF | 6 1/8 | Pistol Grip |

*F-Full, M-Modified, IC-Improved Cylinder, S-Skeet. +Two skeet chokes standard with each shotgun.
**GBF-Gold-Bead Front Sight, GBM-Gold-Bead Middle

# SKB SHOTGUNS

## MODEL 585 and 785 SERIES

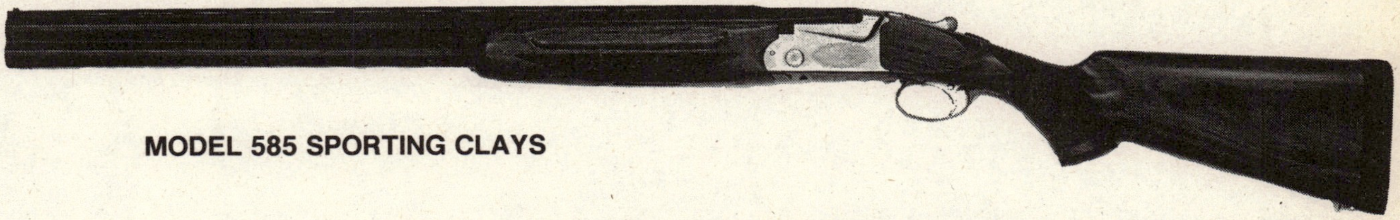

MODEL 585 SPORTING CLAYS

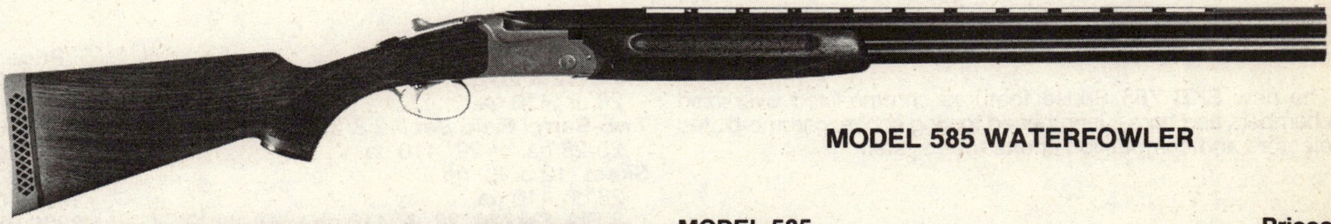

MODEL 585 WATERFOWLER

| **MODEL 585** | **Prices** |
|---|---|
| **Field/Youth** (12 & 20 ga.) | **$1179.00** |
| **Field** (28 or .410 ga.) | **1229.00** |
| **Two-Barrel Field Set** (12 & 20 ga.) | **1929.00** |
| 20/28 ga. or 28/.410 ga. | **1989.00** |
| **Skeet** (12 or 20 ga.) | **1279.00** |
| 28 or .410 ga. | **1319.00** |
| 3-Bbl. Set (20, 28, & .410 ga.) | **2999.00** |
| **Sporting Clays** (12 or 20 ga.) | **1329.00** |
| 28 gauge | **1379.00** |
| **Trap** (Monte Carlo or Std.) | **1279.00** |
| 2-Barrel Trap Combo | **1929.00** |
| **Waterfowler** | **1329.00** |

### FIELD MODELS

| GAUGE | CHAMBER | BARREL LENGTH | OVERALL LENGTH | INTER CHOKE | SIGHTS✓ | RIB WIDTH | AVERAGE WEIGHT * 785 | AVERAGE WEIGHT * 585 |
|---|---|---|---|---|---|---|---|---|
| 12 | 3" | 28" | 45 3/8" | COMP. | MFB | 3/8" | 8 lb. 0 oz. | 7 lb. 12 oz. |
| 12 | 3" | 26" | 43 3/8" | COMP. | MFB | 3/8" | 8 lb. 0 oz. | 7 lb. 11 oz. |
| 20 | 3" | 28" | 45 3/8" | STND-A | MFB | 5/16" | 7 lb. 4 oz. | 6 lb. 12 oz. |
| 20 | 3" | 26" | 43 3/8" | STND-B | MFB | 5/16" | 7 lb. 3 oz. | 6 lb. 10 oz. |
| 28 | 2 3/4" | 28" | 45 3/8" | STND-A | MFB | 5/16" | 7 lb. 4 oz. | 6 lb. 14 oz. |
| 28 | 2 3/4" | 26" | 43 3/8" | STND-B | MFB | 5/16" | 7 lb. 3 oz. | 6 lb. 13 oz. |
| 410 | 3" | 28" | 45 3/8" | M / F | MFB | 5/16" | 7 lb. 4 oz. | 7 lb. 0 oz. |
| 410 | 3" | 26" | 43 3/8" | IC / M | MFB | 5/16" | 7 lb. 3 oz. | 6 lb. 14 oz. |

### 2 BARREL FIELD SETS

| GAUGE | CHAMBER | BARREL LENGTH | OVERALL LENGTH | INTER CHOKE | SIGHTS✓ | RIB WIDTH | AVERAGE WEIGHT * 785 | AVERAGE WEIGHT * 585 |
|---|---|---|---|---|---|---|---|---|
| 12 | 3" | 28" | 45 3/8" | COMP. | MFB | 3/8" | 8 lb. 1 oz. | 7 lb. 11 oz. |
| 20 | 3" | 26" | 43 3/8" | STND-B | MFB | 3/8" | 8 lb. 4 oz. | 7 lb. 12 oz. |
| 20 | 3" | 28" | 45 3/8" | STND-A | MFB | 5/16" | 7 lb. 5 oz. | 7 lb. 2 oz. |
| 28 | 2 3/4" | 28" | 45 3/8" | STND-A | MFB | 5/16" | 7 lb. 5 oz. | 7 lb. 1 oz. |
| 20 | 3" | 26" | 43 3/8" | STND-B | MFB | 5/16" | 7 lb. 3 oz. | 7 lb. 1 oz. |
| 28 | 2 3/4" | 26" | 43 3/8" | STND-B | MFB | 5/16" | 7 lb. 3 oz. | 7 lb. 0 oz. |
| 28 | 2 3/4" | 28" | 45 3/8" | STND-A | MFB | 5/16" | 7 lb. 6 oz. | 7 lb. 1 oz. |
| 410 | 3" | 26" | 43 3/8" | IC / M | MFB | 5/16" | 7 lb. 5 oz. | 7 lb. 0 oz. |

*Weights may vary due to wood density. Specifications may vary.

*INTER-CHOKE SYSTEMS
COMP. - Competition series includes Mod., Full, Imp. Cyl.
STND A - Standard series includes Mod., Full, Imp. Cyl.
STND B - Standard series includes Imp. Cyl. Mod., Skeet

STOCK DIMENSIONS
Length of Pull - 14 1/8"
Drop at Comb - 1 1/2"
Drop at Heel - 2 3/16"
✓ MFB - Metal Front Bead

*NOTE: 785's Are Equipped With Step-Up Style Ribs*

### SPORTING CLAY MODELS

| GAUGE | CHAMBER | BARREL LENGTH | OVERALL LENGTH | INTER CHOKE | SIGHTS✓ | RIB WIDTH | AVERAGE WEIGHT * 785 | AVERAGE WEIGHT * 585 |
|---|---|---|---|---|---|---|---|---|
| 12 | 3" | 32" | 49 3/8" | COMP. | CP/WFB | 15/32" CH/STP | 8 lb. 14 oz. | [illegible] |
| 12 | 3" | 30" | 47 3/8" | COMP. | CP/WFB | 15/32" CH/STP | 8 lb. 12 oz. | [illegible] |
| 12 | 3" | 30" | 47 3/8" | COMP. | CP/WFB | 3/8" SW | 8 lb [illegible] | [illegible] |
| 12 | 3" | 28" | 45 3/8" | COMP. | CP/WFB | 15/32" CH/STP | [illegible] | [illegible] |
| 12 | 3" | 28" | 45 3/8" | COMP. | CP/WFB | 3/8" S[illegible] | [illegible] | [illegible] |
| 20 | 3" | 28" | 45 3/8" | STND-B | CP/WFB | [illegible] | [illegible] | [illegible] |
| 28 | 2 3/4" | 28" | 45 3/8" | STND-B | CP/WF[illegible] | [illegible] | [illegible] | [illegible] |

### 2 BARR[illegible] SET

| GAUGE | CHAMBER | BARREL LENGTH | OVERALL LENGTH | INTER CHOKE | SIGHTS | RIB WIDTH | 785 | 585 |
|---|---|---|---|---|---|---|---|---|
| 12 | 3" | 30" | 47·3/8" | C[illegible] | [illegible] | [illegible] | 8 lb. 14 oz. | [illegible] |
| 20 | 3" | 28" | 45 3/8" | [illegible] | [illegible] | [illegible]32" CH/STP | 8 lb. 10 oz. | [illegible] |

*Weights may vary due to wood density. Specificatio[illegible]

*INTER-CHOKE SYSTEMS
COMP. - Competition series includes S[illegible]
SK I/SC I and MOD/SC IV
STND B - Standard series include[illegible]

STOCK DIMENSIONS
Length of Pull - 14 1/4"
Drop at Comb - 1 7/16"
Drop at Heel - 1 7/8"

✓ CP/WFB - Center Post White Front Bead
✓ CH/STP - Center Channeled, Semi Wide Step Up Rib
SW - Semi Wide Step Up Rib

## MODEL 585 and 785 SERIES

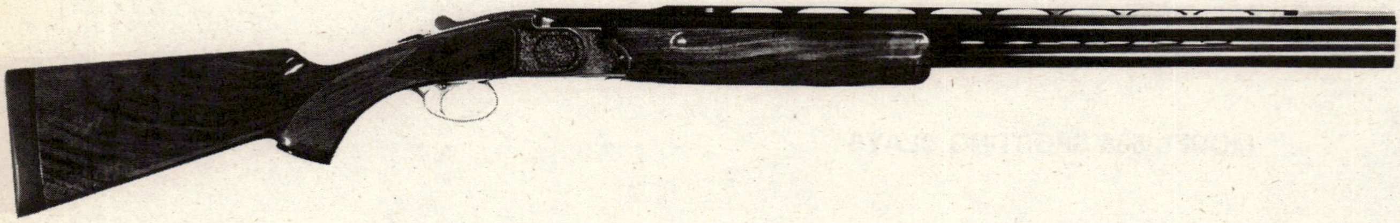

### MODEL 785 OVER/UNDER

The new SKB 785 Series features chrome-lined oversized chambers and bores, lengthened forcing cones, chrome-plated ejectors and competition choke tube system.

| MODEL 785 | Prices |
|---|---|
| **Field** (12 & 20 ga.) | **$1899.00** |
| 28 or .410 ga. | **1949.00** |
| **Two-Barrel Field Set** (12 & 20 ga.) | **2749.00** |
| 20/28 ga. or 28/.410 ga. | **2819.00** |
| **Skeet** (12 or 20 ga.) | **1949.00** |
| 28 or .410 ga. | **1999.00** |
| 3-Bbl. Set (20, 28, & .410 ga.) | **3929.00** |
| **Sporting Clays** (12 or 20 ga.) | **2029.00** |
| 28 gauge | **2079.00** |
| 2-Barrel Set (12 & 20 ga.) | **2889.00** |
| **Trap** (Monte Carlo or Std.) | **1949.00** |
| 2-Barrel Trap Combo | **2719.00** |

**TRAP MODELS**

| GAUGE | STOCK | BARREL✓ LENGTH | OVERALL LENGTH | INTER CHOKE | SIGHTS✓ | 785 RIB WIDTH | 585 RIB WIDTH | AVERAGE WEIGHT* 785 | AVERAGE WEIGHT* 585 | MANUFACTURES ID # 785 | MANUFACTURES ID # 585 |
|---|---|---|---|---|---|---|---|---|---|---|---|
| 12 | STND | 30" | 47 3/8" | COMP-A | CP/WFB | 15/32" CH/STP | 3/8" STP | 8 lb. 15 oz. | 8 lb. 7 oz. | A7820CVTN | A5820CVTN |
| 12 | MONTE | 30" | 47 3/8" | COMP-A | CP/WFB | 15/32" CH/STP | 3/8" STP | 9 lb. 0 oz. | 8 lb. 7 oz. | A7820CVTM | A5820CVTM |
| 12 | STND | 32" | 49 3/8" | COMP-A | CP/WFB | 15/32" CH/STP | 3/8" STP | 9 lb. 1 oz. | 8 lb. 10 oz. | A7822CVTN | A5822CVTN |
| 12 | MONTE | 32" | 49 3/8" | COMP-A | CP/WFB | 15/32" CH/STP | 3/8" STP | 9 lb. 1 oz. | 8 lb. 9 oz. | A7822CVTM | A5822CVTM |

**TRAP COMBO'S — STANDARD**

| ...ALL ...H | INTER CHOKE | SIGHTS✓ | 785 RIB WIDTH | 585 RIB WIDTH | AVERAGE WEIGHT* 785 | AVERAGE WEIGHT* 585 | MANUFACTURES ID # 785 | MANUFACTURES ID # 585 |
|---|---|---|---|---|---|---|---|---|
| | COMP. | CP/WFB | 15/32" CH/STP | 3/8" STP | 8 lb. 15 oz. | 8 lb. 6 oz. | A7820TN / 7822 | A5820TN / 5822 |
| | ...OMP. | CP/WFB | 15/32" CH/STP | 3/8" STP | 9 lb. 0 oz. | 8 lb. 6 oz. | | |
| | | CP/WFB | 15/32" CH/STP | 3/8" STP | 9 lb. 0 oz. | 8 lb. 4 oz. | A7820TN / 7824 | A5820TN / 5824 |
| | | CP/WFB | 15/32" CH/STP | 3/8" STP | 9 lb. 1 oz. | 8 lb. 6 oz. | | |
| | | ...WFB | 15/32" CH/STP | 3/8" STP | 9 lb. 0 oz. | 8 lb. 7 oz. | A7822TN / 7824 | A5822TN / 5824 |
| | | ...B | 15/32" CH/STP | 3/8" STP | 9 lb. 1 oz. | 8 lb. 8 oz. | | |

| | | | | | | |
|---|---|---|---|---|---|---|
| 12 | MONTE | O/U-30" | 47 3/8" | | | |
| 12 | MONTE | S/O-32" | 49 3/8" | COM... | | |
| 12 | MONTE | O/U-30" | 47 3/8" | COMP. | | |
| 12 | MONTE | S/O-34" | 51 3/8 | COMP. | CP/WFB | |
| 12 | MONTE | O/U-32" | 49 3/8" | COMP. | CP/WFB | |
| 12 | MONTE | S/O-34" | 51 3/8 | COMP. | CP/WFB | 15/32" CH/STP |

*Weights may vary due to wood density. Specifications may vary.
*INTER-CHOKE SYSTEMS
COMP. - Competition series includes Full, Mod., Imp. Cyl.
STND. B - Standard series includes Imp. Cyl., Mod. and Skeet

**...MONTE CARLO**

| | | | | |
|---|---|---|---|---|
| ...STP | 8 lb. 15 oz. | 8 lb. 6 oz. | A7820TM / 7822 | A5820TM / 5822 |
| | 9 lb. 0 oz. | 8 lb. 6 oz. | | |
| CH/S... | ...lb. 15 oz. | 8 lb. 4 oz. | A7820TM / 7824 | A5820TM / 5824 |
| | ...1 oz. | 8 lb. 6 oz. | | |
| | | 8 lb. 7 oz. | A7822TM / 7824 | A5822TM / 5824 |
| | | 8 lb. 9 oz. | | |

STOCK DIMENSIONS
Length of Pull - 13 1/2"
Drop at Comb - 1 1/2"
Drop at Heel - 2 1/4"
✓ MFB - Metal Front Bead

**YOUTH & LADIES**

| GAUGE | CHAMBER | BARREL LENGTH | OVERALL LENGTH | INTER CHOKE | SIGHTS✓ | RIB WIDTH | AVERAGE WEIGHT* 785 | AVERAGE WEIGHT* 585 | MANUFACTURES ID # 785 | MANUFACTURES ID # 585 |
|---|---|---|---|---|---|---|---|---|---|---|
| 12 | 3" | 28" | 44 1/2" | COMP. | MFB | 3/8" | | 7 lb. 11 oz. | | A5828CFY |
| 12 | 3" | 26" | 42 1/2" | COMP. | MFB | 3/8" | | 7 lb. 9 oz. | | A5826CFY |
| 20 | 3" | 26" | 42 1/2" | STND-B | MFB | 3/8" | | 6 lb. 7 oz. | | A5806CFY |

**SKEET MODELS**

| GAUGE | CHAMBER | BARREL LENGTH | OVERALL LENGTH | INTER CHOKE | SIGHTS✓ | RIB WIDTH | AVERAGE WEIGHT* 785 | AVERAGE WEIGHT* 585 | MANUFACTURES ID # 785 | MANUFACTURES ID # 585 |
|---|---|---|---|---|---|---|---|---|---|---|
| 12 | 3" | 30" | 47 1/4" | COMP. | CP/WFB | 3/8" | 8 lb. 9 oz. | 8 lb. 1 oz. | A7820CV | A5820CV |
| 12 | 3" | 28" | 45 1/4" | COMP. | CP/WFB | 3/8" | 8 lb. 6 oz. | 7 lb. 12 oz. | A7828CV | A5828CV |
| 20 | 3" | 28" | 45 1/4" | STND. | CP/WFB | 5/16" | 7 lb. 2 oz. | 6 lb. 15 oz. | A7808CV | A5808CV |
| 28 | 2 3/4" | 28" | 45 1/4" | STND. | CP/WFB | 5/16" | 7 lb. 5 oz. | 6 lb. 15 oz. | A7888CV | A5888CV |
| 410 | 3" | 28" | 45 1/4" | SK/SK | CP/WFB | 5/16" | 7 lb. 5 oz. | 7 lb. 0 oz. | A7848V | A5848V |

**3 BARREL SKEET SETS**

| | | | | | | | | | | |
|---|---|---|---|---|---|---|---|---|---|---|
| 20 | 3" | 28" | 45 1/4" | STND. | CP/WFB | 5/16" | 7 lb. 2 oz. | 6 lb. 15 oz. | | |
| 28 | 2 3/4" | 28" | 45 1/4" | STND. | CP/WFB | 5/16" | 7 lb. 5 oz. | 7 lb. 0 oz. | A78088 | A58088 |
| 410 | 3" | 28" | 45 1/4" | SK/SK | CP/WFB | 5/16" | 7 lb. 5 oz. | 7 lb. 0 oz. | | |

*Weights may vary due to wood density. Specifications may vary.
*INTER-CHOKE SYSTEMS
COMP. - Competition series includes 2-SKI/SCI, 1-Mod/SCIV
STND. - Standard series includes Skeet, Skeet and Imp. Cyl.

STOCK DIMENSIONS
Length of Pull - 14 1/8"
Drop at Comb - 1 1/2"
Drop at Heel - 2 3/16"
✓ CP/WFB - Center Post/White Front Bead

*NOTE: 785's Are Equipped With Step-Up Style Ribs*

# TIKKA SHOTGUNS

## (Formerly Valmet)

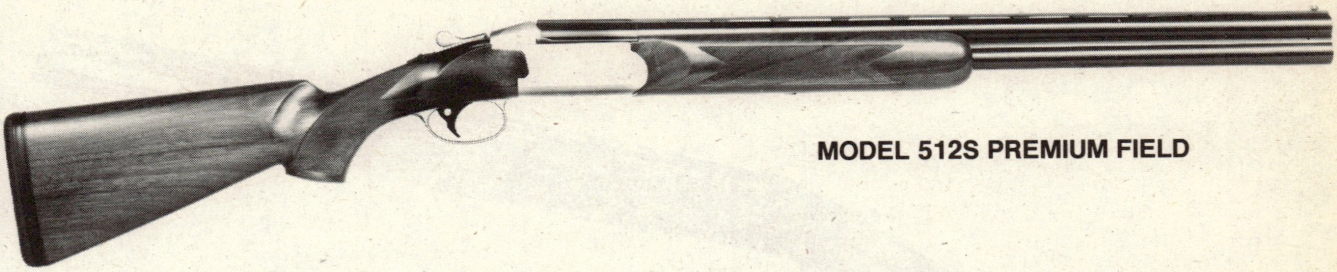

MODEL 512S PREMIUM FIELD

### TIKKA 512S OVER/UNDER
### PREMIUM FIELD GRADE $1275.00

Designed for the experienced hunter, TIKKA's 512S represents the pride and skill of "Old World" European craftsmanship. The barrels are polished to a mirror finish and deeply blued. Select semi-fancy American walnut stock and forearm highlight fine, deep-cut checkering. Other features include:

**Time-proven action:** Designed to handle large centerfire calibers for more durability and reliability.

**Mechanical trigger:** Fires two shots as fast as you can pull the trigger. Does not rely on the inertia from the recoil of the first shot to set the trigger for the second. In the event of a faulty primer or light hit, inertia trigger shotguns cannot function on the second round.

**Single selective trigger:** Selector button is located on the trigger for fast, easy selection.

**Large trigger guard opening:** Designed for cold weather shooting; permits easy finger movement when wearing gloves.

**Semi-fancy European walnut stock and forearm:** Add greatly to overall appearance.

**Superior stock design:** A palm swell provides additional hand comfort. Length and angle (pitch) can be adjusted for a perfect fit with addition of factory spacers. Fine, deep-cut checkering.

**Palm-filling forearm:** Rounded and tapered for comfort and smooth, true swing, plus fine, deep-cut checkering.

**Automatic ejectors:** Select and eject fired rounds. Raise unfired shells for safe removal.

**Chrome-lined barrels:** For more consistent patterns. Eliminates pitting and corrosion, extends barrel life even with steel shot.

**Stainless steel choke tubes:** Added strength over regular carbon and alloy materials. Easily handles steel shot. Recessed so as not to detract from appearance. Tight tolerances enable truer patterns and enhance choke versatility.

**Sliding locking bolt:** Secure lockup between receiver and barrels. Wears in, not loose.

**Polished blue receiver:** Fully engraved with gold inlay.

**Wide vent rib:** Cross-file pattern reduces glare. Fluorescent front and middle beads.

**Automatic safety:** Goes to safe position automatically when gun is opened.

**Cocking indicators:** Allow shooter to determine (through sight or feel) which barrel has been fired.

**Steel receiver:** Forged and machined for durability.

**Chamber:** 3-inch on all models

**Two-piece firing pin:** For more durability

**Versatility:** Change from over/under shotgun to shotgun/rifle, trap, skeet or double rifle. Precision tolerances require only minor initial fitting.

**SPECIFICATIONS**
**Gauge:** 12
**Chambers:** 3″
**Weight:** 7¼ lbs. w/26″ barrels; 7½ lbs. w/28″ barrels
**Barrel lengths/chokes:**
26″, 5 chokes (F, M, IM, IC & Skeet)
28″, 5 chokes (F, M, IM, IC & Skeet)

### SPORTING CLAYS SHOTGUN (not shown)
### $1315.00

Designed to accommodate the specific requirements of the shooter in this, the fastest growing shooting sport in America today. The Sporting Clays shotgun features a specially designed American walnut stock with a double palm swell finished with a soft satin lacquer for maximum protection with minimum maintenance. Available in 12 gauge with a selection of 5 recessed choke tubes. Other features include a 3″ chamber, manual safety, customized sporting clay recoil pad, single selective trigger, blued receiver and 28″ and 30″ barrel with ventilated side and top rib with two iridescent beads. In addition, the shotgun is furnished with an attractive carrying case.

Manufactured in Italy, TIKKA is designed and crafted by SAKO of Finland, which has enjoyed international acclaim for the manufacture of precision sporting firearms since 1918.

SHOTGUNS

# TIKKA SHOTGUNS

## (Formerly Valmet)

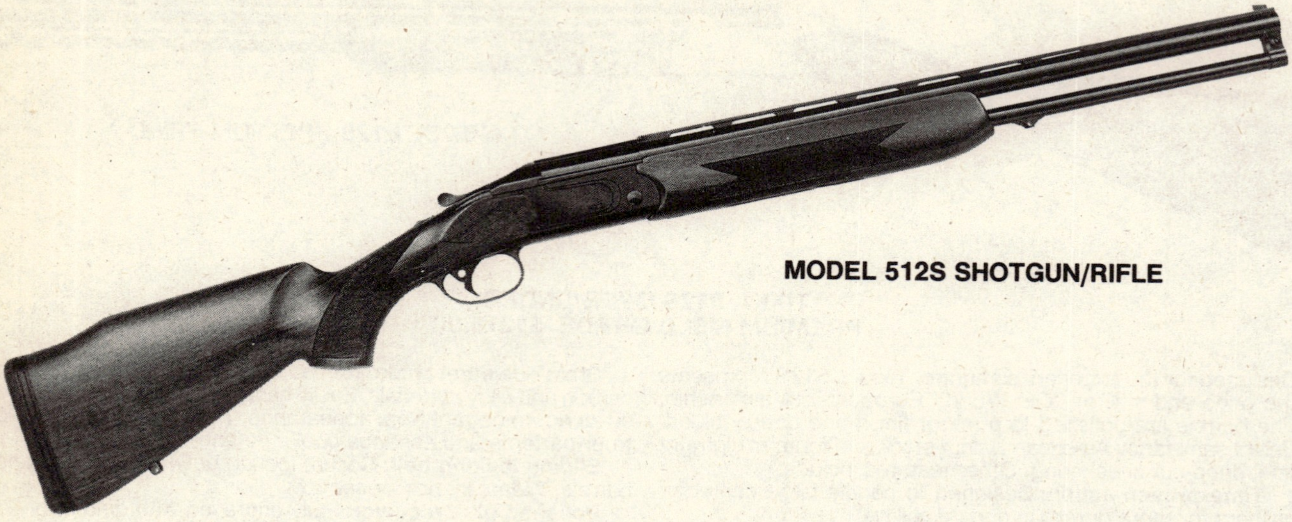

MODEL 512S SHOTGUN/RIFLE

**TIKKA 512S SHOTGUN/RIFLE**
**$1350.00**

TIKKA's unique 512S Shotgun/Rifle combination continues to be the most popular gun of its type in the U.S. Its features are identical to the 512S Field Grade over/under shotguns, including strong steel receiver, superior sliding locking mechanism with automatic safety, cocking indicators, mechanical triggers and two-piece firing pin. In addition, note the other features of this model—

**Barrel regulation:** Adjusts for windage simply by turning the screw on the muzzle. Elevation is adjustable by regulating the sliding wedge located between the barrels.

**Compact:** 24-inch barrels mounted on the low-profile receiver limit the overall length to 40 inches (about 5″ less than most bolt-action rifles with similar 24-inch barrels).

**Single selective trigger:** A barrel selector is located on the trigger for quick, easy selection. Double triggers are also available.

**Choice of rifle calibers:** Choose from 222, 30-06, 308 or 9.3×74R for the under barrel to complement the 12-gauge upper barrel with 3″ chamber and Improved Modified choke.

**Sighting options:** The vent rib is cross-filed to reduce glare. The rear sight is flush-folding and permits rapid alignment with the large blade front sight. The rib is milled to accommodate TIKKA's one-piece scope mount with 1″ rings. The "quick-release" design of the scope mount enables the shooter to remove it without altering zero.

**European walnut stock:** Stock is of semi-Monte Carlo design, available with palm swell for greater control and comfort. Equipped with quick-detachable sling swivels. Length or pitch adjustable with factory spacers.

**Interchangeability:** Receiver will accommodate TIKKA's over/under shotgun barrels and double-rifle barrels with minor initial fitting.

**SPECIFICATIONS**
**Gauge/Caliber:** 12/222, 12/30-06, 12/308 and 12/9.3×74R
**Chamber:** 3″ with Improved Modified choke
**Barrel length:** 24″
**Overall length:** 40″
**Weight:** 8 lbs.
**Stock:** European walnut with semi-Monte Carlo design

**Extra Barrel Sets:**

| | |
|---|---|
| Over/Under | **$650.00** |
| Shotgun/Rifle | **725.00** |
| Double Rifle | **825.00** |
| Sporting Clays | **715.00** |

# WEATHERBY SHOTGUNS

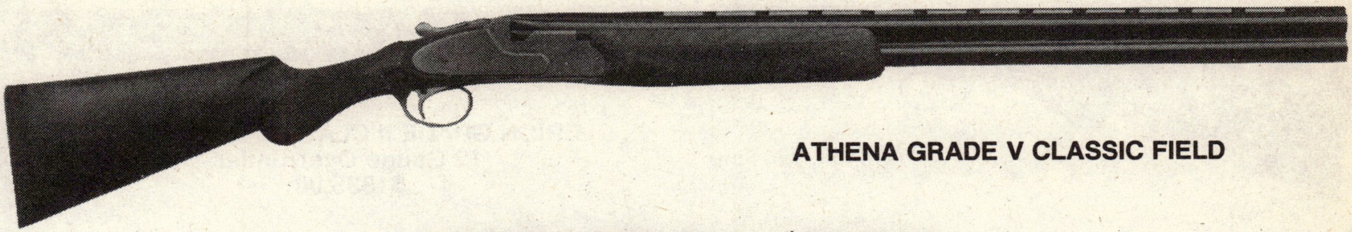

ATHENA GRADE V CLASSIC FIELD

## ATHENA GRADE IV $2200.00
## ATHENA GRADE V $2575.00

**Receiver:** The Athena receiver houses a strong, reliable box-lock action, yet it features side lock-type plates to carry through the fine floral engraving. The hinge pivots are made of a special high-strength steel alloy. The locking system employs the time-tested Greener cross-bolt design.

**Single selective trigger:** It is mechanically rather than recoil operated. This provides a fully automatic switchover, allowing the second barrel to be fired on a subsequent trigger pull, even during a misfire. A flick of the trigger finger and the selector lever, located just in front of the trigger, is all the way to the left, enabling you to fire the lower barrel first, or to the right for the upper barrel. The Athena trigger is selective as well.

**Barrels:** The breech block is hand-fitted to the receiver, providing closest possible tolerances. Every Athena is equipped with a matted, ventilated rib and bead front sight.

**Selective automatic ejectors:** The Athena contains ejectors that are fully automatic both in selection and action.

**Slide safety:** The safety is the traditional slide type located conveniently on the upper tang atop the pistol grip.

**Stock:** Each stock is carved from specially selected Claro walnut, with fine line hand-checkering and high-luster finish. Trap model has Monte Carlo stock only.

See the Athena and Orion table on the following page for additional information and specifications.

**GRADE IV CHOKES**
**Fixed Choke**
Field, .410 Gauge
Skeet, 12 or 20 Gauge
**IMC Multi-Choke**
Field, 12, 20 or 28 Gauge
Trap, 12 Gauge
Trap, single barrel, 12 Gauge
Trap Combo, 12 Gauge

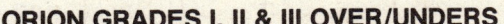

ORION GRADE II CLASSIC FIELD

## ORION GRADES I, II & III OVER/UNDERS

For greater versatility, the Orion incorporates the integral multichoke (IMC) system. Available in Extra-full, Full, Modified, Improved Modified, Improved Cylinder and Skeet, the choke tubes fit flush with the muzzle without detracting from the beauty of the gun. Three tubes are furnished with each gun. The precision hand-fitted monobloc and receiver are machined from high-strength steel with a highly polished finish. The box-lock design uses the Greener cross-bolt locking system and special sears maintain hammer engagement. Pistol grip stock and forearm are carved of Claro walnut with hand-checkered diamond inlay pattern and high-gloss finish. Chrome-moly steel barrels, and the receiver, are deeply blued. The Orion also features selective automatic ejectors, single selective trigger, front bead sight and ventilated rib. The trap model boasts a curved trap-style recoil pad and is available with Monte Carlo stock only. **Weight:** 12 ga. Field, 7½ lbs.; 20 ga. Field, 7½ lbs.; Trap, 8 lbs.

See following page for prices and additional specifications.

**ORION CHOKES**
**Grade I**
IMC Multi-Choke, Field, 12 or 20 Gauge
**Grade II**
Fixed Choke, Field, .410 Gauge
Fixed Choke, Skeet, 12 or 20 Gauge
IMC Multi-Choke, Field, 12, 20 or 28 Gauge
IMC Multi-Choke, Trap, 12 Gauge
**Grade II Sporting Clays**
12 Gauge only
**Grade III**
IMC Multi-Choke, Field, 12 or 20 Gauge

# WEATHERBY SHOTGUNS

**ORION GRADE II CLASSIC SPORTING**
**12 Gauge Over/Under**
**$1335.00**

**ORION GRADES I, II, III**
**Prices:**

| | |
|---|---|
| **Orion I** | **$1225.00** |
| **Orion II Classic Field** | **1295.00** |
| **Orion II Sporting Clays** | **1395.00** |
| **Orion III Field & Classic Field** | **1545.00** |

**ATHENA & ORION OVER/UNDER SHOTGUN SPECIFICATIONS**

| Model | Gauge | Chamber | Barrel Length | Overall Length | Length of Pull | Drop at Heel | Drop at Comb | Bead Sight | Approx. Weight |
|---|---|---|---|---|---|---|---|---|---|
| Athena Grade V Classic Field | 12<br>20 | 3″<br>3″ | 30″, 28″ or 26″<br>28″ or 26″ | 47″, 45″ or 43″<br>45″ or 43″ | 14¼″<br>14¼″ | 2.5″<br>2.5″ | 1.5″<br>1.5″ | Brilliant front<br>Brilliant front | 6½–8 lbs.<br>6½–8 lbs. |
| Athena Grade IV Field | 12<br>20 | 3″<br>3″ | 30″, 28″ or 26″<br>28″ or 26″ | 47″, 45″ or 43″<br>45″ or 43″ | 14¼″<br>14¼″ | 2.5″<br>2.5″ | 1.5″<br>1.5″ | Brilliant front<br>Brilliant front | 6½–8 lbs.<br>6½–8 lbs. |
| Orion Grade III Classic Field | 12<br>20 | 3″<br>3″ | 28″<br>26″ | 45″<br>43″ | 14¼″<br>14¼″ | 2.5″<br>2.5″ | 1.5″<br>1.5″ | Brilliant front<br>Brilliant front | 6½–8 lbs.<br>6½–8 lbs. |
| Orion Grade III Field | 12<br>20 | 3″<br>3″ | 30″, 28″ or 26″<br>28″ or 26″ | 47″, 45″ or 43″<br>45″ or 43″ | 14¼″<br>14¼″ | 2.5″<br>2.5″ | 1.5″<br>1.5″ | Brilliant front<br>Brilliant front | 6½–8 lbs.<br>6½–8 lbs. |
| Orion Grade II Classic Field | 12<br>20<br>28 | 3″<br>3″<br>2¾″ | 30″, 28″ or 26″<br>28″ or 26″<br>26″ | 47″, 45″ or 43″<br>45″ or 43″<br>43″ | 14¼″<br>14¼″<br>14¼″ | 2.5″<br>2.5″<br>2.5″ | 1.5″<br>1.5″<br>1.5″ | Brilliant front<br>Brilliant front<br>Brilliant front | 6½–8 lbs.<br>6½–8 lbs.<br>6½–8 lbs. |
| Orion Grade I | 12<br>20 | 3″<br>3″ | 30″, 28″ or 26″<br>28″ or 26″ | 47″, 45″ or 43″<br>45″ or 43″ | 14¼″<br>14¼″ | 2.5″<br>2.5″ | 1.5″<br>1.5″ | Brilliant front<br>Brilliant front | 6½–8 lbs.<br>6½–8 lbs. |
| Orion Grade II Classic Sporting | 12 | 2¾″ | 28″ | 45″ | 14¼″ | 2.25″ | 1.5″ | Midpoint w/ white front | 7½ lbs. |
| Orion Grade II Sporting | 12 | 2¾″ | 30″ or 28″ | 47″ or 45″ | 14¼″ | 2.25″ | 1.5″ | Midpoint w/ white front | 7½–8 lbs. |

# WINCHESTER SECURITY SHOTGUNS

These tough 12-gauge shotguns provide backup strength for security and police work as well as all-around utility. The action is one of the fastest second-shot pumps made. It features a front-locking rotating bolt for strength and secure, single-unit lockup into the barrel. Twin-action slide bars prevent binding.

The shotguns are chambered for 3-inch shotshells. They handle 3-inch Magnum, 2 3/4-inch Magnum and standard 2 3/4-inch shotshells interchangeably. They have a crossbolt safety, walnut-finished hardwood stock and forearm, black rubber buttpad and plain 18-inch barrel with Cylinder Bore choke. All are ultra-reliable and easy to handle.

Special chrome finish on Police and Marine guns are actually triple-plated: first with copper for adherence, then with nickel for rust protection, and finally with chrome for a hard finish. This triple-plating assures durability and quality. Both guns have a forend cap with swivel to accommodate sling.

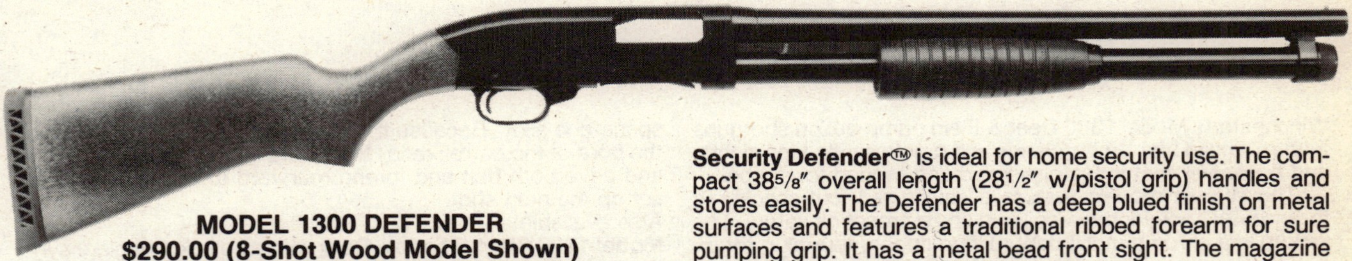

**MODEL 1300 DEFENDER**
**$290.00 (8-Shot Wood Model Shown)**
**$393.00 DEFENDER/FIELD COMBO**

**Security Defender**™ is ideal for home security use. The compact 38 5/8″ overall length (28 1/2″ w/pistol grip) handles and stores easily. The Defender has a deep blued finish on metal surfaces and features a traditional ribbed forearm for sure pumping grip. It has a metal bead front sight. The magazine holds eight 12-gauge. 3″ Magnum shells.

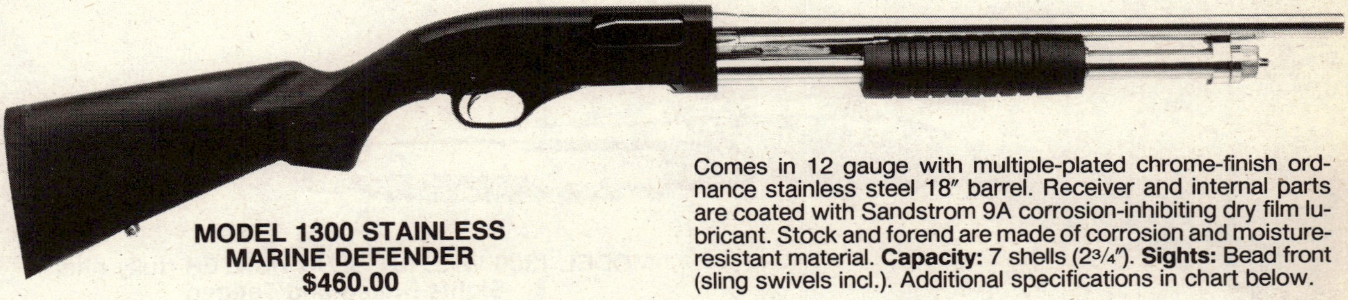

**MODEL 1300 STAINLESS**
**MARINE DEFENDER**
**$460.00**

Comes in 12 gauge with multiple-plated chrome-finish ordnance stainless steel 18″ barrel. Receiver and internal parts are coated with Sandstrom 9A corrosion-inhibiting dry film lubricant. Stock and forend are made of corrosion and moisture-resistant material. **Capacity:** 7 shells (2 3/4″). **Sights:** Bead front (sling swivels incl.). Additional specifications in chart below.

SHOTGUNS

### SPECIFICATIONS MODEL 1300 DEFENDER

| Model | Gauge | Barrel Length | Chamber | Capacity* | Choke | Overall Length | Length of Pull | Drop At Comb/Heel | Weight (Lbs.) | Sights |
|---|---|---|---|---|---|---|---|---|---|---|
| **Combo, Hardwood** Stock and Pistol Grip | 12<br>12 | 18″<br>28 VR | 3″ Mag.<br>3″ Mag. | 5<br>5 | Cyl.<br>W1M | 38 5/8″<br>48 5/8 | 14″<br>14″ | 1 1/2″ 2 1/2″<br>1 1/2 2 1/2 | 6 1/2″<br>7 1/4 | MBF<br>MBF |
| **Hardwood Stock** 5 Shot | 12 | 18″ | 3″ Mag. | 5 | Cyl. | 38 5/8″ | 14″ | 1 1/2″ 2 1/2″ | 6 1/2 | MBF |
| **Hardwood Stock** 8 Shot | 12 | 18″ | 3″ Mag. | 8¹ | Cyl. | 38 5/8″ | 14″ | 1 1/2″ 2 1/2″ | 6 1/2 | MBF |
| **Synthetic** Pistol Grip | 12 | 18″ | 3″ Mag. | 8¹ | Cyl. | 28 1/2″ | — | — — | 5 3/4 | MBF |
| **Synthetic Stock** 12 Gauge | 12 | 18″ | 3″ Mag. | 8¹ | Cyl. | 38 5/8″ | 14″ | 1 3/8″ 2 3/4″ | 6 1/4 | MBF |
| **Synthetic Stock** 20 Gauge | 20 | 18″ | 3″ Mag. | 5 | Cyl. | 38 5/8″ | 14″ | 1 1/2″ 2 1/2″ | 6 | MBP |
| **Stainless Marine** | 12 | 18″ | 3″ Mag. | 7¹ | Cyl. | 38 5/8 | 14″ | 1 1/2″ 2 1/2″ | 6 3/4 | MBF |
| **Pistol Grip (Stainless)** | 12 | 18″ | 3″ Mag. | 7¹ | Cyl. | 28 5/8 | — | — — | 5 3/4 | MBF |

* Includes one shotshell in chamber when ready to fire. ¹ Subtract one shell capacity for 3″ shells. VR = Ventilated rib. Cyl. = Cylinder Bore. MBF = Metal bead front.

# WINCHESTER SHOTGUNS

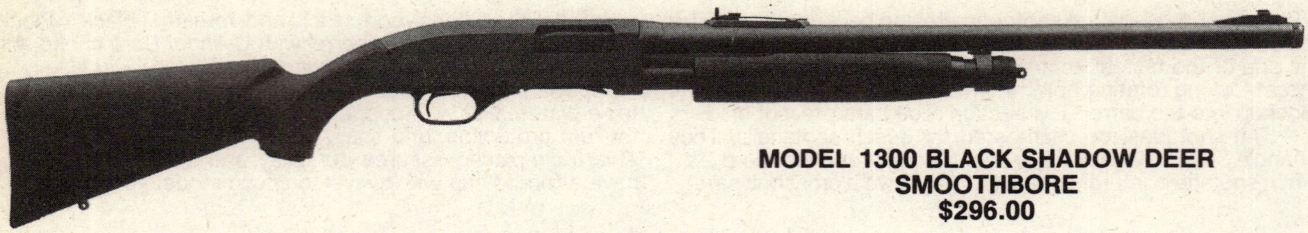

**MODEL 1300 BLACK SHADOW DEER SMOOTHBORE**
**$296.00**

**MODEL 1300 DEER & FIELD**

Winchester's Model 1300 Deer & Field pump-action shotguns feature a rifled barrel with 8 lands and grooves, rifle-type sights, and a receiver that is factory-drilled and tapped for scope.

The Walnut models feature a sculptured, cut-checkered forend with honeycomb recoil pad and a crossbolt safety. The lockup is a chrome molybdenum high-speed, four-slug rotary bolt and barrel extension system (lockup does not require use of the receiver top as part of the locking system). The Model 1300 receiver is made of lightweight, corrosion-resistant, space-age alloy. Because the rotary lockup is concentric with the bore of the barrel, recoil forces are used to unlock the bolt and drive both bolt and forend rearward to help the shooter set up the next shot.

Also available:
**Model 1300 Black Shadow Deer** with all-black, nonglare synthetic stock and forearm. Improved Cylinder Winchoke is standard. Additional specifications appear on the following page.

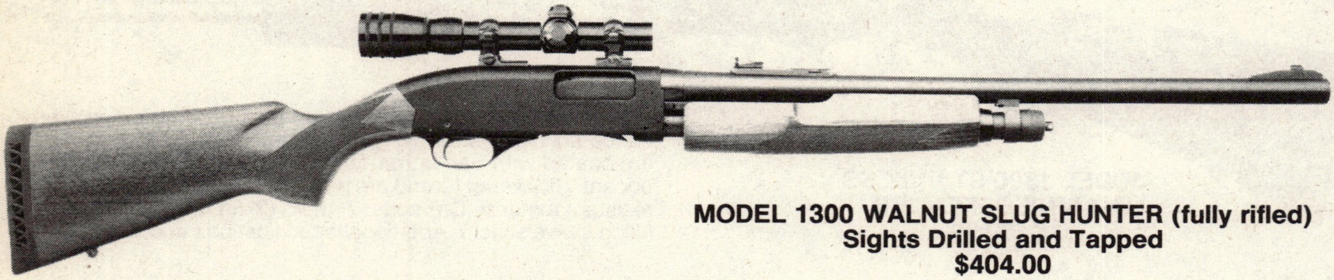

**MODEL 1300 WALNUT SLUG HUNTER (fully rifled)**
**Sights Drilled and Tapped**
**$404.00**

**MODEL 1300 DEER/ADVANTAGE**
**$432.00 (Rifled) $410.00 (Smooth)**
(See table of specifications on following page)

# WINCHESTER SHOTGUNS



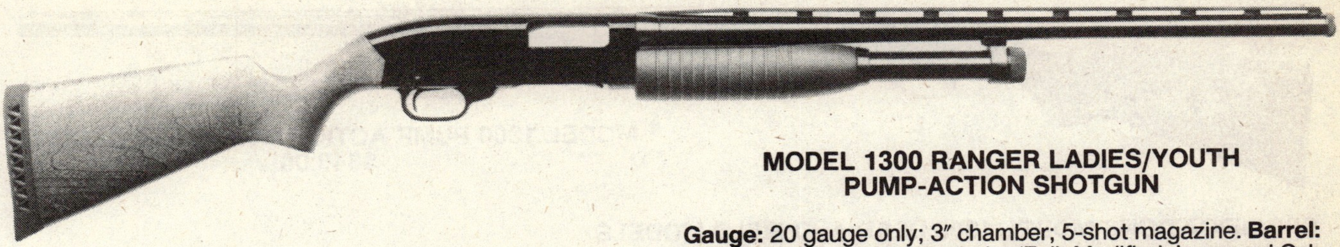

**MODEL 1300 RANGER LADIES/YOUTH PUMP-ACTION SHOTGUN**

**Gauge:** 20 gauge only; 3″ chamber; 5-shot magazine. **Barrel:** 22″ barrel w/vent rib; Winchoke (Full, Modified, Improved Cylinder). **Weight:** 6 1/2 lbs. **Length:** 41 5/8″. **Stock:** Walnut or American hardwood with ribbed forend. **Sights:** Metal bead front. **Features:** Crossbolt safety; black rubber buttpad; twin-action slide bars; front-locking rotating bolt; removable segmented magazine plug to limit shotshell capacity for training purposes

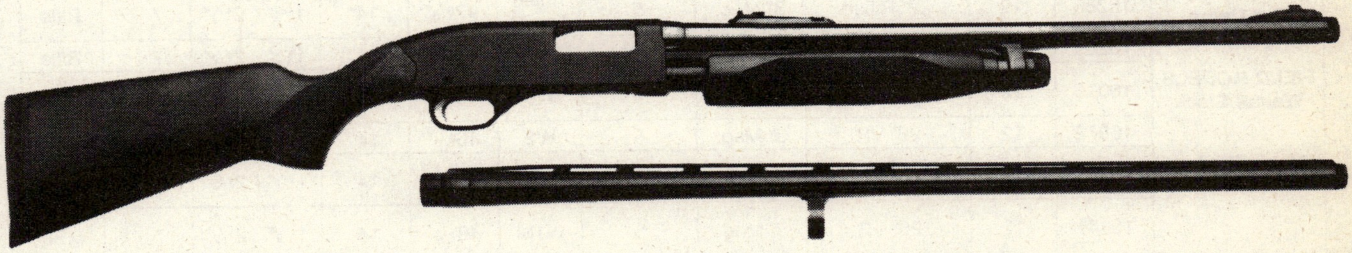

**MODEL 1300 RANGER 12 GAUGE DEER COMBO**
**22″ Rifled w/Sights & 28″ Vent Rib Barrels**

**SPECIFICATIONS MODEL 1300 RANGER, RANGER DEER & LADIES/YOUTH**

| Model | Gauge | Choke | Barrel Length & Type | Overall Length | Nominal Length of Pull | Nominal Weight (Lbs.) | Sights | Prices |
|---|---|---|---|---|---|---|---|---|
| **1300 Ranger** | 12 | W3 | 28″ VR | 48 5/8″ | 14″ | 7 1/4 | MBF | **$309.00** |
| | 20 | W3 | 28 VR | 48 5/8 | 14 | 7 | MBF | |
| | 12 | W3 | 26 VR | 46 5/8 | 14 | 7 1/4 | MBF | |
| | 20 | W3 | 26 VR | 46 5/8 | 14 | 7 | MBF | |
| **1300 Ranger Deer Combo** | 12 | Cyl. | 22 Smooth | 42 5/8 | 14 | 6 3/4 | Rifle | **401.00*** |
| 12 ga. Extra Barrel | 12 | W1M | 28 VR | 48 5/8 | 14 | 7 1/2 | MBF | |
| **1300 Ranger Deer** | 12 | Rifled Barrel | 22 Rifled | 42 5/8 | 14 | 7 1/4 | Rifle | **343.00** |
| **1300 Ranger Ladies/Youth** | 20 | W3 | 22 VR | 41 5/8 | 13 | 6 3/4 | MBF | **309.00** |

All models have 3″ Mag. chambers and 5-shot shell capacity, including one shotshell in chamber when ready to fire. VR-Ventilated rib. Cyl.-Cylinder Bore, R-Rifled Barrel. MBF-Metal bead front. RT-Rifle type front and rear sights. Model 1300 and Ranger pump-action shotguns have factory-installed plug which limits capacity to three shells. Ladies/Youth has factory-installed plug that limits capacity to one, two or three shells as desired. Extra barrels for Model 1300 and Ranger shotguns are available in 12 gauge, plain or vent rib, in a variety of barrel lengths and chokes; interchangeable with gauge. Winchoke sets with wrench come with gun as follows: W3W-Extra Full, Full, Modified tubes. W3-Full, Modified, Improved Cylinder tubes. W1M-Modified tube. Nominal drop at comb: 1 1/2″; nominal drop at heel: 2 1/2″ (2 3/8″-Ladies' models).

# WINCHESTER SHOTGUNS

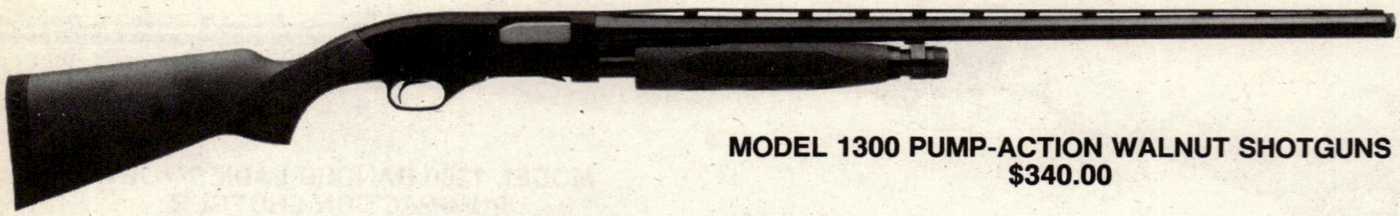

**MODEL 1300 PUMP-ACTION WALNUT SHOTGUNS**
**$340.00**

### SPECIFICATIONS MODEL 1300 DEER AND FIELD MODELS

| Model | Symbol Number | Gauge | Barrel Length & Type | Chamber | Shotshell Capacity* | Choke | Overall Length | Length of Pull | Drop At Comb/Heel | Weight (Lbs.) | Sights |
|---|---|---|---|---|---|---|---|---|---|---|---|
| DEER MODELS Walnut Stock | 16205 | 12 | 22″ Rifled | 3″ Mag. | 5 | Rifled | 42 5/8″ | 14″ | 1 1/2″ 2 1/2″ | 7 1/4 | Rifle |
| Black Shadow (Syn.) | 16275 | 12 | 22″ Smooth | 3″ Mag. | 5 | W1C | 42 5/8″ | 14″ | 1 1/2″ 2 1/2″ | 7 | Rifle |
| Advantage® Full Camo | 16285 | 12 | 22″ Rifled | 3″ Mag. | 5 | Rifled Barrel | 42 5/8″ | 14″ | 1 1/2″ 2 1/2″ | 7 | Rifle |
| | 16289 | 12 | 22″ Smooth | 3″ Mag. | 5 | W1C | 42 5/8″ | 14″ | 1 1/2″ 2 1/2″ | 7 | Rifle |
| FIELD MODELS Walnut Stock | 16015 | 12 | 28″ VR | 3″ Mag. | 5 | W3 | 48 5/8″ | 14″ | 1 1/2″ 2 1/2″ | 7 1/4 | MBF |
| | 16072 | 12 | 26″ VR | 3″ Mag. | 5 | W3 | 46 5/8″ | 14″ | 1 1/2″ 2 1/2″ | 7 1/4 | MBF |
| Black Shadow (Syn.) | 16339 | 12 | 28″ VR | 3″ Mag. | 5 | W1M | 48 5/8″ | 14″ | 1 1/2″ 2 1/2″ | 7 | MBF |
| | 16341 | 12 | 26″ VR | 3″ Mag. | 5 | W1M | 46 5/8″ | 14″ | 1 1/2″ 2 1/2″ | 7 | MBF |

* Includes one shotshell in chamber when ready to fire. VR-Vent rib. Winchoke sets with wrench come with gun as follows: W3-Full, Mod., Imp. Cyl. tubes. W1M-Mod. tube.

**MODEL 1300 ALL-PURPOSE REALTREE® TURKEY**
**$370.00 ($432.00 Full Camo, shown)**

**MODEL 1300 BLACK SHADOW TURKEY**
**$296.00**

### SPECIFICATIONS MODEL 1300 TURKEY

| Model | Gauge | Barrel Length & Type | Chamber | Shotshell Capacity | Choke | Overall Length | Length of Pull | Drop At Comb/Heel | Weight (Lbs.) | Sights |
|---|---|---|---|---|---|---|---|---|---|---|
| Realtree® All-Purpose Full Camo | 12 | 22″ VR | 3″ Mag. | 5 | W3W | 42 5/8″ | 14″ | 1 1/2″ 2 1/2″ | 7 | MBF |
| Realtree® All-Purpose (Matte Metal) | 12 | 22″ VR | 3″ Mag. | 5 | W3W | 42 5/8″ | 14″ | 1 1/2″ 2 1/2″ | 7 | MBF |
| Black Shadow (Syn. Stock) | 12 | 22″ VR | 3″ Mag. | 5 | W1F | 42 5/8″ | 14″ | 1 1/2″ 2 1/2″ | 7 | MBF |

VR-Vent rib. MBF-Metal bead front. Winchoke sets with wrench come with gun as follows: W3W-Extra Full, Full, Mod. tubes.

# Black Powder



For addresses and phone numbers of manufacturers and distributors included in this section, turn to *DIRECTORY OF MANUFACTURERS AND SUPPLIERS* at the back of the book.

1847 WALKER

## 1847 WALKER
## $296.00 (Percussion)

This replica of the Texas Ranger's and Mexican War's "Horse Pistol" was designed by Capt. Samuel Walker and built by Samuel Colt.

**SPECIFICATIONS**
**Caliber:** 44
**Capacity:** 6 shots
**Barrel length:** 9″ round w/hinged loading lever
**Overall length:** 15 1/2″ **Weight:** 72 oz.
**Features:** Engraved blued steel cylinder; color casehardened steel frame and backstrap; solid brass trigger guard; one-piece walnut grip

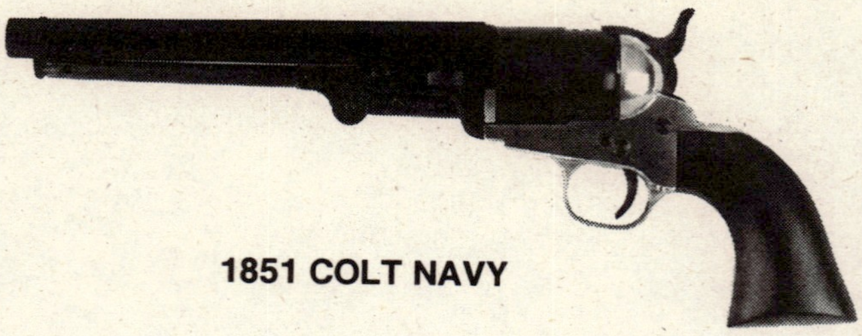

1851 COLT NAVY

## 1851 COLT NAVY
## $145.00 (Percussion)

This replica of the most famous revolver of the percussion era was used extensively during the Civil War and on the Western frontier.

**SPECIFICATIONS**
**Caliber:** 36 **Capacity:** 6 shots
**Barrel length:** 7 1/2″ octagonal w/hinged loading lever
**Overall length:** 13″ **Weight:** 44 oz.
**Features:** Solid brass frame, trigger guard and backstrap; one-piece walnut grip; engraved blued steel cylinder

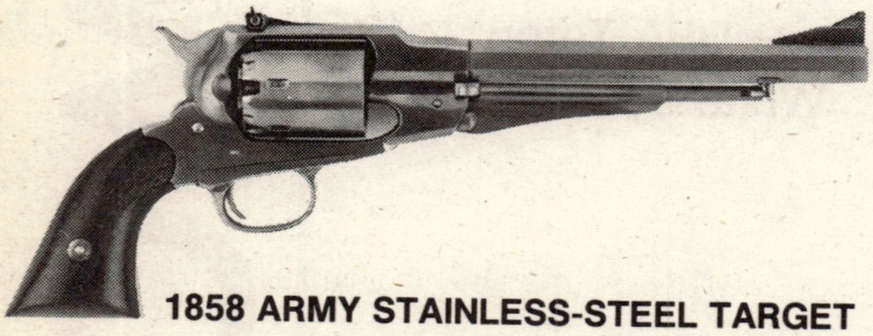

1858 ARMY STAINLESS-STEEL TARGET

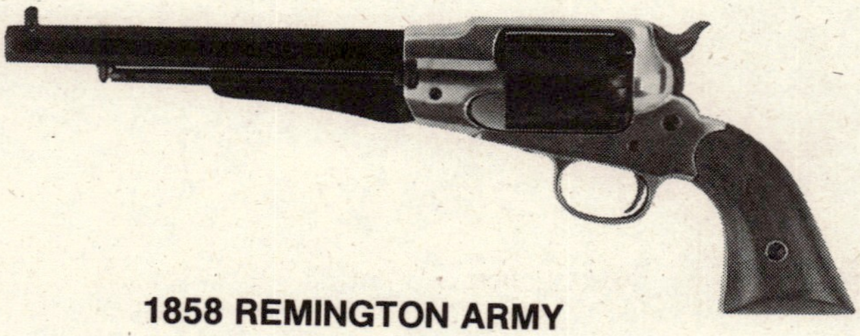

1858 REMINGTON ARMY

## 1858 REMINGTON ARMY
## $156.00 (Percussion)

This replica of the last of Remington's percussion revolvers saw extensive use in the Civil War.

**SPECIFICATIONS**
**Caliber:** 44 **Capacity:** 6 shots
**Barrel length:** 8″ octagonal w/creeping loading lever
**Overall length:** 13″ **Weight:** 38 oz.
**Features:** Two-piece walnut grips
Also available w/stainless-steel frame, barrel and cylinder, adj. rear target sight and ramp blade. **Price: $343.00**

## 1860 COLT ARMY
## $156.00 (Percussion)

Union troops issued this sidearm during the Civil War and subsequent Indian Wars.

**SPECIFICATIONS**
**Caliber:** 44 **Capacity:** 6 shots
**Barrel length:** 8″ round w/creeping loading lever
**Overall length:** 13 1/2″ **Weight:** 44 oz.
**Features:** Solid brass frame, trigger guard and backstrap; one-piece walnut grip; engraved blued steel cylinder

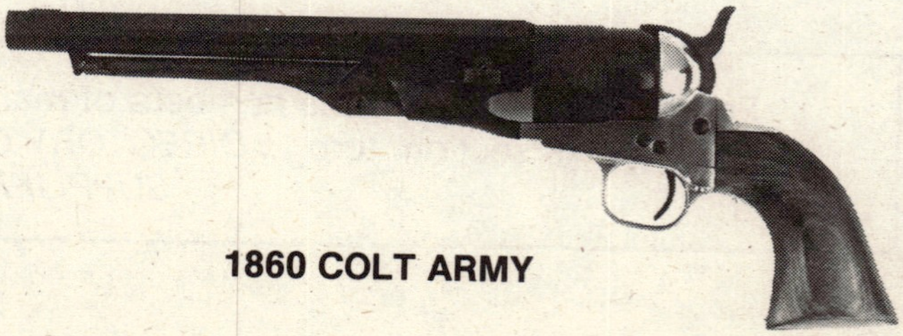

1860 COLT ARMY

# ARMSPORT

## REPLICA REVOLVERS

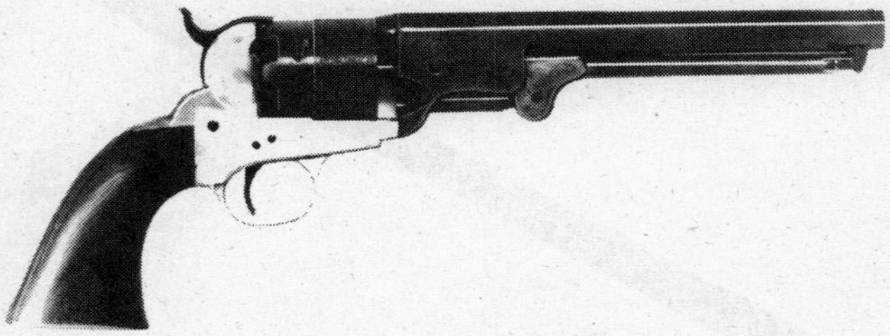

### MODEL 5133
### COLT 1851 NAVY "REB"

A modern replica of a Confederate percussion revolver in 36 or 44 caliber, this has a polished brass frame, rifled blued barrel and polished walnut grips.
**Price:** . . . . . . . . . . . . . . . . . . . . . . . . . . . . . . . . . . . . . . . . **$145.00**

### MODEL 5138
### REMINGTON ARMY STAINLESS STEEL

This stainless-steel version of the 44-caliber Remington New Army Revolver is made for the shooter who seeks the best. Its stainless-steel frame assures lasting good looks and durability.
**Price:** . . . . . . . . . . . . . . . . . . . . . . . . . . . . . . . . . . . . . . . . **$375.00**

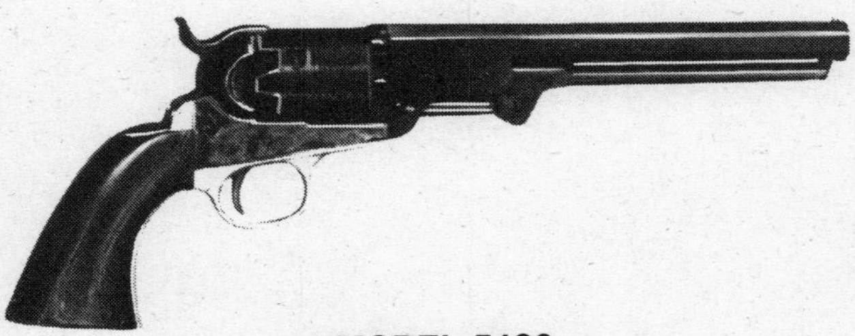

### MODEL 5136
### COLT 1851 NAVY STEEL

This authentic reproduction of the Colt Navy Revolver in 36 or 44 caliber, which helped shape the history of America, features a rifled barrel, casehardened steel frame, engraved cylinder, polished brass trigger guard and walnut grips.
**Price:** . . . . . . . . . . . . . . . . . . . . . . . . . . . . . . . . . . . . . . . . **$197.00**

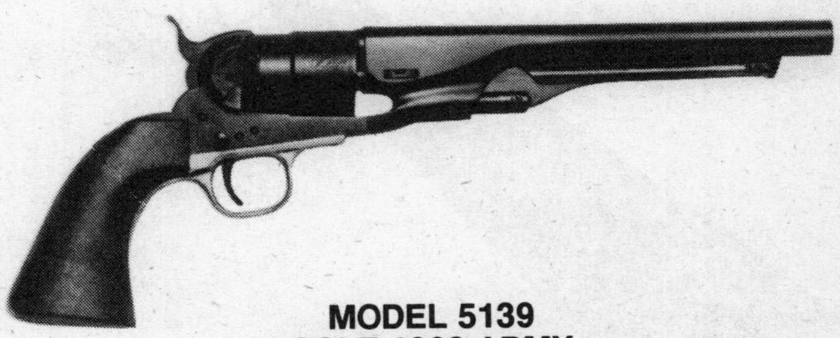

### MODEL 5139
### COLT 1860 ARMY

This authentic 44-caliber reproduction offers the same balance and ease of handling for fast shooting as the original 1860 Army model.
**Price:** . . . . . . . . . . . . . . . . . . . . . . . . . . . . . . . . . . . . . . . . **$230.00**
Also available:
**Model 5150 Stainless Steel** . . . . . . . . . . . . . . . . . . . . . . **395.00**

### MODEL 5120
### NEW REMINGTON ARMY
### STEEL REVOLVER

One of the most accurate cap-and-ball revolvers of the 1860s. Its rugged steel frame and top strap made this 44 caliber the favorite of all percussion cap revolvers.
**Price:** . . . . . . . . . . . . . . . . . . . . . . . . . . . . . . . . . . . . . . . . **$230.00**
**Model 5121** with brass frame: . . . . . . . . . . . . . . . . . **170.00**
Also available:
**Stainless Target Model 5149** . . . . . . . . . . . . . . . . . . **415.00**

### MODEL 5140
### COLT 1860 ARMY

Same as the Model 5139 Colt Army replica, but with brightly polished brass frame.
**Price:** . . . . . . . . . . . . . . . . . . . . . . . . . . . . . . . . . . . . . . . . **$165.00**

# CUMBERLAND MOUNTAIN ARMS

PLATEAU RIFLE

**PLATEAU RIFLE**
**$1085.00**

**SPECIFICATIONS**
**Calibers:** 40-65, 45-70 (and others as requested)
**Action:** CMA falling block; 4140 heat-treated steel (regular blue)
**Barrel length:** Up to 32″ (round)
**Weight:** 10½ lbs.
**Sights:** Marble
**Stock:** Grade #1 walnut stock with lacquer finish; smooth semibeavertail forearm; crescent buttplate

Also available:

| | |
|---|---|
| Half-round or half-octagonal barrel | **$115.00** |
| Octagonal barrel | **97.00** |
| Grade #2 walnut stock/forearm | **$ 86.00–$293.00** |
| Grade #3 walnut stock | **172.00– 402.00** |
| Standard checkering pattern | **207.00** |
| CMA Long-range Vernier Tang Sight | **365.00** |
| **MOUNTAIN MUZZLELOADER** | **931.50** |

# CVA REVOLVERS

1858 ARMY REVOLVER
STEEL FRAME

**Caliber:** 44
**Cylinder:** 6-shot
**Barrel length:** 8″ octagonal
**Overall length:** 13″
**Weight:** 38 oz.
**Sights:** Blade front; adjustable target
**Grip:** Two-piece walnut
**Prices:**
Brass Frame: . . . . . . . . . . . . . . . . . . . . . . . . . . . . . . . . . . . . . . **$139.95**
Steel Frame: . . . . . . . . . . . . . . . . . . . . . . . . . . . . . . . . . . . . . . **189.95**

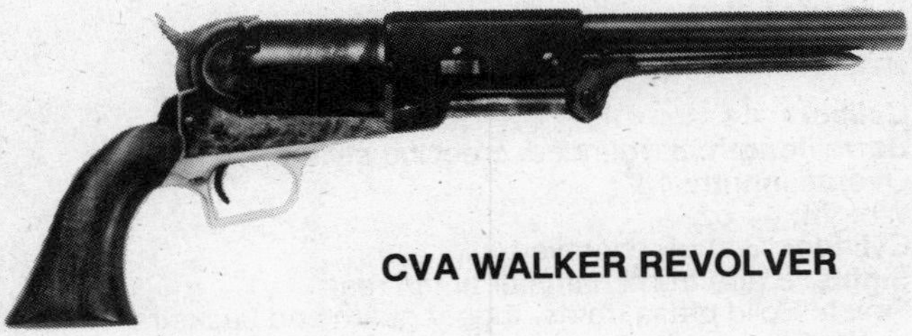

CVA WALKER REVOLVER

**Caliber:** 44
**Barrel:** 9″ rounded with hinged-style loading lever
**Cylinder:** 6-shot engraved
**Overall length:** 15 1/2″
**Weight:** 72 oz.
**Grip:** One-piece walnut
**Front sight:** Blade
**Finish:** Solid brass trigger guard
**Price:** . . . . . . . . . . . . . . . . . . . . . . . . . . . . . . . . . . . . . . . . . . . **$259.95**

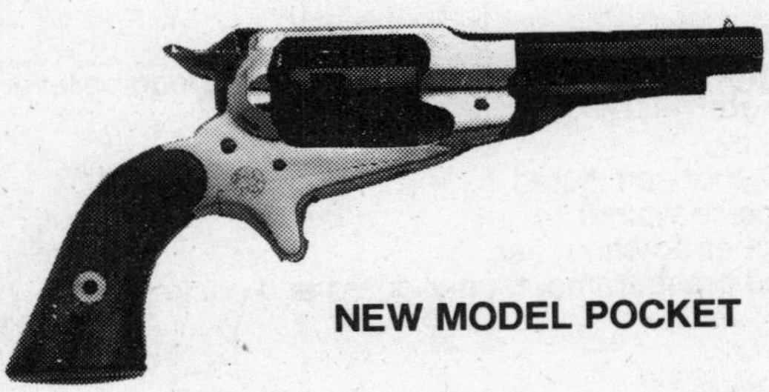

NEW MODEL POCKET

**Caliber:** 31 percussion
**Barrel length:** 4″ octagonal
**Cylinder:** 5 shots
**Overall length:** 7 1/2″
**Sights:** Post in front; groove in frame in rear
**Weight:** 15 oz.
**Finish:** Solid brass frame
**Price:** . . . . . . . . . . . . . . . . . . . . . . . . . . . . . . . . . . . . . . . . . . . **$139.95**

REMINGTON BISON

**Caliber:** 44
**Cylinder:** 6-shot
**Barrel length:** 10 1/4″ octagonal
**Overall length:** 18″
**Weight:** 48 oz.
**Sights:** Fixed blade front; screw adjustable target rear
**Grip:** Two-piece walnut
**Finish:** Solid brass frame
**Price:** . . . . . . . . . . . . . . . . . . . . . . . . . . . . . . . . . . . . . . . . . . . **$187.95**

# CVA REVOLVERS

**1851 NAVY REVOLVER
BRASS FRAME**

**Caliber:** 36 and 44
**Barrel length:** 7 1/2″ octagonal; hinged-style loading lever
**Overall length:** 13″
**Weight:** 44 oz.
**Cylinder:** 6-shot, engraved
**Sights:** Post front; hammer notch rear
**Grip:** One-piece walnut
**Finish:** Solid brass frame, trigger guard and backtrap; blued barrel and cylinder; color casehardened loading lever and hammer
**Prices:**
Finished . . . . . . . . . . **$139.95**
Kit (44 cal. only) . . . . . . . . . . **115.95**

**1861 NAVY REVOLVER
BRASS FRAME**

**Calibers:** 44
**Barrel length:** 8″ rounded; creeping style
**Overall length:** 13″
**Weight:** 44 oz.
**Cylinder:** 6-shot, engraved
**Sights:** Blade front; hammer notch rear
**Finish:** Solid brass frame, trigger guard and backstrap; blued barrel and cylinder
**Grip:** One-piece walnut
**Price:** Finished . . . . . . . . . . **$139.95**

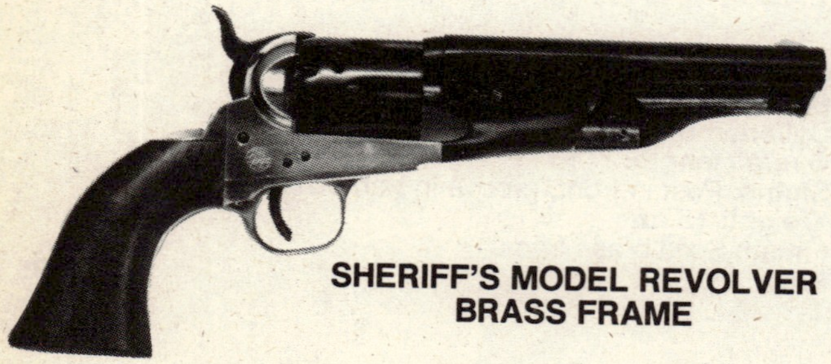

**SHERIFF'S MODEL REVOLVER
BRASS FRAME**

**Caliber:** 36
**Barrel length:** 5 1/2″ (octagonal w/creeping-style loading lever)
**Overall length:** 11 1/2″
**Weight:** 40 oz.
**Cylinder:** 6-shot semifluted
**Grip:** One-piece walnut
**Sight:** Hammer notch in rear
**Finish:** Solid brass frame, trigger guard and backstrap
**Price:** . . . . . . . . . . **$156.95**

Also available:
**Engraved Nickel-Plated Model** with matching flask
**Price:** . . . . . . . . . . **$194.95**

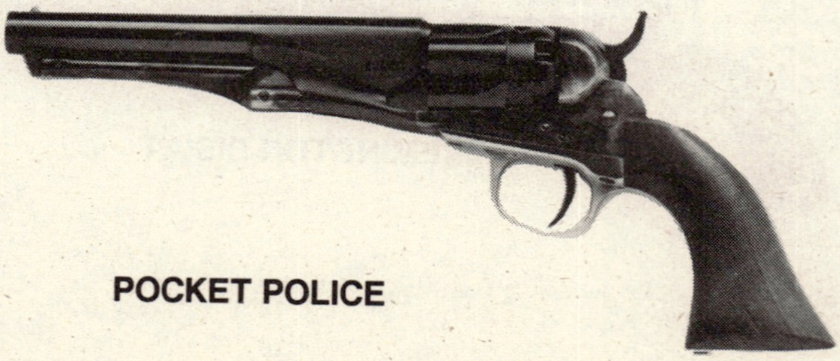

**POCKET POLICE**

**Caliber:** 36
**Capacity:** 5-shot cylinder
**Barrel length:** 5 1/2″ octagonal, with creeping-style loading lever
**Overall length:** 10 1/2″
**Weight:** 26 oz.
**Sights:** Post front; hammer notch rear
**Price:** w/Brass Frame . . . . . . . . . . **$139.95**

# CVA PISTOLS

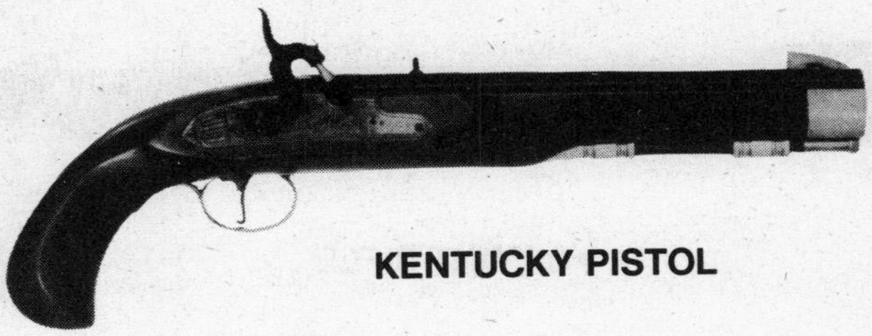

KENTUCKY PISTOL

**Caliber:** 50 percussion
**Barrel:** 9 3/4″, rifled, octagonal
**Overall length:** 15 1/2″
**Weight:** 40 oz.
**Finish:** Blued barrel, brass hardware
**Sights:** Brass blade front; fixed open rear
**Stock:** Select hardwood
**Ignition:** Engraved, color casehardened percussion lock, screw adjustable sear engagement
**Accessories:** Brass-tipped, hardwood ramrod; stainless-steel nipple or flash hole liner
**Prices:**
Finished . . . . . . . . . . **$149.95**
Percussion Kit . . . . . . . . . . **109.95**

HAWKEN PISTOL

**Caliber:** 50 percussion
**Barrel length:** 9 3/4″, octagonal
**Overall length:** 16 1/2″
**Weight:** 50 oz.
**Trigger:** Early-style brass
**Sights:** Beaded steel blade front; fully adjustable rear (click adj. screw settings lock into position)
**Stock:** Select hardwood
**Finish:** Solid brass wedge plate, nose cap, ramrod thimbles, trigger guard and grip cap
**Prices:**
Finished . . . . . . . . . . **$139.95**
Kit . . . . . . . . . . **119.95**
Laminated stock . . . . . . . . . . **159.95**

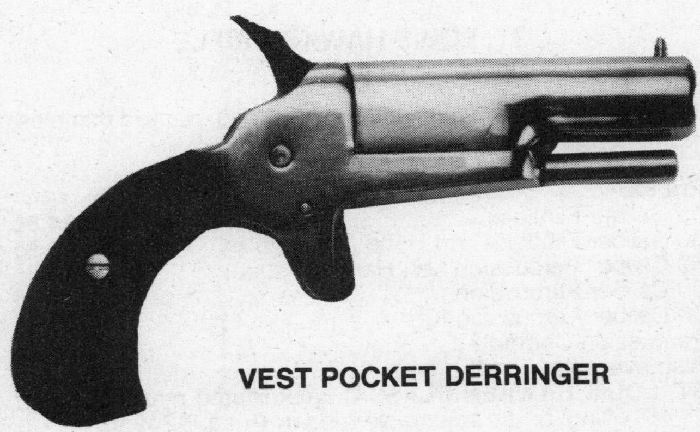

VEST POCKET DERRINGER

**Caliber:** 31 Derringer
**Barrel length:** 2 1/2″ (single shot) brass
**Overall length:** 5″
**Weight:** 16 oz.
**Grip:** Two-piece walnut
**Frame:** Brass
**Price:** Finished . . . . . . . . . . **$69.95**

# CVA RIFLES

## VARMINT RIFLE

**Caliber:** 32 percussion
**Barrel length:** 24″ octagonal; $^7/_8$″ across flats
**Rifling:** 1 in 56″
**Overall length:** 40″
**Weight:** $6^3/_4$ lbs.
**Lock:** Color casehardened with 45° offset hammer
**Trigger:** Single trigger
**Sights:** Steel blade front; Patridge-style click-adjustable rear
**Stock:** Select hardwood
**Features:** Brass trigger guard, nose cap, wedge plate, thimble and buttplate
**Price:** . . . . . . . . . . . . . . . . . . . . . . . . . . . . . . . . . . **$219.95**

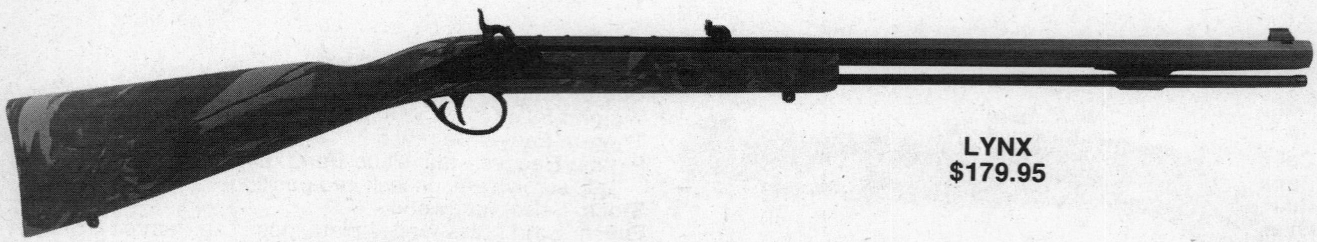

## LYNX
## $179.95

**Calibers:** 50 and 54 percussion
**Barrel length:** 26″ ($^{15}/_{16}$″ octagonal)
**Rifling:** 1:32″
**Overall length:** 40″
**Weight:** $7^1/_2$ lbs.
**Sights:** Blue beaded blade front; economy rear
**Stock:** Dura-Grip; checkered forend and trigger
**Finish:** RealTree all-purpose gray

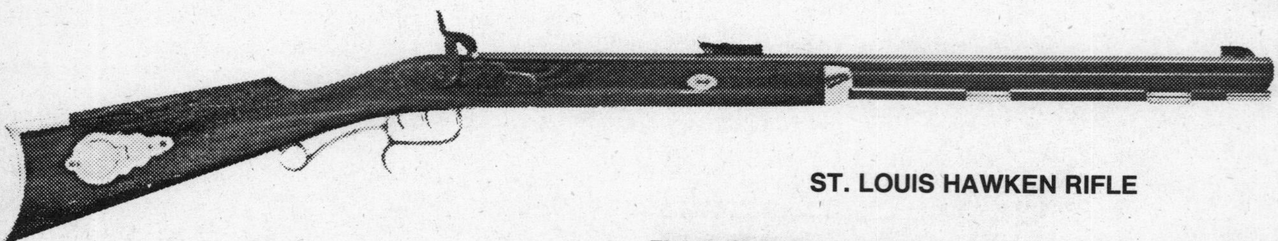

## ST. LOUIS HAWKEN RIFLE

**Calibers:** 50 and 54 percussion or flintlock (50 cal. only)
**Barrel:** 28″ octagonal $^{15}/_{16}$″ across flats; hooked breech; rifling one turn in 66″, 8 lands and deep grooves
**Overall length:** 44″
**Weight:** 8 lbs.
**Sights:** Dovetail, beaded blade front; adjustable open hunting-style dovetail rear
**Stock:** Select hardwood with beavertail cheekpiece
**Triggers:** Double set; fully adjustable trigger pull
**Finish:** Solid brass wedge plates, nose cap, ramrod thimbles, trigger guard and patchbox

**Prices:**

| | |
|---|---|
| 50 Caliber Flintlock . . . . . . . . . . . . . . . . . . . . . . | **$234.95** |
| 50 Caliber Flintlock Left Hand (finished) . . . . . . . . . | **249.95** |
| 50 Caliber Percussion Left Hand (finished) . . . . . . . | **234.95** |
| 50 Caliber Percussion . . . . . . . . . . . . . . . . . . . . . | **209.95** |
| 50 Caliber Percussion Kit . . . . . . . . . . . . . . . . . . | **169.95** |
| Percussion Combo Kit . . . . . . . . . . . . . . . . . . . . . | **229.95** |

Also available:
**ST. LOUIS HAWKEN CLASSIC** w/laminated matte finish; 1:48″ rifling; brass adjustable trigger. **Price: $249.95**

# CVA RIFLES

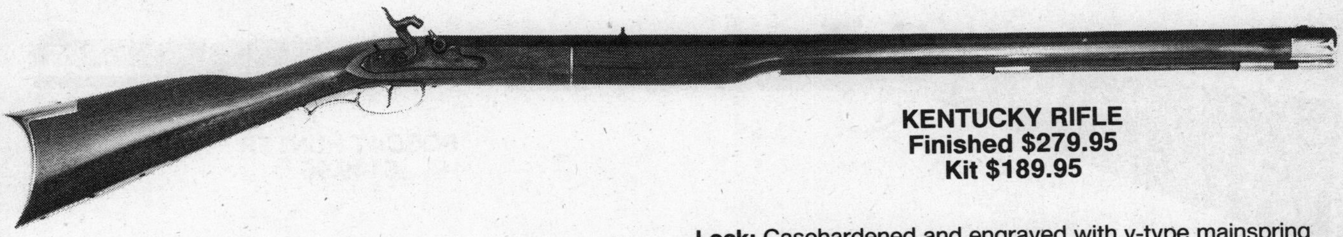

**KENTUCKY RIFLE**
**Finished $279.95**
**Kit $189.95**

**Caliber:** 50 percussion
**Barrel length:** 33 1/2″ octagonal; 7/8″ across flats
**Rifling:** 1 in 66″
**Overall length:** 48″ **Weight:** 7 1/2 lbs.
**Lock:** Casehardened and engraved with v-type mainspring
**Trigger:** Early brass-style single trigger
**Sights:** Brass blade front; fixed open rear
**Features:** Solid brass trigger guard, buttplate, toe plate, nose cap and thimble; select hardwood stock

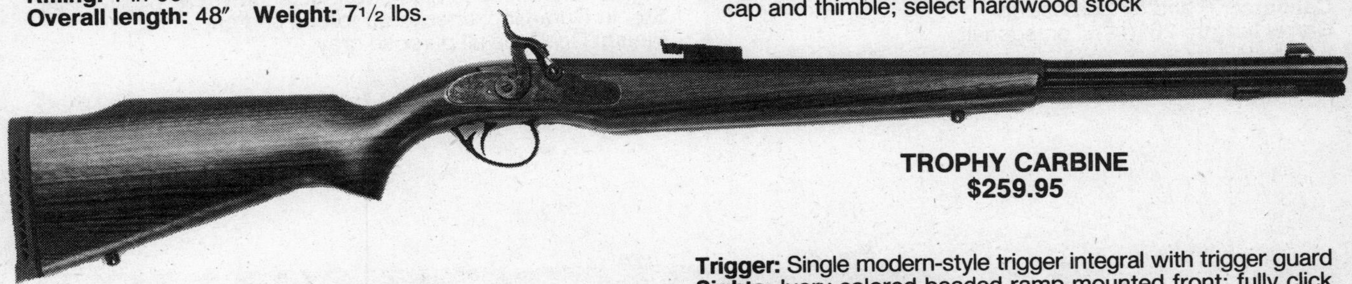

**TROPHY CARBINE**
**$259.95**

**Calibers:** 50 and 54 percussion
**Barrel length:** 24″ half-round, half-octagonal; 15/16″ across flats
**Rifling:** 1 in 32″
**Overall length:** 40″ **Weight:** 6 3/4 lbs.
**Lock:** Hawken-style with bridle and fly; engraved
**Trigger:** Single modern-style trigger integral with trigger guard
**Sights:** Ivory-colored beaded ramp mounted front; fully click adjustable rear
**Stock:** Walnut with Monte Carlo comb, pistol grip and formed cheekpiece
**Features:** Ventilated rubber recoil pad, molded black oversized trigger guard and blued thimble

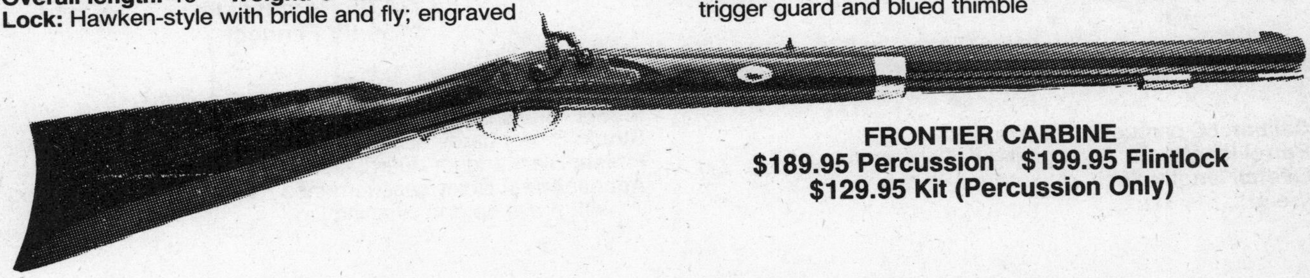

**FRONTIER CARBINE**
**$189.95 Percussion $199.95 Flintlock**
**$129.95 Kit (Percussion Only)**

**Caliber:** 50 percussion or flintlock
**Barrel length:** 24″ octagonal; 15/16″ across flats
**Rifling:** 1 turn in 48″ (8 lands and deep grooves)
**Overall length:** 40″ **Weight:** 6 lbs. 12 oz.
**Sights:** Steel-beaded blade front; hunting-style fully adjustable rear
**Trigger:** Early-style brass with tension spring
**Features:** Solid brass buttplate, trigger guard, wedge plate, nose cap and thimble, select hardwood stock
**Accessories:** Stainless steel nipple, hardwood ramrod with brass tips and cleaning jag

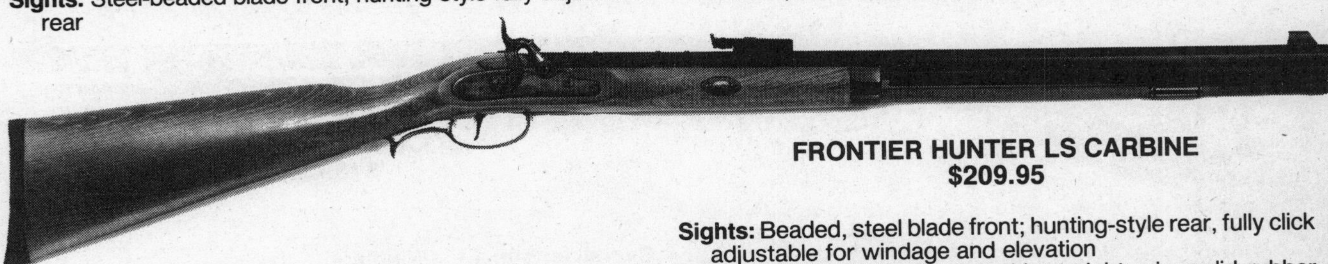

**FRONTIER HUNTER LS CARBINE**
**$209.95**

**Calibers:** 50 and 54 percussion
**Barrel length:** 24″, blued, 15/16″ octagonal
**Overall length:** 40″ **Weight:** 6 1/2 lbs.
**Sights:** Beaded, steel blade front; hunting-style rear, fully click adjustable for windage and elevation
**Stock:** Laminated hardwood with straight grip; solid rubber recoil pad
**Trigger:** Early-style blue
**Features:** Black-chromed nose cap, trigger guard and blued wedge plate

**BOBCAT HUNTER**
**$149.95**

**SPECIFICATIONS**
**Calibers:** 50 and 54 percussion
**Barrel length:** 26″ (15/16″ octagonal)
**Rifling:** 1:48″
**Overall length:** 40″
**Trigger:** Oversized trigger guard
**Sights:** Blue beaded blade front; economy rear
**Stock:** Dura-Grip; checkered forend and grip
**Finish:** RealTree all-purpose gray

**PLAINSMAN RIFLE**
**$174.95 Percussion**
**$159.95 Flintlock**

**Caliber:** 50 percussion and flintlock
**Barrel length:** 26″ octagonal (15/16″ across flats)
**Overall length:** 40″
**Weight:** 6 1/2 lbs.
**Trigger:** Single trigger with large trigger guard
**Sights:** Brass blade front; adjustable rear
**Stock:** Select hardwood
**Finish:** Black trigger guard, wedge plate and thimble
**Accessories:** Color casehardened nipple, hardwood ramrod with brass tip and cleaning jag

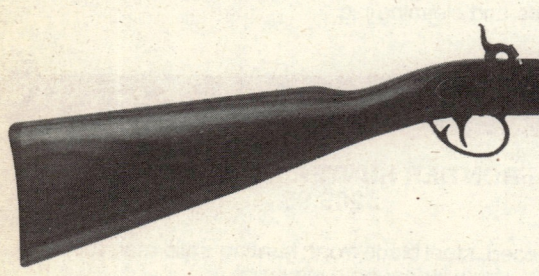

**WOODSMAN RIFLE LS**
**$189.95**

**SPECIFICATIONS**
**Calibers:** 50 and 54 percussion
**Barrel length:** 26″ blued octagon
**Overall length:** 40″ **Weight:** 6 1/2 lbs.
**Trigger:** Single trigger w/oversized trigger guard
**Stock:** Dark brown stained laminated hardwood
**Features:** Blued wedge plate and ramp-mounted thimble; black polymer buttplate; synthetic ramrod with black tip and cleaning jag

# CVA RIFLES

**APOLLO COMET**
**$259.95**

**Caliber:** 50 percussion
**Barrel length:** 24″
**Rifling:** 1 in 32″
**Overall length:** 42″
**Sights:** Blue beaded blade front; micro-adjustable rear
**Stock:** Synthetic; black matte finish
**Features:** Removable breech plug; synthetic ramrod

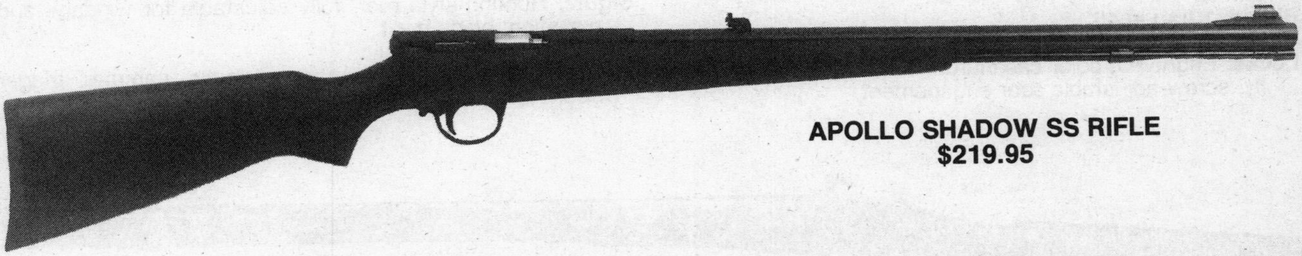

**APOLLO SHADOW SS RIFLE**
**$219.95**

**Calibers:** 50 and 54 percussion
**Barrel length:** 24″ blued round taper with octagonal one-piece receiver
**Overall length:** 42″ **Weight:** 9 lbs.
**Trigger:** Box-style with hooking tumbler; auto safety system
**Sights:** Ramp-mounted, blue beaded blade with hood front; fully click micro-adjustable rear; drilled and tapped for scope mounting
**Stock:** Synthetic; black, textured epoxicoat Dura-Grip synthetic with raised comb and pistol grip
**Features:** Solid rubber recoil pad; bottom screw attachment and blued thimble
Also available:
**APOLLO ECLIPSE** with weatherproof Dura-Grip synthetic stock, sling swivel studs, sporter adjustable rear sight. **Price: $189.95**

**APOLLO ECLIPSE**

**APOLLO CLASSIC**
**$259.95**

**Calibers:** 50 and 54 percussion
**Barrel length:** 24″ blued round taper with octagonal one-piece receiver
**Overall length:** 42″ **Weight:** 9 lbs.
**Trigger:** Box-style with hooking tumbler; auto safety system
**Sights:** Steel ramp-mounted beaded blade front; click adjustable-style rear; drilled and tapped for scope mounting
**Stock:** Laminated hardwood with pistol grip, raised comb and recoil pad; sling swivel stud on buttstock
**Features:** Molded black oversized trigger guard; bottom screw attachment, blued thimble and fiberglass ramrod

# CVA RIFLES/SHOTGUNS

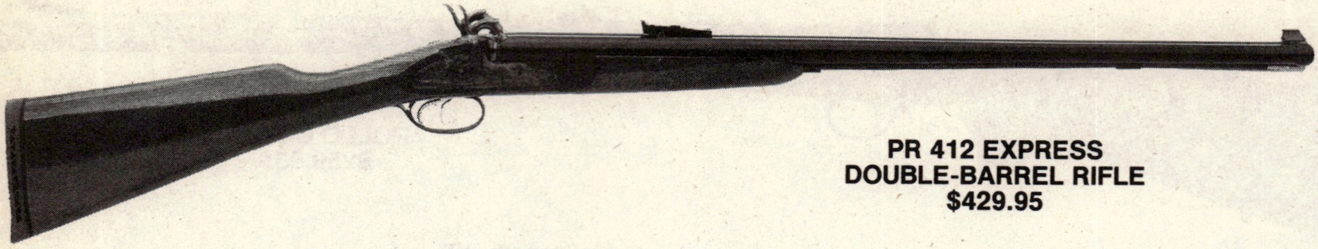

**PR 412 EXPRESS DOUBLE-BARREL RIFLE**
**$429.95**

**Caliber:** 50 percussion
**Barrels:** Two laser-aligned, tapered 28″ round; button-style breech
**Rifling:** 1 turn in 48″
**Overall length:** 44″ **Weight:** 10 lbs.
**Locks:** Engraved, color casehardened plate; includes bridle, fly, screw-adjustable sear engagement
**Triggers:** Double, gold tone
**Sights:** Hunting-style rear, fully adjustable for windage and elevation; blade front
**Stock:** Select hardwood
**Features:** Casehardened engraved locks, hammer, trigger guard and tang

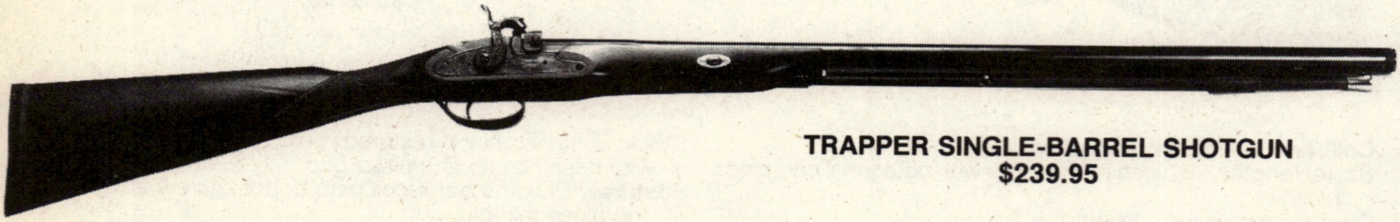

**TRAPPER SINGLE-BARREL SHOTGUN**
**$239.95**

**Gauge:** 12 percussion
**Barrel length:** 28″ round, chrome-lined bore; hooked breech; three Modified interchangeable chokes
**Overall length:** 46″ **Weight:** 6 lbs.
**Trigger:** Early-style steel
**Lock:** Color casehardened; engraved with v-type mainspring, bridle and fly
**Sights:** Brass bead front (no rear sight)
**Stock:** Select hardwood
**Features:** Color casehardened engraved lockplate; ventilated recoil pad, fiberglass ramrod and rear sling swivel

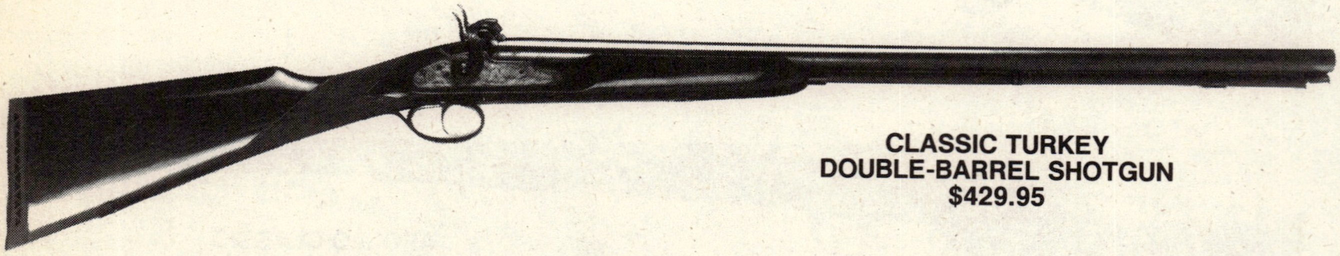

**CLASSIC TURKEY DOUBLE-BARREL SHOTGUN**
**$429.95**

**Gauge:** 12 percussion
**Barrel length:** 28″ round, chrome-lined bore; double button-style breech, Modified choke
**Overall length:** 45″ **Weight:** 9 lbs.
**Triggers:** Hinged, gold-tone double triggers
**Lock:** Color casehardened; engraved with v-type mainspring, bridle and fly
**Sights:** Brass bead front (no rear sight)
**Stock:** Select hardwood; wraparound forearm with bottom screw attachment
**Features:** Ventilated recoil pad; rear sling swivel; fiberglass ramrod

# DIXIE

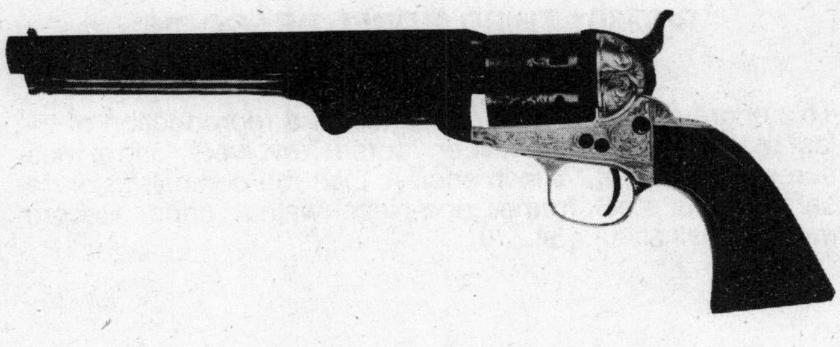

**DIXIE NAVY REVOLVER**
**Plain Model $135.00**
**Engraved Model $139.95**
**Kit $114.00**

This 36-caliber revolver was a favorite of the officers of the Civil War. Although called a Navy type, it is somewhat misnamed since many more of the Army personnel used it. Made in Italy; uses .376 mold or ball to fit and number 11 caps. Blued steel barrel and cylinder with brass frame.

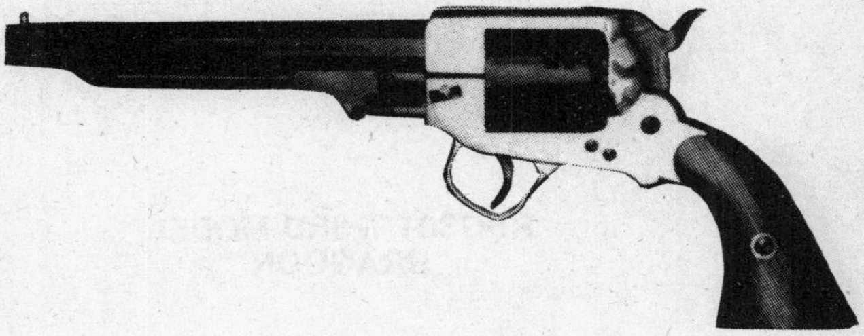

**SPILLER & BURR 36 CALIBER BRASS-FRAME REVOLVER**
**$125.00 Kit $115.00**

The 36-caliber octagonal barrel on this revolver is 7 inches long. The six-shot cylinder chambers mike .378, and the hammer engages a slot between the nipples on the cylinder as an added safety device. It has a solid brass trigger guard and frame with backstrap cast integral with the frame, two-piece walnut grips and Whitney-type casehardened loading lever.

**REMINGTON 44 ARMY REVOLVER**
**$169.95**

All steel external surfaces finished bright blue, including 8″ octagonal barrel (hammer is casehardened). Polished brass guard and two-piece walnut grips are standard.

**DIXIE 1860 ARMY REVOLVER**
**$169.95**

The Dixie 1860 Army has a half-fluted cylinder and its chamber diameter is .447. Use .451 round ball mold to fit this 8-inch barrel revolver. Cut for shoulder stock.

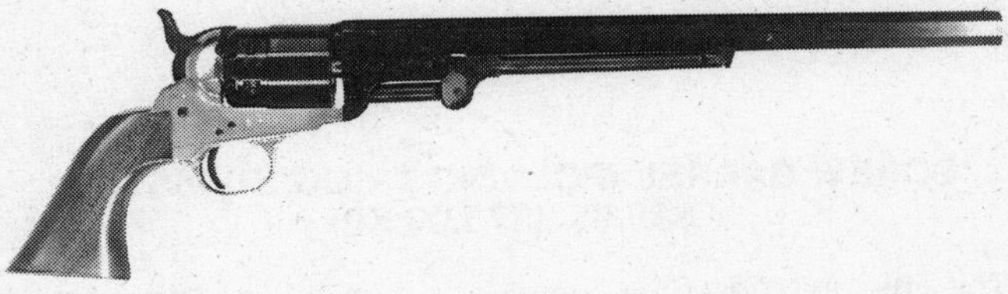

**"WYATT EARP" REVOLVER**
**$130.00**

This 44-caliber revolver has a 12-inch octagon rifled barrel and rebated cylinder. Highly polished brass frame, backstrap and trigger guard. The barrel and cylinder have a deep blue luster finish. Hammer, trigger, and loading lever are casehardened. Walnut grips. Recommended ball size is .451.

**RHO200 WALKER REVOLVER**
**$225.95 Kit $184.95**

This 4½-pound, 44-caliber pistol is the largest ever made. Steel backstrap; guard is brass with Walker-type rounded-to-frame walnut grips; all other parts are blued. Chambers measure .445 and take a .450 ball slightly smaller than the originals.

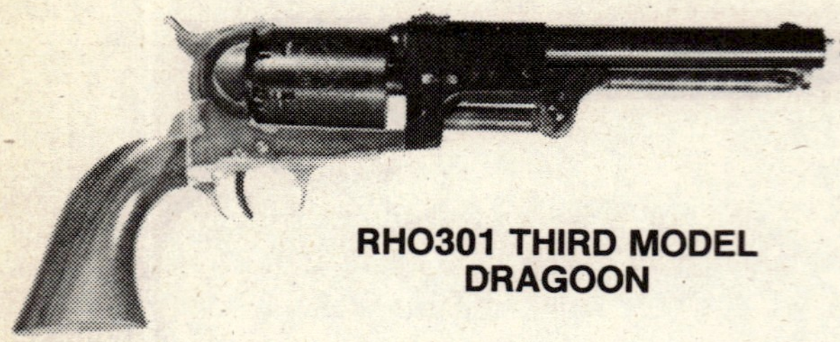

RHO301 THIRD MODEL DRAGOON

## RHO301 THIRD MODEL DRAGOON
**$199.95**

This engraved-cylinder, $4\frac{1}{2}$-pounder is a reproduction of the last model of Colt's 44-caliber "horse" revolvers. Barrel measures $7\frac{3}{8}$ inches, $\frac{1}{8}$ inch shorter than the original; color casehardened steel frame, one-piece walnut grips. Recommended ball size: .454.

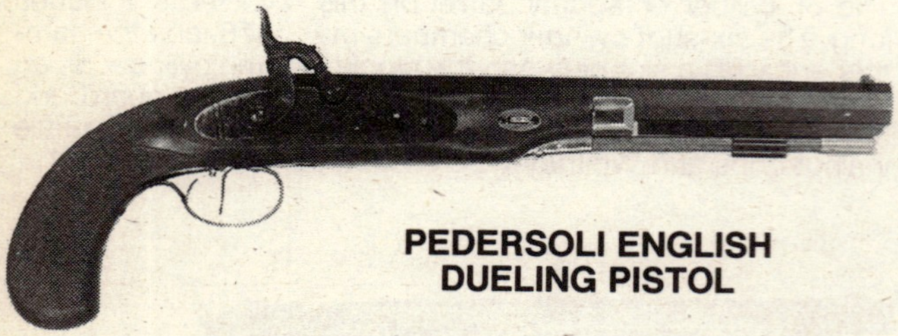

PEDERSOLI ENGLISH DUELING PISTOL

## PEDERSOLI ENGLISH DUELING PISTOL
**$265.00**

This reproduction of an English percussion dueling pistol, created by Charles Moore of London, features a European walnut halfstock with oil finish and checkered grip. The 45-caliber octagonal barrel is 11″ with 12 grooves and a twist of 1 in 15″. Nose cap and thimble are silver. Barrel is blued; lock and trigger guard are color casehardened.

PEDERSOLI MANG TARGET PISTOL

## PEDERSOLI MANG TARGET PISTOL
**$749.00**

Designed specifically for the precision target shooter, this 38-caliber pistol has a $10\frac{7}{16}$″ octagonal barrel with 7 lands and grooves. Twist is 1 in 15″. **Sights:** Blade front dovetailed into barrel; rear mounted on breechplug tang, adjustable for windage. **Overall length:** $17\frac{1}{4}$″. **Weight:** $2\frac{1}{2}$ lbs.

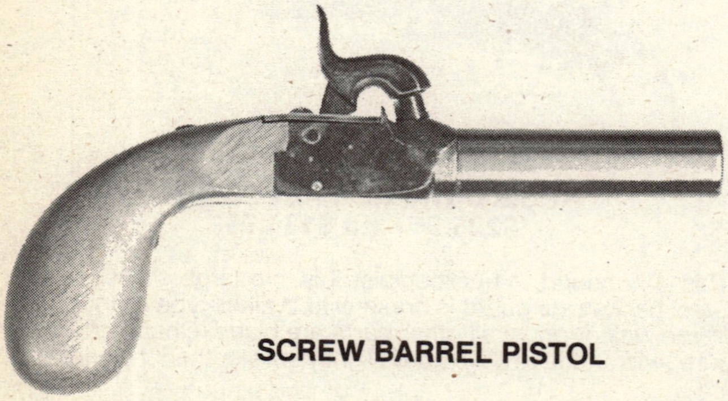

SCREW BARREL PISTOL

## SCREW BARREL (FOLDING TRIGGER) PISTOL
**$89.95 ($75.00 Kit)**

This little gun, only $6\frac{1}{2}$″ overall, has a unique loading system that eliminates the need for a ramrod. The barrel is loosened with a barrel key, then unscrewed from the frame by hand. The recess is then filled with 10 grains of FFFg black powder, the .445 round ball is seated in the dished area, and the barrel is then screwed back into place. The .245×32 nipple uses #11 percussion caps. The pistol also features a sheath trigger that folds into the frame, then drops down for firing when the hammer is cocked. Comes with color casehardened frame, trigger and center-mounted hammer.

# DIXIE

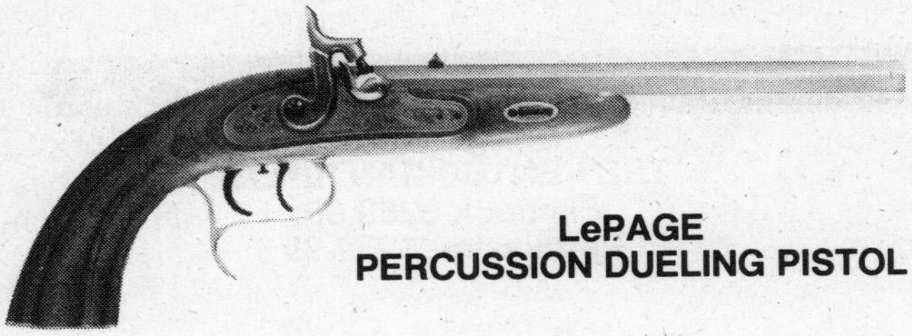

LePAGE
PERCUSSION DUELING PISTOL

## LePAGE PERCUSSION DUELING PISTOL
**$259.95**

This 45-caliber percussion pistol features a blued 10″ octagonal barrel with 12 lands and grooves; a brass-bladed front sight with open rear sight dovetailed into the barrel; polished silver-plated trigger guard and butt cap. Right side of barrel is stamped "LePage á Paris." Double-set triggers are single screw adjustable. **Overall length:** 16″. **Weight:** $2\frac{1}{2}$ lbs.

## DIXIE PENNSYLVANIA PISTOL
**Percussion $149.95 Kit $129.95**
**Flintlock $149.95 Kit $119.95**

Available in 44-caliber percussion or flintlock. The bright luster blued barrel measures 10″ long; rifled, $\frac{7}{8}$-inch octagonal and takes .430 ball; barrel is held in place with a steel wedge and tang screw; brass front and rear sights. The brass trigger guard, thimbles, nose cap, wedge plates and side plates are highly polished. Locks are fine quality with early styling. Plates measure $4\frac{3}{4}$ inches $\times$ $\frac{7}{8}$ inch. Percussion hammer is engraved and both plates are left in the white. The flint is an excellent style lock with the gooseneck hammer having an early wide thumbpiece. The stock is walnut stained and has a wide bird's-head-type grip.

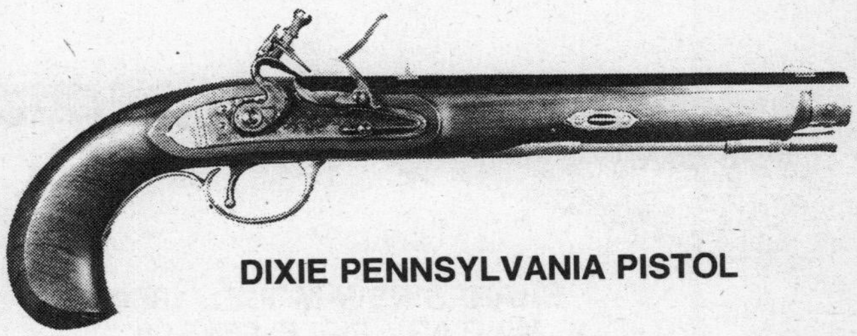

DIXIE PENNSYLVANIA PISTOL

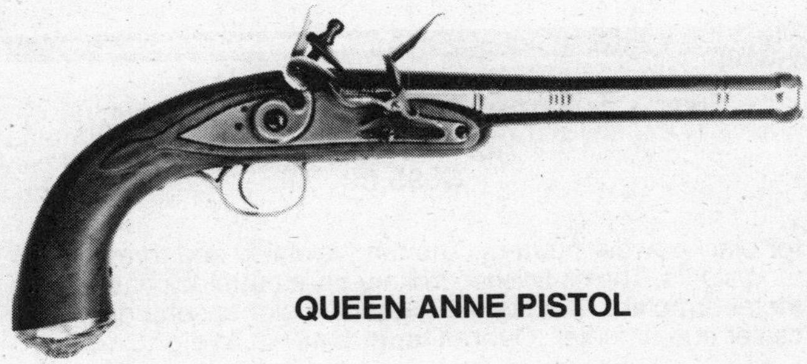

QUEEN ANNE PISTOL

## QUEEN ANNE PISTOL
**$189.95**
**Kit $154.95**

Named for the Queen of England (1702–1714), this flintlock pistol has a $7\frac{1}{2}$″ barrel that tapers from rear to front with a cannon-shaped muzzle. The brass trigger guard is fluted and the brass butt on the walnut stock features a grotesque mask worked into it. **Overall length:** 13″. **Weight:** $2\frac{1}{4}$ lbs.

## FHO201 FRENCH CHARLEVILLE FLINT PISTOL (Not shown)
**$195.00**

Reproduction of the Model 1777 Cavalry, Revolutionary War-era pistol. Has reversed frizzen spring; forend and lock housing are all in one; casehardened, round-faced, double-throated hammer; walnut stock; casehardened frizzen and trigger; shoots .680 round ball loaded with about 40 grains FFg black powder.

## DOUBLE-BARREL MAGNUM MUZZLELOADING SHOTGUN (not shown)

A full 12-gauge, high-quality, double-barreled percussion shotgun with 30-inch browned barrels. Will take the plastic shot cups for better patterns. Bores are Choked, Modified and Full. Lock, barrel tang and trigger are casehardened in a light gray color and are nicely engraved.

**12 Gauge** . . . . . . . . . . . . . . . . . . . . . . . . . . . . . . . . . **$399.00**
**12-Gauge Kit** . . . . . . . . . . . . . . . . . . . . . . . . . . . . . . 350.00
**10-Gauge Magnum** (double barrel—right-hand = cyl. bore, left-hand = Mod.) . . . . . . . . . . . . . . . . 495.00
**10-Gauge Magnum Kit** . . . . . . . . . . . . . . . . . . . . . . . . 375.00

# DIXIE

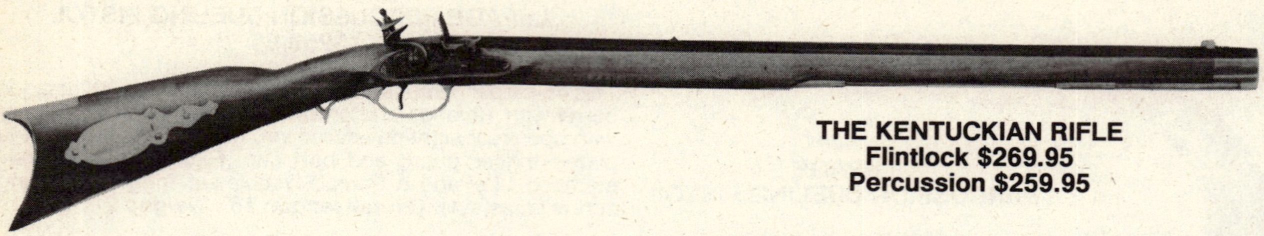

**THE KENTUCKIAN RIFLE**
**Flintlock $269.95**
**Percussion $259.95**

This 45-caliber rifle, in flintlock or percussion, has a $33\frac{1}{2}$-inch blued octagonal barrel that is $\frac{13}{16}$ inch across the flats. The bore is rifled with 6 lands and grooves of equal width and about .006″ deep. Land-to-land diameter is .453 with groove-to-groove diameter of .465. Ball size ranges from .445 to .448.

The rifle has a brass blade front sight and a steel open rear sight. The Kentuckian is furnished with brass buttplate, trigger guard, patchbox, sideplate, thimbles and nose cap plus casehardened and engraved lock plate. Highly polished and finely finished stock in European walnut. **Overall length:** 48″. **Weight:** Approx. $6\frac{1}{4}$ lbs.

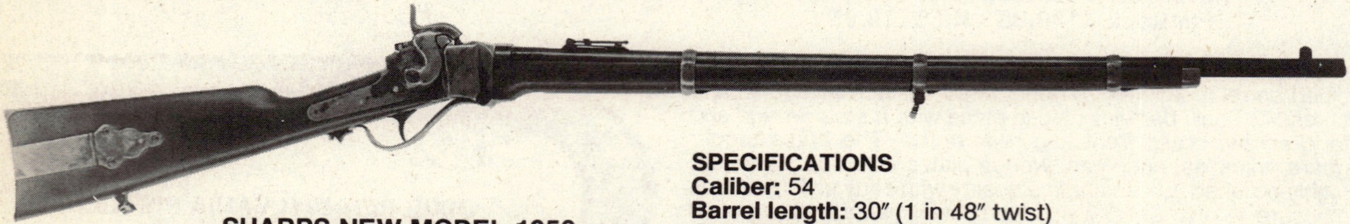

**SHARPS NEW MODEL 1859**
**MILITARY RIFLE $895.00**

Initially used by the First Connecticut Volunteers, this rifle is associated mostly with the 1st U.S. (Berdan's) Sharpshooters. There were 6,689 made with most going to the Sharpshooters (2,000) and the U.S. Navy (2,780). Made in Italy by David Pedersoli & Co.

**SPECIFICATIONS**
**Caliber:** 54
**Barrel length:** 30″ (1 in 48″ twist)
**Overall length:** $45\frac{1}{2}$″
**Weight:** 9 lbs.
**Sights:** Blade front; rear sight adjustable for elevation and windage
**Features:** Buttstock and forend straight-grained and oilfinished walnut; three barrel bands, receiver, hammer, nose cap, lever, patchbox cover and butt are all color casehardened; sling swivels attached to middle band and butt

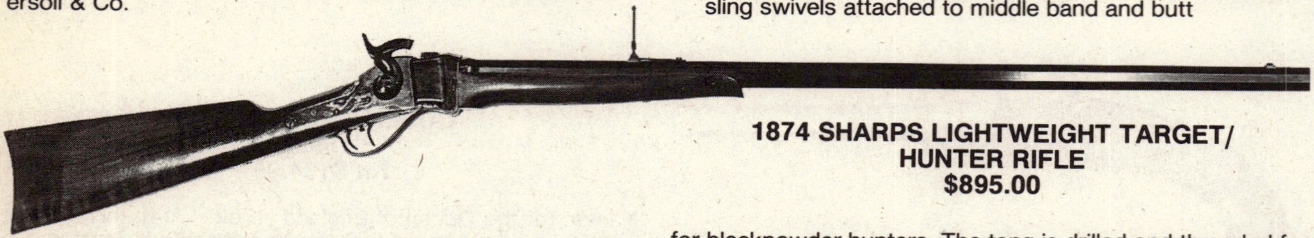

**1874 SHARPS LIGHTWEIGHT TARGET/**
**HUNTER RIFLE**
**$895.00**

This Sharps rifle in 45-70 Government caliber has a 30″ octagon barrel with blued matte finish (1:18″ twist). It also features an adjustable hunting rear sight and blade front, making it ideal for blackpowder hunters. The tang is drilled and threaded for tang sights. The oil-finished military-style buttstock has a blued metal buttplate. Double-set triggers. Color casehardened receiver and hammer. **Overall length:** $49\frac{1}{2}$″. **Weight:** 10 lbs.

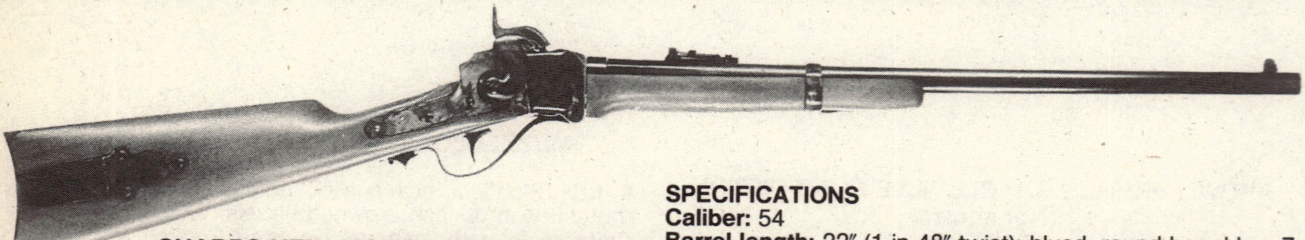

**SHARPS NEW MODEL 1859 CARBINE**
**$775.00**

About 115,000 Sharps New Model 1859 carbines and its variants were made during the Civil War. Characterized by durability and accuracy, they became a favorite of cavalrymen on both sides. Made in Italy by David Pedersoli & Co.

**SPECIFICATIONS**
**Caliber:** 54
**Barrel length:** 22″ (1 in 48″ twist); blued, round barrel has 7-groove rifling
**Overall length:** $37\frac{1}{2}$″
**Weight:** $7\frac{3}{4}$ lbs.
**Sights:** Blade front; adjustable rear
**Stock:** Oil-finished walnut
**Features:** Barrel band, hammer, receiver, saddle bar and ring all color casehardened

# DIXIE RIFLES

TENNESSEE MOUNTAIN FLINTLOCK RIFLE

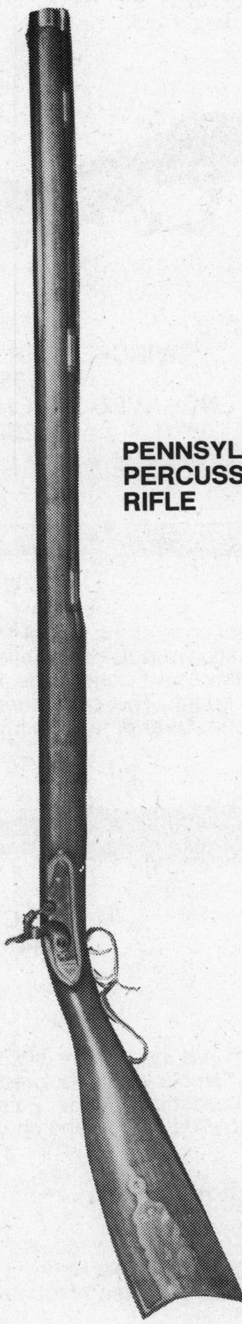

PENNSYLVANIA PERCUSSION RIFLE

**HAWKEN RIFLE (not shown)**
**$250.00 Kit $220.00**

Blued barrel is 15/16″ across the flats and 30″ in length with a twist of 1 in 64″. Stock is of walnut with a steel crescent buttplate, halfstock with brass nosecap. Double-set triggers, front-action lock and adjustable rear sight. Ramrod is equipped with jag. **Overall length:** 46 1/2″. Average actual **weight:** about 8 lbs., depending on the caliber; shipping weight is 10 lbs. Available in either finished gun or kit. **Calibers:** 45, 50 and 54.

**DIXIE TENNESSEE MOUNTAIN RIFLE**
**$575.00 Percussion or Flintlock**

This 50-caliber rifle features double-set triggers with adjustable set screw, bore rifled with 6 lands and grooves, barrel of 15/16 inch across the flats, brown finish and cherry stock. **Overall length:** 41 1/2 inches. Right- and left-hand versions in flint or percussion. **Kit:** . . . . . . . . . . . . . . . . . . . . . . . . . . . **$495.00**

**DIXIE TENNESSEE SQUIRREL RIFLE**
**$575.00 (not shown)**

In 32-caliber flint or percussion, right hand only, cherry stock.
**Kit:** . . . . . . . . . . . . . . . . . . . . . . . . . . . . . . . . . . . **$495.00**

**PENNSYLVANIA RIFLE**
**Percussion or Flintlock $395.00**
**Kit (Flint or Perc.) $345.00**

A lightweight at just 8 pounds, the 41 1/2″ blued rifle barrel is fitted with an open buckhorn rear sight and front blade. The walnut one-piece stock is stained a medium darkness that contrasts with the polished brass buttplate, toe plate, patchbox, sideplate, trigger guard, thimbles and nose cap. Featuring double-set triggers, the rifle can be fired by pulling only the front trigger, which has a normal trigger pull of 4 to 5 pounds; or the rear trigger can first be pulled to set a spring-loaded mechanism that greatly reduces the amount of pull needed for the front trigger to kick off the sear in the lock. The land-to-land measurement of the bore is an exact .450 and the recommended ball size is .445. **Overall length:** 51 1/2″.

**PEDERSOLI WAADTLANDER RIFLE (not shown)**
**$1295.00**

This authentic re-creation of a Swiss muzzleloading target rifle features a heavy octagonal barrel (31″) that has 7 lands and grooves. **Caliber:** 45. Rate of twist is 1 turn in 48″. Double-set triggers are multilever type and are easily removable for adjustment. Sights are fitted post front and tang-mounted Swiss-type diopter rear. Walnut stock, color casehardened hardware, classic buttplate and curved trigger guard complete this reproduction. The original was made between 1839 and 1860 by Marc Bristlen, Morges, Switzerland.

# DIXIE

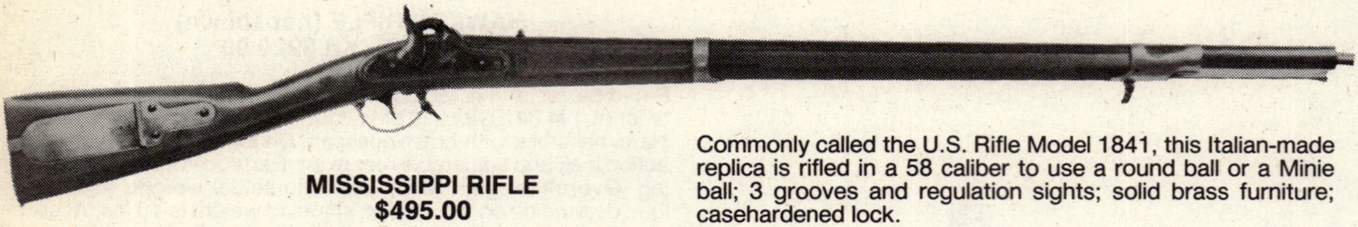

**MISSISSIPPI RIFLE**
**$495.00**

Commonly called the U.S. Rifle Model 1841, this Italian-made replica is rifled in a 58 caliber to use a round ball or a Minie ball; 3 grooves and regulation sights; solid brass furniture; casehardened lock.

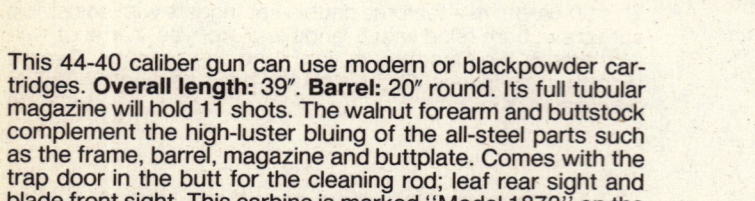

This 44-40 caliber gun can use modern or blackpowder cartridges. **Overall length:** 39″. **Barrel:** 20″ round. Its full tubular magazine will hold 11 shots. The walnut forearm and buttstock complement the high-luster bluing of the all-steel parts such as the frame, barrel, magazine and buttplate. Comes with the trap door in the butt for the cleaning rod; leaf rear sight and blade front sight. This carbine is marked "Model 1873" on the tang and caliber "44-40" on the brass carrier block.

**WINCHESTER '73 CARBINE**
**$895.00**
**ENGRAVED WINCHESTER '73 RIFLE**
**$1250.00**

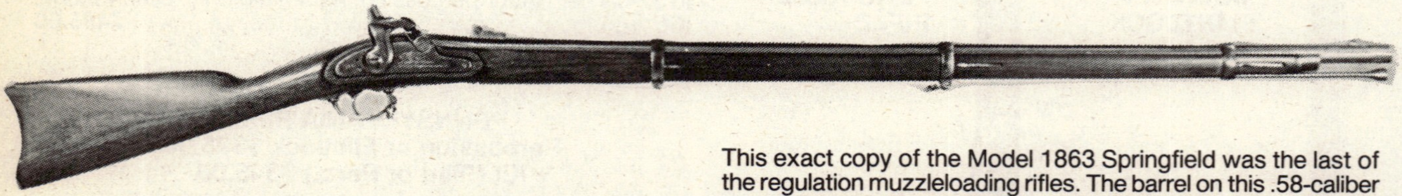

**1863 SPRINGFIELD CIVIL WAR MUSKET**
**$595.00 Kit $525.00**

This exact copy of the Model 1863 Springfield was the last of the regulation muzzleloading rifles. The barrel on this .58-caliber gun measures 40 inches. The action and all-metal furniture is finished bright. The oil-finished walnut-stained stock is 53 inches long. **Overall length:** 56″. **Weight:** 9 1/2 lbs.

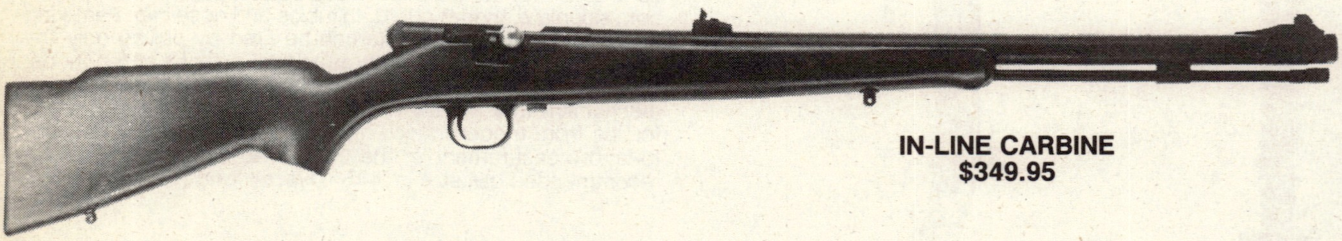

**IN-LINE CARBINE**
**$349.95**

Made in Italy by D. Pedersoli, this rifle in 50 or 54 caliber features a sliding "bolt" that completely encloses cap and nipple, making it the most weatherproof muzzleloader available. **Barrel length:** 24″. **Overall length:** 41″. **Weight:** 6 1/2 lbs. **Sights:** Ramp front with red insert; rear sight adjustable for windage and elevation. **Stock:** Walnut-colored wood with Monte Carlo comb and black plastic buttplate. Features include fully adj. trigger, automatic slide safety, and chromed bolt and handle.

**TRYON CREEDMOOR RIFLE (not shown)**
**$595.00**

This Tryon rifle features a high-quality back-action lock, double-set triggers, steel buttplate, patchbox, toe plate and curved trigger guard. **Caliber:** 45. **Barrel:** 32 3/4″, octagonal, with 1 twist in 20.87″. **Sights:** Hooded post front fitted with replaceable inserts; rear is tang-mounted and adjustable for windage and elevation.

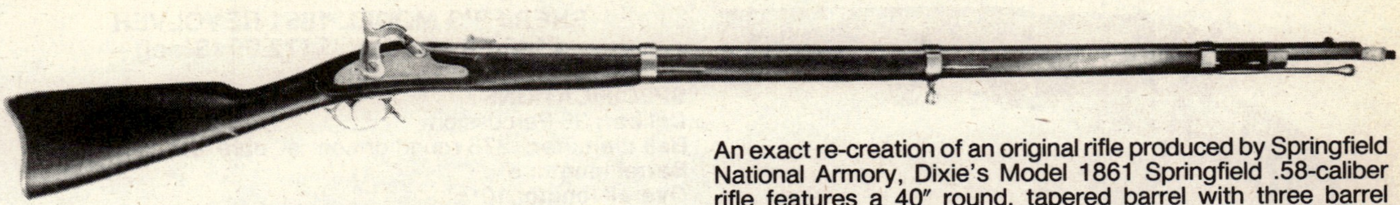

**U.S. MODEL 1861 SPRINGFIELD PERCUSSION RIFLE-MUSKET**
**$550.00 Kit $472.00**

An exact re-creation of an original rifle produced by Springfield National Armory, Dixie's Model 1861 Springfield .58-caliber rifle features a 40″ round, tapered barrel with three barrel bands. Sling swivels are attached to the trigger guard bow and middle barrel band. The ramrod has a trumpet-shaped head with swell; sights are standard military rear and bayonet-attachment lug front. The percussion lock is marked "1861" on the rear of the lockplate with an eagle motif and "U.S. Springfield" in front of the hammer. "U.S." is stamped on top of buttplate. All furniture is "National Armory Bright." **Overall length:** 55 13/16″. **Weight:** 8 lbs.

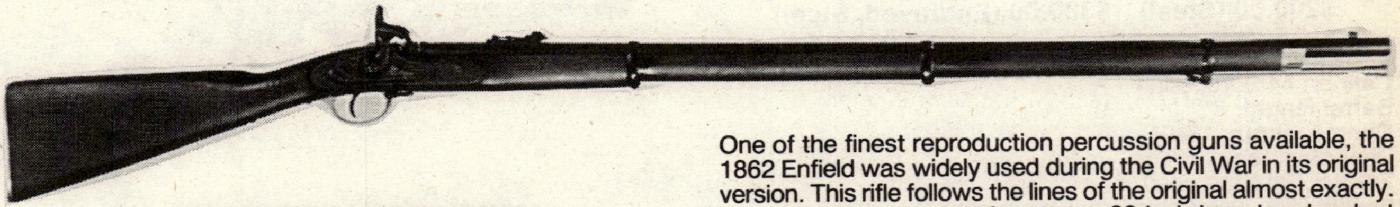

**1862 THREE-BAND ENFIELD RIFLED MUSKET**
**$485.00 Kit $425.00**

One of the finest reproduction percussion guns available, the 1862 Enfield was widely used during the Civil War in its original version. This rifle follows the lines of the original almost exactly. The .58-caliber musket features a 39-inch barrel and walnut stock. Three steel barrel bands and the barrel itself are blued; the lockplate and hammer are case colored and the remainder of the furniture is highly polished brass. The lock is marked, "London Armory Co." **Weight:** 10 1/2 lbs. **Overall length:** 55″.

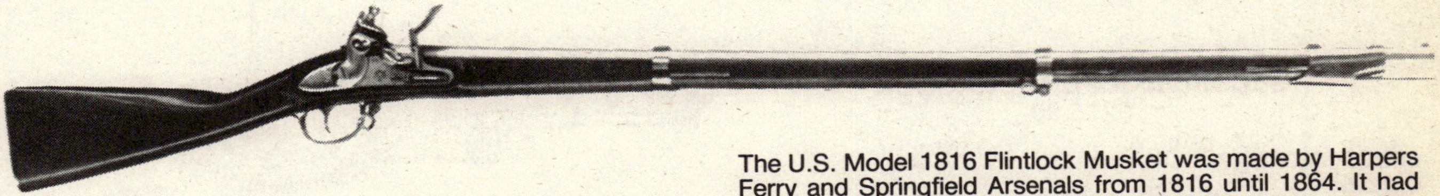

**U.S. MODEL 1816 FLINTLOCK MUSKET**
**$725.00**

The U.S. Model 1816 Flintlock Musket was made by Harpers Ferry and Springfield Arsenals from 1816 until 1864. It had the highest production of any U.S. flintlock musket and after conversion to percussion saw service in the Civil War. It has a .69-caliber, 42″ smoothbore barrel held by three barrel bands with springs. All metal parts are finished in "National Armory Bright." The lockplate has a brass pan and is marked "Harpers Ferry" vertically behind the hammer, with an American eagle placed in front of the hammer. The bayonet lug is on top of the barrel and the steel ramrod has a button-shaped head. Sling swivels are mounted on the trigger guard and middle barrel band. **Overall length:** 56 1/2″. **Weight:** 9 3/4 lbs.

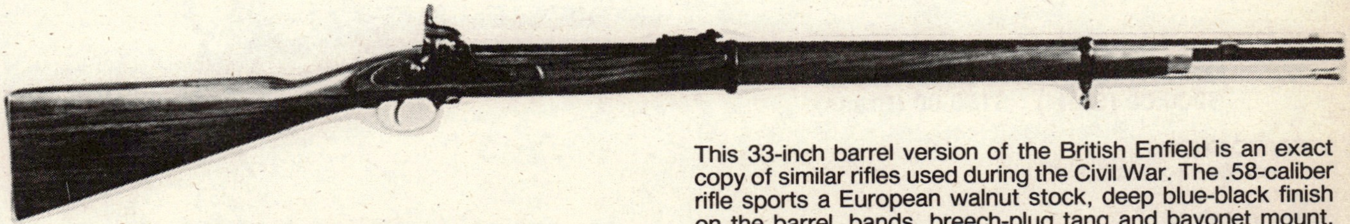

**1858 TWO-BAND ENFIELD RIFLE**
**$450.00**

This 33-inch barrel version of the British Enfield is an exact copy of similar rifles used during the Civil War. The .58-caliber rifle sports a European walnut stock, deep blue-black finish on the barrel, bands, breech-plug tang and bayonet mount. The percussion lock is color casehardened and the rest of the furniture is brightly polished brass.

# EMF REVOLVERS

SHERIFF'S MODEL 1851

### SHERIFF'S MODEL 1851 REVOLVER
**$140.00 (Brass) $172.00 (Steel)**

**SPECIFICATIONS**
**Caliber:** 36 Percussion
**Ball diameter:** .376 round or conical, pure lead
**Barrel length:** 5″
**Overall length:** 10 1/2″
**Weight:** 39 oz.
**Sights:** V-notch groove in hammer (rear); truncated cone in front
**Percussion cap size:** #11

### MODEL 1860 ARMY REVOLVER
**$145.00 (Brass) $173.00 (Engraved, Brass)**
**$200.00 (Steel) $330.00 (Engraved, Steel)**

**SPECIFICATIONS**
**Caliber:** 44 Percussion
**Barrel length:** 8″
**Overall length:** 13 5/8″
**Weight:** 41 oz.
**Frame:** Casehardened
**Finish:** High-luster blue with walnut grips
Also available:
**Cased set** with steel frame, wood case, flask and mold . . . . . **$303.00**
Engraved cased set . . . . . **438.00**
**Fluted cylinder model** (steel frame only) . . . . . **245.00**

MODEL 1860 ARMY

### SECOND MODEL 44 DRAGOON
**$275.00**

**SPECIFICATIONS**
**Caliber:** 44
**Barrel length:** 7 1/2″ (round)
**Overall length:** 14″
**Weight:** 4 lbs.
**Finish:** Steel casehardened frame
Also available:
**Third Model Dragoon** . . . . . **$275.00**
**Texas Dragoon** . . . . . **290.00**

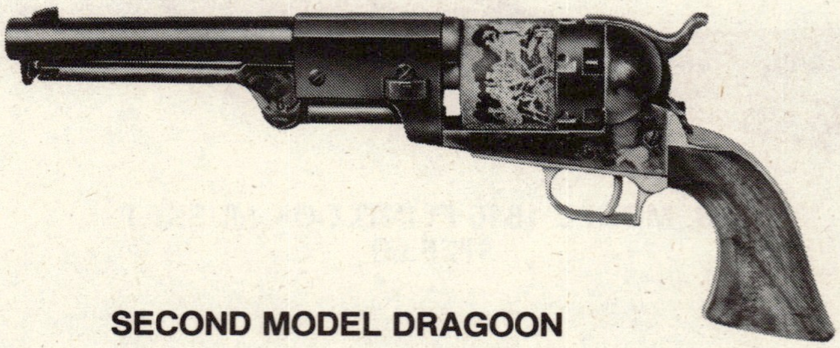

SECOND MODEL DRAGOON

### MODEL 1862 POLICE REVOLVER
**$200.00 (Steel) $150.00 (Brass)**

**SPECIFICATIONS**
**Caliber:** 36 Percussion
**Capacity:** 5-shot
**Barrel length:** 6 1/2″
Also available:
**Cased set** (steel only) . . . . . **$297.00**

MODEL 1862 POLICE

# EUROARMS OF AMERICA

**COOK & BROTHER CONFEDERATE CARBINE**
**Model 2300: $440.00**

Classic re-creation of the rare 1861, New Orleans-made Artillery Carbine. The lockplate is marked "Cook & Brother N.O. 1861" and is stamped with a Confederate flag at the rear of the hammer.

**SPECIFICATIONS**
**Caliber:** 58 percussion
**Barrel length:** 24″ **Overall length:** 40⅓″
**Weight:** 7½ lbs.
**Sights:** Fixed blade front and adjustable dovetailed rear
**Ramrod:** Steel
**Finish:** Barrel is antique brown; buttplate, trigger guard, barrel bands, sling swivels and nose cap are polished brass; stock is walnut
**Recommended ball sizes:** .575 r.b., .577 Minie and .580 maxi; uses musket caps

Also available:
**MODEL 2301 COOK & BROTHER FIELD** with 33″ barrel
**Price:** . . . . . . . . . . . . . . . . . . . . . . . . . . . . . . **$470.60**

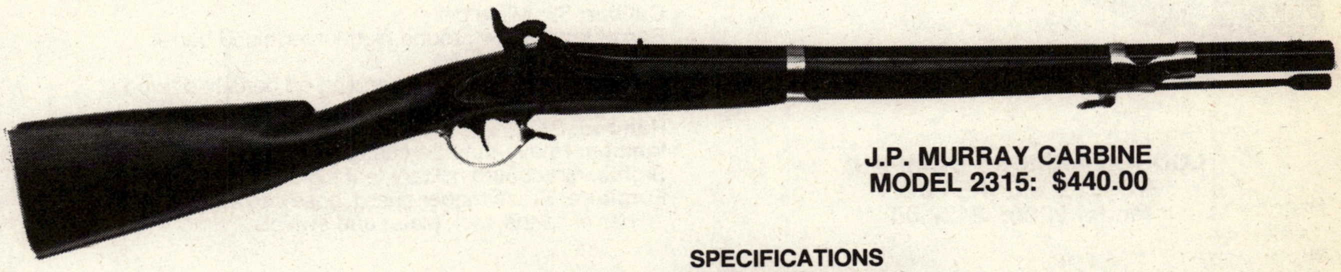

**J.P. MURRAY CARBINE**
**MODEL 2315: $440.00**

Replica of an extremely rare CSA Cavalry Carbine based on an 1841 design of parts and lock.

**SPECIFICATIONS**
**Caliber:** 58 percussion
**Barrel length:** 23″
**Features:** Brass barrel bands and buttplate; oversized trigger guard; sling swivels

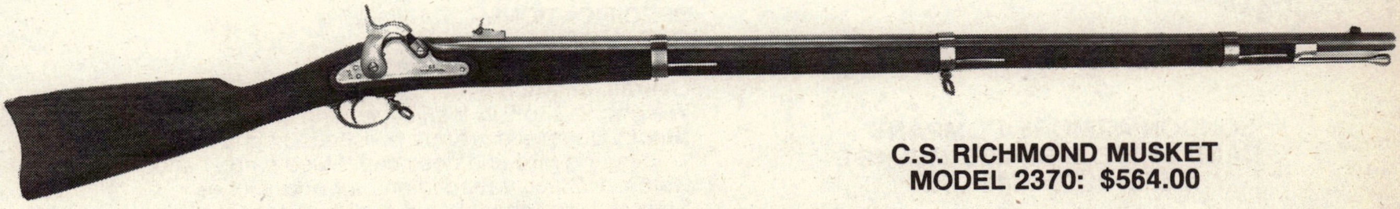

**C.S. RICHMOND MUSKET**
**MODEL 2370: $564.00**

**SPECIFICATIONS**
**Caliber:** 58 percussion. **Barrel length:** 40″ with three bands.

# EUROARMS OF AMERICA

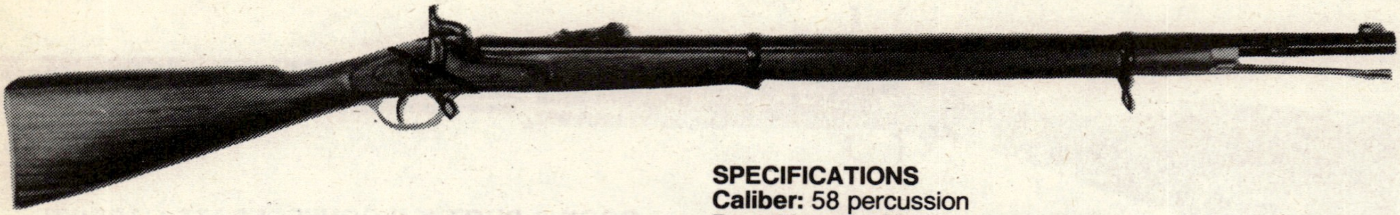

LONDON ARMORY COMPANY
2-BAND RIFLE MUSKET
Model 2270: $467.00

**SPECIFICATIONS**
**Caliber:** 58 percussion
**Barrel length:** 33″, blued and rifled
**Overall length:** 49″
**Weight:** 8½ to 8¾ lbs., depending on wood density
**Stock:** One-piece walnut; polished "bright" brass butt plate, trigger guard and nose cap; blued barrel bands
**Sights:** Inverted 'V' front sight; Enfield folding ladder rear
**Ramrod:** Steel

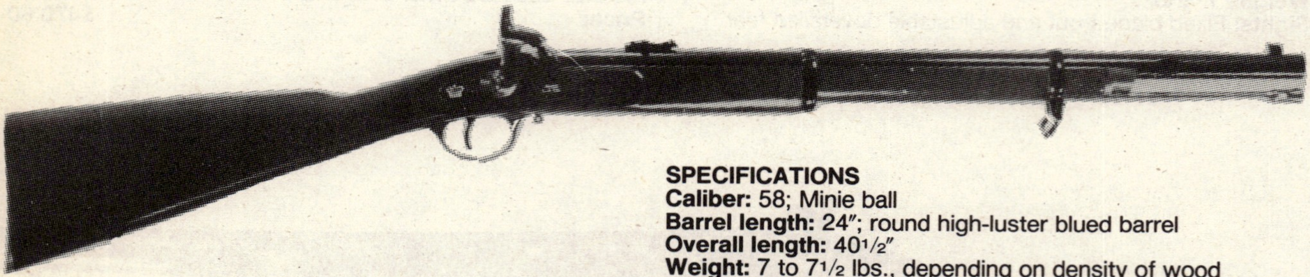

LONDON ARMORY COMPANY
ENFIELD MUSKETOON
Model 2280: $427.00

**SPECIFICATIONS**
**Caliber:** 58; Minie ball
**Barrel length:** 24″; round high-luster blued barrel
**Overall length:** 40½″
**Weight:** 7 to 7½ lbs., depending on density of wood
**Stock:** Seasoned walnut stock with sling swivels
**Ramrod:** Steel
**Ignition:** Heavy-duty percussion lock
**Sights:** Graduated military-leaf sight
**Furniture:** Brass trigger guard, nose cap and butt plate; blued barrel bands, lock plate, and swivels

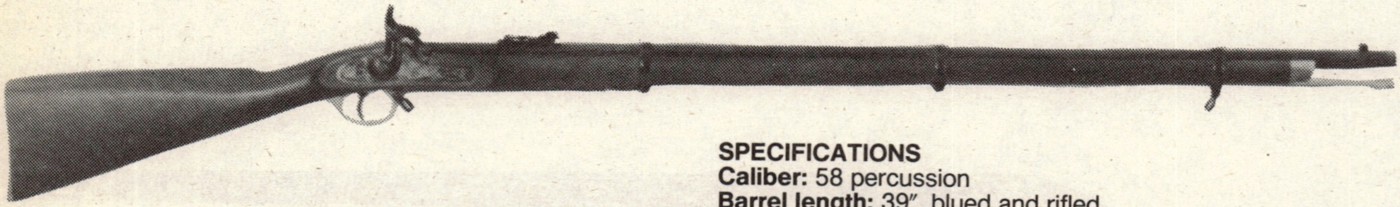

LONDON ARMORY COMPANY
3-BAND ENFIELD RIFLED MUSKET
Model 2260: $484.00

**SPECIFICATIONS**
**Caliber:** 58 percussion
**Barrel length:** 39″, blued and rifled
**Overall length:** 54″
**Weight:** 9½ to 9¾ lbs., depending on wood density
**Stock:** One-piece walnut; polished "bright" brass butt plate, trigger guard and nose cap; blued barrel bands
**Ramrod:** Steel; threaded end for accessories
**Sights:** Traditional Enfield folding ladder rear sight; inverted 'V' front sight
Also available:
**MODEL 2261** with white barrel . . . . . . . . . . . . . . . . **$507.00**

# EUROARMS OF AMERICA

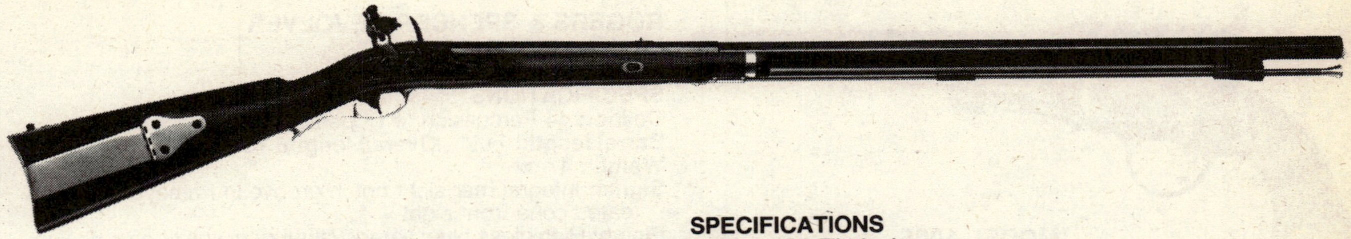

**1803 HARPERS FERRY FLINTLOCK RIFLE**
**Model 2305: $567.00**

**SPECIFICATIONS**
**Caliber:** 54 Flintlock
**Barrel length:** 35″, octagonal
**Features:** Walnut half stock with cheekpiece; browned barrel

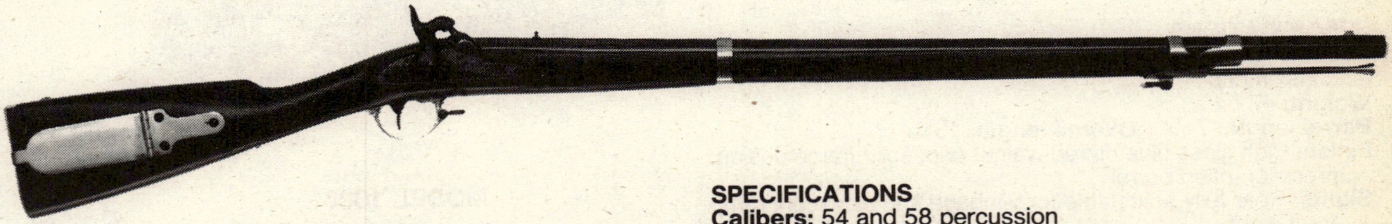

**1841 MISSISSIPPI RIFLE**
**Model 2310: $487.00**

**SPECIFICATIONS**
**Calibers:** 54 and 58 percussion
**Barrel length:** 33″, octagonal
**Features:** Walnut stock; brass barrel bands and buttplate; sling swivels

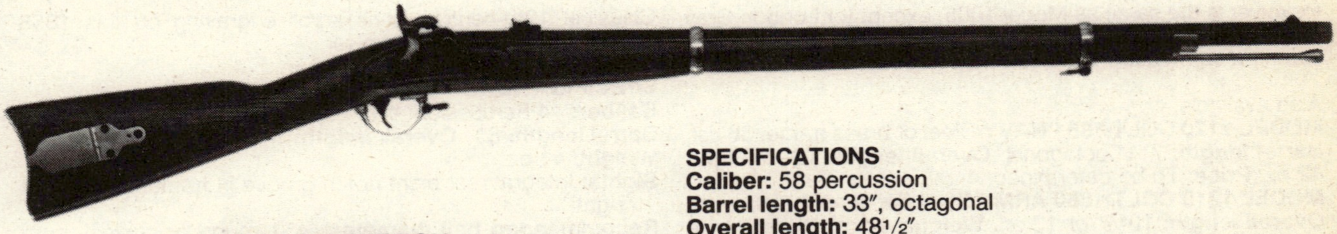

**1863 REMINGTON**
**ZOUAVE RIFLE (2-Barrel Bands)**
**Model 2255: $460.00 (Range Grade)**
**Model 2250: $340.00 (Field Grade)**

**SPECIFICATIONS**
**Caliber:** 58 percussion
**Barrel length:** 33″, octagonal
**Overall length:** 48 1/2″
**Weight:** 9 1/2 to 9 3/4 lbs.
**Sights:** U.S. Military 3-leaf rear; blade front
**Features:** Two brass barrel bands; brass buttplate and nose cap; sling swivels

**1861 SPRINGFIELD RIFLE**
**Model 2360: $564.00**

**SPECIFICATIONS**
**Caliber:** 58 percussion
**Barrel length:** 40″
**Features:** 3 barrel bands

# EUROARMS OF AMERICA

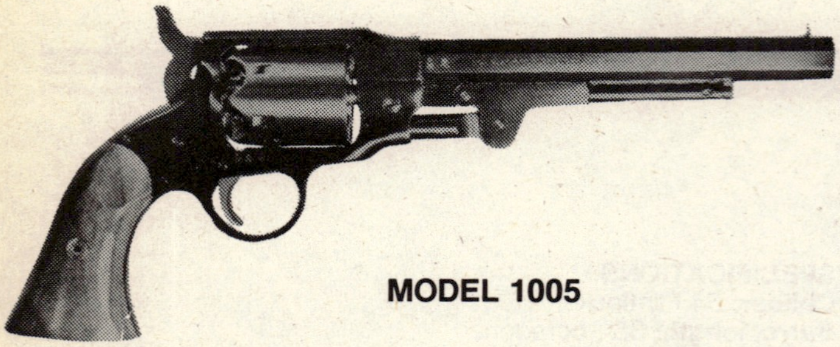

MODEL 1005

**ROGERS & SPENCER REVOLVER**
**Model 1005: $227.00**

**SPECIFICATIONS**
**Caliber:** 44 Percussion; #11 percussion cap
**Barrel length:** 7 1/2″ **Overall length:** 13 3/4″
**Weight:** 47 oz.
**Sights:** Integral rear sight notch groove in frame; brass truncated cone front sight
**Finish:** High gloss blue; flared walnut grip; solid frame design; precision-rifled barrel
**Recommended ball diameter:** .451 round or conical, pure lead

**ROGERS & SPENCER ARMY REVOLVER**
**Model 1006 (Target): $239.00**

**SPECIFICATIONS**
**Caliber:** 44; takes .451 round or conical lead balls; #11 percussion cap
**Weight:** 47 oz.
**Barrel length:** 7 1/2″ **Overall length:** 13 3/4″
**Finish:** High gloss blue; flared walnut grip; solid frame design; precision-rifled barrel
**Sights:** Rear fully adjustable for windage and elevation; ramp front sight

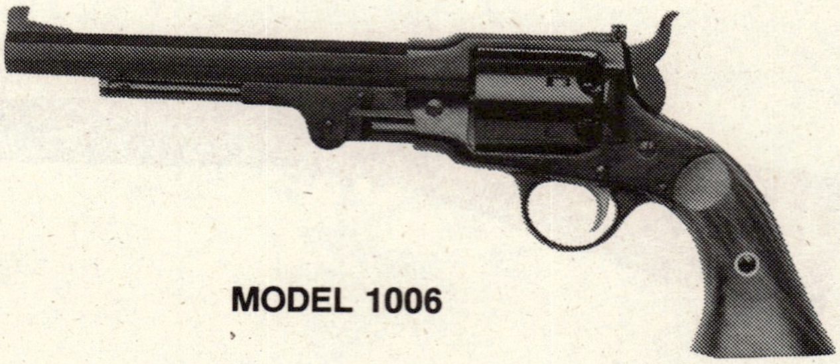

MODEL 1006

**ROGERS & SPENCER REVOLVER**
**LONDON GRAY (Not shown)**
**Model 1007: $245.00**

Revolver is the same as Model 1005, except for London Gray finish, which is heat treated and buffed for rust resistance; same recommended ball size and percussion caps.

Also available:
**MODEL 1120 COLT 1851 NAVY** Steel or brass frame. 36 cal. **Barrel length:** 7 1/2″ octagonal. **Overall length:** 13″. **Weight:** 42 oz. **Price:** To be determined.
**MODEL 1210 COLT 1860 ARMY** Steel frame. 44 percussion. **Overall length:** 10 5/8″ or 13 5/8″. **Weight:** 41 oz. **Price:** To be determined.

**REMINGTON 1858**
**NEW MODEL ARMY ENGRAVED (Not shown)**
**Model 1040: $275.00**

Classical 19th-century style scroll engraving on this 1858 Remington New Model revolver.

**SPECIFICATIONS**
**Caliber:** 44 Percussion; #11 cap
**Barrel length:** 8″ **Overall length:** 14 3/4″
**Weight:** 41 oz.
**Sights:** Integral rear sight notch groove in frame; blade front sight
**Recommended ball diameter:** .451 round or conical, pure lead

**REMINGTON 1858**
**NEW MODEL ARMY REVOLVER**
**Model 1020: $213.00**

This model is equipped with blued steel frame, brass trigger guard in 44 caliber.

**SPECIFICATIONS**
**Weight:** 40 oz.
**Barrel length:** 8″ **Overall length:** 14 3/4″
**Finish:** Deep luster blue rifled barrel; polished walnut stock; brass trigger guard.
Also available:
**MODEL 1010.** Same as Model 1020, except with 6 1/2″ barrel and in 36 caliber: .................... **$213.00**

MODEL 1010
(36 Cal. w/6 1/2″ barrel)

# GONIC ARMS

**MODEL GA-87 RIFLE**
**$569.50 Standard Walnut**
**$616.00 (Open Sights) $621.50 (Peep Sights)**

**SPECIFICATIONS**
**Calibers:** 30, 38, 44, 45, 50 Mag., 54 and 20 ga. smoothbore
**Barrel length:** 26″ **Overall length:** 43″
**Weight:** 6½ lbs.
**Sights:** Bead front; open rear (adjustable for windage and elevation); drilled and tapped for scope bases
**Stock:** American walnut (grey or brown laminated stock optional). **Length of pull:** 14″

**Trigger:** Single stage (4-lb. pull)
**Mechanism type:** Closed-breech muzzleloader
**Features:** Ambidextrous safety; nonglare satin finish; newly designed loading system; all-weather performance guaranteed; faster lock time
Also available:

| | |
|---|---|
| **Brown or Gray Laminated Stock Models** (Std.) | **$618.95** |
| With open sights | **665.50** |
| With peep sights | **669.50** |

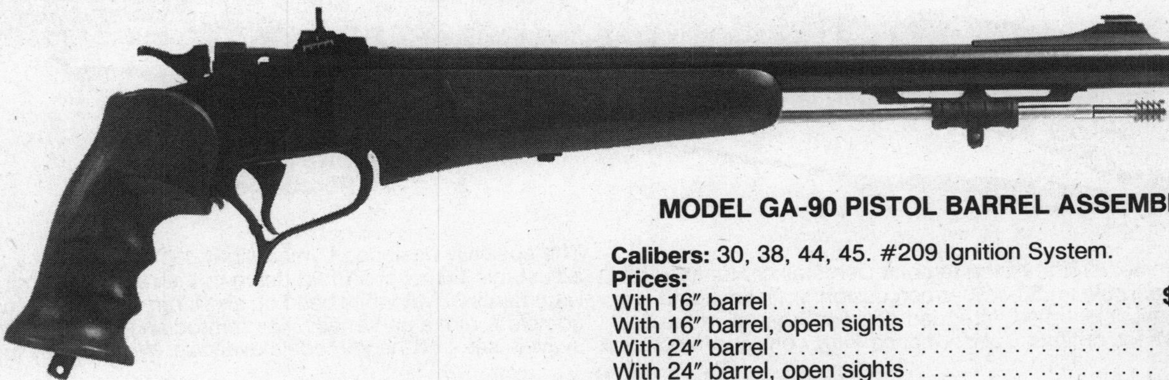

**MODEL GA-90 PISTOL BARREL ASSEMBLY**

**Calibers:** 30, 38, 44, 45. #209 Ignition System.
**Prices:**

| | |
|---|---|
| With 16″ barrel | **$184.00** |
| With 16″ barrel, open sights | **227.00** |
| With 24″ barrel | **200.00** |
| With 24″ barrel, open sights | **243.00** |
| With 24″ barrel, peep sights | **248.00** |

**MODEL 93 MAGNUM RIFLE**
**$460.00**
**$542.00 (Stainless w/Black Stock)**

Gonic Arms' new blackpowder rifle has a unique loading system that produces better consistency and utilizes the full powder charge of the specially designed penetrator bullet (ballistics = 2,650 foot-pounds at 1,600 fps w/465-grain .500 bullet).

**SPECIFICATIONS**
**Caliber:** 50 Magnum
**Barrel length:** 26″ **Overall length:** 43″
**Weight:** 6 to 6½ lbs.
**Sights:** Open hunting sights (adjustable)

**Features:** Walnut-stained hardwood stock; adjustable trigger; nipple wrench; drilled and tapped for scope bases; ballistics and instruction manual
Also available:
**Brown or Gray Laminated Thumbhole Stock**

| | |
|---|---|
| **Blued Barrel** | **$784.00** |
| With open sights | **820.00** |
| With peep sights | **823.00** |
| **Stainless Barrel** | **621.00** |
| With thumbhole stock | **866.00** |
| Same as above w/open sights | **903.00** |
| With peep sights | **905.00** |

# LYMAN CARBINES/RIFLES

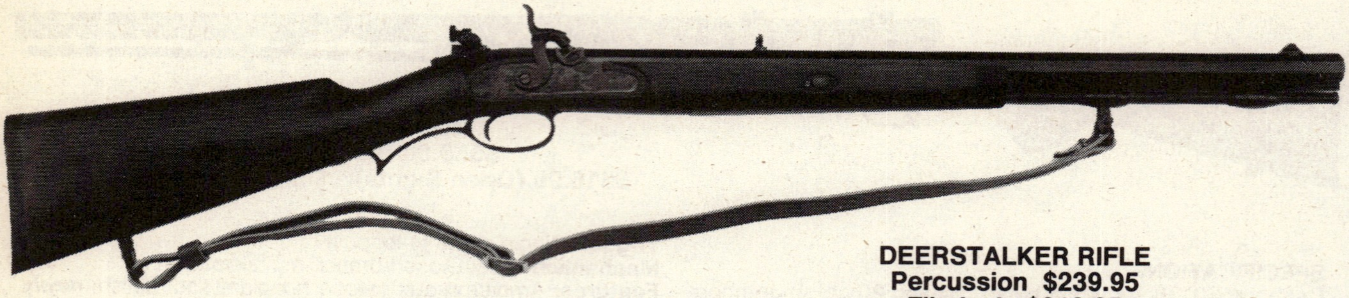

**DEERSTALKER RIFLE**
**Percussion $239.95**
**Flintlock $319.95**

Lyman's Deerstalker rifle incorporates many features most desired by muzzleloading hunters: higher comb for better sighting plane • nonglare hardware • 24″ octagonal barrel • casehardened sideplate • Q.D. sling swivels • Lyman sight package (37MA beaded front; fully adjustable fold-down 16A rear) • walnut stock with 1/2″ black recoil pad • single trigger. Left-hand models available (same price). **Calibers:** 50 and 54, flintlock or percussion. **Weight:** 7 1/2 lbs.

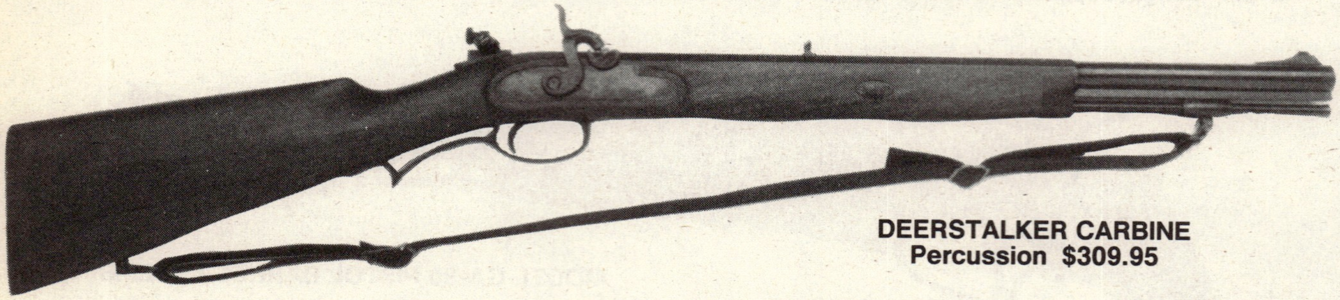

**DEERSTALKER CARBINE**
**Percussion $309.95**

This carbine version of the famous Deerstalker Hunting Rifle is now available in .50-caliber percussion or flintlock and features a precision-rifled "stepped octagon" barrel with a 1 in 24″ twist for optimum performance with conical projectiles. The specially designed Lyman sight package features a fully adjustable Lyman 16A fold-down in the rear. The front sight is Lyman's 37MA white bead on an 18 ramp. Each rifle comes complete with a darkened nylon ramrod and modern sling and swivels set. Left-hand models available. **Weight:** 6 3/4 lbs.

**GREAT PLAINS RIFLE**
**Percussion $416.00 (Kit $329.95)**
**Flintlock $445.00 (Kit $359.95)**

The Great Plains Rifle has a 32-inch deep-grooved barrel and 1 in 66-inch twist to shoot patched round balls. Blued steel furniture including the thick steel wedge plates and steel toe plate; correct lock and hammer styling with coil spring dependability; and a walnut stock without a patchbox. A Hawken-style trigger guard protects double-set triggers. Steel front sight and authentic buckhorn styling in an adjustable rear sight. Fixed primitive rear sight also included. Left-hand models available (same price). **Calibers:** 50 and 54.

**LYMAN TRADE RIFLE**
**Percussion $299.95**
**Flintlock $319.95**

The Lyman Trade Rifle features a 28-inch octagonal barrel, rifled 1 turn at 48 inches, designed to fire both patched round balls and the popular maxistyle conical bullets. Polished brass furniture with blued finish on steel parts; walnut stock; hook breech; single spring-loaded trigger; coil-spring percussion lock; fixed steel sights; adjustable rear sight for elevation also included. Steel barrel rib and ramrod ferrrule. **Caliber:** 50 or 54 percussion and flint. **Overall length:** 45″.

## KNIGHT RIFLES

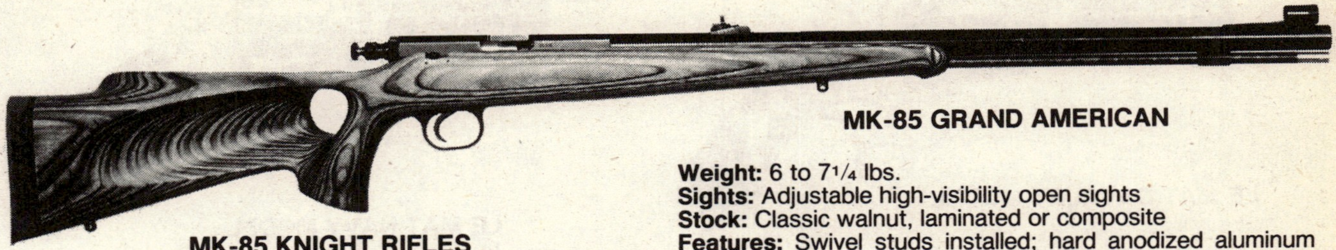

### MK-85 KNIGHT RIFLES

The MK-85 muzzleloading rifles (designed by William A. "Tony" Knight) are handcrafted, lightweight rifles capable of 1½-inch groups at 100 yards. They feature a one-piece, in-line bolt assembly, patented double-safety system, Timney featherweight deluxe trigger system, recoil pad, and Green Mountain barrels (1 in 28″ twist in 50 and 54 caliber).

**Calibers:** 50 and 54
**Barrel length:** 24″ **Overall length:** 43″

### MK-85 GRAND AMERICAN

**Weight:** 6 to 7¼ lbs.
**Sights:** Adjustable high-visibility open sights
**Stock:** Classic walnut, laminated or composite
**Features:** Swivel studs installed; hard anodized aluminum ramrod; combo tool; hex keys, and more.
**Prices:**

| | |
|---|---|
| **MK-85 HUNTER** (Walnut) | $ 559.95 |
| **MK-85 KNIGHT HAWK** (24″ Blued barrel) | 759.95 |
| Stainless barrel | 849.95 |
| **MK-85 PREDATOR** (Stainless) | 709.95 |
| **MK-85 STALKER** (Laminated) | 669.95 |
| **MK-85 GRAND AMERICAN** (Blued barrel, Shadow brown or black) | 995.95 |
| In Stainless Steel | 1095.95 |

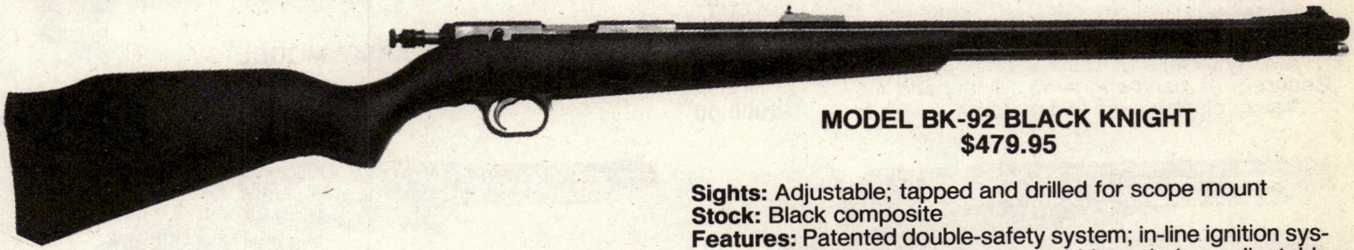

**Calibers:** 50 and 54
**Barrel length:** 24″ (tapered nonglare w/open breech system)

### MODEL BK-92 BLACK KNIGHT
### $479.95

**Sights:** Adjustable; tapped and drilled for scope mount
**Stock:** Black composite
**Features:** Patented double-safety system; in-line ignition system; 1 in 28″ twist; stainless-steel breechplug; adjustable trigger; ½″ recoil pad; Knight precision loading ramrod; Monte Carlo stock

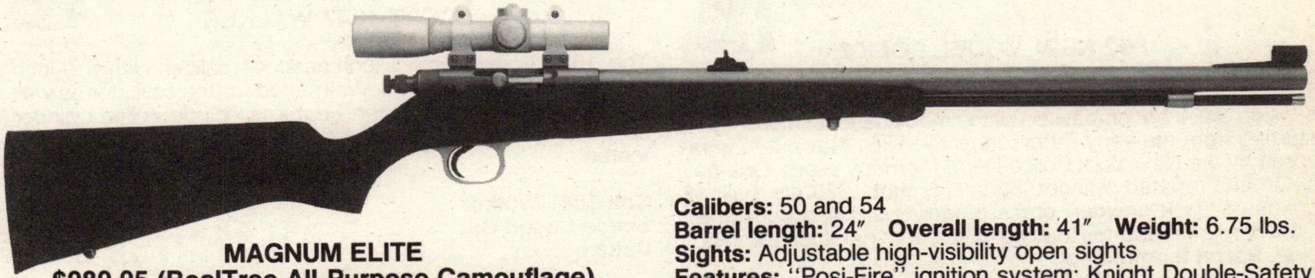

### MAGNUM ELITE
**$989.95 (RealTree All-Purpose Camouflage)**
**$929.95 (Black Composite Stock, shown)**

**Calibers:** 50 and 54
**Barrel length:** 24″ **Overall length:** 41″ **Weight:** 6.75 lbs.
**Sights:** Adjustable high-visibility open sights
**Features:** "Posi-Fire" ignition system; Knight Double-Safety System; aluminum ramrod; sling swivel studs

**Caliber:** 50
**Barrel length:** 22″; blued rifle-grade steel (1:28″ twist)
**Overall length:** 41″ **Weight:** 6 lbs.

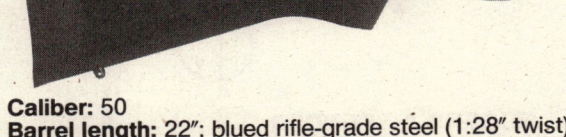

### WOLVERINE
**$269.95 (Blued) $369.95 (Stainless)**

**Sights:** Adjustable high-visibility rear sight; Quick-Detachable scope bases and rings
**Stock:** Lightweight Fiber-Lite molded stock
**Features:** Patented double-safety system; adjustable Accu-Lite trigger; removable breechplug; stainless-steel hammer

# NAVY ARMS REVOLVERS

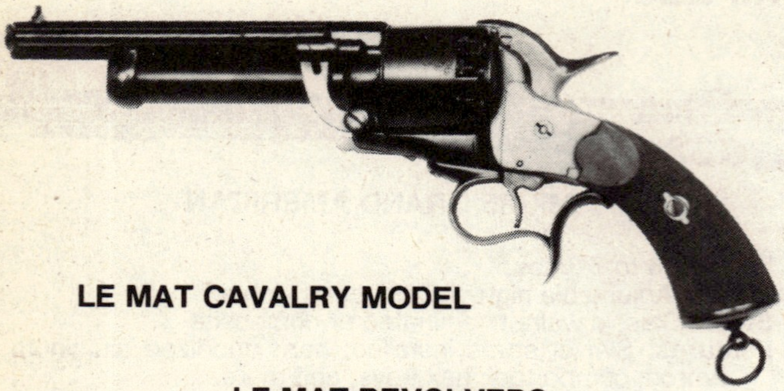

LE MAT CAVALRY MODEL

LE MAT NAVY MODEL

LE MAT ARMY MODEL

### LE MAT REVOLVERS

Once the official sidearm of many Confederate cavalry officers, this 9-shot .44-caliber revolver with a central single-shot barrel of approx. 65 caliber gave the cavalry man 10 shots to use against the enemy. **Barrel length:** 7 5/8″. **Overall length:** 14″. **Weight:** 3 lbs. 7 oz.

**Cavalry Model** . . . . . . . . . . . . . . . . . . . . . . . . . . . . **$ 595.00**
**Navy Model** . . . . . . . . . . . . . . . . . . . . . . . . . . . . . . **595.00**
**Army Model** . . . . . . . . . . . . . . . . . . . . . . . . . . . . . . **595.00**
**18th Georgia** (engraving on cylinder, display case) . . . . . . . . . . . . . . . . . . . . . **795.00**
**Beauregard** (hand-engraved cylinder and frame; display case and mold) . . . . . . . . . . . . . **1000.00**

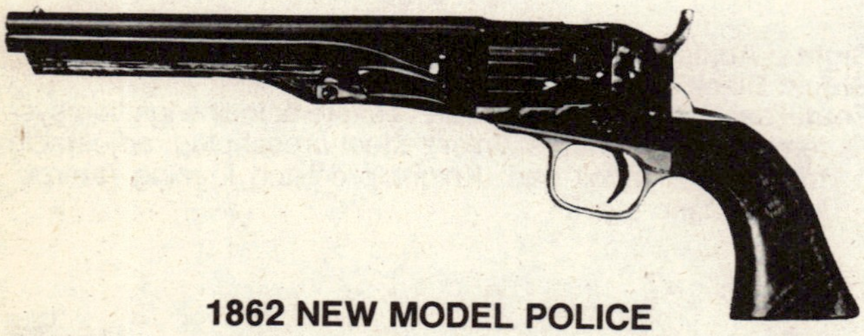

### 1862 NEW MODEL POLICE

This is the last gun manufactured by the Colt plant in the percussion era. It encompassed all the modifications of each gun, starting from the early Paterson to the 1861 Navy. It was favored by the New York Police Dept. for many years. One-half fluted and rebated cylinder, 36 cal., 5 shot, .375 dia. ball, 18 grains of black powder, brass trigger guard and backstrap. Casehardened frame, loading lever and hammer—balance blue. **Barrel length:** 5 1/2″.

**1862 Police** . . . . . . . . . . . . . . . . . . . . . . . . . . . . . **$290.00**
**Law and Order Set** . . . . . . . . . . . . . . . . . . . . . . . . **365.00**

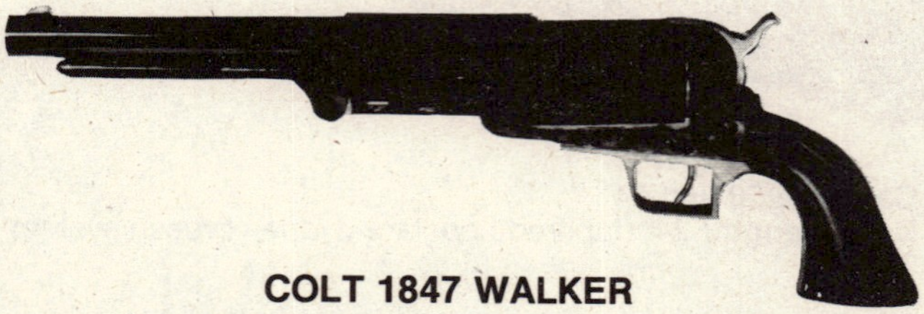

### COLT 1847 WALKER

The 1847 Walker replica comes in 44 caliber with a 9-inch barrel. **Weight:** 4 lbs. 8 oz. Well suited for the collector as well as the blackpowder shooter. Features include: rolled cylinder scene; blued and casehardened finish; and brass guard. Proof tested.

**Colt 1847 Walker** . . . . . . . . . . . . . . . . . . . . . . . . . **$275.00**
**Single Cased Set** . . . . . . . . . . . . . . . . . . . . . . . . . . **405.00**
**Deluxe** . . . . . . . . . . . . . . . . . . . . . . . . . . . . . . . . . **505.00**

### ROGERS & SPENCER REVOLVER

This revolver features a six-shot cylinder, octagonal barrel, hinged-type loading lever assembly, two-piece walnut grips, blued finish and casehardened hammer and lever. **Caliber:** 44. **Barrel length:** 7 1/2″. **Overall length:** 13 3/4″. **Weight:** 3 lbs.

**Rogers & Spencer** . . . . . . . . . . . . . . . . . . . . . . . . . **$245.00**
London Gray . . . . . . . . . . . . . . . . . . . . . . . . . . . . . **270.00**
Target Model (w/adjustable sights) . . . . . . . . . . . . **270.00**

ROGERS & SPENCER REVOLVER

# NAVY ARMS REVOLVERS

REB MODEL 1860

A modern replica of the confederate Griswold & Gunnison percussion Army revolver. Rendered with a polished brass frame and a rifled steel barrel finished in a high-luster blue with genuine walnut grips. All Army Model 60s are completely proof-tested by the Italian government to the most exacting standards. **Calibers:** 36 and 44. **Barrel length:** 7¼". **Overall length:** 13". **Weight:** 2 lbs. 10 oz.–11 oz. **Finish:** Brass frame, backstrap and trigger guard, round barrel, hinged rammer on the 44 cal. rebated cylinder.

| | |
|---|---|
| **Reb Model 1860** | **$115.00** |
| **Single Cased Set** | **235.00** |
| **Double Cased Set** | **365.00** |
| **Kit** | **90.00** |

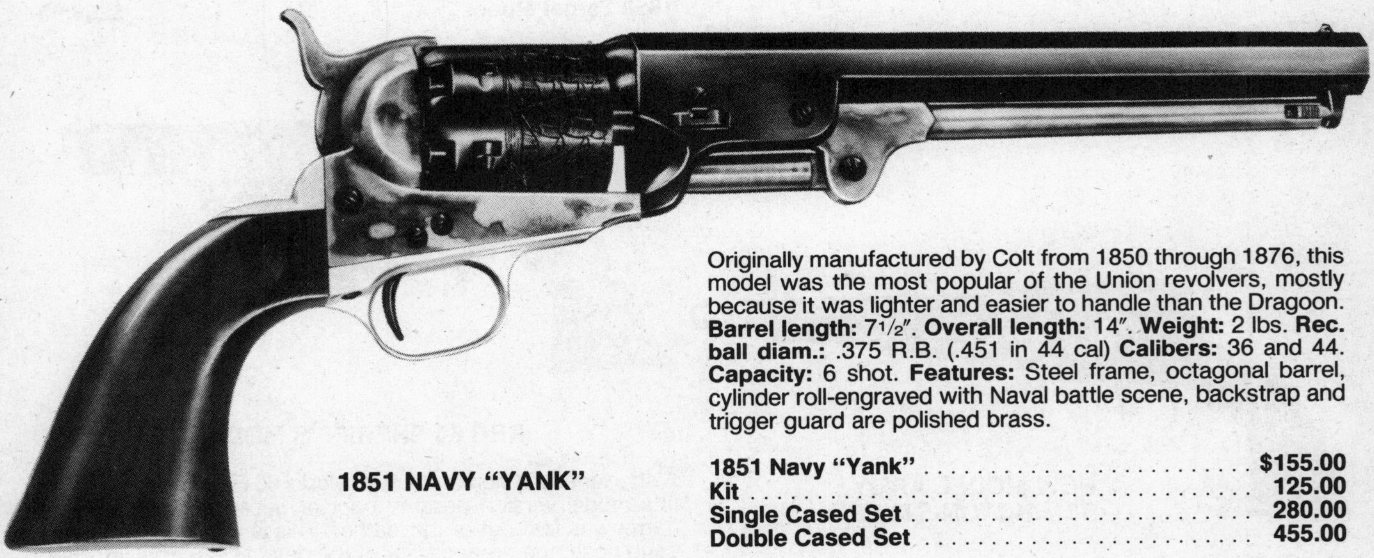

1851 NAVY "YANK"

Originally manufactured by Colt from 1850 through 1876, this model was the most popular of the Union revolvers, mostly because it was lighter and easier to handle than the Dragoon. **Barrel length:** 7½". **Overall length:** 14". **Weight:** 2 lbs. **Rec. ball diam.:** .375 R.B. (.451 in 44 cal) **Calibers:** 36 and 44. **Capacity:** 6 shot. **Features:** Steel frame, octagonal barrel, cylinder roll-engraved with Naval battle scene, backstrap and trigger guard are polished brass.

| | |
|---|---|
| **1851 Navy "Yank"** | **$155.00** |
| **Kit** | **125.00** |
| **Single Cased Set** | **280.00** |
| **Double Cased Set** | **455.00** |

The 1860 Army satisfied the Union Army's need for a more powerful .44-caliber revolver. The cylinder on this replica is roll engraved with a polished brass trigger guard and steel strap cut for shoulder stock. The frame, loading lever and hammer are finished in high-luster color case-hardening. Walnut grips. **Weight:** 2 lbs. 9 oz. **Barrel length:** 8". **Overall length:** 13⅝". **Caliber:** 44. **Finish:** Brass trigger guard, steel backstrap, round barrel, creeping lever, rebated cylinder, engraved Navy scene. Frame cut for s/stock (4 screws).

| | |
|---|---|
| **1860 Army** | **$175.00** |
| **Single Cased Set** | **300.00** |
| **Double Cased Set** | **490.00** |
| **Kit** | **155.00** |

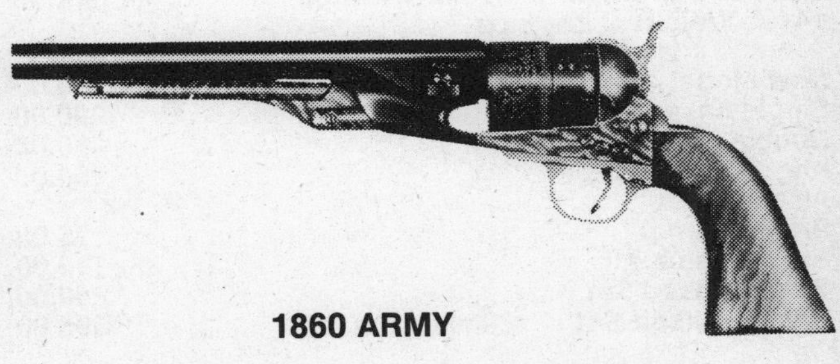

1860 ARMY

# NAVY ARMS REVOLVERS

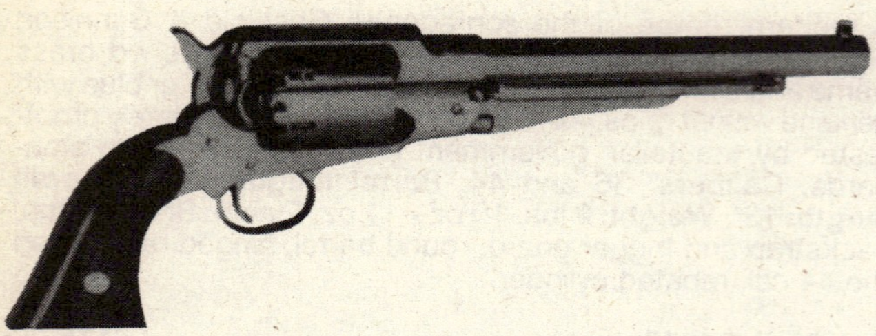

## 1858 NEW MODEL ARMY REMINGTON-STYLE, STAINLESS STEEL

Exactly like the standard 1858 Remington (below) except that every part except for the grips and trigger guard is manufactured from corrosion-resistant stainless steel. This gun has all the style and feel of its ancestor with all of the conveniences of stainless steel. **Caliber:** 44.

| | |
|---|---|
| **1858 Remington Stainless** | **$270.00** |
| **Single Cased Set** | **395.00** |
| **Double Cased Set** | **680.00** |

**NEW MODEL ARMY REMINGTON-STYLE**

## NEW MODEL ARMY REMINGTON-STYLE REVOLVER

This rugged, dependable, battle-proven Civil War veteran with its top strap and rugged frame was considered the Magnum of C.W. revolvers, ideally suited for the heavy 44 charges. Blued finish. **Caliber:** 44. **Barrel length:** 8″. **Overall length:** 14¼″. **Weight:** 2 lbs. 8 oz.

| | |
|---|---|
| **New Model Army Revolver** | **$170.00** |
| **Single cased set** | **290.00** |
| **Double cased set** | **480.00** |
| **Kit** | **150.00** |
| Also available: | |
| **Brass Frame** | **125.00** |
| **Brass Frame Kit** | **115.00** |
| **Single Cased Set** | **250.00** |
| **Double Cased Set** | **395.00** |

## 1858 TARGET MODEL

With its top strap solid frame, the Remington Percussion Revolver is considered the Magnum of Civil War revolvers and is ideally suited to the heavy 44-caliber charges. Based on the Army Model, the target gun has target sights for controlled accuracy. Ruggedly built from modern steel and proof tested.

| | |
|---|---|
| **1858 Target Model** | **$205.00** |

## REB 60 SHERIFF'S MODEL

A shortened version of the Reb Model 60 Revolver. The Sheriff's model version became popular because the shortened barrel was fast out of the leather. This is actually the original snub nose, the predecessor of the detective specials or belly guns designed for quick-draw use. **Calibers:** 36 and 44.

| | |
|---|---|
| **Reb 60 Sheriff's Model** | **$115.00** |
| **Kit** | **90.00** |
| **Single Cased Set** | **235.00** |
| **Double Cased Set** | **365.00** |

## DELUXE NEW MODEL 1858 REMINGTON-STYLE 44 CALIBER (not shown)

Built to the exact dimensions and weight of the original Remington 44, this model features an 8″ barrel with progressive rifling, adjustable front sight for windage, all-steel construction with walnut stocks and silver-plated trigger guard. Steel is highly polished and finished in rich charcoal blue. **Barrel length:** 8″. **Overall length:** 14¼″. **Weight:** 2 lbs. 14 oz.

| | |
|---|---|
| **Deluxe New Model 1858** | **$415.00** |

# NAVY ARMS PISTOLS

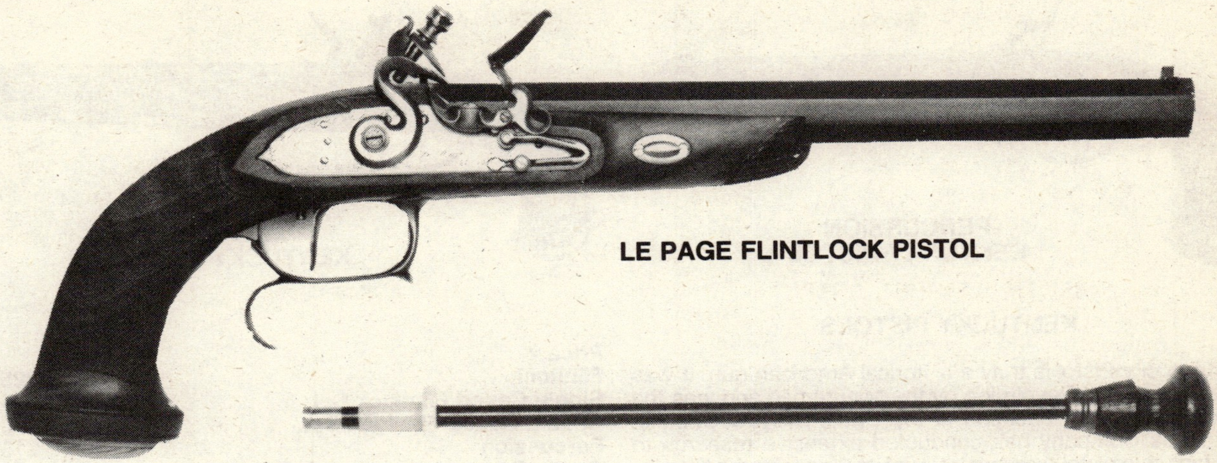

LE PAGE FLINTLOCK PISTOL

## LE PAGE FLINTLOCK PISTOL (44 Caliber)

The Le Page pistol is a beautifully hand-crafted reproduction featuring hand-checkered walnut stock with hinged buttcap and carved motif of a shell at the forward portion of the stock. Single-set trigger and highly polished steel lock and furniture together with a brown-finished rifled barrel make this a highly desirable target pistol. **Barrel length:** 10 1/2″. **Overall length:** 17″. **Weight:** 2 lbs. 2 oz.

**Le Page Flintlock** (rifled or smoothbore) . . . . . . . . **$625.00**

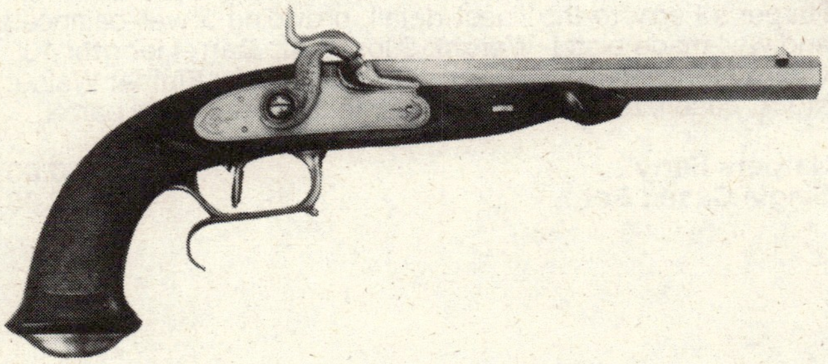

## LE PAGE PERCUSSION PISTOL (44 Caliber)

The tapered octagonal rifled barrel is in the traditional style with 7 lands and grooves. Fully adjustable single-set trigger. Engraved overall with traditional scrollwork. The European walnut stock is in the Boutet style. Spur-style trigger guard. Fully adjustable elevating rear sight. Dovetailed front sight adjustable for windage. **Barrel length:** 9″. **Overall length:** 15″. **Weight:** 2 lbs. 2 oz. **Rec. ball diameter:** 424 R.B.

**Le Page Percussion** . . . . . . . . . . . . . . . . . . . . . . . . **$500.00**

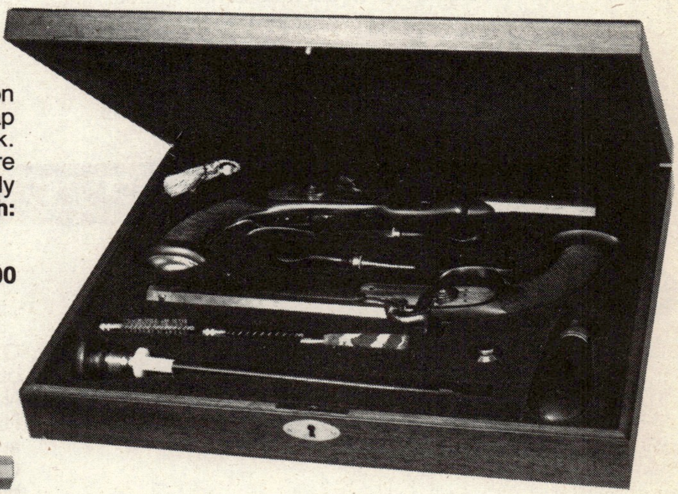

## CASED LE PAGE PISTOL SETS

The case is French-fitted and the accessories are the finest quality to match.

**Double Cased Sets**
French-fitted double cased set comprising two Le Page pistols, turn screw, nipple key, oil bottle, cleaning brushes, leather covered flask and loading rod. Rifled or smoothbore barrel.

**Double Cased Flintlock Set** . . . . . . . . . . . . . . . . . **$1575.00**
**Double Cased Percussion Set** . . . . . . . . . . . . . . . **1300.00**

**Single Cased Sets**
French-fitted single cased set comprising one Le Page pistol, turn screw, nipple key, oil bottle, cleaning brushes, leather covered flask and loading rod. Rifled or smoothbore barrel.

**Single Cased Flintlock Set** . . . . . . . . . . . . . . . . . . **$900.00**
**Single Cased Percussion Set** . . . . . . . . . . . . . . . . **775.00**

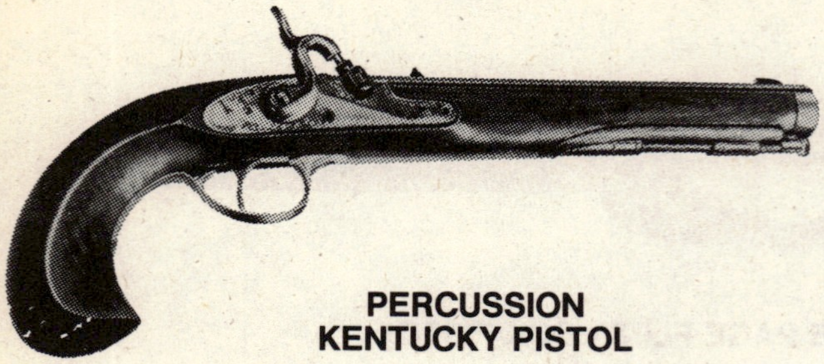

PERCUSSION
KENTUCKY PISTOL

FLINTLOCK
KENTUCKY PISTOL

## KENTUCKY PISTOLS

The Kentucky Pistol is truly a historical American gun. It was carried during the Revolution by the Minutemen and was the sidearm of "Andy" Jackson in the Battle of New Orleans. Navy Arms Company has conducted extensive research to manufacture a pistol representative of its kind, with the balance and handle of the original for which it became famous.

**Prices:**

| | |
|---|---|
| **Flintlock** | **$225.00** |
| **Single Cased Flintlock Set** | **325.00** |
| **Double Cased Flintlock Set** | **550.00** |
| **Percussion** | **215.00** |
| **Single Cased Percussion Set** | **310.00** |
| **Double Cased Percussion Set** | **525.00** |

1806 HARPERS FERRY
FLINTLOCK PISTOL

## 1806 HARPERS FERRY PISTOL

Of all the early American martial pistols, Harpers Ferry is one of the best known and was carried by both the Army and the Navy. Navy Arms Company has authentically reproduced the Harper's Ferry to the finest detail, providing a well-balanced and well-made pistol. **Weight:** 2 lbs. 9 oz. **Barrel length:** 10″. **Overall length:** 16″. **Caliber:** 58 smoothbore. **Finish:** Walnut stock; casehardened lock; brass-mounted browned barrel.

| | |
|---|---|
| **Harpers Ferry** | **$290.00** |
| **Single Cased Set** | **335.00** |

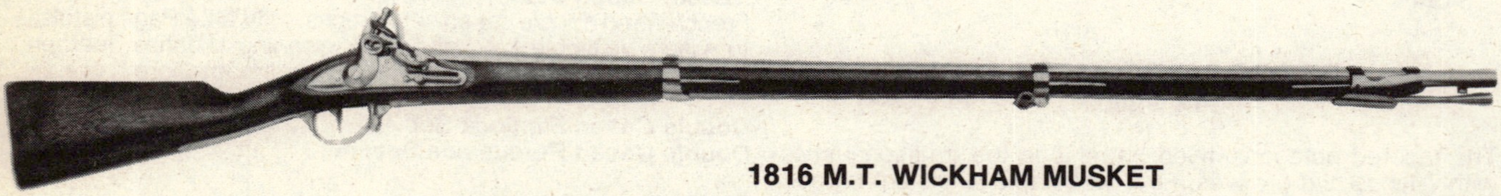

## 1816 M.T. WICKHAM MUSKET

This version of the French 1777 Charleville musket was chosen by the U.S. Army in 1816 to replace the 1808 Springfield. Manufactured in Philadelphia by M.T. Wickham, it was one of the last contract models. **Caliber:** 69. **Barrel length:** $44\frac{1}{2}$″. **Overall length:** $56\frac{1}{4}$″. **Weight:** 10 lbs. **Sights:** Brass blade front. **Stock:** European walnut. **Feature:** Brass flashpan.

| | |
|---|---|
| **1816 M.T. Wickham Musket** | **$765.00** |

# NAVY ARMS RIFLES

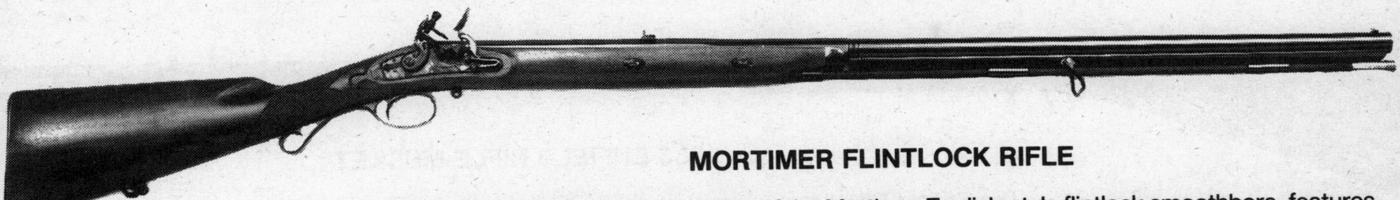

### MORTIMER FLINTLOCK RIFLE

This big-bore flintlock rifle, a replica of the Mortimer English-style flintlock smoothbore, features a waterproof pan, roller frizzen and external safety. **Caliber:** 54. **Barrel length:** 36″. **Overall length:** 53″. **Weight:** 7 lbs. **Sights:** Blade front; notch rear. **Stock:** Walnut.

**Mortimer Flintlock Rifle** . . . . . . . . . . . . . . . . . . . . **$725.00**
12-gauge drop-in barrel . . . . . . . . . . . . . . . . . . . . **300.00**

### MORTIMER FLINTLOCK MATCH RIFLE

This is the sleek match version of the large-bore rifle above. **Caliber:** .54. **Barrel length:** 36″. **Overall length:** 52 1/4″. **Weight:** 9 lbs. **Sights:** Precision aperture match rear; globe-style front. **Stock:** Walnut with cheekpiece, checkered wrist, sling swivels. **Features:** Waterproof pan; roller frizzen; external safety.

**Mortimer Flintlock Match Rifle** . . . . . . . . . . . . . . . . . . . . **$875.00**

### 1863 SHARPS CAVALRY CARBINE

This percussion version of the Sharps is a copy of the popular breechloading Cavalry Carbine of the Civil War. It features a patchbox and bar and saddle ring on left side of the stock. **Caliber:** 54. **Barrel length:** 22″. **Overall length:** 39″. **Weight:** 7 3/4 lbs. **Sights:** Blade front; military ladder rear. **Stock:** Walnut.

**Sharps Cavalry Carbine** . . . . . . . . . . . . . . . . . . . . **$835.00**
Also available:
**1859 Sharps Infantry Rifle** (54 cal.) . . . . . . . . . . . . . . . . . . . . **890.00**

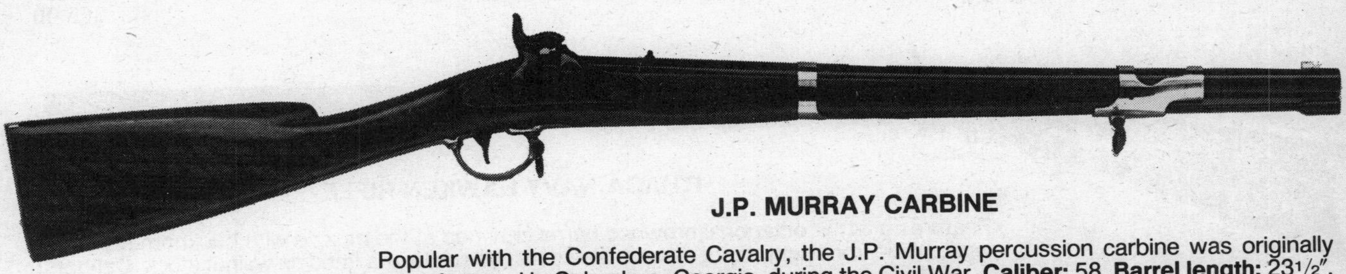

### J.P. MURRAY CARBINE

Popular with the Confederate Cavalry, the J.P. Murray percussion carbine was originally manufactured in Columbus, Georgia, during the Civil War. **Caliber:** 58. **Barrel length:** 23 1/2″. **Overall length:** 39 1/4″. **Weight:** 8 lbs. 5 oz. **Finish:** Walnut stock with polished brass.

**J.P. Murray Carbine** . . . . . . . . . . . . . . . . . . . . **$405.00**

BLACK POWDER

# NAVY ARMS RIFLES

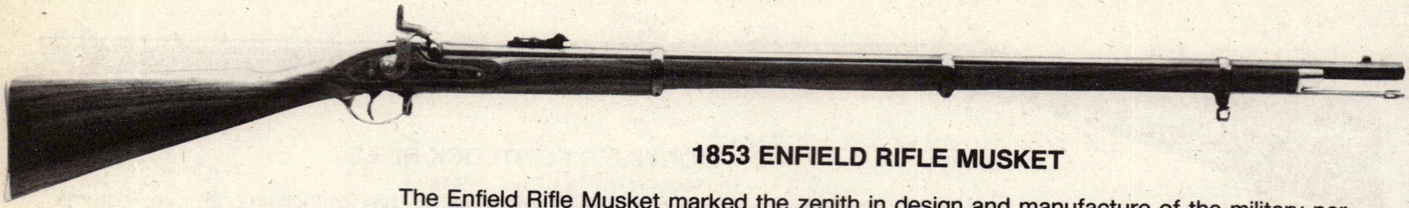

### 1853 ENFIELD RIFLE MUSKET

The Enfield Rifle Musket marked the zenith in design and manufacture of the military percussion rifle, and this perfection has been reproduced by Navy Arms Company. This and other Enfield muzzleloaders were the most coveted rifles of the Civil War, treasured by Union and Confederate troops alike for their fine quality and deadly accuracy. **Caliber:** 58. **Barrel length:** 39″. **Weight:** 10 lbs. 6 oz. **Overall length:** 55″. **Sights:** Fixed front; graduated rear. **Stock:** Seasoned walnut with solid brass furniture.

**1853 Enfield Rifle Musket** .................................................... **$480.00**

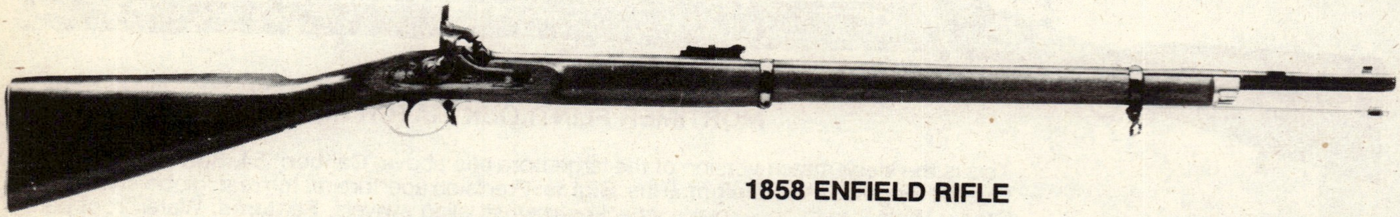

### 1858 ENFIELD RIFLE

In the late 1850s the British Admiralty, after extensive experiments, settled on a pattern rifle with a 5-groove barrel of heavy construction, sighted to 1,100 yards, designated the Naval rifle, Pattern 1858. **Caliber:** 58. **Barrel length:** 33″. **Weight:** 9 lbs. 10 oz. **Overall length:** 48.5″. **Sights:** Fixed front; graduated rear. **Stock:** Seasoned walnut with solid brass furniture.

**1858 Enfield Rifle** .................................................... **$450.00**

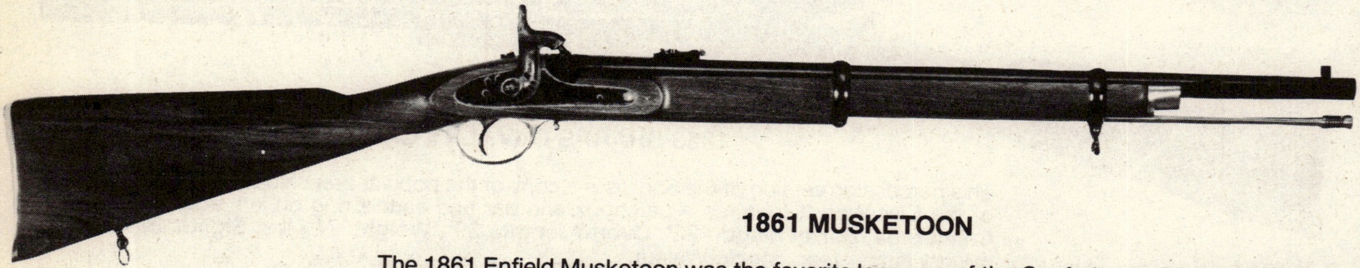

### 1861 MUSKETOON

The 1861 Enfield Musketoon was the favorite long arm of the Confederate Cavalry. **Caliber:** 58. **Barrel length:** 24″. **Weight:** 7 lbs. 8 oz. **Overall length:** 40.25″. **Sights:** Fixed front; graduated rear. **Stock:** Seasoned walnut with solid brass furniture.

**1861 Musketoon** .................................................... **$405.00**
**Kit** .................................................... **365.00**

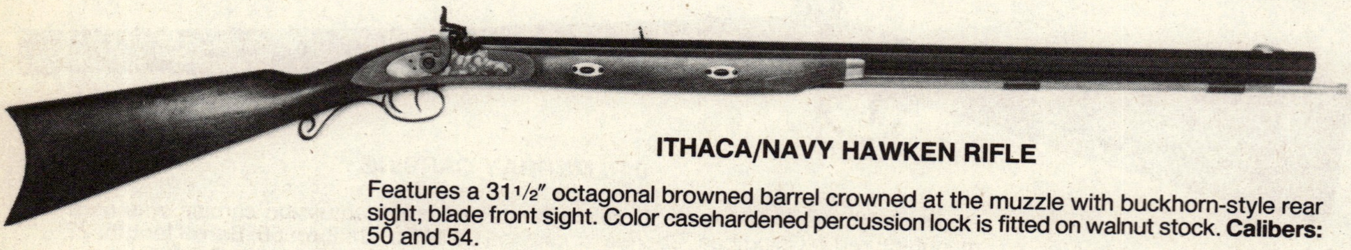

### ITHACA/NAVY HAWKEN RIFLE

Features a 31½″ octagonal browned barrel crowned at the muzzle with buckhorn-style rear sight, blade front sight. Color casehardened percussion lock is fitted on walnut stock. **Calibers:** 50 and 54.

**Ithaca/Navy Hawken Rifle** .................................................... **$400.00**
**Kit** .................................................... **360.00**

# NAVY ARMS RIFLES

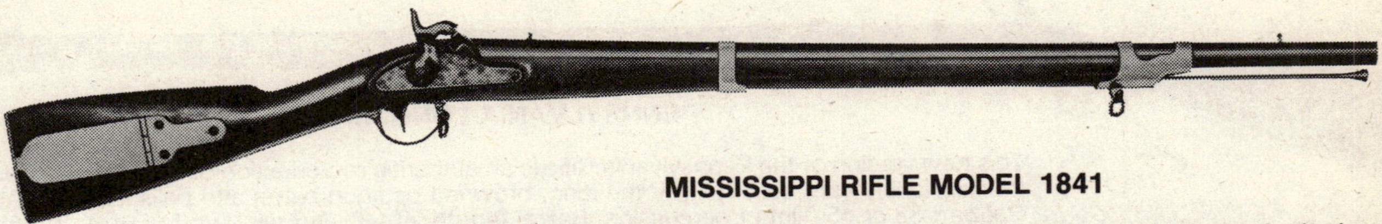

### MISSISSIPPI RIFLE MODEL 1841

This historic percussion weapon gained its name because of its performance in the hands of Jefferson Davis' Mississippi Regiment during the heroic stand at the Battle of Buena Vista. Also known as the "Yager" (a misspelling of the German Jaeger), this was one of the first percussion rifles adopted by Army Ordnance. The Mississippi is handsomely furnished in brass, including patchbox for tools and spare parts. **Weight:** $9\frac{1}{2}$ lbs. **Barrel length:** $32\frac{1}{2}$″. **Overall length:** $48\frac{1}{2}$″. **Calibers:** 54 and 58. **Finish:** Walnut finish stock, brass mounted.

**Mississippi Rifle Model 1841** . . . . . . . . . . . . . . . . . . . . . . . . . . . . **$465.00**

### SMITH CARBINE

The Smith Carbine was considered one of the finest breechloading carbines of the Civil War period. The hinged breech action allowed fast reloading for cavalry units. Available in either the **Cavalry Model** (with saddle ring and bar) or **Artillery Model** (with sling swivels). **Caliber:** 50. **Barrel length:** $21\frac{1}{2}$″. **Overall length:** 39″. **Weight:** $7\frac{3}{4}$ lbs. **Sights:** Brass blade front; folding ladder rear. **Stock:** American walnut.

**Smith Carbine** . . . . . . . . . . . . . . . . . . . . . . . . . . . . . . . . . . . . **$600.00**

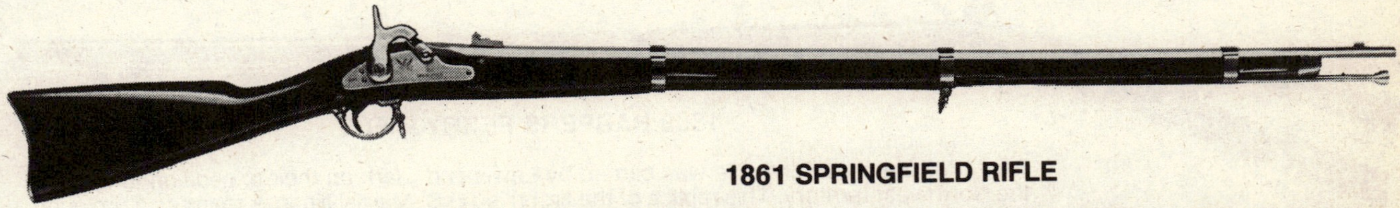

### 1861 SPRINGFIELD RIFLE

One of the most popular Union rifles of the Civil War, the 1861 used the 1855-style hammer. The lockplate on this replica is marked "1861, U.S. Springfield." **Caliber:** 58. **Barrel length:** 40″. **Overall length:** 56″. **Weight:** 10 lbs. **Finish:** Walnut stock with polished metal lock and stock fitting.

**1861 Springfield Rifle** . . . . . . . . . . . . . . . . . . . . . . . . . . . . . . . **$550.00**

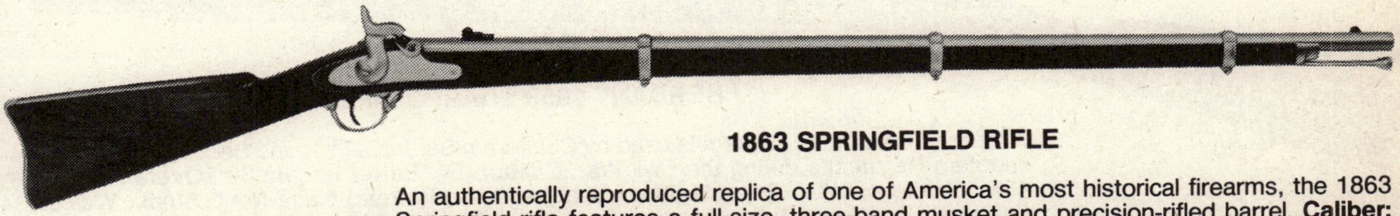

### 1863 SPRINGFIELD RIFLE

An authentically reproduced replica of one of America's most historical firearms, the 1863 Springfield rifle features a full-size, three-band musket and precision-rifled barrel. **Caliber:** 58. **Barrel length:** 40″. **Overall length:** 56″. **Weight:** $9\frac{1}{2}$ lbs. **Finish:** Walnut stock with polished metal lock and stock fittings. Casehardened lock available upon request.

**1863 Springfield Rifle** . . . . . . . . . . . . . . . . . . . . . . . . . . . . . . . **$550.00**

# NAVY ARMS

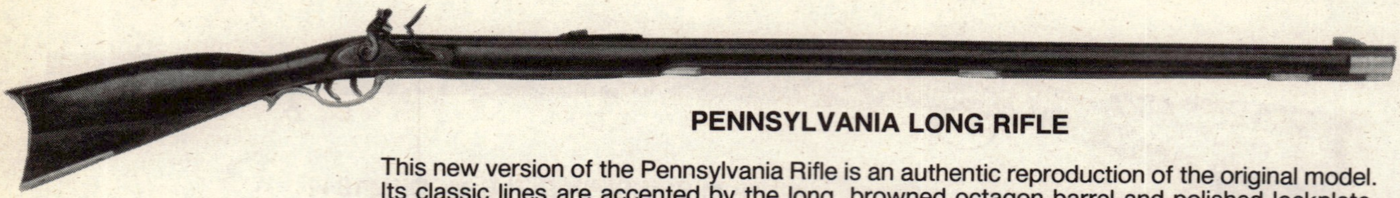

## PENNSYLVANIA LONG RIFLE

This new version of the Pennsylvania Rifle is an authentic reproduction of the original model. Its classic lines are accented by the long, browned octagon barrel and polished lockplate. **Caliber:** 32 or 45 (flint or percussion. **Barrel length:** 40½″. **Overall length:** 56½″. **Weight:** 7½ lbs. **Sights:** Blade front; adjustable Buckhorn rear. **Stock:** Walnut.

**Pennsylvania Long Rifle** Flintlock . . . . . . . . **$435.00**
Percussion . . . . . . . . **425.00**

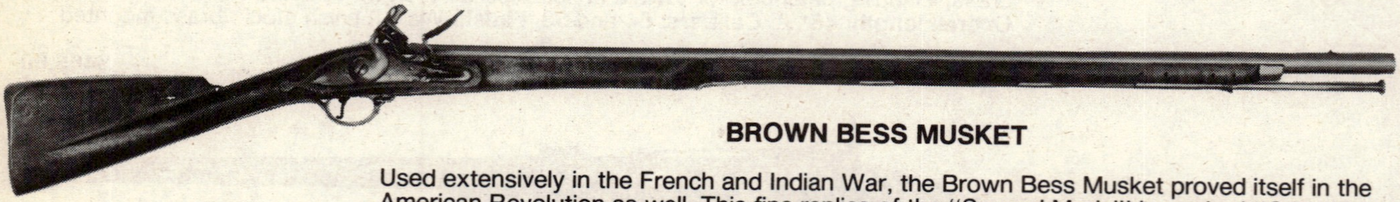

## BROWN BESS MUSKET

Used extensively in the French and Indian War, the Brown Bess Musket proved itself in the American Revolution as well. This fine replica of the "Second Model" is marked "Grice" on the lockplate. **Caliber:** 75. **Barrel length:** 42″. **Overall length:** 59″. **Weight:** 9½ lbs. **Sights:** Lug front. **Stock:** Walnut.

**Brown Bess Musket** . . . . . . . . **$705.00**
**Kit** . . . . . . . . **580.00**

Also available:
**Brown Bess Carbine**
**Caliber:** 75. **Barrel length:** 30″. **Overall length:** 47″. **Weight:** 7¾ lbs.
**Price** . . . . . . . . **$705.00**

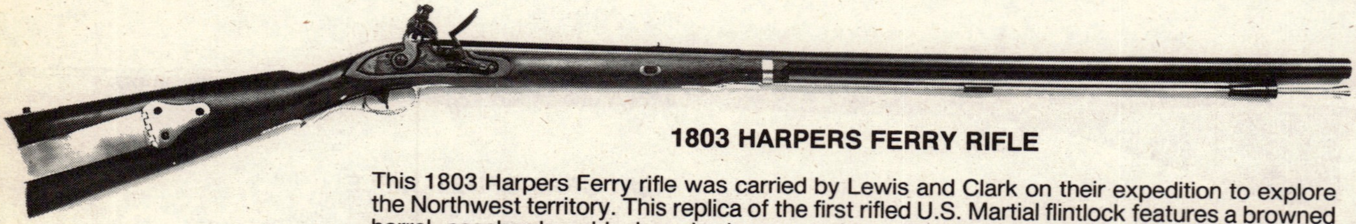

## 1803 HARPERS FERRY RIFLE

This 1803 Harpers Ferry rifle was carried by Lewis and Clark on their expedition to explore the Northwest territory. This replica of the first rifled U.S. Martial flintlock features a browned barrel, casehardened lock and a brass patchbox. **Caliber:** 54. **Barrel length:** 35″. **Overall length:** 50½″. **Weight:** 8½ lbs.

**1803 Harpers Ferry Rifle** . . . . . . . . **$615.00**

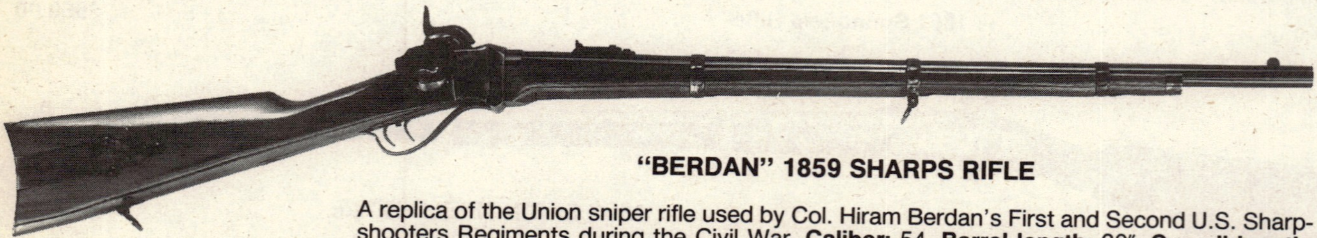

## "BERDAN" 1859 SHARPS RIFLE

A replica of the Union sniper rifle used by Col. Hiram Berdan's First and Second U.S. Sharpshooters Regiments during the Civil War. **Caliber:** 54. **Barrel length:** 30″. **Overall length:** 46¾″. **Weight:** 8 lbs. 8 oz. **Sights:** Military-style ladder rear; blade front. **Stock:** Walnut. **Features:** Double set triggers, casehardened receiver; patchbox and furniture

**"Berdan" 1859 Sharps Rifle** . . . . . . . . **$1020.00**
Also available:
**Single Trigger Infantry Model** . . . . . . . . **890.00**

# NAVY ARMS RIFLES

## 1862 C.S. RICHMOND RIFLE

This model was manufactured by the Confederacy at the Richmond Armory utilizing 1855 Rifle Musket parts captured from the Harpers Ferry Arsenal. This replica features the unusual 1855 lockplate, stamped "1862 C.S. Richmond, V.A." **Caliber:** 58. **Barrel length:** 40". **Overall length:** 56". **Weight:** 10 lbs. **Finish:** Walnut stock with polished metal lock and stock fittings.

**1862 C.S. Richmond Rifle** . . . . . . . . . . . . . . . . . . . . . . . . . . . . . . . . . **$550.00**

## TRYON CREEDMOOR RIFLE

This replica of the Tryon Creedmoor match rifle won a Gold Medal at the 13th World Shoot in Germany. It features a blued octagonal heavy match barrel, hooded target front sight, adjustable Vernier tang sight, double-set triggers, sling swivels and a walnut stock. **Caliber:** 451. **Barrel length:** 33". **Overall length:** $48^{1}/_{4}$". **Weight:** $9^{1}/_{2}$ lbs.

**Tryon Creedmoor Rifle** . . . . . . . . . . . . . . . . . . . . . . . . . . . . . . . . . **$740.00**
**Brass telescopic sight** . . . . . . . . . . . . . . . . . . . . . . . . . . . . . . . . . **125.00**

## KODIAK DOUBLE RIFLE

The powerful double-barreled Kodiak percussion rifle has fully adjustable sights mounted on blued steel barrels. The lockplates are engraved and highly polished. **Calibers:** 50, 54 and 58. **Barrel length:** $28^{1}/_{2}$". **Overall length:** 45". **Weight:** 11 lbs. **Sights:** Folding notch rear; ramp bead front. **Stock:** Hand-checkered walnut.

**Kodiak Double Rifle** . . . . . . . . . . . . . . . . . . . . . . . . . . . . . . . . . **$775.00**

BLACK POWDER

# NAVY ARMS SHOTGUNS

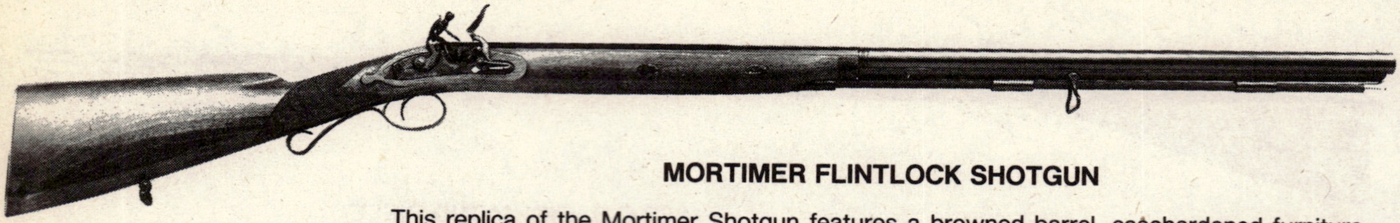

## MORTIMER FLINTLOCK SHOTGUN

This replica of the Mortimer Shotgun features a browned barrel, casehardened furniture, sling swivels and checkered walnut stock. The lock contains waterproof pan, roller frizzen and external safety. **Gauge:** 12. **Barrel length:** 36″. **Overall length:** 53″. **Weight:** 7 lbs.

**Mortimer Flintlock Shotgun** . . . . . . . . . . . . . . . . . . . . . . . . . . . . **$700.00**

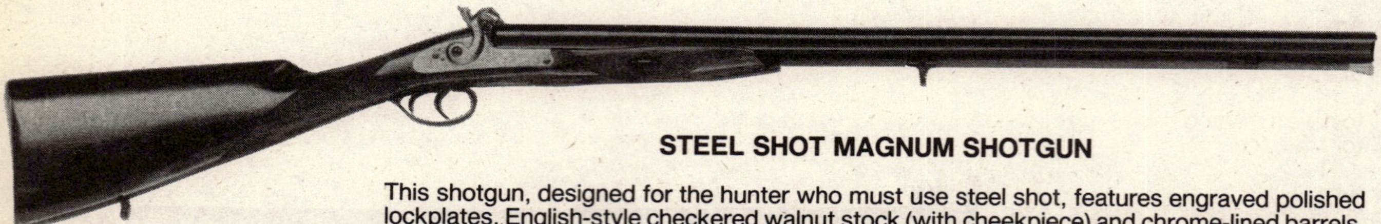

## STEEL SHOT MAGNUM SHOTGUN

This shotgun, designed for the hunter who must use steel shot, features engraved polished lockplates, English-style checkered walnut stock (with cheekpiece) and chrome-lined barrels. **Gauge:** 10. **Barrel length:** 28″. **Overall length:** 45 1/2″. **Weight:** 7 lbs. 9 oz. **Choke:** Cylinder/Cylinder.

**Steel-Shot Magnum Shotgun** . . . . . . . . . . . . . . . . . . . . . . . . . . . . **$560.00**

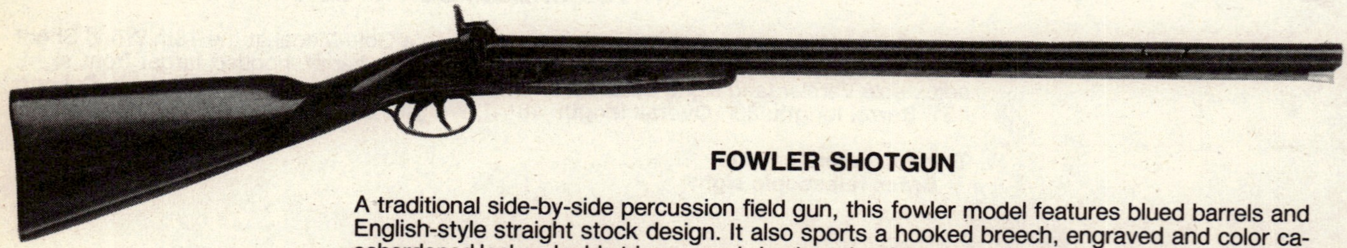

## FOWLER SHOTGUN

A traditional side-by-side percussion field gun, this fowler model features blued barrels and English-style straight stock design. It also sports a hooked breech, engraved and color casehardened locks, double triggers and checkered walnut stock. **Gauge:** 12. **Chokes:** Cylinder/Cylinder. **Barrel length:** 28″. **Overall length:** 44 1/2″. **Weight:** 7 1/2 lbs.

**Fowler Shotgun** . . . . . . . . . . . . . . . . . . . . . . . . . . . . **$340.00**
**Kit** . . . . . . . . . . . . . . . . . . . . . . . . . . . . **310.00**

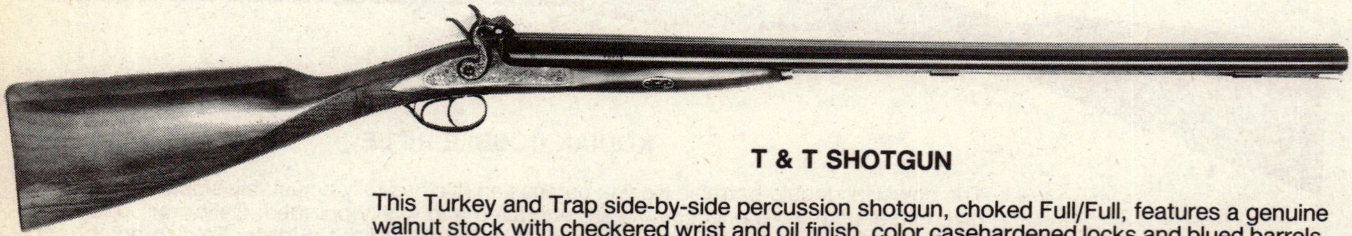

## T & T SHOTGUN

This Turkey and Trap side-by-side percussion shotgun, choked Full/Full, features a genuine walnut stock with checkered wrist and oil finish, color casehardened locks and blued barrels. **Gauge:** 12. **Barrel length:** 28″. **Overall length:** 44″. **Weight:** 7 1/2 lbs.

**T & T Shotgun** . . . . . . . . . . . . . . . . . . . . . . . . . . . . **$540.00**

# REMINGTON

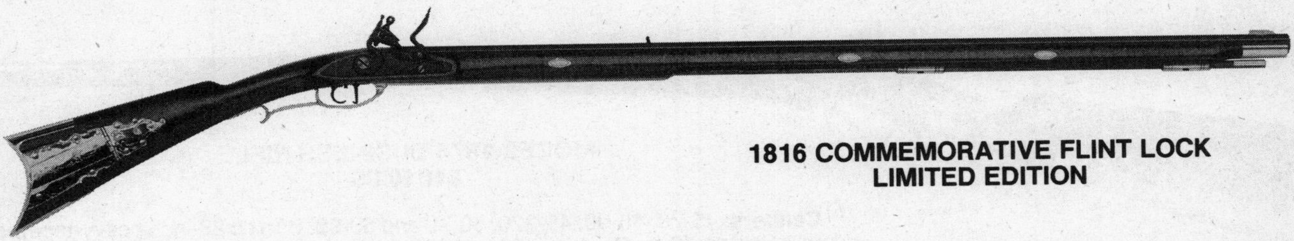

1816 COMMEMORATIVE FLINT LOCK
LIMITED EDITION

## 1816 COMMEMORATIVE FLINT LOCK RIFLE LIMITED EDITION $1899.00

America's oldest gunmaker celebrates its history with this authentic commemorative of the first flintlock rifle made by Eliphalet Remington in 1816 in Ilion, New York. Remington carried his first rifle barrel blank to the nearby town of Utica to have it reamed and rifled. His barrels soon became renowned for their accuracy, and his barrel business flourished.

The new 50-caliber Remington 1816 Flint Lock Rifle features a 39″ octagonal barrel with deep cut-rifling and a 1-in-66″ slow twist, plus six hand-engraved brass escutcheons and a Ketland-style lock mechanism. The rifle comes with a set trigger and polished brass trigger guard. The front blade sight is matched to a small rear sight (V-leaf design). Other features include a full-length extra-fancy, curly maple stock, hand-rubbed with 25 coats of Tru Oil, polished brass buttplate, toe, nosecap and fancy hand-engraved patchbox. Each rifle comes with a brief history of the product.

# RUGER

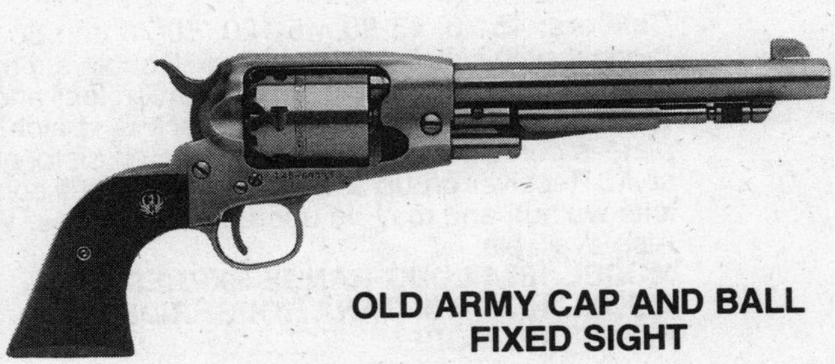

OLD ARMY CAP AND BALL
FIXED SIGHT

## OLD ARMY CAP AND BALL $398.00 ($450.00 Stainless Steel)

This Old Army cap-and-ball revolver with fixed sights is reminiscent of the Civil War era martial revolvers and those used by the early frontiersmen in the 1800s. This Ruger model comes in both blued and stainless-steel finishes and features modern materials, technology and design throughout, including steel music-wire coil springs.

**SPECIFICATIONS**
**Caliber:** 45 (.443″ bore; .45″ groove)
**Barrel length:** $7^1/_2$″
**Rifling:** 6 grooves, R.H. twist (1:16″)
**Weight:** $2^7/_8$ lbs.
**Sights:** Fixed, ramp front; topstrap channel rear
**Percussion cap nipples:** Stainless steel (#11)

BLACK POWDER

# SHILOH SHARPS

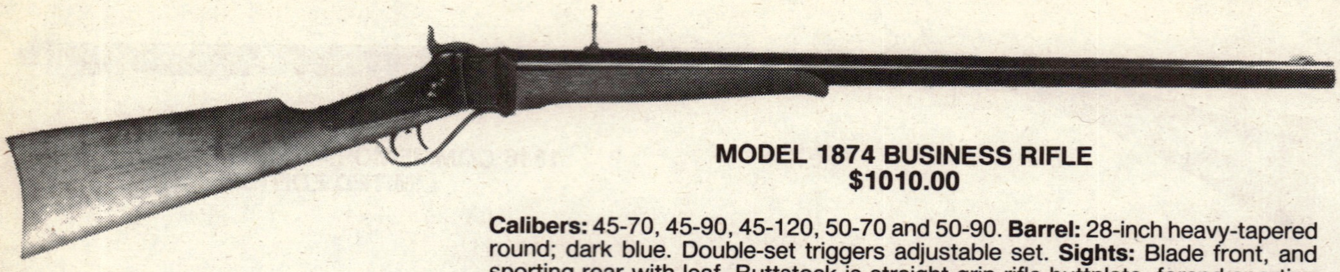

### MODEL 1874 BUSINESS RIFLE
### $1010.00

**Calibers:** 45-70, 45-90, 45-120, 50-70 and 50-90. **Barrel:** 28-inch heavy-tapered round; dark blue. Double-set triggers adjustable set. **Sights:** Blade front, and sporting rear with leaf. Buttstock is straight grip rifle buttplate, forend sporting schnabel style. Receiver group and buttplate case-colored; wood is American walnut oil-finished. **Weight:** 9 lbs. 8 oz.

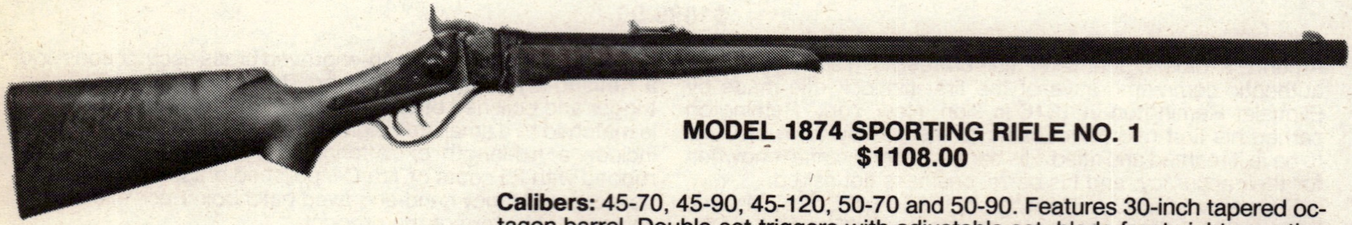

### MODEL 1874 SPORTING RIFLE NO. 1
### $1108.00

**Calibers:** 45-70, 45-90, 45-120, 50-70 and 50-90. Features 30-inch tapered octagon barrel. Double-set triggers with adjustable set, blade front sight, sporting rear with elevation leaf and sporting tang sight adjustable for elevation and windage. Buttstock is pistol grip, shotgun butt, sporting forend style. Receiver group and buttplate case colored. Barrel is high-finish blue-black; wood is American walnut oil finish.

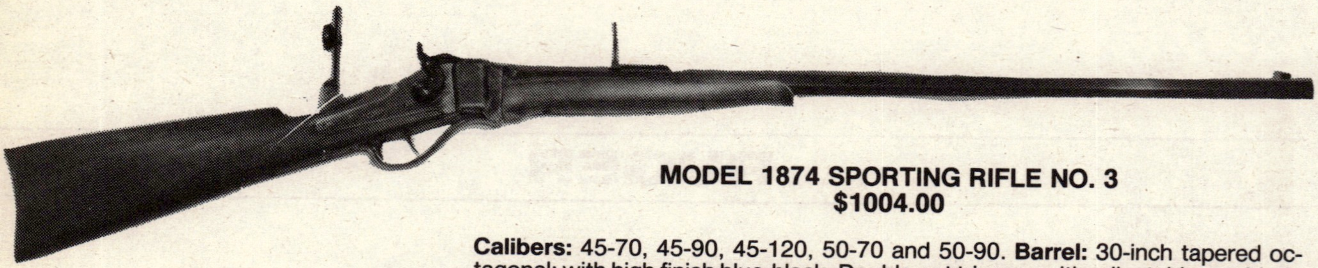

### MODEL 1874 SPORTING RIFLE NO. 3
### $1004.00

**Calibers:** 45-70, 45-90, 45-120, 50-70 and 50-90. **Barrel:** 30-inch tapered octagonal; with high finish blue-black. Double-set triggers with adjustable set, blade front sight, sporting rear with elevation leaf and sporting tang sight adjustable for elevation and windage. Buttstock is straight grip with rifle buttplate; trigger plate is curved and checkered to match pistol grip. Forend is sporting schnabel style. Receiver group and buttplate are case colored. Wood is oil-finished American walnut, and may be upgraded in all rifles. **Weight:** 9 lbs. 8 oz.
Also available:
**MODEL 1874 LONG-RANGE EXPRESS** .......... **$1134.00**
**MODEL 1874 MONTANA ROUGHRIDER** .......... **1004.00**
**HARTFORD MODEL** .......... **1174.00**

### SHILOH SHARPS RIFLE CARTRIDGE AVAILABILITY

The **Long-Range Express, No. 1 Sporting, No. 3 Sporting, Business, Montana Roughrider** and **Hartford Model rifles** all are available in the following cartridges: 30-40, 38-55, 38-56, 40-50 ($1\frac{11}{16}$ B.N.), 40-60 Maynard ST, 40-65 WIN, 40-70 ($2\frac{1}{10}$ B.N.), 40-70 ($2\frac{1}{4}$ B.N.), 40-70 ($2\frac{1}{2}$ ST), 40-82 Shiloh, 40-90 ($3\frac{1}{4}$ ST), 40-90 ($2\frac{5}{8}$ B.N.), 44-77 B.N., 44-90 B.N., 45-70 ($2\frac{1}{10}$ ST), 45-90 ($2\frac{4}{10}$ ST), 45-100 ($2\frac{6}{10}$ ST), 45-110 ($2\frac{7}{8}$ ST), 45-120 ($3\frac{1}{4}$ ST), 50-70 ($1\frac{3}{4}$ ST) and 50-100 ($2\frac{1}{2}$ ST). The **1874 Saddle Rifle** is available in all of the above calibers, except the 40-82 Shiloh, 44-90, 45-100, 45-110 and 45-120.(B.N.=Bottleneck; ST=Straight)

# STONE MOUNTAIN ARMS

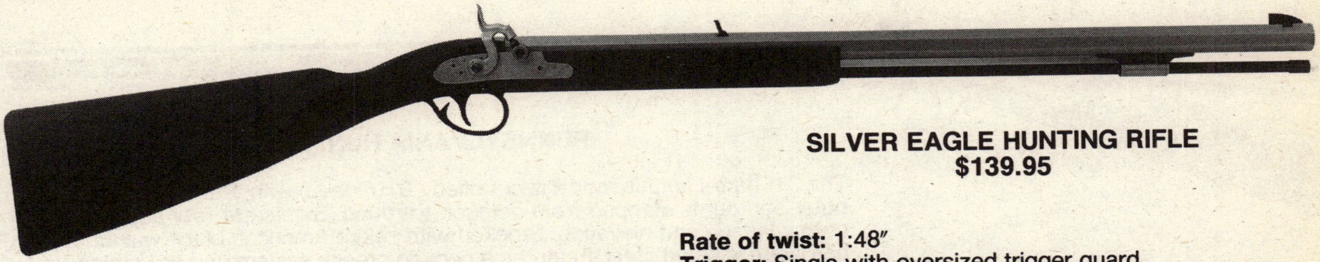

## SILVER EAGLE HUNTING RIFLE
**$139.95**

**SPECIFICATIONS**
**Caliber:** 50 percussion
**Barrel length:** 26″ (Weatherguard nickel), octagonal
**Overall length:** 40″
**Rate of twist:** 1:48″
**Trigger:** Single with oversized trigger guard
**Sights:** Fixed
**Stock:** Duragrip synthetic stock with checkered grip surfaces
**Features:** Weatherguard tang, thimble and lock; blued ramp and sights

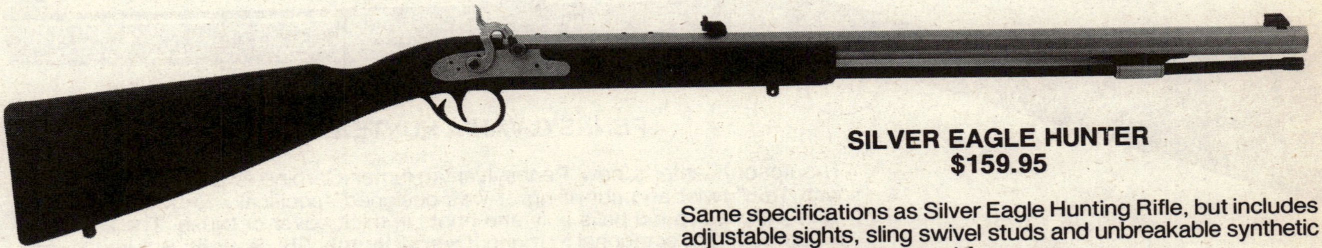

## SILVER EAGLE HUNTER
**$159.95**

Same specifications as Silver Eagle Hunting Rifle, but includes adjustable sights, sling swivel studs and unbreakable synthetic ramrod; drilled and tapped for scope.

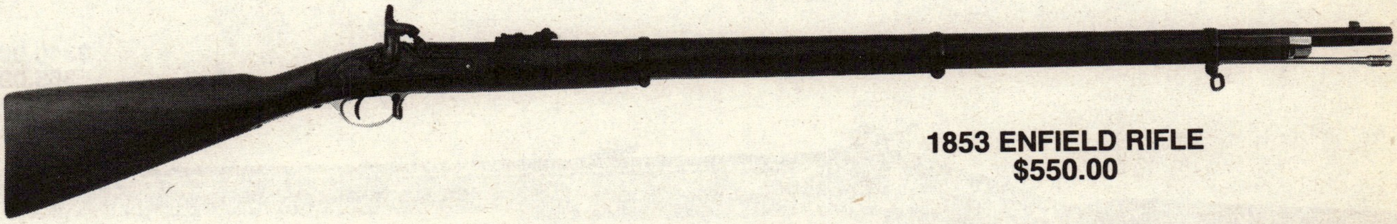

## 1853 ENFIELD RIFLE
**$550.00**

**SPECIFICATIONS**
**Caliber:** 58 percussion
**Barrel length:** 39″ w/3 blued steel bands
**Overall length:** 54″
**Sights:** Folding ladder rear; inverted "V" front
**Stock:** Walnut
**Features:** Blued barrel tang, breech plug and bayonet mount; polished brass furniture; color casehardened lock and sideplates

Also available:
**HARPERS FERRY 1803 FLINTLOCK.** 54 cal. with 32½″ browned barrel and 1:60″ twist. **Overall length:** 49″. **Weight:** 9½ lbs. **Price:** .......... **$729.00**
**1861 SPRINGFIELD RIFLE.** 58 cal. 40″ barrel fitted with three-tier rear sight. **Overall length:** 56″. **Weight:** 9½ lbs. **Price:** .......... **$599.00**

## ROGERS & SPENCER REVOLVER
**$289.00**

**SPECIFICATIONS**
**Caliber:** 44 percussion
**Capacity:** 6 shots
**Barrel length:** 8″, octagonal
**Grips:** Two-piece walnut
**Features:** Steel frame with top-strap design; blue-black finish
Also available:
**1858 REMINGTON TARGET REVOLVER.** 44 cal. with adjustable rear sights. **Price:** .......... **$219.95**

## PENNSYLVANIA HUNTER

The 31″ barrel on this model is cut rifled (.010″ deep) with 1 turn in 66″ twist. Its outer contour is stepped from octagon to round. Sights are fully adjustable for both windage and elevation. Stocked with select American black walnut; metal hardware is blued steel. Features a hooked breech system and coil-spring lock. **Caliber:** 50. **Overall length:** 48″. **Weight:** Approx. 7.6 lbs.

**Pennsylvania Hunter Caplock** .......... **$350.00**
**Pennsylvania Hunter Flintlock** .......... **365.00**

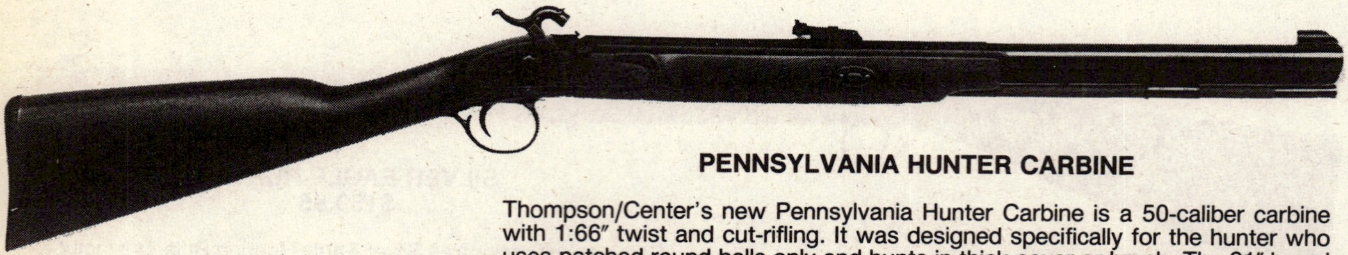

## PENNSYLVANIA HUNTER CARBINE

Thompson/Center's new Pennsylvania Hunter Carbine is a 50-caliber carbine with 1:66″ twist and cut-rifling. It was designed specifically for the hunter who uses patched round balls only and hunts in thick cover or brush. The 21″ barrel is stepped from octagonal to round. **Overall length:** 38″. **Weight:** 6½ lbs. **Sights:** Fully adjustable open hunting-style rear with bead front. **Stock:** Select American walnut. **Trigger:** Single hunting-style trigger. **Lock:** Color cased, coil spring, with floral design.

**Pennsylvania Hunter Carbine Caplock** .......... **$340.00**
**Pennsylvania Hunter Carbine Flintlock** .......... **355.00**

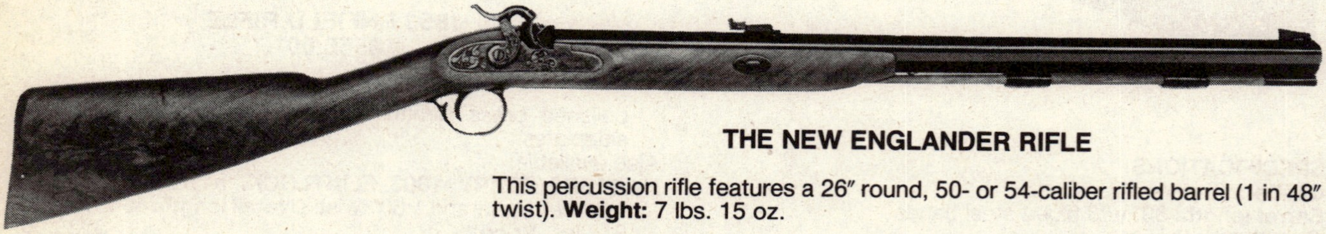

## THE NEW ENGLANDER RIFLE

This percussion rifle features a 26″ round, 50- or 54-caliber rifled barrel (1 in 48″ twist). **Weight:** 7 lbs. 15 oz.

**New Englander Rifle** .......... **$295.00**
With Rynite stock (24″ barrel, right-hand only) .......... **280.00**
**Left-Hand Model** .......... **315.00**

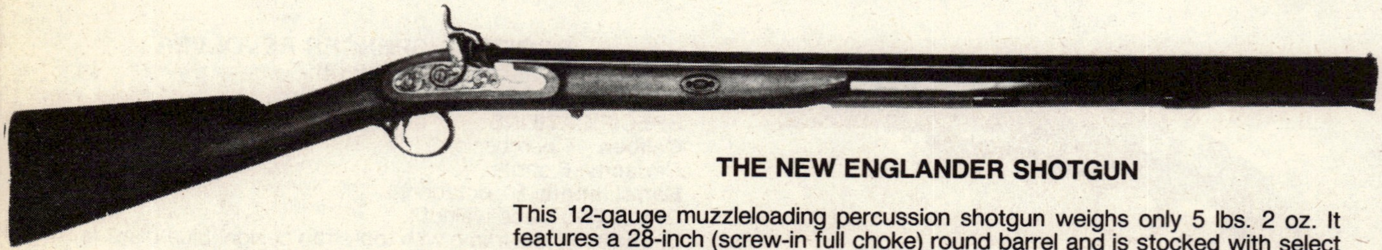

## THE NEW ENGLANDER SHOTGUN

This 12-gauge muzzleloading percussion shotgun weighs only 5 lbs. 2 oz. It features a 28-inch (screw-in full choke) round barrel and is stocked with select American black walnut.

**New Englander Shotgun** .......... **$315.00**

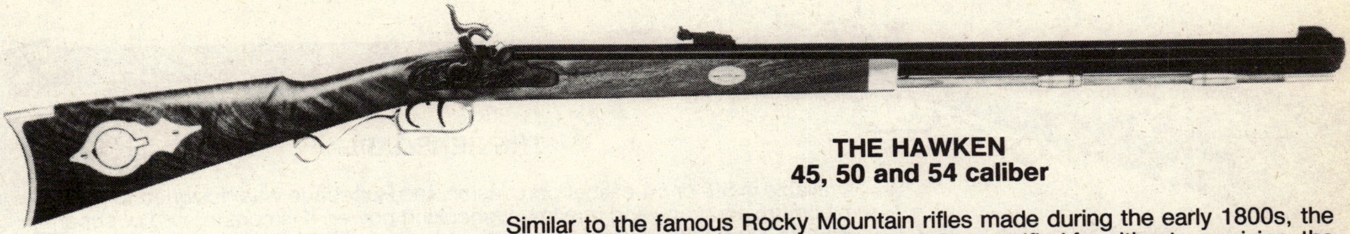

## THE HAWKEN
### 45, 50 and 54 caliber

Similar to the famous Rocky Mountain rifles made during the early 1800s, the Hawken is intended for serious shooting. Button-rifled for ultimate precision, the Hawken is available in 45, 50 or 54 caliber, flintlock or percussion. It features a hooked breech, double-set triggers, first-grade American walnut stock, adjustable hunting sights, solid brass trim and color casehardened lock. Beautifully decorated. **Weight:** Approx. 8½ lbs.

**Hawken Caplock** 45, 50 or 54 caliber . . . . . . . . . . . . . . . . . . . . . . . . . . **$405.00**
**Hawken Flintlock** 50 caliber . . . . . . . . . . . . . . . . . . . . . . . . . . . . . . . . **415.00**
**Kit:** Caplock . . . . . . . . . . . . . . . . . . . . . . . . . . . . . . . . . . . . . . . . . . . . **300.00**
**Kit:** Flintlock . . . . . . . . . . . . . . . . . . . . . . . . . . . . . . . . . . . . . . . . . . . **320.00**

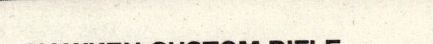

## HAWKEN CUSTOM RIFLE

T/C's Hawken Custom features a crescent buttplate inletted in a select American walnut stock. The barrel, lockplate, buttplate, trigger guard and forend cap are all polished and buffed to a high-luster sheen with a deep blue finish. The 50-caliber 28-inch octagonal barrel has a 1:48″ twist and handles patched round balls and conical projectiles. **Overall length:** 45¼″. **Weight:** 8½ lbs. **Sights:** Fully adjustable open hunting-style rear; bead-style front. **Features:** Hooked-breech system; heavy-duty, coil-type internal springs; fully adjustable trigger (functions as double set or single stage).

**Hawken Custom Rifle** . . . . . . . . . . . . . . . . . . . . . . . . . . . . . . . . . . . . . . . **$495.00**

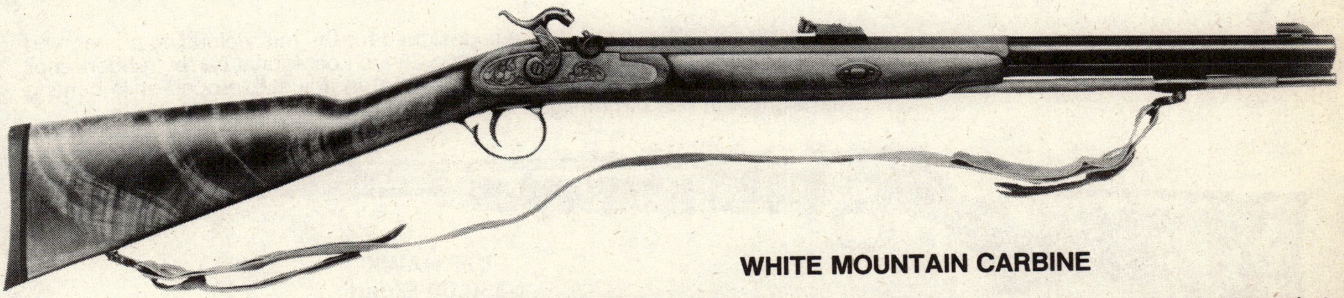

WHITE MOUNTAIN CAPLOCK CARBINE

## WHITE MOUNTAIN CARBINE

This hunter's rifle with single trigger features a wide trigger guard bow that allows the shooter to fire the rifle in cold weather without removing his gloves. Its stock is of select American black walnut with a rifle-type rubber recoil pad, and is equipped with swivel studs and quick detachable sling swivels. A soft leather hunting-style sling is included. The barrel is stepped from octagonal to round. **Calibers:** 50 and 54 (Hawken or Renegade loads). **Barrel length:** 21″. **Overall length:** 38″. **Weight:** 6½ lbs. **Sights:** Open hunting (Patridge) style, fully adjustable. **Lock:** Heavy-duty coil springs; decorated with floral design and color-cased. **Breech:** Hooked-breech system.

**White Mountain Carbine–Caplock** (right-hand only) . . . . . . . . . . . . . . **$350.00**

# THOMPSON/CENTER

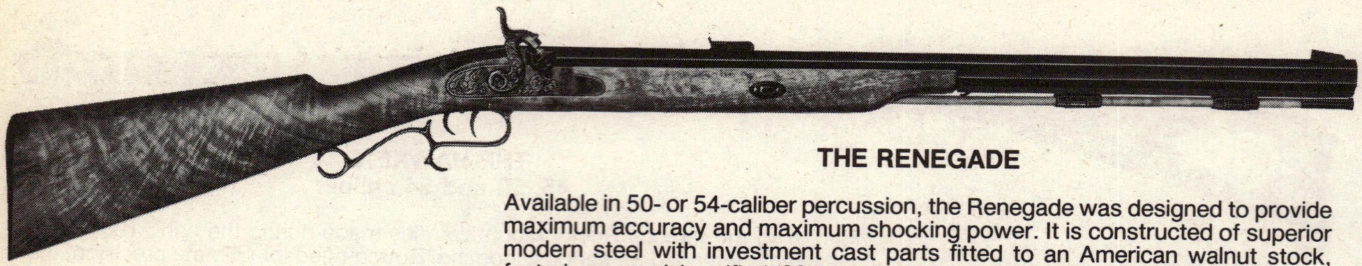

## THE RENEGADE

Available in 50- or 54-caliber percussion, the Renegade was designed to provide maximum accuracy and maximum shocking power. It is constructed of superior modern steel with investment cast parts fitted to an American walnut stock, featuring a precision-rifled (26-inch carbine-type) octagonal barrel, hooked-breech system, coil spring lock, double-set triggers, adjustable hunting sights and steel trim. **Weight:** Approx. 8 lbs.

**Renegade Caplock** 50 and 54 caliber . . . . . . . . . . **$360.00**
**Renegade Caplock** Left Hand . . . . . . . . . . **370.00**
**Renegade Caplock Kit** Right Hand . . . . . . . . . . **260.00**

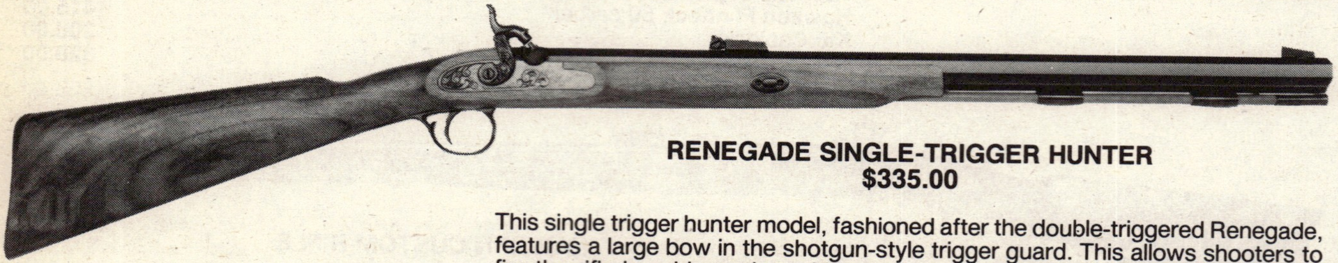

## RENEGADE SINGLE-TRIGGER HUNTER
**$335.00**

This single trigger hunter model, fashioned after the double-triggered Renegade, features a large bow in the shotgun-style trigger guard. This allows shooters to fire the rifle in cold weather without removing their gloves. The octagon barrel measures 26 inches and the stock is made of select American walnut. **Weight:** About 8 pounds. **Calibers:** 50 and 54.

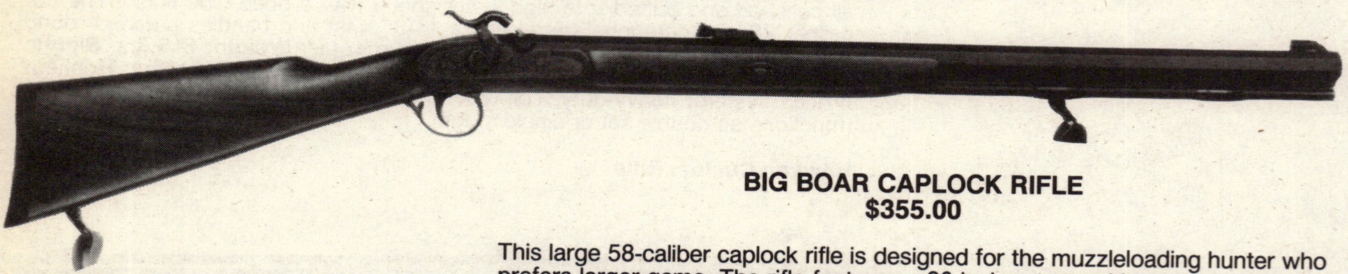

## BIG BOAR CAPLOCK RIFLE
**$355.00**

This large 58-caliber caplock rifle is designed for the muzzleloading hunter who prefers larger game. The rifle features a 26-inch octagonal barrel, rubber recoil pad, leather sling with QD sling swivels, and an adjustable open-style hunting rear sight with bead front sight. Stock is of American black walnut.

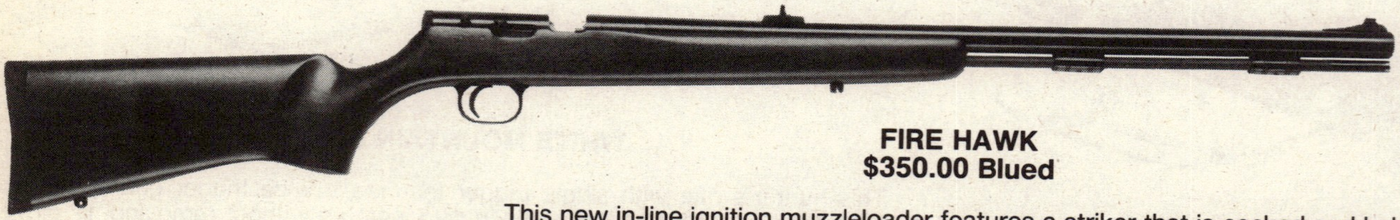

## FIRE HAWK
**$350.00 Blued**

This new in-line ignition muzzleloader features a striker that is cocked and held rearward, locked in place when the thumb safety is in the rearward position. By sliding the thumb safety forward, the striker is free to fire the percussion cap when the trigger is pulled. The Fire Hawk's free-floated 24″ barrel is rifled with a 1:38″ twist and is designed for use with modern conical or sabot projectiles. **Calibers:** 50 and 54. **Overall length:** 41 3/4″. **Weight:** 7 lbs. **Sights:** Adj. leaf-style rear; ramp-style white bead front. **Stock:** American black walnut or Rynite. Also available:

**Stainless Steel w/Rynite stock** . . . . . . . . . . **$370.00**
**Stainless Steel w/walnut stock** . . . . . . . . . . **385.00**

# THOMPSON/CENTER

**SCOUT CARBINE with Rynite Stock**

## SCOUT RIFLE, CARBINE & PISTOL

Thompson/Center's Scout Carbine & Pistol uses the in-line ignition system with a special vented breechplug that produces constant pressures from shot to shot, thereby improving accuracy. The patented trigger mechanism consists of only two moving parts—the trigger and the hammer—thus providing ease of operation and low maintenance. Both the carbine and pistol are available in 50 and 54 caliber. The carbine's 21″ and 24″ (stepped) barrels and the pistol's 12-inch barrel (overall length: 17″) are easily removable and readily interchangeable in either caliber. Their lines are reminiscent of the saddle guns and pistols of the "Old West," combining modern-day engineering with the flavor of the past. Both are suitable for left-handed shooters.

| | |
|---|---|
| **Rifle** | $425.00 |
| With Rynite stock | 340.00 |
| **Scout Carbine** | 415.00 |
| With Rynite Stock | 325.00 |
| **Scout Pistol** (45, 50, 54 cal.) | 340.00 |

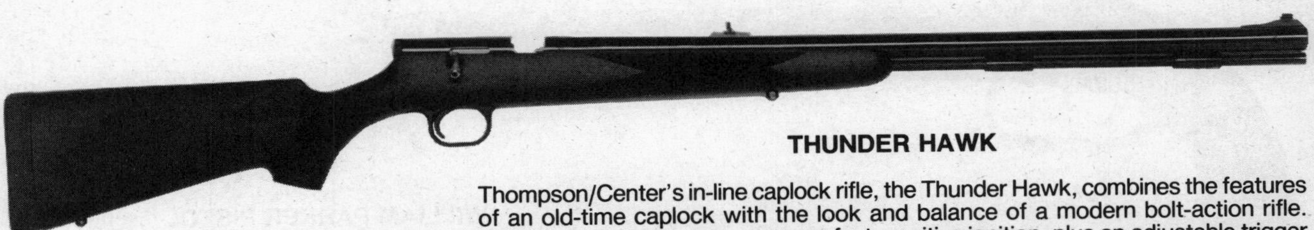

**THUNDER HAWK with 24″ Barrel, Rynite Stock**

## THUNDER HAWK

Thompson/Center's in-line caplock rifle, the Thunder Hawk, combines the features of an old-time caplock with the look and balance of a modern bolt-action rifle. The in-line ignition system ensures fast, positive ignition, plus an adjustable trigger for a crisp trigger pull. The 21-inch and 24-inch barrels have an adjustable rear sight and bead-style front sight (barrel is drilled and tapped to accept T/C's Thunder Hawk scope rings or Quick-Release Mounting System). The stock is American black walnut with rubber recoil pad and sling swivel studs. Rifling is 1:38″ twist, designed to fire patched round balls, conventional conical projectiles and sabot bullets. **Weight:** Approx. 6¾ lbs. **Calibers:** 50 and 54.

| | |
|---|---|
| **Thunder Hawk** w/21″ barrel | $300.00 |
| Stainless steel with Rynite stock | 320.00 |
| **Thunder Hawk** w/24″ barrel | |
| Stainless steel with Rynite stock | 330.00 |
| Blued steel with Rynite stock | 290.00 |
| Blued steel with walnut stock | 310.00 |

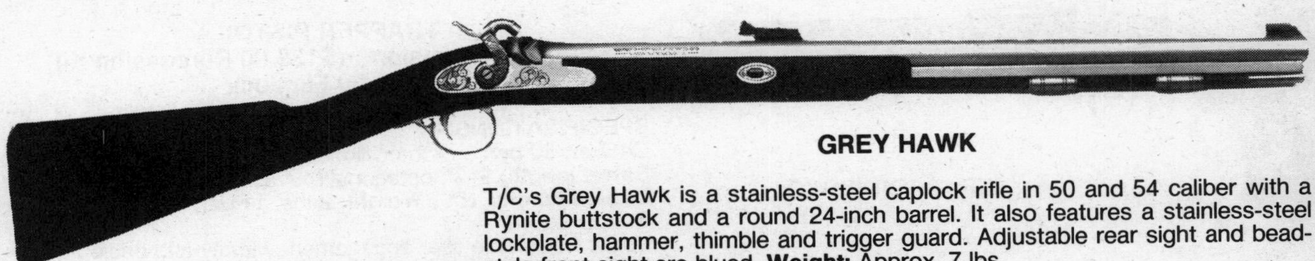

## GREY HAWK

T/C's Grey Hawk is a stainless-steel caplock rifle in 50 and 54 caliber with a Rynite buttstock and a round 24-inch barrel. It also features a stainless-steel lockplate, hammer, thimble and trigger guard. Adjustable rear sight and bead-style front sight are blued. **Weight:** Approx. 7 lbs.

| | |
|---|---|
| **Grey Hawk** | $330.00 |

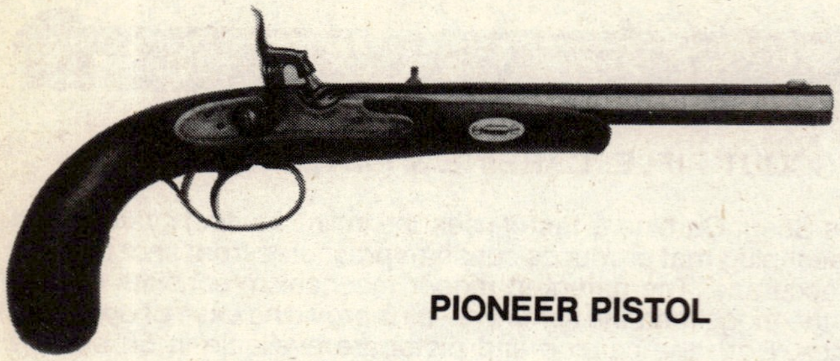

PIONEER PISTOL

## PIONEER PISTOL
**$160.00 ($126.50 Kit)**

**SPECIFICATIONS**
**Caliber:** 45 percussion
**Barrel length:** 9 5/8" octagonal with tenon; 13/16" across flats, rifled 1 in 16"; hooked breech
**Overall length:** 15" **Weight:** 1 lb. 15 oz.
**Sights:** Blade front; fixed rear
**Trigger:** Single
**Stock:** Beech, rounded
**Lock:** V-type mainspring
**Features:** German silver furniture; blackened hardware

WILLIAM PARKER PISTOL

## WILLIAM PARKER PISTOL
**$274.00**

**SPECIFICATIONS**
**Caliber:** 50 percussion
**Barrel length:** 10 3/8" octagonal (15/16" across flats)
**Overall length:** 17 1/2" **Weight:** 2 lbs. 5 oz.
**Sights:** Brass blade front; fixed rear
**Stock:** Walnut, checkered at wrist
**Triggers:** Double set; will fire set and unset
**Lock:** Adjustable sear engagement with fly and bridle; V-type mainspring
**Features:** Brass percussion cap guard; polished hardware, brass inlays and separate ramrod

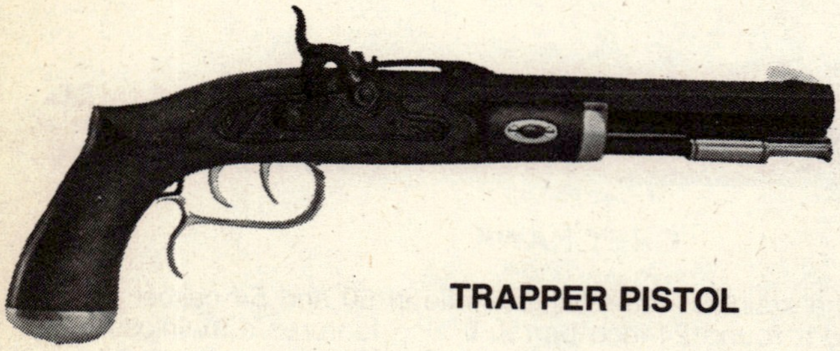

TRAPPER PISTOL

## TRAPPER PISTOL
**$178.00 Percussion ($139.00 Percussion Kit)**
**$198.00 Flintlock**

**SPECIFICATIONS**
**Caliber:** 50 percussion or flintlock
**Barrel length:** 9 3/4"; octagonal (7/8" across flats) with tenon
**Overall length:** 16" **Weight:** 2 lbs. 11 oz.
**Stock:** Beech
**Lock:** Adjustable sear engagement with fly and bridle
**Triggers:** Double set, will fire set and unset
**Sights:** Primitive-style adjustable rear; brass blade front
**Furniture:** Solid brass; blued steel on assembled pistol

# TRADITIONS

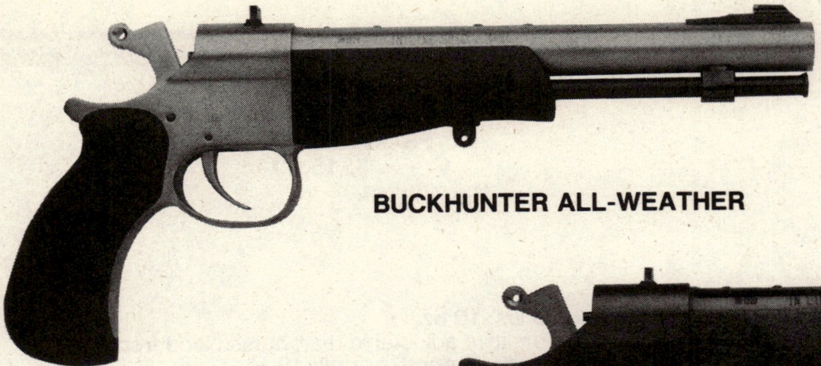

**BUCKHUNTER ALL-WEATHER**

**BUCKHUNTER BLUED**
**w/Walnut Stock**

## BUCKHUNTER IN-LINE PISTOL
**$215.00 ($231.00 w/All-Weather Stock)**

**SPECIFICATIONS**
**Calibers:** 50 and 54 Percussion
**Barrel length:** 10″ round (closed breech); 1:20″ twist
**Overall length:** 13 7/8″
**Weight:** 3 lbs.
**Trigger:** Single
**Sights:** Fixed rear; blade front
**Stock:** Walnut or All-Weather
**Features:** Blued or C-Nickel furniture; PVC ramrod; drilled and tapped for scope mounting; coil mainspring

## BUCKSKINNER PISTOL (not shown)
**$165.00 ($182.00 Laminated)**

**SPECIFICATIONS**
**Caliber:** 50 percussion
**Barrel length:** 10″ octagonal (15/16″ across flats)
**Overall length:** 15″
**Weight:** 2 lbs. 9 oz.
**Trigger:** Single
**Sights:** Fixed rear; blade front
**Stock:** Beech or laminated
**Features:** Blackened furniture; wood ramrod

## KENTUCKY PISTOL
**$142.00 ($106.50 Kit)**

**SPECIFICATIONS**
**Caliber:** 50 Percussion
**Barrel length:** 9.75″ octagon (7/8″ flats); closed breech; 1:16″ twist
**Overall length:** 15 1/2″
**Weight:** 2 lbs. 8 oz.
**Trigger:** Single
**Sights:** Fixed rear; ramp front
**Stock:** Beechwood
**Features:** Brass furniture; wood ramrod; kit available

# TRADITIONS

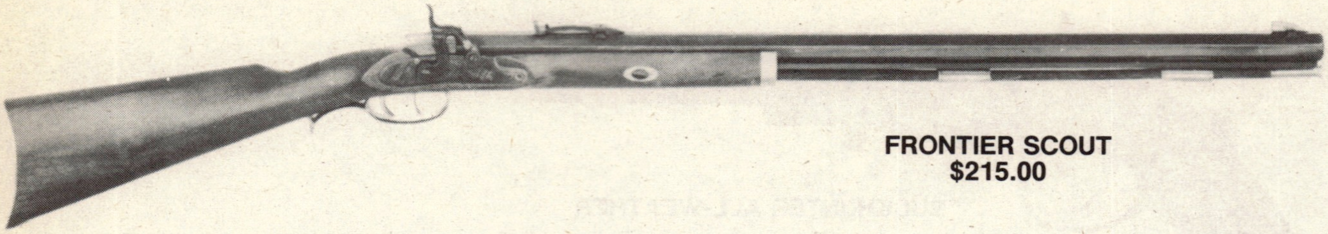

**FRONTIER SCOUT**
**$215.00**

**SPECIFICATIONS**
**Calibers:** 36 and 50 percussion
**Barrel length:** 24″ (36 caliber); 26″ (50 caliber); octagonal (7/8″ across flats) with tenon; rifled 1:48″ (36 cal.) and 1:66″ (50 cal.); hooked breech
**Overall length:** 39 1/8″ (36 caliber); 41 1/8″ (50 caliber)
**Weight:** 5 lbs. 10 oz.
**Sights:** Primitive adjustable rear; brass blade front
**Stock:** Beech **Length of pull:** 12 1/4″
**Lock:** Adjustable sear engagement with fly and bridle
**Furniture:** Solid brass, blued steel

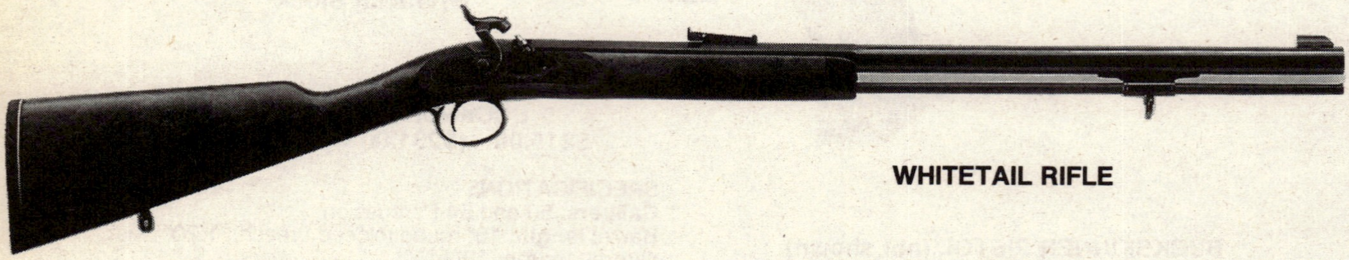

**WHITETAIL RIFLE**

**WHITETAIL RIFLE & CARBINE**
**$240.00 (Percussion) $256.00 (Flintlock)**

**SPECIFICATIONS**
**Calibers:** 50 (flintlock or perc.) and 54 (percussion only)
**Barrel length:** 24″ octagonal tapering to round
**Overall length:** 39 1/4″ **Weight:** 5 lbs. 12 oz.
**Sights:** Hunting-style rear, click adjustable for windage and elevation; beaded blade front with fluorescent dot
**Trigger:** Single
**Stock:** Select hardwood w/walnut stain, rubber recoil pad
**Features:** Sling swivels; oversized trigger guard; inletted wedge plates; engraved and color casehardened lock

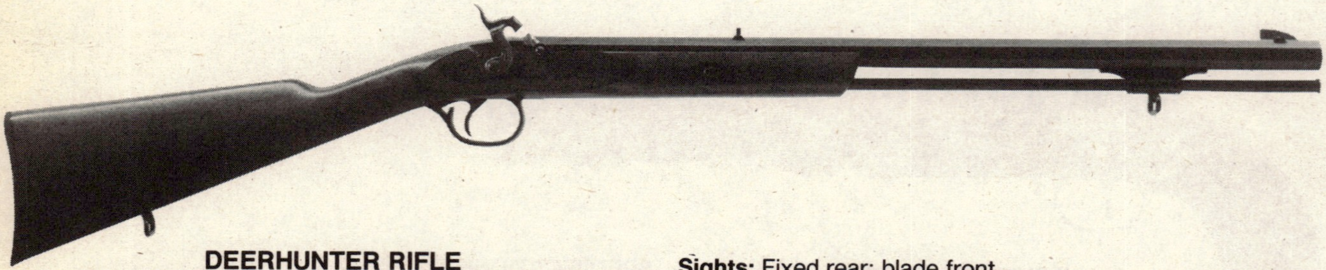

**DEERHUNTER RIFLE**
**$173.00 (Percussion) $190.00 (Flintlock)**

**SPECIFICATIONS**
**Calibers:** 32 (Hunter Package only), 50 and 54 percussion
**Barrel length:** 24″ octagonal
**Rifling twist:** 1:48″ (percussion only); 1:66″ (flint or percussion)
**Overall length:** 39 1/4″
**Weight:** 6 lbs. (6.25 lbs. in All-Weather Model)
**Trigger:** Single
**Sights:** Fixed rear; blade front
**Features:** Wooden ramrod; blackened furniture; inletted wedge plates
Also available:
**DEERHUNTER ALL-WEATHER MODEL.** Epoxy-covered beech stock and C-Nickel finish. **Price: $215.00** (1:66″ twist flintlock); **$198.00** (1:48″ twist, percussion, 50 or 54 caliber, drilled and tapped).
**HUNTER PACKAGE** (32, 50 and 54 cal.) **SMALL GAME RIFLE: $190.00** (**$152.75** percussion kit)

# TRADITIONS

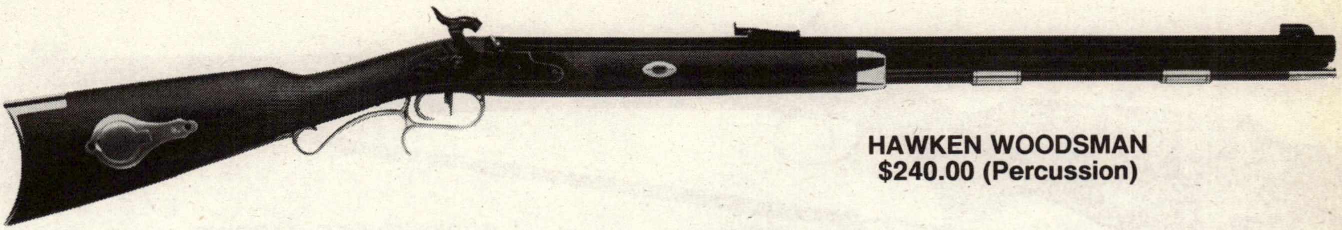

## HAWKEN WOODSMAN
**$240.00 (Percussion)**

**SPECIFICATIONS**
**Calibers:** 50 and 54 percussion or flintlock
**Barrel length:** 26″ (octagonal); hooked breech; rifled 1 turn in 66″ (1 turn in 48″ in 50 or 54 caliber also available)
**Overall length:** 45 3/4″ (Brass); 42″ (Blackened)
**Weight:** 6 lbs. 14 oz.
**Triggers:** Double set; will fire set or unset
**Lock:** Adjustable sear engagement with fly and bridle

**Stock:** Beech
**Sights:** Beaded blade front; hunting-style rear, fully screw adjustable for windage and elevation
**Furniture:** Solid brass, blued steel or blackened (50 cal. only); unbreakable ramrod
Also available:

| | |
|---|---|
| Left-Hand model w/brass furniture | **$260.00** |
| 50 Caliber Flintlock w/blackened furniture | **256.00** |
| 50 and 54 Cal. Perc. w/blackened furniture (1:48″) | **240.00** |

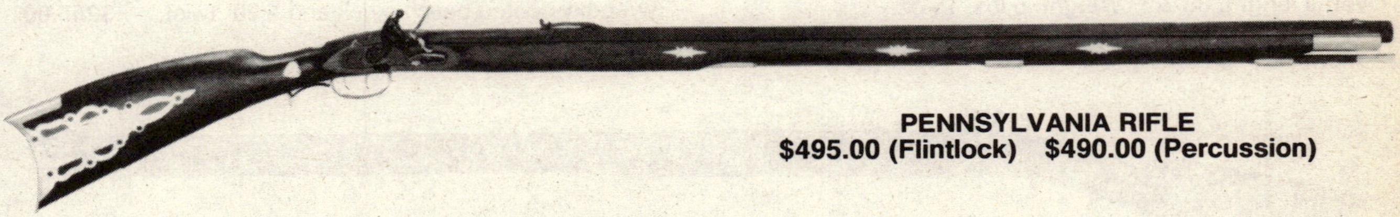

## PENNSYLVANIA RIFLE
**$495.00 (Flintlock) $490.00 (Percussion)**

**SPECIFICATIONS**
**Caliber:** 50
**Barrel length:** 40 1/4″; octagonal (7/8″ across flats) with 3 tenons; rifled 1 turn in 66″
**Overall length:** 57 1/2″ **Weight:** 9 lbs.
**Lock:** Adjustable sear engagement with fly and bridle

**Stock:** Walnut, beavertail style
**Triggers:** Double set; will fire set and unset
**Sights:** Primitive-style adjustable rear; brass blade front
**Furniture:** Solid brass, blued steel

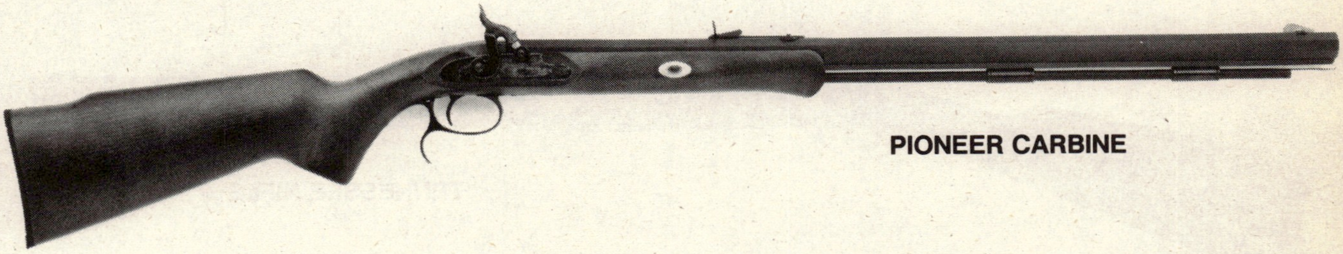

**PIONEER CARBINE**

## PIONEER RIFLE & CARBINE
**$208.00**

**SPECIFICATIONS**
**Calibers:** 50 and 54 percussion (rifle only)
**Barrel length:** Carbine—24″ (1:32″); Rifle—28″ (1:48″ or 1:66″), octagonal w/tenon
**Overall length:** 40 1/2″ (carbine); 44″ (rifle)

**Weight:** 6 lbs. 3 oz. (carbine); 6 lbs. 14 oz. (rifle)
**Trigger:**Single
**Stock:** Beech
**Sights:** Buckhorn rear with elevation ramp, ajustable for windage and elevation; German silver blade front
**Lock:** Adjustable sear engagement; V-type mainspring
**Features:** Blackened hardware; German silver furniture; unbreakable ramrod; inletted wedge plates

### BUCKSKINNER CARBINE

**$250.00 (Percussion) $274.00 (Flintlock)**
**$315.00 (Laminated Stock, Percussion)**
**$331.00 (Laminated Stock, Flintlock)**

**SPECIFICATIONS**
**Caliber:** 50 percussion or flintlock
**Barrel length:** 21″ octagonal-to-round with tenon; 15/16″ across flats; 1:66″ twist (1:20″ twist also available)
**Overall length:** 36 1/4″ **Weight:** 5 lbs. 15 oz.

**BUCKSKINNER CARBINE**
**Laminated Stock**

**Sights:** Hunting-style, click adjustable rear; beaded blade front with white dot
**Trigger:** Single
**Features:** Blackened furniture; German silver ornamentation; belting leather sling and sling swivels; unbreakable ramrod
Also available:
**BUCKSKINNER CARBINE DELUXE.** Percussion with 1:20″ twist .......... **$352.00**
Flintlock with 1:66″ twist .......... **337.00**
**BUCKSKINNER CARBINE ALL-WEATHER.** 50 cal. percussion w/epoxy-coated beech stock and 1:20″ twist: .. **$265.00**

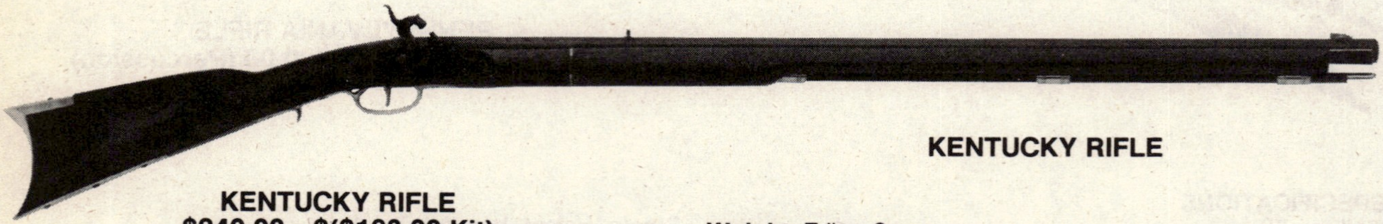

**KENTUCKY RIFLE**

### KENTUCKY RIFLE

**$240.00 $($198.00 Kit)**

**SPECIFICATIONS**
**Caliber:** 50 percussion
**Barrel length:** 33 1/2″ octagon (7/8″ flats); closed breech; 1:66″ twist
**Overall length:** 48″
**Weight:** 7 lbs. 8 oz.
**Trigger:** Single
**Tenons:** 2 pins
**Stock:** Beechwood
**Sights:** Fixed rear; blade front
**Features:** Brass furniture; wood ramrod; inletted wedge plates; toe plate; V-mainspring

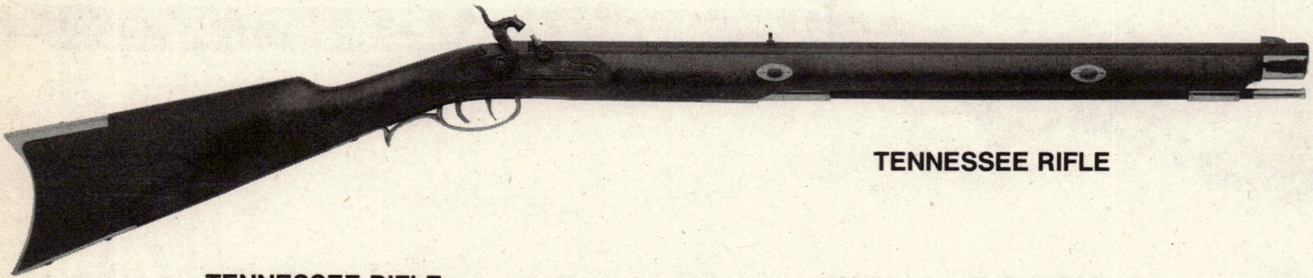

**TENNESSEE RIFLE**

### TENNESSEE RIFLE

**$314.00 (Flintlock) $298.00 (Percussion)**

**SPECIFICATIONS**
**Caliber:** 50 flintlock or percussion
**Barrel length:** 24″ octagon (15/16″ across flats); hooked breech; 1:32″ twist
**Overall length:** 40 1/2″
**Weight:** 6 lbs.
**Sights:** Fixed rear; blade front
**Stock:** Beechwood
**Features:** Brass furniture; wood ramrod; inletted wedge plate; stock inlays; toe plate; V-mainspring

# TRADITIONS

## BUCKHUNTER™ IN-LINE RIFLE SERIES

This new family of hunting rifles is designed for serious black-powder hunters as well as those who are just getting started in muzzleloading. These rifles deliver the balance, fast handling and long-range accuracy of a modern hunting gun. They shoulder naturally, pick up the target quickly, and hold the point of aim. A unique three-position safety (1) allows the bolt to be placed forward without engaging the nipple or cap; (2) allow the bolt to lock open in an elevated notch position, preventing the trigger from being engaged; or (3) locks the bolt with a push of the bolt handle to prevent any bolt movement during stalking. The breech design disperses ignition gases safely to the side. No special tools are needed for cleaning. All rifles have rubber recoil pads, are drilled and tapped (with 8-40 plug screws) for easy scoping and come with clickadjustable hunting sights and PVC ramrod. Specifications and prices for all models in the series are listed in the table below.

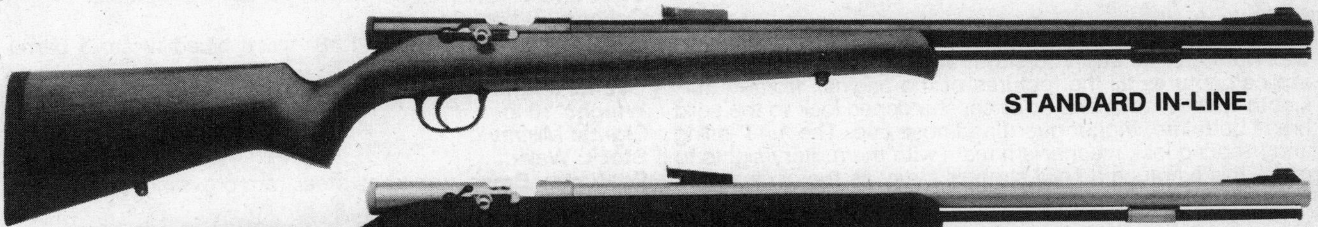

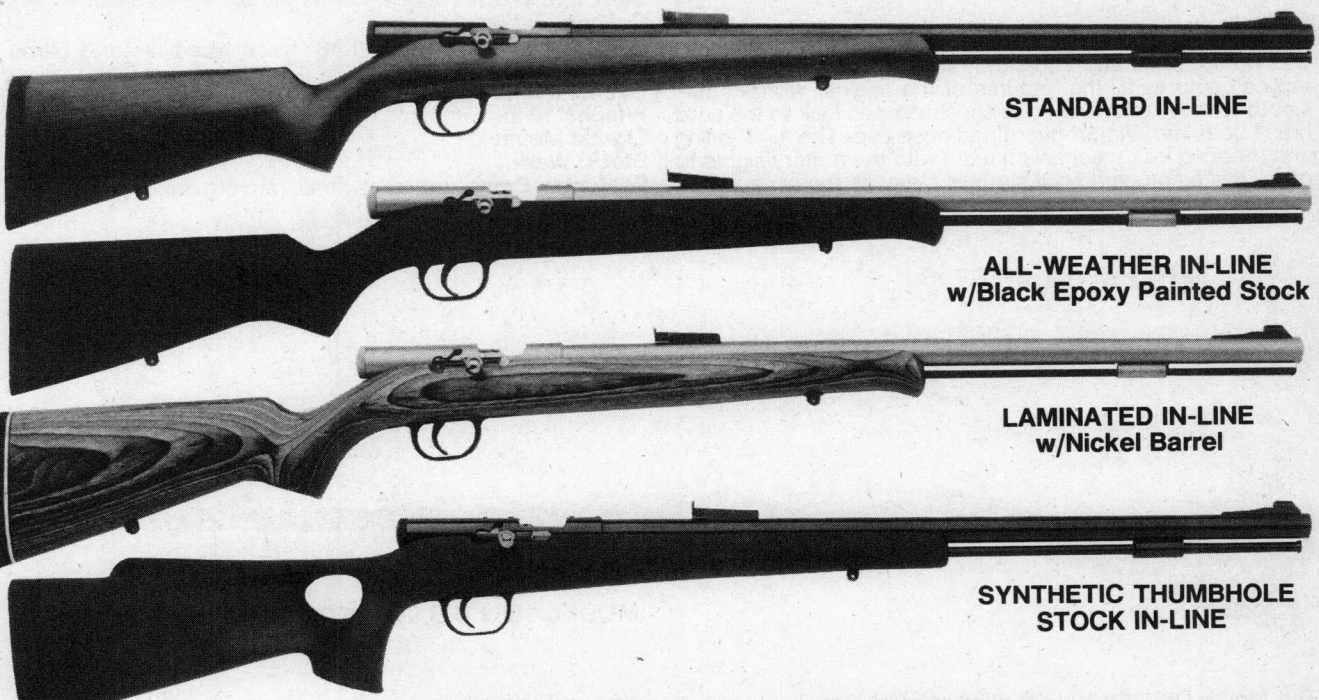

**STANDARD IN-LINE**

**ALL-WEATHER IN-LINE**
**w/Black Epoxy Painted Stock**

**LAMINATED IN-LINE**
**w/Nickel Barrel**

**SYNTHETIC THUMBHOLE STOCK IN-LINE**

**Buckhunter In-Line Rifles**

| | | Standard | Blackened | Laminated | All-Weather | Thumbhole |
|---|---|---|---|---|---|---|
| **Lock:** | ignition | in-line percussion | in-line percussion | in-line percussion | in-line percussion | in-line percussion |
| **Stock:** | | beech | epoxy coated beech | laminated | epoxy coated beech | fiberglass |
| **Calibers:** | rifling twist | .50p (1:32")<br>.54p (1:48") | .50p (1:32")<br>.54p (1:48") | .50p (1:32")<br>.54p (1:48") | .50p (1:32")<br>.54p (1:48") | .50p (1:32")<br>.54p (1:48") |
| **Barrel:** | length/shape<br>finish<br>breech<br>other | 24" round<br>blued<br>open<br>drilled/tapped | 24" round<br>blued<br>open<br>drilled/tapped | 24" round<br>blued or C-Nickel<br>open<br>drilled/tapped | 24" round<br>C-Nickel<br>open<br>drilled/tapped | 24" round<br>blued or C-Nickel<br>open<br>drilled/tapped |
| **Trigger:** | | single | single | single | single | single |
| **Sights:** | rear<br>front | click adjustable<br>beaded blade | click adjustable<br>beaded blade | click adjustable<br>beaded blade | click adjustable<br>beaded blade | click adjustable<br>beaded blade |
| **Features:** | furniture<br>ramrod<br>other | blued<br>PVC<br>sling swivel studs | blackened<br>PVC<br>sling swivel studs | blued<br>PVC<br>sling swivel studs | blued<br>PVC<br>sling swivel studs | blued<br>PVC<br>sling swivel studs |
| **Overall length:** | | 41" | 41" | 41" | 41" | 41" |
| **Weight:** | | 7 lbs. 8 oz. | 7 lbs. 9 oz. | 8 lbs. 1 oz. | 7 lbs. 9 oz. | 7 lbs. 6 oz. |
| **Models/prices:** | | R40002 .50p $255<br>R40048 .54p $255 | R41102 .50p $250<br>R41148 .54p $250<br>*R41302 .50p $222<br>*R41348 .54p $222<br>**R41302S .50p $274<br>**R41348S .54p $274 | R40202 .50p blk $331<br>R40248 .54p blk $331<br>R40302 .50p brn $315<br>R40348 .54p brn $315 | R40102 .50p $274<br>R40148 .54p $274 | R42202 blued .50p $331<br>R42248 blued .54p $331<br>R42302 C-Nic. .50p $364<br>R42348 C-Nic. .54p $364 |

*No sights option **Scope & mount option

**MODEL 1853 3-BAND ENFIELD RIFLED MUSKET**
**$580.00**

Carried by Northern and Southern troops alike, the 1853 Enfield was noted for its ability to shoot straight and hard. This fine replica captures all the features of the original, from its full-length walnut stock and color casehardened lock to the solid brass buttplate, trigger guard and nose cap. The 1:48″ rifling and V-spring lock mechanism team with the military sights to make this as much a solid shooter today as the original was in its day.

**SPECIFICATIONS**
**Caliber:** 58 percussion
**Barrel length:** 39″ round; 1:48″ twist; blued finish; 3 barrel bands
**Overall length:** 55″
**Weight:** 10 lbs.
**Sights:** Military
**Stock:** Walnut
**Features:** Brass furniture; steel ramrod; sling swivels; V-mainspring

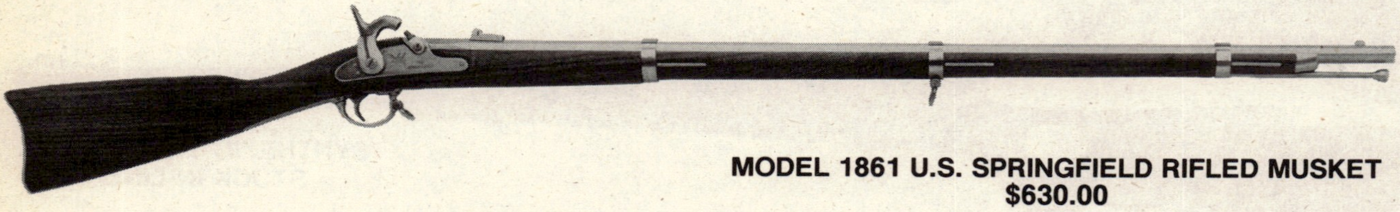

**MODEL 1861 U.S. SPRINGFIELD RIFLED MUSKET**
**$630.00**

The Model 1861 Springfield rifled musket was the principal firearm of the Civil War. By the end of 1863, most Federal infantrymen were armed with either this musket or the Enfield 58-caliber rifled barrel. This faithful replica glows "in the white" as was the original, with a full-length walnut military stock. The authentic sidelock action is accented by markings of "1861 U.S. Springfield" to complement the steel buttplate, wide trigger guard, barrel bands and sling hardware. The steel ramrod, like the original, is of the swelled design. Military-style sights and a long sighting plane make this an accurate long gun approved for use by the North-South Skirmish Association.

**SPECIFICATIONS**
**Caliber:** 58 percussion
**Barrel length:** 40″ round; 1:66″ twist; white steel finish; 3 barrel bands
**Overall length:** 56″
**Weight:** 10.3 lbs.
**Trigger:** Single
**Sights:** Military
**Stock:** Walnut
**Features:** Steel furniture and ramrod; sling swivels; V-mainspring

## PERCUSSION RIFLES/SHOTGUN

**CREEDMORE MATCH RIFLE**
**$1150.00**

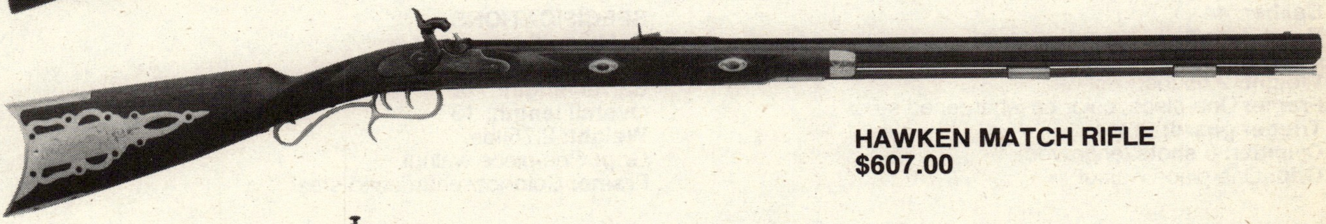

**HAWKEN MATCH RIFLE**
**$607.00**

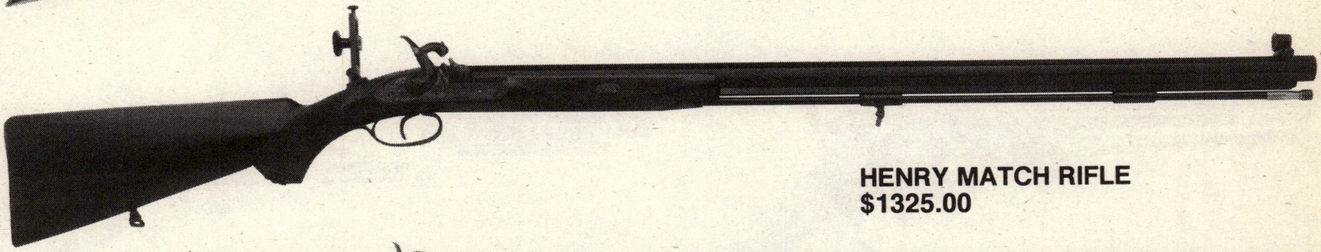

**HENRY MATCH RIFLE**
**$1325.00**

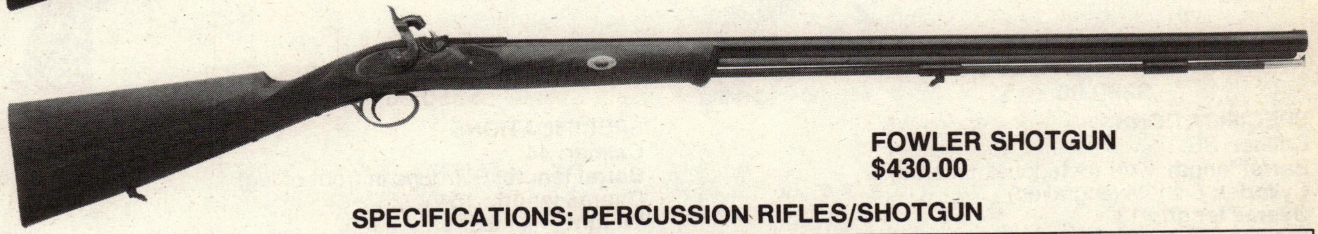

**FOWLER SHOTGUN**
**$430.00**

### SPECIFICATIONS: PERCUSSION RIFLES/SHOTGUN

| | | Creedmore Match | Henry Match | Hawken Match | Fowler Shotgun |
|---|---|---|---|---|---|
| **Lock:** | ignition | percussion | percussion | percussion | percussion |
| | mainspring | V | V | V | V |
| **Stock:** | | walnut | walnut | walnut | walnut |
| **Caliber:** | rifling twist | .451 (1:20") | .451 (1:20") | .451 (1:20") | 12 ga (cylinder) |
| **Barrel:** | length | 32" | 32" | 32" | 32" |
| | shape | octagon-to-round | octagon | octagon | octagon-to-round |
| | flats | n/a | 15/16" | 15/16" | n/a |
| | tenons | 1 | 1 | 2 | 1 |
| | breech | hook | hook | hook | hook |
| **Triggers:** | | single | single | double | single |
| **Sights:** | rear | diopter | diopter | buckhorn | n/a |
| | front | tunnel | tunnel | blade | bead |
| **Features:** | furniture | color case hardened/blued | color case hardened/blued | engraved brass | German silver/ blued |
| | ramrod | n/a | metal w/jag | wood | wood |
| | wedge plates | inletted | inletted | inletted | inletted |
| | other | tool kit | tool kit/swivels | toe plate | |
| **Overall length:** | | 50" | 49 ¾" | 50" | 48 ¼" |
| **Weight:** | | 8 lbs. 8 oz. | 11 lbs. 2 oz. | 9 lbs. 14 oz. | 5 lbs. 6 oz. |
| **Models/prices:** | | R27051 $1150 | R28051 $1325 | R3081 $607 | S5002 $430 |

# A. UBERTI

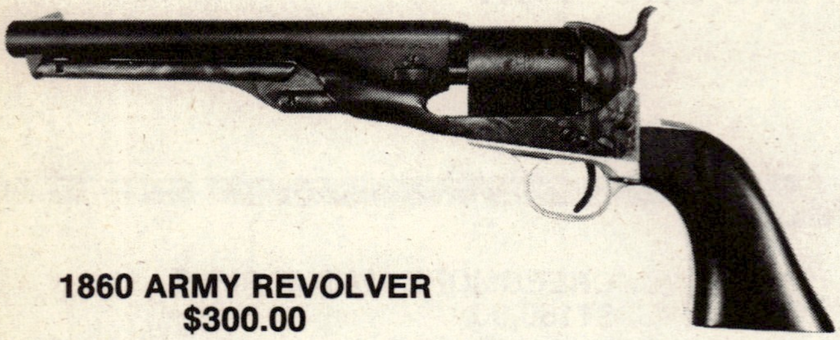

### 1860 ARMY REVOLVER
### $300.00

**SPECIFICATIONS**
**Caliber:** 44
**Barrel length:** 8″ (round, tapered)
**Overall length:** 13$\frac{3}{4}$″
**Weight:** 2.65 lbs.
**Frame:** One-piece, color casehardened steel
**Trigger guard:** Brass
**Cylinder:** 6 shots (engraved)
**Grip:** One-piece walnut

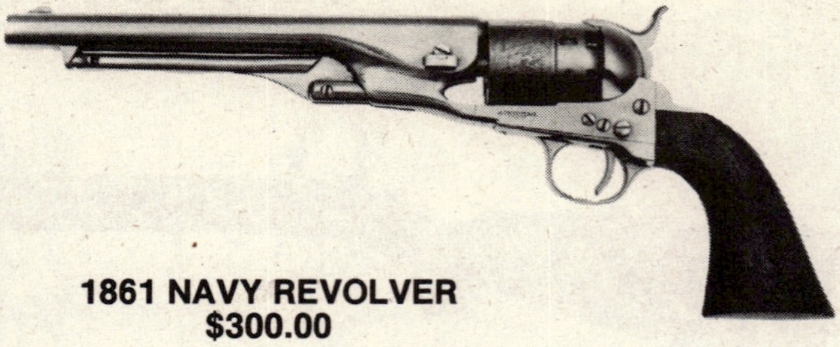

### 1861 NAVY REVOLVER
### $300.00

**SPECIFICATIONS**
**Caliber:** 36
**Capacity:** 6 shots
**Barrel length:** 7$\frac{1}{2}$″
**Overall length:** 13″
**Weight:** 2.75 lbs.
**Grip:** One-piece walnut
**Frame:** Color casehardened steel

### 1851 NAVY REVOLVER
### $280.00

**SPECIFICATIONS**
**Caliber:** 36
**Barrel length:** 7$\frac{1}{2}$″ (octagonal, tapered)
**Cylinder:** 6 shots (engraved)
**Overall length:** 13″
**Weight:** 2$\frac{3}{4}$ lbs.
**Frame:** Color casehardened steel
**Backstrap and trigger guard:** Brass
**Grip:** One-piece walnut

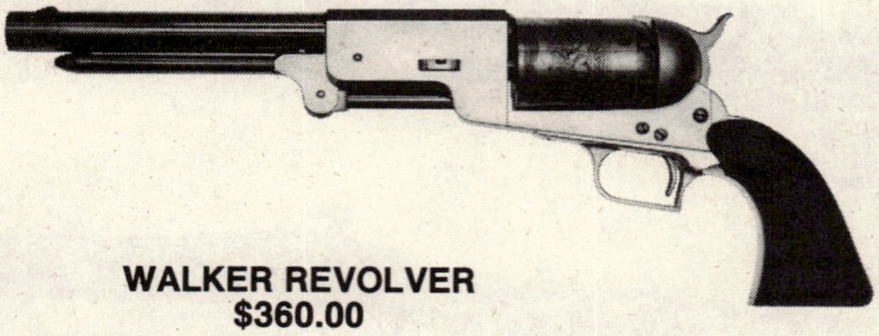

### WALKER REVOLVER
### $360.00

**SPECIFICATIONS**
**Caliber:** 44
**Barrel length:** 9″ (round in front of lug)
**Overall length:** 15$\frac{3}{4}$″
**Weight:** 4.41 lbs.
**Frame:** Color casehardened steel
**Backsstrap:** Steel
**Cylinder:** 6 shots (engraved with "Fighting Dragoons" scene)
**Grip:** One-piece walnut

### 1st MODEL DRAGOON REVOLVER

**SPECIFICATIONS**
**Caliber:** 44
**Capacity:** 6 shots
**Barrel length:** 7$\frac{1}{2}$″ round forward of lug
**Overall length:** 13$\frac{1}{2}$″
**Weight:** 4 lbs.
**Frame:** Color casehardened steel
**Grip:** One-piece walnut
Also available:
**2nd Model Dragoon** w/square cylinder bolt shot . . **$325.00**
**3rd Model Dragoon** w/loading lever latch, steel backstrap, cut for shoulder stock . . . . . . . . . . . . **330.00**

### 1st MODEL DRAGOON REVOLVER
### $325.00

# A. UBERTI

## 1858 REMINGTON NEW ARMY 44 REVOLVER

**Prices:**

| | |
|---|---|
| 8″ barrel, open sights | **$280.00** |
| With stainless steel and open sights | **380.00** |
| **Target Model** w/black finish | **330.00** |
| **Target Model** w/stainless steel | **399.00** |

Also available:

| | |
|---|---|
| **1858 New Navy** (36 cal.) | **280.00** |
| **1858 New Army Revolving Carbine** (18″ barrel) | **425.00** |

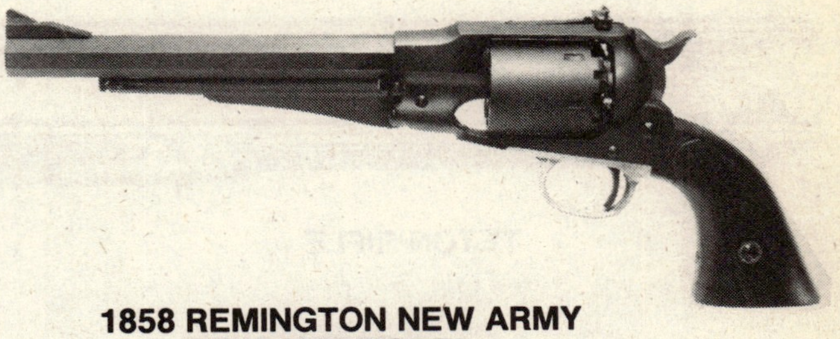

**1858 REMINGTON NEW ARMY TARGET MODEL**

## PATERSON REVOLVER

Manufactured at Paterson, New Jersey, by the Patent Arms Manufacturing Company from 1836 to 1842, these were the first revolving pistols created by Samuel Colt. All early Patersons featured a five-shot cylinder, roll-engraved with one or two scenes, octagon barrel and folding trigger that extends when the hammer is cocked.

**SPECIFICATIONS**
**Caliber:** 36
**Capacity:** 5 shots (engraved cylinder)
**Barrel length:** 7½″ octagonal
**Overall length:** 11½″
**Weight:** 2.552 lbs.
**Frame:** Color casehardened steel
**Grip:** One-piece walnut

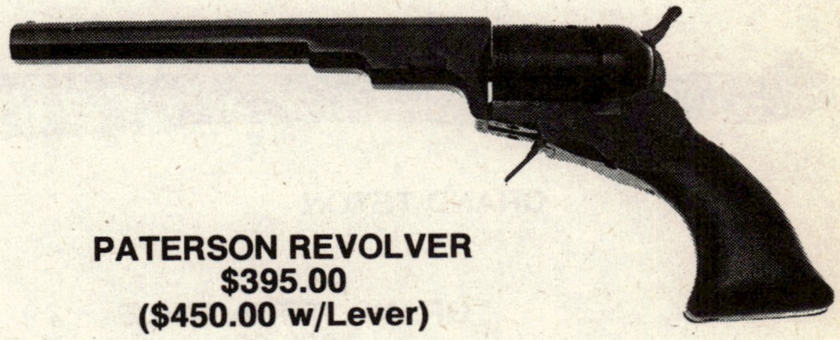

**PATERSON REVOLVER**
**$395.00**
**($450.00 w/Lever)**

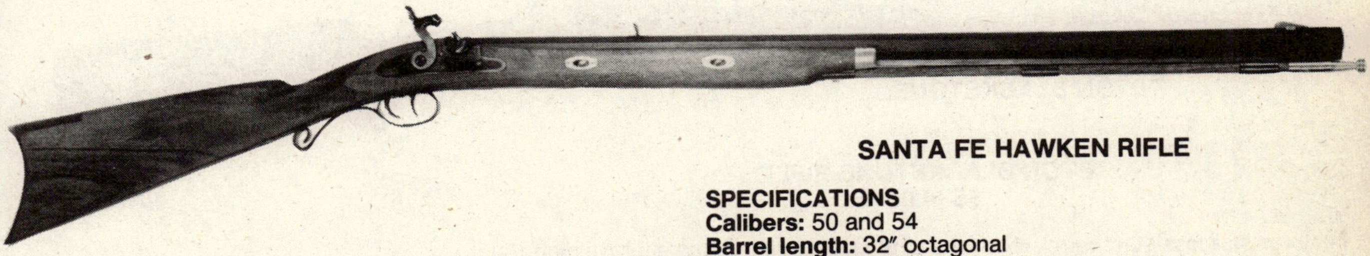

**SANTA FE HAWKEN RIFLE**
**$495.00**

## SANTA FE HAWKEN RIFLE

**SPECIFICATIONS**
**Calibers:** 50 and 54
**Barrel length:** 32″ octagonal
**Overall length:** 50″
**Weight:** 9½ lbs.
**Stock:** Walnut with beavertail cheekpiece
**Features:** Brown finish; double-set trigger; color casehardened lockplate; German silver wedge plates

# UFA TETON RIFLES

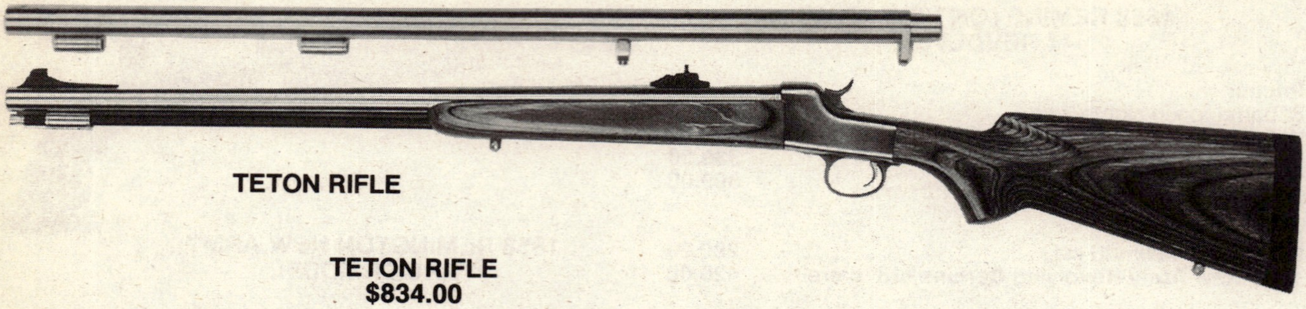

TETON RIFLE

**TETON RIFLE**
**$834.00**

Available in stainless steel or blued chromemoly, black or brown laminate wood and matte or dull finish. It has a 1″ Pachmayr decelerator pad, all-steel Marble sight and high-grade wood finish. Barrel lengths are 26″ (standard) and 30″ (stainless steel). The 30″ model features a 12-gauge cylinder bore barrel above the standard 26″ barrel. Also available is a 26″ 12-bore rifled barrel (.72 caliber) designed to shoot shotgun slugs as well as lead conical bullets. **Calibers:** 45 and 50. All barrels interchange easily.

GRAND TETON

**GRAND TETON RIFLE**
**$995.00**

This model features a 30″ tapered octagonal barrel and a choice of all-stainless or chromemoly steel, brushed or matte finish, premium recoil pad and brown or black laminate stock. Options include upgraded sights and scope mount, plus premium figured walnut or maple stocks (Add **$150.00). Calibers:** 45 or 50.

TETON BLACKSTONE

**TETON BLACKSTONE RIFLE**
**$534.00**

Features stainless-steel barrel, receiver and trigger housing in nonreflective matte finish. Stock is straight-grain hardwood, epoxy-coated with tough black-textured finish and 1″ ventilated recoil pad. Other features include Williams adjustable sights, full-length ramrod and sling swivel studs. The Blackstone has a 1 in 24″ twist, shallow-groove rifled 26″ barrel. Uses either conical or sabot bullets. **Caliber:** 50 only.

# WHITE SYSTEMS

## G & W SERIES RIFLES

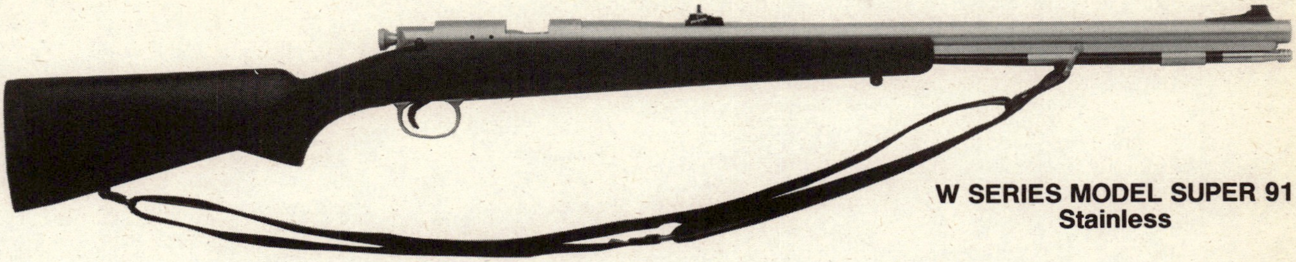

**W SERIES MODEL SUPER 91**
**Stainless**

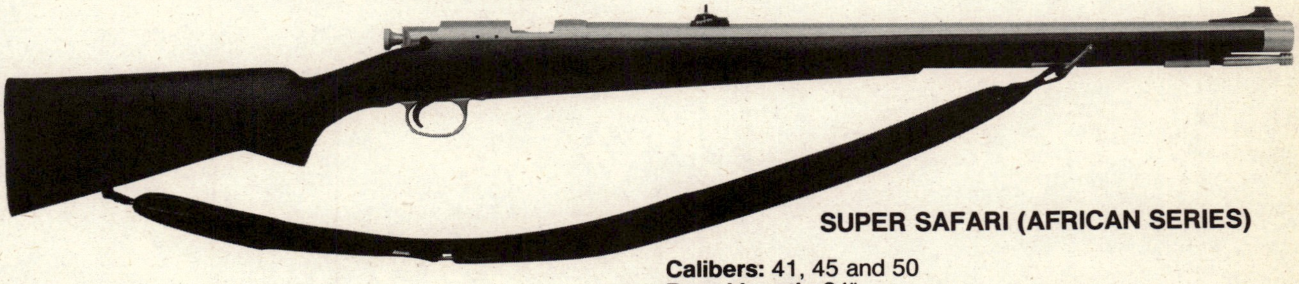

**SUPER SAFARI (AFRICAN SERIES)**

### MODEL SUPER 91

This modern muzzleloading system features the following: Ordnance-grade stainless-steel construction • Fast twist, shallow groove rifling • Stainless-steel nipple and breechplug • Side swing safety (locks the striker, not just the trigger) • Classic stock configuration (fits right- or left-handed shooters • Fast second shot and easy access to nipple from either side for quick capping • Fully adjustable trigger

**Calibers:** 41, 45 and 50
**Barrel length:** 24″
**Rifling:** 1 in 20″ (45 cal.); 1 in 24″ (50 cal.)
**Weight:** 7¾ lbs.
**Sights:** Fully adjustable Williams sights
**Prices:**

| | |
|---|---|
| Blued | **$599.00** |
| Stainless Steel | **699.00** |
| w/Black Laminate stock | **749.00** |
| **Sporting** (Green River Series) | **799.00** |

Also available:
**SUPER SAFARI SS TAPERED** (African Series)

| | |
|---|---|
| 41, 45, 50 caliber Mannlicher | **$799.00** |

**G SERIES**
**WHITETAIL MUZZLELOADER SS**

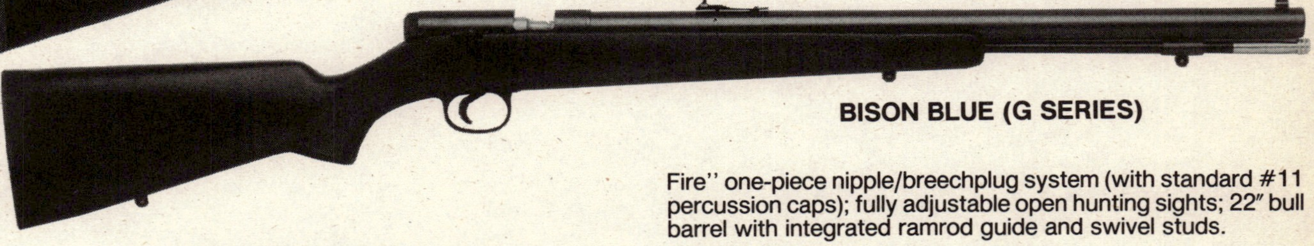

**BISON BLUE (G SERIES)**

### WHITETAIL AND BISON MUZZLELOADING RIFLES

White's "G Series" rifles feature straight-line action with easy no-tool takedown in the field. A stainless-steel hammer system has an ambidextrous cocking handle that doubles as a sure-safe hammer-lock safety. Other features include the "Insta-Fire" one-piece nipple/breechplug system (with standard #11 percussion caps); fully adjustable open hunting sights; 22″ bull barrel with integrated ramrod guide and swivel studs.

**Calibers:** 41, 45, 50 and 54 (Bison only)
**Prices:**

| | |
|---|---|
| **Bison** (50 and 54 cal.) Blued | **$349.00** |
| **Whitetail** (45 and 50 cal.) | |
| Blued | **399.00** |
| Stainless steel | **499.00** |
| w/Black Laminate stock | **549.00** |

# Sights & Scopes



For addresses and phone numbers of manufacturers and distributors included in this section, turn to *DIRECTORY OF MANUFACTURERS AND SUPPLIERS* at the back of the book.

# AIMPOINT SIGHTS

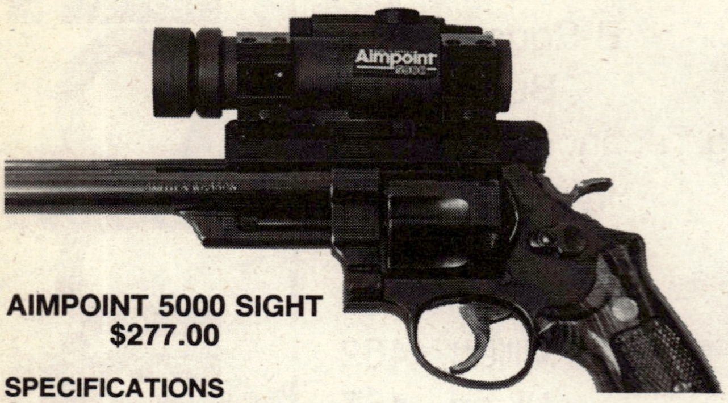


## AIMPOINT 5000 SIGHT
## $277.00

**SPECIFICATIONS**
**System:** Parallax free
**Optical:** Anti-reflex coated lenses
**Adjustment:** 1 click = ¼-inch at 100 yards
**Length:** 5½″
**Weight:** 5.8 oz.
**Objective diameter:** 36mm
**Mounting system:** 30mm rings
**Magnification:** 1X
**Material:** Anodized aluminum; black or stainless finish
**Diameter of dot:** 3″ at 100 yds. or Mag Dot reticle, 10″ at 100 yards.

## AIMPOINT COMP
## $308.00

**SPECIFICATIONS**
**System:** 100% Parallax free
**Optics:** Anti-reflex coated lenses
**Eye relief:** Unlimited
**Batteries:** 3 × Mercury SP 675
**Adjustment:** 1 click = ¼-inch at 100 yards
**Length:** 4⅜″
**Weight:** 4.75 oz.
**Objective diameter:** 36mm
**Dot diameter:** 2″ at 30 yds. (7 MOA); 3″ at 30 yds. (10 MOA)
**Mounting system:** 30mm rings
**Magnification:** 1X
**Material:** Anodized aluminum, blue or stainless finish

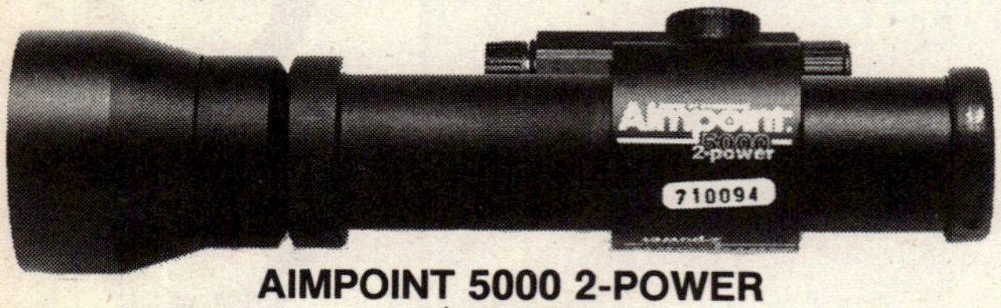


## AIMPOINT 5000 2-POWER
## $367.00

**SPECIFICATIONS**
**System:** Parallax free
**Optical:** Anti-reflex coated lens
**Adjustment:** clock = ¼″ at 100 yards
**Length:** 7″
**Weight:** 9 oz.
**Objective diameter:** 46mm
**Diameter of dot:** 1½″ at 100 yards
**Mounting system:** 30mm rings
**Magnification:** 2X
**Material:** Anodized aluminum; blue finish

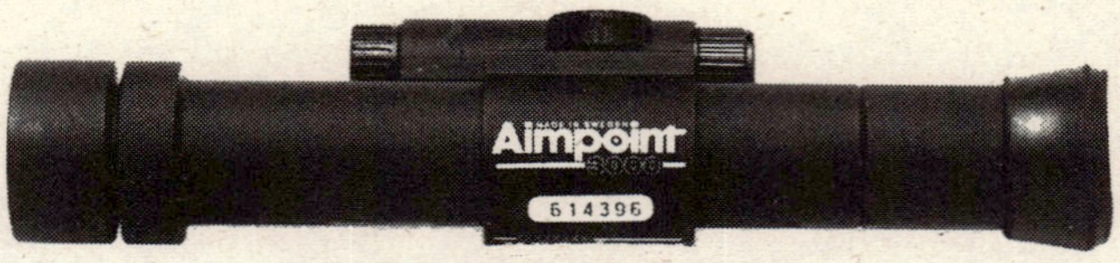


## SERIES 3000 UNIVERSAL
## $232.00 (Black or Stainless)

**SPECIFICATIONS**
**System: 100% parallax free**
**Weight:** 5.8 oz.
**Length:** 6.15″
**Magnification:** 1X
**Scope attachment:** 3X
**Eye relief:** Unlimited
**Battery choices:** 2X Mercury SP 675 1X Lithium or DL 1/3N
**Material:** Anodized aluminum, black or stainless finish
**Mounting:** 1″ Rings (Medium or High)

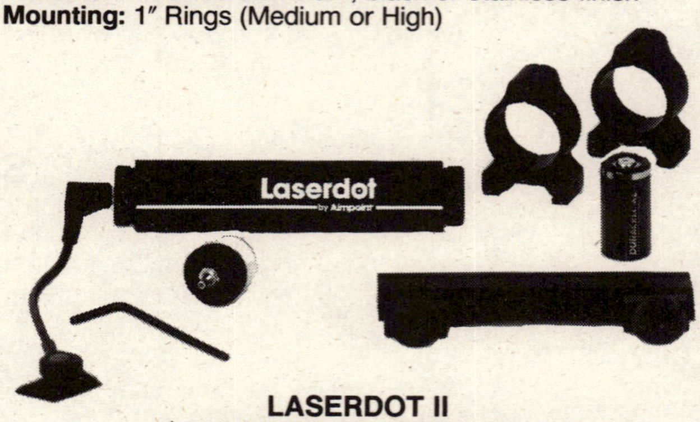


## LASERDOT II
## $319.00 (Black or Stainless)

**SPECIFICATIONS**
**Length:** 3.5″
**Weight:** 2.9 oz.
**Diameter:** 1″
**Switch pad:** 5.5″ long cable and pressure switch (optional toggle switch available)
**Material:** 6061T aluminum
**Finish:** Black or stainless
**Output beam:** Wavelength 670 nm; Class IIIa limit; output aperture approx. ¼″ (6mm); beam divergence 0.5 Rad
**Batteries:** 1 X 3v Lithium
**Battery life:** Up to 15 hours continuous
**Environmental:** 0-30 C. operating 0-95% rh.; will withstand 2 meter drop; one meter immersion proof

## LASERDOT AUTO LASER (not shown)
## $370.00 (w/Mounts)

**SPECIFICATIONS**
**Length:** 1.6″–3.5″
**Weight:** 2.5–3.9 oz.
**Dot diameter:** 1½″ at 100 yards
**Switch pad:** Toggle
**Material:** 6061T aluminum
**Finish:** Black or stainless
**Batteries:** 1x6v Lithium
**Mounting:** Integrated on trigger guard
Also available: Laser Sights for Revolvers: **$348.00**

# BAUSCH & LOMB RIFLESCOPES

**ELITE 4000**
**2.5–10X40**

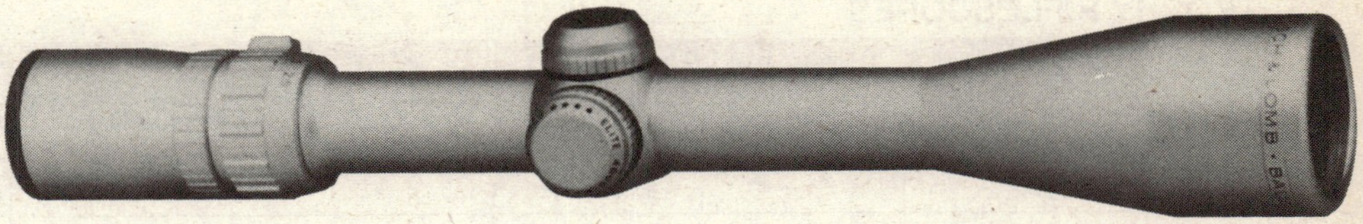

## ELITE™ 4000 RIFLESCOPES

| Model | Special Feature | Actual Magni-fication | Obj. Lens Aperature (mm) | Field of View @100yds (ft) | Weight (oz.) | Length (in.) | Eye Relief (in.) | Exit Pupil (mm) | Click @100yds (in.) | Adjust Range @100yds (in.) | Selection | Suggested Retail |
|---|---|---|---|---|---|---|---|---|---|---|---|---|
| ELITE® 4000 | | | | | | | | | | | | |
| 40-1040 | Ranging reticle 30mm body tube | 10x | 40 | 10.5 | 22.1 | 13.8 | 3.6 | 4 | .25 | 120 | The ultimate for precise pinpoint accuracy w/parallax focus & target adustment knobs. | 1,729.00 |
| 40-1636G | (40-1636M Matte Finish) | 1.5x-6x | 36 | 61.8-16.1 | 15.4 | 12.8 | 3 | 14.6-6 | .25 | 60 | Compact wide angle for close-in & brush hunting. Max. brightness. Excel. for shotguns | 561.00 (G) 584.00 (M) |
| 40-2104G | (40-2104M Matte Finish 40-2104S Silver Finish) | 2.5x-10x | 40 | 41.5-10.8 | 16 | 13.5 | 3 | 15.6-4 | .25 | 50 | All purpose hunting scope w/ 4x zoom range for close-in brush & long range shooting | 599.00 (G) 626.00 (M) 626.00 (S) |
| 40-3640A | Adjustable Objective | 36x | 40 | 3 | 17.6 | 15 | 3.2 | 1.1 | .125 | 30 | Ideal benchrest scope. | 851.00 (A) |
| 40-6244A | Adjustable Objective, Sunshade (40-6244M Matte Finish) | 6x-24x | 40 | 18-4.5 | 20.2 | 16.9 | 3 | 6.7-1.7 | .125 | 26 | Varmit, target & silhouette long range shooting. Parallax focus adjust. for pinpoint accuracy. | 696.00 (A) 720.00 (M) |

## ELITE™ 3000 RIFLESCOPES

| Model | Special Feature | Actual Magni-fication | Obj. Lens Aperature (mm) | Field of View @100yds (ft) | Weight (oz.) | Length (in.) | Eye Relief (in.) | Exit Pupil (mm) | Click @100yds (in.) | Adjust Range @100yds (in.) | Selection | Suggested Retail |
|---|---|---|---|---|---|---|---|---|---|---|---|---|
| ELITE® 3000 | | | | | | | | | | | | |
| 30-1545G | (30-1545M Matte Finish) | 1.5x-4.5x | 32 | 73-24 | 10 | 9.7 | 3.3 | 21-7 | .25 | 100 | Low power variable ideal for brush, medium range slug gun hunting. | 411.95 (G) 430.95 (M) |
| 30-1642E | European Reticle Matte Finish | 1.5x-6x | 42 | 57.7-15 | 21 | 14.4 | 3 | 17.6-7 | .36 | 60 | Large exit pupil & 30mm tube for max. brightness. | 638.95 |
| 30-2028G | Handgun (30-2028S Silver Finish) | 2x | 28 | 23 | 6.9 | 8.4 | 9-26 | 14 | .25 | 40 | Excellent short to medium range hunting & target scope w/ max. recoil resistance. | 299.95 (G) 318.95 (S) |
| 30-2632G | Handgun (30-2632S Silver Finish) | 2x-6x | 32 | 10-4 | 10 | 9 | 20 | 16-5.3 | .25 | 50 | Constant eye relief at all powers w/ max. recoil resistance. | 409.95 (G) 428.95 (S) |
| 30-2732G | (30-2732M Matte Finish) | 2x-7x | 32 | 44.6-12.7 | 12 | 11.6 | 3 | 12.2-4.6 | .25 | 50 | Compact variable for close-in brush or medium range shooting. Excellent for shotguns. | 339.95 (G) 358.95 (M) |
| 30-3940G | (30-3940M Matte Finish 30-3940S Silver Finish) | 3x-9x | 40 | 33.8-11.5 | 13 | 12.6 | 3 | 13.3-4.4 | .25 | 50 | For the full range of hunting. From varmint to big game. Tops in versatility. | 348.95 (G) 370.95 (M) 370.95 (S) |
| 30-3950G | ( 30-3950M Matte Finish) | 3x-9x | 50 | 31.5-10.5 | 19 | 15.7 | 3 | 12.5-5.6 | .25 | 50 | All purpose variable with extra brightness. | 430.95 (G) 449.95 (M) |
| 30-3955E | European Reticle Matte Finish | 3x-9x | 50 | 31.5-10.5 | 22 | 15.6 | 3 | 12.5-5.6 | .36 | 70 | Large exit pupil & 30mm tube for max. brightness. | 628.95 |
| 30-4124A | Adjustable Objective | 4x-12x | 40 | 26.9-9 | 15 | 13.2 | 3 | 10-3.33 | .25 | 50 | Medium to long-range variable makes a superb choice for varmint or big game. | 418.95 |

# BAUSCH & LOMB/BUSHNELL

## TROPHY RIFLESCOPES

| Model | Special Feature | Actual Magni-fication | Obj. Lens Aperature (mm) | Field of View @100yds (ft) | Weight (oz.) | Length (in.) | Eye Relief (in.) | Exit Pupil (mm) | Click @100yds (in.) | Adjust Range @100yds (in.) | Selection | Suggested Retail |
|---|---|---|---|---|---|---|---|---|---|---|---|---|
| TROPHY® RIFLESCOPES | | | | | | | | | | | | |
| 73-0440 | Wide angle | 4x | 40 | 36 | 12.5 | 12.5 | 3 | 10 | .25 | 100 | General purpose. | 151.95 |
| 73-1500 | Wide angle | 1.75x-5x | 32 | 68@1.75x 23@5x | 12.3 | 10.8 | 3.5 | 18.3@1.75x 6.4@5x | .25 | 120 | Shotgun, black powder or center-fire. Close-in brush hunting. | 257.95 |
| 73-2545 | 45mm objective for maximum light transmission | 2.5x-10x | 45 | 39@2.5x 10@10x | 14 | 13.75 | 3 | 18@2.5x 4.5@10x | .25 | 60 | All purpose hunting with 4 times zoom for close-in and long range shooting. | 307.95 |
| 73-2733 | Wide angle | 2x-7x | 32 | 63@2x 18@7x | 11.3 | 10 | 3 | 16@2x 4.6@7x | .25 | 110 | Low power variable for close-in brush and medium range shooting. Ideal for slug gun shooting. | 254.95 |
| 73-3940 | Wide angle (73-3940S Silver, 73-3948 Matte) | 3x-9x | 40 | 42@3x 14@9x | 13.2 | 11.7 | 3 | 13.3@3x 4.4@9x | .25 | 60 | All purpose variable, excellent for use from close to long range. Circular view provides a definite advantage over "TV screen" type scopes for running game uphill or down. | 184.95 195.95 (S) 195.95 (M) |
| 73-3941* | Illuminated Dot reticle with back-up crosshairs | 3x-9x | 40 | 37@3x 12.5@9x | 16 | 13 | 3 | 13.3@3x 4.4@9x | .25 | 70 | Variable intensity light control. | 382.95 |
| 73-3942* | Long mounting length designed for long-action rifles | 3x-9x | 42 | 42@3x 14@9x | 13.8 | 12 | 3 | 14@3x 4.7@9x | .25 | 40 | 7" mounting length. | 195.95 |
| 73-3949* | Wide angle with Circle-x™ Reticle | 3x-9x | 40 | 42@3x 14@9x | 13.2 | 11.7 | 3 | 13.3@3x 4.4@9x | .25 | 60 | Matte finish, Ideal low light reticle. | 204.95 |
| 73-3950M | Large objective for enhanced low light viewing | 3x-9x | 50 | 33@3x 11@9x | 19 | 15.5 | 3 | 16.7@3x 5.6@9x | .25 | 50 | Matte finish. | 392.95 |
| 73-4124 | Wide angle, adjustable objective (73-4124M* Matte) | 4x-12x | 40 | 32@4x 11@12x | 16.1 | 12.6 | 3 | 10@4x 3.3@12x | .25 | 60 | Medium to long range variable for varmint and big game. Range focus adjustment. Excellent air riflescope. | 286.95 295.95 (M) |
| 73-6184 | Semi-turret target adjustments, adjustable objective | 6x-18x | 40 | 17.3@6x 6@18x | 17.9 | 14.8 | 3 | 6.6@6x 2.2@18x | .125 | 40 | Long range variable for varmint centerfire or short range air rifle target precision accuracy. | 335.95 |

## TROPHY HANDGUN, SHOTGUN AND AIR RIFLESCOPES

| Model | Special Feature | Actual Magni-fication | Obj. Lens Aperature (mm) | Field of View @100yds (ft) | Weight (oz.) | Length (in.) | Eye Relief (in.) | Exit Pupil (mm) | Click @100yds (in.) | Adjust Range @100yds (in.) | Selection | Suggested Retail |
|---|---|---|---|---|---|---|---|---|---|---|---|---|
| TROPHY® HANDGUN SCOPES | | | | | | | | | | | | |
| 73-0232 | (73-0232S Silver) | 2x | 32 | 20 | 7.7 | 8.7 | 9-26 | 16 | .25 | 90 | Designed for target and short to medium range hunting. Magnum recoil resistant. | 189.95 204.95 (S) |
| 73-2632 | (73-2632S Silver) | 2x-6x | 32 | 11@2x 4@6x | 10.9 | 9.1 | 18 | 16@2x 5.3@6x | .25 | 50 | 18 inches of eye relief at all powers. | 244.95 257.95 (S) |
| TROPHY® SHOTGUN/HANDGUN SCOPES | | | | | | | | | | | | |
| 73-0130 | Illuminated dot reticle | 1x | 25 | 61 | 5.5 | 5.25 | Unltd. | 18 | 1.0 | 80 | 30mm tube with rings, ext. tube polarization filter, amber coating. For black powder, shotgun and handgun shooting. | 280.95 |
| 73-1420 | Turkey Scope w/Circle-x™ Reticle | 1.75x-4x | 32 | 73@1.75x 30@4x | 10.9 | 10.8 | 3.5 | 18@1.75x 8@4x | .25 | 120 | Ideal for turkey hunting, slug guns or blackpowder guns. Matte finish. | 263.95 |
| 73-1421 | Brush Scope w/Circle-x™ Reticle | 1.75x-4x | 32 | 73@1.75x 30@4x | 10.9 | 10.8 | 3.5 | 18@1.75x 8@4x | .25 | 120 | Ideal for turkey hunting, slug guns or blackpowder guns. Matte finish. | 263.95 |
| TROPHY® AIR RIFLESCOPES | | | | | | | | | | | | |
| 73-4124 | Wide angle adjustable objective | 4x-12x | 40 | 32@4x 11@12x | 16.1 | 12.6 | 3 | 10@4x 3.3@12x | .25 | 60 | Medium to long range variable for varmint and big game. Range focus adjustment. Excellent air riflescope. | 286.95 295.95 (M) |
| 73-6184 | Semi-turret target adjustments, adjustable objective | 6x-18x | 40 | 17.3@6x 6@18x | 17.9 | 14.8 | 3 | 6.6@6x 2.2@18x | .125 | 40 | Long range varmint centerfire or short range air rifle, target precision accuracy. | 335.95 |

# BAUSCH & LOMB/BUSHNELL

**ELITE 4000
1.5X–6X36**

## SPORTVIEW RIFLESCOPES

| Model | Special Feature | Actual Magni-fication | Obj. Lens Aperature (mm) | Field of View @100yds (ft) | Weight (oz.) | Length (in.) | Eye Relief (in.) | Exit Pupil (mm) | Click @100yds (in.) | Adjust Range @100yds (in.) | Selection | Suggested Retail |
|---|---|---|---|---|---|---|---|---|---|---|---|---|
| SPORTVIEW® RIFLESCOPES | | | | | | | | | | | | |
| 79-0412 | *NEW* Adjustable objective | 4x-12x | 40 | 27@4x<br>9@12x | 14.6 | 13.1 | 3.2 | 10@4x<br>3.3@12x | .25 | 60 | Long range. | 131.95 |
| 79-0640 | *NEW* | 6X | 40 | 20.5 | 10.4 | 12.25 | 3 | 6.6 | .25 | 50 | Medium range shooting centerfire and rimfire rifles. | 91.95 |
| 79-1393 | *NEW* (79-1398 Matte) 79-1393S Matte Silver) | 3x-9x | 32 | 35@3x<br>12@9x | 10 | 11.75 | 3.5 | 10.7@3x<br>3.6@9x | .25 | 50 | All purpose variable. | 66.95<br>68.95(S)(M) |
| 79-1403 | *NEW* (79-1403S Silver) | 4x | 32 | 29 | 9.2 | 11.75 | 4 | 8 | .25 | 60 | General purpose. | 53.95<br>56.95(S) |
| 79-1545 | *NEW* | 1.5x-4.5x | 21 | 69@1.5x<br>24@4.5x | 8.6 | 10.7 | 3 | 14@1.5x<br>4.7@4.5x | .25 | 60 | Low power variable ideal for close-in brush or medium range shooting. | 88.95 |
| 79-2532 | *NEW* | 2.5x | 32 | 44 | 9 | 10.75 | 3.5 | 12.8 | .25 | 80 | Shotgun. | 88.95 |
| 79-3145 | *NEW* Larger objective | 3.5x-10x | 45 | 36@3.5x<br>13@10x | 13.9 | 12.75 | 3 | 12.9@3.5x<br>4.5@10x | .25 | 60 | Large objective for low light use. | 144.95 |
| 79-3929 | *NEW* T.V. View | 3x-9x | 40 | 40@3x<br>13@9x | 12 | 12.25 | 3 | 13.3@3x<br>4.4@9x | .25 | 45 | T.V. View | 99.95 |
| 79-3938 | *NEW* Wide angle | 3x-9x | 38 | 42@3x<br>14@9x | 12.5 | 12.7 | 3 | 12.7@3x<br>4.2@9x | .25 | 50 | Excellent for use at any range. | 105.95 |
| 79-4389 | *NEW* Wide angle | 4x | 38 | 34 | 11.7 | 12.5 | 3 | 9.5 | .25 | 50 | General purpose. Wide angle. | 91.95 |

## BANNER RIFLESCOPES

| Model | Special Feature | Actual Magni-fication | Obj. Lens Aperature (mm) | Field of View @100yds (ft) | Weight (oz.) | Length (in.) | Eye Relief (in.) | Exit Pupil (mm) | Click @100yds (in.) | Adjust Range @100yds (in.) | Selection | Suggested Retail |
|---|---|---|---|---|---|---|---|---|---|---|---|---|
| BANNER® | | | | | | | | | | | | |
| 71-2520 | | 2.5x | 20 | 44 | 7.5 | 10 | 3.6 | 8 | .25 | 80 | Shotgun use. | 84.95 |
| 71-3956 | Extra large objective | 3x-9x | 56 | 37@3x<br>12@9x | 17.3 | 13.7 | 3.5 | 10.3@3x<br>6.2@9x | .25 | 50 | All purpose variable with maximum brightness. | 286.95 |
| 71-4220 | With .22 rings | 4x | 20 | 28 | 8.1 | 11.7 | 3 | 5 | .25 | 60 | All purpose .22 with a 1-inch body tube for increased brightness | 70.95 |
| 71-6102 | BDC, Wide angle | 3x-9x | 40 | 42@3x<br>14@9x | 13.1 | 12 | 3.3 | 13.3@3x<br>4.4@9x | .25 | 70 | All purpose variable, excellent for use from close or long range. Circular view provides a definite advantage over "TV screen" type scopes for running game uphill or down. | 134.95 |
| LITE-SITE® | | | | | | | | | | | | |
| 71-3940 | Illuminated dot reticle | 3x-9x | 40 | 36@3x<br>13@9x | 15.5 | 12.8 | 3.1 | 13.3@3x<br>4.4@9x | .25 | 60 | Illuminated dot reticle with back-up cross hairs. All purpose variable. Excellent for use at any range. | 365.95 |

# BEEMAN SCOPES

**BEEMAN SS-2 W/FIREARM**

## SS-2 SERIES

Beeman SS-1 and SS-2 short scopes are extra compact and rugged, largely due to breakthroughs in optical engineering and computer programming of lens formulas. Less than 7 inches long, both scopes pack 11 lenses that actually gather light for bigger, brighter targets than "projected spot" targets. Scope body and built-in mounts are milled as a single unit from a solid block of hi-tensile aircraft aluminum.

**SS-2 Series** .................... **from $290.00–305.00**

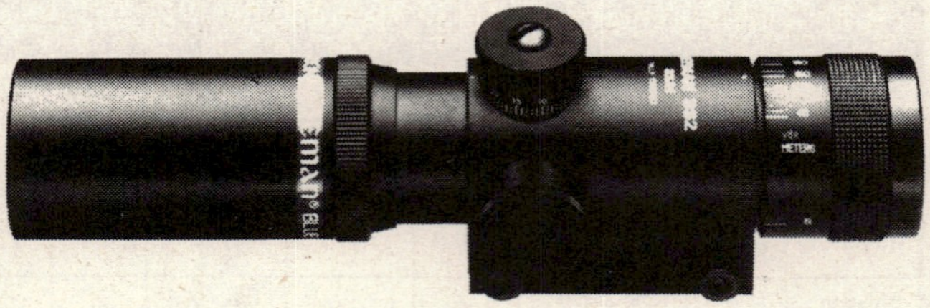

**BEEMAN SS-2**

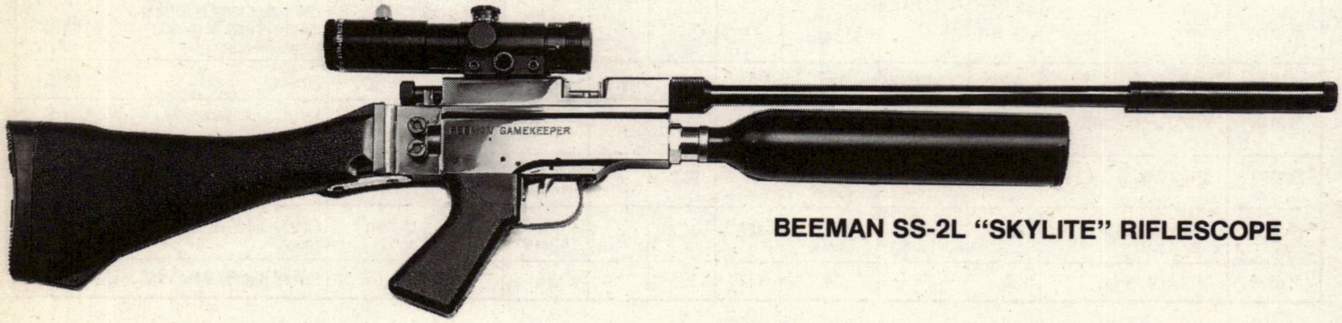


**BEEMAN SS-2L "SKYLITE" RIFLESCOPE**

## BEEMAN SS-2L "SKYLITE" RIFLESCOPE

Features a brightly illuminated reticle powered by daylight and even moonlight (no batteries necessary). In addition to standard black reticle, supplementary color filters are available for different lighting and shooting situations. Filter options include: white (for silhouette or target); red (for twilight and general purpose); yellow (for haze, fog and low light); green (for bright light and snow). A small electrical illuminator is also available for use in total darkness.

| | |
|---|---|
| **Beeman SS-2L** w/color reticle, 3x | **$340.00** |
| **Beeman SS-2L** w/color reticle, 4x | **370.00** |
| **Micro Lamp** | **35.00** |
| **Filter Kit** (green or yellow) | **19.50** |

**BEEMAN SS-3**

## SS-3 SERIES

Offers 1.5-4x zoom power for greater flexibility. Glare-free black matte finish is anodized into metal for deep sheen and extra toughness. Instant action dial around front of scope dials away parallax error and dials in perfect focus from 10 feet to infinity. Scope measures only 5¾ inches in length and weighs only 8.5 ounces. **SS-3 Series** ................ **$300.00**

# BEEMAN SCOPES



## BLUE RIBBON

### BEEMAN MODEL 66R

Every feature of the Model 66R has been carefully developed to make it the ultimate scope for centerfire, .22-caliber rimfire and adult air rifles. It can zoom instantly from 2 to 7X—an excellent range of magnification that provides sufficient high power for long-range shots requiring pinpoint accuracy, and very low power for times when speed and a broad field of view are needed. Speed Dials (with full saddle) with 1/2-minute adjustments per click and Range Focus are two of the 66R's star features. The 32mm objective lens up front provides a bright, wide field view, extends daily shooting time, and affords better viewing into shadows.

**Model 66R 2-7X32** with Range Focus .......... **$315.00**

### BEEMAN MODEL 66RL

The ultimate scope for centerfire, rimfire and adult airguns. Zoom instantly from 2X to 7X—range that provides sufficient high power for long shots as well as very low power when a broad field of view is demanded. Features speed dials, Range Focus and 32mm objective lens.

**Model 66RL** w/Color Reticle Scope ............ **$355.00**

### BEEMAN MODEL 25
### (Shown on Beeman P1 Air Pistol)

Beeman has improved upon the modified domestic pistol scope that was formerly recommended. Starting with the same dedication to quality, special Beeman Blue Ribbon® Scope features have been added to produce one of the finest scopes for air pistols (and a variety of other pistols). Features include Speed Dial elevation and windage knobs and the brightness and performance that only a 1″ tube, top-quality lens system can offer. Full saddle. Especially recommended for Beeman P1/P2 air pistols.

**Model 25 2X20 Blue Ribbon Pistol Scope** ...... **$155.00**

BEEMAN MODEL 25 SCOPE

# B-SQUARE

**MINI-LASERS**
**$239.95 (Blue) $259.95 (Stainless)**

**SPECIFICATIONS**
**Power:** 5mW max (class IIIA)
**Size:** 1.1″×1.1″×.6″
**Batteries:** Common A76 (lithium or alkaline)
**Aiming method:** Omnidirectional
**Visibility:** 1″ at 25 yds.
**Min. Life:** 60 min.
**Features:** Quick detachable laser allows holstering; moisture proof and shock resistant; "Aim-Lock" screw type; windage and elevation adjustable; no trigger finger interference; cord or integral switch; on-off switch optional; wide selection of mounts available

**BSL-1 LASER SIGHT**
**$199.95 (Blue) $209.95 (Stainless)**

**SPECIFICATIONS**
**Power:** 5mW max (class IIIA)
**Size:** .75″; dia.×2.65″
**Aiming method:** Omnidirectional (screw type, lockable)
**Visibility:** Pulsed dot 1″ at 100 yds.
**Features:** "Aim-Lock" no-slip mounts; T-Slot cap; cord or integral switch; wide selection of mounts

# BURRIS SCOPES

**6X HBR**
**$294.00 (Fine Plex)**

Engineered and designed to meet Hunter Benchrest specifications, this scope has precise 1/8″ minute click adjustments with re-zeroable target-style knobs. Complete with parallax adjustment from 25 yards to infinity. Weighs only 13 ounces.

**1.5X GUNSITE SCOUT SCOPE**

**GUNSITE SCOUT SCOPES**

Made for hunters who need a 7- to 14-inch eye relief to mount just in front of the ejection port opening, allowing hunters to shoot with both eyes open. The 15-foot field of view and 2 3/4X magnification are ideal for brush guns and handgunners.

| | |
|---|---|
| 1.5X Plex XER | **$218.00** |
| 1.5X Plex XER Safari Finish | **236.00** |
| 1.5X Heavy Plex | **227.00** |
| 1.5X Heavy Plex Safari | **245.00** |
| 2.75X Heavy Plex | **222.95** |
| 2.75X Heavy Plex Safari | **232.00** |
| 2.75X Plex XER | **223.00** |

# BURRIS SCOPES

## SIGNATURE SERIES

All models in the Signature Series have **Hi-Lume** (multi-coated) lenses for maximum light transmission. Also features new **Posi-Lock** to prevent recoil and protect against rough hunting use and temperature change. Allows shooter to lock internal optics of scope in position after rifle has been sighted in.

**8X-32X SIGNATURE**

| Models | Prices |
|---|---|
| 4X Plex (black) | $336.00 |
| 6X Plex (black) | 353.00 |
| 6X Plex (matte) | 372.00 |
| 1.5X-6X Plex (black) | 413.00 |
| 1.5X-6X Plex (matte) | 431.00 |
| 1.5X-6X Plex (silver) | 441.00 |
| 1.5X-6X Heavy Plex (black) | 422.00 |
| 1.5X-6X Heavy Plex (matte) | 441.00 |
| 1.5X-6X Plex Posi-Lock (black) | 493.00 |
| 1.5X-6X Plex Posi-Lock (matte) | 511.00 |
| 2X-8X Plex (black) | 480.00 |
| 2X-8X Plex (matte) | 497.00 |
| 2X-8X Plex (silver) | 506.00 |
| 2X-8X Plex Posi-Lock (black) | 551.00 |
| 2X-8X Plex Posi-Lock (matte)lf | 568.00 |
| 2X-8X Plex Posi-Lock (silver) | 577.00 |
| 3X-9X Plex (black) | 489.00 |
| 3X-9X Plex (matte) | 508.00 |
| 3X-9X Plex (silver) | 517.00 |
| 3X-9X Plex Posi-Lock (black) | 561.00 |
| 3X-9X Plex Posi-Lock (matte) | 579.00 |
| 3X-9X Plex Posi-Lock (silver) | 588.00 |
| 2.5X-10X Plex Parallax Adjustment (black) | 552.00 |
| 2.5X-10X Plex Parallax Adjustment (matte) | 571.00 |
| 2.5X-10X Plex Parallax Adjustment (silver) | 580.00 |
| 2.5X-10X Peep Plex Parallax Adjustment (black) | 561.00 |
| 2.5X-10X Plex Posi-Lock Parallax Adjustment (black) | 624.00 |
| 2.5X-10X Plex Posi-Lock Parallax Adjustment (matte) | 642.00 |
| 2.5X-10X Plex Posi-Lock Parallax Adjustment (silver) | 651.00 |
| 3X-12X Plex | 612.00 |
| 3X-12X Plex Parallax Adjustment (matte) | 629.00 |
| 3X-12X Peep Plex Parallax Adjustment (black) | 621.00 |
| 3X-12X Peep Plex Parallax Adjustment (matte) | 638.00 |
| 3X-12X Plex Posi-Lock Parallax Adjustment (black) | 683.00 |
| 3X-12X Plex Posi-Lock Parallax Adjustment (matte) | 701.00 |
| 4X-16X Plex Parallax Adjustment (black) | 624.00 |
| 4X-16X Plex Parallax Adjustment) (matte) | 642.00 |
| 4X-16X Peep Plex Parallax Adjustment (black) | 633.00 |
| 4X-16X Plex Posi-Lock Parallax Adjustment (black) | 695.00 |
| 4X-16X Plex Posi-Lock Parallax Adjustment (matte) | 713.00 |
| 6X-24X Plex Parallax Adjustment (black) | 638.00 |
| 6X-24X Plex Parallax Adjustment (matte) | 656.00 |
| 6X-24X Fine Flex Target (black) | 662.00 |
| 6X-24X Fine Plex Target (matte) | 679.00 |
| 6X-24X Peep Parallax Adjustment (black) | 647.00 |
| 6X-24X Peep Plex Parallax Adjustment (matte) | 666.00 |
| 6X-24X 2″-.5″ Dot Target (black) | 679.00 |
| 6X-24X Plex Posi-Lock Parallax Adjustment (black) | 710.00 |
| 6X-24XP Plex Posi-Lock Parallax Adjustment (matte) | 728.00 |
| 8X-32X Fine Plex Target (black) | 699.00 |
| 8X-32X Peep Plex Target (black) | 708.00 |
| 8X-32X 2″-5″ Dot Target (black) | 718.00 |
| 8X-32X Fine Plex Posi-Lock Parallax Adjustment (black) | 792.00 |

**2.5X10X SIGNATURE**

**3X-9X SIGNATURE**

**3X-9X RAC SCOPE**
**w/Automatic Rangefinder & Hi-Lume Lenses**

When the crosshair is zeroed at 200 yards (or 1.8″ high at 100 yards), it will remain zeroed at 200 yards regardless of the power ring setting. The Range Reticle automatically moves to zero at ranges up to 500 yards as power is increased to fit the target between the stadia range wires. No need to adjust the elevation knob; bullet drop compensation is automatic. See also **Fullfield** listings below.

| | |
|---|---|
| 3X-9X RAC CHP (black) | $385.00 |
| 3X-9X RAC Crosshair Dot (black) | 385.00 |
| 3X-9X RAC Crosshair Plex (matte) | 402.00 |

## FULLFIELD SCOPES
**Fixed Power with Hi-Lume Lenses**

**12X FULLFIELD**

| Models | Prices |
|---|---|
| 1X XER Heavy Plex (black) | $247.00 |
| 1X XER Heavy Plex (matte) | 265.00 |
| 1X XER Plex (matte) | 282.00 |
| 1½X Plex (black) | 247.00 |

(cont. on next page)

# BURRIS FULLFIELD SCOPES

## FULLFIELD (cont.)

| Models | Prices |
|---|---|
| 1½X Heavy Plex (black) | $256.00 |
| 2½X Plex (black) | 258.00 |
| 2½X Heavy Plex (black) | 268.00 |
| 4X Plex (black) | 277.00 |
| 4X Plex (matte) | 296.00 |
| 6X Plex (black) | 297.00 |
| 6X Plex (matte) | 315.00 |
| 12X Plex Parallax Adjustment (black) | 374.00 |
| 12X Fine Plex Parallax Adjustment (black) | 374.00 |
| 12X Fine Plex Target (black) | 402.00 |
| 12X ½″ Dot Target (black) | 420.00 |
| 1X-4X XER Heavy Plex (black) | 325.00 |
| 1X-4X XER Heavy Plex (matte) | 343.00 |
| 1.75X-5X Plex (black) | 323.00 |
| 1.75X-5X Plex (matte) | 341.00 |
| 1.75X-5X Heavy Plex (black) | 332.00 |
| 1.75X-5X Heavy Plex (matte) | 350.00 |
| 1.75x-5X Plex Posi-Lock (black) | 395.00 |
| 1.75X-5X Plex Safari Posi-Lock (matte) | 413.00 |
| 1.75X-5X Plex Posi-Lock (silver) | 422.00 |
| 2X-7X Plex (black) | 348.00 |
| 2X-7X Plex (matte) | 365.00 |
| 2X-7X Plex (silver) | 374.00 |
| 2X-7X Post Crosshair (black) | 356.00 |
| 3X-9X Plex (black) | 332.00 |
| 3X-9X Plex (matte) | 363.00 |
| 3X-9X Plex (silver) | 372.00 |
| 3X-9X Peep Plex (black) | 359.00 |
| 3X-9X Post Crosshair (black) | 359.00 |
| 3X-9X 3.″-1.″ Dot (black) | 363.00 |
| 3X-9X Plex Posi-Lock (black) | 416.00 |
| 3X-9X Plex Posi-Lock (silver) | 443.00 |
| 3.5X-10X-50mm Plex (black) | 429.00 |
| 3.5X-10X-50mm Plex (matte) | 458.00 |
| 3.5X-10X-50mm Plex (silver) | 467.00 |
| 3.5X-10X-50mm Peep Plex (black) | 449.00 |
| 3.5X-10X-50mm Plex Posi-Lock (black) | 511.00 |
| 3.5X-10X-50mm Plex Posi-Lock (matte) | 529.00 |
| 3.5X-10X-50mm Plex Posi-Lock (silver) | 538.00 |
| 4X-12X Plex Parallex Adjustment (black) | 437.00 |
| 4X-12X Fine Plex Parallex Adjustment (black) | 437.00 |
| 4X-12X Peep Plex Parallax Adjustment (black) | 445.00 |
| 6X-18X Plex Parallax Adjustment (black) | 455.00 |
| 6X-18X Plex Parallax Adjustment (matte) | 474.00 |
| 6X-18X Fine Plex Parallax Adjustment (black) | 455.00 |
| 6X-18X Fine Plex Target (black) | 483.00 |
| 6X-18X Peep Plex Parallax Adjustment (black) | 465.00 |
| 6X-18X Peep Plex Parallax Adjustment (matte) | 483.00 |
| 6X-18X 2.″-.7″ Dot Target (black) | 501.00 |

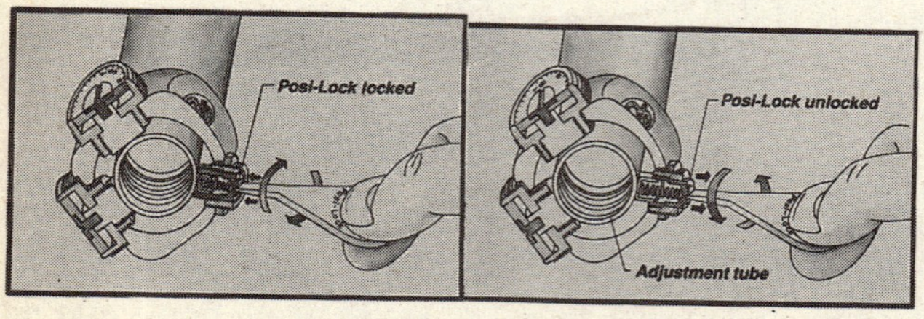


BURRIS POSI-LOCK

## COMPACT SCOPES

| | |
|---|---|
| 4X Plex (black) | $223.00 |
| 4X Plex (silver) | 250.00 |
| 4X Plex Parallax Adjustment (black) | 258.00 |
| 6X Plex Target (black) | 238.00 |
| 6X Plex Target Parallax Adjustment (black) | 273.00 |
| 6X HBR Fine Plex Target (black) | 307.00 |
| 6X HBR FCH Target (black) | 307.00 |
| 6X HBR FCH Target (silver) | 335.00 |
| 6X HBR .375 Dot Target (black) | 325.00 |
| 6X HBR .375 Dot Target (silver) | 352.00 |
| 2X-7X Plex (black) | 305.00 |
| 2X-7X Plex (matte) | 323.00 |
| 2X-7X Plex (silver) | 333.00 |
| 3X-9X Plex (black) | 312.00 |
| 3X-9X Plex (matte) | 331.00 |
| 3X-9X Plex (silver) | 340.00 |
| 4X-12X Plex Parallax Adjustment (black) | 413.00 |
| 4X-12X Plex Target (black) | 440.00 |

3X LER

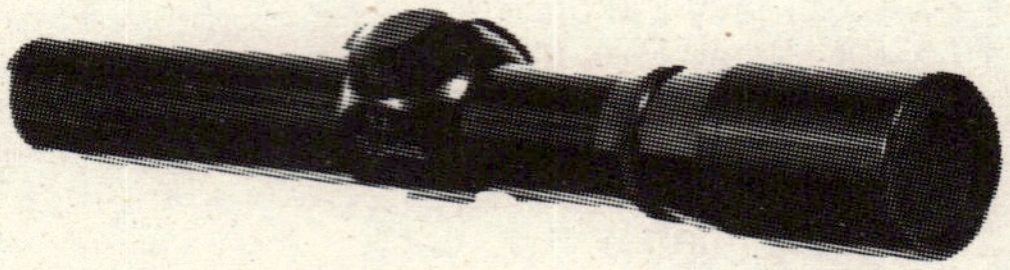

## HANDGUN LONG EYE RELIEF SCOPE with Plex Reticle:

| | |
|---|---|
| 1X Plex (black) | $212.00 |
| 2X Plex (black) | 219.00 |
| 2X Plex (silver) | 247.00 |
| 2X Heavy Plex (black) | 229.00 |
| 2X Plex Posi-Lock (black) | 291.00 |
| 2X-Plex Posi-Lock (silver) | 318.00 |
| 3X Plex (black) | 236.00 |
| 4X Plex (black) | 245.00 |
| 4X Plex (silver) | 272.00 |
| 4X Plex Parallax Adjustment (black) | 281.00 |
| 4X Plex Posi-Lock (black) | 316.00 |
| 4X Plex Posi-Lock (silver) | 343.00 |
| 7X Plex Parallax Adjustment (black) | 307.00 |
| 7X Plex Parallax Adjustment (silver) | 334.00 |
| 10X Plex Target (black) | 363.00 |
| 1.5X-4X Plex (black) | 342.00 |
| 1.5X-4X Plex (silver) | 368.00 |
| 1.5X-4X Plex Posi-Lock (black) | 413.00 |
| 1.5X-4X Plex Posi-Lock (silver) | 440.00 |
| 2X-7X Plex Target (black) | 334.00 |
| 2X-7X Plex (matte) | 352.00 |
| 2X-7X Plex (silver) | 361.00 |
| 2X-7X Plex Parallax Adjustment (black) | 370.00 |
| 2X-7X Plex Posi-Lock (black) | 406.00 |
| 2X-7X Plex Posi-Lock (silver) | 433.00 |
| 3X-9X Plex (black) | 376.00 |
| 3X-9X Plex (matte) | 394.00 |
| 3X-9X Plex (silver) | 402.00 |
| 3X-9X Plex (black) | 385.00 |
| 3X-9X Plex Parallax Adjustment (black) | 411.00 |
| 3X-9X Plex Posi-Lock (black) | 447.00 |
| 3X-9X Plex Posi-Lock (silver) | 474.00 |

# BURRIS SCOPES



## LONG EYE-RELIEF HANDGUN SCOPES

### 1X LONG EYE RELIEF (LER)

This model has been tested and proved in numerous competitions over the years. The 1X magnification eliminates any parallax. Has super crisp optics and the widest field of view of all our handgun scopes.

### 2X-7X LONG EYE-RELIEF (LER)

The perfect handgun scope for varmint or big game hunters. Versatile, compact and available with parallax adjustment.

### 1.5X-4X LONG EYE RELIEF (LER)

Designed especially for hunting with a handgun. At 1½X there is a big field of view for those fast, close shots. 4X magnification permits precision, long range shots. Eye relief is 11 inches minimum, 24 inches maximum. Weight is 11 ounces, overall length is 10¼ inches. Burris mounts recommended for this scope.

### 3X-9X LONG EYE RELIEF (LER)

The highest variable powered handgun scope made. Compact and versatile, this scope is the ultimate for hunting game or testing loads. Fog proof and magnum proof. Also available with parallax adjustment.

## INTERMEDIATE EYE-RELIEF HANDGUN SCOPES

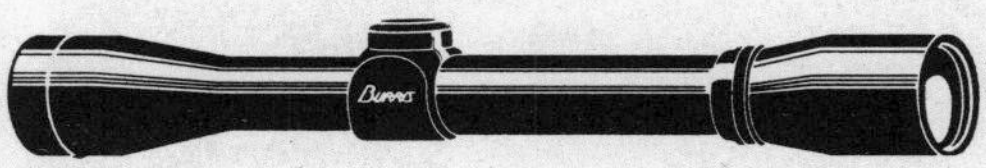


### 7X INTERMEDIATE EYE RELIEF (IER)

Developed for the long range, accurate handgunner. Requires a two handed hold. Eye relief is 10 inches minimum, 16 inches maximum. Weight is 10 ounces. Overall length is 11¼ inches. Burris mounts recommended for mounting this scope. Also available with parallax adjustment.

### 10X IER P.A.

Designed for the precision shooting handgunner to be shot from a rest or a two handed hold. Handgun should have a 14 inch barrel minimum. Overall length of scope is 13.6 inches. Weight is 14 ounces. Parallax adjustment is 50 yards to infinity.

MODEL LA16
HOTDOT MIGHTY SIGHT

## HOTDOT LASERAIM LASER SIGHTS

Ten times brighter than other laser sights, Laseraim's Hotdot Lasersights include a rechargeable NICad battery and in-field charger. Produce a 2″ dot at 100 yards with a 500-yard range. **Length:** 2″. **Diameter:** .75″. Feature pressure switch and 4-way microlock windage and elevation adjustments. Can be used with handguns, rifles, shotguns and bows. Fit all Laseraim mounts. Available in black or satin.

**Prices:**

**MODEL LA16 HOTDOT MIGHTY SIGHT** . . . . . . . . **$169.00**

**MODEL LA17 CLIP SIGHT** w/wireless pushbutton switch . . . . . . . . . . . . . . . . . . . . . . . . . . . . . . . . . **278.00**

**MODEL LA19** laser integrated w/rosewood grips (1½″ longer than standard grips) . . . . . . . . . . . . **249.00**

**MODEL LA14 HOTDOT TRIGGER GUARD SIGHT** w/integrated laser & mount, wireless toggle switch . . . . . . . . . . . . . . . . . . . . . . . . . . . . . . . . . **319.00**

## LASERAIM ILLUSION ELECTRONIC RED DOT SIGHTS

**LA9750B GRAND ILLUSION 2″**

6 MOA Medium Dot . . . . . . . . . . . . . . . . . . . . . . . **$230.00**

Same as above with 10 MOA Large Dot . . . . . . **230.00**

MODEL LA19
Laser Integrated w/Rosewood Grips

MODEL LA17 CLIP SIGHT

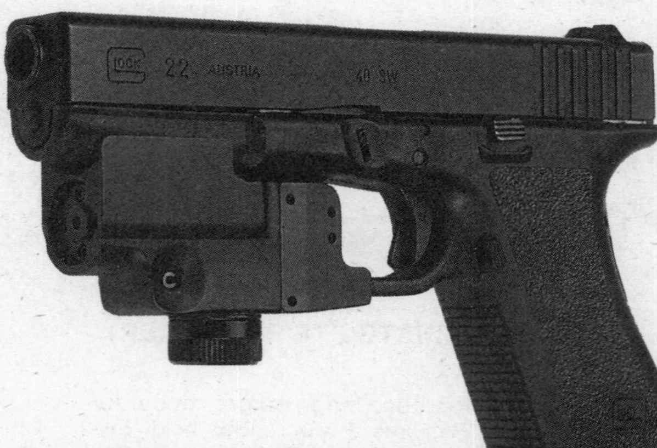

MODEL LA14 HOTDOT
TRIGGER GUARD SIGHT

# INTERAIMS SIGHTS

SCOPES

## RED DOT ELECTRONIC SIGHTS

**The following features are incorporated into each model, including the MONO TUBE:**

**—5 YEAR WARRANTY—**

- Sharp Red Dot
- Lightweight
- Compact
- Wide Field of View
- Parallaxfree
- True 1X for Unlimited Eye Relief
- Nitrogen Filled Tube
- Waterproof, Moisture Proof, Shockproof
- Rugged Aluminum Body
- Easy 1″ and 30mm Ring Mounting
- Manually Adjustable Light Intensity
- Windage and Elevation Adjustments
- Dielectrical Coated Lenses
- Battery—Polarized Filter—Extension Tube—Protective Rubber Eye Piece—All included

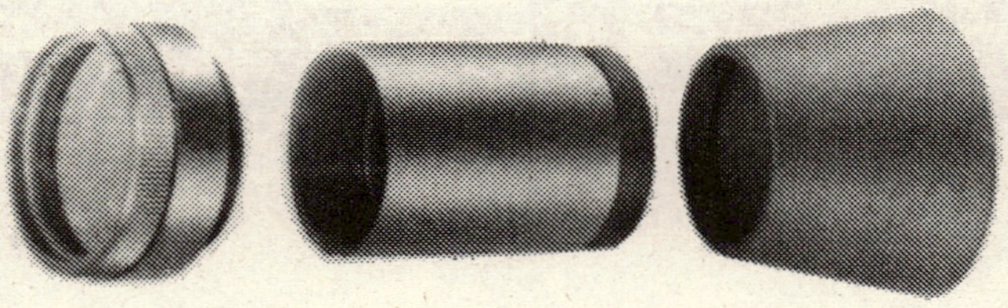

**MONOTUBE CONSTRUCTIONS ONE V**

| Weight | Length | Battery | Finish |
|---|---|---|---|
| 3.9 oz. | 4½″ | (1) 3 V Lithium | Black or Satin Nickel |

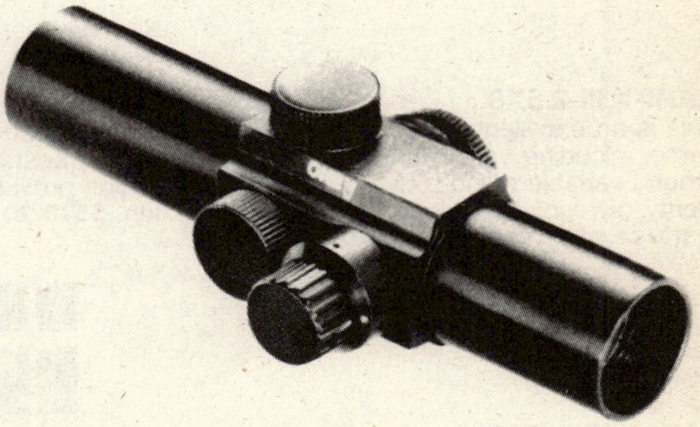

**ONE V 1″ MODEL**
**$159.00**

Also available:
1″ or 30mm rings in black or satin nickel .......... **$11.95**

**ONE V 30**
**$176.00**

**MONOTUBE CONSTRUCTIONS ONE V 30**

| Weight | Length | Battery | Finish |
|---|---|---|---|
| 5.5 oz. | 5.4″ | (1) 3 V Lithium DL 2032 | Black or Satin Nickel |

# LEUPOLD RIFLE SCOPES

## VARI-X III LINE

The Vari-X III scopes feature a power-changing system that is similar to the sophisticated lens systems in today's finest cameras. Some of the improvements include an extremely accurate internal control system and a sharp, superb-contrast sight picture. All lenses are coated with **Multicoat 4**. Reticles are the same apparent size throughout power range, stay centered during elevation/windage adjustments. Eyepieces are adjustable and fog-free.

**VARI-X III 1.5X5**
Here's a fine selection of hunting powers for ranges varying from very short to those at which big game is normally taken. The exceptional field at 1.5X lets you get on a fast-moving animal quickly. With the generous magnification at 5X, you can hunt medium and big game around the world at all but the longest ranges. Duplex or Heavy Duplex **$532.10** In black matte finish: **$553.60**
Also available:
**VARI-X III 1.75X6-32mm: $555.40.** With matte finish: **$576.80**

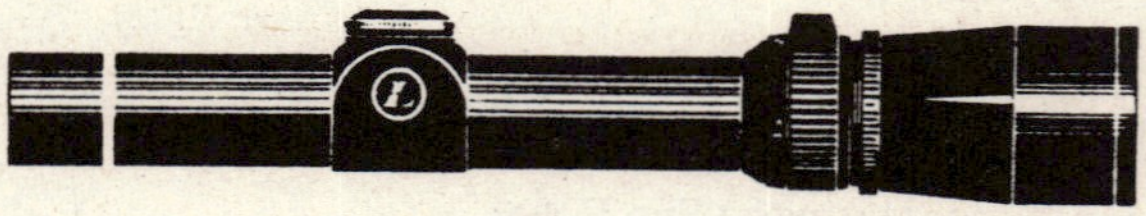

**VARI-X III 1.5X5**

**VARI-X III 2.5X8**

**VARI-X III 2.5X8**
This is an excellent range of powers for almost any kind of game, inlcuding varmints. In fact, it possibly is the best all-around variable going today. The top magnification provides plenty of resolution for practically any situation. **$573.20** In matte or silver finish: **$594.60.**

**VARI-X III 3.5X10**

**VARI-X III 3.5X10**
The extra power range makes these scopes the optimum choice for year-around big game and varmint hunting. The adjustable objective model, with its precise focusing at any range beyond 50 yards, also is an excellent choice for some forms of target shooting. **$594.60**. With matte finish: **$616.10**. With silver: **$616.10**

**VARI-X III 3.5X10–50mm**

**VARI-X III 3.5X10–50mm**
Leupold announces its first hunting scope designed specifically for low-light situations. The 3.5X10–50mm scope, featuring lenses coated with Multicoat 4, is ideal for twilight hunting (especially whitetail deer) because of its efficient light transmission. The new scope delivers maximum available light through its large 50mm objective lens, which translates into an exit pupil that transmits all the light the human eye can handle in typical low-light circumstances, even at the highest magnification: **$692.90**. With matte or silver finish: **$714.30**

Also available:
**VARI-X III 3.5X10-50mm Adj. Objective: $748.20.** With matte finish: **$769.60.**

**VARI-X III 4.5X14 (Adj. Objective)**
This new model has enough range to double as a hunting scope and as a varmint scope. Duplex or Heavy Duplex: **$667.90**
Same as above with 50mm adj. obj., Duplex or Heavy Duplex: **$789.30**

**VARI-X III 6.5X20**
**(With Adjustable Objective)**

**VARI-X III 6.5X20 (Adj. Objective)**
This scope has the widest range of power settings in our variable line, with magnifications that are especially useful to hunters of all types of varmints. In addition, it can be used for any kind of big-game hunting where higher magnifications are an aid: **$694.60**. With matte finish: **$716.10**

# LEUPOLD RIFLE SCOPES

## VARIABLE POWER SCOPES

VARI-X II 1X4

**VARI-X II 1X4 DUPLEX**
This scope, the smallest of Leupold's VARI-X II line, is reintroduced in response to consumer demand for its large field of view: 70 feet at 100 yards. . . . . . . . . . . . . . . . . . . **$357.10**

VARI-X II 2X7

**VARI-X II 2X7 DUPLEX**
A compact scope, no larger than the Leupold M8-4X, offering a wide range of power. It can be set at 2X for close ranges in heavy cover or zoomed to maximum power for shooting or identifying game at longer ranges. . . . . . . . . . . . . . . . **$387.50**

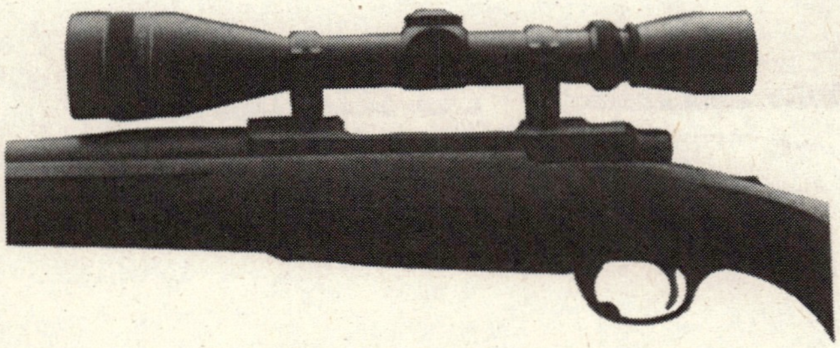

VARI-X II 4X12 MATTE FINISH

**VARI-X II 4X12 (Adj. Objective)**
The ideal answer for big game and varmint hunters alike. At 12.25 inches, the 4X12 is virtually the same length as Vari-X II 3X9. . . . . . . . . . . . . . . . . . . . . . . . . . . . . . . . . . . **$530.40**
With matte or silver finish: . . . . . . . . . . . . . . . . . . . . **551.80**

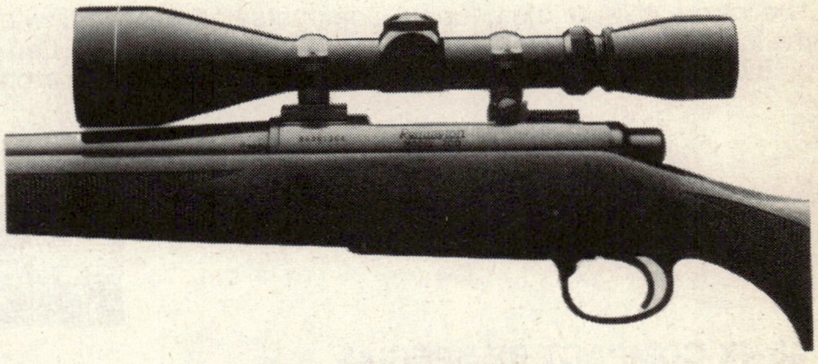

VARI-X II 3X9–50mm

**VARI-X II 3X9–50mm**
This LOV scope delivers a 5.5mm exit pupil, providing excellent low-light visibility. . . . . . . . . . . . . . . . . . . . . . . . . . . . . **$469.60**
With matte finish: . . . . . . . . . . . . . . . . . . . . . . . . . . . . **491.10**

**VARI-X II 3X9 DUPLEX**
A wide selection of powers lets you choose the right combination of field of view and magnification to fit the particular conditions you are hunting at the time. Many hunters use the 3X or 4X setting most of the time, cranking up to 9X for positive identification of game or for extremely long shots. The adjustable objective eliminates parallax and permits precise focusing on any object from less than 50 yards to infinity for extra-sharp definition. . . . . . . . . . . . . . . . . . . . . . . . . . . **$391.10**
Also available in matte or silver: . . . . . . . . . . . . . . . . **412.50**

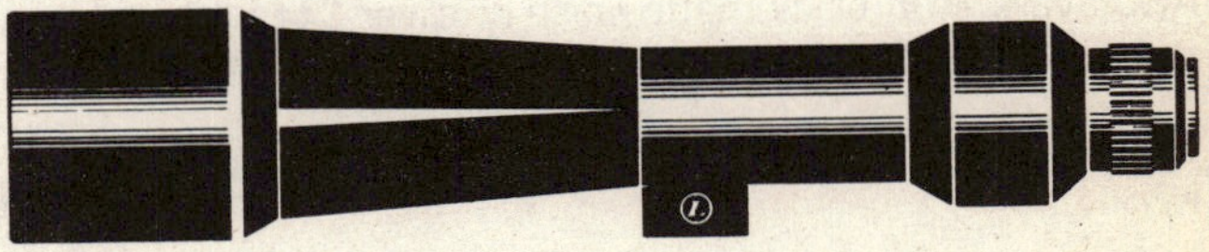

ARMORED SPOTTING SCOPE

**SPOTTING SCOPES**
Leupold's Golden Ring Armored Spotting Scopes feature extraordinary eye relief and crisp, bright roof prism optics housed in a lightweight, sealed, waterproof body. The Spotting Scopes come complete with a self-storing screw-on sunshade, lens caps, and a green canvas case. Now available in 12X40-60mm variable power with 30.8mm eye relief at 20X.

**Prices:**
**20X50mm Compact Armored** . . . . . . . . . . . . . . . **$646.40**
**25X50mm Compact Armored** . . . . . . . . . . . . . . . **689.30**
**30X60mm** . . . . . . . . . . . . . . . . . . . . . . . . . . . . . . . **710.70**
**12X40-60mm Variable Power** . . . . . . . . . . . . . . . **1026.80**

## THE COMPACT SCOPE LINE

The introduction of the Leupold Compacts has coincided with the increasing popularity of the new featherweight rifles. Leupold Compact scopes give a more balanced appearance atop these new scaled-down rifles and offer generous eye relief, magnification and field of view, yet are smaller inside and out. Fog-free.

4X COMPACT & 4X RF SPECIAL

### M8-4X COMPACT RF SPECIAL

The 4X RF Special is focused to 75 yards and has a Duplex reticle with finer crosshairs. **$326.80**

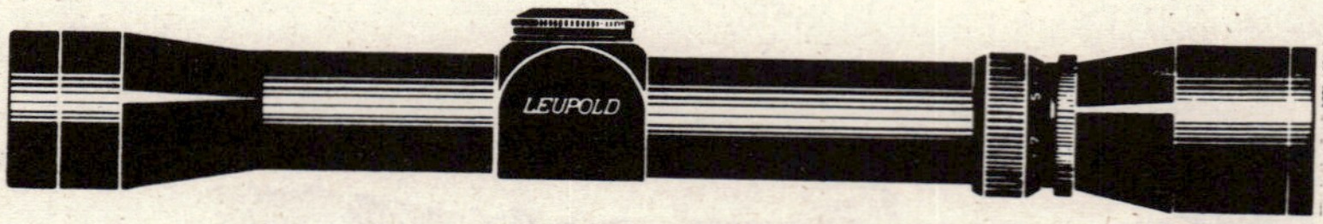


2X7 COMPACT

### 2X7 COMPACT

Two ounces lighter and a whole inch shorter than its full-size counterpart, this 2X7 is one of the world's most compact variable power scopes. It's the perfect hunting scope for today's trend toward smaller and lighter rifles. **$405.40**

3X9 COMPACT

### 3X9 COMPACT

The 3X9 Compact is a full-blown variable that's 3½ ounces lighter and 1.3 inches shorter than a standard 3X9. **$419.60** Also available in black matte finish or silver **$441.10**

3X9 COMPACT SILVER

### SHOTGUN SCOPES (not shown)

Leupold shotgun scopes are parallax-adjusted to deliver precise focusing at 75 yards (as opposed to 150 yards usually prescribed for rifle scopes). Each scope features a special Heavy Duplex reticle that is more effective against heavy, brushy backgrounds.

**Prices:**

| | |
|---|---|
| **Vari-X II 1X4 Model Heavy Duplex** | **$378.60** |
| **M8-4X Heavy Duplex** | **348.20** |
| **Vari-X III 2X7 Heavy Duplex** | **408.90** |

# LEUPOLD SCOPES

SCOPES

## HANDGUN SCOPES

**M8-2X EER**
With an optimum eye relief of 12–24 inches, the 2X EER is an excellent choice for most handguns. It is equally favorable for carbines and other rifles with top ejection that calls for forward mounting of the scope. Available in black anodized or silver finish to match stainless steel and nickel-plated handguns. **$264.30**. In silver finish: **$285.70**

**LASERLIGHT HANDGUN SIGHT (not shown)**
This advanced electronic device projects a laser dot, the result of a collimated coherent laser beam. Micro circuitry pulses the diode thousands of times per second, placing a dot of light where the bullet will impact the target: **$266.10**

**2X EER**

**M8-4X EER**
Only 8.4 inches long and 7.6 ounces. Optimum eye relief 12–24 inches. Available in black anodized or silver finish to match stainless steel and nickel-plated handguns. In matte or silver finish: **$357.10**

Also available:
**VARI-X 2.5X8 EER w/Multicoat 4: $514.30.** In silver: **$535.70**

## FIXED-POWER SCOPES

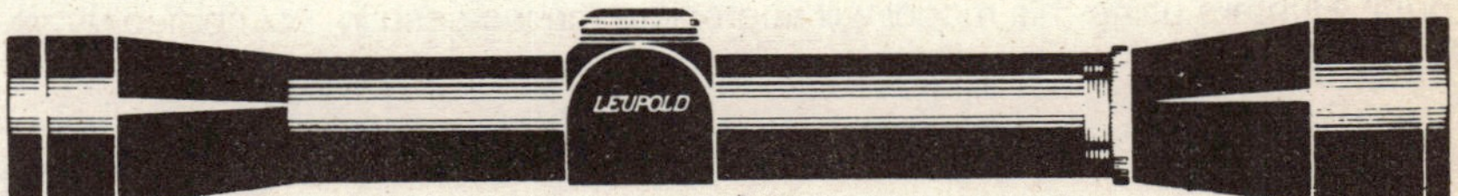

**4X**

**M8-4X**
The all-time favorite is the 4X, which delivers a widely used magnification and a generous field of view. **$326.80.** In black matte finish: **$348.20**

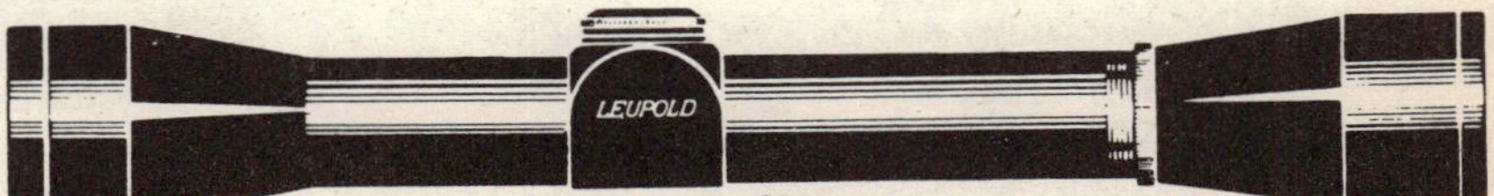

**6X**

**M8-6X**
Gaining popularity fast among fixed power scopes is the 6X, which can extend the range for big-game hunting and double, in some cases, as a varmint scope: **$348.20**

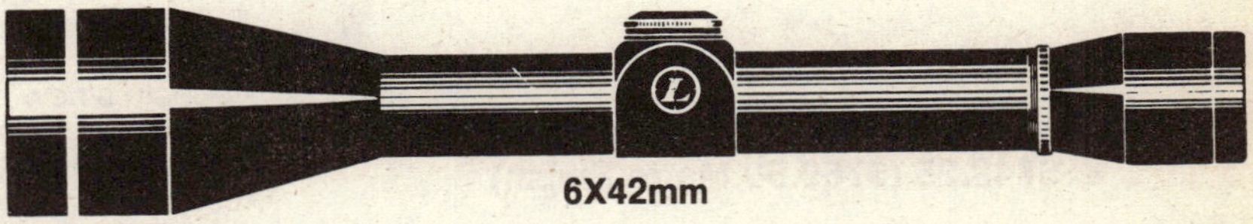
**6X42mm**

**M8-6X42mm W/Multicoat 4**
Large 42mm objective lens features increased light gathering capability and a 7mm exit pupil. Great for varmint shooting at night. Duplex or Heavy Duplex: **$432.10.** In matte finish: **$453.60**

## VARMINT SCOPES

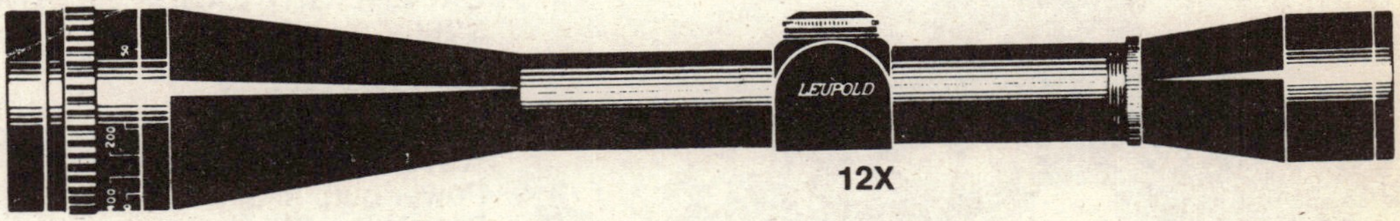

**12X**

**M8-12X STANDARD (Adj. Obj.)**
Superlative optical qualities, outstanding resolution and magnification make the 12X a natural for the varmint shooter. Adjustable objective is standard for parallax-free focusing. Duplex: **$478.60.** With CPC reticle or Dot: **$532.10**

Also available:
**VARI-X III 6.5X20 VARMINT** (Adj. Obj.) Target Dot w/Multicoat 4: **$775.00**

# LEUPOLD SCOPES

## NEW PRODUCTS FOR 1996

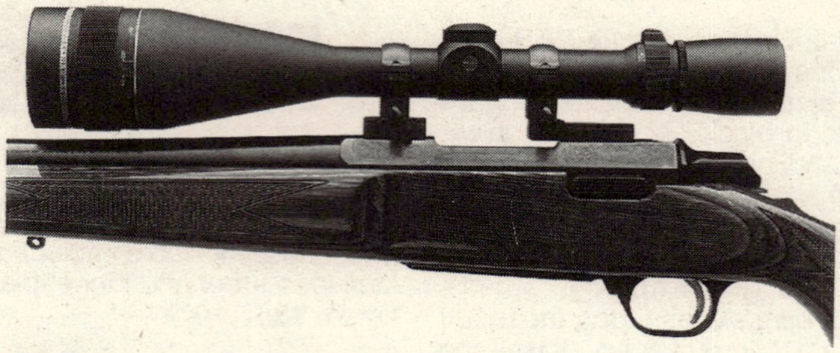

### LEUPOLD VARI-X III 6.5X20-50mm
### $814.50

Leupold has added a 6.5X20 with a 50mm objective lens to its Vari-X III line of riflescopes. The benefit of the 50mm objective to varmint and silhouette competitors is its larger exit pupil. Hunters using this model will appreciate the increase in light energy at lower powers. The new 6.5X20-50mm has all the features found in Leupold's Vari-X III line, including Multicoat 4 lens coating for increased light transmission, tactile and audible clicks in windage and elevation adjustments, a simplified range estimating feature and one-piece construction.

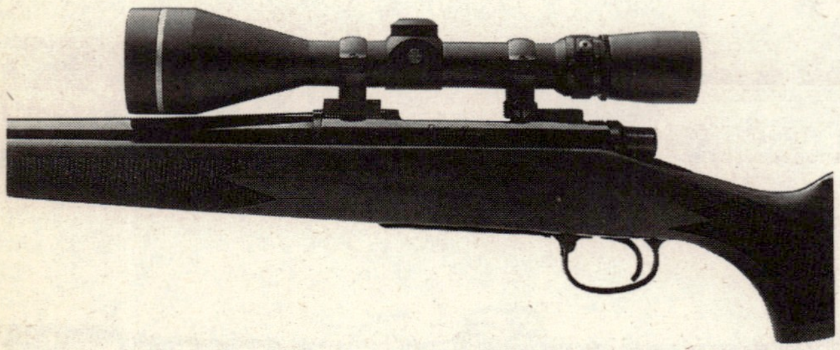

**LEUPOLD VARI-X 3.5X10-50mm**
**$748.25 ($769.50 Matte Finish)**

### LEUPOLD VARI-X III 1.75X6-32mm
### $576.80

Leupold's new scope has a maintube that extends to accommodate Magnum-action rifles. An additional 3/4-inch of mounting space on the front end of the maintube makes it easier to mount on big and dangerous game rifles. This new model also retains all the positive features of the original Vari-X III 1.75X6 (introduced in 1993), including Multicoat 4 for efficient light transmission, tactile and audible clicks on the windage and elevation adjustments, range estimating and one-piece maintube construction.

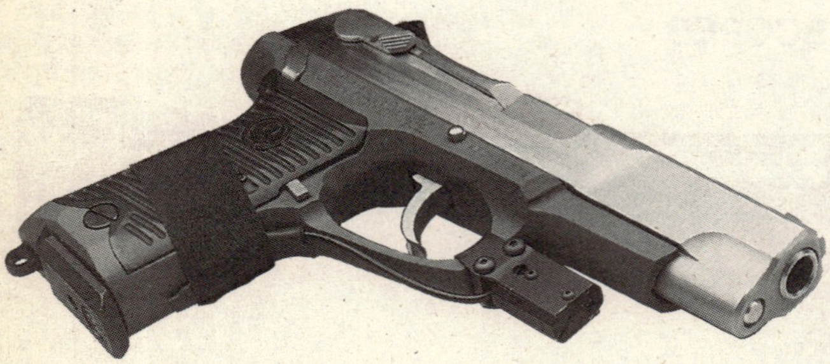

**LASERLIGHT LASER SIGHTING SYSTEM**

### LASERLIGHT LASER SIGHTING SYSTEM
### $266.00

**SPECIFICATIONS**
**Laser source:** Laser emitting diode
**Wave length:** 670nM
**Power output:** 5mW
**Dot size at 25 yds.:** 3/8″
**Battery type:** #393 silver oxide (4)
**Weight:** 1/2 ounce
**Length:** 1 3/16″ **Width:** 3/4″
**Finish:** Black matte
**Windage/elevation travel:** 100 minutes each axis
**Adjustment type:** Friction

# LYMAN SIGHTS

### 93 MATCH SIGHT

Lyman's globe front sight, the "93 Match," adapts to any rifle with a standard dovetail mounting block. The sight has a diameter of 7/8″ and comes complete with 7 target inserts. The 93 Match has a special hooked locking bolt and nut to allow quick removal or installation. Bases are available in.860 (European) and .562 (American) hole spacing. The sight height is .550 from the top of the dovetail to the center of the aperture. . . . . . . . . . . . . . . . . . . . . . . . . . . . . . . . . . . . . **$48.00**

### 90 MJT UNIVERSAL TARGET RECEIVER SIGHT (Not shown)

Designed to mount on a Marlin Model 2000 Target Rifle using standard Williams FP bases, the Target Sight features target knobs scribed with audible click detents in minute and quarter-minute graduations, plus elevation and windage direction arrows. Adjustable zero scales allow adjustments to be made without disturbing pre-set zero; quick release slide allows slide to be removed with a press of the release button. Large 7/8″ diameter non-glare .040 target aperture disk is standard. Adjustable from 1.060 to 1.560 above centerline of bore. **$79.95**

### 20 MJT 7/8″ DIAMETER GLOBE FRONT SIGHT

Machined from one solid piece of steel designed for use with dovetail slot mounting in the barrel or with Lyman's 25A dovetail base. Height is .700″ from bottom of dovetail to center of aperture. Supplied with 7 Anschutz-size steel apertures. . . . . . . . . . . . . . . . . . . . . . . . . . **$36.00**

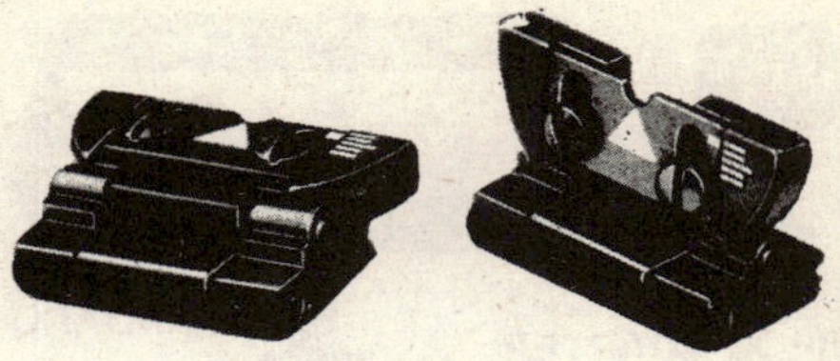

### NO. 16 FOLDING LEAF SIGHT

Designed primarily as open rear sights with adjustable elevation, leaf sights make excellent auxiliary sights for scope-mounted rifles. They fold close to the barrel when not in use, and they can be installed and left on the rifle without interfering with scope or mount. Two lock screws hold the elevation blade adjustments firmly in place. Leaf sights are available in the following heights. . . . . . . . . . . . . . . . . . . . . . . . . . . . . **$13.50**

**16A**—.400″ high; elevates to .500″
**16B**—.345″ high; elevates to .445″
**16C**—.500″ high; elevates to .600″

### LYMAN NO.2 TANG SIGHT

Recreated for the Special Edition Winchester 1894 100th Anniversary Edition, this version of the tang sight features high index marks on the aperture post with a maximum elevation of .800 for long-range shooting. Comes with both .093 quick-sighting aperture and .040 large disc aperture, plus replacement stock screw and front tang screw.

**Prices:**
For Winchester 94 Centennial . . . . . . . . . . . . . . . . . . . . . . . . . **$75.00**
For Marlin lever actions . . . . . . . . . . . . . . . . . . . . . . . . . . . . . **79.95**

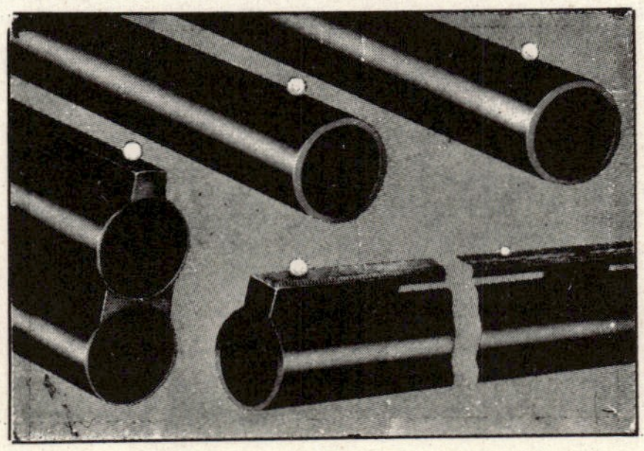

### PEEP SIGHT

The 66-MK "peep" sight fits all versions of the Knight MK-85 rifle with flat-sided receiver. The 57 SME and 57 SMET are designed for White Systems Model 91 and Whitetail models with round receivers. Both sights feature quick release slides, adjustable windage and elevation scales.

**66 MK or 57 SME/57 SMET** . . . . . . . . . . . . . . . . . . . . . . . . . . . . . . . . . . . **$68.00**

### SHOTGUN SIGHTS

**No. 10 Front Sight** (press fit) for use on double barrel, or ribbed single -barrel guns . . . . . . . . . . . . . . . . . . . . . . . . . . . . . . . . . . . . . . **$5.00**
**No. 10D Front Sight** (screw fit) for use on non-ribbed single-barrel guns; supplied with a wrench . . . . . . . . . . . . . . . . . . . . . . . . . . . . . . . . **6.50**
**No. 11 Middle Sight** (press fit). This small middle sight is intended for use on double-barrel and ribbed single-barrel guns . . . . . . . . . . . . . . . . . . . . **5.30**

# MILLETT SIGHTS

HARRIS BIPOD ADAPTER

STANDARD LOOP 1″

### FLUSH-MOUNT HARRIS BIPOD ADAPTER

Millett's flush-mount sling swivels have a simple-to-use adapter for the Harris bipod that detaches quickly so the loop can then be installed in the bipod loop receptacle. Will also fit Pachmayr flush-mount bases.

| | | |
|---|---|---|
| Harris Bipod Adapter | SS00004 | **$9.15** |

### DUAL-CRIMP INSTALLATION TOOL KIT

The Dual-Crimp System is a new revolutionary way of installing front sights on autos. Now it is not necessary to heliarc or silver solder to get a good secure job. Dual-Crimp has a two-post, hollow rivet design that works very much like an aircraft rivet and withstands the heavy abuse of hardball ammo. Your choice of four styles and nine heights. Dual-Crimp is the quick and easy system for professionals. Requires a drill press.

| | |
|---|---|
| Dual-Crimp Tool Set, Complete | **$150.00** |
| Application Tool | **80.80** |
| Reverse counterbore (solid carbide) | **38.70** |
| 3/16″ Drill (solid carbide) | **17.90** |
| Drill Jig | **23.05** |

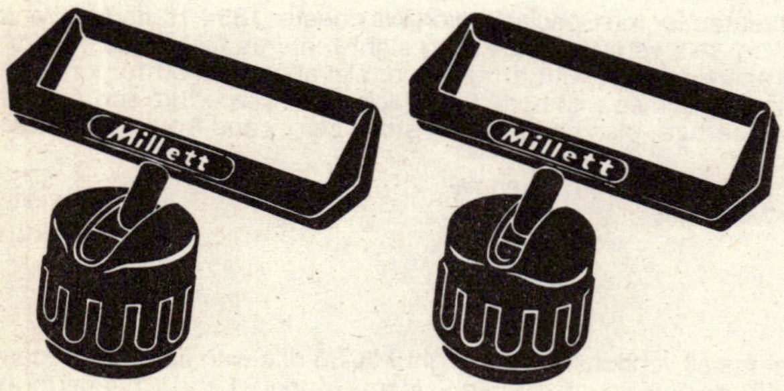


### FLUSH-MOUNT SLING SWIVELS

Millett's flush-mount redesigned Pachmayr sling swivels are quick detachable and beautifully styled in heat-treated nickel steel. The sling swivel loop has been redesigned to guide the sling into the loop, eliminating twisitng and fraying on edges of sling. Millett flush-mount bases are much easier to install than the old Pachmayr design, with no threading and an easy to use step drill.

| | | |
|---|---|---|
| Flush-Mount Swivels (pair) | SS00001 | **$16.45** |
| Loops Only | SS00002 | **9.15** |
| Installation Drill | SS00003 | **17.58** |

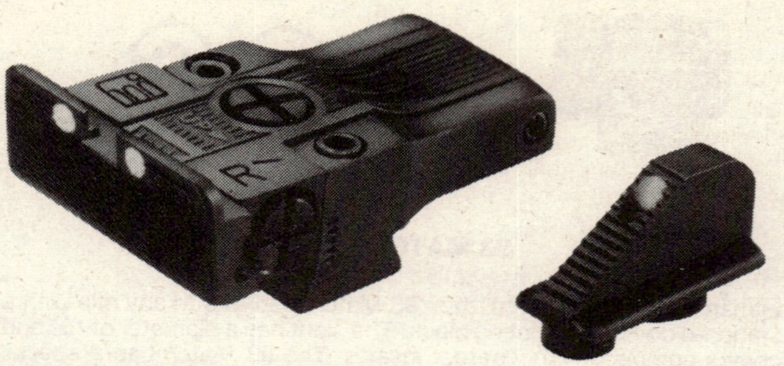

### 3-DOT SYSTEM SIGHTS

Millett announces 3-Dot System sights for a wide variety of popular handguns.

**3-Dot System Front and Rear Sight Selection Chart (partial listing only)**

**DUAL-CRIMP™ FRONTS (White Dot)** . . . . . . . . . . . . **$16.00**

| | |
|---|---|
| DC 18500 | .185 Height |
| DC 20004 | .200 Height |
| DC 22512 | .225 Height |
| DC31216 | .312 Height |
| DC34020 | .340 Height |
| DC36024 | .360 Height |

**WIDE STAKE-ON FRONTS (White Dot)** . . . . . . . . . . **$16.00**
**(for Colt pistols only, after June 1988)**

| | |
|---|---|
| WS18504 | .185 Height |
| WS20008 | .200 Height |
| WS31220 | .312 Height |
| WS22504 | .225 Height |

**SPECIAL-APPLICATION PISTOL FRONTS** . . . . . . . **$16.00**

| | | |
|---|---|---|
| GL00006 | Glock 17, 17L & 19 | |
| RP85009 | Ruger-P-85 | |
| RS22015 | Ruger Std. Auto (Fixed Model) | |
| SP22567 | Sig Sauer P225/226, Dovetail | |
| SW40513 | S&W 3rd Generation, Dovetail | |
| SW46913 | S&W 3rd Generation, Dovetail | |
| BE00010 | Beretta Accurizer | **25.14** |

**AUTOPISTOL REAR SIGHTS**

| | | |
|---|---|---|
| BE00003 | Beretta | **$56.40** |
| BA00008 | Browning Hi-Power, Adjustable | **55.60** |
| BF00008 | Browning Hi-Power, Fixed | **55.60** |
| CA00008 | Colt-Hi-Profile | **55.60** |
| CC00008 | Colt Custom Combat Lo-Profile | **55.60** |
| GC00008 | Colt Gold Cup | **49.30** |
| RP85008 | Ruger P-85 | **55.60** |
| RS22003 | Ruger Std. Auto | **55.60** |
| SP22005 | Sig P220, 225, 226 | **55.60** |
| SW40504 | Smith & Wesson, ALL Factory Adjustable (incl. 2nd & 3rd Generation)* | **55.60** |
| SW46904 | Smith & Wesson, ALL Factory Fixed (incl. 2nd & 3rd Generation)* | **55.60** |

** 2nd Generation use DC Fronts; 3rd Generation use Dovetail Fronts*

# MILLETT REVOLVER SIGHTS

## COLT REVOLVER

The Series 100 Adjustable Sight System offers today's discriminating Colt owner the finest quality replacement sight available. 12 crisp click stops for each turn of adjustment, delivers 5/8″ of adjustment per click at 100 yards with a 6″ barrel. For Colt Python, Trooper, Diamond Back and new Frontier single action army.

| | | |
|---|---|---|
| Rear Only (White Outline) | CR00001 | **$49.30** |
| Rear Only (Target Blade) | CR00002 | **49.30** |
| Rear Only (Silhouette) | CR00003 | **49.30** |

Colt owners will really appreciate the high-visability feature of Colt front sights. Easy to install—just drill 2 holes in the new sight and pin on. All steel. Your choice of blaze orange or white bar. Fits 4″, 6″ & 8″ barrels only.

| | | |
|---|---|---|
| Colt Python & Anaconda (White or Orange Bar) | FB00007-8 | **$13.60** |
| Diamond Back, King Cobra, Peacemaker | FB00015-16 | **13.60** |

## SMITH & WESSON

The Series 100 Adjustable Sight System for Smith & Wesson revolvers provides the sight picture and crisp click adjustments desired by the discriminating shooter. 1/2″ of adjustment per click, at 100 yards on elevation, and 5/8″ on windage, with a 6″ barrel. Can be installed in a few minutes, using factory front sight.

**Smith & Wesson N Frame:**
**N.312**—Model 25-5, all bbl., 27-3 1/2″ & 5″, 28-4″ & 6″
**N.360**—Model 25, 27, 29, 57, & 629-4, 6 & 6 1/2″ bbl.
**N.410**—Model 27, 29, 57, 629 with 8 3/8″ bbl.

**Smith & Wesson K&L Frame:**
**K.312**—Models 14, 15, 18, 48-4″, & 53
**K&L360**—Models 16, 17, 19, 48-6″, 8 3/8″, 66, 686, 586

**Smith & Wesson K&L-Frame $49.30**

| | |
|---|---|
| Rear Only .312 (White Outline) | SK00001 |
| Rear Only .312 (Target Blade) | SK00002 |
| Rear Only .360 (White Outline) | SK00003 |
| Rear Only .360 (Target Blade) | SK00004 |
| Rear Only .410 (White Outline) | SK00005 |
| Rear Only .410 (Target Blade) | SK00006 |

**Smith & Wesson K&N Old Style $49.30**

| | |
|---|---|
| Rear Only .312 (White Outline) | KN00001 |
| Rear Only .312 (Target Blade) | KN00002 |
| Rear Only .360 (White Outline) | KN00003 |
| Rear Only .360 (Target Blade) | KN00004 |
| Rear Only .410 (White Outline) | KN00005 |
| Rear Only .410 (Target Blade) | KN00006 |

**Smith & Wesson N-Frame $49.30**

| | |
|---|---|
| Rear Only .312 (White Outline) | SN00001 |
| Rear Only .312 (Target Blade) | SN00002 |
| Rear Only .360 (White Outline) | SN00003 |
| Rear Only .360 (Target Blade) | SN00001 |
| Rear Only .410 (White Outline) | SN00005 |
| Rear Only .410 (Target Blade) | KN00006 |

## RUGER

The high-visibility white outline sight picture and precision click adjustments of the Series 100 Adjustable Sight System will greatly improve the accuracy and fast sighting capability of your Ruger. 3/4″ per click at 100 yard for elevation, 5/8″ per click for windage, with 6″ barrel. Can be easily installed, using factory front sight or all-steel replacement front sight which is a major improvement over the factory front. Visibility is greatly increased for fast sighting. Easy to install by drilling one hole in the new front sight.

The Red Hawk all-steel replacement front sight is highly visible and easy to pick up under all lighting conditions. Easy to install. Fits the factory replacement system.

**SERIES 100 Ruger Double Action Revolver Sights**

| | |
|---|---|
| Rear Sight (fits all adjustable models) | **$49.30** |
| Front Sight (Security Six, Police Six, Speed Six) | **13.60** |
| Front Sight (Redhawk) | **9.60** |

**SERIES 100 Ruger Single Action Revolver Sights**

| | |
|---|---|
| Rear Sight (Black Hawk Standard & Super; Bisley Large Frame, Single-Six | **$49.30** |
| Front Sight (Millett Replacement sights not available for Ruger single action revolvers). | |

**TAURUS**

| | |
|---|---|
| Rear, .360 White Outline | **$49.30** |
| Rear, .360 Target Blade | **49.30** |

## DAN WESSON

This sight is exactly what every Dan Wesson owner has been looking for. The Series 100 Adjustable Sight System provides 12 crisp click stops for each turn of adjustment, with 5/8″ per click for windage, with a 6″ barrel. Can be easily installed, using the factory front or new Millett high-visibility front sights.

Choice of white outline or target blade.

| | | |
|---|---|---|
| Rear Only (White Outline) | DW00001 | **$49.30** |
| Rear Only (Target Blade) | DW00002 | **49.30** |
| Rear Only (White Outline) 44 Mag. | DW00003 | **49.30** |
| Rear Only (Target Blade) 44 Mag. | DW00004 | **49.30** |

If you want super-fast sighting capability for your Dan Wesson, the new Millett blaze orange or white bar front is the answer. Easy to install. Fits factory quick-change system. All steel, no plastic. Available in both heights.

| | | |
|---|---|---|
| Dan Wesson .44 Mag (White Bar) (high) | FB00009 | **$12.95** |
| Dan Wesson .44 Mag (Orange Bar) (high) | FB00010 | **13.60** |
| Dan Wesson 22 Caliber (White Bar) (low) | FB00011 | **13.60** |
| Dan Wesson 22 Caliber (Orange Bar) (low) | FB00012 | **13.60** |

# MILLETT AUTO PISTOL SIGHTS

### RUGER STANDARD AUTO

The Ruger Standard Auto Combo provides a highly visible sight picture even under low-light conditions. The blaze orange or white bar front sight allows the shooter to get on target fast. Great for target use or plinking. Uses Factory Front Sight on adjustable model guns when using Millett target rear only. All other installations use Millett Front Sight. Easy to install.

| | |
|---|---|
| Rear Only (White Outline) | **$55.60** |
| Rear Only (Silhouette Target Blade) | **55.60** |
| Rear Only (Target Blade) | **55.60** |
| Front Only (White), Fixed Model | **16.00** |
| Front Only (Orange), Fixed Model | **16.00** |
| Front Only (Serrated Ramp), Fixed Model | **16.00** |
| Front Only (Target-Adjustable Model/White Bar) | **16.00** |
| Front Only (Target-Adjustable Model/Orange Bar) | **16.00** |
| Front Only Bull Barrel (White or Orange Ramp) | **17.60** |

### RUGER P85

| | |
|---|---|
| Rear (White Outline) | **$55.60** |
| Rear (Target Blade) | **55.60** |
| Front (White Ramp) | **16.00** |
| Front (Orange Ramp) | **16.00** |
| Front (Serrated Ramp) | **16.00** |

### TAURUS PT92

| | |
|---|---|
| Rear (White Outline, use Beretta Front) | **$55.60** |
| Rear (Target Blade, use Beretta Front) | **55.60** |
| Front (White Bar) | **25.14** |
| Front (Orange Bar) | **25.14** |
| Front (Serrated Ramp) | **25.14** |

### GLOCK 17, 17L & 19

| | |
|---|---|
| Rear (White Outline) | **$55.60** |
| Rear (Target Blade) | **55.60** |
| Rear (3-Dot) | **55.60** |

### GLOCK STAKE-ON FRONT SIGHTS

| | |
|---|---|
| Front .340 White Bar | **$16.00** |
| Front .340 Orange Bar | **16.00** |
| Front .340 Serrated Ramp | **16.00** |
| Front .340 White Dot | **16.00** |

### COLT

| | |
|---|---|
| Colt Gold Cup Marksman Speed Rear Only (Target .410 Blade) | **$49.30** |
| Custom Combat Low Profile Marksman Speed Rear Only (Target .410 Blade) | **55.60** |
| Colt Gold Cup Rear (use DC or WS 200 Frt) | **49.30** |
| Colt Mark I Fixed Rear Only (use .200 front) | **19.75** |
| Colt Mark II Fixed Rear Only (use .200 front) | **34.60** |

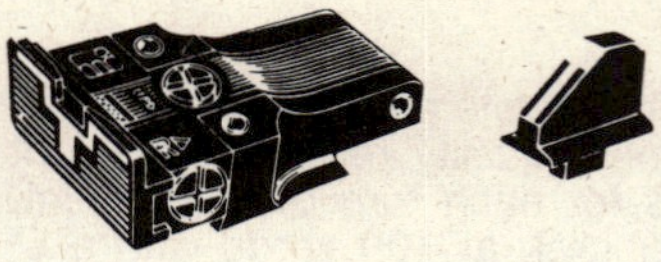

**RUGER**

**COLT**

**COLT GOLD CUP**

**MARK II HI-PROFILE**

### COLT WIDE STAKE FRONT SIGHTS (POST 6/88) $16.00

.185 WS White Bar
.185 WS Orange Bar
.185 WS Serrated Ramp
.185 WS White Dot
.200 WS White Bar
.200 WS Orange Bare with Skirt
.200 WS Serrated Ramp with Skirt
.200 WS White Dot with Skirt
.312 WS White Bar with Skirt
.312 WS Orange Bar with Skirt
.312 WS Serrated Ramp with Skirt
.312 WS White Dot with Skirt

### SIG/SAUER P-220, P-225, P-226

Now Sig Pistol owners can obtain a Series-100 adjustable sight system for their guns. Precision click adjustment for windage and elevation makes it easy to zero when using different loads. The high-visibility features assures fast sight acquisition when under the poorest light conditions. Made of high-quality heat-treated nickel steel and built to last. Extremely easy to install on P-225 and P-226. The P-220 and Browning BDA 45 require the Dual-Crimp front sight installation.

| | | |
|---|---|---|
| Sig P220-25-26 Rear Only (White)* | SP22003 | **$55.60** |
| Sig P220-25-26 Rear Only (Target)* | SP22004 | **55.60** |
| Sig P225-6 (White) Dovetail Front* | SP22565 | **16.00** |
| Sig P225-6 (Orange) Dovetail Front* | SP22566 | **16.00** |

** The Sig P220 Uses .360 Dual-Crimp Front Sight. The Sig P225-6 Uses a Dovetail Mount Front Sight*

# MILLETT AUTO PISTOL SIGHTS

## SMITH & WESSON 39/59

This sight system provides fast and accurate sighting capability even under low-light conditions. The unique white outline rear blade teamed up with the blaze orange or white bar front sight creates a highly visible sight picture, ideal for match or duty use.

| | | |
|---|---|---|
| Rear Only (White outline) | SW39595 | **$59.30** |
| Rear Only (Target Blade) | SW39596 | **59.30** |

*Requires .340 Dual-Crimp Front*

**SMITH & WESSON 2ND AND 3RD GENERATION**
**FITS FACTORY ADJUSTABLE $56.80**
Rear (3-Dot)
Rear (White Outline)
Rear (Target Blade)
**FITS FACTORY FIXED $55.60**
Rear (3-Dot)
Rear (White Outline)
Rear (Target Blade)
**THIRD GENERATION FRONT SIGHTS $16.00**
Front Dovetail White Bar .260
Front Dovetail Orange Bar .260
Front Dovetail Serrated Ramp .260
Front Dovetail White Dot .260
Front Dovetail White Bar .385
Front Dovetail Orange Bar .385
Front Dovetail Serrated Ramp .385
Front Dovetail White Dot .385

## BROWNING HI-POWER

The Series 100 Adjustable Sight System for Browning Hi-Power will provide accurate high-visibility sighting for both fixed and adjustable slides with no machine modifications required to the dovetail. Most adjustable slide model Hi-Powers can use the factory front sight as shown in the photo. The fixed slide model requires a new front sight installation. We highly recommend the Dual-Crimp front sight installation on this gun.

**BROWNING HI-POWER (Adjustable Slide Model)**

| | | |
|---|---|---|
| Rear Only (White Outline) | BA00009 | **$55.60** |
| Rear Only (Target Blade) | BA00010 | **55.60** |

*High-Power Requires .340 High Front Sight.*

**BROWNING HI-POWER (Fixed Slide Model)**

| | | |
|---|---|---|
| Rear Only (White Outline) | BF00009 | **$55.60** |
| Rear Only (Target Blade) | BF00010 | **55.60** |

*High-Power Requires .340 High Front Sight.*

**MODELS CZ75/TZ75/TA90 AUTOPISTOL SIGHTS**

| | |
|---|---|
| Rear Sight (White Outline or Target Blade) | **$55.60** |

## COLT 45

This Series 100 High Profile Adjustable Sight is rugged, all steel, precision sight which fits the standard factory dovetail with no machine modifications required. This sight provides a highly visible sight picture even under low-light conditions. Blaze orange or white bar front sight, precision click adjustments for windage and elevation makes the Colt .45 Auto Combo the handgunner's choice.

| | | |
|---|---|---|
| Rear Only (White Outline) | CA00009 | **$55.60** |
| Rear Only (Target Blade) | CA00010 | **55.60** |
| Rear (Marksman, .410 Blade) | CA00018 | **55.60** |

*Colt Gov. and Com. Require .312 High Front Sight.*

## BERETTA ACCURIZER

This amazing new sight system not only provides a highly visible sight picture but also tunes the barrel lockup to improve your accuracy and reduce your group size by as much as 50%. The Beretta Accurizer sight system fits the 92S, 92SB, 84 and 85 models. Easy to install. Requires the drilling of one hole for installation. Your choice of rear blade styles. Front sight comes in white bar, serrated ramp or blaze orange.

| | | |
|---|---|---|
| Rear Only (White Outline) | BE00005 | **$56.40** |
| Rear Only (Target Blade) | BE00006 | **56.40** |
| Front Only (White Bar) | BE00007 | **25.14** |
| Front Only (Orange Bar) | BE00008 | **25.14** |
| Front Only (Serrated Ramp) | BE00009 | **25.14** |

*Fits Models 92S, 92SB, 85, 84*

**NEW BAR-DOT-BAR™ TRITIUM NIGHT SIGHT COMBOS**

| | |
|---|---|
| **Ruger** P-85, 89, 90 Combo | **$135.00** |
| **Sig Sauer** P225/226/228 & New P220 Combo | **135.00** |
| **Sig Sauer** P220 (Prior to 10-90) Combo | **135.00** |
| **Browning Hi-Power** (Fixed Model) Combo | **135.00** |
| **Browning Hi-Power** (Fixed Model Dovetail Front) | **135.00** |
| **Colt Auto Combo** | **135.00** |
| **Colt Custom Combat** Low Profile Combo | **135.00** |
| **CZ-75**/TZ-75, TA-90 Combo | **135.00** |
| **Glock** 17, 19, 20, 21, 22, 23 Combo | **135.00** |
| **S & W** 3rd Generation Fixed Combo | **135.00** |
| **S & W** 2nd Generation Fixed Combo | **135.00** |
| **Beretta** 92SB, 85, 84 Combo | **143.50** |
| **Taurus** PT-92 Combo | **143.50** |

# MILLETT

**BENCHMASTER PISTOL REST**
**$39.95**

**BENCHMASTER RIFLE REST**
**$39.95**

**BENCHMASTER WINDOW REST (not shown)**
**$19.95**

**ELECTRONIC RED DOT SIGHTS**
**$189.95 (1″ Compact, Blue or Silver)**
**$289.95 (30mm Wide View)**

## ONE-PIECE COMBO PAKS $56.25

| Model | Smooth Turn-In Med | Smooth Angle-Loc™ Weaver-Style Med |
|---|---|---|
| Browning A-Bolt | CP00041 | CP00052 |
| Interarms Mk X, FN Mauser 98 | CP00043 | CP00054 |
| Remington 700 (LA-RH) | CP00040 | CP00051 |
| Remington 700 (SA-RH) 600, 7, XP-100 | CP00039 | CP00050 |
| Remington 7400/7600/4/6 | CP00044 | CP00055 |
| Winchester 70 (LA-RH) | CP00045 | CP00056 |

## MAGAZINES

| Description | Price |
|---|---|
| Ruger Double 10, 10/22, M77, AMT Lighting | $28.95 |
| Remington Short Action .308, .243, 10 rounds; | 19.95 |
| Auto & Pumps 740, 742, 760, 7400, 7600, 4 & 6 | 19.95 |
| Remington Long Action .30-06, .270, .280, 7mm, | |
| 10 rounds; Auto and Pumps 740, 742, 760, 7400, | |
| 7600, 4 and 6 | 19.95 |
| 45 ACP, 7 rounds, flush fit, blued steel | 24.95 |
| 45 ACP, 7 rounds, flush fit, stainless steel | 29.95 |
| 45 ACP, 8 rounds, flush fit, follower, fixed | |
| base, blued steel | 24.95 |
| 45 ACP, 8 rounds, flush fit, safety orange | |
| follower, fixed base, stainless steel | 29.95 |
| Mini-14, 10 round Lexan | 20.00 |
| Mini-30, 10 round Lexan | 20.00 |

## TWO-PIECE COMBO PACKS

| Model | Low | Med | Price |
|---|---|---|---|
| Browning A-Bolt | CP00017 (Smooth) | CP00018 (Smooth) | $56.25 |
| | CP00019 (Engraved) | CP00020 (Engraved) | 71.30 |
| | CP00037 (Nickel) | CP00038 (Nickel) | 68.15 |
| | CP00717 (Matte) | CP00718 (Matte) | 56.25 |
| Browning BAR/BLR | CP00013 (Smooth) | CP00014 (Smooth) | 56.25 |
| | CP00015 (Engraved) | CP00016 (Engraved) | 71.30 |
| Interarms Mk X, FN | CP00005 (Smooth) | CP00006 (Smooth) | 56.25 |
| | CP00007 (Engraved) | CP00008 (Engraved) | 71.30 |
| Marlin 336 | CP00025 (Smooth) | CP00026 (Smooth) | 56.25 |
| | CP00027 (Engraved) | CP00028 (Engraved) | 71.30 |
| Remington 700 | CP00001 (Smooth) | CP00002 (Smooth) | 56.25 |
| | CP00023 (Engraved) | CP00024 (Engraved) | 71.30 |
| | CP00901 (Nickel) | CP00902 (Nickel) | 68.15 |
| | | CP00702 (Matte) | 56.25 |
| Remington 7400/7600/4/6 | CP00021 (Smooth) | CP00022 (Smooth) | 56.25 |
| | CP00003 (Engraved) | CP00004 (Engraved) | 71.30 |
| Savage 110 | CP00033 (Smooth) | CP00034 (Smooth) | 56.25 |
| | CP00035 (Engraved) | CP00036 (Engraved) | 71.30 |
| | | CP00934 (Nickel) | 68.15 |
| | | CP00734 (Matte) | 56.25 |
| Winchester 70 | CP00009 (Smooth) | CP00010 (Smooth) | 56.25 |
| | CP00011 (Engraved) | CP00012 (Engraved) | 71.30 |
| | CP00909 (Nickel) | CP00910 (Nickel) | 68.15 |
| Winchester 94 | CP00029 (Smooth) | CP00030 (Smooth) | 56.25 |
| | CP00031 (Engraved) | CP00032 (Engraved) | 71.30 |

# NIKON SCOPES

## PISTOL SCOPES

**Key Features:**
- Edge to edge sharpness for precise detection of camouflaged game
- Super multicoating and blackened internal metal parts provide extreme reduction of flare and image ghost-out
- Aluminum alloy one-piece 1″ tube provides lightweight but rugged construction (fully tested on Magnum calibers)
- 1/4 MOA windage/elevation adjustment
- Extended eye relief
- Nitrogen gas filled and 0-ring sealed for water and fogproofing
- Black Lustre or satin silver finish

**Prices:**

| | |
|---|---|
| **2X20 EER** | **$213.00** |
| **1.5-4.5X24 EER** | **352.00** |

**2X20 EER PISTOL SCOPE**

**1.5-4.5X24 EER PISTOL SCOPE**

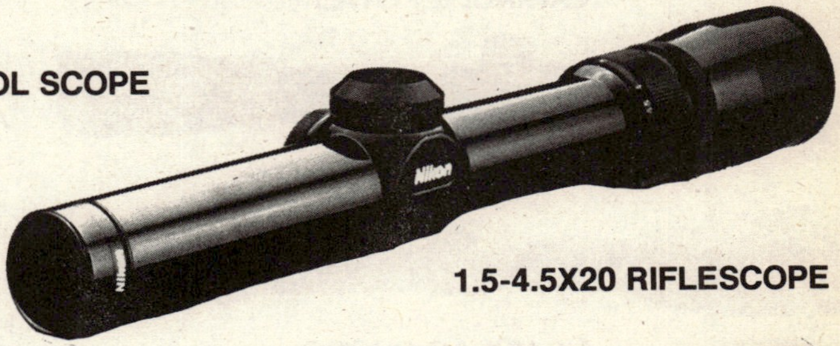
**1.5-4.5X20 RIFLESCOPE**

## RIFLESCOPES

**Key Features:** Essentially the same as the **Pistol Scopes** (above). Available in black lustre and black matte finishes (3-9 available and 4X40 in silver).

**Prices:**

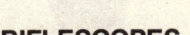

| | |
|---|---|
| **4X40** | **$284.00** |
| **1.5-4.5X20** | **352.00** |
| **2-7X32** | **367.00** |
| **3-9X40** | **371.00** |
| **4-12X40 AO** | **476.00** |
| **6.5-20X44 AO** | **591.00** |
| **3.5-10X50** | **489.00** |
| **4-12X50** | **578.00** |

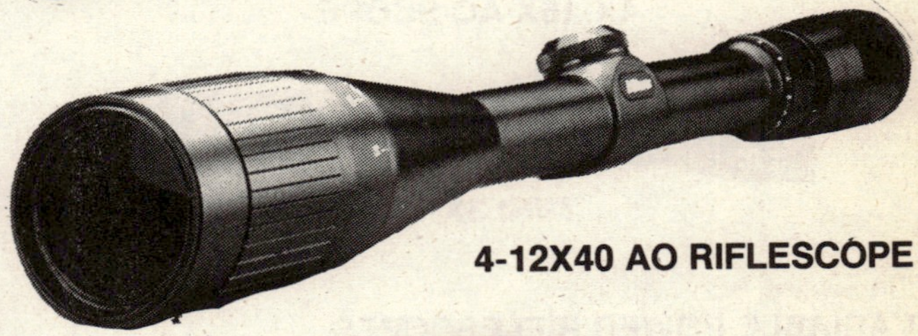
**4-12X40 AO RIFLESCOPE**

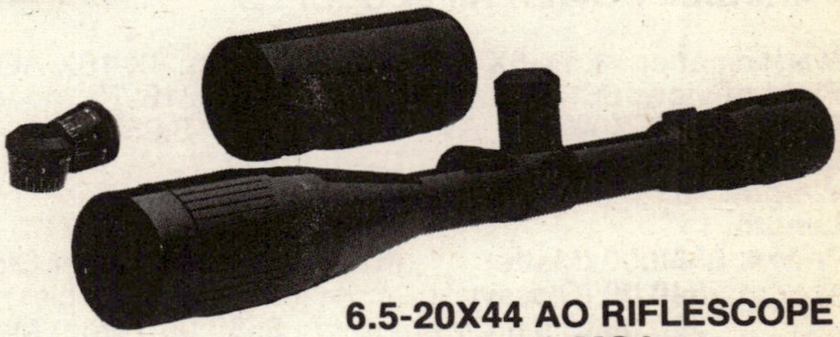
**6.5-20X44 AO RIFLESCOPE**
**1/8 MOA**

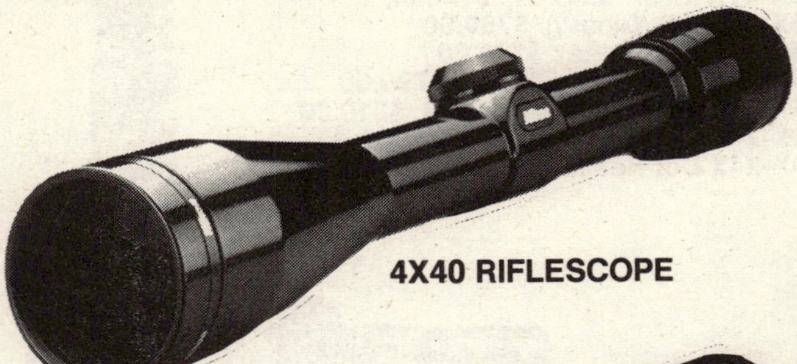
**4X40 RIFLESCOPE**

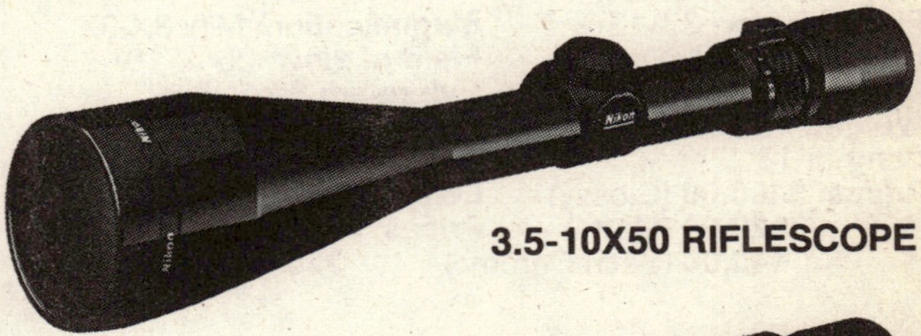
**3.5-10X50 RIFLESCOPE**

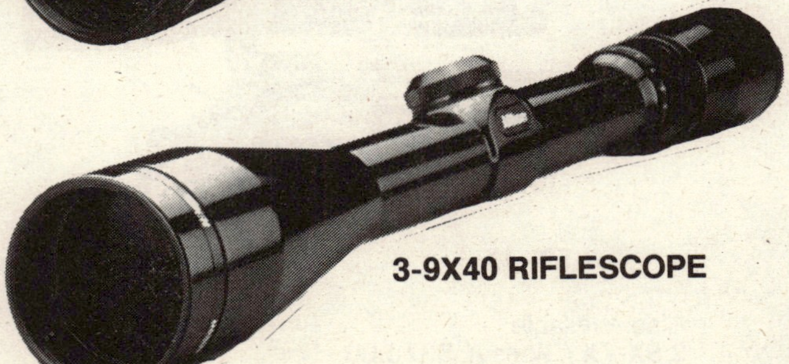
**3-9X40 RIFLESCOPE**

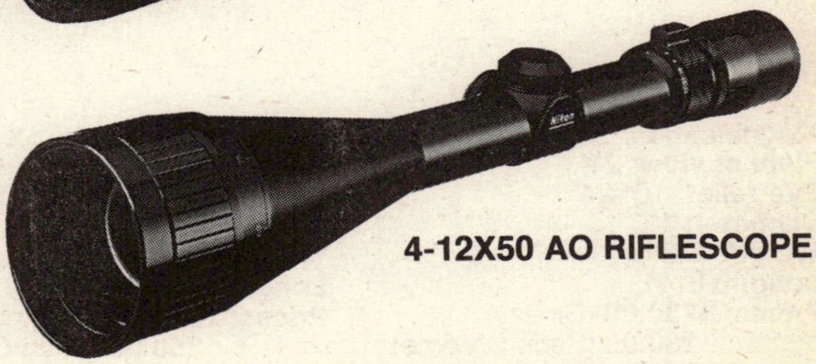
**4-12X50 AO RIFLESCOPE**

# PENTAX SCOPES

ZERO-XSG

VARIABLE POWER

3X-9X

4X-16X AO SCOPE

MINI 3X-9X

## LIGHTSEEKER SG PLUS

**Magnification:** 2½X SG Plus
**Field of view:** 55′
**Eye relief:** 3.25″
**Diameter:** 1″
**Weight:** 9 oz.
**Length:** 10″
**Prices: $290.00** (Glossy)
**310.00** (Matte)
**$330.00** (Mossy Oak)

**Magnification:** Zero-X
**Field of view:** 51′
**Eye relief:** 4.5″-15″
**Diameter:** 1″
**Weight:** 7.9 oz.
**Length:** 8.9″
**Prices: $348.00** (Glossy)
**360.00** (Matte)

Also available: **Zero-X/V $420.00** (glossy); **$440.00** (matte)

## LIGHTSEEKER 3X-9X RIFLESCOPE

**Field of view:** 36-14′
**Eye relief:** 3″
**Diameter:** 1″
**Weight:** 15 oz.
**Length:** 12.7″
**Prices: $540.00** (Glossy)
**560.00** (Matte)
**580.00** (Satin)

Also available:
**2X-8X** (Glossy): **$510.00**
**2X-8X** (Matte): **$530.00**
**2X-8X** (Satin Chrome): **$550.00**
**3.5X-10X** (Glossy): **$560.00**
**3.5X-10X** (Pro Matte): **$580.00**
**3.5X-10X** (Chrome): **$600.00**
**3X-11X** (Glossy-XL): **$700.00**
**3X-11X** (Pro Matte): **$720.00**
**3X-11X** (Satin Chrome): **$740.00**
**4X-16X AO** (Glossy): **$750.00**
**4X-16X AO** (matte): **$770.00**
**6X-24X Fine Plex** (Glossy): **$790.00**
**6X-24X Fine Plex** (Pro Matte): **$810.00**
**6X-24X Dot Reticle** (Glossy): **$800.00**
**6X-24X Dot Reticle** (Pro Matte): **$820.00**

LIGHTSEEKER 3X-11X

## VARIABLE POWER RIFLESCOPES

**Magnification:** 1.5X-5X
**Field of view:** 66′-25′
**Eye relief:** 3″-3¼″
**Diameter:** 1″
**Weight:** 13 oz.
**Length:** 11″
**Prices: $360.00** (Matte)
**340.00** (Glossy)
**380.00** (Satin Chrome)

**Magnification:** 6X-18X AO
**Field of view:** 16′-7′
**Eye relief:** 3″-3.25″
**Diameter:** 1″
**Weight:** 18.5 oz.
**Length:** 15.8″
**Prices: $540.00** Target Glossy (fine plex)
**$560.00** Target Matte (fine plex)

**Magnification:** 3X-9X
**Field of view:** 33′-13½′
**Eye relief:** 3″-3¼″
**Diameter:** 1″
**Weight:** 15 oz.
**Length:** 13″
**Prices: $400.00** (Glossy)
**420.00** (Matte)
**440.00** (Satin Chrome)

**Magnification:** Mini 3X-9X
**Field of view:** 26½′-10½′
**Eye relief:** 3¼″
**Diameter:** 1″
**Weight:** 13 oz.
**Length:** 10.4″
**Prices: $340.00** (Mini Glossy)
**360.00** (Matte)

## PISTOL SCOPES

**Magnification:** 2X
**Field of view:** 21′
**Eye relief:** 10″-24″
**Diameter:** 1″
**Weight:** 6.8 oz.
**Length:** 8¼″
**Prices: $230.00** (Glossy)
**260.00** (Satin Chrome)

**Magnification:** 1.5X-4X
**Field of view:** 16′-11′
**Eye relief:** 11″-25″/11″-18″
**Diameter:** 1″
**Weight:** 11 oz.
**Length:** 10″
**Prices: $350.00** (Glossy)
**380.00** (Satin Chrome)

1.5X-4X

Also available:
**2.5X-7X** (Glossy): **$370.00**
**2.5X-7X** (Chrome-Matte): **$390.00**

# QUARTON BEAMSHOT SIGHTS

1000 (PLUS RV2 MOUNT)

## BEAMSHOT 1000 ULTRA/SUPER

**SPECIFICATIONS**
**Size:** 3/4″×2 3/5″ (overall length)
**Weight:** 3.8 oz. (incl. battery & mount)
**Construction:** Aluminum 6061 T6
**Finish:** Black anodized
**Cable length:** 5″
**Range:** 500 yards
**Power:** <5mW Class IIIA Laser
**Wave length:** 650nm (Beamshot 1000U-635nm)
**Power supply:** 3V Lithium battery
**Battery life:** Approx. 20 hrs. (continuous)
**Dot size:** 5″ at 10 yds.; 4″ at 100 yds.
**Prices: $149.00** (Ultra) **$99.00** (Super) **$89.00** (Standard)

1000 (PLUS P1A MOUNT)

## BEAMSHOT 3000

**SPECIFICATIONS**
**Size:** 3/5″×2″ (overall length)
**Weight:** 2 oz. (incl. battery)
**Construction:** Aluminum 6061 T6
**Finish:** Black
**Cable length:** 5″
**Range:** 300 yards
**Power:** <5mW Class IIIA Laser
**Wave length:** 670nm
**Power supply:** 3 SR44 silver oxide watch battery
**Battery life:** Approx. 4 hrs. (continuous)
**Dot size:** 0.5″ at 10 yds.; 4″ at 100 yds.
**Prices: $79.00**

3000 (PLUS P4 MOUNT

# REDFIELD SCOPES

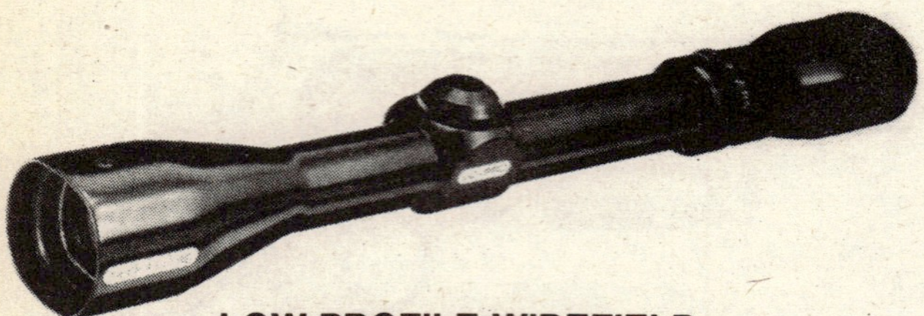

LOW PROFILE WIDEFIELD
3X-9X VARIABLE

GOLDEN FIVE STAR TARGET
ADJUST KNOBS (6X-18X)

## GOLDEN FIVE STAR SCOPES

This series of seven scopes incorporates the latest variable and fixed power scope features, including multicoated and Magnum recoil-resistant optical system, plus maximum light-gathering ability. Positive quarter-minute click adjustments for ease of sighting and optimum accuracy. Anodized finish provides scratch-resistant surface.

| **Golden Five Star Scopes:** | |
|---|---|
| 4X Fixed Power | **$259.95** |
| 6X Fixed Power | **282.95** |
| 6X Fixed Power Matte | **290.95** |
| 1X-4X Variable Power | **317.95** |
| 1X-4X Black Matte Variable Power | **326.95** |
| 2X-7X Variable Power | **333.95** |
| 3X-9X Variable Power | **357.95** |
| 3X-9X Black Matte Variable Power | **321.95** |
| 3X-9X Nickel Matte Variable Power | **331.95** |
| 3X-9X Accu-Trac Variable Power | **409.95** |
| 4X-12X Variable Power (Adj. Objective) | **455.95** |
| 4X-12X Black Matte | **462.95** |
| 4X-12X w/Target Knob (AO) | **475.95** |
| 4X-12X Black Matte Target Knob | **480.95** |
| 4X-12X Accu-Trac (AO) | **505.95** |
| 4X-12X Accu-Trac (AO) | **512.95** |
| 6X-18X Accu-Trac Black Matte | **471.95** |
| 6X-18X Variable Power (Adj. Objective) | **483.95** |
| 6X-18X Accu-Trac Variable Power (Adj. Obj.) | **533.95** |
| 6X-18X Black Matte (AO) | **493.95** |
| 6X-18X w/Target Knob (AO) | **439.95** |
| 6X-18X Black Matte w/Targt Knob (AO) | **446.95** |

| **50mm Golden Five Star Scopes:** | |
|---|---|
| 3X-9X 50mm Five Star Variable<br>116500 4 Plex | **$429.95** |
| 3X-9X 50mm Five Star Matte Finish<br>116508 4 Plex | **440.95** |
| 3X-9X 50mm Five Star Nickel Matte Finish<br>116900 4 Plex | **394.95** |

## LOW PROFILE WIDEFIELD

The Widefield®, with 25% more field of view than conventional scopes, lets you spot game quicker, stay with it and see other animals that might be missed.

The patented Low Profile design means a low mounting on the receiver, allowing you to keep your cheek tight on the stock for a more natural and accurate shooting stance, especially when swinging on running game.

The one-piece, fog-proof tube is machined with high-tensile strength aluminum alloy and is anodized to a lustrous finish that's rust-free and virtually scratch-proof. Available in seven models.

### WIDEFIELD LOW PROFILE SCOPES

| | |
|---|---|
| **1¾X-5X Low Profile Black Matte Variable Power**<br>113807 1¾X-5X 4 Plex | **$397.95** |
| **1¾X-5X Low Profile Variable Power**<br>113806 1¾X-5X 4 Plex | **389.95** |
| **2X-7X Low Profile Variable Power**<br>111806 2X-7X 4 Plex | **400.95** |
| **2X-7X Low Profile Nickel Matte Variable Power**<br>111808 2X-7X 4 Plex | **417.95** |
| **3X-9X Low Profile Variable Power**<br>112806 3X-9X 4 Plex | **445.95** |
| **3X-9X Low Profile Accu-Trac Variable Power**<br>112810 3X-9X 4 Plex AT | **515.95** |
| **2¾X Low Profile Fixed Power**<br>141807 2¾X 4 Plex | **283.95** |
| **4X Low Profile Fixed Power**<br>143806 4X 4 Plex | **317.95** |
| **6X Low Profile Fixed Power**<br>146806 6X 4 Plex | **340.95** |
| **3X-9X Low Profile Nickel Matte Variable Power**<br>112814 4 Plex | **404.95** |
| **3X-9X Low Profile Black Matte Variable Power**<br>112812 4 Plex | **396.95** |

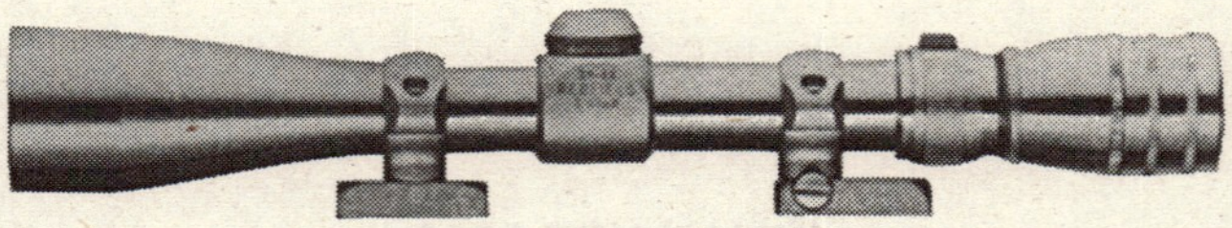

3X-9X NICKEL-PLATED GOLDEN
FIVE STAR SCOPE

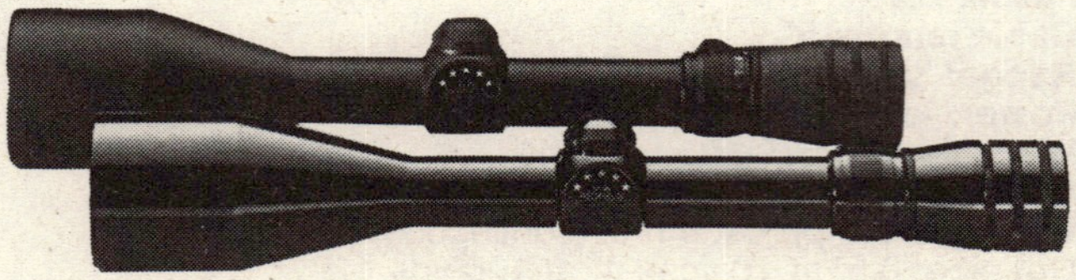

50mm GOLDEN FIVE STAR SCOPE

# REDFIELD SCOPES

**3X-9X WIDEFIELD® ILLUMINATOR w/Nickel Matte Finish**

## THE ILLUMINATOR

With the Illuminator series, you can add precious minutes to morning and evening hunting. These scopes actually compensate for the low light, letting you "see" contrasts between field and game.

Optimum resolution, contrast, color correction, flatness of field, edge-to-edge sharpness and absolute fidelity are improved by the unique air-spaced, triplet objective, and the advanced 5-element erector lens system.

The Illuminators also feature a zero tolerance nylon cam follower and thrust washers to provide absolute point of impact hold through all power ranges. The one-piece tube construction is virtually indestructible, tested at 1200g acceleration forces, and fog-free through the elimination of potential leak paths.

Offered in both the Traditional and Widefield® variable power configurations, the Illuminator is also available with the Accu-Trac® feature.

Also offered in 30mm 3X-12X with a 56mm adj. obj.

**ILLUMINATOR SCOPES**

| | |
|---|---|
| **2X-7X Widefield Variable Power** | |
| 112910 4 Plex | **$539.95** |
| **3X-9X Widefield Variable Power** | |
| 112886 3X-9X 4 Plex | **609.95** |
| **3X-9X Widefield Accu-Trac Variable Power** | |
| 112880 3X-9X 4 Plex | **665.95** |
| **3X9 Widefield Var. Power Black Matte Finish** | |
| 112888 | **619.95** |
| **3X-9X Widefield Nickel Matte Variable Power** | |
| 112892 4 Plex AT | **629.95** |
| **3X-9X Widefield Accu-Trac Black Matte Variable** | |
| 112890 4 Plex AT | **590.95** |
| **3X-10X Widefield 50mm Black** | |
| 112700 | **681.95** |
| **3X-10X 50mm Black Matte** | **689.95** |

## GOLDEN FIVE STAR EXTENDED EYE RELIEF HANDGUN SCOPES

| | |
|---|---|
| **2X Fixed** | |
| 140002 4 Plex | **$223.95** |
| **2X Nickel Plated Fixed** | |
| 14003 4 Plex | **239.95** |
| **4X Fixed** | |
| 140005 4 Plex | **223.95** |
| **4X Nickel Plated Fixed** | |
| 140006 4 Plex | **239.95** |
| **2-1/2X-7X Variable** | |
| 140008 4 Plex | **303.95** |
| **21/2X-7X Nickel Plated Variable** | |
| 140009 4 Plex | **322.95** |
| **21/2X-7X Black Matte Variable** | |
| 140010 4 Plex | **322.95** |

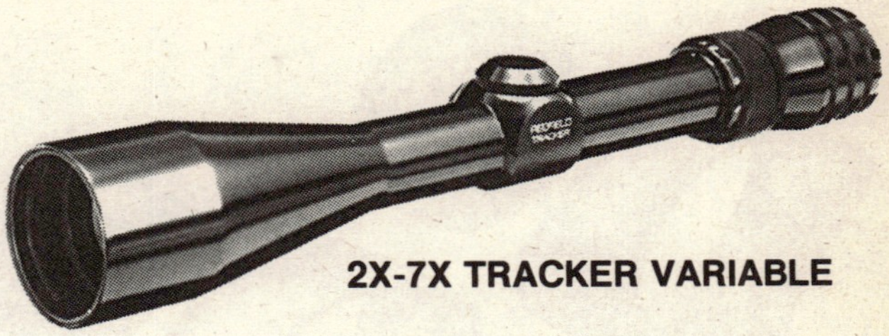

**2X-7X TRACKER VARIABLE**

## THE TRACKER

The Tracker series brings you a superior combination of price and value. It provides the same superb quality, precision and strength of construction found in all Redfield scopes, but at an easily affordable price. Features include the tough, one-piece tube, machined and hand-fitted internal parts, excellent optical quality and traditional Redfield styling.

**TRACKER SCOPES:**

| | |
|---|---|
| **2X-7X Tracker Variable Power** | |
| 122300 2X-7X 4 Plex | **$239.95** |
| **2X-7X Tracker Nickel Matte Variable Power** | |
| 122310 4 Plex | **226.95** |
| **3X-9X Tracker Variable Power** | |
| 123300 3X-9X 4 Plex | **269.95** |
| **3X-9X Tracker Nickel Matte Variable Power** | |
| 123320 4 Plex | **290.95** |
| **4X Tracker Fixed Power** | |
| 135300 4X 4 Plex | **187.95** |
| **4X 40mm Tracker Nickel Matte Fixed Power** | |
| 135312 4 Plex | **189.95** |
| **4X40mm Black** | |
| 135310 4 Plex | **197.95** |
| **4X 40mm Tracker Black Matte Fixed Power** | |
| 135320 4 Plex | **181.95** |
| **6X Tracker Fixed Power** | |
| 135600 6X 4 Plex | **217.95** |
| **8X40mm Black** | |
| 135800 | **237.95** |
| **Matte Finish** | |
| 122308 2X-7X 4 Plex | **250.95** |
| 123308 3X-9X 4 Plex | **279.95** |
| 135608 6X 4 Plex | **226.95** |
| 135308 4X 32mm | **197.95** |
| 135808 8X 40mm | **246.95** |

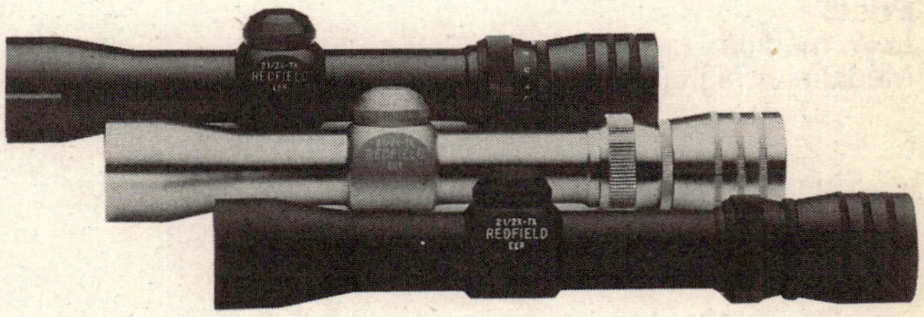

**VARIABLE GOLDEN FIVE STAR (21/2X-7X) HANDGUN SCOPES (Black, Nickel, Black Matte)**

# SAKO SCOPE MOUNTS

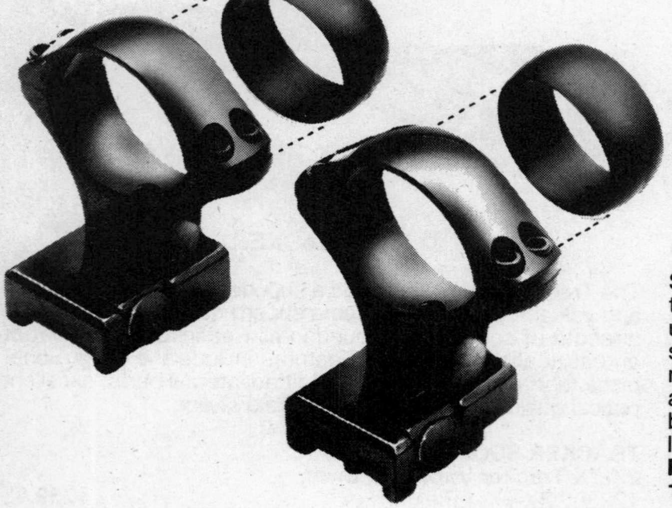

"ORIGINAL" SCOPE MOUNTS

### "ORIGINAL" SCOPE MOUNTS

Sako's "Original" scope mounts are designed and engineered to exacting specifications, which is traditional to all Sako products. The dovetail mounting system provides for a secure and stable system that is virtually immovable. Unique to this Sako mount is a synthetic insert that provides maximum protection against possible scope damage. It also affords additional rigidity by compressing itself around the scope. Manufactured in Finland.

**Prices:**

**1″ Medium & High** (Short, Medium & Long Action) . . . . . . . . . . . . . . . . . . . . . . . . **$130.00**

**30mm Medium & High** (Short, Medium & Long Action) . . . . . . . . . . . . . . . . . . . . . . . . **145.00**

### SCOPE MOUNTS

These new Sako scope mounts are lighter, yet stronger than ever. Tempered steel allows the paring of every last gram of unnecessary weight without sacrificing strength. Like the original mount, these rings clamp directly to the tapered dovetails on Sako rifles, thus eliminating the need for separate bases. Grooves inside the rings preclude scope slippage even under the recoil of the heaviest calibers. Nicely streamlined and finished in a rich blue-black to complement any Sako rifle.

**Price:**

Low, medium, or high (1″) . . . . . . . . . . . . . . . . . . . . . . . . **$70.00**

Medium or high (30mm) . . . . . . . . . . . . . . . . . . . . . . . . **85.00**

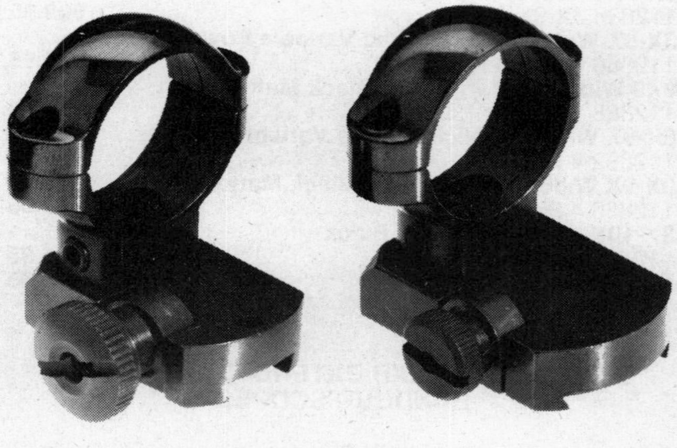

"NEW" SCOPE MOUNTS

# SCHMIDT & BENDER SCOPES



## VARIABLE POWER

**2½-10X56 VARIABLE POWER SCOPE**
**$1117.00 ($1228.00 w/Glass Reticle)**

**1½-6X42 VARIABLE POWER SCOPE**
**$977.00**

Also available:
**1¼-4X20 VARIABLE POWER SCOPE $919.00**
**3-12X50 VARIABLE POWER SCOPE $1183.00**

## FIXED POWER

**4X36 FIXED POWER SCOPE**
**(Steel Tube w/o Mounting Rail)**
**$680.00**

**6X42 FIXED POWER SCOPE**
**(Steel Tube w/o Mounting Rail)**
**$743.00**

**10X42 FIXED POWER SCOPE**
**(Steel Tube w/o Mounting Rail)**
**$850.00**

**8X56 FIXED POWER SCOPE**
**(Steel Tube w/o Mounting Rail)**
**$857.00**

# SIMMONS SCOPES

## 44 MAG RIFLESCOPES

MODEL 1045

**MODEL 1044**
**3-10X44mm**
**Field of view:** 38′-12′
**Eye relief:** 3″
**Length:** 12.8″
**Weight:** 16.9 oz.
**Price: $259.95**

**MODEL 1045**
**4-12X44mm**
**Field of view:** 27′-9′
**Eye relief:** 3″
**Length:** 12.8″
**Weight:** 19.5 oz.
**Price: $279.95**

**MODEL 1047**
**6.5-20X44mm**
**Field of view:** 14′-5′
**Eye relief:** 2.6″-3.4″
**Length:** 12.8″
**Weight:** 19½ oz.
**Price: $289.95**

Also available:
**MODEL M1048**
6.5-20X44 Target Turrets
Black Matte (1/8″ MOA) **$329.95**

**MODEL 3044**
**3-10X44mm**
**Field of view:** 38′-11′
**Eye relief:** 3″
**Length:** 13.1″
**Weight:** 16.4 oz.
**Price: $269.95**

## PROHUNTER RIFLESCOPES

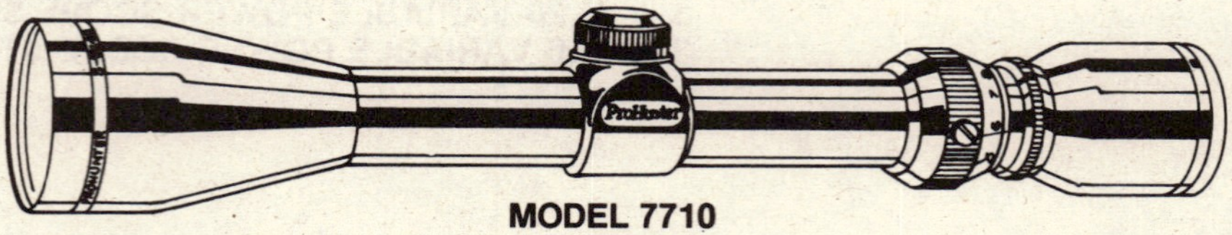


MODEL 7710

MODELS 7711/7712

**MODEL 7710**
**3-9X40mm Wide Angle Riflescope**
**Field of view:** 40′-15′ at 100 yards
**Eye relief:** 3″
**Length:** 12.6″
**Weight:** 11.6 oz.
**Features:** Triplex reticle; silver finish
**Price: $169.95** (Same in black matte or black polish, Models 7711 and 7712)

Also available:
**Model 7700/7701** 2-7X32 Black Matte or Black Polish . . . **$169.95**
**Models 7710/7711** 3-9X40 WA Black, Black Polished or Silver Matte . . . **179.95**
**Model 7716** 4-12X40 Black Matte . . . **$199.95**
**Model 7720** 6-18X40 (adj. obj. Black) . . . **224.95**
**Model 7740** 6X40 Black Matte . . . **144.95**

**#1401** **#1403** **#1406**

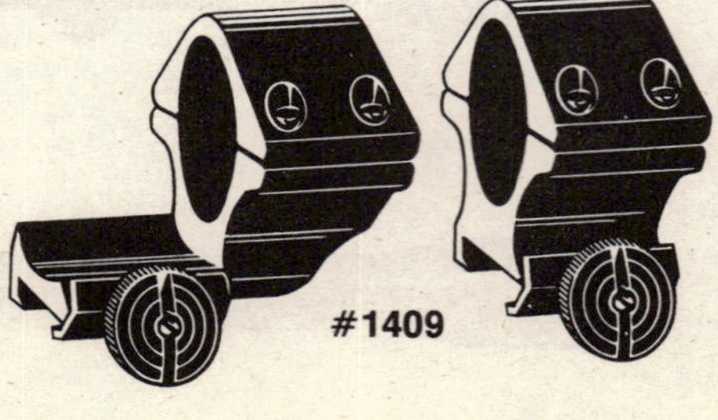

**#1409**

### RIFLESCOPE ALLOY RINGS

**Model 1401** Low 1″ Set . . . **$11.95**
**Model 1403** Medium 1″ Set . . . **11.95**
**Model 1404** High 1″ Set . . . **11.95**
**Model 1405** 1″ See-Thru Set . . . **13.95**
**Model 1406** 1″ Rings for 22 Grooved Receiver . . . **11.95**
**Model 1409** 1″ Rings extention for Compact Scopes . . . **20.95**

# SIMMONS SCOPES

## WHITETAIL CLASSIC RIFLESCOPES

Simmons' Whitetail Classic Series features fully coated lenses and glare-proof BlackGranite finish. The Mono-Tube construction means that front bell and tube, saddle and rear tube are all turned from one piece of aircraft aluminum. This system eliminates 3 to 5 joints found in most other scopes in use today, making the Whitetail Classic up to 400 times stronger than comparably priced scopes.

**MODEL WTC9**
**3X28** Lighted Reticle Black Granite
**Field of view:**11.5′
**Eye relief:** 11″-20″
**Length:** 9″
**Weight:** 9.2 oz.
**Price: $329.95**

**MODEL WTC11**

**MODEL WTC11**
**1.5-5X20mm**
**Field of view:** 80′-23.5′
**Eye relief:** 3.5″
**Length:** 9 1/2″
**Weight:** 9.9 oz.
**Price: $184.95**

**MODEL WTC12**

**MODEL WTC12**
**2.5-8X36mm**
**Field of view:** 48′-14.8′
**Eye relief:** 3″
**Length:** 12.8″
**Weight:** 12.9 oz.
**Price: $199.95**

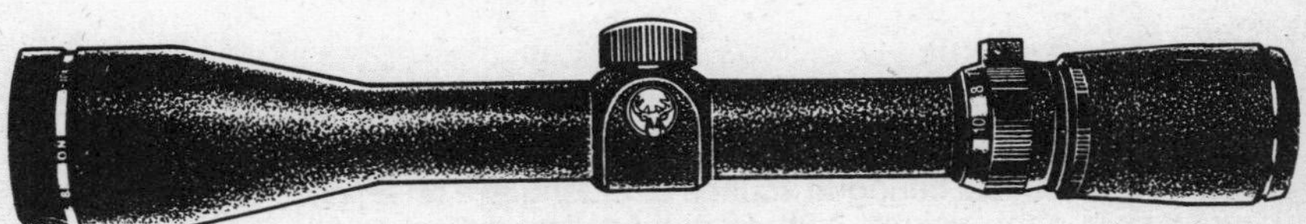

**MODEL WTC13**

**MODEL WTC13**
**3.5-10X40mm**
**Field of view:** 35′-12′
**Eye relief:** 3″
**Length:** 12.8″
**Weight:** 16.9 oz.
**Price: $219.95**

**MODEL WTC15/35**
**3.5-10X50** Black or Silver Granite
**Field of view:** 30.3′-11.3′
**Eye relief:** 3.2″
**Length:** 12.25″
**Weight:** 13.6 oz.
**Price: $329.95**

**MODEL WTC16**
**4X40** Black Granite
**Field of view:** 36.8′
**Eye relief:** 4″
**Length:** 9.9″
**Weight:** 12 oz.
**Price: $149.95**

**MODEL WTC 17**
**4-12X44 WA/AO** Black Granite
**Field of view:** 26′-7.9′
**Eye relief:** 3″
**Length:** 12.8″
**Weight:** 19.5 oz.
**Price: $329.95**

**MODEL WTC 18**
**6.5-20X50 WA/AO** Black Granite
**Field of view:** 17′-6′
**Eye relief:** 2.8-3.7″
**Length:** 14.5″
**Weight:** 22.1 oz.
**Price: $349.95**

**MODEL WTC23**
**3.5-10X40**
**Field of view:** 34′-11.5′
**Eye relief:** 3.2″
**Length:** 12.4″
**Weight:** 12.8 oz.
**Price: $219.95**

**MODEL WTC33**
**3.5-10X40 Silver**
Same specifications as Model WTC23
**Price: $219.95**

# SIMMONS SCOPES

## GOLD MEDAL SILHOUETTE SERIES

Simmons Gold Medal Silhouette Riflescopes are made of state-of-the-art drive train and erector tube design, a new windage and elevation indexing mechanism, camera-quality 100% multicoated lenses, and a super smooth objective focusing device. High silhouette-type windage and elevation turrets house 1/8 minute click adjustments. The scopes have a black matte finish and crosshair reticle and are fogproof, waterproof and shockproof.

MODEL 23000/23001

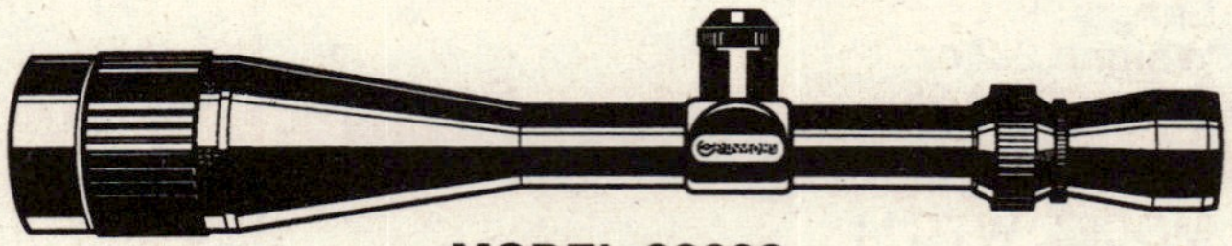

MODEL 23002

**MODEL #23000/23010**
**12X44mm**
**Field of view:** 8.7′
**Eye relief:** 3.17″
**Length:** 14.5″
**Weight:** 18.3 oz.
**Feature:** Truplex Reticle, 100% Multi-Coat Lens system, black matte finish, obj. focus
**Price: $469.95** (Crosshair)
**479.95** (Dot Reticle)

**MODEL #23001/23011**
**24X44mm**
**Field of view:** 4.3′
**Eye relief:** 3″
**Length:** 14.5″
**Weight:** 18.3 oz.
**Feature:** Truplex reticle, 100% Multi-Coat Lens System, black matte finish, obj. focus
**Price: $479.95** (Crosshair)
**479.95** (Dot Reticle)

**MODEL #23002/23012**
**6-20X44mm**
**Field of view:** 17.4′-5.4′
**Eye relief:** 3″
**Length:** 14.5″
**Weight:** 18.3 oz.
**Feature:** Truplex reticle, 100% Multi-Coat Lens System, black matte finish, obj. focus
**Price: $529.95** (Crosshair)
**529.95** (Dot Reticle)

## GOLD MEDAL HANDGUN SERIES

Simmons gold medal handgun scopes offer long eye relief, no tunnel vision, light weight, high resolution, non-critical head alignment, compact size and durability to withstand the heavy recoil of today's powerful handguns. In black and silver finishes, all have fully multicoated lenses and a Truplex reticle.

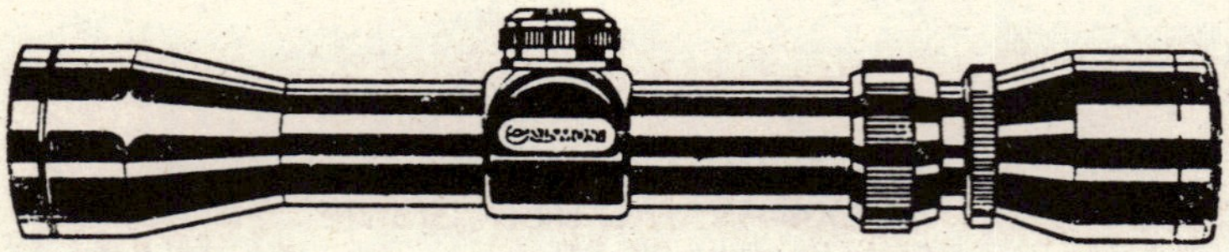

MODEL 22001

**MODEL #22001**
**2.5-7X28mm**
**Field of view:** 9.7′-4.0′
**Eye relief:** 8.9″-19.4″
**Length:** 9.2″
**Weight:** 9 oz.
**Feature:** Truplex reticle, 100% Multi-Coat Lens System, black polished finish.
**Price: $329.95**

**MODEL #22002**
**2.5-7X28mm**
**Field of view:** 9.7′-4.0′
**Eye relief:** 8.9″-19.4″
**Length:** 9.2″
**Weight:** 9 oz.
**Feature:** Truplex reticle, 100% Multi-Coat Lens System, black polished finish.
**Price: $329.95**

Also Available:
**MODEL #22003**
**2X20** . . . . . . . . . . . . . . **$229.95**
**MODEL #22004**
**2X20** . . . . . . . . . . . . . . **229.95**
**MODEL #22005**
**4X32** . . . . . . . . . . . . . . **269.95**
**MODEL #22006**
**4X32** . . . . . . . . . . . . . . **269.95**

# SIMMONS SCOPES

**MASTER RED DOT SCOPES**
**$269.95**

**MODELS 51004/51005**
**Magnification:** 1X30
**Finish:** Black or silver matte
**Field of view:** 40′
100 yards
**Eye relief:** Infinite **Reticle:** 4 MOA Dot
**Length:** 5.25″ **Weight:** 4.8 oz.
Also available:
**MODELS 51012/51032.** Same specifications as Models 51004/51005 w/ 12 MOA Dot reticle

**MASTER RED DOT SCOPES**

## BLACKPOWDER SCOPES

**MODEL BP2732M**

**MODEL BP2732S**

**MODELS BP2520M**
**Magnification:** 2.5X20
**Finish:** Black or silver matte
**Field of view:** 24′
100 yards
**Eye relief:** 6″ **Reticle:** Truplex
**Length:** 7.4″ **Weight:** 7.3 oz.
**Price: $109.95**

**MODELS BP420M/420S**
**Magnification:** 4X20
**Finish:** Black or silver matte
**Field of view:** 19.5′
100 yards
**Eye relief:** 4″ **Reticle:** Truplex
**Length:** 7.5″ **Weight:** 8.3 oz.
**Price: $109.95**

**MODELS BP2732M/2732S**
**Magnification:** 2-7X32
**Finish:** Black or silver matte
**Field of view:** 57.7′-16.6′
100 yards
**Eye relief:** 3″ **Reticle:** Truplex
**Length:** 11.6″ **Weight:** 12.4 oz.
**Price: $129.95**

## SHOTGUN SCOPES

**MODELS 21004/7790D/7793 DCP**
**Magnification:** 4X32
**Finish:** Black matte
**Field of view:** 16′ (Model 21004); 17′ (Models 7790D/7793 DCP)
**Eye relief:** 5.5″
**Reticle:** Truplex (Model 21004); Pro-Diamond (Models 7790D/7793 DCP)
**Length:** 8.5″ (8.8″ Model 21004)
**Weight:** 8.75 oz. (9.1 oz. Models 7790D/7793 DCP)
**Prices:**

| | |
|---|---|
| **Model 21004** | **$109.95** |
| **Model 7790D** | **139.95** |
| **Model 7793 DCP** | **179.95** |

**MODEL 7790D**

Also available:

| | |
|---|---|
| **Model 21005** 2.5X20 Black matte (Truplex reticle) | **$ 99.95** |
| **Model 1091** 1X20 WA Black matte (Truplex reticle) | **119.95** |
| **Model 7788** 1X32 Black matte (Truplex reticle) | **129.95** |
| **Model 7789D** 2X32 Black matte (ProDiamond reticle) | **129.95** |
| **Model 7791** 1.5-5X20 WA Black matte (Truplex reticle) | **139.95** |
| **Model 7792 DCP** 2X32 Black matte w/mount (ProDiamond reticle) | **179.95** |

# SWAROVSKI RIFLESCOPES

## PH SERIES

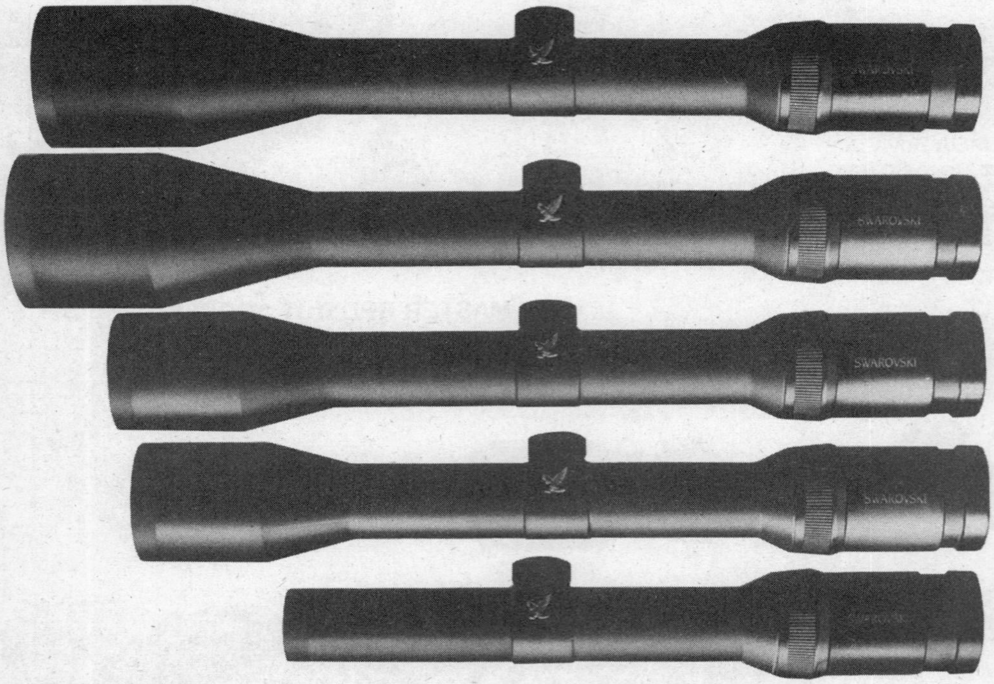

3-12X50 $1265.60

2.5-10X56 $1276.67

2.5-10X42 $1216.67

1.5-6X42 $1043.33

1.25-4X24 $943.33

### SPECIFICATIONS PROFESSIONAL HUNTER PH SERIES

| Type | Maintube | Magnification | Max. effective objective lens ø in/mm | Exit pupil ø in/mm | Exit pupil distance in/mm | Field of view ft/100yds m/100 m | Twilight performance acc. to DIN 58388 | Middle tube ø standard in/mm a | Objective lens tube ø in/mm b | Total length in/mm c | 1 click in/100 yds mm/100 m | Max. adjustment range in/100 yds m/100 m | Weight S/LS (approx.) oz/g | Licencenumber |
|---|---|---|---|---|---|---|---|---|---|---|---|---|---|---|
| 1.25-4x24 | S<br>L<br>LS | 1.25-4 | 0.94<br>24 | 0.49-0.24<br>12.5-6 | 3.15<br>80 | 10.8-3.5<br>32.8-10.4 | 3.5-9.8 | 1.18<br>30 | 1.18<br>30 | 10.6<br>270 | 0.54<br>15 | 119<br>3.3 | 450<br>350<br>385 | 15.9<br>12.3<br>13.6 |
| 1.5-6x42 | S<br>L<br>LS | 1.5-6 | 1.65<br>42 | 0.52-0.28<br>13.1-7 | 3.15<br>80 | 7.3-2.3<br>21.8-7 | 4.2-15.9 | 1.18<br>30 | 1.89<br>48 | 13.0<br>330 | 0.36<br>10 | 79<br>2.2 | 580<br>450<br>485 | 20.5<br>15.9<br>17.1 |
| 2.5-10x42 | S<br>L<br>LS | 2.5-10 | 1.65<br>42 | 0.52-0.17<br>13.1-4.2 | 3.15<br>80 | 4.4-1.4<br>13.2-4.1 | 7.1-20.5 | 1.18<br>30 | 1.89<br>48 | 13.2<br>336 | 0.36<br>10 | 47<br>1.3 | 550<br>420<br>455 | 19.4<br>14.8<br>16.0 |
| 2.5-10x56 | S<br>L<br>LS | 2.5-10 | 2.20<br>56 | 0.52-0.22<br>13.1-5.6 | 3.15<br>80 | 4.4-1.4<br>13.2-4.1 | 7.1-23.7 | 1.18<br>30 | 2.44<br>62 | 14.7<br>374 | 0.36<br>10 | 47<br>1.3 | 690<br>520<br>560 | 24.3<br>18.3<br>19.8 |
| 3-12x50 | S<br>L<br>LS | 3-12 | 1.97<br>50 | 0.52-0.17<br>13.1-4.2 | 3.15<br>80 | 3.7-1.2<br>11-3.5 | 8.5-24.5 | 1.18<br>30 | 2.20<br>56 | 14.3<br>364 | 0.36<br>10 | 40<br>1.1 | 625<br>470<br>510 | 22.0<br>16.6<br>18.0 |

S = steel body, L = light alloy body, LS = light alloy body with mounting rail

# SWAROVSKI RIFLESCOPES

## TRADITIONAL RIFLESCOPES

6X42 $832.22

FIXED POWER (STEEL TUBES ONLY)

8X56 $910.00

These fine Austrian-made sights feature brilliant optics with high-quality lens coating and optimal sighting under poor light and weather conditions. The Nova ocular system with telescope recoil damping reduces the danger of injury, especially with shots aimed in an upward direction.

**SPECIFICATIONS TRADITIONAL RIFLESCOPES**

| Telescopic Sights | 6X42 | 8X56 | 10X42* |
|---|---|---|---|
| Magnification | 6X | 8X | 10X |
| Max. effective objective dia. | 42mm | 56mm | 42mm |
| Exit pupil dia. | 7mm | 7mm | 4.2mm |
| Field of view at 100m | 7m | 5.2m | 4 |
| Twilight effective factor (DIN 58388) | 15.9 | 21.1 | 20.5 |
| Intermediary tube dia. Steel-Standard | 26mm | 26mm | 30mm |
| Objective tube dia. | 48mm | 62mm | 48mm |
| Ocular tube dia. | 40mm | 40mm | NA |
| Scope length | 322mm | 370mm | 341mm |
| Weight Steel | 500g | 660g | 420g |
| (approx.) Light metal with rail | NA | NA | NA |
| A change of the impact point per click in mm/100m | 6 | 4 | 6 |

*Aluminum tube

Price: 10X42: $998.89

### AMERICAN LIGHTWEIGHT RIFLESCOPE

This model features precision ground, coated and aligned optics sealed in a special aluminum alloy tube to withstand heavy recoil. Eye relief is 85mm and the recoiling eyepiece protects the eye. Positive click adjustments for elevation and windage change the impact point (approx. 1/4") per click at 100 yards, with parallax also set at 100 yards. Weight is only 13 ounces.

**Prices:**
**1.5-4.5X20** with duplex reticle . . . . . . **$643.33**
**4X32** with duplex reticle . . . . . . **521.11**
**6X36** with duplex reticle . . . . . . **550.00**
**3-9X36** with duplex reticle . . . . . . **665.00**

# SWIFT RIFLESCOPES

**MODEL 650 $80.00**
**(Matte $99.50 Silver $100.00)**

**MODEL 653 $98.00**

## RIFLESCOPE SPECIFICATIONS

| MODEL# | DESCRIPTION | FIELD OF VIEW AT 100 YDS. (FT') | ZERO PARALLAX AT | EYE RELIEF (INCH) | TUBE DIAMETER (INCH) | CLICK ADJUST-MENT (INCH) | LENGTH (INCH) | WEIGHT (OZ.) | LENS ELEMENT (PC'E) |
|---|---|---|---|---|---|---|---|---|---|
| 650 | 4x,32mm | 26' | 100 YDS. | 4 | 1" | 1/4" | 12" | 9.1 | 9 |
| 653 | 4x,40mm, W.A. | 35' | 100 YDS. | 4 | 1" | 1/4" | 12.2" | 12.6 | 11 |
| 660 | 4x,20mm | 25' | 35 YDS. | 4 | 1" | 1/4" | 11.8" | 9 | 9 |
| 666 | 1x,20mm | 113' | - | 3.2 | 1" | 1/4" | 7.5" | 9.6 | - |
| 654 | 3-9x,32mm | 35' @ 3x<br>12' @ 9x | 100 YDS. | 3.4 @ 3x<br>2.9 @ 9x | 1" | 1/4" | 12" | 9.8 | 11 |
| 656 | 3-9x,40mm, W.A. | 40' @ 3x<br>14' @ 9x | 100 YDS. | 3.4 @ 3x<br>2.8 @ 9x | 1" | 1/4" | 12.6" | 12.3 | 11 |
| 664R | 4-12x,40mm | 27' / 9' | Adjust-able | 3.0 / 2.8 | 1" | 1/4" | 13.3" | 14.8 | - |
| 665 | 1.5-4.5x,21mm | 69' / 24.5' | 100 YDS. | 3.5 / 3.0 | 1" | 1/4" | 10.9" | 9.6 | - |
| 659 | 3.5-10x,44mm, W.A. | 34' @ 3.5x<br>12' @ 10x | - | 3.0 / 2.8 | 1" | 1/4" | 12.8" | 13.5 | - |
| 649 | 4-12x,50mm, W.A. | 30' @ 4x<br>10' @ 12x | - | 3.2 / 3.0 | 1" | 1/4" | 13.2" | 14.6 | - |
| 658 | 2-7x,40mm, W.A. | 55' @ 2x<br>18' @ 7x | - | 3.3 / 3.0 | 1" | 1/4" | 11.6" | 12.5 | - |
| 667 | FIRE-FLY, 1x,30mm | 40' | 100YDS. | Unlimited | 30mm | 1/2" | 5 3/8" | 5 | - |

Also available:
**Model 649** . . . . . . . . . . . . . . . . . . . . . . . . . . . . . . . . . . **$215.00**
**Model 649M** . . . . . . . . . . . . . . . . . . . . . . . . . . . . . . . . **218.00**
**Model 657 Mark I 6X, 40mm** . . . . . . . . . . . . . . . . . . **99.50**

**MODEL 667 FIRE-FLY SCOPE**
**1X30 RED-DOT**
**$215.00**

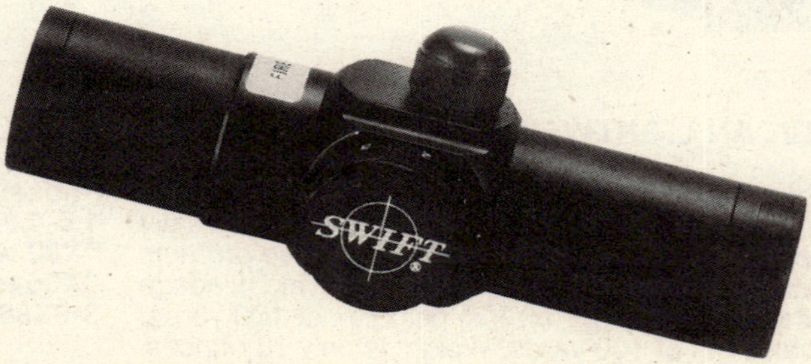

# SWIFT RIFLESCOPES

For complete specifications, please see preceding page.

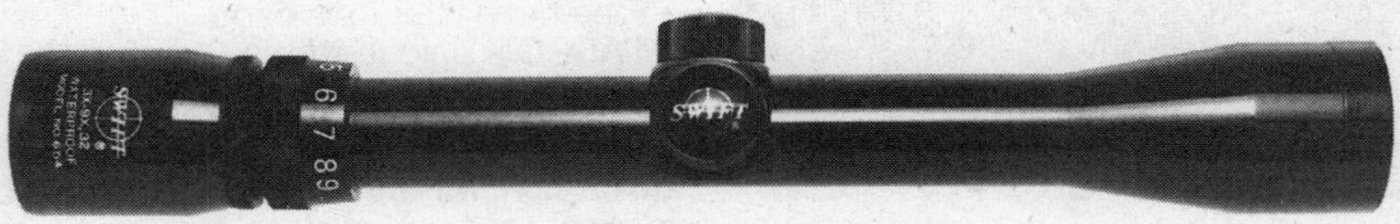


**MODEL 654 $95.00**

**MODEL 656 $103.00**
**(Matte $105.00 Silver $106.00)**

**MODEL 658 $136.50**
**(Matte $138.00)**

**MODEL 659**
**$212.00**
**(Matte $213.00 Silver $214.00)**

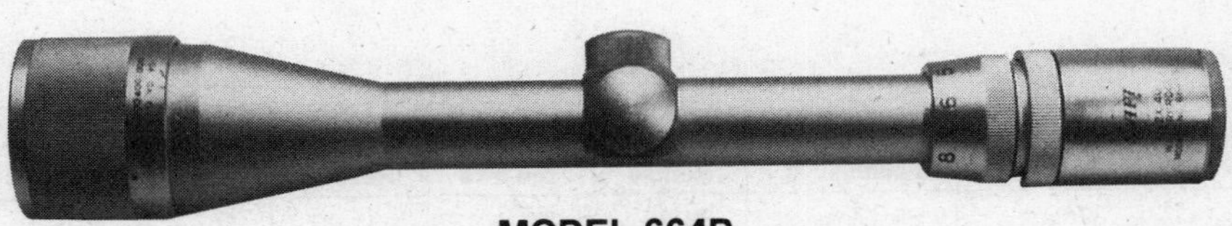

**MODEL 664R**
**$144.00**
**(Silver $145.00)**

# TASCO SCOPES

**MODEL WA1.35×20**

## WORLD-CLASS WIDE-ANGLE® RIFLESCOPES

**Features:**
- 25% larger field of view
- Exceptional optics
- Fully coated for maximum light transmission
- Waterproof, shockproof, fogproof
- Non-removable eye bell
- Free haze filter lens caps
- TASCO's unique World Class Lifetime Warranty

This member of Tasco's World Class Wide Angle line offers a wide field of view—115 feet at 1X and 31 feet at 3.5X—and quick sighting without depending on a critical view. The scope is ideal for hunting deer and dangerous game, especially in close quarters or in heavily wooded and poorly lit areas. Other features include 1/2-minute positive click stops, fully coated lenses (including Supercon process), nonremovable eyebell and windage/elevation screws. Length is 9 3/4″, with 1″ diameter tube. Weight is 10.5 ounces.

### WORLD-CLASS, WIDE-ANGLE VARIABLE ZOOM RIFLESCOPES

| Model No. | Power | Objective Diameter | Finish | Reticle | Field of View @100 Yds. | Eye Relief | Tube Diameter | Scope Length | Scope Weight | Price |
|---|---|---|---|---|---|---|---|---|---|---|
| **WA4X40** | 4X | 40mm | Black Gloss | 30/30 | 36′ | 3″ | 1″ | 13″ | 11.5 oz | **$161.30** |
| **WA6X40** | 6X | 40mm | Black Gloss | 30/30 | 23′ | 3″ | 1″ | 12.75″ | 11.5 oz. | **169.80** |
| **WA13.5X20** | 1X-3.5X | 20mm | Black Gloss | 30/30 | 103′–31′ | 3″ | 1″ | 9.6″ | 12 oz. | **305.60** |
| **WA1.755X20** | 1.75X–5X | 20mm | Black Gloss | 30/30 | 72′–24′ | 3″ | 1″ | 10.5″ | 10 oz. | **305.60** |
| **WA2.58X40** | 2.5X8X | 40mm | Black Gloss | 30/30 | 44′–14′ | 3″ | 1″ | 11.75″ | 14.25 oz. | **220.70** |
| **WA2.58X40ST** | 2.5X–8X | 40mm | Stainless | 30/30 | 44′–14′ | 3″ | 1″ | 11.75″ | 14.25 oz. | **220.70** |
| **WA27X32** | 2X-7X | 32mm | Black Gloss | 30/30 | 56′–17′ | 3.25″ | 1″ | 11.5″ | 12 oz. | **191.00** |
| **DWC39X40** | 3X-9X | 40mm | Black Matte | 30/30 | 41′-15′ | 3″ | 1″ | 12.75″ | 13 oz. | **198.45** |
| **WA39X40** | 3X-9X | 40mm | Black Gloss | 30/30 | 41′-15′ | 3″ | 1″ | 12.75″ | 13 oz. | **198.65** |
| **WA39X40TV** | 3X-9X | 40mm | Black Gloss | 30/30 TV | 41′-15′ | 3″ | 1″ | 12.75″ | 13 oz. | **206.30** |
| **WA39X40ST** | 3X-9X | 40mm | Stainless | 30/30 | 41′-15′ | 3″ | 1″ | 12.75″ | 13 oz. | **198.65** |

## WORLD-CLASS 1″ PISTOL SCOPES

Built to withstand the most punishing recoil, these scopes feature a 1″ tube that provides long eye relief to accommodate all shooting styles safely, along with fully coated optics for a bright, clear image and shot-after-shot durability. The 2X22 model is recommended for target shooting, while the 4X28 model and 1.25X-4X28 are used for hunting as well. All are fully waterproof, fogproof, shockproof and include haze filter caps.

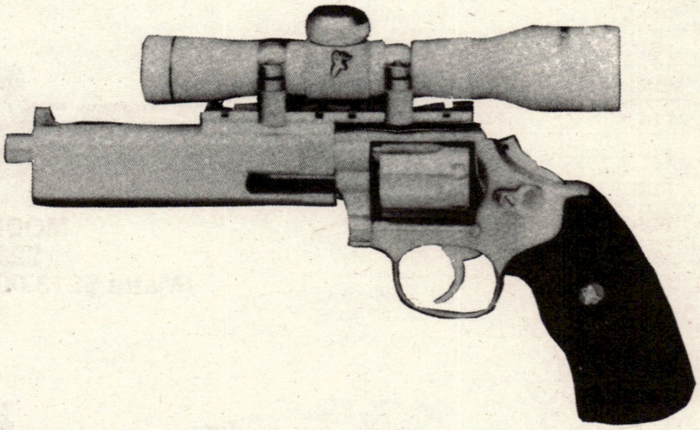

### SPECIFICATIONS

| Model | Power | Objective Diameter | Finish | Reticle | Field of View @ 100 Yds | Eye Relief | Tube Diam. | Scope Length | Scope Weight | Prices |
|---|---|---|---|---|---|---|---|---|---|---|
| **PWC2X22** | 2X | 22mm | Blk Gloss | 30/30 | 25′ | 11″–20″ | 1″ | 8.75″ | 7.3 oz. | **$288.60** |
| **PWC2X22MA** | 2X | 22mm | Matte Alum. | 30/30 | 25′ | 11″–20″ | 1″ | 8.75″ | 7.3 oz. | **288.60** |
| **PWC4X28** | 4X | 28mm | Blk Gloss | 30/30 | 8′ | 12″–19″ | 1″ | 9.45″ | 7.9 oz. | **339.55** |
| **PWC4X28MA** | 4X | 28mm | Matte Alum. | 30/30 | 8′ | 12″–19″ | 1″ | 9.45″ | 7.9 oz. | **339.55** |
| **P1.254X28** | 1.25X-4X | 28mm | Blk Gloss | 30/30 | 23′-9′ | 15″-23″ | 1″ | 9.25″ | 8.2 oz. | **339.55** |
| **P1.254X28MA** | 1.25X-4X | 28mm | Matte Alum. | 30/30 | 23′-9′ | 15″-23″ | 1″ | 9.25″ | 8.2 oz. | **339.55** |

# TASCO SCOPES

## PROPOINT MULTI-PURPOSE SCOPES

Tasco's ProPoint is a true 1X-30mm scope with electronic red dot reticle that features unlimited eye relief, enabling shooters to shoot with both eyes open. It is available with a 3X booster, plus a special, open T-shaped electronic reticle with a dot in the center, making it ideal for fast-action pistol competition and bull's-eye marksmanship. It also has application for rifle, shotgun, bow and black powder. The compact version (PDP2) houses a lithium battery pack, making it 1¼ inches narrower than previous models and lighter as well (5.5 oz.). A mercury battery converter is provided for those who prefer standard batteries.

Tasco's 3X booster with crosshair reticle weighs 6.1 oz. and is 5½ inches long. Model PB2 fits the new PDP2/PDP2MA, and because both units include separate windage and elevation systems the electronic red dot is movable within the crosshair. That means it can be set for two different distances, making it the ultimate rangefinder. Another 3X booster—the PB1—has no crosshairs and fits all other Pro-Point models. Specifications and prices are listed below.

**3X BOOSTER**

### SPECIFICATIONS PROPOINT SCOPES*

| Model | Power | Objective Diameter | Finish | Reticle | Field of View @ 100 Yds. | Eye Relief | Tube Diam. | Scope Length | Scope Weight | Prices |
|---|---|---|---|---|---|---|---|---|---|---|
| **PDP2** | 1X | 25mm | Black Matte | 5 M.O.A. Dot | 40′ | Unlimited | 30mm | 5″ | 5.5 oz. | **$305.60** |
| **PDP2ST** | 1X | 25mm | Stainless | 5 M.O.A. Dot | 40′ | Unlimited | 30mm | 5″ | 5.5 oz. | **305.60** |
| **PDP2BD** | 1X | 25mm | Black Matte | 10 M.O.A. Dot | 40′ | Unlimited | 30mm | 5″ | 5.5 oz. | **305.60** |
| **PDP2BDST** | 1X | 25mm | Stainless | 10 M.O.A. Dot | 40′ | Unlimited | 30mm | 5″ | 5.5 oz. | **305.60** |
| **PDP3** | 1X | 25mm | Black Matte | 5 M.O.A. Dot | 52′ | Unlimited | 30mm | 5″ | 5.5 oz. | **382.00** |
| **PDP3ST** | 1X | 25mm | Stainless | 5 M.O.A. Dot | 52′ | Unlimited | 30mm | 5″ | 5.5 oz. | **382.00** |
| **PDP3BD** | 1X | 25mm | Black Matte | 10 M.O.A. Dot | 52′ | Unlimited | 30mm | 5″ | 5.5 oz. | **382.00** |
| **PDP3BDST** | 1X | 25mm | Stainless | 10 M.O.A. Dot | 52′ | Unlimited | 30mm | 5″ | 5.5 oz. | **382.00** |
| **PDP45** | 1X | 40mm | Black Matte | 5 M.O.A. Dot | 82′ | Unlimited | 45mm | 4.8″ | 6.1 oz. | **509.30** |
| **PDP45ST** | 1X | 40mm | Stainless | 5 M.O.A. Dot | 82′ | Unlimited | 45mm | 4.8″ | 6.1 oz. | **509.30** |
| **PDP410** | 1X | 40mm | Black Matte | 10 M.O.A. Dot | 82′ | Unlimited | 45mm | 4.8″ | 6.1 oz. | **509.30** |
| **PDP410ST** | 1X | 40mm | Stainless | 10 M.O.A. Dot | 82′ | Unlimited | 45mm | 4.8″ | 6.1 oz. | **509.30** |
| **PDP415** | 1X | 40mm | Black Matte | 15 M.O.A. Dot | 82′ | Unlimited | 45mm | 4.8″ | 6.1 oz. | **509.30** |
| **PDP415ST** | 1X | 40mm | Stainless | 15 M.O.A. Dot | 82′ | Unlimited | 45mm | 4.8″ | 6.1 oz. | **509.30** |
| **PDP420** | 1X | 40mm | Black Matte | 20 M.O.A. Dot | 82′ | Unlimited | 45mm | 4.8″ | 6.1 oz. | **509.30** |
| **PDP420ST** | 1X | 40mm | Stainless | 20 M.O.A. Dot | 82′ | Unlimited | 45mm | 4.8″ | 6.1 oz. | **509.30** |
| **PDP420SG** | 1X | 40mm | Black Matte | 20 M.O.A. Dot | 82′ | Unlimited | 45mm | 4.8″ | 6.1 oz. | **534.75** |

* **Model PDP4-10** (1X40) available. Specifications to be announced. **$458.00**

# TASCO SCOPES

## WORLD-CLASS PLUS RIFLESCOPES

WORLD-CLASS TARGET SCOPE 36X50mm

### SPECIFICATIONS WORLD CLASS PLUS RIFLESCOPES

| Model | Power | Objective Diameter | Finish | Reticle | Field of View @ 100 Yds. | Eye Relief | Tube Diam. | Scope Length | Scope Weight | Prices |
|---|---|---|---|---|---|---|---|---|---|---|
| WCP4X44 | 4X | 44mm | Black Gloss | 30/30 | 32′ | 3 1/4″ | 1″ | 12.75″ | 13.5 oz. | $392.50 |
| WCP6X44 | 6X | 44mm | Black Gloss | 30/30 | 21′ | 3 1/4″ | 1″ | 12.75″ | 13.6 oz. | 407.45 |
| WCP39X44 | 3X-9X | 44mm | Black Gloss* | 30/30 | 39′-14′ | 3 1/2″ | 1″ | 12.75″ | 15.8 oz. | 407.45 |
| DWCP39X44 | 3X-9X | 44mm | Black Matte | 30/30 | 39′-14′ | 3 1/2″ | 1″ | 12.75″ | 15.8 oz. | 407.45 |
| WCP39X44ST | 3X-9X | 44 mm | Stainless | 30/30 | 39′-14′ | 3 1/2″ | 1″ | 12.75″ | 15.8 oz. | 407.45 |
| WCP3.510X50 | 3.5X-10X | 50mm | Black Gloss | 30/30 | 30′-10.5′ | 3 3/4″ | 1″ | 13″ | 17.1 oz. | 492.35 |
| DWCP3.510X50 | 3.5X-10X | 50mm | Black Matte | 30/30 | 30′-10.5′ | 3 3/4″ | 1″ | 13″ | 17.1 oz. | 492.35 |
| WCP24X50 | 24X | 50mm | Black Gloss | Crosshair | 4.8′ | 3 1/2″ | 1″ | 13.25″ | 15.9 oz. | 730.00 |
| WCP36X50 | 36X | 50mm | Black Gloss | Crosshair | 3′ | 3 1/2″ | 1″ | 14″ | 15.9 oz. | 760.90 |

## RUBBER ARMORED SCOPES

| Model | Power | Objective Diameter | Finish | Reticle | Field of View @ 100 Yards | Eye Relief | Tube Diam. | Scope Length | Scope Weight | Price |
|---|---|---|---|---|---|---|---|---|---|---|
| RC39X40 A,B | 3-9 | 40mm | Green Rubber | 30/30 | 35′-14′ | 3 1/4″ | 1″ | 12 5/8″ | 14.3 oz. | $229.20 |

"A" fits standard dove tail base. "B" fits 3/8″ grooved receivers—most 22 cal. and airguns.

## MAG IV RIFLESCOPES (not shown)

MAG IV scopes yield four times magnification range in a standard size riflescope and one-third more zooming range than most variable scopes. Features include: Fully coated optics and large objective lens to keep target in low light . . . Non-removable eye bell . . . 1/4-minute positive click stops . . . Non-removable windage and elevation screws. . . Opticentered 30/30 rangefinding reticle . . . Waterproof, fogproof, shockproof.

### SPECIFICATIONS

| Model | Power | Objective Diameter | Finish | Reticle | Field of View @ 100 Yds. | Eye Relief | Tube Diam. | Scope Length | Scope Weight | Price |
|---|---|---|---|---|---|---|---|---|---|---|
| W312X40 | 3–12 | 40mm | Black | 30/30 | 35′–9′ | 3 1/8″ | 1″ | 12 3/16″ | 12 oz. | $183.35 |
| W416X40†* | 4–16 | 40mm | Black | 30/30 | 26′–6′ | 3 1/8″ | 1″ | 14 1/8″ | 15.6 oz. | 263.15 |
| W624X40† | 6–24 | 40mm | Black | 30/30 | 17′–4′ | 3″ | 1″ | 15 3/8″ | 16.75 oz. | 305.60 |

† Indicates focusing objective. *Also available: **Model V416X40ST** in stainless. **$263.15**

# TASCO SCOPES

## HIGH COUNTRY RIFLESCOPES

3X-9X40mm

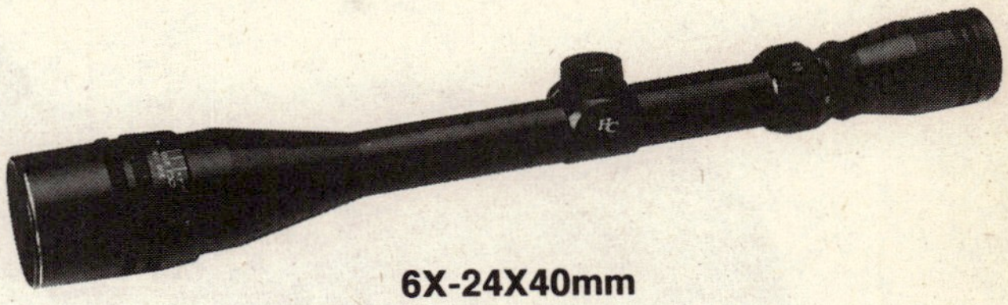

6X-24X40mm

4X-16X40mm

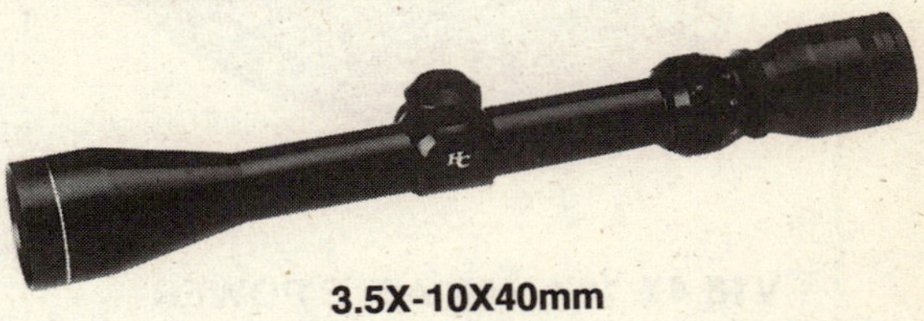

3.5X-10X40mm

### SPECIFICATIONS HIGH COUNTRY RIFLESCOPES $195.00–$280.00

| Model | Power | Objective Diameter | Field of view @ 100 yds. | Reticle | Eye Relief | Tube Diam. | Finish | Length | Weight |
|---|---|---|---|---|---|---|---|---|---|
| HC416X40 | 4X-16X | 40mm | 26′-7′ | 30/30 | 3.25″ | 1″ | Black gloss | 14.25″ | 15.6 oz. |
| HC624X40 | 6X-24X | 40mm | 17′-4′ | 30/30 | 3″ | 1″ | Black gloss | 15.25″ | 16.8 oz. |
| HC39X40 | 3X-9X | 40mm | 41′-15′ | 30/30 | 3″ | 1″ | Black gloss | 12.75″ | 13 oz. |
| HC3.510X40 | 3.5X-10X | 40mm | 30′-10.5′ | 30/30 | 3″ | 1″ | Black gloss | 11.75″ | 14.25 oz. |

### LASER POINT

Tasco's LaserPoint model is the first compact to have a multi-mode red dot (one second continuous followed by one second pulsating), making it the fastest and easiest dot to locate on the target. An index-guided diode designed with minimum astigmatism, maximum efficiency and battery life results in a much improved laser dot. Additional features include adjustable windage and elevation system, waterproofing and several optional mounts that require no gunsmithing.

**Price:** . . . . . . . . . . . . . . . . . . . . . . . . . . . . . . . . **$373.50**

# WEAVER SCOPES

V16 4X-16X

### V16 4X-16X VARIABLE POWER

Offers large magnification for extreme long shots like varmint or benchrest shooting. Or twist it down for close-range shots that require a large field of view. The adjustable objective allows a parallax-free view at any distance. Its single piece tube design offers strength and moisture resistance in the foulest of conditions. Multicoated lenses provide clear, crisp images from dawn to dusk, while the matte finish eliminates glare.

**Model V16** (dual X reticle) .................... **$364.57**
**Model V16 MFC** (fine crosshair reticle) .......... **364.57**
**Model V16 MDT** (1/4-minute dot reticle) .......... **364.57**

### K2.5 2.5X FIXED POWER

Optimum power, field of view and size for close-range hunting with slug or brush guns.

**Model K2.5** .............................. **$138.47**

### K4 4X FIXED POWER

The K4's 4X magnification and wide field of view make it the ideal all-purpose scope. Especially good for medium-range small- and big-game hunting.

**Model K4** ................................ **$150.13**
**Model K4** Matte Finish ...................... **157.71**

### K6 6X FIXED POWER

Identical to the K4, except with more power. Use the K6 for longer distance shooting in wide-open country.

**Model K6** ................................ **$163.61**

### KT15 TARGET SILHOUETTE

The KT15's range-focus mechanism allows parallax-free sighting at almost any distance. This is an ideal scope for precise target and varmint shooting.

**Model KT15** .............................. **$326.00**
**Model T-36** (36-40) ......................... **773.81**
**Model T-24** (24-40) ......................... **767.86**
**Model T-16** (16-40) ......................... **762.00**
**Model T-10** (10-40) ......................... **756.00**

### WEAVER HANDGUN SCOPE

One-piece aircraft grade aluminum alloy construction keeps water out and lenses locked. Audible "click" windage and elevation adjustments. Nitrogen charged and scaled. Multi-coated optics, precision ground for clear target image in low light. Adjustable ocular lens puts reticle clearly in focus.

**Model 2x28** Gloss Blued ..................... **$196.80**
**Model 2x28** Stainless ....................... **207.71**
**Model 4x28** Gloss Blued ..................... **207.71**
**Model 4x28** Stainless ....................... **218.64**
**Model 5-4x20** Variable Gloss Blued ............ **253.00**
**Model 1.5-4x20** Variable Stainless ............ **263.83**

### V3 1X-3X VARIABLE POWER

At 1X the V3 provides excellent field of view. At 3X you get the crisp magnification needed for critical shot placement. With extra eye relief for big recoils and fast targeting, giant exit pupil for dim light and moving game.

**Model V3** ................................ **$181.49**
**Model V3** Matte Finish ...................... **490.56**

### V9 3X-9X VARIABLE POWER

Easy adjustment ring lets you dial the magnification. Precision ground lenses offer crystal clear resolution. Long eye relief and rubber guards protect against facial impact from recoil.

**Model V9** ................................ **$195.56**
**Model V9** Matte Finish ...................... **205.33**
**Model V9x50** .............................. **281.73**

### V10 2X-10X VARIABLE POWER

The 5 to 1 magnification range of the V10 lets it handle a variety of situations, from close-in moving game to long-distance varmint or target shooting.

**Model V10** ............................... **$208.00**
**Model V10** Matte Finish ..................... **218.47**
**Model V10** Stainless ........................ **218.47**

# WIDEVIEW SCOPE MOUNTS

## PREMIUM SEE-THRU SCOPE MOUNTS

| Rifle/Model | Prices |
|---|---|
| Browning A-Bolt NN | $22.00 |
| Browning Semi-Auto AA | 22.00 |
| Browning Lever Action AA | 22.00 |
| Browning F.N. Bolt Action CB | 22.00 |
| BSA, Medium & Long Action DB | 22.00 |
| Glenfield 30 by Marlin GG | 22.00 |
| H & R Bolt Action F.N. 300, 301, 317, 330, 370 CB | 22.00 |
| Husquvarna F.N. Action CB | 22.00 |
| Interarms Mark X CB | 22.00 |
| Ithaca Bolt Action DB | 22.00 |
| Marlin 336, 62, 36, 444 GG | 22.00 |
| Marlin 1893, 1894, 1895, 9, 45 CG | 22.00 |
| Marlin 465 F.N. Action CB | 22.00 |
| Mauser F.N. 98, 2000, 3000 CB | 22.00 |
| Mossberg 800, 500 AA | 22.00 |
| Parker Hale 1000, 1000c, 1100, 1200, 1200C CB | 22.00 |
| Parker Hale 2100 CB | 22.00 |
| Remington 7 JB | 22.00 |
| Remington 700, 721, 722, 725 DB | 22.00 |
| Remington 740, 742, 600 EB | 22.00 |
| Remington 788 FH | 22.00 |
| Remington 4, 6, 7400, 7600 EB8 | 22.00 |
| Remington XP-100 Pistol 600, 660 HB | 22.00 |
| Revelation 200 Lever Action GG | 22.00 |
| Ruger M-77 Round Receiver DB | 22.00 |
| Ruger 44 Rifle QO | 22.00 |
| Ruger 10/22 OP | 22.00 |
| Savage 99 KM | 22.00 |
| Savage 110, 111, 112 IB | 22.00 |
| Savage 170 EB | 22.00 |
| Smith & Wesson 1500 Bolt DB | 22.00 |
| Weatherby Mark V & Vanguard DB | 22.00 |
| Western Field 740 GG | 22.00 |
| Winchester 88, 100 BB | 22.00 |
| Winchester 70, 70A, 670, 770 and ser. #700 (except 375 H & H) FB | 22.00 |
| Winchester 94AE Angle Eject 94 AE | 24.00 |
| Winchester 94 Side Mount 94 | 26.00 |

## SHOTGUNS (Must Be Drilled and Tapped)

Ithaca, Remington, Winchester, Mossberg, etc. Note: Remington 1100 and Browning 5 Auto not recommended by Wideview for top mounts. Receivers should be .150 thousands or more in thickness BB . . . . $22.00

## FOR WEAVER-STYLE BASES

| | |
|---|---|
| Savage 24V U-20 | $24.00 |
| Straight Cut U-10 | 22.00 |
| 20 Degree Angle Cut U-20 | 24.00 |
| Straight Cut 30 Millimeter U-1030 | 24.62 |
| 20 Degree Angle Cut 30 Millimeter U-2030 | 24.62 |

## RING-STYLE MOUNTS

| | |
|---|---|
| Dove Tail Solid Lock Ring Fits Any Redfield, Tasco or Weaver-Style Base SR | $16.00 |
| Dove Tail Solid Lock 30 Millimeter SR30 | 18.65 |
| True-Fit Lo Ring L-Ring | 16.00 |

| Rifle/Model | Prices |
|---|---|
| Tru-Fit Hi Ring H-Ring | $16.00 |
| Tru-Fit Grooved Receiver GR-Ring | 16.00 |
| Ruger High Rings M77R, M77RS, M77V TU | 26.20 |
| Ruger High Rings No. 1-A, RSI. , S, H, 3. 77/22 TU | 26.20 |
| Ruger Redhawk Hunter UU | 26.20 |
| Ruger Mini-14/5R, K-Mini Thirty TU | 26.20 |
| Ruger Redhawk, Hunter 30 Millimeter UU30 | 29.00 |

## PREMIUM FLASHLIGHT MOUNT

Site Lite Mount SL . . . . $26.00

## 22 RIMFIRE SEE-THRU MOUNT

For All 22-Caliber Rimfire Rifles With Grooved Receiver. Designed for 1/4 and 1″ Diameter Scopes. Also Used On Air Rifles 22R . . $18.00

## BLACK POWDER MOUNTS (See Thru)
Barrels Must Be Drilled and Tapped

| | |
|---|---|
| CVA Frontier Carbine, Plainsman, Pennsylvania Long Rifle CVA Hawken, GG | $22.00 ea. |
| CVA Hawken, Hunter Hawken, Mountain Rifle, Blazer GG | 22.00 ea. |
| CVA Squirrel Rifle, Kentucky, Kentucky Hunter & Kit Rifles GG | 22.00 ea. |
| Thompson Center, Renegade, Hawken, White Mountain, New Englander GG | 22.00 ea. |
| Traditions Frontier Carbine, Pioneer Rifle GG | 22.00 ea. |
| Traditions Pennsylvania Rifle, Hawken Woodsman, Frontier Rifle GG | 22.00 ea. |
| Traditions Trapper, Frontier Scout Kits for Hawken GG | 22.00 ea. |
| Woodsman, Frontier Rifle, Frontier Carbine GG | 22.00 ea. |

## BLACK POWDER SEE-THRU MOUNTS
NO DRILLING OR TAPPING

| | |
|---|---|
| Thompson Center Hawken (Ultra Precision See-Thru Mount Included) TEC | $44.00 |
| Thompson Center Renegade (Ultra Precision See-Thru Mounts Included) TCR | 44.00 |
| CVA Stalker Rifle/Carbine ii | 22.00 ea. |
| CVA Apollo 90 Rifle/Carbine ii | 22.00 ea. |
| CVA Apollo Sporter ii | 22.00 ea. |
| CVA Shadow Rifle ii | 22.00 ea. |
| CVA Tracker Carbine ii | 22.00 ea. |
| CVA Hawken Deerslayer Rifle/Carbine ii | 22.00 ea. |
| CVA Trophy Carbine ii | 22.00 ea. |
| CVA Frontier Hunter Carbine ii | 22.00 ea. |
| Knight MK-85, BK-90 ii | 22.00 ea. |

## SHOTGUN MOUNTS (No Drilling or Tapping)

| | |
|---|---|
| Mossberg 500 500 | $34.95 |
| Remington 870 870 | 34.95 |
| Remington 1100 1100 | 34.95 |

# WILLIAMS SCOPES

**1.5X-5X (and 2X-6X): $221.00**

**2½X: $156.00**

**4X: $164.00**

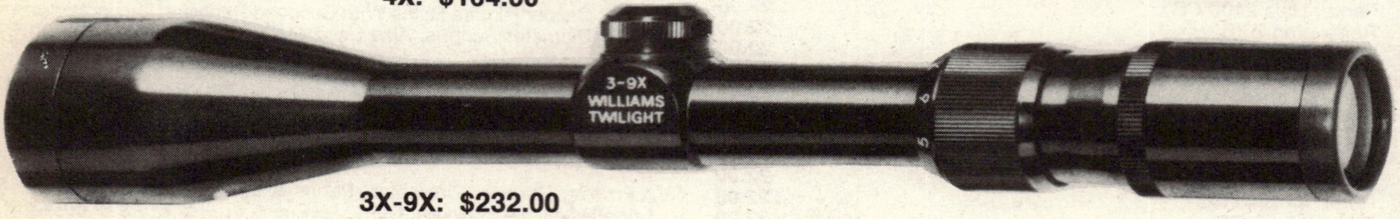


**3X-9X: $232.00**

The "Twilight" and "Guideline II" series of scopes are waterproof and shockproof, have coated lenses and are nitrogen-filled. Resolution is sharp and clear.

There are five models available: the 2½x, the 4x, the 1.5x-5x, the 2x-6x, and the 3x-9x. They are available in T-N-T reticle only (which stands for "thick and thin").

Patterned after the popular Twilight Series, Williams' Guideline II Series features silent adjustment screws, streamlined adjustment caps and power adjustment rings. Fully multi-coated lenses ensure superior light gathering and brightness. Comes equipped with T-N-T reticle and a choice of matte or glossy black finish. Prices range from **$238.00** (4X) to **$317.00** (3X-9X).

## WILLIAMS TWILIGHT & GUIDELINE II SERIES

| | | 1.5X–5X | | 2X–6X | | 3X–9X | |
|---|---|---|---|---|---|---|---|
| **OPTICAL SPECIFICATIONS** | **4X** | **At 1.5X** | **At 5X** | **At 2X** | **At 6X** | **At 3X** | **At 9X** |
| Clear aperture of objective lens | 32mm | 20mm | Same | 32mm | Same | 40mm | Same |
| Clear aperture of ocular lens | 32mm | 32mm | Same | 32mm | Same | 32mm | Same |
| Exit Pupil | 8mm | 13.3mm | 4mm | 16mm | 5.3mm | 13.3mm | 44.4mm |
| Relative Brightness | 64 | 177 | 16 | 256 | 28 | 161.2 | 17.6 |
| Field of view (degree of angle) | 5°30′ | 11° | 4° | 8°30′ | 3°10′ | 7° | 2°20′ |
| Field of view at 100 yards | 29′ | 57¾′ | 21′ | 45½′ | 16¾′ | 36½′ | 12¾′ |
| Eye Relief | 3.6″ | 3.5″ | 3.5″ | 3″ | 3″ | 3.1″ | 2.9″ |
| Parallax Correction (at) | 100 yds. | 100 yds. | Same | 100 yds. | Same | 100 yds. | Same |
| Lens Construction | 9 | 10 | Same | 11 | Same | 11 | Same |
| **MECHANICAL SPECIFICATIONS** | | | | | | | |
| Outside diameter of objective end | 1.525″ | 1.00″ | Same | 1.525″ | Same | 1.850″ | 1.850″ |
| Outside diameter of ocular end | 1.455″ | 1.455″ | Same | 1.455″ | Same | 1.455″ | Same |
| Outside diameter of tube | 1″ | 1″ | Same | 1″ | Same | 1″ | Same |
| Internal adjustment graduation | ¼ min. | ¼ min. | Same | ¼ min. | Same | ¼ min. | Same |
| Minimum internal adjustment | 75 min. | 75 min. | Same | 75 min. | Same | 60 min. | Same |
| Finish | | | | Glossy Hard Black Anodized | | | |
| Length | 11¾″ | 10¾″ | Same | 11½″ | 11½″ | 12¾″ | 12¾″ |
| Weight | 9½ oz. | 10 oz. | Same | 11½ oz. | Same | 13½ oz. | Same |

# ZEISS RIFLESCOPES

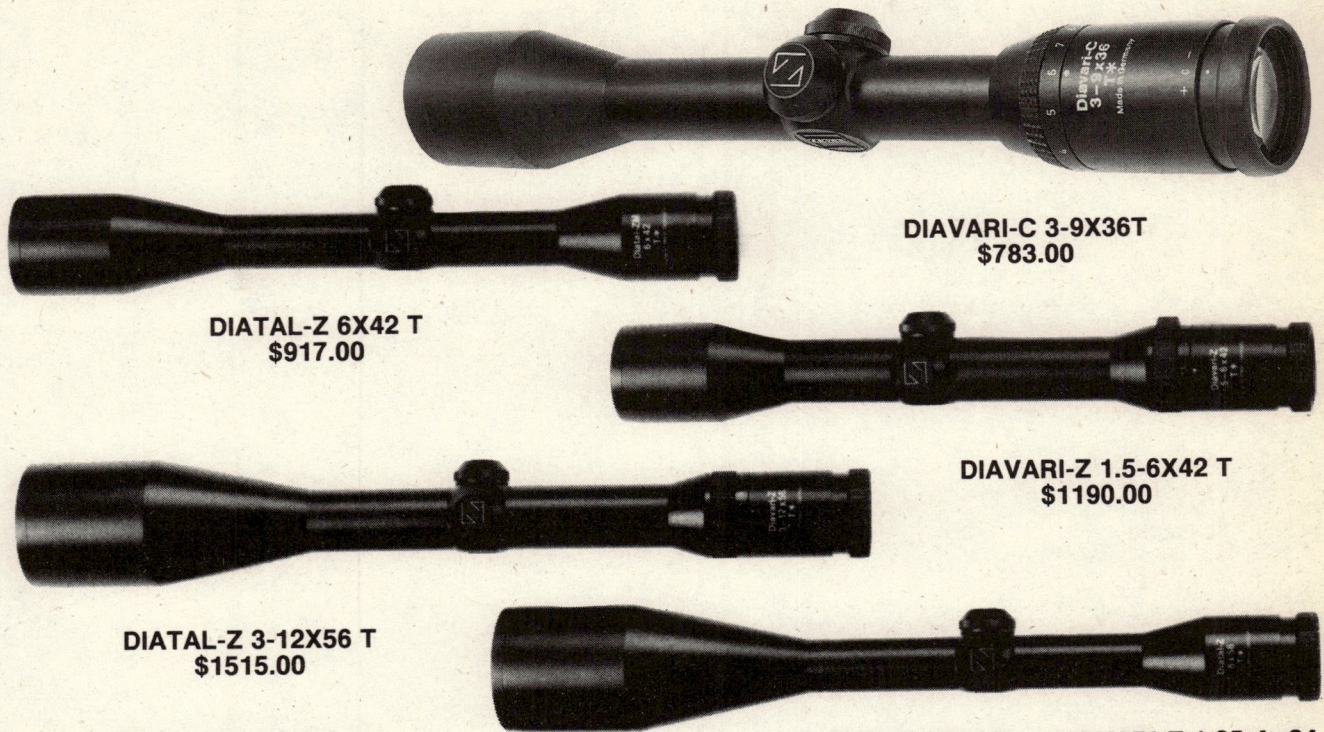

## THE "Z" SERIES

DIAVARI-C 3-9X36T
$783.00

DIATAL-Z 6X42 T
$917.00

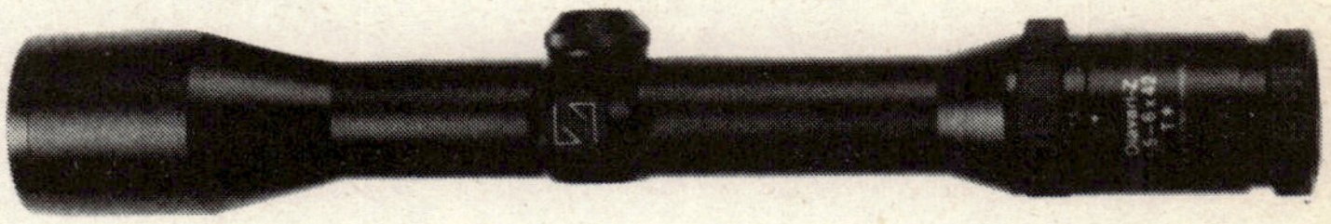

DIAVARI-Z 1.5-6X42 T
$1190.00

DIATAL-Z 3-12X56 T
$1515.00

DIAVARI-Z 2.5-10X48 T
(not shown)
$1407.00

DIATAL-Z 8X56 T
$1092.00

DIAVARI-Z 1.25-4×24
(not shown)
$1041.00

## ZM/Z SERIES RIFLESCOPE SPECIFICATIONS

| Model | Diatal-ZM/Z 6X42 T | Diavari-ZM/Z 1.5-6X42 T | Diavari-ZM/Z 3-12X56 T | Diatal-ZM/Z 8X56 T | Diavari-ZM/Z 2.5-10X48 T | Diavera-ZM/Z 1.25-4X24 | Diavari-C 3-9X36 |
|---|---|---|---|---|---|---|---|
| Magnification | 6X | 1.5X 6X | 3X 12X | 8X | 2.5X-10X | 1.25-4X | 3X 9X |
| Effective obj. diam. | 42mm/1.7″ | 19.5/0.8″ 42/1.7″ | 38/1.5″ 56/2.2″ | 56mm/2.2″ | 33/1.30″ 48/1.89″ | NA | 30.0/1.2″ 36.0/1.4″ |
| Diameter of exit pupil | 7mm | 13mm 7mm | 12.7mm 4.7mm | 7mm | 13.2mm 4.8mm | 12.6mm 6.3mm | 10.0 4.0mm |
| Twilight factor | 15.9 | 4.2 15.9 | 8.5 25.9 | 21.2 | 7.1 21.9 | 3.54 9.6 | 8.5 18.0 |
| Field of view at 100 m/ ft. at 100 yds. | 6.7m/20.1′ | 18/54.0′ 6.5/19.5′ | 9.2/27.6′ 3.3/9.9′ | 5m/15.0′ | 11.0/33.0 3.9/11.7 | 32 10 | 12.0/36.0 4.3/12.9 |
| Approx. eye relief | 8cm/3.2″ | 8cm/3.2″ | 8cm/3.2″ | 8cm/3.2″ | 8cm/3.2″ | 8cm/3.2″ | 3.5″ |
| Click-stop adjustment 1 click = (cm at 100 m)/ (inch at 100 yds.) | 1cm/0.36″ | 1cm/0.36″ | 1cm/0.36″ | 1cm/0.36″ | 1cm/0.36″ | 1cm/0.36″ | 107/0.25″ |
| Max. adj. (elev./wind.) at 100 m (cm)/at 100 yds. | 187 | 190 | 95 | 138 | 110/39.6 | 300 | 135/49 |
| Center tube dia. | 25.4mm/1″ | 30mm/1.18″ | 30mm/1.18″ | 25.4mm/1″ | 30mm/1.18″ | 30mm/1.18″ | 25.4/1.0″ |
| Objective bell dia. | 48mm/1.9″ | 48mm/1.9″ | 62mm/2.44″ | 62mm/2.44″ | 54mm/2.13″ | NA | 44.0/1.7 |
| Ocular bell dia. | 40mm/1.57″ | 40mm/1.57″ | 40mm/1.57″ | 40mm/1.57″ | 40mm/1.57″ | NA | 42.5/1.8 |
| Length | 324mm/12.8″ | 320mm/12.6″ | 388mm/15.3″ | 369mm/14.5″ | 370mm/14.57″ | 290mm/11.46″ | |
| Approx. weight: ZM | 350g/15.3 oz. | 586g/20.7 oz. | 765g/27.0 oz. | 550g/19.4 oz. | 715g/25.2 oz. | 490g/17.3 oz. | NA |
| Z | 400g/14.1 oz. | 562g/19.8 | 731g/25.8 oz. | 520g/18.3 oz. | 680g/24 oz. | NA | 430g/15.2 oz. |

# Ammunition



For addresses and phone numbers of manufacturers and distributors included in this section, turn to *DIRECTORY OF MANUFACTURERS AND SUPPLIERS* at the back of the book.

# FEDERAL AMMUNITION

Federal's new or recent lines of cartridges and shotshells for 1995–96 are featured below. For a complete listing of Federal ammunition, call or write the Federal Cartridge Company (*see* Directory of Manufacturers and Suppliers in the Reference section for address and phone number). *See* also Federal ballistics tables.

**STEEL MAGNUMS**
***New Higher Velocity Loads***

| | | | | |
|---|---|---|---|---|
| W102 - BBB, BB | 10 gauge | $3^1/_2$″ | $1^3/_8$ ounce | 1425 FPS |
| W133 - BBB, BB, 2 | 12 gauge | $3^1/_2$″ | $1^3/_8$ ounce | 1450 FPS |
| W143 - BBB, BB, 2 | 12 gauge | 3″ | $1^1/_8$ ounce | 1450 FPS |

**STEEL HI-BRASS (*New Shot Sizes)***

| | | | | |
|---|---|---|---|---|
| W146 - 6,7 | 12 gauge | $2^3/_4$″ | 1 ounce | 1375 FPS |

**PREMIUM® STEEL MAGNUMS**

| | | | | |
|---|---|---|---|---|
| PW102 - BBB, BB | 10 gauge | $3^1/_2$″ | $1^3/_8$ ounce | 1425 FPS |
| PW133 - BBB, BB, 2 | 12 gauge | $3^1/_2$″ | $1^3/_8$ ounce | 1450 FPS |
| PW143 - BBB, BB, 2 | 12 gauge | 3″ | $1^1/_8$ ounce | 1450 FPS |
| PW148 - BB, 2 | 12 gauge | $2^3/_4$″ | $1^1/_4$ ounce | 1275 FPS |

**PREMIUM® STEEL HI-BRASS**

| | | | | |
|---|---|---|---|---|
| PW147- 2 | 12 gauge | $2^3/_4$″ | $1^1/_8$ ounce | 1365 FPS |

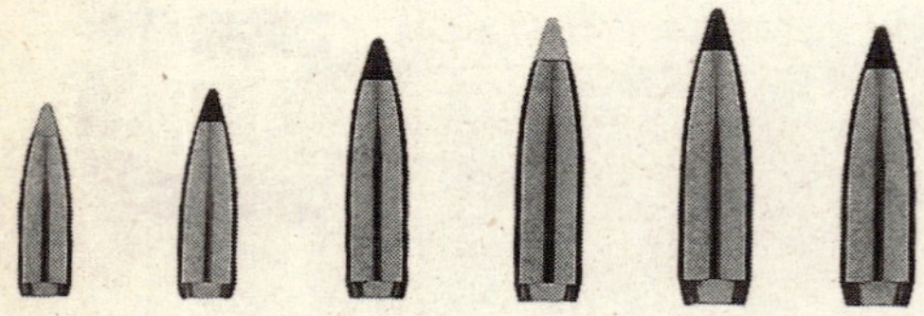

223 REM. 243 WIN. 25-06 REM. 270 WIN. 30-06 SPRING. 308 WIN.

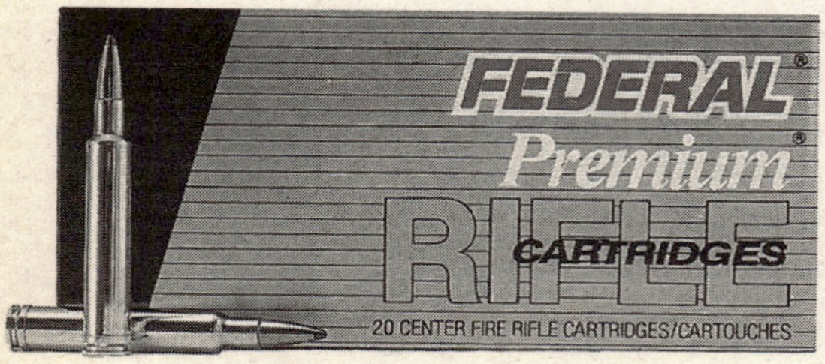


**NEW PREMIUM® NOSLER BALLISTIC TIP**

| | | | |
|---|---|---|---|
| P223F | 223 Rem. | 55 grain | Nosler Ballistic Tip |
| P243F | 243 Win. | 70 grain | Nosler Ballistic Tip |
| P2506D | 25-06 Rem. | 100 grain | Nosler Ballistic Tip |
| P270F | 270 Win. | 130 grain | Nosler Ballistic Tip |
| P308F | 308 Win. | 150 grain | Nosler Ballistic Tip |
| P3006P | 30-06 Springfield | 150 grain | Nosler Ballistic Tip |
| P3006Q | 30-06 Springfield | 165 grain | Nosler Ballistic Tip |

**PREMIUM® NOSLER PARTITION**
***Now Available in Weatherby Calibers***

| | | |
|---|---|---|
| P270WBA | 270 Weatherby Magnum | 130 grain Nosler Partition |
| P7WBA | 7mm Weatherby Magnum | 160 grain Nosler Partition |
| P300WBA | 300 Weatherby Magnum | 180 grain Nosler Partition |

# HORNADY AMMUNITION

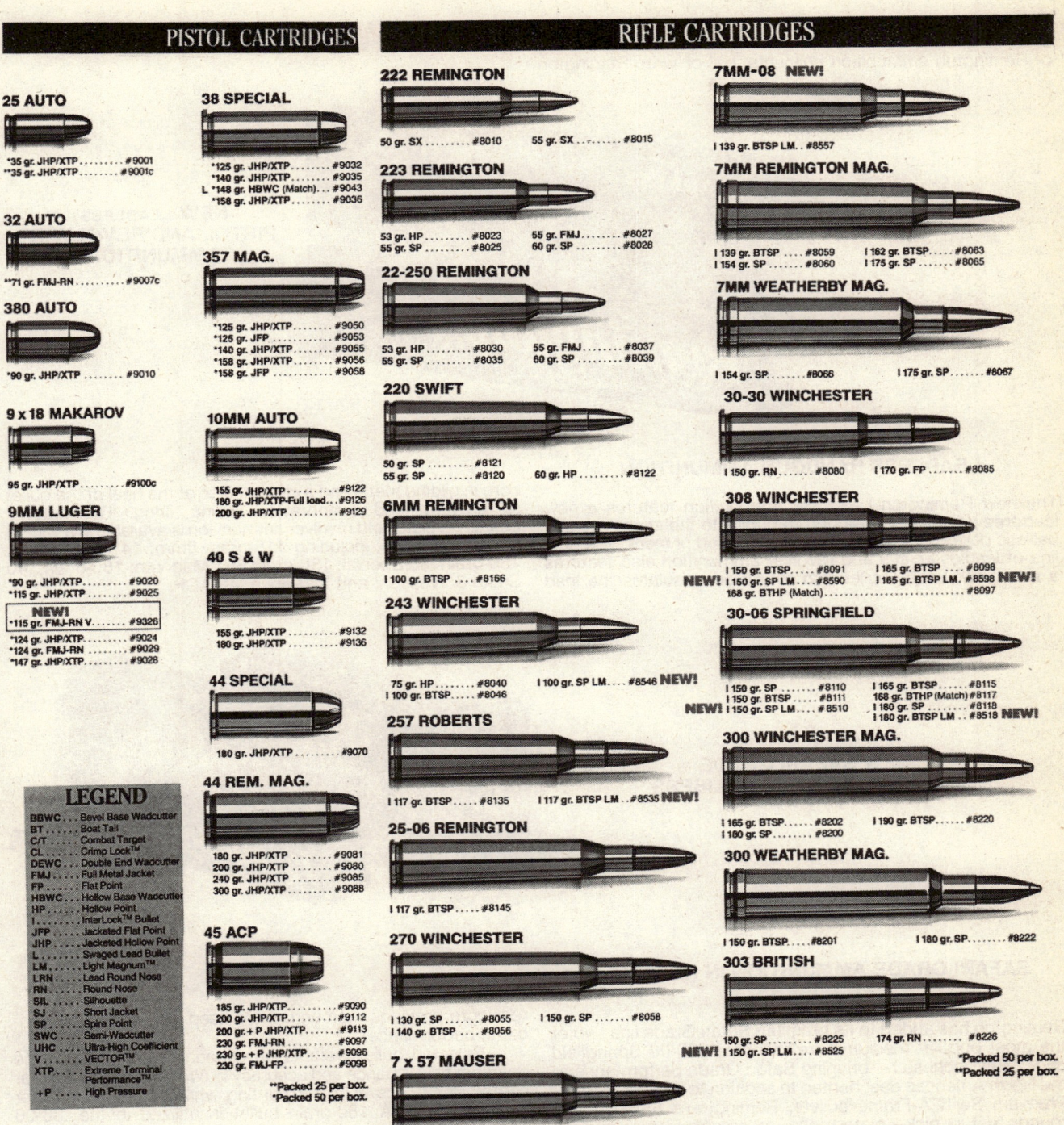

## PISTOL CARTRIDGES

### 25 AUTO

*35 gr. JHP/XTP ......... #9001
**35 gr. JHP/XTP ........ #9001c

### 32 AUTO

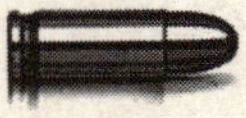

**71 gr. FMJ-RN .......... #9007c

### 380 AUTO

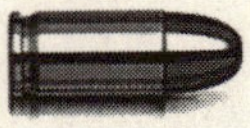

*90 gr. JHP/XTP ........ #9010

### 9 x 18 MAKAROV

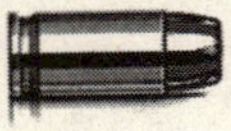

95 gr. JHP/XTP ......... #9100c

### 9MM LUGER

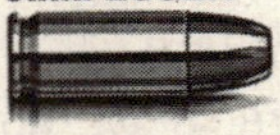

*90 gr. JHP/XTP ......... #9020
*115 gr. JHP/XTP ........ #9025

**NEW!**
*115 gr. FMJ-RN V ....... #9326

*124 gr. JHP/XTP ......... #9024
*124 gr. FMJ-RN ......... #9029
*147 gr. JHP/XTP ......... #9028

### 38 SPECIAL

*125 gr. JHP/XTP ........ #9032
*140 gr. JHP/XTP ........ #9035
L *148 gr. HBWC (Match) ... #9043
*158 gr. JHP/XTP ........ #9036

### 357 MAG.

*125 gr. JHP/XTP ........ #9050
*125 gr. JFP ............ #9053
*140 gr. JHP/XTP ........ #9055
*158 gr. JHP/XTP ........ #9056
*158 gr. JFP ............ #9058

### 10MM AUTO

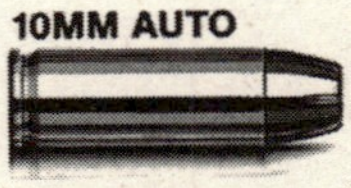

155 gr. JHP/XTP .......... #9122
180 gr. JHP/XTP-Full load ... #9126
200 gr. JHP/XTP .......... #9129

### 40 S & W

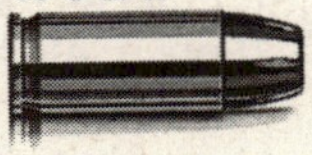

155 gr. JHP/XTP .......... #9132
180 gr. JHP/XTP .......... #9136

### 44 SPECIAL

180 gr. JHP/XTP .......... #9070

### 44 REM. MAG.

180 gr. JHP/XTP ......... #9081
200 gr. JHP/XTP ......... #9080
240 gr. JHP/XTP ......... #9085
300 gr. JHP/XTP .......... #9088

### 45 ACP

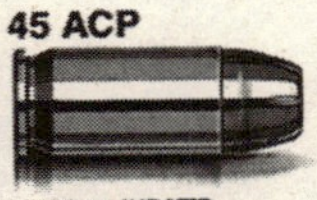

185 gr. JHP/XTP .......... #9090
200 gr. JHP/XTP .......... #9112
200 gr. + P JHP/XTP ....... #9113
230 gr. FMJ-RN .......... #9097
230 gr. + P JHP/XTP ...... #9096
230 gr. FMJ-FP ........... #9098

**Packed 25 per box.
*Packed 50 per box.

### LEGEND

BBWC ... Bevel Base Wadcutter
BT ...... Boat Tail
C/T ..... Combat Target
CL ...... Crimp Lock™
DEWC ... Double End Wadcutter
FMJ ..... Full Metal Jacket
FP ...... Flat Point
HBWC ... Hollow Base Wadcutter
HP ...... Hollow Point
I ........ InterLock™ Bullet
JFP ..... Jacketed Flat Point
JHP ..... Jacketed Hollow Point
L ........ Swaged Lead Bullet
LM ...... Light Magnum™
LRN ..... Lead Round Nose
RN ...... Round Nose
SIL ..... Silhouette
SJ ...... Short Jacket
SP ...... Spire Point
SWC .... Semi-Wadcutter
UHC .... Ultra-High Coefficient
V ....... VECTOR™
XTP ..... Extreme Terminal Performance™
+P ..... High Pressure

## RIFLE CARTRIDGES

### 222 REMINGTON

50 gr. SX ......... #8010
55 gr. SX ......... #8015

### 223 REMINGTON

53 gr. HP ......... #8023
55 gr. SP ......... #8025
55 gr. FMJ ........ #8027
60 gr. SP ......... #8028

### 22-250 REMINGTON

53 gr. HP ......... #8030
55 gr. SP ......... #8035
55 gr. FMJ ........ #8037
60 gr. SP ......... #8039

### 220 SWIFT

50 gr. SP ......... #8121
55 gr. SP ......... #8120
60 gr. HP ......... #8122

### 6MM REMINGTON

I 100 gr. BTSP .... #8166

### 243 WINCHESTER

75 gr. HP ........ #8040
I 100 gr. BTSP ..... #8046
I 100 gr. SP LM .... #8546 **NEW!**

### 257 ROBERTS

I 117 gr. BTSP ..... #8135
I 117 gr. BTSP LM .. #8535 **NEW!**

### 25-06 REMINGTON

I 117 gr. BTSP ..... #8145

### 270 WINCHESTER

I 130 gr. SP ....... #8055
I 140 gr. BTSP .... #8056
I 150 gr. SP ....... #8058

### 7 x 57 MAUSER

I 139 gr. BTSP ..... #8155
I 139 gr. BTSP LM .. #8555 **NEW!**

### 7MM-08 **NEW!**

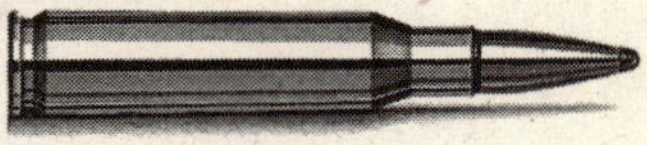

I 139 gr. BTSP LM .. #8557

### 7MM REMINGTON MAG.

I 139 gr. BTSP .... #8059
I 154 gr. SP ....... #8060
I 162 gr. BTSP ..... #8063
I 175 gr. SP ....... #8065

### 7MM WEATHERBY MAG.

I 154 gr. SP ....... #8066
I 175 gr. SP ....... #8067

### 30-30 WINCHESTER

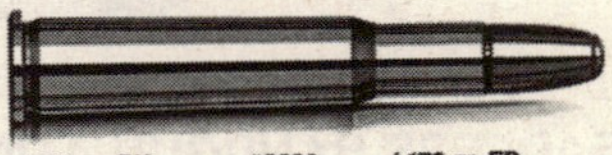

I 150 gr. RN ....... #8080
I 170 gr. FP ....... #8085

### 308 WINCHESTER

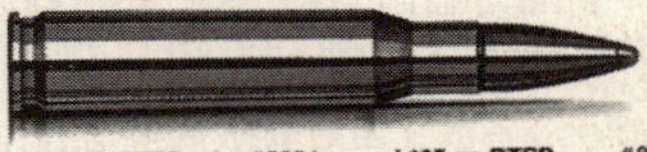

I 150 gr. BTSP ..... #8091
**NEW!** I 150 gr. SP LM .... #8590
I 165 gr. BTSP .... #8098
I 165 gr. BTSP LM. #8598 **NEW!**
168 gr. BTHP (Match) ............................ #8097

### 30-06 SPRINGFIELD

I 150 gr. SP ....... #8110
I 150 gr. BTSP ..... #8111
**NEW!** I 150 gr. SP LM .... #8510
I 165 gr. BTSP ...... #8115
168 gr. BTHP (Match) #8117
I 180 gr. SP ........ #8118
I 180 gr. BTSP LM .. #8518 **NEW!**

### 300 WINCHESTER MAG.

I 165 gr. BTSP ...... #8202
I 180 gr. SP ........ #8200
I 190 gr. BTSP ...... #8220

### 300 WEATHERBY MAG.

I 150 gr. BTSP ..... #8201
I 180 gr. SP ........ #8222

### 303 BRITISH

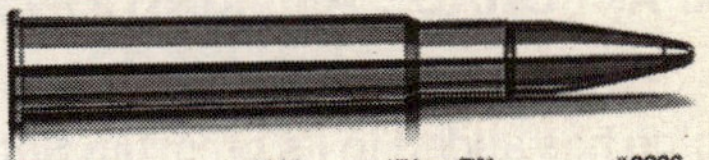

150 gr. SP ......... #8225
**NEW!** I 150 gr. SP LM .... #8525
174 gr. RN ........ #8226

*Packed 50 per box.
**Packed 25 per box.

# REMINGTON AMMUNITION

The following pages include Remington's new or recent lines of cartridges and shotshells for 1995–96. For a complete listing of Remington ammunition products, call or write Remington (*see* Directory of Manufacturers and Suppliers in the reference section for address and phone number).

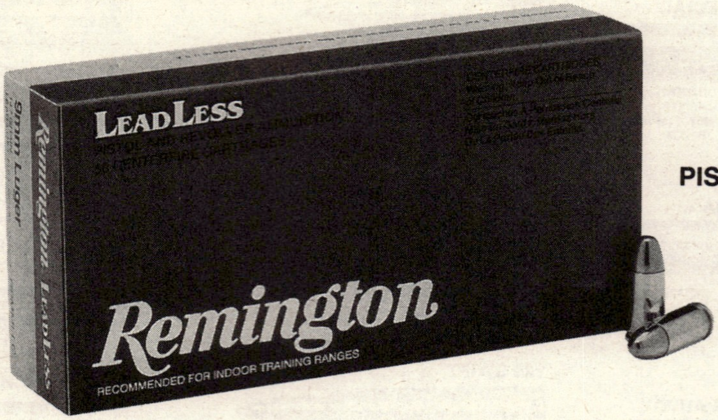


**NEW LEADLESS PISTOL AND REVOLVER AMMUNITION**

### LEADLESS HANDGUN AMMUNITION

The new Remington LeadLess ammunition features a new lead-free primer mix designed to duplicate the sensitivity and ballistic performance of current lead-based primers. The new line of leadless pistol and revolver ammunition also features a new Lead-Lokt® bullet that totally encapsulates the lead core in gilding metal and a closure disc at the heel of the bullet to prevent lead evaporation during firing. Remington's LeadLess pistol and revolver ammunition is available in a variety of specifications, including 115-gram 9mm; 147-grain 9mm; 130-grain .38 Special; 130-grain 357 Magnum; 180-grain, .40 Smith & Wesson; and 230-grain .45 ACP.

**NEW SAFARI GRADE CENTERFIRE RIFLE CALIBERS**

### SAFARI GRADE AMMUNITION IN NEW DEER CALIBERS

Remington has added to its premium Safari Grade line two of the most popular medium-bore calibers—.30-06 Springfield and .270 Winchester—bringing Safari Grade performance to the North American deer hunter. In addition to the use of Ultra-Premium Swift A-Frame bullets, Remington's Safari Grade rounds feature nickel-plated cases for reliable feeding and extraction. Swift bonded-core A-Frame bullets have a bullet weight retention of nearly 100 percent. The unique dual-core bullets feature a cross member that stops bullet expansion at twice bullet diameter. The pure lead core is physically bonded to the copper jacket to prevent core separation. The protected rear core provides momentum for deep penetration and on-game performance.

Selected bullet weights have been designed to create optimum performance and accuracy in two of the most popular centerfire calibers used for hunting whitetail deer and other midsize game. A 180-grain bullet is utilized in the .30-06 Springfield cartridge, providing a velocity of 2700 fps at the muzzle. The .270 cartridge features a 140-grain bullet with a muzzle velocity of 2925 fps. Both rounds expand the caliber options to seven: 270 Win., .30-06, 7mm Remington Magnum, .338 Win. Mag., 300 Win. Mag., 375 H&H Mag., and .416 Rem. Mag.

**NEW SHURSHOT® 12 GAUGE HEAVY FIELD LOADS**

## NEW REMINGTON SHURSHOT® HEAVY FIELD LOADS

Remington's Shurshot® Heavy Field loads now feature a 3¼ dram powder equivalent loading with a full 1¼ ounces of shot—more than Heavy Dove loads. These new field loads, designed for upland and small-game hunters, utilize one-piece unibody hulls and feature the proven Power Piston wad and mid-height cap for extra strength. Loaded to a velocity of 1220 fps, Shurshot® Heavy Field loads are available with # 6, #7½ and #8 shot.

## HANDICAP TRAP LOAD FOR PREMIER® NITRO 27 SHOTSHELLS

Remington's new Premier® Nitro 27 shotshells utilize slower burning powders that optimize the pressure/time curve for gentler acceleration of shot. The result is enhanced performance with less shot deformation and reduced recoil sensation. These loads have improved-pattern center core density at 40 yards that is 4 to 5 percent more dense than in current target loads. The result: target loads break targets more consistently at handicap distances. They are also recommended for other clay target sports in which long shots such as sporting clays second shots are possible.

Premier® Nitro 27 shotshells are available in 12 gauge 2¾″ with 1⅛ oz. of lead shot loaded to 3 dram. Both #7½ and #8 shot are available.

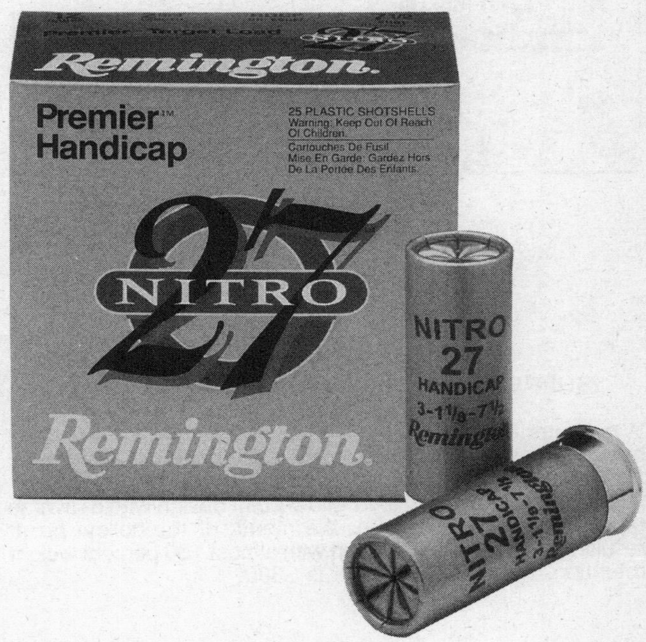


**PREMIER® NITRO 27™ HANDICAP TRAP LOADS**

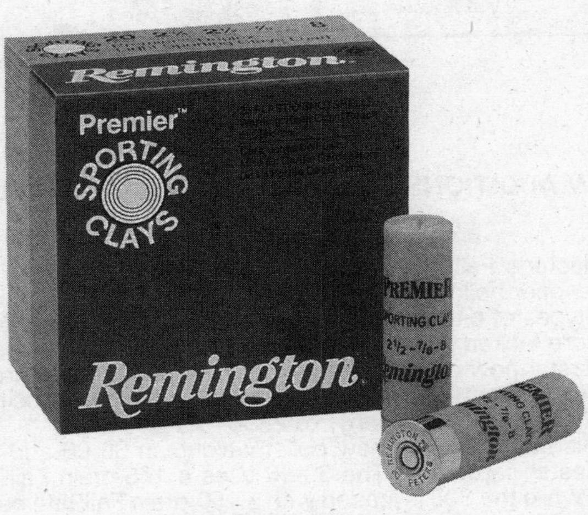


**PREMIER® 20 GAUGE SPORTING CLAYS LOADS**

## 20-GAUGE SPORTING CLAYS LOAD

Remington's Premier® 20-gauge Sporting Clays load features the 2½ dram ⅞ oz. offering of #8 high-antimony lead shot loaded to 1200 fps. This new load utilizes the same high-tensile one-piece Hardbody® hull as the 12-gauge target loads. The smooth hull promotes positive ejection and greater reloading ease, featuring an all-brass head for longer reloading life. The Premier Target Load line includes the new .410 gauge #8½ and specialty application loads.

# WINCHESTER AMMUNITION

The following pages include Winchester's new or recent lines of cartridges and shotshells for 1995–96. For a complete listing of Winchester ammunition products, call or write Winchester (*see* Directory of Manufacturers and Suppliers in the reference section for address and phone number).

## SUPER-X SUPER UNLEADED LINE

Pistol shooters who use a .45 Automatic can now shoot a lead-free load that uses a 230-grain FMJ encapsulated bullet in Winchester's Super-X Unleaded handgun ammunition line. The .45 Auto round has a muzzle velocity of 835 fps and a muzzle energy of 356 foot-pounds (virtually the same ballistics as the Super-X 230-grain FMJ load). It features a primer containing no lead, barium, antimony or strontium and a totally encapsulated lead core FMJ bullet. Symbol number is X45ASU.

## SUPREME SXT 380 AUTO HANDGUN LOAD

Winchester has added a 380 Auto load to its Supreme SXT handgun ammunition line. It uses a 95-grain SXT bullet with a muzzle velocity of 955 fps and muzzle energy of 192 foot-pounds. The SXT bullet is a hollow-point design with a reverse taper jacket extending over the mouth of the hollow point, resulting in excellent expansion with almost 100 percent weight retention. The symbol number is S380.

## NEW ADDITIONS TO SUPREME FAILSAFE RIFLE LINE

Winchester's FailSafe bullet, introduced in 1993, features a solid copper hollow-point nose section that expands quickly on all types of big game. The rear section of the bullet has a lead core locked in place and is supported by a steel insert. Winchester now offers a 280 Remington load in its Supreme Rifle line with a 160-grain FailSafe bullet, a muzzle velocity of 2840 fps and muzzle energy of 2866 foot-pounds.

Also available are new bullet weights in 30-06 and 308 Winchester cartridges. The 30-06 uses a 165-grain FailSafe bullet, while the 308 is loaded with a 150-grain FailSafe bullet. The 30-06 has a muzzle velocity of 2800 fps, and the 308 reaches 2820 fps. Symbol numbers are S280X (280 Rem.), S3006XA (30-06) and S308XA (308 Win.).

# WINCHESTER AMMUNITION

## AA/DOUBLE A 12-GAUGE 1 OZ. TARGET LOAD

Winchester's new 1 oz. AA load, which contains a full 3-dram equivalent of powder, is fast, hard-hitting and low on recoil. It's available in shot sizes 7½, 8 or 9 with a muzzle velocity of 1234 fps. It also uses the famous one-piece solver handicap AA hull, AA wad, BALL POWDER® propellant and extra-hard shot. The symbol number for the 1 oz. AA Target Load is AAHL12.

## NEW SHOT SIZES IN AA .410- & 28-GAUGE LOADS

Winchester's new 2½" .410 load uses ½ oz. of #8½ hard shot with a muzzle velocity of 1200 fps. In the new 28-gauge AA load, Winchester offers a ¾-oz. load of #8 hard shot, which is designed especially for skeet and sporting clay shooters. The 28-gauge load has a muzzle velocity of 1200 fps. Symbol numbers are AA4185 (.410 load) and AA288 (28-gauge load).

## POWER-POINT 22 RIMFIRE LOAD

The power-point 22 is more effective on varmints and small game than any other 22-rimfire load previously developed. At 100 yards, the Power-Point 22 bullet retains excellent velocity and energy. The copper-plated bullet works well in all types of 22-rimfire firearms, including semiauto pistols and rifles. This hard-hitting hollow-point bullet mushrooms much like a big-game bullet. Its symbol number is X22LRPP.

# WINCHESTER AMMUNITION

## SHOTSHELL GUIDE

### SHOTSHELL GAME GUIDE

| | SHELL | | SHOT SIZE | CHOKE | GAUGE |
|---|---|---|---|---|---|
| **GEESE** | STEEL: | Super-X® Drylok™ | T, BBB, BB, | Mod. | 10,12 |
| | | | 1, 2 | Mod., Imp. Mod. | 10, 12 |
| **DUCKS** | STEEL: | Super-X Drylok | 1, 2, 3, 4, 6 | Imp. Cyl. Mod., Imp. Mod. | 10, 12, 20 |
| **TURKEY** | LEAD: | Super-X | 4, 5, 6 | Full | 12, 16, 20 |
| | | Double X® | 4, 5, 6 | Full | 10, 12, 16, 20 |
| **PHEASANT** | LEAD: | Super-X | 4, 5, 6, 7½ | Imp. Cyl., Mod., Imp. Mod. | 12, 16, 20 |
| | | Double X | 4, 6 | Imp. Cyl., Mod., Imp. Mod. | 12, 16, 20 |
| | | Small Game Hunter™ | 6 | Imp. Cyl., Mod., Imp. Mod. | 12, 20 |
| | | AA® Super Pigeon | 7½ | Mod., Imp. Mod., Full | 12 |
| | STEEL: | Super-X Drylok | 4, 6 | Mod., Imp. Mod.,Full | 12, 20 |
| **PARTRIDGE** | LEAD: | Super-X | 5, 6, 7½, 8 | Imp. Cyl., Mod. | 12, 16, 20, 28 |
| | | Small Game Hunter | 6, 7½, 8 | Imp. Cyl., Mod. | 12, 20 |
| **WOODCOCK SNIPE RAIL** | LEAD: | Super-X | 6, 7½, 8 | Imp. Cyl., Mod. | 12, 16, 20, 28 |
| | | Small Game Hunter | 7½, 8 | Imp. Cyl., Mod. | 12, 20 |
| | STEEL: | Super-X Drylok | 4, 6 | Imp. Cyl., Mod. | 12, 16, 20 |
| **QUAIL** | LEAD: | Super-X | 7½, 8, 9 | Imp. Cyl., Mod. | 12, 16, 20, 28 |
| | | Small Game Hunter | 7½, 8 | Imp. Cyl., Mod. | 12, 20 |
| **DOVE** | LEAD: | Super-X | 7½, 8, 9 | Imp. Cyl., Mod., Imp. Mod. | 12, 16, 20, 28 |
| | | Small Game Hunter | 7½, 8 | Imp. Cyl., Mod., Imp. Mod. | 12, 20 |
| | STEEL: | Super-X Drylok | 6 | Imp. Cyl., Mod., Imp. Mod. | 12, 16, 20 |
| **RABBIT** | LEAD: | Super-X | 4, 5, 6, 7½ | Imp. Cyl., Mod. | 12, 16, 20, 28, 410 |
| | | Small Game Hunter | 6, 7½ | Imp. Cyl., Mod. | 12, 20 |
| **SQUIRREL** | LEAD: | Super-X | 4, 5, 6 | Mod., Imp. Mod., Full | 12, 16, 20, 28, 410 |
| | | Small Game Hunter | 6 | Mod., Imp. Mod., Full | 12, 20 |

### STANDARD SHOT SIZES

**Buckshot Sizes**

| Shot Number | Diameter in Inches | # Pellets Typical Loads |
|---|---|---|
| #4 | .24 | 27<br>34<br>41 |
| #3 | .25 | 20<br>24 |
| #1 | .30 | 12<br>16<br>20<br>24 |
| 0 | .32 | 12 |
| 00 | .33 | 9<br>12<br>15<br>18 |
| 000 | .36 | 8<br>10 |

**Shot Sizes**

| Shot Number | Diameter in Inches | Pellets/oz., Lead | Pellets/oz., Steel |
|---|---|---|---|
| 9 | .08 | 585 | - |
| 8 | .09 | 410 | - |
| 7½ | .095 | 350 | - |
| 6 | .11 | 225 | 316 |
| 5 | .12 | 170 | 243 |
| 4 | .13 | 135 | 191 |
| 3 | .14 | - | 153 |
| 2 | .15 | 87 | 125 |
| 1 | .16 | - | 103 |
| BB | .18 | 50 | 72 |
| BBB | .19 | - | 61 |
| T | .20 | - | 53 |

### LEAD VS. STEEL

**COMPARISON CHART***

| Shot Type | Wt. | Shot Size | No. Pellets | Muzzle Velocity (FPS) | Retained Energy Per Pellet (Ft. Lbs.) 40 Yds. | 60 Yds. |
|---|---|---|---|---|---|---|
| Lead | 1¼ | 6 | 281 | 1330 | 2.3 | 1.3 |
| Steel | 1⅛ | 4 | 215 | 1365 | 2.5 | 1.4 |
| Lead | 1¼ | 4 | 169 | 1330 | 4.4 | 2.7 |
| Steel | 1⅛ | 2 | 141 | 1365 | 4.4 | 2.6 |
| Lead | 1½ | 4 | 202 | 1260 | 4.1 | 2.6 |
| Steel | 1¼ | 2 | 156 | 1275 | 4.1 | 2.4 |
| Lead | 1½ | 2 | 130 | 1260 | 7.0 | 4.6 |
| Steel | 1¼ | BB | 90 | 1275 | 8.3 | 5.2 |

*Source: SAAMI Exterior Ballistics Tables Adopted 4/23/81
NOTE: Steel shot pellets two sizes larger than lead deliver comparable down range energy.

# Ballistics

# FEDERAL BALLISTICS

## PREMIUM® HUNTING RIFLE BALLISTICS

| USAGE | FEDERAL LOAD NO. | CALIBER | BULLET WGT. IN GRAINS | BULLET WGT. IN GRAMS | BULLET STYLE* | FACTORY PRIMER NO. | VELOCITY IN FEET PER SECOND (TO NEAREST 10 FEET) MUZZLE | 100 YDS. | 200 YDS. | 300 YDS. | 400 YDS. | 500 YDS. | ENERGY IN FOOT-POUNDS (TO NEAREST 5 FOOT-POUNDS) MUZZLE | 100 YDS. | 200 YDS. | 300 YDS. | 400 YDS. | 500 YDS. |
|---|---|---|---|---|---|---|---|---|---|---|---|---|---|---|---|---|---|---|
| 1 | P223E | 223 Rem. (5.56x45mm) | 55 | 3.56 | Boat-tail HP | 205 | 3240 | 2770 | 2340 | 1950 | 1610 | 1330 | 1280 | 935 | 670 | 465 | 315 | 215 |
| 1 NEW | P223F | 223 Rem. (5.56x45mm) | 55 | 3.56 | Nosler Balistic Tip | 205 | 3240 | 2870 | 2530 | 2220 | 1920 | 1660 | 1280 | 1005 | 780 | 600 | 450 | 335 |
| 1 | P22250B | 22-250 Rem. | 55 | 3.56 | Boat-tail HP | 210 | 3680 | 3280 | 2920 | 2590 | 2280 | 1990 | 1655 | 1315 | 1040 | 815 | 630 | 480 |
| 2 | P243C | 243 Win. (6.16x51mm) | 100 | 6.48 | Boat-tail SP | 210 | 2960 | 2760 | 2570 | 2380 | 2210 | 2040 | 1950 | 1690 | 1460 | 1260 | 1080 | 925 |
| 1 | P243D | 243 Win. (6.16x51mm) | 85 | 5.50 | Boat-tail HP | 210 | 3320 | 3070 | 2830 | 2600 | 2380 | 2180 | 2080 | 1770 | 1510 | 1280 | 1070 | 890 |
| 1 NEW | P243F | 243 Win. (6.16x51mm) | 70 | 4.54 | Nosler Ballistic Tip | 210 | 3400 | 3070 | 2760 | 2470 | 2200 | 1950 | 1795 | 1465 | 1185 | 950 | 755 | 590 |
| 2 | P6C | 6mm Rem. | 100 | 6.48 | Nosler Partition | 210 | 3100 | 2830 | 2570 | 2330 | 2100 | 1890 | 2135 | 1775 | 1470 | 1205 | 985 | 790 |
| 2 | P257B | 257 Roberts (High-Velocity + P) | 120 | 7.77 | Nosler Partition | 210 | 2780 | 2560 | 2360 | 2160 | 1970 | 1790 | 2060 | 1750 | 1480 | 1240 | 1030 | 855 |
| 2 | P2506C | 25-06 Rem. | 117 | 7.58 | Boat-tail SP | 210 | 2990 | 2770 | 2570 | 2370 | 2190 | 2000 | 2320 | 2000 | 1715 | 1465 | 1240 | 1045 |
| 2 NEW | P2506D | 25-06 Rem. | 100 | 6.48 | Nosler Ballistic Tip | 210 | 3210 | 2960 | 2720 | 2490 | 2280 | 2070 | 2290 | 1940 | 1640 | 1380 | 1150 | 955 |
| 2 | P6555A | 6.5x55 Swedish | 140 | 9.07 | Nosler Partition | 210 | 2550 | 2350 | 2170 | 1990 | 1820 | 1660 | 2020 | 1725 | 1460 | 1230 | 1030 | 860 |
| 2 | P270C | 270 Win. | 150 | 9.72 | Boat-tail SP | 210 | 2850 | 2660 | 2480 | 2300 | 2130 | 1970 | 2705 | 2355 | 2040 | 1760 | 1510 | 1290 |
| 2 | P270D | 270 Win. | 130 | 8.42 | Boat-tail SP | 210 | 3060 | 2830 | 2620 | 2410 | 2220 | 2030 | 2700 | 2320 | 1980 | 1680 | 1420 | 1190 |
| 2 | P270E | 270 Win. | 150 | 9.72 | Nosler Partition | 210 | 2850 | 2590 | 2340 | 2100 | 1880 | 1670 | 2705 | 2225 | 1815 | 1470 | 1175 | 930 |
| 2 NEW | P270F | 270 Win. | 130 | 8.42 | Nosler Ballistic Tip | 210 | 3060 | 2840 | 2630 | 2430 | 2230 | 2050 | 2700 | 2325 | 1990 | 1700 | 1440 | 1210 |
| 2 | P270T1 | 270 Win. | 140 | 9.07 | Trophy Bonded Bear Claw | 210 | 2940 | 2700 | 2480 | 2260 | 2060 | 1860 | 2685 | 2270 | 1905 | 1590 | 1315 | 1080 |
| 2 NEW | P270WBA | 270 Weatherby Magnum | 130 | 8.42 | Nosler Partition | 210 | 3200 | 2960 | 2740 | 2520 | 2320 | 2120 | 2955 | 2530 | 2160 | 1835 | 1550 | 1300 |
| 2 NEW | P270WBT1 | 270 Weatherby Magnum | 140 | 9.07 | Trophy Bonded Bear Claw | 210 | 3100 | 2880 | 2670 | 2470 | 2280 | 2100 | 2985 | 2575 | 2215 | 1895 | 1610 | 1365 |
| 2 | P730A | 7-30 Waters | 120 | 7.77 | Boat-tail SP | 210 | 2700 | 2300 | 1930 | 1600 | 1330 | 1140 | 1940 | 1405 | 990 | 685 | 470 | 345 |
| 2 | P7C | 7mm Mauser (7x57mm Mauser) | 140 | 9.07 | Nosler Partition | 210 | 2660 | 2450 | 2260 | 2070 | 1890 | 1730 | 2200 | 1865 | 1585 | 1330 | 1110 | 930 |
| 2 | P764A | 7x64 Brenneke | 160 | 10.37 | Nosler Partition | 210 | 2650 | 2480 | 2310 | 2150 | 2000 | 1850 | 2495 | 2180 | 1895 | 1640 | 1415 | 1215 |
| 2 | P280A | 280 Rem. | 150 | 9.72 | Nosler Partition | 210 | 2890 | 2620 | 2370 | 2140 | 1910 | 1710 | 2780 | 2295 | 1875 | 1520 | 1215 | 970 |
| 2 NEW | P280T1 | 280 Rem. | 140 | 9.07 | Trophy Bonded Bear Claw | 210 | 2990 | 2630 | 2310 | 2040 | 1730 | 1480 | 2770 | 2155 | 1655 | 1250 | 925 | 680 |
| 2 | P708A | 7mm-08 | 140 | 9.07 | Nosler Partition | 210 | 2800 | 2590 | 2390 | 2200 | 2020 | 1840 | 2435 | 2085 | 1775 | 1500 | 1265 | 1060 |
| 2 | P7RD | 7mm Rem. Magnum | 150 | 9.72 | Boat-tail SP | 215 | 3110 | 2920 | 2750 | 2580 | 2410 | 2250 | 3220 | 2850 | 2510 | 2210 | 1930 | 1690 |
| 3 | P7RE | 7mm Rem. Magnum | 165 | 10.69 | Boat-tail SP | 215 | 2950 | 2800 | 2650 | 2510 | 2370 | 2230 | 3190 | 2865 | 2570 | 2300 | 2050 | 1825 |
| 3 | P7RF | 7mm Rem. Magnum | 160 | 10.37 | Nosler Partition | 215 | 2950 | 2770 | 2590 | 2420 | 2250 | 2090 | 3090 | 2715 | 2375 | 2075 | 1800 | 1555 |
| 2 | P7RG | 7mm Rem. Magnum | 140 | 9.07 | Nosler Partition | 215 | 3150 | 2930 | 2710 | 2510 | 2320 | 2130 | 3085 | 2660 | 2290 | 1960 | 1670 | 1415 |
| 3 | P7RT1 | 7mm Rem. Magnum | 175 | 11.34 | Trophy Bonded Bear Claw | 215 | 2860 | 2660 | 2470 | 2290 | 2120 | 1950 | 3180 | 2750 | 2375 | 2040 | 1740 | 1475 |
| 2 NEW | P7RT2 | 7mm Rem. Magnum | 160 | 10.37 | Trophy Bonded Bear Claw | 215 | 2940 | 2630 | 2350 | 2080 | 1830 | 1600 | 3070 | 2460 | 1950 | 1530 | 1185 | 905 |
| 3 NEW | P7WBA | 7mm Weatherby Magnum | 160 | 10.37 | Nosler Partition | 215 | 3050 | 2850 | 2650 | 2470 | 2290 | 2120 | 3305 | 2880 | 2505 | 2165 | 1865 | 1600 |
| 3 NEW | P7RWBT1 | 7mm Weatherby Magnum | 160 | 10.37 | Trophy Bonded Bear Claw | 215 | 3050 | 2860 | 2660 | 2480 | 2300 | 2130 | 3305 | 2885 | 2510 | 2175 | 1875 | 1610 |
| 2 | P3030D | 30-30 Win. | 170 | 11.01 | Nosler Partition | 210 | 2200 | 1900 | 1620 | 1380 | 1190 | 1060 | 1830 | 1355 | 990 | 720 | 535 | 425 |
| 2 | P308C | 308 Win. (7.62x51mm) | 165 | 10.69 | Boat-tail SP | 210 | 2700 | 2520 | 2330 | 2160 | 1990 | 1830 | 2670 | 2310 | 1990 | 1700 | 1450 | 1230 |
| 3 | P308E | 308 Win. (7.62x51mm) | 180 | 11.66 | Nosler Partition | 210 | 2620 | 2430 | 2240 | 2060 | 1890 | 1730 | 2745 | 2355 | 2005 | 1700 | 1430 | 1200 |
| 3 NEW | P308F | 308 Win. (7.62x51mm) | 150 | 9.72 | Nosler Ballistic Tip | 210 | 2820 | 2610 | 2410 | 2220 | 2040 | 1860 | 2650 | 2270 | 1935 | 1640 | 1380 | 1155 |
| 3 | P308T1 | 308 Win. | 165 | 10.69 | Trophy Bonded Bear Claw | 210 | 2700 | 2480 | 2280 | 2080 | 1900 | 1720 | 2670 | 2260 | 1900 | 1590 | 1315 | 1085 |
| 2 | P3006D | 30-06 Spring (7.62x63mm) | 165 | 10.69 | Boat-tail SP | 210 | 2800 | 2610 | 2420 | 2240 | 2070 | 1910 | 2870 | 2490 | 2150 | 1840 | 1580 | 1340 |
| 3 | P3006F | 30-06 Spring (7.62x63mm) | 180 | 11.66 | Nosler Partition | 210 | 2700 | 2500 | 2320 | 2140 | 1970 | 1810 | 2915 | 2510 | 2150 | 1830 | 1550 | 1350 |
| 2 | P3006G | 30-06 Spring (7.62x63mm) | 150 | 9.72 | Boat-tail SP | 210 | 2910 | 2690 | 2480 | 2270 | 2070 | 1880 | 2820 | 2420 | 2040 | 1710 | 1430 | 1180 |
| 3 | P3006L | 30-06 Spring (7.62x63mm) | 180 | 11.66 | Boat-tail SP | 210 | 2700 | 2540 | 2380 | 2220 | 2080 | 1930 | 2915 | 2570 | 2260 | 1975 | 1720 | 1495 |
| 3 NEW | P3006P | 30-06 Spring (7.62x63mm) | 150 | 9.72 | Nosler Ballistic Tip | 210 | 2910 | 2700 | 2490 | 2300 | 2110 | 1940 | 2820 | 2420 | 2070 | 1760 | 1485 | 1245 |
| 3 NEW | P3006Q | 30-06 Spring (7.62x63mm) | 165 | 10.69 | Nosler Ballistic Tip | 210 | 2800 | 2610 | 2430 | 2250 | 2080 | 1920 | 2870 | 2495 | 2155 | 1855 | 1585 | 1350 |
| 2 | P3006T1 | 30-06 Spring (7.62x63mm) | 165 | 10.69 | Trophy Bonded Bear Claw | 210 | 2800 | 2540 | 2290 | 2050 | 1830 | 1630 | 2870 | 2360 | 1915 | 1545 | 1230 | 975 |
| 2 NEW | P3006T2 | 30-06 Spring (7.62x63mm) | 180 | 11.66 | Trophy Bonded Bear Claw | 210 | 2700 | 2430 | 2170 | 1930 | 1710 | 1500 | 2915 | 2355 | 1880 | 1485 | 1160 | 905 |
| 3 | P300WC | 300 Win. Magnum | 200 | 12.96 | Boat-tail SP | 215 | 2830 | 2680 | 2530 | 2380 | 2240 | 2110 | 3560 | 3180 | 2830 | 2520 | 2230 | 1970 |

## PREMIUM® SAFARI RIFLE BALLISTICS

| USAGE | FEDERAL LOAD NO. | CALIBER | BULLET WGT. IN GRAINS | BULLET WGT. IN GRAMS | BULLET STYLE* | FACTORY PRIMER NO. | VELOCITY IN FEET PER SECOND (TO NEAREST 10 FEET) MUZZLE | 100 YDS. | 200 YDS. | 300 YDS. | 400 YDS. | 500 YDS. | ENERGY IN FOOT-POUNDS (TO NEAREST 5 FOOT-POUNDS) MUZZLE | 100 YDS. | 200 YDS. | 300 YDS. | 400 YDS. | 500 YDS. |
|---|---|---|---|---|---|---|---|---|---|---|---|---|---|---|---|---|---|---|
| 3 | P300HA | 300 H&H Magnum | 180 | 11.66 | Nosler Partition | 215 | 2880 | 2620 | 2380 | 2150 | 1930 | 1730 | 3315 | 2750 | 2260 | 1840 | 1480 | 1190 |
| 3 | P300WD2 | 300 Win. Magnum | 180 | 11.66 | Nosler Partition | 215 | 2960 | 2700 | 2450 | 2210 | 1990 | 1780 | 3500 | 2905 | 2395 | 1955 | 1585 | 1270 |
| 3 | P300WT1 | 300 Win. Magnum | 200 | 12.96 | Trophy Bonded Bear Claw | 215 | 2800 | 2570 | 2350 | 2150 | 1950 | 1770 | 3480 | 2935 | 2460 | 2050 | 1690 | 1385 |
| 3 NEW | P300WT2 | 300 Win. Magnum | 180 | 11.66 | Trophy Bonded Bear Claw | 215 | 2960 | 2680 | 2410 | 2160 | 1920 | 1700 | 3500 | 2860 | 2315 | 1855 | 1470 | 1155 |
| 3 NEW | P300WBA | 300 Weatherby Magnum | 180 | 11.66 | Nosler Partition | 215 | 3190 | 2980 | 2780 | 2590 | 2400 | 2230 | 4055 | 3540 | 3080 | 2670 | 2305 | 1985 |
| 3 NEW | P300WBT1 | 300 Weatherby Magnum | 180 | 1.66 | Trophy Bonded Bear Claw | 215 | 3190 | 2990 | 2790 | 2610 | 2430 | 2260 | 4065 | 3565 | 3120 | 2720 | 2365 | 2045 |
| 3 | P338A2 | 338 Win. Magnum | 210 | 13.60 | Nosler Partition | 215 | 2830 | 2590 | 2370 | 2160 | 1960 | 1770 | 3735 | 3140 | 2620 | 2170 | 1785 | 1455 |
| 3 | P338B2 | 338 Win. Magnum | 250 | 16.20 | Nosler Partition | 215 | 2660 | 2400 | 2150 | 1910 | 1690 | 1500 | 3925 | 3185 | 2555 | 2055 | 1590 | 1245 |
| 3 | P338T1 | 338 Win. Magnum | 225 | 14.58 | Trophy Bonded Bear Claw | 215 | 2800 | 2560 | 2330 | 2110 | 1900 | 1710 | 3915 | 3265 | 2700 | 2220 | 1800 | 1455 |
| 4 | P375D | 375 H&H Magnum | 300 | 19.44 | Solid | 215 | 2530 | 2170 | 1840 | 1550 | 1310 | 1140 | 4265 | 3140 | 2260 | 1605 | 1140 | 860 |
| 4 | P375F | 375 H&H Magnum | 300 | 19.44 | Nosler Partition | 215 | 2530 | 2320 | 2120 | 1930 | 1750 | 1590 | 4265 | 3585 | 2995 | 2475 | 2040 | 1675 |
| 4 | P375T1 | 375 H&H Magnum | 300 | 19.44 | Trophy Bonded Bear Claw | 215 | 2530 | 2280 | 2040 | 1810 | 1610 | 1425 | 4265 | 3450 | 2765 | 2190 | 1725 | 1350 |
| 3 | P458A | 458 Win. Magnum | 350 | 22.68 | Soft Point | 215 | 2470 | 1990 | 1570 | 1250 | 1060 | 950 | 4740 | 3065 | 1915 | 1205 | 870 | 705 |
| 4 | P458B | 458 Win. Magnum | 510 | 33.04 | Soft Point | 215 | 2090 | 1820 | 1570 | 1360 | 1190 | 1080 | 4945 | 3730 | 2790 | 2080 | 1605 | 1320 |
| 4 | P458C | 458 Win. Magnum | 500 | 32.40 | Solid | 215 | 2090 | 1870 | 1670 | 1480 | 1320 | 1190 | 4850 | 3880 | 3085 | 2440 | 1945 | 1585 |
| 4 | P458T1 | 458 Win. Magnum | 400 | 25.92 | Trophy Bonded Bear Claw | 215 | 2380 | 2170 | 1960 | 1770 | 1590 | 1430 | 5030 | 4165 | 3415 | 2785 | 2255 | 1825 |
| 4 | P458T2 | 458 Win. Magnum | 500 | 32.40 | Trophy Bonded Bear Claw | 215 | 2090 | 1870 | 1660 | 1480 | 1310 | 1180 | 4850 | 3870 | 3065 | 2420 | 1915 | 1550 |
| 4 | P458T3 | 458 Win. Magnum | 500 | 32.40 | Trophy Bonded Solid | 215 | 2090 | 1860 | 1650 | 1460 | 1300 | 1170 | 4850 | 3845 | 3025 | 2365 | 1865 | 1505 |
| 4 | P416A | 416 Rigby | 410 | 26.57 | Weldcore SP | 216 | 2370 | 2110 | 1870 | 1640 | 1440 | 1280 | 5115 | 4050 | 3165 | 2455 | 1895 | 1485 |
| 4 | P416B | 416 Rigby | 410 | 26.57 | Solid | 216 | 2370 | 2110 | 1870 | 1640 | 1440 | 1280 | 5115 | 4050 | 3165 | 2455 | 1895 | 1485 |
| 4 | P416T1 | 416 Rigby | 400 | 25.92 | Trophy Bonded Bear Claw | 216 | 2370 | 2210 | 2050 | 1900 | 1750 | 1620 | 4990 | 4315 | 3720 | 3185 | 2720 | 2315 |
| 4 | P416T2 | 416 Rigby | 400 | 25.92 | Trophy Bonded Solid | 216 | 2370 | 2120 | 1890 | 1660 | 1460 | 1290 | 4990 | 3975 | 3130 | 2440 | 1895 | 1480 |
| 4 | P470A | 470 Nitro Express | 500 | 32.40 | Weldcore SP | 216 | 2150 | 1890 | 1650 | 1440 | 1270 | 1140 | 5130 | 3965 | 3040 | 2310 | 1790 | 1435 |
| 4 | P470B | 470 Nitro Express | 500 | 32.40 | Woodleigh Solid | 216 | 2150 | 1890 | 1650 | 1440 | 1270 | 1140 | 5130 | 3965 | 3040 | 2310 | 1790 | 1435 |
| 4 | P470T1 | 470 Nitro Express | 500 | 32.40 | Trophy Bonded Bear Claw | 216 | 2150 | 1940 | 1740 | 1560 | 1400 | 1260 | 5130 | 4170 | 3360 | 2695 | 2160 | 1750 |
| 4 | P470T2 | 470 Nitro Express | 500 | 32.40 | Trophy Bonded Solid | 216 | 2150 | 1940 | 1740 | 1560 | 1400 | 1260 | 5130 | 4170 | 3360 | 2695 | 2160 | 1750 |

*HP = Hollow Point SP = Soft Point +P ammunition is loaded to a higher pressure. Use only in firearms so recommended by the gun manufacturer.

# FEDERAL BALLISTICS

Usage Key: 1 = Varmints, predators, small game 2 = Medium game 3 = Large, heavy game 4 = Dangerous game 5 = Target shooting, training, practice

| WIND DRIFT IN INCHES 10 MPH CROSSWIND 100 YDS. | 200 YDS. | 300 YDS. | 400 YDS. | 500 YDS. | HEIGHT OF BULLET TRAJECTORY IN INCHES ABOVE OR BELOW LINE OF SIGHT IF ZEROED AT ⊕ YARDS. SIGHTS 1.5 INCHES ABOVE BORE LINE. AVERAGE RANGE 50 YDS. | 100 YDS. | 200 YDS. | 300 YDS. | LONG RANGE 50 YDS. | 100 YDS. | 200 YDS. | 300 YDS. | 400 YDS. | 500 YDS. | TEST BARREL LENGTH INCHES | FEDERAL LOAD NO. |
|---|---|---|---|---|---|---|---|---|---|---|---|---|---|---|---|---|
| 1.3 | 5.8 | 14.2 | 27.7 | 47.6 | -0.3 | ⊕ | -2.7 | -10.8 | +0.4 | +1.4 | ⊕ | -6.7 | -20.5 | -43.4 | 24 | P223E |
| 1.0 | 4.3 | 10.3 | 19.6 | 32.9 | -0.3 | ⊕ | -2.7 | -10.9 | +0.4 | +1.4 | ⊕ | -6.8 | -20.8 | -44.2 | 24 | P223F |
| 0.8 | 3.6 | 8.4 | 15.8 | 26.3 | -0.4 | ⊕ | -1.7 | -7.6 | 0 | +0.9 | ⊕ | -5.0 | -15.1 | -32.0 | 24 | P22250B |
| 0.6 | 2.6 | 6.1 | 11.3 | 18.4 | -0.2 | ⊕ | -3.1 | -11.4 | +0.6 | +1.5 | ⊕ | -6.8 | -19.8 | -39.9 | 24 | P243C |
| 0.7 | 2.7 | 6.3 | 11.6 | 18.8 | -0.3 | ⊕ | -2.2 | -8.8 | +0.2 | +1.1 | ⊕ | -5.5 | -16.1 | -32.8 | 24 | P243D |
| 0.8 | 3.4 | 8.1 | 15.2 | 25.1 | -0.3 | ⊕ | -2.2 | -9.0 | +0.2 | +1.1 | ⊕ | -5.7 | -17.1 | -35.7 | 24 | P243F |
| 0.8 | 3.3 | 7.9 | 14.7 | 24.1 | -0.3 | ⊕ | -2.9 | -11.0 | +0.5 | +1.4 | ⊕ | -6.7 | -19.8 | -39.0 | 24 | P6C |
| 0.8 | 3.3 | 7.7 | 14.3 | 23.5 | -0.1 | ⊕ | -3.8 | -14.0 | +0.8 | +1.9 | ⊕ | -8.2 | -24.0 | -48.9 | 24 | P257B |
| 0.7 | 2.8 | 6.5 | 12.0 | 19.6 | -0.2 | ⊕ | -3.0 | -11.4 | +0.5 | +1.5 | ⊕ | -6.8 | -19.9 | -40.4 | 24 | P2506C |
| 0.7 | 2.9 | 6.7 | 12.4 | 20.2 | -0.3 | ⊕ | -2.5 | -9.7 | +0.3 | +1.2 | ⊕ | -6.0 | -17.5 | -35.8 | 24 | P2506D |
| 0.8 | 3.5 | 8.3 | 15.1 | 25.1 | 0 | ⊕ | -4.8 | -17.1 | +1.2 | +2.4 | ⊕ | -9.8 | -28.2 | -57.7 | 24 | P6555A |
| 0.7 | 2.7 | 6.3 | 11.6 | 18.9 | -0.2 | ⊕ | -3.4 | -12.5 | +0.7 | +1.7 | ⊕ | -7.4 | -21.4 | -43.0 | 24 | P270C |
| 0.7 | 2.8 | 6.6 | 12.1 | 19.7 | -0.2 | ⊕ | -2.8 | -10.7 | +0.5 | +1.4 | ⊕ | -6.5 | -19.0 | -38.5 | 24 | P270D |
| 0.9 | 3.9 | 9.2 | 17.3 | 28.5 | -0.2 | ⊕ | -3.7 | -13.8 | +0.8 | +1.9 | ⊕ | -8.3 | -24.4 | -50.5 | 24 | P270E |
| 0.7 | 2.7 | 6.4 | 11.9 | 19.3 | -0.2 | ⊕ | -2.8 | -10.7 | +0.5 | +1.4 | ⊕ | -6.5 | -18.8 | -38.2 | 24 | P270F |
| 0.8 | 3.2 | 7.6 | 14.2 | 23.0 | -0.2 | ⊕ | -3.3 | -12.2 | +0.6 | +1.6 | ⊕ | -7.3 | -21.5 | -43.7 | 24 | P270T1 |
| 0.7 | 2.7 | 6.3 | 11.7 | 19.0 | -0.3 | ⊕ | -2.5 | -9.6 | +0.3 | +1.2 | ⊕ | -5.9 | -17.3 | -35.1 | 24 | P270WBA |
| 0.6 | 2.66 | 6.17 | 11.38 | 18.6 | -0.3 | ⊕ | -2.7 | -10.3 | +0.4 | +1.4 | ⊕ | -6.2 | -18.1 | -36.9 | 24 | P270WBT1 |
| 1.6 | 7.2 | 17.7 | 34.5 | 58.1 | 0 | ⊕ | -5.2 | -19.8 | +1.2 | +2.6 | ⊕ | -12.0 | -37.6 | -81.7 | 24 | P730A |
| 1.3 | 3.2 | 8.2 | 15.4 | 23.4 | -0.1 | ⊕ | -4.3 | -15.4 | +1.0 | +2.1 | ⊕ | -9.0 | -26.1 | -52.9 | 24 | P7C |
| 0.7 | 2.8 | 6.6 | 12.3 | 19.5 | -0.1 | ⊕ | -4.2 | -14.9 | +0.9 | +2.1 | ⊕ | -8.7 | -24.9 | -49.4 | 24 | P764A |
| 0.9 | 3.8 | 9.0 | 16.8 | 27.8 | -0.2 | ⊕ | -3.6 | -13.4 | +0.7 | +1.8 | ⊕ | -8.0 | -23.8 | -49.2 | 24 | P280A |
| 1.2 | 4.9 | 11.8 | 22.5 | 37.8 | -0.2 | ⊕ | -3.5 | -13.7 | +0.7 | +1.6 | ⊕ | -8.4 | -25.4 | -54.3 | 24 | P280T1 |
| 0.8 | 3.1 | 7.3 | 13.5 | 21.8 | -0.2 | ⊕ | -3.7 | -13.5 | +0.8 | +1.8 | ⊕ | -8.0 | -23.1 | -46.6 | 24 | P708A |
| 0.5 | 2.2 | 5.1 | 9.3 | 15.0 | -0.3 | ⊕ | -2.6 | -9.8 | +0.4 | +1.3 | ⊕ | -5.9 | -17.0 | -34.2 | 24 | P7RD |
| 0.5 | 2.0 | 4.6 | 8.4 | 13.5 | -0.2 | ⊕ | -3.0 | -10.9 | +0.5 | +1.5 | ⊕ | -6.4 | -18.4 | -36.6 | 24 | P7RE |
| 0.6 | 2.5 | 5.6 | 10.4 | 16.9 | -0.2 | ⊕ | -3.1 | -11.3 | +0.6 | +1.5 | ⊕ | -6.7 | -19.4 | -39.0 | 24 | P7RF |
| 0.6 | 2.6 | 6.0 | 11.1 | 18.2 | -0.3 | ⊕ | -2.6 | -9.9 | +0.4 | +1.3 | ⊕ | -6.0 | -17.5 | -35.6 | 24 | P7RG |
| 0.7 | 2.8 | 6.5 | 12.1 | 19.6 | -0.2 | ⊕ | -3.4 | -12.5 | +0.7 | +1.7 | ⊕ | -7.4 | -21.5 | -43.3 | 24 | P7RT1 |
| 1.0 | 4.3 | 10.3 | 19.5 | 32.4 | -0.2 | ⊕ | -3.5 | -13.4 | +0.7 | +1.8 | ⊕ | -8.1 | -24.4 | -51.1 | 24 | P7RT2 |
| 0.6 | 2.5 | 5.8 | 10.7 | 17.3 | -0.2 | ⊕ | -2.8 | -10.5 | +0.4 | +1.4 | ⊕ | -6.3 | -18.4 | -37.1 | 24 | P7WBA |
| 0.56 | 2.49 | 5.74 | 10.53 | 17.18 | -0.3 | ⊕ | -2.8 | -10.5 | +0.5 | +1.4 | ⊕ | -6.3 | -18.3 | -36.9 | 24 | P7RWBT1 |
| 0.9 | 8.0 | 19.4 | 36.7 | 59.8 | -0.3 | ⊕ | -8.3 | -29.8 | +2.4 | +4.1 | ⊕ | -17.4 | -52.4 | -109.4 | 24 | P3030D |
| 0.7 | 3.0 | 7.0 | 13.0 | 21.1 | -0.1 | ⊕ | -4.0 | -14.4 | +0.9 | +2.0 | ⊕ | -8.4 | -24.3 | -49.0 | 24 | P308C |
| 0.8 | 3.3 | 7.7 | 14.3 | 23.3 | -0.1 | ⊕ | -4.4 | -15.8 | +1.0 | +2.2 | ⊕ | -9.2 | -26.5 | -53.6 | 24 | P308E |
| 0.7 | 3.1 | 7.2 | 13.3 | 21.7 | -0.2 | ⊕ | -3.6 | -13.2 | +0.7 | +1.8 | ⊕ | -7.8 | -22.7 | -46.0 | 24 | P308F |
| 0.8 | 3.5 | 8.2 | 15.2 | 24.9 | -0.1 | ⊕ | -4.1 | -15.0 | +0.9 | +2.1 | ⊕ | -8.8 | -25.6 | -52.2 | 24 | P308T1 |
| 0.7 | 2.8 | 6.6 | 12.3 | 19.9 | -0.2 | ⊕ | -3.6 | -13.2 | +0.8 | +1.8 | ⊕ | -7.8 | -22.4 | -45.2 | 24 | P3006D |
| 0.7 | 3.0 | 7.3 | 13.4 | 27.7 | -0.1 | ⊕ | -4.0 | -14.6 | +0.9 | +2.0 | ⊕ | -8.6 | -24.6 | -49.6 | 24 | P3006F |
| 0.7 | 3.0 | 7.1 | 13.4 | 22.0 | -0.2 | ⊕ | -3.3 | -12.4 | +0.6 | +1.7 | ⊕ | -7.4 | -21.5 | -43.7 | 24 | P3006G |
| 0.6 | 2.6 | 6.0 | 11.0 | 17.8 | -0.1 | ⊕ | -3.9 | -13.9 | +0.9 | +1.9 | ⊕ | -8.1 | -23.1 | -46.1 | 24 | P3006L |
| 0.7 | 2.9 | 6.8 | 12.7 | 20.7 | -0.2 | ⊕ | -3.3 | -12.2 | +0.6 | +1.6 | ⊕ | -7.3 | -21.1 | -42.8 | 24 | P3006P |
| 0.7 | 2.8 | 6.6 | 12.1 | 19.7 | -0.2 | ⊕ | -3.6 | -13.2 | +0.7 | +1.8 | ⊕ | -7.7 | -22.3 | -45.0 | 24 | P3006Q |
| 1.0 | 4.0 | 9.6 | 17.8 | 29.7 | -0.1 | ⊕ | -3.9 | -14.5 | +0.8 | +2.0 | ⊕ | -8.7 | -25.4 | -53.1 | 24 | P3006T1 |
| 1.1 | 4.5 | 10.8 | 20.4 | 33.8 | -0.1 | ⊕ | -4.4 | -16.3 | +1.0 | +1.9 | ⊕ | -9.6 | -28.7 | -59.7 | 24 | P3006T2 |
| 0.5 | 2.2 | 5.0 | 9.2 | 14.9 | -0.2 | ⊕ | -3.4 | -12.2 | +0.7 | +1.7 | ⊕ | -7.1 | -20.4 | -40.5 | 24 | P300WC |

| WIND DRIFT IN INCHES 10 MPH CROSSWIND 100 YDS. | 200 YDS. | 300 YDS. | 400 YDS. | 500 YDS. | HEIGHT OF BULLET TRAJECTORY IN INCHES ABOVE OR BELOW LINE OF SIGHT IF ZEROED AT ⊕ YARDS. SIGHTS 1.5 INCHES ABOVE BORE LINE. AVERAGE RANGE 50 YDS. | 100 YDS. | 200 YDS. | 300 YDS. | LONG RANGE 50 YDS. | 100 YDS. | 200 YDS. | 300 YDS. | 400 YDS. | 500 YDS. | TEST BARREL LENGTH INCHES | FEDERAL LOAD NO. |
|---|---|---|---|---|---|---|---|---|---|---|---|---|---|---|---|---|
| 0.9 | 3.7 | 8.8 | 16.3 | 27.1 | -0.3 | ⊕ | -3.5 | -13.3 | +0.7 | +1.8 | ⊕ | -8.0 | -23.4 | -48.6 | 24 | P300HA |
| 0.9 | 3.5 | 8.4 | 15.8 | 25.9 | -0.2 | ⊕ | -3.3 | -12.4 | +0.6 | +1.6 | ⊕ | -7.5 | -22.1 | -45.4 | 24 | P300WD2 |
| 0.9 | 3.4 | 8.1 | 14.9 | 24.5 | -0.1 | ⊕ | -3.7 | -13.8 | +0.8 | +1.9 | ⊕ | -8.2 | -23.9 | -48.8 | 24 | P300WT1 |
| 0.9 | 3.9 | 9.2 | 17.4 | 28.8 | -0.2 | ⊕ | -3.4 | -12.8 | +0.6 | +1.7 | ⊕ | -7.7 | -23.0 | -47.7 | 24 | P300WT2 |
| 0.6 | 2.4 | 5.5 | 10.1 | 16.3 | -0.3 | ⊕ | -2.4 | -9.4 | +0.3 | +1.2 | ⊕ | -5.7 | -16.7 | -33.6 | 24 | P300WBA |
| 0.55 | 2.25 | 5.3 | 9.63 | 15.63 | -0.3 | ⊕ | -2.4 | -9.3 | +0.3 | +1.2 | ⊕ | -5.7 | -16.4 | -33.1 | 24 | P300WBT1 |
| 0.9 | 3.4 | 8.2 | 15.2 | 24.9 | -0.2 | ⊕ | -3.6 | -13.6 | +0.8 | +1.8 | ⊕ | -8.1 | -23.6 | -48.3 | 24 | P338A2 |
| 1.1 | 4.5 | 10.8 | 20.3 | 33.6 | -0.1 | ⊕ | -4.6 | -16.7 | +1.1 | +2.3 | ⊕ | -9.8 | -29.1 | -60.2 | 24 | P338B2 |
| 0.9 | 3.7 | 8.7 | 16.1 | 26.7 | -0.2 | ⊕ | -3.8 | -14.1 | +0.8 | +1.9 | ⊕ | -8.4 | -24.5 | -50.6 | 24 | P338T1 |
| 1.7 | 7.2 | 17.6 | 33.9 | 56.5 | ⊕ | -1.1 | -9.1 | -27.5 | +0.5 | ⊕ | -7.0 | -24.2 | -55.8 | -106.5 | 24 | P375D |
| 0.9 | 3.9 | 9.1 | 17.0 | 27.8 | 0 | ⊕ | -5.0 | -17.7 | +1.2 | +2.5 | ⊕ | -10.3 | -29.9 | -60.8 | 24 | P375F |
| 1.1 | 4.8 | 11.3 | 21.5 | 35.4 | -0.1 | ⊕ | -5.3 | -18.8 | +1.3 | +2.6 | ⊕ | -10.9 | -32.8 | -67.8 | 24 | P375T1 |
| 2.5 | 11.0 | 27.6 | 52.6 | 83.9 | ⊕ | -1.5 | -11.0 | -34.9 | +0.1 | ⊕ | -7.5 | -29.1 | -71.1 | -138.0 | 24 | P458A |
| 1.9 | 7.9 | 18.9 | 35.3 | 56.8 | ⊕ | -1.8 | -13.7 | -39.7 | +0.4 | ⊕ | -9.1 | -32.3 | -73.9 | -138.0 | 24 | P458B |
| 1.5 | 6.1 | 14.5 | 26.9 | 43.7 | ⊕ | -1.7 | -12.9 | -36.7 | +0.4 | ⊕ | -8.5 | -29.5 | -66.2 | -122.0 | 24 | P458C |
| 1.1 | 4.5 | 10.7 | 19.9 | 32.7 | ⊕ | -0.2 | -6.3 | -21.5 | +0.1 | ⊕ | -5.9 | -20.9 | -47.1 | -87.0 | 24 | P458T1 |
| 1.5 | 6.2 | 14.6 | 27.3 | 44.5 | ⊕ | -0.7 | -10.0 | -31.8 | +0.4 | ⊕ | -8.5 | -29.7 | -66.8 | -124.2 | 24 | P458T2 |
| 1.5 | 6.4 | 15.2 | 28.3 | 46.1 | ⊕ | -0.7 | -10.1 | -32.2 | +0.4 | ⊕ | -8.6 | -30.0 | -67.8 | -126.3 | 24 | P458T3 |
| 1.3 | 5.7 | 13.6 | 25.6 | 42.3 | ⊕ | -1.2 | -9.8 | -28.5 | +0.6 | ⊕ | -7.4 | -24.8 | -55.0 | -101.6 | 24 | P416A |
| 1.3 | 5.7 | 13.6 | 25.6 | 42.3 | ⊕ | -1.2 | -9.8 | -28.5 | +0.6 | ⊕ | -7.4 | -24.8 | -55.0 | -101.6 | 24 | P416B |
| 0.8 | 3.4 | 7.9 | 14.7 | 23.8 | ⊕ | -0.2 | -6.0 | -20.1 | +0.1 | ⊕ | -5.7 | -19.6 | -43.3 | -78.4 | 24 | P416T1 |
| 1.3 | 5.5 | 13.2 | 24.8 | 41.0 | ⊕ | -0.2 | -6.8 | -23.2 | +0.1 | ⊕ | -6.3 | -22.5 | -51.5 | -96.7 | 24 | P416T2 |
| 1.6 | 7.0 | 16.6 | 31.1 | 50.6 | ⊕ | -1.6 | -12.6 | -36.2 | +0.8 | ⊕ | -9.3 | -31.3 | -69.7 | -128.6 | 24 | P470A |
| 1.6 | 7.0 | 16.6 | 31.1 | 50.6 | ⊕ | -1.6 | -12.6 | -36.2 | +0.8 | ⊕ | -9.3 | -31.3 | -69.7 | -128.6 | 24 | P470B |
| 1.3 | 5.5 | 13.0 | 24.3 | 39.7 | ⊕ | -0.6 | -9.0 | -28.9 | +0.3 | ⊕ | -7.8 | -27.1 | -60.8 | -112.4 | 24 | P470T1 |
| 1.3 | 5.5 | 13.0 | 24.3 | 39.7 | ⊕ | -0.6 | -9.0 | -28.9 | +0.3 | ⊕ | -7.8 | -27.1 | -60.8 | -112.4 | 24 | P470T2 |

These trajectory tables were calculated by computer using the best available data for each load. Trajectories are representative of the nominal behavior of each load at standard conditions (59°F temperature; barometric pressure of 29.53 inches; altitude at sea level). Shooters are cautioned that actual trajectories may differ due to variations in altitude, atmospheric conditions, guns, sights, and ammunition.

# FEDERAL BALLISTICS

## CENTERFIRE RIFLE

### PREMIUM® VARMINT RIFLE BALLISTICS

| Usage | Federal Load No. | Caliber | Bullet Wgt. in Grains | Bullet Wgt. in Grams | Bullet Style* | Factory Primer No. | Velocity in Feet per Second (to nearest 10 feet) Muzzle | 100 Yds. | 200 Yds. | 300 Yds. | 400 Yds. | 500 Yds. | Energy in Foot-Pounds (to nearest 5 foot-pounds) Muzzle | 100 Yds. | 200 Yds. | 300 Yds. | 400 Yds. | 500 Yds. |
|---|---|---|---|---|---|---|---|---|---|---|---|---|---|---|---|---|---|---|
| [1] | P223V | 223 Rem. (5.56x45mm) | 40 | 2.59 | Hollow Point Varmint | 205 | 3650 | 3010 | 2450 | 1950 | 1530 | 1210 | 1185 | 805 | 535 | 340 | 205 | 130 |
| [1] | P22250V | 22-250 Rem. | 40 | 2.59 | Hollow Point Varmint | 210 | 4000 | 3320 | 2720 | 2200 | 1740 | 1360 | 1420 | 980 | 660 | 430 | 265 | 165 |
| [1] | P243V | 243 Win. (6.16x51mm) | 60 | 3.89 | Hollow Point Varmint | 210 | 3600 | 3110 | 2660 | 2260 | 1890 | 1560 | 1725 | 1285 | 945 | 680 | 475 | 325 |
| [1] | P2506V | 25-06 Rem. | 90 | 5.83 | Hollow Point Varmint | 210 | 3440 | 3040 | 2680 | 2340 | 2030 | 1750 | 2365 | 1850 | 1435 | 1100 | 825 | 610 |

### CLASSIC® HUNTING RIFLE BALLISTICS

Usage Key:

| Usage | Federal Load No. | Caliber | Bullet Wgt. in Grains | Bullet Wgt. in Grams | Bullet Style** | Factory Primer No. | Velocity in Feet per Second (to nearest 10 feet) Muzzle | 100 Yds. | 200 Yds. | 300 Yds. | 400 Yds. | 500 Yds. | Energy in Foot-Pounds (to nearest 5 foot-pounds) Muzzle | 100 Yds. | 200 Yds. | 300 Yds. | 400 Yds. | 500 Yds. |
|---|---|---|---|---|---|---|---|---|---|---|---|---|---|---|---|---|---|---|
| [1] | 222A | 222 Rem. (5.56x43mm) | 50 | 3.24 | Hi-Shok Soft Point | 205 | 3140 | 2600 | 2120 | 1700 | 1350 | 1110 | 1095 | 750 | 500 | 320 | 200 | 135 |
| [5] | 222B | 222 Rem. (5.56x43mm) | 55 | 3.56 | Hi-Shok FMJ Boat-tail | 205 | 3020 | 2740 | 2480 | 2230 | 1990 | 1780 | 1115 | 915 | 750 | 610 | 485 | 385 |
| [1] | 223A | 223 Rem. (5.56x45mm) | 55 | 3.56 | Hi-Shok Soft Point | 205 | 3240 | 2750 | 2300 | 1910 | 1550 | 1270 | 1280 | 920 | 650 | 445 | 295 | 195 |
| [5] | 223B | 223 Rem. (5.56x45mm) | 55 | 3.56 | Hi-Shok FMJ Boat-tail | 205 | 3240 | 2950 | 2670 | 2410 | 2170 | 1940 | 1280 | 1060 | 875 | 710 | 575 | 460 |
| [1] | 22250A | 22-250 Rem. | 55 | 3.56 | Hi-Shok Soft Point | 210 | 3680 | 3140 | 2660 | 2220 | 1830 | 1490 | 1655 | 1200 | 860 | 605 | 410 | 270 |
| [1] | 243A | 243 Win. (6.16x51mm) | 80 | 5.18 | Hi-Shok Soft Point | 210 | 3350 | 2960 | 2590 | 2260 | 1950 | 1670 | 1995 | 1550 | 1195 | 905 | 675 | 495 |
| [2] | 243B | 243 Win. (6.16x51mm) | 100 | 6.48 | Hi-Shok Soft Point | 210 | 2960 | 2700 | 2450 | 2220 | 1990 | 1790 | 1945 | 1615 | 1330 | 1090 | 880 | 710 |
| [1] | 6A | 6mm Rem. | 80 | 5.18 | Hi-Shok Soft Point | 210 | 3470 | 3060 | 2690 | 2350 | 2040 | 1750 | 2140 | 1665 | 1290 | 980 | 735 | 540 |
| [2] | 6B | 6mm Rem. | 100 | 6.48 | Hi-Shok Soft Point | 210 | 3100 | 2830 | 2570 | 2330 | 2100 | 1890 | 2135 | 1775 | 1470 | 1205 | 985 | 790 |
| [2] | 2506B | 25-06 Rem. | 117 | 7.58 | Hi-Shok Soft Point | 210 | 2990 | 2730 | 2480 | 2250 | 2030 | 1830 | 2320 | 1985 | 1645 | 1350 | 1100 | 885 |
| [2] NEW | 6555B | 6.5x55 Swedish | 140 | 9.07 | Hi-Shok Soft Point | 210 | 2600 | 2400 | 2220 | 2040 | 1860 | 1700 | 2100 | 1795 | 1525 | 1285 | 1080 | 900 |
| [2] | 270A | 270 Win. | 130 | 8.42 | Hi-Shok Soft Point | 210 | 3060 | 2800 | 2560 | 2330 | 2110 | 1900 | 2700 | 2265 | 1890 | 1565 | 1285 | 1045 |
| [2] | 270B | 270 Win. | 150 | 9.72 | Hi-Shok Soft Point RN | 210 | 2850 | 2500 | 2180 | 1890 | 1620 | 1390 | 2705 | 2085 | 1585 | 1185 | 870 | 640 |
| [2] | 7A | 7mm Mauser (7x57mm Mauser) | 175 | 11.34 | Hi-Shok Soft Point RN | 210 | 2440 | 2140 | 1860 | 1600 | 1380 | 1200 | 2315 | 1775 | 1340 | 1000 | 740 | 565 |
| [2] | 7B | 7mm Mauser (7x57mm Mauser) | 140 | 9.07 | Hi-Shok Soft Point | 210 | 2660 | 2450 | 2260 | 2070 | 1890 | 1730 | 2200 | 1865 | 1585 | 1330 | 1110 | 930 |
| [2] | 280B | 280 Rem. | 150 | 9.72 | Hi-Shok Soft Point | 210 | 2890 | 2670 | 2460 | 2260 | 2060 | 1880 | 2780 | 2370 | 2015 | 1695 | 1420 | 1180 |
| [2] | 7RA | 7mm Rem. Magnum | 150 | 9.72 | Hi-Shok Soft Point | 215 | 3110 | 2830 | 2570 | 2320 | 2090 | 1870 | 3220 | 2670 | 2200 | 1790 | 1450 | 1160 |
| [3] | 7RB | 7mm Rem. Magnum | 175 | 11.34 | Hi-Shok Soft Point | 215 | 2860 | 2650 | 2440 | 2240 | 2060 | 1880 | 3180 | 2720 | 2310 | 1960 | 1640 | 1370 |
| [1] | 30CA | 30 Carbine (7.62x33mm) | 110 | 7.13 | Hi-Shok Soft Point RN | 205 | 1990 | 1570 | 1240 | 1040 | 920 | 840 | 965 | 600 | 375 | 260 | 210 | 175 |
| [2] | 76239B | 7.62x39mm Soviet | 123 | 7.97 | Hi-Shok Soft Point | 210 | 2300 | 2030 | 1780 | 1550 | 1350 | 1200 | 1445 | 1125 | 860 | 655 | 500 | 395 |
| [2] | 3030A | 30-30 Win. | 150 | 9.72 | Hi-Shok Soft Point FN | 210 | 2390 | 2020 | 1680 | 1400 | 1180 | 1040 | 1900 | 1355 | 945 | 650 | 460 | 355 |
| [2] | 3030B | 30-30 Win. | 170 | 11.01 | Hi-Shok Soft Point RN | 210 | 2200 | 1900 | 1620 | 1380 | 1190 | 1060 | 1830 | 1355 | 990 | 720 | 535 | 425 |
| [1] | 3030C | 30-30 Win. | 125 | 8.10 | Hi-Shok Hollow Point | 210 | 2570 | 2090 | 1660 | 1320 | 1080 | 960 | 1830 | 1210 | 770 | 480 | 320 | 260 |
| [2] | 300A | 300 Savage | 150 | 9.72 | Hi-Shok Soft Point | 210 | 2630 | 2350 | 2100 | 1850 | 1630 | 1430 | 2305 | 1845 | 1460 | 1145 | 885 | 685 |
| [2] | 300B | 300 Savage | 180 | 11.66 | Hi-Shok Soft Point | 210 | 2350 | 2140 | 1940 | 1750 | 1570 | 1410 | 2205 | 1825 | 1495 | 1215 | 985 | 800 |
| [2] | 308A | 308 Win. (7.62x51mm) | 150 | 9.72 | Hi-Shok Soft Point | 210 | 2820 | 2530 | 2260 | 2010 | 1770 | 1560 | 2650 | 2140 | 1705 | 1345 | 1050 | 810 |
| [2] | 308B | 308 Win. (7.62x51mm) | 180 | 11.66 | Hi-Shok Soft Point | 210 | 2620 | 2390 | 2180 | 1970 | 1780 | 1600 | 2745 | 2290 | 1895 | 1555 | 1270 | 1030 |
| [2] | 3006A | 30-06 Springfield (7.62x63mm) | 150 | 9.72 | Hi-Shok Soft Point | 210 | 2910 | 2620 | 2340 | 2080 | 1840 | 1620 | 2820 | 2280 | 1825 | 1445 | 1130 | 875 |
| [3] | 3006B | 30-06 Springfield (7.62x63mm) | 180 | 11.66 | Hi-Shok Soft Point | 210 | 2700 | 2470 | 2250 | 2040 | 1850 | 1660 | 2915 | 2435 | 2025 | 1665 | 1360 | 1105 |
| [1] | 3006C | 30-06 Springfield (7.62x63mm) | 125 | 8.10 | Hi-Shok Soft Point | 210 | 3140 | 2780 | 2450 | 2140 | 1850 | 1600 | 2735 | 2145 | 1660 | 1270 | 955 | 705 |
| [3] | 3006H | 30-06 Springfield (7.62x63mm) | 220 | 14.25 | Hi-Shok Soft Point RN | 210 | 2410 | 2130 | 1870 | 1630 | 1420 | 1250 | 2835 | 2215 | 1705 | 1300 | 985 | 760 |
| [3] | 3006J | 30-06 Springfield (7.62x63mm) | 180 | 11.66 | Hi-Shok Soft Point RN | 210 | 2700 | 2350 | 2020 | 1730 | 1470 | 1250 | 2915 | 2200 | 1630 | 1190 | 860 | 620 |
| [3] | 300WB | 300 Win. Magnum | 180 | 11.66 | Hi-Shok Soft Point | 215 | 2960 | 2750 | 2540 | 2340 | 2160 | 1980 | 3500 | 3010 | 2580 | 2195 | 1860 | 1565 |
| [2] | 303A | 303 British | 180 | 11.66 | Hi-Shok Soft Point | 210 | 2460 | 2230 | 2020 | 1820 | 1630 | 1460 | 2420 | 1995 | 1625 | 1315 | 1060 | 850 |
| [2] | 303B | 303 British | 150 | 9.72 | Hi-Shok Soft Point | 210 | 2690 | 2440 | 2210 | 1980 | 1780 | 1590 | 2400 | 1980 | 1620 | 1310 | 1055 | 840 |
| [2] | 32A | 32 Win. Special | 170 | 11.01 | Hi-Shok Soft Point | 210 | 2250 | 1920 | 1630 | 1370 | 1180 | 1040 | 1910 | 1395 | 1000 | 710 | 520 | 410 |
| [2] | *8A | 8mm Mauser (8x57mm JS Mauser) | 170 | 11.01 | Hi-Shok Soft Point | 210 | 2360 | 1970 | 1620 | 1330 | 1120 | 1000 | 2100 | 1465 | 995 | 670 | 475 | 375 |
| [3] | 338C | 338 Win. Magnum | 225 | 14.58 | Hi-Shok Soft Point | 215 | 2780 | 2570 | 2370 | 2180 | 2000 | 1830 | 3860 | 3305 | 2815 | 2380 | 2000 | 1670 |
| [2] | 357G | 357 Magnum | 180 | 11.66 | Hi-Shok Hollow Point | 100 | 1550 | 1160 | 980 | 860 | 770 | 680 | 960 | 535 | 385 | 295 | 235 | 185 |
| [2] | 35A | 35 Rem. | 200 | 12.96 | Hi-Shok Soft Point | 210 | 2080 | 1700 | 1380 | 1140 | 1000 | 910 | 1920 | 1280 | 840 | 575 | 445 | 370 |
| [3] | 375A | 375 H&H Magnum | 270 | 17.50 | Hi-Shok Soft Point | 215 | 2690 | 2420 | 2170 | 1920 | 1700 | 1500 | 4340 | 3510 | 2810 | 2220 | 1740 | 1355 |
| [4] | 375B | 375 H&H Magnum | 300 | 19.44 | Hi-Shok Soft Point | 215 | 2530 | 2270 | 2020 | 1790 | 1580 | 1400 | 4265 | 3425 | 2720 | 2135 | 1665 | 1295 |
| [2] | 44A | 44 Rem. Magnum | 240 | 15.55 | Hi-Shok Hollow Point | 150 | 1760 | 1380 | 1090 | 950 | 860 | 790 | 1650 | 1015 | 640 | 485 | 395 | 330 |
| [2] | 4570A | 45-70 Government | 300 | 19.44 | Hi-Shok Hollow Point | 210 | 1880 | 1650 | 1430 | 1240 | 1110 | 1010 | 2355 | 1815 | 1355 | 1015 | 810 | 680 |

*Only for use in barrels intended for .323 inch diameter bullets. Do not use in 8x57mm J Commission Rifles (M1888) or in sporting or other military arms of .318 inch bore diameter.
**RN = Round Nose FN = Flat Nose FMJ = Full Metal Jacket HP = Hollow Point

### GOLD MEDAL® MATCH RIFLE BALLISTICS

| Usage | Federal Load No. | Caliber | Bullet Wgt. in Grains | Bullet Wgt. in Grams | Bullet Style* | Factory Primer No. | Velocity in Feet per Second (to nearest 10 feet) Muzzle | 100 Yds. | 200 Yds. | 300 Yds. | 400 Yds. | 500 Yds. | 600 Yds. | 700 Yds. | 800 Yds. | 900 Yds. | 1000 Yds. |
|---|---|---|---|---|---|---|---|---|---|---|---|---|---|---|---|---|---|
| [5] | GM223M | 223 Rem. (5.56x45mm) | 69 | 4.47 | Boat-tail HP Match | 205M | 3000 | 2720 | 2460 | 2210 | 1980 | 1760 | 1560 | 1390 | 1240 | 1130 | 1060 |
| [5] | GM308M | 308 Win. (7.62x51mm) | 168 | 10.88 | Boat-tail HP Match | 210M | 2600 | 2420 | 2240 | 2070 | 1910 | 1760 | 1610 | 1480 | 1360 | 1260 | 1170 |
| [5] | GM3006M | 30-06 Springfield (7.62x63mm) | 168 | 10.88 | Boat-tail HP Match | 210M | 2700 | 2510 | 2330 | 2150 | 1990 | 1830 | 1680 | 1540 | 1410 | 1300 | 1210 |

*HP = Hollow Point

# FEDERAL BALLISTICS

## CENTERFIRE RIFLE

| Wind Drift in Inches, 10 MPH Crosswind: 100 YDS. | 200 YDS. | 300 YDS. | 400 YDS. | 500 YDS. | Height of Bullet Trajectory in Inches Above or Below Line of Sight if Zeroed at ⊕ Yards. Sights 1.5 Inches Above Bore Line. Average Range: 50 YDS. | 100 YDS. | 200 YDS. | 300 YDS. | Long Range: 50 YDS. | 100 YDS. | 200 YDS. | 300 YDS. | 400 YDS. | 500 YDS. | Test Barrel Length Inches | Federal Load No. |
|---|---|---|---|---|---|---|---|---|---|---|---|---|---|---|---|---|
| 1.5 | 6.5 | 16.1 | 32.3 | 56.9 | -0.4 | ⊕ | -2.4 | -10.7 | +0.2 | +1.2 | ⊕ | -7.1 | -23.4 | -54.2 | 24 | P223V |
| 1.3 | 5.7 | 14.0 | 27.9 | 49.2 | -0.4 | ⊕ | -1.7 | -8.1 | 0 | +0.8 | ⊕ | -5.6 | -18.4 | -42.8 | 24 | P22250V |
| 1.1 | 4.8 | 11.7 | 22.6 | 38.7 | -0.4 | ⊕ | -2.1 | -9.2 | +0.2 | +1.1 | ⊕ | -6.0 | -18.9 | -41.6 | 24 | P243V |
| 1.0 | 4.1 | 9.8 | 18.7 | 31.3 | -0.3 | ⊕ | -2.3 | -9.4 | +0.2 | +1.1 | ⊕ | -6.0 | -18.3 | -39.2 | 24 | P2506V |

1 = Varmints, predators, small game  2 = Medium game  3 = Large, heavy game  4 = Dangerous game  5 = Target shooting, training, practice

| Wind Drift in Inches, 10 MPH Crosswind: 100 YDS. | 200 YDS. | 300 YDS. | 400 YDS. | 500 YDS. | Height of Bullet Trajectory in Inches Above or Below Line of Sight if Zeroed at ⊕ Yards. Sights 1.5 Inches Above Bore Line. Average Range: 50 YDS. | 100 YDS. | 200 YDS. | 300 YDS. | Long Range: 50 YDS. | 100 YDS. | 200 YDS. | 300 YDS. | 400 YDS. | 500 YDS. | Test Barrel Length Inches | Federal Load No. |
|---|---|---|---|---|---|---|---|---|---|---|---|---|---|---|---|---|
| 1.7 | 7.3 | 18.3 | 36.4 | 63.1 | -0.2 | ⊕ | -3.7 | -15.3 | +0.7 | +1.9 | ⊕ | -9.7 | -31.6 | -71.3 | 24 | 222A |
| 0.9 | 3.4 | 8.5 | 16.8 | 26.3 | -0.2 | ⊕ | -3.1 | -12.0 | +0.6 | +1.6 | ⊕ | -7.3 | -21.5 | -44.6 | 24 | 222B |
| 1.4 | 6.1 | 15.0 | 29.4 | 50.8 | -0.3 | ⊕ | -3.2 | -12.9 | +0.5 | +1.6 | ⊕ | -8.2 | -26.1 | -58.3 | 24 | 223A |
| 0.8 | 3.3 | 7.8 | 14.5 | 24.0 | -0.3 | ⊕ | -2.5 | -9.9 | +0.3 | +1.3 | ⊕ | -6.1 | -18.3 | -37.8 | 24 | 223B |
| 1.2 | 5.2 | 12.5 | 24.4 | 42.0 | -0.4 | ⊕ | -2.1 | -9.1 | +0.1 | +1.0 | ⊕ | -6.0 | -19.1 | -42.6 | 24 | 22250A |
| 1.0 | 4.3 | 10.4 | 19.8 | 33.3 | -0.3 | ⊕ | -2.5 | -10.2 | +0.3 | +1.3 | ⊕ | -6.4 | -19.7 | -42.2 | 24 | 243A |
| 0.9 | 3.6 | 8.4 | 15.7 | 25.8 | -0.2 | ⊕ | -3.3 | -12.4 | +0.6 | +1.6 | ⊕ | -7.5 | -22.0 | -45.4 | 24 | 243B |
| 1.0 | 4.1 | 9.9 | 18.8 | 31.6 | -0.3 | ⊕ | -2.2 | -9.3 | +0.2 | +1.1 | ⊕ | -5.9 | -18.2 | -39.0 | 24 | 6A |
| 0.8 | 3.3 | 7.9 | 14.7 | 24.1 | -0.3 | ⊕ | -2.9 | -11.0 | +0.5 | +1.4 | ⊕ | -6.7 | -19.8 | -40.6 | 24 | 6B |
| 0.8 | 3.4 | 8.1 | 15.1 | 24.9 | -0.2 | ⊕ | -3.2 | -12.0 | +0.6 | +1.6 | ⊕ | -7.2 | -21.4 | -44.0 | 24 | 2506B |
| 0.8 | 3.4 | 8.0 | 14.8 | 24.1 | -0.1 | ⊕ | -4.5 | -16.2 | +1.1 | +2.3 | ⊕ | -9.4 | -27.2 | -55.0 | 24 | 6555B |
| 0.8 | 3.2 | 7.6 | 14.2 | 23.3 | -0.2 | ⊕ | -2.9 | -11.2 | +0.5 | +1.5 | ⊕ | -6.8 | -20.0 | -41.1 | 24 | 270A |
| 1.2 | 5.3 | 12.8 | 24.5 | 41.3 | -0.1 | ⊕ | -4.1 | -15.5 | +0.9 | +2.0 | ⊕ | -9.4 | -28.6 | -61.0 | 24 | 270B |
| 1.5 | 6.2 | 15.0 | 28.7 | 47.8 | -0.1 | ⊕ | -6.2 | -22.6 | +1.6 | +3.1 | ⊕ | -13.3 | -40.1 | -84.6 | 24 | 7A |
| 1.3 | 3.2 | 8.2 | 15.4 | 23.4 | -0.1 | ⊕ | -4.3 | -15.4 | +1.0 | +2.1 | ⊕ | -9.0 | -26.1 | -52.9 | 24 | 7B |
| 0.7 | 3.1 | 7.2 | 13.4 | 21.9 | -0.2 | ⊕ | -3.4 | -12.6 | +0.7 | +1.7 | ⊕ | -7.5 | -21.8 | -44.3 | 24 | 280B |
| 0.8 | 3.4 | 8.1 | 15.1 | 24.9 | -0.3 | ⊕ | -2.9 | -11.0 | +0.5 | +1.4 | ⊕ | -6.7 | -19.9 | -41.0 | 24 | 7RA |
| 0.7 | 3.1 | 7.2 | 13.3 | 21.7 | -0.2 | ⊕ | -3.5 | -12.8 | +0.7 | +1.7 | ⊕ | -7.6 | -22.1 | -44.9 | 24 | 7RB |
| 3.4 | 15.0 | 35.5 | 63.2 | 96.7 | +0.6 | ⊕ | -12.8 | -46.9 | +3.9 | +6.4 | ⊕ | -27.7 | -81.8 | -167.8 | 18 | 30CA |
| 1.5 | 6.4 | 15.2 | 28.7 | 47.3 | +0.2 | ⊕ | -7.0 | -25.1 | +1.9 | +3.5 | ⊕ | -14.5 | -43.4 | -90.6 | 20 | 76239B |
| 2.0 | 8.5 | 20.9 | 40.1 | 66.1 | +0.2 | ⊕ | -7.2 | -26.7 | +1.9 | +3.6 | ⊕ | -15.9 | -49.1 | -104.5 | 24 | 3030A |
| 1.9 | 8.0 | 19.4 | 36.7 | 59.8 | +0.3 | ⊕ | -8.3 | -29.8 | +2.4 | +4.1 | ⊕ | -17.4 | -52.4 | -109.4 | 24 | 3030B |
| 2.2 | 10.1 | 25.4 | 49.4 | 81.6 | +0.1 | ⊕ | -6.6 | -26.0 | +1.7 | +3.3 | ⊕ | -16.0 | -50.9 | -109.5 | 24 | 3030C |
| 1.1 | 4.8 | 11.6 | 21.9 | 36.3 | 0 | ⊕ | -4.8 | -17.6 | +1.2 | +2.4 | ⊕ | -10.4 | -30.9 | -64.4 | 24 | 300A |
| 1.1 | 4.6 | 10.9 | 20.3 | 33.3 | +0.1 | ⊕ | -6.1 | -21.6 | +1.7 | +3.1 | ⊕ | -12.4 | -36.1 | -73.8 | 24 | 300B |
| 1.0 | 4.4 | 10.4 | 19.7 | 32.7 | -0.1 | ⊕ | -3.9 | -14.7 | +0.8 | +2.0 | ⊕ | -8.8 | -26.3 | -54.8 | 24 | 308B |
| 0.9 | 3.9 | 9.2 | 17.2 | 28.3 | -0.1 | ⊕ | -4.6 | -16.5 | +1.1 | +2.3 | ⊕ | -9.7 | -28.3 | -57.8 | 24 | 308B |
| 1.0 | 4.2 | 9.9 | 18.7 | 31.2 | -0.2 | ⊕ | -3.6 | -13.6 | +0.7 | +1.8 | ⊕ | -8.2 | -24.4 | -50.9 | 24 | 3006A |
| 0.9 | 3.7 | 8.8 | 16.5 | 27.1 | -0.1 | ⊕ | -4.2 | -15.3 | +1.0 | +2.1 | ⊕ | -9.0 | -26.4 | -54.0 | 24 | 3006B |
| 1.1 | 4.5 | 10.8 | 20.5 | 34.4 | -0.3 | ⊕ | -3.0 | -11.9 | +0.5 | +1.5 | ⊕ | -7.3 | -22.3 | -47.5 | 24 | 3006C |
| 1.4 | 6.0 | 14.3 | 27.2 | 45.0 | -0.1 | ⊕ | -6.2 | -22.4 | +1.7 | +3.1 | ⊕ | -13.1 | -39.3 | -82.2 | 24 | 3006H |
| 1.5 | 6.4 | 15.7 | 30.4 | 51.2 | -0.1 | ⊕ | -4.9 | -18.3 | +1.1 | +2.4 | ⊕ | -11.0 | -33.6 | -71.9 | 24 | 3006J |
| 0.7 | 2.8 | 6.6 | 12.3 | 20.0 | -0.2 | ⊕ | -3.1 | -11.7 | +0.6 | +1.6 | ⊕ | -7.0 | -20.3 | -41.1 | 24 | 300WB |
| 1.1 | 4.5 | 10.6 | 19.9 | 32.7 | 0 | ⊕ | -5.5 | -19.6 | +1.4 | +2.8 | ⊕ | -11.3 | -33.2 | -68.1 | 24 | 303A |
| 1.0 | 4.1 | 9.6 | 18.1 | 29.9 | -0.1 | ⊕ | -4.4 | -15.9 | +1.0 | +2.2 | ⊕ | -9.4 | -27.6 | -56.8 | 24 | 303B |
| 1.9 | 8.4 | 20.3 | 38.6 | 63.0 | +0.3 | ⊕ | -8.0 | -29.2 | +2.3 | +4.0 | ⊕ | -17.2 | -52.3 | -109.8 | 24 | 32A |
| 2.1 | 9.3 | 22.9 | 43.9 | 71.7 | +0.2 | ⊕ | -7.6 | -28.5 | +2.1 | +3.8 | ⊕ | -17.1 | -52.9 | -111.9 | 24 | 8A |
| 0.8 | 3.1 | 7.3 | 13.6 | 22.2 | -0.1 | ⊕ | -3.8 | -13.7 | +0.8 | +1.9 | ⊕ | -8.1 | -23.5 | -47.5 | 24 | 338C |
| 5.8 | 21.7 | 45.2 | 76.1 | NA | ⊕ | -3.4 | -29.7 | -88.2 | +1.7 | ⊕ | -22.8 | -77.9 | -173.8 | -321.4 | 18 | 357G |
| 2.7 | 12.0 | 29.0 | 53.3 | 83.3 | +0.5 | ⊕ | -10.7 | -39.3 | +3.2 | +5.4 | ⊕ | -23.3 | -70.0 | -144.0 | 24 | 35A |
| 1.1 | 4.5 | 10.8 | 20.3 | 33.7 | -0.4 | ⊕ | -5.5 | -18.4 | +1.0 | +2.4 | ⊕ | -10.9 | -33.3 | -71.2 | 24 | 375A |
| 1.2 | 5.0 | 11.9 | 22.4 | 37.1 | +0.5 | ⊕ | -6.3 | -21.2 | +1.3 | +2.6 | ⊕ | -11.2 | -33.3 | -69.1 | 24 | 375B |
| 4.2 | 17.8 | 39.8 | 68.3 | 102.5 | ⊕ | -2.2 | -21.7 | -67.2 | +1.1 | ⊕ | -17.4 | -60.7 | -136.0 | -250.2 | 20 | 44A |
| 1.7 | 7.6 | 18.6 | 35.7 | NA | ⊕ | -1.3 | -14.1 | -43.7 | +0.7 | ⊕ | -11.5 | -39.7 | -89.1 | -163.1 | 24 | 4570A |

These trajectory tables were calculated by computer using the best available data for each load. Trajectories are representative of the nominal behavior of each load at standard conditions (59°F temperature:barometric pressure of 29.53 inches; altitude at sea level). Shooters are cautioned that actual trajectories may differ due to variations in altitude, atmospheric conditions, guns, sights, and ammunition.

| Energy in Foot-Pounds (to nearest 5 foot-pounds): Muzzle | 100 YDS. | 200 YDS. | 300 YDS. | 400 YDS. | 500 YDS. | 600 YDS. | 700 YDS. | 800 YDS. | 900 YDS. | 1000 YDS. | Wind Drift in Inches, 10 MPH Crosswind: 100 YDS. | 200 YDS. | 300 YDS. | 400 YDS. | 500 YDS. | 600 YDS. | 700 YDS. | 800 YDS. | 900 YDS. | 1000 YDS. | Height of Bullet Trajectory in Inches Above or Below Line of Sight if Zeroed at ⊕ Yards. Sights 1.5 Inches Above Bore Line: 100 YDS. | 200 YDS. | 300 YDS. | 400 YDS. | 500 YDS. | 600 YDS. | 700 YDS. | 800 YDS. | 900 YDS. | 1000 YDS. | Federal Load No. |
|---|---|---|---|---|---|---|---|---|---|---|---|---|---|---|---|---|---|---|---|---|---|---|---|---|---|---|---|---|---|---|---|
| 1380 | 1135 | 925 | 750 | 600 | 475 | 375 | 295 | 235 | 195 | 170 | 0.9 | 3.7 | 8.7 | 16.3 | 27.0 | 41.3 | 59.5 | 82.2 | 109.2 | 140.0 | +1.6 | ⊕ | -7.4 | -21.9 | -45.3 | -79.8 | -128.7 | -194.1 | -280.2 | -388.7 | GM223M |
| 2520 | 2180 | 1870 | 1600 | 1355 | 1150 | 970 | 815 | 690 | 590 | 510 | 0.8 | 3.1 | 7.4 | 13.6 | 22.2 | 33.3 | 47.1 | 64.1 | 84.2 | 107.5 | +17.5 | +30.5 | +36.6 | +34.5 | +22.9 | ⊕ | -36.1 | -87.8 | -157.5 | -247.4 | GM308M |
| 2720 | 2350 | 2025 | 1730 | 1470 | 1245 | 1050 | 880 | 740 | 630 | 540 | 0.7 | 3.0 | 7.0 | 13.0 | 21.2 | 31.8 | 45.1 | 61.5 | 81.0 | 103.6 | +16.1 | +28.1 | +33.8 | +31.9 | +21.1 | ⊕ | -33.4 | -81.3 | -146.0 | -230.1 | GM3006M |

# FEDERAL BALLISTICS

## CLASSIC® AUTOMATIC PISTOL BALLISTICS

| Usage | Federal Load No. | Caliber | Bullet Wgt. in Grains | Bullet Wgt. in Grams | Bullet Style** | Factory Primer No. | Velocity in Feet per Second: Muzzle | 25 Yds. | 50 Yds. | 75 Yds. | 100 Yds. | Energy in Foot-Pounds: Muzzle | 25 Yds. | 50 Yds. | 75 Yds. | 100 Yds. | Mid-Range Trajectory: 25 Yds. | 50 Yds. | 75 Yds. | 100 Yds. | Test Barrel Length Inches |
|---|---|---|---|---|---|---|---|---|---|---|---|---|---|---|---|---|---|---|---|---|---|
| 3, 4 | 25AP | 25 Auto (6.35mm Browning) | 50 | 3.24 | Full Metal Jacket | 100 | 760 | 750 | 730 | 720 | 700 | 65 | 60 | 59 | 55 | 55 | 0.5 | 1.9 | 4.5 | 8.1 | 2 |
| 3, 4 | 32AP | 32 Auto (7.65mm Browning) | 71 | 4.60 | Full Metal Jacket | 100 | 905 | 880 | 855 | 830 | 810 | 129 | 120 | 115 | 110 | 105 | 0.3 | 1.4 | 3.2 | 5.9 | 4 |
| 3, 4 | 380AP | 380 Auto (9x17mm Short) | 95 | 6.15 | Full Metal Jacket | 100 | 955 | 910 | 865 | 830 | 790 | 190 | 175 | 160 | 145 | 130 | 0.3 | 1.3 | 3.1 | 5.8 | 3¾ |
| 3 | 380BP | 380 Auto (9x17mm Short) | 90 | 5.83 | Hi-Shok JHP | 100 | 1000 | 940 | 890 | 840 | 800 | 200 | 175 | 160 | 140 | 130 | 0.3 | 1.2 | 2.9 | 5.5 | 3¾ |
| 3, 4 | 9AP | 9mm Luger (9x19mm Parabellum) | 124 | 8.03 | Full Metal Jacket | 100 | 1120 | 1070 | 1030 | 990 | 960 | 345 | 315 | 290 | 270 | 255 | 0.2 | 0.9 | 2.2 | 4.1 | 4 |
| 3 | 9BP | 9mm Luger (9x19mm Parabellum) | 115 | 7.45 | Hi-Shok JHP | 100 | 1160 | 1100 | 1060 | 1020 | 990 | 345 | 310 | 285 | 270 | 250 | 0.2 | 0.9 | 2.1 | 3.8 | 4 |
| 3 | 9MS | 9mm Luger (9x19mm Parabellum) | 147 | 9.52 | Hi-Shok JHP | 100 | 975 | 950 | 930 | 900 | 880 | 310 | 295 | 285 | 265 | 255 | 0.3 | 1.2 | 2.8 | 5.1 | 4 |
| 3 NEW | 357S2 | 357 Sig. | 125 | 8.10 | Full Metal Jacket | 100 | 1350 | 1270 | 1190 | 1130 | 1080 | 510 | 445 | 395 | 355 | 325 | 0.2 | 0.7 | 1.6 | 3.1 | 3.9 |
| 3 | 40SWA | 40 S&W | 180 | 11.06 | Hi-Shok JHP | 100 | 985 | 955 | 930 | 905 | 885 | 390 | 365 | 345 | 330 | 315 | 0.3 | 1.2 | 2.8 | 5.0 | 4 |
| 3 | 40SWB | 40 S&W | 155 | 10.04 | Hi-Shok JHP | 100 | 1140 | 1080 | 1030 | 990 | 950 | 445 | 400 | 365 | 335 | 315 | 0.2 | 0.9 | 2.2 | 4.1 | 4 |
| 3 | 10C | 10mm Auto | 180 | 11.06 | Hi-Shok JHP | 150 | 1030 | 995 | 970 | 945 | 920 | 425 | 400 | 375 | 355 | 340 | 0.3 | 1.1 | 2.5 | 4.7 | 5 |
| 3 | 10E | 10mm Auto | 155 | 10.04 | Hi-Shok JHP | 150 | 1325 | 1225 | 1140 | 1075 | 1025 | 605 | 515 | 450 | 400 | 360 | 0.2 | 0.7 | 1.8 | 3.3 | 5 |
| 3 | 45A | 45 Auto | 230 | 14.90 | Full Metal Jacket | 150 | 850 | 830 | 810 | 790 | 770 | 370 | 350 | 335 | 320 | 305 | 0.4 | 1.6 | 3.6 | 6.6 | 5 |
| 4 | 45C | 45 Auto | 185 | 11.99 | Hi-Shok JHP | 150 | 950 | 920 | 900 | 880 | 860 | 370 | 350 | 335 | 315 | 300 | 0.3 | 1.3 | 2.9 | 5.3 | 5 |
| 3 | 45D | 45 Auto | 230 | 14.90 | Hi-Shok JHP | 150 | 850 | 830 | 810 | 790 | 770 | 370 | 350 | 335 | 320 | 300 | 0.4 | 1.6 | 3.7 | 6.7 | 5 |

## CLASSIC® REVOLVER BALLISTICS

| Usage | Federal Load No. | Caliber | Bullet Wgt. in Grains | Bullet Wgt. in Grams | Bullet Style** | Factory Primer No. | Velocity in Feet per Second: Muzzle | 25 Yds. | 50 Yds. | 75 Yds. | 100 Yds. | Energy in Foot-Pounds: Muzzle | 25 Yds. | 50 Yds. | 75 Yds. | 100 Yds. | Mid-Range Trajectory: 25 Yds. | 50 Yds. | 75 Yds. | 100 Yds. | Test Barrel Length Inches |
|---|---|---|---|---|---|---|---|---|---|---|---|---|---|---|---|---|---|---|---|---|---|
| 4 | 32LA | 32 S&W Long | 98 | 6.35 | Lead Wadcutter | 100 | 780 | 700 | 630 | 560 | 500 | 130 | 105 | 85 | 70 | 55 | 0.5 | 2.2 | 5.6 | 11.1 | 4 |
| 4 | 32LB | 32 S&W Long | 98 | 6.35 | Lead Round Nose | 100 | 705 | 690 | 670 | 650 | 640 | 115 | 105 | 98 | 95 | 90 | 0.6 | 2.3 | 5.3 | 9.6 | 4 |
| 3 | 32HRA | 32 H&R Magnum | 95 | 6.15 | Lead Semi-Wadcutter | 100 | 1030 | 1000 | 940 | 930 | 900 | 225 | 210 | 195 | 185 | 170 | 0.3 | 1.1 | 2.5 | 4.7 | 4½ |
| 3 | 32HRB | 32 H&R Magnum | 85 | 5.50 | Hi-Shok JHP | 100 | 1100 | 1050 | 1020 | 970 | 930 | 230 | 210 | 195 | 175 | 165 | 0.2 | 1.0 | 2.3 | 4.3 | 4½ |
| 4 | 38B | 38 Special | 158 | 10.23 | Lead Round Nose | 100 | 755 | 740 | 723 | 710 | 690 | 200 | 190 | 183 | 175 | 170 | 0.5 | 2.0 | 4.6 | 8.3 | 4-V |
| 3, 4 | 38C | 38 Special | 158 | 10.23 | Lead Semi-Wadcutter | 100 | 755 | 740 | 723 | 710 | 690 | 200 | 190 | 183 | 175 | 170 | 0.5 | 2.0 | 4.6 | 8.3 | 4-V |
| 1, 3 | 38E | 38 Special (High-Velocity+P) | 125 | 8.10 | Hi-Shok JHP | 100 | 945 | 920 | 898 | 880 | 860 | 248 | 235 | 224 | 215 | 205 | 0.3 | 1.3 | 2.9 | 5.4 | 4-V |
| 1, 3 | 38F | 38 Special (High-Velocity+P) | 110 | 7.13 | Hi-Shok JHP | 100 | 995 | 960 | 926 | 900 | 870 | 242 | 225 | 210 | 195 | 185 | 0.3 | 1.2 | 2.7 | 5.0 | 4-V |
| 1, 3 | 38G | 38 Special (High-Velocity+P) | 158 | 10.23 | Semi-Wadcutter HP | 100 | 890 | 870 | 855 | 840 | 820 | 278 | 265 | 257 | 245 | 235 | 0.3 | 1.4 | 3.3 | 5.9 | 4-V |
| 3, 4 | 38H | 38 Special (High-Velocity+P) | 158 | 10.23 | Lead Semi-Wadcutter | 100 | 890 | 870 | 855 | 840 | 820 | 270 | 265 | 257 | 245 | 235 | 0.3 | 1.4 | 3.3 | 5.9 | 4-V |
| 1, 3 | 38J | 38 Special (High-Velocity+P) | 125 | 8.10 | Hi-Shok JSP | 100 | 945 | 920 | 898 | 880 | 860 | 248 | 235 | 224 | 215 | 205 | 0.3 | 1.3 | 2.9 | 5.4 | 4-V |
| 2, 3 | 357A | 357 Magnum | 158 | 10.23 | Hi-Shok JSP | 100 | 1235 | 1160 | 1104 | 1060 | 1020 | 535 | 475 | 428 | 395 | 365 | 0.2 | 0.8 | 1.9 | 3.5 | 4-V |
| 1, 3 | 357B | 357 Magnum | 125 | 8.10 | Hi-Shok JHP | 100 | 1450 | 1350 | 1240 | 1160 | 1100 | 583 | 495 | 427 | 370 | 335 | 0.1 | 0.6 | 1.5 | 2.8 | 4-V |
| 4 | 357C | 357 Magnum | 158 | 10.23 | Lead Semi-Wadcutter | 100 | 1235 | 1160 | 1104 | 1060 | 1020 | 535 | 475 | 428 | 395 | 365 | 0.2 | 0.8 | 1.9 | 3.5 | 4-V |
| 1, 3 | 357D | 357 Magnum | 110 | 7.13 | Hi-Shok JHP | 100 | 1295 | 1180 | 1094 | 1040 | 990 | 410 | 340 | 292 | 260 | 235 | 0.2 | 0.8 | 1.9 | 3.5 | 4-V |
| 2, 3 | 357E | 357 Magnum | 158 | 10.23 | Hi-Shok JHP | 100 | 1235 | 1160 | 1104 | 1060 | 1020 | 535 | 475 | 428 | 395 | 365 | 0.2 | 0.8 | 1.9 | 3.5 | 4-V |
| 2 | 357G | 357 Magnum | 180 | 11.66 | Hi-Shok JHP | 100 | 1090 | 1030 | 980 | 930 | 890 | 475 | 425 | 385 | 350 | 320 | 0.2 | 1.0 | 2.4 | 4.5 | 4-V |
| 2, 3 | 357H | 357 Magnum | 140 | 9.07 | Hi-Shok JHP | 100 | 1360 | 1270 | 1200 | 1130 | 1080 | 575 | 500 | 445 | 395 | 360 | 0.2 | 0.7 | 1.6 | 3.0 | 4-V |
| 1, 3 | 41A | 41 Rem. Magnum | 210 | 13.60 | Hi-Shok JHP | 150 | 1300 | 1210 | 1130 | 1070 | 1030 | 790 | 680 | 595 | 540 | 495 | 0.2 | 0.7 | 1.8 | 3.3 | 4-V |
| 1, 3 | 44SA | 44 S&W Special | 200 | 12.96 | Semi-Wadcutter HP | 150 | 900 | 860 | 830 | 800 | 770 | 360 | 330 | 305 | 285 | 260 | 0.3 | 1.4 | 3.4 | 6.3 | 6½-V |
| 2, 3 | 44A | 44 Rem. Magnum | 240 | 15.55 | Hi-Shok JHP | 150 | 1180 | 1130 | 1081 | 1050 | 1010 | 741 | 675 | 623 | 580 | 550 | 0.2 | 0.9 | 2.0 | 3.7 | 6½-V |
| 1, 2 | 44B* | 44 Rem. Magnum | 180 | 11.66 | Hi-Shok JHP | 150 | 1610 | 1480 | 1365 | 1270 | 1180 | 1035 | 875 | 750 | 640 | 555 | 0.1 | 0.5 | 1.2 | 2.3 | 6½-V |
| 1, 3 | 45LCA | 45 Colt | 225 | 14.58 | Semi-Wadcutter HP | 150 | 900 | 880 | 860 | 840 | 820 | 405 | 385 | 369 | 355 | 340 | 0.3 | 1.4 | 3.2 | 5.8 | 5½ |

+P ammunition is loaded to a higher pressure. Use only in firearms so recommended by the gun manufacturer.
"V" indicates vented barrel to simulate service conditions. *Also available in 20-round box (A44B20). **JHP = Jacketed Hollow Point HP = Hollow Point JSP = Jacketed Soft Point

## PREMIUM® NYCLAD® BALLISTICS

| Usage | Federal Load No. | Caliber | Bullet Wgt. in Grains | Bullet Wgt. in Grams | Bullet Style* | Factory Primer No. | Velocity in Feet per Second: Muzzle | 25 Yds. | 50 Yds. | 75 Yds. | 100 Yds. | Energy in Foot-Pounds: Muzzle | 25 Yds. | 50 Yds. | 75 Yds. | 100 Yds. | Mid-Range Trajectory: 25 Yds. | 50 Yds. | 75 Yds. | 100 Yds. | Test Barrel Length Inches |
|---|---|---|---|---|---|---|---|---|---|---|---|---|---|---|---|---|---|---|---|---|---|
| 3 | P9BP | 9mm Luger (9x19mm Parabellum) | 124 | 8.03 | Nyclad Hollow Point | 100 | 1120 | 1070 | 1030 | 990 | 960 | 345 | 315 | 290 | 270 | 255 | 0.2 | 0.9 | 2.2 | 4.1 | 4 |
| 4 | P38B | 38 Special | 158 | 10.23 | Nyclad Round Nose | 100 | 755 | 740 | 723 | 710 | 690 | 200 | 190 | 183 | 175 | 170 | 0.5 | 2.0 | 4.6 | 8.3 | 4-V |
| 1, 3 | P38G | 38 Special (High Velocity +P) | 158 | 10.23 | Nyclad SWC-HP | 100 | 890 | 870 | 855 | 840 | 820 | 270 | 265 | 257 | 245 | 235 | 0.3 | 1.4 | 3.3 | 5.9 | 4-V |
| 3 | P38M | 38 Special | 125 | 8.10 | Nyclad Hollow Point | 100 | 825 | 780 | 730 | 690 | 650 | 190 | 170 | 150 | 130 | 115 | 0.4 | 1.8 | 4.3 | 8.1 | 2-V |
| 1, 3 | P38N | 38 Special (High Velocity +P) | 125 | 8.10 | Nyclad Hollow Point | 100 | 945 | 920 | 898 | 880 | 860 | 248 | 235 | 224 | 215 | 205 | 0.3 | 1.3 | 2.9 | 5.4 | 4-V |
| 2, 3 | P357E | 357 Magnum | 158 | 10.23 | Nyclad SWC-HP | 100 | 1235 | 1160 | 1104 | 1060 | 1020 | 535 | 475 | 428 | 395 | 365 | 0.2 | 0.8 | 1.9 | 3.5 | 4-V |

*HP = Hollow Point

# FEDERAL BALLISTICS

## PISTOL/REVOLVER

### AMERICAN EAGLE PISTOL

| USAGE | FEDERAL LOAD NO. | CALIBER | BULLET WGT. IN GRAINS | BULLET WGT. IN GRAMS | BULLET STYLE* | FACTORY PRIMER NO. | VELOCITY IN FEET PER SECOND MUZZLE | 25 YDS. | 50 YDS. | 75 YDS. | 100 YDS. | ENERGY IN FOOT-POUNDS MUZZLE | 25 YDS. | 50 YDS. | 75 YDS. | 100 YDS. | MID-RANGE TRAJECTORY 25 YDS. | 50 YDS. | 75 YDS. | 100 YDS. | TEST BARREL LENGTH INCHES |
|---|---|---|---|---|---|---|---|---|---|---|---|---|---|---|---|---|---|---|---|---|---|
| [5] | AE25AP | 25 Auto (6.35mm Browning) | 50 | 3.24 | Full Metal Jacket | 100 | 760 | 750 | 730 | 720 | 700 | 65 | 60 | 59 | 58 | 55 | 0.5 | 1.9 | 4.5 | 8.1 | 2 |
| [5] | AE380AP | 380 Auto (9 x 17 short) | 95 | 6.15 | Full Metal Jacket | 100 | 955 | 910 | 865 | 830 | 790 | 190 | 175 | 160 | 145 | 130 | 0.3 | 1.3 | 3.1 | 5.8 | 3¾ |
| [5] | AE9AP | 9mm Luger (9 x 19 Parabellum) | 124 | 8.03 | Full Metal Jacket | 100 | 1120 | 1070 | 1030 | 990 | 960 | 345 | 315 | 290 | 270 | 255 | 0.2 | 0.9 | 2.2 | 4.1 | 4 |
| [5] | AE9FP | 9mm Luger (9 x 19 Parabellum) | 147 | 9.52 | Full Metal Jacket Flat Pt. | 100 | 950 | 930 | 910 | 890 | 870 | 295 | 280 | 270 | 260 | 250 | 0.3 | 1.3 | 2.9 | 5.3 | 4 |
| [5] NEW | AE9MK | 9mm Makarov (9 x 19 Makarov) | 90 | 5.83 | Full Metal Jacket | 100 | 990 | 960 | 920 | 900 | 870 | 195 | 180 | 170 | 160 | 150 | 0.3 | 1.2 | 2.8 | 5.1 | 3¾ |
| [5] NEW | AE38S1 | 38 Super High Velocity +P | 130 | 8.42 | Full Metal Jacket | 200 | 1200 | 1140 | 1100 | 1050 | 1020 | 415 | 380 | 350 | 320 | 300 | 0.2 | 0.8 | 1.9 | 3.6 | 5 |
| [5] NEW | AE38S2 | 38 Super High Velocity +P | 147 | 9.52 | Full Metal Jacket | 200 | 1100 | 1070 | 1050 | 1020 | 1000 | 395 | 375 | 355 | 340 | 325 | 0.2 | 0.9 | 2.2 | 4 | 5 |
| [5] | AE40 | 40 S & W | 180 | 11.06 | Full Metal Jacket | 100 | 990 | 960 | 930 | 910 | 890 | 390 | 365 | 345 | 330 | 315 | 0.3 | 1.2 | 2.8 | 5 | 4 |
| [5] NEW | AE40FP | 40 S & W | 180 | 11.06 | Full Metal Jacket Flat Pt. | 100 | 990 | 960 | 930 | 910 | 880 | 390 | 365 | 345 | 330 | 310 | 0.3 | 1.2 | 2.7 | 5 | 4 |
| [5] NEW | AE40T3 | 40 S & W | 165 | 10.66 | Full Metal Jacket | 100 | 980 | 950 | 930 | 920 | 900 | 350 | 335 | 320 | 305 | 295 | 0.3 | 1.2 | 2.7 | 5 | 4 |
| [5] | AE10 | 10mm Auto | 180 | 11.06 | Full Metal Jacket | 150 | 1030 | 995 | 970 | 945 | 920 | 425 | 400 | 375 | 355 | 340 | 0.3 | 1.1 | 2.5 | 4.7 | 5 |
| [5] | AE45A | 45 Auto | 230 | 14.90 | Full Metal Jacket | 150 | 850 | 830 | 810 | 790 | 770 | 370 | 350 | 335 | 320 | 305 | 0.4 | 1.6 | 3.6 | 6.6 | 5 |

### AMERICAN EAGLE REVOLVER

| USAGE | FEDERAL LOAD NO. | CALIBER | BULLET WGT. IN GRAINS | BULLET WGT. IN GRAMS | BULLET STYLE* | FACTORY PRIMER NO. | VELOCITY IN FEET PER SECOND MUZZLE | 25 YDS. | 50 YDS. | 75 YDS. | 100 YDS. | ENERGY IN FOOT-POUNDS MUZZLE | 25 YDS. | 50 YDS. | 75 YDS. | 100 YDS. | MID-RANGE TRAJECTORY 25 YDS. | 50 YDS. | 75 YDS. | 100 YDS. | TEST BARREL LENGTH INCHES |
|---|---|---|---|---|---|---|---|---|---|---|---|---|---|---|---|---|---|---|---|---|---|
| [5] | AE38B | 38 Special | 158 | 10.23 | Lead Round Nose | 100 | 755 | 740 | 723 | 710 | 690 | 200 | 190 | 183 | 175 | 170 | 0.5 | 2.0 | 4.6 | 8.3 | 4-V |
| [2], [5] | AE357A | 357 Magnum | 158 | 10.23 | Jacketed Soft Point | 100 | 1235 | 1160 | 1104 | 1060 | 1020 | 595 | 475 | 428 | 395 | 365 | 0.2 | 0.8 | 1.0 | 3.5 | 4-V |
| [2], [5] | AE44A | 44 Rem. Magnum | 240 | 15.55 | Jacketed Hollow Point | 150 | 1180 | 1130 | 1081 | 1050 | 1010 | 741 | 675 | 623 | 580 | 550 | 0.2 | 0.9 | 2.0 | 3.7 | 6½-V |

### GOLD MEDAL® MATCH BALLISTICS

| USAGE | FEDERAL LOAD NO. | CALIBER | BULLET WGT. IN GRAINS | BULLET WGT. IN GRAMS | BULLET STYLE* | FACTORY PRIMER NO. | VELOCITY IN FEET PER SECOND MUZZLE | 25 YDS. | 50 YDS. | 75 YDS. | 100 YDS. | ENERGY IN FOOT-POUNDS MUZZLE | 25 YDS. | 50 YDS. | 75 YDS. | 100 YDS. | MID-RANGE TRAJECTORY 25 YDS. | 50 YDS. | 75 YDS. | 100 YDS. | TEST BARREL LENGTH INCHES |
|---|---|---|---|---|---|---|---|---|---|---|---|---|---|---|---|---|---|---|---|---|---|
| [4] | GM9MP | 9mm Luger (9x19mm Parabellum) | 124 | 8.03 | FMJ-SWC Match | 100 | 1120 | 1070 | 1030 | 990 | 960 | 345 | 315 | 290 | 270 | 255 | 0.2 | 0.9 | 2.2 | 4.1 | 4 |
| [4] | GM38A | 38 Special | 148 | 9.59 | Lead Wadcutter Match | 100 | 710 | 670 | 634 | 600 | 560 | 166 | 150 | 132 | 115 | 105 | 0.6 | 2.4 | 5.7 | 10.8 | 4-V |
| [4] NEW | GM356SW | 356 TSW | 147 | 9.52 | FMJ-SWC Match | 100 | 1220 | 1170 | 1120 | 1080 | 1040 | 485 | 445 | 410 | 380 | 355 | 0.2 | 0.8 | 1.9 | 3.5 | 5 |
| [4] | GM44D | 44 Rem. Magnum | 250 | 16.20 | MC Profile Match | 150 | 1180 | 1140 | 1100 | 1070 | 1040 | 775 | 715 | 670 | 630 | 600 | 0.2 | 0.8 | 1.9 | 3.6 | 6½-V |
| [4] | GM45B | 45 Auto | 185 | 11.99 | FMJ-SWC Match | 150 | 775 | 730 | 695 | 660 | 620 | 247 | 220 | 200 | 175 | 160 | 0.5 | 2.0 | 4.8 | 9.0 | 5 |

*MC Profile Match = Metal Case Profile Match   FMJ = Full Metal Jacket   SWC = Semi-Wadcutter

### PREMIUM® HYDRA-SHOK® BALLISTICS

| USAGE | FEDERAL LOAD NO. | CALIBER | BULLET WGT. IN GRAINS | BULLET WGT. IN GRAMS | BULLET STYLE* | FACTORY PRIMER NO. | VELOCITY IN FEET PER SECOND MUZZLE | 25 YDS. | 50 YDS. | 75 YDS. | 100 YDS. | ENERGY IN FOOT-POUNDS MUZZLE | 25 YDS. | 50 YDS. | 75 YDS. | 100 YDS. | MID-RANGE TRAJECTORY 25 YDS. | 50 YDS. | 75 YDS. | 100 YDS. | TEST BARREL LENGTH INCHES |
|---|---|---|---|---|---|---|---|---|---|---|---|---|---|---|---|---|---|---|---|---|---|
| [3] | P380HS1 | 380 Auto (9x17mm Short) | 90 | 5.83 | Hydra-Shok JHP | 100 | 1000 | 940 | 890 | 840 | 800 | 200 | 175 | 160 | 140 | 130 | 0.3 | 1.2 | 2.9 | 5.5 | 3¾ |
| [3] | P9HS1 | 9mm Luger (9x19mm Parabellum) | 124 | 8.03 | Hydra-Shok JHP | 100 | 1120 | 1070 | 1030 | 990 | 960 | 345 | 315 | 290 | 270 | 255 | 0.2 | 0.9 | 2.2 | 4.1 | 4 |
| [3] | P9HS2 | 9mm Luger (9x19mm Parabellum) | 147 | 9.52 | Hydra-Shok JHP | 100 | 1000 | 960 | 920 | 890 | 860 | 325 | 300 | 275 | 260 | 240 | 0.3 | 1.2 | 2.8 | 5.1 | 4 |
| [3] | P40HS1 | 40 S&W | 180 | 11.06 | Hydra-Shok JHP | 100 | 985 | 955 | 930 | 910 | 890 | 390 | 365 | 345 | 330 | 315 | 0.3 | 1.2 | 2.8 | 5.0 | 4 |
| [3] | P40HS2 | 40 S&W | 155 | 10.04 | Hydra-Shok JHP | 100 | 1140 | 1080 | 1030 | 990 | 950 | 445 | 400 | 365 | 335 | 315 | 0.2 | 0.9 | 2.2 | 4.1 | 4 |
| [3] | P40HS3 | 40 S&W | 165 | 10.66 | Hydra-Shok JHP | 100 | 975 | 950 | 927 | 906 | 887 | 348 | 331 | 315 | 301 | 288 | 0.3 | 1.2 | 2.7 | 5.1 | 4 |
| [3] | P10HS1 | 10mm Auto | 180 | 11.06 | Hydra-Shok JHP | 150 | 1030 | 995 | 970 | 945 | 920 | 425 | 400 | 375 | 355 | 340 | 0.3 | 1.1 | 2.5 | 4.7 | 5 |
| [3] | P45HS1 | 45 Auto | 230 | 14.90 | Hydra-Shok JHP | 150 | 850 | 830 | 810 | 790 | 770 | 370 | 350 | 335 | 320 | 305 | 0.4 | 1.6 | 3.6 | 6.6 | 5 |
| [3] | P38HS1 | 38 Special (High Velocity +P) | 129 | 8.36 | Hydra-Shok JHP | 100 | 945 | 930 | 910 | 890 | 870 | 255 | 245 | 235 | 225 | 215 | 0.3 | 1.3 | 2.9 | 5.3 | 4-V |
| [3] | P357HS1 | 357 Magnum | 158 | 10.23 | Hydra-Shok JHP | 100 | 1235 | 1160 | 1104 | 1060 | 1020 | 535 | 475 | 428 | 395 | 365 | 0.2 | 0.8 | 1.9 | 3.5 | 4-V |
| [3] | P44HS1 | 44 Rem. Magnum | 240 | 15.55 | Hydra-Shok JHP | 150 | 1180 | 1130 | 1081 | 1050 | 1010 | 741 | 675 | 623 | 580 | 550 | 0.2 | 0.9 | 2.0 | 3.7 | 6½-V |

+P ammunition is loaded to a higher pressure. Use only in firearms so recommended by the gun manufacturer. "V" indicates vented barrel to simulate service conditions.
*HP = Hollow Point   SWC = Semi-Wadcutter

# HORNADY BALLISTICS

| RIFLE | MUZZLE VELOCITY | VELOCITY FEET PER SECOND | | | | | ENERGY FOOT - POUNDS | | | | | | TRAJECTORY TABLES | | | | |
|---|---|---|---|---|---|---|---|---|---|---|---|---|---|---|---|---|---|
| Caliber | Muzzle | 100 yds. | 200 yds. | 300 yds. | 400 yds. | 500 yds. | Muzzle | 100 yds. | 200 yds. | 300 yds. | 400 yds. | 500 yds. | 100 yds. | 200 yds. | 300 yds. | 400 yds. | 500 yds. |
| 222 Rem., 50 gr. SX | 3140 | 2602 | 2123 | 1700 | 1350 | 1107 | 1094 | 752 | 500 | 321 | 202 | 136 | +2.2 | -0- | -10.0 | -32.3 | -73.8 |
| 222 Rem., 55 gr. SX | 3020 | 2562 | 2147 | 1773 | 1451 | 1201 | 1114 | 801 | 563 | 384 | 257 | 176 | +2.2 | -0- | -9.9 | -31.0 | -68.7 |
| 223 Rem., 53 gr. HP | 3330 | 2882 | 2477 | 2106 | 1710 | 1475 | 1305 | 978 | 722 | 522 | 369 | 356 | +1.7 | -0- | -7.4 | -22.7 | -49.1 |
| 223 Rem., 55 gr. SP | 3240 | 2747 | 2304 | 1905 | 1554 | 1270 | 1282 | 921 | 648 | 443 | 295 | 197 | +1.9 | -0- | -8.5 | -26.7 | -59.6 |
| 223 Rem., 55 gr. FMJ | 3240 | 2759 | 2326 | 1933 | 1587 | 1301 | 1282 | 929 | 660 | 456 | 307 | 207 | +1.9 | -0- | -8.4 | -26.2 | -57.9 |
| 223 Rem., 60 gr. SP | 3150 | 2782 | 2442 | 2127 | 1837 | 1575 | 1322 | 1031 | 795 | 603 | 450 | 331 | +1.6 | -0- | -7.5 | -22.5 | -48.1 |
| 22-250 Rem., 53 gr. HP | 3680 | 3185 | 2743 | 2341 | 1974 | 1646 | 1594 | 1194 | 886 | 645 | 459 | 319 | +1.0 | -0- | -5.7 | -17.8 | -38.8 |
| 22-250 Rem., 55 gr. SP | 3680 | 3137 | 2656 | 2222 | 1832 | 1439 | 1654 | 1201 | 861 | 603 | 410 | 272 | +1.1 | -0- | -6.0 | -19.2 | -42.6 |
| 22-250 Rem., 55 gr. FMJ | 3680 | 3137 | 2656 | 2222 | 1836 | 1439 | 1654 | 1201 | 861 | 603 | 410 | 273 | +1.1 | -0- | -6.0 | -19.2 | -42.6 |
| 22-250 Rem., 60 gr. SP | 3600 | 3195 | 2826 | 2485 | 2169 | 1878 | 1727 | 1360 | 1064 | 823 | 627 | 470 | +1.0 | -0- | -5.4 | -16.3 | -34.8 |
| 220 Swift, 50 gr. SP | 3850 | 3327 | 2862 | 2442 | 2060 | 1716 | 1645 | 1228 | 909 | 662 | 471 | 327 | +0.8 | -0- | -5.1 | -16.1 | -35.3 |
| 220 Swift, 55 gr. SP | 3650 | 3194 | 2772 | 2384 | 2035 | 1724 | 1627 | 1246 | 939 | 694 | 506 | 363 | +1.0 | -0- | -5.6 | -17.4 | -37.5 |
| 220 Swift, 60 gr. HP | 3600 | 3199 | 2824 | 2475 | 2156 | 1868 | 1727 | 1364 | 1063 | 816 | 619 | 465 | +1.0 | -0- | -5.4 | -16.3 | -34.8 |
| 243 Win., 75 gr. HP | 3400 | 2970 | 2578 | 2219 | 1890 | 1595 | 1926 | 1469 | 1107 | 820 | 595 | 425 | +1.2 | -0- | -6.5 | -20.3 | -43.8 |
| 243 Win., 100 gr. BTSP | 2960 | 2728 | 2508 | 2299 | 2099 | 1910 | 1945 | 1653 | 1397 | 1174 | 979 | 810 | +1.6 | -0- | -7.2 | -21.0 | -42.8 |
| 243 Win., 100 gr. SP LM | 3100 | 2839 | 2592 | 2358 | 2138 | 1936 | 2133 | 1790 | 1491 | 1235 | 1014 | 832 | +1.5 | -0- | -6.81 | -19.8 | -40.2 |
| 6MM Rem., 100 gr. BTSP | 3100 | 2861 | 2634 | 2419 | 2231 | 2018 | 2134 | 1818 | 1541 | 1300 | 1088 | 904 | +1.3 | -0- | -6.5 | -18.9 | -38.5 |
| 257 Roberts, 117 gr. BTSP | 2780 | 2550 | 2331 | 2122 | 1925 | 1740 | 2007 | 1689 | 1411 | 1170 | 963 | 787 | +1.9 | -0- | -8.3 | -24.4 | -49.9 |
| 257 Roberts, 117 gr. BTSP LM | 2940 | 2694 | 2460 | 2240 | 2031 | 1844 | 2245 | 1885 | 1572 | 1303 | 1071 | 883 | +1.7 | -0- | -7.6 | -21.8 | -44.7 |
| 25-06 117 gr. BTSP | 2990 | 2749 | 2520 | 2302 | 2096 | 1900 | 2322 | 1962 | 1649 | 1377 | 1141 | 938 | +1.6 | -0- | -7.0 | -20.7 | -42.2 |
| 270 Win., 130 gr. SP | 3060 | 2800 | 2560 | 2330 | 2110 | 1900 | 2700 | 2265 | 1890 | 1565 | 1285 | 1045 | +1.8 | -0- | -7.1 | -20.6 | -42.0 |
| 270 Win., 140 gr. BTSP | 2940 | 2747 | 2562 | 2385 | 2214 | 2050 | 2688 | 2346 | 2041 | 1769 | 1524 | 1307 | +1.6 | -0- | -7.0 | -20.2 | -40.3 |
| 270 Win., 150 gr. SP | 2800 | 2684 | 2478 | 2284 | 2100 | 1927 | 2802 | 2400 | 2046 | 1737 | 1469 | 1237 | +1.7 | -0- | -7.4 | -21.6 | -43.9 |
| 7 x 57 Mau., 139 gr. BTSP | 2700 | 2504 | 2316 | 2137 | 1965 | 1802 | 2251 | 1936 | 1656 | 1410 | 1192 | 1002 | +2.0 | -0- | -8.5 | -24.9 | -50.3 |
| 7 x 57 Mau., 139 gr. BTSP LM | 2830 | 2620 | 2450 | 2250 | 2070 | 1910 | 2475 | 2135 | 1835 | 1565 | 1330 | 1115 | +1.8 | -0- | -7.6 | -22.1 | -45.0 |
| 7MM-08, 139 gr. BTSP LM | 3000 | 2790 | 2590 | 2399 | 2216 | 2041 | 2777 | 2403 | 2071 | 1776 | 1515 | 1285 | +1.5 | -0- | -6.7 | -19.4 | -39.2 |
| 7MM Rem. Mag., 139 gr. BTSP | 3150 | 2933 | 2727 | 2530 | 2341 | 2160 | 3063 | 2656 | 2296 | 1976 | 1692 | 1440 | +1.2 | -0- | -6.1 | -17.7 | -35.5 |
| 7MM Rem. Mag., 154 gr. SP | 3035 | 2814 | 2604 | 2404 | 2212 | 2029 | 3151 | 2708 | 2319 | 1977 | 1674 | 1408 | +1.3 | -0- | -6.7 | -19.3 | -39.3 |
| 7MM Rem. Mag., 162 gr. BTSP | 2940 | 2757 | 2582 | 2413 | 2251 | 2094 | 3110 | 2735 | 2399 | 2095 | 1823 | 1578 | +1.6 | -0- | -6.7 | -19.7 | -39.3 |
| 7MM Rem. Mag., 175 gr. SP | 2860 | 2650 | 2440 | 2240 | 2060 | 1880 | 3180 | 2720 | 2310 | 1960 | 1640 | 1370 | +2.0 | -0- | -7.9 | -22.7 | -45.8 |
| 7MM Wby. Mag., 154 gr. SP | 3200 | 2971 | 2753 | 2546 | 2348 | 2159 | 3501 | 3017 | 2592 | 2216 | 1885 | 1593 | +1.2 | -0- | -5.8 | -17.0 | -34.5 |
| 7MM Wby. Mag., 175 gr. SP | 2910 | 2709 | 2516 | 2331 | 2154 | 1985 | 3290 | 2850 | 2459 | 2111 | 1803 | 1531 | +1.6 | -0- | -7.1 | -20.6 | -41.7 |
| 30-30 Win., 150 gr. RN | 2390 | 1973 | 1605 | 1303 | 1095 | 974 | 1902 | 1296 | 858 | 565 | 399 | 316 | -0- | -8.2 | -30.0 | | |
| 30-30 Win., 170 gr. FP | 2200 | 1895 | 1619 | 1381 | 1191 | 1064 | 1827 | 1355 | 989 | 720 | 535 | 425 | -0- | -8.9 | -31.1 | | |
| 308 Win., 150 gr. BTSP | 2820 | 2560 | 2315 | 2084 | 1866 | 1644 | 2648 | 2183 | 1785 | 1447 | 1160 | 922 | +2.0 | -0- | -8.5 | -25.2 | -51.8 |
| 308 Win., 150 gr. SP LM | 2980 | 2703 | 2442 | 2195 | 1964 | 1748 | 2959 | 2433 | 1986 | 1606 | 1285 | 1018 | +1.6 | -0- | -7.5 | -22.2 | -46.0 |
| 308 Win., 165 gr. BTSP | 2700 | 2496 | 2301 | 2115 | 1937 | 1770 | 2670 | 2283 | 1940 | 1639 | 1375 | 1148 | +2.0 | -0- | -8.7 | -25.2 | -51.0 |
| 308 Win., 165 gr. BTSP LM | 2870 | 2658 | 2456 | 2263 | 2078 | 1903 | 3019 | 2589 | 2211 | 1877 | 1583 | 1327 | +1.7 | -0- | -7.5 | -21.8 | -44.1 |
| 308 Win., 168 gr. BTHP MATCH | 2700 | 2524 | 2354 | 2191 | 2035 | 1885 | 2720 | 2377 | 2068 | 1791 | 1545 | 1326 | +2.0 | -0- | -8.4 | -23.9 | -48.0 |
| 30-06 150 gr. SP | 2910 | 2617 | 2342 | 2083 | 1843 | 1622 | 2820 | 2281 | 1827 | 1445 | 1131 | 876 | +2.1 | -0- | -8.5 | -25.0 | -51.8 |
| 30-06 150 gr. BTSP | 2910 | 2683 | 2467 | 2262 | 2066 | 1880 | 2820 | 2397 | 2027 | 1706 | 1421 | 1177 | +2.0 | -0- | -7.7 | -22.2 | -44.9 |
| 30-06 150 gr. SP LM | 3100 | 2815 | 2548 | 2295 | 2058 | 1835 | 3200 | 2639 | 2161 | 1755 | 1410 | 1121 | +1.4 | -0- | -6.8 | -20.3 | -42.0 |
| 30-06 165 gr. BTSP | 2800 | 2591 | 2392 | 2202 | 2020 | 1848 | 2873 | 2460 | 2097 | 1777 | 1495 | 1252 | +1.8 | -0- | -8.0 | -23.3 | -47.0 |
| 30-06 168 gr. BTHP MATCH | 2790 | 2620 | 2447 | 2280 | 2120 | 1966 | 2925 | 2561 | 2234 | 1940 | 1677 | 1442 | +1.7 | -0- | -7.7 | -22.2 | -44.3 |
| 30-06 180 gr. SP | 2700 | 2469 | 2258 | 2042 | 1846 | 1663 | 2913 | 2436 | 2023 | 1666 | 1362 | 1105 | +2.4 | -0- | -9.3 | -27.0 | -54.9 |
| 30-06 180 gr. BTSP LM | 2880 | 2676 | 2480 | 2293 | 2114 | 1943 | 3316 | 2862 | 2459 | 2102 | 1786 | 1509 | +1.7 | -0- | -7.3 | -21.3 | -43.1 |
| 300 Wby. Mag., 180 gr. SP | 3120 | 2891 | 2673 | 2466 | 2268 | 2079 | 3890 | 3340 | 2856 | 2430 | 2055 | 1727 | +1.3 | -0- | -6.2 | -18.1 | -36.8 |
| 300 Win. Mag., 150 gr. BTSP | 3275 | 2988 | 2718 | 2464 | 2224 | 1998 | 3573 | 2974 | 2461 | 2023 | 1648 | 1330 | +1.2 | -0- | -6.0 | -17.8 | -36.5 |
| 300 Win. Mag., 165 gr. BTSP | 3100 | 2877 | 2665 | 2462 | 2269 | 2084 | 3522 | 3033 | 2603 | 2221 | 1887 | 1592 | +1.3 | -0- | -6.5 | -18.5 | -37.3 |
| 300 Win. Mag., 180 gr. SP | 2960 | 2745 | 2540 | 2344 | 2157 | 1979 | 3501 | 3011 | 2578 | 2196 | 1859 | 1565 | +1.9 | -0- | -7.3 | -20.9 | -41.9 |
| 300 Win. Mag., 190 gr. BTSP | 2900 | 2711 | 2529 | 2355 | 2187 | 2026 | 3549 | 3101 | 2699 | 2340 | 2018 | 1732 | +1.6 | -0- | -7.1 | -20.4 | -41.0 |
| 303 British, 150 gr. SP | 2685 | 2441 | 2210 | 1992 | 1787 | 1598 | 2401 | 1984 | 1627 | 1321 | 1064 | 500 | +2.2 | -0- | -9.3 | -27.4 | -56.5 |
| 303 British, 150 gr. SP LM | 2830 | 2570 | 2325 | 2094 | 1884 | 1690 | 2667 | 2199 | 1800 | 1461 | 1185 | 952 | +2.0 | -0- | -8.4 | -24.6 | -50.3 |
| 303 British, 174 gr. RN | 2500 | 2181 | 1886 | 1669 | 1387 | 1201 | 2414 | 1837 | 1374 | 1012 | 743 | 557 | +2.9 | -0- | -12.8 | -39.0 | -83.4 |

| BARREL LENGTH | PISTOL | MUZZLE VELOCITY | VELOCITY FT. PER SECOND | | ENERGY | | |
|---|---|---|---|---|---|---|---|
| | Caliber | Muzzle | 50 yds. | 100 yds. | Muzzle | 50 yds. | 100 yds. |
| 2″ | 25 Auto, 35 gr. JHP/XTP | 900 | 813 | 742 | 63 | 51 | 43 |
| 4″ | 32 Auto, 71 gr. FMJ | 900 | 845 | 797 | 128 | 112 | 100 |
| 3¾″ | 380 Auto, 90 gr. JHP/XTP | 1000 | 902 | 823 | 200 | 163 | 135 |
| 4″ | 9MM Luger, 90 gr. JHP/XTP | 1360 | 1112 | 978 | 370 | 247 | 191 |
| 4″ | 9MM Luger, 115 gr. JHP/XTP | 1155 | 1047 | 971 | 341 | 280 | 241 |
| 4″ | 9MM Luger, 115 gr. FMJ V | 1155 | 1047 | 971 | 341 | 280 | 241 |
| 4″ | 9MM Luger, 124 gr. JHP/XTP | 1110 | 1030 | 971 | 339 | 292 | 259 |
| 4″ | 9MM Luger, 147 gr. JHP/XTP | 975 | 935 | 899 | 310 | 285 | 264 |
| 4″ | 9 x 18 Makarov, 95 gr. JHP/XTP | 1000 | 930 | 874 | 211 | 182 | 161 |
| 4″V | 38 Special, 125 gr. JHP/XTP | 900 | 856 | 817 | 225 | 203 | 185 |
| 4″V | 38 Special, 140 gr. JHP/XTP | 900 | 850 | 806 | 252 | 225 | 202 |
| 4″V | 38 Special, 148 gr. HBWC | 800 | 697 | 610 | 210 | 160 | 122 |
| 4″V | 38 Special, 158 gr. JHP/XTP | 800 | 765 | 731 | 225 | 205 | 188 |
| 8″V | 357 Mag., 125 gr. JHP/XTP | 1500 | 1314 | 1166 | 624 | 479 | 377 |
| 8″V | 357 Mag., 125 gr. JFP/XTP | 1500 | 1311 | 1161 | 624 | 477 | 374 |
| 8″V | 357 Mag., 140 gr. JHP/XTP | 1400 | 1249 | 1130 | 609 | 485 | 397 |
| 8″V | 357 Mag., 158 gr. JHP/XTP | 1250 | 1150 | 1073 | 548 | 464 | 404 |
| 8″V | 357 Mag., 158 gr. JFP | 1250 | 1147 | 1068 | 548 | 461 | 400 |

| BARREL LENGTH | PISTOL | MUZZLE VELOCITY | VELOCITY FT. PER SECOND | | ENERGY | | |
|---|---|---|---|---|---|---|---|
| | Caliber | Muzzle | 50 yds. | 100 yds. | Muzzle | 50 yds. | 100 yds. |
| 5″ | 10MM Auto, 155 gr. JHP/XTP | 1265 | 1119 | 1020 | 551 | 431 | 358 |
| 5″ | 10MM Auto, 180 gr. JHP/XTP Full | 1180 | 1077 | 1004 | 556 | 464 | 403 |
| 5″ | 10MM Auto, 200 gr. JHP/XTP | 1050 | 994 | 948 | 490 | 439 | 399 |
| 4″ | 40 S&W, 155 gr. JHP/XTP | 1180 | 1061 | 980 | 479 | 388 | 331 |
| 4″ | 40 S&W, 180 gr. JHP/XTP | 950 | 903 | 862 | 361 | 326 | 297 |
| 7½″V | 44 Special, 180 gr. JHP/XTP | 1000 | 935 | 882 | 400 | 350 | 311 |
| 7½″V | 44 Rem. Mag., 180 gr. JHP/XTP | 1550 | 1340 | 1173 | 960 | 717 | 550 |
| 7½″V | 44 Rem. Mag., 200 gr. JHP/XTP | 1500 | 1284 | 1128 | 999 | 732 | 565 |
| 7½″V | 44 Rem. Mag., 240 gr. JHP/XTP | 1350 | 1188 | 1078 | 971 | 753 | 619 |
| 7½″V | 44 Rem. Mag., 300 gr. JHP/XTP | 1150 | 1084 | 1031 | 881 | 782 | 708 |
| 5″ | 45 ACP, 185 gr. JHP/XTP | 950 | 880 | 819 | 371 | 318 | 276 |
| 5″ | 45 ACP, 200 gr. JHP/XTP | 900 | 938 | 885 | 444 | 391 | 348 |
| 5″ | 45 ACP+P, 200 gr. HP/XTP | 1055 | 982 | 925 | 494 | 428 | 380 |
| 5″ | 45 ACP+P, 230 gr. HP/XTP | 950 | 904 | 865 | 462 | 418 | 382 |
| 5″ | 45 ACP, 230 gr. FMJ/RN | 850 | 809 | 771 | 369 | 334 | 304 |
| 5″ | 45 ACP, 230 gr. FMJ/FP | 850 | 809 | 771 | 369 | 334 | 304 |

LM . . . . . . Light Magnum™ V . . . . . . . VECTOR™

# REMINGTON BALLISTICS

| Caliber | Order No. | Primer No. | Weight (grs.) | Bullet Style | Velocity (ft./sec.) Muzzle | Velocity 50 Yds. | Velocity 100 Yds. | Energy (ft.-lb.) Muzzle | Energy 50 Yds. | Energy 100 Yds. | Mid-range Trajectory 50 Yds. | Mid-range Trajectory 100 Yds. | B.L. |
|---|---|---|---|---|---|---|---|---|---|---|---|---|---|
| 221 REM. FIREBALL | R221F | 7½ | 50 | Pointed Soft Point | 2650 | 2380 | 2130 | 780 | 630 | 505 | 0.2" | 0.8" | 10" |
| 25 (6.35MM) AUTO. PISTOL | R25AP | 1½ | 50 | Metal Case | 760 | 707 | 659 | 64 | 56 | 48 | 2.0" | 8.7" | 2" |
| 6MM BR REM. | R6MMBR | 7½ | 100 | Pointed Soft Point | Refer to page 30 for ballistics. | | | | | | | | |
| 7MM BR REM. | R7MMBR | 7½ | 140 | Pointed Soft Point | Refer to page 30 for ballistics. | | | | | | | | |
| 32 S. & W. | R32SW | 1½ | 88 | Lead | 680 | 645 | 610 | 90 | 81 | 73 | 2.5" | 0.5" | 3" |
| 32 S. & W. LONG | R32SWL | 1½ | 98 | Lead | 705 | 670 | 635 | 115 | 98 | 88 | 2.3" | 10.5" | 4" |
| 32 (7.65MM) AUTO. PISTOL | R32AP | 1½ | 71 | Metal Case | 905 | 855 | 810 | 129 | 115 | 97 | 1.4" | 5.8" | 4" |
| 357 MAG. | R357M7 | 5½ | 110 | Semi-Jacketed H.P. | 1295 | 1094 | 975 | 410 | 292 | 232 | 0.8" | 3.5" | 4" |
| Vented Barrel Ballistics | R357M1 | 5½ | 125 | Semi-Jacketed H.P. | 1450 | 1240 | 1090 | 583 | 427 | 330 | 0.6" | 2.8" | 4" |
| | GS357MA | 5½ | 125 | Brass-Jacketed Hollow Point | 1220 | 1095 | 1009 | 413 | 333 | 283 | 0.8" | 3.5" | 4" |
| | RH357MA★ | 5½ | 165 | JHP Core-Lokt® | 1290 | 1189 | 1108 | 610 | 518 | 450 | 0.7" | 3.1" | 8⅜" |
| | LL357MB★ | 5½ | 130 | TEMC, Lead-Lokt™ | 1400 | 1239 | 1116 | 566 | 443 | 360 | 0.6" | 2.8" | 4" |
| (Refer to page 42 for test details) | R357M2 | 5½ | 158 | Semi-Jacketed H.P. | 1235 | 1104 | 1015 | 535 | 428 | 361 | 0.8" | 3.5" | 4" |
| | R357M3 | 5½ | 158 | Soft Point | 1235 | 1104 | 1015 | 535 | 428 | 361 | 0.8" | 3.5" | 4" |
| | R357M5 | 5½ | 158 | Semi-Wadcutter | 1235 | 1104 | 1015 | 535 | 428 | 361 | 0.8" | 3.5" | 4" |
| | R357M9 | 5½ | 140 | Semi-Jacketed H.P. | 1360 | 1195 | 1076 | 575 | 444 | 360 | 0.7" | 3.0" | 4" |
| | R357M10 | 5½ | 180 | Semi-Jacketed H.P. | 1145 | 1053 | 985 | 524 | 443 | 388 | 0.9" | 3.9" | 8⅜" |
| | R357M11 | 5½ | 125 | Semi-Jacketed H.P. (Med. Vel.) | 1220 | 1077 | 984 | 413 | 322 | 269 | 0.8" | 3.7" | 4" |
| 357 REM. MAXIMUM* | 357MX1 | 7½ | 158 | Semi-Jacketed H.P. | 1825 | 1588 | 1381 | 1168 | 885 | 669 | 0.4" | 1.7" | 10" |
| 9MM LUGER | R9MM1 | 1½ | 115 | Jacketed H.P. | 1155 | 1047 | 971 | 341 | 280 | 241 | 0.9" | 3.9" | 4" |
| | R9MM10 | 1½ | 124 | Jacketed H.P. | 1120 | 1028 | 960 | 346 | 291 | 254 | 1.0" | 4.1" | 4" |
| AUTO. PISTOL | R9MM2 | 1½ | 124 | Metal Case | 1110 | 1030 | 971 | 339 | 292 | 259 | 1.0" | 4.1" | 4" |
| | R9MM3 | 1½ | 115 | Metal Case | 1135 | 1041 | 973 | 329 | 277 | 242 | 0.9" | 4.0" | 4" |
| | R9MM5§ | 1½ | 88 | Jacketed H.P. | 1500 | 1191 | 1012 | 440 | 277 | 200 | 0.6" | 3.1" | 4" |
| | R9MM6 | 1½ | 115 | Jacketed H.P. (+P)‡ | 1250 | 1113 | 1019 | 399 | 316 | 265 | 0.8" | 3.5" | 4" |
| | R9MM8 | 1½ | 147 | Jacketed H.P. (Subsonic) | 990 | 941 | 900 | 320 | 289 | 264 | 1.1" | 4.9" | 4" |
| | R9MM9 | 1½ | 147 | Metal Case (Match) | 990 | 941 | 900 | 320 | 289 | 264 | 1.1" | 4.9" | 4" |
| | LL9MMA★ | 1½ | 115 | TEMC, Lead-Lokt™ | 1135 | 1041 | 973 | 329 | 277 | 242 | 0.9" | 4.0" | 4" |
| | LL9MC★ | 1½ | 147 | TEMC, Lead-Lokt™ | 990 | 941 | 900 | 320 | 289 | 264 | 1.1" | 4.9" | 4" |
| | GS9MMB | 1½ | 124 | Brass-Jacketed Hollow Point | 1125 | 1031 | 963 | 349 | 293 | 255 | 1.0" | 4.0" | 4" |
| | GS9MMC | 1½ | 147 | Brass-Jacketed Hollow Point | 990 | 941 | 900 | 320 | 289 | 264 | 1.1" | 4.9" | 4" |
| | GS9MMD★ | 1½ | 124 | BJHP (+P)‡ | 1180 | 1089 | 1021 | 384 | 327 | 287 | 0.8" | 3.8" | 4" |
| 380 AUTO. PISTOL | R380AP | 1½ | 95 | Metal Case | 955 | 865 | 785 | 190 | 160 | 130 | 1.4" | 5.9" | 4" |
| | R380A1 | 1½ | 88 | Jacketed H.P. | 990 | 920 | 868 | 191 | 165 | 146 | 1.2" | 5.1" | 4" |
| | GS380B★ | 1½ | 102 | BJHP | 940 | 901 | 866 | 200 | 184 | 170 | 1.2" | 5.1" | 4" |
| 38 SUPER AUTO. COLT PISTOL (A) | R38SU1 | 1½ | 115 | Jacketed H.P. (+P)‡ | 1300 | 1147 | 1041 | 431 | 336 | 277 | 0.7" | 3.3" | 5" |
| 38 S. & W. | R38SW | 1½ | 146 | Lead | 685 | 650 | 620 | 150 | 135 | 125 | 2.4" | 10.0" | 4" |
| 38 SPECIAL | R38S1§ | 1½ | 95 | Semi-Jacketed H.P. (+P)‡ | 1175 | 1044 | 959 | 291 | 230 | 194 | 0.9" | 3.9" | 4" |
| Vented Barrel Ballistics | R38S10 | 1½ | 110 | Semi-Jacketed H.P. (+P)‡ | 995 | 926 | 871 | 242 | 210 | 185 | 1.2" | 5.1" | 4" |
| | R38S16 | 1½ | 110 | Semi-Jacketed H.P. | 950 | 890 | 840 | 220 | 194 | 172 | 1.4" | 5.4" | 4" |
| | R38S2 | 1½ | 125 | Semi-Jacketed H.P. (+P)‡ | 945 | 898 | 858 | 248 | 224 | 204 | 1.3" | 5.4" | 4" |
| | LL38SB★ | 1½ | 130 | TEMC, Lead-Lokt™ | 950 | 901 | 859 | 261 | 235 | 213 | 1.4" | 5.0" | 4" |
| | GS38SB | 1½ | 125 | Brass-Jacketed Hollow Point (+P) | 975 | 929 | 885 | 264 | 238 | 218 | 1.0" | 5.2" | 4" |
| | R38S3 | 1½ | 148 | Targetmaster Lead W.C. Match | 710 | 634 | 566 | 166 | 132 | 105 | 2.4" | 10.8" | 4" |
| | R38S4 | 1½ | 158 | Targetmaster Lead | 755 | 723 | 692 | 200 | 183 | 168 | 2.0" | 8.3" | 4" |
| | R38S5 | 1½ | 158 | Lead (Round Nose) | 755 | 723 | 692 | 200 | 183 | 168 | 2.0" | 8.3" | 4" |
| | R38S14 | 1½ | 158 | Semi-Wadcutter (+P)‡ | 890 | 855 | 823 | 278 | 257 | 238 | 1.4" | 6.0" | 4" |
| | R38S6 | 1½ | 158 | Semi-Wadcutter | 755 | 723 | 692 | 200 | 183 | 168 | 2.0" | 8.3" | 4" |
| | R38S12 | 1½ | 158 | Lead H.P. (+P)‡ | 890 | 855 | 823 | 278 | 257 | 238 | 1.4" | 6.0" | 4" |
| 38 SHORT COLT | R38SC | 1½ | 125 | Lead | 730 | 685 | 645 | 150 | 130 | 115 | 2.2" | 9.4" | 6" |
| 40 S. & W. | R40SW1 | 5½ | 155 | Jacketed H.P. | 1205 | 1095 | 1017 | 499 | 413 | 356 | 0.8" | 3.6" | 4" |
| | R40SW2 | 5½ | 180 | Jacketed H.P. | 1015 | 960 | 914 | 412 | 368 | 334 | 1.3" | 4.5" | 4" |
| | LL40SWB★ | 5½ | 180 | TEMC, Lead-Lokt™ | 985 | 936 | 893 | 388 | 350 | 319 | 1.4" | 5.0" | 4" |
| | GS40SWA | 5½ | 165 | Brass-Jacketed Hollow Point | 1150 | 1040 | 964 | 485 | 396 | 340 | 1.0" | 4.0" | 4" |
| | GS40SWB | 5½ | 180 | Brass-Jacketed Hollow Point | 1015 | 960 | 914 | 412 | 368 | 334 | 1.3" | 4.5" | 4" |
| 10MM AUTO. | R10MM2§ | 2½ | 200 | Metal Case | 1050 | 994 | 948 | 490 | 439 | 399 | 1.0" | 4.2" | 5" |
| | R10MM3 | 2½ | 180 | Jacketed H. P. (Subsonic) | 1055 | 997 | 951 | 445 | 397 | 361 | 1.0" | 4.6" | 5" |
| | R10MM4 | 21/2 | 180 | Jacketed H. P. (High Vel.) | 1160 | 1079 | 1017 | 538 | 465 | 413 | 0.9" | 3.8" | 5" |
| 41 REM. MAG. | R41MG1 | 2½ | 210 | Soft Point | 1300 | 1162 | 1062 | 788 | 630 | 526 | 0.7" | 3.2" | 4" |
| Vented Barrel Ballistics | R41MG2 | 2½ | 210 | Lead | 965 | 898 | 842 | 434 | 376 | 331 | 1.3" | 5.4" | 4" |
| | R41MG3 | 2½ | 170 | Semi-Jacketed H.P. | 1420 | 1166 | 1014 | 761 | 513 | 388 | 0.7" | 3.2" | 4" |
| 44 REM. MAG. | R44MG5 | 2½ | 180 | Semi-Jacketed H.P. | 1610 | 1365 | 1175 | 1036 | 745 | 551 | 0.5" | 2.3" | 4" |
| Vented Barrel Ballistics | R44MG1§ | 2½ | 240 | Lead Gas Check | 1350 | 1186 | 1069 | 971 | 749 | 608 | 0.7" | 3.1" | 4" |
| | R44MG2 | 2½ | 240 | Soft Point | 1180 | 1081 | 1010 | 741 | 623 | 543 | 0.9" | 3.7" | 4" |
| | R44MG3 | 2½ | 240 | Semi-Jacketed H.P. | 1180 | 1081 | 1010 | 741 | 623 | 543 | 0.9" | 3.7" | 4" |
| | R44MG4 | 2½ | 240 | Lead (Med. Vel.) | 1000 | 947 | 902 | 533 | 477 | 433 | 1.1" | 4.8" | 6½" |
| | R44MG6 | 2½ | 210 | Semi-Jacketed H.P. | 1495 | 1312 | 1167 | 1042 | 803 | 634 | 0.6" | 2.5" | 6½" |
| | RH44MGA★ | 2½ | 275 | JHP Core-Lokt® | 1235 | 1142 | 1070 | 931 | 797 | 699 | 0.8" | 3.3" | 6½" |
| 44 S. & W. SPECIAL | R44SW | 2½ | 246 | Lead | 755 | 725 | 695 | 310 | 285 | 265 | 2.0" | 8.3" | 6" |
| | R44SW1 | 2½ | 200 | Semi-Wadcutter | 1035 | 938 | 866 | 476 | 391 | 333 | 1.1" | 4.9" | 6" |
| 45 COLT | R45C | 2½ | 250 | Lead | 860 | 820 | 780 | 410 | 375 | 340 | 1.6" | 6.6" | 5" |
| | R45C1 | 21/2 | 225 | Semi-Wadcutter (Keith) | 960 | 890 | 832 | 460 | 395 | 346 | 1.3" | 5.5" | 5" |
| 45 AUTO. | R45AP1 | 2½ | 185 | Targetmaster M.C. W.C. Match | 770 | 707 | 650 | 244 | 205 | 174 | 2.0" | 8.7" | 5" |
| | R45AP2 | 2½ | 185 | Jacketed H.P. | 1000 | 939 | 889 | 411 | 362 | 324 | 1.1" | 4.9" | 5" |
| | R45AP4 | 2½ | 230 | Metal Case | 835 | 800 | 767 | 356 | 326 | 300 | 1.6" | 6.8" | 5" |
| | R45AP6 | 2½ | 185 | Jacketed H.P. (+P)‡ | 1140 | 1040 | 971 | 534 | 445 | 387 | 0.9" | 4.0" | 5" |
| | LL45APB★ | 2½ | 230 | TEMC, Lead-Lokt™ | 835 | 800 | 767 | 356 | 326 | 300 | 1.6" | 6.8" | 5" |
| | GS45APA | 2½ | 185 | Brass-Jacketed Hollow Point | 1015 | 951 | 899 | 423 | 372 | 332 | 1.1" | 4.5" | 5" |
| | GS45APB | 2½ | 230 | Brass-Jacketed Hollow Point | 875 | 833 | 795 | 391 | 355 | 323 | 1.5" | 6.1" | 5" |

★NEW FOR 1995

*Will not chamber in 357 Mag. or 38 Special handguns. ‡Ammunition with (+P) on the case headstamp is loaded to higher pressure. Use only in firearms designated for this cartridge and so recommended by the gun manufacturer. §Subject to stock on hand. (A)Adapted only for 38 Colt Super and Colt Commander automatic pistols. Not for use in sporting, military and pocket models.

# REMINGTON BALLISTICS

## CENTERFIRE RIFLE BALLISTICS

These tables were calculated by computer. A standard scientific technique was used to predict trajectories from the best available data for each round. Trajectories shown typify the ammunition's performance at sea level, but note that they may vary due to atmospheric conditions, and the equipment.

All velocity and energy figures in these charts have been derived by using test barrels of indicated lengths.

Ballistics shown are for 24″ barrels, except those for 30 carbine, 350 Rem. Mag. and .44 Rem. Mag., which are for 20″ barrels, and the 6mm BR Remington and 7mm BR Remington which have a 15″ barrel. These barrel lengths were chosen as representative, as it's impractical to show performance figures for all barrel lengths.

The muzzle velocities, muzzle energies and trajectory data in these tables represent the approximate performance expected of each specified loading. Differences in barrel lengths, internal firearm dimensions, temperature and test procedures can produce actual velocities that vary from those given here.

Specifications are nominal. Ballistics figures established in test barrels. Individual rifles may vary from test-barrel specifications.

* Inches above or below line of sight. Hold low for positive numbers, high for negative numbers.

† 280 Rem. and 7mm Express Rem. are interchangeable.

‡ Interchangeable in 244 Rem.

§ Subject to stock on hand

[1] Bullet does not rise more than 1″ above line of sight from muzzle to sighting in range.

[2] Bullet does not rise more than 3″ above line of sight from muzzle to sighting in range.

★ NEW for 1995–96

*Note:* 0.0 indicates yardage at which rifle was sighted in.

| Caliber | Remington Order No. | Bullet Wt.(grs.) | Style | Primer No. | Velocity – Feet Per Second Muzzle | 100 Yds. | 200 Yds. | 300 Yds. | 400 Yds. | 500 Yds. |
|---|---|---|---|---|---|---|---|---|---|---|
| 17 Rem. | R17REM | 25 | Hollow Point Power-Lokt® | 7 ½ | 4040 | 3284 | 2644 | 2086 | 1606 | 1235 |
| 22 Hornet | R22HN1 | 45 | Pointed Soft Point | 6 ½ | 2690 | 2042 | 1502 | 1128 | 948 | 840 |
| | R22HN2 | 45 | Hollow Point | 6 ½ | 2690 | 2042 | 1502 | 1128 | 948 | 840 |
| 220 Swift | R220S1 | 50 | Pointed Soft Point | 9 ½ | 3780 | 3158 | 2617 | 2135 | 1710 | 1357 |
| 222 Rem. | R222R1 | 50 | Pointed Soft Point | 7 ½ | 3140 | 2602 | 2123 | 1700 | 1350 | 1107 |
| | R222R3 | 50 | Hollow Point Power-Lokt® | 7 ½ | 3140 | 2635 | 2182 | 1777 | 1432 | 1172 |
| 222 Rem. Mag. | R222M1 | 55 | Pointed Soft Point | 7 ½ | 3240 | 2748 | 2305 | 1906 | 1556 | 1272 |
| 223 Rem. | R223R1 | 55 | Pointed Soft Point | 7 ½ | 3240 | 2747 | 2304 | 1905 | 1554 | 1270 |
| | R223R2 | 55 | Hollow Point Power-Lokt® | 7½ | 3240 | 2773 | 2352 | 1969 | 1627 | 1341 |
| | R223R3 | 55 | Metal Case | 7 ½ | 3240 | 2759 | 2326 | 1933 | 1587 | 1301 |
| | R223R4 | 60 | Hollow Point Match | 7 ½ | 3100 | 2712 | 2355 | 2026 | 1726 | 1463 |
| 22-250 Rem. | R22501 | 55 | Pointed Soft Point | 9 ½ | 3680 | 3137 | 2656 | 2222 | 1832 | 1493 |
| | R22502 | 55 | Hollow Point Power-Lokt® | 9 ½ | 3680 | 3209 | 2785 | 2400 | 2046 | 1725 |
| 243 Win. | R243W1 | 80 | Pointed Soft Point | 9 ½ | 3350 | 2955 | 2593 | 2259 | 1951 | 1670 |
| | R243W2 | 80 | Hollow Point Power-Lokt® | 9 ½ | 3350 | 2955 | 2593 | 2259 | 1951 | 1670 |
| | R243W3 | 100 | Pointed Soft Point Core-Lokt® | 9 ½ | 2960 | 2697 | 2449 | 2215 | 1993 | 1786 |
| | ER243WA | 105 | Extended Range | 9 ½ | 2920 | 2689 | 2470 | 2261 | 2062 | 1874 |
| 6MM Rem. | R6MM1 | 80 | Pointed Soft Point | 9 ½ | 3470 | 3064 | 2694 | 2352 | 2036 | 1747 |
| | R6MM4 | 100 | Pointed Soft Point Core-Lokt® | 9 ½ | 3100 | 2829 | 2573 | 2332 | 2104 | 1889 |
| | ER6MMRA§ | 105 | Extended Range | 9 ½ | 3060 | 2822 | 2596 | 2381 | 2177 | 1982 |
| 6MM BR Rem. | R6MMBR§ | 100 | Pointed Soft Point | 7 ½ | 2550 | 2310 | 2083 | 1870 | 1671 | 1491 |
| 25-20 Win. | R25202 | 86 | Soft Point | 6 ½ | 1460 | 1194 | 1030 | 931 | 858 | 797 |
| 250 Sav. | R250SV | 100 | Pointed Soft Point | 9 ½ | 2820 | 2504 | 2210 | 1936 | 1684 | 1461 |
| 257 Roberts | R257 | 117 | Soft Point Core-Lokt® | 9 ½ | 2650 | 2291 | 1961 | 1663 | 1404 | 1199 |
| | ER257A§ | 122 | Extended Range | 9 ½ | 2600 | 2331 | 2078 | 1842 | 1625 | 1431 |
| 25-06 Rem. | R25062 | 100 | Pointed Soft Point Core-Lokt® | 9 ½ | 3230 | 2893 | 2580 | 2287 | 2014 | 1762 |
| | R25063 | 120 | Pointed Soft Point Core-Lokt® | 9 ½ | 2990 | 2730 | 2484 | 2252 | 2032 | 1825 |
| | ER2506A | 122 | Extended Range | 9 ½ | 2930 | 2706 | 2492 | 2289 | 2095 | 1911 |
| 6.5x55 Swedish | R65SWE1 | 140 | Pointed Soft Point Core-Lokt® | 9 ½ | 2550 | 2353 | 2164 | 1984 | 1814 | 1654 |
| 264 Win. Mag. | R264W2 | 140 | Pointed Soft Point Core-Lokt® | 9 ½M | 3030 | 2782 | 2548 | 2326 | 2114 | 1914 |
| 270 Win. | R270W1 | 100 | Pointed Soft Point | 9 ½ | 3320 | 2924 | 2561 | 2225 | 1916 | 1636 |
| | R270W2 | 130 | Pointed Soft Point Core-Lokt® | 9 ½ | 3060 | 2776 | 2510 | 2259 | 2022 | 1801 |
| | R270W3 | 130 | Bronze Point | 9 ½ | 3060 | 2802 | 2559 | 2329 | 2110 | 1904 |
| | R270W4 | 150 | Soft Point Core-Lokt® | 9 ½ | 2850 | 2504 | 2183 | 1886 | 1618 | 1385 |
| | RS270WA★ | 140 | Swift A-Frame® PSP | 9 ½ | 2925 | 2652 | 2394 | 2152 | 1923 | 1711 |
| | ER270WB§ | 135 | Extended Range | 9 ½ | 3000 | 2780 | 2570 | 2369 | 2178 | 1995 |
| | ER270WA | 140 | Extended Range Boat Tail | 9 ½ | 2960 | 2749 | 2548 | 2355 | 2171 | 1995 |
| 7MM BR Rem. | R7MMBR§ | 140 | Pointed Soft Point | 7 ½ | 2215 | 2012 | 1821 | 1643 | 1481 | 1336 |
| 7MM Mauser (7 x 57) | R7MSR1 | 140 | Pointed Soft Point | 9 ½ | 2660 | 2435 | 2221 | 2018 | 1827 | 1648 |
| 7 x 64 | R7X641 | 140 | Pointed Soft Point | 9 ½ | 2950 | 2714 | 2489 | 2276 | 2073 | 1881 |
| | R7X642 | 175 | Pointed Soft Point Core-Lokt® | 9 ½ | 2650 | 2445 | 2248 | 2061 | 1883 | 1716 |
| 7MM-08 Rem. | R7M081 | 140 | Pointed Soft Point | 9 ½ | 2860 | 2625 | 2402 | 2189 | 1988 | 1798 |
| | R7M083 | 120 | Hollow Point | 9 ½ | 3000 | 2725 | 2467 | 2223 | 1992 | 1778 |
| | ER7M08A | 154 | Extended Range | 9 ½ | 2715 | 2510 | 2315 | 2128 | 1950 | 1781 |
| 280 Rem. | R280R3 | 140 | Pointed Soft Point | 9 ½ | 3000 | 2758 | 2528 | 2309 | 2102 | 1905 |
| | R280R1 | 150 | Pointed Soft Point Core-Lokt® | 9 ½ | 2890 | 2624 | 2373 | 2135 | 1912 | 1705 |
| | R280R2 | 165 | Soft Point Core-Lokt® | 9 ½ | 2820 | 2510 | 2220 | 1950 | 1701 | 1479 |
| | ER280RA | 165 | Extended Range | 9 ½ | 2820 | 2623 | 2434 | 2253 | 2080 | 1915 |
| 7MM Rem. Mag. | R7MM2 | 150 | Pointed Soft Point Core-Lokt® | 9 ½M | 3110 | 2830 | 2568 | 2320 | 2085 | 1866 |
| | R7MM3 | 175 | Pointed Soft Point Core-Lokt® | 9 ½M | 2860 | 2645 | 2440 | 2244 | 2057 | 1879 |
| | R7MM4 | 140 | Pointed Soft Point | 9 ½M | 3175 | 2923 | 2684 | 2458 | 2243 | 2039 |
| | RS7MMA | 160 | Swift A-Frame™ PSP | 9 ½M | 2900 | 2659 | 2430 | 2212 | 2006 | 1812 |
| | ER7MMA | 165 | Extended Range | 9 ½M | 2900 | 2699 | 2507 | 2324 | 2147 | 1979 |
| 7MM Wby. Mag. | R7MWB1§ | 140 | Pointed Soft Point | 9 ½M | 3225 | 2970 | 2729 | 2501 | 2283 | 2077 |
| | R7MWB2 | 175 | Pointed Soft Point Core-Lokt® | 9 ½M | 2910 | 2693 | 2486 | 2288 | 2098 | 1918 |
| | ER7MWBA§ | 165 | Extended Range | 9 ½M | 2950 | 2747 | 2553 | 2367 | 2189 | 2019 |
| 30 Carbine | R30CAR | 110 | Soft Point | 6 ½ | 1990 | 1567 | 1236 | 1035 | 923 | 842 |
| 30 Rem. | R30REM | 170 | Soft Point Core-Lokt® | 9 ½ | 2120 | 1822 | 1555 | 1328 | 1153 | 1036 |
| 30-30 Win. Accelerator® | R3030A | 55 | Soft Point | 9 ½ | 3400 | 2693 | 2085 | 1570 | 1187 | 986 |
| 30-30 Win. | R30301 | 150 | Soft Point Core-Lokt® | 9 ½ | 2390 | 1973 | 1605 | 1303 | 1095 | 974 |
| | R30302 | 170 | Soft Point Core-Lokt® | 9 ½ | 2200 | 1895 | 1619 | 1381 | 1191 | 1061 |
| | R30303 | 170 | Hollow Point Core-Lokt® | 9 ½ | 2200 | 1895 | 1619 | 1381 | 1191 | 1061 |
| | ER3030A | 160 | Extended Range | 9 ½ | 2300 | 1997 | 1719 | 1473 | 1268 | 1116 |
| 300 Savage | R30SV3 | 180 | Soft Point Core-Lokt® | 9 ½ | 2350 | 2025 | 1728 | 1467 | 1252 | 1098 |
| | R30SV2 | 150 | Pointed Soft Point Core-Lokt® | 9 ½ | 2630 | 2354 | 2095 | 1853 | 1631 | 1432 |

# REMINGTON BALLISTICS

| | Energy – Foot-Pounds | | | | | Short Range[1] Trajectory* | | | | | | Long Range[2] Trajectory* | | | | | | | |
|---|---|---|---|---|---|---|---|---|---|---|---|---|---|---|---|---|---|---|---|
| Muzzle | 100 Yds. | 200 Yds. | 300 Yds. | 400 Yds. | 500 Yds. | 50 Yds. | 100 Yds. | 150 Yds. | 200 Yds. | 250 Yds. | 300 Yds. | 100 Yds. | 150 Yds. | 200 Yds. | 250 Yds. | 300 Yds. | 400 Yds. | 500 Yds | Barrel Length |
| 906 | 599 | 388 | 242 | 143 | 85 | 0.1 | 0.5 | 0.0 | -1.5 | -4.2 | -8.5 | 2.1 | 2.5 | 1.9 | 0.0 | -3.4 | -17.0 | -44.3 | 24" |
| 723 | 417 | 225 | 127 | 90 | 70 | 0.3 | 0.0 | -2.4 | -7.7 | -16.9 | -31.3 | 1.6 | 0.0 | -4.5 | -12.8 | -26.4 | -75.6 | -163.4 | 24" |
| 723 | 417 | 225 | 127 | 90 | 70 | 0.3 | 0.0 | -2.4 | -7.7 | -16.9 | -31.3 | 1.6 | 0.0 | -4.5 | -12.8 | -26.4 | -75.6 | -163.4 | |
| 1586 | 1107 | 760 | 506 | 325 | 204 | 0.2 | 0.5 | 0.0 | -1.6 | -4.4 | -8.8 | 1.3 | 1.2 | 0.0 | -2.5 | -6.5 | -20.7 | -47.0 | 24" |
| 1094 | 752 | 500 | 321 | 202 | 136 | 0.5 | 0.9 | 0.0 | -2.5 | -6.9 | -13.7 | 2.2 | 1.9 | 0.0 | -3.8 | -10.0 | -32.3 | -73.8 | 24" |
| 1094 | 771 | 529 | 351 | 228 | 152 | 0.5 | 0.9 | 0.0 | -2.4 | -6.6 | -13.1 | 2.1 | 1.8 | 0.0 | -3.6 | -9.5 | -30.2 | -68.1 | |
| 1282 | 922 | 649 | 444 | 296 | 198 | 0.4 | 0.8 | 0.0 | -2.2 | -6.0 | -11.8 | 1.9 | 1.6 | 0.0 | -3.3 | -8.5 | -26.7 | -59.5 | 24" |
| 1282 | 921 | 648 | 443 | 295 | 197 | 0.4 | 0.8 | 0.0 | -2.2 | -6.0 | -11.8 | 1.9 | 1.6 | 0.0 | -3.3 | -8.5 | -26.7 | -59.6 | |
| 1282 | 939 | 675 | 473 | 323 | 220 | 0.4 | 0.8 | 0.0 | -2.1 | -5.8 | -11.4 | 1.8 | 1.6 | 0.0 | -3.2 | -8.2 | -25.5 | -56.0 | 24" |
| 1282 | 929 | 660 | 456 | 307 | 207 | 0.4 | 0.8 | 0.0 | -2.1 | -5.9 | -11.6 | 1.9 | 1.6 | 0.0 | -3.2 | -8.4 | -26.2 | -57.9 | |
| 1280 | 979 | 739 | 547 | 397 | 285 | 0.5 | 0.8 | 0.0 | -2.2 | -6.0 | -11.5 | 1.9 | 1.6 | 0.0 | -3.2 | -8.3 | -25.1 | -53.6 | |
| 1654 | 1201 | 861 | 603 | 410 | 272 | 0.2 | 0.5 | 0.0 | -1.6 | -4.4 | -8.7 | 2.3 | 2.6 | 1.9 | 0.0 | -3.4 | -15.9 | -38.9 | 24" |
| 1654 | 1257 | 947 | 703 | 511 | 363 | 0.2 | 0.5 | 0.0 | -1.5 | -4.1 | -8.0 | 2.1 | 2.5 | 1.8 | 0.0 | -3.1 | -14.1 | -33.4 | |
| 1993 | 1551 | 1194 | 906 | 676 | 495 | 0.3 | 0.7 | 0.0 | -1.8 | -4.9 | -9.4 | 2.6 | 2.9 | 2.1 | 0.0 | -3.6 | -16.2 | -37.9 | |
| 1993 | 1551 | 1194 | 906 | 676 | 495 | 0.3 | 0.7 | 0.0 | -1.8 | -4.9 | -9.4 | 2.6 | 2.9 | 2.1 | 0.0 | -3.6 | -16.2 | -37.9 | 24" |
| 1945 | 1615 | 1332 | 1089 | 882 | 708 | 0.5 | 0.9 | 0.0 | -2.2 | -5.8 | -11.0 | 1.9 | 1.6 | 0.0 | -3.1 | -7.8 | -22.6 | -46.3 | |
| 1988 | 1686 | 1422 | 1192 | 992 | 819 | 0.5 | 0.9 | 0.0 | -2.2 | -5.8 | -11.0 | 2.0 | 1.6 | 0.0 | -3.1 | -7.7 | -22.2 | -44.8 | |
| 2139 | 1667 | 1289 | 982 | 736 | 542 | 0.3 | 0.6 | 0.0 | -1.6 | -4.5 | -8.7 | 2.4 | 2.7 | 1.9 | 0.0 | -3.3 | -14.9 | -35.0 | |
| 2133 | 1777 | 1470 | 1207 | 983 | 792 | 0.4 | 0.8 | 0.0 | -1.9 | -5.2 | -9.9 | 1.7 | 1.5 | 0.0 | -2.8 | -7.0 | -20.4 | -41.7 | |
| 2183 | 1856 | 1571 | 1322 | 1105 | 916 | 0.4 | 0.8 | 0.0 | -2.0 | -5.2 | -9.8 | 1.7 | 1.5 | 0.0 | -2.7 | -6.9 | -20.0 | -40.4 | |
| 1444 | 1185 | 963 | 776 | 620 | 494 | 0.3 | 0.0 | -1.9 | -5.6 | -11.4 | -19.3 | 2.8 | 2.3 | 0.0 | -4.3 | -10.9 | -31.7 | -65.1 | 15" |
| 407 | 272 | 203 | 165 | 141 | 121 | 0.0 | -4.1 | -14.4 | -31.8 | -57.3 | -92.0 | 0.0 | -8.2 | -23.5 | -47.0 | -79.6 | -175.9 | -319.4 | 24" |
| 1765 | 1392 | 1084 | 832 | 630 | 474 | 0.2 | 0.0 | -1.6 | -4.7 | -9.6 | -16.5 | 2.3 | 2.0 | 0.0 | -3.7 | -9.5 | -28.3 | -59.5 | 24" |
| 1824 | 1363 | 999 | 718 | 512 | 373 | 0.3 | 0.0 | -1.9 | -5.8 | -11.9 | -20.7 | 2.9 | 2.4 | 0.0 | -4.7 | -12.0 | -36.7 | -79.2 | 24" |
| 1831 | 1472 | 1170 | 919 | 715 | 555 | 0.3 | 0.0 | -1.9 | -5.5 | -11.2 | -19.1 | 2.8 | 2.3 | 0.0 | -4.3 | -10.9 | -32.0 | -66.4 | |
| 2316 | 1858 | 1478 | 1161 | 901 | 689 | 0.4 | 0.7 | 0.0 | -1.9 | -5.0 | -9.7 | 1.6 | 1.4 | 0.0 | -2.7 | -6.9 | -20.5 | -42.7 | |
| 2382 | 1985 | 1644 | 1351 | 1100 | 887 | 0.5 | 0.8 | 0.0 | -2.1 | -5.6 | -10.7 | 1.9 | 1.6 | 0.0 | -3.0 | -7.5 | -22.0 | -44.8 | 24" |
| 2325 | 1983 | 1683 | 1419 | 1189 | 989 | 0.5 | 0.9 | 0.0 | -2.2 | -5.7 | -10.8 | 1.9 | 1.6 | 0.0 | -3.0 | -7.5 | -21.7 | -43.9 | |
| 2021 | 1720 | 1456 | 1224 | 1023 | 850 | 0.3 | 0.0 | -1.8 | -5.4 | -10.8 | -18.2 | 2.7 | 2.2 | 0.0 | -4.1 | -10.1 | -29.1 | -58.7 | 24" |
| 2854 | 2406 | 2018 | 1682 | 1389 | 1139 | 0.5 | 0.8 | 0.0 | -2.0 | -5.4 | -10.2 | 1.8 | 1.5 | 0.0 | -2.9 | -7.2 | -20.8 | -42.2 | 24" |
| 2448 | 1898 | 1456 | 1099 | 815 | 594 | 0.3 | 0.7 | 0.0 | -1.8 | -5.0 | -9.7 | 2.7 | 3.0 | 2.2 | 0.0 | -3.7 | -16.6 | -39.1 | |
| 2702 | 2225 | 1818 | 1472 | 1180 | 936 | 0.5 | 0.8 | 0.0 | -2.0 | -5.5 | -10.4 | 1.8 | 1.5 | 0.0 | -2.9 | -7.4 | -21.6 | -44.3 | |
| 2702 | 2267 | 1890 | 1565 | 1285 | 1046 | 0.4 | 0.8 | 0.0 | -2.0 | -5.3 | -10.1 | 1.8 | 1.5 | 0.0 | -2.8 | -7.1 | -20.6 | -42.0 | 24" |
| 2705 | 2087 | 1587 | 1185 | 872 | 639 | 0.7 | 1.0 | 0.0 | -2.6 | -7.1 | -13.6 | 2.3 | 2.0 | 0.0 | -3.8 | -9.7 | -29.2 | -62.2 | |
| 2659 | 2186 | 1782 | 1439 | 1150 | 910 | 0.6 | 0.9 | 0.0 | -2.3 | -6.0 | -11.5 | 2.0 | 1.7 | 0.0 | -3.2 | -8.1 | -23.8 | -48.9 | |
| 2697 | 2315 | 1979 | 1682 | 1421 | 1193 | 0.5 | 0.8 | 0.0 | -2.0 | -5.3 | -10.1 | 1.8 | 1.5 | 0.0 | -2.8 | -7.1 | -20.4 | -41.0 | |
| 2723 | 2349 | 2018 | 1724 | 1465 | 1237 | 0.5 | 0.8 | 0.0 | -2.1 | -5.5 | -10.3 | 1.9 | 1.5 | 0.0 | -2.9 | -7.2 | -20.7 | -41.6 | |
| 1525 | 1259 | 1031 | 839 | 681 | 555 | 0.5 | 0.0 | -2.7 | -7.7 | -15.4 | -25.9 | 1.8 | 0.0 | -4.1 | -10.9 | -20.6 | -50.0 | -95.2 | 15" |
| 2199 | 1843 | 1533 | 1266 | 1037 | 844 | 0.2 | 0.0 | -1.7 | -5.0 | -10.0 | -17.0 | 2.5 | 2.0 | 0.0 | -3.8 | -9.6 | -27.7 | -56.3 | 24" |
| 2705 | 2289 | 1926 | 1610 | 1336 | 1100 | 0.5 | 0.9 | 0.0 | -2.1 | -5.7 | -10.7 | 1.9 | 1.6 | 0.0 | -3.0 | -7.6 | -21.8 | -44.2 | 24" |
| 2728 | 2322 | 1964 | 1650 | 1378 | 1144 | 0.2 | 0.0 | -1.7 | -4.9 | -9.9 | -16.8 | 2.5 | 2.0 | 0.0 | -3.9 | -9.4 | -26.9 | -54.3 | |
| 2542 | 2142 | 1793 | 1490 | 1228 | 1005 | 0.6 | 0.9 | 0.0 | -2.3 | -6.1 | -11.6 | 2.1 | 1.7 | 0.0 | -3.2 | -8.1 | -23.5 | -47.7 | |
| 2398 | 1979 | 1621 | 1316 | 1058 | 842 | 0.5 | 0.8 | 0.0 | -2.1 | -5.7 | -10.8 | 1.9 | 1.6 | 0.0 | -3.0 | -7.6 | -22.3 | -45.8 | 24" |
| 2520 | 2155 | 1832 | 1548 | 1300 | 1085 | 0.7 | 1.0 | 0.0 | -2.5 | -6.7 | -12.6 | 2.3 | 1.9 | 0.0 | -3.5 | -8.8 | -25.3 | -51.0 | |
| 2797 | 2363 | 1986 | 1657 | 1373 | 1128 | 0.5 | 0.8 | 0.0 | -2.1 | -5.5 | -10.4 | 1.8 | 1.5 | 0.0 | -2.9 | -7.3 | -21.1 | -42.9 | |
| 2781 | 2293 | 1875 | 1518 | 1217 | 968 | 0.6 | 0.9 | 0.0 | -2.3 | -6.2 | -11.8 | 2.1 | 1.7 | 0.0 | -3.3 | -8.3 | -24.2 | -49.7 | |
| 2913 | 2308 | 1805 | 1393 | 1060 | 801 | 0.2 | 0.0 | -1.5 | -4.6 | -9.5 | -16.4 | 2.3 | 1.9 | 0.0 | -3.7 | -9.4 | -28.1 | -58.8 | 24" |
| 2913 | 2520 | 2171 | 1860 | 1585 | 1343 | 0.6 | 0.9 | 0.0 | -2.3 | -6.1 | -11.4 | 2.1 | 1.7 | 0.0 | -3.2 | -8.0 | -22.8 | -45.6 | |
| 3221 | 2667 | 2196 | 1792 | 1448 | 1160 | 0.4 | 0.8 | 0.0 | -1.9 | -5.2 | -9.9 | 1.7 | 1.5 | 0.0 | -2.8 | -7.0 | -20.5 | -42.1 | |
| 3178 | 2718 | 2313 | 1956 | 1644 | 1372 | 0.6 | 0.9 | 0.0 | -2.3 | -6.0 | -11.3 | 2.0 | 1.7 | 0.0 | -3.2 | -7.9 | -22.7 | -45.8 | 24" |
| 3133 | 2655 | 2240 | 1878 | 1564 | 1292 | 0.4 | 0.7 | 0.0 | -1.8 | -4.8 | -9.1 | 2.6 | 2.9 | 2.0 | 0.0 | -3.4 | -14.5 | -32.6 | |
| 2987 | 2511 | 2097 | 1739 | 1430 | 1166 | 0.6 | 0.9 | 0.0 | -2.2 | -5.9 | -11.3 | 2.0 | 1.7 | 0.0 | -3.2 | -7.9 | -23.0 | -46.7 | |
| 3081 | 2669 | 2303 | 1978 | 1689 | 1434 | 0.5 | 0.9 | 0.0 | -2.1 | -5.7 | -10.7 | 1.9 | 1.6 | 0.0 | -3.0 | -7.5 | -21.4 | -42.9 | |
| 3233 | 2741 | 2315 | 1943 | 1621 | 1341 | 0.3 | 0.7 | 0.0 | -1.7 | -4.6 | -8.8 | 2.5 | 2.8 | 2.0 | 0.0 | -3.2 | -14.0 | -31.5 | |
| 3293 | 2818 | 2401 | 2033 | 1711 | 1430 | 0.5 | 0.9 | 0.0 | -2.2 | -5.7 | -10.8 | 1.9 | 1.6 | 0.0 | -3.0 | -7.6 | -21.8 | -44.0 | 24" |
| 3188 | 2765 | 2388 | 2053 | 1756 | 1493 | 0.5 | 0.8 | 0.0 | -2.1 | -5.5 | -10.3 | 1.9 | 1.6 | 0.0 | -2.9 | -7.2 | -20.6 | -41.3 | |
| 967 | 600 | 373 | 262 | 208 | 173 | 0.9 | 0.0 | -4.5 | -13.5 | -28.3 | -49.9 | 0.0 | -4.5 | -13.5 | -28.3 | -49.9 | -118.6 | -228.2 | 20" |
| 1696 | 1253 | 913 | 666 | 502 | 405 | 0.7 | 0.0 | -3.3 | -9.7 | -19.6 | -33.8 | 2.2 | 0.0 | -5.3 | -14.1 | -27.2 | -69.0 | -136.9 | 24" |
| 1412 | 886 | 521 | 301 | 172 | 119 | 0.4 | 0.8 | 0.0 | -2.4 | -6.7 | -13.8 | 2.0 | 1.8 | 0.0 | -3.8 | -10.2 | -35.0 | -84.4 | 24" |
| 1902 | 1296 | 858 | 565 | 399 | 316 | 0.5 | 0.0 | -2.7 | -8.2 | -17.0 | -30.0 | 1.8 | 0.0 | -4.6 | -12.5 | -24.6 | -65.3 | -134.9 | |
| 1827 | 1355 | 989 | 720 | 535 | 425 | 0.6 | 0.0 | -3.0 | -8.9 | -18.0 | -31.1 | 2.0 | 0.0 | -4.8 | -13.0 | -25.1 | -63.6 | -126.7 | 24" |
| 1827 | 1355 | 989 | 720 | 535 | 425 | 0.6 | 0.0 | -3.0 | -8.9 | -18.0 | -31.1 | 2.0 | 0.0 | -4.8 | -13.0 | -25.1 | -63.6 | -126.7 | |
| 1879 | 1416 | 1050 | 771 | 571 | 442 | 0.5 | 0.0 | -2.7 | -7.9 | -16.1 | -27.6 | 1.8 | 0.0 | -4.3 | -11.6 | -22.3 | -56.3 | -111.9 | |
| 2207 | 1639 | 1193 | 860 | 626 | 482 | 0.5 | 0.0 | -2.6 | -7.7 | -15.6 | -27.1 | 1.7 | 0.0 | -4.2 | -11.3 | -21.9 | -55.8 | -112.0 | 24" |
| 2303 | 1845 | 1462 | 1143 | 806 | 685 | 0.3 | 0.0 | -1.8 | -5.4 | 11.0 | 18.8 | 2.7 | 2.2 | 0.0 | -4.2 | -10.7 | -31.5 | -65.6 | |

# REMINGTON BALLISTICS

## CENTERFIRE RIFLE BALLISTICS

| | | | | | Velocity – Feet per second | | | | | |
|---|---|---|---|---|---|---|---|---|---|---|
| Caliber | Remington Order No. | Bullet Wt.(grs.) | Style | Primer No. | Muzzle | 100 Yds. | 200 Yds. | 300 Yds. | 400 Yds. | 500 Yds. |
| 30-40 Krag | R30402 | 180* | Pointed Soft Point Core-Lokt® | 9 ½ | 2430 | 2213 | 2007 | 1813 | 1632 | 1468 |
| 308 Win. | R308W1 | 150 | Pointed Soft Point Core-Lokt® | 9 ½ | 2820 | 2533 | 2263 | 2009 | 1774 | 1560 |
| | R308W2 | 180 | Soft Point Core-Lokt® | 9 ½ | 2620 | 2274 | 1955 | 1666 | 1414 | 1212 |
| | R308W3 | 180 | Pointed Soft Point Core-Lokt® | 9 ½ | 2620 | 2393 | 2178 | 1974 | 1782 | 1604 |
| | R308W7 | 168 | Boat Tail H.P. Match | 9 ½ | 2680 | 2493 | 2314 | 2143 | 1979 | 1823 |
| | ER308WA | 165 | Extended Range Boat Tail | 9 ½ | 2700 | 2497 | 2303 | 2117 | 1941 | 1773 |
| | ER308WB§ | 178 | Extended Range | 9 ½ | 2620 | 2415 | 2220 | 2034 | 1857 | 1691 |
| 30-06 Accelerator® | R30069 | 55 | Pointed Soft Point | 9 ½ | 4080 | 3485 | 2965 | 2502 | 2083 | 1709 |
| 30-06 Springfield | R30061 | 125 | Pointed Soft Point | 9 ½ | 3140 | 2780 | 2447 | 2138 | 1853 | 1595 |
| | R30062 | 150 | Pointed Soft Point Core-Lokt® | 9 ½ | 2910 | 2617 | 2342 | 2083 | 1843 | 1622 |
| | R30063 | 150 | Bronze Point | 9 ½ | 2910 | 2656 | 2416 | 2189 | 1974 | 1773 |
| | R3006B | 165 | Pointed Soft Point Core-Lokt® | 9 ½ | 2800 | 2534 | 2283 | 2047 | 1825 | 1621 |
| | R30064 | 180 | Soft Point Core-Lokt® | 9 ½ | 2700 | 2348 | 2023 | 1727 | 1466 | 1251 |
| | R30065 | 180 | Pointed Soft Point Core-Lokt® | 9 ½ | 2700 | 2469 | 2250 | 2042 | 1846 | 1663 |
| | R30066 | 180 | Bronze Point | 9 ½ | 2700 | 2485 | 2280 | 2084 | 1899 | 1725 |
| | R30067 | 220 | Soft Point Core-Lokt® | 9 ½ | 2410 | 2130 | 1870 | 1632 | 1422 | 1246 |
| | RS3006A★ | 180 | Swift A-Frame™ PSP | 9½ | 2700 | 2465 | 2243 | 2032 | 1833 | 1648 |
| | ER3006A | 152 | Extended Range | 9 ½ | 2910 | 2654 | 2413 | 2184 | 1968 | 1765 |
| | ER3006B | 165 | Extended Range Boat Tail | 9 ½ | 2800 | 2592 | 2394 | 2204 | 2023 | 1852 |
| | ER3006C§ | 178 | Extended Range | 9 ½ | 2720 | 2511 | 2311 | 2121 | 1939 | 1768 |
| 300 H&H Mag. | R300HH | 180 | Pointed Soft Point Core-Lokt® | 9 ½M | 2880 | 2640 | 2412 | 2196 | 1990 | 1798 |
| 300 Win. Mag. | R300W1 | 150 | Pointed Soft Point Core-Lokt® | 9 ½M | 3290 | 2951 | 2636 | 2342 | 2068 | 1813 |
| | R300W2 | 180 | Pointed Soft Point Core-Lokt® | 9 ½M | 2960 | 2745 | 2540 | 2344 | 2157 | 1979 |
| | RS300WA | 200 | Swift A-Frame™ PSP | 9 ½M | 2825 | 2595 | 2376 | 2167 | 1970 | 1783 |
| | ER300WB | 190 | Extended Range Boat Tail | 9 ½M | 2885 | 2691 | 2506 | 2327 | 2156 | 1993 |
| 300 Wby Mag. | R300WB1 | 180 | Pointed Soft Point Core-Lokt® | 9 ½M | 3120 | 2866 | 2627 | 2400 | 2184 | 1979 |
| | R300WB2§ | 220 | Soft Point Core-Lokt® | 9 ½M | 2850 | 2541 | 2283 | 1984 | 1736 | 1512 |
| | ER30WBA§ | 178 | Extended Range | 9 ½M | 3120 | 2902 | 2695 | 2497 | 2308 | 2126 |
| | ER30WBB | 190 | Extended Range Boat Tail | 9 ½M | 3030 | 2830 | 2638 | 2455 | 2279 | 2110 |
| 303 British | R303B1 | 180 | Soft Point Core-Lokt® | 9 ½ | 2460 | 2124 | 1817 | 1542 | 1311 | 1137 |
| 7.62 x 39MM | R762391 | 125 | Pointed Soft Point | 7 ½ | 2365 | 2062 | 1783 | 1533 | 1320 | 1154 |
| 32-20 Win. | R32201 | 100 | Lead | 6 ½ | 1210 | 1021 | 913 | 834 | 769 | 712 |
| | R32202 | 100 | Soft Point | 6 ½ | 1210 | 1021 | 913 | 834 | 769 | 712 |
| 32 Win. Special | R32WS2 | 170 | Soft Point Core-Lokt® | 9 ½ | 2250 | 1921 | 1626 | 1372 | 1175 | 1044 |
| 8MM Mauser | R8MSR | 170 | Soft Point Core-Lokt® | 9 ½ | 2360 | 1969 | 1622 | 1333 | 1123 | 997 |
| 338 Win. Mag. | R338W1 | 225 | Pointed Soft Point | 9 ½M | 2780 | 2572 | 2374 | 2184 | 2003 | 1832 |
| | R338W2 | 250 | Pointed Soft Point | 9 ½M | 2660 | 2456 | 2261 | 2075 | 1898 | 1731 |
| | RS338WA | 225 | Swift A-Frame PSP | 9 ½M | 2785 | 2517 | 2266 | 2029 | 1808 | 1605 |
| 35 Rem. | R35R1 | 150 | Pointed Soft Point Core-Lokt® | 9 ½ | 2300 | 1874 | 1506 | 1218 | 1039 | 934 |
| | R35R2 | 200 | Soft Point Core-Lokt® | 9 ½ | 2080 | 1698 | 1376 | 1140 | 1001 | 911 |
| 350 Rem. Mag. | R350M1 | 200 | Pointed Soft Point Core-Lokt® | 9 ½M | 2710 | 2410 | 2130 | 1870 | 1631 | 1421 |
| 35 Whelen | R35WH1 | 200 | Pointed Soft Point | 9 ½M | 2675 | 2378 | 2100 | 1842 | 1606 | 1399 |
| | R35WH2§ | 250 | Soft Point | 9 ½M | 2400 | 2066 | 1761 | 1492 | 1269 | 1107 |
| | R35WH3 | 250 | Pointed Soft Point | 9 ½M | 2400 | 2197 | 2005 | 1823 | 1652 | 1496 |
| 375 H&H Mag. | R375M1 | 270 | Soft Point | 9 ½M | 2690 | 2420 | 2166 | 1928 | 1707 | 1507 |
| | RS375MA | 300 | Swift A-Frame PSP | 9 ½M | 2530 | 2245 | 1979 | 1733 | 1512 | 1321 |
| 416 Rem. Mag. | R416R1§ | 400 | Solid | 9 ½M | 2400 | 2042 | 1718 | 1436 | 1212 | 1062 |
| | R416R2 | 400 | Swift A-Frame PSP | 9 ½M | 2400 | 2175 | 1962 | 1763 | 1579 | 1414 |
| | R416R3§ | 350 | Swift A-Frame PSP | 9 ½M | 2520 | 2270 | 2034 | 1814 | 1611 | 1429 |
| 44-40 Win. | R4440W | 200 | Soft Point | 2 ½ | 1190 | 1006 | 900 | 822 | 756 | 699 |
| 44 Rem. Mag. | R44MG2 | 240 | Soft Point | 2 ½ | 1760 | 1380 | 1114 | 970 | 878 | 806 |
| | R44MG3 | 240 | Semi-Jacketed Hollow Point | 2 ½ | 1760 | 1380 | 1114 | 970 | 878 | 806 |
| | R44MG6 | 210 | Semi-Jacketed Hollow Point | 2 ½ | 1920 | 1477 | 1155 | 982 | 880 | 802 |
| | RH44MGA | 275 | JHP Core-Lokt® | 2 ½ | 1580 | 1293 | 1093 | 976 | 896 | 832 |
| 444 Mar. | R444M | 240 | Soft Point | 9 ½ | 2350 | 1815 | 1377 | 1087 | 941 | 846 |
| 45-70 Government | R4570G | 405 | Soft Point | 9 ½ | 1330 | 1168 | 1055 | 977 | 918 | 869 |
| | R4570L | 300 | Jacketed Hollow Point | 9 ½ | 1810 | 1497 | 1244 | 1073 | 969 | 895 |
| 458 Win. Mag. | R458W1§ | 500 | Metal Case | 9 ½M | 2040 | 1823 | 1623 | 1442 | 1237 | 1161 |
| | R458W2 | 510 | Soft Point | 9 ½M | 2040 | 1770 | 1527 | 1319 | 1157 | 1046 |

# REMINGTON BALLISTICS

| Energy – Foot-pounds | | | | | | Short Range[1] Trajectory* | | | | | | Long Range[2] Trajectory* | | | | | | | |
|---|---|---|---|---|---|---|---|---|---|---|---|---|---|---|---|---|---|---|---|
| Muzzle | 100 Yds. | 200 Yds. | 300 Yds. | 400 Yds. | 500 Yds. | 50 Yds. | 100 Yds. | 150 Yds. | 200 Yds. | 250 Yds. | 300 Yds. | 100 Yds. | 150 Yds. | 200 Yds. | 250 Yds. | 300 Yds. | 400 Yds. | 500 Yds. | Barrel Length |
| 2360 | 1957 | 1610 | 1314 | 1064 | 861 | 0.4 | 0.0 | -2.1 | -6.2 | -12.5 | -21.1 | 1.4 | 0.0 | -3.4 | -8.9 | -16.8 | -40.9 | -78.1 | 24" |
| 2648 | 2137 | 1705 | 1344 | 1048 | 810 | 0.2 | 0.0 | -1.5 | -4.5 | -9.3 | -15.9 | 2.3 | 1.9 | 0.0 | -3.6 | -9.1 | -26.9 | -55.7 | |
| 2743 | 2066 | 1527 | 1109 | 799 | 587 | 0.3 | 0.0 | -2.0 | -5.9 | -12.1 | -20.9 | 2.9 | 2.4 | 0.0 | -4.7 | -12.1 | -36.9 | -79.1 | |
| 2743 | 2288 | 1896 | 1557 | 1269 | 1028 | 0.2 | 0.0 | -1.8 | -5.2 | -10.4 | -17.7 | 2.6 | 2.1 | 0.0 | -4.0 | -9.9 | -28.9 | -58.8 | 24" |
| 2678 | 2318 | 1998 | 1713 | 1460 | 1239 | 0.2 | 0.0 | -1.6 | -4.7 | -9.4 | -15.9 | 2.4 | 1.9 | 0.0 | -3.5 | -8.9 | -25.3 | -50.6 | |
| 2670 | 2284 | 1942 | 1642 | 1379 | 1152 | 0.2 | 0.0 | -1.6 | -4.7 | -9.4 | -16.0 | 2.3 | 1.9 | 0.0 | -3.5 | -8.9 | -25.6 | -51.5 | |
| 2713 | 2306 | 1948 | 1635 | 1363 | 1130 | 0.2 | 0.0 | -1.7 | -5.1 | -10.2 | -17.2 | 2.5 | 2.1 | 0.0 | -3.8 | -9.6 | -27.6 | -55.8 | |
| 2033 | 1483 | 1074 | 764 | 530 | 356 | 0.4 | 1.0 | 0.9 | 0.0 | -1.9 | -5.0 | 1.8 | 2.1 | 1.5 | 0.0 | -2.7 | -12.5 | -30.5 | 24" |
| 2736 | 2145 | 1662 | 1269 | 953 | 706 | 0.4 | 0.8 | 0.0 | -2.1 | -5.6 | -10.7 | 1.8 | 1.5 | 0.0 | -3.0 | -7.7 | -23.0 | -48.5 | |
| 2820 | 2281 | 1827 | 1445 | 1131 | 876 | 0.6 | 0.9 | 0.0 | -2.3 | -6.3 | -12.0 | 2.1 | 1.8 | 0.0 | -3.3 | -8.5 | -25.0 | -51.8 | |
| 2820 | 2349 | 1944 | 1596 | 1298 | 1047 | 0.6 | 0.9 | 0.0 | -2.2 | -6.0 | -11.4 | 2.0 | 1.7 | 0.0 | -3.2 | -8.0 | -23.3 | -47.5 | |
| 2872 | 2352 | 1909 | 1534 | 1220 | 963 | 0.7 | 1.0 | 0.0 | -2.5 | -6.7 | -12.7 | 2.3 | 1.9 | 0.0 | -3.6 | -9.0 | -26.3 | -54.1 | |
| 2913 | 2203 | 1635 | 1192 | 859 | 625 | 0.2 | 0.0 | -1.8 | -5.5 | -11.2 | -19.5 | 2.7 | 2.3 | 0.0 | -4.4 | -11.3 | -34.4 | -73.7 | |
| 2913 | 2436 | 2023 | 1666 | 1362 | 1105 | 0.2 | 0.0 | -1.6 | -4.8 | -9.7 | -16.5 | 2.4 | 2.0 | 0.0 | -3.7 | -9.3 | -27.0 | -54.9 | 24" |
| 2913 | 2468 | 2077 | 1736 | 1441 | 1189 | 0.2 | 0.0 | -1.6 | -4.7 | -9.6 | -16.2 | 2.4 | 2.0 | 0.0 | -3.6 | -9.1 | -26.2 | -53.0 | |
| 2837 | 2216 | 1708 | 1301 | 988 | 758 | 0.4 | 0.0 | -2.3 | -6.8 | -13.8 | -23.6 | 1.5 | 0.0 | -3.7 | -9.9 | -19.0 | -47.4 | -93.1 | |
| 2913 | 2429 | 2010 | 1650 | 1343 | 1085 | 0.2 | 0.0 | -1.6 | -4.8 | -9.8 | -16.6 | 2.4 | 2.0 | 0.0 | -3.7 | -9.4 | -27.2 | -55.3 | |
| 2858 | 2378 | 1965 | 1610 | 1307 | 1052 | 0.6 | 0.9 | 0.0 | -2.3 | -6.0 | -11.4 | 2.0 | 1.7 | 0.0 | -3.2 | -8.0 | -23.3 | -47.7 | |
| 2872 | 2462 | 2100 | 1780 | 1500 | 1256 | 0.6 | 1.0 | 0.0 | -2.4 | -6.2 | -11.8 | 2.1 | 1.8 | 0.0 | -3.3 | -8.2 | -23.6 | -47.5 | |
| 2924 | 2491 | 2111 | 1777 | 1486 | 1235 | 0.7 | 1.0 | 0.0 | -2.6 | -6.7 | -12.7 | 2.3 | 1.9 | 0.0 | -3.5 | -8.8 | -25.4 | -51.2 | |
| 3315 | 2785 | 2325 | 1927 | 1583 | 1292 | 0.6 | 0.9 | 0.0 | -2.3 | -6.0 | -11.5 | 2.1 | 1.7 | 0.0 | -3.2 | -8.0 | -23.3 | -47.4 | 24" |
| 3605 | 2900 | 2314 | 1827 | 1424 | 1095 | 0.3 | 0.7 | 0.0 | -1.8 | -4.8 | -9.3 | 2.6 | 2.9 | 2.1 | 0.0 | -3.5 | -15.4 | -35.5 | |
| 3501 | 3011 | 2578 | 2196 | 1859 | 1565 | 0.5 | 0.8 | 0.0 | -2.1 | -5.5 | -10.4 | 1.9 | 1.6 | 0.0 | -2.9 | -7.3 | -20.9 | -41.9 | 24" |
| 3544 | 2989 | 2506 | 2086 | 1722 | 1412 | 0.6 | 1.0 | 0.0 | -2.4 | -6.3 | -11.9 | 2.1 | 1.8 | 0.0 | -3.3 | -8.3 | -24.0 | -48.8 | |
| 3511 | 3055 | 2648 | 2285 | 1961 | 1675 | 0.5 | 0.9 | 0.0 | -2.2 | -5.7 | -10.7 | 1.9 | 1.6 | 0.0 | -3.0 | -7.5 | -21.4 | -42.9 | |
| 3890 | 3284 | 2758 | 2301 | 1905 | 1565 | 0.4 | 0.7 | 0.0 | -1.9 | -5.0 | -9.5 | 2.7 | 3.0 | 2.1 | 0.0 | -3.5 | -15.2 | -34.2 | |
| 3967 | 3155 | 2480 | 1922 | 1471 | 1117 | 0.6 | 1.0 | 0.0 | -2.5 | -6.7 | -12.9 | 2.3 | 1.9 | 0.0 | -3.6 | -9.1 | -27.2 | -56.8 | 24" |
| 3847 | 3329 | 2870 | 2464 | 2104 | 1787 | 0.4 | 0.7 | 0.0 | -1.8 | -4.8 | -9.1 | 2.6 | 2.9 | 2.0 | 0.0 | -3.3 | -14.3 | -31.8 | |
| 3873 | 3378 | 2936 | 2542 | 2190 | 1878 | 0.4 | 0.8 | 0.0 | -1.9 | -5.1 | -9.6 | 1.7 | 1.4 | 0.0 | -2.7 | -6.7 | -19.2 | -38.4 | |
| 2418 | 1803 | 1319 | 950 | 687 | 517 | 0.4 | 0.0 | -2.3 | -6.9 | -14.1 | -24.4 | 1.5 | 0.0 | -3.8 | -10.2 | -19.8 | -50.5 | -101.5 | 24" |
| 1552 | 1180 | 882 | 652 | 483 | 370 | 0.4 | 0.0 | -2.5 | -7.3 | -14.3 | -25.7 | 1.7 | 0.0 | -4.8 | -10.8 | -20.7 | -52.3 | -104.0 | 24" |
| 325 | 231 | 185 | 154 | 131 | 113 | 0.0 | -6.3 | -20.9 | -44.9 | -79.3 | -125.1 | 0.0 | -11.5 | -32.3 | -63.8 | -106.3 | -230.3 | -413.3 | 24" |
| 325 | 231 | 185 | 154 | 131 | 113 | 0.0 | -6.3 | -20.9 | -44.9 | -79.3 | -125.1 | 0.0 | -11.5 | -32.3 | -63.6 | -106.3 | -230.3 | -413.3 | |
| 1911 | 1393 | 998 | 710 | 521 | 411 | 0.6 | 0.0 | -2.9 | -8.6 | -17.6 | -30.5 | 1.9 | 0.0 | -4.7 | -12.7 | -24.7 | -63.2 | -126.9 | 24" |
| 2102 | 1463 | 993 | 671 | 476 | 375 | 0.5 | 0.0 | -2.7 | -8.2 | -17.0 | -29.8 | 1.8 | 0.0 | -4.5 | -12.4 | -24.3 | -63.8 | -130.7 | 24" |
| 3860 | 3305 | 2815 | 2383 | 2004 | 1676 | 0.6 | 1.0 | 0.0 | -2.4 | -6.3 | -12.0 | 2.2 | 1.8 | 0.0 | -3.3 | -8.4 | -24.0 | -48.4 | |
| 3927 | 3348 | 2837 | 2389 | 1999 | 1663 | 0.2 | 0.0 | -1.7 | -4.9 | -9.8 | -16.6 | 2.4 | 2.0 | 0.0 | -3.7 | -9.3 | -26.6 | -53.6 | 24" |
| 3871 | 3165 | 2565 | 2057 | 1633 | 1286 | 0.2 | 0.0 | -1.5 | -4.6 | -9.4 | -16.0 | 2.3 | 1.9 | 0.0 | -3.6 | -9.1 | -26.7 | -54.9 | |
| 1762 | 1169 | 755 | 494 | 359 | 291 | 0.6 | 0.0 | -3.0 | -9.2 | -19.1 | -33.9 | 2.0 | 0.0 | -5.1 | -14.1 | -27.8 | -74.0 | -152.3 | 24" |
| 1921 | 1280 | 841 | 577 | 445 | 369 | 0.8 | 0.0 | -3.8 | -11.3 | -23.5 | -41.2 | 2.5 | 0.0 | -6.3 | -17.1 | -33.6 | -87.7 | -176.4 | |
| 3261 | 2579 | 2014 | 1553 | 1181 | 897 | 0.2 | 0.0 | -1.7 | -5.1 | -10.4 | -17.9 | 2.6 | 2.1 | 0.0 | -4.0 | -10.3 | -30.5 | -64.0 | 20" |
| 3177 | 2510 | 1958 | 1506 | 1145 | 869 | 0.2 | 0.0 | -1.8 | -5.3 | -10.8 | -18.5 | 2.6 | 2.2 | 0.0 | -4.2 | -10.6 | -31.5 | -65.9 | |
| 3197 | 2369 | 1722 | 1235 | 893 | 680 | 0.4 | 0.0 | -2.5 | -7.3 | -15.0 | -26.0 | 1.6 | 0.0 | -4.0 | -10.9 | -21.0 | -53.8 | -108.2 | 24" |
| 3197 | 2680 | 2230 | 1844 | 1515 | 1242 | 0.4 | 0.0 | -2.2 | -6.3 | -12.6 | -21.3 | 1.4 | 0.0 | -3.4 | -9.0 | -17.0 | -41.0 | -77.8 | |
| 4337 | 3510 | 2812 | 2228 | 1747 | 1361 | 0.2 | 0.0 | -1.7 | -5.1 | -10.3 | -17.6 | 2.5 | 2.1 | 0.0 | -3.9 | -10.0 | -29.4 | -60.7 | 24" |
| 4262 | 3357 | 2608 | 2001 | 1523 | 1163 | 0.3 | 0.0 | -2.0 | -6.0 | -12.3 | -21.0 | 3.0 | 2.5 | 0.0 | -4.7 | -12.0 | -35.6 | -74.5 | |
| 5115 | 3702 | 2620 | 1832 | 1305 | 1001 | 0.4 | 0.0 | -2.5 | -7.5 | -15.5 | -27.0 | 1.7 | 0.0 | -4.2 | -11.3 | -21.9 | -56.7 | -115.1 | |
| 5115 | 4201 | 3419 | 2760 | 2214 | 1775 | 0.4 | 0.0 | -2.2 | -6.5 | -13.0 | -22.0 | 1.5 | 0.0 | -3.5 | -9.3 | -17.6 | -42.9 | -82.2 | 24" |
| 4935 | 4004 | 3216 | 2557 | 2017 | 1587 | 0.3 | 0.0 | -2.0 | -5.9 | -11.9 | -20.2 | 2.9 | 2.4 | 0.0 | -4.5 | -11.4 | -33.4 | -68.7 | |
| 629 | 449 | 360 | 300 | 254 | 217 | 0.0 | -6.5 | -21.6 | -46.3 | -81.8 | -129.1 | 0.0 | -11.8 | -33.3 | -65.5 | -109.5 | -237.4 | -426.2 | 24" |
| 1650 | 1015 | 661 | 501 | 411 | 346 | 0.0 | -2.7 | -10.0 | -23.0 | -43.0 | -71.2 | 0.0 | -5.9 | -17.6 | -36.3 | -63.1 | -145.5 | -273.0 | |
| 1650 | 1015 | 661 | 501 | 411 | 346 | 0.0 | -2.7 | -10.0 | -23.0 | -43.0 | -71.2 | 0.0 | -5.9 | -17.6 | -36.3 | -63.1 | -145.5 | -273.0 | 20" |
| 1719 | 1017 | 622 | 450 | 361 | 300 | 0.0 | -2.2 | -8.3 | -19.7 | -37.6 | -63.2 | 0.0 | -5.1 | -15.4 | -32.1 | -56.7 | -134.0 | -256.2 | |
| 1524 | 1020 | 730 | 582 | 490 | 422 | 1.7 | 0.0 | -6.9 | -20.0 | -40.1 | -68.7 | 0.0 | -6.9 | -20.0 | -40.1 | -68.7 | -153.8 | -283.0 | |
| 2942 | 1755 | 1010 | 630 | 472 | 381 | 0.6 | 0.0 | -3.2 | -9.9 | -21.3 | -38.5 | 2.1 | 0.0 | -5.6 | -15.9 | -32.1 | -87.8 | -182.7 | 24" |
| 1590 | 1227 | 1001 | 858 | 758 | 679 | 0.0 | -4.7 | -15.8 | -34.0 | -60.0 | -94.5 | 0.0 | -8.7 | -24.6 | -48.2 | -80.3 | -172.4 | -305.9 | 24" |
| 2182 | 1492 | 1031 | 767 | 625 | 533 | 0.0 | -2.3 | -8.5 | -19.4 | -35.9 | -59.0 | 0.0 | -5.0 | -14.8 | -30.1 | -52.1 | -119.5 | — | |
| 4620 | 3689 | 2924 | 2308 | 1839 | 1469 | 0.7 | 0.0 | -3.3 | -9.6 | -19.2 | -32.5 | 2.2 | 0.0 | -5.2 | -13.6 | -25.8 | -63.2 | -121.7 | 24" |
| 4712 | 3547 | 2640 | 1970 | 1516 | 1239 | 0.8 | 0.0 | -3.5 | -10.3 | -20.8 | -35.6 | 2.4 | 0.0 | -5.6 | -14.9 | -28.5 | -71.5 | -140.4 | |

# WEATHERBY BALLISTICS

| SUGGESTED USAGE | CARTRIDGE | BULLET | | VELOCITY in Feet per Second | | | | | | ENERGY in Foot-Pounds | | | | | | PATH OF BULLET Above or below line-of-sight of riflescopes mounted 1.5" above bore | | | | |
|---|---|---|---|---|---|---|---|---|---|---|---|---|---|---|---|---|---|---|---|---|
| | Cartridge | Weight Grains | Bullet Type | Muzzle | 100 Yards | 200 Yards | 300 Yards | 400 Yards | 500 Yards | Muzzle | 100 Yards | 200 Yards | 300 Yards | 400 Yards | 500 Yards | 100 Yards | 200 Yards | 300 Yards | 400 Yards | 500 Yards |
| V | .224 WM | 55 | Pt-Ex | 3650 | 3192 | 2780 | 2403 | 2057 | 1742 | 1627 | 1244 | 944 | 705 | 516 | 370 | 2.8 | 3.7 | 0.0 | -9.7 | -27.7 |
| V | .240 WM | 87 | Pt-Ex | 3523 | 3233 | 2943 | 2680 | 2432 | 2197 | 2398 | 2007 | 1673 | 1388 | 1143 | 933 | 2.5 | 3.3 | 0.0 | -8.0 | -22.0 |
| M | | 100 | Pt-Ex | 3406 | 3116 | 2844 | 2588 | 2346 | 2117 | 2577 | 2156 | 1796 | 1488 | 1222 | 996 | 2.8 | 3.5 | 0.0 | -8.6 | -23.6 |
| | | 100 | Partition | 3406 | 3136 | 2881 | 2641 | 2413 | 2196 | 2577 | 2184 | 1843 | 1549 | 1293 | 1071 | 2.7 | 3.5 | 0.0 | -8.3 | -22.7 |
| V | .257 WM | 87 | Pt-Ex | 3825 | 3456 | 3118 | 2803 | 2511 | 2236 | 2827 | 2308 | 1878 | 1518 | 1218 | 966 | 2.1 | 2.8 | 0.0 | -7.2 | -20.0 |
| M | | 100 | Pt-Ex | 3602 | 3280 | 2980 | 2701 | 2438 | 2190 | 2882 | 2389 | 1973 | 1620 | 1320 | 1065 | 2.4 | 3.2 | 0.0 | -7.8 | -21.6 |
| | | 100 | *Partition® | 3555 | 3270 | 3004 | 2753 | 2516 | 2290 | 2806 | 2374 | 2053 | 1683 | 1405 | 1165 | 2.5 | 3.2 | 0.0 | -7.8 | -21.0 |
| | | 120 | Partition | 3305 | 3045 | 2800 | 2568 | 2348 | 2139 | 2911 | 2472 | 2090 | 1758 | 1469 | 1219 | 3.0 | 3.7 | 0.0 | -8.8 | -24.0 |
| V | .270 WM | 100 | Pt-Ex | 3760 | 3380 | 3033 | 2712 | 2412 | 2133 | 3139 | 2537 | 2042 | 1633 | 1292 | 1010 | 2.3 | 3.0 | 0.0 | -7.8 | -21.6 |
| M | | 130 | Pt-Ex | 3375 | 3100 | 2842 | 2598 | 2367 | 2147 | 3287 | 2773 | 2330 | 1948 | 1616 | 1331 | 2.9 | 3.6 | 0.0 | -8.7 | -23.7 |
| | | 130 | Partition | 3375 | 3127 | 2893 | 2670 | 2458 | 2257 | 3287 | 2822 | 2415 | 2058 | 1714 | 1470 | 2.8 | 3.5 | 0.0 | -8.3 | -22.4 |
| | | 150 | Pt-Ex | 3245 | 3019 | 2803 | 2598 | 2402 | 2215 | 3507 | 3034 | 2617 | 2248 | 1922 | 1634 | 3.0 | 3.7 | 0.0 | -8.9 | -23.8 |
| | | 150 | Partition | 3245 | 3029 | 2823 | 2627 | 2439 | 2259 | 3507 | 3055 | 2655 | 2298 | 1981 | 1699 | 3.0 | 3.7 | 0.0 | -8.7 | -23.3 |
| M | 7MM WM | 139 | Pt-Ex | 3340 | 3082 | 2838 | 2608 | 2389 | 2180 | 3443 | 2931 | 2486 | 2099 | 1761 | 1467 | 2.9 | 3.6 | 0.0 | -8.7 | -23.6 |
| | | 140 | Partition | 3303 | 3069 | 2847 | 2636 | 2434 | 2241 | 3391 | 2927 | 2519 | 2159 | 1842 | 1562 | 2.9 | 3.6 | 0.0 | -8.6 | -23.1 |
| | | 154 | Pt-Ex | 3260 | 3022 | 2797 | 2583 | 2379 | 2184 | 3633 | 3123 | 2675 | 2281 | 1934 | 1630 | 3.0 | 3.7 | 0.0 | -9.0 | -24.1 |
| | | 160 | Partition | 3200 | 2991 | 2791 | 2600 | 2417 | 2241 | 3637 | 3177 | 2767 | 2401 | 2075 | 1784 | 3.1 | 3.8 | 0.0 | -8.9 | -23.8 |
| B | | 175 | Pt-Ex | 3070 | 2879 | 2696 | 2520 | 2351 | 2188 | 3662 | 3220 | 2824 | 2467 | 2147 | 1861 | 3.4 | 4.1 | 0.0 | -9.6 | -25.4 |
| M | .300 WM | 150 | Pt-Ex | 3600 | 3297 | 3016 | 2751 | 2502 | 2266 | 4316 | 3621 | 3028 | 2520 | 2084 | 1709 | 2.4 | 3.1 | 0.0 | -7.7 | -21.0 |
| | | 150 | Partition | 3600 | 3319 | 3057 | 2809 | 2575 | 2353 | 4316 | 3669 | 3111 | 2628 | 2208 | 1843 | 2.4 | 3.0 | 0.0 | -7.5 | -20.1 |
| | | 165 | Boat Tail | 3450 | 3220 | 3003 | 2796 | 2598 | 2409 | 4360 | 3799 | 3303 | 2863 | 2473 | 2146 | 2.5 | 3.2 | 0.0 | -7.6 | -20.4 |
| B | | 180 | Pt-Ex | 3300 | 3064 | 2841 | 2629 | 2426 | 2233 | 4352 | 3753 | 3226 | 2762 | 2352 | 1992 | 2.9 | 3.6 | 0.0 | -8.6 | -23.2 |
| | | 180 | Partition | 3300 | 3085 | 2881 | 2686 | 2499 | 2319 | 4352 | 3804 | 3317 | 2882 | 2495 | 2150 | 2.8 | 3.5 | 0.0 | -8.3 | -22.3 |
| | | 220 | Rn-Ex | 2905 | 2498 | 2125 | 1787 | 1491 | 1250 | 4122 | 3047 | 2206 | 1560 | 1085 | 763 | 5.3 | 6.6 | 0.0 | -17.6 | -51.3 |
| B | .340 WM | 200 | Pt-Ex | 3260 | 3011 | 2775 | 2552 | 2339 | 2137 | 4719 | 4025 | 3420 | 2892 | 2430 | 2027 | 3.1 | 3.8 | 0.0 | -9.1 | -24.7 |
| | | 210 | Partition | 3250 | 3000 | 2763 | 2539 | 2325 | 2122 | 4924 | 4195 | 3559 | 3004 | 2520 | 2098 | 3.1 | 3.8 | 0.0 | -9.2 | -24.9 |
| | | 250 | Rn-Ex | 3002 | 2672 | 2365 | 2079 | 1814 | 1574 | 5002 | 3963 | 3105 | 2399 | 1827 | 1375 | 1.7 | 0.0 | -7.9 | -24.0 | -50.7 |
| | | 250 | Partition | 2980 | 2780 | 2588 | 2404 | 2228 | 2059 | 4931 | 4290 | 3719 | 3209 | 2756 | 2354 | 3.7 | 4.4 | 0.0 | -10.3 | -27.5 |
| B | .378 WM | 270 | Pt-Ex | 3180 | 2976 | 2781 | 2594 | 2415 | 2243 | 6062 | 5308 | 4635 | 4034 | 3496 | 3015 | 1.2 | 0.0 | -5.7 | -16.6 | -33.5 |
| | | | | | | | | | | | | | | | | 3.1 | 3.8 | 0.0 | -9.0 | -23.9 |
| | | 300 | Rn-Ex | 2925 | 2603 | 2303 | 2024 | 1764 | 1531 | 5701 | 4516 | 3535 | 2729 | 2074 | 1563 | 1.8 | 0.0 | -8.3 | -25.2 | -53.5 |
| A | | 300 | FMJ | 2925 | 2580 | 2262 | 1972 | 1710 | 1482 | 5701 | 4434 | 3408 | 2592 | 1949 | 1463 | 1.84 | 0.0 | -8.6 | -26.1 | -55.9 |
| A | .416 WM | 400 | Swift P | 2650 | 2411 | 2185 | 1971 | 1770 | 1585 | 6239 | 5165 | 4242 | 3450 | 2783 | 2233 | 5.4 | 6.3 | 0.0 | -15.1 | -41.7 |
| | | | | | | | | | | | | | | | | 2.2 | 0.0 | -9.5 | -27.7 | -57.5 |
| | | 400 | Rn-Ex | 2700 | 2390 | 2101 | 1834 | 1591 | 1379 | 6474 | 5073 | 3921 | 2986 | 2247 | 1688 | 5.7 | 6.8 | 0.0 | -17.2 | -48.4 |
| | | | | | | | | | | | | | | | | 2.3 | 0.0 | -10.2 | -30.9 | -65.4 |
| | | 400 | **Mono Solid® | 2700 | 2397 | 2115 | 1852 | 1613 | 1402 | 6474 | 5104 | 3971 | 3047 | 2310 | 1747 | 5.7 | 6.7 | 0.0 | -17.0 | -47.4 |
| | | | | | | | | | | | | | | | | 2.3 | 0.0 | -10.1 | -30.4 | -64.3 |
| A | .460 WM | 500 | RNSP | 2600 | 2310 | 2039 | 1787 | 1559 | 1359 | 7507 | 5926 | 4618 | 3545 | 2701 | 2050 | 2.5 | 0.0 | -10.8 | -32.7 | -69.2 |
| | | 500 | FMJ | 2600 | 2330 | 2077 | 1839 | 1623 | 1426 | 7507 | 6030 | 4791 | 3755 | 2924 | 2258 | | | | | |

**LEGEND:** Pt-Ex = Pointed-Expanding Rn-Ex = Round nose-Expanding FMJ = Full Metal Jacket P = Divided Lead Cavity or "H" Type

*Note:* These tables were calculated by computer using a standard modern scientific technique to predict trajectories and recoil energies from the best available cartridge data. Figures shown are expected to be reasonably accurate; however, the shooter is cautioned that performance will vary because of variations in rifles, ammunition, atmospheric conditions and altitude. Velocities were determined using 26-inch barrels; shorter barrels will reduce velocity by 30 to 65 fps per inch of barrel removed. Trajectories were computed with the line-of-sight 1.5 inches above the bore centerline. *B.C.:* Ballistic Coefficients supplied by the bullet manufacturers. * Partition is a registered trademark of Nosler, Inc. ** Monolithic Solid is a registered trademark of A-Square, Inc.

# WINCHESTER BALLISTICS

## CENTERFIRE PISTOL/REVOLVER

| | Cartridge | Symbol | Bullet Wt. Grs. | Bullet Type | Velocity (fps) Muzzle | Velocity (fps) 50 Yds. | Velocity (fps) 100 Yds. | Energy (ft-lbs.) Muzzle | Energy (ft-lbs.) 50 Yds. | Energy (ft-lbs.) 100 Yds. | Mid Range Traj. (in.) 50 Yds. | Mid Range Traj. (in.) 100 Yds. | Barrel Length Inches |
|---|---|---|---|---|---|---|---|---|---|---|---|---|---|
| | 25 Automatic | X25AXP | 45 | Expanding Point** | 815 | 729 | 655 | 66 | 53 | 42 | 1.8 | 7.7 | 2 |
| | 25 Automatic | X25AP | 50 | Full Metal Jacket | 760 | 707 | 659 | 64 | 56 | 48 | 2.0 | 8.7 | 2 |
| | 30 Luger (7.65mm) | X30LP | 93 | Full Metal Jacket | 1220 | 1110 | 1040 | 305 | 255 | 225 | 0.9 | 3.5 | 4-1/2 |
| | 30 Carbine # | X30M1 | 110 | Hollow Soft Point | 1790 | 1601 | 1430 | 783 | 626 | 500 | 0.4 | 1.7 | 10 |
| | 32 Smith & Wesson | X32SWP | 85 | Lead-Round Nose | 680 | 645 | 610 | 90 | 81 | 73 | 2.5 | 10.5 | 3 |
| | 32 Smith & Wesson Long | X32SWLP | 98 | Lead-Round Nose | 705 | 670 | 635 | 115 | 98 | 88 | 2.3 | 10.5 | 4 |
| | 32 Short Colt | X32SCP | 80 | Lead-Round Nose | 745 | 665 | 590 | 100 | 79 | 62 | 2.2 | 9.9 | 4 |
| | 32 Automatic | X32ASHP | 60 | Silvertip® Hollow Point | 970 | 895 | 835 | 125 | 107 | 93 | 1.3 | 5.4 | 4 |
| | 32 Automatic | X32AP | 71 | Full Metal Jacket | 905 | 855 | 810 | 129 | 115 | 97 | 1.4 | 5.8 | 4 |
| | 38 Smith & Wesson | X38SWP | 145 | Lead-Round Nose | 685 | 650 | 620 | 150 | 135 | 125 | 2.4 | 10.0 | 4 |
| | 380 Automatic | X380ASHP | 85 | Silvertip Hollow Point | 1000 | 921 | 860 | 189 | 160 | 140 | 1.2 | 5.1 | 3-3/4 |
| New | 380 Automatic SXT® | S380 | 95 | SXT | 955 | 889 | 835 | 192 | 167 | 147 | 1.3 | 5.5 | 3-3/4 |
| | 380 Automatic | X380AP | 95 | Full Metal Jacket | 955 | 865 | 785 | 190 | 160 | 130 | 1.4 | 5.9 | 3-3/4 |
| | 38 Special | X38S9HP | 110 | Silvertip Hollow Point | 945 | 894 | 850 | 218 | 195 | 176 | 1.3 | 5.4 | 4V |
| | 38 Special Super Unleaded™ | X38SSU | 130 | Full Metal Jacket Encapsulated | 775 | 743 | 712 | 173 | 159 | 146 | 1.9 | 7.9 | 4V |
| | 38 Special Super Match® | X38SMRP | 148 | Lead-Wad Cutter | 710 | 634 | 566 | 166 | 132 | 105 | 2.4 | 10.8 | 4V |
| | 38 Special | X38S1P | 158 | Lead-Round Nose | 755 | 723 | 693 | 200 | 183 | 168 | 2.0 | 8.3 | 4V |
| | 38 Special | X38WCPSV | 158 | Lead-Semi Wad Cutter | 755 | 721 | 689 | 200 | 182 | 167 | 2.0 | 8.4 | 4V |
| | 38 Special + P | X38SSHP | 95 | Silvertip Hollow Point | 1100 | 1002 | 932 | 255 | 212 | 183 | 1.0 | 4.3 | 4V |
| | 38 Special + P# | X38S6PH | 110 | Jacketed Hollow Point | 995 | 926 | 871 | 242 | 210 | 185 | 1.2 | 5.1 | 4V |
| | 38 Special + P# | X38S7PH | 125 | Jacketed Hollow Point | 945 | 898 | 858 | 248 | 224 | 204 | 1.3 | 5.4 | 4V |
| | 38 Special + P# | X38S8HP | 125 | Silvertip Hollow Point | 945 | 898 | 858 | 248 | 224 | 204 | 1.3 | 5.4 | 4V |
| | 38 Special Subsonic® + P | XSUB38S | 147 | Jacketed Hollow Point | 860 | 830 | 802 | 241 | 225 | 210 | 1.5 | 6.3 | 4V |
| | 38 Special + P | X38SPD | 158 | Lead-Semi Wad Cutter Hollow Point | 890 | 855 | 823 | 278 | 257 | 238 | 1.4 | 6.0 | 4V |
| | 38 Special + P | X38WCP | 158 | Lead-Semi Wad Cutter | 890 | 855 | 823 | 278 | 257 | 238 | 1.4 | 6.0 | 4V |
| | 9mm Luger Super Unleaded | X9MMSU | 115 | Full Metal Jacket Encapsulated | 1155 | 1047 | 971 | 341 | 280 | 241 | 0.9 | 3.9 | 4 |
| | 9mm Luger | X9LP | 115 | Full Metal Jacket | 1155 | 1047 | 971 | 341 | 280 | 241 | 0.9 | 3.9 | 4 |
| | 9mm Luger | X9MMSHP | 115 | Silvertip Hollow Point | 1225 | 1095 | 1007 | 383 | 306 | 259 | 0.8 | 3.6 | 4 |
| New | 9mm Luger SXT | S9 | 147 | SXT | 990 | 947 | 909 | 320 | 293 | 270 | 1.2 | 4.8 | 4 |
| | 9mm Luger Subsonic | XSUB9MM | 147 | Jacketed Hollow Point | 990 | 945 | 907 | 320 | 292 | 268 | 1.2 | 4.8 | 4 |
| | 9mm Luger | X9MMST147 | 147 | Silvertip Hollow Point | 1010 | 962 | 921 | 333 | 302 | 277 | 1.1 | 4.7 | 4 |
| | 9mm Luger Super Match | X9MMTCM | 147 | Full Metal Jacket-Truncated Cone-Match | 990 | 945 | 907 | 320 | 292 | 268 | 1.2 | 4.8 | 4 |
| | 38 Super Automatic + P* | X38ASHP | 125 | Silvertip Hollow Point | 1240 | 1130 | 1050 | 427 | 354 | 306 | 0.8 | 3.4 | 5 |
| | 38 Super Automatic + P* | X38A1P | 130 | Full Metal Jacket | 1215 | 1099 | 1017 | 426 | 348 | 298 | 0.8 | 3.6 | 5 |
| | 357 Magnum # | X3573P | 110 | Jacketed Hollow Point | 1295 | 1095 | 975 | 410 | 292 | 232 | 0.8 | 3.5 | 4V |
| | 357 Magnum # | X3576P | 125 | Jacketed Hollow Point | 1450 | 1240 | 1090 | 583 | 427 | 330 | 0.6 | 2.8 | 4V |
| | 357 Magnum # | X357SHP | 145 | Silvertip Hollow Point | 1290 | 1155 | 1060 | 535 | 428 | 361 | 0.8 | 3.5 | 4V |
| | 357 Magnum | X3571P | 158 | Lead-Semi Wad Cutter** | 1235 | 1104 | 1015 | 535 | 428 | 361 | 0.8 | 3.5 | 4V |
| | 357 Magnum # | X3574P | 158 | Jacketed Hollow Point | 1235 | 1104 | 1015 | 535 | 428 | 361 | 0.8 | 3.5 | 4V |
| | 357 Magnum # | X3575P | 158 | Jacketed Soft Point | 1235 | 1104 | 1015 | 535 | 428 | 361 | 0.8 | 3.5 | 4V |
| | 40 Smith & Wesson | X40SWSTHP | 155 | Silvertip Hollow Point | 1205 | 1096 | 1018 | 500 | 414 | 357 | 0.8 | 3.6 | 4 |
| | 40 Smith & Wesson Super Match | X40SWTCM | 155 | Full Metal Jacket-Truncated Cone-Match | 1125 | 1046 | 986 | 436 | 377 | 335 | 0.9 | 3.9 | 4 |
| | 40 Smith & Wesson Super Unleaded | X40SWSU | 180 | Full Metal Jacket Encapsulated | 990 | 933 | 886 | 392 | 348 | 314 | 1.2 | 5.0 | 4 |
| New | 40 Smith & Wesson SXT | S40 | 180 | SXT | 1015 | 959 | 912 | 412 | 367 | 333 | 1.1 | 4.7 | 4 |
| | 40 Smith & Wesson Subsonic | XSUB40SW | 180 | Jacketed Hollow Point | 1010 | 954 | 909 | 408 | 364 | 330 | 1.1 | 4.8 | 4 |
| | 10mm Automatic | X10MMSTHP | 175 | Silvertip Hollow Point | 1290 | 1141 | 1037 | 649 | 506 | 418 | 0.7 | 3.3 | 5-1/2 |
| | 10mm Automatic Subsonic | XSUB10MM | 180 | Jacketed Hollow Point | 990 | 936 | 891 | 390 | 350 | 317 | 1.2 | 4.9 | 5 |
| | 41 Remington Magnum # | X41MSTHP2 | 175 | Silvertip Hollow Point | 1250 | 1120 | 1029 | 607 | 488 | 412 | 0.8 | 3.4 | 4V |
| | 41 Remington Magnum # | X41MHP2 | 210 | Jacketed Hollow Point | 1300 | 1162 | 1062 | 788 | 630 | 526 | 0.7 | 3.2 | 4V |
| | 44 Smith & Wesson Special # | X44STHPS2 | 200 | Silvertip Hollow Point | 900 | 860 | 822 | 360 | 328 | 300 | 1.4 | 5.9 | 6-1/2 |
| | 44 Smith & Wesson Special | X44SP | 246 | Lead-Round Nose | 755 | 725 | 695 | 310 | 285 | 265 | 2.0 | 8.3 | 6-1/2 |
| | 44 Remington Magnum | X44MSTHP2 | 210 | Silvertip Hollow Point | 1250 | 1106 | 1010 | 729 | 570 | 475 | 0.8 | 3.5 | 4V |
| | 44 Remington Magnum | X44MHSP2 | 240 | Hollow Soft Point | 1180 | 1081 | 1010 | 741 | 623 | 543 | 0.9 | 3.7 | 4V |
| | 45 Automatic | X45ASHP2 | 185 | Silvertip Hollow Point | 1000 | 938 | 888 | 411 | 362 | 324 | 1.2 | 4.9 | 5 |
| | 45 Automatic Super Match | X45AWCP | 185 | Full Metal Jacket - Semi Wad Cutter | 770 | 707 | 650 | 244 | 205 | 174 | 2.0 | 8.7 | 5 |
| New | 45 Automatic SXT | S45 | 230 | SXT | 880 | 846 | 816 | 396 | 366 | 340 | 1.5 | 6.1 | 5 |
| New | 45 Automatic | X45ASU | 230 | Full Metal Jacket - Encapsulated | 835 | 800 | 767 | 356 | 326 | 300 | 1.6 | 6.8 | 5 |
| | 45 Automatic Subsonic | XSUB45A | 230 | Jacketed Hollow Point | 925 | 880 | 840 | 437 | 396 | 361 | 1.3 | 5.6 | 5 |
| | 45 Automatic | X45A1P2 | 230 | Full Metal Jacket | 835 | 800 | 767 | 356 | 326 | 300 | 1.6 | 6.8 | 5 |
| | 45 Colt # | X45CSHP2 | 225 | Silvertip Hollow Point | 920 | 877 | 839 | 423 | 384 | 352 | 1.4 | 5.6 | 5-1/2 |
| | 45 Colt | X45CP2 | 255 | Lead-Round Nose | 860 | 820 | 780 | 420 | 380 | 345 | 1.5 | 6.1 | 5-1/2 |
| | 45 Winchester Magnum | X45WMA | 260 | Jacketed Soft Point | 1250 | 1137 | 1053 | 902 | 746 | 640 | 0.8 | 3.3 | 5 |

+P Ammunition with (+P) on the case head stamp is loaded to higher pressure. Use only in firearms designated for this cartridge and so recommended by the gun manufacturer.

V-Data is based on velocity obtained from 4" vented test barrels for revolver cartridges (38 Special, 357 Magnum, 41 Rem. Mag. and 44 Rem. Mag.)

Specifications are nominal. Test barrels are used to determine ballistics figures. Individual firearms may differ from test barrel statistics.

Specifications subject to change without notice.

**Lubaloy® Coated
*For use only in 38 Super Automatic Pistols.
#Acceptable for use in rifles also.

# CENTERFIRE RIFLE BALLISTICS

| Game Selector | CXP Class | Examples |
|---|---|---|
| V-Varmint | 1 | Prairie dog, coyote, woodchuck |
| D-Deer | 2 | Antelope, deer, black bear |
| O/P-Open or Plains | 3 | Elk, moose |
| M-Medium Game | 3D | All game in category 3 plus large dangerous game (i.e. Kodiak bear) |
| L-Large Game | 4 | Cape Buffalo, elephant |
| XL-Extra Large Game | M | Match |

# Acceptable for use in pistols and revolvers also.
Bold type indicates Supreme® product line

*Intended for use in fast twist barrels (e.g., 1 in 7 to 1 in 9).
Slower twist barrels may not sufficiently stabilize bullet.

| Cartridge | Symbol | Game Selector Guide | CXP Guide Number | Bullet Wt. Grs. | Bullet Type | Barrel Length (In.) | Velocity in Feet Per Second (fps) Muzzle | 100 | 200 | 300 | 400 | 500 | Energy in Foot Pounds (ft-lbs.) Muzzle | 100 | 200 | 300 | 400 | 500 | Trajectory, Short Range Yards 50 | 100 | 150 | 200 | 250 | 300 | Trajectory, Long Range Yards 100 | 150 | 200 | 250 | 300 | 400 | 500 |
|---|---|---|---|---|---|---|---|---|---|---|---|---|---|---|---|---|---|---|---|---|---|---|---|---|---|---|---|---|---|---|---|
| 218 Bee | X218B | V | 1 | 46 | Hollow Point | 24 | 2760 | 2102 | 1550 | 1155 | 961 | 850 | 778 | 451 | 245 | 136 | 94 | 74 | 0.3 | 0 | -2.3 | -7.2 | -15.8 | -29.4 | 1.5 | 0 | -4.2 | -12.0 | -24.8 | -71.4 | -155.6 |
| **22 Hornet** | **X22H1** | V | 1 | 45 | Soft Point | 24 | 2690 | 2042 | 1502 | 1128 | 948 | 840 | 723 | 417 | 225 | 127 | 90 | 70 | 0.3 | 0 | -2.4 | -7.7 | -16.9 | -31.3 | 1.6 | 0 | -4.5 | -12.8 | -26.4 | -75.6 | -163.4 |
| **22 Hornet** | **X22H2** | V | 1 | 46 | Hollow Point | 24 | 2690 | 2042 | 1502 | 1128 | 948 | 841 | 739 | 426 | 230 | 130 | 92 | 72 | 0.3 | 0 | -2.4 | -7.7 | -16.9 | -31.3 | 1.6 | 0 | -4.5 | -12.8 | -26.4 | -75.5 | -163.3 |
| **22-250 Remington** | **S22250** | **V** | **1** | **52** | **Hollow Point Boattail** | **24** | **3750** | **3268** | **2835** | **2442** | **2082** | **1755** | **1624** | **1233** | **928** | **689** | **501** | **356** | **0.1** | **0** | **-0.7** | **-2.4** | **-5.1** | **-9.1** | **1.2** | **1.1** | **0** | **-2.1** | **-5.5** | **-16.9** | **-36.3** |
| 22-250 Remington | X222501 | V | 1 | 55 | Pointed Soft Point | 24 | 3680 | 3137 | 2656 | 2222 | 1832 | 1493 | 1654 | 1201 | 861 | 603 | 410 | 272 | 0.2 | 0.5 | 0 | -1.6 | -4.4 | -8.7 | 2.3 | 2.6 | 1.9 | 0 | -3.4 | -15.9 | -38.9 |
| **222 Remington** | **X222R** | V | 1 | 50 | Pointed Soft Point | 24 | 3140 | 2602 | 2123 | 1700 | 1350 | 1107 | 1094 | 752 | 500 | 321 | 202 | 136 | 0.5 | 0.9 | 0 | -2.5 | -6.9 | -13.7 | 2.2 | 1.9 | 0 | -3.8 | -10.0 | -32.3 | -73.8 |
| **222 Remington** | **X222R1** | V | 1 | 55 | Full Metal Jacket | 24 | 3020 | 2675 | 2355 | 2057 | 1783 | 1537 | 1114 | 874 | 677 | 517 | 388 | 288 | 0.5 | 0.9 | 0 | -2.2 | -6.1 | -11.7 | 2.0 | 1.7 | 0 | -3.3 | -8.3 | -24.9 | -52.5 |
| 223 Remington | X223RH | V | 1 | 53 | Hollow Point | 24 | 3330 | 2882 | 2477 | 2106 | 1770 | 1475 | 1305 | 978 | 722 | 522 | 369 | 256 | 0.3 | 0.7 | 0 | -1.9 | -5.3 | -10.3 | 1.7 | 1.4 | 0 | -2.9 | -7.4 | -22.7 | -49.1 |
| 223 Remington | X223R | V | 1 | 55 | Pointed Soft Point | 24 | 3240 | 2747 | 2304 | 1905 | 1554 | 1270 | 1282 | 921 | 648 | 443 | 295 | 197 | 0.4 | 0.8 | 0 | -2.2 | -6.0 | -11.8 | 1.9 | 1.6 | 0 | -3.3 | -8.5 | -26.7 | -59.6 |
| 223 Remington | X223R1 | V | 1 | 55 | Full Metal Jacket | 24 | 3240 | 2877 | 2543 | 2232 | 1943 | 1679 | 1282 | 1011 | 790 | 608 | 461 | 344 | 0.4 | 0.7 | 0 | -1.9 | -5.1 | -9.9 | 1.7 | 1.4 | 0 | -2.8 | -7.1 | -21.2 | -44.6 |
| 223 Remington | X223R2 | D | 2 | 64 | Power-Point® | 24 | 3020 | 2621 | 2256 | 1920 | 1619 | 1362 | 1296 | 977 | 723 | 524 | 373 | 264 | 0.6 | 0.9 | 0 | -2.4 | -6.5 | -12.5 | 2.1 | 1.8 | 0 | -3.5 | -9.0 | -27.4 | -59.6 |
| **223 Remington Match** | **S223M*** | **–** | **M** | **69** | **Hollow Point Boattail** | **24** | **3060** | **2740** | **2442** | **2164** | **1904** | **1665** | **1435** | **1151** | **914** | **717** | **555** | **425** | **-0.2** | **0** | **-0.9** | **-3.1** | **-6.8** | **-12.1** | **1.6** | **1.4** | **0** | **-2.9** | **-7.4** | **-22.3** | **-46.7** |
| **225 Winchester** | **X2251** | V | 1 | 55 | Pointed Soft Point | 24 | 3570 | 3066 | 2616 | 2208 | 1838 | 1514 | 1556 | 1148 | 836 | 595 | 412 | 280 | 0.2 | 0.6 | 0 | -1.7 | -4.6 | -9.0 | 2.4 | 2.8 | 2.0 | 0 | -3.5 | -16.3 | -39.5 |
| 243 Winchester | X2431 | V | 1 | 80 | Pointed Soft Point | 24 | 3350 | 2955 | 2593 | 2259 | 1951 | 1670 | 1993 | 1551 | 1194 | 906 | 676 | 495 | 0.3 | 0.7 | 0 | -1.8 | -4.9 | -9.4 | 2.6 | 2.9 | 2.1 | 0 | -3.6 | -16.2 | -37.9 |
| 243 Winchester | X2432 | D,O/P | 2 | 100 | Power-Point | 24 | 2960 | 2697 | 2449 | 2215 | 1993 | 1786 | 1945 | 1615 | 1332 | 1089 | 882 | 708 | 0.5 | 0.9 | 0 | -2.2 | -5.8 | -11.0 | 1.9 | 1.6 | 0 | -3.1 | -7.8 | -22.6 | -46.3 |
| **243 Winchester** | **S243** | **D,O/P** | **2** | **100** | **Soft Point Boattail** | **24** | **2960** | **2712** | **2477** | **2254** | **2042** | **1843** | **1946** | **1633** | **1363** | **1128** | **926** | **754** | **0.1** | **0** | **-1.3** | **-3.8** | **-7.8** | **-13.3** | **1.9** | **1.6** | **0** | **-3.0** | **-7.6** | **-22.0** | **-44.8** |
| **6mm Remington** | **X6MMR2** | D,O/P | 2 | 100 | Power-Point | 24 | 3100 | 2829 | 2573 | 2332 | 2104 | 1889 | 2133 | 1777 | 1470 | 1207 | 983 | 792 | 0.4 | 0.8 | 0 | -1.9 | -5.2 | -9.9 | 1.7 | 1.5 | 0 | -2.8 | -7.0 | -20.4 | -41.7 |
| 25-06 Remington | X25061 | V | 1 | 90 | Positive Expanding Point | 24 | 3440 | 3043 | 2680 | 2344 | 2034 | 1749 | 2364 | 1850 | 1435 | 1098 | 827 | 611 | 0.3 | 0.6 | 0 | -1.7 | -4.5 | -8.8 | 2.4 | 2.7 | 2.0 | 0 | -3.4 | -15.0 | -35.2 |
| 25-06 Remington | X25062 | D,O/P | 2 | 120 | Positive Expanding Point | 24 | 2990 | 2730 | 2484 | 2252 | 2032 | 1825 | 2382 | 1985 | 1644 | 1351 | 1100 | 887 | 0.5 | 0.8 | 0 | -2.1 | -5.6 | -10.7 | 1.9 | 1.6 | 0 | -3.0 | -7.5 | -22.0 | -44.8 |
| **25-20 Winchester #** | **X25202** | V | 1 | 86 | Soft Point | 24 | 1460 | 1194 | 1030 | 931 | 858 | 798 | 407 | 272 | 203 | 165 | 141 | 122 | 0 | -4.1 | -14.4 | -31.8 | -57.3 | -92.0 | 0 | -8.2 | -23.5 | -47.0 | -79.6 | -175.9 | -319.4 |
| 25-35 Winchester | X2535 | D | 2 | 117 | Soft Point | 24 | 2230 | 1866 | 1545 | 1282 | 1097 | 984 | 1292 | 904 | 620 | 427 | 313 | 252 | 0.6 | 0 | -3.1 | -9.2 | -19.0 | -33.1 | 2.1 | 0 | -5.1 | -13.8 | -27.0 | -70.1 | -142.0 |
| **250 Savage** | **X2503** | D,O/P | 2 | 100 | Silvertip® | 24 | 2820 | 2467 | 2140 | 1839 | 1569 | 1339 | 1765 | 1351 | 1017 | 751 | 547 | 398 | 0.2 | 0 | -1.6 | -4.9 | -10.0 | -17.4 | 2.4 | 2.0 | 0 | -3.9 | -10.1 | -30.5 | -65.2 |
| 257 Roberts + P | X257P3 | D,O/P | 2 | 117 | Power-Point | 24 | 2780 | 2411 | 2071 | 1761 | 1488 | 1263 | 2009 | 1511 | 1115 | 806 | 576 | 415 | 0.8 | 1.1 | 0 | -2.9 | -7.8 | -15.1 | 2.6 | 2.2 | 0 | -4.2 | -10.8 | -33.0 | -70.0 |
| **264 Winchester Mag.** | **X2642** | D,O/P | 2 | 140 | Power-Point | 24 | 3030 | 2782 | 2548 | 2326 | 2114 | 1914 | 2854 | 2406 | 2018 | 1682 | 1389 | 1139 | 0.5 | 0.8 | 0 | -2.0 | -5.4 | -10.2 | 1.8 | 1.5 | 0 | -2.9 | -7.2 | -20.8 | -42.2 |
| 6.5 x 55 Swedish | X6555 | D,O/P | 2 | 140 | Soft Point | 24 | 2550 | 2359 | 2176 | 2002 | 1836 | 1680 | 2022 | 1731 | 1473 | 1246 | 1048 | 878 | 0 | 0 | -1.5 | -4.8 | -9.8 | -16.9 | 2.4 | 2 | 0 | -3.9 | -9.7 | -28.1 | -56.8 |
| **270 Winchester** | **X2705** | D,O/P | 2 | 130 | Power-Point | 24 | 3060 | 2802 | 2559 | 2329 | 2110 | 1904 | 2702 | 2267 | 1890 | 1565 | 1285 | 1046 | 0.4 | 0.8 | 0 | -2.0 | -5.3 | -10.1 | 1.8 | 1.5 | 0 | -2.8 | -7.1 | -20.6 | -42.0 |
| **270 Winchester** | **X2703** | D,O/P | 2 | 130 | Silvertip | 24 | 3060 | 2776 | 2510 | 2259 | 2022 | 1801 | 2702 | 2225 | 1818 | 1472 | 1180 | 936 | 0.5 | 0.8 | 0 | -2.0 | -5.5 | -10.4 | 1.8 | 1.5 | 0 | -2.9 | -7.4 | -21.6 | -44.3 |
| **270 Winchester** | **S270** | **D,O/P** | **2** | **140** | **Silvertip Boattail** | **24** | **2960** | **2753** | **2554** | **2365** | **2183** | **2009** | **2724** | **2356** | **2029** | **1739** | **1482** | **1256** | **0.1** | **0** | **-1.2** | **-3.7** | **-7.5** | **-12.7** | **1.8** | **1.5** | **0** | **-2.9** | **-7.2** | **-20.6** | **-41.3** |
| **270 Winchester** | **S270X** | **D,O/P** | **2** | **140** | **Fail Safe®** | **24** | **2920** | **2671** | **2435** | **2211** | **1999** | **1799** | **2651** | **2218** | **1843** | **1519** | **1242** | **1007** | **-0.2** | **0** | **-1** | **-3.4** | **-7.2** | **-12.6** | **1.7** | **1.5** | **0** | **-3** | **-7.6** | **-22.3** | **-45.7** |
| 270 Winchester | X2704 | D,M | 3 | 150 | Power-Point | 24 | 2850 | 2585 | 2336 | 2100 | 1879 | 1673 | 2705 | 2226 | 1817 | 1468 | 1175 | 932 | 0.6 | 1.0 | 0 | -2.4 | -6.4 | -12.2 | 2.2 | 1.8 | 0 | -3.4 | -8.6 | -25.0 | -51.4 |
| 280 Remington | X280R | D,O/P | 2 | 140 | Power-Point | 24 | 3050 | 2705 | 2428 | 2167 | 1924 | 1698 | 2799 | 2274 | 1833 | 1461 | 1151 | 897 | 0.5 | 0.8 | 0 | -2.2 | -5.8 | -11.1 | 1.9 | 1.6 | 0 | -3.1 | -7.8 | -23.1 | -47.8 |
| **280 Remington** | **S280R** | **D,O/P** | **3** | **160** | **Silvertip Boattail** | **24** | **2840** | **2637** | **2442** | **2256** | **2078** | **1909** | **2866** | **2471** | **2120** | **1809** | **1535** | **1295** | **0.1** | **0** | **-1.4** | **-4.1** | **-8.3** | **-14.0** | **2.1** | **1.7** | **0** | **-3.2** | **-7.9** | **-22.6** | **-45.4** |
| **NEW 280 Remington** | **S280X** | **D,O/P,M** | **3** | **160** | **Fail Safe** | **24** | **2840** | **2600** | **2372** | **2156** | **1951** | **1759** | **2866** | **2402** | **2000** | **1652** | **1353** | **1100** | **-0.2** | **0** | **-1.1** | **-3.7** | **-7.7** | **-13.5** | **1.8** | **1.6** | **0** | **-3.2** | **-8** | **-23.5** | **-48.2** |
| 284 Winchester | X2842 | D,O/P,M | 3 | 150 | Power-Point | 24 | 2860 | 2595 | 2344 | 2108 | 1886 | 1680 | 2724 | 2243 | 1830 | 1480 | 1185 | 940 | 0.6 | 1.0 | 0 | -2.4 | -6.3 | -12.1 | 2.1 | 1.8 | 0 | -3.4 | -8.5 | -24.8 | -51.0 |
| 7mm Mauser (7x57) | X7MM1 | D | 2 | 145 | Power-Point | 24 | 2660 | 2413 | 2180 | 1959 | 1754 | 1564 | 2279 | 1875 | 1530 | 1236 | 990 | 788 | 0.2 | 0 | -1.7 | -5.1 | -10.3 | -17.5 | 1.1 | 0 | -2.8 | -7.4 | -14.1 | -34.4 | -66.1 |
| 7mm Remington Mag. | X7MMR1 | D,O/P,M | 2 | 150 | Power-Point | 24 | 3110 | 2830 | 2568 | 2320 | 2085 | 1866 | 3221 | 2667 | 2196 | 1792 | 1448 | 1160 | 0.4 | 0.8 | 0 | -1.9 | -5.2 | -9.9 | 1.7 | 1.5 | 0 | -2.8 | -7.0 | -20.5 | -42.1 |
| **7mm Remington Mag.** | **S7MAGA** | **D,O/P,M,L** | **3** | **160** | **Silvertip Boattail** | **24** | **2950** | **2745** | **2550** | **2363** | **2184** | **2012** | **3093** | **2679** | **2311** | **1984** | **1694** | **1439** | **0.1** | **0** | **-1.2** | **-3.7** | **-7.5** | **-12.8** | **1.9** | **1.5** | **0** | **-2.9** | **-7.2** | **-20.6** | **-41.4** |
| **7mm Remington Mag.** | **S7MAGX** | **D,O/P,M,L** | **3** | **160** | **Fail Safe** | **24** | **2920** | **2678** | **2449** | **2231** | **2025** | **1830** | **3030** | **2549** | **2131** | **1769** | **1457** | **1190** | **-0.2** | **0** | **-1** | **-3.4** | **-7.1** | **-12.5** | **1.7** | **1.5** | **0** | **-2.9** | **-7.5** | **-22** | **-44.9** |
| 7mm Remington Mag. | X7MMR2 | D,O/P,M | 3 | 175 | Power-Point | 24 | 2860 | 2645 | 2440 | 2244 | 2057 | 1879 | 3178 | 2718 | 2313 | 1956 | 1644 | 1372 | 0.6 | 0.9 | 0 | -2.3 | -6.0 | -11.3 | 2.0 | 1.7 | 0 | -3.2 | -7.9 | -22.7 | -45.8 |
| 7.62 x 39mm Russian | X76239 | D,V | 2 | 123 | Soft Point | 20 | 2365 | 2033 | 1731 | 1465 | 1248 | 1093 | 1527 | 1129 | 818 | 586 | 425 | 327 | 0.5 | 0 | -2.6 | -7.6 | -15.4 | -26.7 | 3.8 | 3.1 | 0 | -6.0 | -15.4 | -46.3 | -98.4 |
| **30 Carbine #** | **X30M1** | V | 1 | 110 | Hollow Soft Point | 20 | 1990 | 1567 | 1236 | 1035 | 923 | 842 | 967 | 600 | 373 | 262 | 208 | 173 | 0.9 | 0 | -4.5 | -13.5 | -28.3 | -49.9 | 0 | -4.5 | -13.5 | -28.3 | -49.9 | -118.6 | -228.2 |
| 30-30 Winchester | X30301 | D | 2 | 150 | Hollow Point | 24 | 2390 | 2018 | 1684 | 1398 | 1177 | 1036 | 1902 | 1356 | 944 | 651 | 461 | 357 | 0.5 | 0 | -2.6 | -7.7 | -16.0 | -27.9 | 1.7 | 0 | -4.3 | -11.6 | -22.7 | -59.1 | -120.5 |
| 30-30 Winchester | X30306 | D | 2 | 150 | Power-Point | 24 | 2390 | 2018 | 1684 | 1398 | 1177 | 1036 | 1902 | 1356 | 944 | 651 | 461 | 357 | 0.5 | 0 | -2.6 | -7.7 | -16.0 | -27.9 | 1.7 | 0 | -4.3 | -11.6 | -22.7 | -59.1 | -120.5 |
| 30-30 Winchester | X30302 | D | 2 | 150 | Silvertip | 24 | 2390 | 2018 | 1684 | 1398 | 1177 | 1036 | 1902 | 1356 | 944 | 651 | 461 | 357 | 0.5 | 0 | -2.6 | -7.7 | -16.0 | -27.9 | 1.7 | 0 | -4.3 | -11.6 | -22.7 | -59.1 | -120.5 |
| 30-30 Winchester | X30303 | D | 2 | 170 | Power-Point | 24 | 2200 | 1895 | 1619 | 1381 | 1191 | 1061 | 1827 | 1355 | 989 | 720 | 535 | 425 | 0.6 | 0 | -3.0 | -8.9 | -18.0 | -31.1 | 2.0 | 0 | -4.8 | -13.0 | -25.1 | -63.6 | -126.7 |
| 30-30 Winchester | X30304 | D | 2 | 170 | Silvertip | 24 | 2200 | 1895 | 1619 | 1381 | 1191 | 1061 | 1827 | 1355 | 989 | 720 | 535 | 425 | 0.6 | 0 | -3.0 | -8.9 | -18.0 | -31.1 | 2.0 | 0 | -4.8 | -13.0 | -25.1 | -63.6 | -126.7 |
| **30-06 Springfield** | **X30062** | V | 1 | 125 | Pointed Soft Point | 24 | 3140 | 2780 | 2447 | 2138 | 1853 | 1595 | 2736 | 2145 | 1662 | 1269 | 953 | 706 | 0.4 | 0.8 | 0 | -2.1 | -5.6 | -10.7 | 1.8 | 1.5 | 0 | -3.0 | -7.7 | -23.0 | -48.5 |
| **30-06 Springfield** | **X30061** | D,O/P | 2 | 150 | Power-Point | 24 | 2920 | 2580 | 2265 | 1972 | 1704 | 1466 | 2839 | 2217 | 1708 | 1295 | 967 | 716 | 0.6 | 1.0 | 0 | -2.4 | -6.6 | -12.7 | 2.2 | 1.8 | 0 | -3.5 | -9.0 | -27.0 | -57.1 |
| **30-06 Springfield** | **X30063** | D,O/P | 2 | 150 | Silvertip | 24 | 2910 | 2617 | 2342 | 2083 | 1843 | 1622 | 2820 | 2281 | 1827 | 1445 | 1131 | 876 | 0.6 | 0.9 | 0 | -2.3 | -6.3 | -12.0 | 2.1 | 1.8 | 0 | -3.3 | -8.5 | -25.0 | -51.8 |
| **30-06 Springfield** | **S3006** | **D,O/P,M** | **2** | **165** | **Silvertip Boattail** | **24** | **2800** | **2597** | **2402** | **2216** | **2038** | **1869** | **2873** | **2421** | **2114** | **1799** | **1522** | **1280** | **0.1** | **0** | **-1.4** | **-4.3** | **-8.6** | **-14.6** | **2.1** | **1.8** | **0** | **-3.3** | **-8.2** | **-23.4** | **-47.0** |

# WINCHESTER BALLISTICS

| | | | | | | | | | | | | | | | | | | | | | | | | | | | | | | | |
|---|---|---|---|---|---|---|---|---|---|---|---|---|---|---|---|---|---|---|---|---|---|---|---|---|---|---|---|---|---|---|---|
| 30-06 Springfield | X30065 | D,O/P,M | 2 | 165 | Soft Point | 24 | 2800 | 2573 | 2357 | 2151 | 1956 | 1772 | 2873 | 2426 | 2036 | 1696 | 1402 | 1151 | 0.7 | 1.0 | 0 | -2.5 | -6.5 | -12.2 | 2.2 | 1.9 | 0 | -3.6 | -8.4 | -24.4 | -49.6 |
| NEW 30-06 Springfield | S3006XA | - | - | 165 | Fail Safe | | | | | | | | | | *under development* | | | | | | | | | | | | | | | | |
| 30-06 Springfield | S3006X | D,O/P,M,L | 3 | 180 | Fail Safe | 24 | 2700 | 2486 | 2283 | 2089 | 1904 | 1731 | 2914 | 2472 | 2083 | 1744 | 1450 | 1198 | -0.1 | 0 | -1.3 | -4.1 | -8.6 | -14.9 | 2.1 | 1.8 | 0 | -3.5 | -8.7 | -25.5 | -51.8 |
| 30-06 Springfield | X30064 | D,O/P,M | 2 | 180 | Power-Point | 24 | 2700 | 2348 | 2023 | 1727 | 1466 | 1251 | 2913 | 2203 | 1635 | 1192 | 859 | 625 | 0.2 | 0 | -1.8 | -5.5 | -11.2 | -19.5 | 2.7 | 2.3 | 0 | -4.4 | -11.3 | -34.4 | -73.7 |
| 30-06 Springfield | X30066 | D,O/P,M,L | 3 | 180 | Silvertip | 24 | 2700 | 2469 | 2250 | 2042 | 1846 | 1663 | 2913 | 2436 | 2023 | 1666 | 1362 | 1105 | 0.2 | 0 | -1.6 | -4.8 | -9.7 | -16.5 | 2.4 | 2.0 | 0 | -3.7 | -9.3 | -27.0 | -54.9 |
| 30-06 Springfield | X30069 | M,L | 3 | 220 | Silvertip | 24 | 2410 | 2192 | 1985 | 1791 | 1611 | 1448 | 2837 | 2347 | 1924 | 1567 | 1268 | 1024 | 0.4 | 0 | -2.2 | -6.4 | -12.7 | -21.6 | 1.5 | 0 | -3.5 | -9.1 | -17.2 | -41.8 | -79.9 |
| 30-40 Krag | X30401 | D | 2 | 180 | Power-Point | 24 | 2430 | 2099 | 1795 | 1525 | 1298 | 1128 | 2360 | 1761 | 1288 | 929 | 673 | 508 | 0.4 | 0 | -2.4 | -7.1 | -14.5 | -25.0 | 1.6 | 0 | -3.9 | -10.5 | -20.3 | -51.7 | -103.9 |
| 300 Winchester Mag. | X30WM1 | D,O/P | 2 | 150 | Power-Point | 24 | 3290 | 2951 | 2636 | 2342 | 2068 | 1813 | 3605 | 2900 | 2314 | 1827 | 1424 | 1095 | 0.3 | 0.7 | 0 | -1.8 | -4.8 | -9.3 | 2.6 | 2.9 | 2.1 | 0 | -3.5 | -15.4 | -35.5 |
| 300 Winchester Mag. | S300WX | M,L | 3D | 180 | Fail Safe | 24 | 2960 | 2732 | 2514 | 2307 | 2110 | 1923 | 3503 | 2983 | 2528 | 2129 | 1780 | 1478 | -0.2 | 0 | -1.0 | -3.2 | -6.8 | -11.8 | 1.6 | 1.4 | 0 | -2.8 | -7.1 | -20.7 | -42.1 |
| 300 Winchester Mag. | X30WM2 | O/P,M,L | 3 | 180 | Power-Point | 24 | 2960 | 2745 | 2540 | 2344 | 2157 | 1979 | 3501 | 3011 | 2578 | 2196 | 1859 | 1565 | 0.5 | 0.8 | 0 | -2.1 | -5.5 | -10.4 | 1.9 | 1.6 | 0 | -2.9 | -7.3 | -20.9 | -41.9 |
| 300 Winchester Mag. | X30WM3 | M,L,XL | 3D | 220 | Silvertip | 24 | 2680 | 2448 | 2228 | 2020 | 1823 | 1640 | 3508 | 2927 | 2424 | 1993 | 1623 | 1314 | 0.2 | 0 | -1.7 | -4.9 | -9.9 | -16.9 | 2.5 | 2.0 | 0 | -3.8 | -9.5 | -27.5 | -56.1 |
| 300 H&H Magnum | X300H2 | O/P,M,L | 3 | 180 | Silvertip | 24 | 2880 | 2640 | 2412 | 2196 | 1991 | 1798 | 3315 | 2785 | 2325 | 1927 | 1584 | 1292 | 0.6 | 0.9 | 0 | -2.3 | -6.0 | -11.5 | 2.1 | 1.7 | 0 | -3.2 | -8.0 | -23.3 | -47.4 |
| 300 Savage | X3001 | D,O/P | 2 | 150 | Power-Point | 24 | 2630 | 2311 | 2015 | 1743 | 1500 | 1295 | 2303 | 1779 | 1352 | 1012 | 749 | 558 | 0.3 | 0 | -1.9 | -5.7 | -11.6 | -19.9 | 2.8 | 2.3 | 0 | -4.5 | -11.5 | -34.4 | -73.0 |
| 300 Savage | X3003 | D,O/P | 2 | 150 | Silvertip | 24 | 2630 | 2354 | 2095 | 1853 | 1631 | 1434 | 2303 | 1845 | 1462 | 1143 | 886 | 685 | 0.3 | 0 | -1.8 | -5.4 | -11.0 | -18.8 | 2.7 | 2.2 | 0 | -4.2 | -10.7 | -31.5 | -65.5 |
| 300 Savage | X3004 | D | 2 | 180 | Power-Point | 24 | 2350 | 2025 | 1728 | 1467 | 1252 | 1098 | 2207 | 1639 | 1193 | 860 | 626 | 482 | 0.5 | 0 | -2.6 | -7.7 | -15.6 | -27.1 | 1.7 | 0 | -4.2 | -11.3 | -21.9 | -55.8 | -112.0 |
| 303 Savage | X3032 | D | 2 | 190 | Silvertip | 24 | 1890 | 1612 | 1372 | 1183 | 1055 | 970 | 1507 | 1096 | 794 | 591 | 469 | 397 | 1.0 | 0 | -4.3 | -12.6 | -25.5 | -43.7 | 2.9 | 0 | -6.8 | -18.3 | -35.1 | -88.2 | -172.5 |
| 303 British | X303B1 | D | 2 | 180 | Power-Point | 24 | 2460 | 2233 | 2018 | 1816 | 1629 | 1459 | 2418 | 1993 | 1627 | 1318 | 1060 | 851 | 0.3 | 0 | -2.1 | -6.1 | -12.2 | -20.8 | 1.4 | 0 | -3.3 | -8.8 | -16.6 | -40.4 | -77.4 |
| 307 Winchester | X3076 | D,M | 2 | 180 | Power-Point | 24 | 2510 | 2179 | 1874 | 1599 | 1362 | 1177 | 2519 | 1898 | 1404 | 1022 | 742 | 554 | 0.3 | 0 | -2.2 | -6.5 | -13.3 | -22.9 | 1.5 | 0 | -3.6 | -9.6 | -18.6 | -47.1 | -93.7 |
| 308 Winchester | S308 | D,O/P | 2 | 150 | Silvertip Boattail | 24 | 2820 | 2559 | 2312 | 2080 | 1861 | 1659 | 2649 | 2182 | 1782 | 1441 | 1154 | 917 | 0.2 | 0 | -1.5 | -4.4 | -9.0 | -15.4 | 2.2 | 1.8 | 0 | -3.5 | -8.7 | -25.5 | -52.3 |
| 308 Winchester | X3085 | D,O/P | 2 | 150 | Power-Point | 24 | 2820 | 2488 | 2179 | 1893 | 1633 | 1405 | 2648 | 2061 | 1581 | 1193 | 888 | 657 | 0.2 | 0 | -1.6 | -4.8 | -9.8 | -16.9 | 2.4 | 2.0 | 0 | -3.8 | -9.8 | -29.3 | -62.0 |
| 308 Winchester | X3082 | D,O/P | 2 | 150 | Silvertip | 24 | 2820 | 2533 | 2263 | 2009 | 1774 | 1560 | 2648 | 2137 | 1705 | 1344 | 1048 | 810 | 0.2 | 0 | -1.5 | -4.5 | -9.3 | -15.9 | 2.3 | 1.9 | 0 | -3.6 | -9.1 | -26.9 | -55.7 |
| NEW 308 Winchester | S308XA | – | – | 150 | Fail Safe | 24 | | | | | | | | | *under development* | | | | | | | | | | | | | | | | |
| 308 Winchester Match | S308M | – | M | 168 | Hollow Point Boattail | 24 | 2680 | 2485 | 2297 | 2118 | 1948 | 1786 | 2680 | 2303 | 1970 | 1674 | 1415 | 1190 | -0.1 | 0 | -1.3 | -4.1 | -8.6 | -14.9 | 2.1 | 1.8 | 0 | -3.4 | -8.7 | -25.1 | -50.7 |
| 308 Winchester | S308X | D,O/P,M,L | 3 | 180 | Fail Safe | 24 | 2590 | 2357 | 2137 | 1929 | 1734 | 1555 | 2682 | 2222 | 1826 | 1487 | 1202 | 966 | 0 | 0 | -1.5 | -4.8 | -9.9 | -18.2 | 2.4 | 2.1 | 0 | -4.0 | -10.0 | -29.4 | -60.3 |
| 308 Winchester | X3086 | D,O/P,M | 2 | 180 | Power-Point | 24 | 2620 | 2274 | 1955 | 1666 | 1414 | 1212 | 2743 | 2066 | 1527 | 1109 | 799 | 587 | 0.3 | 0 | -2.0 | -5.9 | -12.1 | -20.9 | 2.9 | 2.4 | 0 | -4.7 | -12.1 | -36.9 | -79.1 |
| 308 Winchester | X3083 | M,L | 3 | 180 | Silvertip | 24 | 2620 | 2393 | 2178 | 1974 | 1782 | 1604 | 2743 | 2288 | 1896 | 1557 | 1269 | 1028 | 0.2 | 0 | -1.8 | -5.2 | -10.4 | -17.7 | 2.6 | 2.1 | 0 | -4.0 | -9.9 | -28.9 | -58.8 |
| 32 Win Special | X32WS2 | D | 2 | 170 | Power-Point | 24 | 2250 | 1870 | 1537 | 1267 | 1082 | 971 | 1911 | 1320 | 892 | 606 | 442 | 356 | 0.6 | 0 | -3.1 | -9.2 | -19.0 | -33.2 | 2.0 | 0 | -5.1 | -13.8 | -27.1 | -70.9 | -144.3 |
| 32 Win Special | X32WS3 | D | 2 | 170 | Silvertip | 24 | 2250 | 1870 | 1537 | 1267 | 1082 | 971 | 1911 | 1320 | 892 | 606 | 442 | 356 | 0.6 | 0 | -3.1 | -9.2 | -19.0 | -33.2 | 2.0 | 0 | -5.1 | -13.8 | -27.1 | -70.9 | -144.3 |
| 32-20 Winchester # | X32201 | V | 1 | 100 | Lead | 24 | 1210 | 1021 | 913 | 834 | 769 | 712 | 325 | 231 | 185 | 154 | 131 | 113 | 0 | -6.3 | -20.9 | -44.9 | -79.3 | -125.1 | 0 | -11.5 | -32.3 | -63.6 | -106.3 | -230.3 | -413.3 |
| 8mm Mauser (8 x 57) | X8MM | D | 2 | 170 | Power-Point | 24 | 2360 | 1969 | 1622 | 1333 | 1123 | 997 | 2102 | 1463 | 993 | 671 | 476 | 375 | 0.5 | 0 | -2.7 | -8.2 | -17.0 | -29.8 | 1.8 | 0 | -4.5 | -12.4 | -24.3 | -63.8 | -130.7 |
| 338 Winchester Mag. | X3381 | D,O/P,M | 3 | 200 | Power-Point | 24 | 2960 | 2658 | 2375 | 2110 | 1862 | 1635 | 3890 | 3137 | 2505 | 1977 | 1539 | 1187 | 0.5 | 0.9 | 0 | -2.3 | -6.1 | -11.6 | 2.0 | 1.7 | 0 | -3.2 | -8.2 | -24.3 | -50.4 |
| 338 Winchester Mag. | X3383 | M,L,XL | 3D | 225 | Soft Point | 24 | 2780 | 2572 | 2374 | 2184 | 2003 | 1832 | 3862 | 3306 | 2816 | 2384 | 2005 | 1677 | 1.2 | 1.3 | 0 | -2.7 | -7.1 | -12.9 | 2.7 | 2.1 | 0 | -3.6 | -9.4 | -25.0 | -49.9 |
| 338 Winchester Mag. | S338XA | M,L,XL | 3D | 230 | Fail Safe | 24 | 2780 | 2573 | 2375 | 2186 | 2005 | 1834 | 3948 | 3382 | 2881 | 2441 | 2054 | 1719 | -0.1 | 0 | -1.2 | -3.8 | -7.9 | -13.7 | 1.9 | 1.7 | 0 | -3.2 | -8.1 | -23.4 | -47.4 |
| 348 Winchester | Q3167 | D,M | 3 | 200 | Silvertip | 24 | 2520 | 2215 | 1931 | 1672 | 1443 | 1253 | 2820 | 2178 | 1656 | 1241 | 925 | 697 | 0.3 | 0 | -2.1 | -6.2 | -12.7 | -21.9 | 1.4 | 0 | -3.4 | -9.2 | -17.7 | -44.4 | -87.9 |
| 35 Remington | X35R1 | D | 2 | 200 | Power-Point | 24 | 2020 | 1646 | 1335 | 1114 | 985 | 901 | 1812 | 1203 | 791 | 551 | 431 | 360 | 0.9 | 0 | -4.1 | -12.1 | -25.1 | -43.9 | 2.7 | 0 | -6.7 | -18.3 | -35.8 | -92.8 | -185.5 |
| 356 Winchester | X3561 | D,M | 2 | 200 | Power-Point | 24 | 2460 | 2114 | 1797 | 1517 | 1284 | 1113 | 2688 | 1985 | 1434 | 1022 | 732 | 550 | 0.4 | 0 | -2.3 | -7.0 | -14.3 | -24.7 | 1.6 | 0 | -3.8 | -10.4 | -20.1 | -51.2 | -102.3 |
| 357 Magnum # | X3575P | V,D | 2 | 158 | Jacketed Soft Point | 20 | 1830 | 1427 | 1138 | 980 | 883 | 809 | 1175 | 715 | 454 | 337 | 274 | 229 | 0 | -2.4 | -9.1 | -21.0 | -39.2 | -64.3 | 0 | -5.5 | -16.2 | -33.1 | -57.0 | -128.3 | -235.8 |
| 358 Winchester | X3581 | D,M | 3 | 200 | Silvertip | 24 | 2490 | 2171 | 1876 | 1610 | 1379 | 1194 | 2753 | 2093 | 1563 | 1151 | 844 | 633 | 0.4 | 0 | -2.2 | -6.5 | -13.3 | -23.0 | 1.5 | 0 | -3.6 | -9.7 | -18.6 | -47.2 | -94.1 |
| 375 Winchester | X375W | D,M | 2 | 200 | Power-Point | 24 | 2200 | 1841 | 1526 | 1268 | 1089 | 980 | 2150 | 1506 | 1034 | 714 | 527 | 427 | 0.6 | 0 | -3.2 | -9.5 | -19.5 | -33.8 | 2.1 | 0 | -5.2 | -14.1 | -27.4 | -70.1 | -138.1 |
| 375 H&H Magnum | X375H2 | M,L,XL | 3D | 300 | Silvertip | 24 | 2530 | 2268 | 2022 | 1793 | 1583 | 1397 | 4263 | 3426 | 2723 | 2141 | 1669 | 1300 | 0.3 | 0 | -2.0 | -5.9 | -11.9 | -20.3 | 2.9 | 2.4 | 0 | -4.5 | -11.5 | -33.8 | -70.1 |
| 375 H&H Magnum | X375H3 | XL | 4 | 300 | Full Metal Jacket | 24 | 2530 | 2171 | 1843 | 1551 | 1307 | 1126 | 4263 | 3139 | 2262 | 1602 | 1138 | 844 | 0.3 | 0 | -2.2 | -6.5 | -13.5 | -23.4 | 1.5 | 0 | -3.6 | -9.8 | -19.1 | -49.1 | -99.5 |
| 38-40 Winchester # | X3840 | D | 2 | 180 | Soft Point | 24 | 1160 | 999 | 901 | 827 | 764 | 710 | 538 | 399 | 324 | 273 | 233 | 201 | 0 | -6.7 | -22.2 | -47.3 | -83.2 | -130.8 | 0 | -12.1 | -33.9 | -66.4 | -110.6 | -238.3 | -425.6 |
| 38-55 Winchester | X3855 | D | 2 | 255 | Soft Point | 24 | 1320 | 1190 | 1091 | 1018 | 963 | 917 | 987 | 802 | 674 | 587 | 525 | 476 | 0 | -4.7 | -15.4 | -32.7 | -57.2 | -89.3 | 0 | -8.4 | -23.4 | -45.6 | -75.2 | -158.8 | -277.4 |
| 44 Remington Magnum # | X44MSTHP2 | V,D | 2 | 210 | Silvertip Hollow Point | 20 | 1580 | 1198 | 993 | 879 | 795 | 725 | 1164 | 670 | 460 | 361 | 295 | 245 | 0 | -3.7 | -13.3 | -29.8 | -54.2 | -87.3 | 0 | -7.7 | -22.4 | -44.9 | -76.1 | -168.0 | -305.8 |
| 44 Remington Magnum # | X44MHSP2 | D | 2 | 240 | Hollow Soft Point | 20 | 1760 | 1362 | 1094 | 953 | 861 | 789 | 1650 | 988 | 638 | 484 | 395 | 332 | 0 | -2.7 | -10.2 | -23.6 | -44.2 | -73.3 | 0 | -6.1 | -18.1 | -37.4 | -65.1 | -150.3 | -282.5 |
| 44-40 Winchester # | X4440 | D | 2 | 200 | Soft Point | 24 | 1190 | 1006 | 900 | 822 | 756 | 699 | 629 | 449 | 360 | 300 | 254 | 217 | 0 | -6.5 | -21.6 | -46.3 | -81.8 | -129.1 | 0 | -11.8 | -33.3 | -65.5 | -109.5 | -237.4 | -426.2 |
| 45-70 Government | X4570H | D,M | 2 | 300 | Jacketed Hollow Point | 24 | 1880 | 1650 | 1425 | 1235 | 1105 | 1010 | 2355 | 1815 | 1355 | 1015 | 810 | 680 | 0 | -2.4 | -8.2 | -17.6 | -31.4 | -51.5 | 0 | -4.6 | -12.8 | -25.4 | -44.3 | -95.5 | – |
| 458 Winchester Magnum | X4581 | L,XL | 3D | 510 | Soft Point | 24 | 2040 | 1770 | 1527 | 1319 | 1157 | 1046 | 4712 | 3547 | 2640 | 1970 | 1516 | 1239 | 0.8 | 0 | -3.5 | -10.3 | -20.8 | -35.6 | 2.4 | 0 | -5.6 | -14.9 | -28.5 | -71.5 | -140.4 |

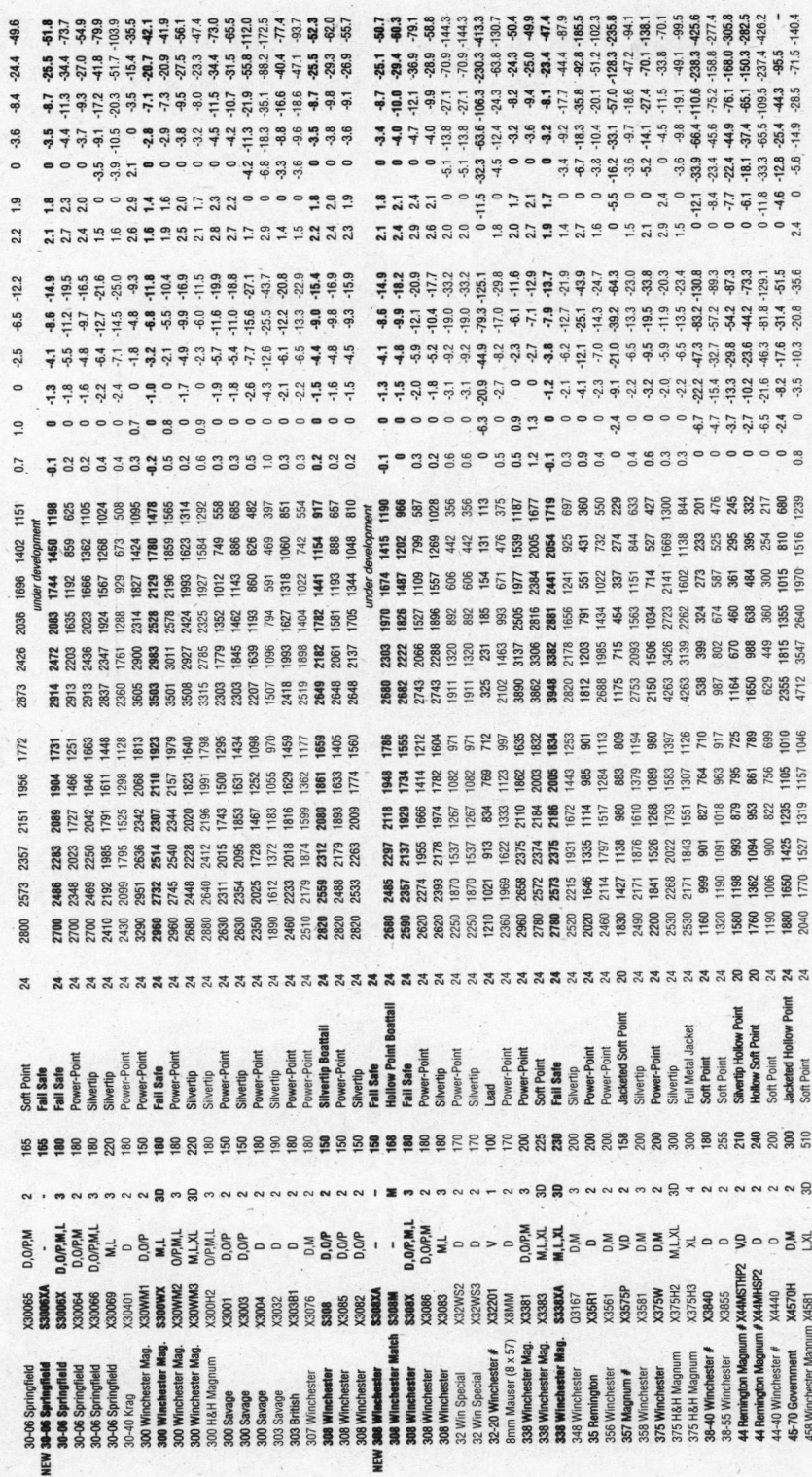

# Reloading



For addresses and phone numbers of manufacturers and distributors included in this section, turn to *DIRECTORY OF MANUFACTURERS AND SUPPLIERS* at the back of the book.

# HORNADY BULLETS

## RIFLE BULLETS

### 17 CALIBER (.172)
- 25 gr. HP #1710

### 22 CALIBER (.222)
- 40 gr. Jet #2210

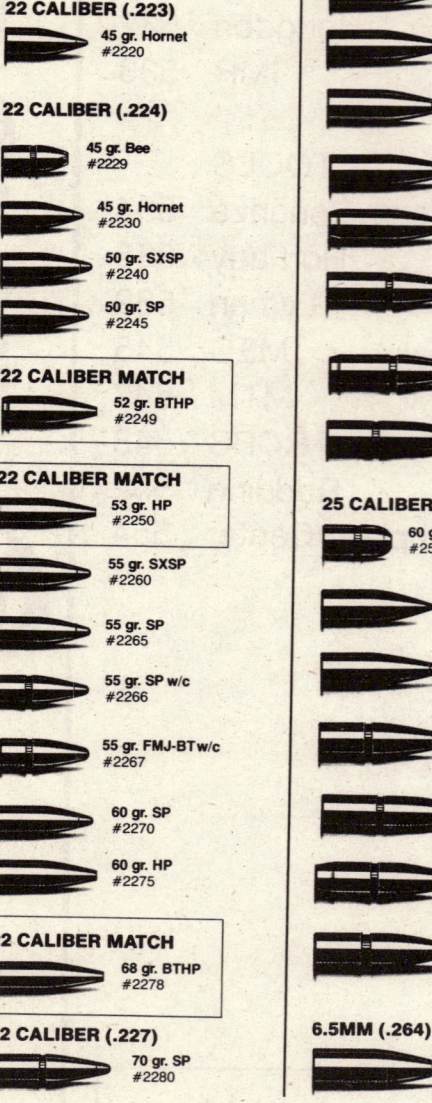

### 22 CALIBER (.223)
- 45 gr. Hornet #2220

### 22 CALIBER (.224)
- 45 gr. Bee #2229
- 45 gr. Hornet #2230
- 50 gr. SXSP #2240
- 50 gr. SP #2245

### 22 CALIBER MATCH
- 52 gr. BTHP #2249

### 22 CALIBER MATCH
- 53 gr. HP #2250
- 55 gr. SXSP #2260
- 55 gr. SP #2265
- 55 gr. SP w/c #2266
- 55 gr. FMJ-BT w/c #2267
- 60 gr. SP #2270
- 60 gr. HP #2275

### 22 CALIBER MATCH
- 68 gr. BTHP #2278

### 22 CALIBER (.227)
- 70 gr. SP #2280

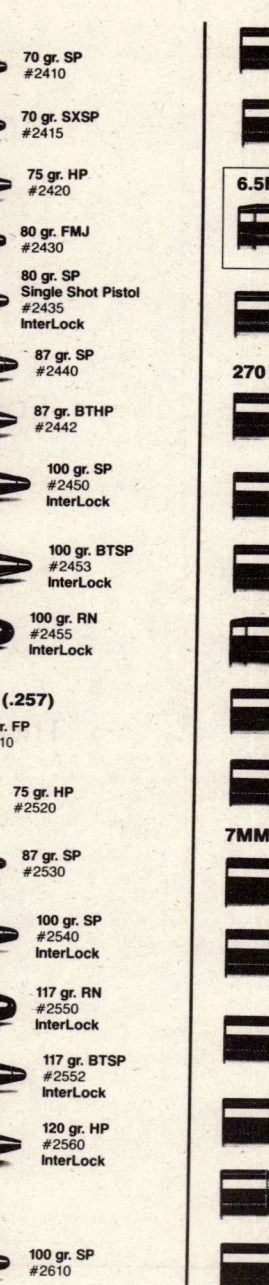

### 6MM (.243)
- 70 gr. SP #2410
- 70 gr. SXSP #2415
- 75 gr. HP #2420
- 80 gr. FMJ #2430
- 80 gr. SP Single Shot Pistol #2435 InterLock
- 87 gr. SP #2440
- 87 gr. BTHP #2442
- 100 gr. SP #2450 InterLock
- 100 gr. BTSP #2453 InterLock
- 100 gr. RN #2455 InterLock

### 25 CALIBER (.257)
- 60 gr. FP #2510
- 75 gr. HP #2520
- 87 gr. SP #2530
- 100 gr. SP #2540 InterLock
- 117 gr. RN #2550 InterLock
- 117 gr. BTSP #2552 InterLock
- 120 gr. HP #2560 InterLock

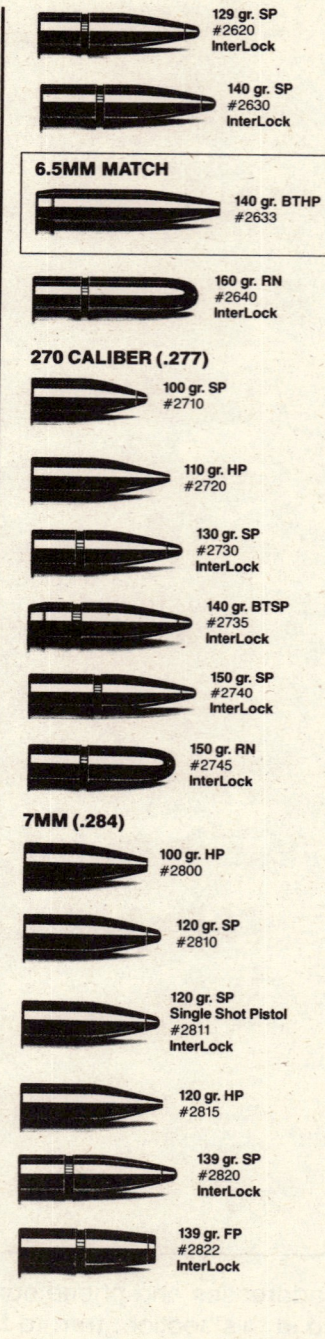

### 6.5MM (.264)
- 100 gr. SP #2610
- 129 gr. SP #2620 InterLock
- 140 gr. SP #2630 InterLock

### 6.5MM MATCH
- 140 gr. BTHP #2633

- 160 gr. RN #2640 InterLock

### 270 CALIBER (.277)
- 100 gr. SP #2710
- 110 gr. HP #2720
- 130 gr. SP #2730 InterLock
- 140 gr. BTSP #2735 InterLock
- 150 gr. SP #2740 InterLock
- 150 gr. RN #2745 InterLock

### 7MM (.284)
- 100 gr. HP #2800
- 120 gr. SP #2810
- 120 gr. SP Single Shot Pistol #2811 InterLock
- 120 gr. HP #2815
- 139 gr. SP #2820 InterLock
- 139 gr. FP #2822 InterLock

# HORNADY BULLETS

## RIFLE BULLETS

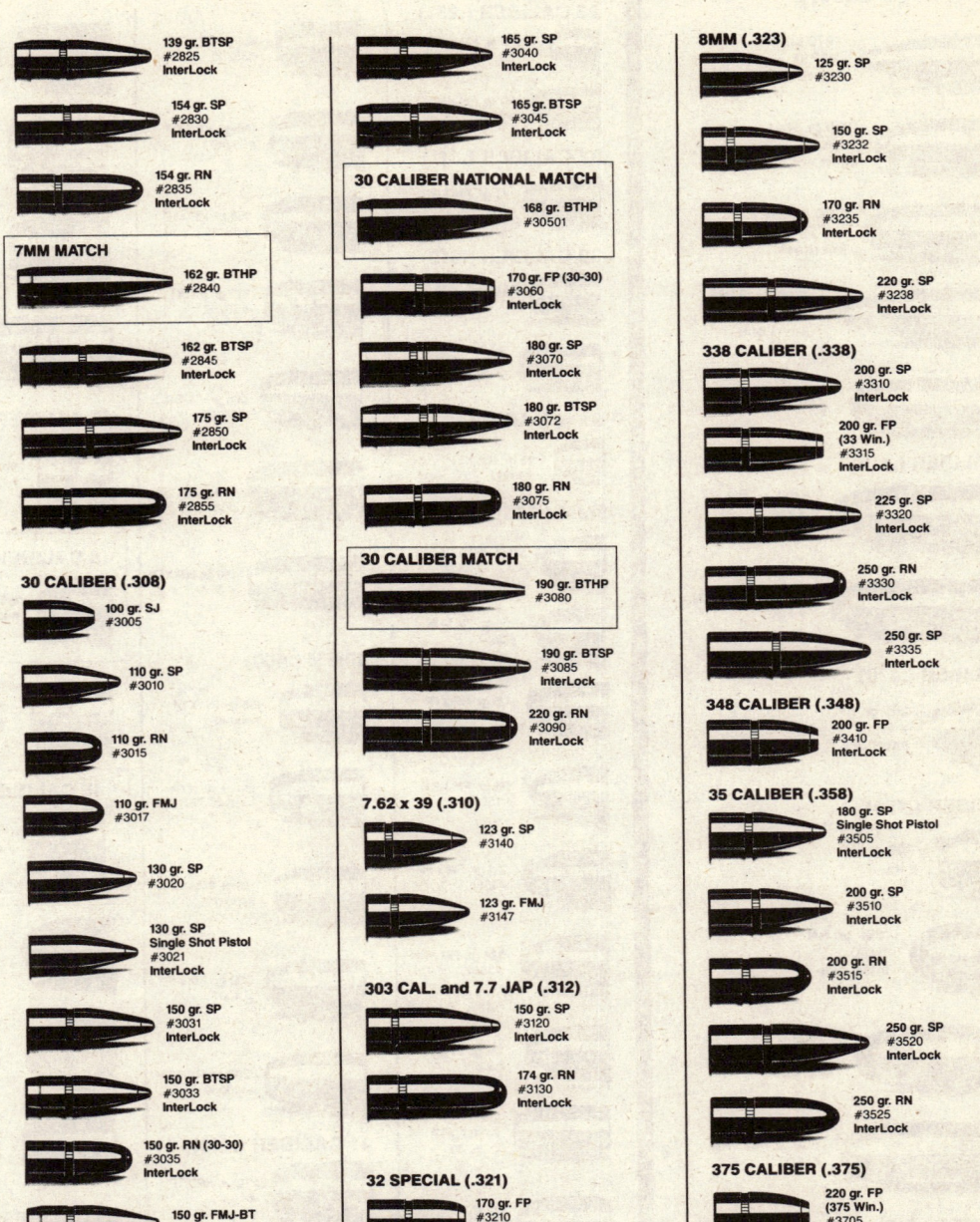

139 gr. BTSP
#2825
InterLock

154 gr. SP
#2830
InterLock

154 gr. RN
#2835
InterLock

**7MM MATCH**

162 gr. BTHP
#2840

162 gr. BTSP
#2845
InterLock

175 gr. SP
#2850
InterLock

175 gr. RN
#2855
InterLock

**30 CALIBER (.308)**

100 gr. SJ
#3005

110 gr. SP
#3010

110 gr. RN
#3015

110 gr. FMJ
#3017

130 gr. SP
#3020

130 gr. SP
Single Shot Pistol
#3021
InterLock

150 gr. SP
#3031
InterLock

150 gr. BTSP
#3033
InterLock

150 gr. RN (30-30)
#3035
InterLock

150 gr. FMJ-BT
#3037

165 gr. SP
#3040
InterLock

165 gr. BTSP
#3045
InterLock

**30 CALIBER NATIONAL MATCH**

168 gr. BTHP
#30501

170 gr. FP (30-30)
#3060
InterLock

180 gr. SP
#3070
InterLock

180 gr. BTSP
#3072
InterLock

180 gr. RN
#3075
InterLock

**30 CALIBER MATCH**

190 gr. BTHP
#3080

190 gr. BTSP
#3085
InterLock

220 gr. RN
#3090
InterLock

**7.62 x 39 (.310)**

123 gr. SP
#3140

123 gr. FMJ
#3147

**303 CAL. and 7.7 JAP (.312)**

150 gr. SP
#3120
InterLock

174 gr. RN
#3130
InterLock

**32 SPECIAL (.321)**

170 gr. FP
#3210
InterLock

**8MM (.323)**

125 gr. SP
#3230

150 gr. SP
#3232
InterLock

170 gr. RN
#3235
InterLock

220 gr. SP
#3238
InterLock

**338 CALIBER (.338)**

200 gr. SP
#3310
InterLock

200 gr. FP
(33 Win.)
#3315
InterLock

225 gr. SP
#3320
InterLock

250 gr. RN
#3330
InterLock

250 gr. SP
#3335
InterLock

**348 CALIBER (.348)**

200 gr. FP
#3410
InterLock

**35 CALIBER (.358)**

180 gr. SP
Single Shot Pistol
#3505
InterLock

200 gr. SP
#3510
InterLock

200 gr. RN
#3515
InterLock

250 gr. SP
#3520
InterLock

250 gr. RN
#3525
InterLock

**375 CALIBER (.375)**

220 gr. FP
(375 Win.)
#3705
InterLock

# HORNADY BULLETS

## RIFLE BULLETS (cont.)

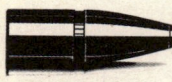

*270 gr. SP
#3710
InterLock

*270 gr. RN
#3715
InterLock

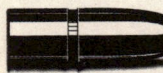

*300 gr. RN
#3720
InterLock

*300 gr. BTSP
#3725
InterLock

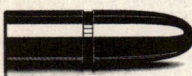

*300 gr. FMJ-RN
#3727

### 416 CALIBER (.416)

*400 gr. RN
#4165
InterLock

*400 gr. FMJ-RN
#4167

### 44 CALIBER (.430)

265 gr. FP
#4300
InterLock

### 45 CALIBER (.458)

*300 gr. HP
#4500

*350 gr. RN
#4502
InterLock

*500 gr. RN
#4504
InterLock

*500 gr. FMJ-RN
#4507

### 50 CALIBER (.510)

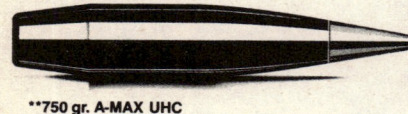

**750 gr. A-MAX UHC
#5165

*340 gr. BTSP
#4163

## PISTOL BULLETS

### 25 CALIBER (.251)

35 gr. HP/XTP
#35450

50 gr. FMJ-RN
#3545

### 32 CALIBER (.311)

71 gr. FMJ-RN
#3200

### 32 CALIBER (.312)

85 gr. HP/XTP
#32050

100 gr. HP/XTP
#32070

### 9 x 18 MAKAROV

95 gr. HP/XTP
#36500

### 9MM (.355)

90 gr. HP/XTP
#35500

100 gr. FMJ-RN
#3552

115 gr. HP/XTP
#35540

115 gr. FMJ-RN
#3555

124 gr. FMJ-FP
#3556

124 gr. FMJ-RN
#3557

124 gr. HP/XTP
#35571

147 gr.
HP-BT/XTP
# 35580

147 gr.
FMJ-RN-BT
# 3559

### 38 CALIBER (.357)

110 gr. HP/XTP
#35700

125 gr. HP/XTP
#35710

125 gr. FP/XTP
#35730

140 gr. HP/XTP
#35740

158 gr. HP/XTP
#35750

158 gr. FP/XTP
#35780

160 gr. CL-SIL
#3572

180 gr. CL-SIL
#3577

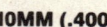

180 gr. HP/XTP
# 35771

### 10MM (.400)

155 gr. HP/XTP
#40000

180 gr. HP/XTP
#40040

180 gr. FMJ-FP
#40041

200 gr. FMJ-FP
#4007

200 gr. HP/XTP
#40060

### 41 CALIBER (.410)

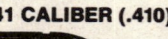

210 gr. HP/XTP
#41000

210 gr. CL-SIL
#4105

### 44 CALIBER (.430)

180 gr. HP/XTP
#44050

200 gr. HP/XTP
#44100

240 gr. HP/XTP
#44200

240 gr. CL-SIL
#4425

*300 gr. HP/XTP
#44280

### 45 CALIBER (.451)

185 gr. HP/XTP
#45100

**45 CALIBER MATCH**

185 gr. SWC
#4513

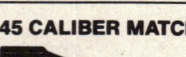

200 gr. HP/XTP
#45140

**45 CALIBER MATCH**

200 gr. FMJ-C/T
#4515

230 gr. FMJ-RN
#4517

230 gr. FMJ-FP
#4518

230 gr. HP/XTP
# 45160

### 45 CALIBER (.452)

250 gr. Long
Colt HP/XTP
#45200

*300 gr. HP/XTP
# 45230

*Packed 50 per box.
All others packed 100 per box.

# NOSLER BULLETS

## HANDGUN

| Caliber/ Diameter | Bullet Weight and Style | Sectional Density | Ballistic Coefficient | Part Number |
|---|---|---|---|---|
| 9mm/ .355" | 90 Gr. Hollow Point | .102 | .086 | 42050 |
| | 115 Gr. Full Metal Jacket | .130 | .103 | 42059 |
| | 115 Gr. Hollow Point 250 Quantity Bulk Pack | .130 | .110 | 43009 44848 |
| 38/ .357" | 125 Gr. Hollow Point 250 Quantity Bulk Pack | .140 | .143 | 42055 44840 |
| | 135 Gr. IPSC 250 Quantity Bulk Pack | .151 | .149 | 44836 |
| | 150 Gr. Soft Point | .168 | .153 | 42056 |
| | 150 Gr. IPSC 250 Quantity Bulk Pack | .168 | .157 | 44839 |
| | 158 Gr. Hollow Point 250 Quantity Bulk Pack | .177 | .182 | 42057 44841 |
| | 180 Gr. Silhouette 250 Quantity Bulk Pack | .202 | .210 | 42058 44851 |
| 10mm/ .400" | 135 Gr. Hollow Point 250 Quantity Bulk Pack | .121 | .093 | 44838 44852 |
| | 150 Gr. Hollow Point | .134 | .106 | 44849 |
| | 170 Gr. Hollow Point | .152 | .137 | 44844 |
| | 180 Gr. Hollow Point | .161 | .147 | 44837 |
| 41/ .410" | 210 Gr. Hollow Point | .178 | .170 | 43012 |
| 44/ .429" | 200 Gr. Hollow Point 250 Quantity Bulk Pack | .155 | .151 | 42060 44846 |
| | 240 Gr. Soft Point | .186 | .177 | 42068 |
| | 240 Gr. Hollow Point 250 Quantity Bulk Pack | .186 | .173 | 42061 44842 |
| | 300 Gr. Hollow Point | .233 | .206 | 42069 |
| 45/ .451" | 185 Gr. Hollow Point 250 Quantity Bulk Pack | .130 | .142 | 42062 44847 |
| | 230 Gr. Full Metal Jacket | .162 | .183 | 42064 |
| 45 Colt/ .451" | 250 Gr. Hollow Point | .176 | .177 | 43013 |

## BALLISTIC TIP®

| Caliber/ Diameter | Bullet Weight and Style | Sectional Density | Ballistic Coefficient | Part Number |
|---|---|---|---|---|
| 22/ .224" | 40 Gr. Spitzer (Orange Tip) Varmint | .114 | .221 | 39510 |
| | 50 Gr. Spitzer (Orange Tip) Varmint | .142 | .238 | 39522 |
| | 55 Gr. Spitzer (Orange Tip) Varmint | .157 | .267 | 39526 |
| 6mm/ .243" | 70 Gr. Spitzer (Purple Tip) Varmint | .169 | .310 | 39532 |
| | 95 Gr. Spitzer (Purple Tip) | .230 | .379 | 39534 |
| 25/ .257" | 85 Gr. Spitzer (Blue Tip) Varmint | .183 | .331 | 43004 |
| | 100 Gr. Spitzer (Blue Tip) | .216 | .393 | 43005 |
| 6.5mm/ .264" | 100 Gr. Spitzer (Brown Tip) | .205 | .350 | 43008 |
| | 120 Gr. Spitzer (Brown Tip) | .246 | .458 | 43007 |
| 270/ .277" | 130 Gr. Spitzer (Yellow Tip) | .242 | .433 | 39589 |
| | 140 Gr. Spitzer (Yellow Tip) | .261 | .456 | 43983 |
| | 150 Gr. Spitzer (Yellow Tip) | .279 | .496 | 39588 |
| 7mm/ .284" | 120 Gr. Spitzer (Red Tip) | .213 | .417 | 39550 |
| | 140 Gr. Spitzer (Red Tip) | .248 | .485 | 39587 |
| | 150 Gr. Spitzer (Red Tip) | .266 | .493 | 39586 |
| 30/ .308" | 125 Gr. Spitzer (Green Tip) | .188 | .366 | 43980 |
| | 150 Gr. Spitzer (Green Tip) | .226 | .435 | 39585 |
| | 165 Gr. Spitzer (Green Tip) | .248 | .475 | 39584 |
| | 180 Gr. Spitzer (Green Tip) | .271 | .507 | 39583 |
| 338/ .338" | 200 Gr. Spitzer (Maroon Tip) | .250 | .414 | 39595 |

# NOSLER BULLETS

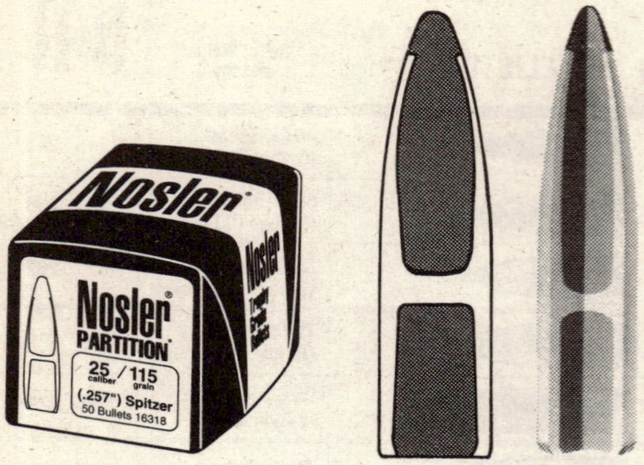


## Nosler Partition® Bullets

The Nosler Partition® bullet earned its reputation among professional guides and serious hunters for one reason: it doesn't fail. The patented Partition® design offers a dual core that is unequalled in mushrooming, weight retention and hydrostatic shock.

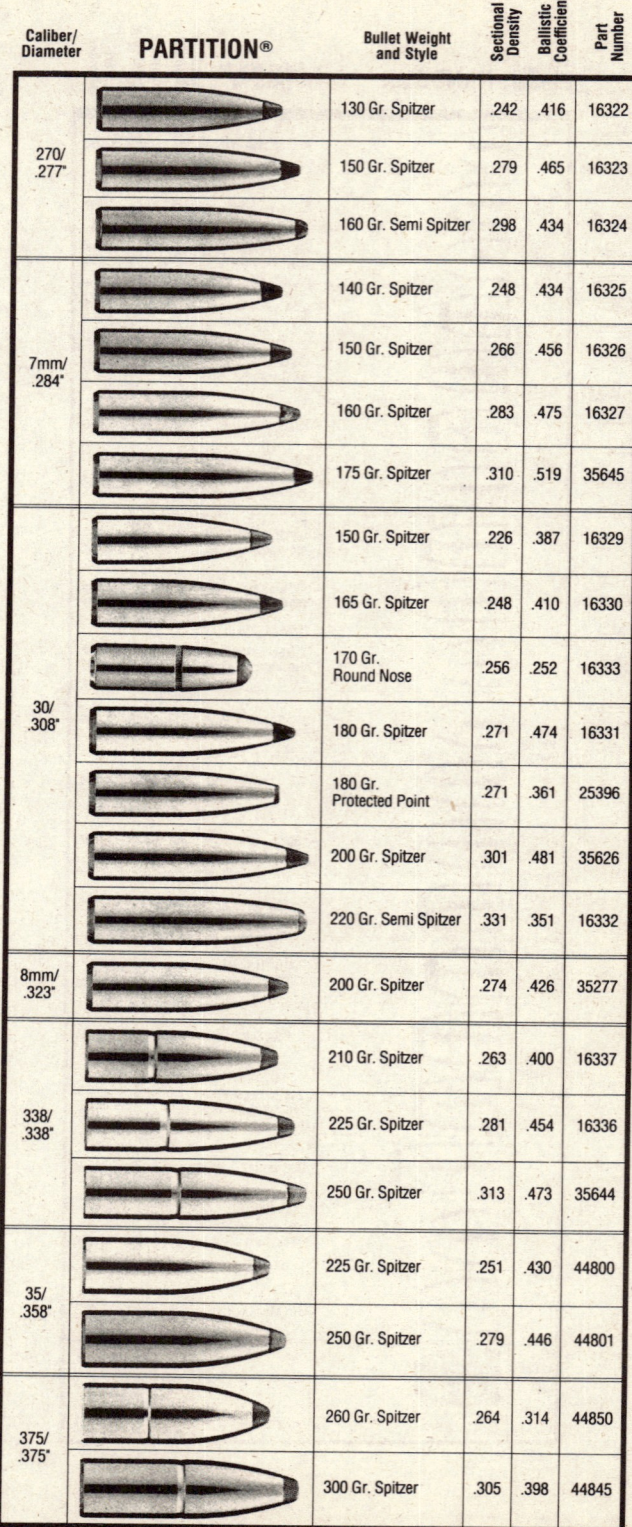

| Caliber/ Diameter | PARTITION® Bullet Weight and Style | Sectional Density | Ballistic Coefficient | Part Number |
|---|---|---|---|---|
| 6mm/ .243" | 85 Gr. Spitzer | .206 | .315 | 16314 |
| | 95 Gr. Spitzer | .230 | .365 | 16315 |
| | 100 Gr. Spitzer | .242 | .384 | 35642 |
| 25/ .257" | 100 Gr. Spitzer | .216 | .377 | 16317 |
| | 115 Gr. Spitzer | .249 | .389 | 16318 |
| | 120 Gr. Spitzer | .260 | .391 | 35643 |
| 6.5mm/ .264" | 125 Gr. Spitzer | .256 | .449 | 16320 |
| | 140 Gr. Spitzer | .287 | .490 | 16321 |

| Caliber/ Diameter | PARTITION® Bullet Weight and Style | Sectional Density | Ballistic Coefficient | Part Number |
|---|---|---|---|---|
| 270/ .277" | 130 Gr. Spitzer | .242 | .416 | 16322 |
| | 150 Gr. Spitzer | .279 | .465 | 16323 |
| | 160 Gr. Semi Spitzer | .298 | .434 | 16324 |
| 7mm/ .284" | 140 Gr. Spitzer | .248 | .434 | 16325 |
| | 150 Gr. Spitzer | .266 | .456 | 16326 |
| | 160 Gr. Spitzer | .283 | .475 | 16327 |
| | 175 Gr. Spitzer | .310 | .519 | 35645 |
| 30/ .308" | 150 Gr. Spitzer | .226 | .387 | 16329 |
| | 165 Gr. Spitzer | .248 | .410 | 16330 |
| | 170 Gr. Round Nose | .256 | .252 | 16333 |
| | 180 Gr. Spitzer | .271 | .474 | 16331 |
| | 180 Gr. Protected Point | .271 | .361 | 25396 |
| | 200 Gr. Spitzer | .301 | .481 | 35626 |
| | 220 Gr. Semi Spitzer | .331 | .351 | 16332 |
| 8mm/ .323" | 200 Gr. Spitzer | .274 | .426 | 35277 |
| 338/ .338" | 210 Gr. Spitzer | .263 | .400 | 16337 |
| | 225 Gr. Spitzer | .281 | .454 | 16336 |
| | 250 Gr. Spitzer | .313 | .473 | 35644 |
| 35/ .358" | 225 Gr. Spitzer | .251 | .430 | 44800 |
| | 250 Gr. Spitzer | .279 | .446 | 44801 |
| 375/ .375" | 260 Gr. Spitzer | .264 | .314 | 44850 |
| | 300 Gr. Spitzer | .305 | .398 | 44845 |

# SIERRA BULLETS

## RIFLE BULLETS

### .22 Caliber Hornet (.223/5.66MM Diameter)

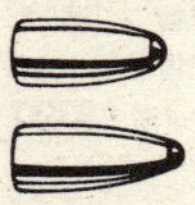

40 gr. Hornet Varminter #1100
45 gr. Hornet Varminter #1110

### .22 Caliber Hornet (.224/5.69MM Diameter)

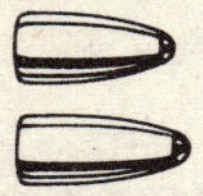

40 gr. Hornet Varminter #1200
45 gr. Hornet Varminter #1210

### .22 Caliber (.224/5.69MM Diameter)

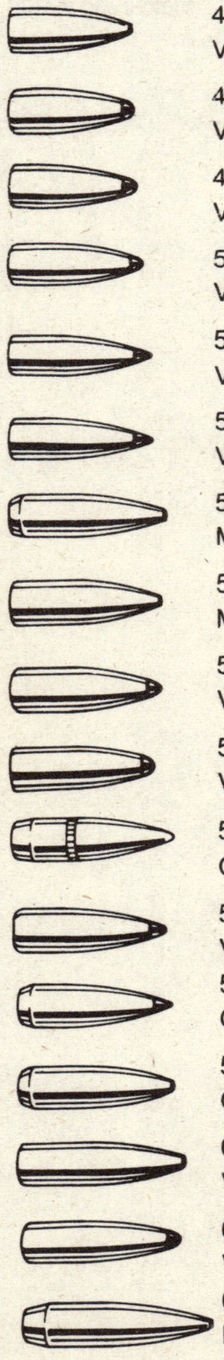

40 gr. HP Varminter #1385
45 gr. SMP Varminter #1300
45 gr. SPT Varminter #1310
50 gr. SMP Varminter #1320
50 gr. SPT Varminter #1330
50 gr. Blitz Varminter #1340
52 gr. HPBT MatchKing #1410
53 gr. HP MatchKing #1400
55 gr. Blitz Varminter #1345
55 gr. SMP Varminter #1350
55 gr. FMJBT GameKing #1355
55 gr. SPT Varminter #1360
55 gr. SBT GameKing #1365
55 gr. HPBT GameKing #1390
60 gr. HP Varminter #1375
63 gr. SMP Varminter #1370
69 gr. HPBT MatchKing #1380
***7"-10" TWST BBLS***

### 6MM .243 Caliber (.243/6.17MM Diameter)

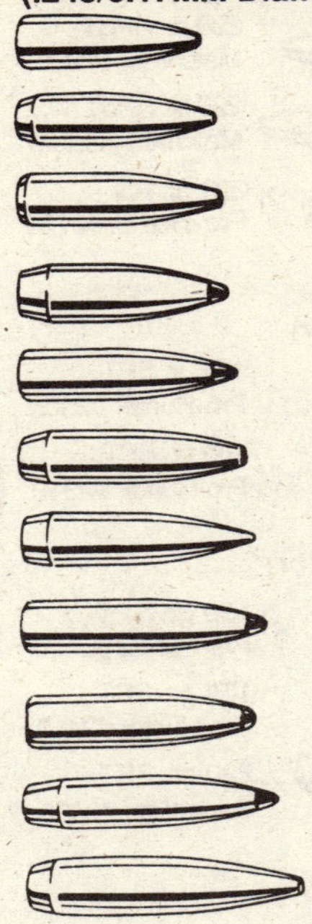

60 gr. HP Varminter #1500
70 gr. HPBT MatchKing #1505
75 gr. HP Varminter #1510
**80 gr. Blitz Varminter #1515**
85 gr. SPT Varminter #1520
85 gr. HPBT GameKing #1530
90 gr. FMJBT GameKing #1535
100 gr. SPT Pro-Hunter #1540
100 gr. SMP Pro-Hunter #1550
100 gr. SBT GameKing #1560
107 gr. HPBT MatchKing #1570
***7"-8" TWST BBLS***

### .25 Caliber (.257/6.53MM Diameter)

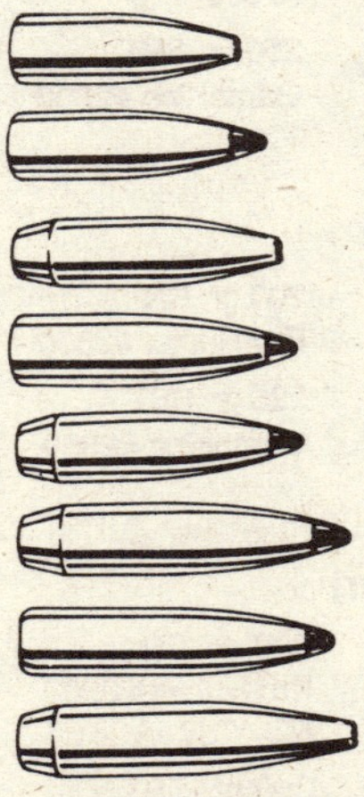

75 gr. HP Varminter #1600
87 gr. SPT Varminter #1610
90 gr. HPBT GameKing #1615
100 gr. SPT Pro-Hunter #1620
100 gr. SBT GameKing #1625
117 gr. SBT GameKing #1630
117 gr. SPT Pro-Hunter #1640
120 gr. HPBT GameKing #1650

### 6.5MM .264 Caliber (.264/6.71MM Diameter)

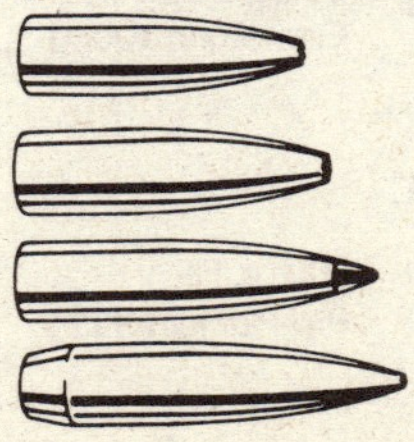

85 gr. HP Varminter #1700
100 gr. HP Varminter #1710
120 gr. SPT Pro-Hunter #1720
120 gr. HPBT MatchKing #1725

### 6.5MM .264 Caliber (cont.) (.264/6.71MM Diameter)

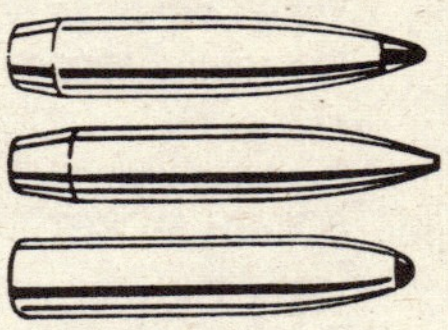

140 gr. SBT GameKing #1730
140 gr. HPBT MatchKing #1740
160 gr. SMP Pro-Hunter #1750

### .270 Caliber (.277/7.04MM Diameter)

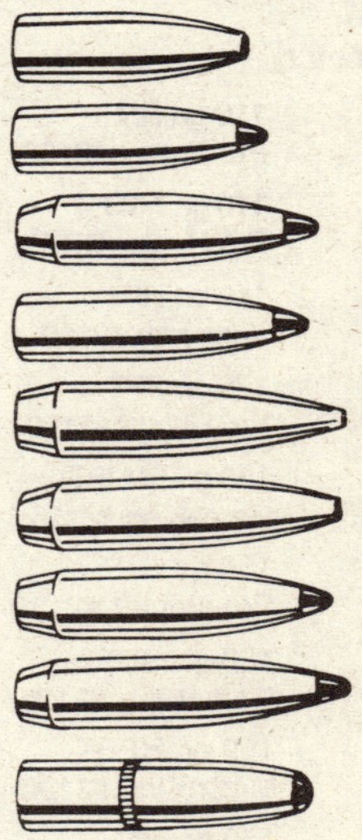

90 gr. HP Varminter #1800
110 gr. SPT Pro-Hunter #1810
130 gr. SBT GameKing #1820
130 gr. SPT Pro-Hunter #1830
**135 gr. HPBT MatchKing #1833**
140 gr. HPBT GameKing #1835
140 gr. SBT GameKing #1845
150 gr. SBT GameKing #1840
150 gr. RN Pro-Hunter #1850

### 7MM .284 Caliber (.284/7.21MM Diameter)

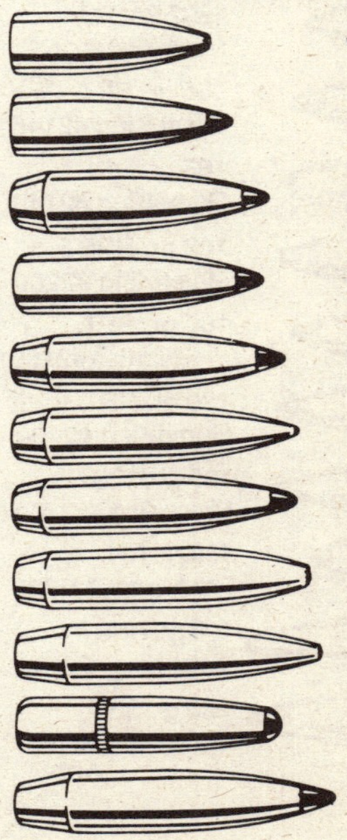

100 gr. HP Varminter #1895
120 gr. SPT Pro-Hunter #1900
140 gr. SBT GameKing #1905
140 gr. SPT Pro-Hunter #1910
150 gr. SBT GameKing #1913
150 gr. HPBT MatchKing #1915
160 gr. SBT GameKing #1920
160 gr. HPBT GameKing #1925
168 gr. HPBT MatchKing #1930
170 gr. RN Pro-Hunter #1950
175 gr. SBT GameKing #1940

# SIERRA BULLETS

## RIFLE BULLETS

### .30 (30-30) Caliber (.308/7.82MM Diameter)

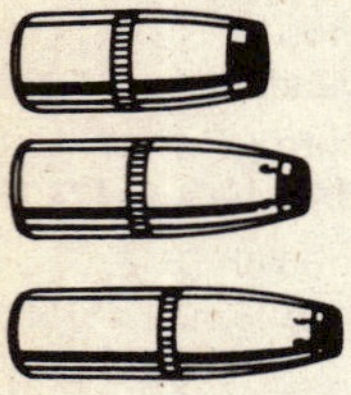

125 gr. HP Pro-Hunter #2020

150 gr. FN Pro-Hunter #2000 POWER JACKET

170 gr. FN Pro-Hunter #2010 POWER JACKET

### 30 Caliber 7.62MM (.308/7.82MM Diameter)

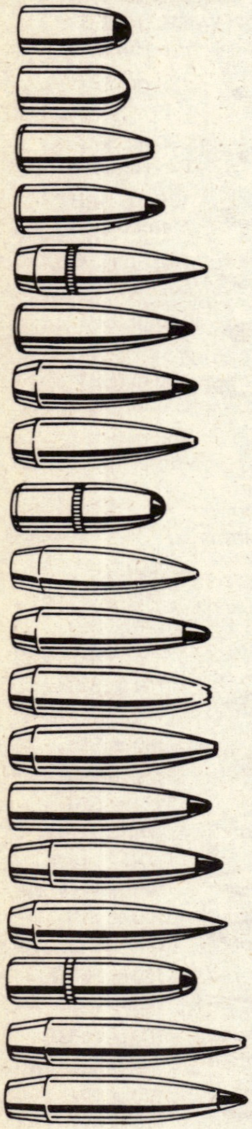

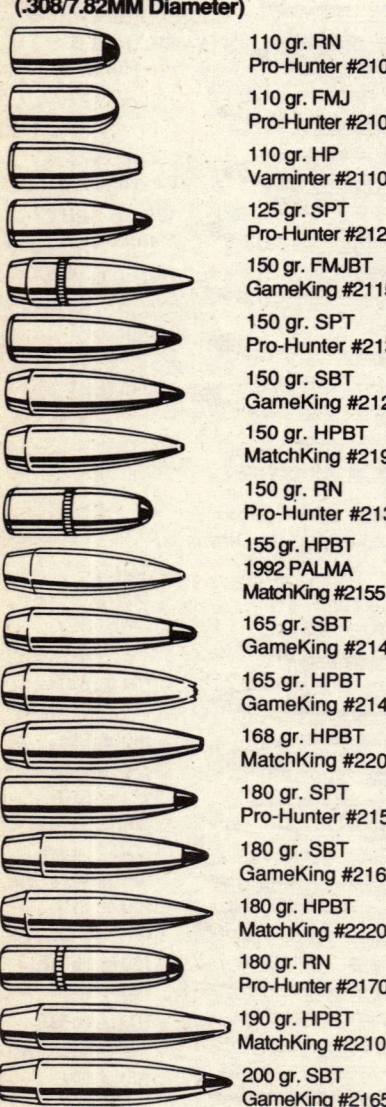

110 gr. RN Pro-Hunter #2100

110 gr. FMJ Pro-Hunter #2105

110 gr. HP Varminter #2110

125 gr. SPT Pro-Hunter #2120

150 gr. FMJBT GameKing #2115

150 gr. SPT Pro-Hunter #2130

150 gr. SBT GameKing #2125

150 gr. HPBT MatchKing #2190

150 gr. RN Pro-Hunter #2135

155 gr. HPBT 1992 PALMA MatchKing #2155

165 gr. SBT GameKing #2145

165 gr. HPBT GameKing #2140

168 gr. HPBT MatchKing #2200

180 gr. SPT Pro-Hunter #2150

180 gr. SBT GameKing #2160

180 gr. HPBT MatchKing #2220

180 gr. RN Pro-Hunter #2170

190 gr. HPBT MatchKing #2210

200 gr. SBT GameKing #2165

### 30 Caliber 7.62MM (cont.) (.308/7.82MM Diameter)

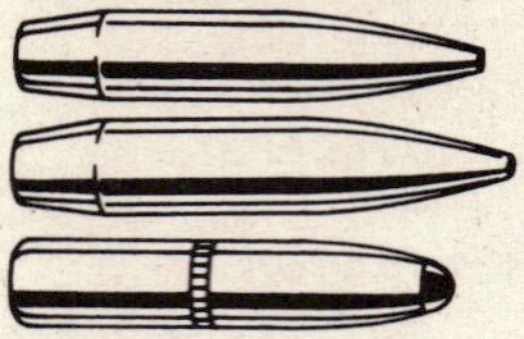

200 gr. HPBT MatchKing #2230

220 gr. HPBT MatchKing #2240

220 gr. RN Pro-Hunter #2180

### .303 Caliber 7.7MM (.311/7.90MM Diameter)

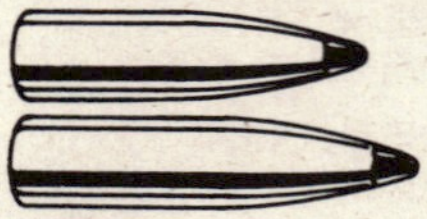

150 gr. SPT Pro-Hunter #2300

180 gr. SPT Pro-Hunter #2310

### 8MM (.323/8.20MM Diameter)

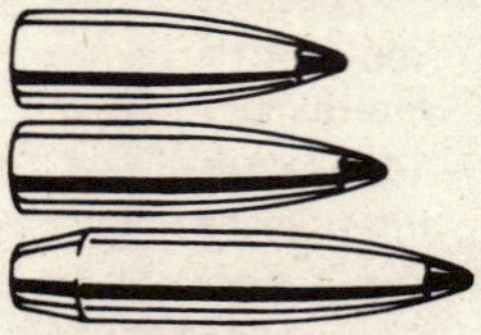

150 gr. SPT Pro-Hunter #2400

175 gr. SPT Pro-Hunter #2410

220 gr. SBT GameKing #2420

### .338 Caliber (.338/8.59MM Diameter)

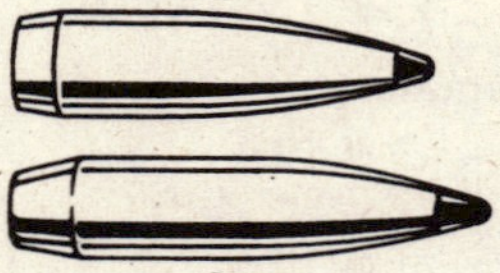

**215 gr. SBT GameKing #2610**

250 gr. SBT GameKing #2600

### .35 Caliber (.358/9.09MM Diameter)

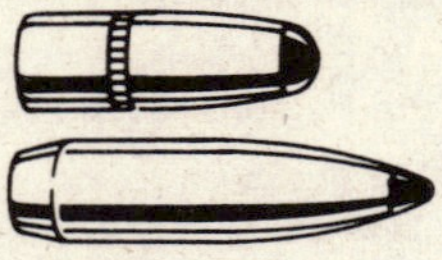

200 gr. RN Pro-Hunter #2800

225 gr. SBT GameKing #2850

### .375 Caliber (.375/9.53MM Diameter)

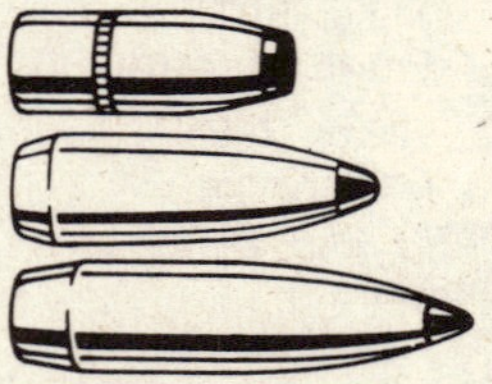

200 gr. FN Pro-Hunter #2900 POWER JACKET

250 gr. SBT GameKing #2950

300 gr. SBT GameKing #3000

### .45 Caliber (45.70) (.458/11.63MM Diameter)

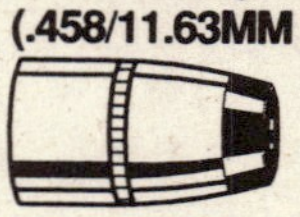

300 gr. HP Pro-Hunter #8900

### *Long Range & Specialty Bullets*

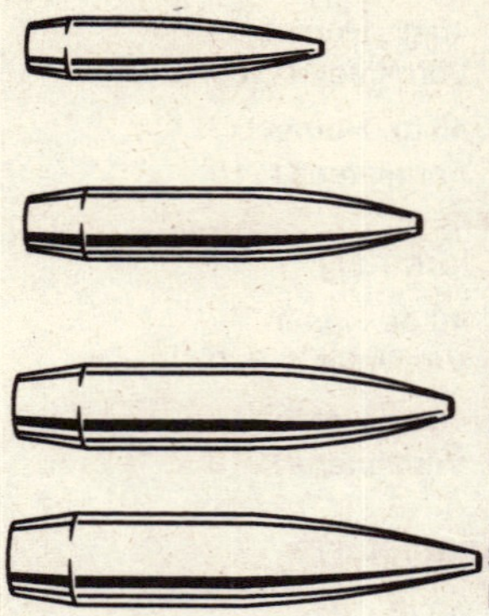

22 Caliber Diameter 80 gr. HPBT MatchKing #9390

6.5MM 264 Caliber 155 gr. HPBT MatchKing #9570

.30 Caliber 7.62MM 240 gr. HPBT MatchKing #9245

.338 Caliber 300 gr. HPBT MatchKing #9300

# SIERRA BULLETS

## HANDGUN BULLETS

**Single Shot Pistol Bullets**

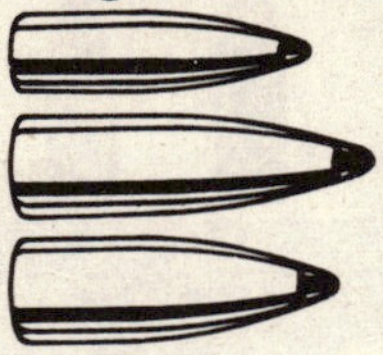

6MM .243 Dia. 80 gr. SPT
Pro-Hunter #7150

7MM .284 Dia. 130 gr. SPT
Pro-Hunter #7250

.30 cal. .308 Dia. 135 gr. SPT
Pro-Hunter #7350

**.25 Caliber**
**(.251/6.38MM Diameter)**

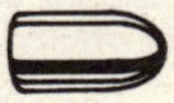

50 gr. FMJ
Tournament Master #8000

**.32 Caliber 7.65MM**
**(.312/7.92MM Diameter)**

71 gr. FMJ
Tournament Master #8010

**.32 Mag.**
**(.312/7.92MM Diameter)**

90 gr. JHC
Sports Master #8030
POWER JACKET

**9MM .355 Caliber**
**(.355/9.02MM Diameter)**

90 gr. JHP
Sports Master #8100
POWER JACKET

95 gr. FMJ
Tournament Master #8105

115 gr. JHP
Sports Master #8110
POWER JACKET

115 gr. FMJ
Tournament Master #8115

125 gr. FMJ
Tournament Master #8120

130 gr. FMJ
Tournament Master #8345

**9MM Makarov**
**(.363 Diameter)**

95 gr. JHP
Makarov #8200

100 gr. FPJ
Makarov #8210

**.38 Super**
**(.356 Diameter)**

.38 SUPER 150 gr. FPJ
Tournament Master #8250

**.38 Caliber**
**(.357/9.07MM Diameter)**

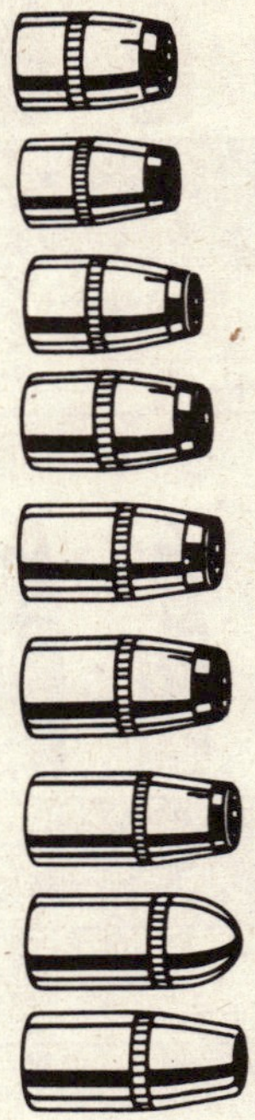

110 gr. JHC Blitz
Sports Master #8300
POWER JACKET

125 gr. JSP
Sports Master #8310

25 gr. JHC
Sports Master #8320
POWER JACKET

140 gr. JHC
Sports Master #8325
POWER JACKET

158 gr. JSP
Sports Master #8340

158 gr. JHC
Sports Master #8360
POWER JACKET

170 gr. JHC
Sports Master #8365
POWER JACKET

170 gr. FMJ Match
Tournament Master #8350

180 gr. FPJ Match
Tournament Master #8370

**10MM .400 Caliber**
**(.400/10.16MM Diameter)**

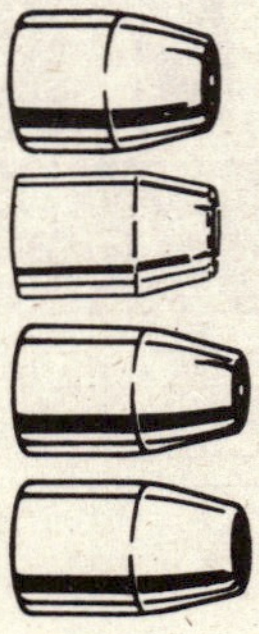

150 gr. JHP
Sports Master #8430
POWER JACKET

165 gr. JHP
Sports Master #8445
POWER JACKET

180 gr. JHP
Sports Master #8460
POWER JACKET

190 gr. FPJ
Tournament Master #8480

**.41 Caliber**
**(.410/10.41MM Diameter)**

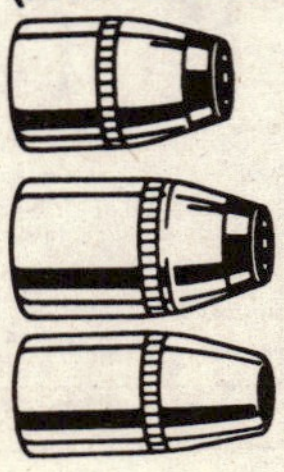

170 gr. JHC
Sports Master #8500
POWER JACKET

210 gr. JHC
Sports Master #8520
POWER JACKET

220 gr. FPJ Match
Tournament Master #8530

**.44 Magnum**
**(.4295/10.91MM Diameter)**

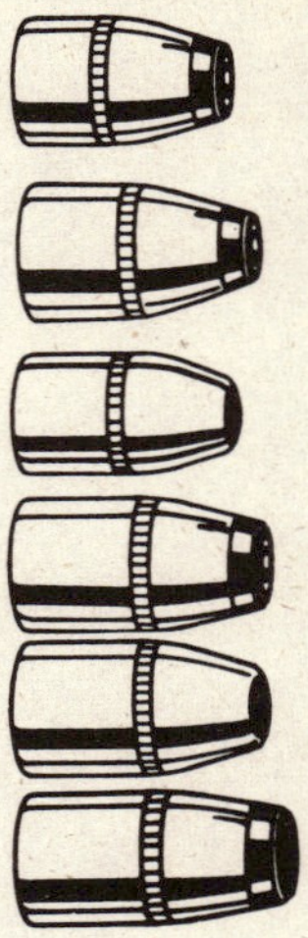

180 gr. JHC
Sports Master #8600
POWER JACKET

210 gr. JHC
Sports Master #8620
POWER JACKET

220 gr. FPJ Match
Tournament Master #8605

240 gr. JHC
Sports Master #8610
POWER JACKET

250 gr. FPJ Match
Tournament Master #8615

300 gr. JSP
Sports Master #8630

**.45 Caliber**
**(.4515/11.47MM Diameter)**

185 gr. JHP
Sports Master #8800
POWER JACKET

185 gr. FPJ Match
Tournament Master #8810

200 gr. FPJ Match
Tournament Master #8825

230 gr. FMJ Match
Tournament Master #8815

240 gr. JHC
Sports Master #8820
POWER JACKET

300 gr. JSP
Sports Master #8830

# SPEER RIFLE BULLETS

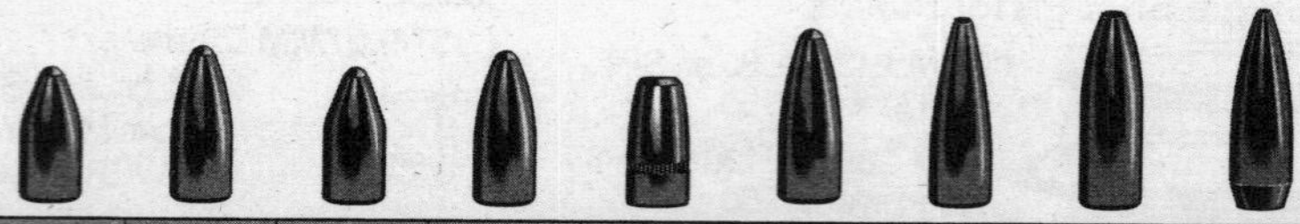

| Bullet Caliber & Type | 22 Spire Soft Point | 22 Spitzer Soft Point | 22 Spire Soft Point | 22 Spitzer Soft Point | 22 218 Bee Flat Soft Point w/Cann. | 22 Spitzer Soft Point | 22 "TNT" Hollow Point | 22 Hollow Point | 22 Hollow Point B.T. Match |
|---|---|---|---|---|---|---|---|---|---|
| Diameter | .223" | .223" | .224" | .224" | .224" | .224" | .224" | .224" | .224" |
| Weight (grs.) | 40 | 45 | 40 | 45 | 46 | 50 | 50 | 52 | 52 |
| Ballist. Coef. | 0.145 | 0.166 | 0.144 | 0.167 | 0.094 | 0.231 | 0.223 | 0.225 | 0.253 |
| Part Number | 1005 | 1011 | 1017 | 1023 | 1024 | 1029 | 1030 | 1035 | 1036 |
| Box Count | 100 | 100 | 100 | 100 | 100 | 100 | 100 | 100 | 100 |

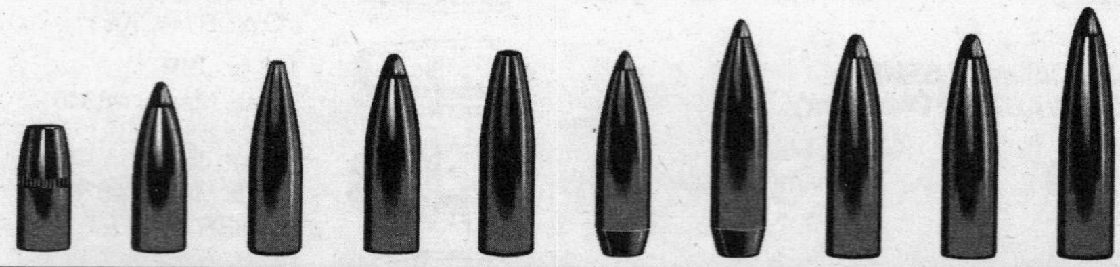

| 25-20 Win. Flat Soft Point w/Cann. | 25 Spitzer Soft Point | 25 "TNT" Hollow Point | 25 Spitzer Soft Point | 25 Hollow Point | 25 Spitzer Soft Point B.T. | 25 Spitzer Soft Point B.T. | 25 Spitzer Soft Point | 6.5mm Spitzer Soft Point | 6.5mm Spitzer Soft Point |
|---|---|---|---|---|---|---|---|---|---|
| .257" | .257" | .257" | .257" | .257" | .257" | .257" | .257" | .263" | .263" |
| 75 | 87 | 87 | 100 | 100 | 100 | 120 | 120 | 120 | 140 |
| 0.133 | 0.300 | 0.310 | 0.369 | 0.255 | 0.393 | 0.435 | 0.41 | 0.433 | 0.496 |
| 1237 | 1241 | 1246 | 1405 | 1407 | 1408 | 1410 | 1411 | 1435 | 1441 |
| 100 | 100 | 100 | 100 | 100 | 100 | 100 | 100 | 100 | 100 |

| 7mm Spitzer Soft Point | 7mm Match Hollow Point B.T. | 7mm Spitzer Soft Point B.T. | 7mm Spitzer Soft Point | 7mm Mag-Tip™ Soft Point | 7mm Mag-Tip™ Soft Point | 30 Round Soft Point Plinker™ | 30 Hollow Point | 30 Round Soft Point | 30 Carbine Round FMJ | 30 Spire Soft Point | 30 "TNT" Hollow Point | 30 Hollow Point |
|---|---|---|---|---|---|---|---|---|---|---|---|---|
| .284" | .284" | .284" | .284" | .284" | .284" | .308" | .308" | .308" | .308" | .308" | .308" | .308" |
| 145 | 145 | 160 | 160 | 160 | 175 | 100 | 110 | 110 | 110 | 110 | 125 | 130 |
| 0.457 | 0.465 | 0.556 | 0.502 | 0.354 | 0.385 | 0.124 | 0.136 | 0.144 | 0.179 | 0.273 | 0.326 | 0.263 |
| 1629 | 1631 | 1634 | 1635 | 1637 | 1641 | 1805 | 1835 | 1845 | 1846 | 1855 | 1986 | 2005 |
| 100 | 100 | 100 | 100 | 100 | 100 | 100 | 100 | 100 | 100 | 100 | 100 | 100 |

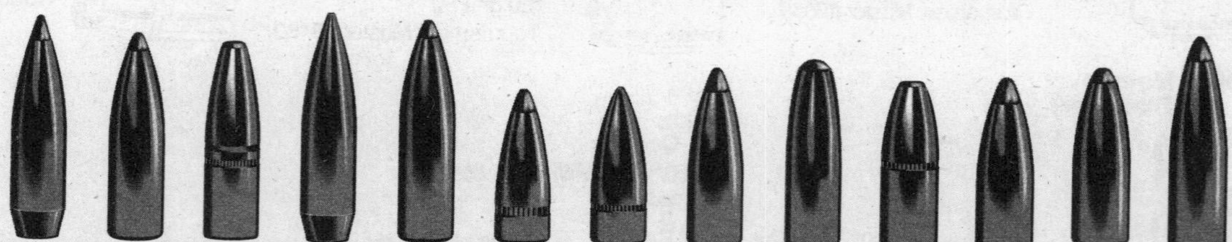

| 30 Spitzer Soft Point B.T. | 30 Spitzer Soft Point | 30 Mag-Tip™ Soft Point | 30 Match Hollow Point B.T. | 30 Spitzer Soft Point | 303 Spitzer Soft Point w/Cann. | 303 (7.62x39) FMJ w/Cann. | 303 Spitzer Soft Point | 303 Round Soft Point | 32 Flat Soft Point | 8mm Spitzer Soft Point | 8mm Semi-Spitzer Soft Point | 8mm Spitzer Soft Point |
|---|---|---|---|---|---|---|---|---|---|---|---|---|
| .308" | .308" | .308" | .308" | .308" | .311" | .311" | .311" | .311" | .321" | .323" | .323" | .323" |
| 180 | 180 | 180 | 190 | 200 | 125 | 123 | 150 | 180 | 170 | 150 | 170 | 200 |
| 0.540 | 0.483 | 0.352 | 0.540 | 0.556 | 0.292 | 0.256 | 0.411 | 0.328 | 0.297 | 0.369 | 0.354 | 0.411 |
| 2052 | 2053 | 2059 | 2080 | 2211 | 2213 | 2214 | 2217 | 2223 | 2259 | 2277 | 2283 | 2285 |
| 100 | 100 | 100 | 50 | 50 | 100 | 100 | 100 | 100 | 100 | 100 | 100 | 50 |

# SPEER RIFLE BULLETS

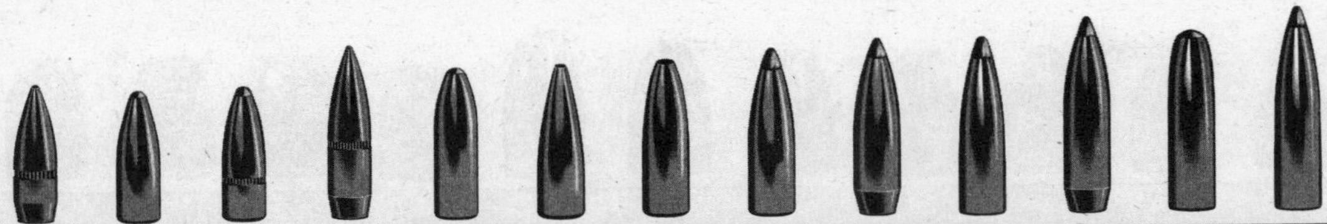

| 22 FMJ B.T. w/Cann. | 22 Spitzer Soft Point | 22 Spitzer S.P. w/Cann. | 22 FMJ B.T. w/Cann. | 22 Semi-Spitzer Soft Point | 6mm "TNT" Hollow Point | 6mm Hollow Point | 6mm Spitzer Soft Point | 6mm Spitzer Soft Point B.T. | 6mm Spitzer Soft Point | 6mm Spitzer Soft Point B.T. | 6mm Round Soft Point | 6mm Spitzer Soft Point |
|---|---|---|---|---|---|---|---|---|---|---|---|---|
| .224" | .224" | .224" | .224" | .224" | .243" | .243" | .243" | .243" | .243" | .243" | .243" | .243" |
| 55 | 55 | 55 | 62 | 70 | 70 | 75 | 80 | 85 | 90 | 100 | 105 | 105 |
| 0.269 | 0.255 | 0.241 | 0.307 | 0.214 | 0.282 | 0.234 | 0.365 | 0.404 | 0.385 | 0.430 | 0.207 | 0.443 |
| 1044 | 1047 | 1049 | 1050 | 1053 | 1206 | 1205 | 1211 | 1213 | 1217 | 1220 | 1223 | 1229 |
| 100 | 100 | 100 | 100 | 100 | 100 | 100 | 100 | 100 | 100 | 100 | 100 | 100 |

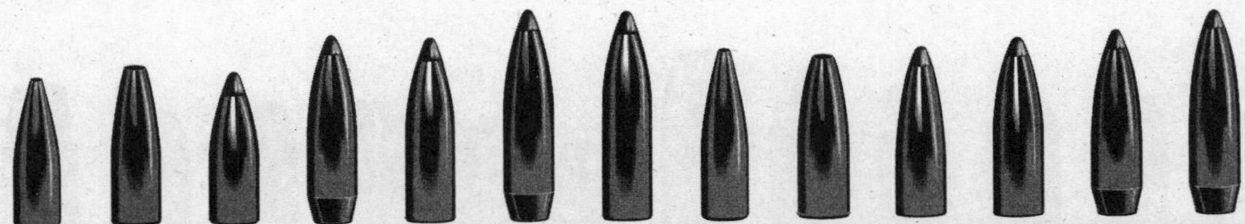

| 270 "TNT" Hollow Point | 270 Hollow Point | 270 Spitzer Soft Point | 270 Spitzer Soft Point B.T. | 270 Spitzer Soft Point | 270 Spitzer Soft Point B.T. | 270 Spitzer Soft Point | 7mm "TNT" Hollow Point | 7mm Hollow Point | 7mm Spitzer Soft Point | 7mm Spitzer Soft Point | 7mm Spitzer Soft Point B.T. | 7mm Spitzer Soft Point B.T. |
|---|---|---|---|---|---|---|---|---|---|---|---|---|
| .277" | .277" | .277" | .277" | .277" | .277" | .277" | .284" | .284" | .284" | .284" | .284" | .284" |
| 90 | 100 | 100 | 130 | 130 | 150 | 150 | 110 | 115 | 120 | 130 | 130 | 145 |
| 0.275 | 0.225 | 0.319 | 0.449 | 0.408 | 0.496 | 0.481 | 0.338 | 0.257 | 0.386 | 0.394 | 0.411 | 0.502 |
| 1446 | 1447 | 1453 | 1458 | 1459 | 1604 | 1605 | 1616 | 1617 | 1620 | 1623 | 1624 | 1628 |
| 100 | 100 | 100 | 100 | 100 | 100 | 100 | 100 | 100 | 100 | 100 | 100 | 100 |

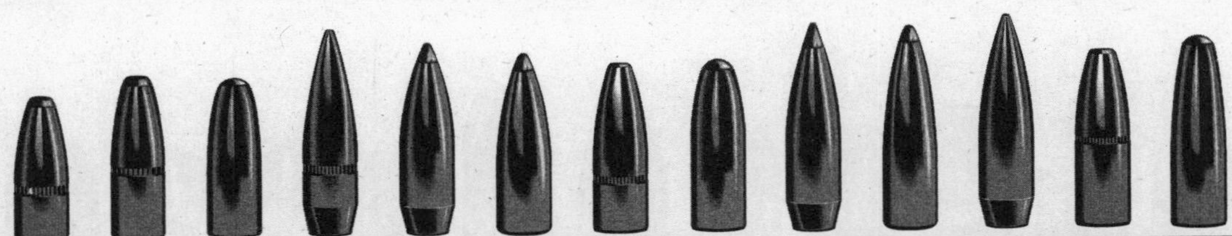

| 30 Flat Soft Point | 30 Flat Soft Point | 30 Round Soft Point | 30 FMJ B.T. w/Cann. | 30 Spitzer Soft Point B.T. | 30 Spitzer Soft Point | 30 Mag-Tip™ Soft Point | 30 Round Soft Point | 30 Spitzer Soft Point B.T. | 30 Spitzer Soft Point | 30 Match Hollow Point B.T. | 30 Flat Soft Point | 30 Round Soft Point |
|---|---|---|---|---|---|---|---|---|---|---|---|---|
| .308" | .308" | .308" | .308" | .308" | .308" | .308" | .308" | .308" | .308" | .308" | .308" | .308" |
| 130 | 150 | 150 | 150 | 150 | 150 | 150 | 165 | 165 | 165 | 168 | 170 | 180 |
| 0.248 | 0.268 | 0.266 | 0.425 | 0.423 | 0.389 | 0.301 | 0.274 | 0.477 | 0.433 | 0.480 | 0.304 | 0.304 |
| 2007 | 2011 | 2017 | 2018 | 2022 | 2023 | 2025 | 2029 | 2034 | 2035 | 2040 | 2041 | 2047 |
| 100 | 100 | 100 | 100 | 100 | 100 | 100 | 100 | 100 | 100 | 100 | 100 | 100 |

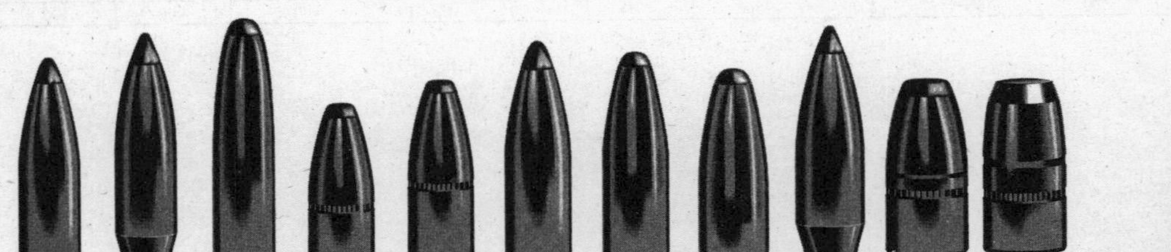

| 338 Spitzer Soft Point | 338 Spitzer Soft Point B.T. | 338 Semi-Spitzer Soft Point | 35 Flat Soft Point | 35 Flat Soft Point | 35 Spitzer Soft Point | 9.3mm Semi-Spitzer Soft Point | 375 Semi-Spitzer Soft Point | 375 Spitzer Soft Point B.T. | 45 Flat Soft Point | 45 Flat Soft Point | 50 BMG FMJ |
|---|---|---|---|---|---|---|---|---|---|---|---|
| .338" | .338" | .338" | .358" | .358" | .358" | .366" | .375" | .375" | .458" | .458" | .510" |
| 200 | 225 | 275 | 180 | 220 | 250 | 270 | 235 | 270 | 350 | 400 | 647 |
| 0.448 | 0.484 | 0.456 | 0.245 | 0.316 | 0.446 | 0.361 | 0.317 | 0.429 | 0.232 | 0.214 | 0.701 |
| 2405 | 2406 | 2411 | 2435 | 2439 | 2453 | 2459 | 2471 | 2472 | 2478*** | 2479 | 2491 |
| 50 | 50 | 50 | 100 | 50 | 50 | 50 | 50 | 50 | 50 | 50 | 20 |

# SPEER HANDGUN BULLETS

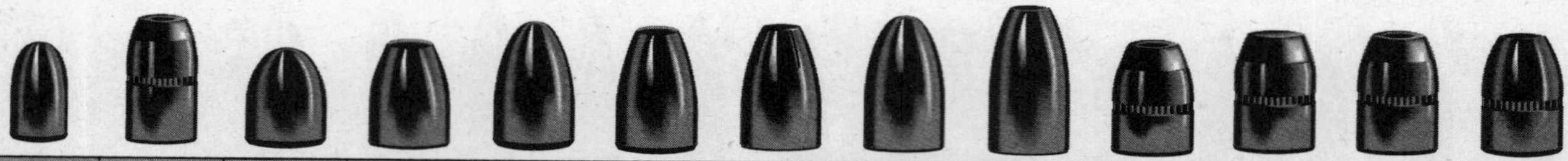

| 25 TMJ | 32 JHP | 9mm TMJ | 9mm JHP | 9mm TMJ | 9mm JHP | 9mm SP | 9mm TMJ | 9mm TMJ | 38 JHP | 38 JSP | 38 JHP | 38 TMJ |
|---|---|---|---|---|---|---|---|---|---|---|---|---|
| .251" | .312" | .355" | .355" | .355" | .355" | .355" | .355" | .355" | .357" | .357" | .357" | .357" |
| 50 | 100 | 95 | 100 | 115 | 115 | 124 | 124 | 147 | 110 | 125 | 125 | 125 |
| 0.110 | 0.167 | 0.131 | 0.111 | 0.177 | 0.118 | 0.115 | 0.114 | 0.208 | 0.122 | 0.14 | 0.135 | 0.146 |
| 3982 | 3981 | 4001 | 3983 | 3995* | 3996 | 3997 | 4004 | 4006 | 4007 | 4011 | 4013 | 4015 |
| 100 | 100 | 100 | 100 | 100 | 100 | 100 | 100 | 100 | 100 | 100 | 100 | 100 |

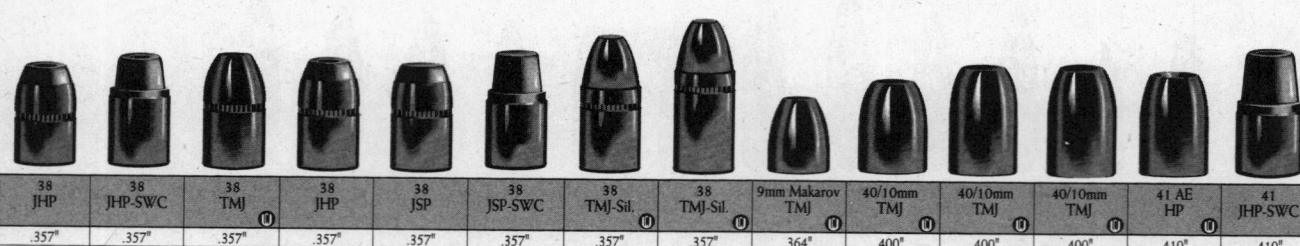

| 38 JHP | 38 JHP-SWC | 38 TMJ | 38 JHP | 38 JSP | 38 JSP-SWC | 38 TMJ-Sil. | 38 TMJ-Sil. | 9mm Makarov TMJ | 40/10mm TMJ | 40/10mm TMJ | 40/10mm TMJ | 41 AE HP | 41 JHP-SWC |
|---|---|---|---|---|---|---|---|---|---|---|---|---|---|
| .357" | .357" | .357" | .357" | .357" | .357" | .357" | .357" | .364" | .400" | .400" | .400" | .410" | .410" |
| 140 | 146 | 158 | 158 | 158 | 160 | 180 | 200 | 95 | 155 | 180 | 200 | 180 | 200 |
| 0.152 | 0.159 | 0.173 | 0.158 | 0.15 | 0.17 | 0.23 | 0.236 | 0.127 | 0.125 | 0.143 | 0.208 | 0.138 | 0.113 |
| 4203 | 4205 | 4207 | 4211 | 4217 | 4223 | 4229 | 4231 | 4375 | 4399 | 4402 | 4403 | 4404 | 4405 |
| 100 | 100 | 100 | 100 | 100 | 100 | 100 | 100 | 100 | 100 | 100 | 100 | 100 | 100 |

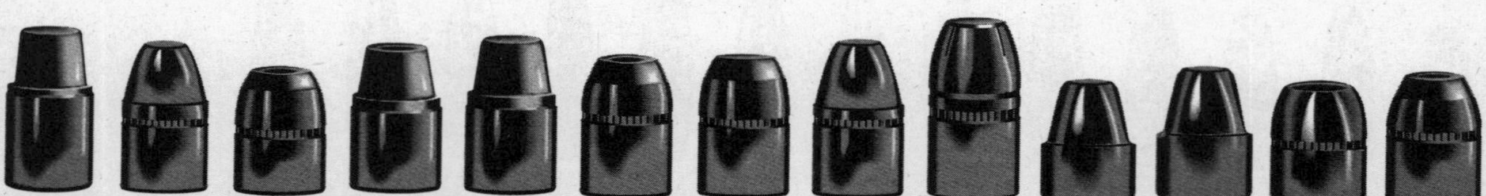

| 41 JSP-SWC | 41 TMJ-Sil. | 44 Mag. JHP | 44 JHP-SWC | 44 JSP-SWC | 44 Mag.JHP | 44 Mag.JSP | 44 TMJ-Sil. | 44 Mag. SP | 45 TMJ-Match | 45 TMJ-Match | 45 JHP | 45 Mag. JHP |
|---|---|---|---|---|---|---|---|---|---|---|---|---|
| .410" | .410" | .429" | .429" | .429" | .429" | .429" | .429" | .429" | .451" | .451" | .451" | .451" |
| 220 | 210 | 200 | 225 | 240 | 240 | 240 | 240 | 300 | 185 | 200 | 200 | 225 |
| 0.137 | 0.216 | 0.122 | 0.146 | 0.157 | 0.165 | 0.164 | 0.206 | 0.213 | 0.090 | 0.129 | 0.138 | 0.169 |
| 4417 | 4420 | 4425 | 4435 | 4447 | 4453 | 4457 | 4459 | 4463 | 4473 | 4475 | 4477 | 4479 |
| 100 | 100 | 100 | 100 | 100 | 100 | 100 | 100 | 50 | 100 | 100 | 100 | 100 |

| 45 TMJ | 45 Mag. JHP | 45 SP | 50 AE HP |
|---|---|---|---|
| .451" | .451" | .451" | .500" |
| 230 | 260 | 300 | 325 |
| 0.153 | 0.183 | 0.199 | 0.149 |
| 4480 | 4481 | 4485 | 4495 |
| 100 | 100 | 50 | 50 |

# SPEER HANDGUN BULLETS

Gold Dot Hollow Point Bullets

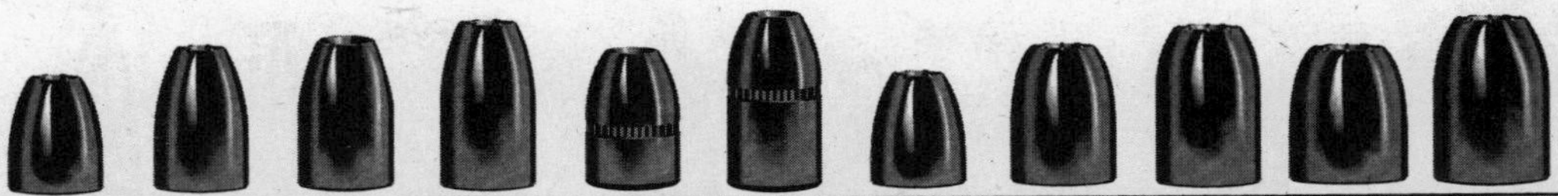

| Caliber & Type | 9mm Gold Dot Hollow Point | 9mm Gold Dot Hollow Point | 9mm Gold Dot Hollow Point | 9mm Gold Dot Hollow Point | 38 Gold Dot Hollow Point | 38 Gold Dot Hollow Point | 9mm Makarov Gold Dot Hollow Point | 40/10mm Gold Dot Hollow Point | 40/10mm Gold Dot Hollow Point | 45 Gold Dot Hollow Point | 45 Gold Dot Hollow Point |
|---|---|---|---|---|---|---|---|---|---|---|---|
| Diameter | .355" | .355" | .355" | .355" | .357" | .357" | .364" | .400" | .400" | .451" | .451" |
| Weight (grs.) | 90 | 115 | 124 | 147 | 125 | 158 | 90 | 155 | 180 | 185 | 230 |
| Ballist. Coef. | 0.101 | 0.125 | 0.134 | 0.164 | 0.140 | 0.168 | 0.107 | 0.123 | 0.143 | 0.109 | 0.143 |
| Part Number | 3992 | 3994 | 3998 | 4002 | 4012 | 4215 | 3999 | 4400 | 4406 | 4470 | 4483 |
| Box Count | 100 | 100 | 100 | 100 | 100 | 100 | 100 | 100 | 100 | 100 | 100 |

HAND-GUN BULLETS LEAD

| Caliber & Type | 32 HB-WC | 9mm | 38 BB-WC | 38 DE-WC | 38 HB-WC | 38 SWC | 38 HP-SWC | 38 RN | 44 SWC | 45 SWC | 45 RN | 45 SWC |
|---|---|---|---|---|---|---|---|---|---|---|---|---|
| Diameter | .314" | .356" | .358" | .358" | .358" | .358" | .358" | .358" | .430" | .452" | .452" | .452" |
| Weight (grs.) | 98 | 125 | 148 | 148 | 148 | 158 | 158 | 158 | 240 | 200 | 230 | 250 |
| Part Number | | 4601 | 4605 | | 4617 | 4623 | 4627 | 4647 | 4660 | 4677 | 4690 | 4683 |
| Bulk Pkg | 4600 | 4602 | 4606 | 4611 | 4618 | 4624 | 4628 | 4648 | 4661 | 4678 | 4691 | 4684 |

**PLASTIC INDOOR AMMO**

| | | Bullets | Cases |
|---|---|---|---|
| No. Per Box | | 50 | 50 |
| Part No. | 38 Cal. | 8510 | 8515 |
| | 44 Cal. | 8520 | 8525 |
| | 45 Cal. | 8530 | See Note |

Note: Shown are 38 bullet and 38 case. 45 bullet is used with regular brass case.

**SHOT SHELL CAPSULES**

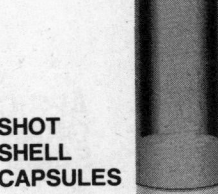

| Empty Capsules with Base Plugs | | |
|---|---|---|
| No. Per Box | | 50 |
| Part No. | 38/357 | 8780 |
| | 44 | 8782 |
| | | |

# SPEER BIG-GAME BULLETS

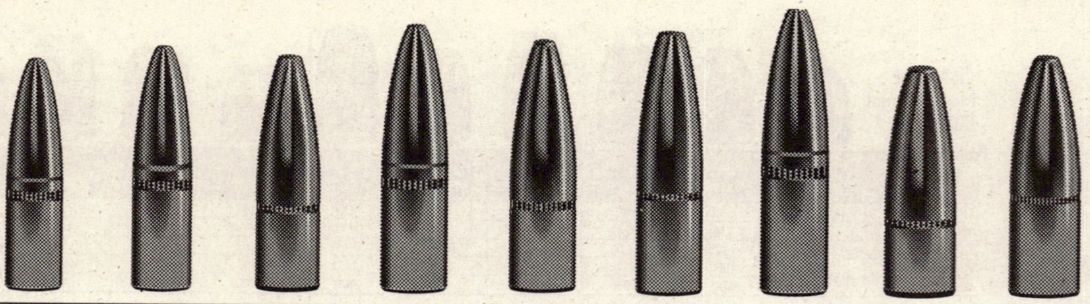

## GRAND SLAM

| Bullet Caliber & Type | 6mm GS Soft Point | 25 GS Soft Point | 270 GS Soft Point | 270 GS Soft Point | 7mm GS Soft Point | 7mm GS Soft Point | 7mm GS Soft Point | 30 GS Soft Point | 30 GS Soft Point |
|---|---|---|---|---|---|---|---|---|---|
| Diameter | .243" | .257" | .277" | .277" | .284" | .284" | .284" | .308" | .308" |
| Weight (grs.) | 100 | 120 | 130 | 150 | 145 | 160 | 175 | 150 | 165 |
| Ballist. Coef. | 0.351 | 0.328 | 0.345 | 0.385 | 0.327 | 0.387 | 0.465 | 0.305 | 0.393 |
| Part Number | 1222 | 1415 | 1465 | 1608 | 1632 | 1638 | 1643 | 2026 | 2038 |
| Box Count | 50 | 50 | 50 | 50 | 50 | 50 | 50 | 50 | 50 |

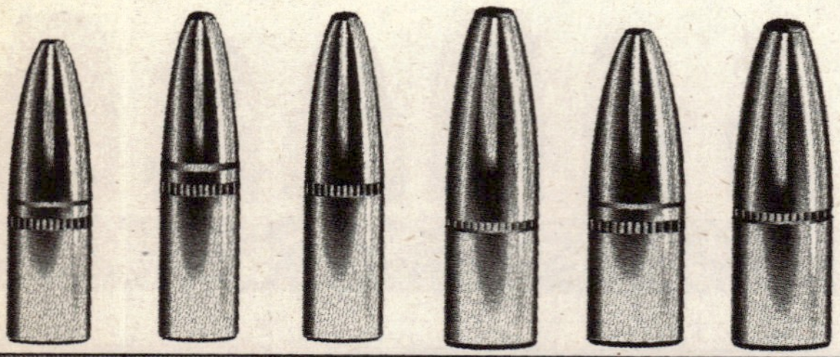

| 30 GS Soft Point | 30 GS Soft Point | 311 GS Soft Point | 338 GS Soft Point | 35 GS Soft Point | 375 GS Soft Point |
|---|---|---|---|---|---|
| .308" | .308" | .311" | .338" | .358" | .375" |
| 180 | 200 | 200 | 250 | 250 | 285 |
| 0.416 | 0.448 | 0.441 | 0.431 | 0.335 | 0.354 |
| 2063 | 2212 | 2226 | 2408 | 2455 | 2473 |
| 50 | 50 | 50 | 50 | 50 | 50 |

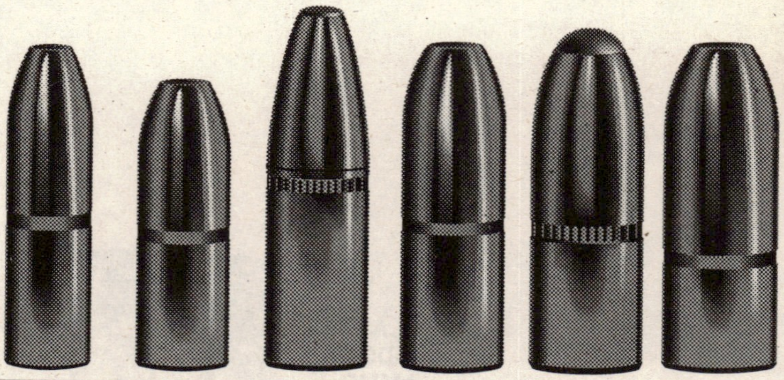

## AFRICAN GRAND SLAM

| Bullet Caliber & Type | 338 AGS Tungsten Solid | 375 AGS Tungsten Solid | 416 AGS Soft Point | 416 AGS Tungsten Solid | 45 AGS Soft Point | 45 AGS Tungsten Solid |
|---|---|---|---|---|---|---|
| Diameter | 338" | .375" | .416" | .416" | .458" | .458" |
| Weight (grs.) | 275 | 300 | 400 | 400 | 500 | 500 |
| Ballist. Coef. | 0.291 | 0.258 | 0.381 | 0.262 | 0.285 | 0.277 |
| Part Number | 2414 | 2474 | 2475 | 2476 | 2485 | 2486 |
| Box Count | 25 | 25 | 25 | 25 | 25 | 25 |

# HERCULES SMOKELESS POWDERS

Twelve types of Hercules smokeless sporting powders are available to the handloader. These have been selected from the wide range of powders produced for factory loading to provide at least one type that can be used efficiently and economically for each type of ammunition. These include:

***BULLSEYE®*** A high-energy, quick-burning powder especially designed for pistol and revolver. The most popular powder for .38 special target loads. Can also be used for 12 gauge-1 oz. shotshell target loads.

***RED DOT®*** The preferred powder for light-to-medium shotshells; specifically designed for 12-gauge target loads. Can also be used for handgun loads.

***GREEN DOT®*** Designed for 12-gauge medium shotshell loads. Outstanding in 20-gauge skeet loads.

***UNIQUE®*** Has an unusually broad application from light to heavy shotshell loads. As a handgun powder, it is our most versatile, giving excellent performance in many light to medium-heavy loads.

***HERCO®*** A long-established powder for high velocity shotshell loads. Designed for heavy and magnum 10-, 12-, 16- and 20-gauge loads. Can also be used in high-performance handgun loads.

***BLUE DOT®*** Designed for use in magnum shotshell loads, 10-, 12-, 16-, 20- and 28-gauge. Also provides top performance with clean burning in many magnum handgun loads.

***HERCULES 2400®*** For use in small-capacity rifle cartridges and .410-Bore shotshell loads. Can also be used for large-caliber magnum handgun cartridges.

***RELODER® SERIES*** Designed for use in center-fire rifle cartridges. Reloder 7, 12, 15, 19 and 22 provide the right powder for the right use. From small capacity to magnum loads. All of them deliver high velocity, clean burn, round-to-round consistency, and economy.

***PACKAGING***

| POWDER | 1-LB CANISTERS | 4-LB CANISTERS | 5-LB CANISTERS | 8-LB KEG |
|---|---|---|---|---|
| Bullseye | ● | ● | | ● |
| Red Dot | ● | ● | | ● |
| Green Dot | ● | ● | | ● |
| Unique | ● | ● | | ● |
| Herco | ● | ● | | ● |
| Blue Dot | ● | | ● | |
| Hercules 2400 | ● | ● | | ● |
| Reloder Series | ● | | ● | |

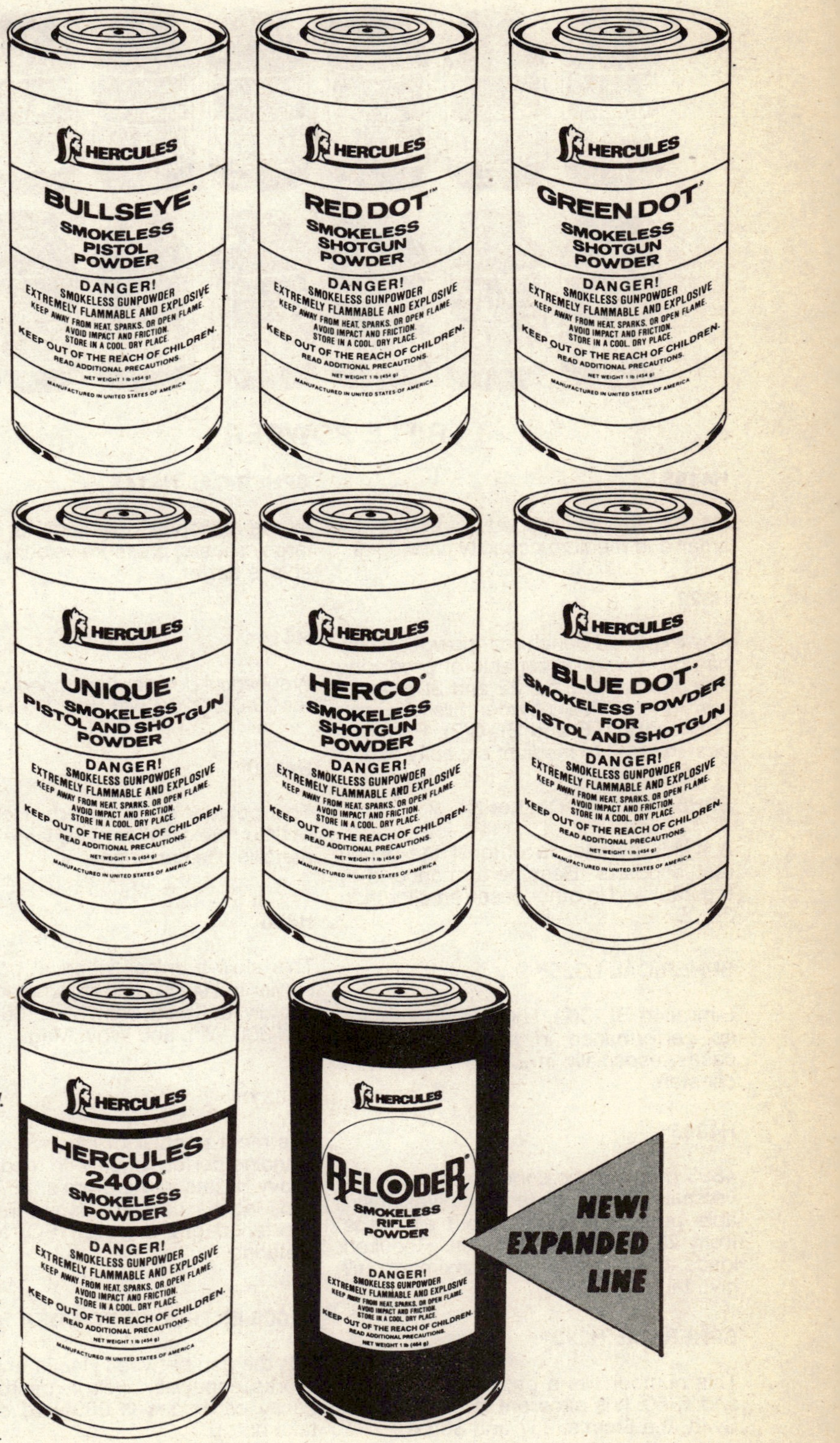

# HODGDON SMOKELESS POWDER

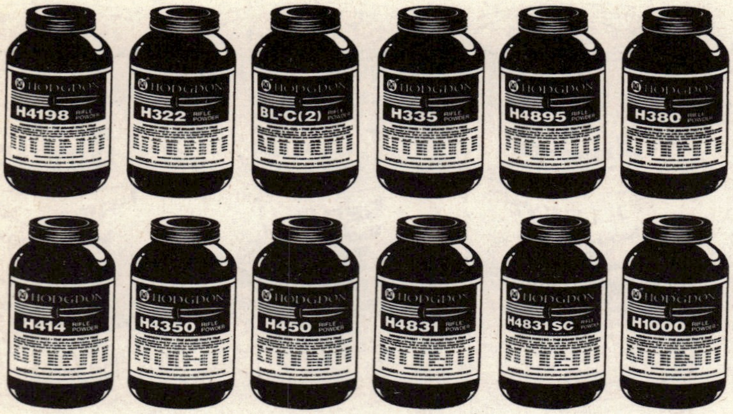


## RIFLE POWDER

### H4198

H4198 was developed especially for small and medium capacity cartridges.

### H322

Any extruded bench rest powder which has proved to be capable of producing fine accuracy in the 22 and 308 bench rest guns. This powder fills the gap betweenH4198 and BL-C(2). Performs best in small to medium capacity cases.

### SPHERICAL BL-C®, Lot No. 2

A highly popular favorite of the bench rest shooters. Best performance is in the 222, and in other cases smaller than 30/06.

### SPHERICAL H335®

Similar to BL-C(2), H335 is popular for its performance in medium capacity cases, especially in 222 and 308 Winchesters.

### H4895®

4895 may well be considered the most versatile of all propellants. It gives desirable performance in almost all cases from 222 Rem. to 458 Win. Reduced loads, to as low as 3/5 of maximum, still give target accuracy.

### SPHERICAL H380®

This number fills a gap between 4320 and 4350. It is excellent in 22/250, 220 Swift, the 6mm's, 257 and 30/06.

### SPHERICAL H414®

In many popular medium to medium-large calibers, pressure velocity relationship is better.

### H414®

A spherical powder developed especially for 30-06, 220 Swift and 375 H&H.

### H4350

This powder gives superb accuracy at optimum velocity for many large capacity metallic rifle cartridges.

### H450

This slow-burning spherical powder is similar to H4831. It is recommended especially for 25-06, 7mm Mag., 30-06, 270 and 300 Win. and Wby. Mag.

### H4831®

The most popular of all powders. Outstanding performance with medium and heavy bullets in the 6mm's, 25/06, 270 and Magnum calibers. Also available with shortened grains (H4831SC) for easy metering.

### H1000 EXTRUDED POWDER

Fills the gap between H4831 and H870. Works especially well in overbore capacity cartridges (1,000-yard shooters take note).

**VARGET®**

- New small extruded grain powder for uniform metering.
- Similar to 4064 in burning speed.
- Higher velocities /normal pressures in popular calibers such as .223, 22-250, .308, .30-06, .375 H&H.
- Ideal use in .22-250.

Available in 1 lb. cans, 5 lb. caddies, and 8 lb. kegs.

## VARGET RIFLE POWDER

### HP38

A fast pistol powder for most pistol loading. Especially recommended for mid-range 38 specials.

### CLAYS

A powder developed for 12-gauge clay target shooters. Also performs well in many handgun applications, including .38 Special, .40 S&W and 45 ACP. Perfect for 1 1/8 and 1 oz. loads.
Now available:
**Universal Clays.** Loads nearly all of the straight-wall pistol cartridges as well as 12 ga. 1 1/4 oz. thru 28 ga. 3/4 oz. target loads.
**International Clays.** Perfect for 12 and 20 ga. autoloaders who want reduced recoil.

### HS-6 and HS-7

HS-6 and HS-7 for Magnum field loads are unsurpassed, since they do not pack in the measure. They deliver uniform charges and are dense to allow sufficient wad column for best patterns.

### H110

A spherical powder made especially for the 30 M1 carbine. H110 also does very well in 357, 44 Spec., 44 Mag. or .410 ga. shotshell. Magnum primers are recommended for consistent ignition.

### H4227

An extruded powder similar to H110, it is the fastest burning in Hodgdon's line. Recommended for the 22 Hornet and some specialized loading in the 45-70 caliber. Also excellent in magnum pistol and .410 shotgun.

# IMR SMOKELESS POWDERS

## SHOTSHELL POWDER

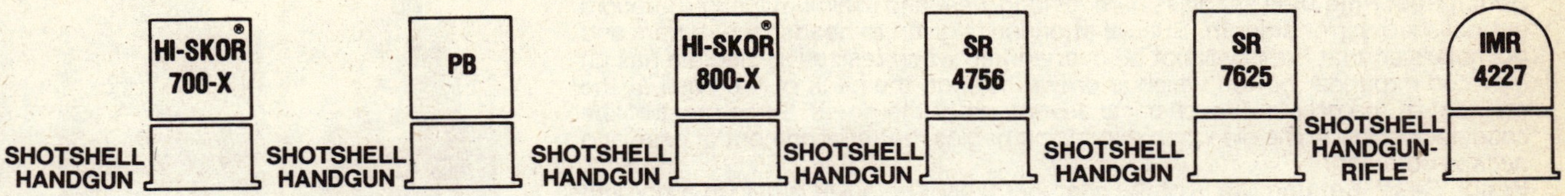


**Hi-Skor 700-X Double-Base Shotshell Powder.** Specifically designed for today's 12-gauge components. Developed to give optimum ballistics at minimum charge weight (which means more reloads per pounds of powder). 700-X is dense, easy to load, clean to handle and loads uniformly.
**PB Shotshell Powder.** Produces exceptional 20 and 28-gauge skeet reloads; preferred by many in 12-gauge target loads, it gives 3-dram equivalent velocity at relatively low chamber pressures.
**Hi-Skor 800-X Shotshell Powder.** An excellent powder for 12-gauge field loads and 20 and 28-gauge loads.
**SR-4756 Powder.** Great all-around powder for target and field loads.
**SR-7625.** A fast-growing favorite for reloading target as well as light and heavy field loads in 4 gauges. Excellent velocity-chamber pressure.
**IMR-4227 Powder.** Can be used effectively for reloading .410-gauge shotshell ammunition.

## RIFLE POWDER

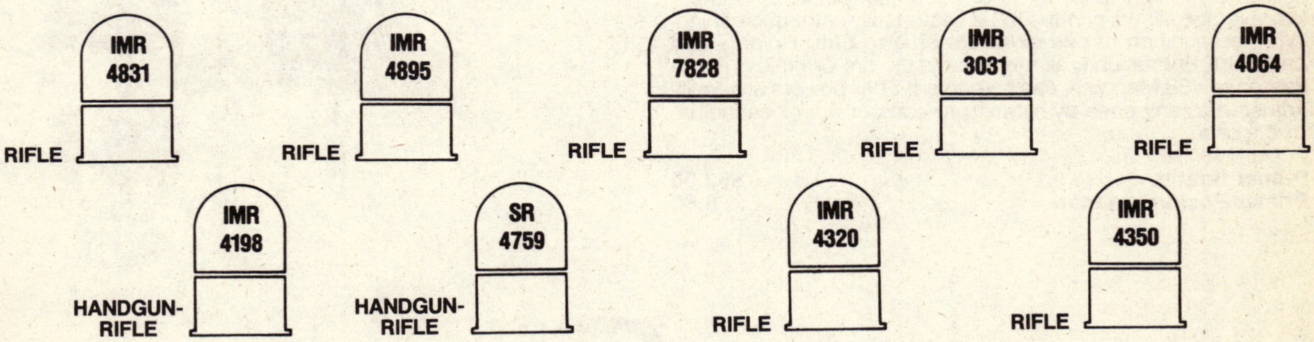


**IMR-3031 Rifle Powder.** Specifically recommended for medium-capacity cartridges.
**IMR-4064 Rifle Powder.** Has exceptionally uniform burning qualities when used in medium and large-capacity cartridges.
**IMR-4198.** Made the Remington 222 cartridge famous. Developed for small and medium-capacity cartridges.
**IMR-4227 Rifle Powder.** Fastest burning of the IMR Series. Specifically designed for the 22 Hornet class of cartridges.
**SR-4759.** Brought back by shooter demand. Available for cast bullet loads.
**IMR-4320.** Recommended for high-velocity cartridges.
**IMR-4350 Rifle Powder.** Gives unusually uniform results when loaded in Magnum cartridges.
**IMR-4831.** Produced as a canister-grade handloading powder. Packaged in 1 lb. canister, 8 lb. caddy and 20 lb. kegs.
**IMR-4895 Rifle Powder.** The time-tested standard for caliber 30 military ammunition; slightly faster than IMR-4320. Loads uniformly in all powder measures. One of the country's favorite powder.
**IMR-7828 Rifle Powder.** The slowest burning DuPont IMR canister powder, intended for large-capacity and magnum-type cases with heavy bullets.

## PISTOL POWDER

**PB Powder.** Another powder for reloading a wide variety of centerfire handgun ammunition.
**IMR-4227 Powder.** Can be used effectively for reloading Magnum handgun ammunition.
**Hi-Skor 700-X Powder.** The same qualities that make it a superior powder contribute to its excellent performance in all the popular handguns.
**Hi-Skor 800-X Powder.** Good powder for heavier bullet handgun calibers.
**SR-7625 Powder.** For reloading a wide variety of centerfire handgun ammunition.
**SR-4756.** Clean burning with uniform performance. Can be used in a variety of handgun calibers.

# FORSTER/BONANZA RELOADING

## CO-AX® BENCH REST® RIFLE DIES

**Bench Rest Rifle Dies** are glass hard for long wear and minimum friction. Interiors are polished mirror smooth. Special attention is given to headspace, tapers and diameters so that brass will not be overworked when resized. Sizing die has an elevated expander button which is drawn through the neck of the case at the moment of the greatest mechanical advantage of the press. Since most of the case neck is still in the die when expanding begins, better alignment of case and neck is obtained.
**Bench Rest® Seating Die** is of the chamber type. The bullet is held in alignment in a close-fitting channel. The case is held in a tight-fitting chamber. Both bullet and case are held in alignment while the bullet is being seated. Crossbolt lock ring included at no charge.

| | |
|---|---|
| **Bench Rest® Die Set** | $65.00 |
| **Weatherby Bench Rest Die Set** | 72.00 |
| **Ultra Bench Rest Die Set** | 80.00 |
| **Full Length Sizer** | 30.00 |
| **Bench Rest Seating Die** | 36.00 |

## PRIMER SEATER
## With "E-Z-Just" Shellholder

The Bonanza Primer Seater is designed so that primers are seated Co-Axially (primer in line with primer pocket). Mechanical leverage allows primers to be seated fully without crushing. With the addition of one extra set of Disc Shell Holders and one extra Primer Unit, all modern cases, rim or rimless, from 222 up to 458 Magnum, can be primed. Shell holders are easily adjusted to any case by rotating to contact rim or cannelure of the case.

| | |
|---|---|
| **Primer Seater** | $62.00 |
| **Primer Pocket Cleaner** | 6.60 |

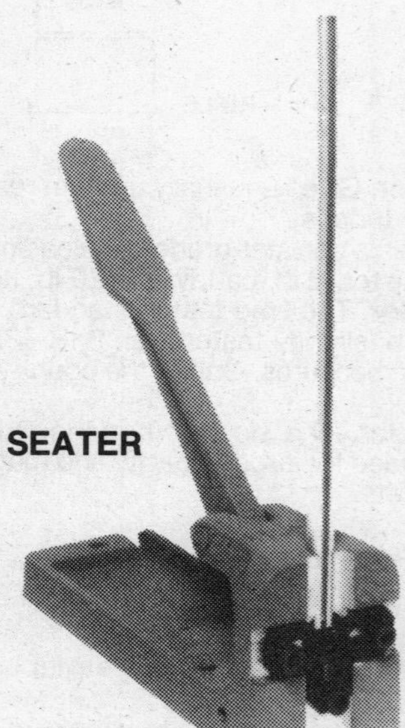

**PRIMER SEATER**

## CO-AX® INDICATOR

Bullets will not leave a rifle barrel at a uniform angle unless they are started uniformly. The Co-Ax Indicator provides a reading of how closely the axis of the bullet corresponds to the axis of the cartridge case. The Indicator features a spring-loaded plunger to hold cartridges against a recessed, adjustable rod while the cartridge is supported in a "V" block. To operate, simply rotate the cartridge with the fingers; the degree of misalignment is transferred to an indicator which measures in one-thousandths.

| | | |
|---|---|---|
| **Price:** | Without dial | $50.00 |
| | Indicator Dial | 58.00 |

# FORSTER/BONANZA RELOADING

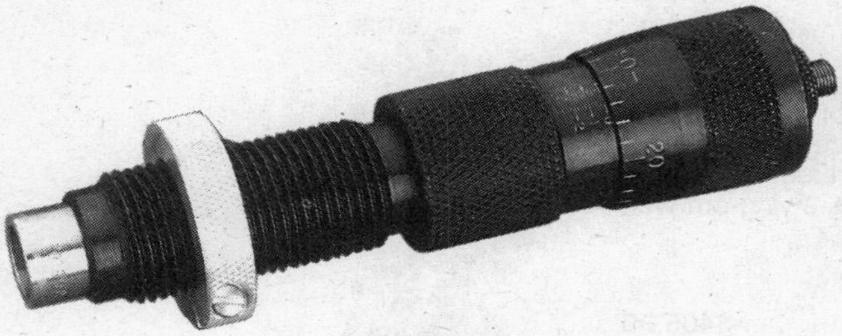

## ULTRA BULLET SEATER DIE

Forster's new Ultra Die is available in 51 calibers, more than any other brand of micrometer-style seater. Adjustment is identical to that of a precision micrometer—the head is graduated to .001″ increments with .025″ bullet movement per revolution. The cartridge case, bullet and seating stem are completely supported and perfectly aligned in a close-fitting chamber before and during the bullet seating operation.
**Price:** . . . . . . . . . . . . . . . . . . . . . . . . . . . . . . . . . . . . **$53.50**

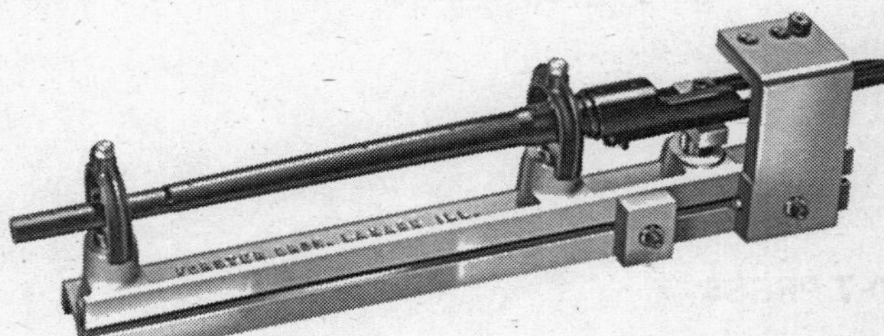

CO-AX LOADING PRESS B-2

## UNIVERSAL SIGHT MOUNTING FIXTURE

This product fills the exacting requirements needed for drilling and tapping holes for the mounting of scopes, receiver sights, shotgun beads, etc. The fixture handles any single-barrel gun—bolt-action, lever-action or pump-action—as long as the barrel can be laid into the "V" blocks of the fixture. Tubular guns are drilled in the same manner by removing the magazine tube. The fixture's main body is made of aluminum casting. The two "V" blocks are adjustable for height and are made of hardened steel ground accurately on the "V" as well as the shaft.
**Price:** . . . . . . . . . . . . . . . . . . . . . . . . . . . . . . . . . . . . **$344.00**

## CO-AX® LOADING PRESS MODEL B-2

Designed to make reloading easier and more accurate, this press offers the following features: Snap-in and snap-out die change • Positive spent primer catcher • Automatic self-acting shell holder • Floating guide rods • Working room for right- or left-hand operators • Top priming device seats primers to factory specifications • Uses any standard 7/8″×14 dies • No torque on the head • Perfect alignment of die and case • Three times the mechanical advantage of a "C" press
**Price:** . . . . . . . . . . . . . . . . . . . . . . . . . . . . . . . . . . . . . . . . . . **$276.00**

BENCH REST POWDER MEASURE

## BENCH REST POWDER MEASURE

When operated uniformly, this measure will throw uniform charges from 2½ grains Bullseye to 95 grains #4320. No extra drums are needed. Powder is metered from the charge arm, allowing a flow of powder without extremes in variation while minimizing powder shearing. Powder flows through its own built-in baffle so that powder enters the charge arm uniformly.
**Price:** . . . . . . . . . . . . . . . . . . . . . . . . . . . . . . . . . . . . . . . . . . **$100.00**

# HORNADY

## APEX 3.0 SHOTSHELL RELOADER

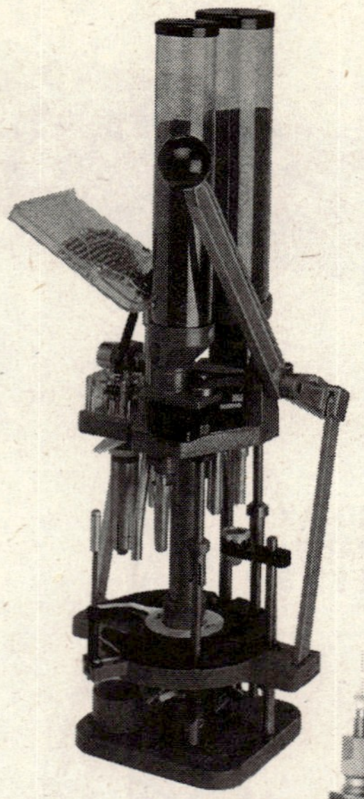

This versatile shotshell reloader has all the features of a progressive press along with the control, accuracy, easy operation and low price tag of a single-stage loader. You can load one shell at a time or seven shells at once, turning out a fully loaded shell with every pull of the handle. Other features include: extra-large shot hopper, short linkage arm, automatic dual-action crimp die, swing-out wad guide, and extra-long shot and powder feed tubes.

**Apex 3.0 Shotshell Reloader (Automatic)**
In 12 and 20 gauge . . . . . . . . . . $405.30
**Apex Shotshell Reloader (Standard)**
In 12 and 20 gauge . . . . . . . . . . 144.95

## 00-7 PRESS

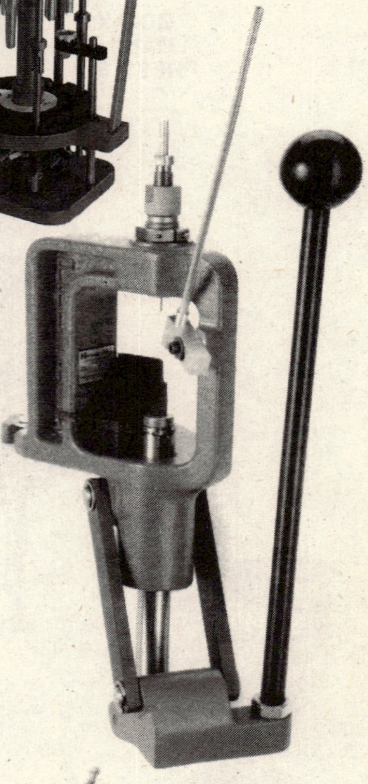

- "Power-Pac" linkage multiplies lever-to-arm power.
- Frame of press angled 30° to one side, making the "O" area of press totally accessible.
- More mounting area for rock-solid attachment to bench.
- Special strontium-alloy frame provides greater stress resistance. Won't spring under high pressures needed for full-length resizing.

**00-7 Press** (does not include dies or shell holder) . . . . . . . . . . $63.25
**00-7 Automatic Primer Feed** (complete with large and small primer tubes) . . . . . . . . . . 19.25

## THE 00-7 PRESS PACKAGE
### A reloading press complete with dies and shell holder

Expanded and improved to include Automatic Primer Feed. It sets you up to load many calibers and includes choice of a basic 00-7 complete with: • Set of New Dimension Dies • Primer catcher • Removable head shell holder • Positive Priming System • Automatic Primer Feed.

**00-7 Package** with Series I & II Dies (14 lbs.) . . . . . . . . . . $158.00
**00-7 Package Series II Titanium Nitride** (15 lbs.) . . . . . . . . . . 170.00
**00-7 Kit** with Series I & II Dies . . . . . . . . . . 325.00
**00-7 Kit** with Titanium Nitride Dies . . . . . . . . . . 339.00

## THE HANDLOADER'S ACCESSORY PACK I

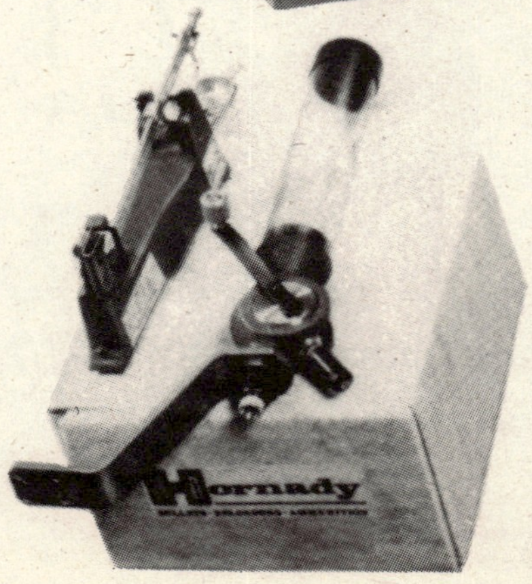


Here's everything you need in one money-saving pack. It includes: • Deluxe powder measure • Powder scale • Two non-static powder funnels • Universal loading block • Primer turning plate • Case lube • Chamfering and deburring tool • 3 case neck brushes • Large and small primer pocket cleaners • Accessory handle. Plus one copy of the *Hornady Handbook of Cartridge Reloading*.

**Handloader's Accessory Pack I** No. 030300 . . . . . . . . . . $175.00

# HORNADY

## NEW DIMENSION CUSTOM GRADE RELOADING DIES

Features an Elliptical Expander that minimizes friction and reduces case neck stretch, plus the need for a tapered expander for "necking up" to the next larger caliber. Other recent design changes include a hardened steel decap pin that will not break, bend or crack even when depriming stubborn military cases. A bullet seater alignment sleeve guides the bullet and case neck into the die for in-line benchrest alignment. All New Dimension Reloading Dies include: collar and collar lock to center expander precisely; one-piece expander spindle with tapered bottom for easy cartridge insertion; wrench flats on die body, Sure-Loc™ lock rings and collar lock for easy tightening; and built-in crimper.

**New Dimension Custom Grade Reloading Dies:**

| | |
|---|---|
| **Series I Two-die Rifle Set** | **$25.95** |
| **Series I Three-die Rifle Set** | **27.95** |
| **Series II Three-die Pistol Set** (w/Titanium Nitride) | **37.00** |
| **Series III Two-die Rifle Set** | **31.50** |
| **Series IV Specialty Die Set** | **52.65** |

## PRO-JECTOR PRESS PACKAGE

- Includes Pro-Jector Press, set of New Dimension dies, automatic primer feed, brass kicker, primer catcher, shell plate, and automatic primer shut-off
- Just place case in shell plate, start bullet, pull lever and drop powder. Automatic rotation of shell plate prepares next round.
- Fast inexpensive changeover requires only shell plate and set of standard 7/8 × 14 threaded dies.
- Primes automatically.
- Power-Pac Linkage assures high-volume production even when full-length sizing.
- Uses standard powder measures and dies.

| | |
|---|---|
| **Series I & II** | **$400.00** |
| **Series II Titanium Nitride Dies** | **415.80** |
| **Extra Shell Plates** | **23.15** |
| **Pro-Jector Kit** with Series I & II Dies | **577.90** |
| **Kit Series III** with Titanium Nitride Dies | **589.50** |

## MODEL 366 AUTO SHOTSHELL RELOADER

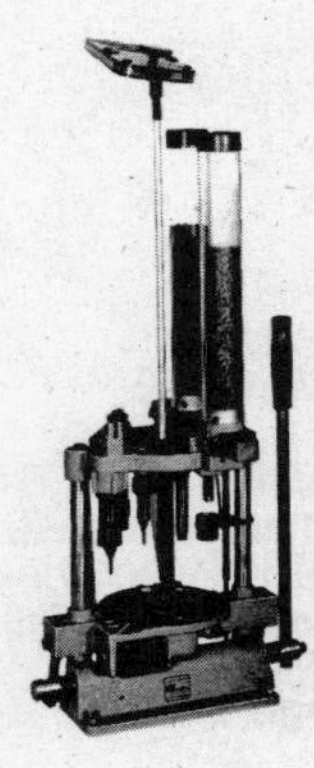

The 366 Auto features full-length resizing with each stroke, automatic primer feed, swing-out wad guide, three-stage crimping featuring Taper-Loc for factory tapered crimp, automatic advance to the next station and automatic ejection. The turntable holds 8 shells for 8 operations with each stroke. The primer tube filler is fast. The automatic charge bar loads shot and powder. Right- or left-hand operation; interchangeable charge bushings, die sets and Magnum dies and crimp starters for 6 point, 8 point and paper crimps.

**Model 366 Auto Shotshell Reloader:**

| | |
|---|---|
| 12, 20, 28 gauge or .410 bore | **$463.00** |
| **Model 366 Auto Die Set** | **93.65** |
| **Auto Advance** | **52.95** |
| **Swing-out Wad Guide & Shell Drop Combo** | **131.60** |

# HORNADY

## M-3 CASE TUMBLER
## $129.00

Twice as large as the M-2 Tumbler, this product will hold up to 1,000 cases (38 Special) for cleaning. Available in 110V and 220C models. A Case Tumbler Sifter (**$11.95**) conveniently separates tumbler media from cleaned shells.

## HORNADY BULLET DISPLAY
## $165.00

This display features every one of Hornady's jacketed and lead bullets currently in production, along with muzzleloading bullets. Contains over 175 bullets in all, including the new A/MAX 50-caliber target bullet. Moulded from handcrafted oak, highlighting target shooters, a muzzleloader, whitetail deer, bighorn sheep and Hornady's slogan: "Our reputation rides on every shot."

## TRIMMER PACKAGE

Combines Hornady's Case Trimmer with the new Metric Caliper and Steel Dial Caliper, which measures case and bullet lengths plus inside/outside diameters. Made from machined steel, the caliper provides extremely accurate measurements with an easy-to-read large dial gauge.

**Trimmer Package** . . . . . . . . . . . . . . . . . . . . . . . . . . . . . . . . . . . . . . . . **$89.95**

# LYMAN BULLET SIZING EQUIPMENT

## MAG 20 ELECTRIC FURNACE

The MAG 20 is a new furnace offering several advantages to cast bullet enthusiasts. It features a steel crucible of 20-pound capacity and incorporates a proven bottom-pour valve system and a fully adjustable mould guide. The improved design of the MAG 20 makes it equally convenient to use the bottom-pour valve, or a ladle. A new heating coil design reduces the likelihood of pour spout "freeze." Heat is controlled from "Off" to nominally 825° F by a calibrated thermostat which automatically increases temperature output when alloy is added to the crucible. A pre-heat shelf for moulds is attached to the back of the crucible. Availalbe for 100 V and 200 V systems.

**Price:** 110 V . . . . . . . . . . . . . . . . . . . . . . . . . . . . . . **$236.00**
220 V . . . . . . . . . . . . . . . . . . . . . . . . . . . . . . **240.00**

## BULLET-MAKING EQUIPMENT

**Deburring Tool**
Lyman's deburring tool can be used for chamfering or deburring of cases up to 45 caliber. For precise bullet seating, use the pointed end of the tool to bevel the inside of new or trimmed cases. To remove burrs left by trimming, place the other end of the deburring tool over the mouth of the case and twist. The tool's centering pin will keep the case aligned . . **$10.50**

**Mould Handles**
These large hardwood handles are available in three sizes single-, double- and four-cavity.
**Single-cavity handles** (for small block, black powder and specialty moulds; 12 oz.) . . . . . . . . . . . . . . . . . **$23.00**
**Double-cavity handles** (for two-cavity and large-block single-cavity moulds; 12 oz.) . . . . . . . . . . . . . . **23.00**
**Four-cavity handles** (1 lb.) . . . . . . . . . . . . . . . . . . . . . **27.00**

**Rifle Moulds**
All Lyman rifle moulds are available in double cavity only, except those moulds where the size of the bullet necessitates a single cavity (12 oz.) . . . . . . . . . . . . . . . . . . . . . . . . . . . . . **$46.95**

**Hollow-Point Bullet Moulds**
Hollow-point moulds are cut in single-cavity blocks only and require single-cavity handles (9 oz.) . . . . . . . . . . . . . . **$46.95**

**Shotgun Slug Moulds**
Available in 12 or 20 gauge; do not require rifling. Moulds are single cavity only, cut on the larger double-cavity block and require double-cavity handles (14 oz.) . . . . . . . . . . . . **$46.95**

**Pistols Moulds**
Cover all popular calibers and bullet designs in double-cavity blocks and, on a limited basis, four-cavity blocks.
**Double-cavity mould block** . . . . . . . . . . . . . . . . . . **$46.95**
**Four-cavity mould block** . . . . . . . . . . . . . . . . . . . . **72.50**

**Lead Casting Dipper**
Dipper with cast-iron head. The spout is shaped for easy, accurate pouring that prevents air pockets in the finished bullet . . . . . . . . . . . . . . . . . . . . . . . . . . . . . . . . . . . **$12.95**

**Gas Checks**
Gas checks are gilding metal caps which fit to the base of cast bullets. These caps protect the bullet base from the burning effect of hot powder gases and permit higher velocities. Easily seated during the bullet-sizing operation. Only Lyman gas checks should be used with Lyman cast bullets.

**22 through 35 caliber** (per 1000) . . . . . . . . . . . . . . . **$23.50**
**375 through 45 caliber** (per 1000) . . . . . . . . . . . . . . **28.50**
**Gas check seater** . . . . . . . . . . . . . . . . . . . . . . . . . . . . **7.00**

**Lead Pot**
The cast-iron pot allows the bullet caster to use any source of heat. Pot capacity is about 8 pounds of alloy and the flat bottom prevents tipping . . . . . . . . . . . . . . . . . . . . . . . **$12.95**

**Universal Decapping Die**
Covers all calibers .22 through .45 (except .378 and .460 Weatherby). Can be used before cases are cleaned or lubricated. Requires no adjustment when changing calibers; fits all popular makes of 7/8×14 presses, single station or progressive, and is packaged with 10 replacement pins **$18.50**

## UNIVERSAL CARBIDE FOUR-DIE SET

Lyman's new 4-die carbide sets allow simultaneous neck expanding and powder charging. They feature specially designed hollow expanding plugs that utilize Lyman's 2-step neck-expansion system, while allowing powder to flow through the die into the cartridge case after expanding. Includes taper crimp die. All popular pistol calibers. . . . . . . . . . . **$46.50**

# LYMAN RELOADING TOOLS

### MAG TUMBLER

This new Mag Tumbler features an industrial strength motor and large 14-inch bowl design. With a working capacity of 2¾ gallons, it cleans more than 1,500 pistol cases in each cycle. The Mag Tumbler is also suitable for light industrial use in deburring and polishing metal parts. Available in 110V or 220V, with standard on/off switch.

**Mag Tumbler** . . . . . . . . . . . . . . . . . . . . . . . . . . . . . . . . . . **$229.95**
**Super Mag AutoFlo** . . . . . . . . . . . . . . . . . . . . . . . . . . . . **230.00**

### TUBBY TUMBLER

This popular tumbler now features a clear plastic "see thru" lid that fits on the outside of the vibrating tub. The Tubby has a polishing action that cleans more than 100 pistol cases in less than two hours. The built-in handle allows easy dumping of cases and media. An adjustable tab also allows the user to change the tumbling speed for standard or fast action.

**Tubby Tumbler** . . . . . . . . . . . . . . . . . . . . . . . . . . . . . . . . . **$58.50**

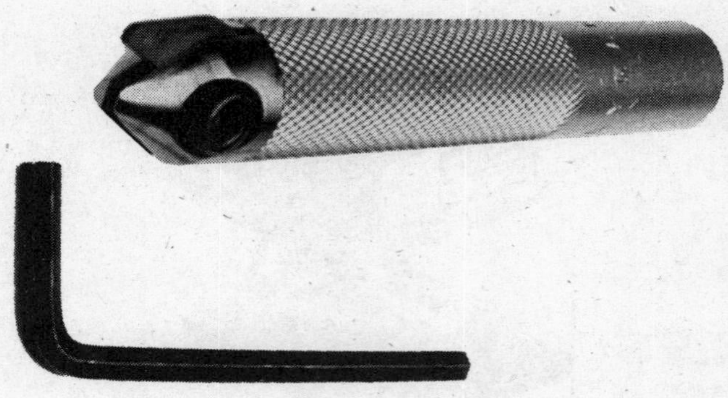

### "INSIDE/OUTSIDE" DEBURRING TOOL

This unique new tool features an adjustable cutting blade that adapts easily to any rifle or pistol case from 22 caliber to 45 caliber with a simple hex wrench adjustment. Inside deburring is completed by a conical internal section with slotted cutting edges, thus providing uniform inside and outside deburring in one simple operation. The deburring tool is mounted on an anodized aluminum handle that is machine-knurled for a sure grip.

**Deburring Tool** . . . . . . . . . . . . . . . . . . . . . . . . . . . . . . . . . . **$13.25**

### MASTER CASTING KIT

Designed especially to meet the needs of blackpowder shooters, this new kit features Lyman's combination round ball and maxi ball mould blocks. It also contains a combination double cavity mould, mould handle, mini-mag furnace, lead dipper, bullet lube, a user's manual and a cast bullet guide. Kits are available in 45, 50 and 54 caliber.

**Master Casting Kit** . . . . . . . . . . . . . . . . . . . . . . . . . . . . . **$144.95**

# LYMAN RELOADING TOOLS

## FOR RIFLE OR PISTOL CARTRIDGES

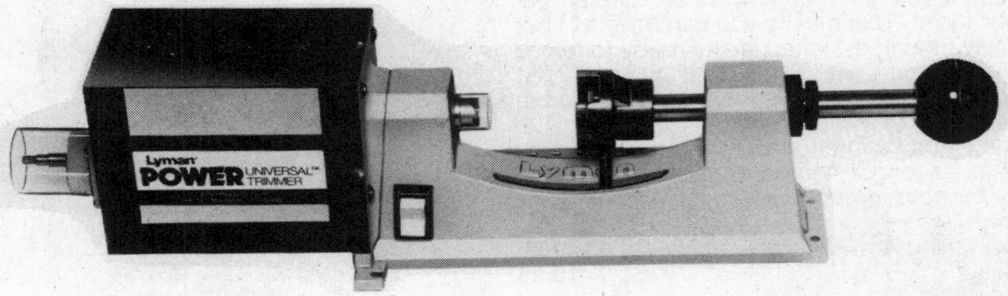


### POWER CASE TRIMMER

The new Lyman Power Trimmer is powered by a fan-cooled electric motor designed to withstand the severe demands of case trimming. The unit, which features the Universal™ Chuckhead, allows cases to be positioned for trimming or removed with fingertip ease. The Power Trimmer package includes Nine Pilot Multi-Pack. In addition to two cutter heads, a pair of wire end brushes for cleaning primer pockets are included. Other features include safety guards, on-off rocker switch, heavy cast base with receptacles for nine pilots, and bolt holes for mounting on a work bench. Available for 110 V or 220 V systems.

**Prices:** 110 V Model . . . . . . . . . . . . . . . . . . . . . . . . **$174.95**
220 V Model . . . . . . . . . . . . . . . . . . . . . . . . **175.00**

### ACCULINE OUTSIDE NECK TURNER (not shown)

To obtain perfectly concentric case necks, Lyman's Outside Neck Turner assures reloaders of uniform neck wall thickness and outside neck diameter. The unit fits Lyman's Universal Trimmer and AccuTrimmer. In use, each case is run over a mandrel, which centers the case for the turning operation. The cutter is carefully adjusted to remove a minimum amount of brass. Rate of feed is adjustable and a mechanical stop controls length of cut. Mandrels are available for calibers from .17 to .375; cutter blade can be adjusted for any diameter from .195″ to .405″.

**Outside Neck Turner** w/extra blade, 6 mandrels . . . **$27.50**
**Individual Mandrels** . . . . . . . . . . . . . . . . . . . . . . . . **4.00**

### ORANGE CRUSHER KIT

Includes "Orange Crusher" Press, loading block, case lube kit, primer tray, Model 500 Pro scale, powder funnel and Lyman Reloading Handbook.

**Starter Kit** . . . . . . . . . . . . . . . . . . . . . . . . . . . . **$149.95**

### LYMAN "ORANGE CRUSHER" RELOADING PRESS (see photo below)

The only press for rifle or pistol cartridges that offers the advantage of powerful compound leverage combined with a true Magnum press opening. A unique handle design transfers power easily where you want it to the center of the ram. A 4½-inch press opening accommodates even the largest cartridges.

**"Orange Crusher" Press:**
With Priming Arm and Catcher . . . . . . . . . . . . . . . . . **$99.95**

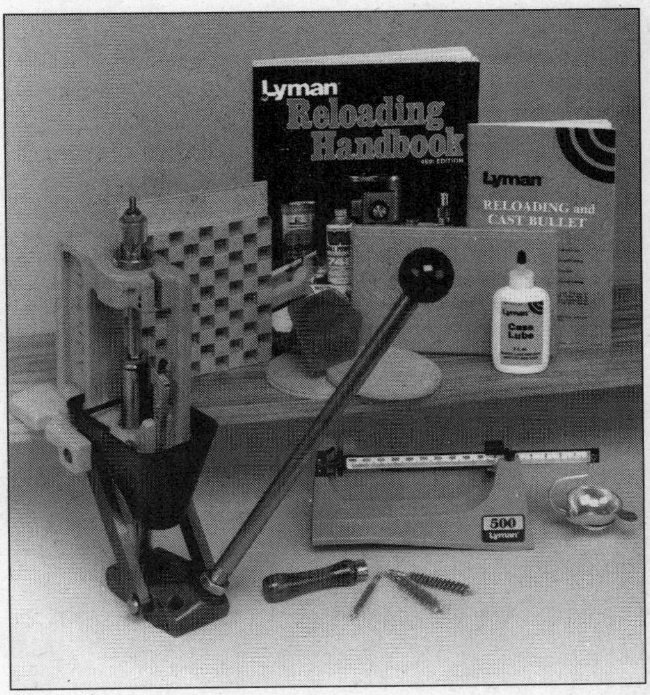


STARTER KIT

# LYMAN RELOADING TOOLS

## T-MAG II TURRET RELOADING PRESS

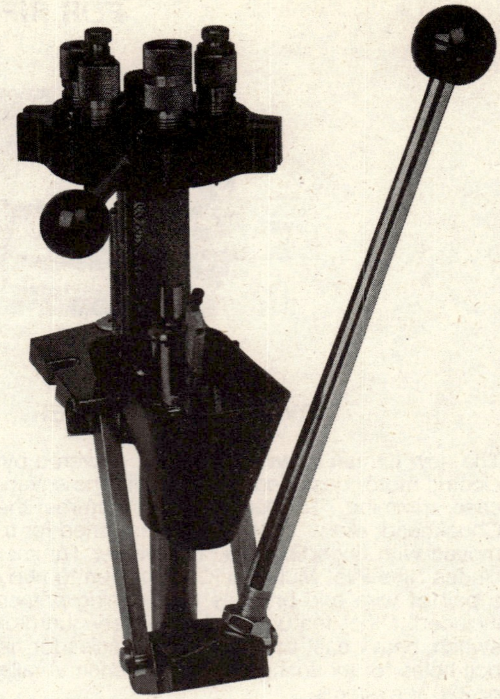

With the new T-Mag II you can mount up to six different reloading dies on our turret. This means you can have all your dies set up, precisely mounted, locked in and ready to reload at all times. The T-Mag works with all $\frac{7}{8} \times 14$ dies. The T-Mag II turret with its quick-disconnect release system is held in rock-solid alignment by a $\frac{3}{4}$-inch steel stud.

Also featured is Lyman's Orange Crusher compound leverage system. It has a longer handle with a ball-type knob that mounts easily for right- or left-handed operation.

**T-Mag II Press** w/Priming Arm & Catcher ....... **$144.95**
Extra Turret Head ........................ **19.95**

Also available:
**EXPERT KIT** that includes T-MAG II Press, Universal Case Trimmer and pilot Multi-Pak, Model 500 powder scale and Model 50 powder measure, plus accessories and Reloading Manual.

Available in calibers 9mm Luger, 38/357, 44 Mag., 45 ACP and 30-06 .................. **$330.00**

## ELECTRONIC SCALE MODEL LE: 1000

Accurate to $\frac{1}{10}$ grain, Lyman's new LE: 1000 measures up to 1000 grains of powder and easily converts to the gram mode for metric measurements. The push-botton automatic calibration feature eliminates the need for calibrating with a screwdriver. The scale works off a single 9V battery or AC power adaptor (included with each scale). Its compact design allows the LE: 1000 to be carried to the field easily. A sculpted carrying case is optional. 110 Volt or 220 Volt.

**Model LE: 1000 Electronic Scale** .............. **$283.25**
**Model LE: 300 Electronic Scale** ............... **165.00**

## PISTOL ACCUMEASURE

Lyman's Pistol AccuMeasure uses changeable brass rotors pre-drilled to drop precise charges of ball and flake pistol propellants (the tool is not intended for use with long grain IMR-type powders). Most of the rotors are drilled with two cavities for maximum accuracy and consistency. The brass operating handle, which can be shifted for left or right hand operation, can be removed. The Pistol AccuMeasure can be mounted on all turret and single station presses; it can also be hand held with no loss of accuracy.

**Pistol AccuMeasure** w/3-rotor starter kit ......... **$33.25**

Also available:
**ROTOR SELECTION SET** including 12 dual-cavity rotors and 4 single-cavity units. Enables reloaders to throw a variety of charges for all pistol calibers through 45 .......... **$46.00**

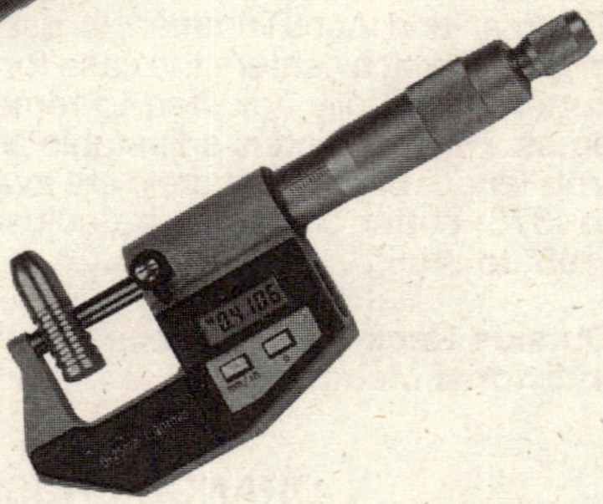

**ELECTRONIC DIGITAL MICROMETER**
**$84.95**

# LYMAN RELOADING TOOLS

**DRILL PRESS CASE TRIMMER**

Intended for competitive shooters, varmint hunters, and other sportsmen who use large amounts of reloaded ammunition, this new drill press case trimmer consists of the Universal® Chuckhead, a cutter shaft adapted for use in a drill press, and two quick-change cutter heads. Its two major advantages are speed and accuracy. An experienced operator can trim several hundred cases in a hour, and each will be trimmed to a precise length.

**Drill Press Case Trimmer** . . . . . . . . . . . . . . . . . . . . **$44.00**

## AUTO TRICKLER (not shown)

This unique device allows reloaders to trickle the last few grains of powder automatically into their scale powder pans. The Auto-Trickler features vertical and horizontal height adjustments, enabling its use with both mechanical and the new electronic scales. It also offers a simple push-button operation. The powder reservoir is easily removed for cleaning. Handles all conventional ball, stick or flare powder types.

**Auto-Trickler** . . . . . . . . . . . . . . . . . . . . . . . . . . . **$36.50**

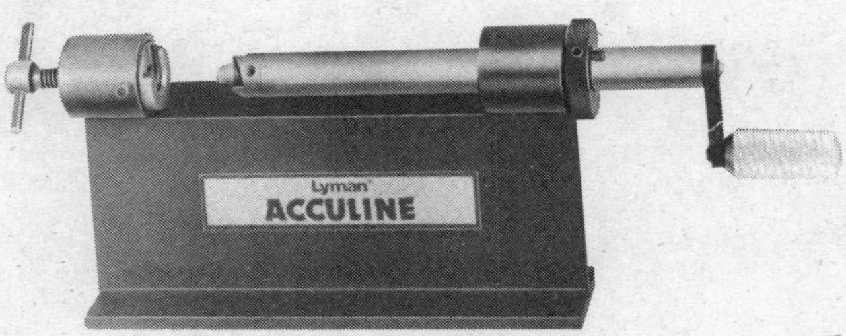


## ACCU TRIMMER

Lyman's Accu Trimmer can be used for all rifle and pistol cases from 22 to 458 Winchester Magnum. Standard shellholders are used to position the case, and the trimmer incorporates standard Lyman cutter heads and pilots. Mounting options include bolting to a bench, C-clamp or vise.

**Accu Trimmer** w/9-pilot multi-pak . . . . . . . . . . . . . **$38.95**

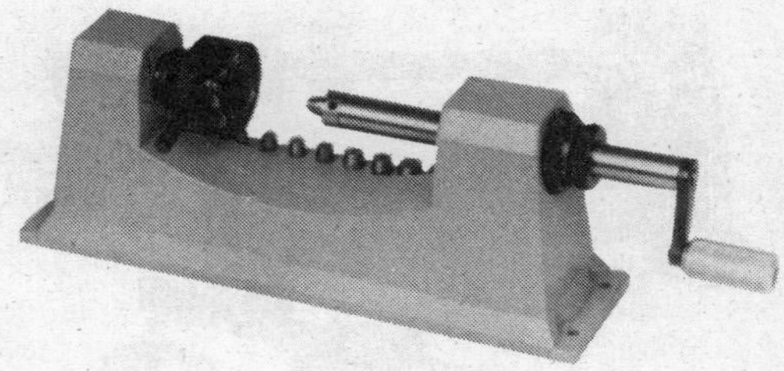

## UNIVERSAL TRIMMER WITH NINE PILOT MULTI-PACK

This trimmer with patented chuckhead accepts all metallic rifle or pistol cases, regardless of rim thickness. To change calibers, simply change the case head pilot. Other features include coarse and fine cutter adjustments, an oil-impregnated bronze bearing, and a rugged cast base to assure precision alignment and years of service. Optional carbide cutter available. Trimmer Stop Ring includes 20 indicators as reference marks.

Replacement carbide cutter . . . . . . . . . . . . . . . . . . . **$39.95**
**Trimmer Multi-Pack** (incl. 9 pilots: 22, 24, 27, 28/7mm, 30, 9mm, 35, 44 and 45A . . . . . . . . . . . . . . . . . . . . **63.95**
**Nine Pilot Multi-Pack** . . . . . . . . . . . . . . . . . . . . . . **9.95**
**Power Pack Trimmer** . . . . . . . . . . . . . . . . . . . . . . **74.95**
**Universal Trimmer Power Adapter** . . . . . . . . . . . . . **15.95**

## UNIVERSAL TRIMMER POWER ADAPTER

## ELECTRONIC DIGITAL CALIPER (not shown)

Lyman's 6″ electronic caliper gives a direct digital readout for both inches and millimeters and can perform both inside and outside depth measurements. Its zeroing function allows the user to select zeroing dimensions and sort parts or cases by their plus or minus variation. The caliper works on a single, standard 1.5 volt silver oxide battery and comes with a fitted wooden storage case.

**Electronic Caliper** . . . . . . . . . . . . . . . . . . . . . . . . . **$84.95**

# LYMAN RELOADING TOOLS

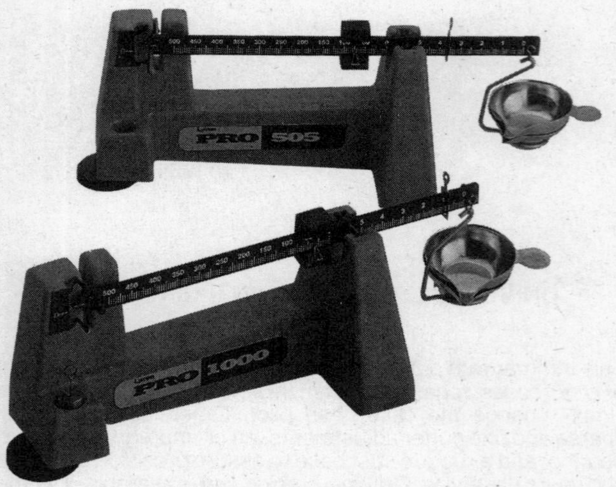


## PRO 1000 & 505 RELOADING SCALES

Features include improved platform system; hi-tech base design of high-impact styrene; extra-large, smooth leveling wheel; dual agate bearings; larger damper for fast zeroing; built-in counter weight compartment; easy-to-read beam.

**PRO 1000 SCALE** . . . . . . . . . . . . . . . . . . . . . . . . **$54.95**
**PRO 505 SCALE** . . . . . . . . . . . . . . . . . . . . . . . . . . **37.50**

## AUTOSCALE

After setting this new autoscale to the desired powder charge, it dispenses the exact amount of powder with the push of a button, over and over again. Features solid-state electronics and is controlled by a photo transistor to ensure accurate powder charges.

**AUTOSCALE** . . . . . . . . . . . . . . . . . . . . . . . . . . . . **$296.00**

## POWER DEBURRING KIT

Features a high torque, rechargeable power driver plus a complete set of accessories, including inside and outside deburr tools, large and small reamers and cleaners and case neck brushes. No threading or chucking required. Set also includes battery recharger and standard flat and phillips driver bits.

**POWER DEBURRING KIT** . . . . . . . . . . . . . . . . . . . . **$54.95**

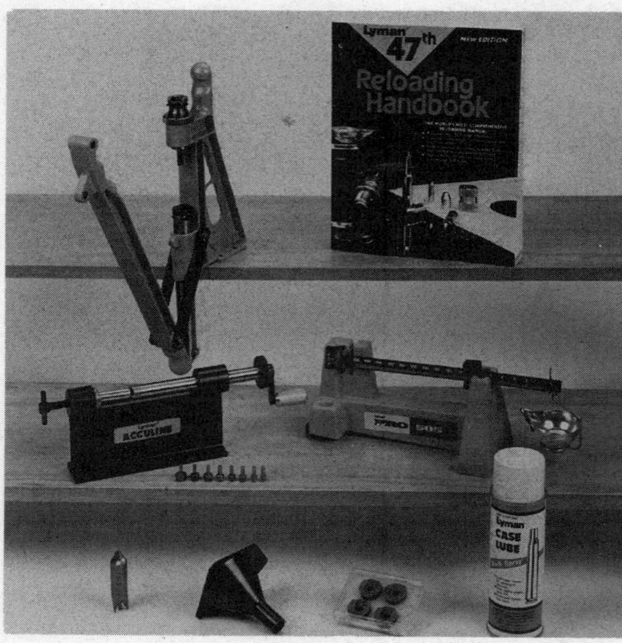


## DELUXE RELOADERS PRO KIT

Includes Accupress with compound leverage; Pro 505 Scale; Accutrimmer with 9 popular pilots; ram prime die; deburr tool; powder funnel; Quick Spray case lube; shellholders (4); Lyman's 47th Reloading Handbook.

**DELUXE RELOADERS PRO KIT** . . . . . . . . . . . . . . . **$129.95**

# MEC SHOTSHELL RELOADERS

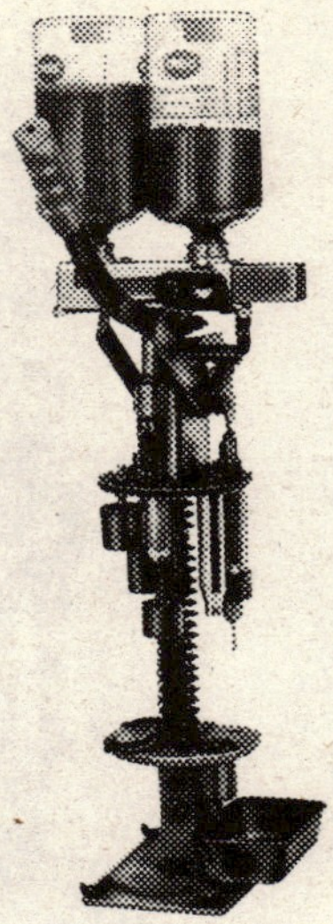

**MODEL 600 JR. MARK 5**
**$162.62**

This single-stage reloader features a cam-action crimp die to ensure that each shell returns to its original condition. MEC's 600 Jr. Mark 5 can load 8 to 10 boxes per hour and can be updated with the 285 CA primer feed. Press is adjustable for 3″ shells. Die sets are available in all gauges at: . . . . **$59.50**

**MODEL 8567 GRABBER**
**$458.78**

This reloader features 12 different operations at all 6 stations, producing finished shells with each stroke of the handle. It includes a fully automatic primer feed and Auto-Cycle charging, plus MEC's exclusive 3-stage crimp. The "Power Ring" resizer ensures consistent, accurately sized shells without interrupting the reloading sequence. Simply put in the wads and shell casings, then remove the loaded shells with each pull of the handle. Optional kits to load 3″ shells and steel shot make this reloader tops in its field. Resizes high and low base shells. Available in 12, 16, 20, 28 gauge and.410 bore. No die sets are available.

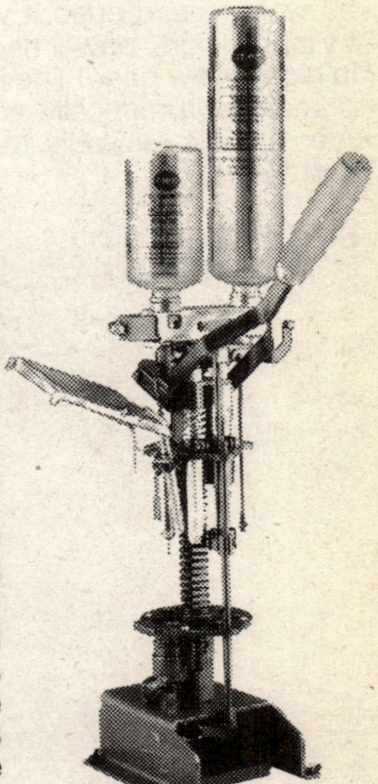

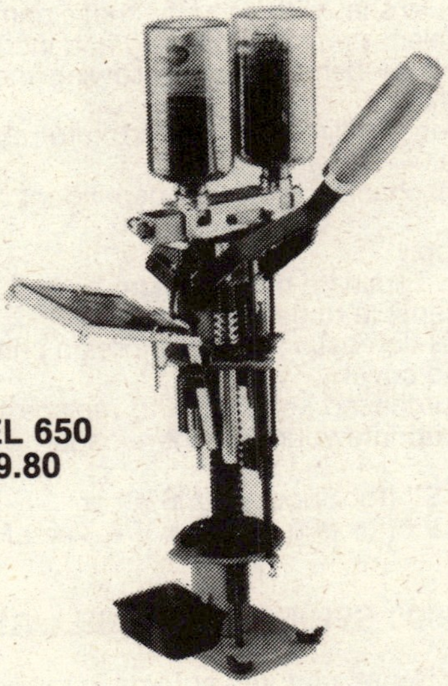

**MODEL 650**
**$319.80**

This reloader works on 6 shells at once. A reloaded shell is completed with every stroke. The MEC 650 does not resize except as a separate operation. Automatic Primer feed is standard. Simply fill it with a full box of primers and it will do the rest. Reloader has 3 crimping stations: the first one starts the crimp, the second closes the crimp, and the third places a taper on the shell. Available in 12, 16, 20 and 28 gauge and .410 bore. No die sets are available.

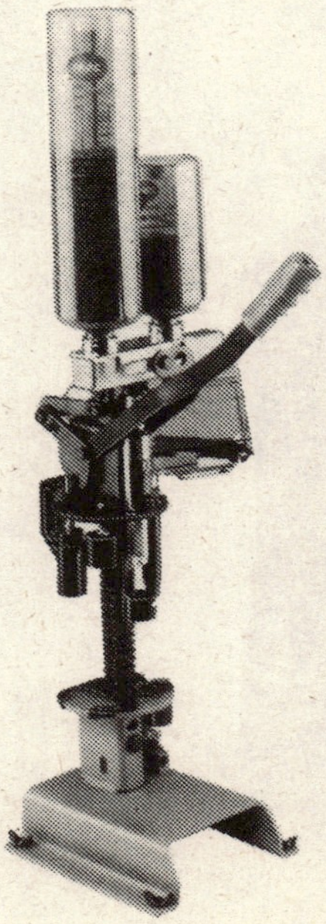

**MODEL 8120 SIZEMASTER**
**$245.00**

Sizemaster's "Power Ring" collet resizer returns each base to factory specifications. This new generation resizing station handles brass or steel heads, both high and low base. An 8-fingered collet squeezes the base back to original dimensions, then opens up to release the shell easily. The E-Z Prime auto primer feed is standard equipment. Press is adjustable for 3″ shells and is available in 12, 16, 20, 28 gauge and .410 bore. Die sets are available at: **$88.65 ($104.00** in 10 ga.).

# MEC RELOADING

## STEELMASTER SINGLE STAGE

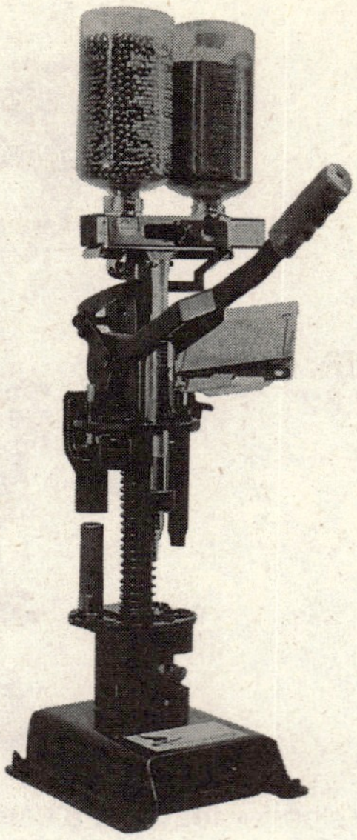

The only shotshell relaoder equipped to load steel shotshells as well as lead ones. Every base is resized to factory specs by a precision "power ring" collet. Handles brass or steel heads in high or low base. The E-Z prime auto primer feed dispenses primers automatically and is standard equipment. Separate presses are available for 12 gauge 2 3/4", 3", 12 gauge 3 1/2" and 10 gauge.

**Steelmaster** . . . . . . . . . . . . . . . . . . . . . . . . . . . . . **$255.00**
In 12 ga. 3 1/2" only . . . . . . . . . . . . . . . . . . . . . . . . . **280.66**

GRABBER
9000G

HUSTLER
9000H

## E-Z PRIME "S" AND "V" AUTOMATIC PRIMER FEEDS

From carton to shell with security, these primer feeds provide safe, convenient primer positioning and increase rate of production. Reduce bench clutter, allowing more free area for wads and shells.

- Primers transfer directly from carton to reloader, tubes and tube fillers
- Positive mechanical feed (not dependent upon agitation of press)
- Visible supply
- Automatic. Eliminate hand motion
- Less susceptible to damage
- Adapt to all domestic and most foreign primers with adjustment of the cover
- May be purchased separately to replace tube-type primer feed or to update your present reloader

**E-Z Prime "S"** (for Super 600, 650) or
**E-Z Prime "V"** (for 600 Jr. Mark V & VersaMEC) . . . **$38.50**

## MEC 9000 SERIES SHOTSHELL RELOADER

MEC's 9000 Series features automatic indexing and finished shell ejection for quicker and easier reloading. The factory set speed provides uniform movement through every reloading stage. Dropping the primer into the reprime station no longer requires operator "feel." The reloader requires only a minimal adjustment from low to high brass domestic shells, any one of which can be removed for inspection from any station.

**MEC 9000H Hustler** . . . . . . . . . . . . . . . . . . . . . . . . **$1345.72**
**MEC 9000G Grabber** . . . . . . . . . . . . . . . . . . . . . . . . **557.00**

# MTM RELOADING

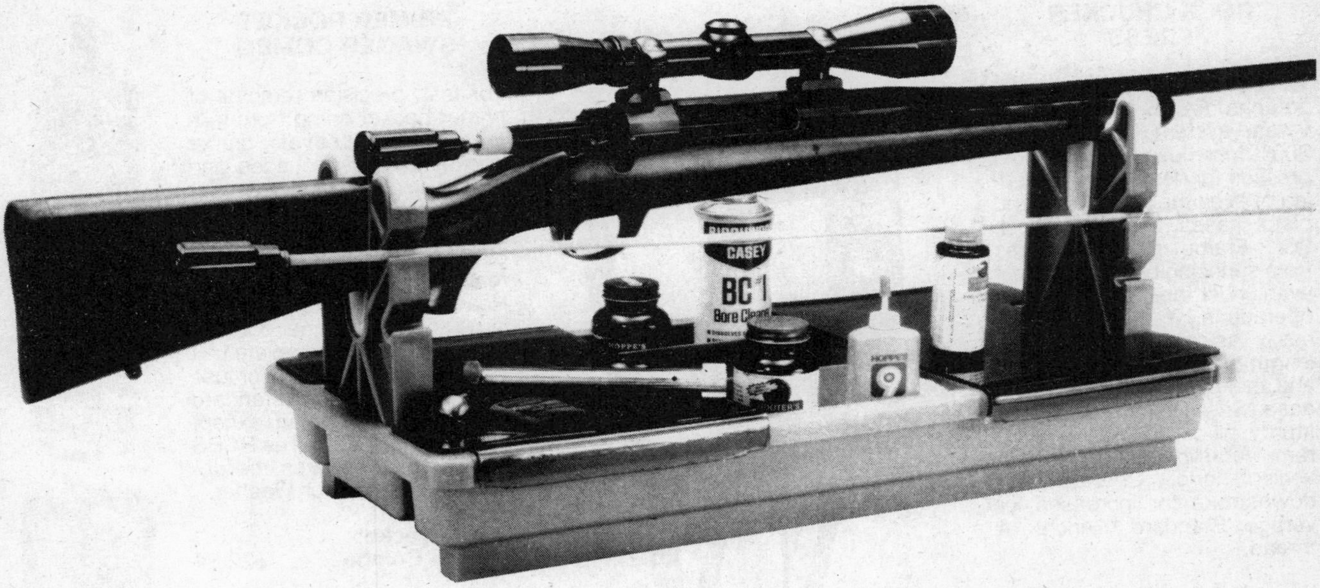


## PORTABLE RIFLE MAINTENANCE CENTER

Holds rifles and shotguns for easy cleaning and maintenance (can also be used as a shooting rest). Features gun forks with built-in cleaning rod holders; sliding see-through dust covers; tough polypropylene material; fits conveniently on top of Case-Gard A-760.

**Price:** . . . . . . . . . . . . . . . . . . . . . . . . . . . . . . . . . . . . **$29.15**

## MTM HANDLOADER'S LOG (not shown)

MEC's revised handloaders log has 150 pages for recording shotshell loading data, firearms inventory, ammo performance, plus an assortment of targets for quick anaylsis.

**HL-95** . . . . . . . . . . . . . . . . . . . . . . . . . . . . . . . . . . . . **$14.99**

## FUNNELS (not shown)

**MTM Benchrest Funnel Set** is designed specifically for the bench-rest shooter. One fits 222 and 243 cases only; the other 7mm and 308 cases. Both can be used with pharmaceutical vials popular with bench-rest competitors for storage of pre-weighed charges. Funnel design prevents their rolling off the bench.

**MTM Universal Funnel** fits all calibers from 222 to 45.
**UF-1** . . . . . . . . . . . . . . . . . . . . . . . . . . . . . . . . . . . . **$2.87**

**Patented MTM Adapto 5-in-1 Funnel Kit** includes funnel, adapters for 17 Rem., 222 Rem. and 30 through 45. Long drop tube facilitates loading of maximum charges: 222 to 45.
**AF-5** . . . . . . . . . . . . . . . . . . . . . . . . . . . . . . . . . . . . **$4.14**

## PORTABLE RANGE ORGANIZER

MTM's Portable Range Organizer is a portable utility platform that makes outdoor shooting with shotguns, rifles, pistols, black powder and archery more convenient and organized. As a rifle or shotgun stand, it holds four long guns with room left on top for ammo and extra shooting gear. Pistol shooters can use the troughs to hold an extra handgun or accessories like eye and ear protection. Blackpowder shooters can use the top platform to hold powder flask, caps and patches. A special slot in the side holds cleaning or slave rods. The platform is 13″ by 13″ and stands 32″ tall, allowing the shooter easy access to shooting equipment. Collapsible for storing. Uses two steel stakes for insertion into ground.

**PRO-1-30** . . . . . . . . . . . . . . . . . . . . . . . . . . . . . . . . . . . . **$22.90**

# RCBS RELOADING TOOLS

## ROCK CHUCKER PRESS

The Rock Chucker Press, with patented RCBS compound leverage system, delivers up to 200% more leverage than most presses for heavy-duty reloading of even the largest rifle and pistol cases. Rugged, Block "O" Frame prevents press from springing out of alignment even under the most strenuous operations. It case-forms as easily as most presses full-length size; it full-length sizes and makes bullets with equal ease. Shell holders snap into sturdy, all-purpose shell holder ram. Non-slip handle with convenient grip. Operates on downstroke for increased leverage. Standard 7/8-inch×14 thread.

**Rock Chucker Press**
(Less dies) . . . . . . . . **$121.90**

## PRIMER POCKET SWAGER COMBO

For fast, precision removal of primer pocket crimp from military cases. Leaves primer pocket perfectly rounded and with correct dimensions for seating of American Boxer-type primers. Will not leave oval-shaped primer pocket that reaming produces. Swager Head Assemblies furnished for large and small primer pockets no need to buy a complete unit for each primer size. For use with all presses with standard 7/8-inch×14 top thread, except RCBS "A-3" Press. The RCBS "A-2" Press requires the optional Case Stripper Washer.

**Primer Pocket**
**Swager Combo** . . . . . **$22.54**

## ROCK CHUCKER MASTER RELOADING KIT

For reloaders who want the best equipment, the Rock Chucker Master Reloading Kit includes all the tools and accessories needed. Included are the following: • Rock Chucker Press • RCBS 505 Reloading Scale • Speer Reloading Manual #11 • Uniflow Powder Measure • RCBS Rotary Case Trimmer-2 • deburring tool • case loading block • Primer Tray-2 • Automatic Primer Feed Combo • powder funnel • case lube pad • case neck brushes • fold-up hex ket set.

**Rock Chucker Master Reloading Kit** . . . . . **$336.81**

## PRIMER POCKET BRUSH COMBO

A slight twist of this tool thoroughly cleans residue out of primer pockets. Interchangeable stainless steel brushes for large and small primer pockets attach easily to accessory handle.

**Primer Pocket Brush Combo** . . . . . . . . . . . **$11.19**

# RCBS RELOADING TOOLS

## RELOADER SPECIAL-5

This RCBS Reloader Special-5 Press is the ideal setup to get started reloading your own rifle and pistol ammo from 12 gauge shotshells and the largest Magnums down to 22 Hornets. This press develops ample leverage and pressure to perform all reloading tasks including: (1) resizing cases their full length; (2) forming cases from one caliber into another; (3) making bullets. Rugged Block "O" Frame, designed by RCBS, prevents press from springing out of alignment even under tons of pressure. Frame is offset 30° for unobstructed front access, and is made of 48,000 psi aluminum alloy. Compound leverage system allows you to swage bullets, full-length resize cases, form 30-06 cases into other calibers. Counter-balanced handle prevents accidental drop. Extra-long ram-bearing surface minimizes wobble and side play. Standard 7/8-inch-14 thread accepts all popular dies and reloading accessories.

**Reloader Special-5**
(Less dies) . . . . . . . . . . . . . . **$94.94**

**RELOADER SPECIAL-5**

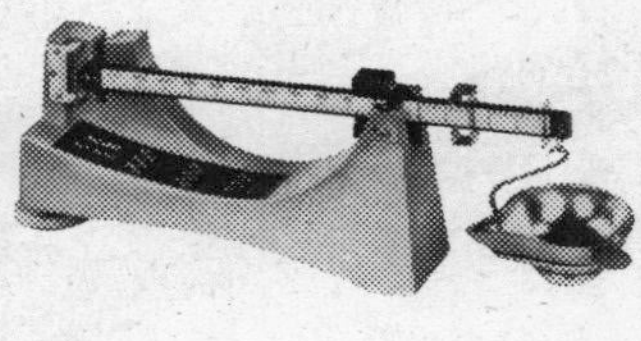

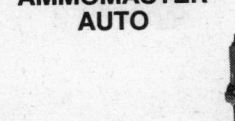

**RELOADING SCALE MODEL 5-0-5**

This 511-grain capacity scale has a three-poise system with widely spaced, deep beam notches to keep them in place. Two smaller poises on right side adjust from 0.1 to 10 grains, larger one on left side adjusts in full 10-grain steps. The first scale to use magnetic dampening to eliminate beam oscillation, the 5-0-5 also has a sturdy die-cast base with large leveling legs for stability. Self-aligning agate bearings support the hardened steel beam pivots for a guaranteed sensitivity to 0.1 grains.

**Model 5-0-5** . . . . . . . . . . . . . . **$68.79**

**AMMOMASTER SINGLE STAGE**

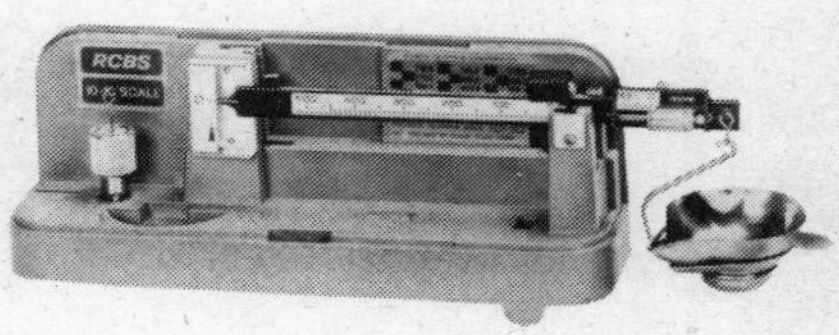


**RELOADING SCALE MODEL 10-10**

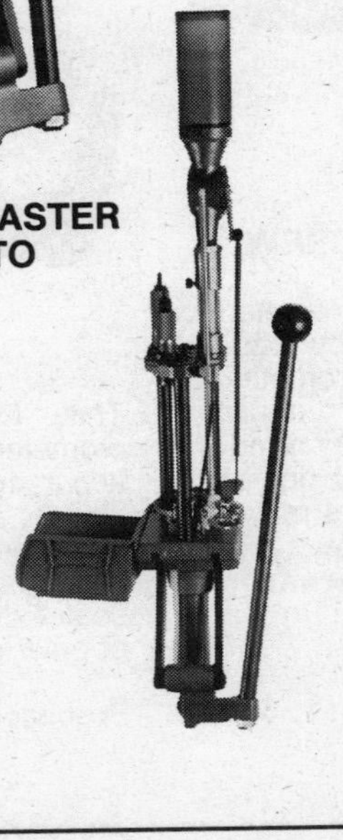

**AMMOMASTER AUTO**

## AMMOMASTER RELOADING SYSTEM

The AmmoMaster offers the handloader the freedom to configure a press to his particular needs and preferences. It covers the complete spectrum of reloading, from single stage through fully automatic progressive reloading, from .32 Auto to .50 caliber. The **AmmoMaster Auto** has all the features of a five-station press.

**AmmoMaster** Single stage . . **$169.09**
**AmmoMaster Auto** . . . . . . . . 374.19

**Up to 1010 Grain Capacity**
Normal capacity is 510 grains, which can be increased, without loss in sensitivity, by attaching the included extra weight.

Features include micrometer poise for quick, precise weighing, special approach-to-weight indicator, easy-to-read graduations, magnetic dampener, agate bearings, anti-tip pan, and dustproof lid snaps on to cover scale for storage. Sensitivity is guaranteed to 0.1 grains.

**Model 10-10 Scale** . . . . . . . . **$109.16**

# RCBS RELOADING TOOLS

## ELECTRONIC SCALE

This new RCBS Electronic Scale brings solid state electronic accuracy and convenience to handloaders. The LCD digital readings are ideal for weighing bullets and cases. The balance gives readings in grains, from zero to 500. The tare feature allows direct reading of the sample's weight with or without using the scale pan. The scale can be used on the range, operating on 8 AA batteries (approx. 50 hours).

**Electronic Scale** . . . . . . . . . . . . . . . . . . . . . . . . . . . . **$395.00**

## POWDER CHECKER

Operates on a free-moving rod for simple, mechanical operation with nothing to break. Standard 7/8×14 die body can be used in any progressive loader that takes standard dies. Black oxide finish provides corrosion resistance with good color contrast for visibility.

**Powder Checker** . . . . . . . . . . . . . . . . . . . . . . . . . . . . **$22.15**

## UPM MICROMETER ADJUSTMENT SCREW

Handloaders who want the convenience of a micrometer adjustment on their Uniflow Powder Measure can now add that feature to their powder measure. The RCBS Micrometer Adjustment Screw fits any Uniflow Powder Measure equipped with a large or small cylinder. It is easily installed by removing the standard metering screw, lock ring and bushing, which are replaced by the micrometer unit. Handloaders may then record the micrometer reading for a specific charge of a given powder and return to that setting at a later date when the same charge is used again.

**UPM Micrometer Adjustment Screw**
(large or small) . . . . . . . . . . . . . . . . . . . . . . . . . . . . **$31.33**

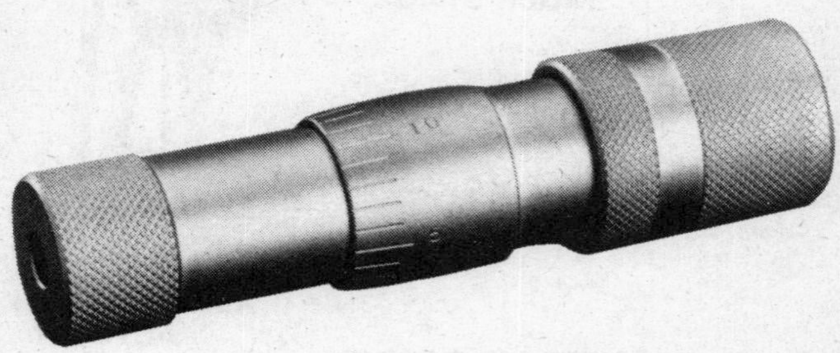

## PRECISION MIC

This "Precisioneered Cartridge Micrometer" provides micrometer readings of case heads to shoulder lengths, improving accuracy by allowing the best possible fit of cartridge to chamber. By allowing comparison of the chamber to SAAMI specifications, it alerts the handloader to a long chamber or excess headspace situation. It also ensures accurate adjustment of seater die to provide optimum seating depth. Available in 19 popular calibers.

**Precision MIC** . . . . . . . . . . . . . . . . . . . . . . . . . . . . **$35.64**

# RCBS RELOADING TOOLS

**HAND-PRIMING TOOL**
**$23.99**

This hand-priming tool features a patented shielding mechanism that separates the seating operation from the primer supply, virtually ending the possibility of primer tray detonation. This tool fits comfortably in the palm of the hand for portable primer seating with a simple squeeze. The primer tray is easily removed, installed and filled, requiring no hand contact with the primers. Uses standard RCBS shell holders. Made of durable cast material and comes with large and small primer feed set ups.

**TRIM PRO™ POWER CASE TRIMMER**

**TRIM PRO™ MANUAL CASE TRIMMER**

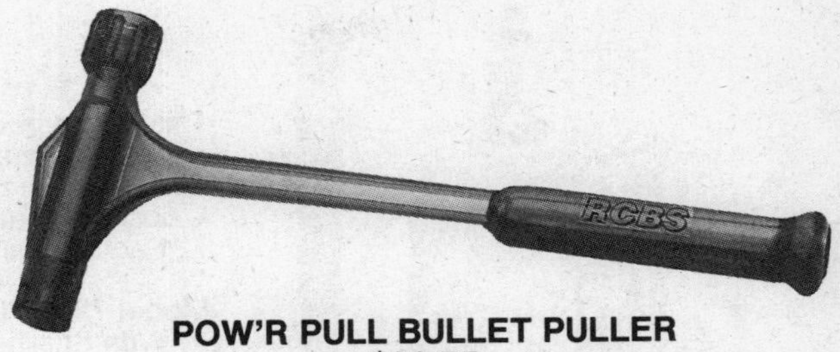


**POW'R PULL BULLET PULLER**
**$23.75**

The RCBS Pow'r Pull bullet puller features a three-jaw chuck that grips the case rim—just rap it on any solid surface like a hammer, and powder and bullet drop into the main chamber for re-use. A soft cushion protects bullets from damage. Works with most centerfire cartridges from .22 to .45 (not for use with rimfire cartridges).

**CARTRIDGE COUNTER**
**$16.66**

The RCBS Cartridge Counter enables reloaders to compare the number of cartridges actually loaded. It attaches to the RCBS Uniflow powder measure and registers each time the drum dispenses a charge. The cartridge counter also features a reset knob for quick return to zero.

**TRIM PRO CASE TRIMMER**
**$198.50 (Power) $66.00 (Manual)**

Cartridge cases are trimmed quickly and easily with a few turns of the RCBS Trim Pro case trimmer. The lever-type handle is more accurate to use than draw collet systems. A flat plate shell holder keeps cases locked in place and aligned. A micrometer fine adjustment bushing offers trimming accuracy to within .001″. Made of die-cast metal with hardened cutting blades. The power model is like having a personal lathe, delivering plenty of torque. Positive locking handle and in-line power switch make it simple and safe.

Also available:

**TRIM PRO CASE TRIMMER STAND** . . . . . . . . . . . . $13.99
**CASE HOLDER ACCESSORY** . . . . . . . . . . . . . . . . . 29.75

# REDDING RELOADING TOOLS

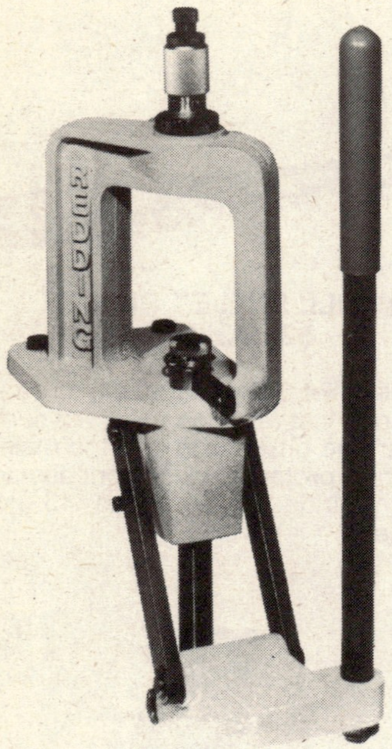

## MODEL 721
## "THE BOSS" PRESS

This "O" type reloading press features a rigid cast iron frame whose 36° offset provides the best visibility and access of comparable presses. Its "Smart" primer arm moves in and out of position automatically with ram travel. The priming arm is positioned at the bottom of ram travel for lowest leverage and best feel. Model 721 accepts all standard 7/8-14 threaded dies and universal shell holders.

**Model 721 "The Boss"** . . . . . . . . . . **$124.50**
With Shellholder and 10A Dies . . . . . . . . . . **159.00**

**Also available:**
**Boss Pro-Pak Deluxe Reloading Kit.** Includes Boss Reloading Press, #2 Powder and Bullet Scale, Powder Trickler, Reloading Dies, and more . . . . . . . . . . **$315.00**

## ULTRAMAG MODEL 700

Unlike other reloading presses that connect the linkage to the lower half of the press, the Ultramag's compound leverage system is connected at the top of the press frame. This allows the reloader to develop tons of pressure without the usual concern about press frame deflection. Huge frame opening will handle 50 × 3¼-inch Sharps with ease.

**No. 700 Press,** complete . . . . . . . . . . **$279.00**
**No. 700K Kit,** includes shell holder and one set of dies . . . . . . . . . . **312.00**

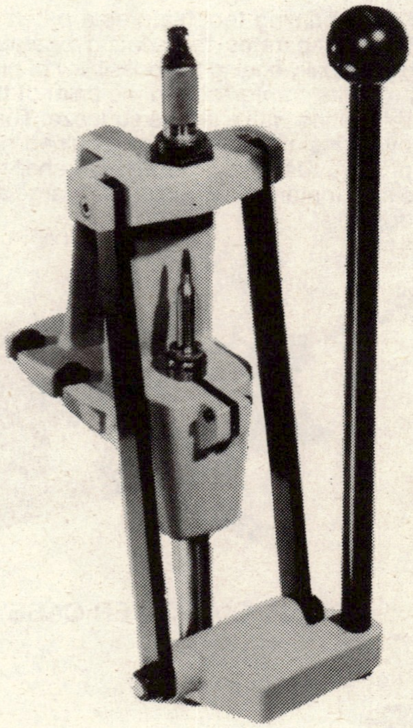

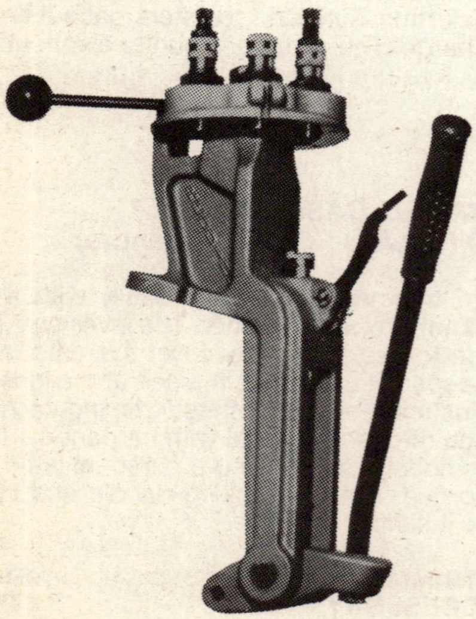

## METALLIC TURRET RELOADING PRESS
## MODEL 25

Extremely rugged, ideal for production reloading. No need to move shell, just rotate turret head to positive alignment. Ram accepts any standard snap-in shell holder. Includes primer arm for seating both small and large primers.

**No. 25 Press,** complete . . . . . . . . . . **$279.00**
**No. 25K Kit,** includes press, shell holder, and one set of dies . . . . . . . . . . **312.00**

# REDDING RELOADING TOOLS

## MASTER POWDER MEASURE MODEL 3

Universal- or pistol-metering chambers interchange in seconds. Measures charges from 1/2 to 100 grains. Unit is fitted with lock ring for fast dump with large "clear" plastic reservoir. "See-thru" drop tube accepts all calibers from 22 to 600. Precision-fitted rotating drum is critically honed to prevent powder escape. Knife-edged powder chamber shears coarse-grained powders with ease, ensuring accurate charges.

**No. 3 Master Powder Measure** (specify Universal- or Pistol-Metering chamber) . . . . . . **$108.00**
**No. 3K Kit Form,** includes both Universal and Pistol chambers . . . . . . . . . . . . . . . **129.00**
**Bench Stand** . . . . . . . . . . . . . . . **24.00**

## MASTER CASE TRIMMER MODEL 1400

This unit features a universal collet that accepts all rifle and pistol cases. The frame is solid cast iron with storage holes in the base for extra pilots. Both coarse and fine adjustments are provided for case length.

The case-neck cleaning brush and primer pocket cleaners attached to the frame of this tool make it a very handy addition to the reloading bench. Trimmer comes complete with:

- New speed cutter shaft
- Six pilots (22, 6mm, 25, 270, 7mm and 30 cal.)
- Universal collet
- Two neck cleaning brushes (22 thru 30 cal.)
- Two primer pocket cleaners (large and small)

**No. 1400 Master Case Trimmer** complete . . . . . . . . **$89.50**
**No. 1500 Pilots** . . . . . . . . . . . . . . . . . . . . . . . . . . . . **3.60**

## MATCH GRADE POWDER MEASURE MODEL 3BR

Designed for the most demanding reloaders—bench rest, silhouette and varmint shooters. The Model 3BR is unmatched for its precision and repeatability. Its special features include a powder baffle and zero backlash micrometer.

**No. 3BR** with Universal or Pistol Metering Chamber . . . . . . . **$144.00**
**No. 3 BRK** includes both metering chambers . . . . . . . **174.00**

## COMPETITION MODEL BR-30 POWDER MEASURE (not shown)

This powder measure features a new drum and micrometer that limit the overall charging range from a low of 10 grains (depending on powder density) to a maximum of approx. 50 grains. For serious competitive shooters whose loading requirements are between 10 and 50 grains, this is the measure to choose. The diameter of Model 3BR's metering cavity has been reduced, and the metering plunger on the new model has a unique hemispherical or cup shape, creating a powder cavity that resembles the bottom of a test tube. The result: irregular powder setting is alleviated and charge-to-charge uniformity is enhanced.

**Competition Model BR-30 Powder Measure** . . . . . **$165.00**

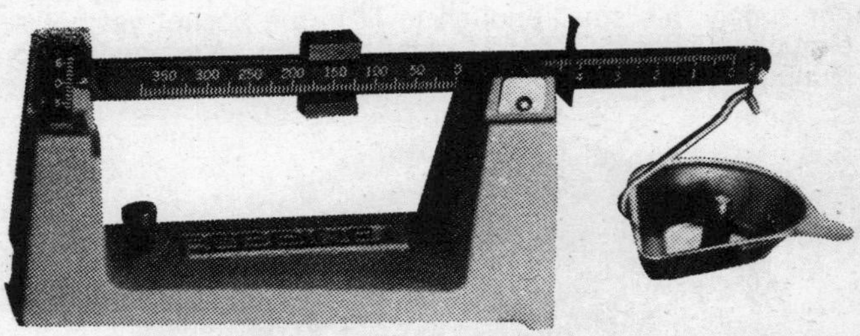

## STANDARD POWDER AND BULLET SCALE MODEL RS-1

For the beginner or veteran reloader. Only two counterpoises need to be moved to obtain the full capacity range of 1/10 grain to 380 grains. Clearly graduated with white numerals and lines on a black background. Total capacity of this scale is 380 grains. An over-and-under plate graduate in 10th grains allows checking of variations in powder charges or bullets without further adjustments.

**Model No. RS-1** . . . . . . . . . . . . . . . . . . . . . . . . . . . . . **$49.50**

Also available: **Master Powder & Bullet Scale.** Same as standard model, but includes a magnetic dampened beam swing for extra fast readings. 505-grain capacity . . . . . . . . **$72.00**

## BLACKPOWDER TOOLS

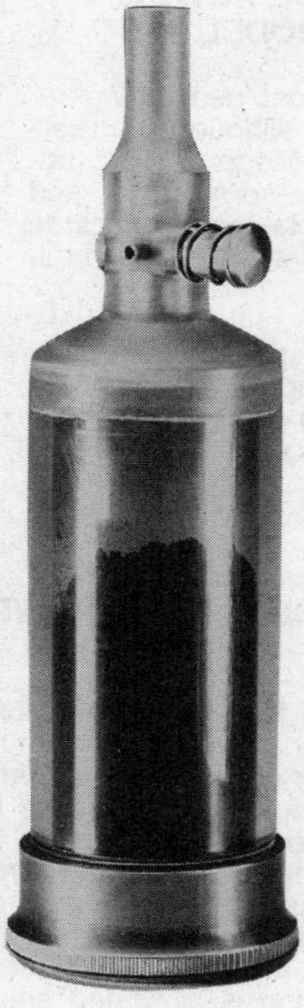

### U-VIEW POWDER FLASK
**$21.90**

This see-through powder flask makes it easy to monitor powder supply. It's small enough to fit in the pocket yet holds enough powder for a dozen reloads or more. A spring-loaded plunger helps to control dispensing operation.

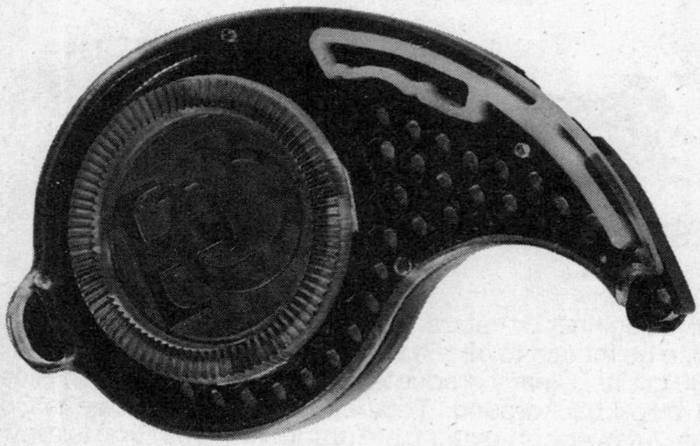

### U-VIEW CAPPER
**$22.90**

Holds an entire box of 100 caps. Traditional shape makes it easy to use with both inline ignition muzzleloaders and sidelock actions. Simple thumb-actuated mechanism. Rugged construction.

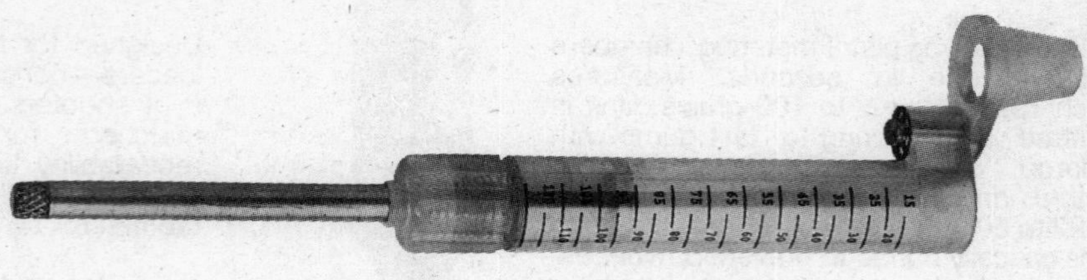

### U-VIEW POWDER MEASURE
**$16.90**

This measure shows the exact level of powder in the tube. Eliminates the guesswork of loading consistent charges. Includes loading spout that swivels out of the way to fill measure. Locking shaft is easy to adjust.

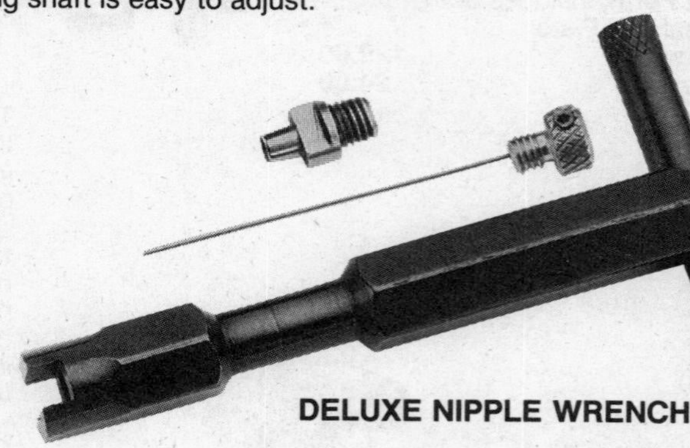

DELUXE NIPPLE WRENCH

HOT SHOT NIPPLE

### HOT SHOT NIPPLE
**$425.00**

Allows more even and controlled flow of pressurized gases from cap into ignition channel. Also releases gases through the side ports to prevent gas blowback. Made of hardened stainless steel to tight tolerances. Use with 1/4-28 threads for T/C caplocks (except T/C Scout).
Also available:
**DELUXE NIPPLE WRENCH: . . . . . . . . . . . . . . . . . . . . . $12.90**

### MAXI-SHOK BULLET PERFORMANCE TOOLS
**$24.95**

Seat bullet or round ball with one of 4 tips on the end of the ramrod to improve terminal ballistics. By changing front of the soft lead bullet, maximum energy transfer is assured through increase in projectile expansion. Includes 3 bore guides: .45, .50 & .54 cal., plus 5/16 adapter.

# Reference

# THE SHOOTER'S BOOKSHELF

The following is a current listing of recently published titles of special interest to shooters and gun enthusiasts. Most of these books can be found at your local library, bookstore or gunshop. If not available, contact the publisher directly. For a complete listing of in-print titles covering all subjects of interest to shooters, use the *Subject Guide to Books in Print,* which is updated annually and is available at most public libraries. The following entries are listed alphabetically by author and include year of publication, number of pages, publisher and retail price.


***ARMS AND ARMOR***

Bottomley, I. **Arms & Armor of the Samurai.** 1993. Random House. $17.99

Brown, Stuart, Jr. **The Guns of Harpers Ferry** (Illus.). 158 p. 1993. Clearfield Co. pap. $14.95

DuPuy, Trevor N. **The Evolution of Weapons & Warfare.** Repr. of 1984 ed. Books on Demand Pub. $102.70

Foss, C. **Jane's Armour & Artillery.** 1994-95. Jane's Info Group. $255.00

Hogg, I., ed. **Jane's Infantry Weapons.** 1994-95. Jane's Info Group. text ed. $255.00

Moller, George D. **American Military Shoulder Arms. Vol. II: From the 1790s to the End of the Flintlock Period** (Illus.). 496 p. 1993. University of Colorado Press. $75.00

***DECOYS***

Aziz, Laura. **Decoys: A Celebration of Contemporary Wildlife Carving** (Illus.). 120 p. 1994. Camden House. $34.95

**Decoys Calendar.** 120 p. (Illus.). 1996. Camden House. $34.95

***DEER & ELK HUNTING***

Deer & Deer Hunting Magazine staff. **Deer Hunters Almanac.** 1994. Krause Pub. pap. $6.95

Mostoller, Ed. **Deer Hunting: The Guide to Doing it Right.** (Illus.) 97 p. Logo Press. $16.95

Patent, Dorothy. **Deer and Elk.** (Illus.). 1994. Clarion book (HM). $15.95

Phillips, John E. **The Master's Secrets of Bowhunting Deer: Secret Tactics from Master Bowmen.** (Illus.) 160 p. Larsens Outdoor Pub. pap. $9.95

Prothro, Walter. **Stalking Trophy Mule Deer.** 240 p. 1993. Horizon Utah. $18.98

van Zwoll, Wayne. **The Elk Hunter's Handbook.** (Illus.). 416 p. 1992. Larsens Outdoor Pub. $24.95

***FIREARMS***

Briggs, Doug. **The Consumer's Guide to Handguns, Defensive Shotguns & Rifles.** (Illus.). 224 p. 1993. Beverly Books. $14.95

Gangarosa, Gene, Jr. **Modern Beretta Firearms.** (Illus.). 288 p. 1994. Stoeger Pub. co. pap. $16.95

Hogg, Ian. **Small Arms: Pistols & Rifles.** (Illus.). 1994. 160 p. Stackpole. $19.95

Karns, John A. and Traister, John E. **Firearms Disassembly With Exploded Views.** 320 p. (Illus). 1995. Stoeger Pub. co. $19.95

**News Media Guide to Firearms.** (Illus.). 52 p. 1994. Diane Pub. pap. $25.00

Phillips, John. **Black Powder Hunting Secrets.** (Illus.). 160 p. 1993. Larsens Outdoor Pub. pap. $11.95

Thompson, Leroy & Smeets, Rene. **Great Combat Handguns.** (Illus.). 250 p. 1993. Sterling. $29.95

Wood, J.B. **Gun Digest Book of Firearms Assembly-Disassembly, Part III: Rimfire Rifles.** rev. ed. (Illus.). 480 p. 1994. DBI. pap. $18.95

Workman, William. **Ruger 10-22.** 1994. Krause Pub. pap. $19.95

***FIREARMS—CATALOGS***

Fjestad, J.P. **Blue Book of Gun Values.** 15th ed. (Illus.). 1,256 p. 1994. Blue Book Pub. pap. $24.95

**Gun Traders Guide. 18th ed.** 1995. 576 p. Stoeger Pub. Co. pap. $19.95

Quetermous, Steve. **Pocket Guide to Handguns: Identification and Values, 1900 to Present.** 1993. Collector Books. pap. $9.95

**Shooter's Bible 1996 Edition.** 576 p. (Illus.). 1995. Stoeger Pub. Co. $21.95

Traister, John E. **Antique Guns, The Collector's Guide. 2nd ed.** (Illus.). 1994. Stoeger Pub. Co. pap. $18.95

Wilson, R. L. **The Book of Colt Firearms.** 2nd ed. (Illus.) 624 p. 1993. Blue Book Pub. $14.95

***FIREARMS—HISTORY***

Wilson, K. L. & Eberhart, L.D. **The Derringer in America, Vol. II: The Cartridge Period.** (Illus.). 1993. A. Mowbray Pub. $65.00

***FIREARMS—IDENTIFICATION***

Briggs, Doug. **The Writer's Complete Guide to Firearms.** (Illus.). 1993. 224 p. Beverly books. $14.95

***FIREARMS—LAW & LEGISLATION***

Gottlieb, Alan & Kopel, David. **Things You Can Do to Defend Your Gun Rights.** 192 p. 1995. Merrill Press (price not set)

Halbrook, Stephen P. **That Every Man Be Armed: The Evolution of a Constitutional Right.** 1994. Independent Inst. Press. pap. $16.95

**Identification of Firearms Within the Purview of the National Firearms Act.** 1994. Gordon Press. $259.95

Malcolm, Joyce L. **To Keep and Bear Arms: The Origin of Our Anglo-American Right.** 1994. HUP. $29.95

Schulman, J. Neil. **Stopping Power: Why Seventy Million Americans Own Guns.** 288 p. 1994. Snyapse Cent. $22.95

***GAME & GAME BIRDS***

DeBastyai, L. **All My Life With Hunting Birds.** (Illus.). 256 p. 1994. Saifer. $45.00

***GAME COOKERY***

Cox, Nicola. **Nicola Cox on Game Cookery.** 1994. (Illus.). 224 p. Trafalgar. pap. $24.95

Dobson, Ned. **Venison: As You Like It.** 112 p. 1994. Dobson Enterprise. pap. $7.95

Little, Carolyn. **The Game Cook.** (Illus.). 224 p. 1994. Trafalgar. $24.95

***HUNTING** (see also* FIREARMS)

Boddington, D. **Shots at Big Game** (Illus.) 198 p. 1993. Safari Press. pap. $15.95

Butler, Bill. **The Versatile Trophy Hunter.** 208 p. 1993. Bill Butler Pub. pap. $12.95

Poole, R. W. **Hunting: An Introductory Handbook.** (Illus.). 192 p. 1993. Trafalgar Pub. pap. $29.95

Taylor, J. **Big Game and Big Game Rifles.** 215 p. 1993. Safari Press. $24.95

Lawrence, Len. **The Small Game and Varmint Hunter's Bible.** 1994. Doubleday. $12.00

***HUNTING DOGS***

Deeley, Martin. **Advanced Gundog Training: Practical Field Work and Competition.** (Illus.). 176 p. 1994. Trafalgar. $34.95

***PISTOLS & REVOLVERS** (see also* FIREARMS)

Gangarosa, Gene, Jr. **P-38 Automatic Pistol.** (Illus.). 288 p. 1993 Stoeger Pub. Co. $16.95

Zhuk, A.B. **Illustrated Encyclopedia of Twentieth Century Handguns. Pistols and Revolvers of the World from 1870 to the Present.** 256 p. 1994. Stackpole. $49.95

***RELOADING***

**Lyman's Shotshell Reloading Handbook, 4th ed.** 1995. Lyman Products Corp. $24.95

***RIFLES** (see also* FIREARMS, FIREARMS—CATALOGS, HUNTING)

O'Connor, J. **The Big Game Rifles.** (Illus) 370 p. 1994. Safari Press. $37.50

Riesch, Craig. **U.S. M1 Carbines: Wartime Production.** (Illus.) 124 p. 1994. N.Cape Pub. pap. $15.95

***SHOOTING***

Edie, George. **The Art of English Shooting.** (Collector's ed.). 48 p. 1993. Arion Pres. $125.00

Garfit, Will. **Will's Shoot.** (Illus.) 128 p. 1994. Trafalgar. $34.95

Jarrett, William S., ed. **Shooter's Bible 1996.** (Illus.). 576 p. 1995. Stoeger Pub. Co. $21.95

***SHOTGUNS** (see also* FIREARMS, SHOOTING)

Boothroyd, G. **The Shotgun.** (Illus.). 240 p. 1993. Safari Press. $35.00

Burrard. **The Modern Shotgun.** 3 vols. (Illus.). 1081 p. (set). Safari Press. $125.00

Garwood, G.T. **Gough Thomas's Gun Book: Shotgun Lore for the Sportsman.** (Illus.). 273 p. 1994. rep. of 1969 ed. Gunnerman Press. $34.95

**Lyman's Shotshell Reloading Handbook, 4th ed.** 1995. Lyman Products Corp. $24.95

Matunas, Ed. **Guide to Big Game Cartridges & Rifles.** 288 p. (Illus.). 1994. Lyman Products Corp. $17.95

Quertermous, Steve. **Pocket Guide to Shotguns: Identifications and Values 1900 to Present.** 1993. Collector Books. pap. $9.95

***WILDLIFE CONSERVATION, MANAGEMENT & PRESERVATION***

Baldessare, Guy A. and Bolen, Eric. **Waterfowl Ecology and Management.** 1994. Wiley. $59.95

Bellrose, Frank & Holme, Daniel. **Ecology and Management of the Wood Duck.** (Illus.). 636 p. 1994. Stackpole. $59.95

Dizard, Jan. **Going Wild: Hunting, Animal Rights and the Contested Meaning of Nature.** 200 p. 1994. Univ. of Mass. Press. Library binding. $35.00

Hochbaun, H. Albert. **Wings Over the Prairie.** (Illus.). 116 p. 1994. Sterling. $24.95

Johna, Dina J. **Attitudes Toward the Outdoors: An Annotated Bibliography of U.S. Survey and Poll Research Concerning the Environment, Wildlife and Recreation.** 256 p. 1994. McFarland. Library binding. $45.00

Olney, P.J. et al, eds. **Creative Conservation: Interactive Management of Wild and Captive Animals.** 1993. Chapman & Hall. $94.95

White, Jan. **Basic Wildlife Rehabilitation.** 150 p. 1992. JWRC. $25.00

# DIRECTORY OF MANUFACTURERS AND SUPPLIERS

The following manufacturers, suppliers and distributors of firearms, ammunition, reloading equipment, sights, scopes and accessories all appear with their products in the catalog and/or "Manufacturers' Showcase" sections of this edition of SHOOTER'S BIBLE.

**Accurate Arms, Ltd.** (smokeless powder)
5891 Highway 230 West
McEwen, Tennessee 37101
Ph: 615-729-4207 Fax: 615-729-4217

**Action Arms, Ltd.** (Brno handguns, rifles, Timber Wolf rifles, sights, scopes)
P.O. Box 9573
Philadelphia, Pennsylvania 19124
Ph: 215-744-0100 Fax: 215-533-2188

**Aimpoint** (sights, scopes, mounts)
580 Herndon Parkway, Suite 500
Herndon, Virginia 22070
Ph: 703-471-6828 Fax: 703-689-0575

**Lou Alessandri & Son, Ltd.** (Rizzini shotguns, rifles, extension tubes)
24 French Street
Rehoboth, Massachusetts 02769
Ph: 508-252-5590 Fax: 508-252-3436

**American Arms** (handguns, rifles, blackpowder; Franchi shotguns; Uberti handguns and rifles)
715 E. Armour Road
N. Kansas City, Missouri 64116
Ph: 816-474-3161 Fax: 816-474-1225

**American Derringer Corp.** (handguns)
127 North Lacy Drive
Waco, Texas 76705
Ph: 817-799-9111 Fax: 817-799-7935

**Anschutz** (handguns, rifles)
Available through Precision Sales International

**Arcadia Machine & Tool Inc.** (AMT handguns, rifles)
6226 Santos Diaz Street
Irwindale, California 91702
Ph: 818-334-6629 Fax: 818-969-5247

**Armes de Chasse** (rifles, shotguns)
P.O. Box 86
Hertford, North Carolina 27944-0086

**Armsport, Inc.** (blackpowder arms, Bernardelli handguns, shotguns)
3590 NW 49th Street, P.O. Box 523066
Miami, Florida 33142
Ph: 305-635-7850 Fax: 305-633-2877

**A-Square Company Inc.** (rifles)
One Industrial Park
Bedford, Kentucky 40006
Ph: 502-255-7456 Fax: 502-255-7657

**Astra** (handguns)
Available through European American Armory

**Auto-Ordnance Corp.** (handguns, rifles)
Williams Lane
West Hurley, New York 12491
Ph: 914-679-7225 Fax: 914-679-2698

**AYA** (shotguns)
Available through Armes de Chasse

**Bausch & Lomb** (scopes)
Sports Optics Division
9200 Cody
Overland Park, Kansas 66214
Ph: 913-752-3433 Fax: 913-752-3489

**Beeman Precision Airguns** (scopes, mounts)
5454 Argosy Avenue
Huntington Beach, California 92649
Ph: 714-890-4800 Fax: 714-890-4808

**Benelli** (shotguns)
Available through Heckler & Koch; (handguns) Available through European American Armory

**Benton & Brown Firearms** (handguns, rifles)
311 West First, P.O. Box 326
Delhi, Louisiana 71232-0326
Ph: 318-878-2499 Fax: 817-284-9300

**Beretta U.S.A. Corp.** (handguns, shotguns)
17601 Beretta Drive
Accokeek, Maryland 20607
Ph: 301-283-2191 Fax: 301-375-7677

**Bernardelli** (handguns, shotguns)
Available through Armsport

**Bersa** (handguns)
Available through Eagle Imports Inc.

**Blaser USA, Inc.** (rifles)
c/o Autumn Sales, Inc.
1320 Lake Street
Fort Worth, Texas 76102
Ph: 817-335-1634 Fax: 817-338-0119

**Blount, Inc.** (RCBS reloading equipment, Speer and CCI bullets, Weaver scopes)
P.O. Box 856
Lewiston, Idaho 83501
Ph: 208-746-2351 Fax: 208-746-2915

**Bonanza** (reloading tools)
See Forster Products

**Brno** (rifles)
Available through Magnum Research

**Brown Precision, Inc.** (custom rifles)
7786 Molinos Avenue; P.O. Box 270 W.
Los Molinos, California 96055
Ph: 916-384-2506 Fax: 916-384-1638

**Browning** (handguns, rifles, shotguns)
Route One
Morgan, Utah 84050
Ph: 801-876-2711 Fax: 801-876-3331

**B-Square Co.** (sights, mounts)
P.O. Box 11281
Fort Worth, Texas 76110
Ph: 817-923-0964 Fax: 817-926-7012

**Burris Company, Inc.** (scopes)
331 East Eighth Street, P.O. Box 1747
Greeley, Colorado 80631
Ph: 303-356-1670 Fax: 303-356-8702

**Butler Creek Corp.** (stocks, scope covers, slings)
290 Arden Drive
Belgrade, Montana 59714
Ph: 406-388-1356 Fax: 406-388-7204

**Charco Inc.** (Charter Arms handguns)
26 Beaver Street
Ansonia, Connecticut 06401
Ph: 203-735-4686 Fax: 203-378-2846

**Charter Arms Corp.** (handguns)
Available through Charco Inc.

**Clifton Arms** (custom rifles)
P.O. Box 1471
Medina, Texas 78055
Ph: 210-589-2666

**Colt's Manufacturing Co., Inc.** (handguns, rifles)
P.O. Box 1868
Hartford, Connecticut 06144-1868
PH: 203-236-6311 Fax: 203-244-1449

**Connecticut Shotgun Manufacturing Co.** (A. H. Fox shotguns)
35 Woodland Street, P.O. Box 1692
New Britain, Connecticut 06051-1692
Ph: 203-225-6682 Fax: 203-832-8707

**Connecticut Valley Classics** (shotguns)
12 Taylor Lane
P.O. Box 2068
Westport, Connecticut 06880
Ph: 203-254-7864 Fax: 203-254-7866

**Coonan Arms** (handguns)
1465 Selby Ave.
St. Paul, Minnesota 55104
Ph: 612-641-1263

**Cooper Firearms** (rifles)
P.O. Box 114
Stevensville, Montana 59870
Ph: 406-777-5534

**County** (shotguns)
10020 Whitman Lane
Tamarac, Florida 33321
Ph: 305-720-2066 Fax: 305-722-6353

**CVA** (blackpowder guns)
5988 Peachtree Corners East
Norcross, Georgia 30071
Ph: 404-449-4687 Fax: 404-242-8546

**Cumberland Mountain Arms** (blackpowder rifles)
1045 Dinah Shore Blvd., P.O. Box 710
Winchester, Tennessee 37398
Ph: 615-967-2676 Fax: 615-967-9199

**CZ** (handguns, rifles)
Available through Magnum Research

**Daewoo Precision Industries, Ltd.** (handguns)
Available through Kimber of America

**Dakota** (handguns, rifles)
Available through E.M.F. Co., Inc.

**Dakota Arms, Inc.** (rifles)
HC 55, Box 326
Sturgis, South Dakota 57785
Ph: 605-347-4686 Fax: 605-347-4459

**Davis Industries** (handguns)
11186 Venture Drive
Mira Loma, California 91752
Ph: 909-360-5598 Fax: 909-360-1749

**Dixie Gun Works** (blackpowder guns)
P.O. Box 130, Highway 51 S.
Union City, Tennessee 38261
Ph: 901-885-0561 Fax: 901-885-0440

**Docter Optic Technologies** (binoculars)
4685 Boulder Highway, Suite A
Las Vegas, Nevada 89121
Ph: 800-290-3634 Fax: 702-898-3737

**Dynamit Nobel/RWS** (Rottweil shotguns)
81 Ruckman Road
Closter, New Jersey 07624
Ph: 201-767-1995 Fax: 201-767-1589

**Eagle Imports, Inc.** (Bersa handguns, Lanber shotguns)
1750 Brielle Avenue, Unit B1
Wanamassa, New Jersey 07712
Ph: 908-493-0333 Fax: 908-493-0301

**Emerging Technologies Inc.** (handguns, sights)
P.O. Box 3548
Little Rock, Arkansas 72203
Ph: 501-375-2227 Fax: 501-372-1445

**E.M.F. Company, Inc.** (Dakota handguns, blackpowder arms)
1900 East Warner Avenue 1-D
Santa Ana, California 92705
Ph: 714-261-6611 Fax: 714-756-0133

**Erma** (handguns)
Available through Precision Sales

**Euroarms of America Inc.** (blackpowder guns)
1501 Lenoir Drive, P.O. Box 3277
Winchester, Virginia 22601
Ph: 703-662-1863

**European American Armory** (Astra and Benelli handguns, E.A.A. handguns, rifles)
P.O. Box 1299
Sharpes, Florida 32959
Ph: 407-639-4842 Fax: 407-639-7006

**Feather Industries, Inc.** (handguns, rifles)
2300 Central Avenue, Unit K
Boulder, Colorado 80301
Ph: 303-442-7021 Fax: 303-447-0944

**Federal Cartridge Co.** (ammunition)
900 Ehlen Drive
Anoka, Minnesota 55303-7503
Ph: 612-323-2506 Fax: 612-323-2506

**Fiocchi of America** (ammunition)
5030 Fremont Road
Ozark, Missouri 65721
Ph: 417-725-4118 Fax: 417-725-1039

**Flintlocks, Etc.** (Pedersoli replica rifles)
160 Rossiter Road
Richmond, Massachusetts 01254
Ph: 413-698-3822 Fax: 413-698-3866

**Forster Products** (Bonanza and Forster reloading)
82 East Lanark Avenue
Lanark, Illinois 61046
Ph: 815-493-6360 Fax: 815-493-2371

**A. H. Fox** (shotguns)
Available thru Connecticut Shotgun Mfg. Co.

**Franchi** (shotguns)
Available through American Arms

**Francotte** (rifles and shotguns)
Available through Armes de Chasse

**Freedom Arms** (handguns)
One Freedom Lane, P.O. Box 1776
Freedom, Wyoming 83120
Ph: 307-883-2468

**Garbi** (shotguns)
Available through W. L. Moore & Co.

**Gibbs Rifle Co.** (Mauser handguns, rifles)
Cannon Hill Industrial Park
Hoffman Road
Martinsburg, West Virginia 25401
Ph: 304-274-0458

**Glaser Safety Slug, Inc.** (ammunition and gun accessories)
P.O. Box 8223
Foster City, California 94404
Ph: 415-345-7677 Fax: 415-345-8217

**Glock, Inc.** (handguns)
6000 Highlands Parkway
Smyrna, Georgia 30082
Ph: 404-432-1202 Fax: 404-433-8719

**Gonic Arms** (blackpowder rifles)
134 Flagg Road
Gonic, New Hampshire 03839
603-332-8456 Fax: 603-332-8457

**Grendel, Inc.** (handguns)
550 St. Johns Street
Cocoa, Florida 32922
Ph: 407-636-1211

**Gun South Inc.** (Merkel shotguns, Steyr-Mannlicher rifles)
108 Morrow Ave., P.O. Box 129
Trussville, Alabama 35173
Ph: 205-655-8299 Fax: 205-655-7078

**Hämmerli U.S.A.** (handguns)
19296 Oak Grove Circle
Groveland, California 95321
Ph: 209-962-5311 Fax: 209-962-5931

**Harrington & Richardson** (handguns, rifles, shotguns)
60 Industrial Rowe
Gardner, Massachusetts 01440
Ph: 508-632-9393 Fax: 508-632-2300

**Heckler & Koch** (handguns, rifles, Benelli shotguns)
21480 Pacific Boulevard
Sterling, Virginia 20166
Ph: 703-450-1900 Fax: 703-450-8160

**Hercules Inc.** (gunpowder)
Hercules Plaza
Wilmington, Delaware 19894
Ph: 302-594-5000 Fax: 302-594-5305

**Heritage Manufacturing** (handguns)
4600 NW 135 St.
Opa Locka, Florida 33054
Ph: 305-685-5966 Fax: 305-687-6721

**Hi-Point Firearms** (handguns)
174 South Mulberry
Mansfield, Ohio 44902
Ph: 419-522-8330

**High-Standard Manufacturing Co.** (handguns)
264 Whitney Street
Hartford, Connecticut 06105-2270
Ph: 203-586-8220 Fax: 203-231-0411

**Hodgdon Powder Co., Inc.** (gunpowder)
6231 Robinson, P.O. Box 2932
Shawnee Mission, Kansas 66201
Ph: 913- 362-9455 Fax: 913-362-1307

**Hornady Manufacturing Company** (reloading, ammunition)
P.O. Box 1848
Grand Island, Nebraska 68802-1848
Ph: 308-382-1390 Fax: 308-382-5761

**Howa** (rifles)
Available through Interarms

**IGA Shotguns**
Available through Stoeger Industries

**IMR Powder Company** (gunpowder)
R.D. 5, Box 247E
Plattsburgh, New York 12901
Ph: 518-561-9530

**InterAims** (sights)
Available through Stoeger Industries

**Interarms** (handguns, shotguns and rifles, including Howa, Mark X, Rossi, Star, Walther)
10 Prince Street
Alexandria, Virginia 22314
Ph: 703-548-1400 Fax: 703-549-7826

**Ithaca Gun Co.** (shotguns)
891 Route 34B
King Ferry, New York 13081
Ph: 315-364-7171 Fax: 315-364-5134

**JägerSport** (Voere rifles)
1 Wholesale Way
Cranston, Rhode Island 02920
Ph: 401-942-3380 Fax: 401-946-2587

**Jarrett Rifles Inc.** (custom rifles and accessories)
383 Brown Road
Jackson, South Carolina 29831
Ph: 803-471-3616

**Kahr Arms** (handguns)
P.O. Box 220
Blauvelt, New York 10913
Ph: 914-353-5996

**K.B.I., Inc.** (handguns, shotguns)
P.O. Box 6346
Harrisburg, Pennsylvania 17112
Ph: 717-540-8518 Fax: 717-540-8567

**Kimber of America, Inc.** (rifles, handguns; Daewoo rifles and handguns)
9039 Southeast Jannsen Road
Clackamas, Oregon 97015
Ph: 503-656-1704 Fax: 503-657-5695

**Krieghoff International Inc.** (rifles, shotguns)
337A Route 611, P.O. Box 549
Ottsville, Pennsylvania 18942
Ph: 610-847-5173 Fax: 610-847-8691

**LakeField Arms Ltd.** (rifles)
P.O. Box 129
Lakefield, Ontario K0L 2H0 Canada
Ph: 705-652-8000 Fax: 705-652-8431

**L.A.R. Manufacturing, Inc.** (Grizzly handguns, rifles)
4133 West Farm Road
West Jordan, Utah 84084
Ph: 801-255-7106 Fax: 801-569-1972

**Leupold & Stevens, Inc.** (scopes, mounts)
P.O. Box 688
Beaverton, Oregon 97075
Ph: 503-646-9171 Fax: 503-526-1455

**Llama** (handguns)
Available through SGS Importers International

**Luger, American Eagle** (pistols)
Available through Stoeger Industries

**Lyman Products Corp.** (blackpowder guns, sights, reloading tools)
Route 147
Middlefield, Connecticut 06455
Ph: 203-349-3421 Fax: 203-349-3586

**Magnum Research Inc.** (Desert Eagle handguns; CZ and Brno rifles, handguns)
7110 University Avenue N.E.
Minneapolis, Minnesota 55432
Ph: 612-574-1868 Fax: 612-574-0109

**Magtech Recreational Products** (shotguns)
5030 Paradise Rd., Ste C-211
Las Vegas, Nevada 89119
Ph: 702-795-7191 Fax: 702-795-2769

**Mark X** (rifles)
Available through Interarms

**Marlin Firearms Company** (rifles, shotguns)
100 Kenna Drive
North Haven, Connecticut 06473
Ph: 203-239-5621 Fax: 203-234-2991

**Marocchi** (Conquista shotguns)
Available through Precision Sales

**Mauser** (handguns, rifles)
Available through Gibbs Rifle Co.

**Maverick of Mossberg** (shotguns)
Available through O. F. Mossberg

**McMillan Gun Works** (rifles)
302 W. Melinda Lane
Phoenix, Arizona 85027
Ph: 602-582-9627 Fax: 602-582-5178

**MEC Inc.** (reloading tools)
c/o Mayville Engineering Co.
715 South Street
Mayville, Wisconsin 53050
Ph: 414-387-4500 Fax: 414-387-2682

**Merit Corp.** (sights)
P.O. Box 9044
Schenectady, New York 12309
Ph: 518-346-1420

**Merkel** (shotguns)
Available through Gun South Inc.

**Midway Arms, Inc.** (reloading tools, shooting accessories)
5875 West Van Horn Tavern Road
Columbia, Missouri 65203
Ph: 314-455-6363 Fax: 314-446-1018

**Millett Sights** (sights and mounts)
16131 Gothard Street
Huntington Beach, California 92647
Ph: 714-842-5575 Fax: 714-843-5707

**Mitchell Arms** (handguns, rifles)
3400-1 West MacArthur Blvd.
Santa Ana, California 92704
Ph: 714-957-5711 Fax: 714-957-5732

**M.O.A. Corp.** (handguns)
2451 Old Camden Pike
Eaton, Ohio 45302
Ph: 513-456-3669

**Modern Muzzle Loading Inc.** (blackpowder guns)
P.O. Box 130, 234 Airport Rd.,
Centerville, Iowa 52544
Ph: 515-856-2626 Fax :515-856-2628

**William L. Moore & Co.** (Garbi and Piotti shotguns)
31360 Via Colinas, No. 109
Westlake Village, California 91361
Ph: 818-889-4160

**O. F. Mossberg & Sons, Inc.** (shotguns)
7 Grasso Avenue; P.O. Box 497
North Haven, Connecticut 06473
Ph: 203-230-5361 Fax: 203-230-5420

**MTM Molded Products** (reloading tools)
P.O. Box 14117
Dayton, Ohio 45413
Ph: 513-890-7461 Fax: 513-890-1747

**Navy Arms Company, Inc.** (handguns, rifles, blackpowder guns)
689 Bergen Boulevard
Ridgefield, New Jersey 07657
Ph: 201-945-2500

**New England Firearms Co., Inc.** (handguns, rifles, shotguns; Harrington & Richardson handguns, shotguns)
Industrial Rowe
Gardner, Massachusetts 01440
Ph: 508-632-9393 Fax: 508-632-2300

**Nikon Inc.** (scopes)
1300 Walt Whitman Road
Melville, New York 11747
Ph: 516-547-4381 Fax: 516-547-0309

**North American Arms** (handguns)
1800 North 300 West
P.O. Box 707
Spanish Fork, Utah 84660
Ph: 800-821-5783 Fax: 801-798-9418

**Nosler Bullets, Inc.** (bullets)
P.O. Box 671
Bend, Oregon 97709
Ph: 503-382-3921 Fax: 503-388-4667

**Nygord Precision Products** (Unique handguns, rifles)
P.O. Box 8394
La Crescenta, California 91224
Ph: 818-352-3027

**Olin/Winchester** (ammunition, primers, cases)
427 North Shamrock
East Alton, Illinois 62024
Ph: 618-258-2000

**Palsa Outdoor Products** (recoil pads)
P.O. Box 81336
Lincoln, Nebraska 68501-1336
Ph: 402-488-5288 Fax: 402-488-2321

**Para-Ordnance** (handguns)
3411 McNicoll Avenue #14
Scarborough, Ontario, Canada M1V 2V6
Ph: 416-297-7855 Fax: 416-297-1289

**Parker Reproductions** (shotguns)
124 River Road
Middlesex, New Jersey 08846
Ph: 908-469-0100 Fax: 908-469-9692

**Pedersoli, Davide** (replica firearms)
Available through Flintlocks Etc.

**Peltor Inc.** (hearing protection products)
41 Commercial Way
East Providence, Rhode Island 02914
Ph: 401-438-4800 Fax: 401-434-1708

**Pentax** (scopes)
35 Inverness Drive East
Englewood, Colorado 80112
Ph: 303-799-8000 Fax: 303-790-1131

**Perazzi U.S.A.** (shotguns)
1207 S. Shamrock Ave.
Monrovia, California 91016
Ph: 818-303-0068 Fax: 818-303-2081

**Piotti** (shotguns)
Available through W. L. Moore & Co.

**Precision Sales International** (Anschutz pistols and rifles; Erma pistols; Marocchi shotguns)
P.O. Box 1776
Westfield, Massachusetts 01086
Ph: 413-562-5055

**Precision Small Arms** (handguns)
155 Carleton Rd.
Charlottesville, Virginia 22902
Ph: 804-293-6124 Fax: 804-295-0780

**Quarton USA** (sights)
7042 Alamo Downs Parkway, Suite 250
San Antonio, Texas 78238-4518
Ph: 210-520-8430 Fax: 210-520-8433

**RCBS, Inc.** (reloading tools)
See Blount, Inc.

**Redding Reloading Equipment** (reloading tools)
1089 Starr Road
Cortland, New York 13045
Ph: 607-753-3331 Fax: 607-756-8445

**Redfield** (scopes)
5800 East Jewell Avenue
Denver, Colorado 80227
Ph: 303-757-6411 Fax: 303-756-2338

**Remington Arms Company, Inc.** (rifles, shotguns, blackpowder, ammunition)
1007 Market Street
Wilmington, Delaware 19898
Ph: 302-773-5291 Fax: 302-774-5776

**Rizzini** (shotguns)
Available through Lou Alessandri & Sons, Ltd.

**Rossi** (handguns, rifles, shotguns)
Available through Interarms

**Rottweil** (shotguns)
Available through Dynamit Nobel/RWS

**Ruger** (handguns, rifles, shotguns, blackpowder guns)
See Sturm, Ruger & Company, Inc.

**Ruko Products, Inc.** (rifles)
2245 Kenmore Avenue, Suite 102
Buffalo, New York 14207
Ph: 716-874-2707 Fax: 416-826-1353

**Sako** (rifles, actions, scope mounts)
Available through Stoeger Industries

**Sauer** (rifles)
c/o Paul Company, Inc.
27385 Pressonville Road
Wellsville, Kansas 66092
Ph: 913-883-4444 Fax: 913-883-2525

**Savage Arms** (rifles)
Springdale Road
Westfield, Massachusetts 01085
Ph: 413-568-7001 Fax: 413-562-7764

**Schmidt and Bender** (scopes)
Schmidt & Bender U.S.A.
P.O. Box 134
Meriden, New Hampshire 03770
Ph: 800-468-3450 Fax: 603-469-3471

**SGS Importers International Inc.** (Bersa and Llama handguns)
1750 Brielle Avenue
Wanamassa, New Jersey 07712
Ph: 908-493-0302 Fax: 908-493-0301

**Shiloh Rifle Mfg. Co., Inc.** (Shiloh Sharps blackpowder rifles)
P.O. Box 279, Industrial Park
Big Timber, Montana 59011
Ph: 406-932-4454 Fax: 406-932-5627

**Shooting Systems Group, Inc.** (gun holsters, cases)
1075 Headquarters Park
Fenton, Missouri 63026
Ph: 314-343-3575 Fax: 314-349-3311

**Sierra Bullets** (bullets)
P.O. Box 818
1400 West Henry St.
Sedalia, Missouri 65301
Ph: 816-827-6300 Fax: 816-827-6300

**Sigarms Inc.** (SIG-Sauer handguns)
Corporate Park
Exeter, New Hampshire 03862
Ph: 603-772-2302 Fax: 603-772-9082

**Simmons Outdoor Corp.** (scopes)
2571 Executive Center Circle East, Suite 100
Tallahassee, Florida 32301
Ph: 904-878-5100 Fax: 904-878-0300

**SKB Shotguns** (shotguns)
4325 South 120th Street
P.O. Box 37669
Omaha, Nebraska 68137
Ph: 800-752-2767 Fax: 402-330-8029

**Smith & Wesson** (handguns)
2100 Roosevelt Avenue
Springfield, Massachusetts 01102-2208
Ph: 413-781-8300 Fax: 413-731-8980

**Speer** (bullets)
See Blount, Inc.

**Springfield Inc.** (handguns, rifles)
420 West Main Street
Geneseo, Illinois 61254
Ph: 309-944-5631 Fax: 309-944-3676

**Star** (handguns)
Available through Interarms

**Steyr-Mannlicher** (rifles)
Available through Gun South Inc.

**Stoeger Industries** (American Eagle Luger; Pro Series handguns®; IGA shotguns; InterAims sights; Sako actions, mounts & rifles; Tikka rifles & shotguns)
5 Mansard Court
Wayne, New Jersey 07470
Ph: 201-872-9500 Fax: 201-872-2230

**Stone Mountain Arms** (blackpowder rifles, handguns)
c/o CVA, 5988 Peachtree Corners East
Norcross, Georgia 30071
Ph: 404-449-4687 Fax: 404-242-8546

**Sturm, Ruger and Company, Inc.** (Ruger handguns, rifles, shotguns)
Lacey Place
Southport, Connecticut 06490
Ph: 203-259-4537 Fax: 203-259-2167

**Swarovski Optik North America** (scopes)
One Wholesale Way
Cranston, Rhode Island 02920
Ph: 401-942-3380 Fax: 401-946-2587

**Swift Instruments, Inc.** (scopes and mounts)
952 Dorchester Avenue
Boston, Massachusetts 02125
Ph; 800-446-1116 Fax: 617-436-3232

**Tasco** (scopes and mounts)
7600 N.W. 26th Street
Miami, Florida 33122
Ph: 305-591-3670 Fax: 305-592-5895

**Taurus International, Inc.** (handguns)
16175 N.W. 49th Avenue
Miami, Florida 33014
Ph: 305-624-1115 Fax: 305-623-7506

**Texas Arms** (handguns)
P.O. Box 154906
Waco, Texas 76715
Ph: 817-867-6972

**Thompson/Center Arms** (handguns, rifles, blackpowder guns)
Farmington Road, P.O. Box 5002
Rochester, New Hampshire 03867
Ph: 603-332-2394 Fax: 603-332-5133

**Tikka** (rifles, shotguns)
Available through Stoeger Industries

**Traditions, Inc.** (blackpowder guns)
P.O. Box 235
Deep River, Connecticut 06417
Ph: 203-526-9555 Fax: 203-526-4564

**Trius Products, Inc.** (traps, clay targets)
221 South Miami Avenue, P.O. Box 25
Cleves, Ohio 45002
Ph: 513-941-5682 Fax: 513-941-7970

**Uberti USA, Inc.** (blackpowder rifles, revolvers)
362 Limerock Rd., P.O. Box 469
Lakeville, Connecticut 06039
Ph: 203-435-8068

**UFA Inc.** (Teton blackpowder rifles)
7655 E. Evans Rd. #2
Scottsdale, Arizona 85260
Ph: 602-998-3941 Fax: 602-922-0148

**Ultra Light Arms Company** (rifles)
214 Price Street, P.O. Box 1270
Granville, West Virginia 26505
Ph: 304-599-5687 Fax: 304-599-5687

**Unique** (handguns, rifles)
Available through Nygord Precision Products

**U.S. Repeating Arms Co.** (Winchester rifles, shotguns)
275 Winchester Avenue
New Haven, Connecticut 06511
Ph: 203-789-5000 Fax: 203-789-5071

**Voere** (rifles)
Available through JägerSport

**Walther** (handguns, rifles)
Available through Interarms

**Weatherby, Inc.** (rifles, shotguns, ammunition)
2781 Firestone Boulevard
South Gate, California 90280
Ph: 213-569-7186 Fax: 213-569-5025

**Weaver** (scopes, mount rings)
See Blount, Inc.

**Wesson Firearms Co., Inc.** (handguns)
Maple Tree Industrial Center, Route 20
Wilbraham Road
Palmer, Massachusetts 01069
Ph: 413-267-4081 Fax: 413-267-3601

**White Shooting Systems** (blackpowder rifles)
25 East Highway 40, Box 330-12
Roosevelt, Utah 84066
Ph: 801-277-3085 Fax: 801-722-3054

**Wichita Arms** (handguns)
P.O. Box 11371
Wichita, Kansas 67211
Ph: 316-265-0661

**Wideview Scope Mount Corp.** (mounts, rings)
13535 S. Hwy. 16
Rapid City, South Dakota 57701
Ph: 605-341-3220 Fax: 605-341-9142

**Wildey Inc.** (handguns)
P.O. Box 475
Brookfield, Connecticut 06804
Ph: 203-355-9000

**Williams Gun Sight Co.** (sights, scopes, mounts)
7389 Lapeer Road, P.O. Box 329
Davison, Michigan 48423
Ph: 313-653-2131 Fax: 313-658-2140

**Winchester** (ammunition, primers, cases)
See Olin/Winchester

**Winchester** (domestic rifles, shotguns)
See U.S. Repeating Arms Co.

**Winslow Arms Co.** (rifles)
P.O. Box 783
Camden, South Carolina 29020
PH: 803-432-2938

**Zeiss Optical, Inc.** (scopes)
1015 Commerce Street
Petersburg, Virginia 23803
Ph: 804-861-0033 Fax: 804-733-4024

# CALIBERFINDER

How to use this guide: To find a 22 LR handgun, look under that heading in the **HANDGUNS** section below. You'll find several models of that description, including the Beretta Model 89. Next, turn to the **GUNFINDER** section and locate the heading for **Beretta** (pistols, in this case). Beretta's Model 89 Gold Standard appears on page 107.

## HANDGUNS

### 22 LONG

**Harrington & Richardson** Models 939 Premier Target, 949 Classic Western, Sportsman 999
**Mitchell Arms** Olympic I.S.U.
**New England Firearms** Standard and Ultra Revolvers

### 22 LONG RIFLE

**American Arms** Models CX-22, PK-22 and PX-22, Model P-98
**American Derringer** Models 1, 7, 11
**Anschutz** Exemplar and Exemplar XIV
**Benelli** Models MP90S Target and MP95E
**Beretta** Models 21, 87 and 89 Gold Standard
**Bernardelli** Model PO10 Target Pistol
**Bersa** Model Thunder 22
**Browning** Buck Mark 22 and 5.5 Target Series, Micro Buck Mark
**Charter Arms** Off-Duty
**Colt** Cadet and .22 Target
**Daewoo** Model DP52
**Davis** D-Series Derringers
**EMF/Dakota** Dakota Target, Hartford Scroll-Engraved Single Action Revolver
**Erma** ESP 85A Competition Pistols
**European American Armory** Windicator DA
**Feather** Guardian Angel
**Freedom Arms** Model 252
**Hämmerli** Models 160 Free Pistol, 162 Electronic, 208S Standard Pistol, 212 Hunter, 280 Target Pistol
**Harrington & Richardson** Models 939 Premier Target, 949 Classic Western, Sportsman 999
**Heckler and Koch** Model P7K3
**Heritage** Rough Rider SA, Sentry DA
**Hi-Standard** Supermatic Citation, Citation MS, Trophy and Tournament Models; Victor, Sport King, Olympic I.S.U.
**KBI** Model FEG SMC-22
**Magnum Research** Mountain Eagle
**Mitchell Arms** Target Pistols (Citation II, Sharpshooter II, Victor II, Trophy II); Sport King II
**New England Firearms** Standard and Ultra Revolvers
**North American Arms** Mini-Revolvers and Mini-Master Series
**Rossi** Model 518
**Ruger** New Bearcat SA, Bisley SA Target, Mark II Pistols, New Model Super Single-Six, Model SP101 Revolver
**Smith & Wesson** Models 41, 63, 422, 617 (K-22 Masterpiece), 2206, 2206 Target, 2213/2214
**Stoeger** Pro Series 95
**Taurus** Models 94, 96, PT-22
**Thompson/Center** Contender Bull Barrel, Octagon Barrel and "Super 14"
**A. Uberti** 1871 Rolling Block Target Pistol
**Unique** Models DES 69U, Int'l Silhouette and Sport
**Walther** Model TPH Double Action
**Dan Wesson** Models 22 and 722; 22 Silhouette Revolver
**Wichita Arms** International Pistol

### 22 HORNET

**Anschutz** Exemplar Hornet
**Magnum Research** Lone Eagle SS
**MOA** Maximum
**Thompson/Center** Contender Bull Barrel and Super "14"
**Uberti** 1871 Rolling Block Target Pistol

### 22 MAG./22 WIN. MAG. (WMR)

**American Derringer** Models 6, 7 and 11
**AMT** 22 Automag II
**Charter Arms** Off-Duty
**Davis** Long-Bore D-Series and D-Series Derringers
**European American Armory** Windicator DA Revolver
**Feather** Guardian Angel
**Freedom Arms** Model 252
**Heritage** Rough Rider SA, Sentry DA
**New England Firearms** Ultra Mag. Revolver
**North American** Mini-Revolvers and Mini-Master Series
**Rossi** Model 515
**Ruger** New Bearcat
**Smith & Wesson** Model 651
**Taurus** Model 941
**Thompson/Center** Contender Bull Barrel
**Uberti** 1871 Rolling Block Target Pistol
**Unique** International Silhouette and Sport
**Wichita Arms** International Pistol

### 22 SHORT

**Harrington & Richardson** Models 939 Premier Target, 949 Classic Western, Sportsman 999
**Hi-Standard** Military
**Mitchell Arms** Olympic I.S.U.
**New England Firearms** Standard and Ultra Revolvers
**Unique** Model DES 2000U

### 22-250

**Magnum Research** Lone Eagle

### 223 REMINGTON

**American Derringer** Model 1
**Magnum Research** Lone Eagle SS
**Thompson/Center** Contender Bull Barrel, Hunter, "Super 14"

### 243

**Magnum Research** Lone Eagle

### 25 AUTO (ACP)

**Beretta** Model 21 Bobcat, Model 950 BS Jetfire
**Davis** D-Series Derringers
**Heritage** Model H25B/H25G Semiauto
**KBI** Model PSP-25
**Precision Small Arms** Model PSP-25
**Taurus** Model PT-25
**Walther** DA Model TPH

### 7mm BR

**Magnum Research** Lone Eagle
**Wichita** Silhouette

### 7mm SUPER MAG.

**Wichita Arms** International Pistols

### 7mm T.C.U.

**Thompson/Center** Contender Bull Barrel
**Unique** International Silhouette

### 7mm-08

**Magnum Research** Model Lone Eagle

### 7-30 WATERS

**Thompson/Center** Contender Hunter, Super "14"
**Wichita Arms** International Pistol

### 30 CARBINE

**American Derringer** Model 1
**AMT** Automag III
**Ruger** New Model Blackhawk SA

### 30-06

**Magnum Research** Lone Eagle

### 30-30 WIN.

**American Derringer** Model 1
**Magnum Research** Lone Eagle
**Thompson/Center** Contender Bull Barrel and Hunter, Super "14"
**Wichita Arms** International Pistol

### 300 WHISPER

**Thompson/Center** Contender Super "14" and Bull Barrel

### 308 WINCHESTER

**Magnum Research** Lone Eagle
**Wichita Arms** Silhouette

### 32 AUTO

**Davis** D-Series Derringers, Model P-32
**European American Armory** SA Compacts
**Walther** Model PP Double Action

### 32 H&H MAGNUM

**Wichita** International Pistol

### 32 H&R MAG.

**Charter Arms** Police Undercover
**Davis** Big-Bore D-Series
**New England Firearms** Lady Ultra Revolver, Standard Revolver
**Dan Wesson** Models 32 and 732 Six Shot

### 32 MAGNUM

**American Derringer** Models 1, 7, 11, Lady Derringer
**Charter Arms** Police Undercover
**Ruger** Model SP101, Bisley SA Target, New Model Single Six SSM

### 32 S&W/32 S&W LONG

**American Derringer** Models 1 and 7
**Charter Arms** Lady On-Duty
**Hämmerli** Model 280 Target Pistol
**New England** Standard Revolver
**Ruger** New Model Single-Six SSM
**Dan Wesson** Models 32 and 732 Six Shot

### 32 S&W WADCUTTER

**Erma** ESP 85A Competition Pistols, Model 773 Match
**Benelli** Models MP90S and MP95E

**New England** Standard Revolver
**Ruger** New Model Single-Six

**32-20**

**American Derringer** Model 1
**EMF/Dakota** Hartford SA Models
**Thompson/Center** Contender Bull Barrel

**35 REMINGTON**

**Magnum Research** Lone Eagle
**Thompson/Center** Contender Hunter and Super "14"

**357 MAGNUM**

**American Arms** Regulator SA
**American Derringer** Models 1, 4, 6, 38 DA, Lady Derringer
**Charter Arms** Bulldog Special
**Colt** King Cobra, Python Premium
**Coonan Arms** 357 Magnum, Cadet Compact
**EMF/Dakota** Model 1873, Model 1873 Dakota SA, 1875 Outlaw, 1890 Remington Police, Hartford Scroll-Engraved SA, Target
**Erma** Model 777 Sporting Revolver
**European American Armory** Big Bore Bounty Hunter, Windicator DA
**Freedom Arms** Model 353, Silhouette/Competition Models
**L.A.R.** Grizzly Mark I
**Magnum Research** Desert Eagle
**Mitchell Arms** Titan DA Series
**Rossi** Models 971 and 971 Compact
**Ruger** Bisley SA Target, New Model Blackhawk and Blackhawk Convertible, Model GP-100, Model SP101
**Sig-Sauer** Model P229
**Smith & Wesson** Models 13, 19, 65 LadySmith, 66, 586, 640, 686 and 686 Powerport
**Taurus** Models 65, 66, 605, 607, 669, 689
**Texas Arms** Defender Derringer
**Thompson/Center** Contender Bull Barrel
**Uberti** 1871 Rolling Block Target Pistol, 1873 Cattleman, 1875 Outlaw/1890 Police
**Unique** Model International Silhouette
**Dan Wesson** Models 14, 15, 714 and 715; Fixed Barrel Revolvers
**Wichita Arms** International Pistol

**357 MAXIMUM/SUPER MAG.**

**American Derringer** Models 1 and 4
**Magnum Research** Lone Eagle
**Thompson/Center** Contender Bull Barrel
**Dan Wesson** Model 740, 357 Super Mag., Hunter Series (Varmint), Super Ram Silhouette
**Wichita Arms** International Pistol

**358 WINCHESTER**

**Magnum Research** Lone Eagle
**MOA** Maximum

**36**

**EMF** Colt 1851 Navy

**375 WINCHESTER**

**Thompson/Center** Contender Hunter and Super "14"

**38 SPECIAL**

**American Derringer** Models 1, 7, 10, 11, 38 DA, Lady Derringer, 125th Anniversary Double Derringers
**Charter Arms** Off-Duty, Lady On-Duty and Police Undercover
**Colt** Detective Special, King Cobra DA, Python Premium DA, Model 38 SF-VI, Police Positive
**Davis** Big-Bore D-Series
**Heritage** Sentry DA
**Mitchell Arms** Guardian II Revolver
**Rossi** Models 68S and M88S Series, 851, 971, Lady Rossi
**Ruger** GP-100 DA, New Model Blackhawk, SP101
**Smith & Wesson** (38 S&W Special) Models 10, 13, 14, 15, 36, 37, 38, 49, 60, 64, 65, 442, Model 649 Bodyguard, LadySmith Models 36-LS and 60-LS and 65-LS
**Springfield** PDP Series
**Taurus** Models 80, 82, 83, 85, 605, 607
**Texas Arms** Defender Derringer
**Dan Wesson** Models 8, 9, 708, 709; Fixed Barrel Revolvers

**38 SUPER**

**American Derringer** Model 1
**AMT** Backup
**Auto-Ordnance** Models 1911A1 Thompson and Competition
**Colt** Combat Commander MK Series 80, Gold Cup Combat Elite, Gov't. Model Series 80
**European American Armory** Witness, Witness Gold Team and Subcompact, Windicator
**McMillan** Wolverine
**Sig-Sauer** Model P220 "American"
**Springfield** Model 1911-A1 Standard, 38 Super, 1911-A1 Factory Comp, Hi-Capacity Raceguns

**38 Wadcutter**

**McMillan** Wolverine

**38 + P**

**Ruger** Model SP101 Spurless
**Dan Wesson** Model 738+P "L'il Dan"

**38-40**

**Colt** Single Action Army
**EMF/Dakota** Model 1873, Hartford SA Model
**Uberti** 1873 Cattleman

**380 AUTO (ACP)**

**American Arms** Escort
**American Derringer** Models 1, 7 and 11
**AMT** Models 380 Backup and Backup II
**Beretta** Cheetah Models 84, 85 and 86
**Bernardelli** PO18 Compact Target Pistol
**Bersa** Model Thunder 380, Series 95
**Browning** Model BDA-380
**Colt** Government Model 380, Mustang, Mustang Plus II, Mustang PocketLite 380
**CZ** Model 83
**Daewoo** Model DH380
**Davis** P-380
**European American Armory** European SA Compacts
**Grendel** Model P-12
**Heckler and Koch** Model P7K3
**Hi-Point** Model 380 Polymer
**KBI** FEG Model SMC-380, Baikal IJ-70
**Llama** Automatic (Small Frame)
**Sig-Sauer** Model P230
**Springfield** Models MD-1
**Taurus** Model PT-58
**Walther** Models PP, PPK and PPK/S

**9mm×18**

**KBI** Baikal IJ-70 and FEG Model SMC-918

**9mm PARABELLUM (LUGER)/9mm × 19**

**American Derringer** 38 DA
**Auto-Ordnance** Model 1911A1 Thompson
**Astra** Models A-70, A-75 and A-100
**Beretta** Models 92D, 92FS, 920, Brigadier, Centurion, Cougar Series
**Bernardelli** Model PO18 Target and Compact
**Bersa** Thunder 9 DA
**Browning** Hi-Power, BDM Double Action
**CZ** Models 75, 75 Compact, 85, 85 Compact
**Daewoo** Model DP51, DP51C (Compact), DP51S
**Davis** Long-Bore D-Series
**European American Armory** Witness, Witness FAB, Gold Team, Witness Subcompact
**Glock** Models 17, 17L Competition, Model 19 Compact
**Heckler and Koch** Models HK USP, P7M8, P7M13
**Heritage** Senty DA
**Hi-Point Firearms** Model 9mm and Compact
**Kahr Arms** Model K9
**KBI** FEG Model PJK-9HP
**Llama** Max-I Pistol
**Luger,** American Eagle P-08
**Magnum Research** Baby Eagle
**McMillan** Wolverine
**Ruger** Blackhawk Convertible, Model SP101 Spurless, P-Series
**Sig-Sauer** Models P225, P226, P228, P229
**Smith & Wesson** Models 909, 910, 940 Centennial, Model 3900 and 6900 Compact Series, Model 5900 Series, Sigma Series
**Springfield** Model 1911-A1 Standard, Hi-Capacity Raceguns
**Star** Models Firestar M43, Firestar Plus and Ultrastar
**Taurus** Models PT-92 AF, PT-92AFC, PT-99, PT-99AFD, PT-908
**Texas Arms** Defender Derringer
**Walther** Models P-38, P-5 DA

**9mm×21**

**European American Armory** Witness Gold Team

**10mm**

**American Derringer** Model 1
**Auto-Ordnance** Model 1911A1 Thompson
**Colt** Delta Elite, Delta Gold Cup
**Emerging Technologies** Laseraim Series I, II, III
**Glock** Model 20
**L.A.R. Grizzly** Mark I
**McMillan** Wolverine

**40 AUTO**

**Beretta** Cougar Series
**Ruger** P-Series Pistols

**40 S&W**

**American Derringer** Model 1, 38 DA Derringer
**AMT** Backup
**Astra** Models A-70, A-75, A-100
**Beretta** Brigadier, Centurion, Models 96, 96D
**Browning** Hi-Power
**Daewoo** Model DH40
**European American Armory** Witness, Witness FAB, Subcompact and Gold Team
**Glock** Models 22, 23, 24
**Heckler and Koch** Model HK USP, Model P7M10
**Hi-Point Firearms** Model 40
**KBI** FEG GKK-45
**Magnum Research** Baby Eagle
**Para-Ordnance** Model P16
**Sig-Sauer** Model P229
**Smith & Wesson** Model 411, Model 4000 Series Compact and Full Size, Sigma Series
**Star** Model Firestar M40, Firestar Plus
**Taurus** Models PT-100/101

**41 ACTION EXPRESS**

**Magnum Research** Baby Eagle

**41 MAGNUM**

**American Derringer** Model 1
**Magnum Research** Desert Eagle

**Ruger** Bisley SA Target, New Model Blackhawk
**Smith & Wesson** Model 657
**Dan Wesson** Models 41 and 741, Hunter (Boar) Series, Super Ram Silhouette

**.410**

**American Derringer** Models 1, 4 and 6
**Texas Arms** Defender Derringer
**Thompson/Center** Contender Bull Barrel, Super "14" and "16"

**44 MAG./44 REM. MAG.**

**American Arms** Buckhorn SA
**American Derringer** Models 1, 4
**Colt** Anaconda Revolver
**European American Armory** Big Boar Bounty Hunter
**Freedom Arms** Models 454 Field and Premier Grades, Silhouette/Competition Models
**L.A.R.** Grizzly Mark 4
**Magnum Research** Desert Eagle, Lone Eagle
**Ruger** Bisley SA Target, Redhawk, Super Redhawk, New Model Super Blackhawk SA, Vaquero SA
**Smith & Wesson** Models 29, 629, 629 Classic
**Taurus** Model 44
**Texas Arms** Defender Derringer
**Thompson/Center** Contender Bull Barrel, Hunter, Super "14"
**Uberti** Buckhorn 1873 SA Target
**Unique** Model Int'l Silhouette
**Dan Wesson** Models 44, 744 and Fixed Barrel Revolvers, Hunter (Buck) Series, Super Ram Silhouette

**44 SPECIAL/44 S&W SPECIAL**

**American Derringer** Models 1, 7
**Charter Arms** Bulldog Pug 44 Special
**Colt** Anaconda
**EMF/Dakota** Hartford Models
**Rossi** Model 720, 720 Covert Special DA
**Ruger** New Model Super Blackhawk
**Smith & Wesson** Model 629, 629 Classic
**Taurus** Models 431 and 441
**Uberti** 1873 Cattleman
**Dan Wesson** Fixed Barrel Revolvers

**44-40**

**American Arms** Regulator SA
**American Derringer** Model 1, 125th Anniversary Commemorative
**Colt** Single Action Army
**EMF/Dakota** Models 1851 Colt Navy, 1873, 1873 Dakota SA, 1875 Outlaw, 1890 Remington Police, Hartford Models, Hartford Scroll-Engraved SA
**Navy Arms** 1873 SA, 1875 Schofield
**Ruger** Vaquero SA Revolver
**Uberti** Buckhorn 1873 SA Target, 1873 Cattleman, 1875 Outlaw/1890 Police

**444 MARLIN**

**Magnum Research** Lone Eagle

**445 SUPERMAG**

**Dan Wesson** Models 445 and 7445 Supermag, Hunter Series (Grizzly)

**45 AUTO (ACP)**

**American Derringer** Models 1, 4, 6, 10
**AMT** Backup, Longslide, 1911 Government and Hardballer Models
**Astra** Models A-75 and A-100
**Auto-Ordnance** Model 1911 "The General," 1911A1 Competition, 1911A1 Thompson, Deluxe, Pit Bull, WWII Parkerized
**Colt** Anaconda, Combat Commander MK IV Series 80, Double Eagle MK Series 90, Gold Cup National Match, Government Model, Model 1991A1 (Compact and Commander), Officer's 45 ACP
**Emerging Technologies** Laseraim Series I, II, III
**European American Armory** Witness, Witness FAB/Gold Team/Subcompact
**Glock** Model 21 Pistol
**Heckler and Koch** Model HK USP
**Hi-Point Firearms** Model 45
**KBI** FEG GKK-45
**Kimber** Model Classic Series .45
**L.A.R.** Grizzly Mark I
**Laseraim** Series I, II and III
**Llama** MAX-I Compact IX-D, IX-C Government Model
**McMillan** Wolverine
**Mitchell Arms** Alpha Series, 1911 Gold Series
**Para-Ordnance** Models P12, P13 and P14
**Ruger** P-Series
**Sig-Sauer** Model P220 "American"
**Smith & Wesson** Model 625, Model 4500 Series Compact and Full Size
**Springfield** Model 1911-A1 Standard, Champion, Compact, Defender, Factory Comp, Trophy Match; Hi-Capacity Full-House Custom Racegun, Model PDP Series High Capacity Carry Gun
**Star** Model Firestar M45 and Firestar Plus
**Taurus** Model PT-945
**Texas Arms** Defender Derringer
**Uberti** 1873 Cattleman, 1875 Outlaw/1890 Police
**Wesson** Pin Gun

**45 COLT/LONG COLT**

**American Arms** Regulator SA
**American Derringer** Models 1, 4, 6, 10, 125th Anniversary Commemorative, Lady Derringer, M-4 Alaskan Survival
**Colt** Single Action Army Revolver, Anaconda
**EMF/Dakota** Hartford Models (Artillery, Cavalry Colt, Single Action, Scroll Engraved); Models 1873, 1873 Dakota SA, 1875 "Outlaw," Model 1890 Remington Police, Pinkerton Detective SA, Target
**European American Armory** Big Bore Bounty Hunter
**Navy Arms** 1873 SA, 1895 Artillery and Calvary, 1875 Schofield
**Ruger** Model Bisley SA Target, New Model Blackhawk, Vaquero
**Texas Arms** Defender Derringer
**Thompson/Center** Contender Bull Barrel, Super "14" and "16"
**Uberti** 1871 Rolling Block Target Pistol, 1873 Cattleman, 1875 Outlaw/1890 Police
**Wesson** Model 745 Colt Revolver

**45 ITALIAN**

**McMillan** Wolverine

**45 WIN. MAG.**

**American Derringer** Model 1
**AMT** Automag IV
**L.A.R.** Grizzly Mark I
**Wildey** Hunter and Survivor Pistols

**45-70 GOV'T.**

**American Derringer** Models 1, 4, and M-4 Alaskan Survival
**Thompson/Center** Contender Hunter

**454 CASULL**

**Freedom Arms** Casull Field and Premier

**475 WILDEY MAG.**

**Wildey** Hunter and Survivor Pistols

**50 MAG. AE**

**AMT** Automag V
**Freedom Arms** Model 555 Premier
**L.A.R.** Grizzly 50 Mark 5
**Magnum Research** Desert Eagle 50

# RIFLES

## CENTERFIRE—AUTOLOADING

**223 REMINGTON**

**Colt** Match Target Lightweight and Match Target Competition H-Bar, H-Bar II Competition, Match H-Bar
**Ruger** Mini-14, Mini-14 Ranch
**Steyr-Mannlicher** Aug S.A.

**243 WINCHESTER**

**Browning** BAR Mark II
**Remington** Model 7400
**Springfield** M1A Standard, Bush, Super Match, National Match

**270 WIN./WBY.**

**Browning** BAR Mark II
**Remington** Model 7400 (also caliber 280 Rem.)

**30-06**

**Browning** BAR Mark II
**Remington** Model 7400

**300 WIN. MAG.**

**Browning** BAR Mark II

**308 WINCHESTER**

**Browning** BAR Mark II
**Heckler and Koch** PSG-1 Marksman
**Remington** Model 7400
**Springfield** M1A Standard, National Match, Super Match, M1A-A1 Bush

**338 WIN. MAG.**

**Browning** BAR Mark II

**35 WHELEN**

**Remington** Model 7400

**45 AUTO**

**Auto-Ordnance** Thompson Models M1, 1927A1
**Marlin** Model 45

**7mm REM. MAG.**

**Browning** BAR Mark II

**7mm-08**

**Springfield** M1A Standard, Bush, Super Match, National Match

**7.62×39**

**Ruger** Mini-30

**375 H&H MAG.**

**Laurona** Model 2000X Express

**9mm**

**Colt** Match Target Lightweight
**Feather** Model AT-9
**Marlin** Model 9 Camp Carbine

**10mm**

**Auto-Ordnance** Model 1927-A1

## CENTERFIRE—BOLT ACTION

### STANDARD CALIBERS

**7 ACKLEY HORNET, 17 CCM**

**Cooper Arms** Model 40 Classic

**17 BEE**

**Francotte** Bolt Action

**17 REMINGTON**

**Cooper Arms** Model 21 Varmint Extreme
**Remington** Model 700 ADL, BDL, Model Seven
**Sako** Deluxe, Hunter Lightweight, Super Deluxe, Varmint
**Ultra Light** Model 20 Series
**Winslow** Varmint

**22 CCM, 22K HORNET**

**Cooper Arms** Model 40 Classic

**22 HORNET**

**Anschutz** Models 1700 Bavarian, 1700D Custom and Graphite Custom, Mannlicher Model 1733D
**Browning** A-Bolt II Short Action
**Cooper Arms** Model 40 Classic
**CZ** Model CZ 527
**Dakota Arms** Model 76 Varmint
**Ruger** Model 77/22RH
**Ultra Light** Model 20 Series

**22 PPC**

**Cooper Arms** Model 21 Varmint Extreme and Model 21 Benchrest
**Dakota Arms** Model 76 Varmint

**22-250**

**A-Square** Ghenghis Kahn
**Blaser** Model R93
**Browning** Short Action A-Bolt II, Stalker Varmint
**Cooper Arms** Model 22 Pro Varmint Extreme
**Dakota** 76 Classic and Varmint
**Howa** Lightning
**Kimber** Swedish Mauser 98
**McMillan** Classic & Stainless Sporters, Talon Sporter, Varminter
**Remington** Model 700 ADL, BDL, Varmint LS and Synthetic
**Ruger** Model M-77 Mark II All-Weather
**Sako** Deluxe, Hunter Lightweight, Laminated, Left-Handed Models, Super Deluxe, Varmint
**Savage** Model 111G Classic Hunter, Model 112FV and FVSS
**Tikka** Whitetail Hunter
**Ultra Light** Model 20 Series
**Weatherby** Mark V Deluxe, Varmintmaster
**Winchester** Model 70 Featherweight, Classic Stainless, Heavy Barrel Varmint
**Winslow** Basic

**220 SWIFT**

**Cooper Arms** Model 22 Pro Varmint Extreme
**Dakota Arms** Model 76 Varmint
**Remington** Model 700 Varmint Synthetic
**Ruger** Mark II HB
**Winchester** Model 70 Varmint HB

**221 FIREBALL**

**Cooper Arms** Model 21 Varmint Extreme

**222 REM.**

**Blaser** Model R93
**Cooper Arms** Model 21 Varmint Extreme
**CZ** Model ZKM 527
**Francotte** Bolt Action
**Remington** Model 700 ADL, BDL, Varmint LS
**Sako** Deluxe, Hunter Lightweight, Super Deluxe, Varmint
**Steyr-Mannlicher** Models SL, Varmint, Jagd Match
**Ultra Light** Model 20 Series
**Winslow** Varmint

**223 REM.**

**Blaser** Model R 93
**Browning** A-Bolt II Short Action, Stalker, Varmint
**Brown Precision** High Country Youth and Tactical Elite
**Cooper Arms** Model 21 Varmint Extreme and Model 21 Benchrest
**CZ** Model ZKM 527
**Dakota Arms** Model 76 Varmint
**Howa** Lightning
**Jarrett** Lightweight Varmint
**McMillian** Varminter
**Remington** Models 700 ADL, BDL, BDL Stainless, Varmint LS and Synthetic, Model Seven
**Ruger** M-77 RL Ultra Light, M-77 VT Mark II HB, All-Weather, M-77 R
**Sako** Deluxe, Hunter Lightweight, Super Deluxe, Varmint
**Savage** Model 110 Series, Model 111G and 111F Classic Hunter, Model 112 BT Competition, 112FVSS, 116FCS and 116FSS
**Steyr-Mannlicher** Model SL Sporter
**Tikka** Whitetail Hunter
**Ultra Light** Model 20 Series
**Winchester** Models 70 Featherweight, FWT Classic, Lightweight, Ranger, Heavy Barrel Varmint, Classic Stainless
**Winslow** Varmint

**223 UCC CASELESS**

**Voere** Model VEC 91 Lightning Bolt

**243 WINCHESTER**

**A-Square** Ghenghis Khan
**Benton & Brown** Model 93
**Blaser** Model R93
**Brown Precision** High Country Youth
**Browning** A-Bolt II Short Action
**Clifton Arms** Scout
**Cooper Arms** Model 22 Pro Varmint Extreme
**CZ** Models CZ550, ZKK 601, ZKM 537
**Francotte** Bolt Action
**Howa** Lightning
**Kimber** Swedish Mauser Sporter
**McMillan** Benchrest, Talon Sporter, Varminter
**Remington** Model Seven, Models 700 ADL, BDL, BDL (DM), BDL SS, Mountain, Varmint Laminated, 7400, 7600
**Ruger** M-77 VT Mark II HB and All-Weather, M-77RS, M-77RL Ultra Light, M-77RSI International Mannlicher
**Sako** Classic, Deluxe, Hunter Lightweight, Left-Handed Models, LS, Mannlicher-Style Carbine, Super Deluxe, Varmint
**Savage** Models 110 Series, Model 111G and 111F Classic Hunter, Model 116FCS and 116FSS
**Steyr-Mannlicher** Models Luxus, Sporter L, SSG, Jagd Match
**Tikka** Whitetail Hunter
**Ultra Light** Model 20 Series
**Unique** Model TGC
**Winchester** Models 70 Featherweight, FWT Classic, Classic Stainless, DBM, Lightweight, Ranger and Ranger Ladies/Youth, Heavy Barrel Varmint
**Winslow** Basic

**244 REMINGTON**

**Winslow** Basic

**6mm BR**

**McMillan** Benchrest Rifle, Classic, Stainless & Talon Sporters

**6mm PPC**

**Cooper Arms** Model 22 Pro Varmint Extreme
**Dakota Arms** Model 76 Varmint
**McMillan** Benchrest
**Ruger** M-77 VT Mark II HB

**6mm REMINGTON**

**A-Square** Ghenghis Khan
**Benton & Brown** Model 93
**Brown Precision** High Country Youth and Tactical Elite
**McMillan** Benchrest, Classic, Stainless & Talon Sporters, Varminter
**Remington** Model Seven, Models 700 BDL SS, BDL DM
**Ruger** Model M-77R MK II
**Ultra Light** Model 20 Series

**6.5×55mm**

**Kimber** Swedish Mauser 98
**Steyr-Mannlicher** Luxus and Sporter

**25-06**

**A-Square** Ghenghis Khan and Hamilcar
**Benton & Brown** Model 93
**Browning** A-Bolt II
**Cooper Arms** Model 22 Pro Varmint Extreme
**McMillan** Classic, Stainless & Talon Sporters, Varminter
**Remington** Models 700 ADL, BDL, BDL SS, BLD (DM), Mountain, Sendero
**Ruger** Models 77RS, M-77V1 HB
**Sako** Deluxe, Fiberclass, Hunter Lightweight, LS, Left-Handed Models, TRG-S Magnum
**Sauer** Model 90
**Savage** Model 110FP, 111G and 111F Classic Hunter, 112 FV Varmint
**Steyr-Mannlicher** Model MIII Professional
**Tikka** Whitetail Hunter
**Ultra Light** Model 24 Series
**Winslow** Basic

**250 SAVAGE**

**Savage** Model 111G and 111F Classic Hunter
**Ultra Light** Model 20 Series

**257 ACKLEY**

**Ruger** Model M-77RL Ultra Light
**Ultra Light** Model 20 Series

**257 ROBERTS**

**Browning** A-Bolt II Short Action
**Dakota Arms** Model 76 Classic
**Ruger** Model M-77R MK II
**Ultra Light** Model 20 Series
**Winslow** Basic

**264 WINCHESTER**

**A-Square** Hamilcar
**Ultra Light Arms** Model 28 Series

**270 WINCHESTER**

**A-Square** Hamilcar
**Benton & Brown** Model 93
**Blaser** Model R93
**Browning** A-Bolt II Long Action
**CZ** Models CZ550, ZKK 600, ZKM 537
**Dakota Arms** Model 76 Classic
**Francotte** Bolt Action
**Howa** Lightning
**Magnum Research** Mountain Eagle

**McMillan** Alaskan; Classic Stainless & Talon Sporters, Titanium Mountain
**Remington** Models 700 ADL and BDL, BDL SS, BDL Synthetic, BDL (DM), Mountain, 7400, 7600, Sendero
**Ruger** Mark II Series (M-77R, M-77RL, M-77RS, M-77RL Ultralight, 77RSI International, M77 All-Weather, M-77 EXP MK II Express)
**Sako** Classic, Deluxe, Fiberclass, Hunter Lightweight, LS, Mannlicher-Style Carbine, Left-Handed Models, Super Deluxe, TRG-S
**Sauer** Model 90
**Savage** Model 110 Series, Model 111GC and 111FC Classic Hunter, Model 114CU, 116FCS, 116FSK and 116FSS
**Steyr-Mannlicher** Luxus Model M, MIII Professional, Luxus M
**Tikka** Whitetail Hunter
**Ultra Light** Model 24 Series
**Unique** Model TGC
**Weatherby** Models Mark V Alaskan, Sporter, Weathermark
**Winchester** Models 70 Featherweight, FWT Classic, Classic SM, Classic Super Grade, Classic Sporter, DBM, Lightweight, Ranger
**Winslow** Basic

**280 IMP**

**Jarrett** Standard Hunting

**280 REMINGTON**

**A-Square** Hamilcar
**Benton & Brown** Model 93
**Browning** A-Bolt II Long Action
**Dakota Arms** Model 76 Classic
**Magnum Research** Mountain Eagle
**McMillan** Alaskan, Classic, Stainless & Talon Sporters, Titanium Mountain
**Remington** Models 700 ADL, 700 BDL, BDL Synthetic, BDL (DM), BDL SS, Mountain, 7400, 7600
**Ruger** Model M-77R MK II, M-77 All-Weather
**Sako** Deluxe, Fiberclass, Hunter Lightweight, LS, Left-Handed Models, Super Deluxe
**Winchester** Models 70 Featherweight, FWT Classic Lightweight
**Winslow** Basic

**284 WINCHESTER**

**Browning** A-Bolt II Short Action
**McMillan** Classic, Stainless & Talon Sporters
**Ultra Light** Model 20 Series
**Winslow** Basic

**7mm ACKLEY**

**Ultra Light** Model 20 Series

**7mm BR**

**McMillan** Classic Sporter, Talon Sporter

**7mm EXPRESS**

**Ultra Light** Model 24 Series

**7mm MAUSER**

**Remington** Model 700 Mountain
**Ultra Light** Model 20 Series
**Winslow** Basic

**7mm REM./WBY.**

**A-Square** Hamilcar
**CZ** Model CZ 550
**Ultra Light Arms** Model 28 Series

**7mm STW**

**A-Square** Hamilcar
**Jarrett** Model 3

**7mm-08**

**Brown Precision** High Country Youth
**Browning** A-Bolt II Short Action
**Clifton Arms** Scout
**McMillan** Classic, Stainless & Talon Sporters, National Match Varminter
**Remington** Model Seven, Models 700 ADL, BDL, BDL (DM), BDL SS Synthetic, Mountain
**Sako** Deluxe, Hunter Lightweight, LS, Left-Handed Models, Super Deluxe, Varmint
**Savage** Model 111G and 111F Classic Hunter
**Ultra Light** Model 20 Series
**Unique** Model TGC
**Winchester** Model 70 Featherweight, FWT Classic

**7×57**

**CZ** Model CZ 550
**Ruger** Model M-77R MKII

**30-06**

**A-Square** Hamilcar
**Benton & Brown** Model 93
**Browning** A-Bolt II Long Action
**Clifton Arms** Scout
**CZ** Models ZKK 600, ZKM 537
**Dakota Arms** Model 76 Classic
**Francotte** Bolt Action
**Howa** Lightning
**Magnum Research** Mountain Eagle
**McMillan** Alaskan; Classic, Stainless & Talon Sporters; Titanium Mountain
**Remington** Models 700 ADL, BDL, BDL Stainless Synthetic and BDL (DM), Mountain, 7400, 7400 Carbine, 7600
**Ruger** M-77 All-Weather, M-77EXP Express, Model 77R, 77RL Ultra Light, M-77RS
**Sako** Classic, Deluxe, Mannlicher-Style Carbine, Fiberclass, Hunter Lightweight, LS, Left-Handed Models, Super Deluxe, TRG-S
**Sauer** Model 90
**Savage** Model 111FC and 111GC Classic Hunter, Model 114CU, 116FSS, 116FCS, 116FSK
**Steyr-Mannlicher** Model Sporter M, Luxus M, M111 Professional
**Tikka** Whitetail Hunter
**Ultra Light** Model 24 Series
**Unique** Model TGC
**Weatherby** Mark V Alaskan, Deluxe, Lazermark, Sporter, Weathermark
**Winchester** Models 70 Featherweight, Classic Stainless, Classic SM, DBM, FWT Classic, Lightweight, Ranger, Super Grade, Classic Sporter
**Winslow** Basic

**30-06 CARBINE**

**Remington** Models 7400 and 7600 Carbines

**300 SAVAGE**

**Savage** 110 Series, Model 111G and 111F Classic Hunter
**Ultra Light** Model 20 Series

**300 WINCHESTER**

**A-Square** Hamilcar
**Ultra Light Arms** Model 28 Series

**308 WINCHESTER**

**Benton & Brown** Model 93
**Blaser** Model R 93
**Browning** A-Bolt II Short Action
**Brown Precision** High Country Youth and Tactical Elite
**Clifton Arms** Scout
**Cooper Arms** Model 22 Pro Varmint Extreme
**CZ** Models CZ 550, ZKK 601, ZKM 537
**Francotte** Bolt Action
**Howa** Lightning
**Kimber** Swedish Mauser
**McMillan** Benchrest, Classic, Stainless & Talon Sporters, National Match, Varminter
**Remington** Models 700 ADL, BDL, BDL Synthetic, BDL Laminated, BDL (DM), Mountain, Varmint Synthetic, 7400, 7600
**Ruger** Models M-77 All Weather, M-77R, M-77RL Ultra Light, M-77RS, Mannlicher, M-77VT HB
**Sako** Deluxe, Hunter Lightweight, LS, Left-Handed Models, Mannlicher-Style Carbine, TRG-21, Super Deluxe, Varmint
**Savage** Model 110 Series, Model 111G and 111F Classic Hunter, Model 112BT Competition, Model 116 FSS and FCS "Weather Warrior"
**Steyr-Mannlicher** Luxus L, Match UIT, Sporter L, Jagd Match, SSG
**Tikka** Whitetail Hunter
**Ultra Light** Model 20 Series
**Unique** Model TGC
**Winchester** Model 70 Featherweight, FWT Classic Stainless, Classic DBM, Lightweight, Ladies Ranger Youth, Heavy Barrel Varmint
**Winslow** Basic

**338-06**

**A-Square** Hamilcar

**35 WHELEN**

**Remington** Models 7400, 7600

**358 WINCHESTER**

**Ultra Light** Model 20 Series
**Winslow** Basic

## CENTERFIRE—BOLT ACTION

## MAGNUM CALIBERS

**222 REM. MAG.**

**Cooper Arms** Model 21 Varmint Extreme
**Dakota Arms** Model 76 Varmint
**Steyr-Mannlicher** Model Sporter (SL)
**Ultra Light** Model 20 Series
**Winslow** Varmint

**240 WBY. MAG.**

**Weatherby** Mark V Deluxe, Lazermark

**257 WBY./ROBERTS**

**A-Square** Hamilcar
**Benton & Brown** Model 93
**Blaser** Model R93
**Weatherby** Mark V, Deluxe, Euromark, Eurosport, Lazermark, Sporter, Stainless, Synthetic
**Winslow** Basic

**264 WIN. MAG.**

**Benton & Brown** Model 93
**Blaser** Model R93
**Winchester** Model 70 Sporter
**Winslow** Basic

**270 WBY./WIN. MAG.**

**Weatherby** Mark V, Deluxe, Euromark, Eurosport, Lazermark, Sporter, Stainless, Synthetic
**Winchester** Model 70 Sporter
**Winslow** Basic

**7mm REM./WBY. MAG.**

**A-Square** Caesar
**Benton & Brown** Model 93
**Blaser** Model R93
**Browning** A-Bolt II Long Action Mag.

**Dakota Arms** Model 76 Classic
**Howa** Lightning
**Magnum Research** Mountain Eagle
**McMillan** Alaskan; Classic, Stainless & Talon Sporters; Long Range Rifle, Titanium Mountain
**Remington** African Plains, Alaskan Wilderness, Models 700 ADL, BDL, BDL (DM), BDL SS Synthetic, Sendero
**Ruger** Models M-77 All-Weather, M-77EXP Express, 77R, M-77RS, M-77LR
**Sako** Classic, Deluxe, Fiberclass, Hunter Lightweight, LS, Left-Handed Models, Super Deluxe, TRG-S
**Sauer** Model 90
**Savage** Model 114 CU, 116 FCS, 116FSK, 116FSS, 111GC and 111FC, Classic Hunter, 112 FV Varmint
**Steyr-Mannlicher** Luxus S, Sporter S
**Tikka** Whitetail Hunter
**Unique** Model TGC
**Weatherby** Mark V Deluxe, Euromark, Eurosport, Lazermark, Sporter, Stainless, Synthetic
**Winchester** Model 70 Classic SM, Classic Stainless, Classic Super Grade, DBM, Sporter, Super Grade, Winlite
**Winslow** Basic

### 8mm REM. MAG.

**A-Square** Caesar and Hannibal

### 300 PHOENIX

**McMillan** .300 Phoenix, Long Range, Safari Super Magnum

### 300 WBY. MAG.

**A-Square** Caesar and Hannibal, Hamilcar
**Blaser** Model 93
**McMillan** Alaskan; Classic, Stainless & Talon Sporters; Safari
**Remington** Model 700 BDL SS Synthetic, African Plains, Alaskan Wilderness
**Sako** Deluxe, Hunter Lightweight, Left-Handed Models, Super Deluxe, TRG-S
**Sauer** Model 90
**Ultra Light Arms** Model 40 Series
**Weatherby** Mark V Deluxe, Euromark, Eurosport, Lazermark, Sporter, Stainless, Synthetic, Weathermark
**Winchester** Model 70 Classic Stainless, Sporter
**Winslow** Basic

### 300 WIN. MAG.

**A-Square** Caesar
**Benton & Brown** Model 93
**Blaser** Model R93
**Brown Precision** Tactical Elite
**Browning** A-Bolt II Long Action Mag.
**CZ** Model CZ 550
**Dakota Arms** Model 76 Classic and Safari
**Magnum Research** Mountain Eagle
**McMillan** Alaskan; Classic, Stainless & Talon Sporters; Long Range Rifle, Safari, Titanium Mountain
**Remington** African Plains, Alaskan Wilderness, Models 700 ADL, BDL, BDL SS, Sendero, BDL (DM), Classic
**Ruger** M-77 All-Weather, M-77EXP Express, M-77R, M-77RS, 77R
**Sako** Deluxe, Fiberclass, L. H. Models, Hunter Lightweight, LS, Super Deluxe, TRG-S
**Sauer** Model 90
**Savage** Model 114CU, 116FCS, 116 FSSK, 116SE Safari Express and 116FSS, 111GC and 111FC Classic Hunter, 112 FV Varmint
**Steyr-Mannlicher** Luxus S, Sporter S
**Tikka** Whitetail Hunter
**Unique** Model TGC
**Weatherby** Mark V Sporter, Eurosport, Stainless, Synthetic
**Winchester** Model 70, Classic SM, Classic Stainless, Classic Super Grade, DBM, Sporter
**Winslow** Basic

### 300 H&H

**McMillan** Alaskan; Classic, Stainless & Talon Sporters; Safari

### 308 NORMA

**Remington** Model 700
**Winslow** Basic

### 338 LAPUA

**McMillan** Long Range, Safari Super Magnum
**Sako** Model TRG-S

### 338 WIN. MAG.

**A-Square** Caesar, Hamilcar and Hannibal
**Benton & Brown** Model 93
**Blaser** Model R93
**Browning** A-Bolt II Long Action Mag.
**Dakota Arms** Model 76 Classic, Safari
**Howa**Lightning
**Magnum Research** Mountain Eagle
**McMillan** Classic, Stainless & Talon Sporters, Safari
**Remington** African Plains, Alaskan Wilderness, Models 700 ADL, BDL, BDL Synthetic, BDL (DM)
**Ruger** Models M-77 All-Weather, M-77EXP Express, 77R, M-77RS
**Sako** Deluxe, Hunter Lightweight, Fiberclass, Left-Handed Models, LS, Mannlicher-Style Carbine, Safari Grade, Super Deluxe, TRG-S
**Sauer** Model 90
**Savage** Model 116FCS, 116FSK, 116FSS and 116SE
**Tikka** Whitetail Hunter
**Weatherby** Mark V Sporter, Eurosport, Stainless, Synthetic
**Winchester** Model 70 Classic SM, Classic Stainless, Sporter, Super Grade
**Winslow** Basic

### 340 WBY. MAG.

**A-Square** Caesar and Hannibal
**Benton & Brown** Model 93
**McMillan** Alaskan; Classic, Stainless & Talon Sporters, Safari
**Weatherby** Mark V Deluxe, Euromark, Eurosport, Lazermark, Sporter, Stainless, Synthetic

### 35 WHELEN

**Remington** Models 7400 and 7600

### 350 REM. MAG.

**Clifton Arms** Scout
**McMillan** Classic, Stainless & Talon Sporters, Varminter

### 358 WIN./NORMA

**A-Square** Caesar and Hannibal
**McMillan** Alaskan MA
**Winslow** Basic

### 375 H&H

**A-Square** Caesar and Hannibal
**Benton & Brown** Model 93
**Blaser** Model R93
**Browning** A-Bolt II Long Action Mag. and Composite Stalker (stainless)
**CZ** Model ZKK 602
**Dakota Arms** Model 76 Safari, Classic
**Francotte** Bolt Action
**McMillan** Alaskan; Classic, Stainless & Talon Sporters; Safari
**Remington** African Plains, Alaskan Wilderness
**Ruger** 77RSM MKII Magnum
**Sako** Deluxe, Fiberclass, Hunter Lightweight, LS, Left-Handed Models, Mannlicher-Style Carbine, Safari Grade, Super Deluxe, TRG-S
**Sauer** Model 90
**Steyr-Mannlicher** Sporter Models S and S/T
**Weatherby** Mark V Eurosport, Sporter, Stainless, Synthetic
**Winchester** Model 70 Classic SM, Classic Stainless
**Winslow** Basic

### 375 WEATHERBY

**A-Square** Caesar and Hannibal

### 378 WIN./WBY. MAG.

**A-Square** Hannibal
**McMillan** Safari Super Magnum
**Weatherby** Mark V Deluxe, Lazermark

### 404 JEFFERY

**A-Square** Caesar and Hannibal
**Dakota Arms** 76 African
**McMillan** Safari

### 416 REM./WBY. MAG.

**A-Square** Caesar and Hannibal
**Blaser** Model R93
**McMillan** Alaskan; Classic, Stainless & Talon Sporters; Safari and Safari Super Magnum
**Sako** Deluxe, Fiberclass, Hunter Lightweight, Laminated Stock Models, Left-Handed Models, Safari Grade
**Weatherby** Mark V Deluxe, Euromark, Lazermark

### 416 RIGBY/DAKOTA

**A-Square** Hannibal
**Dakota Arms** 76 African
**Francotte** Bolt Action
**McMillan** Safari Super Magnum
**Ruger** 77 Model RSM MKII Magnum
**Ultra Light Arms** Model 40 Series

### 416 TAYLOR and HOFFMAN

**A-Square** Caesar and Hannibal

### 425 EXPRESS

**A-Square** Caesar and Hannibal
**Savage** Model 116SE Safari Express

### 450 ACKLEY/DAKOTA

**A-Square** Caesar and Hannibal
**Dakota Arms** 76 African

### 45-70

**Pedersoli** Replica Rolling Block Target Rifle

### 458 WIN. MAG./LOTT

**A-Square** Caesar and Hannibal
**CZ** Model ZKK 602
**Dakota Arms** Model 76 Classic, Safari
**McMillan** Safari
**Ruger** Model M-77RS MKII
**Sauer** Safari, Model 90
**Savage** Model 116SE Safari Express
**Steyr-Mannlicher** Sporter Model S/T
**Winslow** Basic

### 460 WIN./WBY. MAG.

**A-Square** Hannibal
**Francotte** Bolt Action
**McMillan** Safari Super Magnum
**Weatherby** Mark V Deluxe, Lazermark

**470 CAPSTICK**

**A-Square** Caesar and Hannibal

**495 A-SQUARE MAG.**

**A-Square** Caesar and Hannibal

**500 A-SQUARE**

**A-Square** Hannibal

**505 GIBBS**

**Francotte** Bolt Action

## CENTERFIRE—LEVER ACTION

**22 HORNET**

**Uberti** Model 1871 Rolling Block Baby Carbine

**22-250**

**Browning** Model 81 BLR

**222 REM./223 REM.**

**Browning** Model 81 BLR

**243 WINCHESTER**

**Browning** Model 81 BLR
**Savage** Model 99C

**270**

**Browning** Model 81 BLR LA

**284 WINCHESTER**

**Browning** Model 81 BLR

**7mm MAGNUM**

**Browning** Model 81 BLR LA

**7mm-08**

**Browning** Model 81 BLR

**7-30 WATERS**

**Winchester** Model 94 Standard Walnut

**30-06**

**Browning** Model 81 BLR Long Action

**30-30 WINCHESTER**

**Marlin** Models 30AS, 336CS
**Winchester** Models 94 Ranger, Standard, Trapper Carbine, Walnut, Win-Tuff, Wrangler

**307 WINCHESTER**

**Winchester** Model 94 Big Bore Walnut

**308 WINCHESTER**

**Browning** Model 81 BLR
**Savage** Model 99C

**35 REMINGTON**

**Marlin** Model 336CS

**356 WINCHESTER**

**Winchester** Model 94 Big Bore Walnut

**357 MAGNUM**

**EMF** Model 1873 Sporting
**Marlin** Model 1894CS
**Rossi** Models M92 SRS and SRC
**Uberti** Models 1871 Rolling Block Baby Carbine, 1873 Sporting and Carbine
**Winchester** Model 94 Trapper Carbine

**38 SPECIAL**

**EMF** Model 1866 Yellow Boy Rifle/Carbine
**Marlin** Model 1894CS
**Rossi** Model M92 SRC and SRS
**Uberti** Models 1866 Sporting, 1866 Yellowboy Carbine

**44 REM. MAG.**

**Marlin** Model 1894S
**Winchester** Model 94 Trapper Carbine, Wrangler

**44 SPECIAL**

**Marlin** Model 1894S
**Winchester** Model 94 Trapper Carbine, Wrangler

**44-40**

**EMF** Model 1860 Henry, 1866 Yellow Boy Rifle/Carbine, Model 1873 Sporting
**Navy Arms** 1866 Yellowboy (rifle and carbine), Henry Military, Carbine, Iron Frame and Trapper Models, 1873 Winchester-Style and Sporting Rifles
**Rossi** Model M92
**Uberti** Model 1866 Sporting and Yellowboy Carbine, 1873 Sporting Rifle/Carbine, Henry Rifle/Carbine

**444 MARLIN**

**Marlin** Model 444SS

**45 COLT**

**EMF** Model 1860 Henry, 1866 Yellow Boy Rifle/Carbine, 1873 Sporting, Carbine, 1875 Outlaw Revolving Carbine
**Marlin** Model 1894S
**Navy Arms** 1873 Winchester Sporting Rifles
**Rossi** Model M92
**Uberti** Model 1873 Sporting and Carbine, Henry Rifle
**Winchester** Model 94 Trapper Carbine

**45-70 GOV'T.**

**Marlin** Model 1895SS, 1895CLTD

## CENTERFIRE—DOUBLE RIFLES

**308 WIN.**

**Krieghoff** Models Ulm, Teck and Classic
**Tikka** Model 512S

**30-06**

**Krieghoff** Models Ulm, Teck and Classic
**Laurona** Model 2000X Express
**Tikka** Model 512S

**300 WIN. MAG.**

**Krieghoff** Models Ulm and Teck

**9.3×74R**

**Francotte** Sidelock S/S and Boxlock S/S
**Krieghoff** Classic
**Pedersoli** Kodiak Mark IV
**Tikka** Model 512S

**375 H&H**

**Krieghoff** Classic and Classic Big Boar
**Laurona** Model 2000X Express

**416 RIGBY**

**Krieghoff** Classic Big Boar

**45-70**

**Pedersoli** Kodiak Mark IV

**458 WIN. MAG.**

**Krieghoff** Models Ulm, Teck, Classic and Classic Big Boar

**470 N.E., 500 N.E.**

**Krieghoff** Classic Big Boar

## CENTERFIRE/RIMFIRE—PUMP ACTION

**22 S, L, LR (RF)**

**Remington** Model 572 BDL Deluxe Fieldmaster
**Rossi** Models M62 SAC and SA

**22 MAGNUM (RF)**

**Rossi** Model 59

**243 WIN./270 WIN. (CF)**

**Remington** Model 7600 Rifle/Carbine (also calibers 280 Rem., 30-06, 308 Win., 35 Whelen, 30-06 Carbine)

## CENTERFIRE/RIMFIRE—SINGLE SHOT

**17 REMINGTON**

**Thompson/Center** Contender

**218 BEE**

**Ruger** No. 1B Standard, No. 1S Medium Sporter

**22 S, L, LR**

**Dakota Arms** Model 10
**European American Armory** HW 60 Target, HW 660 Match
**Lakefield** Mark I, Model 91T
**Marlin** 15YN "Little Buckaroo," Model 2000 Target
**Thompson/Center** Contender
**Ultra Light Arms** Model 20RF

**22 HORNET**

**New England** Handi-Rifle
**Ruger** No. 1B Standard
**Thompson/Center** Contender

**22 PPC**

**Ruger** No.1V Special Varminter

**22-250 REM.**

**Browning** Model 1885 High Wall
**New England** Handi-Rifle
**Ruger** No. 1B Standard, Special Varminter
**Ruger** No. 1B Standard No. 1V Special Varminter

**220 SWIFT**

**Savage** Model 112FVSS Varmint and 112FV

**222 REMINGTON**

**Remington** Models 40-XB Bench Rest, Rangemaster

**223 REM.**

**Browning** Model 1885 Low Wall
**Harrington & Richardson** Ultra Single Shot Varmint
**New England** Handi-Rifle
**Ruger** No. 1B Standard, No. 1V Special Varminter
**Thompson/Center** Contender

**243 WINCHESTER**

**New England** Handi-Rifle
**Ruger** No. 1A Light Sporter, No. 1B Standard, No. 1 RSI International Standard

**25-06**

**Ruger** No. 1B Standard, No. 1V Special Varminter

**6mm PPC**

**Ruger** No. 1V Special Varminter

**6mm REMINGTON**

**Ruger** No. 1B Standard, No. 1V Special Varminter

**257 ROBERTS**

**Ruger** No. 1B Standard

**270 WEATHERBY**

**Ruger** No. 1B Standard

**270 WINCHESTER**

**Browning** Model 1885 High Wall
**New England** Handi-Rifle
**Ruger** No. 1A Light Sporter, No. 1B Standard, RSI International

**280 REMINGTON**

**Ruger** No. 1B Standard

**30-06**

**Browning** Model 1885 High Wall
**New England** Handi-Rifle
**Remington** Model 40XB Rangemaster
**Ruger** No. 1A Light Sporter, No. 1B Standard, RSI International

**300 WBY. MAG.**

**Ruger** No. 1B Standard

**300 WIN. MAG.**

**Ruger** No. 1B Standard, No. 1S Medium Sporter
**Savage** Model 112 BT

**30-30 WIN.**

**New England** Handi-Rifle
**Thompson/Center** Contender

**7mm REM. MAG.**

**Browning** Model 1885 High Wall
**Ruger** No. 1S Medium Sporter, No. 1B Standard

**7-30 WATERS**

**Thompson/Center** Contender

**338 WIN. MAG.**

**Ruger** No. 1S Medium Sporter, No. 1B Standard

**357 WIN.**

**Pedersoli** Rolling Block Target
**Thompson/Center** Contender

**375 H&H/WIN.**

**Ruger** No. 1H Tropical
**Thompson/Center** Contender

**404 JEFFERY**

**Ruger** No. 1H Tropical

**.410 BORE**

**Thompson/Center** Contender Carbine SS and Conversion Kit

**416 REM./RIGBY**

**Ruger** No. 1H Tropical

**45-70 GOV'T.**

**Browning** Model 1885 High Wall
**Navy Arms** No. 2 Creedmoor Target, 1874 Sharps Sniper, Remington-Style Rolling Block Buffalo, 1874 Sharps Cavalry Carbine
**New England** Handi-Rifle
**Pedersoli** Rolling Block Target
**Ruger** No. 1S Medium Sporter

**458 WIN. MAG.**

**Ruger** No. 1H Tropical

**50 BMG**

**L.A.R. Grizzly** Big Boar Competitor

**54**

**Pedersoli** Sharps Carbine Model 766

## CENTERFIRE/RIMFIRE—RIFLE/SHOTGUN COMBOS

**22 LR, 22 HORNET, 223 REM./12 or 20 Ga.**

**Savage** Model 24F

**30-30/12 or 20 Ga.**

**Savage** Model 24F

**30-30/12 or 20 Ga.**

**Savage** Model 24F

## RIMFIRE—AUTOLOADING

**22 S, L, LR**

**AMT** Challenge Edition
**Anschutz** Model 525
**Browning** Model 22 (Grades I and VI)
**Cooper Arms** Models 36 Sportsman, Featherweight, 36 BR-50, Custom Classic
**European American Armory** Sabatti SP1822H Bull Barrel
**Feather** Models AT-22 and F2 AT-22
**Lakefield** Model 64B
**Marlin** Models 60, 60SS, 70HC, 70PSS "Papoose," 995SS
**Mitchell Arms** Models 15/22, 20/22
**Remington** Model 522 Viper, Model 552 BDL Deluxe Speedmaster
**Ruger** Model 10/22 Series, 77/22 Series
**Ruko-Armscor** Models M20C, M20P, M2000

**22 WIN. MAG. (WMR)**

**AMT** Rimfire Magnum
**Brno** Model ZKM 611
**Marlin** Models 882L, 922 Mag.
**Ruger** Model 922 Mag.

## RIMFIRE—BOLT ACTION

**22 S, L, LR**

**Anschutz** Achiever; BR-50 Bench Rest, Match 64 Sporters: Models 1416D, 1418D and 1516D, 1518D Mannlicher; 64MS, 1903, 1907, 1910, 1911, 1913; Models 1700 Custom, 1700D FWT, 1700D FWT Deluxe, 1700D Bavarian, Graphite Custom, 1827 B/BT Biathlon, 2007 Super Match 54, 2013 Super Match 54, Model 54.18MS, 1808 DRT
**Browning** Model A-Bolt (Grade I and Gold Medallion)
**CZ** Model ZKM 452
**Dakota** Sporter
**European American Armory** HW 660 Match, Target/Silhouette
**Kimber** Model 82C Series
**Lakefield Sporting** Models 90B, 91T, 91TR, 92S, Mark I, Mark II
**Marlin** Models 15YN, 880, 881, Model 2000 Target
**Mitchell Arms** Models 9301–9304
**Remington** Models 541-T and 581-S
**Ruger** Model 77/22R Series and K77/22VBZ Varmint
**Sako** Finnfire
**Ultra Light Arms** Model 20 RF
**Unique** Model T Dioptra Sporter, T UIT Standard, T/SM Silhouette

**22 MAGNUM**

**Anschutz** Match 64 Sporter Models, Models 1516 DCL, 1516D, 1516D Custom, 1518D Mannlicher
**Mitchell Arms** Models 9301–9304

**22 WIN. MAG. (WMR)**

**Browning** A-Bolt (Grade I)
**CZ** Model ZKM 452
**Marlin** Models 25MN, 25N, 882 and 882L, 883, 883SS
**Ruko-Armscor** M1500

## RIMFIRE—LEVER ACTION

**22 S, L, LR**

**Browning** Model BL-22 (Grades I and II)
**Marlin** Models 39TDS, Golden 39AS
**Uberti** Models 1866 Sporting Rifle and Yellowboy Carbine, 1871 Rolling Block Baby Carbine
**Winchester** Model 9422 (Walnut, Win-Tuff)

**22 MAG. (WMR)**

**Winchester** Model 9422 (Walnut, Win-Cam, Win-Tuff)

**44**

**Navy Arms** Henry Military and Iron Frame Rifles

# BLACK POWDER

## HANDGUNS

**30**

**Gonic Arms** Model GA-90

**31**

**CVA** New Model Pocket, Vest Pocket Derringer

**36**

**American Arms** 1851 Colt Navy
**Armsport** Models 5133, 5136
**CVA** Model 1851 Navy, Pocket Police, Sheriff's Model Revolver Brass Frame
**Dixie** Navy Revolver, Spiller and Burr Revolver
**EMF** 1851 Sheriff's Model, Model 1862 Police
**Euroarms** Model 1120 Colt 1851 Navy, Model 1010 Remington 1858 New Model Army Revolver
**Navy Arms** 1851 Navy "Yank" Revolver, Reb Model 1860, Reb 60 Sheriff's Model, 1862 New Police Revolver
**Uberti** 1851 and 1861 Navy, 1858 New Navy, Paterson

**38**

**Dixie** Pedersoli Mang Target Pistol
**Gonic Arms** Model GA-90

**44**

**American Arms** 1847 Walker, 1858 Remington Army and Army SS Target, 1860 Colt Army
**Armsport** Models 5120, 5121, 5133, 5136, 5138, 5139, 5140, 5149, 5150
**CVA** 1851 and 1861 Navy Brass-Framed Revolvers, Remington Bison, 1858 Remington Target Model and Army Steel Frame Revolver (also Brass Frame), Walker
**Dixie** 1860 Army Revolver, Pennsylvania Pistol, Remington Army Revolver, Screw Barrel Pistol, Third Model Dragoon, Walker Revolver, Wyatt Earp Revolver
**EMF** Model 1860 Army, Second Model 44 Dragoon
**Euroarms** Rogers and Spencer Models 1005, 1006 and 1007, Models 1020 and 1040, Remington 1858 New Model Army, Model 1210 Colt 1860 Army
**Gonic Arms** Model GA-90
**Navy Arms** Colt Walker 1847, 1851 Navy "Yank", Reb Model 1860 Revolver, 1860 Army Revolver, Reb 60 Sheriff's Model, Rogers and Spencer Revolver, 1858 Target Remington and Deluxe New Model Revolvers, 1858 Remington New Model Army and SS, Kentucky Pistols, LeMat Revolvers, Le Page Flintlock/Percussion Pistols and Cased Sets
**Stone Mountain Arms** 1858 Remington Target and Rogers & Spencer Revolvers
**Uberti** 1st, 2nd and 3rd Model Dragoon, Walker, 1858 Remington New Army, 1860 Army

**45**

**Dixie** LePage Dueling Pistol, Pedersoli English Dueling Pistol
**Gonic Arms** Model GA-90
**Ruger** Old Army Cap and Ball
**Thompson/Center** Scout Pistol
**Traditions** Pioneer Pistol

**50**

**CVA** Kentucky Pistol, Hawken Pistol
**Thompson/Center** Scout Pistol
**Traditions** Buckhunter In-Line Pistol, Buckskinner, Kentucky Pistols, William Parker Pistol, Trapper Pistol

**54**

**Thompson/Center** Scout Pistol
**Traditions** Buckhunter In-Line Pistol

**58**

**Navy Arms** Harpers Ferry Pistol

## RIFLES and CARBINES

**30**

**Gonic Arms** Model GA-87

**32**

**CVA** Varmint
**Dixie** Tennessee Squirrel
**Navy Arms** Pennsylvania Long
**Traditions** Deerhunter

**36**

**Traditions** Frontier Scout

**38**

**Gonic Arms** Model GA-87

**40-65**

**Cumberland Mountain Arms** Plateau Rifle

**41**

**White Systems** Model Super 91, Super Safari and G Series

**44**

**Gonic Arms** Model GA-87

**44-40**

**Dixie** Winchester '73 Carbine

**45**

**Dixie** Hawken, Kentuckian, Pedersoli Waadtlander, Pennsylvania, Tryon Creedmoor
**Gonic Arms** Model GA-87
**Navy Arms** Pennsylvania Long
**Thompson/Center** Hawken
**UFA** Teton and Grand Teton Rifles
**White Systems** Model Super 91, Super Safari and "G" Series Whitetail

**451**

**Navy Arms** Tryon Creedmoor
**Traditions** Creedmore Match, Hawken Match and Henry Match Percussion Rifles

**45-70**

**Cumberland Mountain Arms** Plateau Rifle
**Dixie** 1874 Sharps Lightweight Target/Hunter
**Shiloh Sharps** Model 1874 Business, 1874 Sporting Rifle #1 and #3,

**45-90**

**Shiloh Sharps** Model 1874 Business, Sporting Rifle #1 and #3,

**45-120**

**Shiloh Sharps** Model 1874 Business, Sporting Rifle #1 and #3

**50**

**CVA** Apollo Shadow, Eclipse, Comet, Classic; Bobcat Hunter, Bushwacker, Express Double Rifle and Carbine, Frontier and Hunter Carbine, Kentucky, Lynx, Plainsman, St. Louis Hawken, Trophy Carbine, Woodsman
**Dixie** Hawken, In-Line Carbine, Tennessee Mountain
**Gonic Arms** GA-87 and Model 93 Rifles
**Lyman** Deerstalker Rifle and Carbine, Great Plains, Trade Rifle
**Modern Muzzleloading** Knight MK-85 Series, Model BK-92 Black Knight, Magnum Elite, Wolverine
**Navy Arms** Ithaca-Navy Hawken, Smith Carbine
**Remington** 1816 Flint Lock Rifle
**Stone Mountain Arms** Silver Eagle Hunting Rifle
**Thompson/Center** Grey Hawk, Hawken, Hawken Custom, New Englander, Pennsylvania Hunter (rifle and carbine), Renegade, Renegade Single Trigger Hunter, Scout Rifle and Carbine, Thunder Hawk, Fire Hawk, White Mountain Carbine
**Traditions** Buckskinner Carbine, Deerhunter, Frontier Scout, Hawken Woodsman, In-Line Rifle Series, Pennsylvania, Pioneer, Whitetail (rifle and carbine), Kentucky, Tennessee
**Uberti** Santa Fe Hawken
**UFA** Teton and Grand Teton rifles, Teton Blackstone
**White Systems** Model Super 91, Super Safari and "G" Series

**50-70**

**Shiloh Sharps** Model 1874 Business, Sporting Rifle #1 and #3

**50-90**

**Shiloh Sharps** Model 1874 Business, Sporting #1 and #3

**54**

**CVA** Apollo Classic and Shadow; Woodsman, Frontier Hunter LS Carbine, St. Louis Hawken, Trophy Carbine, Lynx, Bobcat Hunter
**Dixie** Hawken, In-Line Carbine, Sharps New Model 1859 Carbine and 1859 Military Rifle
**Euroarms** 1803 Harpers Ferry, 1841 Mississippi
**Gonic Arms** Model GA-87
**Lyman** Deerstalker Rifle, Great Plains, Trade Rifle
**Modern Muzzleloading** Knight MK-85 Series, BK-92 Black Knight, Magnum Elite
**Navy Arms** 1803 Harpers Ferry, 1841 Mississippi, 1859 Berdan Sharps, 1863 Sharps Cavalry Carbine, Ithaca/Navy Hawken, Mortimer Flintlock and Match Flintlock
**Stone Mountain Arms** Harpers Ferry 1803 Flintlock
**Thompson/Center** Grey Hawk, Hawken, New Englander, Renegade, Renegade Single Trigger Hunter, Scout Carbine and Rifle, Thunder Hawk, White Mountain Carbine, Fire Hawk
**Traditions** Deerhunter, Hawken Woodsman, Hunter, In-Line Rifle Series, Pioneer and Whitetail (rifle and carbine)
**Uberti** Sante Fe Hawken
**White Systems** G Series Bison

**58**

**Dixie** 1858 Two-Band Enfield Rifle, U.S. Model 1861 Springfield, Mississippi, 1862 Three-Band Enfield Rifle Musket, 1863 Springfield Civil War Musket
**Euroarms** Model 2260 London Armory Company Enfield 3-Band Rifle Musket, Models 2270 and 2280 London Armory Company Enfield Rifled Muskets, Model 2300 Cook and Brother Confederate Carbine, J. P. Murray Carbine, 1861 Springfield, 1863 Remington Zouave, C. S. Richmond Musket, 1841 Mississippi
**Navy Arms** Mississippi Model 1841, 1853 Enfield Rifle and Musket, 1861 Enfield Musketoon, 1861 Springfield, 1863 Springfield, J.P. Murray Carbine, 1862 C. S. Richmond
**Stone Mountain Arms** 1861 Springfield and 1853 Enfield Rifles
**Thompson/Center** Big Boar Caplock
**Traditions** Model 1853 3-Band Enfield Rifled Musket, Model 1861 U. S. Springfield Rifled Musket

**69**

**Dixie** U.S. Model 1816 Flintlock Musket
**Navy Arms** 1816 M.T. Wickham Musket

**75**

**Navy Arms** Brown Bess Musket and Carbine

## DOUBLE RIFLE (Black Powder)

**50, 54, 58**

**Navy Arms** Kodiak

## SHOTGUNS (Black Powder)

**CVA** Trapper Single Barrel and Classic Turkey Double Barrel (12 Ga.)
**Dixie** Double Barrel Magnum (12 Ga.)
**Navy Arms** Model TandT, Fowler (12 Ga.), Mortimer Flintlock 12 Ga., Steel Shot Magnum 10 Ga.
**Thompson/Center** New Englander (12 Ga.)
**Traditions** Fowler Shotgun

# GUNFINDER

To help you find the model of your choice, the following list includes each gun found in the catalog section of SHOOTER'S BIBLE 1996. The **Caliberfinder** and a supplemental listing of **Discontinued Models** precede this section.

## HANDGUNS

### PISTOLS

## REVOLVERS



# RIFLES

## CENTERFIRE—AUTOLOADING and SLIDE ACTION



## CENTERFIRE—BOLT ACTION

## CENTERFIRE—LEVER ACTION



## CENTERFIRE—SINGLE SHOT



## RIMFIRE—AUTOLOADING and SLIDE ACTION



## RIMFIRE—BOLT ACTION and SINGLE SHOT

## RIMFIRE—LEVER ACTION



## DOUBLE RIFLES, ACTIONS and DRILLINGS



## RIFLE/SHOTGUN COMBINATIONS (*see* Shotgun Section)

## REPLICA RIFLES



# SHOTGUNS

## AUTOLOADING



## BOLT ACTION



## OVER-UNDER



## SIDE-BY-SIDE

# DISCONTINUED MODELS

The following models that appeared in the 1995 edition of SHOOTER'S BIBLE have been discontinued by their manufacturers or are no longer imported by U.S. distributors or are now listed under a different manufacturer/distributor.

## *HANDGUNS*

**AMERICAN DERRINGER** Model 4 Alaskian
**AMT** On Duty
**AUTO-ORDNANCE** Model 1927A5
**BERSA** Models 23DA, 83DA, 85DA, 86 Custom Undercover
**ERMA** Model ESP Golden Target, Model 772 Match
**GRENDEL** Model P-31
**HELWAN** Brigadier
**HIGH-STANDARD** Model 2 "Pen" Pistol, Cop & Mini-Cop, Semmerling LM-4, Model 3
**LLAMA** 22 LR Small Frame Auto Pistols
**MITCHELL ARMS** SA Army and High Standard Signature Series Competition
**NAVY ARMS** TT-Olympia Pistol
**REMINGTON** Model XP-100 Series
**SPRINGFIELD** Model XM4 High-Capacity 1911-A1, Compact Comp. 1911-A1 and Lighweight Compact Raceguns
**SMITH & WESSON** Model 915, Model 27
**STAR** Megastar
**TAURUS** Models 741 and 761, Model 86 Target Master
**WALTHER** Model P-88DA
**DAN WESSON** Hunter Pacs

## *RIFLES*

**ACTION ARMS** IMI Timber Wolf
**AMT** Small Game Hunter II
**ANSCHUTZ** Model 1808 DRT
**AUTO-ORDNANCE** Thompson Model 1927A3
**BRNO** Models 452, 527, 537, 600/601/602 (replaced by CZ models)
**EAGLE ARMS** EA-15 Models
**CARL GUSTAF** Model 2000
**HEYM EXPRESS** Models 55B and 88B
**KDF** Model K15
**MAGTECH** Model MT-122.2
**MARK X** Actions and Rifles (Mini-Mark, Viscount, Sporter, Whitworth)
**MARLIN** Models 881, 990L, 1894 Century Ltd.
**MITCHELL ARMS** 1858 Henry, 1866 Winchester, 1873 Winchester
**NAVY ARMS** Models TU-KKW (Training Rifle), TT-33/40 (Sniper Trainer) and EM-331 Sporting Rifle
**NORINCO** Models 22 ATD and JW-15
**PARKER-HALE** Models M81 Classic & African, M-85 Sniper, Models 1000 Clip, 1100 Lightweight & African Magnum, 1200 Super, 1300 C Scout, 2100 Midland
**REMINGTON** Models 700 ADL LS, BDL European
**RUKO-ARMSCOR** Model M14P
**TIKKA** New Generation Premium Grade Continental, Whitetail/Battue
**SAKO** Left-Hand Model Deluxe and Classic Models 2155, 2165, 2185
**VOERE** Models 2115 and 2150
**WINCHESTER** Model 52B Rimfire, Models 70 Featherweight and Featherweight Classic, 70 DBM and Classic DBM

## *SHOTGUNS*

**AMERICAN ARMS** Franchi Spas-12 and Law-12
**BERETTA** Model 303 Competition Trap/Skeet
**BROWNING** Model B-125 Custom A Style, Model BPS Pigeon Grades, Model GTI Sporting Clay
**CHURCHILL** Turkey Automatic
**CONNECTICUT VALLEY CLASSICS** Field and Waterfowler
**EUROPEAN AMERICAN ARMORY** Sabatti Sporting Clay & Trap, Scirocco Lu-Mar Field Grade & Sporting Clay
**LANBER** Models 82 Field Grade, 87 Deluxe Field Grade, 97 Sporting Clays
**LAURONA** Model 85X/New Classic X, Silhouette Model 600X, Olympic 92X
**MAGTECH** Models 586 Slug Gun and VR
**MAROCCHI** Avanza Series
**REMINGTON** Models 870 Express Security and Small Gauge; 870 "TC" Trap, Brushmaster Deer Gun; 870 Wingmaster; 11-87 SPS Big Game; Models 1100 Tournament Skeet and Autoloader (28 and .410 guage); SP-10 Magnum Combo
**SKB** Model 685 Series
**WINCHESTER** Model 12 (Grades I and IV), Model 1001, Model 1300 Walnut Deer, Pump Deluxe Walnut, 1400 Semiauto

## *BLACK POWDER*

**ARMSPORT** Models 5145 (Colt 1847 Walker), 5152 (Engraved Remington 44), 5153 (Engraved Colt Army 44), 5154 (Engraved Colt Navy 36)
**CVA** Revolver Models 1856 Target, 1860 Army, 3rd Model Dragoon, Wells Fargo; Rifle Models Apollo Carbelite, Bushwacker, Panther Carbine, Tracker Carbine LS
**DIXIE** Lincoln Derringer, 2nd Model Brown Bess Musket
**PARKER-HALE** Models 1853 (Three-Band Musket), 1858 (Two- Band Musket), 1861 Musketoon; Volunteer and Whitworth Military Target Rifles
**SHILOH SHARPS** Model 1874 Saddle Rifle
**TRADITIONS** Frontier Rifle and Carbine
**ULTRA LIGHT ARMS** Model 90